Windows Internals
Seventh Edition
Part 1

System architecture, processes, threads, memory management, and more

Pavel Yosifovich, Alex Ionescu,
Mark E. Russinovich, and David A. Solomon

To my family–my wife Idit and our children Danielle, Amit, and Yoav–
thank you for your patience and encouragement during this demanding work.

Pavel Yosifovich

To my parents, who guided and inspired me to follow my dreams, and to my family,
who stood by me all those countless nights.

Alex Ionescu

To our parents, who guided and inspired us to follow our dreams.

Mark E. Russinovich and David A. Solomon

PUBLISHED BY
Microsoft Press
A division of Microsoft Corporation
One Microsoft Way
Redmond, Washington 98052-6399

Library of Congress Control Number: 2014951935

ISBN: 978-0-7356-8418-8

Printed and bound in Great Britain by Ashford Colour Press Ltd.

First Printing

Microsoft Press books are available through booksellers and distributors worldwide. If you need support related to this book, email Microsoft Press Support at *mspinput@microsoft.com*. Please tell us what you think of this book at *https://aka.ms/tellpress*.

Acquisitions Editor: Devon Musgrave
Editorial Production: Polymath Publishing
Technical Reviewer: Christophe Nasarre
Layout Services: Shawn Morningstar
Indexing Services: Kelly Talbot Editing Services
Proofreading Services: Corina Lebegioara
Cover: Twist Creative • Seattle

Contents

Chapter 3   Processes and jobs   101

Chapter 4   Threads   193

Chapter 5   Memory management   301

Chapter 7   Security   605

Introduction

Windows Internals, Seventh Edition is intended for advanced computer professionals (developers, security researchers, and system administrators) who want to understand how the core components of the Microsoft Windows 10 and Windows Server 2016 operating systems work internally. With this knowledge, developers can better comprehend the rationale behind design choices when building applications specific to the Windows platform. Such knowledge can also help developers debug complex problems. System administrators can benefit from this information as well, because understanding how the operating system works "under the hood" facilitates an understanding of the performance behavior of the system and makes troubleshooting system problems much easier when things go wrong. Security researchers can figure out how software applications and the operating system can misbehave and be misused, causing undesirable behavior, while also understanding the mitigations and security features modern Windows offers against such scenarios. After reading this book, you should have a better understanding of how Windows works and why it behaves as it does.

History of the book

This is the seventh edition of a book that was originally called *Inside Windows NT* (Microsoft Press, 1992), written by Helen Custer (prior to the initial release of Microsoft Windows NT 3.1). *Inside Windows NT* was the first book ever published about Windows NT and provided key insights into the architecture and design of the system. *Inside Windows NT, Second Edition* (Microsoft Press, 1998) was written by David Solomon. It updated the original book to cover Windows NT 4.0 and had a greatly increased level of technical depth.

Inside Windows 2000, Third Edition (Microsoft Press, 2000) was authored by David Solomon and Mark Russinovich. It added many new topics, such as startup and shutdown, service internals, registry internals, file-system drivers, and networking. It also covered kernel changes in Windows 2000, such as the Windows Driver Model (WDM), Plug and Play, power management, Windows Management Instrumentation (WMI), encryption, the job object, and Terminal Services. *Windows Internals, Fourth Edition* (Microsoft Press, 2004) was the Windows XP and Windows Server 2003 update and added more content focused on helping IT professionals make use of their knowledge of Windows internals, such as using key tools from Windows SysInternals and analyzing crash dumps.

Windows Internals, Fifth Edition (Microsoft Press, 2009) was the update for Windows Vista and Windows Server 2008. It saw Mark Russinovich move on to a full-time job at

Microsoft (where he is now the Azure CTO) and the addition of a new co-author, Alex Ionescu. New content included the image loader, user-mode debugging facility, Advanced Local Procedure Call (ALPC), and Hyper-V. The next release, *Windows Internals, Sixth Edition* (Microsoft Press, 2012), was fully updated to address the many kernel changes in Windows 7 and Windows Server 2008 R2, with many new hands-on experiments to reflect changes in the tools as well.

Seventh edition changes

Since this book's last update, Windows has gone through several releases, coming up to Windows 10 and Windows Server 2016. Windows 10 itself, being the current going-forward name for Windows, has had several releases since its initial release to manufacturing (RTM). Each is labeled with a four-digit version number indicating the year and month of release, such as *Windows 10, version 1703*, which was completed in March 2017. This implies that Windows has gone through at least six versions since Windows 7 (at the time of this writing).

Starting with Windows 8, Microsoft began a process of OS convergence, which is beneficial from a development perspective as well as for the Windows engineering team. Windows 8 and Windows Phone 8 had converged kernels, with modern app convergence arriving in Windows 8.1 and Windows Phone 8.1. The convergence story was complete with Windows 10, which runs on desktops/laptops, servers, XBOX One, phones (Windows Mobile 10), HoloLens, and various Internet of Things (IoT) devices.

With this grand unification completed, the time was right for a new edition of the series, which could now finally catch up with almost half a decade of changes in what will now be a more stable kernel architecture going forward. As such, this latest book covers aspects of Windows from Windows 8 to Windows 10, version 1703. Additionally, this edition welcomes Pavel Yosifovich as its new co-author.

Hands-on experiments

Even without access to the Windows source code, you can glean much about Windows internals from the kernel debugger, tools from SysInternals, and the tools developed specifically for this book. When a tool can be used to expose or demonstrate some aspect of the internal behavior of Windows, the steps for trying the tool yourself are listed in special "EXPERIMENT" sections. These appear throughout the book, and we encourage you to try them as you're reading. Seeing visible proof of how Windows works internally will make much more of an impression on you than just reading about it will.

Topics not covered

Windows is a large and complex operating system. This book doesn't cover everything relevant to Windows internals but instead focuses on the base system components. For example, this book doesn't describe COM+, the Windows distributed object-oriented programming infrastructure, or the Microsoft .NET Framework, the foundation of managed code applications. Because this is an "internals" book and not a user, programming, or system-administration book, it doesn't describe how to use, program, or configure Windows.

A warning and a caveat

Because this book describes undocumented behavior of the internal architecture and the operation of the Windows operating system (such as internal kernel structures and functions), this content is subject to change between releases.

By "subject to change," we don't necessarily mean that details described in this book will change between releases, but you can't count on them not changing. Any software that uses these undocumented interfaces, or insider knowledge about the operating system, might not work on future releases of Windows. Even worse, software that runs in kernel mode (such as device drivers) and uses these undocumented interfaces might experience a system crash when running on a newer release of Windows, resulting in potential loss of data to users of such software.

In short, you should never use any internal Windows functionality, registry key, behavior, API, or other undocumented detail mentioned in this book during the development of any kind of software designed for end-user systems, or for any other purpose other than research and documentation. Always check with the Microsoft Software Development Network (MSDN) for official documentation on a particular topic first.

Assumptions about you

The book assumes the reader is comfortable with working on Windows at a power-user level, and has a basic understanding of operating system and hardware concepts, such as CPU registers, memory, processes, and threads. Basic understanding of functions, pointers, and similar C programming language constructs is beneficial in some sections.

Organization of this book

The book is divided into two parts (as was the sixth edition), the first of which you're holding in your hands.

- Chapter 1, "Concepts and tools," provides a general introduction to Windows internals concepts and introduces the main tools used throughout the book. It's critical to read this chapter first, as it provides the necessary background needed for the rest of the book.

- Chapter 2, "System architecture," shows the architecture and main components that comprise Windows and discusses them in some depth. Several of these concepts are dealt with in greater detail in subsequent chapters.

- Chapter 3, "Processes and jobs," details how processes are implemented in Windows and the various ways of manipulating them. Jobs are also discussed as a means for controlling a set of processes and enabling Windows Container support.

- Chapter 4, "Threads," details how threads are managed, scheduled, and otherwise manipulated in Windows.

- Chapter 5, "Memory management," shows how the memory manager uses physical and virtual memory, and the various ways that memory can be manipulated and used by processes and drivers alike.

- Chapter 6, "I/O system," shows how the I/O system in Windows works and integrates with device drivers to provide the mechanisms for working with I/O peripherals.

- Chapter 7, "Security," details the various security mechanisms built into Windows, including mitigations that are now part of the system to combat exploits.

Conventions

The following conventions are used in this book:

- **Boldface** type is used to indicate text that you type as well as interface items that you are instructed to click or buttons that you are instructed to press.

- *Italic* type is used to indicate new terms.

- Code elements appear in a monospaced font.

- The first letters of the names of dialog boxes and dialog box elements are capitalized—for example, the Save As dialog box.

- Keyboard shortcuts are indicated by a plus sign (+) separating the key names. For example, Ctrl+Alt+Delete mean that you press Ctrl, Alt, and Delete keys at the same time.

About the companion content

We have included companion content to enrich your learning experience. The companion content for this book can be downloaded from the following page:

https://aka.ms/winint7ed/downloads

We have also placed the source code for the tools written specifically for this book at *https://github.com/zodiacon/windowsinternals*.

Acknowledgments

First, thanks to Pavel Yosifovich for joining us on this project. His involvement with the book was crucial to its release, and his many nights spent studying Windows details and writing about six releases' worth of changes is the reason this book exists.

This book wouldn't contain the depth of technical detail or the level of accuracy it has without the review, input, and support of key members of the Microsoft Windows development team and other experts at Microsoft. Therefore, we want to thank the following people, who provided technical review and/or input to the book, or were simply a source of support and help to the authors: Akila Srinivasan, Alessandro Pilotti, Andrea Allievi, Andy Luhrs, Arun Kishan, Ben Hillis, Bill Messmer, Chris Kleynhans, Deepu Thomas, Eugene Bak, Jason Shirk, Jeremiah Cox, Joe Bialek, John Lambert, John Lento, Jon Berry, Kai Hsu, Ken Johnson, Landy Wang, Logan Gabriel, Luke Kim, Matt Miller, Matthew Woolman, Mehmet Iyigun, Michelle Bergeron, Minsang Kim, Mohamed Mansour, Nate Warfield, Neeraj Singh, Nick Judge, Pavel Lebedynskiy, Rich Turner, Saruhan Karademir, Simon Pope, Stephen Finnigan, and Stephen Hufnagel.

We would like to again thank Ilfak Guilfanov of Hex-Rays (*http://www.hex-rays.com*) for the IDA Pro Advanced and Hex-Rays licenses they granted to Alex Ionescu more than a decade ago, so that he could speed up his reverse engineering of the Windows kernel, and for the continued support and development of decompiler features which make writing such a book possible without source code access.

Finally, the authors would like to thank the great staff at Microsoft Press who have been behind turning this book into a reality. Devon Musgrave served his last tour as our acquisitions editor, while Kate Shoup oversaw the title as its project editor. Shawn Morningstar, Kelly Talbot, and Corina Lebegioara also contributed to the quality of this book.

Errata and book support

We have made every effort to ensure the accuracy of this book and its companion content. Any errors that have been reported since this book was published are listed on our Microsoft Press site at:

https://aka.ms/winint7ed/errata

If you find an error that is not already listed, you can report it to us through the same page.

If you need additional support, email Microsoft Press Book Support at *mspinput@ microsoft.com*.

Please note that product support for Microsoft software is not offered through the addresses above.

We want to hear from you

At Microsoft Press, your satisfaction is our top priority and your feedback our most valuable asset. Please tell us what you think of this book at:

https://aka.ms/tellpress

The survey is short, and we read every one of your comments and ideas. Thanks in advance for your input!

Stay in touch

Let's keep the conversation going! We're on Twitter: @MicrosoftPress.

CHAPTER 1

Concepts and tools

I n this chapter, we'll introduce the key Microsoft Windows operating system (OS) concepts and terms
we'll be using throughout this book, such as the Windows API, processes, threads, virtual memory,
kernel mode and user mode, objects, handles, security, and the registry. We'll also introduce the tools
that you can use to explore Windows internals, such as the kernel debugger, the Performance Monitor,
and key tools from Windows Sysinternals (*http://www.microsoft.com/technet/sysinternals*). In addition,
we'll explain how you can use the Windows Driver Kit (WDK) and the Windows Software Development
Kit (SDK) as resources for finding further information on Windows internals.

Be sure that you understand everything in this chapter; the remainder of the book is written assuming that you do.

Windows operating system versions

This book covers the most recent version of the Microsoft Windows client and server operating
systems: Windows 10 (32-bit on x86 and ARM, and 64-bit version on x64) and Windows Server 2012
R2 (which exists as 64-bit version only). Unless specifically stated, the text applies to all versions. As
background information, Table 1-1 lists the Windows product names, their internal version number,
and their release date.

TABLE 1-1   Windows operating system releases

Product Name	Internal Version Number	Release Date
Windows NT 3.1	3.1	July 1993
Windows NT 3.5	3.5	September 1994
Windows NT 3.51	3.51	May 1995
Windows NT 4.0	4.0	July 1996
Windows 2000	5.0	December 1999
Windows XP	5.1	August 2001
Windows Server 2003	5.2	March 2003

Product Name	Internal Version Number	Release Date (continued)
Windows Server 2003 R2	5.2	December 2005
Windows Vista	6.0	January 2007
Windows Server 2008	6.0 (Service Pack 1)	March 2008
Windows 7	6.1	October 2009
Windows Server 2008 R2	6.1	October 2009
Windows 8	6.2	October 2012
Windows Server 2012	6.2	October 2012
Windows 8.1	6.3	October 2013
Windows Server 2012 R2	6.3	October 2013
Windows 10	10.0 (build 10240)	July 2015
Windows 10 version 1511	10.0 (build 10586)	November 2015
Windows 10 version 1607 (Anniversary Update)	10.0 (build 14393)	July 2016
Windows Server 2016	10.0 (build 14393)	October 2016

The version numbers seem to have strayed from a well-defined path starting with Windows 7. Its version number was 6.1 and not 7. Because of the popularity of Windows XP, when Windows Vista bumped the version number to 6.0, some applications failed to detect the correct (OS) because developers checked major numbers greater than or equal to 5 and minor numbers greater than or equal to 1, which was not the case with Windows Vista. Having learned the lesson, Microsoft chose to leave the major version number as 6 and the minor version number as 2 (greater than 1) to minimize such incompatibilities. However, with Windows 10, the version number has been updated to 10.0.

Note   Starting with Windows 8, the GetVersionEx Windows API function returns the OS version number as 6.2 (Windows 8) by default, regardless of the actual OS. (The function is also declared as deprecated.) This is done to minimize compatibility issues but also as an indicator that checking for the OS version is not the best approach in most cases. This is because some components can be installed out of band, without coinciding with an official Windows release. Still, if you need the actual OS version, you can obtain it indirectly by using the VerifyVersionInfo function or the newer version helper APIs, such as IsWindows8OrGreater, IsWindows8Point1OrGreater, IsWindows10OrGreater, IsWindowsServer, and similar. Also, OS compatibility can be indicated in the executable's manifest, which changes the results of this function. (See Chapter 8, "System mechanisms," in *Windows Internals Part 2* for details.)

You can view the Windows version information using the ver command-line tool or graphically by running winver. Here's a screenshot of winver on Windows 10 Enterprise version 1511:

The graphic also shows the Windows build number (10586.218 in this example), which could be useful for Windows Insiders (those who registered for getting earlier previews of Windows). It's also helpful for managing security updates because it shows which patch level is installed.

Windows 10 and future Windows versions

With Windows 10, Microsoft declared it will update Windows at a faster cadence than before. There will not be an official "Windows 11"; instead, Windows Update (or another enterprise servicing model) will update the existing Windows 10 to a new version. At the time of writing, two such updates have occurred, in November 2015 (also known as *version 1511*, referring to the year and month of servicing) and July 2016 (*version 1607*, also known by the marketing name of *Anniversary Update*).

Note   Internally, Microsoft still builds Windows versions in waves. For example, the initial Windows 10 release was code-named *Threshold 1*, while the November 2015 update was called *Threshold 2*. The next three phases of update are called *Redstone 1* (version 1607) to be followed by *Redstone 2* and *Redstone 3*.

Windows 10 and OneCore

Over the years, several flavors of Windows have evolved. Apart from mainstream Windows running on PCs, there is the Xbox 360 game console that runs a fork off Windows 2000. Windows Phone 7 runs a variant based on Windows CE (Microsoft's real-time OS). Maintaining and extending all these code bases is clearly difficult. Therefore, Microsoft decided to converge the kernels and base platform support binaries into one. This started with Windows 8 and Windows Phone 8 having a shared kernel (and Windows 8.1 and Windows Phone 8.1 having a converged Windows Runtime API). With Windows 10, the convergence is complete; this shared platform is known as OneCore, and it runs on PCs, phones, the Xbox One game console, the HoloLens and Internet of Things (IoT) devices such as the Raspberry Pi 2.

Clearly, all these device form factors are very different from one another. Some features simply don't exist on some devices. For example, supporting a mouse or a physical keyboard on a HoloLens device may not make sense, so you can't expect those parts to be present on the Windows 10 version for such a device. But the kernel, drivers, and base platform binaries are essentially the same (with registry-based and/or policy-based settings where they make sense for performance or other reasons). You'll see one such policy example in the section "API Sets" in Chapter 3, "Processes and jobs."

This book delves into the internals of the OneCore kernel, on whatever device it's running on. The experiments in the book, however, are targeted to a desktop machine with a mouse and keyboard mostly for convenience, as it's not easy (and sometimes officially impossible) to perform the experiments on other devices such as phones or the Xbox One.

Foundation concepts and terms

The following sections introduce the most fundamental concepts in Windows, which are essential to understanding the topics discussed in the rest of the book. Many of the concepts such as processes, threads, and virtual memory are discussed at length in subsequent chapters.

Windows API

The Windows application programming interface (API) is the user-mode system programming interface to the Windows OS family. Prior to the introduction of 64-bit versions of Windows, the programming interface to the 32-bit versions of the Windows OS was called the *Win32 API* to distinguish it from the original 16-bit Windows API, which was the programming interface to the original 16-bit versions of Windows. In this book, the term *Windows API* refers to both the 32-bit and 64-bit programming interfaces to Windows.

 Note We sometimes use the term *Win32 API* in lieu of *Windows API*. Either way, it still refers to the 32-bit and 64-bit variants.

 Note The Windows API is described in the Windows SDK documentation. (See the section "Windows Software Development Kit" later in this chapter.) This documentation is available free online at *https://developer.microsoft.com/en-us/windows/desktop/develop*. It is also included with all subscription levels to the Microsoft Developer Network (MSDN), Microsoft's support program for developers. An excellent description of how to program the Windows base API is in the book *Windows via C/C++, Fifth Edition* by Jeffrey Richter and Christophe Nasarre (Microsoft Press, 2007).

Windows API flavors

The Windows API originally consisted of C-style functions only. Today, thousands of such functions exist for developers to use. C was the natural choice at the time of the inception of Windows because it was the lowest common denominator (that is, it could be accessed from other languages as well) and was low level enough to expose OS services. The downside was the sheer number of functions coupled with the lack of naming consistency and logical groupings (for example, C++ namespaces). One outcome of these difficulties resulted in some newer APIs using a different API mechanism: the Component Object Model (COM).

COM was originally created to enable Microsoft Office applications to communicate and exchange data between documents (such as embedding an Excel chart inside a Word document or a PowerPoint presentation). This ability is called Object Linking and Embedding (OLE). OLE was originally implemented using an old Windows messaging mechanism called Dynamic Data Exchange (DDE). DDE was inherently limited, which is why a new way of communication was developed: COM. In fact, COM initially was called OLE 2, released to the public circa 1993.

COM is based on two foundational principles. First, clients communicate with objects (sometimes called COM server objects) through interfaces—well-defined contracts with a set of logically related methods grouped under the virtual table dispatch mechanism, which is also a common way for C++ compilers to implement virtual functions dispatch. This results in binary compatibility and removal of compiler name mangling issues. Consequently, it is possible to call these methods from many languages (and compilers), such as C, C++, Visual Basic, .NET languages, Delphi and others. The second principle is that component implementation is loaded dynamically rather than being statically linked to the client.

The term *COM server* typically refers to a Dynamic Link Library (DLL) or an executable (EXE) where the COM classes are implemented. COM has other important features related to security, cross-process marshalling, threading model, and more. A comprehensive treatment of COM is beyond the scope of this book; an excellent treatment of COM can be found in the book *Essential COM* by Don Box (Addison-Wesley, 1998).

Note Examples of APIs accessed through COM include DirectShow, Windows Media Foundation, DirectX, DirectComposition, Windows Imaging Component (WIC), and the Background Intelligent Transfer Service (BITS).

The Windows Runtime

Windows 8 introduced a new API and supporting runtime called the *Windows Runtime* (sometimes abbreviated *WinRT*, not to be confused with Windows RT, the discontinued ARM-based Windows OS version). The Windows Runtime consists of platform services aimed particularly at app developers for the so-called *Windows Apps* (formerly known as *Metro Apps*, *Modern Apps*, *Immersive Apps*, and *Windows Store Apps*). Windows Apps may target multiple device form factors, from small IoT devices to phones, tablets, laptops, desktops, and even devices such as the Xbox One and Microsoft HoloLens.

From an API perspective, WinRT is built on top of COM, adding various extensions to the base COM infrastructure. For example, complete type metadata is available in WinRT (stored in WINMD files and based on the .NET metadata format) that extends a similar concept in COM known as type libraries. From an API design perspective, it's much more cohesive than classic Windows API functions, with namespace hierarchies, consistent naming, and programmatic patterns.

Windows Apps are subject to new rules, unlike the normal Windows applications (now called *Windows desktop applications* or *Classic Windows applications*). These rules are described in Chapter 9, "Management mechanisms," in Part 2.

The relationship between the various APIs and applications is not straightforward. Desktop apps can use a subset of the WinRT APIs. Conversely, Windows Apps can use a subset of Win32 and COM APIs. Refer to the MSDN documentation for the details of which APIs are available from each application platform. Note, however, that at the basic binary level, the WinRT API is still based on top of the legacy Windows binaries and APIs, even though the availability of certain APIs may not be documented or supported. It is not a new "native" API for the system, much like .NET still leverages the traditional Windows API.

Applications written in C++, C# (or other .NET languages), and JavaScript can consume WinRT APIs easily thanks to language projections developed for these platforms. For C++, Microsoft created a non-standard extension known as C++/CX that makes it simpler to consume WinRT types. The normal COM interop layer for .NET (with some supporting run-time extensions) allows any .NET language to consume WinRT APIs naturally and simply just as if it were pure .NET. For JavaScript developers, an extension called *WinJS* was developed for accessing WinRT, although JavaScript developers must still use HTML to build their app's user interface.

Note Even though HTML can be used in Windows Apps, it's still a local client app and not a web application retrieved from a web server.

The .NET Framework

The .NET Framework is part of Windows. Table 1-2 shows the .NET Framework version installed as part of a given Windows version. However, a later version of the .NET Framework can be installed on older OS versions.

TABLE 1-2   Default .NET Framework installations on Windows

Windows Version	.NET Framework Version
Windows 8	4.5
Windows 8.1	4.5.1
Windows 10	4.6
Windows 10 version 1511	4.6.1
Windows 10 version 1607	4.6.2

The .NET Framework consists of two major components:

- **The Common Language Runtime (CLR)**   This is the run-time engine for .NET and includes a Just In Time (JIT) compiler that translates Common Intermediate Language (CIL) instructions to the underlying hardware CPU machine language, a garbage collector, type verification, code access security, and more. It's implemented as a COM in-process server (DLL) and uses various facilities provided by the Windows API.

- **The .NET Framework Class Library (FCL)**   This is a large collection of types that implement functionality typically needed by client and server applications, such as user interface services, networking, database access, and much more.

By offering these features and others, including new high-level programming languages (C#, Visual Basic, F#) and supporting tools, the .NET Framework improves developer productivity and increases safety and reliability within applications that target it. Figure 1-1 shows the relationship between the .NET Framework and the OS.

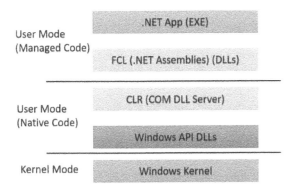

FIGURE 1-1   This diagram shows the relationship between .NET and the Windows OS.

Services, functions, and routines

Several terms in the Windows user and programming documentation have different meanings in different contexts. For example, the word *service* can refer to a callable routine in the OS, a device driver, or a server process. The following list describes what certain terms mean in this book:

- **Windows API functions**   These are documented, callable subroutines in the Windows API. Examples include CreateProcess, CreateFile, and GetMessage.

- **Native system services (or system calls)**   These are the undocumented, underlying services in the OS that are callable from user mode. For example, NtCreateUserProcess is the internal system service the Windows CreateProcess function calls to create a new process.

- **Kernel support functions (or routines)**   These are the subroutines inside the Windows OS that can be called only from kernel mode (defined later in this chapter). For example, ExAllocatePoolWithTag is the routine that device drivers call to allocate memory from the Windows system heaps (called *pools*).

- **Windows services**   These are processes started by the Windows service control manager. For example, the Task Scheduler service runs in a user-mode process that supports the schtasks command (which is similar to the UNIX commands at and cron). (Note that although the registry defines Windows device drivers as "services," they are not referred to as such in this book.)

- **Dynamic link libraries (DLLs)**   These are callable subroutines linked together as a binary file that can be dynamically loaded by applications that use the subroutines. Examples include Msvcrt.dll (the C run-time library) and Kernel32.dll (one of the Windows API subsystem libraries). Windows user-mode components and applications use DLLs extensively. The advantage DLLs provide over static libraries is that applications can share DLLs, and Windows ensures that there is only one in-memory copy of a DLL's code among the applications that are referencing it. Note that library .NET assemblies are compiled as DLLs but without any unmanaged exported subroutines. Instead, the CLR parses compiled metadata to access the corresponding types and members.

Processes

Although programs and processes appear similar on the surface, they are fundamentally different. A *program* is a static sequence of instructions, whereas a *process* is a container for a set of resources used when executing the instance of the program. At the highest level of abstraction, a Windows process comprises the following:

- **A private virtual address space**   This is a set of virtual memory addresses that the process can use.

- **An executable program**   This defines initial code and data and is mapped into the process's virtual address space.

- **A list of open handles**   These map to various system resources such as semaphores, synchronization objects, and files that are accessible to all threads in the process.

- **A security context**   This is an *access token* that identifies the user, security groups, privileges, attributes, claims, capabilities, User Account Control (UAC) virtualization state, session, and limited user account state associated with the process, as well as the AppContainer identifier and its related sandboxing information.

- **A process ID**   This is a unique identifier, which is internally part of an identifier called a *client ID*.

- **At least one thread of execution**   Although an "empty" process is possible, it is (mostly) not useful.

A number of tools for viewing (and modifying) processes and process information are available. The following experiments illustrate the various views of process information you can obtain with some of these tools. While many of these tools are included within Windows itself, and within the Debugging Tools for Windows and the Windows SDK, others are stand-alone tools from Sysinternals. Many of these tools show overlapping subsets of the core process and thread information, sometimes identified by different names.

Probably the most widely used tool to examine process activity is Task Manager. (Because there is no such thing as a "task" in the Windows kernel, the name of this tool, Task Manager, is a bit odd.) The following experiment shows some of the basic features of Task Manager.

EXPERIMENT: Viewing process information with Task Manager

The built-in Windows Task Manager provides a quick list of the processes on the system. You can start Task Manager in one of four ways:

- Press **Ctrl+Shift+Esc**.

- Right-click the taskbar and click **Start Task Manager**.

- Press **Ctrl+Alt+Delete** and click the **Start Task Manager** button.

- Start the executable Taskmgr.exe.

The first time Task Manager shows up, it's in "less details" mode, where only processes that have a visible top-level window are shown, as in the following screenshot:

There's little you can do from this window, so click the **More Details** expander button to show Task Manager's full view. The Processes tab should be selected by default:

The Processes tab shows the list of processes, with four columns: CPU, Memory, Disk, and Network. You can show more columns by right-clicking the header. Available columns are Process (Image) Name, Process ID, Type, Status, Publisher, and Command Line. Some processes can be further expanded, showing top-level visible windows created by the process.

To get even more process details, click the **Details** tab. Or, right-click a process and choose **Go to Details** to switch to the Details tab and select that specific process.

 Note The Windows 7 Task Manager's Processes tab is roughly equivalent to Windows 8+ Task Manager's Details tab. The Windows 7 Task Manager's Applications tab shows top-level visible Windows and not processes per se. This information is now contained in the Processes tab of the new Windows 8+ Task Manager.

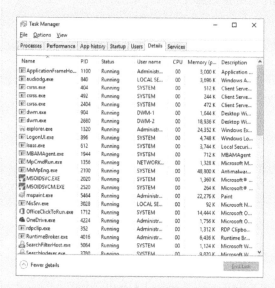

The Details tab shows processes as well, but does so in a more compact manner. It does not show windows created by processes, and provides more diverse information columns.

Notice that processes are identified by the name of the image of which they are an instance. Unlike some objects in Windows, processes can't be given global names. To display additional details, right-click the header row and click **Select Columns**. A list of columns appears as shown here:

Some key columns are as follows:

- **Threads**   The Threads column shows the number of threads in each process. This number should normally be at least one, as there's no direct way of creating a process with no threads (and such a process is pretty useless anyway). If a process shows zero threads, it usually means the process can't be deleted for some reason—probably because of some buggy driver code.

- **Handles**   The Handles column shows the number of handles to kernel objects opened by threads running within the process. (This is described later in this chapter and in detail in Chapter 8 in Part 2.)

- **Status**   The Status column is a little bit tricky. For processes that don't have any user interface, Running should be the normal case, although the threads may all be waiting for something, such as a kernel object being signaled or some I/O operation to complete. The other option for such processes is Suspended, and this happens if all the threads in the process are in a suspended state. This is unlikely to occur by the process itself, but can be achieved programmatically by calling the undocumented NtSuspendProcess native API on the process, typically through a tool (for example, Process Explorer, described later, has such an option). For processes that create a user interface, the Running status value means that the UI is responsive. In other words, the thread that created the window(s) is waiting for UI input (technically, the message queue associated with the thread). The Suspended state is possible just like in the non-UI case, but for Windows Apps (those hosting the Windows Runtime), Suspended normally occurs when the app loses its foreground status by being minimized by the user. Such processes are suspended after 5 seconds so that they don't consume any CPU or networking resources, thus allowing the new foreground app to get all machine resources. This is especially important for battery-powered devices, such as tablets and phones. This and other related mechanisms are described more fully in Chapter 9 in Part 2. The third possible value for Status is Not Responding. This can happen if a thread within the process that created the user interface has not checked its message queue for UI-related activity for at least 5 seconds. The process (actually the thread that owns the window) may be busy doing some CPU-intensive work or waiting on something else entirely (such as an I/O operation to complete). Either way, the UI freezes up, and Windows indicates that by fading the window(s) in question and appending "(Not Responding)" to its title.

Each process also points to its parent or creator process (which may be, but is not always, its creator process). If the parent no longer exists, this information is not updated. Therefore, it is possible for a process to refer to a nonexistent parent. This is not a problem, because nothing relies on this information being kept current. In the case of the Process Explorer tool, the start time of the parent process is taken into account to avoid attaching a child process based on a reused process ID. The following experiment illustrates this behavior.

Note Why would a parent process not be the same as its creator? In certain cases, some processes that appear to be created by a certain user application might involve the help of a broker, or helper, process, which is responsible for calling the process creation API. In such cases, it would be confusing (and sometimes incorrect, if handle or address space inheritance is needed) to display the broker process as the creator, and a "re-parenting" is done. You'll learn about one such example in Chapter 7, "Security."

EXPERIMENT: Viewing the process tree

One unique attribute about a process that most tools don't display is the parent or creator process ID. You can retrieve this value with the Performance Monitor (or programmatically) by querying the Creating Process ID. You can use the Tlist.exe tool in the Debugging Tools for Windows to show the process tree by using the /t switch. Here's an example of output from `tlist /t`:

```
System Process (0)
System (4)
  smss.exe (360)
csrss.exe (460)
wininit.exe (524)
  services.exe (648)
    svchost.exe (736)
      unsecapp.exe (2516)
      WmiPrvSE.exe (2860)
      WmiPrvSE.exe (2512)
      RuntimeBroker.exe (3104)
      SkypeHost.exe (2776)
      ShellExperienceHost.exe (3760) Windows Shell Experience Host
      ApplicationFrameHost.exe (2848) OleMainThreadWndName
      SearchUI.exe (3504) Cortana
      WmiPrvSE.exe (1576)
      TiWorker.exe (6032)
      wuapihost.exe (5088)
    svchost.exe (788)
    svchost.exe (932)
    svchost.exe (960)
    svchost.exe (976)
    svchost.exe (68)
    svchost.exe (380)
    VSSVC.exe (1124)
    svchost.exe (1176)
      sihost.exe (3664)
      taskhostw.exe (3032) Task Host Window
    svchost.exe (1212)
    svchost.exe (1636)
    spoolsv.exe (1644)
    svchost.exe (1936)
    OfficeClickToRun.exe (1324)
    MSOIDSVC.EXE (1256)
```

```
      MSOIDSVCM.EXE (2264)
    MBAMAgent.exe (2072)
    MsMpEng.exe (2116)
    SearchIndexer.exe (1000)
      SearchProtocolHost.exe (824)
    svchost.exe (3328)
    svchost.exe (3428)
    svchost.exe (4400)
    svchost.exe (4360)
    svchost.exe (3720)
    TrustedInstaller.exe (6052)
  lsass.exe (664)
csrss.exe (536)
winlogon.exe (600)
  dwm.exe (1100) DWM Notification Window
explorer.exe (3148) Program Manager
  OneDrive.exe (4448)
  cmd.exe (5992) C:\windows\system32\cmd.exe - tlist  /t
    conhost.exe (3120) CicMarshalWnd
    tlist.exe (5888)
SystemSettingsAdminFlows.exe (4608)
```

The list indents each process to show its parent/child relationship. Processes whose parents aren't alive are left-justified (as explorer.exe is in the preceding example) because even if a grandparent process exists, there's no way to find that relationship. Windows maintains only the creator process ID, not a link back to the creator of the creator, and so forth.

The number in parentheses is the process ID, and the text that follows some processes is the title of a window that was created by that process.

To prove that Windows doesn't keep track of more than just the parent process ID, follow these steps:

1. Press **WinKey+R**, type **cmd**, and press **Enter** to open a Command Prompt window.

2. Type **title Parent** to change the title of the window to *Parent*.

3. Type **start cmd** to open a second Command Prompt window.

4. Type **title Child** in the second Command Prompt window.

5. Type **mspaint** in the second Command Prompt window to start Microsoft Paint.

6. Go back to the second Command Prompt window and type **exit**. Notice that Paint remains.

7. Press **Ctrl+Shift+Esc** to open Task Manager.

8. If Task Manager is in "less details" mode, click **More Details**.

9. Click the **Processes** tab.

10. Find the Windows Command Processor app and expand its node. You should see the title *Parent*, as in the following screenshot:

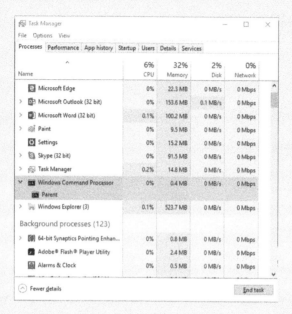

11. Right-click the **Windows Command Processor** entry and select **Go to details**.

12. Right-click this **cmd.exe** process and select **End Process Tree**.

13. Click **End Process Tree** in the Task Manager confirmation dialog box.

The first Command Prompt window will disappear, but you should still see the Paint window because it was the grandchild of the command prompt process you terminated. Because the intermediate process (the parent of Paint) was terminated, there was no link between the parent and the grandchild.

Process Explorer, from Sysinternals, shows more details about processes and threads than any other available tool, which is why you will see it used in a number of experiments throughout the book. Following are some of the unique things that Process Explorer shows or enables:

- A process security token, such as lists of groups and privileges and the virtualization state

- Highlighting to show changes in the process, thread, DLLs, and handles list

- A list of services inside service-hosting processes, including the display name and description

- A list of additional process attributes, such as mitigation policies and their process protection level

- Processes that are part of a job and job details

- Processes hosting .NET applications and .NET-specific details, such as the list of AppDomains, loaded assemblies, and CLR performance counters

- Processes that host the Windows Runtime (immersive processes)

- The start time for processes and threads

- A complete list of memory-mapped files (not just DLLs)

- The ability to suspend a process or a thread

- The ability to kill an individual thread

- Easy identification of which processes were consuming the most CPU over a period of time

 Note The Performance Monitor can display process CPU utilization for a given set of processes, but it won't automatically show processes created after the performance-monitoring session has started. Only a manual trace in binary output format can do that.

Process Explorer also provides easy access to information in one place, such as the following:

- A process tree, with the ability to collapse parts of the tree

- Open handles in a process, including unnamed handles

- A list of DLLs (and memory-mapped files) in a process

- Thread activity within a process

- User-mode and kernel-mode thread stacks, including the mapping of addresses to names using the Dbghelp.dll that comes with the Debugging Tools for Windows

  - More accurate CPU percentage using the thread cycle count—an even better representation of precise CPU activity, as explained in Chapter 4, "Threads."

  - Integrity level

- Memory manager details such as peak commit charge and kernel memory paged and non-paged pool limits (other tools show only current size)

An introductory experiment using Process Explorer follows.

EXPERIMENT: Viewing process details with Process Explorer

Download the latest version of Process Explorer from Sysinternals and run it. You can run it with standard user privileges. Alternatively, right-click the executable and select **Run as Administrator** to run it with administrator privileges. Running with admin privileges causes Process Explorer to install a driver that provides more features. The following description works the same regardless of how you launch Process Explorer.

The first time you run Process Explorer, you should configure symbols. If you don't, you will receive a message that symbols are not currently configured when you double-click a process and click the **Threads** tab. If properly configured, Process Explorer can access symbol information to display the symbolic name of the thread start function as well as functions on a thread's call stack. This is useful for identifying what threads are doing within a process. To access symbols, you must have Debugging Tools for Windows installed (described later in this chapter). Then click **Options**, choose **Configure Symbols**, and fill in the path to Dbghelp.dll in the Debugging Tools folder and a valid symbol path. For example, on a 64-bit system, this configuration is correct if Debugging Tools for Windows are installed in the default location as part of the WDK:

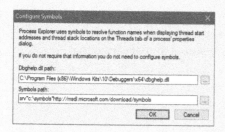

In the preceding example, the on-demand symbol server is used to access symbols and a copy of the symbol files is stored on the local machine in the C:\symbols folder. (You can replace this folder with some other folder, such as on another drive, if free disk space is an issue.) For more information on configuring the use of the symbol server, see *https://msdn.microsoft.com/en-us/library/windows/desktop/ee416588.aspx*.

 Tip You can configure the Microsoft symbol server by setting an environment variable named _NT_SYMBOL_PATH to the value shown in the preceding graphic. Various tools look for this variable automatically, such as Process Explorer, the debuggers that are part of the Debugging Tools for Windows, Visual Studio, and others. This will help you avoid having to configure each tool separately.

When Process Explorer starts, it shows the process tree view by default. You can expand the lower pane to display open handles or mapped DLLs and memory-mapped files. (These are explored in Chapter 5, "Memory management," and in Chapter 8 in Part 2.) It also shows a tooltip for the process command line and path, which becomes visible when you hover the mouse over the process name. For some types of processes, the tooltip also shows extra information, including the following:

- The services inside a service-hosting process (for example, Svchost.exe)

- The tasks inside a task-hosting process (for example, TaskHostw.exe)

- The target of a Rundll32.exe process, used for Control Panel items and other features

- The COM class information when being hosted inside a Dllhost.exe process (also known as the default COM+ surrogate)

- Provider information for Windows Management Instrumentation (WMI) host processes such as WMIPrvSE.exe (see Chapter 8 in Part 2 for more on WMI)

- Package information for Windows Apps processes (processes hosting the Windows Runtime, briefly discussed in "The Windows Runtime" section earlier in this chapter)

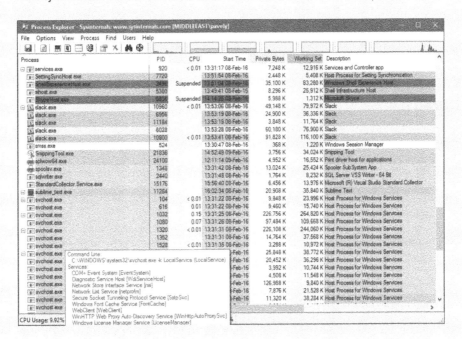

Here are a few steps to walk you through some basic capabilities of Process Explorer:

1. Notice that processes hosting services are highlighted by default in pink. Your own processes are highlighted in blue. You can change these colors by opening the drop-down menu, selecting **Options**, and choosing **Configure Colors**.

2. Hover your mouse pointer over the image name for processes. Notice that the tooltip displays the full path. As noted, certain types of processes have additional details in the tooltip.

3. In the Process Image tab, click **View**, choose **Select Columns**, and add the image path.

4. Click the **Process** column head to sort the processes. Notice that the tree view disappears. (You can either display the tree view or sort by any of the columns shown.) Click the **Process** column head again to sort from Z to A. Click it a third time to return the display to tree view.

5. Open the **View** menu and deselect **Show Processes from All Users** to show only your processes.

6. Click the **Options** menu, choose **Difference Highlight Duration**, and change the value to 3 seconds. Then launch a new process (anything). Notice that the new process is highlighted in green for 3 seconds. Exit this new process, and notice that the process is highlighted in red for 3 seconds before disappearing from the display. This can be useful for seeing processes being created and exiting on your system.

7. Double-click a process and explore the various tabs available from the process properties display. (These will be referenced in various experiments throughout the book where the information being shown is being explained.)

Threads

A *thread* is an entity within a process that Windows schedules for execution. Without it, the process's program can't run. A thread includes the following essential components:

- The contents of a set of CPU registers representing the state of the processor

- Two stacks—one for the thread to use while executing in kernel mode and one for executing in user mode

- A private storage area called *thread-local storage* (*TLS*) for use by subsystems, run-time libraries, and DLLs

- A unique identifier called a *thread ID* (part of an internal structure called a *client ID*; process IDs and thread IDs are generated out of the same namespace, so they never overlap)

In addition, threads sometimes have their own security context, or token, which is often used by multithreaded server applications that impersonate the security context of the clients that they serve.

The volatile registers, stacks, and private storage area are called the thread's *context*. Because this information is different for each machine architecture that Windows runs on, this structure, by necessity, is architecture-specific. The Windows GetThreadContext function provides access to this architecture-specific information (called the CONTEXT block).

Because switching execution from one thread to another involves the kernel scheduler, it can be an expensive operation, especially if two threads are often switching between each other. Windows implements two mechanisms to reduce this cost: *fibers* and *user-mode scheduling* (*UMS*).

Note The threads of a 32-bit application running on a 64-bit version of Windows will contain both 32-bit and 64-bit contexts, which Wow64 (Windows on Windows) will use to switch the application from running in 32-bit to 64-bit mode when required. These threads will have two user stacks and two CONTEXT blocks, and the usual Windows API functions will return the 64-bit context instead. The Wow64GetThreadContext function, however, will return the 32-bit context. See Chapter 8 in Part 2 for more information on Wow64.

Fibers

Fibers allow an application to schedule its own threads of execution rather than rely on the priority-based scheduling mechanism built into Windows. Fibers are often called *lightweight threads*. In terms of scheduling, they're invisible to the kernel because they're implemented in user mode in Kernel32.dll. To use fibers, you first make a call to the Windows ConvertThreadToFiber function. This function converts the thread to a running fiber. Afterward, the newly converted fiber can create additional fibers via the CreateFiber function. (Each fiber can have its own set of fibers.) Unlike a thread, however, a fiber doesn't begin execution until it's manually selected through a call to the SwitchToFiber function. The new fiber runs until it exits or until it calls SwitchToFiber, again selecting another fiber to run. For more information, see the Windows SDK documentation on fiber functions.

Note Using fibers is usually not a good idea. This is because they are invisible to the kernel. They also have issues such as sharing thread local storage (TLS) because several fibers can be running on the same thread. Although fiber local storage (FLS) exists, this does not solve all sharing issues, and I/O-bound fibers will perform poorly regardless. Additionally, fibers cannot run concurrently on more than one processor, and are limited to cooperative multitasking only. In most scenarios, it's best to let the Windows kernel handle scheduling by using the appropriate threads for the task at hand.

User-mode scheduling threads

User-mode scheduling (UMS) threads, which are available only on 64-bit versions of Windows, provide the same basic advantages as fibers—and only a few of the disadvantages. UMS threads have their own kernel thread state and are therefore visible to the kernel, which allows multiple UMS threads to issue blocking system calls and share and contend on resources. Or, when two or more UMS threads need to perform work in user mode, they can periodically switch execution contexts (by yielding from one thread to another) in user mode rather than involving the scheduler. From the kernel's perspective, the same kernel thread is still running and nothing has changed. When a UMS thread performs an operation that requires entering the kernel (such as a system call), it switches to its dedicated kernel-mode thread (called a *directed context switch*). While concurrent UMS threads still cannot run on multiple processors, they do follow a pre-emptible model that's not solely cooperative.

Although threads have their own execution context, every thread within a process shares the process's virtual address space (in addition to the rest of the resources belonging to the process), meaning that all the threads in a process have full read-write access to the process virtual address space. Threads cannot accidentally reference the address space of another process, however, unless the other process makes available part of its private address space as a shared memory section (called a *file mapping object* in the Windows API) or unless one process has the right to open another process to use cross-process memory functions, such as ReadProcessMemory and WriteProcessMemory (which a process that's running with the same user account, and not inside of an AppContainer or other type of sandbox, can get by default unless the target process has certain protections).

In addition to a private address space and one or more threads, each process has a security context and a list of open handles to kernel objects such as files, shared memory sections, or one of the synchronization objects such as mutexes, events, or semaphores, as illustrated in Figure 1-2.

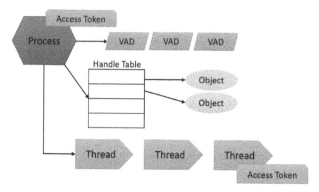

FIGURE 1-2 A process and its resources.

Each process's security context is stored in an object called an *access token*. The process access token contains the security identification and credentials for the process. By default, threads don't have their own access token, but they can obtain one, thus allowing individual threads to impersonate the security context of another process—including processes on a remote Windows system—without affecting other threads in the process. (See Chapter 7 for more details on process and thread security.)

The *virtual address descriptors* (*VADs*) are data structures that the memory manager uses to keep track of the virtual addresses the process is using. These data structures are described in more depth in Chapter 5.

Jobs

Windows provides an extension to the process model called a *job*. A job object's main function is to allow the management and manipulation of groups of processes as a unit. A job object allows control of certain attributes and provides limits for the process or processes associated with the job. It also records basic accounting information for all processes associated with the job and for all processes that were associated with the job but have since terminated. In some ways, the job object compensates for the lack of a structured process tree in Windows—yet in many ways it is more powerful than a UNIX-style process tree.

> **Note** Process Explorer can show processes managed by a job using a default color of brown, but it's not enabled by default (to enable it, open the **Options** menu and choose **Configure Colors**). Furthermore, the property pages of such a process have an additional Job tab that gives information on the job object itself.

You'll find out much more about the internal structure of processes and jobs in Chapter 3 and about threads and thread-scheduling algorithms in Chapter 4.

Virtual memory

Windows implements a virtual memory system based on a flat (linear) address space that provides each process with the illusion of having its own large, private address space. Virtual memory provides a logical view of memory that might not correspond to its physical layout. At run time, the memory manager—with assistance from hardware—translates, or *maps*, the virtual addresses into physical addresses, where the data is actually stored. By controlling the protection and mapping, the OS can ensure that individual processes don't bump into each other or overwrite OS data.

Because most systems have much less physical memory than the total virtual memory in use by the running processes, the memory manager transfers, or *pages*, some of the memory contents to disk. Paging data to disk frees physical memory so that it can be used for other processes or for the OS itself. When a thread accesses a virtual address that has been paged to disk, the virtual memory manager loads the information back into memory from disk.

Applications don't have to be altered in any way to take advantage of paging because hardware support enables the memory manager to page without the knowledge or assistance of processes or threads. Figure 1-3 shows two processes using virtual memory in which parts are mapped to physical memory (RAM) while other parts are paged to disk. Notice that contiguous virtual memory chunks may be mapped to non-contiguous chunks in physical memory. These chunks are called pages, and have a default size of 4 KB.

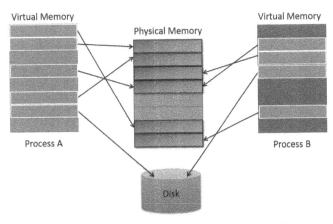

FIGURE 1-3 Mapping virtual memory to physical memory with paging.

The size of the virtual address space varies for each hardware platform. On 32-bit x86 systems, the total virtual address space has a theoretical maximum of 4 GB. By default, Windows allocates the lower half of this address space (addresses 0x00000000 through 0x7FFFFFFF) to processes for their unique private storage and the upper half (addresses 0x80000000 through 0xFFFFFFFF) for its own protected OS memory utilization. The mappings of the lower half change to reflect the virtual address space of the currently executing process, but (most of) the mappings of the upper half always consist of the OS's virtual memory. Windows supports boot-time options, such as the `increaseuserva` qualifier in the Boot Configuration Database (described in Chapter 5), that give processes running specially marked programs the ability to use up to 3 GB of private address space, leaving 1 GB for the OS. (By "specially marked," we mean the large address space–aware flag must be set in the header of the executable image.) This option allows applications such as database servers to keep larger portions of a database in the process address space, thus reducing the need to map subset views of the database on disk and therefore increasing overall performance (although in certain cases, the loss of 1 GB for the system can cause more pronounced system-wide performance losses). Figure 1-4 shows the two typical virtual address space layouts supported by 32-bit Windows. (The `increaseuserva` option allows executable images marked with the large address space–aware flag to use anywhere from 2 to 3 GB.)

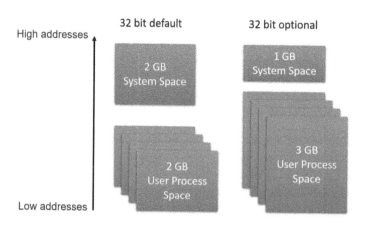

FIGURE 1-4 Typical address space layouts for 32-bit Windows.

Although 3 GB is better than 2 GB, it's still not enough virtual address space to map very large (multi-gigabyte) databases. To address this need on 32-bit systems, Windows provides a mechanism called *Address Windowing Extensions* (*AWE*), which allows a 32-bit application to allocate up to 64 GB of physical memory and then map views, or windows, into its 2 GB virtual address space. Although using AWE puts the burden of managing the mapping of virtual to physical memory on the developer, it does address the need to directly access more physical memory than can be mapped at any one time in a 32-bit process address space.

64-bit Windows provides a much larger address space for processes: 128 TB on Windows 8.1, Server 2012 R2, and later systems. Figure 1-5 shows a simplified view of the 64-bit system address space layouts. (For a detailed description, see Chapter 5.) Note that these sizes do not represent the architectural limits for these platforms. Sixty-four bits of address space is 2 to the 64th power, or 16 EB (where 1 EB equals 1,024 PB, or 1,048,576 TB), but current 64-bit hardware limits this to smaller values. The unmapped region marked in figure 1-5 is much larger than the possible mapped region (about one million times larger on Windows 8), which means the images are (by far) not to scale.

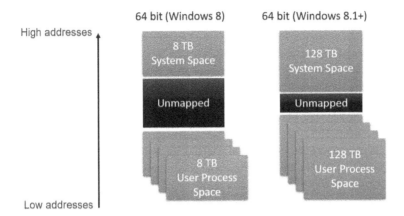

FIGURE 1-5 Address space layouts for 64-bit Windows.

Details of the implementation of the memory manager, including how address translation works and how Windows manages physical memory, are described in Chapter 5.

Kernel mode vs. user mode

To protect user applications from accessing and/or modifying critical OS data, Windows uses two processor access modes (even if the processor on which Windows is running supports more than two): *user mode* and *kernel mode*. User application code runs in user mode, whereas OS code (such as system services and device drivers) runs in kernel mode. Kernel mode refers to a mode of execution in a processor that grants access to all system memory and all CPU instructions. Some processors differentiate between such modes by using the term *code privilege level* or *ring level*, while others use terms such as *supervisor mode* and *application mode*. Regardless of what it's called, by providing the operating system kernel with a higher privilege level than user mode applications have, the processor provides a necessary foundation for OS designers to ensure that a misbehaving application can't disrupt the stability of the system as a whole.

Note The architectures of the x86 and x64 processors define four privilege levels (or rings) to protect system code and data from being overwritten either inadvertently or maliciously by code of lesser privilege. Windows uses privilege level 0 (or ring 0) for kernel mode and privilege level 3 (or ring 3) for user mode. The reason Windows uses only two levels is that some hardware architectures, such as ARM today and MIPS/Alpha in the past, implemented only two privilege levels. Settling on the lowest minimum bar allowed for a more efficient and portable architecture, especially as the other x86/x64 ring levels do not provide the same guarantees as the ring 0/ring 3 divide.

Although each Windows process has its own private memory space, the kernel-mode OS and device-driver code share a single virtual address space. Each page in virtual memory is tagged to indicate what access mode the processor must be in to read and/or write the page. Pages in system space can be accessed only from kernel mode, whereas all pages in the user address space are accessible from user mode and kernel mode. Read-only pages (such as those that contain static data) are not writable from any mode. Additionally, on processors that support no-execute memory protection, Windows marks pages containing data as non-executable, thus preventing inadvertent or malicious code execution in data areas (if this feature, Data Execution Prevention [DEP] is enabled).

Windows doesn't provide any protection for private read/write system memory being used by components running in kernel mode. In other words, once in kernel mode, OS and device-driver code has complete access to system-space memory and can bypass Windows security to access objects. Because the bulk of the Windows OS code runs in kernel mode, it is vital that components that run in kernel mode be carefully designed and tested to ensure they don't violate system security or cause system instability.

This lack of protection also emphasizes the need to remain vigilant when loading a third-party device driver, especially if it's unsigned, because once in kernel mode, the driver has complete access to all OS data. This risk was one of the reasons behind the driver-signing mechanism introduced in Windows 2000, which warns (and, if configured as such, blocks) the user if an attempt is made to add an unsigned plug-and-play driver (see Chapter 6, "I/O system," for more information on driver signing), but does not affect other types of drivers. Also, a mechanism called Driver Verifier helps device-driver writers find bugs, such as buffer overruns or memory leaks, that can cause security or reliability issues. (Chapter 6 also discusses Driver Verifier.)

On 64-bit and ARM versions of Windows 8.1, the kernel-mode code-signing (KMCS) policy dictates that all device drivers (not just plug-and-play) must be signed with a cryptographic key assigned by one of the major code certification authorities. The user cannot explicitly force the installation of an unsigned driver, even as an administrator. As a one-time exception, however, this restriction can be disabled manually. This allows drivers to be self-signed and tested, places a watermark on the desktop wallpaper labeled "Test Mode," and disables certain digital rights management (DRM) features.

On Windows 10, Microsoft implemented an even more significant change, which was enforced starting one year after release as part of the July Anniversary Update (version 1607). As of that time, all new Windows 10 drivers must be signed by only two of the accepted certification authorities with a SHA-2 Extended Validation (EV) Hardware certificate instead of the regular file-based SHA-1 certificate and its 20 authorities. Once EV-signed, the hardware driver must be submitted to Microsoft through the System Device (SysDev) portal for attestation signing, which will see the driver receive a Microsoft signature. As such, the kernel will sign only Microsoft-signed Windows 10 drivers with no exemptions except the aforementioned Test Mode. Drivers signed before the release date of Windows 10 (July 2015) can continue to load with their regular signature for the time being.

With Windows Server 2016, the operating system takes its strongest stance yet. On top of the aforementioned EV requirements, mere attestation signing is insufficient. For a Windows 10 driver to load on a server system, it must pass through stringent Windows Hardware Quality Labs (WHQL) certification as part of the Hardware Compatibility Kit (HCK) and be submitted for formal evaluation. Only WHQL-signed drivers—which provide certain compatibility, security, performance, and stability assurances to system administrators

—will be allowed to load on such systems. All in all, the reduction of third-party drivers that are allowed to load in kernel mode memory should result in significant stability and security improvements.

Certain vendors, platforms, and even enterprise configurations of Windows can have any number of these signing policies customized, such as through the Device Guard technology, which we'll briefly describe in the upcoming "Hypervisor" section, and later in Chapter 7. As such, an enterprise might require WHQL signatures even on Windows 10 client systems, or might request the omission of this requirement on a Windows Server 2016 system.

As you'll see in Chapter 2, "System architecture," user applications switch from user mode to kernel mode when they make a system service call. For example, a Windows `ReadFile` function eventually needs to call the internal Windows routine that actually handles reading data from a file. That routine, because it accesses internal system data structures, must run in kernel mode. The use of a special processor instruction triggers the transition from user mode to kernel mode and causes the processor to enter the system service dispatching code in the kernel. This in turn calls the appropriate internal function in Ntoskrnl.exe or Win32k.sys. Before returning control to the user thread, the processor mode is switched back to user mode. In this way, the OS protects itself and its data from perusal and modification by user processes.

 Note A transition from user mode to kernel mode (and back) does not affect thread scheduling *per se*. A mode transition is *not* a context switch. Further details on system service dispatching are included in Chapter 2.

Thus, it's normal for a user thread to spend part of its time executing in user mode and part in kernel mode. In fact, because the bulk of the graphics and windowing system also runs in kernel mode, graphics-intensive applications spend more of their time in kernel mode than in user mode. An easy way to test this is to run a graphics-intensive application such as Microsoft Paint and watch the time split between user mode and kernel mode using one of the performance counters listed in Table 1-3. More advanced applications can use newer technologies such as Direct2D and DirectComposition, which perform bulk computations in user mode and send only the raw surface data to the kernel. This reduces the time spent transitioning between user and kernel modes.

TABLE 1-3 Mode-related performance counters

Object: Counter	Function
Processor: % Privileged Time	Percentage of time that an individual CPU (or all CPUs) has run in kernel mode during a specified interval
Processor: % User Time	Percentage of time that an individual CPU (or all CPUs) has run in user mode during a specified interval
Process: % Privileged Time	Percentage of time that the threads in a process have run in kernel mode during a specified interval
Process: % User Time	Percentage of time that the threads in a process have run in user mode during a specified interval
Thread: % Privileged Time	Percentage of time that a thread has run in kernel mode during a specified interval
Thread: % User Time	Percentage of time that a thread has run in user mode during a specified interval

EXPERIMENT: Kernel mode vs. user mode

You can use the Performance Monitor to see how much time your system spends executing in kernel mode versus in user mode. Follow these steps:

1. Open the **Start** menu and type **Run Performance Monitor** (it should be suggested before you finish typing) to run Performance Monitor.

2. Select the **Performance Monitor** node under Performance/Monitoring Tools in the tree on the left side.

3. To delete the default counter showing the total CPU time, click the **Delete** button on the toolbar or press the **Suppr** key on the keyboard.

4. Click the **Add (+)** button on the toolbar.

5. Expand the **Processor** counter section, click the **% Privileged Time** counter, and, while holding down the **Ctrl** key, click the **% User Time** counter.

6. Click **Add**, and then click **OK**.

7. Open a command prompt and type **dir \\%computername%\c$ /s** to run a directory scan of your C drive.

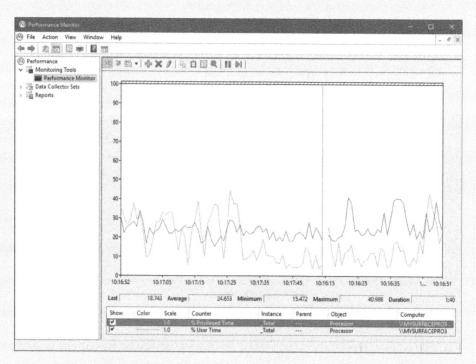

8. When you're finished, close the tool.

You can also quickly see this by using Task Manager. Just click the **Performance** tab, right-click the CPU graph, and select **Show Kernel Times**. The CPU usage bar will show kernel-mode CPU time usage in a darker shade of light blue.

To see how the Performance Monitor itself uses kernel time and user time, run it again, but add the individual process counters % User Time and % Privileged Time for every process in the system:

1. If it's not already running, run the Performance Monitor again. (If it is already running, start with a blank display by right-clicking in the graph area and selecting **Remove All Counters**.)

2. Click the **Add** button on the toolbar.

3. In the available counters area, expand the **Process** section.

4. Select the **% Privileged Time** and **% User Time** counters.

5. Select a few processes in the Instance box (such as **mmc**, **csrss**, and **Idle**).

6. Click **Add**, and then click **OK**.

7. Move the mouse rapidly back and forth.

8. Press **Ctrl+H** to turn on highlighting mode. This highlights the currently selected counter in black.

9. Scroll through the counters at the bottom of the display to identify the processes whose threads were running when you moved the mouse, and note whether they were running in user mode or kernel mode.

When you move the mouse, you should see the kernel-mode *and* user-mode time increase in the Instance column of the mmc process in the Process Monitor. This is because the process is executing application code in user mode and calling Windows functions that run in kernel mode. You'll also notice kernel-mode thread activity in a process named *csrss* when you move the mouse. This activity occurs because the Windows subsystem's kernel-mode raw input thread, which handles keyboard and mouse input, is attached to this process. (See Chapter 2 for more information about system threads and subsystems.) Finally, the Idle process that you see spending nearly 100 percent of its time in kernel mode isn't really a process—it's a fake process used to account for idle CPU cycles. As you can observe from the mode in which the threads in the Idle process run, when Windows has nothing to do, it does it in kernel mode.

Hypervisor

Recent shifts in application and software models, such as the introduction of cloud-based services and the pervasiveness of IoT devices, have resulted in the need for operating systems and hardware vendors to figure out more efficient ways to virtualize other OS guests on the host hardware of the machine, whether to allow for hosting multiple tenants on a server farm and run 100 isolated websites on a single server or to permit developers to test dozens of different OS varieties without buying dedicated hardware. The need for fast, efficient, and secure virtualization has driven new models of computing and reasoning about software. In fact, today, certain software—such as Docker, which is supported in Windows 10 and Server 2016—runs in containers, which provide fully isolated virtual machines solely designed for running a single application stack or framework, pushing the boundaries of a guest/host even further.

To provide such virtualization services, almost all modern solutions employ the use of a *hypervisor*, which is a specialized and highly privileged component that allows for the virtualization and isolation of all resources on the machine, from virtual to physical memory, to device interrupts, and even to PCI and USB devices. Hyper-V is an example of such a hypervisor, which powers the Hyper-V client functionality exposed in Windows 8.1 and later. Competing products such as Xen, KVM, VMware, and VirtualBox all implement their own hypervisors, each with their own strengths and weaknesses.

Due to its highly privileged nature, and because it has access even greater than the kernel itself, a hypervisor has a distinct advantage that goes beyond merely running multiple guest instances of other operating systems: It can protect and monitor a single host instance to offer assurances and guarantees beyond what the kernel provides. In Windows 10, Microsoft now leverages the Hyper-V hypervisor to provide a new set of services known as *virtualization-based security* (*VBS*):

- **Device Guard** This provides Hypervisor Code Integrity (HVCI) for stronger code-signing guarantees over KMCS alone, and allows for the customization of the signature policy of the Windows OS, for both user-mode and kernel-mode code.

- **Hyper Guard** This protects key kernel-related and hypervisor-related data structures and code.

- **Credential Guard** This prevents unauthorized access to domain account credentials and secrets, combined with secure biometrics.

- **Application Guard** This provides an even stronger sandbox for the Microsoft Edge browser.

- **Host Guardian and Shielded Fabric** These leverage a virtual TPM (v-TPM) to protect a virtual machine from the infrastructure it's running on.

Additionally, the Hyper-V hypervisor enables certain key kernel mitigations against exploits and other attackers. The key advantage of all these technologies is that unlike previous kernel-based security improvements, they are not vulnerable to malicious or badly written drivers, regardless of whether they are signed or not. This makes them highly resilient against today's advanced adversaries. This is possible due to the hypervisor's implementation of Virtual Trust Levels (VTLs). Because the normal operating system and its components are in a less privileged mode (VTL 0), but these VBS technologies run at VTL 1 (a higher privilege), they cannot be affected even by kernel mode code. As such, code remains within the realm of the VTL 0 privilege space. In this way, you can think of VTLs as orthogonal to the processor's privilege levels: kernel and user mode exist *within* each VTL, and the hypervisor manages privileges *across* VTLs. Chapter 2 covers additional details on the hypervisor-assisted architecture, and Chapter 7 discusses these VBS security mechanisms in detail.

Firmware

Windows components increasingly rely on the security of the operating system and its kernel, and the latter now relies on the protection of the hypervisor. A question arises of what can ensure these components are loaded securely and can authenticate their contents. This is typically the job of the boot loader, but it, too, needs the same level of authenticity checking, creating an increasingly complicated hierarchy of trust.

What, then, provides a root chain of trust that can guarantee an unencumbered boot process? In modern Windows 8 and later systems, this falls under the purview of the system firmware, which must be UEFI-based on certified systems. As part of the UEFI standard, which Windows dictates (UEFI 2.3.1b; see *http://www.uefi.org* for more information), a secure boot implementation with strong guarantees and requirements around the signature qualities of the boot-related software must be present. Through this verification process, Windows components are guaranteed to load securely from the very beginning of the boot process. In addition, technologies such as Trusted Platform Module (TPM) can measure the process to provide attestation (both local and remote). Through partnerships with the industry, Microsoft manages the whitelist and blacklist of the UEFI secure boot component in case of boot software errors or compromise, and Windows updates now include firmware updates as well. Although we won't talk about firmware again until Chapter 11, "Startup and shutdown," in Part 2, it's important now to state its significance in modern Windows architecture, through the guarantees its meant to provide.

Terminal Services and multiple sessions

Terminal Services refers to the support in Windows for multiple interactive user sessions on a single system. With Windows Terminal Services, a remote user can establish a session on another machine, log in, and run applications on the server. The server transmits the graphical user interface (GUI) to the client (as well as other configurable resources such as audio and clipboard), and the client transmits the user's input back to the server. (Similar to the X Window System, Windows permits running individual applications on a server system with the display remoted to the client instead of remoting the entire desktop.)

The first session is considered the services session, or session zero, and contains system service hosting processes (explained in further detail in Chapter 9 in Part 2). The first login session at the physical console of the machine is session one, and additional sessions can be created through the use of the remote desktop connection program (Mstsc.exe) or through the use of fast user switching.

Windows client editions permit a single remote user to connect to the machine, but if someone is logged in at the console, the workstation is locked. That is, someone can be using the system either locally or remotely, but not at the same time. Windows editions that include Windows Media Center allow one interactive session and up to four Windows Media Center Extender sessions.

Windows server systems support two simultaneous remote connections. This is to facilitate remote management—for example, using management tools that require you to be logged in to the machine being managed. They also support more than two remote sessions if appropriately licensed and configured as a terminal server.

All Windows client editions support multiple sessions, created locally through a feature called *fast user switching*, that can be used one at a time. When a user chooses to disconnect their session instead of log off (for example, by clicking the **Start** button, clicking the current user, and choosing **Switch Account** from the submenu that appears or by holding down the **Windows** key, pressing **L**, and then clicking a different user in the bottom-left corner of the screen), the current session—that is, the processes running in that session and all the session-wide data structures that describe the session—remains active in the system and the system returns to the main logon screen (if it's not already there). If a new user logs in, a new session is created.

For applications that want to be aware of running in a terminal server session, there are a set of Windows APIs for programmatically detecting that as well as for controlling various aspects of Terminal Services. (See the Windows SDK and the Remote Desktop Services API for details.)

Chapter 2 briefly describes how sessions are created and contains some experiments showing how to view session information with various tools, including the kernel debugger. The "Object manager" section in Chapter 8 in Part 2 describes how the system namespace for objects is instantiated on a per-session basis and how applications that need to be aware of other instances of themselves on the same system can accomplish that. Finally, Chapter 5 covers how the memory manager sets up and manages session-wide data.

Objects and handles

In the Windows OS, a *kernel object* is a single, run-time instance of a statically defined object type. An *object type* comprises a system-defined data type, functions that operate on instances of the data type, and a set of object attributes. If you write Windows applications, you might encounter process, thread, file, and event objects, to name just a few examples. These objects are based on lower-level objects that Windows creates and manages. In Windows, a *process* is an instance of the process object type, a *file* is an instance of the file object type, and so on.

An *object attribute* is a field of data in an object that partially defines the object's state. An object of type *process*, for example, would have attributes that include the process ID, a base scheduling priority, and a pointer to an access token object. *Object methods*, the means for manipulating objects, usually read or change object attributes. For example, the *open* method for a process would accept a process identifier as input and return a pointer to the object as output.

> **Note** There is a parameter named ObjectAttributes that a caller supplies when creating an object using the kernel object manager APIs. That parameter shouldn't be confused with the more general meaning of the term as used in this book, however.

The most fundamental difference between an object and an ordinary data structure is that the internal structure of an object is opaque. You must call an object service to get data out of or put data into an object. You can't directly read or change data inside an object. This difference separates the underlying implementation of the object from code that merely uses it, a technique that allows object implementations to be changed easily over time.

Objects, through the help of a kernel component called the *object manager*, provide a convenient means for accomplishing the following four important OS tasks:

- Providing human-readable names for system resources

- Sharing resources and data among processes

- Protecting resources from unauthorized access

- Reference tracking, which allows the system to recognize when an object is no longer in use so that it can be automatically deallocated

Not all data structures in the Windows OS are objects. Only data that needs to be shared, protected, named, or made visible to user-mode programs (via system services) is placed in objects. Structures used by only one component of the OS to implement internal functions are not objects. Objects and handles (references to instances of an object) are discussed in more detail in Chapter 8 in Part 2.

Security

Windows was designed from the start to be secure and to meet the requirements of various formal government and industry security ratings, such as the Common Criteria for Information Technology Security Evaluation (CCITSE) specification. Achieving a government-approved security rating allows an OS to compete in that arena. Of course, many of these capabilities are advantageous features for any multiuser system.

The core security capabilities of Windows include:

- Discretionary (need-to-know) and mandatory protection for all shareable system objects, such as files, directories, processes, threads, and so forth

- Security auditing for accountability of subjects, or users, and the actions they initiate

- User authentication at logon

- The prevention of one user from accessing uninitialized resources, such as free memory or disk space, that another user has deallocated

Windows has three forms of access control over objects:

- **Discretionary access control**   This is the protection mechanism that most people think of when they think of OS security. It's the method by which owners of objects (such as files or printers) grant or deny access to others. When users log in, they are given a set of security credentials, or a security context. When they attempt to access objects, their security context is compared to the access control list on the object they are trying to access to determine whether they have permission to perform the requested operation. With Windows Server 2012 and Windows 8, this form of discretionary control is further improved by implementing attribute-based access control (also called Dynamic Access Control). However, a resource's access control list does not necessarily identify individual users and groups. Instead, it identifies required attributes or claims that grant access to a resource, such as "Clearance Level: Top Secret" or "Seniority: 10 Years." With the ability to populate such attributes automatically by parsing SQL databases and schemas through Active Directory, this significantly more elegant and flexible security model helps organizations avoid cumbersome manual group management and group hierarchies.

- **Privileged access control**   This is necessary for those times when discretionary access control is not enough. It's a method of ensuring that someone can get to protected objects if the owner isn't available. For example, if an employee leaves a company, the administrator needs a way to gain access to files that might have been accessible only to that employee. In that case, under Windows, the administrator can take ownership of the file so that they can manage its rights as necessary.

- **Mandatory integrity control**   This is required when an additional level of security control is needed to protect objects that are being accessed from within the same user account. It's used for everything from providing part of the sandboxing technology for Windows Apps (see the upcoming discussion), to isolating Protected Mode Internet Explorer (and other browsers) from a user's configuration, to protecting objects created by an elevated administrator account from access by a non-elevated administrator account. (See Chapter 7 for more information on User Account Control.)

Starting with Windows 8, a sandbox called an *AppContainer* is used to host Windows Apps, which provides isolation with relation to other AppContainers and non–Windows Apps processes. Code in AppContainers can communicate with brokers (non-isolated processes running with the user's credentials) and sometimes other AppContainers or processes through well-defined contracts provided by the Windows Runtime. A canonical example is the Microsoft Edge browser that runs inside an AppContainer and thus provides better protection against malicious code running within its boundaries. Additionally, third-party developers can leverage AppContainers to isolate their own non–Windows Apps applications in similar ways. The AppContainer model forces a significant shift in traditional programming paradigms, moving from the traditional multithreaded single-process application implementation to a multi-process one.

Security pervades the interface of the Windows API. The Windows subsystem implements object-based security in the same way the OS does: protecting shared Windows objects from unauthorized access by placing Windows security descriptors on them. The first time an application tries to access a shared object, the Windows subsystem verifies the application's right to do so. If the security check succeeds, the Windows subsystem allows the application to proceed.

For a comprehensive description of Windows security, see Chapter 7.

Registry

If you've worked with Windows operating systems, you've probably heard about or looked at the registry. You can't talk much about Windows internals without referring to the registry because it's the system database that contains the information required to boot and configure the system, system-wide software settings that control the operation of Windows, the security database, and per-user configuration settings such as which screen saver to use. In addition, the registry provides a window into in-memory volatile data, such as the current hardware state of the system (what device drivers are loaded, the resources they are using, and so on) as well as the Windows performance counters. The performance counters, which aren't actually *in* the registry, can be accessed through the registry functions (although there is a newer, better API for accessing performance counters). See Chapter 9 in Part 2 for more on how performance counter information is accessed from the registry.

Although many Windows users and administrators will never need to look directly into the registry (because you can view or change most configuration settings with standard administrative utilities), it is still a useful source of Windows internals information because it contains many settings that affect system performance and behavior. You'll find references to individual registry keys throughout this book as they pertain to the component being described. Most registry keys referred to in this book are under the system-wide configuration hive, HKEY_LOCAL_MACHINE, which we'll abbreviate throughout as *HKLM*.

 Caution If you decide to directly change registry settings, you must exercise extreme caution. Any changes might adversely affect system performance or, worse, cause the system to fail to boot successfully.

For further information on the registry and its internal structure, see Chapter 9 in Part 2.

Unicode

Windows differs from most other operating systems in that most internal text strings are stored and processed as 16-bit-wide Unicode characters (technically UTF-16LE; when Unicode is mentioned in this book it refers to UTF-16LE unless otherwise stated). Unicode is an international character set standard that defines unique values for most of the world's known character sets, and provides 8, 16, and even 32-bit encodings for each character.

Because many applications deal with 8-bit (single-byte) ANSI character strings, many Windows functions that accept string parameters have two entry points: a Unicode (wide, 16-bit) version and an ANSI (narrow, 8-bit) version. If you call the narrow version of a Windows function, there is a slight performance impact as input string parameters are converted to Unicode before being processed by the system and output parameters are converted from Unicode to ANSI before being returned to the application. Thus, if you have an older service or piece of code that you need to run on Windows but this code is written using ANSI character text strings, Windows will convert the ANSI characters into Unicode for its own use. However, Windows never converts the *data* inside files—it's up to the application to decide whether to store data as Unicode or as ANSI.

Regardless of language, all versions of Windows contain the same functions. Instead of having separate language versions, Windows has a single worldwide binary so that a single installation can support multiple languages (through the addition of various language packs). Applications can also take advantage of Windows functions that allow single worldwide application binaries that can support multiple languages.

Note The old Windows 9*x* operating systems did not support Unicode natively. This was yet another reason for the creation of two functions for ANSI and Unicode. For example, the Windows API function `CreateFile` is not a function at all; instead, it's a macro that expands to one of two functions: `CreateFileA` (ANSI) or `CreateFileW` (Unicode, where *W* stands for *wide*). The expansion is based on a compilation constant named `UNICODE`. It's defined by default in Visual Studio C++ projects because it's more beneficial to work with the Unicode functions. However, the explicit function name can be used in lieu of the appropriate macro. The following experiment shows these pairs of functions.

EXPERIMENT: Viewing exported functions

In this experiment, you'll use the Dependency Walker tool to view exported functions from a Windows subsystem DLL.

1. Download Dependency Walker from *http://www.dependencywalker.com*. If you have a 32-bit system, download the 32-bit version of Download Dependency. Or, if you have a 64-bit system, download the 64-bit version. Then extract the downloaded ZIP file to a folder of your choice.

2. Run the tool (depends.exe). Then open the **File** menu and choose **Open**, navigate to the C:\Windows\System32 folder (assuming Windows is installed on your C drive), locate the kernel32.dll file and click **Open**.

3. Dependency Walker may show a warning message box. Disregard it and dismiss the message box.

4. You'll see several views with vertical and horizontal splitter bars. Make sure the item selected in the top-left tree view is kernel32.dll.

5. Look at the second view from the top on the right side. This view lists the exported functions available in kernel32.dll. Click the **Function** list header to sort by name. Then locate the function `CreateFileA`. You'll find `CreateFileW` not much farther down, as shown here:

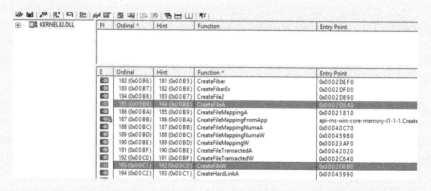

6. As you can see, most functions that have at least one string type argument are in fact pairs of functions. In the preceding graphic, the following are visible: `CreateFileMappingA/W`, `CreateFileTransactedA/W`, and `CreateFileMappingNumaA/W`.

7. You can scroll the list to locate others. You can also open other system files, such as user32.dll and advapi32.dll.

> **Note** The COM-based APIs in Windows typically use Unicode strings, sometimes typed as *BSTR*. This is essentially a null-terminated array of Unicode characters with the length of the string in bytes stored 4 bytes before the start of the array of characters in memory. The Windows Runtime APIs use Unicode strings only, typed as *HSTRING*, which is an immutable array of Unicode characters.

For more information about Unicode, see *http://www.unicode.org* and the programming documentation in the MSDN Library.

Digging into Windows internals

Although much of the information in this book is based on reading Windows source code and talking to developers, you don't have to take *everything* on faith. Many details about the internals of Windows can be exposed and demonstrated by using a variety of available tools, such as those that come with Windows and the Windows debugging tools. These tool packages are briefly described later in this section.

To encourage your exploration of Windows internals, we've included "Experiment" sidebars throughout the book that describe steps you can take to examine a particular aspect of Windows internal behavior. (You already saw a few of these sidebars earlier in this chapter.) We encourage you to try these experiments so you can see in action many of the internals topics described in this book.

Table 1-4 shows a list of the principal tools used in this book and where they come from.

TABLE 1-4 Tools for viewing Windows internals

Tool	Image Name	Origin
Startup Programs Viewer	AUTORUNS	Sysinternals
Access Check	ACCESSCHK	Sysinternals
Dependency Walker	DEPENDS	www.dependencywalker.com
Global Flags	GFLAGS	Debugging tools
Handle Viewer	HANDLE	Sysinternals

Continues...

TABLE 1-4 Tools for viewing Windows internals *(continued)*

Tool	Image Name	Origin
Kernel debuggers	WINDBG, KD	WDK, Windows SDK
Object Viewer	WINOBJ	Sysinternals
Performance Monitor	PERFMON.MSC	Windows built-in tool
Pool Monitor	POOLMON	WDK
Process Explorer	PROCEXP	Sysinternals
Process Monitor	PROCMON	Sysinternals
Task (Process) List	TLIST	Debugging tools
Task Manager	TASKMGR	Windows built-in tool

Performance Monitor and Resource Monitor

We refer to Performance Monitor—which you can access from the Administrative Tools folder in the Control Panel or by typing **perfmon** in the Run dialog box—throughout this book. Specifically, we focus on Performance Monitor and Resource Monitor.

> **Note** Performance Monitor has three functions: system monitoring, viewing performance counter logs, and setting alerts (by using data collector sets, which also contain performance counter logs and trace and configuration data). For simplicity, when we refer to Performance Monitor, we mean the system-monitoring function within that tool.

Performance Monitor provides more information about how your system is operating than any other single utility. It includes hundreds of base and extensible counters for various objects. For each major topic described in this book, a table of the relevant Windows performance counters is included. Performance Monitor contains a brief description for each counter. To see the descriptions, select a counter in the Add Counters window and select the **Show Description** check box.

Although all the low-level system monitoring we'll do in this book can be done with Performance Monitor, Windows also includes a Resource Monitor utility (accessible from the Start menu or from the Task Manager Performance tab) that shows four primary system resources: CPU, disk, network, and memory. In their basic states, these resources are displayed with the same level of information that you would find in Task Manager. However, they also provide sections that can be expanded for more information. Here's a typical view of Resource Monitor:

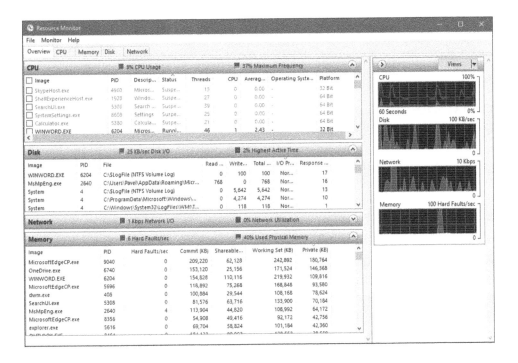

When expanded, the CPU tab displays information about per-process CPU usage, just like Task Manager. However, it adds a column for average CPU usage, which can give you a better idea of which processes are most active. The CPU tab also includes a separate display of services and their associated CPU usage and average. Each service-hosting process is identified by the service group it is hosting. As with Process Explorer, selecting a process (by clicking its associated check box) will display a list of named handles opened by the process, as well as a list of modules (such as DLLs) that are loaded in the process address space. The Search Handles box can also be used to search for which processes have opened a handle to a given named resource.

The Memory tab displays much of the same information that one can obtain with Task Manager, but it is organized for the entire system. A physical memory bar graph displays the current organization of physical memory into either hardware-reserved, in-use, modified, standby, or free memory. See Chapter 5 for the exact meaning of these terms.

The Disk tab, on the other hand, displays per-file information for I/O in a way that makes it easy to identify the most-accessed, the most–written to, or the most–read from files on the system. These results can be further filtered down by process.

The Network tab displays the active network connections, the processes that own them, and how much data is going through them. This information makes it possible to see background network activity that might be hard to detect otherwise. In addition, it shows the TCP connections that are active on the system, organized by process, with data such as the remote and local port and address and packet latency. Finally, it displays a list of listening ports by process, allowing an administrator to see which services or applications are currently waiting for connections on a given port. The protocol and firewall policy for each port and process is also shown.

Note All Windows performance counters are accessible programmatically. For more information, search for "performance counters" in the MSDN documentation.

Kernel debugging

Kernel debugging means examining internal kernel data structures and/or stepping through functions in the kernel. It is a useful way to investigate Windows internals because you can display internal system information not available through any other tools and get a clearer idea of code flows within the kernel. Before describing the various ways in which you can debug the kernel, let's examine a set of files that you'll need in order to perform any type of kernel debugging.

Symbols for kernel debugging

Symbol files contain the names of functions and variables and the layout and format of data structures. They are generated by the linker and used by debuggers to reference and display these names during a debug session. This information is not usually stored in the binary image because it is not needed to execute the code. This means binaries are smaller and faster. However, it also means that when debugging, you must make sure the debugger can access the symbol files associated with the images you are referencing during a debugging session.

To use any of the kernel-debugging tools to examine internal Windows kernel data structures such as the process list, thread blocks, loaded driver list, memory usage information, and so on, you must have the correct symbol files for at least the kernel image, Ntoskrnl.exe. (You can learn more about this file in the section "Architecture overview" in Chapter 2.) Symbol table files must match the version of the image from which they were taken. For example, if you install a Windows service pack or hot fix that updates the kernel, you must obtain the matching updated symbol files.

While it is possible to download and install symbols for various versions of Windows, updated symbols for hot fixes are not always available. The easiest way to obtain the correct version of symbols for debugging is to employ the Microsoft on-demand symbol server by using a special syntax for the symbol path that you specify in the debugger. For example, the following symbol path causes the debugging tools to load required symbols from the Internet symbol server and keep a local copy in the C:\symbols folder:

```
srv*c:\symbols*http://msdl.microsoft.com/download/symbols
```

Debugging Tools for Windows

The Debugging Tools for Windows package contains advanced debugging tools, which are used in this book to explore Windows internals. The latest version is included as part of the Windows SDK. (See *https://msdn.microsoft.com/en-us/library/windows/hardware/ff551063.aspx* for more details about the different installation types.) These tools can be used to debug user-mode processes as well as the kernel.

There are four debuggers included in the tools: cdb, ntsd, kd, and WinDbg. All are based on a single debugging engine implemented in DbgEng.dll, which is documented fairly well in the help file for the tools. Here's a brief overview of the debuggers:

- cdb and ntsd are user-mode debuggers based on a console user interface. The only difference between them is that ntsd opens a new console window if activated from an existing console window, while cdb does not.

- kd is a kernel-mode debugger based on a console user interface.

- WinDbg can be used as a user-mode or kernel-mode debugger, but not both at the same time. It provides a GUI for the user.

- The user-mode debuggers (cdb, ntsd, and WinDbg, when used as such) are essentially equivalent. Usage of one or the other is a matter of preference.

- The kernel-mode debuggers (kd and WinDbg, when used as such) are equivalent as well.

User-mode debugging　The debugging tools can also be used to attach to a user-mode process and to examine and/or change process memory. There are two options when attaching to a process:

- **Invasive**　Unless specified otherwise, when you attach to a running process, you use the DebugActiveProcess Windows function to establish a connection between the debugger and the debugee. This permits you to examine and/or change process memory, set breakpoints, and perform other debugging functions. Windows allows you to stop debugging without killing the target process as long as the debugger is detached, not killed.

- **Noninvasive**　With this option, the debugger simply opens the process with the OpenProcess function. It does not attach to the process as a debugger. This allows you to examine and/or change memory in the target process, but you cannot set breakpoints. This also means it's possible to attach noninvasively even if another debugger is attached invasively.

You can also open user-mode process dump files with the debugging tools. User-mode dump files are explained in Chapter 8 in Part 2 in the section on exception dispatching.

Kernel-mode debugging　As mentioned, there are two debuggers that can be used for kernel debugging: a command-line version (Kd.exe) and a GUI version (Windbg.exe). You can perform three types of kernel debugging with these tools:

- Open a crash dump file created as a result of a Windows system crash. (See Chapter 15, "Crash dump analysis," in Part 2 for more information on kernel crash dumps.)

- Connect to a live, running system and examine the system state (or set breakpoints if you're debugging device driver code). This operation requires two computers: a target (the system being debugged) and a host (the system running the debugger). The target system can be connected to the host via a null modem cable, an IEEE 1394 cable, a USB 2.0/3.0 debugging cable, or the local network. The target system must be booted in debugging mode. You can configure the system to boot in debugging mode using Bcdedit.exe or Msconfig.exe. (Note that you may have to disable secure boot in the UEFI BIOS settings.) You can also connect through a named pipe—which is useful when debugging Windows 7 or earlier versions through a virtual machine product such as Hyper-V, Virtual Box, or VMWare Workstation—by exposing the guest operating system's serial port as a named pipe device. For Windows 8 and later guests, you should instead use local network debugging by exposing a host-only network using a virtual NIC in the guest operating system. This will result in 1,000x performance gain.

■ Windows systems also allow you to connect to the local system and examine the system state. This is called *local kernel debugging*. To initiate local kernel debugging with WinDbg, first make sure the system is set to debug mode (for example, by running msconfig.exe, clicking the **Boot** tab, selecting **Advanced Options**, selecting **Debug**, and restarting Windows). Launch WinDbg with admin privileges and open the **File** menu, choose **Kernel Debug**, click the **Local** tab, and then click **OK** (or use bcdedit.exe). Figure 1-6 shows a sample output screen on a 64-bit Windows 10 machine. Some kernel debugger commands do not work when used in local kernel debugging mode, such as setting breakpoints or creating a memory dump with the `.dump` command. However, the latter can be done with LiveKd, described later in this section.

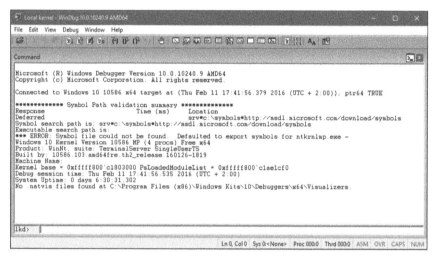

FIGURE 1-6 Local kernel debugging.

Once connected in kernel-debugging mode, you can use one of the many debugger extension commands—also known as *bang* commands, which are commands that begin with an exclamation point (!)—to display the contents of internal data structures such as threads, processes, I/O request packets, and memory management information. Throughout this book, the relevant kernel debugger commands and output are included as they apply to each topic being discussed. An excellent companion reference is the Debugger.chm help file, contained in the WinDbg installation folder, which documents all the kernel debugger functionality and extensions. In addition, the `dt` (display type) command can format more than 1,000 kernel structures because the kernel symbol files for Windows contain type information that the debugger can use to format structures.

EXPERIMENT: Displaying type information for kernel structures

To display the list of kernel structures whose type information is included in the kernel symbols, type **dt nt!_*** in the kernel debugger. A sample partial output is shown here. (ntkrnlmp is the internal file name of the 64-bit kernel. For more details, see Chapter 2.)

```
lkd> dt nt!_*
          ntkrnlmp!_KSYSTEM_TIME
          ntkrnlmp!_NT_PRODUCT_TYPE
          ntkrnlmp!_ALTERNATIVE_ARCHITECTURE_TYPE
          ntkrnlmp!_KUSER_SHARED_DATA
          ntkrnlmp!_ULARGE_INTEGER
          ntkrnlmp!_TP_POOL
          ntkrnlmp!_TP_CLEANUP_GROUP
          ntkrnlmp!_ACTIVATION_CONTEXT
          ntkrnlmp!_TP_CALLBACK_INSTANCE
          ntkrnlmp!_TP_CALLBACK_PRIORITY
          ntkrnlmp!_TP_CALLBACK_ENVIRON_V3
          ntkrnlmp!_TEB
```

You can also use the dt command to search for specific structures by using its wildcard lookup capability. For example, if you were looking for the structure name for an interrupt object, you could type **dt nt!_*interrupt***:

```
lkd> dt nt!_*interrupt*
          ntkrnlmp!_KINTERRUPT_MODE
          ntkrnlmp!_KINTERRUPT_POLARITY
          ntkrnlmp!_PEP_ACPI_INTERRUPT_RESOURCE
          ntkrnlmp!_KINTERRUPT
          ntkrnlmp!_UNEXPECTED_INTERRUPT
          ntkrnlmp!_INTERRUPT_CONNECTION_DATA
          ntkrnlmp!_INTERRUPT_VECTOR_DATA
          ntkrnlmp!_INTERRUPT_HT_INTR_INFO
          ntkrnlmp!_INTERRUPT_REMAPPING_INFO
```

Then you can use dt to format a specific structure as shown next (the debugger treats structures as case insensitive):

```
lkd> dt nt!_KINTERRUPT
   +0x000 Type              : Int2B
   +0x002 Size              : Int2B
   +0x008 InterruptListEntry : _LIST_ENTRY
   +0x018 ServiceRoutine    : Ptr64     unsigned char
   +0x020 MessageServiceRoutine : Ptr64     unsigned char
   +0x028 MessageIndex      : Uint4B
   +0x030 ServiceContext    : Ptr64 Void
   +0x038 SpinLock          : Uint8B
   +0x040 TickCount         : Uint4B
   +0x048 ActualLock        : Ptr64 Uint8B
   +0x050 DispatchAddress   : Ptr64     void
   +0x058 Vector            : Uint4B
   +0x05c Irql              : UChar
```

```
+0x05d SynchronizeIrql    : UChar
+0x05e FloatingSave       : UChar
+0x05f Connected          : UChar
+0x060 Number             : Uint4B
+0x064 ShareVector        : UChar
+0x065 EmulateActiveBoth  : UChar
+0x066 ActiveCount        : Uint2B
+0x068 InternalState      : Int4B
+0x06c Mode               : _KINTERRUPT_MODE
+0x070 Polarity           : _KINTERRUPT_POLARITY
+0x074 ServiceCount       : Uint4B
+0x078 DispatchCount      : Uint4B
+0x080 PassiveEvent       : Ptr64 _KEVENT
+0x088 TrapFrame          : Ptr64 _KTRAP_FRAME
+0x090 DisconnectData     : Ptr64 Void
+0x098 ServiceThread      : Ptr64 _KTHREAD
+0x0a0 ConnectionData     : Ptr64 _INTERRUPT_CONNECTION_DATA
+0x0a8 IntTrackEntry      : Ptr64 Void
+0x0b0 IsrDpcStats        : _ISRDPCSTATS
+0x0f0 RedirectObject     : Ptr64 Void
+0x0f8 Padding            : [8] UChar
```

Note that dt does not show substructures (structures within structures) by default. To show substructures, use the -r or -b switches. For example, using one of these switches to display the kernel interrupt object shows the format of the _LIST_ENTRY structure stored in the Interrupt-ListEntry field. (See the documentation for the exact differences between the -r and -b switches.)

```
lkd> dt nt!_KINTERRUPT -r
   +0x000 Type              : Int2B
   +0x002 Size              : Int2B
   +0x008 InterruptListEntry : _LIST_ENTRY
      +0x000 Flink               : Ptr64 _LIST_ENTRY
         +0x000 Flink                : Ptr64 _LIST_ENTRY
         +0x008 Blink                : Ptr64 _LIST_ENTRY
      +0x008 Blink               : Ptr64 _LIST_ENTRY
         +0x000 Flink                : Ptr64 _LIST_ENTRY
         +0x008 Blink                : Ptr64 _LIST_ENTRY
   +0x018 ServiceRoutine    : Ptr64      unsigned char
```

The dt command even lets you specify the level of recursion of structures by appending a number to the -r switch. The following example means one level of recursion:

```
lkd> dt nt!_KINTERRUPT -r1
```

The Debugging Tools for Windows help file explains how to set up and use kernel debuggers. For additional details on using kernel debuggers aimed primarily at device-driver writers, see the WDK documentation.

LiveKd tool

LiveKd is a free tool from Sysinternals that enables you to use the standard Microsoft kernel debuggers just described to examine the running system without booting the system in debugging mode. This approach might be useful when kernel-level troubleshooting is required on a machine that wasn't booted in debugging mode. Certain issues might be hard to reproduce reliably, so a reboot with the *debug* option enabled might not readily exhibit the error.

You run LiveKd just as you would WinDbg or kd. LiveKd passes any command-line options you specify to the debugger you select. By default, LiveKd runs the command-line kernel debugger (kd). To have it run WinDbg, use the -w switch. To see the help files for LiveKd switches, use the -? switch.

LiveKd presents a simulated crash dump file to the debugger so you can perform any operations in LiveKd that are supported on a crash dump. Because LiveKd relies on physical memory to back the simulated dump, the kernel debugger might run into situations in which data structures are in the middle of being changed by the system and are inconsistent. Each time the debugger is launched, it starts with a fresh view of the system state. If you want to refresh the snapshot, enter the **q** command to quit the debugger. LiveKd will ask you whether you want to start it again. If the debugger enters a loop in printing output, press **Ctrl+C** to interrupt the output and quit. If it hangs, press **Ctrl+Break**, which will terminate the debugger process. LiveKd will then ask you whether you want to run the debugger again.

Windows Software Development Kit

The Windows Software Development Kit (SDK) is available as part of the MSDN subscription program. You can also download it for free from *https://developer.microsoft.com/en-US/windows/downloads/windows-10-sdk*. Visual Studio also provides the option of installing the SDK as part of VS installation. The versions contained in the Windows SDK always match the latest version of the Windows operating system, whereas the version that comes with Visual Studio might be an older version that was current when that version was released. Besides the Debugging Tools for Windows, it contains the C header files and the libraries necessary to compile and link Windows applications. From a Windows internals perspective, items of interest in the Windows SDK include the Windows API header files—for example, C:\Program Files (x86)\Windows Kits\10\Include—and the SDK tools (search for the Bin folder). Also of interest is the documentation. It's available online or can be downloaded for offline access. A few of these tools are also shipped as sample source code in both the Windows SDK and the MSDN Library.

Windows Driver Kit

The Windows Driver Kit (WDK) is also available through the MSDN subscription program. Just like the Windows SDK, it is available for free download. The WDK documentation is included in the MSDN Library.

Although the WDK is aimed at developers of device drivers, it is an abundant source of Windows internals information. For example, although Chapter 6 describes the I/O system architecture, driver model, and basic device driver data structures, it does not describe the individual kernel support functions in detail. The WDK documentation contains a comprehensive description of all the Windows kernel support functions and mechanisms used by device drivers in both tutorial and reference form.

In addition to including the documentation, the WDK contains header files (in particular, ntddk.h, ntifs.h, and wdm.h) that define key internal data structures and constants as well as interfaces to many internal system routines. These files are useful when exploring Windows internal data structures with the kernel debugger because although the general layout and content of these structures are shown in this book, detailed field-level descriptions (such as size and data types) are not. A number of these data structures—such as object dispatcher headers, wait blocks, events, mutants, semaphores, and so on—are, however, fully described in the WDK.

If you want to dig into the I/O system and driver model beyond what is presented in this book, read the WDK documentation—especially the *Kernel-Mode Driver Architecture Design Guide* and *Kernel-Mode Driver Reference* manuals. You might also find useful *Programming the Microsoft Windows Driver Model, Second Edition* by Walter Oney (Microsoft Press, 2002) and *Developing Drivers with the Windows Driver Foundation* by Penny Orwick and Guy Smith (Microsoft Press, 2007).

Sysinternals tools

Many experiments in this book use freeware tools that you can download from Sysinternals. Mark Russinovich, coauthor of this book, wrote most of these tools. The most popular tools include Process Explorer and Process Monitor. Note that many of these utilities involve the installation and execution of kernel-mode device drivers and thus require administrator, or elevated, privileges—although some of them can run with limited functionality and output on a standard, or non-elevated, user account.

Because the Sysinternals tools are updated frequently, be make sure you have the latest version. To be notified of tool updates, you can follow the Sysinternals Site Blog (which has an RSS feed). For a description of all the tools, a description of how to use them, and case studies of problems solved, see *Windows Sysinternals Administrator's Reference* by Mark Russinovich and Aaron Margosis (Microsoft Press, 2011). For questions and discussions on the tools, use the Sysinternals Forums.

Conclusion

This chapter introduced key Windows technical concepts and terms that will be used throughout the book. It also offered a glimpse of the many useful tools available for digging into Windows internals. Now you're ready to begin your exploration of the internal design of the system, beginning with an overall view of the system architecture and its key components.

System architecture

N ow that you've learned the terms, concepts, and tools you need to be familiar with, it's time to
start exploring the internal design goals and structure of the Microsoft Windows operating system
(OS). This chapter explains the overall architecture of the system—the key components, how they interact with each other, and the context in which they run. To provide a framework for understanding the
internals of Windows, let's first review the requirements and goals that shaped the original design and
specification of the system.

Requirements and design goals

The following requirements drove the specification of Windows NT back in 1989:

- Provide a true 32-bit, preemptive, reentrant, virtual memory OS.

- Run on multiple hardware architectures and platforms.

- Run and scale well on symmetric multiprocessing systems.

- Be a great distributed computing platform, both as a network client and as a server.

- Run most existing 16-bit MS-DOS and Microsoft Windows 3.1 applications.

- Meet government requirements for POSIX 1003.1 compliance.

- Meet government and industry requirements for OS security.

- Be easily adaptable to the global market by supporting Unicode.

To guide the thousands of decisions that had to be made to create a system that met these requirements, the Windows NT design team adopted the following design goals at the beginning of the project:

- **Extensibility**   The code must be written to comfortably grow and change as market requirements change.

- **Portability**   The system must be able to run on multiple hardware architectures and must be
  able to move with relative ease to new ones as market demands dictate.

- **Reliability and robustness**   The system should protect itself from both internal malfunction
  and external tampering. Applications should not be able to harm the OS or other applications.

- **Compatibility** Although Windows NT should extend existing technology, its user interface and APIs should be compatible with older versions of Windows and with MS-DOS. It should also interoperate well with other systems, such as UNIX, OS/2, and NetWare.

- **Performance** Within the constraints of the other design goals, the system should be as fast and responsive as possible on each hardware platform.

As we explore the details of the internal structure and operation of Windows, you'll see how these original design goals and market requirements were woven successfully into the construction of the system. But before we start that exploration, let's examine the overall design model for Windows and compare it with other modern operating systems.

Operating system model

In most multiuser operating systems, applications are separated from the OS itself. The OS kernel code runs in a privileged processor mode (referred to as *kernel mode* in this book), with access to system data and to the hardware. Application code runs in a non-privileged processor mode (called *user mode*), with a limited set of interfaces available, limited access to system data, and no direct access to hardware. When a user-mode program calls a system service, the processor executes a special instruction that switches the calling thread to kernel mode. When the system service completes, the OS switches the thread context back to user mode and allows the caller to continue.

Windows is similar to most UNIX systems in that it's a monolithic OS in the sense that the bulk of the OS and device driver code shares the same kernel-mode protected memory space. This means that any OS component or device driver can potentially corrupt data being used by other OS system components. However, as you saw in Chapter 1, "Concepts and tools," Windows addresses this through attempts to strengthen the quality and constrain the provenance of third-party drivers through programs such as WHQL and enforcement through KMCS, while also incorporating additional kernel protection technologies such as virtualization-based security and the Device Guard and Hyper Guard features. Although you'll see how these pieces fit together in this section, more details will follow in Chapter 7, "Security," and in Chapter 8, "System mechanisms," in *Windows Internals Part 2*.

All these OS components are, of course, fully protected from errant applications because applications don't have direct access to the code and data of the privileged part of the OS (although they can quickly call other kernel services). This protection is one of the reasons that Windows has the reputation for being both robust and stable as an application server and as a workstation platform, yet fast and nimble from the perspective of core OS services, such as virtual memory management, file I/O, networking, and file and print sharing.

The kernel-mode components of Windows also embody basic object-oriented design principles. For example, in general they don't reach into one another's data structures to access information maintained by individual components. Instead, they use formal interfaces to pass parameters and access and/or modify data structures.

Despite its pervasive use of objects to represent shared system resources, Windows is not an object-oriented system in the strict sense. Most of the kernel-mode OS code is written in C for portability. The C programming language doesn't directly support object-oriented constructs such as polymorphic functions or class inheritance. Therefore, the C-based implementation of objects in Windows borrows from, but doesn't depend on, features of particular object-oriented languages.

Architecture overview

With this brief overview of the design goals and packaging of Windows, let's take a look at the key system components that make up its architecture. A simplified version of this architecture is shown in Figure 2-1. Keep in mind that this diagram is basic. It doesn't show everything. For example, the networking components and the various types of device driver layering are not shown.

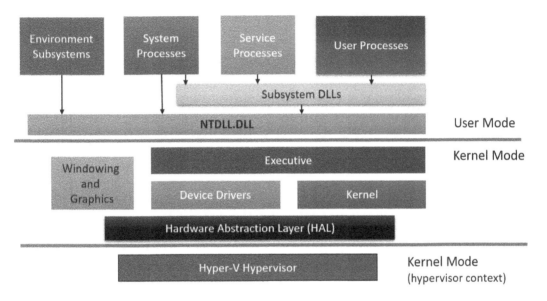

FIGURE 2-1 Simplified Windows architecture.

In Figure 2-1, first notice the line dividing the user-mode and kernel-mode parts of the Windows OS. The boxes above the line represent user-mode processes, and the components below the line are kernel-mode OS services. As mentioned in Chapter 1, user-mode threads execute in a private process address space (although while they are executing in kernel mode, they have access to system space). Thus, system processes, service processes, user processes, and environment subsystems each have their own private process address space. A second dividing line between kernel-mode parts of Windows and the hypervisor is also visible. Strictly speaking, the hypervisor still runs with the same CPU privilege level (0) as the kernel, but because it uses specialized CPU instructions (VT-x on Intel, SVM on AMD), it can both isolate itself from the kernel while also monitoring it (and applications). For these reasons, you may often hear the term *ring -1* thrown around (which is inaccurate).

The four basic types of user-mode processes are described as follows:

- **User processes**   These processes can be one of the following types: Windows 32-bit or 64-bit (Windows Apps running on top of the Windows Runtime in Windows 8 and later are included in this category), Windows 3.1 16-bit, MS-DOS 16-bit, or POSIX 32-bit or 64-bit. Note that 16-bit applications can be run only on 32-bit Windows, and that POSIX applications are no longer supported as of Windows 8.

- **Service processes**   These are processes that host Windows services, such as the Task Scheduler and Print Spooler services. Services generally have the requirement that they run independently of user logons. Many Windows server applications, such as Microsoft SQL Server and Microsoft Exchange Server, also include components that run as services. Chapter 9, "Management mechanisms," in Part 2 describes services in detail.

- **System processes**   These are fixed, or hardwired, processes, such as the logon process and the Session Manager, that are not Windows services. That is, they are not started by the Service Control Manager.

- **Environment subsystem server processes**   These implement part of the support for the OS environment, or personality, presented to the user and programmer. Windows NT originally shipped with three environment subsystems: Windows, POSIX, and OS/2. However, the OS/2 subsystem last shipped with Windows 2000 and POSIX last shipped with Windows XP. The Ultimate and Enterprise editions of Windows 7 client as well as all of the server versions of Windows 2008 R2 include support for an enhanced POSIX subsystem called Subsystem for UNIX-based Applications (SUA). The SUA is now discontinued and is no longer offered as an optional part of Windows (either client or server).

> **Note**   Windows 10 Version 1607 includes a Windows Subsystem for Linux (WSL) in beta state for developers only. However, this is not a true subsystem as described in this section. This chapter will discuss WSL and the related Pico providers in more detail. For information about Pico processes, see Chapter 3, "Processes and jobs."

In Figure 2-1, notice the Subsystem DLLs box below the Service Processes and User Processes boxes. Under Windows, user applications don't call the native Windows OS services directly. Rather, they go through one or more *subsystem dynamic-link libraries* (*DLLs*). The role of subsystem DLLs is to translate a documented function into the appropriate internal (and generally undocumented) native system service calls implemented mostly in Ntdll.dll. This translation might or might not involve sending a message to the environment subsystem process that is serving the user process.

The kernel-mode components of Windows include the following:

- **Executive**   The Windows executive contains the base OS services, such as memory management, process and thread management, security, I/O, networking, and inter-process communication.

- **The Windows kernel**   This consists of low-level OS functions, such as thread scheduling, interrupt and exception dispatching, and multiprocessor synchronization. It also provides a set of routines and basic objects that the rest of the executive uses to implement higher-level constructs.

- **Device drivers**   This includes both hardware device drivers, which translate user I/O function calls into specific hardware device I/O requests, and non-hardware device drivers, such as file system and network drivers.

- **The Hardware Abstraction Layer (HAL)**   This is a layer of code that isolates the kernel, the device drivers, and the rest of the Windows executive from platform-specific hardware differences (such as differences between motherboards).

- **The windowing and graphics system**   This implements the graphical user interface (GUI) functions (better known as the Windows USER and GDI functions), such as dealing with windows, user interface controls, and drawing.

- **The hypervisor layer**   This is composed of a single component: the hypervisor itself. There are no drivers or other modules in this environment. That being said, the hypervisor is itself composed of multiple internal layers and services, such as its own memory manager, virtual processor scheduler, interrupt and timer management, synchronization routines, partitions (virtual machine instances) management and inter-partition communication (IPC), and more.

Table 2-1 lists the file names of the core Windows OS components. (You'll need to know these file names because we'll be referring to some system files by name.) Each of these components is covered in greater detail both later in this chapter and in the chapters that follow.

TABLE 2-1   Core Windows System Files

File Name	Components
Ntoskrnl.exe	Executive and kernel
Hal.dll	HAL
Win32k.sys	Kernel-mode part of the Windows subsystem (GUI)
Hvix64.exe (Intel), Hvax64.exe (AMD)	Hypervisor
.sys files in \SystemRoot\System32\Drivers	Core driver files, such as Direct X, Volume Manager, TCP/IP, TPM, and ACPI support
Ntdll.dll	Internal support functions and system service dispatch stubs to executive functions
Kernel32.dll, Advapi32.dll, User32.dll, Gdi32.dll	Core Windows subsystem DLLs

Before we dig into the details of these system components, though, let's examine some basics about the Windows kernel design, starting with how Windows achieves portability across multiple hardware architectures.

Portability

Windows was designed to run on a variety of hardware architectures. The initial release of Windows NT supported the x86 and MIPS architectures. Support for the Digital Equipment Corporation (which was bought by Compaq, which later merged with Hewlett-Packard) Alpha AXP was added shortly thereafter. (Although Alpha AXP was a 64-bit processor, Windows NT ran in 32-bit mode. During the development of Windows 2000, a native 64-bit version was running on Alpha AXP, but this was never released.) Support for a fourth processor architecture, the Motorola PowerPC, was added in Windows NT 3.51. Because of changing market demands, however, support for the MIPS and PowerPC architectures was dropped before development began on Windows 2000. Later, Compaq withdrew support for the Alpha AXP architecture, resulting in Windows 2000 being supported only on the x86 architecture. Windows XP and Windows Server 2003 added support for two 64-bit processor families: the Intel Itanium IA-64 family and the AMD64 family with its equivalent Intel 64-bit Extension Technology (EM64T). These latter two implementations are called *64-bit extended systems* and in this book are referred to as *x64*. (How Windows runs 32-bit applications on 64-bit Windows is explained in Chapter 8 in Part 2.) Additionally, as of Server 2008 R2, IA-64 systems are no longer supported by Windows.

Newer editions of Windows support the ARM processor architecture. For example, Windows RT was a version of Windows 8 that ran on ARM architecture, although that edition has since been discontinued. Windows 10 Mobile—the successor for Windows Phone 8.*x* operating systems—runs on ARM based processors, such as Qualcomm Snapdragon models. Windows 10 IoT runs on both x86 and ARM devices such as Raspberry Pi 2 (which uses an ARM Cortex-A7 processor) and Raspberry Pi 3 (which uses the ARM Cortex-A53). As ARM hardware has advanced to 64-bit, a new processor family called *AArch64*, or *ARM64*, may also at some point be supported, as an increasing number of devices run on it.

Windows achieves portability across hardware architectures and platforms in two primary ways:

- **By using a layered design** Windows has a layered design, with low-level portions of the system that are processor-architecture–specific or platform-specific isolated into separate modules so that upper layers of the system can be shielded from the differences between architectures and among hardware platforms. The two key components that provide OS portability are the kernel (contained in Ntoskrnl.exe) and the HAL (contained in Hal.dll). Both these components are described in more detail later in this chapter. Functions that are architecture-specific, such as thread context switching and trap dispatching, are implemented in the kernel. Functions that can differ among systems within the same architecture (for example, different motherboards) are implemented in the HAL. The only other component with a significant amount of architecture-specific code is the memory manager, but even that is a small amount compared to the system as a whole. The hypervisor follows a similar design, with most parts shared between the AMD (SVM) and Intel (VT-x) implementation, and some specific parts for each processor—hence the two file names on disk you saw in Table 2-1.

- **By using C** The vast majority of Windows is written in C, with some portions in C++. Assembly language is used only for those parts of the OS that need to communicate directly with system hardware (such as the interrupt trap handler) or that are extremely performance-sensitive (such as context switching). Assembly language code exists not only in the kernel and the HAL but also in a few other places within the core OS (such as the routines that implement interlocked instructions as well as one module in the local procedure call facility), in the kernel-mode part of the Windows subsystem, and even in some user-mode libraries, such as the process startup code in Ntdll.dll (a system library explained later in this chapter).

Symmetric multiprocessing

Multitasking is the OS technique for sharing a single processor among multiple threads of execution. When a computer has more than one processor, however, it can execute multiple threads simultaneously. Thus, whereas a multitasking OS only appears to execute multiple threads at the same time, a multiprocessing OS actually does it, executing one thread on each of its processors.

As mentioned at the beginning of this chapter, one of the key design goals for Windows was that it had to run well on multiprocessor computer systems. Windows is a *symmetric multiprocessing (SMP)* OS. There is no master processor—the OS as well as user threads can be scheduled to run on any processor. Also, all the processors share just one memory space. This model contrasts with *asymmetric multiprocessing (ASMP)*, in which the OS typically selects one processor to execute OS kernel code while other processors run only user code. The differences in the two multiprocessing models are illustrated in Figure 2-2.

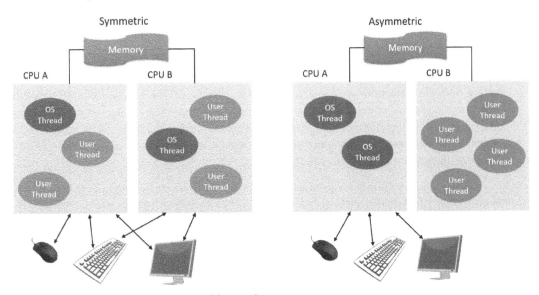

FIGURE 2-2 Symmetric vs. asymmetric multiprocessing.

Windows also supports four modern types of multiprocessor systems: multicore, simultaneous multi-threaded (SMT), heterogeneous, and non-uniform memory access (NUMA). These are briefly mentioned in the following paragraphs. (For a complete, detailed description of the scheduling support for these systems, see the section on thread scheduling in Chapter 4, "Threads.")

SMT was first introduced to Windows systems by adding support for Intel's Hyper-Threading Technology, which provides two logical processors for each physical core. Newer AMD processors under the Zen micro-architecture implement a similar SMT technology, also doubling the logical processor count.

Each logical processor has its own CPU state, but the execution engine and onboard cache are shared. This permits one logical CPU to make progress while the other logical CPU is stalled (such as after a cache miss or branch misprediction). Confusingly, the marketing literature for both companies refers to these additional cores as *threads*, so you'll often see claims such as "four cores, eight threads." This indicates that up to eight threads can be scheduled, hence, the existence of eight logical processors. The scheduling algorithms are enhanced to make optimal use of SMT-enabled machines, such as by scheduling threads on an idle physical processor versus choosing an idle logical processor on a physical processor whose other logical processors are busy. For more details on thread scheduling, see Chapter 4.

In NUMA systems, processors are grouped in smaller units called *nodes*. Each node has its own processors and memory and is connected to the larger system through a cache-coherent interconnect bus. Windows on a NUMA system still runs as an SMP system, in that all processors have access to all memory. It's just that node-local memory is faster to reference than memory attached to other nodes. The system attempts to improve performance by scheduling threads on processors that are in the same node as the memory being used. It attempts to satisfy memory-allocation requests from within the node, but it will allocate memory from other nodes if necessary.

Naturally, Windows also natively supports multicore systems. Because these systems have real physical cores (simply on the same package), the original SMP code in Windows treats them as discrete processors, except for certain accounting and identification tasks (such as licensing, described shortly) that distinguish between cores on the same processor and cores on different sockets. This is especially important when dealing with cache topologies to optimize data-sharing.

Finally, ARM versions of Windows also support a technology known as *heterogeneous multi-processing*, whose implementation on such processors is called *big.LITTLE*. This type of SMP-based design differs from traditional ones in that not all processor cores are identical in their capabilities, yet unlike pure heterogeneous multi-processing, they are still able to execute the same instructions. The difference, then, comes from the clock speed and respective full load/idle power draws, allowing for a collection of slower cores to be paired with faster ones.

Think of sending an e-mail on an older dual-core 1 GHz system connected to a modern Internet connection. It's unlikely this will be any slower than on an eight-core 3.6 GHz machine because bottlenecks are mostly caused by human input typing speed and network bandwidth, not raw processing power. Yet even in its deepest power-saving mode, such a modern system is likely to use significantly more power than the legacy system. Even if it could regulate itself down to 1 GHz, the legacy system has probably set itself to 200 MHz, for example.

By being able to pair such legacy mobile processors with top-of-the-line ones, ARM-based platforms paired with a compatible OS kernel scheduler can maximize processing power when needed (by turning on all cores), strike a balance (by having certain big cores online and other little ones for other tasks), or run in extremely low power modes (by having only a single little core online—enough for SMS and push e-mail). By supporting what are called *heterogeneous scheduling policies*, Windows 10 allows threads to pick and choose between a policy that satisfies their needs, and will interact with the scheduler and power manager to best support it. You'll learn more about these policies in Chapter 4.

Windows was not originally designed with a specific processor number limit in mind, other than the licensing policies that differentiate the various Windows editions. However, for convenience and efficiency, Windows does keep track of processors (total number, idle, busy, and other such details) in a bitmask (sometimes called an *affinity mask*) that is the same number of bits as the native data type of the machine (32-bit or 64-bit). This allows the processor to manipulate bits directly within a register. Due to this fact, Windows systems were originally limited to the number of CPUs in a native word, because the affinity mask couldn't arbitrarily be increased. To maintain compatibility, as well as support larger processor systems, Windows implements a higher-order construct called a *processor group*. The processor group is a set of processors that can all be defined by a single affinity bitmask, and the kernel as well as the applications can choose which group they refer to during affinity updates. Compatible applications can query the number of supported groups (currently limited to 20; the maximum number of logical processors is currently limited to 640) and then enumerate the bitmask for each group. Meanwhile, legacy applications continue to function by seeing only their current group. For more information on how exactly Windows assigns processors to groups (which is also related to NUMA) and legacy processes to groups, see Chapter 4.

As mentioned, the actual number of supported *licensed* processors depends on the edition of Windows being used. (See Table 2-2 later in this chapter.) This number is stored in the system license policy file (essentially a set of name/value pairs) %SystemRoot%\ServiceProfiles\LocalService\AppData\Local\Microsoft\WSLicense\tokens.dat in the variable `kernel-RegisteredProcessors`.

Scalability

One of the key issues with multiprocessor systems is *scalability*. To run correctly on an SMP system, OS code must adhere to strict guidelines and rules. Resource contention and other performance issues are more complicated in multiprocessing systems than in uniprocessor systems and must be accounted for in the system's design. Windows incorporates several features that are crucial to its success as a multiprocessor OS:

- The ability to run OS code on any available processor and on multiple processors at the same time

- Multiple threads of execution within a single process, each of which can execute simultaneously on different processors

- Fine-grained synchronization within the kernel (such as spinlocks, queued spinlocks, and pushlocks, described in Chapter 8 in Part 2) as well as within device drivers and server processes, which allows more components to run concurrently on multiple processors

- Programming mechanisms such as I/O completion ports (described in Chapter 6, "I/O system") that facilitate the efficient implementation of multithreaded server processes that can scale well on multiprocessor systems

The scalability of the Windows kernel has evolved over time. For example, Windows Server 2003 introduced per-CPU scheduling queues with a fine-grained lock, permitting thread-scheduling decisions to occur in parallel on multiple processors. Windows 7 and Windows Server 2008 R2 eliminated global scheduler locking during wait-dispatching operations. This stepwise improvement of the granularity of locking has also occurred in other areas, such as the memory manager, cache manager, and object manager.

Differences between client and server versions

Windows ships in both client and server retail packages. There are six desktop client versions of Windows 10: Windows 10 Home, Windows 10 Pro, Windows 10 Education, Windows 10 Pro Education, Windows 10 Enterprise, and Windows 10 Enterprise Long Term Servicing Branch (LTSB). Other non-desktop editions include Windows 10 Mobile, Windows 10 Mobile Enterprise, and Windows 10 IoT Core, IoT Core Enterprise, and IoT Mobile Enterprise. Still more variants exist that target world regions with specific needs, such as the N series.

There are six different versions of Windows Server 2016: Windows Server 2016 Datacenter, Windows Server 2016 Standard, Windows Server 2016 Essentials, Windows Server 2006 MultiPoint Premium Server, Windows Storage Server 2016, and Microsoft Hyper-V Server 2016.

These versions differ as follows:

- Core-based (rather than socket-based) pricing for the Server 2016 Datacenter and Standard edition

- The number of total logical processors supported

- For server systems, the number of Hyper-V containers allowed to run (client systems support only namespace-based Windows containers)

- The amount of physical memory supported (actually highest physical address usable for RAM; see Chapter 5, "Memory management," for more information on physical memory limits)

- The number of concurrent network connections supported (for example, a maximum of 10 concurrent connections are allowed to the file and print services in client versions)

- Support for multi-touch and Desktop Composition

- Support for features such as BitLocker, VHD booting, AppLocker, Hyper-V, and more than 100 other configurable licensing policy values

- Layered services that come with Windows Server editions that don't come with the client editions (for example, directory services, Host Guardian, Storage Spaces Direct, shielded virtual machines, and clustering)

Table 2-2 lists the differences in memory and processor support for some Windows 10, Windows Server 2012 R2, and Windows Server 2016 editions. For a detailed comparison chart of the different editions of Windows Server 2012 R2, see *https://www.microsoft.com/en-us/download/details.aspx?id=41703*. For Windows 10 and Server 2016 editions and earlier OS memory limits, see *https://msdn.microsoft.com/en-us/library/windows/desktop/aa366778.aspx*.

Although there are several client and server retail packages of the Windows OS, they share a common set of core system files, including the kernel image, Ntoskrnl.exe (and the PAE version, Ntkrnlpa.exe), the HAL libraries, the device drivers, and the base system utilities and DLLs.

TABLE 2-2 Processor and memory limits for some Windows editions

	Number of Sockets Supported (32-Bit Edition)	Physical Memory Supported (32-Bit Edition)	Number of Logical Processors/Sockets Supported (64-Bit Edition)	Physical Memory Supported (x64 Editions)
Windows 10 Home	1	4 GB	1 socket	128 GB
Windows 10 Pro	2	4 GB	2 sockets	2 TB
Windows 10 Enterprise	2	4 GB	2 sockets	2 TB
Windows Server 2012 R2 Essentials	Not available	Not available	2 sockets	64 GB
Windows Server 2016 Standard	Not available	Not available	512 logical processors	24 TB
Windows Server 2016 Datacenter	Not available	Not available	512 logical processors	24 TB

With so many different editions of Windows and each having the same kernel image, how does the system know which edition is booted? By querying the registry values ProductType and ProductSuite under the HKLM\SYSTEM\CurrentControlSet\Control\ProductOptions key. ProductType is used to distinguish whether the system is a client system or a server system (of any flavor). These values are loaded into the registry based on the licensing policy file described earlier. The valid values are listed in Table 2-3. This can be queried from the user-mode VerifyVersionInfo function or from a device driver using the kernel-mode support function RtlGetVersion and RtlVerifyVersionInfo, both documented in the Windows Driver Kit (WDK).

TABLE 2-3 ProductType registry values

Edition of Windows	Value of ProductType
Windows client	WinNT
Windows server (domain controller)	LanmanNT
Windows server (server only)	ServerNT

A different registry value, ProductPolicy, contains a cached copy of the data inside the tokens.dat file, which differentiates between the editions of Windows and the features that they enable.

So if the core files are essentially the same for the client and server versions, how do the systems differ in operation? In short, server systems are optimized by default for system throughput as high-performance application servers, whereas the client version (although it has server capabilities) is optimized for response time for interactive desktop use. For example, based on the product type, several resource-allocation decisions are made differently at system boot time, such as the size and number of OS heaps (or pools), the number of internal system worker threads, and the size of the system data cache. Also, run-time policy decisions, such as the way the memory manager trades off system and process memory demands, differ between the server and client editions. Even some thread-scheduling details have different default behavior in the two families (the default length of the time slice, or thread *quantum*; see Chapter 4 for details). Where there are significant operational differences in the two products, these are highlighted in the pertinent chapters throughout the rest of this book. Unless otherwise noted, everything in this book applies to both the client and server versions.

EXPERIMENT: Determining features enabled by licensing policy

As mentioned, Windows supports more than 100 different features that can be enabled through the software licensing mechanism. These policy settings determine the various differences not only between a client and server installation, but also between each edition (or SKU) of the OS, such as BitLocker support (available on Windows server as well as the Pro and Enterprise editions of Windows client). You can use the SlPolicy tool from the downloads available for the book to display many of these policy values.

Policy settings are organized by a *facility*, which represents the owner module for which the policy applies. You can display a list of all facilities known to the tool by running Slpolicy.exe with the –f switch:

```
C:\>SlPolicy.exe -f
Software License Policy Viewer Version 1.0 (C)2016 by Pavel Yosifovich
Desktop Windows Manager
Explorer
Fax
Kernel
IIS
...
```

You can then add the name of any facility after the switch to display the policy value for that facility. For example, to look at the limitations on CPUs and available memory, use the Kernel facility. Here's the expected output on a machine running Windows 10 Pro:

```
C:\>SlPolicy.exe -f Kernel
Software License Policy Viewer Version 1.0 (C)2016 by Pavel Yosifovich
Kernel
------
Maximum allowed processor sockets: 2
Maximum memory allowed in MB (x86): 4096
Maximum memory allowed in MB (x64): 2097152
Maximum memory allowed in MB (ARM64): 2097152
Maximum physical page in bytes: 4096
Device Family ID: 3
Native VHD boot: Yes
Dynamic Partitioning supported: No
Virtual Dynamic Partitioning supported: No
Memory Mirroring supported: No
Persist defective memory list: No
```

As another example, the output for the kernel facility for a Windows Server 2012 R2 Datacenter edition would look something like this:

```
Kernel
------

Maximum allowed processor sockets: 64
Maximum memory allowed in MB (x86): 4096
Maximum memory allowed in MB (x64): 4194304
Add physical memory allowed: Yes
Add VM physical memory allowed: Yes
Maximum physical page in bytes: 0
Native VHD boot: Yes
Dynamic Partitioning supported: Yes
Virtual Dynamic Partitioning supported: Yes
Memory Mirroring supported: Yes
Persist defective memory list: Yes
```

Checked build

There is a special internal debug version of Windows called the *checked build* (externally available only for Windows 8.1 and earlier with an MSDN Operating Systems subscription). It is a recompilation of the Windows source code with a compile-time flag defined called *DBG*, which causes compile time, conditional debugging, and tracing code to be included. Also, to make it easier to understand the machine code, the post-processing of the Windows binaries to optimize code layout for faster execution is not performed. (See the section "Debugging performance-optimized code" in the Debugging Tools for Windows help file.)

The checked build was provided primarily to aid device driver developers because it performs more stringent error-checking on kernel-mode functions called by device drivers or other system code. For example, if a driver (or some other piece of kernel-mode code) makes an invalid call to a system function that is checking parameters (such as acquiring a spinlock at the wrong interrupt request level), the system will stop execution when the problem is detected rather than allow some data structure to be corrupted and the system to possibly crash at a later time. Because a full checked build was often unstable and impossible to run in most environments, Microsoft provides a checked kernel and HAL only for Windows 10 and later. This enables developers to obtain the same level of usefulness from the kernel and HAL code they interact with without dealing with the issues that a full checked build would cause. This checked kernel and HAL pair is freely available through the WDK, in the \Debug directory of the root installation path. For detailed instructions on how to do this, see the section "Installing Just the Checked Operating System and HAL" in the WDK documentation.

EXPERIMENT: Determining if you are running the checked build

There is no built-in tool to display whether you are running the checked build or the retail build (called the *free build*) of the kernel. However, this information is available through the Debug property of the Windows Management Instrumentation (WMI) Win32_OperatingSystem class.

The following PowerShell script displays this property. (You can try this by opening a PowerShell script host.)

```
PS C:\Users\pavely> Get-WmiObject win32_operatingsystem | select debug
debug
-----
False
```

This system is not running the checked build, because the Debug property shown here says False.

Much of the additional code in the checked-build binaries is a result of using the ASSERT and/or NT_ASSERT macros, which are defined in the WDK header file Wdm.h and documented in the WDK documentation. These macros test a condition, such as the validity of a data structure or parameter. If the expression evaluates to FALSE, the macros either call the kernel-mode function RtlAssert, which calls DbgPrintEx to send the text of the debug message to a debug message buffer, or issue an assertion interrupt, which is interrupt 0x2B on x64 and x86 systems. If a kernel debugger is attached and the appropriate symbols are loaded, this message is displayed automatically followed by a prompt asking the user what to do about the assertion failure (breakpoint, ignore, terminate process, or terminate thread). If the system wasn't booted with the kernel debugger (using the debug option in the Boot Configuration Database) and no kernel debugger is currently attached, failure of an assertion test will bug-check (crash) the system. For a small list of assertion checks made by some of the kernel support routines, see the section "Checked Build ASSERTs" in the WDK documentation (although note this list is unmaintained and outdated).

The checked build is also useful for system administrators because of the additional detailed informational tracing that can be enabled for certain components. (For detailed instructions, see the Microsoft Knowledge Base Article number 314743, titled "HOWTO: Enable Verbose Debug Tracing in Various Drivers and Subsystems.") This information output is sent to an internal debug message buffer using the DbgPrintEx function referred to earlier. To view the debug messages, you can either attach a kernel debugger to the target system (which requires booting the target system in debugging mode), use the !dbgprint command while performing local kernel debugging, or use the Dbgview.exe tool from Sysinternals. Most recent versions of Windows have moved away from this type of debug output, however, and use a combination of either Windows preprocessor (WPP) tracing or TraceLogging technology, both of which are built on top of Event Tracing for Windows (ETW). The advantage of these new logging mechanisms is that they are not solely limited to the checked versions of components (especially useful now that a full checked build is no longer available), and can be seen by using tools such as the Windows Performance Analyzer (WPA), formerly known as XPerf or Windows Perfomance Toolkit, TraceView (from the WDK), or the !wmiprint extension command in the kernel debugger.

Finally, the checked build can also be useful for testing user-mode code only because the timing of the system is different. (This is because of the additional checking taking place within the kernel and the fact that the components are compiled without optimizations.) Often, multithreaded synchronization bugs are related to specific timing conditions. By running your tests on a system running the checked build (or at least the checked kernel and HAL), the fact that the timing of the whole system is different might cause latent timing bugs to surface that do not occur on a normal retail system.

Virtualization-based security architecture overview

As you saw in Chapter 1 and again in this chapter, the separation between user mode and kernel mode provides protection for the OS from user-mode code, whether malicious or not. However, if an unwanted piece of kernel-mode code makes it into the system (because of some yet-unpatched kernel or driver vulnerability or because the user was tricked into installing a malicious or vulnerable driver), the system is essentially compromised because all kernel-mode code has complete access to the entire system. The technologies outlined in Chapter 1, which leverage the hypervisor to provide additional guarantees against attacks, make up a set of virtualization-based security (VBS) capabilities, extending the processor's natural privilege-based separation through the introduction of Virtual Trust Levels (VTLs). Beyond simply introducing a new orthogonal way of isolating access to memory, hardware, and processor resources, VTLs also require new code and components to manage the higher levels of trust. The regular kernel and drivers, running in VTL 0, cannot be permitted to control and define VTL 1 resources; this would defeat the purpose.

Figure 2-3 shows the architecture of Windows 10 Enterprise and Server 2016 when VBS is active. (You'll also sometimes see the term *Virtual Secure Mode*, or *VSM*, used.) With Windows 10 version 1607 and Server 2016 releases, it's always active by default if supported by hardware. For older versions of Windows 10, you can activate it by using a policy or with the Add Windows Features dialog box (select the Isolated User Mode option).

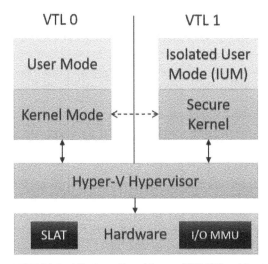

FIGURE 2-3   Windows 10 and Server 2016 VBS architecture.

As shown in Figure 2-3, the user/kernel code discussed earlier is running on top of a Hyper-V hypervisor, just like in Figure 2-1. The difference is that with VBS enabled, a VTL of 1 is now present, which contains its own secure kernel running in the privileged processor mode (that is, ring 0 on x86/x64). Similarly, a run-time user environment mode, called the Isolated User Mode (IUM), now exists, which runs in unprivileged mode (that is, ring 3).

In this architecture, the secure kernel is its own separate binary, which is found under the name se-curekernel.exe on disk. As for IUM, it's both an environment that restricts the allowed system calls that regular user-mode DLLs can make (thus limiting which of these DLLs can be loaded) and a framework that adds special secure system calls that can execute only under VTL 1. These additional system calls are exposed in a similar way as regular system calls: through an internal system library named *Iumdll.dll* (the VTL 1 version of Ntdll.dll) and a Windows subsystem–facing library named *Iumbase.dll* (the VTL 1 version of Kernelbase.dll). This implementation of IUM, mostly sharing the same standard Win32 API libraries, allows for the reduction of the memory overhead of VTL 1 user-mode applications because essentially, the same user-mode code is present as in their VTL 0 counterparts. As an important note, copy-on-write mechanisms, which you'll learn more about in Chapter 5, prevent VTL 0 applications from making changes to binaries used by VTL 1.

With VBS, the regular user versus kernel rules apply, but are now augmented by VTL considerations. In other words, kernel-mode code running at VTL 0 cannot touch user mode running at VTL 1 because VTL 1 is more privileged. Yet, user-mode code running at VTL 1 cannot touch kernel mode running at VTL 0 either because user (ring 3) cannot touch kernel (ring 0). Similarly, VTL 1 user-mode applications must still go through regular Windows system calls and their respective access checks if they wish to access resources.

A simple way of thinking about this is as follows: privilege levels (user versus kernel) enforce *power*. VTLs, on the other hand, enforce *isolation*. Although a VTL 1 user-mode application is not more power-ful than a VTL 0 application or driver, it is isolated from it. In fact, VTL 1 applications aren't just *not* more powerful; in many cases, they're much less so. Because the secure kernel does not implement a full range of system capabilities, it hand-picks which system calls it will forward to the VTL 0 kernel. (Another name for secure kernel is *proxy kernel*.) Any kind of I/O, including file, network, and registry-based, is completely prohibited. Graphics, as another example, are out of the question. Not a single driver is allowed to be communicated with.

The secure kernel however, by both running at VTL 1 and being in kernel mode, does have complete access to VTL 0 memory and resources. It can use the hypervisor to limit the VTL 0 OS access to certain memory locations by leveraging CPU hardware support known as Second Level Address Translation (SLAT). SLAT is the basis of Credential Guard technology, which can store secrets in such locations. Similarly, the secure kernel can use SLAT technology to interdict and control execution of memory locations, a key covenant of Device Guard.

To prevent normal device drivers from leveraging hardware devices to directly access memory, the system uses another piece of hardware known as the *I/O memory management unit* (*MMU*), which effectively virtualizes memory access for devices. This can be used to prevent device drivers from using direct memory access (DMA) to directly access the hypervisor or secure kernel's physical regions of memory. This would bypass SLAT because no virtual memory is involved.

Because the hypervisor is the first system component to be launched by the boot loader, it can pro-gram the SLAT and I/O MMU as it sees fit, defining the VTL 0 and 1 execution environments. Then, while in VTL 1, the boot loader runs again, loading the secure kernel, which can configure the system further to its needs. Only then is the VTL dropped, which will see the execution of the normal kernel, now living in its VTL 0 jail, unable to escape.

Because user-mode processes running in VTL 1 are isolated, potentially malicious code—while not able to exert greater influence over the system—could run surreptitiously, attempt secure system calls (which would allow it to seal/sign its own secrets), and potentially cause bad interactions with other VTL 1 processes or the smart kernel. As such, only a special class of specially signed binaries, called *Trustlets*, are allowed to execute in VTL 1. Each Trustlet has a unique identifier and signature, and the secure kernel has hard-coded knowledge of which Trustlets have been created so far. As such, it is impossible to create new Trustlets without access to the secure kernel (which only Microsoft can touch), and existing Trustlets cannot be patched in any way (which would void the special Microsoft signature). For more information on Trustlets, see Chapter 3.

The addition of the secure kernel and VBS is an exciting step in modern OS architecture. With additional hardware changes to various buses such as PCI and USB, it will soon be possible to support an entire class of secure devices, which, when combined with a minimalistic secure HAL, secure Plug-and-Play manager, and secure User-Mode Device Framework, could allow certain VTL 1 applications direct and segregated access to specially designated devices, such as for biometric or smartcard input. New versions of Windows 10 are likely to leverage such advances.

Key system components

Now that we've looked at the high-level architecture of Windows, let's delve deeper into the internal structure and the role each key OS component plays. Figure 2-4 is a more detailed and complete diagram of the core Windows system architecture and components than was shown in Figure 2-1. Note that it still does not show all components (networking in particular, which is explained in Chapter 10, "Networking," in Part 2).

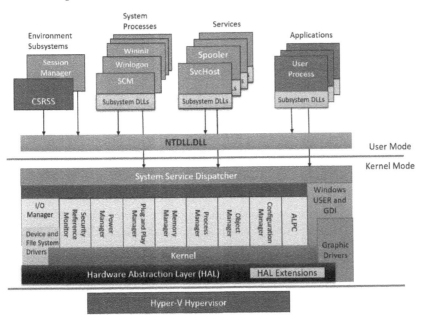

FIGURE 2-4   Windows architecture.

The following sections elaborate on each major element of this diagram. Chapter 8 in Part 2 explains the primary control mechanisms the system uses (such as the object manager, interrupts, and so forth). Chapter 11, "Startup and shutdown," in Part 2 describes the process of starting and shutting down Windows, and Chapter 9 in Part 2 details management mechanisms such as the registry, service processes and WMI. Other chapters explore in even more detail the internal structure and operation of key areas such as processes and threads, memory management, security, the I/O manager, storage management, the cache manager, the Windows file system (NTFS), and networking.

Environment subsystems and subsystem DLLs

The role of an environment subsystem is to expose some subset of the base Windows executive system services to application programs. Each subsystem can provide access to different subsets of the native services in Windows. That means that some things can be done from an application built on one subsystem that can't be done by an application built on another subsystem. For example, a Windows application can't use the SUA fork function.

Each executable image (.exe) is bound to one and only one subsystem. When an image is run, the process creation code examines the subsystem type code in the image header so that it can notify the proper subsystem of the new process. This type code is specified with the /SUBSYSTEM linker option of the Microsoft Visual Studio linker (or through the SubSystem entry in the Linker/System property page in the project's properties).

As mentioned, user applications don't call Windows system services directly. Instead, they go through one or more subsystem DLLs. These libraries export the documented interface that the programs linked to that subsystem can call. For example, the Windows subsystem DLLs (such as Kernel32.dll, Advapi32.dll, User32.dll, and Gdi32.dll) implement the Windows API functions. The SUA subsystem DLL (Psxdll.dll) is used to implement the SUA API functions (on Windows versions that supported POSIX).

EXPERIMENT: Viewing the image subsystem type

You can see the image subsystem type by using the Dependency Walker tool (Depends.exe). For example, notice the image types for two different Windows images, Notepad.exe (the simple text editor) and Cmd.exe (the Windows command prompt):

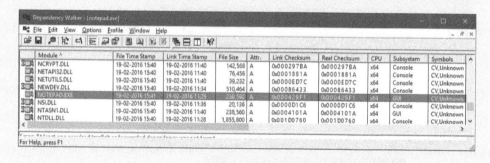

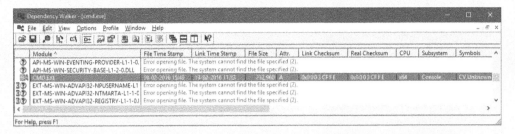

This shows that Notepad is a GUI program, while Cmd is a console, or character-based, program. Although this implies there are two different subsystems for GUI and character-based programs, there is just one Windows subsystem, and GUI programs can have consoles (by calling the AllocConsole function), just like console programs can display GUIs.

When an application calls a function in a subsystem DLL, one of three things can occur:

- The function is entirely implemented in user mode inside the subsystem DLL. In other words, no message is sent to the environment subsystem process, and no Windows executive system services are called. The function is performed in user mode, and the results are returned to the caller. Examples of such functions include GetCurrentProcess (which always returns –1, a value that is defined to refer to the current process in all process-related functions) and GetCurrentProcessId. (The process ID doesn't change for a running process, so this ID is retrieved from a cached location, thus avoiding the need to call into the kernel.)

- The function requires one or more calls to the Windows executive. For example, the Windows ReadFile and WriteFile functions involve calling the underlying internal (and undocumented for user-mode use) Windows I/O system services NtReadFile and NtWriteFile, respectively.

- The function requires some work to be done in the environment subsystem process. (The environment subsystem processes, running in user mode, are responsible for maintaining the state of the client applications running under their control.) In this case, a client/server request is made to the environment subsystem via an ALPC (described in Chapter 8 in Part 2) message sent to the subsystem to perform some operation. The subsystem DLL then waits for a reply before returning to the caller.

Some functions can be a combination of the second and third items just listed, such as the Windows CreateProcess and ExitWindowsEx functions.

Subsystem startup

Subsystems are started by the Session Manager (Smss.exe) process. The subsystem startup information is stored under the registry key HKLM\SYSTEM\CurrentControlSet\Control\Session Manager\SubSystems. Figure 2-5 shows the values under this key (Windows 10 Pro snapshot).

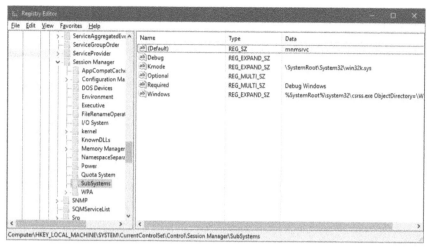

FIGURE 2-5 Registry Editor showing Windows subsystem information.

The Required value lists the subsystems that load when the system boots. The value has two strings: Windows and Debug. The Windows value contains the file specification of the Windows subsystem, Csrss.exe, which stands for *Client/Server Runtime Subsystem*. Debug is blank (this value has not been needed since Windows XP, but the registry value is kept for compatibility) and therefore does nothing. The Optional value indicates optional subsystems, which in this case is blank as well because SUA is no longer available on Windows 10. If it was, a data value of Posix would point to another value pointing to Psxss.exe (the POSIX subsystem process). A value of Optional means "loaded on demand," which means the first time a POSIX image is encountered. The registry value Kmode contains the file name of the kernel-mode portion of the Windows subsystem, Win32k.sys (explained later in this chapter).

Let's take a closer look at the Windows environment subsystems.

Windows subsystem

Although Windows was designed to support multiple independent environment subsystems, from a practical perspective, having each subsystem implement all the code to handle windowing and display I/O would result in a large amount of duplication of system functions that, ultimately, would negatively affect both system size and performance. Because Windows was the primary subsystem, the Windows designers decided to locate these basic functions there and have the other subsystems call on the Windows subsystem to perform display I/O. Thus, the SUA subsystem calls services in the Windows subsystem to perform display I/O.

As a result of this design decision, the Windows subsystem is a required component for any Windows system, even on server systems with no interactive users logged in. Because of this, the process is marked as a critical process (which means if it exits for any reason, the system crashes).

The Windows subsystem consists of the following major components:

- For each session, an instance of the environment subsystem process (Csrss.exe) loads four DLLs (Basesrv.dll, Winsrv.dll, Sxssrv.dll, and Csrsrv.dll) that contain support for the following:

  - Various housekeeping tasks related to creating and deleting processes and threads

  - Shutting down Windows applications (through the ExitWindowsEx API)

  - Containing .ini file to registry location mappings for backward compatibility

  - Sending certain kernel notification messages (such as those from the Plug-and-Play manager) to Windows applications as Window messages (WM_DEVICECHANGE)

  - Portions of the support for 16-bit virtual DOS machine (VDM) processes (32-bit Windows only)

  - Side-by-Side (SxS)/Fusion and manifest cache support

  - Several natural language support functions, to provide caching

 Note Perhaps most critically, the kernel mode code that handles the raw input thread and desktop thread (responsible for the mouse cursor, keyboard input, and handling of the desktop window) is hosted inside threads running inside Winsrv.dll. Additionally, the Csrss.exe instances associated with interactive user sessions contain a fifth DLL called the Canonical Display Driver (Cdd.dll). CDD is responsible for communicating with the DirectX support in the kernel (see the upcoming discussion) on each vertical refresh (VSync) to draw the visible desktop state without traditional hardware-accelerated GDI support.

- A kernel-mode device driver (Win32k.sys) that contains the following:

  - The window manager, which controls window displays; manages screen output; collects input from keyboard, mouse, and other devices; and passes user messages to applications

  - The Graphics Device Interface (GDI), which is a library of functions for graphics output devices and includes functions for line, text, and figure drawing and for graphics manipulation

  - Wrappers for DirectX support that is implemented in another kernel driver (Dxgkrnl.sys)

- The console host process (Conhost.exe), which provides support for console (character cell) applications

- The Desktop Window Manager (Dwm.exe), which allows for compositing visible window rendering into a single surface through the CDD and DirectX

- Subsystem DLLs (such as Kernel32.dll, Advapi32.dll, User32.dll, and Gdi32.dll) that translate documented Windows API functions into the appropriate and undocumented (for user-mode) kernel-mode system service calls in Ntoskrnl.exe and Win32k.sys

- Graphics device drivers for hardware-dependent graphics display drivers, printer drivers, and video miniport drivers

Note As part of a refactoring effort in the Windows architecture called *MinWin*, the subsystem DLLs are now generally composed of specific libraries that implement API Sets, which are then linked together into the subsystem DLL and resolved using a special redirection scheme. For more information on this refactoring, see the "Image loader" section in Chapter 3.

Windows 10 and Win32k.sys

The basic window-management requirements for Windows 10–based devices vary considerably depending on the device in question. For example, a full desktop running Windows needs all the window manager's capabilities, such as resizable windows, owner windows, child windows and so forth. Windows Mobile 10 running on phones or small tablets doesn't need many of these features because there's only one window in the foreground and it cannot be minimized or resized, etc. The same goes for IoT devices, which may not even have a display at all.

For these reasons, the functionality of Win32K.sys has been split among several kernel modules so that not all modules may be required on a specific system. This significantly reduces the attack surface of the window manager by reducing the complexity of the code and eliminating many of its legacy pieces. Here are some examples:

- On phones (Windows Mobile 10) Win32k.sys loads Win32kMin.sys and Win32kBase.sys.
- On full desktop systems Win32k.sys loads Win32kBase.sys and Win32kFull.sys.
- On certain IoT systems, Win32k.sys might only need Win32kBase.sys.

Applications call the standard USER functions to create user-interface controls, such as windows and buttons, on the display. The window manager communicates these requests to the GDI, which passes them to the graphics device drivers, where they are formatted for the display device. A display driver is paired with a video miniport driver to complete video display support.

The GDI provides a set of standard two-dimensional functions that let applications communicate with graphics devices without knowing anything about the devices. GDI functions mediate between applications and graphics devices such as display drivers and printer drivers. The GDI interprets application requests for graphic output and sends the requests to graphics display drivers. It also provides a standard interface for applications to use varying graphics output devices. This interface enables application code to be independent of the hardware devices and their drivers. The GDI tailors its messages to the capabilities of the device, often dividing the request into manageable parts. For example, some devices can understand directions to draw an ellipse; others require the GDI to interpret the command as a series of pixels placed at certain coordinates. For more information about the graphics and video driver architecture, see the "Design Guide" section of the "Display (Adapters and Monitors)" chapter in the WDK.

Because much of the subsystem—in particular, display I/O functionality—runs in kernel mode, only a few Windows functions result in sending a message to the Windows subsystem process: process and thread creation and termination and DOS device drive letter mapping (such as through subst.exe).

In general, a running Windows application won't cause many, if any, context switches to the Windows subsystem process, except as needed to draw the new mouse cursor position, handle keyboard input, and render the screen through CDD.

Console window host

In the original Windows subsystem design, the subsystem process (Csrss.exe) was responsible for managing console windows and each console application (such as Cmd.exe, the command prompt) communicated with Csrss.exe. Starting with Windows 7, a separate process is used for each console window on the system: the console window host (Conhost.exe). (A single console window can be shared by multiple console applications, such as when you launch a command prompt from the command prompt. By default, the second command prompt shares the console window of the first.) The details of the Windows 7 console host are explained in Chapter 2 of the sixth edition of this book.

With Windows 8 and later, the console architecture changed yet again. The Conhost.exe process remains, but is now spawned from the console-based process (rather than from Csrss.exe, as in Windows 7) by the console driver (\Windows\System32\Drivers\ConDrv.sys). The process in question communicates with Conhost.exe using the console driver (ConDrv.sys), by sending read, write, I/O control and other I/O request types. Conhost.exe is designated as a server and the process using the console is the client. This change obviates the need for Csrss.exe to receive keyboard input (as part of the raw input thread), send it through Win32k.sys to Conhost.exe, and then use ALPC to send it to Cmd.exe. Instead, the command-line application can directly receive input from the console driver through read/write I/Os, avoiding needless context switching.

The following Process Explorer screen shows the handle Conhost.exe holds open to the device object exposed by ConDrv.sys named \Device\ConDrv. (For more details on device names and I/O, see Chapter 6.)

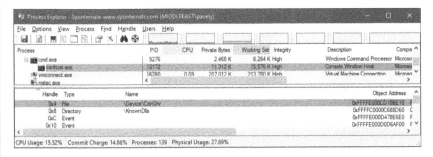

Notice that Conhost.exe is a child process of the console process (in this case, Cmd.exe). Conhost creation is initiated by the image loader for Console subsystem images or on demand if a GUI subsystem image calls the AllocConsole Windows API. (Of course, GUI and Console are essentially the same in the sense both are variants of the Windows subsystem type.) The real workhorse of Conhost.exe is a DLL it loads (\Windows\System32\ConhostV2.dll) that includes the bulk of code that communicates with the console driver.

Other subsystems

As mentioned, Windows originally supported POSIX and OS/2 subsystems. Because these subsystems are no longer provided with Windows, they are not covered in this book. The general concept of subsystems remains, however, making the system extensible to new subsystems if such a need arises in the future.

Pico providers and the Windows subsystem for Linux

The traditional subsystem model, while extensible and clearly powerful enough to have supported POSIX and OS/2 for a decade, has two important technical disadvantages that made it hard to reach broad usage of non-Windows binaries beyond a few specialized use cases:

- As mentioned, because subsystem information is extracted from the Portable Executable (PE) header, it requires the source code of the original binary to rebuild it as a Windows PE executable file (.exe). This will also change any POSIX-style dependencies and system calls into Windows-style imports of the Psxdll.dll library.

- It is limited by the functionality provided either by the Win32 subsystem (on which it sometimes piggybacks) or the NT kernel. Therefore, the subsystem wraps, instead of emulates, the behavior required by the POSIX application. This can sometimes lead to subtle compatibility flaws.

Finally, it's also important to point out, that as the name says, the POSIX subsystem/SUA was designed with POSIX/UNIX applications in mind, which dominated the server market decades ago, not true Linux applications, which are common today.

Solving these issues required a different approach to building a subsystem—one that did not require the traditional user-mode wrapping of the other environments' system call and the execution of traditional PE images. Luckily, the Drawbridge project from Microsoft Research provided the perfect vehicle for an updated take on subsystems. It resulted in the implementation of the Pico model.

Under this model, the idea of a *Pico provider* is defined, which is a custom kernel-mode driver that receives access to specialized kernel interfaces through the `PsRegisterPicoProvider` API. The benefits of these specialized interfaces are two-fold:

- They allow the provider to create Pico processes and threads while customizing their execution contexts, segments, and store data in their respective EPROCESS and ETHREAD structures (see Chapter 3 and Chapter 4 for more on these structures).

- They allow the provider to receive a rich set of notifications whenever such processes or threads engage in certain system actions such as system calls, exceptions, APCs, page faults, termination, context changes, suspension/resume, etc.

With Windows 10 version 1607, one such Pico provider is present: Lxss.sys and its partner Lxcore.sys. As the name suggests, this refers to the Windows Subsystem for Linux (WSL) component, and these drivers make up the Pico provider interface for it.

Because the Pico provider receives almost all possible transitions to and from user and kernel mode (be they system calls or exceptions, for example), as long as the Pico process (or processes) running underneath it has an address space that it can recognize, and has code that can natively execute within it, the "true" kernel below doesn't really matter as long as these transitions are handled in a fully transparent way. As such, Pico processes running under the WSL Pico provider, as you'll see in Chapter 3, are very different from normal Windows processes—lacking, for example, the Ntdll.dll that is always loaded into normal processes. Instead, their memory contains structures such as a vDSO, a special image seen only on Linux/BSD systems.

Furthermore, if the Linux processes are to run transparently, they must be able to execute without requiring recompilation as PE Windows executables. Because the Windows kernel does not know how to map other image types, such images cannot be launched through the `CreateProcess` API by a Windows process, nor do they ever call such APIs themselves (because they have no idea they are running on Windows). Such interoperability support is provided both by the Pico provider and the LXSS Manager, which is a user-mode service. The former implements a private interface that it uses to communicate with the LXSS Manager. The latter implements a COM-based interface that it uses to communicate with a specialized launcher process, currently known as *Bash.exe*, and with a management process, called *Lxrun.exe*. The following diagram shows an overview of the components that make up WSL.

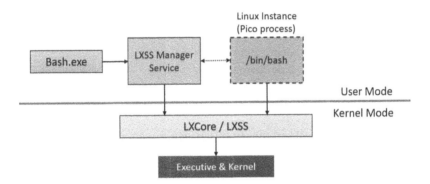

Providing support for a wide variety of Linux applications is a massive undertaking. Linux has hundreds of system calls—about as many as the Windows kernel itself. Although the Pico provider can leverage existing features of Windows—many of which were built to support the original POSIX subsystem, such as `fork()` support—in some cases, it must re-implement functionality on its own. For example, even though NTFS is used to store the actual file system (and not EXTFS), the Pico provider has an entire implementation of the Linux Virtual File System (VFS), including support for inodes, inotify(), and /sys, /dev, and other similar Linux-style file-system–based namespaces with corresponding behaviors. Similarly, while the Pico provider can leverage Windows Sockets for Kernel (WSK) for networking, it has complex wrapping around actual socket behavior, such that it can support UNIX domain sockets, Linux NetLink sockets, and standard Internet sockets.

In other cases, existing Windows facilities were simply not adequately compatible, sometimes in subtle ways. For example, Windows has a named pipe driver (Npfs.sys) that supports the traditional pipe IPC mechanism. Yet, it's subtly different enough from Linux pipes that applications would break. This required a from-scratch implementation of pipes for Linux applications, without using the kernel's Npfs.sys driver.

As the feature is still officially in beta at the time of this writing and subject to significant change, we won't cover the actual internals of the subsystem in this book. We will, however, take another look at Pico processes in Chapter 3. When the subsystem matures beyond beta, you will probably see official documentation on MSDN and stable APIs for interacting with Linux processes from Windows.

Ntdll.dll

Ntdll.dll is a special system support library primarily for the use of subsystem DLLs and native applications. (*Native* in this context refers to images that are not tied to any particular subsystem.) It contains two types of functions:

- System service dispatch stubs to Windows executive system services

- Internal support functions used by subsystems, subsystem DLLs, and other native images

The first group of functions provides the interface to the Windows executive system services that can be called from user mode. There are more than 450 such functions, such as NtCreateFile, Nt-SetEvent, and so on. As noted, most of the capabilities of these functions are accessible through the Windows API. (A number are not, however, and are for use only by specific OS-internal components.)

For each of these functions, Ntdll.dll contains an entry point with the same name. The code inside the function contains the architecture-specific instruction that causes a transition into kernel mode to invoke the system service dispatcher. (This is explained in more detail in Chapter 8 in Part 2.) After verifying some parameters, this system service dispatcher calls the actual kernel-mode system service that contains the real code inside Ntoskrnl.exe. The following experiment shows what these functions look like.

EXPERIMENT: Viewing the system service dispatcher code

Open the version of WinDbg that corresponds to your system's architecture (for example the x64 version bit on 64 bit Windows). Then open the **File** menu and select **Open Executable**. Navigate to **%SystemRoot%\System32** and select **Notepad.exe**.

Notepad should launch and the debugger should break in the initial breakpoint. This is very early in the life of the process, which you can witness by executing the k (call stack) command. You should see a few functions starting with Ldr, which indicates the image loader. The main function for Notepad has not executed yet, which means you won't see Notepad's window.

Set a breakpoint in the NtCreateFile inside Ntdll.dll (the debuggers are not case sensitive):

```
bp ntdll!ntcreatefile
```

Enter the **g** (go) command or press **F5** to let Notepad continue execution. The debugger should break almost immediately, showing something like this (x64):

```
Breakpoint 0 hit
ntdll!NtCreateFile:
00007ffa'9f4e5b10 4c8bd1          mov        r10,rcx
```

You may see the function name as ZwCreateFile. ZwCreateFile and NtCreateFile refer to the same symbol in user mode. Now enter the **u** (unassembled) command to see a few instructions ahead:

```
00007ffa'9f4e5b10 4c8bd1           mov     r10,rcx
00007ffa'9f4e5b13 b855000000       mov     eax,55h
00007ffa'9f4e5b18 f604250803fe7f01 test    byte ptr [SharedUserData+0x308
(00000000'7ffe0308)],1
00007ffa'9f4e5b20 7503             jne     ntdll!NtCreateFile+0x15
(00007ffa'9f4e5b25)
00007ffa'9f4e5b22 0f05             syscall
00007ffa'9f4e5b24 c3               ret
00007ffa'9f4e5b25 cd2e             int     2Eh
00007ffa'9f4e5b27 c3               ret
```

The EAX register is set with the system service number (55 hex in this case). This is the system service number on this OS (Windows 10 Pro x64). Then notice the syscall instruction. This is the one causing the processor to transition to kernel mode, jumping to the system service dispatcher, where that EAX is used to select the NtCreateFile executive service. You'll also notice a check for a flag (1) at offset 0x308 in the Shared User Data (more information on this structure is available in Chapter 4). If this flag is set, execution will take another path, by using the int 2Eh instruction instead. If you enable the specific Credential Guard VBS feature that is described in Chapter 7, this flag will be set on your machine, because the hypervisor can react to the int instruction in a more efficient fashion than the syscall instruction, and this behavior is beneficial to Credential Guard.

As mentioned, more details about this mechanism (and the behavior of both syscall and int) are provided in Chapter 8 in Part 2. For now, you can try to locate other native services such as NtReadFile, NtWriteFile and NtClose.

You saw in the "Virtualization-based security architecture overview" section that IUM applications can leverage another binary similar to Ntdll.dll, called *IumDll.dll*. This library also contains system calls, but their indices will be different. If you have a system with Credential Guard enabled, you can repeat the preceding experiment by opening the **File** menu in WinDbg, choosing **Open Crash Dump**, and choosing **IumDll.dll** as the file. Note how in the following output, the system call index has the high bit set, and no SharedUserData check is done; syscall is always the instruction used for these types of system calls, which are called *secure system calls*:

```
0:000> u iumdll!IumCrypto
iumdll!IumCrypto:
00000001'80001130 4c8bd1           mov     r10,rcx
00000001'80001133 b802000008       mov     eax,8000002h
00000001'80001138 0f05             syscall
00000001'8000113a c3               ret
```

Ntdll.dll also contains many support functions, such as the image loader (functions that start with Ldr), the heap manager, and Windows subsystem process communication functions (functions that start with `Csr`). Ntdll.dll also includes general run-time library routines (functions that start with `Rtl`), support for user-mode debugging (functions that start with `DbgUi`), Event Tracing for Windows (functions starting in `Etw`), and the user-mode asynchronous procedure call (APC) dispatcher and exception dispatcher. (APCs are explained briefly in Chapter 6 and in more detail in Chapter 8 in Part 2, as well as exceptions.)

Finally, you'll find a small subset of the C Run-Time (CRT) routines in Ntdll.dll, limited to those routines that are part of the string and standard libraries (such as `memcpy`, `strcpy`, `sprintf`, and so on); these are useful for native applications, described next.

Native images

Some images (executables) don't belong to any subsystem. In other words, they don't link against a set of subsystem DLLs, such as Kernel32.dll for the Windows subsystem. Instead, they link only to Ntdll.dll, which is the lowest common denominator that spans subsystems. Because the native API exposed by Ntdll.dll is mostly undocumented, these kind of images are typically built only by Microsoft. One example is the Session Manager process (Smss.exe, described in more detail later in this chapter). Smss.exe is the first user-mode process created (directly by the kernel), so it cannot be dependent on the Windows subsystem because Csrss.exe (the Windows subsystem process) has not started yet. In fact, Smss.exe is responsible for launching Csrss.exe. Another example is the Autochk utility that sometimes runs at system startup to check disks. Because it runs relatively early in the boot process (launched by Smss.exe, in fact), it cannot depend on any subsystem.

Here is a screenshot of Smss.exe in Dependency Walker, showing its dependency on Ntdll.dll only. Notice the subsystem type is indicated by `Native`.

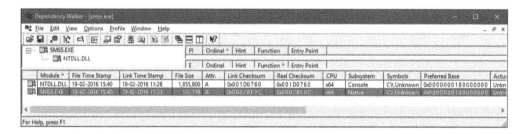

Executive

The Windows executive is the upper layer of Ntoskrnl.exe. (The kernel is the lower layer.) The executive includes the following types of functions:

- **Functions that are exported and callable from user mode** These functions are called *system services* and are exported via Ntdll.dll (such as `NtCreateFile` from the previous experiment). Most of the services are accessible through the Windows API or the APIs of another environment subsystem. A few services, however, aren't available through any documented subsystem function. (Examples include ALPC and various query functions such as `NtQuery-InformationProcess`, specialized functions such as `NtCreatePagingFile`, and so on.)

- **Device driver functions that are called through the *DeviceIoControl* function**   This provides a general interface from user mode to kernel mode to call functions in device drivers that are not associated with a read or write. The driver used for Process Explorer and Process Monitor from Sysinternals are good examples of that as is the console driver (ConDrv.sys) mentioned earlier.

- **Functions that can be called only from kernel mode that are exported and documented in the WDK**   These include various support routines, such as the I/O manager (start with Io), general executive functions (Ex) and more, needed for device driver developers.

- **Functions that are exported and can be called from kernel mode but are not documented in the WDK**   These include the functions called by the boot video driver, which start with Inbv.

- **Functions that are defined as global symbols but are not exported**   These include internal support functions called within Ntoskrnl.dll, such as those that start with Iop (internal I/O manager support functions) or Mi (internal memory management support functions).

- **Functions that are internal to a module that are not defined as global symbols**   These functions are used exclusively by the executive and kernel.

The executive contains the following major components, each of which is covered in detail in a subsequent chapter of this book:

- **Configuration manager**   The configuration manager, explained in Chapter 9 in Part 2, is responsible for implementing and managing the system registry.

- **Process manager**   The process manager, explained in Chapter 3 and Chapter 4, creates and terminates processes and threads. The underlying support for processes and threads is implemented in the Windows kernel; the executive adds additional semantics and functions to these lower-level objects.

- **Security Reference Monitor (SRM)**   The SRM, described in Chapter 7, enforces security policies on the local computer. It guards OS resources, performing run-time object protection and auditing.

- **I/O manager**   The I/O manager, discussed in Chapter 6, implements device-independent I/O and is responsible for dispatching to the appropriate device drivers for further processing.

- **Plug and Play (PnP) manager**   The PnP manager, covered in Chapter 6, determines which drivers are required to support a particular device and loads those drivers. It retrieves the hardware resource requirements for each device during enumeration. Based on the resource requirements of each device, the PnP manager assigns the appropriate hardware resources such as I/O ports, IRQs, DMA channels, and memory locations. It is also responsible for sending proper event notification for device changes (the addition or removal of a device) on the system.

- **Power manager**   The power manager (explained in Chapter 6), processor power management (PPM), and power management framework (PoFx) coordinate power events and generate power management I/O notifications to device drivers. When the system is idle, the PPM can be configured to reduce power consumption by putting the CPU to sleep. Changes in power consumption by individual devices are handled by device drivers but are coordinated by the power manager and PoFx. On certain classes of devices, the terminal timeout manager also manages physical display timeouts based on device usage and proximity.

- **Windows Driver Model (WDM) Windows Management Instrumentation (WMI) routines** These routines, discussed in Chapter 9 in Part 2, enable device drivers to publish performance and configuration information and receive commands from the user-mode WMI service. Consumers of WMI information can be on the local machine or remote across the network.

- **Memory manager** The memory manager, discussed in Chapter 5, implements *virtual memory*, a memory management scheme that provides a large private address space for each process that can exceed available physical memory. The memory manager also provides the underlying support for the cache manager. It is assisted by the prefetcher and Store Manager, also explained in Chapter 5.

- **Cache manager** The cache manager, discussed in Chapter 14, "Cache manager," in Part 2, improves the performance of file-based I/O by causing recently referenced disk data to reside in main memory for quick access. It also achieves this by deferring disk writes by holding the updates in memory for a short time before sending them to the disk. As you'll see, it does this by using the memory manager's support for mapped files.

In addition, the executive contains four main groups of support functions that are used by the executive components just listed. About a third of these support functions are documented in the WDK because device drivers also use them. These are the four categories of support functions:

- **Object manager** The object manager creates, manages, and deletes Windows executive objects and abstract data types that are used to represent OS resources such as processes, threads, and the various synchronization objects. The object manager is explained in Chapter 8 in Part 2.

- **Asynchronous LPC (ALPC) facility** The ALPC facility, explained in Chapter 8 in Part 2, passes messages between a client process and a server process on the same computer. Among other things, ALPC is used as a local transport for *remote procedure call* (*RPC*), the Windows implementation of an industry-standard communication facility for client and server processes across a network.

- **Run-time library functions** These include string processing, arithmetic operations, data type conversion, and security structure processing.

- **Executive support routines** These include system memory allocation (paged and non-paged pool), interlocked memory access, as well as special types of synchronization mechanisms such as executive resources, fast mutexes, and pushlocks.

The executive also contains a variety of other infrastructure routines, some of which are mentioned only briefly in this book:

- **Kernel debugger library** This allows debugging of the kernel from a debugger supporting KD, a portable protocol supported over a variety of transports such as USB, Ethernet, and IEEE 1394, and implemented by WinDbg and the Kd.exe debuggers.

- **User-Mode Debugging Framework**   This is responsible for sending events to the user-mode debugging API and allowing breakpoints and stepping through code to work, as well as for changing contexts of running threads.

- **Hypervisor library and VBS library**   These provide kernel support for the secure virtual machine environment and optimize certain parts of the code when the system knows it's running in a client partition (virtual environment).

- **Errata manager**   The errata manager provides workarounds for nonstandard or noncompliant hardware devices.

- **Driver Verifier**   The Driver Verifier implements optional integrity checks of kernel-mode drivers and code (described in Chapter 6).

- **Event Tracing for Windows (ETW)**   ETW provides helper routines for system-wide event tracing for kernel-mode and user-mode components.

- **Windows Diagnostic Infrastructure (WDI)**   The WDI enables intelligent tracing of system activity based on diagnostic scenarios.

- **Windows Hardware Error Architecture (WHEA) support routines**   These routines provide a common framework for reporting hardware errors.

- **File-System Runtime Library (FSRTL)**   The FSRTL provides common support routines for file system drivers.

- **Kernel Shim Engine (KSE)**   The KSE provides driver-compatibility shims and additional device errata support. It leverages the shim infrastructure and database described in Chapter 8 in Part 2.

Kernel

The kernel consists of a set of functions in Ntoskrnl.exe that provides fundamental mechanisms. These include thread-scheduling and synchronization services, used by the executive components, and low-level hardware architecture–dependent support, such as interrupt and exception dispatching, which is different on each processor architecture. The kernel code is written primarily in C, with assembly code reserved for those tasks that require access to specialized processor instructions and registers not easily accessible from C.

Like the various executive support functions mentioned in the preceding section, a number of functions in the kernel are documented in the WDK (and can be found by searching for functions beginning with Ke) because they are needed to implement device drivers.

Kernel objects

The kernel provides a low-level base of well-defined, predictable OS primitives and mechanisms that allow higher-level components of the executive to do what they need to do. The kernel separates itself from the rest of the executive by implementing OS mechanisms and avoiding policy making. It leaves nearly all policy decisions to the executive, with the exception of thread scheduling and dispatching, which the kernel implements.

Outside the kernel, the executive represents threads and other shareable resources as objects. These objects require some policy overhead, such as object handles to manipulate them, security checks to protect them, and resource quotas to be deducted when they are created. This overhead is eliminated in the kernel, which implements a set of simpler objects, called *kernel objects*, that help the kernel control central processing and support the creation of executive objects. Most executive-level objects encapsulate one or more kernel objects, incorporating their kernel-defined attributes.

One set of kernel objects, called *control objects*, establishes semantics for controlling various OS functions. This set includes the Asynchronous Procedure Call (APC) object, the Deferred Procedure Call (DPC) object, and several objects the I/O manager uses, such as the interrupt object.

Another set of kernel objects, known as *dispatcher objects*, incorporates synchronization capabilities that alter or affect thread scheduling. The dispatcher objects include the kernel thread, mutex (called *mutant* in kernel terminology), event, kernel event pair, semaphore, timer, and waitable timer. The executive uses kernel functions to create instances of kernel objects, to manipulate them, and to construct the more complex objects it provides to user mode. Objects are explained in more detail in Chapter 8 in Part 2, and processes and threads are described in Chapter 3 and Chapter 4, respectively.

Kernel processor control region and control block

The kernel uses a data structure called the *kernel processor control region* (*KPCR*) to store processor-specific data. The KPCR contains basic information such as the processor's interrupt dispatch table (IDT), task state segment (TSS), and global descriptor table (GDT). It also includes the interrupt controller state, which it shares with other modules, such as the ACPI driver and the HAL. To provide easy access to the KPCR, the kernel stores a pointer to it in the fs register on 32-bit Windows and in the gs register on an x64 Windows system.

The KPCR also contains an embedded data structure called the *kernel processor control block* (*KPRCB*). Unlike the KPCR, which is documented for third-party drivers and other internal Windows kernel components, the KPRCB is a private structure used only by the kernel code in Ntoskrnl.exe. It contains the following:

- Scheduling information such as the current, next, and idle threads scheduled for execution on the processor

- The dispatcher database for the processor, which includes the ready queues for each priority level

- The DPC queue

- CPU vendor and identifier information, such as the model, stepping, speed, and feature bits

- CPU and NUMA topology, such as node information, cores per package, logical processors per core, and so on

- Cache sizes

- Time accounting information, such as the DPC and interrupt time.

The KPRCB also contains all the statistics for the processor, such as:

■ I/O statistics

■ Cache manager statistics (see Chapter 14 in Part 2 for a description of these)

■ DPC statistics

■ Memory manager statistics (see Chapter 5 for more information)

Finally, the KPRCB is sometimes used to store cache-aligned, per-processor structures to optimize memory access, especially on NUMA systems. For example, the non-paged and paged-pool system look-aside lists are stored in the KPRCB.

EXPERIMENT: Viewing the KPCR and KPRCB

You can view the contents of the KPCR and KPRCB by using the !pcr and !prcb kernel debugger commands. For the latter, if you don't include flags, the debugger will display information for CPU 0 by default. Otherwise, you can specify a CPU by adding its number after the command—for example, !prcb 2. The former command, on the other hand, will always display information on the current processor, which you can change in a remote debugging session. If doing local debugging, you can obtain the address of the KPCR by using the !pcr extension, followed by the CPU number, then replacing @$pcr with that address. Do not use any of the other output shown in the !pcr command. This extension is deprecated and shows incorrect data. The following example shows what the output of the dt nt!_KPCR @$pcr and !prcb commands looks like (Windows 10 x64):

```
1kd> dt nt!_KPCR @$pcr
    +0x000 NtTib                : _NT_TIB
    +0x000 GdtBase              : 0xfffff802'a5f4bfb0 _KGDTENTRY64
    +0x008 TssBase              : 0xfffff802'a5f4a000 _KTSS64
    +0x010 UserRsp              : 0x0000009b'1a47b2b8
    +0x018 Self                 : 0xfffff802'a280a000 _KPCR
    +0x020 CurrentPrcb          : 0xfffff802'a280a180 _KPRCB
    +0x028 LockArray            : 0xfffff802'a280a7f0 _KSPIN_LOCK_QUEUE
    +0x030 Used_Self            : 0x0000009b'1a200000 Void
    +0x038 IdtBase              : 0xfffff802'a5f49000 _KIDTENTRY64
    +0x040 Unused               : [2] 0
    +0x050 Irql                 : 0 ''
    +0x051 SecondLevelCacheAssociativity : 0x10 ''
    +0x052 ObsoleteNumber       : 0 ''
    +0x053 Fill0                : 0 ''
    +0x054 Unused0              : [3] 0
    +0x060 MajorVersion         : 1
    +0x062 MinorVersion         : 1
    +0x064 StallScaleFactor     : 0x8a0
    +0x068 Unused1              : [3] (null)
    +0x080 KernelReserved       : [15] 0
    +0x0bc SecondLevelCacheSize : 0x400000
    +0x0c0 HalReserved          : [16] 0x839b6800
    +0x100 Unused2              : 0
    +0x108 KdVersionBlock       : (null)
```

```
     +0x110 Unused3           : (null)
     +0x118 PcrAlign1         : [24] 0
     +0x180 Prcb              : _KPRCB
1kd> !prcb
PRCB for Processor 0 at fffff803c3b23180:
Current IRQL -- 0
Threads--  Current ffffe0020535a800 Next 0000000000000000 Idle fffff803c3b99740
Processor Index 0 Number (0, 0) GroupSetMember 1
Interrupt Count -- 0010d637
Times -- Dpc     000000f4 Interrupt 00000119
        Kernel 0000d952 User        0000425d
```

You can also use the dt command to directly dump the _KPRCB data structures because the debugger command gives you the address of the structure (shown in bold for clarity in the previous output). For example, if you wanted to determine the speed of the processor as detected at boot, you could look at the MHz field with the following command:

```
1kd> dt nt!_KPRCB fffff803c3b23180 MHz
    +0x5f4 MHz : 0x893
1kd> ? 0x893
Evaluate expression: 2195 = 00000000'00000893
```

On this machine, the processor was running at about 2.2 GHz during boot-up.

Hardware support

The other major job of the kernel is to abstract or isolate the executive and device drivers from variations between the hardware architectures supported by Windows. This job includes handling variations in functions such as interrupt handling, exception dispatching, and multiprocessor synchronization.

Even for these hardware-related functions, the design of the kernel attempts to maximize the amount of common code. The kernel supports a set of interfaces that are portable and semantically identical across architectures. Most of the code that implements these portable interfaces is also identical across architectures.

Some of these interfaces are implemented differently on different architectures or are partially implemented with architecture-specific code. These architecturally independent interfaces can be called on any machine, and the semantics of the interface will be the same regardless of whether the code varies by architecture. Some kernel interfaces, such as spinlock routines, described in Chapter 8 in Part 2, are actually implemented in the HAL (described in the next section) because their implementation can vary for systems within the same architecture family.

The kernel also contains a small amount of code with x86-specific interfaces needed to support old 16-bit MS-DOS programs (on 32-bit systems). These x86 interfaces aren't portable in the sense that they can't be called on a machine based on any other architecture; they won't be present. This x86-specific code, for example, supports calls to use Virtual 8086 mode, required for the emulation of certain real-mode code on older video cards.

Other examples of architecture-specific code in the kernel include the interfaces to provide translation buffer and CPU cache support. This support requires different code for the different architectures because of the way caches are implemented.

Another example is context switching. Although at a high level the same algorithm is used for thread selection and context switching (the context of the previous thread is saved, the context of the new thread is loaded, and the new thread is started), there are architectural differences among the implementations on different processors. Because the context is described by the processor state (registers and so on), what is saved and loaded varies depending on the architecture.

Hardware abstraction layer

As mentioned at the beginning of this chapter, one of the crucial elements of the Windows design is its portability across a variety of hardware platforms. With OneCore and the myriad device form factors available, this is more important than ever. The hardware abstraction layer (HAL) is a key part of making this portability possible. The HAL is a loadable kernel-mode module (Hal.dll) that provides the low-level interface to the hardware platform on which Windows is running. It hides hardware-dependent details such as I/O interfaces, interrupt controllers, and multiprocessor communication mechanisms—any functions that are both architecture-specific and machine-dependent.

So rather than access hardware directly, Windows internal components and user-written device drivers maintain portability by calling the HAL routines when they need platform-dependent information. For this reason, many HAL routines are documented in the WDK. To find out more about the HAL and its use by device drivers, refer to the WDK.

Although a couple of x86 HALs are included in a standard desktop Windows installation (as shown in Table 2-4), Windows has the ability to detect at boot-up time which HAL should be used, eliminating the problem that existed on earlier versions of Windows when attempting to boot a Windows installation on a different kind of system.

TABLE 2-4 List of x86 HALs

HAL File Name	Systems Supported
Halacpi.dll	Advanced Configuration and Power Interface (ACPI) PCs. Implies uniprocessor-only machine, without APIC support. (The presence of either one would make the system use the HAL below instead.)
Halmacpi.dll	Advanced Programmable Interrupt Controller (APIC) PCs with an ACPI. The existence of an APIC implies SMP support.

On x64 and ARM machines, there is only one HAL image, called Hal.dll. This results from all x64 machines having the same motherboard configuration, because the processors require ACPI and APIC support. Therefore, there is no need to support machines without ACPI or with a standard PIC. Similarly, all ARM systems have ACPI and use interrupt controllers, which are similar to a standard APIC. Once again, a single HAL can support this.

On the other hand, although such interrupt controllers are similar, they are not identical. Additionally, the actual timer and memory/DMA controllers on some ARM systems are different from others.

Finally, in the IoT world, certain standard PC hardware such as the Intel DMA controller may not be present and might require support for a different controller, even on PC-based systems. Older versions of Windows handled this by forcing each vendor to ship a custom HAL for each possible platform combination. This is no longer realistic, however, and results in significant amounts of duplicated code. Instead, Windows now supports modules known as *HAL extensions*, which are additional DLLs on disk that the boot loader may load if specific hardware requiring them is needed (usually through ACPI and registry-based configuration). Your desktop Windows 10 system is likely to include a HalExtPL080.dll and HalExtIntcLpioDMA.dll, the latter of which is used on certain low-power Intel platforms, for example.

Creating HAL extensions requires collaboration with Microsoft, and such files must be custom signed with a special HAL extension certificate available only to hardware vendors. Additionally, they are highly limited in the APIs they can use and interact through a limited import/export table mechanism that does not use the traditional PE image mechanism. For example, the following experiment will not show you any functions if you try to use it on a HAL extension.

EXPERIMENT: Viewing Ntoskrnl.exe and HAL image dependencies

You can view the relationship of the kernel and HAL images by using the Dependency Walker tool (Depends.exe) to examine their export and import tables. To examine an image in the Dependency Walker, open the **File** menu, choose **Open**, and select the desired image file.

Here is a sample of output you can see by viewing the dependencies of Ntoskrnl.exe using this tool (for now, disregard the errors displayed by Dependency Walker's inability to parse the API sets):

Notice that Ntoskrnl.exe is linked against the HAL, which is in turn linked against Ntoskrnl.exe. (They both use functions in each other.) Ntoskrnl.exe is also linked to the following binaries:

- **Pshed.dll** The Platform-Specific Hardware Error Driver (PSHED) provides an abstraction of the hardware error reporting facilities of the underlying platform. It does this by hiding the details of a platform's error-handling mechanisms from the OS and exposing a consistent interface to the Windows OS.

- **Bootvid.dll** The Boot Video Driver on x86 systems (Bootvid) provides support for the VGA commands required to display boot text and the boot logo during startup.

- **Kdcom.dll** This is the Kernel Debugger Protocol (KD) communications library.

- **Ci.dll** This is the integrity library. (See Chapter 8 in Part 2 for more information on code integrity.)

- **Msrpc.sys** The Microsoft Remote Procedure Call (RPC) client driver for kernel mode allows the kernel (and other drivers) to communicate with user-mode services through RPC or to marshal MES-encoded assets. For example, the kernel uses this to marshal data to and from the user-mode Plug-and-Play service.

For a detailed description of the information displayed by this tool, see the Dependency Walker help file (Depends.hlp).

We asked you to disregard the errors that Dependency Walker has parsing API Sets because its authors have not updated it to correctly handle this mechanism. While the implementation of API Sets will be described in Chapter 3 in the "Image loader" section, you should still use the Dependency Walker output to review what other dependencies the kernel may potentially have, depending on SKU, as these API Sets may indeed point to real modules. Note that when dealing with API Sets, they are described in terms of contracts, not DLLs or libraries. It's important to realize that any number (or even all) of these contracts might be absent from your machine. Their presence depends on a combination of factors: SKU, platform, and vendor.

- **Werkernel contract** This provides support for Windows Error Reporting (WER) in the kernel, such as with live kernel dump creation.

- **Tm contract** This is the kernel transaction manager (KTM), described in Chapter 8 in Part 2.

- **Kcminitcfg contract** This is responsible for the custom initial registry configuration that may be needed on specific platforms.

- **Ksr contract** This handles Kernel Soft Reboot (KSR) and the required persistence of certain memory ranges to support it, specifically on certain mobile and IoT platforms.

- **Ksecurity contract** This contains additional policies for AppContainer processes (that is, Windows Apps) running in user mode on certain devices and SKUs.

- **Ksigningpolicy contract** This contains additional policies for user-mode code integrity (UMCI) to either support non-AppContainer processes on certain SKUs or futher configure Device Guard and/or App Locker security features on certain platforms/SKUs.

- **Ucode contract** This is the microcode update library for platforms that can support processor microcode updates, such as Intel and AMD.

- **Clfs contract** This is the Common Log File System driver, used by (among other things) the Transactional Registry (TxR). For more information on TxR, see Chapter 8 in Part 2.

■ **Ium Contract** These are additional policies for IUM Trustlets running on the system, which may be needed on certain SKUs, such as for providing shielded VMs on Datacenter Server. Trustlets are described further in Chapter 3.

Device drivers

Although device drivers are explained in detail in Chapter 6, this section provides a brief overview of the types of drivers and explains how to list the drivers installed and loaded on your system.

Windows supports kernel-mode and user-mode drivers, but this section discussed the kernel drivers only. The term *device driver* implies a hardware device, but there are other device driver types that are not directly related to hardware (listed momentarily). This section focuses on device drivers that are related to controlling a hardware device.

Device drivers are loadable kernel-mode modules (files typically ending with the .sys extension) that interface between the I/O manager and the relevant hardware. They run in kernel mode in one of three contexts:

■ In the context of the user thread that initiated an I/O function (such as a read operation)

■ In the context of a kernel-mode system thread (such as a request from the Plug and Play manager)

■ As a result of an interrupt and therefore not in the context of any particular thread but rather of whichever thread was current when the interrupt occurred

As stated in the preceding section, device drivers in Windows don't manipulate hardware directly. Rather, they call functions in the HAL to interface with the hardware. Drivers are typically written in C and/or C++. Therefore, with proper use of HAL routines, they can be source-code portable across the CPU architectures supported by Windows and binary portable within an architecture family.

There are several types of device drivers:

■ **Hardware device drivers** These use the HAL to manipulate hardware to write output to or retrieve input from a physical device or network. There are many types of hardware device drivers, such as bus drivers, human interface drivers, mass storage drivers, and so on.

■ **File system drivers** These are Windows drivers that accept file-oriented I/O requests and translate them into I/O requests bound for a particular device.

■ **File system filter drivers** These include drivers that perform disk mirroring and encryption or scanning to locate viruses, intercept I/O requests, and perform some added-value processing before passing the I/O to the next layer (or in some cases rejecting the operation).

■ **Network redirectors and servers** These are file system drivers that transmit file system I/O requests to a machine on the network and receive such requests, respectively.

■ **Protocol drivers** These implement a networking protocol such as TCP/IP, NetBEUI, and IPX/SPX.

- **Kernel streaming filter drivers** These are chained together to perform signal processing on data streams, such as recording or displaying audio and video.

- **Software drivers** These are kernel modules that perform operations that can only be done in kernel mode on behalf of some user-mode process. Many utilities from Sysinternals such as Process Explorer and Process Monitor use drivers to get information or perform operations that are not possible to do from user-mode APIs.

Windows driver model

The original driver model was created in the first NT version (3.1) and did not support the concept of Plug and Play (PnP) because it was not yet available. This remained the case until Windows 2000 came along (and Windows 95/98 on the consumer Windows side).

Windows 2000 added support for PnP, Power Options, and an extension to the Windows NT driver model called the Windows Driver Model (WDM). Windows 2000 and later can run legacy Windows NT 4 drivers, but because these don't support PnP and Power Options, systems running these drivers will have reduced capabilities in these two areas.

Originally, WDM provided a common driver model that was (almost) source compatible between Windows 2000/XP and Windows 98/ME. This was done to make it easier to write drivers for hardware devices, since a single code base was needed instead of two. WDM was simulated on Windows 98/ME. Once these operating systems were no longer used, WDM remained the base model for writing drivers for hardware devices for Windows 2000 and later versions.

From the WDM perspective, there are three kinds of drivers:

- **Bus drivers** A bus driver services a bus controller, adapter, bridge, or any device that has child devices. Bus drivers are required drivers, and Microsoft generally provides them. Each type of bus (such as PCI, PCMCIA, and USB) on a system has one bus driver. Third parties can write bus drivers to provide support for new buses, such as VMEbus, Multibus, and Futurebus.

- **Function drivers** A function driver is the main device driver and provides the operational interface for its device. It is a required driver unless the device is used raw, an implementation in which I/O is done by the bus driver and any bus filter drivers, such as SCSI PassThru. A function driver is by definition the driver that knows the most about a particular device, and it is usually the only driver that accesses device-specific registers.

- **Filter drivers** A filter driver is used to add functionality to a device or existing driver, or to modify I/O requests or responses from other drivers. It is often used to fix hardware that provides incorrect information about its hardware resource requirements. Filter drivers are optional and can exist in any number, placed above or below a function driver and above a bus driver. Usually, system original equipment manufacturers (OEMs) or independent hardware vendors (IHVs) supply filter drivers.

In the WDM driver environment, no single driver controls all aspects of a device. A bus driver is concerned with reporting the devices on its bus to PnP manager, while a function driver manipulates the device.

In most cases, lower-level filter drivers modify the behavior of device hardware. For example, if a device reports to its bus driver that it requires 4 I/O ports when it actually requires 16 I/O ports, a lower-level, device-specific function filter driver could intercept the list of hardware resources reported by the bus driver to the PnP manager and update the count of I/O ports.

Upper-level filter drivers usually provide added-value features for a device. For example, an upper-level device filter driver for a disk can enforce additional security checks.

Interrupt processing is explained in Chapter 8 in Part 2 and in the narrow context of device drivers, in Chapter 6. Further details about the I/O manager, WDM, Plug and Play, and power management are also covered in Chapter 6.

Windows Driver Foundation

The Windows Driver Foundation (WDF) simplifies Windows driver development by providing two frameworks: the Kernel-Mode Driver Framework (KMDF) and the User-Mode Driver Framework (UMDF). Developers can use KMDF to write drivers for Windows 2000 SP4 and later, while UMDF supports Windows XP and later.

KMDF provides a simple interface to WDM and hides its complexity from the driver writer without modifying the underlying bus/function/filter model. KMDF drivers respond to events that they can register and call into the KMDF library to perform work that isn't specific to the hardware they are managing, such as generic power management or synchronization. (Previously, each driver had to implement this on its own.) In some cases, more than 200 lines of WDM code can be replaced by a single KMDF function call.

UMDF enables certain classes of drivers—mostly USB-based or other high-latency protocol buses, such as those for video cameras, MP3 players, cell phones, and printers—to be implemented as user-mode drivers. UMDF runs each user-mode driver in what is essentially a user-mode service, and it uses ALPC to communicate to a kernel-mode wrapper driver that provides actual access to hardware. If a UMDF driver crashes, the process dies and usually restarts. That way, the system doesn't become unstable; the device simply becomes unavailable while the service hosting the driver restarts.

UMDF has two major versions: version 1.x is available for all OS versions that support UMDF, the latest and last being version 1.11, available in Windows 10. This version uses C++ and COM for driver writing, which is rather convenient for user-mode programmers, but it makes the UMDF model different from KMDF. Version 2.0 of UMDF, introduced in Windows 8.1, is based around the same object model as KMDF, making the two frameworks very similar in their programming model. Finally, WDF has been open-sourced by Microsoft, and at the time of this writing is available on GitHub at *https://github.com/Microsoft/Windows-Driver-Frameworks*.

Universal Windows drivers

Starting with Windows 10, the term *Universal Windows drivers* refers to the ability to write device drivers once that share APIs and Device Driver Interfaces (DDIs) provided by the Windows 10 common core. These drivers are binary-compatible for a specific CPU architecture (x86, x64, ARM) and can be used as is on a variety of form factors, from IoT devices, to phones, to the HoloLens and Xbox One, to laptops and desktops. Universal drivers can use KMDF, UMDF 2.*x*, or WDM as their driver model.

EXPERIMENT: Viewing the installed device drivers

To list the installed drivers, run the System Information tool (Msinfo32.exe). To launch this tool, click **Start** and then type **Msinfo32** to locate it. Under System Summary, expand **Software Environment** and open **System Drivers**. Here's an example output of the list of installed drivers:

This window displays the list of device drivers defined in the registry, their type, and their state (Running or Stopped). Device drivers and Windows service processes are both defined in the same place: HKLM\SYSTEM\CurrentControlSet\Services. However, they are distinguished by a type code. For example, type 1 is a kernel-mode device driver. For a complete list of the information stored in the registry for device drivers, see Chapter 9 in Part 2.

Alternatively, you can list the currently loaded device drivers by selecting the **System** process in Process Explorer and opening the DLL view. Here's a sample output. (To get the extra columns, right-click a column header and click **Select Columns** to see all the available columns for modules in the DLL tab.)

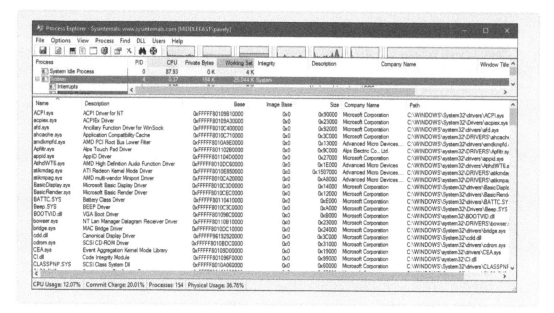

Peering into undocumented interfaces

Examining the names of the exported or global symbols in key system images (such as Ntoskrnl. exe, Hal.dll, or Ntdll.dll) can be enlightening—you can get an idea of the kinds of things Windows can do versus what happens to be documented and supported today. Of course, just because you know the names of these functions doesn't mean that you can or should call them—the interfaces are undocumented and are subject to change. We suggest that you look at these functions purely to gain more insight into the kinds of internal functions Windows performs, not to bypass supported interfaces.

For example, looking at the list of functions in Ntdll.dll gives you the list of all the system services that Windows provides to user-mode subsystem DLLs versus the subset that each subsystem exposes. Although many of these functions map clearly to documented and supported Windows functions, several are not exposed via the Windows API.

Conversely, it's also interesting to examine the imports of Windows subsystem DLLs (such as Kernel32.dll or Advapi32.dll) and which functions they call in Ntdll.dll.

Another interesting image to dump is Ntoskrnl.exe—although many of the exported routines that kernel-mode device drivers use are documented in the WDK, quite a few are not. You might also find it interesting to take a look at the import table for Ntoskrnl.exe and the HAL; this table shows the list of functions in the HAL that Ntoskrnl.exe uses and vice versa.

Table 2-5 lists most of the commonly used function name prefixes for the executive components. Each of these major executive components also uses a variation of the prefix to denote internal functions—either the first letter of the prefix followed by an i (for *internal*) or the full prefix followed by a p (for *private*). For example, Ki represents internal kernel functions, and Psp refers to internal process support functions.

TABLE 2-5 Commonly Used Prefixes

Prefix	Component
Alpc	Advanced Local Procedure Calls
Cc	Common Cache
Cm	Configuration manager
Dbg	Kernel debug support
Dbgk	Debugging Framework for user mode
Em	Errata manager
Etw	Event Tracing for Windows
Ex	Executive support routines
FsRtl	File System Runtime Library
Hv	Hive library
Hvl	Hypervisor library
Io	I/O manager
Kd	Kernel debugger
Ke	Kernel
Kse	Kernel Shim Engine
Lsa	Local Security Authority
Mm	Memory manager
Nt	NT system services (accessible from user mode through system calls)
Ob	Object manager
Pf	Prefetcher
Po	Power manager
PoFx	Power framework
Pp	PnP manager
Ppm	Processor power manager
Ps	Process support
Rtl	Run-time library
Se	Security Reference Monitor
Sm	Store Manager
Tm	Transaction manager
Ttm	Terminal timeout manager
Vf	Driver Verifier

TABLE 2-5   Commonly Used Prefixes (*Continued*)

Prefix	Component
Vsl	Virtual Secure Mode library
Wdi	Windows Diagnostic Infrastructure
Wfp	Windows FingerPrint
Whea	Windows Hardware Error Architecture
Wmi	Windows Management Instrumentation
Zw	Mirror entry point for system services (beginning with Nt) that sets previous access mode to kernel, which eliminates parameter validation, because Nt system services validate parameters only if previous access mode is user

You can decipher the names of these exported functions more easily if you understand the naming convention for Windows system routines. The general format is

<Prefix><Operation><Object>

In this format, *Prefix* is the internal component that exports the routine, *Operation* tells what is being done to the object or resource, and *Object* identifies what is being operated on.

For example, ExAllocatePoolWithTag is the executive support routine to allocate from a paged or non-paged pool. KeInitializeThread is the routine that allocates and sets up a kernel thread object.

System processes

The following system processes appear on every Windows 10 system. One of these (Idle) is not a process at all, and three of them—System, Secure System, and Memory Compression—are not full processes because they are not running a user-mode executable. These types of processes are called *minimal processes* and are described in Chapter 3.

- **Idle process**   This contains one thread per CPU to account for idle CPU time.

- **System process**   This contains the majority of the kernel-mode system threads and handles.

- **Secure System process**   This contains the address space of the secure kernel in VTL 1, if running.

- **Memory Compression process**   This contains the compressed working set of user-mode processes, as described in Chapter 5.

- **Session manager**   (Smss.exe).

- **Windows subsystem**   (Csrss.exe).

- **Session 0 initialization**   (Wininit.exe).

- **Logon process**   (Winlogon.exe).

- **Service Control Manager** (Services.exe) and the child service processes it creates such as the system-supplied generic service-host process (Svchost.exe).

- **Local Security Authentication Service** (Lsass.exe), and if Credential Guard is active, the Isolated Local Security Authentication Server (Lsaiso.exe).

To understand how these processes are related, it is helpful to view the process tree—that is, the parent/child relationship between processes. Seeing which process created each process helps to understand where each process comes from. Figure 2-6 shows the process tree following a Process Monitor boot trace. To conduct a boot trace, open the Process Monitor **Options** menu and select **Enable Boot Logging**. Then restart the system, open Process Monitor again, and open the **Tools** menu and choose **Process Tree** or press **Ctrl+T**. Using Process Monitor enables you to see processes that have since exited, indicated by the faded icon.

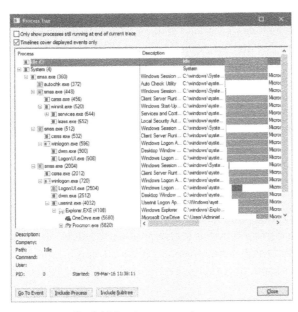

FIGURE 2-6 The initial system process tree.

The next sections explain the key system processes shown in Figure 2-6. Although these sections briefly indicate the order of process startup, Chapter 11 in Part 2, contains a detailed description of the steps involved in booting and starting Windows.

System idle process

The first process listed in Figure 2-6 is the Idle process. As discussed in Chapter 3, processes are identified by their image name. However, this process—as well as the System, Secure System, and Memory Compression processes—isn't running a real user-mode image. That is, there is no "System Idle Process.exe" in the \Windows directory. In addition, because of implementation details, the name shown for this process differs from utility to utility. The Idle process accounts for idle time. That's why the number of "threads" in this "process" is the number of logical processors on the system. Table 2-6 lists several of the names given to the Idle process (process ID 0). The Idle process is explained in detail in Chapter 3.

TABLE 2-6 Names for process ID 0 in various utilities

Utility	Name for Process ID 0
Task Manager	System Idle process
Process Status (Pstat.exe)	Idle process
Process Explorer (Procexp.exe)	System Idle process
Task List (Tasklist.exe)	System Idle process
Tlist (Tlist.exe)	System process

Now let's look at system threads and the purpose of each of the system processes that are running real images.

System process and system threads

The System process (process ID 4) is the home for a special kind of thread that runs only in kernel mode: a *kernel-mode system thread*. System threads have all the attributes and contexts of regular user-mode threads such as a hardware context, priority, and so on, but differ in that they run only in kernel-mode executing code loaded in system space, whether that is in Ntoskrnl.exe or in any other loaded device driver. In addition, system threads don't have a user process address space and hence must allocate any dynamic storage from OS memory heaps, such as a paged or non-paged pool.

> **Note** On Windows 10 Version 1511, Task Manager calls the System process *System and Compressed Memory*. This is because of a new feature in Windows 10 that compresses memory to save more process information in memory rather than page it out to disk. This mechanism is further described in Chapter 5. Just remember that the term *System process* refers to this one, no matter the exact name displayed by this tool or another. Windows 10 Version 1607 and Server 2016 revert the name of the System process to *System*. This is because a new process called *Memory Compression* is used for compressing memory. Chapter 5 discusses this process in more detail.

System threads are created by the PsCreateSystemThread or IoCreateSystemThread functions, both documented in the WDK. These threads can be called only from kernel mode. Windows, as well as various device drivers, create system threads during system initialization to perform operations that require thread context, such as issuing and waiting for I/Os or other objects or polling a device. For example, the memory manager uses system threads to implement such functions as writing dirty pages to the page file or mapped files, swapping processes in and out of memory, and so forth. The kernel creates a system thread called the *balance set manager* that wakes up once per second to possibly initiate various scheduling and memory-management related events. The cache manager also uses system threads to implement both read-ahead and write-behind I/Os. The file server device driver (Srv2.sys) uses system threads to respond to network I/O requests for file data on disk partitions shared to the network. Even the floppy driver has a system thread to poll the floppy device. (Polling is more efficient in this case because an interrupt-driven floppy driver consumes a large amount of system resources.) Further information on specific system threads is included in the chapters in which the corresponding component is described.

By default, system threads are owned by the System process, but a device driver can create a system thread in any process. For example, the Windows subsystem device driver (Win32k.sys) creates a system thread inside the Canonical Display Driver (Cdd.dll) part of the Windows subsystem process (Csrss.exe) so that it can easily access data in the user-mode address space of that process.

When you're troubleshooting or going through a system analysis, it's useful to be able to map the execution of individual system threads back to the driver or even to the subroutine that contains the code. For example, on a heavily loaded file server, the System process will likely consume considerable CPU time. But knowing that when the System process is running, "some system thread" is running isn't enough to determine which device driver or OS component is running.

So if threads in the System process are running, first determine which ones are running (for example, with the Performance Monitor or Process Explorer tools). Once you find the thread (or threads) that is running, look up in which driver the system thread began execution. This at least tells you which driver likely created the thread. For example, in Process Explorer, right-click the **System** process and select **Properties**. Then, in the Threads tab, click the **CPU** column header to view the most active thread at the top. Select this thread and click the **Module** button to see the file from which the code on the top of stack is running. Because the System process is protected in recent versions of Windows, Process Explorer is unable to show a call stack.

Secure System process

The Secure System process (variable process ID) is technically the home of the VTL 1 secure kernel address space, handles, and system threads. That being said, because scheduling, object management, and memory management are owned by the VTL 0 kernel, no such actual entities will be associated with this process. Its only real use is to provide a visual indicator to users (for example, in tools such as Task Manager and Process Explorer) that VBS is currently active (providing at least one of the features that leverages it).

Memory Compression process

The Memory Compression process uses its user-mode address space to store the compressed pages of memory that correspond to standby memory that's been evicted from the working sets of certain processes, as described in Chapter 5. Unlike the Secure System process, the Memory Compression process does actually host a number of system threads, usually seen as SmKmStoreHelperWorker and SmStReadThread. Both of these belong to the Store Manager that manages memory compression.

Additionally, unlike the other System processes in this list, this process actually stores its memory in the user-mode address space. This means it is subject to working set trimming and will potentially have large visible memory usage in system-monitoring tools. In fact, if you view the Performance tab in Task Manager, which now shows both in-use and compressed memory, you should see that the size of the Memory Compression process's working set is equal to the amount of compressed memory.

Session Manager

The Session Manager (%SystemRoot%\System32\Smss.exe) is the first user-mode process created in the system. The kernel-mode system thread that performs the final phase of the initialization of the executive and kernel creates this process. It is created as a Protected Process Light (PPL), as described in Chapter 3.

When Smss.exe starts, it checks whether it is the first instance (the master Smss.exe) or an instance of itself that the master Smss.exe launched to create a session. If command-line arguments are present, it is the latter. By creating multiple instances of itself during boot-up and Terminal Services session creation, Smss.exe can create multiple sessions at the same time—as many as four concurrent sessions, plus one more for each extra CPU beyond one. This ability enhances logon performance on Terminal Server systems where multiple users connect at the same time. Once a session finishes initializing, the copy of Smss.exe terminates. As a result, only the initial Smss.exe process remains active. (For a description of Terminal Services, see the section "Terminal Services and multiple sessions" in Chapter 1.)

The master Smss.exe performs the following one-time initialization steps:

1. It marks the process and the initial thread as critical. If a process or thread marked critical exits for any reason, Windows crashes. See Chapter 3 for more information.

2. It causes the process to treat certain errors as critical, such as invalid handle usage and heap corruption, and enables the Disable Dynamic Code Execution process mitigation.

3. It increases the process base priority to 11.

4. If the system supports hot processor add, it enables automatic processor affinity updates. That way, if new processors are added, new sessions will take advantage of the new processors. For more information about dynamic processor additions, see Chapter 4.

5. It initializes a thread pool to handle ALPC commands and other work items.

6. It creates an ALPC port named \SmApiPort to receive commands.

7. It initializes a local copy of the NUMA topology of the system.

8. It creates a mutex named `PendingRenameMutex` to synchronize file-rename operations.

9. It creates the initial process environment block and updates the `Safe Mode` variable if needed.

10. Based on the `ProtectionMode` value in the HKLM\SYSTEM\CurrentControlSet\Control\Session Manager key, it creates the security descriptors that will be used for various system resources.

11. Based on the `ObjectDirectories` value in the HKLM\SYSTEM\CurrentControlSet\Control\Session Manager key, it creates the object manager directories that are described, such as \ RPC Control and \Windows. It also saves the programs listed under the values `BootExecute`, `BootExecuteNoPnpSync`, and `SetupExecute`.

12. It saves the program path listed in the `S0InitialCommand` value under the HKLM\SYSTEM\CurrentControlSet\Control\Session Manager key.

13. It reads the `NumberOfInitialSessions` value from the HKLM\SYSTEM\CurrentControlSet\ Control\Session Manager key, but ignores it if the system is in manufacturing mode.

14. It reads the file rename operations listed under the `PendingFileRenameOperations` and `PendingFileRenameOperations2` values from the HKLM\SYSTEM\CurrentControlSet\Control\ Session Manager key.

15. It reads the values of the `AllowProtectedRenames`, `ClearTempFiles`, `TempFileDirectory`, and `DisableWpbtExecution` values in the HKLM\SYSTEM\CurrentControlSet\Control\Session Manager key.

16. It reads the list of DLLs in the `ExcludeFromKnownDllList` value found under the HKLM\SYSTEM\ CurrentControlSet\Control\Session Manager key.

17. It reads the paging file information stored in the HKLM\SYSTEM\CurrentControlSet\Control\ Session Manager\Memory Management key, such as the `PagingFiles` and `ExistingPageFiles` list values and the `PagefileOnOsVolume` and `WaitForPagingFiles` configuration values.

18. It reads and saves the values stored in the HKLM\SYSTEM\CurrentControlSet\Control\Session Manager\ DOS Devices key.

19. It reads and saves the `KnownDlls` value list stored in the HKLM\SYSTEM\CurrentControlSet\ Control\Session Manager key.

20. It creates system-wide environment variables as defined in HKLM\SYSTEM\CurrentControlSet\ Control\Session Manager\Environment.

21. It creates the \KnownDlls directory, as well as \KnownDlls32 on 64-bit systems with WoW64.

22. It creates symbolic links for devices defined in HKLM\SYSTEM\CurrentControlSet\Control\Session Manager\DOS Devices under the \Global?? directory in the object manager namespace.

23. It creates a root \Sessions directory in the object manager namespace.

24. It creates protected mailslot and named pipe prefixes to protect service applications from spoofing attacks that could occur if a malicious user-mode application executes before a service does.

25. It runs the programs part of the `BootExecute` and `BootExecuteNoPnpSync` lists parsed earlier. (The default is Autochk.exe, which performs a disk check.)

26. It initializes the rest of the registry (HKLM software, SAM, and security hives).

27. Unless disabled by the registry, it executes the Windows Platform Binary Table (WPBT) binary registered in the respective ACPI table. This is often used by anti-theft vendors to force the execution of a very early native Windows binary that can call home or set up other services for execution, even on a freshly installed system. These processes must link with Ntdll.dll only (that is, belong to the native subsystem).

28. It processes pending file renames as specified in the registry keys seen earlier unless this is a Windows Recovery Environment boot.

29. It initializes paging file(s) and dedicated dump file information based on the HKLM\System\CurrentControlSet\Control\Session Manager\Memory Management and HKLM\System\CurrentControlSet\Control\CrashControl keys.

30. It checks the system's compatibility with memory cooling technology, used on NUMA systems.

31. It saves the old paging file, creates the dedicated crash dump file, and creates new paging files as needed based on previous crash information.

32. It creates additional dynamic environment variables, such as PROCESSOR_ARCHITECTURE, PROCESSOR_LEVEL, PROCESSOR_IDENTIFIER, and PROCESSOR_REVISION, which are based on registry settings and system information queried from the kernel.

33. It runs the programs in HKLM\SYSTEM\CurrentControlSet\Control\Session Manager\SetupExecute. The rules for these executables are the same as for BootExecute in step 11.

34. It creates an unnamed section object that is shared by child processes (for example, Csrss.exe) for information exchanged with Smss.exe. The handle to this section is passed to child processes via handle inheritance. For more on handle inheritance, see Chapter 8 in Part 2.

35. It opens known DLLs and maps them as permanent sections (mapped files) except those listed as exclusions in the earlier registry checks (none listed by default).

36. It creates a thread to respond to session create requests.

37. It creates the Smss.exe instance to initialize session 0 (non-interactive session).

38. It creates the Smss.exe instance to initialize session 1 (interactive session) and, if configured in the registry, creates additional Smss.exe instances for extra interactive sessions to prepare itself in advance for potential future user logons. When Smss.exe creates these instances, it requests the explicit creation of a new session ID using the PROCESS_CREATE_NEW_SESSION flag in NtCreateUserProcess each time. This has the effect of calling the internal memory manager function MiSessionCreate, which creates the required kernel-mode session data structures (such as the Session object) and sets up the Session Space virtual address range that is used by the kernel-mode part of the Windows subsystem (Win32k.sys) and other session-space device drivers. See Chapter 5 for more details.

After these steps have been completed, Smss.exe waits forever on the handle to the session 0 instance of Csrss.exe. Because Csrss.exe is marked as a critical process (and is also a protected process; see Chapter 3), if Csrss.exe exits, this wait will never complete because the system will crash.

A session startup instance of Smss.exe does the following:

■ It creates the subsystem process(es) for the session (by default, the Windows subsystem Csrss.exe).

■ It creates an instance of Winlogon (interactive sessions) or the Session 0 Initial Command, which is Wininit (for session 0) by default unless modified by the registry values seen in the preceding steps. See the upcoming paragraphs for more information on these two processes.

Finally, this intermediate Smss.exe process exits, leaving the subsystem processes and Winlogon or Wininit as parent-less processes.

Windows initialization process

The Wininit.exe process performs the following system initialization functions:

1. It marks itself and the main thread critical so that if it exits prematurely and the system is booted in debugging mode, it will break into the debugger. (Otherwise, the system will crash.)

2. It causes the process to treat certain errors as critical, such as invalid handle usage and heap corruption.

3. It initializes support for state separation, if the SKU supports it.

4. It creates an event named `Global\FirstLogonCheck` (this can be observed in Process Explorer or WinObj under the \BaseNamedObjects directory) for use by Winlogon processes to detect which Winlogon is first to launch.

5. It creates a `WinlogonLogoff` event in the `BasedNamedObjects` object manager directory to be used by Winlogon instances. This event is signaled (set) when a logoff operation starts.

6. It increases its own process base priority to high (13) and its main thread's priority to 15.

7. Unless configured otherwise with the `NoDebugThread` registry value in the HKLM\Software\ Microsoft\Windows NT\CurrentVersion\Winlogon key, it creates a periodic timer queue, which will break into any user-mode process as specified by the kernel debugger. This enables remote kernel debuggers to cause Winlogon to attach and break into other user-mode applications.

8. It sets the machine name in the environment variable COMPUTERNAME and then updates and configures TCP/IP-related information such as the domain name and host name

9. It sets the default profile environment variables USERPROFILE, ALLUSERSPROFILE, PUBLIC, and `ProgramData`.

10. It creates the temp directory by expanding %SystemRoot%\Temp (for example, C:\Windows\ Temp).

11. It sets up font loading and DWM if session 0 is an interactive session, which depends on the SKU.

12. It creates the initial terminal, which is composed of a window station (always named *Winsta0*) and two desktops (Winlogon and Default) for processes to run on in session 0.

13. It initializes the LSA machine encryption key, depending on whether it's stored locally or if it must be entered interactively. See Chapter 7 for more information on how local authentication keys are stored.

14. It creates the Service Control Manager (SCM or Services.exe). See the upcoming paragraphs for a brief description and Chapter 9 in Part 2 for more details.

15. It starts the Local Security Authentication Subsystem Service (Lsass.exe) and, if Credential Guard is enabled, the Isolated LSA Trustlet (Lsaiso.exe). This also requires querying the VBS provisioning key from UEFI. See Chapter 7 for more information on Lsass.exe and Lsaiso.exe.

16. If Setup is currently pending (that is, if this is the first boot during a fresh install or an update to a new major OS build or Insider Preview), it launches the setup program.

17. It waits forever for a request for system shutdown or for one of the aforementioned system processes to terminate (unless the `DontWatchSysProcs` registry value is set in the Winlogon key mentioned in step 7). In either case, it shuts down the system.

Service control manager

Recall that with Windows, *services* can refer to either a server process or a device driver. This section deals with services that are user-mode processes. Services are like Linux daemon processes in that they can be configured to start automatically at system boot time without requiring an interactive logon. They can also be started manually, such as by running the Services administrative tool, using the sc.exe tool, or calling the Windows `StartService` function. Typically, services do not interact with the logged-on user, although there are special conditions when this is possible. Additionally, while most services run in special service accounts (such as SYSTEM or LOCAL SERVICE), others can run with the same security context as logged-in user accounts. (For more, see Chapter 9 in Part 2.)

The Service Control Manager (SCM) is a special system process running the image %SystemRoot%\System32\Services.exe that is responsible for starting, stopping, and interacting with service processes. It is also a protected process, making it difficult to tamper with. Service programs are really just Windows images that call special Windows functions to interact with the SCM to perform such actions as registering the service's successful startup, responding to status requests, or pausing or shutting down the service. Services are defined in the registry under HKLM\SYSTEM\CurrentControlSet\Services.

Keep in mind that services have three names: the process name you see running on the system, the internal name in the registry, and the display name shown in the Services administrative tool. (Not all services have a display name—if a service doesn't have a display name, the internal name is shown.) Services can also have a description field that further details what the service does.

To map a service process to the services contained in that process, use the `tlist /s` (from Debugging Tools for Windows) or `tasklist /svc` (built-in Windows tool) command. Note that there isn't always one-to-one mapping between service processes and running services, however, because some services share a process with other services. In the registry, the Type value under the service's key indicates whether the service runs in its own process or shares a process with other services in the image.

A number of Windows components are implemented as services, such as the Print Spooler, Event Log, Task Scheduler, and various networking components. For more details on services, see Chapter 9 in Part 2.

EXPERIMENT: Listing installed services

To list the installed services, open the Control Panel, select **Administrative Tools**, and select **Services**. Alternatively, click **Start** and run **services.msc**. You should see output like this:

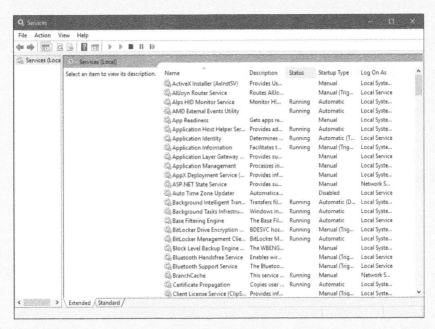

To see the detailed properties of a service, right-click the service and select **Properties**. For example, here are the properties of the Windows Update service:

Notice that the Path to Executable field identifies the program that contains this service and its command line. Remember that some services share a process with other services. Mapping isn't always one-to-one.

EXPERIMENT: Viewing service details inside service processes

Process Explorer highlights processes hosting one service or more. (These processes are shaded pink color by default, but you can change this by opening the **Options** menu and choosing **Configure Colors**.) If you double-click a service-hosting process, you will see a Services tab that lists the services inside the process, the name of the registry key that defines the service, the display name seen by the administrator, the description text for that service (if present), and for Svchost. exe services, the path to the DLL that implements the service. For example, listing the services in one of the Svchost.exe processes running under the System account appears as follows:

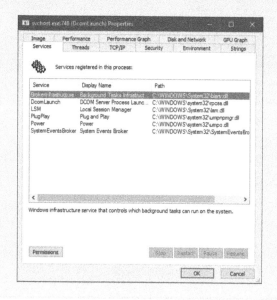

Winlogon, LogonUI, and Userinit

The Windows logon process (%SystemRoot%\System32\Winlogon.exe) handles interactive user logons and logoffs. Winlogon.exe is notified of a user logon request when the user enters the secure attention sequence (SAS) keystroke combination. The default SAS on Windows is Ctrl+Alt+Delete. The reason for the SAS is to protect users from password-capture programs that simulate the logon process because this keyboard sequence cannot be intercepted by a user-mode application.

The identification and authentication aspects of the logon process are implemented through DLLs called *credential providers*. The standard Windows credential providers implement the default Windows authentication interfaces: password and smartcard. Windows 10 provides a biometric credential provider: face recognition, known as *Windows Hello*. However, developers can provide their own credential providers to implement other identification and authentication mechanisms instead of the standard Windows user name/password method, such as one based on a voice print or a biometric device such as a fingerprint reader. Because Winlogon.exe is a critical system process on which the system depends, credential providers and the UI to display the logon dialog box run inside a child process of Winlogon.exe called *LogonUI.exe*. When Winlogon.exe detects the SAS, it launches this process, which initializes the credential providers. When the user enters their credentials (as required by the provider) or dismisses the logon interface, the LogonUI.exe process terminates. Winlogon.exe can also load additional network provider DLLs that need to perform secondary authentication. This capability allows multiple network providers to gather identification and authentication information all at one time during normal logon.

After the user name and password (or another information bundle as the credential provider requires) have been captured, they are sent to the Local Security Authentication Service process (Lsass.exe, described in Chapter 7) to be authenticated. Lsass.exe calls the appropriate authentication package, implemented as a DLL, to perform the actual verification, such as checking whether a password matches what is stored in the Active Directory or the SAM (the part of the registry that contains the definition of the local users and groups). If Credential Guard is enabled, and this is a domain logon, Lsass.exe will communicate with the Isolated LSA Trustlet (Lsaiso.exe, described in Chapter 7) to obtain the machine key required to authenticate the legitimacy of the authentication request.

Upon successful authentication, Lsass.exe calls a function in the SRM (for example, `NtCreateToken`) to generate an access token object that contains the user's security profile. If User Account Control (UAC) is used and the user logging on is a member of the administrators group or has administrator privileges, Lsass.exe will create a second, restricted version of the token. This access token is then used by Winlogon to create the initial process(es) in the user's session. The initial process(es) are stored in the `Userinit` registry value under the HKLM\SOFTWARE\Microsoft\Windows NT\CurrentVersion\Winlogon registry key. The default is Userinit.exe, but there can be more than one image in the list.

Userinit.exe performs some initialization of the user environment, such as running the login script and reestablishing network connections. It then looks in the registry at the `Shell` value (under the same Winlogon key mentioned previously) and creates a process to run the system-defined shell (by default, Explorer.exe). Then Userinit exits. This is why Explorer is shown with no parent. Its parent has exited, and as explained in Chapter 1, tlist.exe and Process Explorer left-justify processes whose parent isn't running. Another way of looking at it is that Explorer is the grandchild of Winlogon.exe.

Winlogon.exe is active not only during user logon and logoff, but also whenever it intercepts the SAS from the keyboard. For example, when you press Ctrl+Alt+Delete while logged on, the Windows Security screen comes up, providing the options to log off, start the Task Manager, lock the workstation, shut down the system, and so forth. Winlogon.exe and LogonUI.exe are the processes that handle this interaction.

For a complete description of the steps involved in the logon process, see Chapter 11 in Part 2. For more details on security authentication, see Chapter 7. For details on the callable functions that interface with Lsass.exe (the functions that start with `Lsa`), see the documentation in the Windows SDK.

Conclusion

This chapter takes a broad look at the overall system architecture of Windows. It examines the key components of Windows and shows how they interrelate. In the next chapter, we'll look in more detail at processes, which are one of the most basic entities in Windows.

CHAPTER 3

Processes and jobs

In this chapter, we'll explain the data structures and algorithms that deal with processes and jobs in Windows. First we'll take a general look at process creation. Then we'll examine the internal structures that make up a process. Next we'll look at protected processes and how they differ from non-protected ones. After that we outline the steps involved in creating a process (and its initial thread). The chapter concludes with a description of jobs.

Because processes touch so many components in Windows, a number of terms and data structures (such as working sets, threads, objects and handles, system memory heaps, and so on) are referred to in this chapter but are explained in detail elsewhere in the book. To fully understand this chapter, you need to be familiar with the terms and concepts explained in Chapter 1, "Concepts and tools," and Chapter 2, "System architecture," such as the difference between a process and a thread, the Windows virtual address space layout, and the difference between user mode and kernel mode.

Creating a process

The Windows API provides several functions for creating processes. The simplest is CreateProcess, which attempts to create a process with the same access token as the creating process. If a different token is required, CreateProcessAsUser can be used, which accepts an extra argument (the first)—a handle to a token object that was already somehow obtained (for example, by calling the LogonUser function).

Other process creation functions include CreateProcessWithTokenW and CreateProcessWithLogonW (both part of advapi32.Dll). CreateProcessWithTokenW is similar to CreateProcessAsUser, but the two differ in the privileges required for the caller. (Check the Windows SDK documentation for the specifics.) CreateProcessWithLogonW is a handy shortcut to log on with a given user's credentials and create a process with the obtained token in one stroke. Both call the Secondary Logon service (seclogon.dll, hosted in a SvcHost.Exe) by making a Remote Procedure Call (RPC) to do the actual process creation. SecLogon executes the call in its internal SlrCreateProcessWithLogon function, and if all goes well, eventually calls CreateProcessAsUser. The SecLogon service is configured by default to start manually, so the first time CreateProcessWithTokenW or CreateProcessWithLogonW is called, the service is started. If the service fails to start (for example, an administrator can configure the service to be disabled), these functions will fail. The runas command-line utility, which you may be familiar with, makes use of these functions.

Figure 3-1 shows the call graph described above.

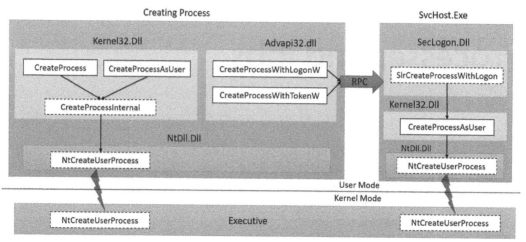

FIGURE 3-1 Process creation functions. Functions marked with dotted boxes are internal.

All the above documented functions expect a proper Portable Executable (PE) file (although the EXE extension is not strictly required), batch file, or 16-bit COM application. Beyond that, they have no knowledge of how to connect files with certain extensions (for example, .txt) to an executable (for example, Notepad). This is something that is provided by the Windows Shell, in functions such as `ShellExecute` and `ShellExecuteEx`. These functions can accept any file (not just executables) and try to locate the executable to run based on the file extensions and the registry settings at HKEY_CLASSES_ROOT. (See Chapter 9, "Management mechanisms," in *Windows Internals Part 2* for more on this.) Eventually, `ShellExecute(Ex)` calls `CreateProcess` with a proper executable and appends appropriate arguments on the command line to achieve the user's intention (such as editing a TXT file by appending the file name to Notepad.exe).

Ultimately, all these execution paths lead to a common internal function, `CreateProcessInternal`, which starts the actual work of creating a user-mode Windows process. Eventually (if all goes well), `CreateProcessInternal` calls `NtCreateUserProcess` in Ntdll.dll to make the transition to kernel mode and continue the kernel-mode part of process creation in the function with the same name (`NtCreateUserProcess`), part of the Executive.

CreateProcess* functions arguments

It's worthwhile to discuss the arguments to the `CreateProcess*` family of functions, some of which will be referred to in the section on the flow of `CreateProcess`. A process created from user mode is always created with one thread within it. This is the thread that eventually will execute the main function of the executable. Here are the important arguments to the `CreateProcess*` functions:

- For `CreateProcessAsUser` and `CreateProcessWithTokenW`, the token handle under which the new process should execute. Similarly, for `CreateProcessWithLogonW`, the username, domain and password are required.

- The executable path and command-line arguments.

- Optional security attributes applied to the new process and thread object that's about to be created.

- A Boolean flag indicating whether all handles in the current (creating) process that are marked inheritable should be inherited (copied) to the new process. (See Chapter 8, "System mechanisms," in Part 2 for more on handles and handle inheritance.)

- Various flags that affect process creation. Here are some examples. (Check the Windows SDK documentation for a complete list.)

  - **CREATE_SUSPENDED** This creates the initial thread of the new process in the suspended state. A later call to ResumeThread will cause the thread to begin execution.

  - **DEBUG_PROCESS** The creating process is declaring itself to be a debugger, creating the new process under its control.

  - **EXTENDED_STARTUPINFO_PRESENT** The extended STARTUPINFOEX structure is provided instead of STARTUPINFO (described below).

- An optional environment block for the new process (specifying environment variables). If not specified, it will be inherited from the creating process.

- An optional current directory for the new process. (If not specified, it uses the one from the creating process.) The created process can later call SetCurrentDirectory to set a different one. The current directory of a process is used in various non-full path searches (such as when loading a DLL with a filename only).

- A STARTUPINFO or STARTUPINFOEX structure that provides more configuration for process creation. STARTUPINFOEX contains an additional opaque field that represents a set of process and thread attributes that are essentially an array of key/value pairs. These attributes are filled by calling UpdateProcThreadAttributes once for each attribute that's needed. Some of these attributes are undocumented and used internally, such as when creating store apps, as described in the next section.

- A PROCESS_INFORMATION structure that is the output of a successful process creation. This structure holds the new unique process ID, the new unique thread ID, a handle to the new process and a handle to the new thread. The handles are useful for the creating process if it wants to somehow manipulate the new process or thread in some way after creation.

Creating Windows modern processes

Chapter 1 described the new types of applications available starting from Windows 8 and Windows Server 2012. The names of these apps have changed over time, but we'll refer to them as modern apps, UWP apps, or immersive processes, to distinguish them from the classic, also known as desktop, applications.

Creating a modern application process requires more than just calling `CreateProcess` with the correct executable path. There are some required command-line arguments. Yet another requirement is adding an undocumented process attribute (using `UpdateProcThreadAttribute`) with a key named `PROC_THREAD_ATTRIBUTE_PACKAGE_FULL_NAME` with the value set to the full store app package name. Although this attribute is undocumented, there are other ways (from an API perspective) to execute a store app. For example, the Windows API includes a COM interface called `IApplicationActivation-Manager` that is implemented by a COM class with a CLSID named `CLSID_ApplicationActivation-Manager`. One of the methods in the interface is `ActivateApplication`, which can be used to launch a store app after obtaining something known as *AppUserModelId* from the store app full package name by calling `GetPackageApplicationIds`. (See the Windows SDK for more information on these APIs.)

Package names and the way a store app is typically created, from a user tapping on a modern app tile, eventually leading to `CreateProcess`, is discussed in Chapter 9 in Part 2.

Creating other kinds of processes

Although Windows applications launch either classic or modern applications, the Executive includes support for additional kinds of processes that must be started by bypassing the Windows API, such as native processes, minimal processes, or Pico processes. For example, we described in Chapter 2 the existence of Smss, the Session Manager, which is an example of a native image. Since it is created directly by the kernel, it obviously does not use the `CreateProcess` API, but instead calls directly into `NtCreateUserProcess`. Similarly, when Smss creates Autochk (the check disk utility) or Csrss (the Windows subsystem process), the Windows API is also not available, and `NtCreateUserProcess` must be used. Additionally, native processes cannot be created from Windows applications, as the `CreateProcessInternal` function will reject images with the native subsystem image type. To alleviate these complications, the native library, Ntdll.dll, includes an exported helper function called `RtlCreateUserProcess`, providing a simpler wrapper around `NtCreateUserProcess`.

As its name suggests, `NtCreateUserProcess` is used for the creation of user-mode processes. However, as we saw in Chapter 2, Windows also includes a number of kernel-mode processes, such as the System process and the Memory Compression processes (which are minimal processes), plus the possibility of Pico processes managed by a provider such as the Windows Subsystem for Linux. The creation of such processes is instead provided by the `NtCreateProcessEx` system call, with certain capabilities reserved solely for kernel-mode callers (such as the creation of minimal processes).

Finally, Pico providers call a helper function, which takes care of both creating the minimal process as well as initializing its Pico provider context—`PspCreatePicoProcess`. This function is not exported, and is only available to Pico providers through their special interface.

As we'll see in the flow section later in this chapter, although `NtCreateProcessEx` and `NtCreate-UserProcess` are different system calls, the same internal routines are used to perform the work: `PspAllocateProcess` and `PspInsertProcess`. All the possible ways we've enumerated so far to create a process, and any ways you can imagine, from a WMI PowerShell cmdlet to a kernel driver, will end up there.

Process internals

This section describes the key Windows process data structures maintained by various parts of the system and describes different ways and tools to examine this data.

Each Windows process is represented by an executive process (EPROCESS) structure. Besides containing many attributes relating to a process, an EPROCESS contains and points to a number of other related data structures. For example, each process has one or more threads, each represented by an executive thread (ETHREAD) structure. (Thread data structures are explained in Chapter 4, "Threads".)

The EPROCESS and most of its related data structures exist in system address space. One exception is the Process Environment Block (PEB), which exists in the process (user) address space (because it contains information accessed by user-mode code). Additionally, some of the process data structures used in memory management, such as the working set list, are valid only within the context of the current process, because they are stored in process-specific system space. (See Chapter 5, "Memory management," for more information on process address space.)

For each process that is executing a Windows program, the Windows subsystem process (Csrss) maintains a parallel structure called the CSR_PROCESS. Additionally, the kernel-mode part of the Windows subsystem (Win32k.sys) maintains a per-process data structure, W32PROCESS, which is created the first time a thread calls a Windows USER or GDI function that is implemented in kernel mode. This happens as soon as the User32.dll library is loaded. Typical functions that cause this library to be loaded are CreateWindow(Ex) and GetMessage.

Since the kernel-mode Windows subsystem makes heavy use of DirectX-based hardware accelerated graphics, the Graphics Device Interface (GDI) component infrastructure causes the DirectX Graphics Kernel (Dxgkrnl.sys) to initialize a structure of its own, DXGPROCESS. This structure contains information for DirectX objects (surfaces, shaders, etc.) and the GPGPU-related counters and policy settings for both computational and memory management–related scheduling.

Except for the idle process, every EPROCESS structure is encapsulated as a process object by the executive object manager (described in Chapter 8 in Part 2). Because processes are not named objects, they are not visible in the WinObj tool (from Sysinternals). You can, however, see the Type object called *Process* in the \ObjectTypes directory (in WinObj). A handle to a process provides, through use of the process-related APIs, access to some of the data in the EPROCESS structure and in some of its associated structures.

Many other drivers and system components, by registering process-creation notifications, can choose to create their own data structures to track information they store on a per-process basis. (The executive functions PsSetCreateProcessNotifyRoutine(Ex, Ex2) allow this and are documented in the WDK.) When one discusses the overhead of a process, the size of such data structures must often be taken into consideration, although it is nearly impossible to obtain an accurate number. Additionally, some of these functions allow such components to disallow, or block, the creation of processes. This provides anti-malware vendors with an architectural way to add security enhancements to the operating system, either through hash-based blacklisting or other techniques.

First let's focus on the Process object. Figure 3-2 shows the key fields in an EPROCESS structure.

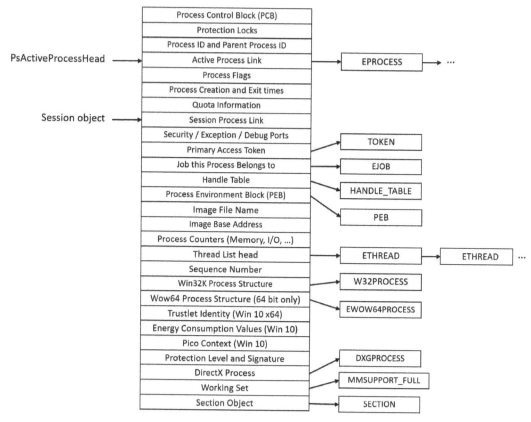

FIGURE 3-2   Important fields of the executive process structure.

Similar to the way the kernel's APIs and components are divided into isolated and layered modules with their own naming conventions, the data structures for a process follow a similar design. As shown in Figure 3-2, the first member of the executive process structure is called *Pcb* (*Process Control Block*). It is a structure of type KPROCESS, for *kernel process*. Although routines in the executive store information in the EPROCESS, the dispatcher, scheduler, and interrupt/time accounting code—being part of the operating system kernel—use the KPROCESS instead. This allows a layer of abstraction to exist between the executive's high-level functionality and its underlying low-level implementation of certain functions, and helps prevent unwanted dependencies between the layers. Figure 3-3 shows the key fields in a KPROCESS structure.

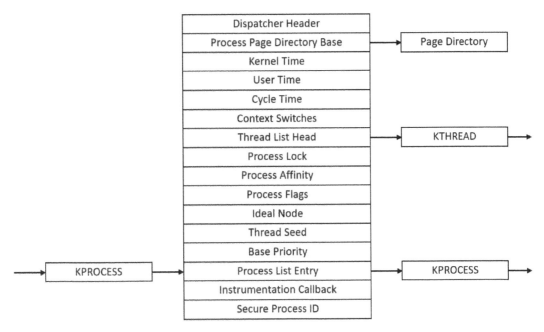

Dispatcher Header	
Process Page Directory Base	→ Page Directory
Kernel Time	
User Time	
Cycle Time	
Context Switches	
Thread List Head	→ KTHREAD →
Process Lock	
Process Affinity	
Process Flags	
Ideal Node	
Thread Seed	
Base Priority	
Process List Entry	→ KPROCESS →
Instrumentation Callback	
Secure Process ID	

→ KPROCESS →

FIGURE 3-3 Important fields of the kernel process structure.

EXPERIMENT: Displaying the format of an EPROCESS structure

For a list of the fields that make up an EPROCESS structure and their offsets in hexadecimal, type **dt nt!_eprocess** in the kernel debugger. (See Chapter 1 for more information on the kernel debugger and how to perform kernel debugging on the local system.) The output (truncated for the sake of space) on a 64-bit Windows 10 system looks like this:

```
lkd> dt nt!_eprocess
   +0x000 Pcb              : _KPROCESS
   +0x2d8 ProcessLock      : _EX_PUSH_LOCK
   +0x2e0 RundownProtect   : _EX_RUNDOWN_REF
   +0x2e8 UniqueProcessId  : Ptr64 Void
   +0x2f0 ActiveProcessLinks : _LIST_ENTRY
...
   +0x3a8 Win32Process     : Ptr64 Void
   +0x3b0 Job              : Ptr64 _EJOB
...
   +0x418 ObjectTable      : Ptr64 _HANDLE_TABLE
   +0x420 DebugPort        : Ptr64 Void
   +0x428 WoW64Process     : Ptr64 _EWOW64PROCESS
...
   +0x758 SharedCommitCharge : Uint8B
   +0x760 SharedCommitLock : _EX_PUSH_LOCK
   +0x768 SharedCommitLinks : _LIST_ENTRY
```

```
+0x778 AllowedCpuSets      : Uint8B
+0x780 DefaultCpuSets      : Uint8B
+0x778 AllowedCpuSetsIndirect : Ptr64 Uint8B
+0x780 DefaultCpuSetsIndirect : Ptr64 Uint8B
```

The first member of this structure (Pcb) is an embedded structure of type KPROCESS. This is where scheduling and time-accounting data is stored. You can display the format of the kernel process structure in the same way as the EPROCESS:

```
lkd> dt nt!_kprocess
   +0x000 Header              : _DISPATCHER_HEADER
   +0x018 ProfileListHead     : _LIST_ENTRY
   +0x028 DirectoryTableBase  : Uint8B
   +0x030 ThreadListHead      : _LIST_ENTRY
   +0x040 ProcessLock         : Uint4B
   ...
   +0x26c KernelTime          : Uint4B
   +0x270 UserTime            : Uint4B
   +0x274 LdtFreeSelectorHint : Uint2B
   +0x276 LdtTableLength      : Uint2B
   +0x278 LdtSystemDescriptor : _KGDTENTRY64
   +0x288 LdtBaseAddress      : Ptr64 Void
   +0x290 LdtProcessLock      : _FAST_MUTEX
   +0x2c8 InstrumentationCallback : Ptr64 Void
   +0x2d0 SecurePid           : Uint8B
```

The dt command also enables you to view the specific contents of one field or multiple fields by typing their names following the structure name. For example, typing **dt nt!_eprocess UniqueProcessId** displays the process ID field. In the case of a field that represents a structure—such as the Pcb field of EPROCESS, which contains the KPROCESS substructure—adding a period after the field name will cause the debugger to display the substructure. For example, an alternative way to see the KPROCESS is to type **dt nt!_eprocess Pcb**. You can continue to recurse this way by adding more field names (within KPROCESS) and so on. Finally, the –r switch of the dt command allows you to recurse through all the substructures. Adding a number after the switch controls the depth of recursion the command will follow.

The dt command used as shown earlier shows the format of the selected structure, not the contents of any particular instance of that structure type. To show an instance of an actual process, you can specify the address of an EPROCESS structure as an argument to the dt command. You can get the addresses of almost all of the EPROCESS structures in the system by using the !process 0 0 command (the exception being the system idle process). Because the KPROCESS is the first thing in the EPROCESS, the address of an EPROCESS will also work as the address of a KPROCESS with dt _kprocess.

EXPERIMENT: Using the kernel debugger !process command

The kernel debugger !process command displays a subset of the information in a process object and its associated structures. This output is arranged in two parts for each process. First you see the information about the process, as shown here. When you don't specify a process address or ID, !process lists information for the process owning the thread currently running on CPU 0, which will be WinDbg itself (or livekd if it's used in lieu of WinDbg) on a single-processor system.

```
1kd> !process
PROCESS ffffe0011c3243c0
    SessionId: 2  Cid: 0e38    Peb: 5f2f1de000  ParentCid: 0f08
    DirBase: 38b3e000  ObjectTable: ffffc000a2b22200  HandleCount: <Data Not Accessible>
    Image: windbg.exe
    VadRoot ffffe0011badae60 Vads 117 Clone 0 Private 3563. Modified 228. Locked 1.
    DeviceMap ffffc000984e4330
    Token                             ffffc000a13f39a0
    ElapsedTime                       00:00:20.772
    UserTime                          00:00:00.000
    KernelTime                        00:00:00.015
    QuotaPoolUsage[PagedPool]         299512
    QuotaPoolUsage[NonPagedPool]      16240
    Working Set Sizes (now,min,max)   (9719, 50, 345) (38876KB, 200KB, 1380KB)
    PeakWorkingSetSize                9947
    VirtualSize                       2097319 Mb
    PeakVirtualSize                   2097321 Mb
    PageFaultCount                    13603
    MemoryPriority                    FOREGROUND
    BasePriority                      8
    CommitCharge                      3994
    Job                               ffffe0011b853690
```

After the basic process output comes a list of the threads in the process. That output is explained in the "Experiment: Using the kernel debugger !thread command" section in Chapter 4.

Other commands that display process information include !handle, which dumps the process handle table (described in more detail in the section "Object handles and the process handle table" in Chapter 8 in Part 2). Process and thread security structures are described in Chapter 7, "Security."

Note that the output gives the address of the PEB. You can use this with the !peb command shown in the next experiment to see a friendly view of the PEB of an arbitrary process or you can use the regular dt command with the _PEB structure. However, because the PEB is in the user-mode address space, it is valid only within the context of its own process. To look at the PEB of another process, you must first switch WinDbg to that process. You can do this with the .process /P command, followed by the EPROCESS pointer.

If you're using the latest Windows 10 SDK, the updated version of WinDbg will include an intuitive hyperlink under the PEB address, which you can click to automatically execute both the `.process` command and the `!peb` command.

The PEB lives in the user-mode address space of the process it describes. It contains information needed by the image loader, the heap manager, and other Windows components that need to access it from user mode; it would be too expensive to expose all that information through system calls. The EPROCESS and KPROCESS structures are accessible only from kernel mode. The important fields of the PEB are illustrated in Figure 3-4 and are explained in more detail later in this chapter.

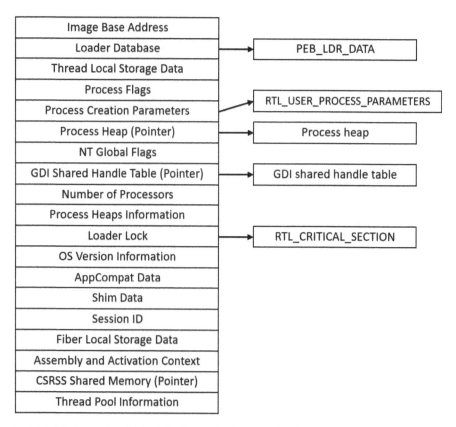

FIGURE 3-4 Important fields of the Process Environment Block.

EXPERIMENT: Examining the PEB

You can dump the PEB structure with the `!peb` command in the kernel debugger, which displays the PEB of the process that owns the currently running thread on CPU 0. By using the information in the previous experiment, you can also use the PEB pointer as an argument to the command.

```
lkd> .process /P ffffe0011c3243c0 ; !peb 5f2f1de000
PEB at 0000003561545000
    InheritedAddressSpace:    No
    ReadImageFileExecOptions: No
    BeingDebugged:            No
    ImageBaseAddress:              00007ff64fa70000
    Ldr                            00007ffdf52f5200
    Ldr.Initialized:               Yes
    Ldr.InInitializationOrderModuleList: 000001d3d22b3630 . 000001d3d6cddb60
    Ldr.InLoadOrderModuleList:           000001d3d22b3790 . 000001d3d6cddb40
    Ldr.InMemoryOrderModuleList:         000001d3d22b37a0 . 000001d3d6cddb50
                  Base TimeStamp                     Module
           7ff64fa70000 56ccafdd Feb 23 21:15:41 2016 C:\dbg\x64\windbg.exe
           7ffdf51b0000 56cbf9dd Feb 23 08:19:09 2016 C:\WINDOWS\SYSTEM32\ntdll.dll
           7ffdf2c10000 5632d5aa Oct 30 04:27:54 2015 C:\WINDOWS\system32\KERNEL32.DLL
    ...
```

The CSR_PROCESS structure contains information about processes that is specific to the Windows subsystem (Csrss). As such, only Windows applications have a CSR_PROCESS structure associated with them (for example, Smss does not). Additionally, because each session has its own instance of the Windows subsystem, the CSR_PROCESS structures are maintained by the Csrss process within each individual session. The basic structure of the CSR_PROCESS is illustrated in Figure 3-5 and is explained in more detail later in this chapter.

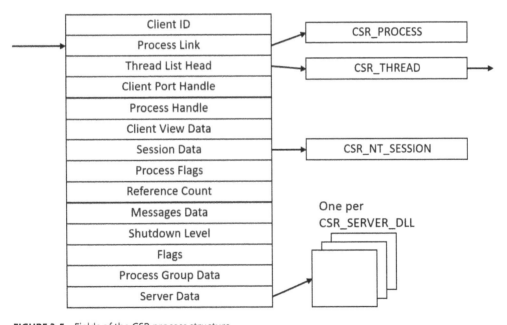

FIGURE 3-5 Fields of the CSR process structure.

EXPERIMENT: Examining the CSR_PROCESS

Csrss processes are protected (see later in this chapter for more on protected processes), so it's not possible to attach a user mode debugger to a Csrss process (not even with elevated privileges or non-invasively). Instead, we'll use the kernel debugger.

First, list the existing Csrss processes:

```
lkd> !process 0 0 csrss.exe
PROCESS ffffe00077ddf080
    SessionId: 0  Cid: 02c0    Peb: c4e3fc0000  ParentCid: 026c
    DirBase:   ObjectTable: ffffc0004d15d040  HandleCount: 543.
    Image: csrss.exe

PROCESS ffffe00078796080
    SessionId: 1  Cid: 0338    Peb: d4b4db4000  ParentCid: 0330
    DirBase:   ObjectTable: ffffc0004ddff040  HandleCount: 514.
    Image: csrss.exe
```

Next, take any one of them and change the debugger context to point to the particular process so that its user mode modules are visible:

```
lkd> .process /r /P ffffe00078796080
Implicit process is now ffffe000'78796080
Loading User Symbols
.............
```

The /p switch changes the process context of the debugger to the provided process object (EPROCESS, mostly needed in live debugging) and /r requests loading of user mode symbols. Now you can look at the modules themselves using the lm command or look at the CSR_PROCESS structure:

```
lkd> dt csrss!_csr_process
    +0x000 ClientId         : _CLIENT_ID
    +0x010 ListLink         : _LIST_ENTRY
    +0x020 ThreadList       : _LIST_ENTRY
    +0x030 NtSession        : Ptr64 _CSR_NT_SESSION
    +0x038 ClientPort       : Ptr64 Void
    +0x040 ClientViewBase   : Ptr64 Char
    +0x048 ClientViewBounds : Ptr64 Char
    +0x050 ProcessHandle    : Ptr64 Void
    +0x058 SequenceNumber   : Uint4B
    +0x05c Flags            : Uint4B
    +0x060 DebugFlags       : Uint4B
    +0x064 ReferenceCount   : Int4B
    +0x068 ProcessGroupId   : Uint4B
    +0x06c ProcessGroupSequence : Uint4B
    +0x070 LastMessageSequence : Uint4B
    +0x074 NumOutstandingMessages : Uint4B
    +0x078 ShutdownLevel    : Uint4B
    +0x07c ShutdownFlags    : Uint4B
    +0x080 Luid             : _LUID
    +0x088 ServerDllPerProcessData : [1] Ptr64 Void
```

The W32PROCESS structure is the final system data structure associated with processes that we'll look at. It contains all the information that the Windows graphics and window management code in the kernel (Win32k) needs to maintain state information about GUI processes (which were defined earlier as processes that have done at least one USER/GDI system call). The basic structure of the W32PROCESS is illustrated in Figure 3-6. Unfortunately, since type information for Win32k structures is not available in public symbols, we can't easily show you an experiment displaying this information. Either way, discussion of graphics-related data structures and concepts is beyond the scope of this book.

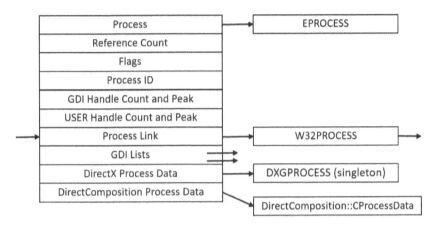

FIGURE 3-6 Fields of the Win32k Process structure.

Protected processes

In the Windows security model, any process running with a token containing the debug privilege (such as an administrator's account) can request any access right that it desires to any other process running on the machine. For example, it can read and write arbitrary process memory, inject code, suspend and resume threads, and query information on other processes. Tools such as Process Explorer and Task Manager need and request these access rights to provide their functionality to users.

This logical behavior (which helps ensure that administrators will always have full control of the running code on the system) clashes with the system behavior for digital rights management requirements imposed by the media industry on computer operating systems that need to support playback of advanced, high-quality digital content such as Blu-ray media. To support reliable and protected playback of such content, Windows Vista and Windows Server 2008 introduced protected processes. These processes exist alongside normal Windows processes, but they add significant constraints to the access rights that other processes on the system (even when running with administrative privileges) can request.

Protected processes can be created by any application. However, the operating system will allow a process to be protected only if the image file has been digitally signed with a special Windows Media Certificate. The Protected Media Path (PMP) in Windows makes use of protected processes to provide protection for high-value media, and developers of applications such as DVD players can make use of protected processes by using the Media Foundation (MF) API.

The Audio Device Graph process (Audiodg.exe) is a protected process because protected music content can be decoded through it. Related to this is the Media Foundation Protected Pipeline (Mfpmp.exe), which is also a protected process for similar reasons (it does not run by default). Similarly, the Windows Error Reporting (WER; discussed in Chapter 8 in Part 2) client process (Werfaultsecure.exe) can also run protected because it needs to have access to protected processes in case one of them crashes. Finally, the System process itself is protected because some of the decryption information is generated by the Ksecdd.sys driver and stored in its user-mode memory. The System process is also protected to protect the integrity of all kernel handles (because the System process's handle table contains all the kernel handles on the system). Since other drivers may also sometimes map memory inside the user-mode address space of the System process (such as Code Integrity certificate and catalog data), it's yet another reason for keeping the process protected.

At the kernel level, support for protected processes is twofold. First, the bulk of process creation occurs in kernel mode to avoid injection attacks. (The flow for both protected and standard process creation is described in detail in the next section.) Second, protected processes (and their extended cousin, Protected Processes Light [PPL], described in the next section) have special bits set in their EPROCESS structure that modify the behavior of security-related routines in the process manager to deny certain access rights that would normally be granted to administrators. In fact, the only access rights that are granted for protected processes are PROCESS_QUERY/SET_LIMITED_INFORMATION, PROCESS_TERMINATE and PROCESS_SUSPEND_RESUME. Certain access rights are also disabled for threads running inside protected processes. We will look at those access rights in Chapter 4 in the section "Thread internals."

Because Process Explorer uses standard user-mode Windows APIs to query information on process internals, it is unable to perform certain operations on such processes. On the other hand, a tool like WinDbg in kernel-debugging mode, which uses kernel-mode infrastructure to obtain this information, will be able to display complete information. See the experiment in the "Thread internals" section in Chapter 4 on how Process Explorer behaves when confronted with a protected process such as Audiodg.exe.

> **Note** As mentioned in Chapter 1, to perform local kernel debugging, you must boot in debugging mode (enabled by using bcdedit /debug on or by using the Msconfig advanced boot options). This mitigates against debugger-based attacks on protected processes and the PMP. When booted in debugging mode, high-definition content playback will not work.

Limiting these access rights reliably allows the kernel to sandbox a protected process from user-mode access. On the other hand, because a protected process is indicated by a flag in the EPROCESS structure, an administrator can still load a kernel-mode driver that modifies this flag. However, this would be a violation of the PMP model and considered malicious, and such a driver would likely eventually be blocked from loading on a 64-bit system because the kernel-mode, code-signing policy prohibits the digital signing of malicious code. Additionally, kernel-mode patch protection, known as PatchGuard (described in Chapter 7), as well as the Protected Environment and Authentication Driver

(Peauth.sys), will recognize and report such attempts. Even on 32-bit systems, the driver has to be recognized by PMP policy or the playback may be halted. This policy is implemented by Microsoft and not by any kernel detection. This block would require manual action from Microsoft to identify the signature as malicious and update the kernel.

Protected Process Light (PPL)

As we just saw, the original model for protected processes focused on DRM-based content. Starting with Windows 8.1 and Windows Server 2012 R2, an extension to the protected process model was introduced, called Protected Process Light (PPL).

PPLs are protected in the same sense as classic protected processes: User-mode code (even running with elevated privileges) cannot penetrate these processes by injecting threads or obtaining detailed information about loaded DLLs. However, the PPL model adds an additional dimension to the quality of being protected: attribute values. The different Signers have differing trust levels, which in turn results in certain PPLs being more, or less, protected than other PPLs.

Because DRM evolved from merely multimedia DRM to also Windows licensing DRM and Windows Store DRM, standard protected processes are now also differentiated based on the Signer value. Finally, the various recognized Signers also define which access rights are denied to lesser protected processes. For example, normally, the only access masks allowed are PROESS_QUERY/SET_LIMITED_INFORMATION and PROCESS_SUSPEND_RESUME. PROCESS_TERMINATE is not allowed for certain PPL signers.

Table 3-1 shows the legal values for the protection flag stored in the EPROCESS structure.

TABLE 3-1 Valid protection values for processes

Internal Protection Process Level Symbol	Protection Type	Signer
PS_PROTECTED_SYSTEM (0x72)	Protected	WinSystem
PS_PROTECTED_WINTCB (0x62)	Protected	WinTcb
PS_PROTECTED_WINTCB_LIGHT (0x61)	Protected Light	WinTcb
PS_PROTECTED_WINDOWS (0x52)	Protected	Windows
PS_PROTECTED_WINDOWS_LIGHT (0x51)	Protected Light	Windows
PS_PROTECTED_LSA_LIGHT (0x41)	Protected Light	Lsa
PS_PROTECTED_ANTIMALWARE_LIGHT (0x31)	Protected Light	Anti-malware
PS_PROTECTED_AUTHENTICODE (0x21)	Protected	Authenticode
PS_PROTECTED_AUTHENTICODE_LIGHT (0x11)	Protected Light	Authenticode
PS_PROTECTED_NONE (0x00)	None	None

As shown in Table 3-1, there are several signers defined, from high to low power. WinSystem is the highest-priority signer and used for the System process and minimal processes such as the Memory Compression process. For user-mode processes, WinTCB (Windows Trusted Computer Base) is the highest-priority signer and leveraged to protect critical processes that the kernel has intimate knowledge of and might reduce its security boundary toward. When interpreting the power of a process, keep in mind that first, protected processes always trump PPLs, and that next, higher-value signer processes have access to lower ones, but not vice versa. Table 3-2 shows the signer levels (higher values denote the signer is more powerful) and some examples of their usage. You can also dump these in the debugger with the _PS_PROTECTED_SIGNER type.

TABLE 3-2 Signers and levels

Signer Name (PS_PROTECTED_SIGNER)	Level	Used For
PsProtectedSignerWinSystem	7	System and minimal processes (including Pico processes).
PsProtectedSignerWinTcb	6	Critical Windows components. PROCESS_TERMINATE is denied.
PsProtectedSignerWindows	5	Important Windows components handling sensitive data.
PsProtectedSignerLsa	4	Lsass.exe (if configured to run protected).
PsProtectedSignerAntimalware	3	Anti-malware services and processes, including third party. PROCESS_TERMINATE is denied.
PsProtectedSignerCodeGen	2	NGEN (.NET native code generation).
PsProtectedSignerAuthenticode	1	Hosting DRM content or loading user-mode fonts.
PsProtectedSignerNone	0	Not valid (no protection).

At this point you may be wondering what prohibits a malicious process from claiming it is a protected process and shielding itself from anti-malware (AM) applications. Because the Windows Media DRM Certificate is no longer necessary to run as a protected process, Microsoft extended its Code Integrity module to understand two special enhanced key usage (EKU) OIDs that can be encoded in a digital code signing certificate: 1.3.6.1.4.1.311.10.3.22 and 1.3.6.4.1.311.10.3.20. Once one of these EKUs is present, hardcoded Signer and Issuer strings in the certificate, combined with additional possible EKUs, are then associated with the various Protected Signer values. For example, the Microsoft Windows Issuer can grant the PsProtectedSignerWindows protected signer value, but only if the EKU for Windows System Component Verification (1.3.6.1.4.1.311.10.3.6) is also present. As an example, Figure 3-7 shows the certificate for Smss.exe, which is permitted to run as WinTcb-Light.

Finally, note that the protection level of a process also impacts which DLLs it will be allowed to load—otherwise, either through a logic bug or simple file replacement or plating, a legitimate protected process could be coerced into loading a third party or malicious library, which would now execute with the same protection level as the process. This check is implemented by granting each process a "Signature Level," which is stored in the SignatureLevel field of EPROCESS, and then using an internal lookup table to find a corresponding "DLL Signature Level," stored as SectionSignatureLevel in EPROCESS. Any DLL loading in the process will be checked by the Code Integrity component in the same way that the main executable is verified. For example, a process with "WinTcb" as its executable signer will only load "Windows" or higher signed DLLs.

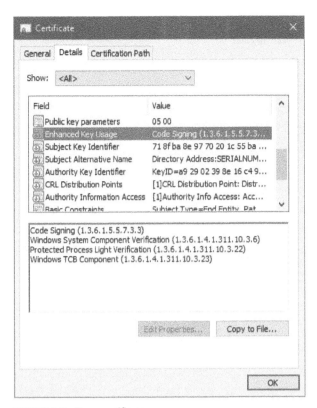

FIGURE 3-7 Smss certificate.

On Windows 10 and Windows Server 2016, the following processes are PPL signed with WinTcb-Lite: smss.exe, csrss.exe, services.exe, and wininit.exe. Lsass.exe is running as PPL on ARM-based Windows (such as Windows mobile 10) and can run as PPL on x86/x64 if configured as such by a registry setting or by policy (see Chapter 7 for more information). Additionally, certain services are configured to run as Windows PPL or protected processes, such as sppsvc.exe (Software Protection Platform). You may also notice certain service-hosting processes (Svchost.exe) running with this protection level, since many services, such as the AppX Deployment Service and the Windows Subsystem for Linux Service, also run protected. More information on such protected services will be described in Chapter 9 in Part 2.

The fact that these core system binaries run as TCB is critical to the security of the system. For example, Csrss.exe has access to certain private APIs implemented by the Window Manager (Win32k.sys), which could give an attacker with Administrator rights access to sensitive parts of the kernel. Similarly, Smss. exe and Wininit.exe implement system startup and management logic that is critical to perform without possible interference from an administrator. Windows guarantees that these binaries will always run as WinTcb-Lite such that, for example, it is not possible for someone to launch them without specifying the correct process protection level in the process attributes when calling `CreateProcess`. This guarantee is known as the *minimum TCB list* and forces any processes with the names in Table 3-3 that are in a System path to have a minimum protection level and/or signing level regardless of the caller's input.

TABLE 3-3 Minimum TCB

Process Name	Minimum Signature Level	Minimum Protection Level
Smss.exe	Inferred from protection level	WinTcb-Lite
Csrss.exe	Inferred from protection level	WinTcb-Lite
Wininit.exe	Inferred from protection level	WinTcb-Lite
Services.exe	Inferred from protection level	WinTcb-Lite
Werfaultsecure.exe	Inferred from protection level	WinTcb-Full
Sppsvc.exe	Inferred from protection level	Windows-Full
Genvalobj.exe	Inferred from protection level	Windows-Full
Lsass.exe	SE_SIGNING_LEVEL_WINDOWS	0
Userinit.exe	SE_SIGNING_LEVEL_WINDOWS	0
Winlogon.exe	SE_SIGNING_LEVEL_WINDOWS	0
Autochk.exe	SE_SIGNING_LEVEL_WINDOWS*	0

*Only on UEFI firmware systems

EXPERIMENT: Viewing protected processes in Process Explorer

In this experiment, we'll look at how Process Explorer shows protected processes (of either type). Run Process Explorer and select the **Protection** check box in the Process Image tab to view the Protection column:

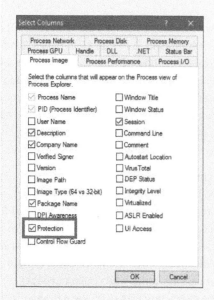

Now sort by the Protection column in descending order and scroll to the top. You should see all protected processes with their protection type. Here's a screenshot from a Windows 10 x64 machine:

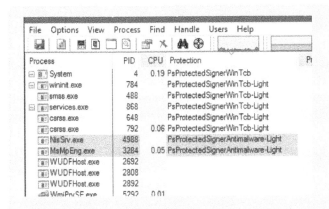

If you select a protected process and look at the lower part when configured to view DLLs, you'll see nothing. That's because Process Explorer uses user-mode APIs to query the loaded modules and that requires access that is not granted for accessing protected processes. The notable exception is the System process, which is protected, but Process Explorer instead shows the list of loaded kernel modules (mostly drivers) since there are no DLLs in system processes. This is done using the EnumDeviceDrivers API, which is a system API that does not require a process handle.

If you switch to Handle view, you'll see complete handle information. The reason is similar: Process Explorer uses an undocumented API that returns all handles on the system, which does not require a specific process handle. Process Explorer can identify the process simply because this information returns the PID associated with each handle.

Third-party PPL support

The PPL mechanism extends the protection possibilities for processes beyond executables created solely by Microsoft. A common example is anti-malware (AM) software. A typical AM product consists of three main components:

- A kernel driver that intercepts I/O requests to the file system and/or the network, and implements blocking capabilities using object, process, and thread callbacks

- A user-mode service (typically running under a privileged account) that configures the driver's policies, receives notifications from the driver regarding "interesting" events (for example, infected file), and may communicate with a local server or the Internet

- A user-mode GUI process that communicates information to the user and optionally allows the user to make decisions where applicable.

One possible way malware can attack a system is by managing to inject code inside a process running with elevated privileges, or better, inject code specifically inside an anti-malware service and thus tamper with it or disable its operation. If, however, the AM service could run as a PPL, no code injection would be possible, and no process termination would be allowed, meaning that the AM software would be better protected from malware that does not employ kernel-level exploits.

To enable this use, the AM kernel driver described above needs to have a corresponding Early-Launch Anti Malware (ELAM) driver. While ELAM is further described in Chapter 7, the key distinction is that such drivers require a special anti-malware certificate provided by Microsoft (after proper verification of the software's publisher). Once such a driver is installed, it can contain a custom resource section in its main executable (PE) file called ELAMCERTIFICATEINFO. This section can describe three additional Signers (identified by their public key), each having up to three additional EKUs (identified by OID). Once the Code Integrity system recognizes any file signed by one of the three Signers, containing one of the three EKUs, it permits the process to request a PPL of PS_PROTECTED_ANTIMALWARE_LIGHT (0x31). A canonical example of this is Microsoft's own AM known as Windows Defender. Its service on Windows 10 (MsMpEng.exe) is signed with the anti-malware certificate for better protection against malware attacking the AM itself, as is its Network Inspection Server (NisSvc.exe).

Minimal and Pico processes

The types of processes we've looked at so far, and their data structures, seem to imply that their use is the execution of user-mode code, and that they contain a great deal of related data structures in memory to achieve this. Yet, not all processes are used for this purpose. For example, as we've seen, the System process is merely used as a container of most of the system threads, such that their execution time doesn't pollute arbitrary user-mode processes, as well as being used as a container of drivers' handles (called kernel handles), such that these don't end up owned by an arbitrary application either.

Minimal processes

When a specific flag is given to the NtCreateProcessEx function, and the caller is kernel-mode, the function behaves slightly differently and causes the execution of the PsCreateMinimalProcess API. In turn, this causes a process to be created without many of the structures that we saw earlier, namely:

- No user-mode address space will be set up, so no PEB and related structures will exist.

- No NTDLL will be mapped into the process, nor will any loader/API Set information.

- No section object will be tied to the process, meaning no executable image file is associated to its execution or its name (which can be empty, or an arbitrary string).

- The Minimal flag will be set in the EPROCESS flags, causing all threads to become minimal threads, and also avoid any user-mode allocations such as their TEB or user-mode stack. (See Chapter 4 for more information on the TEB.)

As we saw in Chapter 2, Windows 10 has at least two minimal processes—the System process and Memory Compression process—and can have a third, the Secure System process, if Virtualization-Based Security is enabled, which is described further in Chapter 2 and Chapter 7.

Finally, the other way to have minimal processes running on a Windows 10 system is to enable the Windows Subsystem for Linux (WSL) optional feature that was also described in Chapter 2. This will install an inbox Pico Provider composed of the Lxss.sys and LxCore.sys drivers.

Pico processes

While minimal processes have a limited use in terms of allowing access to user-mode virtual address space from kernel components and protecting it, Pico processes take on a more important role by permitting a special component, called a *Pico Provider*, to control most aspects of their execution from an operating system perspective. This level of control ultimately allows such a provider to emulate the behavior of a completely different operating system kernel, without the underlying user-mode binary being aware that it is running on a Windows-based operating system. This is essentially an implementation of the Drawbridge project from Microsoft Research, which is also used to support SQL Server for Linux in a similar way (albeit with a Windows-based Library OS on top of the Linux kernel).

To support the existence of Pico processes on the system, a provider must first be present. Such a provider can be registered with the PsRegisterPicoProvider API, but subject to a very specific rule: A Pico provider must be loaded before any other third-party drivers are loaded (including boot drivers). In fact, only one of the limited set of a dozen or so core drivers are allowed to call this API before the functionality is disabled, and these core drivers must be signed with a Microsoft Signer Certificate and Windows Component EKU. On Windows systems with the optional WSL component enabled, this core driver is called Lxss.sys, and serves as a stub driver until another driver, LxCore.sys, loads a bit later and takes over the Pico provider responsibilities by transferring the various dispatch tables over to itself. Additionally, note that at the time of this writing, only one such core driver can register itself as a Pico provider.

When a Pico provider calls the registration API, it receives a set of function pointers, which allow it to create and manage Pico processes:

- One function to create a Pico process and one to create a Pico thread.

- One function to get the context (an arbitrary pointer that the provider can use to store specific data) of a Pico process, one to set it, and another pair of functions to do the same for Pico threads. This will populate the PicoContext field in ETHREAD and/or EPROCESS.

- One function to get the CPU context structure (CONTEXT) of a Pico thread and one to set it.

- A function to change the FS and/or *GS* segments of a Pico thread, which are normally used by user-mode code to point to some thread local structure (such as the TEB on Windows).

- One function to terminate a Pico thread and one to do the same to a Pico process.

- One function to suspend a Pico thread and one to resume it.

As you can see, through these functions, the Pico provider can now create fully custom processes and threads for whom it controls the initial starting state, segment registers, and associate data. However, this alone would not allow the ability to emulate another operating system. A second set of function pointers is transferred, this time from the provider to the kernel, which serve as callbacks whenever certain activities of interest will be performed by a Pico thread or process.

- A callback whenever a Pico thread makes a system call using the SYSCALL instruction

- A callback whenever an exception is raised from a Pico thread

- A callback whenever a fault during a probe and lock operation on a memory descriptor list (MDL) occurs inside a Pico thread

- A callback whenever a caller is requesting the name of a Pico process

- A callback whenever Event Tracing for Windows (ETW) is requesting the user-mode stack trace of a Pico process

- A callback whenever an application attempts to open a handle to a Pico process or Pico thread

- A callback whenever someone requests the termination of a Pico process

- A callback whenever a Pico thread or Pico process terminates unexpectedly

Additionally, a Pico provider also leverages Kernel Patch Protection (KPP), described in Chapter 7, to both protect its callbacks and system calls as well as prevent fraudulent or malicious Pico providers from registering on top of a legitimate Pico provider.

It now becomes clear that with such unparalleled access to any possible user-kernel transition or visible kernel-user interactions between a Pico process/thread and the world, it can be fully encapsulated by a Pico provider (and relevant user-mode libraries) to wrap a completely different kernel implementation than that of Windows (with some exceptions, of course, as thread scheduling rules and memory management rules, such as commit, still apply). Correctly written applications are not supposed to be sensitive to such internal algorithms, as they are subject to change even within the operating system they normally execute on.

Therefore, Pico providers are essentially custom-written kernel modules that implement the necessary callbacks to respond to the list of possible events (shown earlier) that a Pico process can cause to arise. This is how WSL is capable of running unmodified Linux ELF binaries in user-mode, limited only by the completeness of its system call emulation and related functionality.

To complete the picture on regular NT processes versus minimal processes versus Pico processes, we present Figure 3-8, showing the different structures for each.

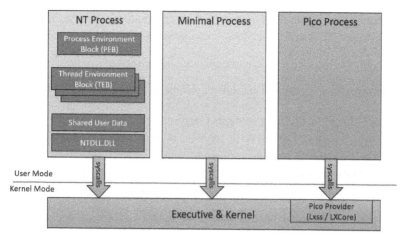

FIGURE 3-8 Process types.

Trustlets (secure processes)

As covered in Chapter 2, Windows contains new virtualization-based security (VBS) features such as Device Guard and Credential Guard, which enhance the safety of the operating system and user data by leveraging the hypervisor. We saw how one such feature, Credential Guard (which is discussed at length in Chapter 7), runs in a new Isolated User Mode environment, which, while still unprivileged (ring 3), has a virtual trust level of 1 (VTL 1), granting it protection from the regular VTL 0 world in which both the NT kernel (ring 0) and applications (ring 3) live. Let's investigate how the kernel sets up such processes for execution, and the various data structures such processes use.

Trustlet structure

To begin with, although Trustlets are regular Windows Portable Executables (PE) files, they contain some IUM-specific properties:

- They can import only from a limited set of Windows system DLLs (C/C++ Runtime, KernelBase, Advapi, RPC Runtime, CNG Base Crypto, and NTDLL) due to the restricted number of system calls that are available to Trustlets. Note that mathematical DLLs that operate only on data structures (such as NTLM, ASN.1, etc.) are also usable, as they don't perform any system calls.

- They can import from an IUM-specific system DLL that is made available to them, called `Iumbase`, which provides the Base IUM System API, containing support for mailslots, storage boxes, cryptography, and more. This library ends up calling into Iumdll.dll, which is the VTL 1 version of Ntdll.dll, and contains secure system calls (system calls that are implemented by the Secure Kernel, and not passed on to the Normal VTL 0 Kernel).

- They contain a PE section named `.tPolicy` with an exported global variable named `s_IumPolicyMetadata`. This serves as metadata for the Secure Kernel to implement policy settings around permitting VTL 0 access to the Trustlet (such as allowing debugging, crash dump support, etc.).

- They are signed with a certificate that contains the Isolated User Mode EKU (1.3.6.1.4.311.10.3.37). Figure 3-9 shows the certificate data for Lsalso.exe, showing its IUM EKU.

Additionally, Trustlets must be launched by using a specific process attribute when using `CreateProcess`—both to request their execution in IUM as well as to specify launch properties. We will describe both the policy metadata and the process attributes in the following sections.

FIGURE 3-9 Trustlet EKU in the certificate.

Trustlet policy metadata

The policy metadata includes various options for configuring how "accessible" the Trustlet will be from VTL 0. It is described by a structure present at the s_IumPolicyMetadata export mentioned earlier, and contains a version number (currently set to 1) as well as the Trustlet ID, which is a unique number that identifies this specific Trustlet among the ones that are known to exist (for example, BioIso.exe is Trustlet ID 4). Finally, the metadata has an array of policy options. Currently, the options listed in Table 3-4 are supported. It should be obvious that as these policies are part of the signed executable data, attempting to modify them would invalidate the IUM signature and prohibit execution.

TABLE 3-4 Trustlet policy options

Policy	Meaning	More Information
ETW	Enables or Disables ETW	
Debug	Configures debugging	Debug can be enabled at all times, only when SecureBoot is disabled, or using an on-demand challenge/response mechanism.
Crash Dump	Enables or disables crash dump	
Crash Dump Key	Specifies Public Key for Encrypting Crash Dump	Dumps can be submitted to Microsoft Product Team, which has the private key for decryption
Crash Dump GUID	Specifies identifier for crash dump key	This allows multiple keys to be used/identified by the product team.

TABLE 3-4 Trustlet policy options *(continued)*

Policy	Meaning	More Information
Parent Security Descriptor	SDDL format	This is used to validate that the owner/parent process is expected.
Parent Security Descriptor Revision	SDDL format revision ID	This is used to validate that the owner/parent process is expected.
SVN	Security version	This is a unique number that can be used by the Trustlet (along its identity) when encrypting AES256/GCM messages.
Device ID	Secure device PCI identifier	The Trustlet can only communicate with a Secure Device whose PCI ID matches.
Capability	Enables powerful VTL 1 capabilities	This enables access to the Create Secure Section API, DMA and user-mode MMIO access to Secure Devices, and Secure Storage APIs.
Scenario ID	Specifies the scenario ID for this binary	Encoded as a GUID, this must be specified by Trustlets when creating secure image sections to ensure it is for a known scenario.

Trustlet attributes

Launching a Trustlet requires correct usage of the PS_CP_SECURE_PROCESS attribute, which is first used to authenticate that the caller truly wants to create a Trustlet, as well as to verify that the Trustlet the caller *thinks* its executing is actually the Trustlet being executed. This is done by embedding a Trustlet identifier in the attribute, which must match the Trustlet ID contained in the policy metadata. Then, one or more attributes can be specified, which are shown in Table 3-5.

TABLE 3-5 Trustlet attributes

Attribute	Meaning	More Information
Mailbox Key	Used to retrieve mailbox data	Mailboxes allow the Trustlet to share data with the VTL 0 world as long as the Trustlet key is known.
Collaboration ID	Sets the collaboration ID to use when using the Secure Storage IUM API	Secure Storage allows Trustlets to share data among each other, as long as they have the same collaboration ID. If no collaboration ID is present, the Trustlet instance ID will be used instead.
TK Session ID	Identifies the session ID used during Crypto	

System built-in Trustlets

At the time of this writing, Windows 10 contains five different Trustlets, which are identified by their identity numbers. They are described in Table 3-6. Note that Trustlet ID 0 represents the Secure Kernel itself.

TABLE 3-6 Built-in Trustlets

Binary Name (Trustlet ID)	Description	Policy Options
Lsalso.exe (1)	Credential and Key Guard Trustlet	Allow ETW, Disable Debugging, Allow Encrypted Crash Dump
Vmsp.exe (2)	Secure Virtual Machine Worker (vTPM Trustlet)	Allow ETW, Disable Debugging, Disable Crash Dump, Enable Secure Storage Capability, Verify Parent Security Descriptor is S-1-5-83-0 (NT VIRTUAL MACHINE\Virtual Machines)
Unknown (3)	vTPM Key Enrollment Trustlet	Unknown
Biolso.exe (4)	Secure Biometrics Trustlet	Allow ETW, Disable Debugging, Allow Encrypted Crash Dump
Fslso.exe (5)	Secure Frame Server Trustlet	Disable ETW, Allow Debugging, Enable Create Secure Section Capability, Use Scenario ID { AE53FC6E-8D89-4488-9D2E-4D008731C5FD}

Trustlet identity

Trustlets have multiple forms of identity that they can use on the system:

- **Trustlet identifier or Trustlet ID**   This is a hard-coded integer in the Trustlet's policy metadata, which also must be used in the Trustlet process-creation attributes. It ensures that the system knows there are only a handful of Trustlets, and that the callers are launching the expected one.

- **Trustlet instance**   This is a cryptographically secure 16-byte random number generated by the Secure Kernel. Without the use of a collaboration ID, the Trustlet instance is what's used to guarantee that Secure Storage APIs will only allow this one instance of the Trustlet to get/put data into its storage blob.

- **Collaboration ID**   This is used when a Trustlet would like to allow other Trustlets with the same ID, or other instances of the same Trustlet, to share access to the same Secure Storage blob. When this ID is present, the instance ID of the Trustlet will be ignored when calling the Get or Put APIs.

- **Security version (SVN)**   This is used for Trustlets that require strong cryptographic proof of provenance of signed or encrypted data. It is used when encrypting AES256/GCM data by Credential and Key Guard, and is also used by the Cryptograph Report service.

- **Scenario ID**   This is used for Trustlets that create named (identity-based) secure kernel objects, such as secure sections. This GUID validates that the Trustlet is creating such objects as part of a predetermined scenario, by tagging them in the namespace with this GUID. As such, other Trustlets wishing to open the same named objects would thus have to have the same scenario ID. Note that more than one scenario ID can actually be present, but no Trustlets currently use more than one.

Isolated user-mode services

The benefits of running as a Trustlet not only include protection from attacks from the normal (VTL 0) world, but also access to privileged and protected secure system calls that are only offered by the Secure Kernel to Trustlets. These include the following services:

- **Secure Devices (`IumCreateSecureDevice`, `IumDmaMapMemory`, `IumGetDmaEnabler`, `IumMap-SecureIo`, `IumProtectSecureIo`, `IumQuerySecureDeviceInformation`, `IopUnmapSecureIo`, `IumUpdateSecureDeviceState`)** These provide access to secure ACPI and/or PCI devices, which cannot be accessed from VTL 0 and are exclusively owned by the Secure Kernel (and its ancillary Secure HAL and Secure PCI services). Trustlets with the relevant capabilities (see the "Trustlet policy metadata" section earlier in this chapter) can map the registers of such a device in VTL 1 IUM, as well as potentially perform Direct Memory Access (DMA) transfers. Additionally, Trustlets can serve as user-mode device drivers for such hardware by using the Secure Device Framework (SDF) located in SDFHost.dll. This functionality is leveraged for Secure Biometrics for Windows Hello, such as Secure USB Smartcard (over PCI) or Webcam/Fingerprint Sensors (over ACPI).

- **Secure Sections (`IumCreateSecureSection`, `IumFlushSecureSectionBuffers`, `IumGetExposed-SecureSection`, `IumOpenSecureSection`)** These provide the ability to both share physical pages with a VTL 0 driver (which would use `Vs1CreateSecureSection`) through exposed secure sections, as well as share data solely within VTL 1 as named secured sections (leveraging the identity-based mechanism described earlier in the "Trustlet identity" section) with other Trustlets or other instances of the same Trustlet. Trustlets require the Secure Section capability described in the "Trustlet policy metadata" section to use these features.

- **Mailboxes (`IumPostMailbox`)** This enables a Trustlet to share up to eight slots of about up to 4 KB of data with a component in the normal (VTL 0) kernel, which can call `Vs1RetrieveMailbox` passing in the slot identifier and secret mailbox key. For example, Vid.sys in VTL 0 uses this to retrieve various secrets used by the vTPM feature from the Vmsp.exe Trustlet.

- **Identity Keys (`IumGetIdk`)** This allows a Trustlet to obtain either a unique identifying decryption key or signing key. This key material is unique to the machine and can be obtained only from a Trustlet. It is an essential part of the Credential Guard feature to uniquely authenticate the machine and that credentials are coming from IUM.

- **Cryptographic Services (`IumCrypto`)** This allows a Trustlet to encrypt and decrypt data with a local and/or per-boot session key generated by the Secure Kernel that is only available to IUM, to obtain a TPM binding handle, to get the FIPS mode of the Secure Kernel, and to obtain a random number generator (RNG) seed only generated by the Secure Kernel for IUM. It also enables a Trustlet to generate an IDK-signed, SHA-2 hashed, and timestamped report with the identity and SVN of the Trustlet, a dump of its policy metadata, whether or not it was ever attached to a debugger, and any other Trustlet-controlled data requested. This can be used as a sort of TPM-like measurement of the Trustlet to prove that it was not tampered with.

- **Secure Storage (`IumSecureStorageGet`, `IumSecureStoragePut`)**   This allows Trustlets that have the Secure Storage capability (described earlier in the "Trustlet policy metadata" section) to store arbitrarily sized storage blobs and to later retrieve them, either based on their unique Trustlet instance or by sharing the same collaboration ID as another Trustlet.

Trustlet-accessible system calls

As the Secure Kernel attempts to minimize its attack surface and exposure, it only provides a subset (less than 50) of all of the hundreds of system calls that a normal (VTL 0) application can use. These system calls are the strict minimum necessary for compatibility with the system DLLs that Trustlets can use (refer to the section "Trustlet structure" to see these), as well as the specific services required to support the RPC runtime (Rpcrt4.dll) and ETW tracing.

- **Worker Factory and Thread APIs**   These support the Thread Pool API (used by RPC) and TLS Slots used by the Loader.

- **Process Information API**   This supports TLS Slots and Thread Stack Allocation.

- **Event, Semaphore, Wait, and Completion APIs**   These support Thread Pool and Synchronization.

- **Advanced Local Procedure Call (ALPC) APIs**   These support Local RPC over the ncalrpc transport.

- **System Information API**   This supports reading Secure Boot information, basic and NUMA system information for Kernel32.dll and Thread Pool scaling, performance, and subsets of time information.

- **Token API**   This provides minimal support for RPC impersonation.

- **Virtual Memory Allocation APIs**   These support allocations by the User-Mode Heap Manager.

- **Section APIs**   These support the Loader (for DLL Images) as well as the Secure Section functionality (once created/exposed through secure system calls shown earlier).

- **Trace Control API**   This supports ETW.

- **Exception and Continue API**   This supports Structured Exception Handling (SEH).

It should be evident from this list that support for operations such as Device I/O, whether on files or actual physical devices, is not possible (there is no `CreateFile` API, to begin with), as is also the case for Registry I/O. Nor is the creation of other processes, or any sort of graphics API usage (there is no Win32k.sys driver in VTL 1). As such, Trustlets are meant to be isolated workhorse back-ends (in VTL 1) of their complex front-ends (in VTL 0), having only ALPC as a communication mechanism, or exposed secure sections (whose handle would have to had been communicated to them through ALPC). In Chapter 7 (Security), we'll look in more detail into the implementation of a specific Trustlet—Lsalso.exe, which provides Credential and Key Guard.

Experiment: Identifying secure processes

Secure processes, other than being known by their name, can be identified in the kernel debugger in two ways. First, each secure process has a secure PID, which represents its handle in the Secure Kernel's handle table. This is used by the normal (VTL 0) kernel when creating threads in the process or requesting its termination. Secondly, the threads themselves have a thread cookie associated with them, which represents their index in the Secure Kernel's thread table.

You can try the following in a kernel debugger:

```
lkd> !for_each_process .if @@(((nt!_EPROCESS*)${@#Process})->Pcb.SecurePid) {
.printf "Trustlet: %ma (%p)\n", @@(((nt!_EPROCESS*)${@#Process})->ImageFileName),
@#Process }
Trustlet: Secure System (ffff9b09d8c79080)
Trustlet: LsaIso.exe (ffff9b09e2ba9640)
Trustlet: BioIso.exe (ffff9b09e61c4640)
lkd> dt nt!_EPROCESS ffff9b09d8c79080 Pcb.SecurePid
   +0x000 Pcb            :
      +0x2d0 SecurePid     : 0x00000001'40000004
lkd> dt nt!_EPROCESS ffff9b09e2ba9640 Pcb.SecurePid
   +0x000 Pcb            :
      +0x2d0 SecurePid     : 0x00000001'40000030
lkd> dt nt!_EPROCESS ffff9b09e61c4640 Pcb.SecurePid
   +0x000 Pcb            :
      +0x2d0 SecurePid     : 0x00000001'40000080
lkd> !process ffff9b09e2ba9640 4
PROCESS ffff9b09e2ba9640
    SessionId: 0  Cid: 0388    Peb: 6cdc62b000  ParentCid: 0328
    DirBase: 2f254000  ObjectTable: ffffc607b59b1040  HandleCount:  44.
    Image: LsaIso.exe
        THREAD ffff9b09e2ba2080  Cid 0388.038c  Teb: 0000006cdc62c000 Win32Thread:
0000000000000000 WAIT
lkd> dt nt!_ETHREAD ffff9b09e2ba2080 Tcb.SecureThreadCookie
   +0x000 Tcb            :
      +0x31c SecureThreadCookie    : 9
```

Flow of CreateProcess

We've shown the various data structures involved in process-state manipulation and management and how various tools and debugger commands can inspect this information. In this section, we'll see how and when those data structures are created and filled out, as well as the overall creation and termination behaviors behind processes. As we've seen, all documented process-creation functions eventually end up calling `CreateProcessInternalW`, so this is where we start.

Creating a Windows process consists of several stages carried out in three parts of the operating system: the Windows client-side library Kernel32.dll (the real work starting with `CreateProcessInternalW`), the Windows executive, and the Windows subsystem process (Csrss). Because of the multiple-environment subsystem architecture of Windows, creating an executive process object (which other subsystems can use) is separated from the work involved in creating a Windows subsystem process. So, although the following description of the flow of the Windows CreateProcess function is complicated, keep in mind that part of the work is specific to the semantics added by the Windows subsystem as opposed to the core work needed to create an executive process object.

The following list summarizes the main stages of creating a process with the Windows CreateProcess* functions. The operations performed in each stage are described in detail in the subsequent sections.

 Note Many steps of CreateProcess are related to the setup of the process virtual address space and therefore refer to many memory-management terms and structures that are defined in Chapter 5.

1. Validate parameters; convert Windows subsystem flags and options to their native counterparts; parse, validate, and convert the attribute list to its native counterpart.

2. Open the image file (.exe) to be executed inside the process.

3. Create the Windows executive process object.

4. Create the initial thread (stack, context, and Windows executive thread object).

5. Perform post-creation, Windows subsystem–specific process initialization.

6. Start execution of the initial thread (unless the CREATE_SUSPENDED flag was specified).

7. In the context of the new process and thread, complete the initialization of the address space (for example, load required DLLs) and begin execution of the program's entry point.

Figure 3-10 shows an overview of the stages Windows follows to create a process.

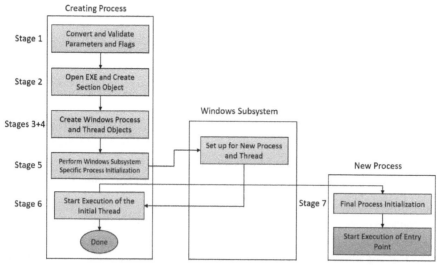

FIGURE 3-10 The main stages of process creation.

Stage 1: Converting and validating parameters and flags

Before opening the executable image to run, `CreateProcessInternalW` performs the following steps:

1. The priority class for the new process is specified as independent bits in the `CreationFlags` parameter to the `CreateProcess*` functions. Thus, you can specify more than one priority class for a single `CreateProcess*` call. Windows resolves the question of which priority class to assign to the process by choosing the lowest-priority class set.

   There are six process priority classes defined, each value mapped to a number:

   - Idle or Low, as Task Manager displays it (4)

   - Below Normal (6)

   - Normal (8)

   - Above Normal (10)

   - High (13)

   - Real-time (24)

   The priority class is used as the base priority for threads created in that process. This value does not directly affect the process itself—only the threads inside it. A description of process priority class and its effects on thread scheduling appears in Chapter 4.

2. If no priority class is specified for the new process, the priority class defaults to Normal. If a Real-time priority class is specified for the new process and the process's caller doesn't have the Increase Scheduling Priority privilege (SE_INC_BASE_PRIORITY_NAME), the High priority class is used instead. In other words, process creation doesn't fail just because the caller has insufficient privileges to create the process in the Real-time priority class; the new process just won't have as high a priority as Real-time.

3. If the creation flags specify that the process will be debugged, Kernel32 initiates a connection to the native debugging code in Ntdll.dll by calling `DbgUiConnectToDbg` and gets a handle to the debug object from the current thread's environment block (TEB).

4. Kernel32.dll sets the default hard error mode if the creation flags specified one.

5. The user-specified attribute list is converted from Windows subsystem format to native format and internal attributes are added to it. The possible attributes that can be added to the attribute list are listed in Table 3-7, including their documented Windows API counterparts, if any.

 Note The attribute list passed on `CreateProcess*` calls permits passing back to the caller information beyond a simple status code, such as the TEB address of the initial thread or information on the image section. This is necessary for protected processes because the parent cannot query this information after the child is created.

TABLE 3-7 Process attributes

Native Attribute	Equivalent Win32 Attribute	Type	Description
PS_CP_PARENT_PROCESS	PROC_THREAD_ATTRIBUTE_ PARENT_PROCESS. Also used when elevating.	Input	Handle to the parent process.
PS_CP_DEBUG_OBJECT	N/A. Used when using DEBUG_ PROCESS as a flag.	Input	Debug object if process is being started debugged.
PS_CP_PRIMARY_TOKEN	N/A. Used when using CreateProcessAsUser/ WithTokenW.	Input	Process token if CreateProcessAsUser was used.
PS_CP_CLIENT_ID	N/A. Returned by Win32 API as a parameter (PROCESS_ INFORMATION).	Output	Returns the TID and PID of the initial thread and the process.
PS_CP_TEB_ADDRESS	N/A. Internally used and not exposed.	Output	Returns the address of the TEB for the initial thread.
PS_CP_FILENAME	N/A. Used as a parameter in CreateProcess APIs.	Input	The name of the process that should be created.
PS_CP_IMAGE_INFO	N/A. Internally used and not exposed.	Output	Returns SECTION_IMAGE_ INFORMATION, which contains information on the version, flags, and subsystem of the executable, as well as the stack size and entry point.
PS_CP_MEM_RESERVE	N/A. Internally used by SMSS and CSRSS.	Input	An array of virtual memory reservations that should be made during initial process address space creation, allowing guaranteed availability because no other allocations have taken place yet.
PS_CP_PRIORITY_CLASS	N/A. Passed in as a parameter to the CreateProcess API.	Input	Priority class that the process should be given.
PS_CP_ERROR_MODE	N/A. Passed in through the CREATE_DEFAULT_ERROR_MODE flag.	Input	Hard error-processing mode for the process.
PS_CP_STD_HANDLE_INFO	None. Used internally.	Input	Specifies whether standard handles should be duplicated or new handles should be created.
PS_CP_HANDLE_LIST	PROC_THREAD_ATTRIBUTE_ HANDLE_LIST	Input	A list of handles belonging to the parent process that should be inherited by the new process.
PS_CP_GROUP_AFFINITY	PROC_THREAD_ATTRIBUTE_ GROUP_AFFINITY	Input	Processor group(s) the thread should be allowed to run on.
PS_CP_PREFERRED_NODE	PROC_THREAD_ATTRIBUTES_ PRFERRED_NODE	Input	The preferred (ideal) NUMA node that should be associated with the process. It affects the node on which the initial process heap and thread stack will be created (see Chapter 5).
PS_CP_IDEAL_PROCESSOR	PROC_THREAD_ATTTRIBUTE_ IDEAL_PROCESSOR	Input	The preferred (ideal) processor that the thread should be scheduled on.
PS_CP_UMS_THREAD	PROC_THREAD_ATTRIBUTE_ UMS_THREAD	Input	Contains the UMS attributes, completion list, and context.

PS_CP_MITIGATION_OPTIONS	PROC_THREAD_MITIGATION_POLICY	Input	Contains information on which mitigations (SEHOP, ATL Emulation, NX) should be enabled/disabled for the process.
PS_CP_PROTECTION_LEVEL	PROC_THREAD_ATTRIBUTE_PROTECTION_LEVEL	Input	Must point to one of the allowed process protection values shown in Table 3-1 or the value PROTECT_LEVEL_SAME to indicate the same protection level as the parent.
PS_CP_SECURE_PROCESS	None. Used internally.	Input	Indicates the process should run as an Isolated User Mode (IUM) Trustlet. See Chapter 8 in Part 2 for more details.
PS_CP_JOB_LIST	None. Used internally.	Input	Assigns the process to a list of jobs.
PS_CP_CHILD_PROCESS_POLICY	PROC_THREAD_ATTRIBUTE_CHILD_PROCESS_POLICY	Input	Specifies whether the new process is allowed to create child processes, either directly or indirectly (such as by using WMI).
PS_CP_ALL_APPLICATION_PACKAGES_POLICY	PROC_THREAD_ATTRIBUTE_ALL_APPLICATION_PACKAGES_POLICY	Input	Specifies if the AppContainer token should be excluded from ACL checks that include the ALL APPLICATION PACKAGES group. The ALL RESTRICTED APPLICATION PACKAGES group will be used instead.
PS_CP_WIN32K_FILTER	PROC_THREAD_ATTRIBUTE_WIN32K_FILTER	Input	Indicates if the process will have many of its GDI/USER system calls to Win32k.sys filtered out (blocked), or if they will be permitted but audited. Used by the Microsoft Edge browser to reduce attack surface.
PS_CP_SAFE_OPEN_PROMPT_ORIGIN_CLAIM	None. Used internally.	Input	Used by the Mark of the Web functionality to indicate the file came from an untrusted source.
PS_CP_BNO_ISOLATION	PROC_THREAD_ATTRIBUTE_BNO_ISOLATION	Input	Causes the primary token of the process to be associated with an isolated BaseNamedObjects directory. (See Chapter 8 in Part 2 for more information on named objects.)
PS_CP_DESKTOP_APP_POLICY	PROC_THREAD_ATTRIBUTE_DESKTOP_APP_POLICY	Input	Indicates if the modern application will be allowed to launch legacy desktop applications, and if so, in what way.
None—used internally	PROC_THREAD_ATTRIBUTE_SECURITY_CAPABILITIES	Input	Specifies a pointer to a SECURITY_CAPABILITIES structure, which is used to create the AppContainer token for the process before calling NtCreateUserProcess.

6. If the process is part of a job object, but the creation flags requested a separate virtual DOS machine (VDM), the flag is ignored.

7. The security attributes for the process and initial thread that were supplied to the CreateProcess function are converted to their internal representation (OBJECT_ATTRIBUTES structures, documented in the WDK).

8. CreateProcessInternalW checks whether the process should be created as modern. The process is to be created modern if specified so by an attribute (PROC_THREAD_ATTRIBUTE_PACKAGE_FULL_NAME) with the full package name or the creator is itself modern (and a parent process has not been explicitly specified by the PROC_THREAD_ATTRIBUTE_PARENT_PROCESS attribute). If so, a call is made to the internal BasepAppXExtension to gather more contextual information on the modern app parameters described by a structure called APPX_PROCESS_CONTEXT. This structure holds information such as the package name (internally referred to as *package moniker*), the capabilities associated with the app, the current directory for the process, and whether the app should have full trust. The option of creating full trust modern apps is not publicly exposed, and is reserved for apps that have the modern look and feel but perform system-level operations. A canonical example is the Settings app in Windows 10 (SystemSettings.exe).

9. If the process is to be created as modern, the security capabilities (if provided by PROC_THREAD_ATTRIBUTE_SECURITY_CAPABILITIES) are recorded for the initial token creation by calling the internal BasepCreateLowBox function. The term *LowBox* refers to the sandbox (AppContainer) under which the process is to be executed. Note that although creating modern processes by directly calling CreateProcess is not supported (instead, the COM interfaces described earlier should be used), the Windows SDK and MSDN do document the ability to create AppContainer legacy desktop applications by passing this attribute.

10. If a modern process is to be created, then a flag is set to indicate to the kernel to skip embedded manifest detection. Modern processes should never have an embedded manifest as it's simply not needed. (A modern app has a manifest of its own, unrelated to the embedded manifest referenced here.)

11. If the debug flag has been specified (DEBUG_PROCESS), then the Debugger value under the Image File Execution Options registry key (discussed in the next section) for the executable is marked to be skipped. Otherwise, a debugger will never be able to create its debuggee process because the creation will enter an infinite loop (trying to create the debugger process over and over again).

12. All windows are associated with desktops, the graphical representation of a workspace. If no desktop is specified in the STARTUPINFO structure, the process is associated with the caller's current desktop.

 Note The Windows 10 Virtual Desktop feature does not use multiple desktop objects (in the kernel object sense). There is still one desktop, but windows are shown and hidden as required. This is in contrast to the Sysinternals desktops.exe tool, which really creates up to four desktop objects. The difference can be felt when trying to move a window from one desktop to another. In the case of desktops.exe, it can't be done, as such an operation is not supported in Windows. On the other hand, Windows 10's Virtual Desktop allows it, since there is no real "moving" going on.

13. The application and command-line arguments passed to `CreateProcessInternalW` are analyzed. The executable path name is converted to the internal NT name (for example, c:\temp\a.exe turns into something like \device\harddiskvolume1\temp\a.exe) because some functions require it in that format.

14. Most of the gathered information is converted to a single large structure of type RTL_USER_ PROCESS_PARAMETERS.

Once these steps are completed, `CreateProcessInternalW` performs the initial call to `NtCreate-UserProcess` to attempt creation of the process. Because Kernel32.dll has no idea at this point whether the application image name is a real Windows application or a batch file (.bat or .cmd), 16-bit, or DOS application, the call might fail, at which point `CreateProcessInternalW` looks at the error reason and attempts to correct the situation.

Stage 2: Opening the image to be executed

At this point, the creating thread has switched into kernel mode and continues the work within the `NtCreateUserProcess` system call implementation.

1. `NtCreateUserProcess` first validates arguments and builds an internal structure to hold all creation information. The reason for validating arguments again is to make sure the call to the executive did not originate from a hack that managed to simulate the way Ntdll.dll makes the transition to the kernel with bogus or malicious arguments.

2. As illustrated in Figure 3-11, the next stage in `NtCreateUserProcess` is to find the appropriate Windows image that will run the executable file specified by the caller and to create a section object to later map it into the address space of the new process. If the call fails for any reason, it returns to `CreateProcessInternalW` with a failure state (look ahead to Table 3-8) that causes `CreateProcessInternalW` to attempt execution again.

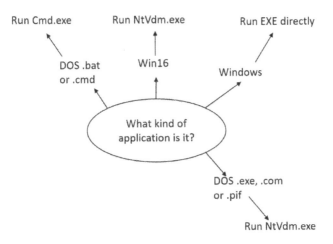

FIGURE 3-11 Choosing a Windows image to activate.

3. If the process needs to be created protected, it also checks the signing policy.

4. If the process to be created is modern, a licensing check is done to make sure it's licensed and allowed to run. If the app is inbox (preinstalled with Windows), it's allowed to run regardless of license. If sideloading apps is allowed (configured through the Settings app), then any signed app can be executed, not just from the store.

5. If the process is a Trustlet, the section object must be created with a special flag that allows the secure kernel to use it.

6. If the executable file specified is a Windows EXE, `NtCreateUserProcess` tries to open the file and create a section object for it. The object isn't mapped into memory yet, but it is opened. Just because a section object has been successfully created doesn't mean the file is a valid Windows image, however. It could be a DLL or a POSIX executable. If the file is a POSIX executable, the call fails, because POSIX is no longer supported. If the file is a DLL, `CreateProcessInternalW` fails as well.

7. Now that `NtCreateUserProcess` has found a valid Windows executable image, as part of the process creation code described in the next section, it looks in the registry under HKLM\SOFTWARE\Microsoft\Windows NT\CurrentVersion\Image File Execution Options to see whether a subkey with the file name and extension of the executable image (but without the directory and path information—for example, Notepad.exe) exists there. If it does, `PspAllocate-Process` looks for a value named `Debugger` for that key. If this value is present, the image to be run becomes the string in that value and `CreateProcessInternalW` restarts at stage 1.

> **Tip** You can take advantage of this process-creation behavior and debug the startup code of Windows services processes before they start rather than attach the debugger after starting a service, which doesn't allow you to debug the startup code.

8. On the other hand, if the image is not a Windows EXE (for example, if it's an MS-DOS or a Win16 application), `CreateProcessInternalW` goes through a series of steps to find a Windows support image to run it. This process is necessary because non-Windows applications aren't run directly. Windows instead uses one of a few special support images that, in turn, are responsible for actually running the non-Windows program. For example, if you attempt to run an MS-DOS or a Win16 executable (32-bit Windows only), the image to be run becomes the Windows executable Ntvdm.exe. In short, you can't directly create a process that is not a Windows process. If Windows can't find a way to resolve the activated image as a Windows process (as shown in Table 3-8), `CreateProcessInternalW` fails.

TABLE 3-8 Decision tree for stage 1 of `CreateProcess`

If the Image...	Create State Code	This Image Will Run...	...and This Will Happen
Is an MS-DOS application with an .exe, .com, or .pif extension	`PsCreateFailOnSectionCreate`	Ntvdm.exe	`CreateProcessInternalW` restarts stage 1.
Is a Win16 application	`PsCreateFailOnSectionCreate`	Ntvdm.exe	`CreateProcessInternalW` restarts stage 1.
Is a Win64 application on a 32-bit system (or a PPC, MIPS, or Alpha binary)	`PsCreateFailMachineMismatch`	N/A	`CreateProcessInternalW` will fail.
Has a Debugger value with another image name	`PsCreateFailExeName`	Name specified in the Debugger value	`CreateProcessInternalW` restarts stage 1.
Is an invalid or damaged Windows EXE	`PsCreateFailExeFormat`	N/A	`CreateProcessInternalW` will fail.
Cannot be opened	`PsCreateFailOnFileOpen`	N/A	`CreateProcessInternalW` will fail.
Is a command procedure (application with a .bat or .cmd extension)	`PsCreateFailOnSectionCreate`	Cmd.exe	`CreateProcessInternalW` restarts Stage 1.

Specifically, the decision tree that `CreateProcessInternalW` goes through to run an image is as follows:

- If it's x86 32-bit Windows, and the image is an MS-DOS application with an .exe, .com, or .pif extension, a message is sent to the Windows subsystem to check whether an MS-DOS support process (Ntvdm.exe, specified in the HKLM\SYSTEM\CurrentControlSet\Control\WOW\ cmdline registry value) has already been created for this session. If a support process has been created, it is used to run the MS-DOS application. (The Windows subsystem sends the message to the virtual DOS machine [VDM] process to run the new image.) Then `CreateProcessInternalW` returns. If a support process hasn't been created, the image to be run changes to Ntvdm.exe and `CreateProcessInternalW` restarts at stage 1.

- If the file to run has a .bat or .cmd extension, the image to be run becomes Cmd.exe, the Windows command prompt, and `CreateProcessInternalW` restarts at stage 1. (The name of the batch file is passed as the second parameter to Cmd.exe after the /c switch.)

- For an x86 Windows system, if the image is a Win16 (Windows 3.1) executable, `CreateProcessInternalW` must decide whether a new VDM process must be created to run it or whether it should use the default session-wide shared VDM process (which might not yet have been created). The `CreateProcess` flags CREATE_SEPARATE_WOW_VDM and CREATE_SHARED_WOW_VDM control this decision. If these flags aren't specified, the HKLM\SYSTEM\CurrentControlSet\ Control\WOW\DefaultSeparateVDM registry value dictates the default behavior. If the application is to be run in a separate VDM, the image to be run changes to Ntvdm.exe followed by some configuration parameters and the 16-bit process name, and `CreateProcess-InternalW` restarts at stage 1. Otherwise, the Windows subsystem sends a message to see whether the shared VDM process exists and can be used. (If the VDM process is running on a different desktop or isn't running under the same security as the caller, it can't be used, and a new VDM process must be created.) If a shared VDM process can be used, the Windows subsystem sends a message to it to run the new image and `CreateProcessInternalW` returns. If the VDM process hasn't yet been created (or if it exists but can't be used), the image to be run changes to the VDM support image and `CreateProcessInternalW` restarts at stage 1.

Stage 3: Creating the Windows executive process object

At this point, `NtCreateUserProcess` has opened a valid Windows executable file and created a section object to map it into the new process address space. Next, it creates a Windows executive process object to run the image by calling the internal system function `PspAllocateProcess`. Creating the executive process object (which is done by the creating thread) involves the following sub-stages:

3A. Setting up the EPROCESS object

3B. Creating the initial process address space

3C. Initializing the kernel process structure (KPROCESS)

3D. Concluding the setup of the process address space

3E. Setting up the PEB

3F. Completing the setup of the executive process object

 Note The only time there won't be a parent process is during system initialization (when the System process is created). After that point, a parent process is always required to provide a security context for the new process.

Stage 3A: Setting up the EPROCESS object

This sub-stage involves the following steps:

1. Inherit the affinity of the parent process unless it was explicitly set during process creation (through the attribute list).

2. Choose the ideal NUMA node that was specified in the attribute list, if any.

3. Inherit the I/O and page priority from the parent process. If there is no parent process, the default page priority (5) and I/O priority (Normal) are used.

4. Set the new process exit status to `STATUS_PENDING`.

5. Choose the hard error processing mode selected by the attribute list. Otherwise, inherit the parent's processing mode if none was given. If no parent exists, use the default processing mode, which is to display all errors.

6. Store the parent process's ID in the `InheritedFromUniqueProcessId` field in the new process object.

7. Query the Image File Execution Options (IFEO) key to check if the process should be mapped with large pages (`UseLargePages` value in the IFEO key), unless the process is to run under Wow64, in which case large pages will not be used. Also, query the key to check if NTDLL has been listed as a DLL that should be mapped with large pages within this process.

8. Query the performance options key in IFEO (`PerfOptions`, if it exists), which may consist of any number of the following possible values: `IoPriority`, `PagePriority`, `CpuPriorityClass`, and `WorkingSetLimitInKB`.

9. If the process would run under Wow64, then allocate the Wow64 auxiliary structure (`EWOW64PROCESS`) and set it in the `WoW64Process` member of the EPROCESS structure.

10. If the process is to be created inside an `AppContainer` (in most cases a modern app), validate that the token was created with a LowBox. (See Chapter 7 for more on AppContainers.)

11. Attempt to acquire all the privileges required for creating the process. Choosing the Real-time process priority class, assigning a token to the new process, mapping the process with large pages, and creating the process within a new session are all operations that require the appropriate privilege.

12. Create the process's primary access token (a duplicate of its parent's primary token). New processes inherit the security profile of their parents. If the `CreateProcessAsUser` function is being used to specify a different access token for the new process, the token is then changed appropriately. This change might happen only if the parent token's integrity level dominates the integrity level of the access token, and if the access token is a true child or sibling of the parent token. Note that if the parent has the `SeAssignPrimaryToken` privilege, this will bypass these checks.

13. The session ID of the new process token is now checked to determine if this is a cross-session create. If so, the parent process temporarily attaches to the target session to correctly process quotas and address space creation.

14. Set the new process's quota block to the address of its parent process's quota block, and increment the reference count for the parent's quota block. If the process was created through `CreateProcessAsUser`, this step won't occur. Instead, the default quota is created, or a quota matching the user's profile is selected.

15. The process minimum and maximum working set sizes are set to the values of `PspMinimumWorkingSet` and `PspMaximumWorkingSet`, respectively. These values can be overridden if performance options were specified in the `PerfOptions` key part of Image File Execution Options, in which case the maximum working set is taken from there. Note that the default working set limits are soft limits and are essentially hints, while the `PerfOptions` working set maximum is a hard limit. (That is, the working set will not be allowed to grow past that number.)

16. Initialize the address space of the process. (See stage 3B.) Then detach from the target session if it was different.

17. The group affinity for the process is now chosen if group-affinity inheritance was not used. The default group affinity will either inherit from the parent if NUMA node propagation was set earlier (the group owning the NUMA node will be used) or be assigned round-robin. If the system is in forced group-awareness mode and group 0 was chosen by the selection algorithm, group 1 is chosen instead, as long as it exists.

18. Initialize the KPROCESS part of the process object. (See Stage 3C.)

19. The token for the process is now set.

20. The process's priority class is set to normal unless the parent was using idle or the Below Normal process priority class, in which case the parent's priority is inherited.

21. The process handle table is initialized. If the inherit handles flag is set for the parent process, any inheritable handles are copied from the parent's object handle table into the new process. (For more information about object handle tables, see Chapter 8 in Part 2.) A process attribute can also be used to specify only a subset of handles, which is useful when you are using CreateProcessAsUser to restrict which objects should be inherited by the child process.

22. If performance options were specified through the PerfOptions key, these are now applied. The PerfOptions key includes overrides for the working set limit, I/O priority, page priority, and CPU priority class of the process.

23. The final process priority class and the default quantum for its threads are computed and set.

24. The various mitigation options provided in the IFEO key (as a single 64-bit value named Mitigation) are read and set. If the process is under an AppContainer, add the TreatAs-AppContainer mitigation flag.

25. All other mitigation flags are now applied.

Stage 3B: Creating the initial process address space

The initial process address space consists of the following pages:

- Page directory (it's possible there'll be more than one for systems with page tables more than two levels, such as x86 systems in PAE mode or 64-bit systems)

- Hyperspace page

- VAD bitmap page

- Working set list

To create these pages, the following steps are taken:

1. Page table entries are created in the appropriate page tables to map the initial pages.

2. The number of pages is deducted from the kernel variable MmTotalCommittedPages and added to MmProcessCommit.

3. The system-wide default process minimum working set size (PsMinimumWorkingSet) is deducted from MmResidentAvailablePages.

4. The page table pages for the global system space (that is, other than the process-specific pages we just described, and except session-specific memory) are created.

Stage 3C: Creating the kernel process structure

The next stage of PspAllocateProcess is the initialization of the KPROCESS structure (the Pcb member of the EPROCESS). This work is performed by KeInitializeProcess, which does the following:

1. The doubly linked list, which connects all threads part of the process (initially empty), is initialized.

2. The initial value (or reset value) of the process default quantum (which is described in more detail in the "Thread scheduling" section in Chapter 4) is hard-coded to 6 until it is initialized later (by PspComputeQuantumAndPriority).

 Note The default initial quantum differs between Windows client and server systems. For more information on thread quantums, turn to the discussion in the section "Thread scheduling" in Chapter 4.

3. The process's base priority is set based on what was computed in stage 3A.

4. The default processor affinity for the threads in the process is set, as is the group affinity. The group affinity was calculated in stage 3A or inherited from the parent.

5. The process-swapping state is set to resident.

6. The thread seed is based on the ideal processor that the kernel has chosen for this process (which is based on the previously created process's ideal processor, effectively randomizing this in a round-robin manner). Creating a new process will update the seed in KeNodeBlock (the initial NUMA node block) so that the next new process will get a different ideal processor seed.

7. If the process is a secure process (Windows 10 and Server 2016), then its secure ID is created now by calling HvlCreateSecureProcess.

Stage 3D: Concluding the setup of the process address space

Setting up the address space for a new process is somewhat complicated, so let's look at what's involved one step at a time. To get the most out of this section, you should have some familiarity with the internals of the Windows memory manager, described in Chapter 5.

The routine that does most of the work in setting the address space is `MmInitializeProcess-AddressSpace`. It also supports cloning an address space from another process. This capability was useful at the time to implement the POSIX `fork` system call. It may also be leveraged in the future to support other Unix-style `fork` (this is how `fork` is implemented in Windows Subsystem for Linux in Redstone 1). The following steps do not describe the address space cloning functionality, but rather focus on normal process address space initialization.

1. The virtual memory manager sets the value of the process's last trim time to the current time. The working set manager (which runs in the context of the balance set manager system thread) uses this value to determine when to initiate working set trimming.

2. The memory manager initializes the process's working set list. Page faults can now be taken.

3. The section (created when the image file was opened) is now mapped into the new process's address space, and the process section base address is set to the base address of the image.

4. The Process Environment Block (PEB) is created and initialized (see the section stage 3E).

5. Ntdll.dll is mapped into the process. If this is a Wow64 process, the 32-bit Ntdll.dll is also mapped.

6. A new session, if requested, is now created for the process. This special step is mostly implemented for the benefit of the Session Manager (Smss) when initializing a new session.

7. The standard handles are duplicated and the new values are written in the process parameters structure.

8. Any memory reservations listed in the attribute list are now processed. Additionally, two flags allow the bulk reservation of the first 1 or 16 MB of the address space. These flags are used internally for mapping, for example, real-mode vectors and ROM code (which must be in the low ranges of virtual address space, where normally the heap or other process structures could be located).

9. The user process parameters are written into the process, copied, and fixed up (that is, they are converted from absolute form to a relative form so that a single memory block is needed).

10. The affinity information is written into the PEB.

11. The *MinWin* API redirection set is mapped into the process and its pointer is stored in the PEB.

12. The process unique ID is now determined and stored. The kernel does not distinguish between unique process and thread IDs and handles. The process and thread IDs (handles) are stored in a global handle table (`PspCidTable`) that is not associated with any process.

13. If the process is secure (that is, it runs in IUM), the secure process is initialized and associated with the kernel process object.

Stage 3E: Setting up the PEB

NtCreateUserProcess calls MmCreatePeb, which first maps the system-wide National Language Support (NLS) tables into the process's address space. It next calls MiCreatePebOrTeb to allocate a page for the PEB and then initializes a number of fields, most of them based on internal variables that were configured through the registry, such as MmHeap* values, MmCriticalSectionTimeout, and MmMinimumStackCommitInBytes. Some of these fields can be overridden by settings in the linked executable image, such as the Windows version in the PE header or the affinity mask in the load configuration directory of the PE header.

If the image header characteristics IMAGE_FILE_UP_SYSTEM_ONLY flag is set (indicating that the image can run only on a uniprocessor system), a single CPU (MmRotatingUniprocessorNumber) is chosen for all the threads in this new process to run on. The selection process is performed by simply cycling through the available processors. Each time this type of image is run, the next processor is used. In this way, these types of images are spread evenly across the processors.

Stage 3F: Completing the setup of the executive process object

Before the handle to the new process can be returned, a few final setup steps must be completed, which are performed by PspInsertProcess and its helper functions:

1. If system-wide auditing of processes is enabled (because of either local policy settings or group policy settings from a domain controller), the process's creation is written to the Security event log.

2. If the parent process was contained in a job, the job is recovered from the job level set of the parent and then bound to the session of the newly created process. Finally, the new process is added to the job.

3. The new process object is inserted at the end of the Windows list of active processes (PsActiveProcessHead). Now the process is accessible via functions like EnumProcesses and OpenProcess.

4. The process debug port of the parent process is copied to the new child process unless the NoDebugInherit flag is set (which can be requested when creating the process). If a debug port was specified, it is attached to the new process.

5. Job objects can specify restrictions on which group or groups the threads within the processes part of a job can run on. Therefore, PspInsertProcess must make sure the group affinity associated with the process would not violate the group affinity associated with the job. An interesting secondary issue to consider is if the job's permissions grant access to modify the process's affinity permissions, because a lesser-privileged job object might interfere with the affinity requirements of a more privileged process.

6. Finally, PspInsertProcess creates a handle for the new process by calling ObOpenObjectByPointer, and then returns this handle to the caller. Note that no process-creation callback is sent until the first thread within the process is created, and the code always sends process callbacks before sending object managed–based callbacks.

Stage 4: Creating the initial thread and its stack and context

At this point, the Windows executive process object is completely set up. It still has no thread, however, so it can't do anything yet. It's now time to start that work. Normally, the PspCreateThread routine is responsible for all aspects of thread creation and is called by NtCreateThread when a new thread is being created. However, because the initial thread is created internally by the kernel without user-mode input, the two helper routines that PspCreateThread relies on are used instead: PspAllocate-Thread and PspInsertThread. PspAllocateThread handles the actual creation and initialization of the executive thread object itself, while PspInsertThread handles the creation of the thread handle and security attributes and the call to KeStartThread to turn the executive object into a schedulable thread on the system. However, the thread won't do anything yet. It is created in a suspended state and isn't resumed until the process is completely initialized (as described in stage 5).

> **Note** The thread parameter (which can't be specified in CreateProcess but can be specified in CreateThread) is the address of the PEB. This parameter will be used by the initialization code that runs in the context of this new thread (as described in stage 6).

PspAllocateThread performs the following steps:

1. It prevents user-mode scheduling (UMS) threads from being created in Wow64 processes, as well as preventing user-mode callers from creating threads in the system process.

2. An executive thread object is created and initialized.

3. If energy estimation is enabled for the system (always disabled for XBOX), then it allocates and initializes a THREAD_ENERGY_VALUES structure pointed to by the ETHREAD object.

4. The various lists used by LPC, I/O Management, and the Executive are initialized.

5. The thread's creation time is set, and its thread ID (TID) is created.

6. Before the thread can execute, it needs a stack and a context in which to run, so these are set up. The stack size for the initial thread is taken from the image; there's no way to specify another size. If this is a Wow64 process, the Wow64 thread context will also be initialized.

7. The thread environment block (TEB) is allocated for the new thread.

8. The user-mode thread start address is stored in the ETHREAD (in the StartAddress field). This is the system-supplied thread startup function in Ntdll.dll (RtlUserThreadStart). The user's specified Windows start address is stored in the ETHREAD in a different location (the Win32StartAddress field) so that debugging tools such as Process Explorer can display the information.

9. KeInitThread is called to set up the KTHREAD structure. The thread's initial and current base priorities are set to the process's base priority, and its affinity and quantum are set to that of the process. KeInitThread next allocates a kernel stack for the thread and initializes the machine-dependent hardware context for the thread, including the context, trap, and exception frames.

The thread's context is set up so that the thread will start in kernel mode in KiThreadStartup. Finally, KeInitThread sets the thread's state to Initialized and returns to PspAllocateThread.

10. If this is a UMS thread, PspUmsInitThread is called to initialize the UMS state.

Once that work is finished, NtCreateUserProcess calls PspInsertThread to perform the following steps:

1. The thread ideal processor is initialized if it was specified using an attribute.

2. The thread group affinity is initialized if it was specified using an attribute.

3. If the process is part of a job, a check is made to ensure that the thread's group affinity does not violate job limitations (described earlier).

4. Checks are made to ensure that the process hasn't already been terminated, that the thread hasn't already been terminated, or that the thread hasn't even been able to start running. If any of these are true, thread creation will fail.

5. If the thread is part of a secure process (IUM), then the secure thread object is created and initialized.

6. The KTHREAD part of the thread object is initialized by calling KeStartThread. This involves inheriting scheduler settings from the owner process, setting the ideal node and processor, updating the group affinity, setting the base and dynamic priorities (by copying from the process), setting the thread quantum, and inserting the thread in the process list maintained by KPROCESS (a separate list from the one in EPROCESS).

7. If the process is in a deep freeze (meaning no threads are allowed to run, including new threads), then this thread is frozen as well.

8. On non-x86 systems, if the thread is the first in the process (and the process is not the idle process), then the process is inserted into another system-wide list of processes maintained by the global variable KiProcessListHead.

9. The thread count in the process object is incremented, and the owner process's I/O priority and page priority are inherited. If this is the highest number of threads the process has ever had, the thread count high watermark is updated as well. If this was the second thread in the process, the primary token is frozen (that is, it can no longer be changed).

10. The thread is inserted in the process's thread list, and the thread is suspended if the creating process requested it.

11. The thread object is inserted into the process handle table.

12. If it's the first thread created in the process (that is, the operation happened as part of a Create-Process* call), any registered callbacks for process creation are called. Then any registered thread callbacks are called. If any callback vetoes the creation, it will fail and return an appropriate status to the caller.

13. If a job list was supplied (using an attribute) and this is the first thread in the process, then the process is assigned to all of the jobs in the job list.

14. The thread is readied for execution by calling KeReadyThread. It enters the deferred ready state. (See Chapter 4 for more information on thread states.)

Stage 5: Performing Windows subsystem–specific initialization

Once NtCreateUserProcess returns with a success code, the necessary executive process and thread objects have been created. CreateProcessInternalW then performs various operations related to Windows subsystem–specific operations to finish initializing the process.

1. Various checks are made for whether Windows should allow the executable to run. These checks include validating the image version in the header and checking whether Windows application certification has blocked the process (through a group policy). On specialized editions of Windows Server 2012 R2, such as Windows Storage Server 2012 R2, additional checks are made to see whether the application imports any disallowed APIs.

2. If software restriction policies dictate, a restricted token is created for the new process. Afterward, the application-compatibility database is queried to see whether an entry exists in either the registry or system application database for the process. Compatibility shims will not be applied at this point; the information will be stored in the PEB once the initial thread starts executing (stage 6).

3. CreateProcessInternalW calls some internal functions (for non-protected processes) to get SxS information (see the section "DLL name resolution and redirection" later in this chapter for more information on side-by-side) such as manifest files and DLL redirection paths, as well as other information such as whether the media on which the EXE resides is removable and installer detection flags. For immersive processes, it also returns version information and target platform from the package manifest.

4. A message to the Windows subsystem is constructed based on the information collected to be sent to Csrss. The message includes the following information:

   - Path name and SxS path name
   - Process and thread handles
   - Section handle
   - The access token handle
   - Media information
   - AppCompat and shim data
   - Immersive process information
   - The PEB address
   - Various flags such as whether it's a protected process or whether it is required to run elevated

- A flag indicating whether the process belongs to a Windows application (so that Csrss can determine whether to show the startup cursor)
- UI language information
- DLL redirection and `.local` flags (discussed in the "Image loader" section later in this chapter)
- Manifest file information

When it receives this message, the Windows subsystem performs the following steps:

1. `CsrCreateProcess` duplicates a handle for the process and thread. In this step, the usage count of the process and the thread is incremented from 1 (which was set at creation time) to 2.

2. The Csrss process structure (CSR_PROCESS) is allocated.

3. The new process's exception port is set to be the general function port for the Windows subsystem so that the Windows subsystem will receive a message when a second-chance exception occurs in the process. (For further information on exception handling, see Chapter 8 in Part 2.)

4. If a new process group is to be created with the new process serving as the root (CREATE_NEW_PROCESS_GROUP flag in `CreateProcess`), then it's set in CSR_PROCESS. A process group is useful for sending a control event to a set of processes sharing a console. See the Windows SDK documentation for `CreateProcess` and `GenerateConsoleCtrlEvent` for more information.

5. The Csrss thread structure (CSR_THREAD) is allocated and initialized.

6. `CsrCreateThread` inserts the thread in the list of threads for the process.

7. The count of processes in this session is incremented.

8. The process shutdown level is set to 0x280, the default process shutdown level. (See `SetProcessShutdownParameters` in the Windows SDK documentation for more information.)

9. The new Csrss process structure is inserted into the list of Windows subsystem–wide processes.

After Csrss has performed these steps, `CreateProcessInternalW` checks whether the process was run elevated (which means it was executed through `ShellExecute` and elevated by the `AppInfo` service after the consent dialog box was shown to the user). This includes checking whether the process was a setup program. If it was, the process's token is opened, and the virtualization flag is turned on so that the application is virtualized. (See the information on UAC and virtualization in Chapter 7.) If the application contained elevation shims or had a requested elevation level in its manifest, the process is destroyed and an elevation request is sent to the `AppInfo` service.

Note that most of these checks are not performed for protected processes. Because these processes must have been designed for Windows Vista or later, there's no reason they should require elevation, virtualization, or application-compatibility checks and processing. Additionally, allowing mechanisms such as the shim engine to use its usual hooking and memory-patching techniques on a protected process would result in a security hole if someone could figure how to insert arbitrary shims that modify the behavior of the protected process. Additionally, because the shim engine is installed by the parent process, which might not have access to its child protected process, even legitimate shimming cannot work.

Stage 6: Starting execution of the initial thread

At this point, the process environment has been determined, resources for its threads to use have been allocated, the process has a thread, and the Windows subsystem knows about the new process. Unless the caller specified the CREATE_SUSPENDED flag, the initial thread is now resumed so that it can start running and perform the remainder of the process-initialization work that occurs in the context of the new process (stage 7).

Stage 7: Performing process initialization in the context of the new process

The new thread begins life running the kernel-mode thread startup routine KiStartUserThread. KiStartUserThread lowers the thread's IRQL level from deferred procedure call (DPC) level to APC level and then calls the system initial thread routine, PspUserThreadStartup. The user-specified thread start address is passed as a parameter to this routine. PspUserThreadStartup performs the following actions:

1. It installs an exception chain on x86 architecture. (Other architectures work differently in this regard, see Chapter 8 in Part 2.)

2. It lowers IRQL to PASSIVE_LEVEL (0, which is the only IRQL user code is allowed to run at).

3. It disables the ability to swap the primary process token at runtime.

4. If the thread was killed on startup (for whatever reason), it's terminated and no further action is taken.

5. It sets the locale ID and the ideal processor in the TEB, based on the information present in kernel-mode data structures, and then it checks whether thread creation actually failed.

6. It calls DbgkCreateThread, which checks whether image notifications were sent for the new process. If they weren't, and notifications are enabled, an image notification is sent first for the process and then for the image load of Ntdll.dll.

> **Note** This is done in this stage rather than when the images were first mapped because the process ID (which is required for the kernel callouts) is not yet allocated at that time.

7. Once those checks are completed, another check is performed to see whether the process is a debuggee. If it is and if debugger notifications have not been sent yet, then a create process message is sent through the debug object (if one is present) so that the process startup debug event (CREATE_PROCESS_DEBUG_INFO) can be sent to the appropriate debugger process. This is followed by a similar thread startup debug event and by another debug event for the image load of Ntdll.dll. DbgkCreateThread then waits for a reply from the debugger (via the Continue-DebugEvent function).

8. It checks whether application prefetching is enabled on the system and, if so, calls the prefetcher (and Superfetch) to process the prefetch instruction file (if it exists) and prefetch pages referenced during the first 10 seconds the last time the process ran. (For details on the prefetcher and Superfetch, see Chapter 5.)

9. It checks whether the system-wide cookie in the SharedUserData structure has been set up. If it hasn't, it generates it based on a hash of system information such as the number of interrupts processed, DPC deliveries, page faults, interrupt time, and a random number. This system-wide cookie is used in the internal decoding and encoding of pointers, such as in the heap manager to protect against certain classes of exploitation. (For more information on the heap manager security, see Chapter 5.)

10. If the process is secure (IUM process), then a call is made to HvlStartSecureThread that transfers control to the secure kernel to start thread execution. This function only returns when the thread exits.

11. It sets up the initial thunk context to run the image-loader initialization routine (LdrInitializeThunk in Ntdll.dll), as well as the system-wide thread startup stub (RtlUserThreadStart in Ntdll.dll). These steps are done by editing the context of the thread in place and then issuing an exit from system service operation, which loads the specially crafted user context. The LdrInitializeThunk routine initializes the loader, the heap manager, NLS tables, thread-local storage (TLS) and fiber-local storage (FLS) arrays, and critical section structures. It then loads any required DLLs and calls the DLL entry points with the DLL_PROCESS_ATTACH function code.

Once the function returns, NtContinue restores the new user context and returns to user mode. Thread execution now truly starts.

RtlUserThreadStart uses the address of the actual image entry point and the start parameter and calls the application's entry point. These two parameters have also already been pushed onto the stack by the kernel. This complicated series of events has two purposes:

- It allows the image loader inside Ntdll.dll to set up the process internally and behind the scenes so that other user-mode code can run properly. (Otherwise, it would have no heap, no thread-local storage, and so on.)

- Having all threads begin in a common routine allows them to be wrapped in exception handling so that if they crash, Ntdll.dll is aware of that and can call the unhandled exception filter inside Kernel32.dll. It is also able to coordinate thread exit on return from the thread's start routine and to perform various cleanup work. Application developers can also call SetUnhandledExceptionFilter to add their own unhandled exception-handling code.

EXPERIMENT: Tracing process startup

Now that we've looked in detail at how a process starts up and the different operations required to begin executing an application, we're going to use Process Monitor to look at some of the file I/O and registry keys that are accessed during this process.

Although this experiment will not provide a complete picture of all the internal steps we've described, you'll be able to see several parts of the system in action, notably prefetch and Superfetch, image-file execution options and other compatibility checks, and the image loader's DLL mapping.

We'll look at a very simple executable—Notepad.exe—and launch it from a Command Prompt window (Cmd.exe). It's important that we look both at the operations inside Cmd.exe and those inside Notepad.exe. Recall that a lot of the user-mode work is performed by `CreateProcessInternalW`, which is called by the parent process before the kernel has created a new process object.

To set things up correctly, follow these steps:

1. Add two filters to Process Monitor: one for Cmd.exe and one for Notepad.exe. These are the only two processes you should include. Be sure you don't have any currently running instances of these two processes so that you know you're looking at the right events. The filter window should look like this:

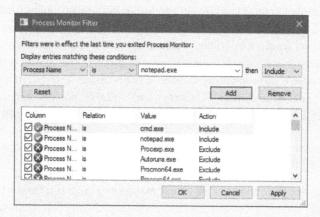

2. Make sure event logging is currently disabled (open the **File** and deselect **Capture Events**) and then start the command prompt.

3. Enable event logging (open the **File** menu and choose **Event Logging**, press **Ctrl+E**, or click the magnifying glass icon on the toolbar) and then type **Notepad.exe** and press **Enter**. On a typical Windows system, you should see anywhere between 500 and 3,500 events appear.

4. Stop capture and hide the Sequence and Time of Day columns so that you can focus your attention on the columns of interest. Your window should look similar to the one shown in the following screenshot.

As described in stage 1 of the `CreateProcess` flow, one of the first things to notice is that just before the process is started and the first thread is created, Cmd.exe does a registry read at HKLM\SOFTWARE\Microsoft\Windows NT\CurrentVersion\Image File Execution Options\Notepad.exe. Because there were no image-execution options associated with Notepad.exe, the process was created as is.

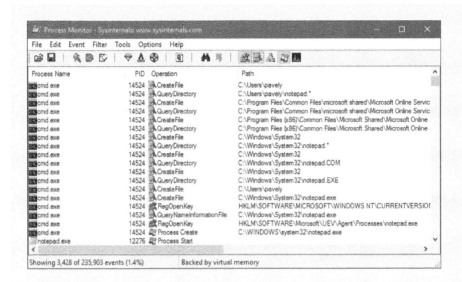

As with this and any other event in Process Monitor's log, you can see whether each part of the process-creation flow was performed in user mode or kernel mode, and by which routines, by looking at the stack of the event. To do this, double-click the RegOpenKey event and switch to the **Stack** tab. The following screenshot shows the standard stack on a 64-bit Windows 10 machine:

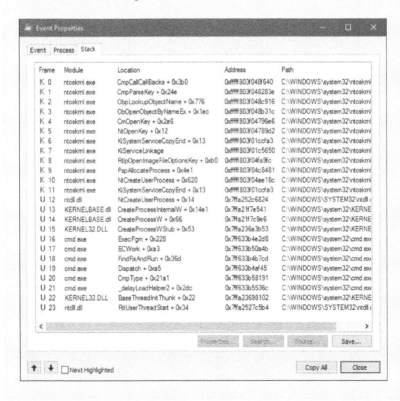

This stack shows that you already reached the part of process creation performed in kernel mode (through `NtCreateUserProcess`) and that the helper routine `PspAllocateProcess` is responsible for this check.

Going down the list of events after the thread and process have been created, you will notice three groups of events:

- A simple check for application-compatibility flags, which will let the user-mode process-creation code know if checks inside the application-compatibility database are required through the shim engine.

- Multiple reads to SxS (search for Side-By-Side), Manifest, and MUI/Language keys, which are part of the assembly framework mentioned earlier.

- File I/O to one or more .sdb files, which are the application-compatibility databases on the system. This I/O is where additional checks are done to see if the shim engine needs to be invoked for this application. Because Notepad is a well-behaved Microsoft program, it doesn't require any shims.

The following screenshot shows the next series of events, which happen inside the Notepad process itself. These are actions initiated by the user-mode thread startup wrapper in kernel mode, which performs the actions described earlier. The first two are the Notepad.exe and Ntdll.dll image load debug notification messages, which can be generated only now that code is running inside Notepad's process context and not inside the context for the command prompt.

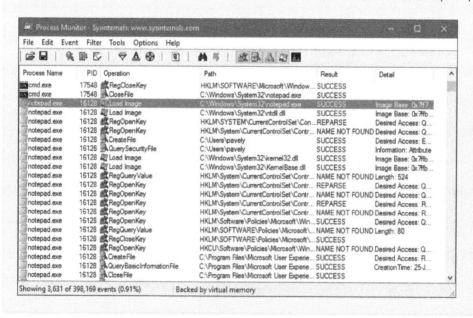

Next, the prefetcher kicks in, looking for a prefetch database file that has already been generated for Notepad. (For more information on the prefetcher, see Chapter 5.) On a system where Notepad has already been run at least once, this database will exist, and the prefetcher will begin executing the commands specified inside it. If this is the case, scrolling down, you will see multiple DLLs being read and queried. Unlike typical DLL loading, which is done by the user-mode image loader by looking at the import tables or when an application manually loads a DLL, these events are being generated by the prefetcher, which is already aware of the libraries that Notepad will require. Typical image loading of the DLLs required happens next, and you will see events similar to the ones shown here:

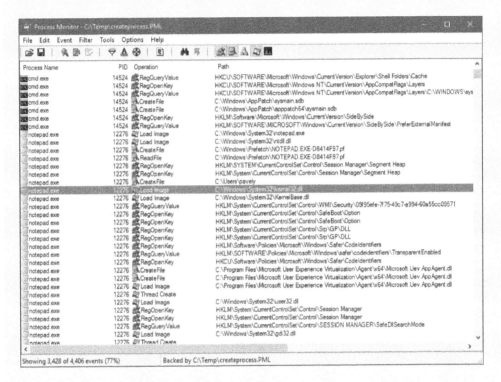

These events are now being generated from code running inside user mode, which was called once the kernel-mode wrapper function finished its work. Therefore, these are the first events coming from LdrpInitializeProcess, which is called by LdrInitializeThunk for the first thread in the process. You can confirm this on your own by looking at the stack of these events—for example, the kernel32.dll image load event, which is shown in the following screenshot.

Further events are generated by this routine and its associated helper functions until you finally reach events generated by the WinMain function inside Notepad, which is where code under the developer's control is now being executed. Describing in detail all the events and user-mode components that come into play during process execution would fill up this entire chapter, so exploration of any further events is left as an exercise for the reader.

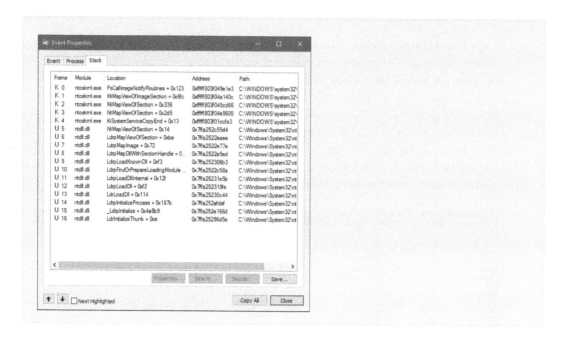

Terminating a process

A process is a container and a boundary. This means resources used by one process are not automatically visible in other processes, so some inter-process communication mechanism needs to be used to pass information between processes. Therefore, a process cannot accidentally write arbitrary bytes on another process's memory. That would require explicit call to a function such as `WriteProcess`Memory. However, to get that to work, a handle with the proper access mask (PROCESS_VM_WRITE) must be opened explicitly, which may or may not be granted. This natural isolation between processes also means that if some exception happens in one process, it will have no effect on other processes. The worst that can happen is that same process would crash, but the rest of the system stays intact.

A process can exit gracefully by calling the `ExitProcess` function. For many processes—depending on linker settings—the process startup code for the first thread calls `ExitProcess` on the process's behalf when the thread returns from its main function. The term *gracefully* means that DLLs loaded into the process get a chance to do some work by getting notified of the process exit using a call to their `DllMain` function with DLL_PROCESS_DETACH.

`ExitProcess` can be called only by the process itself asking to exit. An ungraceful termination of a process is possible using the `TerminateProcess` function, which can be called from outside the process. (For example, Process Explorer and Task Manager use it when so requested.) `TerminateProcess` requires a handle to the process that is opened with the PROCESS_TERMINATE access mask, which may or may not be granted. This is why it's not easy (or it's impossible) to terminate some processes (for example, Csrss)—the handle with the required access mask cannot be obtained by the requesting user.

The meaning of *ungraceful* here is that DLLs don't get a chance to execute code (DLL_PROCESS_DETACH is not sent) and all threads are terminated abruptly. This can lead to data loss in some cases—for example, if a file cache has no chance to flush its data to the target file.

In whatever way a process ceases to exist, there can never be any leaks. That is, all process's private memory is freed automatically by the kernel, the address space is destroyed, all handles to kernel objects are closed, etc. If open handles to the process still exist (the EPROCESS structure still exists), then other processes can still gain access to some process-management information, such as the process exit code (GetExitCodeProcess). Once these handles are closed, the EPROCESS is properly destroyed, and there's truly nothing left of the process.

That being said, if third party drivers make allocations in kernel memory on behalf of a process— say, due to an IOCTL or merely due to a process notification—it is their responsibility to free any such pool memory on their own. Windows does not track or clean-up process-owned kernel memory (except for memory occupied by objects due to handles that the process created). This would typically be done through the IRP_MJ_CLOSE or IRP_MJ_CLEANUP notification to tell the driver that the handle to the device object has been closed, or through a process termination notification. (see Chapter 6, "I/O system," for more on IOCTLs.)

Image loader

As we've just seen, when a process is started on the system, the kernel creates a process object to represent it and performs various kernel-related initialization tasks. However, these tasks do not result in the execution of the application, merely in the preparation of its context and environment. In fact, unlike drivers, which are kernel-mode code, applications execute in user mode. So most of the actual initialization work is done outside the kernel. This work is performed by the *image loader*, also internally referred to as Ldr.

The image loader lives in the user-mode system DLL *Ntdll.dll* and not in the kernel library. Therefore, it behaves just like standard code that is part of a DLL, and it is subject to the same restrictions in terms of memory access and security rights. What makes this code special is the guarantee that it will always be present in the running process (Ntdll.dll is always loaded) and that it is the first piece of code to run in user mode as part of a new process.

Because the loader runs before the actual application code, it is usually invisible to users and developers. Additionally, although the loader's initialization tasks are hidden, a program typically does interact with its interfaces during the run time of a program—for example, whenever loading or unloading a DLL or querying the base address of one. Some of the main tasks the loader is responsible for include:

- Initializing the user-mode state for the application, such as creating the initial heap and setting up the thread-local storage (TLS) and fiber-local storage (FLS) slots.

- Parsing the import table (IAT) of the application to look for all DLLs that it requires (and then recursively parsing the IAT of each DLL), followed by parsing the export table of the DLLs to make sure the function is actually present. (Special *forwarder entries* can also redirect an export to yet another DLL.)

- Loading and unloading DLLs at run time, as well as on demand, and maintaining a list of all loaded modules (the module database).

- Handling manifest files, needed for Windows Side-by-Side (SxS) support, as well as Multiple Language User Interface (MUI) files and resources.

- Reading the application compatibility database for any shims, and loading the shim engine DLL if required.

- Enabling support for API Sets and API redirection, a core part of the One Core functionality that allows creating Universal Windows Platform (UWP) applications.

- Enabling dynamic runtime compatibility mitigations through the *SwitchBack* mechanism as well as interfacing with the shim engine and Application Verifier mechanisms.

As you can see, most of these tasks are critical to enabling an application to actually run its code. Without them, everything from calling external functions to using the heap would immediately fail. After the process has been created, the loader calls the NtContinue special native API to continue execution based on an exception frame located on the stack, just as an exception handler would. This exception frame, built by the kernel as we saw in an earlier section, contains the actual entry point of the application. Therefore, because the loader doesn't use a standard call or jump into the running application, you'll never see the loader initialization functions as part of the call tree in a stack trace for a thread.

EXPERIMENT: Watching the image loader

In this experiment, you'll use global flags to enable a debugging feature called *loader snaps*. This allows you to see debug output from the image loader while debugging application startup.

1. From the directory where you've installed WinDbg, launch the Gflags.exe application, and then click the **Image File** tab.

2. In the Image field, type **Notepad.exe**, and then press the **Tab** key. This should enable the various options. Select the **Show Loader Snaps** option and then click **OK** or **Apply**.

3. Now launch WinDbg, open the **File** menu, choose **Open Executable**, and navigate to c:\windows\system32\notepad.exe to launch it. You should see a couple of screens of debug information similar to that shown here:

```
0f64:2090 @ 02405218 - LdrpInitializeProcess - INFO: Beginning execution of
notepad.exe (C:\WINDOWS\notepad.exe)
    Current directory: C:\Program Files (x86)\Windows Kits\10\Debuggers\
    Package directories: (null)
0f64:2090 @ 02405218 - LdrLoadDll - ENTER: DLL name: KERNEL32.DLL
0f64:2090 @ 02405218 - LdrpLoadDllInternal - ENTER: DLL name: KERNEL32.DLL
0f64:2090 @ 02405218 - LdrpFindKnownDll - ENTER: DLL name: KERNEL32.DLL
0f64:2090 @ 02405218 - LdrpFindKnownDll - RETURN: Status: 0x00000000
```

```
0f64:2090 @ 02405218 - LdrpMinimalMapModule - ENTER: DLL name: C:\WINDOWS\
System32\KERNEL32.DLL
ModLoad: 00007fff'5b4b0000 00007fff'5b55d000   C:\WINDOWS\System32\KERNEL32.DLL
0f64:2090 @ 02405218 - LdrpMinimalMapModule - RETURN: Status: 0x00000000
0f64:2090 @ 02405218 - LdrpPreprocessDllName - INFO: DLL api-ms-win-core-
rtlsupport-l1-2-0.dll was redirected to C:\WINDOWS\SYSTEM32\ntdll.dll by API set
0f64:2090 @ 02405218 - LdrpFindKnownDll - ENTER: DLL name: KERNELBASE.dll
0f64:2090 @ 02405218 - LdrpFindKnownDll - RETURN: Status: 0x00000000
0f64:2090 @ 02405218 - LdrpMinimalMapModule - ENTER: DLL name: C:\WINDOWS\
System32\KERNELBASE.dll
ModLoad: 00007fff'58b90000 00007fff'58dc6000   C:\WINDOWS\System32\KERNELBASE.dll
0f64:2090 @ 02405218 - LdrpMinimalMapModule - RETURN: Status: 0x00000000
0f64:2090 @ 02405218 - LdrpPreprocessDllName - INFO: DLL api-ms-win-
eventing-provider-l1-1-0.dll was redirected to C:\WINDOWS\SYSTEM32\
kernelbase.dll by API set
0f64:2090 @ 02405218 - LdrpPreprocessDllName - INFO: DLL api-ms-win-core-
apiquery-l1-1-0.dll was redirected to C:\WINDOWS\SYSTEM32\ntdll.dll by API set
```

4. Eventually, the debugger breaks somewhere inside the loader code, at a location where the image loader checks whether a debugger is attached and fires a breakpoint. If you press the **g** key to continue execution, you will see more messages from the loader, and Notepad will appear.

5. Try interacting with Notepad and see how certain operations invoke the loader. A good experiment is to open the Save/Open dialog box. That demonstrates that the loader not only runs at startup, but continuously responds to thread requests that can cause *delayed loads* of other modules (which can then be unloaded after use).

Early process initialization

Because the loader is present in Ntdll.dll, which is a native DLL that's not associated with any particular subsystem, all processes are subject to the same loader behavior (with some minor differences). Earlier, we took a detailed look at the steps that lead to the creation of a process in kernel mode, as well as some of the work performed by the Windows function CreateProcess. Here, we'll cover all the *other* work that takes place in user mode, independent of any subsystem, as soon as the first user-mode instruction starts execution.

When a process starts, the loader performs the following steps:

1. It checks if LdrpProcessInitialized is already set to 1 or if the SkipLoaderInit flag is set in the TEB. In this case, skip all initialization and wait three seconds for someone to call LdrpProcess-InitializationComplete. This is used in cases where process reflection is used by Windows Error Reporting, or other process fork attempts where loader initialization is not needed.

2. It sets the LdrInitState to 0, meaning that the loader is uninitialized. Also set the PEB's ProcessInitializing flag to 1 and the TEB's RanProcessInit to 1.

3. It initializes the loader lock in the PEB.

4. It initializes the dynamic function table, used for unwind/exception support in JIT code.

5. It initializes the Mutable Read Only Heap Section (MRDATA), which is used to store security-relevant global variables that should not be modified by exploits (see Chapter 7 for more information).

6. It initializes the loader database in the PEB.

7. It initializes the National Language Support (NLS, for internationalization) tables for the process.

8. It builds the image path name for the application.

9. It captures the SEH exception handlers from the .pdata section and builds the internal exception tables.

10. It captures the system call thunks for the five critical loader functions: `NtCreateSection`, `NtOpenFile`, `NtQueryAttributesFile`, `NtOpenSection`, and `NtMapViewOfSection`.

11. It reads the mitigation options for the application (which are passed in by the kernel through the `LdrSystemDllInitBlock` exported variable). These are described in more detail in Chapter 7.

12. It queries the Image File Execution Options (IFEO) registry key for the application. This will include options such as the global flags (stored in `GlobalFlags`), as well as heap-debugging options (`DisableHeapLookaside`, `ShutdownFlags`, and `FrontEndHeapDebugOptions`), loader settings (`UnloadEventTraceDepth`, `MaxLoaderThreads`, `UseImpersonatedDeviceMap`), ETW settings (`TracingFlags`). Other options include `MinimumStackCommitInBytes` and `MaxDead-ActivationContexts`. As part of this work, the Application Verifier package and related Verifier DLLs will be initialized and Control Flow Guard (CFG) options will be read from `CFGOptions`.

13. It looks inside the executable's header to see whether it is a .NET application (specified by the presence of a .NET-specific image directory) and if it's a 32-bit image. It also queries the kernel to verify if this is a Wow64 process. If needed, it handles a 32-bit IL-only image, which does not require Wow64.

14. It loads any configuration options specified in the executable's Image Load Configuration Directory. These options, which a developer can define when compiling the application, and which the compiler and linker also use to implement certain security and mitigation features such as CFG, control the behavior of the executable.

15. It minimally initializes FLS and TLS.

16. It sets up debugging options for critical sections, creates the user-mode stack trace database if the appropriate global flag was enabled, and queries `StrackTraceDatabaseSizeInMb` from the Image File Execution Options.

17. It initializes the heap manager for the process and creates the first process heap. This will use various load configuration, image file execution, global flags, and executable header options to set up the required parameters.

18. It enables the Terminate process on heap corruption mitigation if it's turned on.

19. It initializes the exception dispatch log if the appropriate global flag has enabled this.

20. It initializes the thread pool package, which supports the Thread Pool API. This queries and takes into account NUMA information.

21. It initializes and converts the environment block and parameter block, especially as needed to support WoW64 processes.

22. It opens the \KnownDlls object directory and builds the known DLL path. For a Wow64 process, \KnownDlls32 is used instead.

23. For store applications, it reads the Application Model Policy options, which are encoded in the WIN://PKG and WP://SKUID claims of the token (see the "AppContainers" section in Chapter 7 for more information).

24. It determines the process's current directory, system path, and default load path (used when loading images and opening files), as well as the rules around default DLL search order. This includes reading the current policy settings for Universal (UWP) versus Desktop Bridge (Centennial) versus Silverlight (Windows Phone 8) packaged applications (or services).

25. It builds the first loader data table entry for Ntdll.dll and inserts it into the module database.

26. It builds the unwind history table.

27. It initializes the parallel loader, which is used to load all the dependencies (which don't have cross-dependencies) using the thread pool and concurrent threads.

28. It builds the next loader data table entry for the main executable and inserts it into the module database.

29. If needed, it relocates the main executable image.

30. If enabled, it initializes Application Verifier.

31. It initializes the Wow64 engine if this is a Wow64 process. In this case, the 64-bit loader will finish its initialization, and the 32-bit loader will take control and re-start most of the operations we've just described up until this point.

32. If this is a .NET image, it validates it, loads Mscoree.dll (.NET runtime shim), and retrieves the main executable entry point (_CorExeMain), overwriting the exception record to set this as the entry point instead of the regular main function.

33. It initializes the TLS slots of the process.

34. For Windows subsystem applications, it manually loads Kernel32.dll and Kernelbase.dll, regardless of actual imports of the process. As needed, it uses these libraries to initialize the SRP/Safer (Software Restriction Policies) mechanisms, as well as capture the Windows subsystem thread initialization thunk function. Finally, it resolves any API Set dependencies that exist specifically between these two libraries.

35. It initializes the shim engine and parses the shim database.

36. It enables the parallel image loader, as long as the core loader functions scanned earlier do not have any system call hooks or "detours" attached to them, and based on the number of loader threads that have been configured through policy and image file execution options.

37. It sets the LdrInitState variable to 1, meaning "import loading in progress."

At this point, the image loader is ready to start parsing the import table of the executable belonging to the application and start loading any DLLs that were dynamically linked during the compilation of the application. This will happen both for .NET images, which will have their imports processed by calling into the .NET runtime, as well as for regular images. Because each imported DLL can also have its own import table, this operation, in the past, continued recursively until all DLLs had been satisfied and all functions to be imported have been found. As each DLL was loaded, the loader kept state information for it and built the module database.

In newer versions of Windows, the loader instead builds a dependency map ahead of time, with specific nodes that describe a single DLL and its dependency graph, building out separate nodes that can be loaded in parallel. At various points when serialization is needed, the thread pool worker queue is "drained," which services as a synchronization point. One such point is before calling all the DLL initialization routines of all the static imports, which is one of the last stages of the loader. Once this is done, all the static TLS initializers are called. Finally, for Windows applications, in between these two steps, the Kernel32 thread initialization thunk function (BaseThreadInitThunk) is called at the beginning, and the Kernel32 post-process initialization routine is called at the end.

DLL name resolution and redirection

Name resolution is the process by which the system converts the name of a PE-format binary to a physical file in situations where the caller has not specified or cannot specify a unique file identity. Because the locations of various directories (the application directory, the system directory, and so on) cannot be hardcoded at link time, this includes the resolution of all binary dependencies as well as LoadLibrary operations in which the caller does not specify a full path.

When resolving binary dependencies, the basic Windows application model locates files in a search path—a list of locations that is searched sequentially for a file with a matching base name—although various system components override the search path mechanism in order to extend the default application model. The notion of a search path is a holdover from the era of the command line, when an application's current directory was a meaningful notion; this is somewhat anachronistic for modern GUI applications.

However, the placement of the current directory in this ordering allowed load operations on system binaries to be overridden by placing malicious binaries with the same base name in the application's current directory, a technique often known as *binary planting*. To prevent security risks associated with this behavior, a feature known as *safe DLL search mode* was added to the path search computation and is enabled by default for all processes. Under safe search mode, the current directory is moved behind the three system directories, resulting in the following path ordering:

1. The directory from which the application was launched

2. The native Windows system directory (for example, C:\Windows\System32)

3. The 16-bit Windows system directory (for example, C:\Windows\System)

4. The Windows directory (for example, C:\Windows)

5. The current directory at application launch time

6. Any directories specified by the %PATH% environment variable

The DLL search path is recomputed for each subsequent DLL load operation. The algorithm used to compute the search path is the same as the one used to compute the default search path, but the application can change specific path elements by editing the %PATH% variable using the SetEnvironmentVariable API, changing the current directory using the SetCurrentDirectory API, or using the SetDllDirectory API to specify a DLL directory for the process. When a DLL directory is specified, the directory replaces the current directory in the search path and the loader ignores the safe DLL search mode setting for the process.

Callers can also modify the DLL search path for specific load operations by supplying the LOAD_WITH_ALTERED_SEARCH_PATH flag to the LoadLibraryEx API. When this flag is supplied and the DLL name supplied to the API specifies a full path string, the path containing the DLL file is used in place of the application directory when computing the search path for the operation. Note that if the path is a relative path, this behavior is undefined and potentially dangerous. When Desktop Bridge (Centennial) applications load, this flag is ignored.

Other flags that applications can specify to LoadLibraryEx include LOAD_LIBRARY_SEARCH_DLL_LOAD_DIR, LOAD_LIBRARY_SEARCH_APPLICATION_DIR, LOAD_LIBRARY_SEARCH_SYSTEM32, and LOAD_LIBRARY_SEARCH_USER_DIRS, in place of the LOAD_WITH_ALTERED_SEARCH_PATH flag. Each of these modifies the search order to only search the specific directory (or directories) that the flag references, or the flags can be combined as desired to search multiple locations. For example, combining the application, system32, and user directories results in LOAD_LIBRARY_SEARCH_DEFAULT_DIRS. Furthermore, these flags can be globally set using the SetDefaultDllDirectories API, which will affect all library loads from that point on.

Another way search-path ordering can be affected is if the application is a packaged application or if it is not a packaged service or legacy Silverlight 8.0 Windows Phone application. In these conditions, the DLL search order will not use the traditional mechanism and APIs, but will rather be restricted to the package-based graph search. This is also the case when the LoadPackagedLibrary API is used instead of the regular LoadLibraryEx function. The package-based graph is computed based on the <PackageDependency> entries in the UWP application's manifest file's <Dependencies> section, and guarantees that no arbitrary DLLs can accidentally load in the package.

Additionally, when a packaged application is loaded, as long as it is not a Desktop Bridge application, all application-configurable DLL search path ordering APIs, such as the ones we saw earlier, will be disabled, and only the default system behavior will be used (in combination with only looking through package dependencies for most UWP applications as per the above).

Unfortunately, even with safe search mode and the default path searching algorithms for legacy applications, which always include the application directory first, a binary might still be copied from its usual location to a user-accessible location (for example, from c:\windows\system32\notepad.exe into c:\temp\notepad.exe, an operation that does not require administrative rights). In this situation, an attacker can place a specifically crafted DLL in the same directory as the application, and due to the ordering above, it will take precedence over the system DLL. This can then be used for persistence or otherwise affecting the application, which might be privileged (especially if the user, unaware of the change, is elevating it through UAC). To defend against this, processes and/or administrators can use a process-mitigation policy (see Chapter 7 for more information on these) called Prefer System32 Images, which inverts the order above between points 1 and 2, as the name suggests.

DLL name redirection

Before attempting to resolve a DLL name string to a file, the loader attempts to apply DLL name redirection rules. These redirection rules are used to extend or override portions of the DLL namespace—which normally corresponds to the Win32 file system namespace—to extend the Windows application model. In order of application, these are:

- **MinWin API Set redirection**   The API set mechanism is designed to allow different versions or editions of Windows to change the binary that exports a given system API in a manner that is transparent to applications, by introducing the concept of contracts. This mechanism was briefly touched upon in Chapter 2, and will be further explained in a later section.

- **.LOCAL redirection**   The .LOCAL redirection mechanism allows applications to redirect all loads of a specific DLL base name, regardless of whether a full path is specified, to a local copy of the DLL in the application directory—either by creating a copy of the DLL with the same base name followed by .*local* (for example, MyLibrary.dll.local) or by creating a file folder with the name .local under the application directory and placing a copy of the local DLL in the folder (for example, C:\\MyApp\.LOCAL\MyLibrary.dll). DLLs redirected by the .LOCAL mechanism are handled identically to those redirected by SxS. (See the next bullet point.) The loader honors .LOCAL redirection of DLLs only when the executable does not have an associated manifest, either embedded or external. It's not enabled by default. To enable it globally, add the DWORD value DevOverrideEnable in the base IFEO key (HKLM\Software\Microsoft\WindowsNT\CurrentVersion\Image File Execution Options) and set it to 1.

- **Fusion (SxS) redirection**   Fusion (also referred to as *side-by-side, or SxS*) is an extension to the Windows application model that allows components to express more detailed binary dependency information (usually versioning information) by embedding binary resources known as *manifests*. The Fusion mechanism was first used so that applications could load the correct version of the Windows common controls package (comctl32.dll) after that binary was split into different versions that could be installed alongside one another; other binaries have since been versioned in the same fashion. As of Visual Studio 2005, applications built with the Microsoft linker use Fusion to locate the appropriate version of the C runtime libraries, while Visual Studio 2015 and later use API Set redirection to implement the idea of the universal CRT.

The Fusion runtime tool reads embedded dependency information from a binary's resource section using the Windows resource loader, and it packages the dependency information into lookup structures known as *activation contexts*. The system creates default activation contexts at the system and process level at boot and process startup time, respectively; in addition, each thread has an associated activation context stack, with the activation context structure at the top of the stack considered active. The per-thread activation context stack is managed both explicitly, via the `ActivateActCtx` and `DeactivateActCtx` APIs, and implicitly by the system at certain points, such as when the DLL main routine of a binary with embedded dependency information is called. When a Fusion DLL name redirection lookup occurs, the system searches for redirection information in the activation context at the head of the thread's activation context stack, followed by the process and system activation contexts; if redirection information is present, the file identity specified by the activation context is used for the load operation.

■ **Known DLL redirection** Known DLLs is a mechanism that maps specific DLL base names to files in the system directory, preventing the DLL from being replaced with an alternate version in a different location.

One edge case in the DLL path search algorithm is the DLL versioning check performed on 64-bit and WoW64 applications. If a DLL with a matching base name is located but is subsequently determined to have been compiled for the wrong machine architecture—for example, a 64-bit image in a 32-bit application—the loader ignores the error and resumes the path search operation, starting with the path element after the one used to locate the incorrect file. This behavior is designed to allow applications to specify both 64-bit and 32-bit entries in the global %PATH% environment variable.

EXPERIMENT: Observing DLL load search order

You can use Sysinternals Process Monitor tool to watch how the loader searches for DLLs. When the loader attempts to resolve a DLL dependency, you will see it perform `CreateFile` calls to probe each location in the search sequence until either it finds the specified DLL or the load fails.

Here's the capture of the loader's search for the OneDrive.exe executable. To re-create the experiment, do the following:

1. If the OneDrive is running, close it from its tray icon. Make sure to close all Explorer windows that are looking at OneDrive content.

2. Open Process Monitor and add filters to show just the process OneDrive.exe. Optionally, show only the operation for `CreateFile`.

3. Go to %LocalAppData%\Microsoft\OneDrive and launch OneDrive.exe or OneDrive Personal.cmd (which launches OneDrive.exe as "personal" rather than "business"). You should see something like the following (note that OneDrive is a 32 bit process, here running on a 64 bit system):

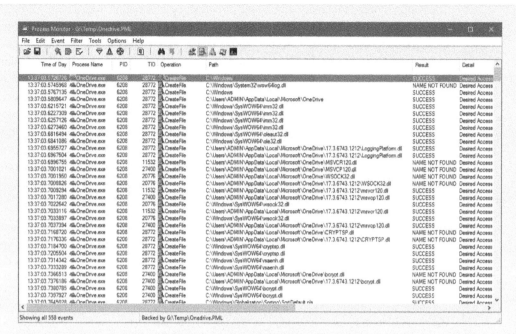

Here are some of the calls shown as they relate to the search order described previously:

- KnownDlls DLLs load from the system location (ole32.dll in the screenshot).

- LoggingPlatform.Dll is loaded from a version subdirectory, probably because OneDrive calls SetDllDirectory to redirect searches to the latest version (17.3.6743.1212 in the screenshot).

- The MSVCR120.dll (MSVC run time version 12) is searched for in the executable's directory, and is not found. Then it's searched in the version subdirectory, where it's located.

- The Wsock32.Dll (WinSock) is searched in the executable's path, then in the version subdirectory, and finally located in the system directory (SysWow64). Note that this DLL is not a KnownDll.

Loaded module database

The loader maintains a list of all modules (DLLs as well as the primary executable) that have been loaded by a process. This information is stored in the PEB—namely, in a substructure identified by *Ldr* and called PEB_LDR_DATA. In the structure, the loader maintains three doubly linked lists, all containing the same information but ordered differently (either by load order, memory location, or initialization order). These lists contain structures called *loader data table entries* (LDR_DATA_TABLE_ENTRY) that store information about each module.

Additionally, because lookups in linked lists are algorithmically expensive (being done in linear time), the loader also maintains two red-black trees, which are efficient binary lookup trees. The first is sorted by base address, while the second is sorted by the hash of the module's name. With these trees, the searching algorithm can run in logarithmic time, which is significantly more efficient and greatly speeds up process-creation performance in Windows 8 and later. Additionally, as a security precaution, the root of these two trees, unlike the linked lists, is not accessible in the PEB. This makes them harder to locate by shell code, which is operating in an environment where address space layout randomization (ASLR) is enabled. (See Chapter 5 for more on ASLR.)

Table 3-9 lists the various pieces of information the loader maintains in an entry.

TABLE 3-9 Fields in a loader data table entry

Field	Meaning
BaseAddressIndexNode	Links this entry as a node in the Red-Black Tree sorted by base address.
BaseDllName/ BaseNameHashValue	The name of the module itself, without the full path. The second field stores its hash using RtlHashUnicodeString.
DdagNode/NodeModuleLink	A pointer to the data structure tracking the distributed dependency graph (DDAG), which parallelizes dependency loading through the worker thread pool. The second field links the structure with the LDR_DATA_TABLE_ENTRYs associated with it (part of the same graph).
DllBase	Holds the base address at which the module was loaded.
EntryPoint	Contains the initial routine of the module (such as DllMain).
EntryPointActivationContext	Contains the SxS/Fusion activation context when calling initializers.
Flags	Loader state flags for this module (see Table 3-10 for a description of the flags).
ForwarderLinks	A linked list of modules that were loaded as a result of export table forwarders from the module.
FullDllName	The fully qualified path name of the module.
HashLinks	A linked list used during process startup and shutdown for quicker lookups.
ImplicitPathOptions	Used to store path lookup flags that can be set with the LdrSetImplicitPathOptions API or that are inherited based on the DLL path.
List Entry Links	Links this entry into each of the three ordered lists part of the loader database.
LoadContext	Pointer to the current load information for the DLL. Typically NULL unless actively being loaded.
ObsoleteLoadCount	A reference count for the module (that is, how many times it has been loaded). This is no longer accurate and has been moved to the DDAG node structure instead.
LoadReason	Contains an enumeration value that explains why this DLL was loaded (dynamically, statically, as a forwarder, as a delay-load dependency, etc.).
LoadTime	Stores the system time value when this module was being loaded.
MappingInfoIndexNode	Links this entry as a node in the red-black tree sorted by the hash of the name.
OriginalBase	Stores the original base address (set by the linker) of this module, before ASLR or relocations, enabling faster processing of relocated import entries.

Continues...

TABLE 3-9 Fields in a loader data table entry *(continued)*

Field	Meaning
ParentDllBase	In case of static (or forwarder, or delay-load) dependencies, stores the address of the DLL that has a dependency on this one.
SigningLevel	Stores the signature level of this image (see Chapter 8, Part 2, for more information on the Code Integrity infrastructure).
SizeOfImage	The size of the module in memory.
SwitchBackContext	Used by SwitchBack (described later) to store the current Windows context GUID associated with this module, and other data.
TimeDateStamp	A time stamp written by the linker when the module was linked, which the loader obtains from the module's image PE header.
TlsIndex	The thread local storage slot associated with this module.

One way to look at a process's loader database is to use WinDbg and its formatted output of the PEB. The next experiment shows you how to do this and how to look at the LDR_DATA_TABLE_ENTRY structures on your own.

EXPERIMENT: Dumping the loaded modules database

Before starting the experiment, perform the same steps as in the previous two experiments to launch Notepad.exe with WinDbg as the debugger. When you get to the initial breakpoint (where you've been instructed to type **g** until now), follow these instructions:

1. You can look at the PEB of the current process with the !peb command. For now, you're interested only in the Ldr data that will be displayed.

```
0:000> !peb
PEB at 000000dd4c901000
    InheritedAddressSpace:    No
    ReadImageFileExecOptions: No
    BeingDebugged:            Yes
    ImageBaseAddress:         00007ff720b60000
    Ldr                       00007ffe855d23a0
    Ldr.Initialized:          Yes
    Ldr.InInitializationOrderModuleList: 0000022815d23d30 . 0000022815d24430
    Ldr.InLoadOrderModuleList:           0000022815d23ee0 . 0000022815d31240
    Ldr.InMemoryOrderModuleList:         0000022815d23ef0 . 0000022815d31250
                    Base TimeStamp                     Module
            7ff720b60000 5789986a Jul 16 05:14:02 2016 C:\Windows\System32\
notepad.exe
            7ffe85480000 5825887f Nov 11 10:59:43 2016 C:\WINDOWS\SYSTEM32\
ntdll.dll
            7ffe84bd0000 57899a29 Jul 16 05:21:29 2016 C:\WINDOWS\System32\
KERNEL32.DLL
            7ffe823c0000 582588e6 Nov 11 11:01:26 2016 C:\WINDOWS\System32\
KERNELBASE.dll
    ...
```

2. The address shown on the Ldr line is a pointer to the PEB_LDR_DATA structure described earlier. Notice that WinDbg shows you the address of the three lists, and dumps the initialization order list for you, displaying the full path, time stamp, and base address of each module.

3. You can also analyze each module entry on its own by going through the module list and then dumping the data at each address, formatted as a LDR_DATA_TABLE_ENTRY structure. Instead of doing this for each entry, however, WinDbg can do most of the work by using the !list extension and the following syntax:

```
!list -x "dt ntdll!_LDR_DATA_TABLE_ENTRY" @@C++(&@$peb->Ldr-
>InLoadOrderModuleList)
```

4. You should then see the entries for each module:

```
+0x000 InLoadOrderLinks : _LIST_ENTRY [ 0x00000228'15d23d10 -
0x00007ffe'855d23b0 ]
   +0x010 InMemoryOrderLinks : _LIST_ENTRY [ 0x00000228'15d23d20 -
0x00007ffe'855d23c0 ]
   +0x020 InInitializationOrderLinks : _LIST_ENTRY [ 0x00000000'00000000 -
0x00000000'00000000 ]
   +0x030 DllBase            : 0x00007ff7'20b60000 Void
   +0x038 EntryPoint         : 0x00007ff7'20b787d0 Void
   +0x040 SizeOfImage        : 0x41000
   +0x048 FullDllName        : _UNICODE_STRING "C:\Windows\System32\notepad.
exe"
   +0x058 BaseDllName        : _UNICODE_STRING "notepad.exe"
   +0x068 FlagGroup          : [4]  "???"
   +0x068 Flags              : 0xa2cc
```

Although this section covers the user-mode loader in Ntdll.dll, note that the kernel also employs its own loader for drivers and dependent DLLs, with a similar loader entry structure called KLDR_DATA_ TABLE_ENTRY instead. Likewise, the kernel-mode loader has its own database of such entries, which is directly accessible through the PsActiveModuleList global data variable. To dump the kernel's loaded module database, you can use a similar !list command as shown in the preceding experiment by replacing the pointer at the end of the command with nt!PsActiveModuleList and using the new structure/module name: !list nt!_KLDR_DATA_TABLE_ENTRY nt!PsActiveModuleList.

Looking at the list in this raw format gives you some extra insight into the loader's *internals*, such as the Flags field, which contains state information that !peb on its own would not show you. See Table 3-10 for their meaning. Because both the kernel and user-mode loaders use this structure, the meaning of the flags is not always the same. In this table, we explicitly cover the user-mode flags only (some of which may exist in the kernel structure as well).

TABLE 3-10 Loader data table entry flags

Flag	Meaning
Packaged Binary (0x1)	This module is part of a packaged application (it can only be set on the main module of an AppX package).
Marked for Removal (0x2)	This module will be unloaded as soon as all references (such as from an executing worker thread) are dropped.
Image DLL (0x4)	This module is an image DLL (and not a data DLL or executable).
Load Notifications Sent (0x8)	Registered DLL notification callouts were notified of this image already.
Telemetry Entry Processed (0x10)	Telemetry data has already been processed for this image.
Process Static Import (0x20)	This module is a static import of the main application binary.
In Legacy Lists (0x40)	This image entry is in the loader's doubly linked lists.
In Indexes (0x80)	This image entry is in the loader's red-black trees.
Shim DLL (0x100)	This image entry represents a DLL part of the shim engine/application compatibility database.
In Exception Table (0x200)	This module's .pdata exception handlers have been captured in the loader's inverted function table.
Load In Progress (0x800)	This module is currently being loaded.
Load Config Processed (0x1000)	This module's image load configuration directory has been found and processed.
Entry Processed (0x2000)	The loader has fully finished processing this module.
Protect Delay Load (0x4000)	Control Flow Guard features for this binary have requested the protection of the delay-load IAT. See chapter 7 for more information.
Process Attach Called (0x20000)	The DLL_PROCESS_ATTACH notification has already been sent to the DLL.
Process Attach Failed (0x40000)	The DllMain routine of the DLL has failed the DLL_PROCESS_ATTACH notification.
Don't Call for Threads (0x80000)	Do not send DLL_THREAD_ATTACH/DETACH notifications to this DLL. Can be set with DisableThreadLibraryCalls.
COR Deferred Validate (0x100000)	The Common Object Runtime (COR) will validate this .NET image at a later time.
COR Image (0x200000)	This module is a .NET application.
Don't Relocate (0x400000)	This image should not be relocated or randomized.
COR IL Only (0x800000)	This is a .NET intermediate-language (IL)-only library, which does not contain native assembly code.
Compat Database Processed (0x40000000)	The shim engine has processed this DLL.

Import parsing

Now that we've explained the way the loader keeps track of all the modules loaded for a process, you can continue analyzing the startup initialization tasks performed by the loader. During this step, the loader will do the following:

1. Load each DLL referenced in the import table of the process's executable image.

2. Check whether the DLL has already been loaded by checking the module database. If it doesn't find it in the list, the loader opens the DLL and maps it into memory.

3. During the mapping operation, the loader first looks at the various paths where it should attempt to find this DLL, as well as whether this DLL is a *known DLL*, meaning that the system has already loaded it at startup and provided a global memory mapped file for accessing it. Certain deviations from the standard lookup algorithm can also occur, either through the use of a .local file (which forces the loader to use DLLs in the local path) or through a manifest file, which can specify a redirected DLL to use to guarantee a specific version.

4. After the DLL has been found on disk and mapped, the loader checks whether the kernel has loaded it somewhere else—this is called *relocation*. If the loader detects relocation, it parses the relocation information in the DLL and performs the operations required. If no relocation information is present, DLL loading fails.

5. The loader then creates a loader data table entry for this DLL and inserts it into the database.

6. After a DLL has been mapped, the process is repeated for this DLL to parse its import table and all its dependencies.

7. After each DLL is loaded, the loader parses the IAT to look for specific functions that are being imported. Usually this is done by name, but it can also be done by ordinal (an index number). For each name, the loader parses the export table of the imported DLL and tries to locate a match. If no match is found, the operation is aborted.

8. The import table of an image can also be bound. This means that at link time, the developers already assigned static addresses pointing to imported functions in external DLLs. This removes the need to do the lookup for each name, but it assumes that the DLLs the application will use will always be located at the same address. Because Windows uses address space randomization (see Chapter 5 for more information on ASLR), this is usually not the case for system applications and libraries.

9. The export table of an imported DLL can use a forwarder entry, meaning that the actual function is implemented in another DLL. This must essentially be treated like an import or dependency, so after parsing the export table, each DLL referenced by a forwarder is also loaded and the loader goes back to step 1.

After all imported DLLs (and their own dependencies, or imports) have been loaded, all the required imported functions have been looked up and found, and all forwarders also have been loaded and processed, the step is complete: All dependencies that were defined at compile time by the application and its various DLLs have now been fulfilled. During execution, delayed dependencies (called *delay load*), as well as run-time operations (such as calling LoadLibrary) can call into the loader and essentially repeat the same tasks. Note, however, that a failure in these steps will result in an error launching the application if they are done during process startup. For example, attempting to run an application that requires a function that isn't present in the current version of the operating system can result in a message similar to the one in Figure 3-12.

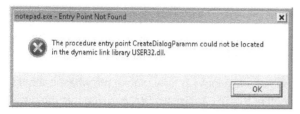

FIGURE 3-12 The dialog box shown when a required (imported) function is not present in a DLL.

Post-import process initialization

After the required dependencies have been loaded, several initialization tasks must be performed to fully finalize launching the application. In this phase, the loader will do the following:

1. These steps begin with the LdrInitState variable set to 2, which means imports have loaded.

2. The initial debugger breakpoint will be hit when using a debugger such as WinDbg. This is where you had to type **g** to continue execution in earlier experiments.

3. Check if this is a Windows subsystem application, in which case the BaseThreadInitThunk function should've been captured in the early process initialization steps. At this point, it is called and checked for success. Similarly, the TermsrvGetWindowsDirectoryW function, which should have been captured earlier (if on a system which supports terminal services), is now called, which resets the System and Windows directories path.

4. Using the distributed graph, recurse through all dependencies and run the initializers for all of the images' static imports. This is the step that calls the DllMain routine for each DLL (allowing each DLL to perform its own initialization work, which might even include loading new DLLs at run time) as well as processes the TLS initializers of each DLL. This is one of the last steps in which loading an application can fail. If all the loaded DLLs do not return a successful return code after finishing their DllMain routines, the loader aborts starting the application.

5. If the image uses any TLS slots, call its TLS initializer.

6. Run the post-initialization shim engine callback if the module is being shimmed for application compatibility.

7. Run the associated subsystem DLL post-process initialization routine registered in the PEB. For Windows applications, this does Terminal Services–specific checks, for example.

8. At this point, write an ETW event indicating that the process has loaded successfully.

9. If there is a minimum stack commit, touch the thread stack to force an in-page of the committed pages.

10. Set LdrInitState to 3, which means initialization done. Set the PEB's ProcessInitializing field back to 0. Then, update the LdrpProcessInitialized variable.

SwitchBack

As each new version of Windows fixes bugs such as race conditions and incorrect parameter validation checks in existing API functions, an application-compatibility risk is created for each change, no matter how minor. Windows makes use of a technology called *SwitchBack*, implemented in the loader, which enables software developers to embed a GUID specific to the Windows version they are targeting in their executable's associated manifest.

For example, if a developer wants to take advantage of improvements added in Windows 10 to a given API, she would include the Windows 10 GUID in her manifest, while if a developer has a legacy application that depends on Windows 7–specific behavior, she would put the Windows 7 GUID in the manifest instead.

SwitchBack parses this information and correlates it with embedded information in SwitchBack-compatible DLLs (in the `.sb_data` image section) to decide which version of an affected API should be called by the module. Because SwitchBack works at the loaded-module level, it enables a process to have both legacy and current DLLs concurrently calling the same API, yet observing different results.

SwitchBack GUIDs

Windows currently defines GUIDs that represent compatibility settings for every version from Windows Vista:

- {e2011457-1546-43c5-a5fe-008deee3d3f0} for Windows Vista

- {35138b9a-5d96-4fbd-8e2d-a2440225f93a} for Windows 7

- {4a2f28e3-53b9-4441-ba9c-d69d4a4a6e38} for Windows 8

- {1f676c76-80e1-4239-95bb-83d0f6d0da78} for Windows 8.1

- {8e0f7a12-bfb3-4fe8-b9a5-48fd50a15a9a} for Windows 10

These GUIDs must be present in the application's manifest file under the `<SupportedOS>` element in the ID attribute in a compatibility attribute entry. (If the application manifest does not contain a GUID, Windows Vista is chosen as the default compatibility mode.) Using Task Manager, you can enable an Operating System Context column in the Details tab, which will show if any applications are running with a specific OS context (an empty value usually means they are operating in Windows 10 mode). Figure 3-13 shows an example of a few such applications, which are operating in Windows Vista and Windows 7 modes, even on a Windows 10 system.

Here is an example of a manifest entry that sets compatibility for Windows 10:

```
<compatibility xmlns="urn:schemas-microsoft-com:compatibility.v1">
  <application>
    <!-- Windows 10 -->
    <supportedOS Id="{8e0f7a12-bfb3-4fe8-b9a5-48fd50a15a9a}" />
  </application>
</compatibility>
```

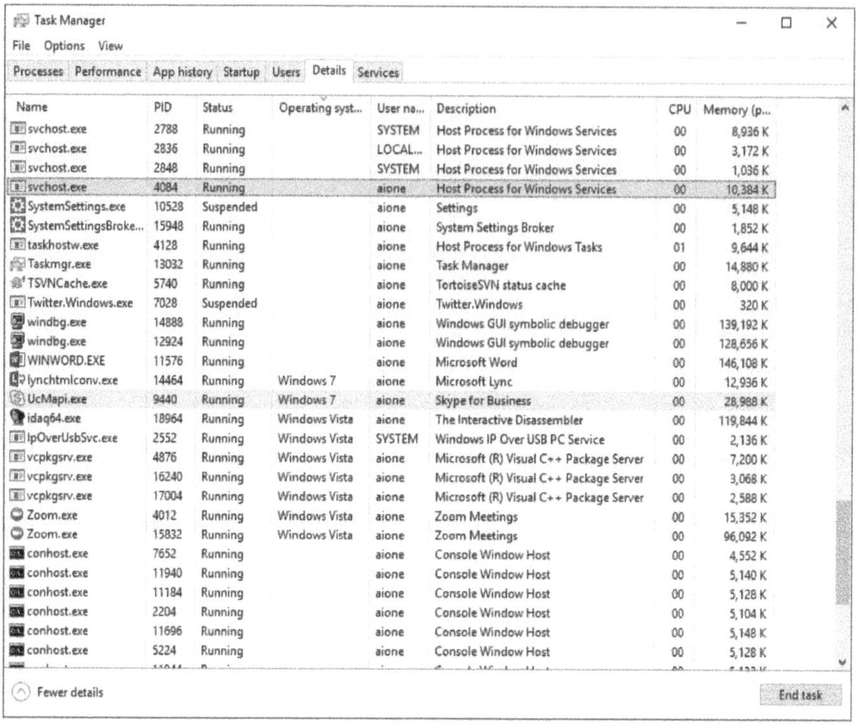

FIGURE 3-13 Some processes that run with compatibility modes.

SwitchBack compatibility modes

As a few examples of what SwitchBack can do, here's what running under the Windows 7 context affects:

- RPC components use the Windows thread pool instead of a private implementation.

- DirectDraw Lock cannot be acquired on the primary buffer.

- Blitting on the desktop is not allowed without a clipping window.

- A race condition in GetOverlappedResult is fixed.

- Calls to CreateFile are allowed to pass a "downgrade" flag to receive exclusive open to a file even when the caller does not have write privilege, which causes NtCreateFile not to receive the FILE_DISALLOW_EXCLUSIVE flag.

Running in Windows 10 mode, on the other hand, subtly affects how the Low Fragmentation Heap (LFH) behaves, by forcing LFH sub-segments to be fully committed and padding all allocations with a header block unless the Windows 10 GUID is present. Additionally, in Windows 10, using the Raise Exception on Invalid Handle Close mitigation (see Chapter 7 for more information) will result in CloseHandle and RegCloseKey respecting the behavior. On the other hand, on previous operating systems, if the debugger is not attached, this behavior will be disabled before calling NtClose, and then re-enabled after the call.

As another example, the Spell Checking Facility will return NULL for languages which don't have a spell checker, while it returns an "empty" spell checker on Windows 8.1. Similarly, the implementation of the function IShellLink::Resolve will return E_INVALIDARG when operating in Windows 8 compatibility mode when given a relative path, but will not contain this check in Windows 7 mode.

Furthermore, calls to GetVersionEx or the equivalent functions in NtDll such as RtlVerifyVersion-Info will return the maximum version number that corresponds to the SwitchBack Context GUID that was specified.

 Note These APIs have been deprecated, and calls to GetVersionEx will return 6.2 on all versions of Windows 8 and later if a higher SwitchBack GUID is not provided.

SwitchBack behavior

Whenever a Windows API is affected by changes that might break compatibility, the function's entry code calls the SbSwitchProcedure to invoke the SwitchBack logic. It passes along a pointer to the SwitchBack *module table*, which contains information about the SwitchBack mechanisms employed in the module. The table also contains a pointer to an array of entries for each SwitchBack point. This table contains a description of each branch-point that identifies it with a symbolic name and a comprehensive description, along with an associated mitigation tag. Typically, there will be several branch-points in a module, one for Windows Vista behavior, one for Windows 7 behavior, etc.

For each branch-point, the required SwitchBack context is given—it is this context that determines which of the two (or more) branches is taken at runtime. Finally, each of these descriptors contains a function pointer to the actual code that each branch should execute. If the application is running with the Windows 10 GUID, this will be part of its SwitchBack context, and the SbSelectProcedure API, upon parsing the module table, will perform a match operation. It finds the module entry descriptor for the context and proceeds to call the function pointer included in the descriptor.

SwitchBack uses ETW to trace the selection of given SwitchBack contexts and branch-points and feeds the data into the Windows AIT (Application Impact Telemetry) logger. This data can be periodically collected by Microsoft to determine the extent to which each compatibility entry is being used, identify the applications using it (a full stack trace is provided in the log), and notify third-party vendors.

As mentioned, the compatibility level of the application is stored in its manifest. At load time, the loader parses the manifest file, creates a context data structure, and caches it in the pShimData member of the PEB. This context data contains the associated compatibility GUIDs that this process is executing under and determines which version of the branch-points in the called APIs that employ SwitchBack will be executed.

API Sets

While SwitchBack uses API redirection for specific application-compatibility scenarios, there is a much more pervasive redirection mechanism used in Windows for all applications, called *API Sets*. Its purpose is to enable fine-grained categorization of Windows APIs into sub-DLLs instead of having large multi-purpose DLLs that span nearly thousands of APIs that might not be needed on all types of Windows systems today and in the future. This technology, developed mainly to support the refactoring of the bottom-most layers of the Windows architecture to separate it from higher layers, goes hand in hand with the breakdown of Kernel32.dll and Advapi32.dll (among others) into multiple, virtual DLL files.

For example, Figure 3-14 shows a screenshot of Dependency Walker where Kernel32.dll, which is a core Windows library, imports from many other DLLs, beginning with API-MS-WIN. Each of these DLLs contains a small subset of the APIs that Kernel32 normally provides, but together they make up the entire API surface exposed by Kernel32.dll. The CORE-STRING library, for instance, provides only the Windows base string functions.

FIGURE 3-14 API sets for kernel32.dll.

In splitting functions across discrete files, two objectives are achieved. First, doing this allows future applications to link only with the API libraries that provide the functionality that they need. Second, if Microsoft were to create a version of Windows that did not support, for example, localization (say, a non-user-facing, English-only embedded system), it would be possible to simply remove the sub-DLL and modify the API Set schema. This would result in a smaller Kernel32 binary, and any applications that ran without requiring localization would still run.

With this technology, a "base" Windows system called *MinWin* is defined (and, at the source level, built), with a minimum set of services that includes the kernel, core drivers (including file systems, basic system processes such as CSRSS and the Service Control Manager, and a handful of Windows services). Windows Embedded, with its Platform Builder, provides what might seem to be a similar technology, as system builders are able to remove select "Windows components," such as the shell, or the network stack. However, removing components from Windows leaves *dangling dependencies*—code paths that, if exercised, would fail because they depend on the removed components. MinWin's dependencies, on the other hand, are entirely self-contained.

When the process manager initializes, it calls the `PspInitializeApiSetMap` function, which is responsible for creating a section object of the API Set redirection table, which is stored in %System-Root%\System32\ApiSetSchema.dll. The DLL contains no executable code, but it has a section called `.apiset` that contains API Set mapping data that maps virtual API Set DLLs to logical DLLs that implement the APIs. Whenever a new process starts, the process manager maps the section object into the process's address space and sets the `ApiSetMap` field in the process's PEB to point to the base address where the section object was mapped.

In turn, the loader's `LdrpApplyFileNameRedirection` function, which is normally responsible for the .local and SxS/Fusion manifest redirection that was mentioned earlier, also checks for API Set redirection data whenever a new import library that has a name starting with *API-* loads (either dynamically or statically). The API Set table is organized by library with each entry describing in which logical DLL the function can be found, and that DLL is what gets loaded. Although the schema data is a binary format, you can dump its strings with the Sysinternals Strings tool to see which DLLs are currently defined:

```
C:\Windows\System32>strings apisetschema.dll
...
api-ms-onecoreuap-print-render-l1-1-0
printrenderapihost.dllapi-ms-onecoreuap-settingsync-status-l1-1-0
settingsynccore.dll
api-ms-win-appmodel-identity-l1-2-0
kernel.appcore.dllapi-ms-win-appmodel-runtime-internal-l1-1-3
api-ms-win-appmodel-runtime-l1-1-2
api-ms-win-appmodel-state-l1-1-2
api-ms-win-appmodel-state-l1-2-0
api-ms-win-appmodel-unlock-l1-1-0
api-ms-win-base-bootconfig-l1-1-0
advapi32.dllapi-ms-win-base-util-l1-1-0
api-ms-win-composition-redirection-l1-1-0
...
api-ms-win-core-com-midlproxystub-l1-1-0
api-ms-win-core-com-private-l1-1-1
api-ms-win-core-comm-l1-1-0
api-ms-win-core-console-ansi-l2-1-0
api-ms-win-core-console-l1-1-0
api-ms-win-core-console-l2-1-0
api-ms-win-core-crt-l1-1-0
api-ms-win-core-crt-l2-1-0
api-ms-win-core-datetime-l1-1-2
api-ms-win-core-debug-l1-1-2
api-ms-win-core-debug-minidump-l1-1-0
```

```
...
api-ms-win-core-firmware-l1-1-0
api-ms-win-core-guard-l1-1-0
api-ms-win-core-handle-l1-1-0
api-ms-win-core-heap-l1-1-0
api-ms-win-core-heap-l1-2-0
api-ms-win-core-heap-l2-1-0
api-ms-win-core-heap-obsolete-l1-1-0
api-ms-win-core-interlocked-l1-1-1
api-ms-win-core-interlocked-l1-2-0
api-ms-win-core-io-l1-1-1
api-ms-win-core-job-l1-1-0
...
```

Jobs

A *job* is a nameable, securable, shareable kernel object that allows control of one or more processes as a group. A job object's basic function is to allow groups of processes to be managed and manipulated as a unit. A process can be a member of any number of jobs, although the typical case is just one. A process's association with a job object can't be broken, and all processes created by the process and its descendants are associated with the same job object (unless child processes are created with the CREATE_BREAKAWAY_FROM_JOB flag and the job itself has not restricted it). The job object also records basic accounting information for all processes associated with the job and for all processes that were associated with the job but have since terminated.

Jobs can also be associated with an I/O completion port object, which other threads might be waiting for, with the Windows GetQueuedCompletionStatus function or by using the Thread Pool API (the native function TpAllocJobNotification). This allows interested parties (typically the job creator) to monitor for limit violations and events that could affect the job's security, such as a new process being created or a process abnormally exiting.

Jobs play a significant role in a number of system mechanisms, enumerated here:

- They manage modern apps (UWP processes), as discussed in more detail in Chapter 9 in Part 2. In fact, every modern app is running under a job. You can verify this with Process Explorer, as described in the "Viewing the job object" experiment later in this chapter.

- They are used to implement Windows Container support, through a mechanism called *server silo*, covered later in this section.

- They are the primary way through which the Desktop Activity Moderator (DAM) manages throttling, timer virtualization, timer freezing, and other idle-inducing behaviors for Win32 applications and services. The DAM is described in Chapter 8 in Part 2.

- They allow the definition and management of scheduling groups for dynamic fair-share scheduling (DFSS), which is described in Chapter 4.

- They allow for the specification of a custom memory partition, which enables usage of the Memory Partitioning API described in Chapter 5.

- They serve as a key enabler for features such as Run As (Secondary Logon), Application Boxing, and Program Compatibility Assistant.

- They provide part of the security sandbox for applications such as Google Chrome and Microsoft Office Document Converter, as well as mitigation from denial-of-service (DoS) attacks through Windows Management Instrumentation (WMI) requests.

Job limits

The following are some of the CPU-, memory-, and I/O-related limits you can specify for a job:

- **Maximum number of active processes**   This limits the number of concurrently existing processes in the job. If this limit is reached, new processes that should be assigned to the job are blocked from creation.

- **Job-wide user-mode CPU time limit**   This limits the maximum amount of user-mode CPU time that the processes in the job can consume (including processes that have run and exited). Once this limit is reached, by default all the processes in the job are terminated with an error code and no new processes can be created in the job (unless the limit is reset). The job object is signaled, so any threads waiting for the job will be released. You can change this default behavior with a call to `SetInformationJobObject` to set the `EndOfJobTimeAction` member of the `JOBOBJECT_END_OF_JOB_TIME_INFORMATION` structure passed with the `JobObjectEnd-OfJobTimeInformation` information class and request a notification to be sent through the job's completion port instead.

- **Per-process user-mode CPU time limit**   This allows each process in the job to accumulate only a fixed maximum amount of user-mode CPU time. When the maximum is reached, the process terminates (with no chance to clean up).

- **Job processor affinity**   This sets the processor affinity mask for each process in the job. (Individual threads can alter their affinity to any subset of the job affinity, but processes can't alter their process affinity setting.)

- **Job group affinity**   This sets a list of groups to which the processes in the job can be assigned. Any affinity changes are then subject to the group selection imposed by the limit. This is treated as a group-aware version of the job processor affinity limit (legacy), and prevents that limit from being used.

- **Job process priority class**   This sets the priority class for each process in the job. Threads can't increase their priority relative to the class (as they normally can). Attempts to increase thread priority are ignored. (No error is returned on calls to `SetThreadPriority`, but the increase doesn't occur.)

- **Default working set minimum and maximum**   This defines the specified working set minimum and maximum for each process in the job. (This setting isn't job-wide. Each process has its own working set with the same minimum and maximum values.)

- **Process and job committed virtual memory limit**   This defines the maximum amount of virtual address space that can be committed by either a single process or the entire job.

- **CPU rate control**   This defines the maximum amount of CPU time that the job is allowed to use before it will experience forced throttling. This is used as part of the scheduling group support described in Chapter 4.

- **Network bandwidth rate control**   This defines the maximum outgoing bandwidth for the entire job before throttling takes effect. It also enables setting a differentiated services code point (DSCP) tag for QoS purposes for each network packet sent by the job. This can only be set for one job in a hierarchy, and affects the job and any child jobs.

- **Disk I/O bandwidth rate control**   This is the same as network bandwidth rate control, but is applied to disk I/O instead, and can control either bandwidth itself or the number of I/O operations per second (IOPS). It can be set either for a particular volume or for all volumes on the system.

For many of these limits, the job owner can set specific thresholds, at which point a notification will be sent (or, if no notification is registered, the job will simply be killed). Additionally, rate controls allow for tolerance ranges and tolerance intervals—for example, allowing a process to go beyond 20 percent of its network bandwidth limit for up to 10 seconds every 5 minutes. These notifications are done by queuing an appropriate message to the I/O completion port for the job. (See the Windows SDK documentation for the details.)

Finally, you can place user-interface limits on processes in a job. Such limits include restricting processes from opening handles to windows owned by threads outside the job, reading and/or writing to the clipboard, and changing the many user-interface system parameters via the Windows `System-ParametersInfo` function. These user-interface limits are managed by the Windows subsystem GDI/USER driver, Win32k.sys, and are enforced through one of the special callouts that it registers with the process manager, the job callout. You can grant access for all processes in a job to specific user handles (for example, window handle) by calling the `UserHandleGrantAccess` function; this can only be called by a process that is not part of the job in question (naturally).

Working with a job

A job object is created using the `CreateJobObject` API. The job is initially created empty of any process. To add a process to a job, call the `AssignProcessToJobObject`, which can be called multiple times to add processes to the job or even to add the same process to multiple jobs. This last option creates a nested job, described in the next section. Another way to add a process to a job is to manually specify a handle to the job object by using the `PS_CP_JOB_LIST` process-creation attribute described earlier in this chapter. One or more handles to job objects can be specified, which will all be joined.

The most interesting API for jobs is `SetInformationJobObject`, which allows the setting of the various limits and settings mentioned in the previous section, and contains internal information classes used by mechanisms such as Containers (Silo), the DAM, or Windows UWP applications. These values can be read back with `QueryInformationJobObject`, which can provide interested parties with the limits set on a job. It's also necessary to call in case limit notifications have been set (as described in the previous section) in order for the caller to know precisely which limits were violated. Another sometimes-useful function is `TerminateJobObject`, which terminates all processes in the job (as if `TerminateProcess` were called on each process).

Nested jobs

Until Windows 7 and Windows Server 2008 R2, a process could only be associated with a single job, which made jobs less useful than they could be, as in some cases an application could not know in advance whether a process it needed to manage happened to be in a job or not. Starting with Windows 8 and Windows Server 2012, a process can be associated with multiple jobs, effectively creating a job hierarchy.

A child job holds a subset of processes of its parent job. Once a process is added to more than one job, the system tries to form a hierarchy, if possible. A current restriction is that jobs cannot form a hierarchy if any of them sets any UI limits (`SetInformationJobObject` with `JobObjectBasicUIRestrictions` argument).

Job limits for a child job cannot be more permissive than its parent, but they can be more restrictive. For example, if a parent job sets a memory limit of 100 MB for the job, any child job cannot set a higher memory limit (such requests simply fail). A child job can, however, set a more restrictive limit for its processes (and any child jobs it has), such as 80 MB. Any notifications that target the I/O completion port of a job will be sent to the job and all its ancestors. (The job itself does not have to have an I/O completion port for the notification to be sent to ancestor jobs.)

Resource accounting for a parent job includes the aggregated resources used by its direct managed processes and all processes in child jobs. When a job is terminated (`TerminateJobObject`), all processes in the job and in child jobs are terminated, starting with the child jobs at the bottom of the hierarchy. Figure 3-15 shows four processes managed by a job hierarchy.

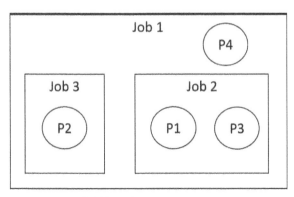

FIGURE 3-15 A job hierarchy.

To create this hierarchy, processes should be added to jobs from the root job. Here are a set of steps to create this hierarchy:

1. Add process P1 to job 1.

2. Add process P1 to job 2. This creates the first nesting.

3. Add process P2 to job 1.

4. Add process P2 to job 3. This creates the second nesting.

5. Add process P3 to job 2.

6. Add process P4 to job 1.

EXPERIMENT: Viewing the job object

You can view named job objects with the Performance Monitor tool. (Look for the Job Object and Job Object Details categories.) You can view unnamed jobs with the kernel debugger !job or dt nt!_ejob commands.

To see whether a process is associated with a job, you can use the kernel debugger !process command or Process Explorer. Follow these steps to create and view an unnamed job object:

1. From the command prompt, use the runas command to create a process running the command prompt (Cmd.exe). For example, type **runas /user:<domain>\< username> cmd**.

2. You'll be prompted for your password. Enter your password, and a Command Prompt window will appear. The Windows service that executes runas commands creates an unnamed job to contain all processes (so that it can terminate these processes at logoff time).

3. Run Process Explorer, open the **Options** menu, choose **Configure Colors**, and check the **Jobs** entry. Notice that the Cmd.exe process and its child ConHost.exe process are highlighted as part of a job, as shown here:

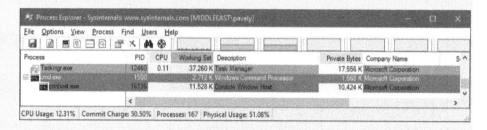

4. Double click the **Cmd.exe** or **ConHost.Exe** process to open its properties dialog box. Then click the **Job** tab to see information about the job this process is part of:

5. From the command prompt, run Notepad.exe.

6. Open Notepad's process and look at the Job tab. Notepad is running under the same job. This is because cmd.exe does not use the CREATE_BREAKAWAY_FROM_JOB creation flag. In the case of nested jobs, the Job tab shows the processes in the direct job this process belongs to and all processes in child jobs.

7. Run the kernel debugger on the live system and type the **!process** command to find the notepad.exe and show its basic info:

```
lkd> !process 0 1 notepad.exe
PROCESS ffffe001eacf2080
    SessionId: 1  Cid: 3078    Peb: 7f4113b000  ParentCid: 05dc
    DirBase: 4878b3000  ObjectTable: ffffc0015b89fd80  HandleCount: 188.
    Image: notepad.exe
    ...
    BasePriority                    8
    CommitCharge                    671
    Job                             ffffe00189aec460
```

8. Note the Job pointer, which is non-zero. To get a summary of the job, type the **!job** debugger command:

```
lkd> !job ffffe00189aec460
Job at ffffe00189aec460
  Basic Accounting Information
    TotalUserTime:              0x0
    TotalKernelTime:            0x0
    TotalCycleTime:             0x0
    ThisPeriodTotalUserTime:    0x0
    ThisPeriodTotalKernelTime:  0x0
    TotalPageFaultCount:        0x0
    TotalProcesses:             0x3
    ActiveProcesses:            0x3
```

```
        FreezeCount:                    0
        BackgroundCount:                0
        TotalTerminatedProcesses:       0x0
        PeakJobMemoryUsed:              0x10db
        PeakProcessMemoryUsed:          0xa56
     Job Flags
     Limit Information (LimitFlags: 0x0)
     Limit Information (EffectiveLimitFlags: 0x0)
```

9. Notice the ActiveProcesses member set to 3 (cmd.exe, conhost.exe, and notepad.exe). You can use flag 2 after the !job command to see a list of the processes that are part of the job:

```
lkd> !job ffffe00189aec460 2
...
Processes assigned to this job:
    PROCESS ffff8188d84dd780
        SessionId: 1 Cid: 5720    Peb: 43bedb6000  ParentCid: 13cc
        DirBase: 707466000  ObjectTable: ffffbe0dc4e3a040  HandleCount:
<Data Not Accessible>
        Image: cmd.exe

    PROCESS ffff8188ea077540
        SessionId: 1 Cid: 30ec    Peb: dd7f17c000  ParentCid: 5720
        DirBase: 75a183000  ObjectTable: ffffbe0dafb79040  HandleCount:
<Data Not Accessible>
        Image: conhost.exe

    PROCESS ffffe001eacf2080
        SessionId: 1 Cid: 3078    Peb: 7f4113b000  ParentCid: 05dc
        DirBase: 4878b3000  ObjectTable: ffffc0015b89fd80  HandleCount: 188.
        Image: notepad.exe
```

10. You can also use the dt command to display the job object and see the additional fields shown about the job, such as its member level and its relations to other jobs in case of nesting (parent job, siblings, and root job):

```
lkd> dt nt!_ejob ffffe00189aec460
    +0x000 Event            : _KEVENT
    +0x018 JobLinks         : _LIST_ENTRY [ 0xffffe001'8d93e548 -
0xffffe001'df30f8d8 ]
    +0x028 ProcessListHead  : _LIST_ENTRY [ 0xffffe001'8c4924f0 -
0xffffe001'eacf24f0 ]
    +0x038 JobLock          : _ERESOURCE
    +0x0a0 TotalUserTime    : _LARGE_INTEGER 0x0
    +0x0a8 TotalKernelTime  : _LARGE_INTEGER 0x2625a
    +0x0b0 TotalCycleTime   : _LARGE_INTEGER 0xc9e03d
    ...
    +0x0d4 TotalProcesses   : 4
    +0x0d8 ActiveProcesses  : 3
    +0x0dc TotalTerminatedProcesses : 0
```

```
...
  +0x428 ParentJob        : (null)
  +0x430 RootJob          : 0xffffe001'89aec460 _EJOB
...
  +0x518 EnergyValues     : 0xffffe001'89aec988 _PROCESS_ENERGY_VALUES
  +0x520 SharedCommitCharge : 0x5e8
```

Windows containers (server silos)

The rise of cheap, ubiquitous cloud computing has led to another major Internet revolution, in which building online services and/or back-end servers for mobile applications is as easy as clicking a button on one of the many cloud providers. But as competition among cloud providers has increased, and as the need to migrate from one to another, or even from a cloud provider to a datacenter, or from a datacenter to a high-end personal server, has grown, it has become increasingly important to have portable back ends, which can be deployed and moved around as needed without the costs associated with running them in a virtual machine.

It is to satisfy this need that technologies such as Docker were created. These technologies essentially allow the deployment of an "application in a box" from one Linux distribution to another without worrying about the complicated deployment of a local installation or the resource consumption of a virtual machine. Originally a Linux-only technology, Microsoft has helped bring Docker to Windows 10 as part of the Anniversary Update. It can work in two modes:

- By deploying an application in a heavyweight, but fully isolated, Hyper-V container, which is supported on both client and server scenarios

- By deploying an application in a lightweight, OS-isolated, server silo container, which is currently supported only in server scenarios due to licensing reasons

This latter technology, which we will investigate in this section, has resulted in deep changes in the operating system to support this capability. Note that, as mentioned, the ability for client systems to create server silo containers exists, but is currently disabled. Unlike a Hyper-V container, which leverages a true virtualized environment, a server silo container provides a second "instance" of all user-mode components while running on top of the same kernel and drivers. At the cost of some security, this provides a much more lightweight container environment.

Job objects and silos

The ability to create a silo is associated with a number of undocumented subclasses as part of the SetJobObjectInformation API. In other words, a silo is essentially a super-job, with additional rules and capabilities beyond those we've seen so far. In fact, a job object can be used for the isolation and resource management capabilities we've looked at as well as used to create a silo. Such jobs are called *hybrid jobs* by the system.

In practice, job objects can actually host two types of silos: application silos (which are currently used to implement the Desktop Bridge are not covered in this section, and are left for Chapter 9 in Part 2) and server silos, which are the ones used for Docker container support.

Silo isolation

The first element that defines a server silo is the existence of a custom object manager root directory object (\). (The object manager is discussed in Chapter 8 in Part 2.) Even though we have not yet learned about this mechanism, suffice it to say that all application-visible named objects (such as files, registry keys, events, mutexes, RPC ports, and more) are hosted in a root namespace, which allows applications to create, locate, and share these objects among themselves.

The ability for a server silo to have its own root means that all access to any named object can be controlled. This is done in one of three ways:

- By creating a new copy of an existing object to provide an alternate access to it from within the silo

- By creating a symbolic link to an existing object to provide direct access to it

- By creating a brand-new object that only exists within the silo, such as the ones a containerized application would use

This initial ability is then combined with the Virtual Machine Compute (Vmcompute) service (used by Docker), which interacts with additional components to provide a full isolation layer:

- **A base Windows image (WIM) file called base OS**   This provides a separate copy of the operating system. At this time, Microsoft provides a Server Core image as well as a Nano Server image.

- **The Ntdll.dll library of the host OS**   This overrides the one in the base OS image. This is due to the fact that, as mentioned, server silos leverage the same host kernel and drivers, and because Ntdll.dll handles system calls, it is the one user-mode component that must be reused from the host OS.

- **A sandbox virtual file system provided by the Wcifs.sys filter driver**   This allows temporary changes to be made to the file system by the container without affecting the underlying NTFS drive, and which can be wiped once the container is shut down.

- **A sandbox virtual registry provided by the VReg kernel component**   This allows for the provision of a temporary set of registry hives (as well as another layer of namespace isolation, as the object manager root namespace only isolates the root of the registry, not the registry hives themselves).

- **The Session Manager (Smss.exe)**   This is now used to create additional service sessions or console sessions, which is a new capability required by the container support. This extends Smss to handle not only additional user sessions, but also sessions needed for each container launched.

The architecture of such containers with the preceding components is shown in Figure 3-16.

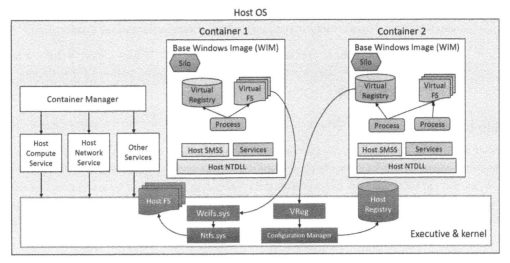

FIGURE 3-16 Containers architecture.

Silo isolation boundaries

The aforementioned components provide the user-mode isolation environment. However, as the host Ntdll.dll component is used, which talks to the host kernel and drivers, it is important to create additional isolation boundaries, which the kernel provides to differentiate one silo from another. As such, each server silo will contain its own isolated:

- **Micro shared user data (SILO_USER_SHARED_DATA in the symbols)** This contains the custom system path, session ID, foreground PID, and product type/suite. These are elements of the original KUSER_SHARED_DATA that cannot come from the host, as they reference information relevant to the host OS image instead of the base OS image, which must be used instead. Various components and APIs were modified to read the silo shared data instead of the user shared data when they look up such data. Note that the original KUSER_SHARED_DATA remains at its usual address with its original view of the host details, so this is one way that host state "leaks" inside container state.

- **Object directory root namespace** This has its own \SystemRoot symlink, \Device directory (which is how all user-mode components access device drivers indirectly), device map and DOS device mappings (which is how user-mode applications access network mapped drivers, for example), \Sessions directory, and more.

- **API Set mapping** This is based on the API Set schema of the base OS WIM, and not the one stored on the host OS file system. As you've seen, the loader uses API Set mappings to determine which DLL, if any, implements a certain function. This can be different from one SKU to another, and applications must see the base OS SKU, not the host's.

- **Logon session** This is associated with the SYSTEM and Anonymous local unique ID (LUID), plus the LUID of a virtual service account describing the user in the silo. This essentially represents the token of the services and application that will be running inside the container service session created by Smss. For more information on LUIDs and logon sessions, see Chapter 7.

- **ETW tracing and logger contexts** These are for isolating ETW operations to the silo and not exposing or leaking states between the containers and/or the host OS itself. (See Chapter 9 in Part 2 for more on ETW.)

Silo contexts

While these are the isolation boundaries provided by the core host OS kernel itself, other components inside the kernel, as well as drivers (including third party), can add contextual data to silos by using the PsCreateSiloContext API to set custom data associated with a silo or by associating an existing object with a silo. Each such silo context will utilize a silo slot index that will be inserted in all running, and future, server silos, storing a pointer to the context. The system provides 32 built-in system-wide storage slot indexes, plus 256 expansion slots, providing lots of extensibility options.

As each server silo is created, it receives its own silo-local storage (SLS) array, much like a thread has thread-local storage (TLS). Within this array, the different entries will correspond to slot indices that have been allocated to store silo contexts. Each silo will have a different pointer at the same slot index, but will always store the same context at that index. (For example, driver "Foo" will own index 5 in all silos, and can use it to store a different pointer/context in each silo.) In some cases, built-in kernel components, such as the object manager, security reference monitor (SRM), and Configuration Manager use some of these slots, while other slots are used by inbox drivers (such as the Ancillary Function Driver for Winsock, Afd.sys).

Just like when dealing with the server silo shared user data, various components and APIs have been updated to access data by getting it from the relevant silo context instead of what used to be a global kernel variable. As an example, because each container will now host its own Lsass.exe process, and since the kernel's SRM needs to own a handle to the Lsass.exe process (see Chapter 7 for more information on Lsass and the SRM), this can no longer be a singleton stored in a global variable. As such, the handle is now accessed by the SRM through querying the silo context of the active server silo, and getting the variable from the data structure that is returned.

This leads to an interesting question: What happens with the Lsass.exe that is running on the host OS itself? How will the SRM access the handle, as there's no server silo for this set of processes and session (that is, session 0 itself)? To solve this conundrum, the kernel now implements a root host silo. In other words, the host itself is presumed to be part of a silo as well! This isn't a silo in the true sense of the word, but rather a clever trick to make querying silo contexts for the current silo work, even when there is no current silo. This is implemented by storing a global kernel variable called PspHostSilo-Globals, which has its own Slot Local Storage Array, as well as other silo contexts used by built-in kernel components. When various silo APIs are called with a NULL pointer, this "NULL" is instead treated as "no silo—i.e., use the host silo."

EXPERIMENT: Dumping SRM silo context for the host silo

As shown, even though your Windows 10 system may not be hosting any server silos, especially if it is a client system, a host silo still exists, which contains the silo-aware isolated contexts used by the kernel. The Windows Debugger has an extension, !silo, which can be used with the –g Host parameters as follows: !silo –g Host. You should see output similar to the one below:

```
1kd> !silo -g Host
Server silo globals fffff801b73bc580:
                      Default Error Port: ffffb30f25b48080
                      ServiceSessionId  : 0
                      Root Directory    : 00007fff00000000 ''
                      State             : Running
```

In your output, the pointer to the silo globals should be hyperlinked, and clicking it will result in the following command execution and output:

```
1kd> dx -r1 (*((nt!_ESERVERSILO_GLOBALS *)0xfffff801b73bc580))
(*((nt!_ESERVERSILO_GLOBALS *)0xfffff801b73bc580))                    [Type: _
ESERVERSILO_GLOBALS]
    [+0x000] ObSiloState         [Type: _OBP_SILODRIVERSTATE]
    [+0x2e0] SeSiloState         [Type: _SEP_SILOSTATE]
    [+0x310] SeRmSiloState       [Type: _SEP_RM_LSA_CONNECTION_STATE]
    [+0x360] CmSiloState         : 0xffffc308870931b0 [Type: _CMP_SILO_CONTEXT *]
    [+0x368] EtwSiloState        : 0xffffb30f236c4000 [Type: _ETW_SILODRIVERSTATE *]
...
```

Now click the SeRmSiloState field, which will expand to show you, among other things, a pointer to the Lsass.exe process:

```
1kd> dx -r1 ((ntkrnlmp!_SEP_RM_LSA_CONNECTION_STATE *)0xfffff801b73bc890)
((ntkrnlmp!_SEP_RM_LSA_CONNECTION_STATE *)0xfffff801b73bc890)          :
0xfffff801b73bc890 [Type: _SEP_RM_LSA_CONNECTION_STATE *]
    [+0x000] LsaProcessHandle : 0xffffffff80000870 [Type: void *]
    [+0x008] LsaCommandPortHandle : 0xffffffff8000087c [Type: void *]
    [+0x010] SepRmThreadHandle : 0x0 [Type: void *]
    [+0x018] RmCommandPortHandle : 0xffffffff80000874 [Type: void *]
```

Silo monitors

If kernel drivers have the capability to add their own silo contexts, how do they first know what silos are executing, and what new silos are created as containers are launched? The answer lies in the silo monitor facility, which provides a set of APIs to receive notifications whenever a server silo is created and/or terminated (PsRegisterSiloMonitor, PsStartSiloMonitor, PsUnregisterSiloMonitor), as well as notifications for any already-existing silos. Then, each silo monitor can retrieve its own slot index by calling PsGetSiloMonitorContextSlot, which it can then use with the PsInsertSiloContext, PsReplaceSiloContext, and PsRemoveSiloContext functions as needed. Additional slots can be allocated with PsAllocSiloContextSlot, but this would be needed only if a component would wish to store two contexts for some reason. Additionally, drivers can also use the PsInsertPermanentSiloContext or

PsMakeSiloContextPermanent APIs to use "permanent" silo contexts, which are not reference counted and are not tied to the lifetime of the server silo or the number of silo context getters. Once inserted, such silo contexts can be retrieved with PsGetSiloContext and/or PsGetPermanentSiloContext.

EXPERIMENT: Silo monitors and contexts

To understand how silo monitors are used, and how they store silo contexts, let's take a look at the Ancillary Function Driver for Winsock (Afd.sys) and its monitor. First, let's dump the data structure that represents the monitor. Unfortunately, it is not in the symbol files, so we must do this as raw data.

```
lkd> dps poi(afd!AfdPodMonitor)
ffffe387'a79fc120  ffffe387'a7d760c0
ffffe387'a79fc128  ffffe387'a7b54b60
ffffe387'a79fc130  00000009'00000101
ffffe387'a79fc138  fffff807'be4b5b10 afd!AfdPodSiloCreateCallback
ffffe387'a79fc140  fffff807'be4bee40 afd!AfdPodSiloTerminateCallback
```

Now get the slot (9 in this example) from the host silo. Silos store their SLS in a field called Storage, which contains an array of data structures (slot entries), each storing a pointer, and some flags. We are multiplying the index by 2 to get the offset of the right slot entry, then accessing the second field (+1) to get the pointer to the context pointer:

```
lkd> r? @$t0 = (nt!_ESERVERSILO_GLOBALS*)@@masm(nt!PspHostSiloGlobals)
lkd> ?? ((void***)@$t0->Storage)[9 * 2 + 1]
void ** 0xffff988f'ab815941
```

Note that the permanent flag (0x2) is ORed into the pointer, mask it out, and then use the !object extension to confirm that this is truly a silo context.

```
lkd> !object (0xffff988f'ab815941 & -2)
Object: ffff988fab815940  Type: (ffff988faaac9f20) PsSiloContextNonPaged
```

Creation of a server silo

When a server silo is created, a job object is first used, because as mentioned, silos are a feature of job objects. This is done through the standard CreateJobObject API, which was modified as part of the Anniversary Update to now have an associated job ID, or JID. The JID comes from the same pool of numbers as the process and thread ID (PID and TID), which is the client ID (CID) table. As such, a JID is unique among not only other jobs, but also other processes and threads. Additionally, a container GUID is automatically created.

Next, the SetInformationJobObject API is used, with the create silo information class. This results in the Silo flag being set inside of the EJOB executive object that represents the job, as well as the allocation of the SLS slot array we saw earlier in the Storage member of EJOB. At this point, we have an *application silo*.

After this, the root object directory namespace is created with another information class and call to `SetInformationJobObject`. This new class requires the trusted computing base (TCB) privilege. As silos are normally created only by the Vmcompute service, this is to ensure that virtual object namespaces are not used maliciously to confuse applications and potentially break them. When this namespace is created, the object manager creates or opens a new Silos directory under the real host root (\) and appends the JID to create a new virtual root (e.g., \Silos\148\). It then creates the `Kernel-Objects`, `ObjectTypes`, `GLOBALROOT`, and `DosDevices` objects. The root is then stored as a silo context with whatever slot index is in `PsObjectDirectorySiloContextSlot`, which was allocated by the object manager at boot.

The next step is to convert this silo into a server silo, which is done with yet another call to `Set-InformationJobObject` and another information class. The `PspConvertSiloToServerSilo` function in the kernel now runs, which initializes the `ESERVERSILO_GLOBALS` structure we saw earlier as part of the experiment dumping the `PspHostSiloGlobals` with the `!silo` command. This initializes the silo shared user data, API Set mapping, SystemRoot, and the various silo contexts, such as the one used by the SRM to identify the Lsass.exe process. While conversion is in progress, silo monitors that have registered and started their callbacks will now receive a notification, such that they can add their own silo context data.

The final step, then, is to "boot up" the server silo by initializing a new service session for it. You can think of this as session 0, but for the server silo. This is done through an ALPC message sent to Smss `SmApiPort`, which contains a handle to the job object created by Vmcompute, which has now become a server silo job object. Just like when creating a real user session, Smss will clone a copy of itself, except this time, the clone will be associated with the job object at creation time. This will attach this new Smss copy to all the containerized elements of the server silo. Smss will believe this is session 0, and will perform its usual duties, such as launching Csrss.exe, Wininit.exe, Lsass.exe, etc. The "boot-up" process will continue as normal, with Wininit.exe then launching the Service Control Manager (Services.exe), which will then launch all the automatic start services, and so on. New applications can now execute in the server silo, which will run with a logon session associated with a virtual service account LUID, as described earlier.

Ancillary functionality

You may have noticed that the short description we've seen so far would obviously not result in this "boot" process actually succeeding. For example, as part of its initialization, it will want to create a named pipe called ntsvcs, which will require communicating with \Device\NamedPipe, or as Services. exe sees it, \Silos\JID\Device\NamedPipe. But no such device object exists!

As such, in order for device driver access to function, drivers must be enlightened and register their own silo monitors, which will then use the notifications to create their own per-silo device objects. The kernel provides an API, `PsAttachSiloToCurrentThread` (and matching `PsDetachSiloFromCurrent-Thread`), which temporarily sets the `Silo` field of the `ETHREAD` object to the passed-in job object. This will cause all access, such as that to the object manager, to be treated as if it were coming from the silo. The named pipe driver, for example, can use this functionality to then create a `NamedPipe` object under the \Device namespace, which will now be part of \Silos\JID\.

Another question is this: If applications launch in essentially a "service" session, how can they be interactive and process input and output? First, it is important to note that there is no GUI possible or permitted when launching under a Windows container, and attempting to use Remote Desktop (RDP) to access a container will also be impossible. As such, only command-line applications can execute. But even such applications normally need an "interactive" session. So how can *those* function? The secret lies in a special host process, CExecSvc.exe, which implements the container execution service. This service uses a named pipe to communicate with the Docker and Vmcompute services on the host, and is used to launch the actual containerized applications in the session. It is also used to emulate the console functionality that is normally provided by Conhost.exe, piping the input and output through the named pipe to the actual command prompt (or PowerShell) window that was used in the first place to execute the docker command on the host. This service is also used when using commands such as docker cp to transfer files from or to the container.

Container template

Even if we take into account all the device objects that can be created by drivers as silos are created, there are still countless *other* objects, created by the kernel as well as other components, with which services running in session 0 are expected to communicate, and vice-versa. In user mode, there is no silo monitor system that would somehow allow components to support this need, and forcing every driver to always create a specialized device object to represent each silo wouldn't make sense.

If a silo wants to play music on the sound card, it shouldn't have to use a separate device object to represent the exact same sound card as every other silo would access, as well as the host itself. This would only be needed if, say, per-silo object sound isolation was required. Another example is AFD. Although it does use a silo monitor, this is to identify which user-mode service hosts the DNS client that it needs to talk to service kernel-mode DNS requests, which will be per-silo, and not to create separate \Silos\JID\Device\Afd objects, as there is a single network/Winsock stack in the system.

Beyond drivers and objects, the registry also contains various pieces of global information that must be visible and exist across all silos, which the VReg component can then provide sandboxing around.

To support all these needs, the silo namespace, registry, and file system are defined by a specialized container template file, which is located in %SystemRoot%\System32\Containers\wsc.def by default, once the Windows Containers feature is enabled in the Add/Remove Windows Features dialog box. This file describes the object manager and registry namespace and rules surrounding it, allowing the definition of symbolic links as needed to the true objects on the host. It also describes which job object, volume mount points, and network isolation policies should be used. In theory, future uses of silo objects in the Windows operating system could allow different template files to be used to provide other kinds of containerized environments. The following is an excerpt from wsc.def on a system for which containers are enabled:

```
<!-- This is a silo definition file for cmdserver.exe -->
<container>
    <namespace>
        <ob shadow="false">
            <symlink name="FileSystem" path="\FileSystem" scope="Global" />
            <symlink name="PdcPort" path="\PdcPort" scope="Global" />
            <symlink name="SeRmCommandPort" path="\SeRmCommandPort" scope="Global" />
            <symlink name="Registry" path="\Registry" scope="Global" />
            <symlink name="Driver" path="\Driver" scope="Global" />
            <objdir name="BaseNamedObjects" clonesd="\BaseNamedObjects" shadow="false"/>
            <objdir name="GLOBAL??" clonesd="\GLOBAL??" shadow="false">
                <!-- Needed to map directories from the host -->
                <symlink name="ContainerMappedDirectories" path="\
ContainerMappedDirectories" scope="Local" />

                <!-- Valid links to \Device -->
                <symlink name="WMIDataDevice" path="\Device\WMIDataDevice" scope="Local"
/>

                <symlink name="UNC" path="\Device\Mup" scope="Local" />
...
            </objdir>
            <objdir name="Device" clonesd="\Device" shadow="false">
                <symlink name="Afd" path="\Device\Afd" scope="Global" />
                <symlink name="ahcache" path="\Device\ahcache" scope="Global" />
                <symlink name="CNG" path="\Device\CNG" scope="Global" />
                <symlink name="ConDrv" path="\Device\ConDrv" scope="Global" />
...
        <registry>
            <load
                key="$SiloHivesRoot$\Silo$TopLayerName$Software_Base"
                path="$TopLayerPath$\Hives\Software_Base"
                ReadOnly="true"
                />
...
            <mkkey
                name="ControlSet001"
                clonesd="\REGISTRY\Machine\SYSTEM\ControlSet001"
                />
            <mkkey
                name="ControlSet001\Control"
                clonesd="\REGISTRY\Machine\SYSTEM\ControlSet001\Control"
                />
```

Conclusion

This chapter examined the structure of processes, including the way processes are created and destroyed. We've seen how jobs can be used to manage a group of processes as a unit and how server silos can be used to usher in a new era of container support to Windows Server versions. The next chapter delves into threads—their structure and operation, how they're scheduled for execution, and the various ways they can be manipulated and used.

CHAPTER 4

Threads

This chapter explains the data structures and algorithms that deal with threads and thread scheduling in Windows. The first section shows how to create threads. Then the internals of threads and thread scheduling are described. The chapter concludes with a discussion of thread pools.

Creating threads

Before discussing the internal structures used to manage threads, let's take a look at creating threads from an API perspective to give a sense of the steps and arguments involved.

The simplest creation function in user mode is `CreateThread`. This function creates a thread in the current process, accepting the following arguments:

- **An optional security attributes structure** This specifies the security descriptor to attach to the newly created thread. It also specifies whether the thread handle is to be created as inheritable. (Handle inheritance is discussed in Chapter 8, "System mechanisms," in *Windows Internals Part 2*.)

- **An optional stack size** If zero is specified, a default is taken from the executable's header. This always applies to the first thread in a user-mode process. (Thread's stack is discussed further in Chapter 5, "Memory management.")

- **A function pointer** This serves as the entry point for the new thread's execution.

- **An optional argument** This is to pass to the thread's function.

- **Optional flags** One controls whether the thread starts suspended (CREATE_SUSPENDED). The other controls the interpretation of the stack size argument (initial committed size or maximum reserved size).

On successful completion, a non-zero handle is returned for the new thread and, if requested by the caller, the unique thread ID.

An extended thread creation function is `CreateRemoteThread`. This function accepts an extra argument (the first), which is a handle to a target process where the thread is to be created. You can use this function to inject a thread into another process. One common use of this technique is for a debugger to force a break in a debugged process. The debugger injects the thread, which immediately causes a breakpoint by calling the DebugBreak function. Another common use of this technique is for one process to obtain internal information about another process, which is easier when running within the target process context (for example, the entire address space is visible). This could be done for legitimate or malicious purposes.

To make CreateRemoteThread work, the process handle must have been obtained with enough access rights to allow such operation. As an extreme example, protected processes cannot be injected in this way because handles to such processes can be obtained with very limited rights only.

The final function worth mentioning here is CreateRemoteThreadEx, which is a superset of Create-Thread and CreateRemoteThread. In fact, the implementation of CreateThread and CreateRemote-Thread simply calls CreateRemoteThreadEx with the appropriate defaults. CreateRemoteThreadEx adds the ability to provide an attribute list (similar to the STARTUPINFOEX structure's role with an additional member over STARTUPINFO when creating processes). Examples of attributes include setting the ideal processor and group affinity (both discussed later in this chapter).

If all goes well, CreateRemoteThreadEx eventually calls NtCreateThreadEx in Ntdll.dll. This makes the usual transition to kernel mode, where execution continues in the executive function NtCreate-ThreadEx. There, the kernel mode part of thread creation occurs (described later in this chapter, in the "Birth of a thread" section).

Creating a thread in kernel mode is achieved with the PsCreateSystemThread function (documented in the WDK). This is useful for drivers that need independent work to be processes within the system process (meaning it's not associated with any particular process). Technically, the function can be used to create a thread under any process, which is less useful for drivers.

Exiting a kernel thread's function does not automatically destroy the thread object. Instead, drivers must call PsTerminateSystemThread from within the thread function to properly terminate the thread. Consequently, this function never returns.

Thread internals

This section discusses the internal structures used within the kernel (and some in user mode) to manage a thread. Unless explicitly stated otherwise, you can assume that anything in this section applies to both user-mode threads and kernel-mode system threads.

Data structures

At the operating-system (OS) level, a Windows thread is represented by an executive thread object. The executive thread object encapsulates an ETHREAD structure, which in turn contains a KTHREAD structure as its first member. These are illustrated in Figure 4-1 (ETHREAD) and Figure 4-2 (KTHREAD). The ETHREAD structure and the other structures it points to exist in the system address space. The only exception is the thread environment block (TEB), which exists in the process address space (similar to a PEB, because user-mode components need to access it).

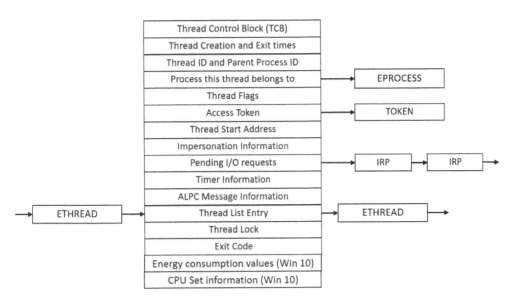

FIGURE 4-1 Important fields of the executive thread structure (ETHREAD).

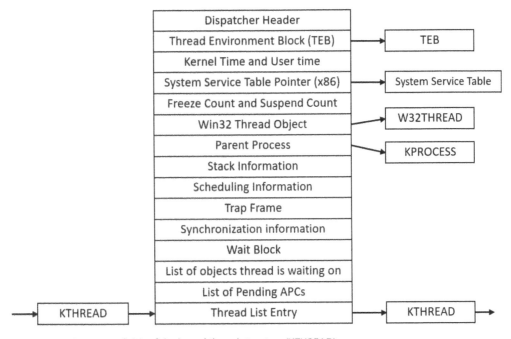

FIGURE 4-2 Important fields of the kernel thread structure (KTHREAD).

The Windows subsystem process (Csrss) maintains a parallel structure for each thread created in a Windows subsystem application, called the CSR_THREAD. For threads that have called a Windows subsystem USER or GDI function, the kernel-mode portion of the Windows subsystem (Win32k.sys) maintains a per-thread data structure (W32THREAD) that the KTHREAD structure points to.

Note The fact that the executive, high-level, graphics-related, Win32k thread structure is pointed to by KTHREAD instead of the ETHREAD appears to be a layer violation or oversight in the standard kernel's abstraction architecture. The scheduler and other low-level components do not use this field.

Most of the fields illustrated in Figure 4-1 are self-explanatory. The first member of the ETHREAD is called Tcb. This is short for *thread control block*, which is a structure of type KTHREAD. Following that are the thread identification information, the process identification information (including a pointer to the owning process so that its environment information can be accessed), security information in the form of a pointer to the access token and impersonation information, fields relating to Asynchronous Local Procedure Call (ALPC) messages, pending I/O requests (IRPs) and Windows 10–specific fields related to power management (described in Chapter 6 , "I/O system") and CPU Sets (described later in this chapter). Some of these key fields are covered in more detail elsewhere in this book. For more details on the internal structure of an ETHREAD structure, you can use the kernel debugger dt command to display its format.

Let's take a closer look at two of the key thread data structures referred to in the preceding text: ETHREAD and KTHREAD. The KTHREAD structure (which is the Tcb member of the ETHREAD) contains information that the Windows kernel needs to perform thread scheduling, synchronization, and time-keeping functions.

EXPERIMENT: Displaying ETHREAD and KTHREAD structures

You can display the ETHREAD and KTHREAD structures with the dt command in the kernel debugger. The following output shows the format of an ETHREAD on a 64-bit Windows 10 system:

```
1kd> dt nt!_ethread
   +0x000 Tcb               : _KTHREAD
   +0x5d8 CreateTime        : _LARGE_INTEGER
   +0x5e0 ExitTime          : _LARGE_INTEGER
...
   +0x7a0 EnergyValues      : Ptr64 _THREAD_ENERGY_VALUES
   +0x7a8 CmCellReferences  : Uint4B
   +0x7b0 SelectedCpuSets   : Uint8B
   +0x7b0 SelectedCpuSetsIndirect : Ptr64 Uint8B
   +0x7b8 Silo              : Ptr64 _EJOB
```

You can display the KTHREAD with a similar command or by typing **dt nt!_ETHREAD Tcb**, as shown in the experiment "Displaying the format of an EPROCESS structure" in Chapter 3, "Processes and jobs."

```
1kd> dt nt!_kthread
   +0x000 Header            : _DISPATCHER_HEADER
   +0x018 SListFaultAddress : Ptr64 Void
   +0x020 QuantumTarget     : Uint8B
   +0x028 InitialStack      : Ptr64 Void
   +0x030 StackLimit        : Ptr64 Void
   +0x038 StackBase         : Ptr64 Void
```

```
    +0x040 ThreadLock       : Uint8B
    +0x048 CycleTime        : Uint8B
    +0x050 CurrentRunTime   : Uint4B
...
    +0x5a0 ReadOperationCount : Int8B
    +0x5a8 WriteOperationCount : Int8B
    +0x5b0 OtherOperationCount : Int8B
    +0x5b8 ReadTransferCount : Int8B
    +0x5c0 WriteTransferCount : Int8B
    +0x5c8 OtherTransferCount : Int8B
    +0x5d0 QueuedScb        : Ptr64 _KSCB
```

EXPERIMENT: Using the kernel debugger !thread command

The kernel debugger !thread command dumps a subset of the information in the thread data structures. Some key elements of the information the kernel debugger displays can't be displayed by any utility, including the following information:

- Internal structure addresses
- Priority details
- Stack information
- The pending I/O request list
- For threads in a wait state, the list of objects the thread is waiting for

To display thread information, use either the !process command (which displays all the threads of a process after displaying the process information) or the !thread command with the address of a thread object to display a specific thread.

Let's find all instances of explorer.exe:

```
lkd> !process 0 0 explorer.exe
PROCESS ffffe00017f3e7c0
    SessionId: 1  Cid: 0b7c    Peb: 00291000  ParentCid: 0c34
    DirBase: 19b264000  ObjectTable: ffffc00007268cc0  HandleCount: 2248.
    Image: explorer.exe


PROCESS ffffe00018c817c0
    SessionId: 1  Cid: 23b0    Peb: 00256000  ParentCid: 03f0
    DirBase: 2d4010000  ObjectTable: ffffc0001aef0480  HandleCount: 2208.
    Image: explorer.exe
```

We'll select one of the instances and show its threads:

```
lkd> !process ffffe00018c817c0 2
PROCESS ffffe00018c817c0
    SessionId: 1  Cid: 23b0    Peb: 00256000  ParentCid: 03f0
    DirBase: 2d4010000  ObjectTable: ffffc0001aef0480  HandleCount: 2232.
    Image: explorer.exe
```

```
        THREAD ffffe0001ac3c080  Cid 23b0.2b88  Teb: 0000000000257000 Win32Thread:
ffffe0001570ca20 WAIT: (UserRequest) UserMode Non-Alertable
        ffffe0001b6eb470  SynchronizationEvent

        THREAD ffffe0001af10800  Cid 23b0.2f40  Teb: 0000000000265000 Win32Thread:
ffffe000156688a0 WAIT: (UserRequest) UserMode Non-Alertable
        ffffe000172ad4f0  SynchronizationEvent
        ffffe0001ac26420  SynchronizationEvent

        THREAD ffffe0001b69a080  Cid 23b0.2f4c  Teb: 0000000000267000 Win32Thread:
ffffe000192c5350 WAIT: (UserRequest) UserMode Non-Alertable
        ffffe00018d83c00  SynchronizationEvent
        ffffe0001552ff40  SynchronizationEvent

...

        THREAD ffffe00023422080  Cid 23b0.3d8c  Teb: 00000000003cf000 Win32Thread:
ffffe0001eccd790 WAIT: (WrQueue) UserMode Alertable
        ffffe0001aec9080  QueueObject

        THREAD ffffe00023f23080  Cid 23b0.3af8  Teb: 00000000003d1000 Win32Thread:
0000000000000000 WAIT: (WrQueue) UserMode Alertable
        ffffe0001aec9080  QueueObject

        THREAD ffffe000230bf800  Cid 23b0.2d6c  Teb: 00000000003d3000 Win32Thread:
0000000000000000 WAIT: (WrQueue) UserMode Alertable
        ffffe0001aec9080  QueueObject

        THREAD ffffe0001f0b5800  Cid 23b0.3398  Teb: 00000000003e3000 Win32Thread:
0000000000000000 WAIT: (UserRequest) UserMode Alertable
        ffffe0001d19d790  SynchronizationEvent
        ffffe00022b42660  SynchronizationTimer
```

The list of threads is truncated for the sake of space. Each thread shows its address (ETHREAD), which can be passed to the `!thread` command; its client ID (`Cid`)–process ID and thread ID (the process ID for all the preceding threads is the same, as they are part of the same explorer.exe process); the Thread Environment Block (TEB, discussed momentarily); and the thread state (most should be in the `Wait` state, with the reason for the wait in parentheses). The next line may show a list of synchronization objects the threads is waiting on.

To get more information on a specific thread, pass its address to the `!thread` command:

```
lkd> !thread ffffe0001d45d800
THREAD ffffe0001d45d800  Cid 23b0.452c  Teb: 000000000026d000 Win32Thread:
ffffe0001aace630 WAIT: (UserRequest) UserMode Non-Alertable
    ffffe00023678350  NotificationEvent
    ffffe00022aeb370  Semaphore Limit 0xffff
    ffffe000225645b0  SynchronizationEvent
Not impersonating
DeviceMap                 ffffc00004f7ddb0
Owning Process            ffffe00018c817c0       Image:        explorer.exe
```

```
Attached Process          N/A            Image:         N/A
Wait Start TickCount      7233205        Ticks: 270 (0:00:00:04.218)
Context Switch Count      6570           IdealProcessor: 7
UserTime                  00:00:00.078
KernelTime                00:00:00.046
Win32 Start Address 0c
Stack Init ffffd000271d4c90 Current ffffd000271d3f80
Base ffffd000271d5000 Limit ffffd000271cf000 Call 0000000000000000
Priority 9 BasePriority 8 PriorityDecrement 0 IoPriority 2 PagePriority 5
GetContextState failed, 0x80004001
Unable to get current machine context, HRESULT 0x80004001
Child-SP          RetAddr          : Args to Child                             : Call Site
ffffd000'271d3fc0 fffff803'bef086ca : 00000000'00000000 00000000'00000001
00000000'00000000 00000000'00000000 : nt!KiSwapContext+0x76
ffffd000'271d4100 fffff803'bef08159 : ffffe000'1d45d800 fffff803'00000000
ffffe000'1aec9080 00000000'0000000f : nt!KiSwapThread+0x15a
ffffd000'271d41b0 fffff803'bef09cfe : 00000000'00000000 00000000'00000000
ffffe000'0000000f 00000000'00000003 : nt!KiCommitThreadWait+0x149
ffffd000'271d4240 fffff803'bf2a445d : ffffd000'00000003 ffffd000'271d43c0
00000000'00000000 fffff960'00000006 : nt!KeWaitForMultipleObjects+0x24e
ffffd000'271d4300 fffff803'bf2fa246 : fffff803'bf1a6b40 ffffd000'271d4810
ffffd000'271d4858 ffffe000'20aeca60 : nt!ObWaitForMultipleObjects+0x2bd
ffffd000'271d4810 fffff803'befdefa3 : 00000000'00000fa0 fffff803'bef02aad
ffffe000'1d45d800 00000000'1e22f198 : nt!NtWaitForMultipleObjects+0xf6
ffffd000'271d4a90 00007ffe'f42b5c24 : 00000000'00000000 00000000'00000000
00000000'00000000 00000000'00000000 : nt!KiSystemServiceCopyEnd+0x13 (TrapFrame @
ffffd000'271d4b00)
00000000'1e22f178 00000000'00000000 : 00000000'00000000 00000000'00000000
00000000'00000000 00000000'00000000 : 0x00007ffe'f42b5c24
```

There is a lot of information about the thread, such as its priority, stack details, user and kernel times, and much more. You'll look at many of these details throughout this chapter and in Chapter 5, "Memory management," and Chapter 6, "I/O system."

EXPERIMENT: Viewing thread information with tlist

The following output is the detailed display of a process produced by using tlist in the Debugging Tools for Windows. (Make sure you run tlist from the same "bitness" as the target process.) Notice that the thread list shows Win32StartAddr. This is the address passed to the CreateThread function by the application. All the other utilities (except Process Explorer) that show the thread start address show the actual start address (a function in Ntdll.dll), not the application-specified start address.

The following output is from running tlist on Word 2016 (truncated):

```
C:\Dbg\x86>tlist winword
 120 WINWORD.EXE       Chapter04.docm - Word
   CWD:     C:\Users\pavely\Documents\
```

```
   CmdLine: "C:\Program Files (x86)\Microsoft Office\Root\Office16\WINWORD.EXE" /n
"D:\OneDrive\WindowsInternalsBook\7thEdition\Chapter04\Chapter04.docm
   VirtualSize:    778012 KB   PeakVirtualSize:    832680 KB
   WorkingSetSize:185336 KB    PeakWorkingSetSize:227144 KB
   NumberOfThreads: 45
   12132 Win32StartAddr:0x00921000 LastErr:0x00000000 State:Waiting
   15540 Win32StartAddr:0x6cc2fdd8 LastErr:0x00000000 State:Waiting
   7096 Win32StartAddr:0x6cc3c6b2 LastErr:0x00000006 State:Waiting
   17696 Win32StartAddr:0x77c1c6d0 LastErr:0x00000000 State:Waiting
   17492 Win32StartAddr:0x77c1c6d0 LastErr:0x00000000 State:Waiting
   4052 Win32StartAddr:0x70aa5cf7 LastErr:0x00000000 State:Waiting
   14096 Win32StartAddr:0x70aa41d4 LastErr:0x00000000 State:Waiting
   6220 Win32StartAddr:0x70aa41d4 LastErr:0x00000000 State:Waiting
   7204 Win32StartAddr:0x77c1c6d0 LastErr:0x00000000 State:Waiting
   1196 Win32StartAddr:0x6ea016c0 LastErr:0x00000057 State:Waiting
   8848 Win32StartAddr:0x70aa41d4 LastErr:0x00000000 State:Waiting
   3352 Win32StartAddr:0x77c1c6d0 LastErr:0x00000000 State:Waiting
   11612 Win32StartAddr:0x77c1c6d0 LastErr:0x00000000 State:Waiting
   17420 Win32StartAddr:0x77c1c6d0 LastErr:0x00000000 State:Waiting
   13612 Win32StartAddr:0x77c1c6d0 LastErr:0x00000000 State:Waiting
   15052 Win32StartAddr:0x77c1c6d0 LastErr:0x00000000 State:Waiting
   ...
   12080 Win32StartAddr:0x77c1c6d0 LastErr:0x00000000 State:Waiting
   9456 Win32StartAddr:0x77c1c6d0 LastErr:0x00002f94 State:Waiting
   9808 Win32StartAddr:0x77c1c6d0 LastErr:0x00000000 State:Waiting
   16208 Win32StartAddr:0x77c1c6d0 LastErr:0x00000000 State:Waiting
   9396 Win32StartAddr:0x77c1c6d0 LastErr:0x00000000 State:Waiting
   2688 Win32StartAddr:0x70aa41d4 LastErr:0x00000000 State:Waiting
   9100 Win32StartAddr:0x70aa41d4 LastErr:0x00000000 State:Waiting
   18364 Win32StartAddr:0x70aa41d4 LastErr:0x00000000 State:Waiting
   11180 Win32StartAddr:0x70aa41d4 LastErr:0x00000000 State:Waiting
  16.0.6741.2037 shp  0x00920000  C:\Program Files (x86)\Microsoft Office\Root\
Office16\WINWORD.EXE
  10.0.10586.122 shp  0x77BF0000  C:\windows\SYSTEM32\ntdll.dll
   10.0.10586.0 shp  0x75540000  C:\windows\SYSTEM32\KERNEL32.DLL
  10.0.10586.162 shp  0x77850000  C:\windows\SYSTEM32\KERNELBASE.dll
   10.0.10586.63 shp  0x75AF0000  C:\windows\SYSTEM32\ADVAPI32.dll
  ...
   10.0.10586.0 shp  0x68540000  C:\Windows\SYSTEM32\VssTrace.DLL
   10.0.10586.0 shp  0x5C390000  C:\Windows\SYSTEM32\adsldpc.dll
  10.0.10586.122 shp  0x5DE60000  C:\Windows\SYSTEM32\taskschd.dll
   10.0.10586.0 shp  0x5E3F0000  C:\Windows\SYSTEM32\srmstormod.dll
   10.0.10586.0 shp  0x5DCA0000  C:\Windows\SYSTEM32\srmscan.dll
   10.0.10586.0 shp  0x5D2E0000  C:\Windows\SYSTEM32\msdrm.dll
   10.0.10586.0 shp  0x711E0000  C:\Windows\SYSTEM32\srm_ps.dll
   10.0.10586.0 shp  0x56680000  C:\windows\System32\OpcServices.dll
                     0x5D240000  C:\Program Files (x86)\Common Files\Microsoft
Shared\Office16\WXPNSE.DLL
  16.0.6701.1023 shp  0x77E80000  C:\Program Files (x86)\Microsoft Office\Root\
Office16\GROOVEEX.DLL
   10.0.10586.0 shp  0x693F0000  C:\windows\system32\dataexchange.dll
```

The TEB, illustrated in Figure 4-3, is one of the data structures explained in this section that exists in the process address space (as opposed to the system space). Internally, it is made up of a header called the *Thread Information Block* (*TIB*), which mainly existed for compatibility with OS/2 and Win9x applications. It also allows exception and stack information to be kept into a smaller structure when creating new threads by using an initial TIB.

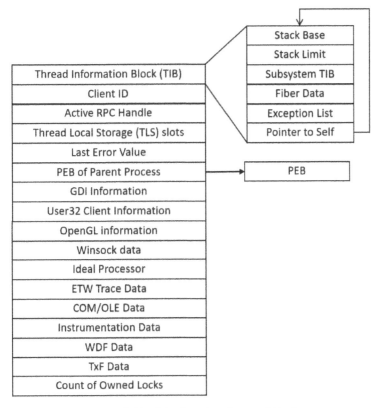

FIGURE 4-3 Important fields of the thread environment block.

The TEB stores context information for the image loader and various Windows DLLs. Because these components run in user mode, they need a data structure writable from user mode. That's why this structure exists in the process address space instead of in the system space, where it would be writable only from kernel mode. You can find the address of the TEB with the kernel debugger !thread command.

EXPERIMENT: Examining the TEB

You can dump the TEB structure with the !teb command in the kernel or user-mode debugger. The command can be used on its own to dump the TEB for the current thread of the debugger or with a TEB address to get it for an arbitrary thread. In case of a kernel debugger, the current process must be set before issuing the command on a TEB address so that the correct process context is used.

To view the TEB with a user-mode debugger, follow these steps. (You'll learn how to view the TEB using a kernel debugger in the next experiment.)

1. Open WinDbg.

2. Open the **File** menu and choose **Run Executable**.

3. Navigate to c:\windows\system32\Notepad.exe. The debugger should break at the initial breakpoint.

4. Issue the **!teb** command to view the TEB of the only thread existing at the moment (the example is from 64 bit Windows):

```
0:000> !teb
TEB at 000000ef125c1000
    ExceptionList:          0000000000000000
    StackBase:              000000ef12290000
    StackLimit:             000000ef1227f000
    SubSystemTib:           0000000000000000
    FiberData:              0000000000001e00
    ArbitraryUserPointer:   0000000000000000
    Self:                   000000ef125c1000
    EnvironmentPointer:     0000000000000000
    ClientId:               00000000000021bc . 0000000000001b74
    RpcHandle:              0000000000000000
    Tls Storage:            00000266e572b600
    PEB Address:            000000ef125c0000
    LastErrorValue:         0
    LastStatusValue:        0
    Count Owned Locks:      0
    HardErrorMode:          0
```

5. Enter the **g** command or press **F5** to proceed with running Notepad.

6. In Notepad, open the **File** menu and choose **Open**. Then click **Cancel** to dismiss the Open File dialog box.

7. Press **Ctrl+Break** or open the **Debug** menu and choose **Break** to forcibly break into the process.

8. Enter the **~** (tilde) command to show all threads in the process. You should see something like this:

```
0:005> ~
   0  Id: 21bc.1b74 Suspend: 1 Teb: 000000ef'125c1000 Unfrozen
   1  Id: 21bc.640 Suspend: 1 Teb: 000000ef'125e3000 Unfrozen
   2  Id: 21bc.1a98 Suspend: 1 Teb: 000000ef'125e5000 Unfrozen
   3  Id: 21bc.860 Suspend: 1 Teb: 000000ef'125e7000 Unfrozen
   4  Id: 21bc.28e0 Suspend: 1 Teb: 000000ef'125c9000 Unfrozen
.  5  Id: 21bc.23e0 Suspend: 1 Teb: 000000ef'12400000 Unfrozen
   6  Id: 21bc.244c Suspend: 1 Teb: 000000ef'125eb000 Unfrozen
   7  Id: 21bc.168c Suspend: 1 Teb: 000000ef'125ed000 Unfrozen
```

```
     8  Id: 21bc.1c90 Suspend: 1 Teb: 000000ef'125ef000 Unfrozen
     9  Id: 21bc.1558 Suspend: 1 Teb: 000000ef'125f1000 Unfrozen
    10  Id: 21bc.a64 Suspend: 1 Teb: 000000ef'125f3000 Unfrozen
    11  Id: 21bc.20c4 Suspend: 1 Teb: 000000ef'125f5000 Unfrozen
    12  Id: 21bc.1524 Suspend: 1 Teb: 000000ef'125f7000 Unfrozen
    13  Id: 21bc.1738 Suspend: 1 Teb: 000000ef'125f9000 Unfrozen
    14  Id: 21bc.f48 Suspend: 1 Teb: 000000ef'125fb000 Unfrozen
    15  Id: 21bc.17bc Suspend: 1 Teb: 000000ef'125fd000 Unfrozen
```

9. Each thread shows its TEB address. You can examine a specific thread by specifying its TEB address to the !teb command. Here's an example for thread 9 from the preceding output:

```
0:005> !teb 000000ef'125f1000
TEB at 000000ef125f1000
    ExceptionList:        0000000000000000
    StackBase:            000000ef13400000
    StackLimit:           000000ef133ef000
    SubSystemTib:         0000000000000000
    FiberData:            0000000000001e00
    ArbitraryUserPointer: 0000000000000000
    Self:                 000000ef125f1000
    EnvironmentPointer:   0000000000000000
    ClientId:             00000000000021bc . 0000000000001558
    RpcHandle:            0000000000000000
    Tls Storage:          00000266ea1af280
    PEB Address:          000000ef125c0000
    LastErrorValue:       0
    LastStatusValue:      c0000034
    Count Owned Locks:    0
    HardErrorMode:        0
```

10. Of course, it's possible to view the actual structure with the TEB address (truncated to conserve space):

```
0:005> dt ntdll!_teb 000000ef'125f1000
    +0x000 NtTib            : _NT_TIB
    +0x038 EnvironmentPointer : (null)
    +0x040 ClientId         : _CLIENT_ID
    +0x050 ActiveRpcHandle  : (null)
    +0x058 ThreadLocalStoragePointer : 0x00000266'ea1af280 Void
    +0x060 ProcessEnvironmentBlock : 0x000000ef'125c0000 _PEB
    +0x068 LastErrorValue   : 0
    +0x06c CountOfOwnedCriticalSections : 0
...
    +0x1808 LockCount       : 0
    +0x180c WowTebOffset    : 0n0
    +0x1810 ResourceRetValue : 0x00000266'ea2a5e50 Void
    +0x1818 ReservedForWdf  : (null)
    +0x1820 ReservedForCrt  : 0
    +0x1828 EffectiveContainerId : _GUID {00000000-0000-0000-0000-000000000000}
```

EXPERIMENT: Examining the TEB with a kernel debugger

Follow these steps to view the TEB with a kernel debugger:

1. Find the process for which a thread's TEB is of interest. For example, the following looks for explorer.exe processes and lists its threads with basic information (truncated):

```
lkd> !process 0 2 explorer.exe
PROCESS ffffe0012bea7840
    SessionId: 2  Cid: 10d8     Peb: 00251000  ParentCid: 10bc
    DirBase: 76e12000  ObjectTable: ffffc000e1ca0c80  HandleCount: <Data Not
Accessible>
    Image: explorer.exe

        THREAD ffffe0012bf53080  Cid 10d8.10dc  Teb: 0000000000252000
Win32Thread: ffffe0012c1532f0 WAIT: (WrUserRequest) UserMode Non-Alertable
            ffffe0012c257fe0  SynchronizationEvent

        THREAD ffffe0012a30f080  Cid 10d8.114c  Teb: 0000000000266000
Win32Thread: ffffe0012c2e9a20 WAIT: (UserRequest) UserMode Alertable
            ffffe0012bab85d0  SynchronizationEvent

        THREAD ffffe0012c8bd080  Cid 10d8.1178  Teb: 000000000026c000
Win32Thread: ffffe0012a801310 WAIT: (UserRequest) UserMode Alertable
            ffffe0012bfd9250  NotificationEvent
            ffffe0012c9512f0  NotificationEvent
            ffffe0012c876b80  NotificationEvent
            ffffe0012c010fe0  NotificationEvent
            ffffe0012d0ba7e0  NotificationEvent
            ffffe0012cf9d1e0  NotificationEvent
...

        THREAD ffffe0012c8be080  Cid 10d8.1180  Teb: 0000000000270000
Win32Thread: 0000000000000000 WAIT: (UserRequest) UserMode Alertable
            fffff80156946440  NotificationEvent

        THREAD ffffe0012afd4040  Cid 10d8.1184  Teb: 0000000000272000
Win32Thread: ffffe0012c7c53a0 WAIT: (UserRequest) UserMode Non-Alertable
            ffffe0012a3dafe0  NotificationEvent
            ffffe0012c21ee70  Semaphore Limit 0xffff
            ffffe0012c8db6f0  SynchronizationEvent

        THREAD ffffe0012c88a080  Cid 10d8.1188  Teb: 0000000000274000
Win32Thread: 0000000000000000 WAIT: (UserRequest) UserMode Alertable
            ffffe0012afd4920  NotificationEvent
            ffffe0012c87b480  SynchronizationEvent
            ffffe0012c87b400  SynchronizationEvent
...
```

2. If more than one explorer.exe process exists, select one arbitrarily for the following steps.

3. Each thread shows the address of its TEB. Because the TEB is in user space, the address has meaning only in the context of the relevant process. You need to switch to the process/thread as seen by the debugger. Select the first thread of explorer because its kernel stack is probably resident in physical memory. Otherwise, you'll get an error.

```
lkd> .thread /p ffffe0012bf53080
Implicit thread is now ffffe001'2bf53080
Implicit process is now ffffe001'2bea7840
```

4. This switches the context to the specified thread (and by extension, the process). Now you can use the !teb command with the TEB address listed for that thread:

```
lkd> !teb 0000000000252000
TEB at 0000000000252000
    ExceptionList:        0000000000000000
    StackBase:            00000000000d0000
    StackLimit:           00000000000c2000
    SubSystemTib:         0000000000000000
    FiberData:            0000000000001e00
    ArbitraryUserPointer: 0000000000000000
    Self:                 0000000000252000
    EnvironmentPointer:   0000000000000000
    ClientId:             00000000000010d8 . 00000000000010dc
    RpcHandle:            0000000000000000
    Tls Storage:          0000000009f73f30
    PEB Address:          0000000000251000
    LastErrorValue:       0
    LastStatusValue:      c0150008
    Count Owned Locks:    0
    HardErrorMode:        0
```

The CSR_THREAD, illustrated in Figure 4-4 is analogous to the data structure of CSR_PROCESS, but it's applied to threads. As you might recall, this is maintained by each Csrss process within a session and identifies the Windows subsystem threads running within it. CSR_THREAD stores a handle that Csrss keeps for the thread, various flags, the client ID (thread ID and process ID), and a copy of the thread's creation time. Note that threads are registered with Csrss when they send their first message to Csrss, typically due to some API that requires notifying Csrss of some operation or condition.

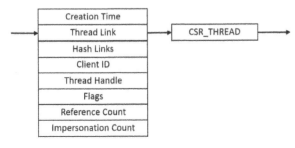

FIGURE 4-4 Fields of the CSR thread.

Finally, the W32THREAD structure, illustrated in Figure 4-5, is analogous to the data structure of W32PROCESS, but it's applied to threads This structure mainly contains information useful for the GDI subsystem (brushes and Device Context attributes) and DirectX, as well as for the User Mode Print Driver (UMPD) framework that vendors use to write user-mode printer drivers. Finally, it contains a rendering state useful for desktop compositing and anti-aliasing.

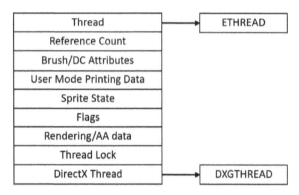

FIGURE 4-5   Fields of the Win32k thread.

Birth of a thread

A thread's life cycle starts when a process (in the context of some thread, such as the thread running the main function) creates a new thread. The request filters down to the Windows executive, where the process manager allocates space for a thread object and calls the kernel to initialize the thread control block (KTHREAD). As mentioned, the various thread-creation functions eventually end up at CreateRemote-ThreadEx. The following steps are taken inside this function in Kernel32.dll to create a Windows thread:

1. The function converts the Windows API parameters to native flags and builds a native structure describing object parameters (OBJECT_ATTRIBUTES, described in Chapter 8 in Part 2).

2. It builds an attribute list with two entries: client ID and TEB address. (For more information on attribute lists, see the section "Flow of CreateProcess" in Chapter 3.)

3. It determines whether the thread is created in the calling process or another process indicated by the handle passed in. If the handle is equal to the pseudo handle returned from GetCurrent-Process (with a value of -1), then it's the same process. If the process handle is different, it could still be a valid handle to the same process, so a call is made to NtQueryInformation-Process (in Ntdll) to find out whether that is indeed the case.

4. It calls NtCreateThreadEx (in Ntdll) to make the transition to the executive in kernel mode and continues inside a function with the same name and arguments.

5. NtCreateThreadEx (inside the executive) creates and initializes the user-mode thread context (its structure is architecture-specific) and then calls PspCreateThread to create a suspended executive thread object. (For a description of the steps performed by this function, see the descriptions of stage 3 and stage 5 in Chapter 3 in the section "Flow of CreateProcess.") Then the function returns, eventually ending back in user mode at CreateRemoteThreadEx.

6. CreateRemoteThreadEx allocates an activation context for the thread used by side-by-side assembly support. It then queries the activation stack to see if it requires activation and activates it if needed. The activation stack pointer is saved in the new thread's TEB.

7. Unless the caller created the thread with the CREATE_SUSPENDED flag set, the thread is now resumed so that it can be scheduled for execution. When the thread starts running, it executes the steps described in Chapter 3 in the section "Stage 7: performing process initialization in the context of the new process" before calling the actual user's specified start address.

8. The thread handle and the thread ID are returned to the caller.

Examining thread activity

Examining thread activity is especially important if you are trying to determine why a process that is hosting multiple services is running (such as Svchost.exe, Dllhost.exe, or Lsass.exe) or why a process has stopped responding.

There are several tools that expose various elements of the state of Windows threads: WinDbg (in user-process attach and kernel-debugging mode), Performance Monitor, and Process Explorer. (The tools that show thread-scheduling information are listed in the section "Thread scheduling.")

To view the threads in a process with Process Explorer, select a process and double-click it to open its Properties dialog box. Alternatively, right-click the process and select the **Properties** menu item.

Then click the **Threads** tab. This tab shows a list of the threads in the process and four columns of information for each thread: its ID, the percentage of CPU consumed (based on the refresh interval configured), the number of cycles charged to the thread, and the thread start address. You can sort by any of these four columns.

New threads that are created are highlighted in green, and threads that exit are highlighted in red. (To configure the highlight duration, open the **Options** menu and choose **Difference Highlight Duration**.) This might be helpful to discover unnecessary thread creation occurring in a process. (In general, threads should be created at process startup, not every time a request is processed inside a process.)

As you select each thread in the list, Process Explorer displays the thread ID, start time, state, CPU time counters, number of cycles charged, number of context switches, the ideal processor and its group, and the I/O priority, memory priority, and base and current (dynamic) priority. There is a Kill button, which terminates an individual thread, but this should be used with extreme care. Another option is the Suspend button, which prevents the thread from forward execution and thus prevents a runaway thread from consuming CPU time. However, this can also lead to deadlocks and should be used with the same care as the Kill button. Finally, the Permissions button allows you to view the security descriptor of the thread. (See Chapter 7, "Security," for more information on security descriptors.)

Unlike Task Manager and all other process/processor monitoring tools, Process Explorer uses the clock cycle counter designed for thread run-time accounting (described later in this chapter) instead of the clock interval timer, so you will see a significantly different view of CPU consumption using Process Explorer. This is because many threads run for such a short time that they are seldom (if ever) the currently running thread when the clock interval timer interrupt occurs. As a result, they are not charged for much of their CPU time, leading clock-based tools to perceive a CPU usage of 0 percent. On the other hand, the total number of clock cycles represents the actual number of processor cycles that each thread in the process accrued. It is independent of the clock interval timer's resolution because the count is maintained internally by the processor at each cycle and updated by Windows at each interrupt entry. (A final accumulation is done before a context switch.)

The thread start address is displayed in the form *module! function*, where *module* is the name of the .EXE or .DLL. The function name relies on access to symbol files for the module (see the section "Experiment: Viewing process details with Process Explorer" in Chapter 1, "Concepts and tools"). If you are unsure what the module is, click the **Module** button to open an Explorer file Properties dialog box for the module containing the thread's start address (for example, the .EXE or .DLL).

 Note For threads created by the Windows `CreateThread` function, Process Explorer displays the function passed to `CreateThread`, not the actual thread start function. This is because all Windows threads start at a common thread startup wrapper function (`RtlUserThreadStart` in Ntdll.dll). If Process Explorer showed the actual start address, most threads in processes would appear to have started at the same address, which would not be helpful in trying to understand what code the thread was executing. However, if Process Explorer can't query the user-defined startup address (such as in the case of a protected process), it will show the wrapper function, so you will see all threads starting at `RtlUserThreadStart`.

The thread start address displayed might not be enough information to pinpoint what the thread is doing and which component within the process is responsible for the CPU consumed by the thread. This is especially true if the thread start address is a generic startup function—for example, if the function name does not indicate what the thread is actually doing. In this case, examining the thread stack might answer the question. To view the stack for a thread, double-click the thread of interest (or select it and click the **Stack** button). Process Explorer displays the thread's stack (both user and kernel, if the thread was in kernel mode).

Note   While the user-mode debuggers (WinDbg, Ntsd, and Cdb) permit you to attach to a process and display the user stack for a thread, Process Explorer shows both the user and kernel stack in one easy click of a button. You can also examine user and kernel thread stacks using WinDbg in local kernel debugging mode, as the next two experiments demonstrate.

When looking at 32-bit processes running on 64-bit systems as a Wow64 process (see Chapter 8 in Part 2 for more information on Wow64), Process Explorer shows both the 32-bit and 64-bit stack for threads. Because at the time of the real (64 bit) system call, the thread has been switched to a 64-bit stack and context, simply looking at the thread's 64-bit stack would reveal only half the story—the 64-bit part of the thread, with Wow64's thunking code. So, when examining Wow64 processes, be sure to take into account both the 32-bit and 64-bit stacks.

EXPERIMENT: Viewing a thread stack with a user-mode debugger

Follow these steps to attach WinDbg to a process and view thread information and its stack:

1. Run notepad.exe and WinDbg.exe.

2. In WinDbg, open the **File** menu and select **Attach to Process**.

3. Find the notepad.exe instance and click **OK** to attach. The debugger should break into Notepad.

4. List the existing threads in the process with the ~ command. Each thread shows its debugger ID, the client ID (*ProcessID. ThreadID*), its suspend count (this should be 1 most of the time, as it is suspended because of the breakpoint), the TEB address, and whether it has been frozen using a debugger command.

```
0:005> ~
   0  Id: 612c.5f68 Suspend: 1 Teb: 00000022'41da2000 Unfrozen
   1  Id: 612c.5564 Suspend: 1 Teb: 00000022'41da4000 Unfrozen
   2  Id: 612c.4f88 Suspend: 1 Teb: 00000022'41da6000 Unfrozen
   3  Id: 612c.5608 Suspend: 1 Teb: 00000022'41da8000 Unfrozen
   4  Id: 612c.cf4 Suspend: 1 Teb: 00000022'41daa000 Unfrozen
.  5  Id: 612c.9f8 Suspend: 1 Teb: 00000022'41db0000 Unfrozen
```

5. Notice the dot preceding thread 5 in the output. This is the current debugger thread. Issue the **k** command to view the call stack:

```
0:005> k
 # Child-SP          RetAddr           Call Site
00 00000022'421ff7e8 00007ff8'504d9031 ntdll!DbgBreakPoint
01 00000022'421ff7f0 00007ff8'501b8102 ntdll!DbgUiRemoteBreakin+0x51
02 00000022'421ff820 00007ff8'5046c5b4 KERNEL32!BaseThreadInitThunk+0x22
03 00000022'421ff850 00000000'00000000 ntdll!RtlUserThreadStart+0x34
```

6. The debugger injected a thread into Notepad's process that issues a breakpoint instruction (DbgBreakPoint). To view the call stack of another thread, use the **~nk** command, where *n* is the thread number as seen by WinDbg. (This does not change the current debugger thread.) Here's an example for thread 2:

```
0:005> ~2k
 # Child-SP          RetAddr           Call Site
00 00000022'41f7f9e8 00007ff8'5043b5e8 ntdll!ZwWaitForWorkViaWorkerFactory+0x14
01 00000022'41f7f9f0 00007ff8'501b8102 ntdll!TppWorkerThread+0x298
02 00000022'41f7fe00 00007ff8'5046c5b4 KERNEL32!BaseThreadInitThunk+0x22
03 00000022'41f7fe30 00000000'00000000 ntdll!RtlUserThreadStart+0x34
```

7. To switch the debugger to another thread, use the **~ns** command (again, *n* is the thread number). Let's switch to thread 0 and show its stack:

```
0:005> ~0s
USER32!ZwUserGetMessage+0x14:
00007ff8'502e21d4 c3                    ret
0:000> k
 # Child-SP          RetAddr           Call Site
00 00000022'41e7f048 00007ff8'502d3075 USER32!ZwUserGetMessage+0x14
01 00000022'41e7f050 00007ff6'88273bb3 USER32!GetMessageW+0x25
02 00000022'41e7f080 00007ff6'882890b5 notepad!WinMain+0x27b
03 00000022'41e7f180 00007ff8'341229b8 notepad!__mainCRTStartup+0x1ad
04 00000022'41e7f9f0 00007ff8'5046c5b4 KERNEL32!BaseThreadInitThunk+0x22
05 00000022'41e7fa20 00000000'00000000 ntdll!RtlUserThreadStart+0x34
```

8. Note that even though a thread might be in kernel mode at the time, a user-mode debugger shows its last function that's still in user mode (ZwUserGetMessage in the preceding output).

EXPERIMENT: Viewing a thread stack with a local kernel-mode debugger

In this experiment, you'll use a local kernel debugger to view a thread's stack (both user mode and kernel mode). The experiment uses one of Explorer's threads, but you can try it with other processes or threads.

1. Show all the processes running the image explorer.exe. (Note that you may see more than one instance of Explorer if the Launch Folder Windows in a Separate Process

option in Explorer options is selected. One process manages the desktop and taskbar, while the other manages Explorer windows.)

```
lkd> !process 0 0 explorer.exe
PROCESS ffffe00197398080
    SessionId: 1  Cid: 18a0    Peb: 00320000  ParentCid: 1840
    DirBase: 17c028000  ObjectTable: ffffc000bd4aa880  HandleCount: <Data
Not Accessible>
    Image: explorer.exe

PROCESS ffffe00196039080
    SessionId: 1  Cid: 1f30    Peb: 00290000  ParentCid: 0238
    DirBase: 24cc7b000  ObjectTable: ffffc000bbbef740  HandleCount: <Data
Not Accessible>
    Image: explorer.exe
```

2. Select one instance and show its thread summary:

```
lkd> !process ffffe00196039080 2
PROCESS ffffe00196039080
    SessionId: 1  Cid: 1f30    Peb: 00290000  ParentCid: 0238
    DirBase: 24cc7b000  ObjectTable: ffffc000bbbef740  HandleCount: <Data
Not Accessible>
    Image: explorer.exe

        THREAD ffffe0019758f080  Cid 1f30.0718  Teb: 0000000000291000
Win32Thread: ffffe001972e3220 WAIT: (UserRequest) UserMode Non-Alertable
        ffffe00192c08150  SynchronizationEvent

        THREAD ffffe00198911080  Cid 1f30.1aac  Teb: 00000000002a1000
Win32Thread: ffffe001926147e0 WAIT: (UserRequest) UserMode Non-Alertable
        ffffe00197d6e150  SynchronizationEvent
        ffffe001987bf9e0  SynchronizationEvent

        THREAD ffffe00199553080  Cid 1f30.1ad4  Teb: 00000000002b1000
Win32Thread: ffffe0019263c740 WAIT: (UserRequest) UserMode Non-Alertable
        ffffe0019ac6b150  NotificationEvent
        ffffe0019a7da5e0  SynchronizationEvent

        THREAD ffffe0019b6b2800  Cid 1f30.1758  Teb: 00000000002bd000
Win32Thread: 0000000000000000 WAIT: (Suspended) KernelMode Non-Alertable
SuspendCount 1
        ffffe0019b6b2ae0  NotificationEvent
...
```

3. Switch to the context of the first thread in the process (you can select other threads):

```
lkd> .thread /p /r ffffe0019758f080
Implicit thread is now ffffe001'9758f080
Implicit process is now ffffe001'96039080
Loading User Symbols
...............................................
```

4. Now look at the thread to show its details and its call stack (addresses are truncated in the shown output):

```
lkd> !thread ffffe0019758f080
THREAD ffffe0019758f080  Cid 1f30.0718  Teb: 0000000000291000 Win32Thread :
ffffe001972e3220 WAIT : (UserRequest)UserMode Non - Alertable
ffffe00192c08150  SynchronizationEvent
Not impersonating
DeviceMap                ffffc000b77f1f30
Owning Process           ffffe00196039080        Image : explorer.exe
Attached Process         N / A           Image : N / A
Wait Start TickCount     17415276        Ticks : 146 (0:00 : 00 : 02.281)
Context Switch Count     2788            IdealProcessor : 4
UserTime                 00 : 00 : 00.031
KernelTime               00 : 00 : 00.000
*** WARNING : Unable to verify checksum for C : \windows\explorer.exe
Win32 Start Address explorer!wWinMainCRTStartup(0x00007ff7b80de4a0)
Stack Init ffffd0002727cc90 Current ffffd0002727bf80
Base ffffd0002727d000 Limit ffffd00027277000 Call 0000000000000000
Priority 8 BasePriority 8 PriorityDecrement 0 IoPriority 2 PagePriority 5

... Call Site
... nt!KiSwapContext + 0x76
... nt!KiSwapThread + 0x15a
... nt!KiCommitThreadWait + 0x149
... nt!KeWaitForSingleObject + 0x375
... nt!ObWaitForMultipleObjects + 0x2bd
... nt!NtWaitForMultipleObjects + 0xf6
... nt!KiSystemServiceCopyEnd + 0x13 (TrapFrame @ ffffd000'2727cb00)
... ntdll!ZwWaitForMultipleObjects + 0x14
... KERNELBASE!WaitForMultipleObjectsEx + 0xef
... USER32!RealMsgWaitForMultipleObjectsEx + 0xdb
... USER32!MsgWaitForMultipleObjectsEx + 0x152
... explorerframe!SHProcessMessagesUntilEventsEx + 0x8a
... explorerframe!SHProcessMessagesUntilEventEx + 0x22
... explorerframe!CExplorerHostCreator::RunHost + 0x6d
... explorer!wWinMain + 0xa04fd
... explorer!__wmainCRTStartup + 0x1d6
```

Limitations on protected process threads

As discussed in Chapter 3, protected processes (classic protected or PPL) have several limitations in terms of which access rights will be granted, even to the users with the highest privileges on the system. These limitations also apply to threads inside such a process. This ensures that the actual code running inside the protected process cannot be hijacked or otherwise affected through standard Windows functions, which require access rights that are not granted for protected process threads. In fact, the only permissions granted are THREAD_SUSPEND_RESUME and THREAD_SET/QUERY_LIMITED_INFORMATION.

EXPERIMENT: Viewing protected process thread information with Process Explorer

In this experiment, you'll view protected process thread information. Follow these steps:

1. Find any protected or PPL process, such as the Audiodg.exe or Csrss.exe process inside the process list.

2. Open the process's Properties dialog box and click the **Threads** tab.

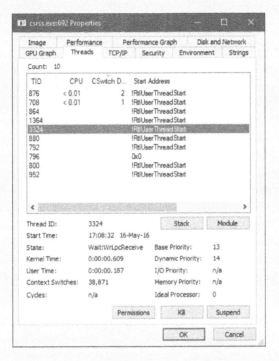

3. Process Explorer doesn't show the Win32 thread start address. Instead, it displays the standard thread start wrapper inside Ntdll.dll. If you click the **Stack** button, you'll get an error, because Process Explorer needs to read the virtual memory inside the protected process, which it can't do.

4. Note that although the base and dynamic priorities are shown, the I/O and memory priorities are not (nor is Cycles), which is another example of the limited access right THREAD_QUERY_LIMITED_INFORMATION versus full query information access right (THREAD_QUERY_INFORMATION).

5. Try to kill a thread inside a protected process. When you do, notice yet another access-denied error: recall the lack of THREAD_TERMINATE access.

Thread scheduling

This section describes the Windows scheduling policies and algorithms. The first subsection provides a condensed description of how scheduling works on Windows and a definition of key terms. Then Windows priority levels are described from both the Windows API and the Windows kernel points of view. After a review of the relevant Windows utilities and tools that relate to scheduling, the detailed data structures and algorithms that make up the Windows scheduling system are presented, including a description of common scheduling scenarios and how thread selection, as well as processor selection, occurs.

Overview of Windows scheduling

Windows implements a priority-driven, preemptive scheduling system. At least one of the highest-priority runnable (ready) threads always runs, with the caveat that certain high-priority threads ready to run might be limited by the processors on which they might be allowed or preferred to run on—phenomenon called *processor affinity*. Processor affinity is defined based on a given processor group, which collects up to 64 processors. By default, threads can run only on available processors within the processor group associated with the process. (This is to maintain compatibility with older versions of Windows, which supported only 64 processors). Developers can alter processor affinity by using the appropriate APIs or by setting an affinity mask in the image header, and users can use tools to change affinity at run time or at process creation. However, although multiple threads in a process can be associated with different groups, a thread on its own can run only on the processors available within its assigned group. Additionally, developers can choose to create group-aware applications, which use extended scheduling APIs to associate logical processors on different groups with the affinity of their threads. Doing so converts the process into a multigroup process that can theoretically run its threads on any available processor within the machine.

After a thread is selected to run, it runs for an amount of time called a *quantum*. A quantum is the length of time a thread is allowed to run before another thread at the same priority level is given a turn to run. Quantum values can vary from system to system and process to process for any of three reasons:

- System configuration settings (long or short quantums, variable or fixed quantums, and priority separation)

- Foreground or background status of the process

- Use of the job object to alter the quantum

These details are explained in the "Quantum" section later in this chapter.

A thread might not get to complete its quantum, however, because Windows implements a preemptive scheduler. That is, if another thread with a higher priority becomes ready to run, the currently running thread might be preempted before finishing its time slice. In fact, a thread can be selected to run next and be preempted before even beginning its quantum!

The Windows scheduling code is implemented in the kernel. There's no single "scheduler" module or routine, however. The code is spread throughout the kernel in which scheduling-related events occur.

The routines that perform these duties are collectively called the kernel's *dispatcher*. The following events might require thread dispatching:

- A thread becomes ready to execute—for example, a thread has been newly created or has just been released from the wait state.

- A thread leaves the running state because its time quantum ends, it terminates, it yields execution, or it enters a wait state.

- A thread's priority changes, either because of a system service call or because Windows itself changes the priority value.

- A thread's processor affinity changes so that it will no longer run on the processor on which it was running.

At each of these junctions, Windows must determine which thread should run next on the logical processor that was running the thread, if applicable, or on which logical processor the thread should now run. After a logical processor has selected a new thread to run, it eventually performs a context switch to it. A *context switch* is the procedure of saving the volatile processor state associated with a running thread, loading another thread's volatile state, and starting the new thread's execution.

As noted, Windows schedules at the thread granularity level. This approach makes sense when you consider that processes don't run; rather, they only provide resources and a context in which their threads run. Because scheduling decisions are made strictly on a thread basis, no consideration is given to what process the thread belongs to. For example, if process A has 10 runnable threads, process B has 2 runnable threads, and all 12 threads are at the same priority, each thread would theoretically receive one-twelfth of the CPU time. That is, Windows wouldn't give 50 percent of the CPU to process A and 50 percent to process B.

Priority levels

To understand the thread-scheduling algorithms, one must first understand the priority levels that Windows uses. As illustrated in Figure 4-6, Windows uses 32 priority levels internally, ranging from 0 to 31 (31 is the highest). These values divide up as follows:

- Sixteen real-time levels (16 through 31)

- Sixteen variable levels (0 through 15), out of which level 0 is reserved for the zero page thread (described in Chapter 5).

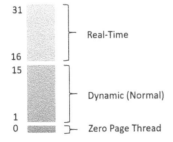

FIGURE 4-6 Thread priority levels.

Thread priority levels are assigned from two different perspectives: those of the Windows API and those of the Windows kernel. The Windows API first organizes processes by the priority class to which they are assigned at creation (the numbers in parentheses represent the internal PROCESS_PRIORITY_CLASS index recognized by the kernel):

- Real-Time (4)
- High (3)
- Above Normal (6)
- Normal (2)
- Below Normal (5)
- Idle (1)

The Windows API SetPriorityClass allows changing a process's priority class to one of these levels.

It then assigns a relative priority of the individual threads within those processes. Here, the numbers represent a priority delta that is applied to the process base priority:

- Time-Critical (15)
- Highest (2)
- Above-Normal (1)
- Normal (0)
- Below-Normal (–1)
- Lowest (–2)
- Idle (–15)

Time-Critical and Idle levels (+15 and –15) are called *saturation values* and represent specific levels that are applied rather than true offsets. These values can be passed to the SetThreadPriority Windows API to change a thread's relative priority.

Therefore, in the Windows API, each thread has a base priority that is a function of its process priority class and its relative thread priority. In the kernel, the process priority class is converted to a base priority by using the PspPriorityTable global array and the PROCESS_PRIORITY_CLASS indices shown earlier, which sets priorities of 4, 8, 13, 14, 6, and 10, respectively. (This is a fixed mapping that cannot be changed.) The relative thread priority is then applied as a differential to this base priority. For example, a Highest thread will receive a thread base priority of two levels higher than the base priority of its process.

This mapping from Windows priority to internal Windows numeric priority is shown graphically in Figure 4-7 and textually in Table 4-1.

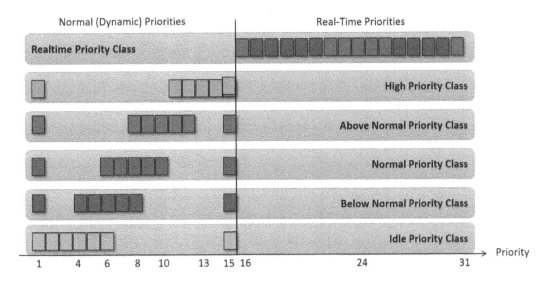

FIGURE 4-7 A graphic view of available thread priorities from a Windows API perspective.

TABLE 4-1 Mapping Windows kernel priorities to the Windows API

Priority Class Relative Priority	Real-Time	High	Above-Normal	Normal	Below-Normal	Idle
Time Critical (+Saturation)	31	15	15	15	15	15
Highest (+2)	26	15	12	10	8	6
Above Normal (+1)	25	14	11	9	7	5
Normal (0)	24	13	10	8	6	4
Below Normal (-1)	23	12	9	7	5	3
Lowest (-2)	22	11	8	6	4	2
Idle (–Saturation)	16	1	1	1	1	1

You'll note that the Time-Critical and Idle relative thread priorities maintain their respective values regardless of the process priority class (unless it is Real-Time). This is because the Windows API requests saturation of the priority from the kernel, by passing in +16 or –16 as the requested relative priority. The formula used to get these values is as follows (HIGH_PRIORITY equals 31):

```
If Time-Critical: ((HIGH_PRIORITY+1) / 2
```

```
If Idle: -((HIGH_PRIORITY+1) / 2
```

These values are then recognized by the kernel as a request for saturation, and the Saturation field in KTHREAD is set. For positive saturation, this causes the thread to receive the highest possible priority within its priority class (dynamic or real-time); for negative saturation, it's the lowest possible one. Additionally, future requests to change the base priority of the process will no longer affect the base priority of these threads because saturated threads are skipped in the processing code.

As shown in Table 4-1, threads have seven levels of possible priorities to set as viewed from the Windows API (six levels for the High priority class). The Real-Time priority class actually allows setting all priority levels between 16 and 31 (as shown in Figure 4-7). The values not covered by the standard constants shown in the table can be specified with the values –7, –6, –5, –4, –3, 3, 4, 5, and 6 as an argument to SetThreadPriority. (See the upcoming section "Real-Time priorities" for more information.)

Regardless of how the thread's priority came to be by using the Windows API (a combination of process priority class and a relative thread priority), from the point of view of the scheduler, only the final result matters. For example, priority level 10 can be obtained in two ways: a Normal priority class process (8) with a thread relative priority of Highest (+2), or an Above-Normal priority class process (10) and a Normal thread relative priority (0). From the scheduler's perspectives, these settings lead to the same value (10), so these threads are identical in terms of their priority.

Whereas a process has only a single base priority value, each thread has two priority values: current (dynamic) and base. Scheduling decisions are made based on the current priority. As explained in the upcoming section called "Priority boosts," under certain circumstances, the system increases the priority of threads in the dynamic range (1 through 15) for brief periods. Windows never adjusts the priority of threads in the Real-Time range (16 through 31), so they always have the same base and current priority.

A thread's initial base priority is inherited from the process base priority. A process, by default, inherits its base priority from the process that created it. You can override this behavior on the Create-Process function or by using the command-line start command. You can also change a process priority after it is created by using the SetPriorityClass function or by using various tools that expose that function, such as Task Manager or Process Explorer. (Right-click on the process and choose a new priority class.) For example, you can lower the priority of a CPU-intensive process so that it does not interfere with normal system activities. Changing the priority of a process changes the thread priorities up or down, but their relative settings remain the same.

Normally, user applications and services start with a normal base priority, so their initial thread typically executes at priority level 8. However, some Windows system processes (such as the Session manager, Service Control Manager, and local security authentication process) have a base process priority slightly higher than the default for the Normal class (8). This higher default value ensures that the threads in these processes will all start at a higher priority than the default value of 8.

Real-Time priorities

You can raise or lower thread priorities within the dynamic range in any application. However, you must have the increase scheduling priority privilege (SeIncreaseBasePriorityPrivilege) to enter the Real-Time range. Be aware that many important Windows kernel-mode system threads run in the Real-Time priority range, so if threads spend excessive time running in this range, they might block critical system functions (such as in the memory manager, cache manager, or some device drivers).

Using the standard Windows APIs, once a process has entered the Real-Time range, all its threads (even Idle ones) must run at one of the Real-Time priority levels. It is thus impossible to mix real-time and dynamic threads within the same process through standard interfaces. This is because the SetThread-Priority API calls the native NtSetInformationThread API with the ThreadBasePriority information class, which allows priorities to remain only in the same range. Furthermore, this information class allows priority changes only in the recognized Windows API deltas of –2 to 2 (or Time-Critical/Idle) unless the request comes from CSRSS or another real-time process. In other words, this means that a real-time process can pick thread priorities anywhere between 16 and 31, even though the standard Windows API relative thread priorities would seem to limit its choices based on the table that was shown earlier.

As mentioned, calling `SetThreadPriority` with one of a set of special values causes a call to `NtSetInformationThread` with the `ThreadActualBasePriority` information class, the kernel base priority for the thread can be directly set, including in the dynamic range for a real-time process.

 Note The name *real-time* does not imply that Windows is a real-time OS in the common definition of the term. This is because Windows doesn't provide true, real-time OS facilities, such as guaranteed interrupt latency or a way for threads to obtain a guaranteed execution time. The term *real-time* really just means "higher than all the others."

Using tools to interact with priority

You can change (and view) the base-process priority with Task Manager and Process Explorer. You can kill individual threads in a process with Process Explorer (which should be done, of course, with extreme care).

You can view individual thread priorities with Performance Monitor, Process Explorer, or WinDbg. Although it might be useful to increase or decrease the priority of a process, it typically does not make sense to adjust individual thread priorities within a process because only a person who thoroughly understands the program (in other words, the developer) would understand the relative importance of the threads within the process.

The only way to specify a starting priority class for a process is with the `start` command in the Windows command prompt. If you want to have a program start every time with a specific priority, you can define a shortcut to use the `start` command by beginning the command with `cmd /c`. This runs the command prompt, executes the command on the command line, and terminates the command prompt. For example, to run Notepad in the Idle-process priority, the command is `cmd /c start /low Notepad.exe`.

EXPERIMENT: Examining and specifying process and thread priorities

To examine and specify process and thread priorities, follow these steps:

1. Run notepad.exe normally—for example, by typing **Notepad** in a command window.

2. Open Task Manager and click to the **Details** tab.

3. Add a column named **Base Priority**. This is the name Task Manager uses for priority class.

4. Find Notepad in the list. You should see something like the following:

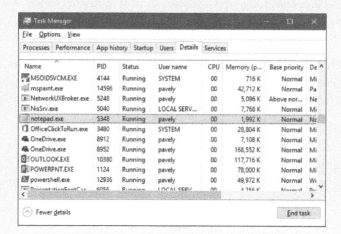

5. Notice the Notepad process running with the Normal priority class (8) and that Task Manager shows the Idle priority class as Low.

6. Open Process Explorer.

7. Double-click the **Notepad** process to show its Properties dialog box and click the **Threads** tab.

8. Select the first thread (if there's more than one). You should see something like this:

9. Notice the thread's priorities. Its base priority is 8 but its current (dynamic) priority is 10. (The reason for this priority boost is discussed in the upcoming "Priority boosts" section).

10. If you want, you can suspend and kill the thread. (Both operations must be used with caution, of course.)

11. In Task Manager, right-click the **Notepad** process, select **Set Priority**, and set the value to **High**, as shown here:

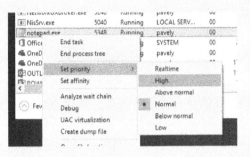

12. Accept the confirmation dialog box change and go back to Process Explorer. Notice that the thread's priority has jumped to the new base for High (13). The dynamic priority has made the same relative jump:

13. In Task Manager, change the priority class to **Realtime**. (You must be an administrator on the machine for this to succeed. Note that you can also make this change in Process Manager.)

14. In Process Manager, notice that the base and dynamic priorities of the thread are now 24. Recall that the kernel never applies priority boosts for threads in the Real-Time priority range.

Windows System Resource Manager

Windows Server 2012 R2 Standard Edition and higher SKUs include an optionally installable component called *Windows System Resource Manager (WSRM)*. It permits the administrator to configure policies that specify CPU utilization, affinity settings, and memory limits (both physical and virtual) for processes. In addition, WSRM can generate resource-utilization reports that can be used for accounting and verification of service-level agreements with users.

Policies can be applied for specific applications (by matching the name of the image with or without specific command-line arguments), users, or groups. The policies can be scheduled to take effect at certain periods or can be enabled all the time.

After you set a resource-allocation policy to manage specific processes, the WSRM service monitors CPU consumption of managed processes and adjusts process base priorities when those processes do not meet their target CPU allocations.

The physical memory limitation uses the function `SetProcessWorkingSetSizeEx` to set a hard-working set maximum. The virtual memory limit is implemented by the service checking the private virtual memory consumed by the processes. (See Chapter 5 for an explanation of these memory limits.) If this limit is exceeded, WSRM can be configured to either kill the processes or write an entry to the event log. This behavior can be used to detect a process with a memory leak before it consumes all the available committed memory on the system. Note that WSRM memory limits do not apply to Address Windowing Extensions (AWE) memory, large page memory, or kernel memory (non-paged or paged pool). (See Chapter 5 for more information on these terms.)

Thread states

Before looking at the thread-scheduling algorithms, you must understand the various execution states that a thread can be in. The thread states are as follows:

- **Ready** A thread in the ready state is waiting to execute or to be in-swapped after completing a wait. When looking for a thread to execute, the dispatcher considers only the threads in the ready state.

- **Deferred ready** This state is used for threads that have been selected to run on a specific processor but have not actually started running there. This state exists so that the kernel can minimize the amount of time the per-processor lock on the scheduling database is held.

- **Standby** A thread in this state has been selected to run next on a particular processor. When the correct conditions exist, the dispatcher performs a context switch to this thread. Only one thread can be in the standby state for each processor on the system. Note that a thread can be preempted out of the standby state before it ever executes (if, for example, a higher-priority thread becomes runnable before the standby thread begins execution).

- **Running** After the dispatcher performs a context switch to a thread, the thread enters the running state and executes. The thread's execution continues until its quantum ends (and another thread at the same priority is ready to run), it is preempted by a higher-priority thread, it terminates, it yields execution, or it voluntarily enters the waiting state.

- **Waiting** A thread can enter the waiting state in several ways: A thread can voluntarily wait for an object to synchronize its execution, the OS can wait on the thread's behalf (such as to resolve a paging I/O), or an environment subsystem can direct the thread to suspend itself. When the thread's wait ends, depending on its priority, the thread either begins running immediately or is moved back to the ready state.

- **Transition** A thread enters the transition state if it is ready for execution but its kernel stack is paged out of memory. After its kernel stack is brought back into memory, the thread enters the ready state. (Thread stacks are discussed in Chapter 5.)

- **Terminated** When a thread finishes executing, it enters this state. After the thread is terminated, the executive thread object (the data structure in system memory that describes the thread) might or might not be deallocated. The object manager sets the policy regarding when to delete the object. For example, the object remains if there are any open handles to the thread. A thread can also enter the terminated state from other states if it's killed explicitly by some other thread—for example, by calling the `TerminateThread` Windows API.

- **Initialized** This state is used internally while a thread is being created.

Figure 4-8 shows the main state transitions for threads. The numeric values shown represent the internal values of each state and can be viewed with a tool such as Performance Monitor. The ready and deferred ready states are represented as one. This reflects the fact that the deferred ready state acts as a temporary placeholder for the scheduling routines. This is true for the standby state as well. These states are almost always very short-lived. Threads in these states always transition quickly to ready, running, or waiting.

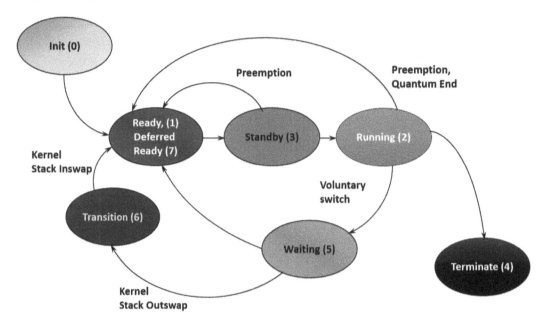

FIGURE 4-8   Thread states and transitions.

EXPERIMENT: Thread-scheduling state changes

You can watch thread-scheduling state changes with the Performance Monitor tool in Windows. This utility can be useful when you're debugging a multithreaded application and you're unsure about the state of the threads running in the process. To watch thread-scheduling state changes by using the Performance Monitor tool, follow these steps:

1. Download the CPU Stress tool from the book's downloadable resources.

2. Run CPUSTRES.exe. Thread 1 should be active.

3. Activate thread 2 by selecting it in the list and clicking the **Activate** button or by right-clicking it and selecting **Activate** from the context menu. The tool should look something like this:

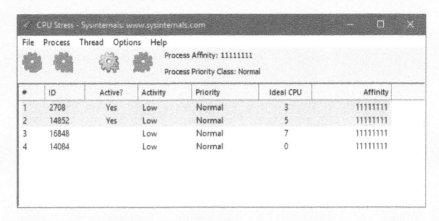

4. Click the **Start** button and type **perfmon** to start the Performance Monitor tool.

5. If necessary, select the chart view. Then remove the existing CPU counter.

6. Right-click the graph and choose **Properties**.

7. Click the **Graph** tab and change the chart vertical scale maximum to 7. (As you saw in Figure 4-8, the various states are associated with numbers 0 through 7.) Then click **OK**.

8. Click the **Add** button on the toolbar to open the Add Counters dialog box.

9. Select the **Thread** performance object and then select the **Thread State** counter.

10. Select the **Show Description** check box to see the definition of the values:

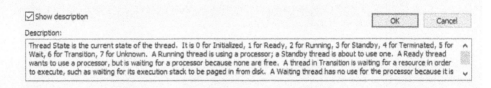

11. In the Instances box, select **<All instances>**. Then type **cpustres** and click **Search**.

12. Select the first three threads of cpustres (**cpustres/0**, **cpustres/1**, and **cpustres/2**) and click the **Add >>** button. Then click **OK**. Thread 0 should be in state 5 (waiting), because that's the GUI thread and it's waiting for user input. Threads 1 and 2 should be alternating between states 2 and 5 (running and waiting). (Thread 1 may be hiding thread 2 as they're running with the same activity level and the same priority.)

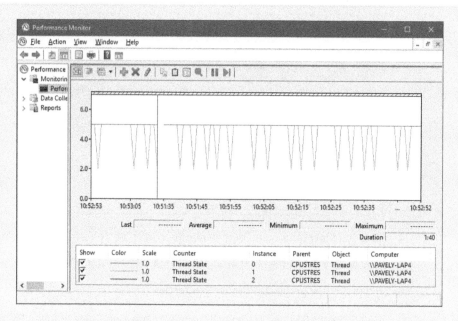

13. Go back to CPU Stress, right-click thread 2, and choose **Busy** from the activity context menu. You should see thread 2 in state 2 (running) more often than thread 1:

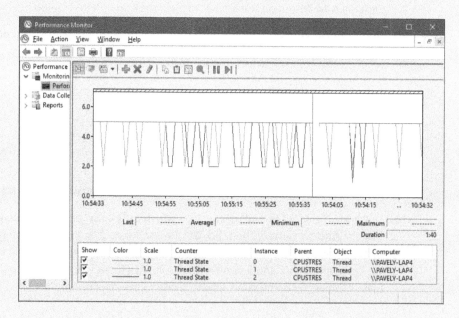

14. Right-click thread 1 and choose an activity level of **Maximum**. Then repeat this step for thread 2. Both threads now should be constantly in state 2 because they're running essentially an infinite loop:

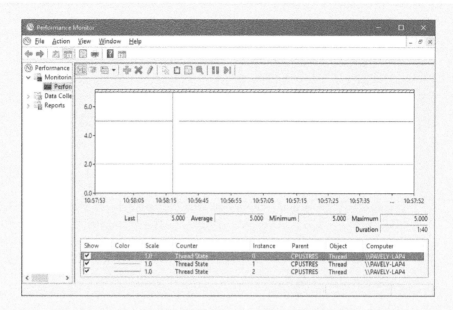

If you're trying this on a single processor system, you'll see something different. Because there is only one processor, only one thread can execute at a time, so you'll see the two threads alternating between states 1 (ready) and 2 (running):

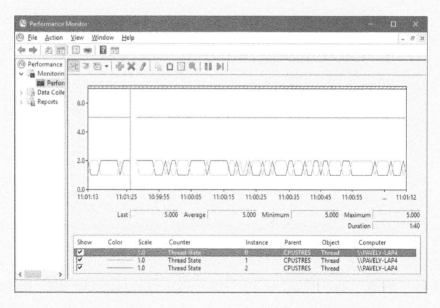

15. If you're on a multiprocessor system (very likely), you can get the same effect by going to Task Manager, right-clicking the CPUSTRES process, selecting **Set Affinity**, and then select just one processor—it doesn't matter which one—as shown here. (You can also do it from CPU Stress by opening the Process menu and selecting **Affinity**.)

16. There's one more thing you can try. With this setting in place, go back to CPU Stress, right-click thread 1, and choose a priority of **Above Normal**. You'll see that thread 1 is running continuously (state 2) and thread 2 is always in the ready state (state 1). This is because there's only one processor, so in general, the higher priority thread wins out. From time to time, however, you'll see a change in thread 1's state to ready. This is because every 4 seconds or so, the starved thread gets a boost that enables it to run for a little while. (Often, this state change is not reflected by the graph because the granularity of Performance Monitor is limited to 1 second, which is too coarse.) This is described in more detail later in this chapter in the section "Priority boosts."

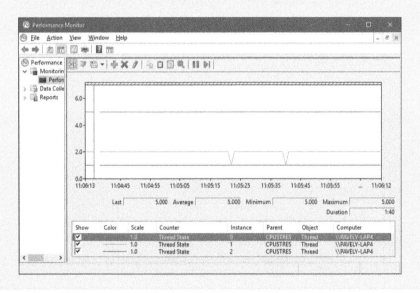

Dispatcher database

To make thread-scheduling decisions, the kernel maintains a set of data structures known collectively as the *dispatcher database*. The dispatcher database keeps track of which threads are waiting to execute and which processors are executing which threads.

To improve scalability, including thread-dispatching concurrency, Windows multiprocessor systems have per-processor dispatcher ready queues and shared processor group queues, as illustrated in Figure 4-9. In this way, each CPU can check its own shared ready queue for the next thread to run without having to lock the system-wide ready queues.

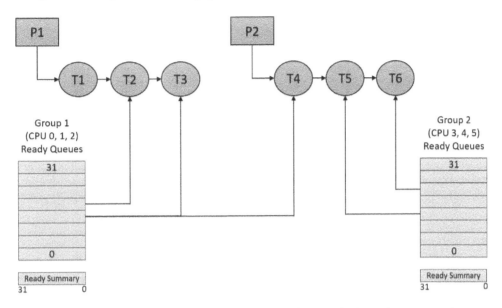

FIGURE 4-9 Windows multiprocessor dispatcher database. (This example shows six processors. *P* represents processes; *T* represents threads.)

Windows versions prior to Windows 8 and Windows Server 2012 used per-processor ready queues and a per-processor ready summary, which were stored as part of processor control block (PRCB) structure. (To see the fields in the PRCB, type **dt nt!_kprcb** in the kernel debugger.) Starting with Windows 8 and Windows Server 2012, a shared ready queue and ready summary are used for a group of processors. This enables the system to make better decisions about which processor to use next for that group of processors. (The per-CPU ready queues are still there and used for threads with affinity constraints.)

Note Because the shared data structure must be protected (by a spinlock), the group should not be too large. That way, contention on the queues is insignificant. In the current implementation, the maximum group size is four logical processors. If the number of logical processors is greater than four, then more than one group would be created, and the available processors spread evenly. For example, on a six-processor system, two groups of three processors each would be created.

The ready queues, ready summary (described next), and some other information is stored in a kernel structure named KSHARED_READY_QUEUE that is stored in the PRCB. Although it exists for every processor, it's used only on the first processor of each processor group, sharing it with the rest of the processors in that group.

The dispatcher ready queues (ReadListHead in KSHARED_READY_QUEUE) contain the threads that are in the ready state, waiting to be scheduled for execution. There is one queue for each of the 32 priority levels. To speed up the selection of which thread to run or preempt, Windows maintains a 32-bit bitmask called the *ready summary* (ReadySummary). Each bit set indicates one or more threads in the ready queue for that priority level (bit 0 represents priority 0, bit 1 priority 1, and so on).

Instead of scanning each ready list to see whether it is empty or not (which would make scheduling decisions dependent on the number of different priority threads), a single bit scan is performed as a native processor command to find the highest bit set. Regardless of the number of threads in the ready queue, this operation takes a constant amount of time.

The dispatcher database is synchronized by raising IRQL to DISPATCH_LEVEL (2). (For an explanation of interrupt priority levels, or IRQLs, see Chapter 6.) Raising IRQL in this way prevents other threads from interrupting thread dispatching on the processor because threads normally run at IRQL 0 or 1. However, more is required than just raising IRQL, because other processors can simultaneously raise to the same IRQL and attempt to operate on their dispatcher database. How Windows synchronizes access to the dispatcher database is explained later in this chapter in the section "Multiprocessor systems."

EXPERIMENT: Viewing ready threads

You can view the list of ready threads with the kernel-debugger !ready command. This command displays the thread or list of threads that are ready to run at each priority level. Here is an example generated on a 32-bit machine with four logical processors:

```
0: kd> !ready
KSHARED_READY_QUEUE 8147e800: (00) ****------------------------------
SharedReadyQueue 8147e800: Ready Threads at priority 8
    THREAD 80af8bc0  Cid 1300.15c4  Teb: 7ffdb000 Win32Thread: 00000000 READY on
processor 80000002
    THREAD 80b58bc0  Cid 0454.0fc0  Teb: 7f82e000 Win32Thread: 00000000 READY on
processor 80000003
SharedReadyQueue 8147e800: Ready Threads at priority 7
    THREAD a24b4700  Cid 0004.11dc  Teb: 00000000 Win32Thread: 00000000 READY on
processor 80000001
    THREAD a1bad040  Cid 0004.096c  Teb: 00000000 Win32Thread: 00000000 READY on
processor 80000001
SharedReadyQueue 8147e800: Ready Threads at priority 6
    THREAD a1bad4c0  Cid 0004.0950  Teb: 00000000 Win32Thread: 00000000 READY on
processor 80000002
    THREAD 80b5e040  Cid 0574.12a4  Teb: 7fc33000 Win32Thread: 00000000 READY on
processor 80000000
SharedReadyQueue 8147e800: Ready Threads at priority 4
    THREAD 80b09bc0  Cid 0004.12dc  Teb: 00000000 Win32Thread: 00000000 READY on
processor 80000003
SharedReadyQueue 8147e800: Ready Threads at priority 0
    THREAD 82889bc0  Cid 0004.0008  Teb: 00000000 Win32Thread: 00000000 READY on
processor 80000000
Processor 0: No threads in READY state
Processor 1: No threads in READY state
Processor 2: No threads in READY state
Processor 3: No threads in READY state
```

The processor numbers have a 0x8000000 added to them, but the actual processor numbers are easy to see. The first line shows the address of the KSHARED_READY_QUEUE with the group number in parentheses (00 in the output) and then a graphic representation of the processors in this particular group (the four asterisks).

The last four lines seem odd, as they appear to indicate no ready threads, contradicting the preceding output. These lines indicate ready threads from the older DispatcherReadyListHead member of the PRCB because the per-processor ready queues are used for threads that have restrictive affinity (set to run on a subset of processors inside that processor group).

You can also dump the KSHARED_READY_QUEUE with the address given by the !ready command:

```
0: kd> dt nt!_KSHARED_READY_QUEUE 8147e800
   +0x000 Lock            : 0
   +0x004 ReadySummary    : 0x1d1
   +0x008 ReadyListHead   : [32] _LIST_ENTRY [ 0x82889c5c - 0x82889c5c ]
   +0x108 RunningSummary  : [32] "???"
   +0x128 Span            : 4
   +0x12c LowProcIndex    : 0
   +0x130 QueueIndex      : 1
   +0x134 ProcCount       : 4
   +0x138 Affinity        : 0xf
```

The ProcCount member shows the processor count in the shared group (4 in this example). Also note the ReadySummary value, 0x1d1. This translates to 111010001 in binary. Reading the binary one bits from right to left, this indicates that threads exist in priorities 0, 4, 6, 7, 8, which match the preceding output.

Quantum

As mentioned earlier in the chapter, a *quantum* is the amount of time a thread is permitted to run before Windows checks to see whether another thread at the same priority is waiting to run. If a thread completes its quantum and there are no other threads at its priority, Windows permits the thread to run for another quantum.

On client versions of Windows, threads run for two clock intervals by default. On server systems, threads runs for 12 clock intervals by default. (We'll explain how to change these values in the "Controlling the quantum" section.) The rationale for the longer default value on server systems is to minimize context switching. By having a longer quantum, server applications that wake up because of a client request have a better chance of completing the request and going back into a wait state before their quantum ends.

The length of the clock interval varies according to the hardware platform. The frequency of the clock interrupts is up to the HAL, not the kernel. For example, the clock interval for most x86 uniprocessors is about 10 milliseconds (note that these machines are no longer supported by Windows and are used here only for example purposes), and for most x86 and x64 multiprocessors it is about 15 milliseconds. This clock interval is stored in the kernel variable KeMaximumIncrement as hundreds of nanoseconds.

Although threads run in units of clock intervals, the system does not use the count of clock ticks as the gauge for how long a thread has run and whether its quantum has expired. This is because thread run-time accounting is based on processor cycles. When the system starts up, it multiplies the processor speed (CPU clock cycles per second) in hertz (Hz) by the number of seconds it takes for one clock tick to fire (based on the KeMaximumIncrement value described earlier) to calculate the number of clock cycles to which each quantum is equivalent. This value is stored in the kernel variable KiCyclesPerClock-Quantum.

The result of this accounting method is that threads do not actually run for a quantum number based on clock ticks. Instead, they run for a quantum target, which represents an estimate of what the number of CPU clock cycles the thread has consumed should be when its turn would be given up. This target should be equal to an equivalent number of clock interval timer ticks. This is because, as you just saw, the calculation of clock cycles per quantum is based on the clock interval timer frequency, which you can check using the following experiment. Note, however, that because interrupt cycles are not charged to the thread, the actual clock time might be longer.

EXPERIMENT: Determining the clock interval frequency

The Windows GetSystemTimeAdjustment function returns the clock interval. To determine the clock interval, run the clockres tool from Sysinternals. Here's the output from a quad-core 64-bit Windows 10 system:

```
C:\>clockres

ClockRes v2.0 - View the system clock resolution
Copyright (C) 2009 Mark Russinovich
SysInternals - www.sysinternals.com

Maximum timer interval: 15.600 ms
Minimum timer interval: 0.500 ms
Current timer interval: 1.000 ms
```

The current interval may be lower than the maximum (default) clock interval because of multimedia timers. Multimedia timers are used with functions such as timeBeginPeriod and timeSetEvent that are used to receive callbacks with intervals of 1 millisecond (ms) at best. This causes a global reprogramming of the kernel interval timer, meaning the scheduler wakes up in more frequent intervals, which can degrade system performance. In any case, this does not affect quantum lengths, as described in the next section.

It's also possible to read the value using the kernel global variable KeMaximumIncrement as shown here (not the same system as the previous example):

```
0: kd> dd nt!KeMaximumIncrement L1
814973b4  0002625a
0: kd> ? 0002625a
Evaluate expression: 156250 = 0002625a
```

This corresponds to the default of 15.6 ms.

Quantum accounting

Each process has a quantum reset value in the process control block (KPROCESS). This value is used when creating new threads inside the process and is duplicated in the thread control block (KTHREAD), which is then used when giving a thread a new quantum target. The quantum reset value is stored in terms of actual quantum units (we'll discuss what these mean soon), which are then multiplied by the number of clock cycles per quantum, resulting in the quantum target.

As a thread runs, CPU clock cycles are charged at different events, such as context switches, interrupts, and certain scheduling decisions. If, at a clock interval timer interrupt, the number of CPU clock cycles charged has reached (or passed) the quantum target, quantum end processing is triggered. If there is another thread at the same priority waiting to run, a context switch occurs to the next thread in the ready queue.

Internally, a quantum unit is represented as one-third of a clock tick. That is, one clock tick equals three quantums. This means that on client Windows systems, threads have a quantum reset value of 6 (2 * 3) and that server systems have a quantum reset value of 36 (12 * 3) by default. For this reason, the KiCyclesPerClockQuantum value is divided by 3 at the end of the calculation previously described, because the original value describes only CPU clock cycles per clock interval timer tick.

The reason a quantum was stored internally as a fraction of a clock tick rather than as an entire tick was to allow for partial quantum decay-on-wait completion on versions of Windows prior to Windows Vista. Prior versions used the clock interval timer for quantum expiration. If this adjustment had not been made, it would have been possible for threads to never have their quantums reduced. For example, if a thread ran, entered a wait state, ran again, and entered another wait state but was never the currently running thread when the clock interval timer fired, it would never have its quantum charged for the time it was running. Because threads now have CPU clock cycles charged instead of quantums, and because this no longer depends on the clock interval timer, these adjustments are not required.

EXPERIMENT: Determining the clock cycles per quantum

Windows doesn't expose the number of clock cycles per quantum through any function. However, with the calculation and description we've given, you should be able to determine this on your own using the following steps and a kernel debugger such as WinDbg in local debugging mode:

1. Obtain your processor frequency as Windows has detected it. You can use the value stored in the PRCB's MHz field, which you can display with the !cpuinfo command. Here is a sample output of a four-processor system running at 2794 megahertz (MHz):

    ```
    lkd> !cpuinfo

    CP  F/M/S Manufacturer  MHz PRCB Signature   MSR 8B Signature Features
     0  6,60,3 GenuineIntel  2794 ffffffff00000000 >ffffffff00000000<a3cd3fff
     1  6,60,3 GenuineIntel  2794 ffffffff00000000                  a3cd3fff
     2  6,60,3 GenuineIntel  2794 ffffffff00000000                  a3cd3fff
     3  6,60,3 GenuineIntel  2794 ffffffff00000000                  a3cd3fff
    ```

2. Convert the number to hertz (Hz). This is the number of CPU clock cycles that occur each second on your system—in this case, 2,794,000,000 cycles per second.

3. Obtain the clock interval on your system by using clockres. This measures how long it takes before the clock fires. On the sample system used here, this interval was 15.625 msec.

4. Convert this number to the number of times the clock interval timer fires each second. One second equals 1,000 ms, so divide the number derived in step 3 by 1,000. In this case, the timer fires every 0.015625 seconds.

5. Multiply this count by the number of cycles each second that you obtained in step 2. In this case, 43,656,250 cycles have elapsed after each clock interval.

6. Remember that each quantum unit is one-third of a clock interval, so divide the number of cycles by 3. This gives you 14,528,083, or 0xDE0C13 in hexadecimal. This is the number of clock cycles each quantum unit should take on a system running at 2,794 MHz with a clock interval of around 15.6 ms.

7. To verify your calculation, dump the value of KiCyclesPerClockQuantum on your system. It should match (or be close enough because of rounding errors).

```
lkd> dd nt!KiCyclesPerClockQuantum L1
8149755c  00de0c10
```

Controlling the quantum

You can change the thread quantum for all processes, but you can choose only one of two settings: short (two clock ticks, which is the default for client machines) or long (12 clock ticks, which is the default for server systems).

> **Note** By using the job object on a system running with long quantums, you can select other quantum values for the processes in the job.

To change this setting, right-click the **This PC** icon on the desktop. Alternatively, in Windows Explorer, choose **Properties**, click the **Advanced System Settings** label, click the **Advanced** tab, click the **Settings** button in the **Performance** section, and click yet another **Advanced** tab. Figure 4-10 shows the resulting dialog box.

FIGURE 4-10 Quantum configuration in the Performance Options dialog box.

This dialog box contains two key options:

- **Programs**   This setting designates the use of short, variable quantums, which is the default for client versions of Windows (and other client-like versions, such as mobile, XBOX, HoloLens, and so on). If you install Terminal Services on a server system and configure the server as an application server, this setting is selected so that the users on the terminal server have the same quantum settings that would normally be set on a desktop or client system. You might also select this manually if you were running Windows Server as your desktop OS.

- **Background Services**   This setting designates the use of long, fixed quantums—the default for server systems. The only reason you might select this option on a workstation system is if you were using the workstation as a server system. However, because changes in this option take effect immediately, it might make sense to use it if the machine is about to run a background or server-style workload. For example, if a long-running computation, encoding, or modeling simulation needs to run overnight, you could select the Background Services option at night and return the system to Programs mode in the morning.

Variable quantums

When variable quantums are enabled, the variable quantum table (PspVariableQuantums), which holds an array of six quantum numbers, is loaded into the PspForegroundQuantum table (a three-element array) that is used by the PspComputeQuantum function. Its algorithm will pick the appropriate quantum index based on whether the process is a foreground process—that is, whether it contains the thread that owns the foreground window on the desktop. If this is not the case, an index of 0 is chosen, which corresponds to the default thread quantum described earlier. If it is a foreground process, the quantum index corresponds to the priority separation.

This priority separation value determines the priority boost (described in the upcoming section "Priority boosts") that the scheduler will apply to foreground threads, and it is thus paired with an appropriate extension of the quantum. For each extra priority level (up to 2), another quantum is given to the thread. For example, if the thread receives a boost of one priority level, it receives an extra quantum as well. By default, Windows sets the maximum possible priority boost to foreground threads, meaning that the priority separation will be 2, which means quantum index 2 is selected in the variable quantum table. This leads to the thread receiving two extra quantums, for a total of three quantums.

Table 4-2 describes the exact quantum value (recall that this is stored in a unit representing one-third of a clock tick) that will be selected based on the quantum index and which quantum configuration is in use.

TABLE 4-2   Quantum values

	Short Quantum Index			Long Quantum Index		
Variable	6	12	18	12	24	36
Fixed	18	18	18	36	36	36

Thus, when a window is brought into the foreground on a client system, all the threads in the process containing the thread that owns the foreground window have their quantums tripled. Threads in the foreground process run with a quantum of six clock ticks, whereas threads in other processes have the default client quantum of two clock ticks. In this way, when you switch away from a CPU-intensive process, the new foreground process will get proportionally more of the CPU. This is because when its threads run, they will have a longer turn than background threads (again, assuming the thread priorities are the same in both the foreground and background processes).

Quantum settings registry value

The user interface that controls quantum settings described earlier modifies the registry value Win32-PrioritySeparation in the key HKLM\SYSTEM\CurrentControlSet\Control\PriorityControl. In addition to specifying the relative length of thread quantums (short or long), this registry value also defines whether variable quantums should be used, as well as the priority separation (which, as you've seen, will determine the quantum index used when variable quantums are enabled). This value consists of 6 bits divided into the three 2-bit fields shown in Figure 4-11.

4	2	0
Short vs. Long	Variable vs. Fixed	Priority Separation

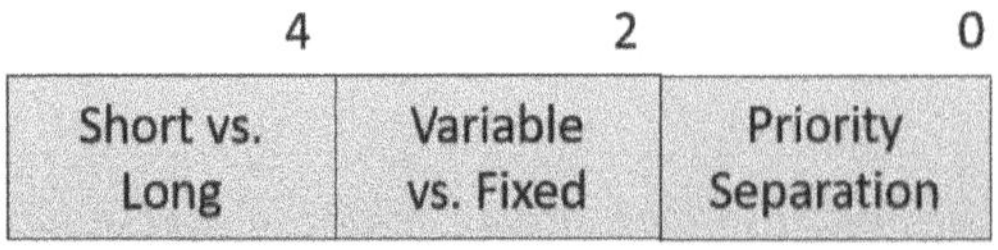

FIGURE 4-11   Fields of the Win32PrioritySeparation registry value.

The fields shown in Figure 4-11 can be defined as follows:

- **Short vs. Long**   A value of 1 specifies long quantums, and a value of 2 specifies short ones. A setting of 0 or 3 indicates that the default appropriate for the system will be used (short for client systems, long for server systems).

- **Variable vs. Fixed**   A value of 1 means to enable the variable quantum table based on the algorithm shown in the "Variable quantums" section. A setting of 0 or 3 means that the default appropriate for the system will be used (variable for client systems, fixed for server systems).

- **Priority Separation**   This field (stored in the kernel variable `PsPrioritySeparation`) defines the priority separation (up to 2), as explained in the "Variable quantums" section.

When you use the Performance Options dialog box (refer to Figure 4-10), you can choose from only two combinations: short quantums with foreground quantums tripled, or long quantums with no quantum changes for foreground threads. However, you can select other combinations by modifying the `Win32PrioritySeparation` registry value directly.

Threads that are part of a process running in the idle process priority class always receive a single thread quantum, ignoring any sort of quantum configuration settings, whether set by default or set through the registry.

On Windows Server systems configured as application servers, the initial value of the `Win32Priori-tySeparation` registry value will be hex 26, which is identical to the value set by the Optimize Performance for Programs option in the Performance Options dialog box. This selects quantum and priority-boost behavior like that on Windows client systems, which is appropriate for a server used primarily to host users' applications.

On Windows client systems and on servers not configured as application servers, the initial value of the `Win32PrioritySeparation` registry setting will be 2. This provides values of 0 for the Short vs. Long and Variable vs. Fixed Bit fields, relying on the default behavior of the system (depending on whether it is a client system or a server system) for these options. However, it provides a value of 2 for the Priority Separation field. After the registry value has been changed via the Performance Options dialog box, it cannot be restored to this original value other than by modifying the registry directly.

EXPERIMENT: Effects of changing the quantum configuration

Using a local kernel debugger, you can see how the two quantum configuration settings, Programs and Background Services, affect the `PsPrioritySeparation` and `PspForegroundQuantum` tables, as well as modify the `QuantumReset` value of threads on the system. Take the following steps:

1. Open the **System** utility in Control Panel or right-click the **This PC** icon on the desktop and choose **Properties**.

2. Click the **Advanced System Settings** label, click the **Advanced** tab, click the **Settings** button in the Performance section, and click the second **Advanced** tab.

3. Select the **Programs** option and click **Apply**. Keep this dialog box open for the duration of the experiment.

4. Dump the values of `PsPrioritySeparation` and `PspForegroundQuantum`, as shown here. The values shown are what you should see on a Windows system after making the change in steps 1–3. Notice how the variable short quantum table is being used and that a priority boost of 2 will apply to foreground applications:

```
lkd> dd nt!PsPrioritySeparation L1
fffff803'75e0e388  00000002
lkd> db nt!PspForegroundQuantum L3

fffff803'76189d28  06 0c 12
```

5. Look at the QuantumReset value of any process on the system. As noted, this is the default full quantum of each thread on the system when it is replenished. This value is cached into each thread of the process, but the KPROCESS structure is easier to look at. Notice in this case it is 6, because WinDbg, like most other applications, gets the quantum set in the first entry of the PspForegroundQuantum table:

```
lkd> .process
Implicit process is now ffffe001'4f51f080
lkd> dt nt!_KPROCESS ffffe001'4f51f080 QuantumReset
    +0x1bd QuantumReset : 6 ''
```

6. Change the Performance option to **Background Services** in the dialog box you opened in steps 1 and 2.

7. Repeat the commands shown in steps 4 and 5. You should see the values change in a manner consistent with our discussion in this section:

```
lkd> dd nt!PsPrioritySeparation L1
fffff803'75e0e388  00000000
lkd> db nt!PspForegroundQuantum L3
fffff803'76189d28  24 24 24
lkd> dt nt!_KPROCESS ffffe001'4f51f080 QuantumReset
    +0x1bd QuantumReset : 36 '$'
```

Priority boosts

The Windows scheduler periodically adjusts the current (dynamic) priority of threads through an internal priority-boosting mechanism. In many cases, it does so to decrease various latencies (that is, to make threads respond faster to the events they are waiting on) and increase responsiveness. In others, it applies these boosts to prevent inversion and starvation scenarios. Here are some of the boost scenarios that will be described in this section (and their purpose):

- Boosts due to scheduler/dispatcher events (latency reduction)

- Boosts due to I/O completion (latency reduction)

- Boosts due to user interface (UI) input (latency reduction/responsiveness)

- Boosts due to a thread waiting on an executive resource (ERESOURCE) for too long (starvation avoidance)

- Boosts when a thread that's ready to run hasn't been running for some time (starvation and priority-inversion avoidance)

Like any scheduling algorithms, however, these adjustments aren't perfect, and they might not benefit all applications.

 Note Windows never boosts the priority of threads in the real-time range (16 through 31). Therefore, scheduling is always predictable with respect to other threads in this range. Windows assumes that if you're using the real-time thread priorities, you know what you're doing.

Client versions of Windows also include a pseudo-boosting mechanism that occurs during multimedia playback. Unlike the other priority boosts, multimedia-playback boosts are managed by a kernel-mode driver called the Multimedia Class Scheduler Service (mmcss.sys). They are not really boosts, however. The driver merely sets new priorities for the threads as needed. Therefore, none of the rules regarding boosts apply. We'll first cover the typical kernel-managed priority boosts and then talk about MMCSS and the kind of "boosting" it performs.

Boosts due to scheduler/dispatcher events

Whenever a dispatch event occurs, the KiExitDispatcher routine is called. Its job is to process the deferred ready list by calling KiProcessThreadWaitList and then call KzCheckForThreadDispatch to check whether any threads on the current processor should not be scheduled. Whenever such an event occurs, the caller can also specify which type of boost should be applied to the thread, as well as what priority increment the boost should be associated with. The following scenarios are considered as AdjustUnwait dispatch events because they deal with a dispatcher (synchronization) object entering a signaled state, which might cause one or more threads to wake up:

- An asynchronous procedure call (APC; described in Chapter 6 and in more detail in Chapter 8 in Part 2) is queued to a thread.
- An event is set or pulsed.
- A timer was set, or the system time was changed, and timers had to be reset.
- A mutex was released or abandoned.
- A process exited.
- An entry was inserted in a queue (KQUEUE), or the queue was flushed.
- A semaphore was released.
- A thread was alerted, suspended, resumed, frozen, or thawed.
- A primary UMS thread is waiting to switch to a scheduled UMS thread.

For scheduling events associated with a public API (such as SetEvent), the boost increment applied is specified by the caller. Windows recommends certain values to be used by developers, which will be described later. For alerts, a boost of 2 is applied (unless the thread is put in an alert wait by calling KeAlertThreadByThreadId, in which case the applied boost is 1), because the alert API does not have a parameter allowing a caller to set a custom increment.

The scheduler also has two special `AdjustBoost` dispatch events, which are part of the lock-ownership priority mechanism. These boosts attempt to fix situations in which a caller that owns the lock at priority x ends up releasing the lock to a waiting thread at priority $< = x$. In this situation, the new owner thread must wait for its turn (if running at priority x), or worse, it might not even get to run at all if its priority is lower than x. This means the releasing thread continues its execution, even though it should have caused the new owner thread to wake up and take control of the processor. The following two dispatcher events cause an `AdjustBoost` dispatcher exit:

- An event is set through the `KeSetEventBoostPriority` interface, which is used by the `ERESOURCE` reader-writer kernel lock.

- A gate is set through the `KeSignalGate` interface, which is used by various internal mechanisms when releasing a gate lock.

Unwait boosts

Unwait boosts attempt to decrease the latency between a thread waking up due to an object being signaled (thus entering the ready state) and the thread actually beginning its execution to process the unwait (thus entering the running state). Generally speaking, it is desirable that a thread that wakes up from a waiting state would be able to run as soon as possible.

The various Windows header files specify recommended values that kernel-mode callers of APIs such as `KeReleaseMutex`, `KeSetEvent` and `KeReleaseSemaphore` should use, which correspond to definitions such as `MUTANT_INCREMENT`, `SEMAPHORE_INCREMENT`, and `EVENT_INCREMENT`. These three definitions have always been set to 1 in the headers, so it is safe to assume that most unwaits on these objects result in a boost of 1. In the user-mode API, an increment cannot be specified, nor do the native system calls such as `NtSetEvent` have parameters to specify such a boost. Instead, when these APIs call the underlying `Ke` interface, they automatically use the default `_INCREMENT` definition. This is also the case when mutexes are abandoned or timers are reset due to a system time change: The system uses the default boost that normally would have been applied when the mutex would have been released. Finally, the APC boost is completely up to the caller. Soon, you'll see a specific usage of the APC boost related to I/O completion.

 Note Some dispatcher objects don't have boosts associated with them. For example, when a timer is set or expires, or when a process is signaled, no boost is applied.

All these boosts of 1 attempt to solve the initial problem by assuming that both the releasing and waiting threads are running at the same priority. By boosting the waiting thread by one priority level, the waiting thread should preempt the releasing thread as soon as the operation completes. Unfortunately, on uniprocessor systems, if this assumption does not hold, the boost might not do much. For example, if the waiting thread is at priority 4 and the releasing thread is at priority 8, waiting at priority 5 won't do much to reduce latency and force preemption. On multiprocessor systems, however, due to the stealing and balancing algorithms, this higher-priority thread may have a better chance of getting picked up by another logical processor. This is due to a design choice made in the initial NT architecture, which is to not track lock ownership (except a few locks). This means the scheduler can't be sure who really owns an event and if it's really being used as a lock. Even with lock-ownership tracking, ownership is not usually passed (to avoid convoy issues) other than in the executive resource case, explained in an upcoming section.

For certain kinds of lock objects that use events or gates as their underlying synchronization object, the lock-ownership boost resolves the dilemma. Also, on a multiprocessor machine, the ready thread might get picked up on another processor (due to the processor-distribution and load-balancing schemes you'll see later), and its high priority might increase the chances of it running on that secondary processor instead.

Lock-ownership boosts

Because the executive-resource (ERESOURCE) and critical-section locks use underlying dispatcher objects, releasing these locks results in an unwait boost as described earlier. On the other hand, because the high-level implementation of these objects tracks the owner of the lock, the kernel can make a more informed decision as to what kind of boost should be applied by using the AdjustBoost reason. In these kinds of boosts, AdjustIncrement is set to the current priority of the releasing (or setting) thread, minus any graphical user interface (GUI) foreground separation boost. In addition, before the KiExitDispatcher function is called, KiRemoveBoostThread is called by the event and gate code to return the releasing thread back to its regular priority. This step is needed to avoid a lock-convoy situation, in which two threads repeatedly passing the lock between one another get ever-increasing boosts.

> **Note** Pushlocks, which are unfair locks because ownership of the lock in a contended acquisition path is not predictable (rather, it's random, like a spinlock), do not apply priority boosts due to lock ownership. This is because doing so only contributes to preemption and priority proliferation, which isn't required because the lock becomes immediately free as soon as it is released (bypassing the normal wait/unwait path).

Other differences between the lock-ownership boost and unwait boost will be exposed in the way the scheduler actually applies boosting, which is the subject of the next section.

Priority boosting after I/O completion

Windows gives temporary priority boosts upon completion of certain I/O operations so that threads that were waiting for an I/O have more of a chance to run right away and process whatever was being waited for. Although you'll find recommended boost values in the Windows Driver Kit (WDK) header files (by searching for #*define IO_* in Wdm.h or Ntddk.h), the actual value for the boost is up to the device driver. (These values are listed in Table 4-3.) It is the device driver that specifies the boost when it completes an I/O request on its call to the kernel function, IoCompleteRequest. In Table 4-3, notice that I/O requests to devices that warrant better responsiveness have higher boost values.

TABLE 4-3 Recommended boost values

Device	Boost
Disk, CD-ROM, parallel, video	1
Network, mailslot, named pipe, serial	2
Keyboard, mouse	6
Sound	8

> **Note** You might intuitively expect better responsiveness from your video card or disk than a boost of 1. However, the kernel is in fact trying to optimize for *latency*, to which some devices (as well as human sensory inputs) are more sensitive than others. To give you an idea, a sound card expects data around every 1 ms to play back music without perceptible glitches, while a video card needs to output at only 24 frames per second, or about once every 40 ms, before the human eye can notice glitches.

As hinted earlier, these I/O completion boosts rely on the unwait boosts seen in the previous section. Chapter 6 shows the mechanism of I/O completion in depth. For now, the important detail is that the kernel implements the signaling code in the `IoCompleteRequest` API through the use of either an APC (for asynchronous I/O) or through an event (for synchronous I/O). When a driver passes in—for example, `IO_DISK_INCREMENT` to `IoCompleteRequest` for an asynchronous disk read—the kernel calls `KeInsertQueueApc` with the boost parameter set to `IO_DISK_INCREMENT`. In turn, when the thread's wait is broken due to the APC, it receives a boost of 1.

Be aware that the boost values given in Table 4-3 are merely recommendations by Microsoft. Driver developers are free to ignore them, and certain specialized drivers can use their own values. For example, a driver handling ultrasound data from a medical device, which must notify a user-mode visualization application of new data, would probably use a boost value of 8 as well, to satisfy the same latency as a sound card. In most cases, however, due to the way Windows driver stacks are built (again, see Chapter 6 for more information), driver developers often write *minidrivers*, which call into a Microsoft-owned driver that supplies its own boost to `IoCompleteRequest`. For example, RAID or SATA controller card developers typically call `StorPortCompleteRequest` to complete processing their requests. This call does not have any parameter for a boost value, because the Storport.sys driver fills in the right value when calling the kernel. Additionally, whenever any file system driver (identified by setting its device type to `FILE_DEVICE_DISK_FILE_SYSTEM` or `FILE_DEVICE_NETWORK_FILE_SYSTEM`) completes its request, a boost of `IO_DISK_INCREMENT` is always applied if the driver passed in `IO_NO_INCREMENT` (0) instead. So this boost value has become less of a recommendation and more of a requirement enforced by the kernel.

Boosts during waiting on executive resources

When a thread attempts to acquire an executive resource (ERESOURCE; see Chapter 8 in Part 2 for more information on kernel-synchronization objects) that is already owned exclusively by another thread, it must enter a wait state until the other thread has released the resource. To limit the risk of deadlocks, the executive performs this wait in intervals of 500 ms instead of doing an infinite wait on the resource.

At the end of these 500 ms, if the resource is still owned, the executive attempts to prevent CPU starvation by acquiring the dispatcher lock, boosting the owning thread or threads to 15 (if the original owner priority is less than the waiter's and not already 15), resetting their quantums, and performing another wait.

Because executive resources can be either shared or exclusive, the kernel first boosts the exclusive owner and then checks for shared owners and boosts all of them. When the waiting thread enters the wait state again, the hope is that the scheduler will schedule one of the owner threads, which will have enough time to complete its work and release the resource. Note that this boosting mechanism is used only if the resource doesn't have the Disable Boost flag set, which developers can choose to set if the priority-inversion mechanism described here works well with their usage of the resource.

Additionally, this mechanism isn't perfect. For example, if the resource has multiple shared owners, the executive boosts all those threads to priority 15. This results in a sudden surge of high-priority threads on the system, all with full quantums. Although the initial owner thread will run first (because it was the first to be boosted and therefore is first on the ready list), the other shared owners will run next because the waiting thread's priority was not boosted. Only after all the shared owners have had a chance to run and their priority has been decreased below the waiting thread will the waiting thread finally get its chance to acquire the resource. Because shared owners can promote or convert their ownership from shared to exclusive as soon as the exclusive owner releases the resource, it's possible for this mechanism not to work as intended.

Priority boosts for foreground threads after waits

As will be described shortly, whenever a thread in the foreground process completes a wait operation on a kernel object, the kernel boosts its current (not base) priority by the current value of `PsPrior\-itySeparation`. (The windowing system is responsible for determining which process is considered to be in the foreground.) As described earlier in this chapter in the section "Controlling the quantum," `PsPrioritySeparation` reflects the quantum-table index used to select quantums for the threads of foreground applications. However, in this case, it is being used as a priority boost value.

The reason for this boost is to improve the responsiveness of interactive applications. By giving the foreground application a small boost when it completes a wait, it has a better chance of running right away, especially when other processes at the same base priority might be running in the background.

EXPERIMENT: Watching foreground priority boosts and decays

Using the CPU Stress tool, you can watch priority boosts in action. Take the following steps:

1. Open the System utility in Control Panel or right-click the **This Computer** icon on the desktop and choose **Properties**.

2. Click the **Advanced System Settings** label, click the **Advanced** tab, click the **Settings** button in the Performance section, and click the **Advanced** tab.

3. Select the **Programs** option. This gives `PsPrioritySeparation` a value of 2.

4. Run CPU Stress, right-click thread 1, and choose **Busy** from the context menu.

5. Start the Performance Monitor tool.

6. Click the **Add Counter** toolbar button or press **Ctrl+I** to open the Add Counters dialog box.

7. Select the **Thread** object and then select the **Priority Current** counter.

8. In the Instances box, select **<All Instances>** and click **Search**.

9. Scroll down to the CPUSTRES process, select the second thread (thread 1; the first thread is the GUI thread) and click the **Add** button. You should see something like this:

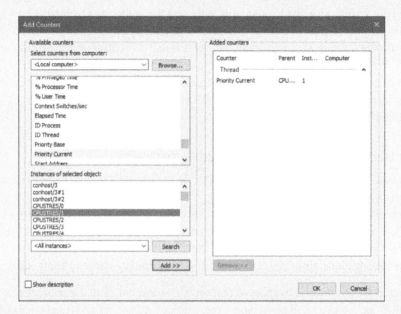

10. Click **OK**.

11. Right-click the counter and select **Properties**.

12. Click the **Graph** tab and change the maximum vertical scale to 16. Then click **OK**.

13. Bring the CPUSTRES process to the foreground. You should see the priority of the CPUSTRES thread being boosted by 2 and then decaying back to the base priority. CPUSTRES periodically receives a boost of 2 because the thread you're monitoring is sleeping about 25 percent of the time and then waking up. (This is the Busy activity level.) The boost is applied when the thread wakes up. If you set the activity level to Maximum, you won't see any boosts because Maximum in CPUSTRES puts the thread into an infinite loop. Therefore, the thread doesn't invoke any wait functions and therefore doesn't receive any boosts.

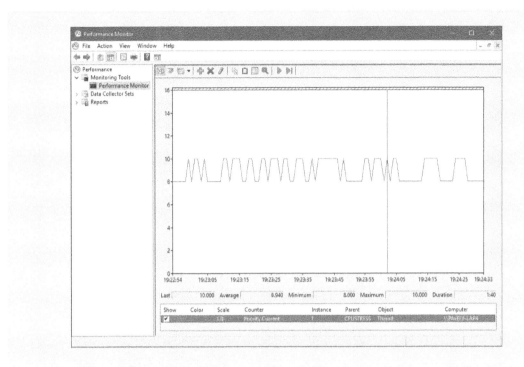

14. When you've finished, exit Performance Monitor and CPU Stress.

Priority boosts after GUI threads wake up

Threads that own windows receive an additional boost of 2 when they wake up because of windowing activity such as the arrival of window messages. The windowing system (Win32k.sys) applies this boost when it calls KeSetEvent to set an event used to wake up a GUI thread. The reason for this boost is similar to the previous one: to favor interactive applications.

EXPERIMENT: Watching priority boosts on GUI threads

You can see the windowing system apply its boost of 2 for GUI threads that wake up to process window messages by monitoring the current priority of a GUI application and moving the mouse across the window. Just follow these steps:

1. Open the **System** utility in Control Panel.

2. Click the **Advanced System Settings** label, click the **Advanced** tab, click the **Settings** button in the Performance section, and click the **Advanced** tab.

3. Select the **Programs** option. This gives PsPrioritySeparation a value of 2.

4. Run Notepad.

5. Start the Performance Monitor tool.

6. Click the **Add Counter** toolbar button or press **Ctrl+I** to open the Add Counters dialog box.

7. Select the **Thread** object and then select the **Priority Current** counter.

8. In the Instances box, type **Notepad**. Then click **Search**.

9. Scroll down to the Notepad/0 entry, click it, click the **Add** button, and then click **OK**.

10. As in the previous experiment, change the maximum vertical scale to 16. You should see the priority of thread 0 in Notepad at 8 or 10. (Because Notepad entered a wait state shortly after it received the boost of 2 that threads in the foreground process receive, it might not yet have decayed from 10 to 8.)

11. With Performance Monitor in the foreground, move the mouse across the Notepad window. (Make both windows visible on the desktop.) Notice that the priority sometimes remains at 10 and sometimes at 9, for the reasons just explained.

> **Note** You won't likely catch Notepad at 8. This is because it runs so little after receiving the GUI thread boost of 2 that it never experiences more than one priority level of decay before waking up again. (This is due to additional windowing activity and the fact that it receives the boost of 2 again.)

12. Bring Notepad to the foreground. You should see the priority rise to 12 and remain there. This is because the thread is receiving two boosts: the boost of 2 applied to GUI threads when they wake up to process windowing input and an additional boost of 2 because Notepad is in the foreground. (Or, you may see it drop to 11 if it experiences the normal priority decay that occurs for boosted threads on the quantum end.)

13. Move the mouse over Notepad while it's still in the foreground. You might see the priority drop to 11 (or maybe even 10) as it experiences the priority decay that normally occurs on boosted threads as they complete their turn. However, the boost of 2 that is applied because it's the foreground process remains as long as Notepad remains in the foreground.

14. Exit Performance Monitor and Notepad.

Priority boosts for CPU starvation

Imagine the following situation: A priority 7 thread is running, preventing a priority 4 thread from ever receiving CPU time. However, a priority 11 thread is waiting for some resource that the priority 4 thread has locked. But because the priority 7 thread in the middle is eating up all the CPU time, the priority 4 thread will never run long enough to finish whatever it's doing and release the resource blocking the priority 11 thread. This scenario is known as *priority inversion*.

What does Windows do to address this situation? An ideal solution (at least in theory) would be to track locks and owners and boost the appropriate threads so that forward progress can be made. This idea is implemented with a feature called *Autoboost*, described later in this chapter in the section "Autoboost." However, for general starvation scenarios, the following mitigation is used.

You saw how the code responsible for executive resources manages this scenario by boosting the owner threads so that they can have a chance to run and release the resource. However, executive resources are only one of the many synchronization constructs available to developers, and the boosting technique will not apply to any other primitive. Therefore, Windows also includes a generic CPU starvation-relief mechanism as part of a thread called the *balance-set manager*. (This is a system thread that exists primarily to perform memory-management functions and is described in more detail in Chapter 5.) Once per second, this thread scans the ready queues for any threads that have been in the ready state (that is, haven't run) for approximately 4 seconds. If it finds such a thread, the balance-set manager boosts the thread's priority to 15 and sets the quantum target to an equivalent CPU clock cycle count of 3 quantum units. After the quantum expires, the thread's priority decays immediately to its original base priority. If the thread wasn't finished and a higher-priority thread is ready to run, the decayed thread returns to the ready queue, where it again becomes eligible for another boost if it remains there for another 4 seconds.

The balance-set manager doesn't actually scan all the ready threads every time it runs. To minimize the CPU time it uses, it scans only 16 ready threads, If there are more threads at that priority level, it remembers where it left off and picks up again on the next pass. Also, it boosts only 10 threads per pass. If it finds more than 10 threads meriting this particular boost (which indicates an unusually busy system), it stops the scan and picks up again on the next pass.

> **Note**   As mentioned, scheduling decisions in Windows are not affected by the number of threads and are made in constant time. Because the balance-set manager must scan ready queues manually, this operation depends on the number of threads on the system; more threads require more scanning time. However, the balance-set manager is not considered part of the scheduler or its algorithms and is simply an extended mechanism to increase reliability. Additionally, because of the cap on threads and queues to scan, the performance impact is minimized and predictable in a worst-case scenario.

EXPERIMENT: Watching priority boosts for CPU starvation

Using the CPU Stress tool, you can watch priority boosts in action. In this experiment, you'll see CPU usage change when a thread's priority is boosted. Take the following steps:

1. Run CPUSTRES.exe.

2. The activity level of thread 1 is Low. Change it to **Maximum**.

3. The thread priority of thread 1 is Normal. Change it to **Lowest**.

4. Click thread 2. Its activity level is Low. Change it to **Maximum**.

5. Change the process affinity mask to a single logical processor. To do so, open the **Process** menu and choose **Affinity**. (It doesn't matter which processor.) Alternatively, use Task Manager to make the change. The screen should look something like this:

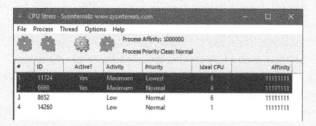

6. Start the Performance Monitor tool.

7. Click the **Add Counter** toolbar button or press **Ctrl+I** to open the Add Counters dialog box.

8. Select the **Thread** object and then select the **Priority Current** counter.

9. In the Instances box, type **CPUSTRES** and click **Search**.

10. Select threads 1 and 2 (thread 0 is the GUI thread), click the **Add** button, and click **OK**.

11. Change the vertical scale maximum to 16 for both counters.

12. Because Performance Monitor refreshes once per second, you may miss the priority boosts. To help with that, press **Ctrl+F** to freeze the display. Then force updates to occur more frequently by pressing and holding down **Ctrl+U**. With some luck, you may see a priority boost for the lower-priority thread to level 15 like so:

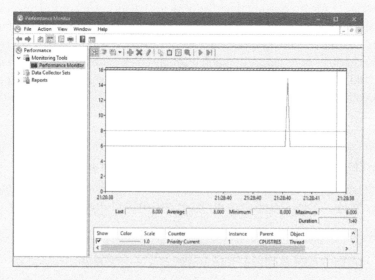

13. Exit Performance Monitor and CPU Stress.

Applying boosts

Back in `KiExitDispatcher`, you saw that `KiProcessThreadWaitList` is called to process any threads in the deferred ready list. It is here that the boost information passed by the caller is processed. This is done by looping through each `DeferredReady` thread, unlinking its wait blocks (only `Active` and `Bypassed` blocks are unlinked), and setting two key values in the kernel's thread control block: `Adjust-Reason` and `AdjustIncrement`. The reason is one of the two `Adjust` possibilities seen earlier, and the increment corresponds to the boost value. `KiDeferredReadyThread` is then called. This makes the thread ready for execution by running two algorithms: the quantum and priority selection algorithm (which you are about to see in two parts) and the processor selection algorithm (which is shown in the "Processor selection" section later in this chapter).

Let's first look at when the algorithm applies boosts, which happens only in cases when a thread is not in the real-time priority range. For an `AdjustUnwait` boost, it will be applied only if the thread is not already experiencing an unusual boost and only if the thread has not disabled boosting by calling `SetThreadPriorityBoost`, which sets the `DisableBoost` flag in the KTHREAD. Another situation that can disable boosting in this case is if the kernel has realized that the thread has actually exhausted its quantum (but the clock interrupt did not fire to consume it) and it has come out of a wait that lasted less than two clock ticks.

If these situations are not currently true, the new priority of the thread will be computed by adding the `AdjustIncrement` to the thread's current base priority. Additionally, if the thread is known to be part of a foreground process (meaning that the memory priority is set to MEMORY_PRIORITY_FOREGROUND, which is configured by Win32k.sys when focus changes), this is where the priority-separation boost (`PsPrioritySeparation`) is applied by adding its value on top of the new priority. This is also known as the *foreground priority boost*, which was explained earlier.

Finally, the kernel checks whether this newly computed priority is higher than the current priority of the thread, and it limits this value to an upper bound of 15 to avoid crossing into the real-time range. It then sets this value as the thread's new current priority. If any foreground separation boost was applied, it sets this value in the `ForegroundBoost` field of the KTHREAD, which results in a `PriorityDecrement` equal to the separation boost.

For `AdjustBoost` boosts, the kernel checks whether the thread's current priority is lower than the `AdjustIncrement` (recall this is the priority of the setting thread) and whether the thread's current priority is below 13. If so, and priority boosts have not been disabled for the thread, the `AdjustIncrement` priority is used as the new current priority, limited to a maximum of 13. Meanwhile, the `UnusualBoost` field of the KTHREAD contains the boost value, which results in a `PriorityDecrement` equal to the lock-ownership boost.

In all cases where a `PriorityDecrement` is present, the quantum of the thread is also recomputed to be the equivalent of only one clock tick, based on the value of `KiLockQuantumTarget`. This ensures that foreground and unusual boosts will be lost after one clock tick instead of the usual two (or other configured value), as will be shown in the next section. This also happens when an `AdjustBoost` is requested but the thread is running at priority 13 or 14 or with boosts disabled.

After this work is complete, `AdjustReason` is now set to `AdjustNone`.

Removing boosts

Removing boosts is done in `KiDeferredReadyThread` as boosts and quantum recomputations are being applied (as shown in the previous section). The algorithm first begins by checking the type of adjustment being done.

For an `AdjustNone` scenario, which means the thread became ready perhaps due to a preemption, the thread's quantum will be recomputed if it already hit its target but the clock interrupt has not yet noticed, as long as the thread was running at a dynamic priority level. Additionally, the thread's priority will be recomputed. For an `AdjustUnwait` or `AdjustBoost` scenario on a non-real-time thread, the kernel checks whether the thread silently exhausted its quantum (as in the prior section). If so, or if the thread was running with a base priority of 14 or higher, or if no `PriorityDecrement` is present and the thread has completed a wait that lasted longer than two clock ticks, the quantum of the thread is recomputed, as is its priority.

Priority recomputation happens on non-real-time threads. It's done by taking the thread's current priority, subtracting its foreground boost, subtracting its unusual boost (the combination of these last two items is the `PriorityDecrement`), and finally subtracting 1. This new priority is bounded with the base priority as the lowest bound and any existing priority decrement is zeroed out (clearing unusual and foreground boosts). This means that in the case of a lock-ownership boost or any of the other unusual boosts explained, the entire boost value is now lost. On the other hand, for a regular `AdjustUnwait` boost, the priority naturally trickles down by 1 due to the subtraction by 1. This lowering eventually stops when the base priority is hit due to the lower bound check.

There is another instance where boosts must be removed, which goes through the `KiRemoveBoost-Thread` function. This is a special-case boost removal that occurs due to the lock-ownership boost rule, which specifies that the setting thread must lose its boost when donating its current priority to the waking thread (to avoid a lock convoy). It is also used to undo the boost due to targeted deferred procedure calls (DPCs) as well as the boost against ERESOURCE lock-starvation boost. The only special detail about this routine is that when computing the new priority, it takes special care to separate the `ForegroundBoost` and `UnusualBoost` components of the `PriorityDecrement` to maintain any GUI foreground-separation boost that the thread accumulated. This behavior, which appeared starting with Windows 7, ensures that threads relying on the lock-ownership boost do not behave erratically when running in the foreground, or vice-versa.

Figure 4-12 displays an example of how normal boosts are removed from a thread as it experiences quantum end.

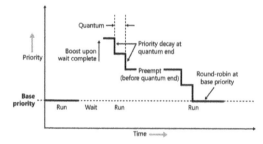

FIGURE 4-12   Priority boosting and decay.

Priority boosts for multimedia applications and games

Although Windows' CPU-starvation priority boosts might be enough to get a thread out of an abnormally long wait state or potential deadlock, they simply cannot deal with the resource requirements imposed by a CPU-intensive application such as Windows Media Player or a 3D computer game.

Skipping and other audio glitches have long been a common source of irritation among Windows users. The Windows user-mode audio stack exacerbates this situation because it offers even more chances for preemption. To address this, client versions of Windows use the MMCSS driver (described earlier in this chapter), implemented in %SystemRoot%\System32\Drivers\MMCSS.sys. Its purpose is to ensure glitch-free multimedia playback for applications that register with it.

> **Note** Windows 7 implements MMCSS as a service (rather than a driver). This posed a potential risk, however. If the MMCSS managing thread blocked for any reason, the threads managed by it would retain their real-time priorities, potentially causing system-wide starvation. The solution was to move the code to the kernel where the managing thread (and other resources used by MMCSS) could not be touched. There are other benefits to being a kernel driver, such as holding a direct pointer to process and thread objects rather than IDs or handles. This bypasses searches based on IDs or handles and allows faster communication with the scheduler and Power Manager.

Client applications can register with MMCSS by calling AvSetMmThreadCharacteristics with a task name that must match one of the subkeys under HKLM\SOFTWARE\Microsoft\Windows NT\CurrentVersion\Multimedia\SystemProfile\Tasks. (The list can be modified by OEMs to include other specific tasks as appropriate.) Out of the box, the following tasks exist:

- Audio
- Capture
- Distribution
- Games
- Low Latency
- Playback
- Pro Audio
- Window Manager

Each of these tasks includes information about the various properties that differentiate them. The most important one for scheduling is called the *Scheduling Category*, which is the primary factor determining the priority of threads registered with MMCSS. Table 4-4 shows the various scheduling categories.

TABLE 4-4 Scheduling categories

Category	Priority	Description
High	23–26	Pro Audio threads running at a higher priority than any other thread on the system except for critical system threads
Medium	16–22	The threads part of a foreground application such as Windows Media Player
Low	8–15	All other threads that are not part of the previous categories
Exhausted	4–6	Threads that have exhausted their share of the CPU and will continue running only if no other higher-priority threads are ready to run

The main mechanism behind MMCSS boosts the priority of threads inside a registered process to the priority level matching their scheduling category and relative priority within this category for a guaranteed period. It then lowers those threads to the exhausted category so that other, non-multimedia threads on the system can also get a chance to execute.

By default, multimedia threads get 80 percent of the CPU time available, while other threads receive 20 percent. (Based on a sample of 10 ms, that would be 8 ms and 2 ms, respectively.) You can change this percentage by modifying the `SystemResponsiveness` registry value under the `HKLM\SOFTWARE\Microsoft\Windows NT\CurrentVersion\Multimedia\SystemProfile` key. The value can range from 10 to 100 percent (20 is the default; setting a value lower than 10 evaluates to 10), which indicates the CPU percentage guaranteed to the system (not the registered audio apps). MMCSS scheduling thread runs at priority 27 because they need to preempt any Pro Audio threads to lower their priority to the exhausted category.

As discussed, changing the relative thread priorities within a process does not usually make sense, and no tool allows this because only developers understand the importance of the various threads in their programs. On the other hand, because applications must manually register with MMCSS and provide it with information about what kind of thread this is, MMCSS does have the necessary data to change these relative thread priorities—and developers are well aware that this will happen.

EXPERIMENT: MMCSS priority boosting

In this experiment, you'll see the effects of MMCSS priority boosting.

1. Run Windows Media Player (wmplayer.exe). (Other playback programs might not take advantage of the API calls required to register with MMCSS.)

2. Play some audio content.

3. Using Task Manager or Process Explorer, set the affinity of the Wmplayer.exe process so that it runs on only one CPU.

4. Start the Performance Monitor tool.

5. Using Task Manager, change Performance Monitor's priority class to **Realtime** so it will have a better chance of recording activity.

6. Click the **Add Counter** toolbar button or press **Ctrl+I** to open the Add Counters dialog box.

7. Select the **Thread** object and then select the **Priority Current**.

8. In the Instances box, type **Wmplayer**, click **Search**, and then select all its threads.

9. Click the **Add** button and click **OK**.

10. Open the **Action** menu and choose **Properties**.

11. On the Graph tab, change the maximum vertical scale to 32. You should see one or more priority-16 threads inside Wmplayer, which will be constantly running unless there is a higher-priority thread requiring the CPU after they are dropped to the exhausted category.

12. Run CPU Stress.

13. Set the activity level of thread 1 to **Maximum**.

14. The priority of thread 1 is Normal. Change it to **Time Critical**.

15. Change the CPUSTRES priority class to **High**.

16. Change the CPUSTRES affinity to use the same CPU used for Wmplayer. The system should slow down considerably, but the music playback should continue. Every so often, you'll be able to get back some responsiveness from the rest of the system.

17. In Performance Monitor, notice that the WmPlayer priority 16 threads drop from time to time as shown here:

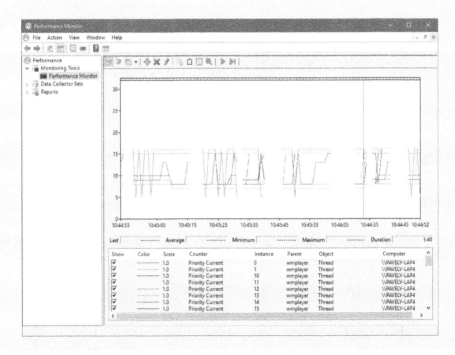

MMCSS' functionality does not stop at simple priority boosting, however. Because of the nature of network drivers on Windows and the NDIS stack, DPCs are quite common mechanisms for delaying work after an interrupt has been received from the network card. Because DPCs run at an IRQL level higher than user-mode code (see Chapter 6 for more information on DPCs and IRQLs), long-running network card driver code can still interrupt media playback—for example, during network transfers or when playing a game.

MMCSS sends a special command to the network stack, telling it to throttle network packets during the duration of the media playback. This throttling is designed to maximize playback performance—at the cost of some small loss in network throughput (which would not be noticeable for network operations usually performed during playback, such as playing an online game). The exact mechanisms behind it do not belong to any area of the scheduler, so we'll leave them out of this description.

MMCSS also supports a feature called *deadline scheduling*. The idea is that an audio-playing program does not always need the highest priority level in its category. If such a program uses buffering (obtaining audio data from disk or network) and then plays the buffer while building the next buffer, deadline scheduling allows a client thread to indicate a time when it must get the high priority level to avoid glitches, but live with a slightly lower priority (within its category) in the meantime. A thread can use the AvTaskIndexYield function to indicate the next time it must be allowed to run, specifying the time it needs to get the highest priority within its category. Until that time arrives, it gets the lowest priority within its category, potentially freeing more CPU time to the system.

Autoboost

Autoboost is a framework targeted at the priority-inversion problem described in the previous section. The idea is to track lock owners and lock waiters in such a way that would allow boosting the appropriate threads' priorities (I/O priority as well if needed) to allow threads to make forward progress. The lock information is stored in a static array of KLOCK_ENTRY objects inside the KTHREAD structure. The current implementation uses a maximum of six entries. Each KLOCK_ENTRY maintains two binary trees: one for locks owned by the thread and the other for locks waited on by the thread. These trees are keyed by priority so that constant time is required to determine the highest priority to which boosting should be applied. If boost is required, the owner's priority is set to the waiter's priority. It may also boost I/O priority if these were issued with low priority. (See Chapter 6 for more on I/O priority.) As with all priority boosts, the maximum priority achievable by Autoboost is 15. (The priority of real-time threads is never boosted.)

Current implementation uses the Autoboost framework for pushlocks and guarded mutexes synchronization primitives, which are exposed to kernel code only. (See Chapter 8 in Part 2 for more on these objects.) The framework is also used by some executive components for specialized cases. Future versions of Windows may implement Autoboost for user-mode accessible objects that have an ownership concept, such as critical sections.

Context switching

A thread's context and the procedure for context switching vary depending on the processor's architecture. A typical context switch requires saving and reloading the following data:

- Instruction pointer
- Kernel stack pointer
- A pointer to the address space in which the thread runs (the process's page table directory)

The kernel saves this information from the old thread by pushing it onto the current (old thread's) kernel-mode stack, updating the stack pointer, and saving the stack pointer in the old thread's KTHREAD structure. The kernel stack pointer is then set to the new thread's kernel stack, and the new thread's context is loaded. If the new thread is in a different process, it loads the address of its page table directory into a special processor register so that its address space is available. (See the description of address translation in Chapter 5.) If a kernel APC that needs to be delivered is pending, an interrupt at IRQL 1 is requested. (For more information on APCs, see Chapter 8 in Part 2.) Otherwise, control passes to the new thread's restored instruction pointer and the new thread resumes execution.

Direct Switch

Windows 8 and Server 2012 introduced an optimization called Direct Switch, that allows a thread to donate its quantum and boost to another thread, which is then immediately scheduled on the same processor. In synchronous client/server scenarios, this can produce significant throughput improvements because the client/server threads are not migrated to other processors that may be idle or parked. Another way to think about this is that at any given time, only the client or the server thread is running, so the thread scheduler should treat them as a single logical thread. Figure 4-13 shows the effect of using Direct Switch.

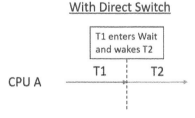

FIGURE 4-13 Direct Switch.

The scheduler has no way of knowing that the first thread (T1 in Figure 4-13) is about to enter a wait state after signaling some synchronization object that the second thread (T2) is waiting on. Therefore, a special function must be called to let the scheduler know that this is the case (atomic signal and wait).

If possible, the `KiDirectSwitchThread` function performs the actual switch. It's called by `KiExit-Dispatcher` if passed a flag indicating to use Direct Switch if possible. Priority donation, in which the first thread's priority is "donated" to the second thread (if the latter's priority is lower than the former), is applied if specified by yet another bit flag to `KiExitDispatcher`. In the current implementation, these two flags are always specified together (or none at all), meaning in any Direct Switch attempt, priority donation is attempted as well. Direct Switch can fail—for example, if the target thread's affinity precludes it from running on the current processor. However, if it succeeds, the quantum of the first thread is transferred to the target thread and the first thread loses its remaining quantum.

Direct Switch is currently used in the following scenarios:

- If a thread calls the `SignalObjectAndWait` Windows API (or its kernel equivalent `NtSignalAndWaitForSingleObject`)

- ALPC (described in Chapter 8 in Part 2)

- Synchronous remote procedure call (RPC) calls

- COM remote calls (currently MTA [multithreaded apartment] to MTA only)

Scheduling scenarios

Windows answers the question of "Who gets the CPU?" based on thread priority, but how does this approach work in practice? The following sections illustrate just how priority-driven preemptive multitasking works on the thread level.

Voluntary switch

A thread might voluntarily relinquish use of the processor by entering a wait state on some object (such as an event, a mutex, a semaphore, an I/O completion port, a process, a thread, and so on) by calling one of the Windows wait functions such as `WaitForSingleObject` or `WaitForMultipleObjects`. (Waiting for objects is described in more detail in Chapter 8 in Part 2.)

Figure 4-14 illustrates a thread entering a wait state and Windows selecting a new thread to run. In Figure 4-14, the top block (thread) is voluntarily relinquishing the processor so that the next thread in the ready queue can run. (This is represented by the halo it has when in the Running column.) Although it might appear from this figure that the relinquishing thread's priority is being reduced, it's not. It's just being moved to the wait queue of the objects the thread is waiting for.

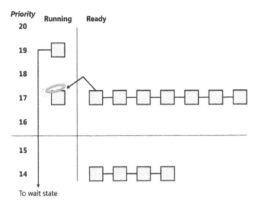

FIGURE 4-14 Voluntary switching.

Preemption

In this scheduling scenario, a lower-priority thread is preempted when a higher-priority thread becomes ready to run. This situation might occur for a couple of reasons:

- A higher-priority thread's wait completes (the event that the other thread was waiting for has occurred).

- A thread priority is increased or decreased.

In either of these cases, Windows must determine whether the currently running thread should continue to run or be preempted to allow a higher-priority thread to run.

> **Note** Threads running in user mode can preempt threads running in kernel mode. The mode in which the thread is running doesn't matter; the thread priority is the determining factor.

When a thread is preempted, it is put at the head of the ready queue for the priority it was running at (see Figure 4-15).

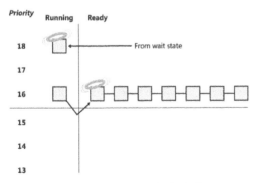

FIGURE 4-15 Preemptive thread scheduling.

In Figure 4-15, a thread with priority 18 emerges from a wait state and repossesses the CPU, causing the thread that had been running (at priority 16) to be bumped to the head of the ready queue. Notice that the bumped thread doesn't go to the end of the queue. Rather, it goes to the beginning. When the preempting thread has finished running, the bumped thread can complete its quantum.

Quantum end

When the running thread exhausts its CPU quantum, Windows must determine whether the thread's priority should be decremented and then whether another thread should be scheduled on the processor.

If the thread priority is reduced (for example, because of some boost it received before), Windows looks for a more appropriate thread to schedule, such as one in a ready queue with a higher priority than the new priority for the currently running thread. If the thread priority isn't reduced and there are other threads in the ready queue at the same priority level, Windows selects the next thread in the ready queue at that same priority level. It then moves the previously running thread to the tail of that queue, giving it a new quantum value and changing its state from running to ready. This is illustrated in Figure 4-16. If no other thread of the same priority is ready to run, the thread gets to run for another quantum.

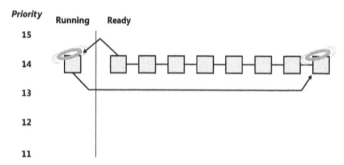

FIGURE 4-16 Quantum-end thread scheduling.

As you saw, instead of simply relying on a clock interval timer–based quantum to schedule threads, Windows uses an accurate CPU clock cycle count to maintain quantum targets. Windows also uses this count to determine whether quantum end is currently appropriate for the thread—something that might have happened previously and is important to discuss.

Using a scheduling model that relies only on the clock interval timer, the following situation can occur:

- Threads A and B become ready to run during the middle of an interval. (Scheduling code runs not just at each clock interval, so this is often the case.)

- Thread A starts running but is interrupted for a while. The time spent handling the interrupt is charged to the thread.

- Interrupt processing finishes and thread A starts running again, but it quickly hits the next clock interval. The scheduler can assume only that thread A had been running all this time and now switches to thread B.

- Thread B starts running and has a chance to run for a full clock interval (barring preemption or interrupt handling).

In this scenario, thread A was unfairly penalized in two different ways. First, the time it spent handling a device interrupt was counted against its own CPU time, even though the thread probably had nothing to do with the interrupt. (Interrupts are handled in the context of whichever thread was running at the time, as discussed in Chapter 6.) It was also unfairly penalized for the time the system was idling inside that clock interval before it was scheduled. Figure 4-17 illustrates this scenario.

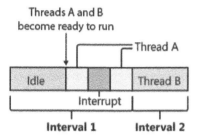

FIGURE 4-17 Unfair time slicing in pre-Vista versions of Windows.

Windows keeps an accurate count of the exact number of CPU clock cycles spent doing work that the thread was scheduled to do (which means excluding interrupts). It also keeps a quantum target of clock cycles that should have been spent by the thread at the end of its quantum. Therefore, both of the unfair decisions that would have been made against thread A as described in the preceding paragraph will not happen in Windows. Instead, the following situation occurs:

- Threads A and B become ready to run during the middle of an interval.

- Thread A starts running but is interrupted for a while. The CPU clock cycles spent handling the interrupt are not charged to the thread.

- Interrupt processing finishes and thread A starts running again, but it quickly hits the next clock interval. The scheduler looks at the number of CPU clock cycles charged to the thread and compares them to the expected CPU clock cycles that should have been charged at quantum end.

- Because the former number is much smaller than it should be, the scheduler assumes that thread A started running in the middle of a clock interval and might have been additionally interrupted.

- Thread A gets its quantum increased by another clock interval, and the quantum target is recalculated. Thread A now has its chance to run for a full clock interval.

- At the next clock interval, thread A has finished its quantum, and thread B now gets a chance to run.

Figure 4-18 illustrates this scenario.

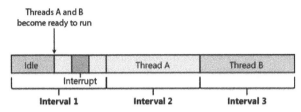

FIGURE 4-18 Fair time slicing in current versions of Windows.

Termination

When a thread finishes running (either because it returned from its main routine, called `ExitThread`, or was killed with `TerminateThread`), it moves from the running state to the terminated state. If there are no handles open on the thread object, the thread is removed from the process thread list and the associated data structures are deallocated and released.

Idle threads

When no runnable thread exists on a CPU, Windows dispatches that CPU's idle thread. Each CPU has its own dedicated idle thread. This is because on a multiprocessor system, one CPU can be executing a thread while other CPUs might have no threads to execute. Each CPU's idle thread is found via a pointer in that CPU's PRCB.

All the idle threads belong to the idle process. The idle process and idle threads are special cases in many ways. They are, of course, represented by EPROCESS/KPROCESS and ETHREAD/KTHREAD structures, but they are not executive manager processes and thread objects. Nor is the idle process on the system process list. (This is why it does not appear in the output of the kernel debugger's `!process 0 0` command.) However, the idle thread or threads and their process can be found in other ways.

EXPERIMENT: Displaying the structures of the idle threads and idle process

You can find the idle thread and process structures in the kernel debugger via the `!pcr` command. (*PCR* is short for *processor control region*.) This command displays a subset of information from the PCR and from the associated PRCB. `!pcr` takes a single numeric argument, which is the number of the CPU whose PCR is to be displayed. The boot processor is processor 0. It is always present, so `!pcr 0` should always work. The following output shows the results of this command from a local kernel debugging session for a 64-bit, eight-processor system:

```
lkd> !pcr
KPCR for Processor 0 at fffff80174bd0000:
    Major 1 Minor 1
      NtTib.ExceptionList: fffff80176b4a000
         NtTib.StackBase: fffff80176b4b070
        NtTib.StackLimit: 000000000108e3f8
      NtTib.SubSystemTib: fffff80174bd0000
          NtTib.Version: 0000000074bd0180
       NtTib.UserPointer: fffff80174bd07f0
```

```
                NtTib.SelfTib: 00000098af072000

                      SelfPcr: 0000000000000000
                         Prcb: fffff80174bd0180
                         Irql: 0000000000000000
                          IRR: 0000000000000000
                          IDR: 0000000000000000
                InterruptMode: 0000000000000000
                          IDT: 0000000000000000
                          GDT: 0000000000000000
                          TSS: 0000000000000000

                CurrentThread: ffffb882fa27c080
                   NextThread: 0000000000000000
                   IdleThread: fffff80174c4c940

                     DpcQueue:
```

This output shows that CPU 0 was executing a thread other than its idle thread at the time the memory dump was obtained because the CurrentThread and IdleThread pointers are different. (On a multi-CPU system you can try !pcr 1, !pcr 2, and so on, until you run out. Observe that each IdleThread pointer is different.)

Now use the !thread command on the indicated idle thread address:

```
lkd> !thread fffff80174c4c940
THREAD fffff80174c4c940  Cid 0000.0000  Teb: 0000000000000000 Win32Thread:
0000000000000000 RUNNING on processor 0
Not impersonating
DeviceMap               ffff800a52e17ce0
Owning Process          fffff80174c4b940        Image:          Idle
Attached Process        ffffb882e7ec7640        Image:          System
Wait Start TickCount    1637993         Ticks: 30 (0:00:00:00.468)
Context Switch Count    25908837        IdealProcessor: 0
UserTime                00:00:00.000
KernelTime              05:51:23.796
Win32 Start Address nt!KiIdleLoop (0xfffff801749e0770)
Stack Init fffff80176b52c90 Current fffff80176b52c20
Base fffff80176b53000 Limit fffff80176b4d000 Call 0000000000000000
Priority 0 BasePriority 0 PriorityDecrement 0 IoPriority 0 PagePriority 5
```

Finally, use the !process command on the owning process shown in the preceding output. For brevity, we'll add a second parameter value of 3, which causes !process to emit only minimal information for each thread:

```
lkd> !process fffff80174c4b940 3
PROCESS fffff80174c4b940
    SessionId: none  Cid: 0000    Peb: 00000000  ParentCid: 0000
    DirBase: 001aa000  ObjectTable: ffff800a52e14040  HandleCount: 2011.
    Image: Idle
    VadRoot ffffb882e7e1ae70 Vads 1 Clone 0 Private 7. Modified 1627. Locked 0.
    DeviceMap 0000000000000000
```

```
Token                                    ffff800a52e17040
ElapsedTime                              07:07:04.015
UserTime                                 00:00:00.000
KernelTime                               00:00:00.000
QuotaPoolUsage[PagedPool]                0
QuotaPoolUsage[NonPagedPool]             0
Working Set Sizes (now,min,max)  (7, 50, 450) (28KB, 200KB, 1800KB)
PeakWorkingSetSize                       1
VirtualSize                              0 Mb
PeakVirtualSize                          0 Mb
PageFaultCount                           2
MemoryPriority                           BACKGROUND
BasePriority                             0
CommitCharge                             0

        THREAD fffff80174c4c940  Cid 0000.0000  Teb: 0000000000000000
Win32Thread: 0000000000000000 RUNNING on processor 0
        THREAD ffff9d81e230ccc0  Cid 0000.0000  Teb: 0000000000000000
Win32Thread: 0000000000000000 RUNNING on processor 1
        THREAD ffff9d81e1bd9cc0  Cid 0000.0000  Teb: 0000000000000000
Win32Thread: 0000000000000000 RUNNING on processor 2
        THREAD ffff9d81e2062cc0  Cid 0000.0000  Teb: 0000000000000000
Win32Thread: 0000000000000000 RUNNING on processor 3
        THREAD ffff9d81e21a7cc0  Cid 0000.0000  Teb: 0000000000000000
Win32Thread: 0000000000000000 RUNNING on processor 4
        THREAD ffff9d81e22ebcc0  Cid 0000.0000  Teb: 0000000000000000
Win32Thread: 0000000000000000 RUNNING on processor 5
        THREAD ffff9d81e2428cc0  Cid 0000.0000  Teb: 0000000000000000
Win32Thread: 0000000000000000 RUNNING on processor 6
        THREAD ffff9d81e256bcc0  Cid 0000.0000  Teb: 0000000000000000
Win32Thread: 0000000000000000 RUNNING on processor 7
```

These process and thread addresses can also be used with dt nt!_EPROCESS, dt nt!_
KTHREAD, and other such commands.

The preceding experiment shows some of the anomalies associated with the idle process and its threads. The debugger indicates an Image name of Idle (which comes from the EPROCESS structure's ImageFileName member), but various Windows utilities report the idle process using different names. Task Manager and Process Explorer call it *System Idle Process*, while tlist calls it *System Process*. The process ID and thread IDs (the client IDs, or Cid in the debugger's output) are 0, as are the PEB and TEB pointers and potentially many other fields in the idle process or its threads. Because the idle process has no user-mode address space and its threads execute no user-mode code, they have no need of the various data required to manage a user-mode environment. Also, the idle process is not an object-manager process object, and its idle threads are not object-manager thread objects. Instead, the initial idle thread and idle process structures are statically allocated and used to bootstrap the system before the process manager and the object manager are initialized. Subsequent idle thread structures are allocated dynamically (as simple allocations from a non-paged pool, bypassing the object manager) as additional processors are brought online. Once process management initializes, it uses the special variable PsIdleProcess to refer to the idle process.

Perhaps the most interesting anomaly regarding the idle process is that Windows reports the priority of the idle threads as 0. In reality, however, the values of the idle threads' priority members are irrelevant because these threads are selected for dispatching only when there are no other threads to run. Their priority is never compared with that of any other thread. Nor is it used to put an idle thread on a ready queue, as idle threads are never part of any ready queues. (Only one thread per Windows system is actually running at priority 0—the zero page thread, explained in Chapter 5.)

Just as the idle threads are special cases in terms of selection for execution, they are also special cases for preemption. The idle thread's routine, KiIdleLoop, performs a number of operations that preclude its being preempted by another thread in the usual fashion. When no non-idle threads are available to run on a processor, that processor is marked as idle in its PRCB. After that, if a thread is selected for execution on the idle processor, the thread's address is stored in the NextThread pointer of the idle processor's PRCB. The idle thread checks this pointer on each pass through its loop.

Although some details of the flow vary between architectures (this is one of the few routines written in assembly and not in C), the basic sequence of operations of the idle thread is as follows:

1. The idle thread briefly enables interrupts, allowing any pending interrupts to be delivered, and then disables them (using the STI and CLI instructions on x86 and x64 processors). This is desirable because significant parts of the idle thread execute with interrupts disabled.

2. On the debug build on some architectures, the idle thread checks whether there is a kernel debugger trying to break into the system. If so, it gives it access.

3. The idle thread checks whether any DPCs (described in Chapter 6) are pending on the processor. DPCs could be pending if a DPC interrupt was not generated when they were queued. If DPCs are pending, the idle loop calls KiRetireDpcList to deliver them. This will also perform timer expiration, as well as deferred ready processing; the latter is explained in the upcoming "Multiprocessor systems" section. KiRetireDpcList must be entered with interrupts disabled, which is why interrupts are left disabled at the end of step 1. KiRetireDpcList exits with interrupts disabled as well.

4. The idle thread checks whether quantum end processing has been requested. If so, KiQuantumEnd is called to process the request.

5. The idle thread checks whether a thread has been selected to run next on the processor. If so, it dispatches that thread. This could be the case if, for example, a DPC or timer expiration processed in step 3 resolved the wait of a waiting thread, or if another processor selected a thread for this processor to run while it was already in the idle loop.

6. If requested, the idle thread checks for threads ready to run on other processors and, if possible, schedules one of them locally. (This operation is explained in the upcoming "Idle scheduler" section).

7. The idle thread calls the registered power-management processor idle routine (in case any power-management functions need to be performed), which is either in the processor power driver (such as intelppm.sys) or in the HAL if such a driver is unavailable.

Thread suspension

Threads can be suspended and resumed explicitly with the `SuspendThread` and `ResumeThread` API functions, respectively. Every thread has a suspend count, which is incremented by suspension and decremented by resuming. If the count is 0, the thread is free to execute. Otherwise, it will not execute.

Suspension works by queuing a kernel APC to the thread. When the thread is switched in to execute, the APC is executed first. This puts the thread in a wait state on event that is signaled when the thread is finally resumed.

This suspension mechanism has a noticeable drawback if the thread is in a wait state while a suspension request comes in, because it means that the thread needs to wake up just to be suspended. This can result in a kernel stack inswap (if the thread's kernel stack was swapped out). Windows 8.1 and Server 2012 R2 added a mechanism called *Lightweight Suspend* to allow for the suspension of a thread that is in a wait state not by using the APC mechanism, but by directly manipulating the thread's object in memory and marking it as suspended.

(Deep) freeze

Freezing is a mechanism by which processes enter a suspended state that cannot be changed by calling `ResumeThread` on threads in the process. This is useful when the system needs to suspend a UWP app. This happens when a Windows app goes to the background—for example, because another app comes to the foreground in Tablet mode or the app is minimized in Desktop mode. In this case, the system gives to the app roughly five seconds to do work, typically to save application state. Saving state is important because Windows apps may be killed without any notice if memory resources become low. If the app is killed, the state can be reloaded on the next launch and the user would have the perception that the app never really went away. Freezing a process means suspending all threads in such a way that `ResumeThread` is not able to wake. A flag in the `KTHREAD` structure indicates whether a thread is frozen. For a thread to be able to execute, its suspend count must be 0 and the `frozen` flag must be clear.

Deep freeze adds another constraint: Newly created threads in the process cannot start as well. For example, if a call to `CreateRemoteThreadEx` is used to create a new thread in a deep-frozen process, the thread will be frozen before actually starting. This is the typical usage of the freezing capability.

Process- and thread-freezing functionality is not exposed directly to user mode. It is used internally by the Process State Manager (PSM) service that is responsible for issuing the requests to the kernel for deep freezing and thawing (unfreezing).

You can also freeze processes using jobs. The ability to freeze and unfreeze a job is not publicly documented, but it's possible to do using the standard `NtSetInformationJobObject` system call. This is typically used for Windows apps, as all Windows apps processes are contained in jobs. Such a job may contain a single process (the Windows app itself), but it can also contain background task-hosting processes related to the same Window app so that freezing or thawing (unfreezing) all processes under that job can be done in a single stroke. (See Chapter 8 in Part 2 for more on Windows apps.)

EXPERIMENT: Deep freeze

In this experiment, you'll watch deep freeze happening by debugging a virtual machine.

1. Open WinDbg with admin privileges and attach to a virtual machine running Windows 10.

2. Press **Ctrl+Break** to break into the VM.

3. Set a breakpoint when deep freeze begins with a command to show the process that is frozen:

```
bp nt!PsFreezeProcess "!process -1 0; g"
```

4. Enter the **g** (go) command or press **F5**. You should see many deep freeze occurrences.

5. Start the Cortana UI from the taskbar and then close the UI. After about 5 seconds you should see something like the following:

```
PROCESS 8f518500  SessionId: 2  Cid: 12c8    Peb: 03945000  ParentCid: 02ac
    DirBase: 054007e0  ObjectTable: b0a8a040  HandleCount: 988.
    Image: SearchUI.exe
```

6. Now break into the debugger and show more info on that process:

```
1: kd> !process 8f518500 1
PROCESS 8f518500  SessionId: 2  Cid: 12c8    Peb: 03945000  ParentCid: 02ac
DeepFreeze
    DirBase: 054007e0  ObjectTable: b0a8a040  HandleCount: 988.
    Image: SearchUI.exe
    VadRoot 95c1ffd8 Vads 405 Clone 0 Private 7682. Modified 201241. Locked 0.
    DeviceMap a12509c0
    Token                             b0a65bd0
    ElapsedTime                       04:02:33.518
    UserTime                          00:00:06.937
    KernelTime                        00:00:00.703
    QuotaPoolUsage[PagedPool]         562688
    QuotaPoolUsage[NonPagedPool]      34392
    Working Set Sizes (now,min,max)   (20470, 50, 345) (81880KB, 200KB, 1380KB)
    PeakWorkingSetSize                25878
    VirtualSize                       367 Mb
    PeakVirtualSize                   400 Mb
    PageFaultCount                    307764
    MemoryPriority                    BACKGROUND
    BasePriority                      8
    CommitCharge                      8908
    Job                               8f575030
```

7. Notice the DeepFreeze attribute written by the debugger. Also notice that the process is part of a job. Use the !job command to see more details:

```
1: kd> !job 8f575030
Job at 8f575030
  Basic Accounting Information
    TotalUserTime:          0x0
```

```
                TotalKernelTime:              0x0
                TotalCycleTime:               0x0
                ThisPeriodTotalUserTime:      0x0
                ThisPeriodTotalKernelTime: 0x0
                TotalPageFaultCount:          0x0
                TotalProcesses:               0x1
                ActiveProcesses:              0x1
                FreezeCount:                  1
                BackgroundCount:              0
                TotalTerminatedProcesses:     0x0
                PeakJobMemoryUsed:            0x38e2
                PeakProcessMemoryUsed:        0x38e2
        Job Flags
          [cpu rate control]
          [frozen]
          [wake notification allocated]
          [wake notification enabled]
          [timers virtualized]
          [job swapped]
        Limit Information (LimitFlags: 0x0)
        Limit Information (EffectiveLimitFlags: 0x3000)
        CPU Rate Control
          Rate = 100.00%
          Scheduling Group: a469f330
```

8. The job is under CPU rate control (see the section "CPU rate limits" later in this chapter for more on CPU rate control) and is frozen. Detach from the VM and close the debugger.

Thread selection

Whenever a logical processor needs to pick the next thread to run, it calls the `KiSelectNextThread` scheduler function. This can happen in a variety of scenarios:

- A hard affinity change has occurred, making the currently running or standby thread ineligible for execution on its selected logical processor. Therefore, another must be chosen.

- The currently running thread reached its quantum end, and the Symmetric Multithreading (SMT) set it was running on has become busy while other SMT sets within the ideal node are fully idle. (*Symmetric Multithreading* is the technical name for the hyper-threading technology described in Chapter 2.) The scheduler performs a quantum-end migration of the current thread, so another must be chosen.

- A wait operation has finished, and there were pending scheduling operations in the wait status register (in other words, the priority and/or affinity bits were set).

In these scenarios, the behavior of the scheduler is as follows:

- The scheduler calls `KiSelectReadyThreadEx` to search for the next ready thread that the processor should run and check whether one was found.

- If a ready thread was not found, the idle scheduler is enabled, and the idle thread is selected for execution. If a ready thread *was* found, it is put in the ready state in the local or shared ready queue, as appropriate.

The `KiSelectNextThread` operation is performed only when the logical processor needs to pick—but not yet run—the next schedulable thread (which is why the thread will enter the Ready state). Other times, however, the logical processor is interested in immediately running the next ready thread or performing another action if one is not available (instead of going idle), such as when the following occurs:

- A priority change causes the current standby or running thread to no longer be the highest-priority ready thread on its selected logical processor, meaning that a higher priority ready thread must now run.

- The thread has explicitly yielded with `YieldProcessor` or `NtYieldExecution` and another thread might be ready for execution.

- The quantum of the current thread has expired, and other threads at the same priority level need their chance to run as well.

- A thread has lost its priority boost, causing a similar priority change to the scenario just described.

- The idle scheduler is running and needs to check whether a ready thread has not appeared in the interval between when the idle scheduling was requested and the idle scheduler ran.

A simple way to remember the difference between which routine runs is to check whether the logical processor *must* run a different thread (in which case `KiSelectNextThread` is called) or if it *should if possible* run a different thread (in which case `KiSelectReadyThreadEx` is called). In either case, because each processor belongs to a shared ready queue (pointed to by the KPRCB), `KiSelectReadyThreadEx` can simply check the current logical processor's (LP's) queues, removing the first highest-priority thread that it finds unless this priority is lower than the one of the currently running thread (depending on whether the current thread is still allowed to run, which would not be the case in the `KiSelectNextThread` scenario). If there is no higher-priority thread (or no threads are ready at all), no thread is returned.

Idle scheduler

Whenever the idle thread runs, it checks whether idle scheduling has been enabled. If so, the idle thread begins scanning other processors' ready queues for threads it can run by calling `KiSearchForNewThread`. The run-time costs associated with this operation are not charged as idle thread time, but are instead charged as interrupt and DPC time (charged to the processor), so idle scheduling time is considered system time. The `KiSearchForNewThread` algorithm, which is based on the functions described earlier in this section, is explained shortly.

Multiprocessor systems

On a uniprocessor system, scheduling is relatively simple: The highest-priority thread that wants to run is always running. On a multiprocessor system, it is more complex. This is because Windows attempts to schedule threads on the most optimal processor for the thread, taking into account the thread's preferred and previous processors as well as the configuration of the multiprocessor system. Therefore, although Windows attempts to schedule the highest-priority runnable threads on all available CPUs, it guarantees only to be running one of the highest-priority threads somewhere. With shared ready queues (for threads with no affinity restrictions), the guarantee is stronger. Each shared group of processors is running at least one of the highest-priority threads.

Before we describe the specific algorithms used to choose which threads run where and when, let's examine the additional information Windows maintains to track thread and processor state on multiprocessor systems and the three different types of multiprocessor systems supported by Windows (SMT, multicore, and NUMA).

Package sets and SMT sets

Windows uses five fields in the KPRCB to determine correct scheduling decisions when dealing with logical processor topologies. The first field, `CoresPerPhysicalProcessor`, determines whether this logical processor is part of a multicore package. It's computed from the CPUID returned by the processor and rounded to a power of 2. The second field, `LogicalProcessorsPerCore`, determines whether the logical processor is part of an SMT set, such as on an Intel processor with hyper-threading enabled, and is also queried through CPUID and rounded. Multiplying these two numbers yields the number of logical processors per package, or an actual physical processor that fits into a socket. With these numbers, each PRCB can then populate its `PackageProcessorSet` value. This is the affinity mask describing which other logical processors within this group (because packages are constrained to a group) belong to the same physical processor. Similarly, the `CoreProcessorSet` value connects other logical processors to the same core, also called an *SMT set*. Finally, the `GroupSetMember` value defines which bitmask within the current processor group identifies this very logical processor. For example, the logical processor 3 normally has a `GroupSetMember` value of 8 (which equals 2 to the third power).

EXPERIMENT: Viewing logical processor information

You can examine the information Windows maintains for SMT processors using the `!smt` command in the kernel debugger. The following output is from a quad-core Intel Core i7 system with SMT (eight logical processors):

```
lkd> !smt
SMT Summary:
------------

KeActiveProcessors:
********-------------------------------------------------------- (00000000000000ff)
IdleSummary:
-****--*-------------------------------------------------------- (000000000000009e)
```

```
No  PRCB                   SMT Set                                                           APIC Id
 0  fffff803d7546180   **------------------------------   (0000000000000003)  0x00000000
 1  ffffba01cb31a180   **------------------------------   (0000000000000003)  0x00000001
 2  ffffba01cb3dd180   --**----------------------------   (000000000000000c)  0x00000002
 3  ffffba01cb122180   --**----------------------------   (000000000000000c)  0x00000003
 4  ffffba01cb266180   ----**--------------------------   (0000000000000030)  0x00000004
 5  ffffba01cabd6180   ----**--------------------------   (0000000000000030)  0x00000005
 6  ffffba01cb491180   ------**------------------------   (00000000000000c0)  0x00000006
 7  ffffba01cb5d4180   ------**------------------------   (00000000000000c0)  0x00000007

Maximum cores per physical processor:    8
Maximum logical processors per core:     2
```

NUMA systems

Another type of multiprocessor system supported by Windows is one with a non-uniform memory architecture (NUMA). In a NUMA system, processors are grouped together in smaller units called *nodes*. Each node has its own processors and memory and is connected to the larger system through a cache-coherent interconnect bus. These systems are called *non-uniform* because each node has its own local high-speed memory. Although any processor in any node can access all of memory, node-local memory is much faster to access.

The kernel maintains information about each node in a NUMA system in a data structure called KNODE. The kernel variable KeNodeBlock is an array of pointers to the KNODE structures for each node. You can reveal the format of the KNODE structure using the dt command in the kernel debugger, as shown here:

```
lkd> dt nt!_KNODE
   +0x000 IdleNonParkedCpuSet : Uint8B
   +0x008 IdleSmtSet       : Uint8B
   +0x010 IdleCpuSet       : Uint8B
   +0x040 DeepIdleSet      : Uint8B
   +0x048 IdleConstrainedSet : Uint8B
   +0x050 NonParkedSet     : Uint8B
   +0x058 ParkLock         : Int4B
   +0x05c Seed             : Uint4B
   +0x080 SiblingMask      : Uint4B
   +0x088 Affinity         : _GROUP_AFFINITY
   +0x088 AffinityFill     : [10] UChar
   +0x092 NodeNumber       : Uint2B
   +0x094 PrimaryNodeNumber : Uint2B
   +0x096 Stride           : UChar
   +0x097 Spare0           : UChar
   +0x098 SharedReadyQueueLeaders : Uint8B
   +0x0a0 ProximityId      : Uint4B
   +0x0a4 Lowest           : Uint4B
   +0x0a8 Highest          : Uint4B
   +0x0ac MaximumProcessors : UChar
   +0x0ad Flags            : _flags
   +0x0ae Spare10          : UChar
   +0x0b0 HeteroSets       : [5] _KHETERO_PROCESSOR_SET
```

EXPERIMENT: Viewing NUMA information

You can examine the information Windows maintains for each node in a NUMA system using the !numa command in the kernel debugger. To experiment with NUMA systems even when such hardware is not available, it's possible to configure a Hyper-V virtual machine to include more than one NUMA node that the guest VM will use. To configure a Hyper-V VM to use NUMA, do the following. (You will need a host machine with more than four logical processors.)

1. Click **Start**, type **hyper**, and click the **Hyper-V Manager** option.

2. Make sure the VM is powered off. Otherwise the following changes cannot be made.

3. Right-click the VM in Hyper-V Manager and select **Settings** to open the VM's settings.

4. Click the **Memory** node and make sure **Dynamic Memory** is unchecked.

5. Click the **Processor** node and enter **4** in the **Number of Virtual Processors** box:

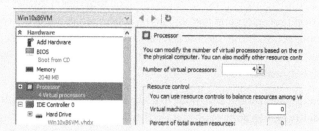

6. Expand the **Processor** node and select the **NUMA** sub-node.

7. Enter **2** in the **Maximum Number of Processors** and **Maximum NUMA Nodes Allowed on a Socket** boxes:

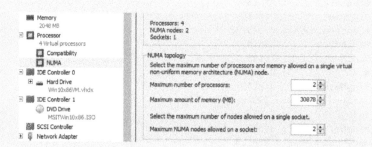

8. Click **OK** to save the settings.

9. Power up the VM.

10. Use a kernel debugger to issue the **!numa** command. Here's an example of output for the previously configured VM:

```
2: kd> !numa
NUMA Summary:
```

```
------------
      Number of NUMA nodes : 2
      Number of Processors : 4
unable to get nt!MmAvailablePages
    MmAvailablePages      : 0x00000000
    KeActiveProcessors    :
    ****--------------------------- (0000000f)

    NODE 0 (FFFFFFFF820510C0):
    Group               : 0 (Assigned, Committed, Assignment Adjustable)
    ProcessorMask       : **----------------------------- (00000003)
    ProximityId         : 0
    Capacity            : 2
    Seed                : 0x00000001
    IdleCpuSet          : 00000003
    IdleSmtSet          : 00000003
    NonParkedSet        : 00000003
Unable to get MiNodeInformation

    NODE 1 (FFFFFFFF8719E0C0):
    Group               : 0 (Assigned, Committed, Assignment Adjustable)
    ProcessorMask       : --**--------------------------- (0000000c)
    ProximityId         : 1
    Capacity            : 2
    Seed                : 0x00000003
    IdleCpuSet          : 00000008
    IdleSmtSet          : 00000008
    NonParkedSet        : 0000000c
Unable to get MiNodeInformation
```

Applications that want to gain the most performance out of NUMA systems can set the affinity mask to restrict a process to the processors in a specific node, although Windows already restricts nearly all threads to a single NUMA node due to its NUMA-aware scheduling algorithms.

How the scheduling algorithms account for NUMA systems is covered later in this chapter in the section "Processor selection." (The optimizations in the memory manager to take advantage of node-local memory are covered in Chapter 5.)

Processor group assignment

While querying the topology of the system to build the various relationships between logical processors, SMT sets, multicore packages, and physical sockets, Windows assigns processors to an appropriate group that will describe their affinity (through the extended affinity mask seen earlier). This work is done by the KePerformGroupConfiguration routine, which is called during initialization before any other phase 1 work is done. The steps of this process are as follows:

1. The function queries all detected nodes (KeNumberNodes) and computes the capacity of each node—that is, how many logical processors can be part of the node. This value is stored in MaximumProcessors in the KeNodeBlock array, which identifies all NUMA nodes on the system.

If the system supports NUMA proximity IDs, the proximity ID is queried for each node and saved in the node block.

2. The NUMA distance array is allocated (KeNodeDistance) and the distance between each NUMA node is computed.

   The next series of steps deal with specific user-configuration options that override default NUMA assignments. For example, consider a system with Hyper-V installed and with the hypervisor configured to auto-start. If the CPU does not support the extended hypervisor interface, then only one processor group will be enabled, and all NUMA nodes (that can fit) will be associated with group 0. Therefore, in this case, Hyper-V cannot take advantage of machines with more than 64 processors.

3. The function checks whether any static group assignment data was passed by the loader (and thus configured by the user). This data specifies the proximity information and group assignment for each NUMA node.

> **Note** Users dealing with large NUMA servers who might need custom control of proximity information and group assignments for testing or validation purposes can enter this data through the Group Assignment and Node Distance registry values. These are found in the HKLM\SYSTEM\ CurrentControlSet\Control\NUMA registry key. The exact format of this data includes a count followed by an array of proximity IDs and group assignments, which are all 32-bit values.

4. Before treating this data as valid, the kernel queries the proximity ID to match the node number and then associates group numbers as requested. It then makes sure that NUMA node 0 is associated with group 0, and that the capacity for all NUMA nodes is consistent with the group size. Finally, the function checks how many groups still have remaining capacity.

> **Note** NUMA node 0 is always assigned to group 0, no matter what.

5. The kernel dynamically attempts to assign NUMA nodes to groups while respecting any statically configured nodes if passed in as just described. Normally, the kernel tries to minimize the number of groups created, combining as many NUMA nodes as possible per group. However, if this behavior is not desired, it can be configured differently with the /MAXGROUP loader parameter, configured through the maxgroup BCD option. Turning this value on overrides the default behavior and causes the algorithm to spread as many NUMA nodes as possible into as many groups as possible, while respecting that the currently implemented group limit is 20. If there is only one node, or if all nodes can fit into a single group (and maxgroup is off), the system performs the default setting of assigning all nodes to group 0.

6. If there is more than one node, Windows checks the static NUMA node distances (if any). It then sorts all the nodes by their capacity so that the largest nodes come first. In the group-minimization mode, the kernel figures out the maximum processors there can be by adding up

all the capacities. By dividing that by the number of processors per group, the kernel assumes there will be this many total groups on the machine (limited to a maximum of 20). In group-maximization mode, the initial estimate is that there will be as many groups as nodes (limited again to 20).

7. The kernel begins the final assignment process. All fixed assignments from earlier are now committed and groups are created for those assignments.

8. All the NUMA nodes are reshuffled to minimize the distance between the different nodes within a group. In other words, closer nodes are put in the same group and sorted by distance.

9. The same process is performed for any dynamically configured node to group assignments.

10. Any remaining empty nodes are assigned to group 0.

Logical processors per group

Generally, Windows assigns 64 processors per group. But you can also customize this configuration by using different load options such as the /GROUPSIZE option, which is configured through the group-size BCD element. By specifying a number that is a power of 2, you can force groups to contain fewer processors than normal for purposes such as testing group awareness in the system. For example, a system with eight logical processors can be made to appear to have one, two, or four groups. To force the issue, the /FORCEGROUPAWARE option (BCD element groupaware) causes the kernel to avoid group 0 whenever possible, assigning the highest group number available in actions such as thread and DPC affinity selection and process group assignment. You should avoid setting a group size of 1 because this will force almost all applications on the system to behave as if they're running on a uniprocessor machine. This is because the kernel sets the affinity mask of a given process to span only one group until the application requests otherwise (which most applications will not do).

In the edge case where the number of logical processors in a package cannot fit into a single group, Windows adjusts these numbers so that a package can fit into a single group. It does so by shrinking the CoresPerPhysicalProcessor number and, if the SMT cannot fit, the LogicalProcessorsPerCore number. The exception to this rule is if the system actually contains multiple NUMA nodes within a single package (uncommon, but possible). In these multi-chip modules (MCMs), two sets of cores as well as two memory controllers are on the same die/package. If the ACPI Static Resource Affinity Table (SRAT) defines the MCM as having two NUMA nodes, Windows might associate the two nodes with two different groups (depending on group-configuration algorithms). In this scenario, the MCM package would span more than one group.

Other than causing significant driver and application compatibility problems—which they are designed to identify and root out, when used by developers—these options have an even greater impact on the machine: They force NUMA behaviors even on a non-NUMA machine. This is because Windows will never allow a NUMA node to span multiple groups, as was shown in the assignment algorithms. So, if the kernel is creating artificially small groups, those two groups must each have their own NUMA node. For example, on a quad-core processor with a group size of 2, this will create two groups, and thus two NUMA nodes, which will be subnodes of the main node. This will affect scheduling and memory-management policies in the same way a true NUMA system would, which can be useful for testing.

Logical processor state

In addition to the shared and local ready queues and summaries, Windows maintains two bitmasks that track the state of the processors on the system. (How these bitmasks are used is explained in the upcoming "Processor selection" section.) Following are the bitmasks that Windows maintains:

- **KeActiveProcessors** This is the active processor mask, which has a bit set for each usable processor on the system. These might be fewer than the number of actual processors if the licensing limits of the version of Windows running supports fewer than the number of available physical processors. Use the KeRegisteredProcessors variable to see how many processors are actually licensed on the machine. In this instance, *processors* refers to physical packages.

- **KeMaximumProcessors** This is the maximum number of logical processors (including all future possible dynamic processor additions) bounded within the licensing limit. It also reveals any platform limitations that are queried by calling the HAL and checking with the ACPI SRAT table, if any.

Part of the node's data (KNODE) is the set of idle CPUs in this node (the IdleCpuSet member), idle CPUs that are not parked (IdleNonParkedCpuSet), and idle SMT sets (IdleSmtSet).

Scheduler scalability

On a multiprocessor system, one processor might need to modify another processor's per-CPU scheduling data structures—for example, inserting a thread that would like to run on a certain processor. For this reason, you synchronize these structures by using a per-PRCB queued spinlock, which is held at DISPATCH_LEVEL. Thus, thread selection can occur while locking only an individual processor's PRCB. If needed, one more processor's PRCB can also be locked, such as in scenarios of thread stealing (described later). Thread context switching is also synchronized by using a finer-grained per-thread spinlock.

There is also a per-CPU list of threads in the deferred ready state (DeferredReadyListHead). These represent threads that are ready to run but have not yet been readied for execution; the actual ready operation has been deferred to a more appropriate time. Because each processor manipulates only its own per-processor deferred ready list, this list is not synchronized by the PRCB spinlock. The deferred ready thread list is processed by KiProcessDeferredReadyList after a function has already done modifications to process or thread affinity, priority (including due to priority boosting), or quantum values.

This function calls KiDeferredReadyThread for each thread on the list, which performs the algorithm shown later in this chapter in the "Processor selection" section. This could cause the thread to run immediately; to be put on the ready list of the processor; or, if the processor is unavailable, to be potentially put on a different processor's deferred ready list, in a standby state or immediately executed. This property is used by the core parking engine when parking a core: All threads are put into the deferred ready list, and it is then processed. Because KiDeferredReadyThread skips parked cores (as will be shown), it causes all of this processor's threads to wind up on other processors.

Affinity

Each thread has an affinity mask that specifies the processors on which the thread is allowed to run. The thread affinity mask is inherited from the process affinity mask. By default, all processes (and therefore all threads) begin with an affinity mask that is equal to the set of all active processors on their assigned group. In other words, the system is free to schedule all threads on any available processor within the group associated with the process. However, to optimize throughput, partition workloads to a specific set of processors, or both, applications can choose to change the affinity mask for a thread. This can be done at several levels:

- By calling the `SetThreadAffinityMask` function to set the affinity for an individual thread.

- By calling the `SetProcessAffinityMask` function to set the affinity for all the threads in a process.

- Task Manager and Process Explorer provide a GUI to this function. To access it, right-click a process and choose **Set Affinity**. In addition, the Psexec tool (from Sysinternals) provides a command-line interface to this function. (See the –a switch in its help output.)

- By making a process a member of a job that has a job-wide affinity mask set using the `SetInformationJobObject` function (described in Chapter 3).

- By specifying an affinity mask in the image header when compiling the application.

> **Tip** For a detailed specification of the Windows images format, search for *Portable Executable and Common Object File Format Specification* on *http://msdn.microsoft.com*.

An image can also have the `uniprocessor` flag set at link time. If this flag is set, the system chooses a single processor at process-creation time (`MmRotatingProcessorNumber`) and assigns that as the process affinity mask, starting with the first processor and then going round-robin across all the processors within the group. For example, on a dual-processor system, the first time an image marked with the `uniprocessor` flag is launched, it is assigned to CPU 0; the second time, CPU 1; the third time, CPU 0; the fourth time, CPU 1; and so on. This flag can be useful as a temporary workaround for programs that have multithreaded synchronization bugs that surface on multiprocessor systems due to race conditions but not on uniprocessor systems. If an image exhibits such symptoms and is unsigned, you can add the flag manually editing the image header with a Portable Executable (PE) image-editing tool. A better solution, also compatible with signed executables, is to use the Microsoft Application Compatibility Toolkit and add a shim to force the compatibility database to mark the image as uniprocessor-only at launch time.

EXPERIMENT: Viewing and changing process affinity

In this experiment, you will modify the affinity settings for a process and see that process affinity is inherited by new processes:

1. Run the command prompt (Cmd.exe).

2. Run Task Manager or Process Explorer and find the Cmd.exe process in the process list.

3. Right-click the process and select **Set Affinity**. A list of processors should be displayed. For example, on a system with eight logical processes, you will see this:

4. Select a subset of the available processors on the system and click **OK**. The process's threads are now restricted to run on the processors you just selected.

5. At the command prompt, type **Notepad** to run Notepad.exe.

6. Go back to Task Manager or Process Explorer and find the new Notepad process.

7. Right-click the process and choose **Affinity**. You should see the same list of processors you chose for the command-prompt process. This is because processes inherit their affinity settings from their parent.

Windows won't move a running thread that could run on a different processor from one CPU to a second processor to permit a thread with an affinity for the first processor to run on the first processor. For example, consider this scenario: CPU 0 is running a priority 8 thread that can run on any processor, and CPU 1 is running a priority 4 thread that can run on any processor. A priority 6 thread that can run on only CPU 0 becomes ready. What happens? Windows won't move the priority 8 thread from CPU 0 to CPU 1 (preempting the priority 4 thread) so that the priority 6 thread can run; the priority 6 thread must stay in the ready state. Therefore, changing the affinity mask for a process or thread can result in threads getting less CPU time than they normally would because Windows is restricted from running the thread on certain processors. Therefore, setting affinity should be done with extreme care. In most cases, it is optimal to let Windows decide which threads run where.

Extended affinity mask

To support more than 64 processors, which is the limit enforced by the original affinity mask structure (composed of 64 bits on a 64-bit system), Windows uses an extended affinity mask, KAFFINITY_EX. This is an array of affinity masks, one for each supported processor group (currently defined at 20).

When the scheduler needs to refer to a processor in the extended affinity masks, it first de-references the correct bitmask by using its group number and then accesses the resulting affinity directly. In the kernel API, extended affinity masks are not exposed; instead, the caller of the API inputs the group number as a parameter and receives the legacy affinity mask for that group. In the Windows API, on the other hand, only information about a single group can usually be queried, which is the group of the currently running thread (which is fixed).

The extended affinity mask and its underlying functionality are also how a process can escape the boundaries of its original assigned processor group. By using the extended affinity APIs, threads in a process can choose affinity masks on other processor groups. For example, if a process has four threads and the machine has 256 processors, thread 1 can run on processor 4, thread 2 can run on processor 68, thread 3 on processor 132, and thread 4 on processor 196, if each thread set an affinity mask of 0x10 (0b10000 in binary) on groups 0, 1, 2, and 3. Alternatively, the threads can each set an affinity of all 1 bits (0xFFFF...) for their given group, and the process then can execute its threads on any available processor on the system (with the limitation that each thread is restricted to running within its own group only).

You can take advantage of extended affinity at creation time by specifying a group number in the thread attribute list (PROC_THREAD_ATTRIBUTE_GROUP_AFFINITY) when creating a new thread or by calling SetThreadGroupAffinity on an existing thread.

System affinity mask

Windows drivers usually execute in the context of the calling thread or an arbitrary thread (that is, not in the safe confines of the System process). Therefore, currently running driver code might be subject to affinity rules set by the application developer. These are not currently relevant to the driver code and might even prevent correct processing of interrupts and other queued work. Driver developers therefore have a mechanism to temporarily bypass user thread affinity settings, by using the KeSetSystemAffinityThread(Ex)/KeSetSystemGroupAffinityThread and KeRevertToUserAffinityThread(Ex)/KeRevertToUserGroupAffinityThread APIs.

Ideal and last processor

Each thread has three CPU numbers stored in the kernel thread control block:

- **Ideal processor**   This is the preferred processor that this thread should run on.

- **Last processor**   This is the processor the thread last ran on.

- **Next processor**   This is the processor that the thread will be or is already running on.

The ideal processor for a thread is chosen when a thread is created using a seed in the process control block. The seed is incremented each time a thread is created so that the ideal processor for each new thread in the process rotates through the available processors on the system. For example, the first thread in the first process on the system is assigned an ideal processor of 0 and the second thread in that process is assigned an ideal processor of 1. However, the next process in the system has its first thread's ideal processor set to 1, the second to 2, and so on. In that way, the threads within each process are spread across the processors. On SMT systems (hyper-threading), the next ideal processor is selected from the next SMT set. For example, on a quad-core, hyper-threaded system, ideal processors for threads in a certain process could be 0, 2, 4, 6, 0, ...; 3, 5, 7, 1, 3, ...; etc. In this way, the threads are spread evenly across the physical processors.

Note that this assumes the threads within a process are doing an equal amount of work. This is typically not the case in a multithreaded process, which normally has one or more housekeeping threads and numerous worker threads. Therefore, a multithreaded application that wants to take full advantage of the platform might find it advantageous to specify the ideal processor numbers for its threads by using the SetThreadIdealProcessor function. To take advantage of processor groups, developers should call SetThreadIdealProcessorEx instead, which allows selection of a group number for the affinity.

In 64-bit Windows, the Stride field in the KNODE is used to balance the assignment of newly created threads within a process. The stride is a scalar number that represents the number of affinity bits within a given NUMA node that must be skipped to attain a new independent logical processor slice, where *independent* means on another core (if dealing with an SMT system) or another package (if dealing with a non-SMT but multicore system). Because 32-bit Windows doesn't support large processor-configuration systems, it doesn't use a stride. It simply selects the next processor number, trying to avoid sharing the same SMT set if possible.

Ideal node

On NUMA systems, when a process is created, an ideal node for the process is selected. The first process is assigned to node 0, the second process to node 1, and so on. Then the ideal processors for the threads in the process are chosen from the process's ideal node. The ideal processor for the first thread in a process is assigned to the first processor in the node. As additional threads are created in processes with the same ideal node, the next processor is used for the next thread's ideal processor, and so on.

CPU sets

You've seen how affinity (sometimes referred to as *hard affinity*) can limit threads to certain processors, which is always honored by the scheduler. The ideal processor mechanism tries to run threads on their ideal processors (sometimes referred to as *soft affinity*), generally expecting to have the thread's state be part of the processor's cache. The ideal processor may or may not be used, and it does not prevent the thread from being scheduled on other processors. Both these mechanisms don't work on system-related activity, such as system threads activity. Also, there is no easy way to set hard affinity to all processes on a system in one stroke. Even walking the process would not work. System processes are generally protected from external affinity changes because they require the PROCESS_SET_INFORMATION access right, which is not granted for protected processes.

Windows 10 and Server 2016 introduce a mechanism called *CPU sets*. These are a form of affinity that you can set for use by the system as a whole (including system threads activity), processes, and even individual threads. For example, a low-latency audio application may want to use a processor exclusively while the rest of the system is diverted to use other processors. CPU sets provide a way to achieve that.

The documented user mode API is somewhat limited at the time of this writing. GetSystemCpuSet-Information returns an array of SYSTEM_CPU_SET_INFORMATION that contains data for each CPU set.

In the current implementation, a CPU set is equivalent to a single CPU. This means the returned array's length is the number of logical processors on the system. Each CPU set is identified by its ID, which is arbitrarily selected to be 256 (0x100) plus the CPU index (0, 1, ...). These IDs are the ones that must be passed to SetProcessDefaultCpuSets and SetThreadSelectedCpuSets functions to set default CPU sets for a process and a CPU set for a specific thread, respectively.

An example for setting thread CPU set would be for an "important" thread that should not be interrupted if possible. This thread could have a CPU set that contains one CPU, while setting the default process CPU set to include all other CPUs.

One missing function in the Windows API is the ability to reduce the system CPU set. This can be achieved by a call to the NtSetSystemInformation system call. For this to succeed, the caller must have SeIncreaseBasePriorityPrivilege.

EXPERIMENT: CPU sets

In this experiment, you'll view and modify CPU sets and watch the resulting effects.

1. Download the CpuSet.exe tool from the book's downloadable resources.

2. Open an administrative command window and navigate to the directory where CPUSET.exe exists.

3. At the command window, type **cpuset.exe** without arguments to see the current system CPU sets. The output should be similar to the following:

```
System CPU Sets
---------------
Total CPU Sets: 8

CPU Set 0
  Id: 256 (0x100)
  Group: 0
  Logical Processor: 0
  Core: 0
  Last Level Cache: 0
  NUMA Node: 0
  Flags: 0 (0x0)  Parked: False  Allocated: False  Realtime: False  Tag: 0

CPU Set 1
  Id: 257 (0x101)
  Group: 0
  Logical Processor: 1
  Core: 0
  Last Level Cache: 0
  NUMA Node: 0
  Flags: 0 (0x0)  Parked: False  Allocated: False  Realtime: False  Tag: 0
...
```

4. Run CPUSTRES.exe and configure it to run a thread or two with maximum activity level. (Aim for something around 25 percent CPU usage.)

5. Open Task Manager, click the **Performance** tab, and select the **CPU** label.

6. Change the CPU graph view to show individual processors (if the view is configured for overall utilization).

7. At the command window, run the following command, replacing the number after -p with the process ID of the CPUSTRES process on your system:

```
CpuSet.exe -p 18276 -s 3
```

The -s argument specifies the processor mask to set as the default for the process. Here, 3 means CPU 0 and 1. You should see Task Manager hard at work on these two CPUs:

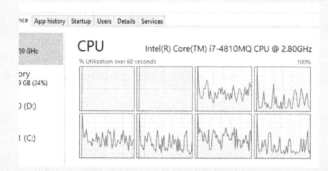

8. Let's look at CPU 0 more closely to see what threads it's running. For this, you'll use Windows Performance Recorder (WPR) and Windows Performance Analyzer (WPA) from the Windows SDK. Click the **Start** button, type **WPR**, and select **Windows Performance Recorder**. Then accept the elevation prompt. You should see the following dialog box:

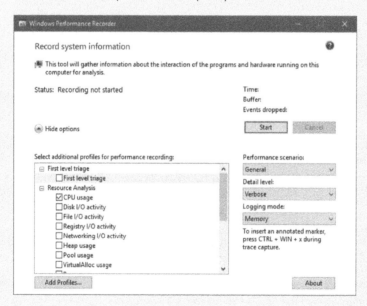

9. The default is to record CPU usage, which is what we want. This tool records Event Tracing for Windows (ETW) events. (See Chapter 8 in Part 2 for more on ETW.) Click the **Start** button in the dialog box and, after a second or two click the same button, now labeled **Save**.

10. WPR will suggest a location to save the recorded data. Accept it or change to some other file/folder.

11. After the file is saved, WPR suggests opening the file with WPA. Accept the suggestion.

12. The WPA tool opens and loads the saved file. (WPA is a rich tool, well beyond the scope of this book). On the left, you'll see the various categories of information captured, something like so:

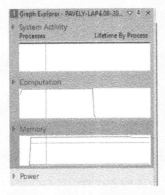

13. Expand the **Computation** node and then expand the **CPU Usage (Precise)** node.

14. Double-click the **Utilization by CPU** graph. It should open in the main display:

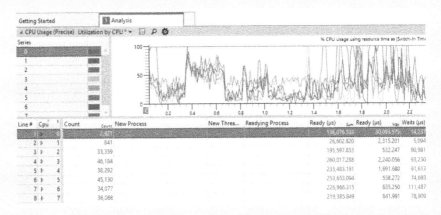

15. At the moment, we're interested in CPU 0. In the next step, you'll make CPU 0 work for CPUSTRES only. To begin, expand the CPU 0 node. You should see various processes, including CPUSTRES, but certainly not exclusively:

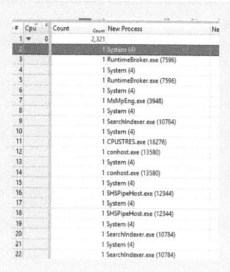

#	Cpu	Count	Count	New Process	Ne
1	▼ 0		2,321		
2				1 System (4)	
3				1 RuntimeBroker.exe (7596)	
4				1 System (4)	
5				1 RuntimeBroker.exe (7596)	
6				1 System (4)	
7				1 MsMpEng.exe (3948)	
8				1 System (4)	
9				1 SearchIndexer.exe (10784)	
10				1 System (4)	
11				1 CPUSTRES.exe (18276)	
12				1 conhost.exe (13580)	
13				1 System (4)	
14				1 conhost.exe (13580)	
15				1 System (4)	
16				1 SHSPipeHost.exe (12344)	
17				1 System (4)	
18				1 SHSPipeHost.exe (12344)	
19				1 System (4)	
20				1 SearchIndexer.exe (10784)	
21				1 System (4)	
22				1 SearchIndexer.exe (10784)	

16. Enter the following command to restrict the system to use all processors except the first. In this system, the number of processors is eight, so a full mask is 255 (0xff). Removing CPU 0 produces 254 (0xfe). Replace the mask with the correct one for your system:

```
CpuSet.exe -s 0xfe
```

17. The view in Task Manager should look about the same. Let's take a closer look at CPU 0. Run WPR again, and record a second or two with the same settings as before.

18. Open the trace in WPA and navigate to **Utilization by CPU**.

19. Expand CPU 0. You should see CPUSTRES almost exclusively, with the System process appearing occasionally:

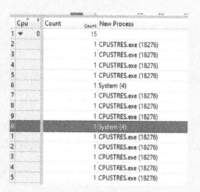

Cpu	Count	Count	New Process
1 ▼ 0		15	
2			1 CPUSTRES.exe (18276)
3			1 CPUSTRES.exe (18276)
4			1 CPUSTRES.exe (18276)
5			1 CPUSTRES.exe (18276)
6			1 System (4)
7			1 CPUSTRES.exe (18276)
8			1 CPUSTRES.exe (18276)
9			1 CPUSTRES.exe (18276)
0			1 System (4)
1			1 CPUSTRES.exe (18276)
2			1 CPUSTRES.exe (18276)
3			1 CPUSTRES.exe (18276)
4			1 CPUSTRES.exe (18276)
5			1 CPUSTRES.exe (18276)

20. Notice in the CPU Usage (in View) (ms) column that the time spent in the System process is very small (micro seconds). Clearly, CPU 0 is dedicated to the CPUSTRES process.

21. Run CPUSET.exe with no arguments again. The first set (CPU 0) is marked Allocated: True because it's now allocated to a particular process and not for general system use.

22. Close CPU Stress.

23. Enter the following command to restore the system CPU set to its default:

    Cpuset -s 0

Thread selection on multiprocessor systems

Before covering multiprocessor systems in more detail, let's summarize the algorithms discussed earlier in the "Thread selection" section. They either continued executing the current thread (if no new candidate was found) or started running the idle thread (if the current thread had to block). However, there is a third algorithm for thread selection called KiSearchForNewThread, which was hinted at earlier. This algorithm is called in one specific instance: when the current thread is about to block due to a wait on an object, including when doing an NtDelayExecutionThread call, also known as the Sleep API in Windows.

> **Note** This shows a subtle difference between the commonly used Sleep(1) call, which makes the current thread block until the next timer tick, and the SwitchToThread call, which was shown earlier. The Sleep(1) call uses the algorithm about to be described, while the SwitchToThread call uses the previously shown logic.

KiSearchForNewThread initially checks whether there is already a thread that was selected for this processor (by reading the NextThread field). If so, it dispatches this thread immediately in the running state. Otherwise, it calls the KiSelectReadyThreadEx routine and, if a thread was found, performs the same steps.

If no thread was found, the processor is marked as idle (even though the idle thread is not yet executing) and a scan of the queues of other logical processors (shared) is initiated (unlike the other standard algorithms, which would now give up). If, however, the processor core is parked, the algorithm will not attempt to check other logical processors, as it is preferable to allow the core to enter the parking state instead of keeping it busy with new work.

Barring these two scenarios, the work-stealing loop now runs. This code looks at the current NUMA node and removes any idle processors (because they shouldn't have threads that need stealing). Then the code looks at the current CPU's shared ready queue and calls KiSearchForNewThreadOnProcessor in a loop. If no thread is found, the affinity is changed to the next group and the function is called again. This time, however, the target CPU points it to the next group's shared queue instead of the current one, causing this processor to find the best ready thread from the other processor group's ready queue. If this fails to find a thread to run, local queues of processors in that group are searched in the same manner. If this is unsuccessful, and if DFSS is enabled, a thread from the idle-only queue of the remote logical processor is released on the current processor instead, if possible.

If no candidate ready thread is found, the next–lower numbered logical processor is attempted, and so on, until all logical processors have been exhausted on the current NUMA node. In this case, the algorithm keeps searching for the next-closest node, and so on, until all nodes in the current group have been exhausted. (Recall that Windows allows a given thread to have affinity only on a single group.) If this process fails to find any candidates, the function returns NULL and the processor enters the idle thread in the case of a wait (which will skip idle scheduling). If this work was already being done from the idle scheduler, the processor enters a sleep state.

Processor selection

We've described how Windows picks a thread when a logical processor needs to make a selection (or when a selection must be made for a given logical processor) and assumed the various scheduling routines have an existing database of ready threads to choose from. Now we'll see how this database gets populated in the first place—in other words, how Windows chooses which LP's ready queues to associate with a given ready thread. Having described the types of multiprocessor systems supported by Windows as well as thread-affinity and ideal processor settings, we're now ready to examine how this information is used for this purpose.

Choosing a processor for a thread when there are idle processors

When a thread becomes ready to run, the KiDeferredReadyThread scheduler function is called. This prompts Windows to perform two tasks:

- Adjust priorities and refresh quantums as needed (as explained in the "Priority boosts" section).
- Pick the best logical processor for the thread.

Windows first looks up the thread's ideal processor and then it computes the set of idle processors within the thread's hard affinity mask. This set is then pruned as follows:

1. Any idle logical processors that have been parked by the core-parking mechanism are removed. (See Chapter 6 for more information on core parking.) If this causes no idle processors to remain, idle processor selection is aborted, and the scheduler behaves as if no idle processors were available (described in the next section).

2. Any idle logical processors that are not on the ideal node (defined as the node containing the ideal processor) are removed (unless this would cause all idle processors to be eliminated).

3. On an SMT system, any non-idle SMT sets are removed, even if this might cause the elimination of the ideal processor itself. In other words, Windows prioritizes a non-ideal, idle SMT set over an ideal processor.

4. Windows checks whether the ideal processor is among the remaining set of idle processors. If not, it must then find the most appropriate idle processor. To do this, it first checks whether the processor that the thread last ran on is part of the remaining idle set. If so, it considers this processor to be a temporary ideal processor and selects it. (Recall that the ideal processor attempts to maximize processor cache hits, and picking the last processor a thread ran on is a good way of doing so.) If the last processor is not part of the remaining idle set, Windows checks whether the current processor (that is, the processor currently executing this scheduling code) is part of this set. If so, it applies the same logic as before.

5. If neither the last nor the current processor is idle, Windows performs one more pruning operation, removing any idle logical processors that are not on the same SMT set as the ideal processor. If there are none left, Windows instead removes any processors not on the SMT set of the current processor (unless this, too, eliminates all idle processors). In other words, Windows prefers idle processors that share the same SMT set as the unavailable ideal processor and/or last processor it would've liked to pick in the first place. Because SMT implementations share the cache on the core, this has nearly the same effect as picking the ideal or last processor from a caching perspective.

6. If after the previous step more than one processor remains in the idle set, Windows picks the lowest-numbered processor as the thread's current processor.

After a processor has been selected for the thread to run on, that thread is put in the standby state and the idle processor's PRCB is updated to point to this thread. If the processor is idle but not halted, a DPC interrupt is sent so that the processor handles the scheduling operation immediately. Whenever such a scheduling operation is initiated, `KiCheckForThreadDispatch` is called. It detects that a new thread has been scheduled on the processor and causes an immediate context switch if possible (as well as notifying Autoboost of the switch and delivering pending APCs). Alternatively, if no thread is pending, it causes a DPC interrupt to be sent.

Choosing a processor for a thread when there are no idle processors

If there are no idle processors when a thread wants to run, or if the only idle processors were eliminated by the first pruning (which got rid of parked idle processors), Windows first checks whether the latter situation has occurred. In this scenario, the scheduler calls `KiSelectCandidateProcessor` to ask the core-parking engine for the best candidate processor. The core-parking engine selects the highest-numbered processor that is unparked within the ideal node. If there are no such processors, the engine forcefully overrides the park state of the ideal processor and causes it to be unparked. Upon returning to the scheduler, it checks whether the candidate it received is idle; if so, it picks this processor for the thread, following the same last steps as in the previous scenario.

If this fails, Windows must decide whether to preempt the currently running thread. First, a target processor needs to be selected. The preference is in order of precedence: the ideal processor of the thread, the last processor the thread ran on, the first available processor in the current NUMA node, the closest processor on another NUMA node, and all these, barring affinity constraints, if any.

After a processor is selected, the next question is whether the new thread should preempt the current one on that processor. This is done by comparing the ranks of the two threads. This is an internal scheduling number that indicates the relative power of a thread based on its scheduling group and other factors. (See the section "Group-based scheduling" later in this chapter for a detailed discussion of group scheduling and rank.) If the rank of the new thread is zero (highest) or lower than the current thread's rank, or the ranks are equal but the priority of the new thread is higher than the currently executing one, then preemption should occur. The currently running thread is marked to be preempted, and Windows queues a DPC interrupt to the target processor to preempt the currently running thread in favor of this new thread.

If the ready thread cannot be run right away, it is moved into the ready state on the shared or local queue (as appropriate based on affinity constraints), where it will await its turn to run. As seen in the scheduling scenarios earlier, the thread will be inserted either at the head or the tail of the queue, based on whether it entered the ready state due to preemption.

> **Note** Regardless of the underlying scenario and various possibilities, threads are mostly put on their ideal processor's per-processor ready queues, guaranteeing the consistency of the algorithms that determine how a logical processor picks a thread to run.

Heterogeneous scheduling (big.LITTLE)

The kernel assumes an SMP system, as previously described. However, some ARM-based processors contain multiple cores that are not the same. A typical ARM CPU (for example, from Qualcomm) contains some powerful cores, which should run for short periods at a time (and consume more energy), and a set of weaker cores, which can run for longer periods (and consume less energy). This is sometimes called *big.LITTLE*.

Windows 10 introduced the ability to distinguish between these cores and schedule threads based on the core's size and policy, including the foreground status of the thread, its priority, and its expected run time. Windows initializes the set of processors when the Power Manager is initialized by calling PopInitializeHeteroProcessors (and if processors are hot-added to the system). The function allows the simulation of hetero systems (for example, for testing purposes) by adding keys under the registry key HKLM\System\CurrentControlSet\Control\Session Manager\Kernel\KGroups as follows:

- A key should use two decimal digits to identify a processor group number. (Recall that each group holds at most 64 processors.) For example, 00 is the first group, 01 is the second, etc. (On most systems, one group would suffice.)

- Each key should contain a DWORD value named SmallProcessorMask that is a mask of processors that would be considered small. For example, if the value is 3 (the first two bits are on) and the group has six total processors, that would mean processors 0 and 1 (3 = 1 or 2) are small, while the other four processors are big. This is essentially the same as an affinity mask.

The kernel has several policy options that can be tweaked when dealing with hetero systems, stored in global variables. Table 4-5 shows some of these variables and their meaning.

TABLE 4-5 Hetero kernel variables

Variable Name	Meaning	Default Value
KiHeteroSystem	Is the system heterogeneous?	False
PopHeteroSystem	System hetero type: None (0) Simulated (1) EfficiencyClass (2) FavoredCore (3)	None (0)

PpmHeteroPolicy	Scheduling policy: None (0) Manual (1) SmallOnly (2) LargeOnly (3) Dynamic (4)	Dynamic (4)
KiDynamicHeteroCpuPolicyMask	Determine what is considered in assessing whether a thread is important	7 (foreground status = 1, priority = 2, expected run time = 4)
KiDefaultDynamicHeteroCpuPolicy	Behavior of Dynamic hetero policy (see above): All (0) (all available) Large (1) LargeOrIdle (2) Small (3) SmallOrIdle (4) Dynamic (5) (use priority and other metrics to decide) BiasedSmall (6) (use priority and other metrics, but prefer small) BiasedLarge (7)	Small (3)
KiDynamicHeteroCpuPolicyImportant	Policy for a dynamic thread that is deemed important (see possible values above)	LargeOrIdle (2)
KiDynamicHeterCpuPolicyImportantShort	Policy for dynamic thread that is deemed important but run a short amount of time	Small (3)
KiDynamicCpuPolicyExpectedRuntime	Run-time value that is considered heavy	5,200 msec
KiDynamicHeteroCpuPolicyImportantPriority	Priority above which threads are considered important if priority-based dynamic policy is chosen	8

Dynamic policies (refer to Table 4-5) must be translated to an importance value based on KiDynamicHeteroPolicyMask and the thread's state. This is done by the KiConvertDynamicHeteroPolicy function, which checks, in order, the foreground state of the thread, its priority relative to KiDynamicHeteroCpuPolicyImportantPriority, and its expected run time. If the thread is deemed important (if running time is the determining factor, then it could be short as well), the important-related policy is used for scheduling decisions. (In Table 4-5, this would be KiDynamicHeteroCpuPolicyImportantShort or KiDynamicHeteroCpuPolicyImportant.)

Group-based scheduling

The previous section described the standard thread-based scheduling implementation of Windows. Since its appearance in the first release of Windows NT (with scalability improvements done with each subsequent release), it has reliably served general user and server scenarios. However, because thread-based scheduling attempts to fairly share the processor or processors only among competing threads of the same priority, it does not account for higher-level requirements such as the distribution of threads to users and the potential for certain users to benefit from more overall CPU time at the expense of other users. This is problematic in terminal-services environments, in which dozens of users compete for CPU time. If only thread-based scheduling is used, a single high-priority thread from a given user has the potential to starve threads from all users on the machine.

Windows 8 and Server 2012 introduced a group-based scheduling mechanism, built around the concept of a scheduling group (KSCHEDULING_GROUP). A scheduling group maintains a policy, scheduling parameters (described shortly), and a list of kernel scheduling control blocks (KSCBs), one per processor, that are part of the scheduling group. The flip side is that a thread points to a scheduling group it belongs to. If that pointer is null, it means the thread is outside any scheduling group's control. Figure 4-19 shows the structure of a scheduling group. In this figure, threads T1, T2, and T3 belong to the scheduling group, while thread T4 does not.

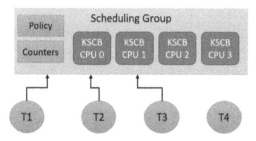

FIGURE 4-19 Scheduling group.

Here are some terms related to group scheduling:

- **Generation**   This is the amount of time over which to track CPU usage.

- **Quota**   This is the amount of CPU usage allowed to a group per generation. *Over quota* means the group has used up all its budget. *Under quota* means the group has not used its full budget.

- **Weight**   This is the relative importance of a group, between 1 and 9, where the default is 5.

- **Fair-share scheduling**   With this type of scheduling, idle cycles can be given to threads that are over quota if no under-quota threads want to run.

The KSCB structure contains CPU-related information as follows:

- Cycle usage for this generation

- Long-term average cycle usage, so that a burst of thread activity can be distinguished from a true hog

- Control flags such as hard capping, which means that even if CPU time is available above the assigned quota, it will not be used to give the thread extra CPU time

- Ready queues, based on the standard priorities (0 to 15 only because real-time threads are never part of a scheduling group)

An important parameter maintained by a scheduling group is called *rank*, which can be considered a scheduling priority of the entire group of threads. A rank with a value of 0 is the highest. A higher-rank number means the group has used more CPU time and so is less likely to get more CPU time.

Rank always trumps priority. This means that given two threads with different ranks, the lower value rank is preferred, regardless of priority. Equal-rank threads are compared based on priority. The rank is adjusted periodically as cycle usage increases.

Rank 0 is the highest (so it always wins out) against a higher number rank, and is implicit for some threads. This can indicate one of the following:

- The thread is not in any scheduling group ("normal" threads)

- Under-quota threads

- Real-time priority threads (16–31)

- Threads executing at IRQL APC_LEVEL (1) within a kernel critical or guarded region (see Chapter 8 in Part 2 for more on APCs and regions)

At various scheduling choices (for example, KiQuantumEnd), the decision of which thread to schedule next accounts for the scheduling group (if any) of the current and ready threads. If a scheduling group exists, the lowest value rank wins out, followed by priority (if ranks are equal), followed by the first arriving thread (if priorities are equal; round-robin at quantum end).

Dynamic fair share scheduling

Dynamic fair share scheduling (DFSS) is a mechanism that can be used to fairly distribute CPU time among sessions running on a machine. It prevents one session from potentially monopolizing the CPU if some threads running under that session have a relatively high priority and run a lot. It's enabled by default on a Windows Server system that has the Remote Desktop role. However, it can be configured on any system, client or server. Its implementation is based on group scheduling described in the previous section.

During the very last parts of system initialization, as the registry SOFTWARE hive is initialized by Smss.exe, the process manager initiates the final post-boot initialization in PsBootPhaseComplete, which calls PspIsDfssEnabled. Here, the system decides which of the two CPU quota mechanisms (DFSS or legacy) will be employed. For DFSS to be enabled, the EnableCpuQuota registry value must be set to a non-zero value in both of the quota keys. The first of these is HKLM\SOFTWARE\Policies\Microsoft\Windows\Session Manager\Quota System, for the policy-based setting. The second is HKLM\SYSTEM\CurrentControlSet\Control\Session Manager\Quota System, under the system key. This determines whether the system supports the functionality (which, by default, is set to TRUE on Windows Server with the Remote Desktop role).

If DFSS is enabled, the PsCpuFairShareEnabled global variable is set to TRUE, which makes all threads belong to scheduling groups (except session 0 processes). DFSS configuration parameters are read from the aforementioned keys by a call to PspReadDfssConfigurationValues and stored in global variables. These keys are monitored by the system. If modified, the notification callback calls PspReadDfssConfigurationValues again to update the configuration values. Table 4-6 shows the values and their meaning.

TABLE 4-6 DFSS registry configuration parameters

Registry Value Name	Kernel Variable Name	Meaning	Default Value
DfssShortTermSharingMS	PsDfssShortTermSharingMS	The time it takes for the group rank to increase within a generation cycle	30 ms
DfssLongTermSharingMS	PsDfssLongTermSharingMS	The time it takes to jump from rank 0 to a non-zero rank when the threads exceed their quota within the generation cycle	15 ms
DfssGenerationLengthMS	PsDfssGenerationLengthMS	The generation time over which to track CPU usage	600 ms
DfssLongTermFraction1024	PsDfssLongTermFraction1024	The value used in a formula for an exponential moving average used for long-term cycles computation	512

After DFSS is enabled, whenever a new session is created (other than session 0), MiSessionObject-Create allocates a scheduling group associated with the session with the default weight of 5, which is the middle ground between the minimum of 1 and the maximum of 9. A scheduling group manages either DFSS or CPU rate-control (see the next section) information based on a policy structure (KSCHEDULING_GROUP_POLICY) that is part of a scheduling group. The Type member indicates whether it's configured for DFSS (WeightBased=0) or rate control (RateControl=1). MiSessionObjectCreate calls KeInsertScheduling Group to insert the scheduling group into a global system list (maintained in the global variable KiSchedulingGroupList, needed for weight recalculation if processors are hot-added). The resulting scheduling group is also pointed to by the SESSION_OBJECT structure for the particular session.

EXPERIMENT: DFSS in action

In this experiment, you'll configure a system to use DFSS and watch it "do its thing".

1. Add the registry keys and values as described in this section to enable DFSS on the system. (You can try this experiment on a VM as well.) Then restart the system for the changes to take effect.

2. To make sure DFSS is active, open a live kernel debug session and inspect the value of PsCpuFairShareEnabled by issuing the following command. A value of 1 indicates DFSS is active.

```
1kd> db nt!PsCpuFairShareEnabled L1
fffff800'5183722a  01
```

3. In the debugger, look at the current thread. (It should be one of the threads running WinDbg.) Notice that the thread is part of a scheduling group and that its KSCB is not NULL because the thread was running at the time of display.

```
1kd> !thread
THREAD ffffd28c07231640  Cid 196c.1a60  Teb: 000000f897f4b000 Win32Thread:
ffffd28c0b9b0b40 RUNNING on processor 1
IRP List:
```

```
     ffffd28c06dfac10: (0006,0118) Flags: 00060000  Mdl: 00000000
Not impersonating
DeviceMap                   ffffac0d33668340
Owning Process              ffffd28c071fd080      Image:        windbg.exe
Attached Process            N/A          Image:          N/A
Wait Start TickCount        6146         Ticks: 33 (0:00:00:00.515)
Context Switch Count        877          IdealProcessor: 0
UserTime                    00:00:00.468
KernelTime                  00:00:00.156
Win32 Start Address 0x00007ff6ac53bc60
Stack Init ffffbf81ae85fc90 Current ffffbf81ae85f980
Base ffffbf81ae860000 Limit ffffbf81ae85a000 Call 0000000000000000
Priority 8 BasePriority 8 PriorityDecrement 0 IoPriority 2 PagePriority 5
Scheduling Group: ffffd28c089e7a40 KSCB: ffffd28c089e7c68 rank 0
```

4. Enter the **dt** command to view the scheduling group:

```
lkd> dt nt!_kscheduling_group ffffd28c089e7a40
   +0x000 Policy            : _KSCHEDULING_GROUP_POLICY
   +0x008 RelativeWeight    : 0x80
   +0x00c ChildMinRate      : 0x2710
   +0x010 ChildMinWeight    : 0
   +0x014 ChildTotalWeight  : 0
   +0x018 QueryHistoryTimeStamp : 0xfed6177
   +0x020 NotificationCycles : 0n0
   +0x028 MaxQuotaLimitCycles : 0n0
   +0x030 MaxQuotaCyclesRemaining : 0n-73125382369
   +0x038 SchedulingGroupList : _LIST_ENTRY [ 0xfffff800'5179b110 -
0xffffd28c'081b7078 ]
   +0x038 Sibling           : _LIST_ENTRY [ 0xfffff800'5179b110 -
0xffffd28c'081b7078 ]
   +0x048 NotificationDpc   : 0x0002eaa8'0000008e _KDPC
   +0x050 ChildList         : _LIST_ENTRY [ 0xffffd28c'062a7ab8 -
0xffffd28c'05c0bab8 ]
   +0x060 Parent            : (null)
   +0x080 PerProcessor      : [1] _KSCB
```

5. Create another local user on the machine.

6. Run CPU Stress in the current session.

7. Make a few threads run at maximum activity, but not enough to overwhelm the machine. For example, the following image shows two threads running at maximum activity on a three-processor virtual machine:

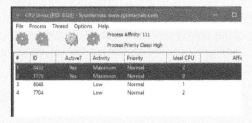

8. Press **Ctrl+Alt+Del** and select **Switch User**. Then select and log in to the account for the other user you created.

9. Run CPU Stress again, making the same number of threads run with maximum activity.

10. For the CPUSTRES process, open the **Process** menu, choose **Priority Class**, and select **High** to change the process priority class. Without DFSS, that higher-priority process should consume most of the CPU. This is because there are four threads competing for three processors. One of these will lose out, and it should be from the lower-priority process.

11. Open Process Explorer, double-click both CPUSTRES processes, and select the **Performance Graph** tab.

12. Place both windows side by side. You should see the CPU consumed roughly evenly between the processes, even though their priorities are not the same:

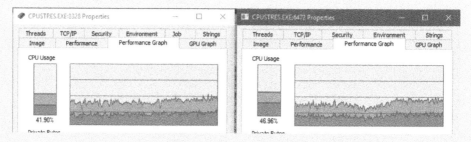

13. Disable DFSS by removing the registry keys. Then restart the system.

14. Rerun the experiment. You should clearly see the difference with the higher-priority process receiving the most CPU time.

CPU rate limits

DFSS works by automatically placing new threads inside the session-scheduling group. This is fine for a terminal-services scenario, but is not good enough as a general mechanism to limit the CPU time of threads or processes.

The scheduling-group infrastructure can be used in a more granular fashion by using a job object. Recall from Chapter 3 that a job can manage one or more processes. One of the limitations you can place on a job is a CPU rate control, which you do by calling SetInformationJobObject with JobObjectCpuRateControlInformation as the job information class and a structure of type JOBOBJECT_CPU_RATE_CONTROL_INFORMATION containing the actual control data. The structure contains a set of flags that enable you to apply one of three settings to limit CPU time:

- **CPU rate** This value can be between 1 and 10000 and represents a percent multiplied by 100 (for example, for 40 percent the value should be 4000).

- **Weight-based** This value can be between 1 and 9, relative to the weight of other jobs. (DFSS is configured with this setting.)

- **Minimum and maximum CPU rates** These values are specified similarly to the first option. When the threads in the job reach the maximum percentage specified in the measuring interval (600 ms by default), they cannot get any more CPU time until the next interval begins. You can use a control flag to specify whether to use hard capping to enforce the limit even if there is spare CPU time available.

The net result of setting these limits is to place all threads from all processes that are in the job in a new scheduling group and configuring the group as specified.

EXPERIMENT: CPU rate limit

In this experiment, you'll look at CPU rate limit using a job object. It's best to perform this experiment on a virtual machine and attach to its kernel rather than using the local kernel because of a debugger bug at the time of writing.

1. Run CPU Stress on the test VM and configure a few threads to consume about 50 percent of CPU time. For example, on an eight-processor system, activate four threads that run with maximum activity level:

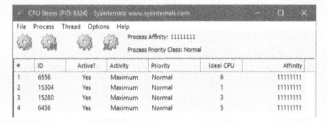

2. Open Process Explorer, find the CPUSTRES instance, open its properties, and select the **Performance Graph** tab. The CPU usage should be roughly 50 percent.

3. Download the CPULIMIT tool from the book's downloadable resources. This is a simple tool that allows you to limit the CPU usage of a single process through hard capping.

4. Run the command shown to limit the CPU usage to 20 percent for the CPUSTRES process. (Replace the number 6324 with your process ID.)

```
CpuLimit.exe 6324 20
```

5. Look at the Process Explorer window. You should see the drop to around 20 percent:

6. Open WinDbg on the host system.

7. Attach to the kernel of the test system and break into it.

8. Enter the following command to locate the CPUSTRES process:

```
0: kd> !process 0 0 cpustres.exe
PROCESS ffff9e0629528080
    SessionId: 1  Cid: 18b4    Peb: 009e4000  ParentCid: 1c4c
    DirBase: 230803000  ObjectTable: ffffd78d1af6c540  HandleCount: <Data
Not Accessible>
    Image: CPUSTRES.exe
```

9. Type the following command to list basic information for the process:

```
0: kd> !process ffff9e0629528080 1
PROCESS ffff9e0629528080
    SessionId: 1  Cid: 18b4    Peb: 009e4000  ParentCid: 1c4c
    DirBase: 230803000  ObjectTable: ffffd78d1af6c540  HandleCount: <Data
Not Accessible>
    Image: CPUSTRES.exe
    VadRoot ffff9e0626582010 Vads 88 Clone 0 Private 450. Modified 4. Locked 0.
    DeviceMap ffffd78cd8941640
    Token                             ffffd78cfe3db050
    ElapsedTime                       00:08:38.438
    UserTime                          00:00:00.000
    KernelTime                        00:00:00.000
    QuotaPoolUsage[PagedPool]         209912
    QuotaPoolUsage[NonPagedPool]      11880
    Working Set Sizes (now,min,max)   (3296, 50, 345) (13184KB, 200KB, 1380KB)
    PeakWorkingSetSize                3325
    VirtualSize                       108 Mb
    PeakVirtualSize                   128 Mb
    PageFaultCount                    3670
    MemoryPriority                    BACKGROUND
    BasePriority                      8
    CommitCharge                      568
    Job                               ffff9e06286539a0
```

10. Notice there is a non-NULL job object. Show its properties with the **!job** command. The tool creates a job (CreateJobObject), adds the process to the job (AssignProcessTo-JobObject), and calls SetInformationJobObject with the CPU rate information class and rate value of 2000 (20 percent).

```
0: kd> !job ffff9e06286539a0
Job at ffff9e06286539a0
  Basic Accounting Information
    TotalUserTime:              0x0
    TotalKernelTime:            0x0
    TotalCycleTime:             0x0
    ThisPeriodTotalUserTime:    0x0
    ThisPeriodTotalKernelTime:  0x0
```

```
        TotalPageFaultCount:        0x0
        TotalProcesses:             0x1
        ActiveProcesses:            0x1
        FreezeCount:                0
        BackgroundCount:            0
        TotalTerminatedProcesses:   0x0
        PeakJobMemoryUsed:          0x248
        PeakProcessMemoryUsed:      0x248
     Job Flags
       [close done]
       [cpu rate control]
     Limit Information (LimitFlags: 0x0)
     Limit Information (EffectiveLimitFlags: 0x800)
     CPU Rate Control
       Rate = 20.00%
       Hard Resource Cap
       Scheduling Group: ffff9e0628d7c1c0
```

11. Rerun the CPULIMIT tool on the same process and again set the CPU rate to 20 percent. You should see the CPU consumption of CPUSTRES drop down to around 4 percent. This is because of job nesting. A new job is created, as is the process assigned to it, nested under the first job. The net result is 20 percent of 20 percent, which is 4 percent.

Dynamic processor addition and replacement

As you've seen, developers can fine-tune which threads are allowed to (and in the case of the ideal processor, should) run on which processor. This works fine on systems that have a constant number of processors during their run time. For example, desktop machines require shutting down the computer to make any sort of hardware changes to the processor or their count. Today's server systems, however, cannot afford the downtime that CPU replacement or addition normally requires. In fact, you may be required to add a CPU at times of high load that is above what the machine can support at its current level of performance. Having to shut down the server during a period of peak usage would defeat the purpose.

To address this requirement, the latest generation of server motherboards and systems support the addition of processors (as well as their replacement) while the machine is still running. The ACPI BIOS and related hardware on the machine have been specifically built to allow and be aware of this need, but OS participation is required for full support.

Dynamic processor support is provided through the HAL, which notifies the kernel of a new processor on the system through the `KeStartDynamicProcessor` function. This routine does similar work to that performed when the system detects more than one processor at startup and needs to initialize the structures related to them. When a dynamic processor is added, various system components perform some additional work. For example, the memory manager allocates new pages and memory structures optimized for the CPU. It also initializes a new DPC kernel stack while the kernel initializes the global descriptor table (GDT), the interrupt dispatch table (IDT), the processor control region (PCR), the process control block (PRCB), and other related structures for the processor.

Other executive parts of the kernel are also called, mostly to initialize the per-processor look-aside lists for the processor that was added. For example, the I/O manager, executive look-aside list code, cache manager, and object manager all use per-processor look-aside lists for their frequently allocated structures.

Finally, the kernel initializes threaded DPC support for the processor and adjusts exported kernel variables to report the new processor. Different memory-manager masks and process seeds based on processor counts are also updated, and processor features need to be updated for the new processor to match the rest of the system—for example, enabling virtualization support on the newly added processor. The initialization sequence completes with the notification to the Windows Hardware Error Architecture (WHEA) component that a new processor is online.

The HAL is also involved in this process. It is called once to start the dynamic processor after the kernel is aware of it, and called again after the kernel has finished initialization of the processor. However, these notifications and callbacks only make the kernel aware and respond to processor changes. Although an additional processor increases the throughput of the kernel, it does nothing to help drivers.

To handle drivers, the system has a default executive callback object, `ProcessorAdd`, with which drivers can register for notifications. Similar to the callbacks that notify drivers of power state or system time changes, this callback allows driver code to, for example, create a new worker thread if desirable so that it can handle more work at the same time.

Once drivers are notified, the final kernel component called is the Plug and Play manager, which adds the processor to the system's device node and rebalances interrupts so that the new processor can handle interrupts that were already registered for other processors. CPU-hungry applications are also able to take advantage of the new processors.

However, a sudden change of affinity can have potentially breaking changes for a running application—especially when going from a single-processor to a multiprocessor environment—through the appearance of potential race conditions or simply misdistribution of work (because the process might have calculated the perfect ratios at startup, based on the number of CPUs it was aware of). As a result, applications do not take advantage of a dynamically added processor by default. They must request it.

The `SetProcessAffinityUpdateMode` and `QueryProcessAffinityUpdateMode` Windows APIs, which use the undocumented `NtSet/QueryInformationProcess` system call) tell the process manager that these applications should have their affinity updated (by setting the `AffinityUpdateEnable` flag in EPROCESS) or that they do not want to deal with affinity updates (by setting the `AffinityPermanent` flag in EPROCESS). This is a one-time change. After an application has told the system that its affinity is permanent, it cannot later change its mind and request affinity updates.

As part of `KeStartDynamicProcessor`, a new step has been added after interrupts are rebalanced: calling the process manager to perform affinity updates through `PsUpdateActiveProcessAffinity`. Some Windows core processes and services already have affinity updates enabled, while third-party software will need to be recompiled to take advantage of the new API call. The System process, Svchost processes, and Smss are all compatible with dynamic processor addition.

Worker factories (thread pools)

Worker factories are the internal mechanism used to implement user-mode thread pools. The legacy thread-pool routines were completely implemented in user mode inside the Ntdll.dll library. In addition, the Windows API provided several functions for developers to call, which provided waitable timers (`CreateTimerQueue`, `CreateTimerQueueTimer`, and friends), wait callbacks (`RegisterWaitForSingleObject`), and work item processing with automatic thread creation and deletion (`QueueUserWorkItem`), depending on the amount of work being done.

One issue with the old implementation was that only one thread pool could be created in a process, which made some scenarios difficult to implement. For example, trying to prioritize work items by building two thread pools which would serve a different set of requests was not directly possible. The other issue was the implementation itself, which was in user mode (in Ntdll.dll). Because the kernel can have direct control over thread scheduling, creation, and termination without the typical costs associated with doing these operations from user mode, most of the functionality required to support the user-mode thread pool implementation in Windows is now located in the kernel. This also simplifies the code that developers need to write. For example, creating a worker pool in a remote process can be done with a single API call instead of the complex series of virtual memory calls this normally requires. Under this model, Ntdll.dll merely provides the interfaces and high-level APIs required for interfacing with the worker factory kernel code.

This kernel thread pool functionality in Windows is managed by an object manager type called `TpWorkerFactory`, as well as four native system calls for managing the factory and its workers (`NtCreateWorkerFactory`, `NtWorkerFactoryWorkerReady`, `NtReleaseWorkerFactoryWorker`, and `NtShutdownWorkerFactory`); two query/set native calls (`NtQueryInformationWorkerFactory` and `NtSetInformationWorkerFactory`); and a wait call (`NtWaitForWorkViaWorkerFactory`). Just like other native system calls, these calls provide user mode with a handle to the `TpWorkerFactory` object, which contains information such as the name and object attributes, the desired access mask, and a security descriptor. Unlike other system calls wrapped by the Windows API, however, thread-pool management is handled by Ntdll.dll's native code. This means developers work with opaque descriptors: a TP_POOL pointer for a thread pool and other opaque pointers for object created from a pool, including TP_WORK (work callback), TP_TIMER (timer callback), TP_WAIT (wait callbacks), etc. These structures hold various pieces of information, such as the handle to the `TpWorkerFactory` object.

As its name suggests, the worker factory implementation is responsible for allocating worker threads (and calling the given user-mode worker thread entry point) and maintaining a minimum and maximum thread count (allowing for either permanent worker pools or totally dynamic pools) as well as other accounting information. This enables operations such as shutting down the thread pool to be performed with a single call to the kernel because the kernel has been the only component responsible for thread creation and termination.

Because the kernel dynamically creates new threads as needed (based on minimum and maximum numbers provided), this increases the scalability of applications using the new thread-pool implementation. A worker factory will create a new thread whenever all of the following conditions are met:

- Dynamic thread creation is enabled.

- The number of available workers is lower than the maximum number of workers configured for the factory (default of 500).

- The worker factory has bound objects (for example, an ALPC port that this worker thread is waiting on) or a thread has been activated into the pool.

- There are pending I/O request packets (IRPs; see Chapter 6 for more information) associated with a worker thread.

In addition, it will terminate threads whenever they've become idle—that is, they haven't processed any work item—for more than 10 seconds (by default). Furthermore, although developers have always been able to take advantage of as many threads as possible (based on the number of processors on the system) through the old implementation, it's now possible for applications using thread pools to automatically take advantage of new processors added at run time. This is through its support for dynamic processors in Windows Server (as discussed earlier in this chapter).

Worker factory creation

The worker factory support is merely a wrapper to manage mundane tasks that would otherwise have to be performed in user mode (at a loss of performance). Much of the logic of the new thread-pool code remains in the Ntdll.dll side of this architecture. (Theoretically, by using undocumented functions, a different thread-pool implementation can be built around worker factories.) Also, it is not the worker factory code that provides the scalability, wait internals, and efficiency of work processing. Instead, it is a much older component of Windows: I/O completion ports or, more correctly, kernel queues (KQUEUE). In fact, when creating a worker factory, an I/O completion port must have already been created by user mode, and the handle needs to be passed in.

It is through this I/O completion port that the user-mode implementation will queue and wait for work—but by calling the worker factory system calls instead of the I/O completion port APIs. Internally, however, the "release" worker factory call (which queues work) is a wrapper around `IoSetIoCompletionEx`, which increases pending work, while the "wait" call is a wrapper around `IoRemoveIoCompletion`. Both these routines call into the kernel queue implementation. Therefore, the job of the worker factory code is to manage either a persistent, static, or dynamic thread pool; wrap the I/O completion port model into interfaces that try to prevent stalled worker queues by automatically creating dynamic threads; and simplify global cleanup and termination operations during a factory shutdown request (as well as easily block new requests against the factory in such a scenario).

The executive function that creates the worker factory, `NtCreateWorkerFactory`, accepts several arguments that allow customization of the thread pool, such as the maximum threads to create and the initial committed and reserved stack sizes. The `CreateThreadpool` Windows API, however, uses the default stack sizes embedded in the executable image (just like a default `CreateThread` would). The Windows API does not, however, provide a way to override these defaults. This is somewhat unfortunate, as in many cases thread-pool threads don't require deep call stacks, and it would be beneficial to allocate smaller stacks.

The data structures used by the worker factory implementation are not in the public symbols, but it is still possible to look at some worker pools, as you'll see in the next experiment. Additionally, the NtQueryInformationWorkerFactory API dumps almost every field in the worker factory structure.

EXPERIMENT: Looking at thread pools

Because of the advantages of the thread-pool mechanism, many core system components and applications use it, especially when dealing with resources such as ALPC ports (to dynamically process incoming requests at an appropriate and scalable level). One of the ways to identify which processes are using a worker factory is to look at the handle list in Process Explorer. Follow these steps to look at some details behind them:

1. Run Process Explorer.

2. Open the **View** menu and select **Show Unnamed Handles and Mappings**. (Unfortunately, worker factories aren't named by Ntdll.dll, so you need to take this step to see the handles.)

3. Select an instance of svchost.exe from the list of processes.

4. Open the **View** menu and choose **Show Lower Pane** to display the lower pane of the handle table.

5. Open the **View** menu, choose **Lower Pane View**, and select **Handles** to display the table in handle mode.

6. Right-click the lower pane column headers and choose **Select Columns**.

7. Make sure the **Type** and **Handle Value** columns are checked.

8. Click the **Type** header to sort by type.

9. Scroll down the handles, looking at the Type column, until you find a handle of type TpWorkerFactory.

10. Click the **Handle** header to sort by handle value. You should see something similar to the following screenshot. Notice how the TpWorkerFactory handle is immediately preceded by an IoCompletion handle. As discussed, this occurs because a handle to an I/O completion port on which work will be sent must be created before creating a worker factory.

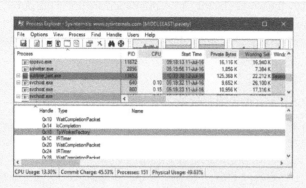

11. Double-click the selected process in the list of processes, click the **Threads** tab, and click the **Start Address** column. You should see something similar to the following screenshot. Worker factory threads are easily identified by their Ntdll.dll's entry point, TppWorkerThread. (*Tpp* stands for *thread pool private*.)

If you look at other worker threads, you'll see some are waiting for objects such as events. A process can have multiple thread pools, and each thread pool can have a variety of threads doing completely unrelated tasks. It's up to the developer to assign work and to call the thread-pool APIs to register this work through Ntdll.dll.

Conclusion

This chapter examined the structure of threads, how they are created and managed, and how Windows decides which threads should run, for how long, and on which processor or processors. In the next chapter, you'll look at one of the most important aspects of any OS: memory management.

CHAPTER 5

Memory management

In this chapter, you'll learn how Windows implements virtual memory and how it manages the subset of virtual memory kept in physical memory. We'll also describe the internal structure and components that make up the memory manager, including key data structures and algorithms. Before examining these mechanisms, we'll review the basic services provided by the memory manager and key concepts such as reserved memory versus committed memory and shared memory.

Introduction to the memory manager

By default, the virtual size of a process on 32-bit Windows is 2 GB. If the image is marked specifically as large address space–aware, and the system is booted with a special option (described in the section "x86 address space layouts" later in this chapter), a 32-bit process can grow to be up to 3 GB on 32-bit Windows and to 4 GB on 64-bit Windows. The process virtual address space size on 64-bit Windows 8 and Server 2012 is 8192 GB (8 TB) and on 64 bit Windows 8.1 (and later) and Server 2012 R2 (and later), it is 128 TB.

As you saw in Chapter 2, "System architecture"—specifically in Table 2-2—the maximum amount of physical memory currently supported by Windows ranges from 2 GB to 24 TB, depending on which version and edition of Windows you are running. Because the virtual address space might be larger or smaller than the physical memory on the machine, the memory manager has two primary tasks:

- Translating, or mapping, a process's virtual address space into physical memory so that when a thread running in the context of that process reads or writes to the virtual address space, the correct physical address is referenced. (The subset of a process's virtual address space that is physically resident is called the *working set*. Working sets are described in more detail in the section "Working sets" later in this chapter.)

- Paging some of the contents of memory to disk when it becomes overcommitted—that is, when running threads try to use more physical memory than is currently available—and bringing the contents back into physical memory when needed.

In addition to providing virtual memory management, the memory manager provides a core set of services on which the various Windows environment subsystems are built. These services include memory-mapped files (internally called *section objects*), copy-on-write memory, and support for applications using large, sparse address spaces. The memory manager also provides a way for a process to allocate and use larger amounts of physical memory than can be mapped into the process virtual address space at one time—for example, on 32-bit systems with more than 3 GB of physical memory. This is explained in the section "Address Windowing Extensions" later in this chapter.

> **Note** There is a Control Panel applet (System) that provides control over the size, number, and locations of paging files. Its nomenclature suggests that virtual memory is the same thing as the paging file. This is not the case. The paging file is only one aspect of virtual memory. In fact, even if you run with no page file at all, Windows will still be using virtual memory. This distinction is explained in more detail later in this chapter.

Memory manager components

The memory manager is part of the Windows executive and therefore exists in the file Ntoskrnl.exe. It's the largest component in the executive, hinting at its importance and complexity. No parts of the memory manager exist in the HAL. The memory manager consists of the following components:

- A set of executive system services for allocating, deallocating, and managing virtual memory, most of which are exposed through the Windows API or kernel-mode device driver interfaces

- A translation-not-valid and access fault trap handler for resolving hardware-detected memory-management exceptions and making virtual pages resident on behalf of a process

- Six key top-level routines, each running in one of six different kernel-mode threads in the System process:

  - **The balance set manager (KeBalanceSetManager, priority 17)** This calls an inner routine, the working set manager (MmWorkingSetManager), once per second as well as when free memory falls below a certain threshold. The working set manager drives the overall memory-management policies, such as working set trimming, aging, and modified page writing.

  - **The process/stack swapper (KeSwapProcessOrStack, priority 23)** This performs both process and kernel thread stack inswapping and outswapping. The balance set manager and the thread-scheduling code in the kernel awaken this thread when an inswap or outswap operation needs to take place.

  - **The modified page writer (MiModifiedPageWriter, priority 18)** This writes dirty pages on the modified list back to the appropriate paging files. This thread is awakened when the size of the modified list needs to be reduced.

  - **The mapped page writer (MiMappedPageWriter, priority 18)** This writes dirty pages in mapped files to disk or remote storage. It is awakened when the size of the modified list needs to be reduced or if pages for mapped files have been on the modified list for more than 5 minutes. This second modified page writer thread is necessary because it can generate page faults that result in requests for free pages. If there were no free pages and only one modified page writer thread, the system could deadlock waiting for free pages.

  - **The segment dereference thread (MiDereferenceSegmentThread, priority 19)** This is responsible for cache reduction as well as for page file growth and shrinkage. For example, if there is no virtual address space for paged pool growth, this thread trims the page cache so that the paged pool used to anchor it can be freed for reuse.

- **The zero page thread (MiZeroPageThread, priority 0)**   This zeroes out pages on the free list so that a cache of zero pages is available to satisfy future demand-zero page faults. In some cases, memory zeroing is done by a faster function called MiZeroInParallel. See the note in the "Page list dynamics" section later in this chapter.

Each of these components is covered in more detail later in the chapter except for the segment dereference thread, which is covered in Chapter 14, "Cache manager," in Part 2.

Large and small pages

Memory management is done in distinct chunks called *pages*. This is because the hardware memory management unit translates virtual to physical addresses at the granularity of a page. Hence, a page is the smallest unit of protection at the hardware level. (The various page-protection options are de-scribed in the section "Protecting memory" later in this chapter.) The processors on which Windows runs support two page sizes: small and large. The actual sizes vary based on the processor architecture, and they are listed in Table 5-1.

TABLE 5-1   Page sizes

Architecture	Small Page Size	Large Page Size	Small Pages per Large Page
x86 (PAE)	4 KB	2 MB	512
x64	4 KB	2 MB	512
ARM	4 KB	4 MB	1024

Note   Some processors support configurable page sizes, but Windows does not use this feature.

The primary advantage of large pages is speed of address translation for references to data within the large page. This advantage exists because the first reference to any byte within a large page will cause the hardware's translation look-aside buffer (TLB) (described in the section "Address translation" later in this chapter), to have in its cache the information necessary to translate references to any other byte within the large page. If small pages are used, more TLB entries are needed for the same range of virtual addresses, thus increasing the recycling of entries as new virtual addresses require translation. This, in turn, means having to go back to the page table structures when references are made to virtual addresses outside the scope of a small page whose translation has been cached. The TLB is a very small cache; thus, large pages make better use of this limited resource.

To take advantage of large pages on systems with more than 2 GB of RAM, Windows maps with large pages the core operating system images (Ntoskrnl.exe and Hal.dll) as well as core operating system data (such as the initial part of non-paged pool and the data structures that describe the state of each physical memory page). Windows also automatically maps I/O space requests (calls by device drivers to MmMapIoSpace) with large pages if the request is of a satisfactorily large page length and alignment. In addition, Windows allows applications to map their images, private memory, and page file–backed sections with large pages (see the MEM_LARGE_PAGES flag on the VirtualAlloc, Virtual-AllocEx, and VirtualAllocExNuma functions). You can also specify other device drivers to be mapped with large pages by adding a multistring registry value LargePageDrivers to the key HKLM\SYSTEM\CurrentControlSet\Control\Session Manager\Memory Management and specifying the names of the drivers as separately null-terminated strings.

Attempts to allocate large pages may fail after the operating system has been running for an extended period because the physical memory for each large page must occupy a significant number (refer to Table 5-1) of physically contiguous small pages. This extent of physical pages must furthermore begin on a large page boundary. For example, physical pages 0–511 could be used as a large page on an x64 system, as could physical pages 512–1,023, but pages 10–521 could not. Free physical memory does become fragmented as the system runs. This is not a problem for allocations using small pages but can cause large page allocations to fail.

The memory is also always non-pageable because the page file system does not support large pages. Because the memory is non-pageable, the caller is required to have the SeLockMemoryPrivilege to be able to allocate using large pages. Also, the allocated memory is not considered part of the process working set (described in the section "Working sets" later in this chapter); nor are large page allocations subject to job-wide limits on virtual memory usage.

On Windows 10 version 1607 x64 and Server 2016 systems, large pages may also be mapped with huge pages, which are 1 GB in size. This is done automatically if the allocation size requested is larger than 1 GB, but it does not have to be a multiple of 1 GB. For example, an allocation of 1040 MB would result in using one huge page (1024 MB) plus 8 "normal" large pages (16 MB divided by 2 MB).

There is an unfortunate side effect of large pages. Each page (whether huge, large, or small) must be mapped with a single protection that applies to the entire page. This is because hardware memory protection is on a per-page basis. If a large page contains, for example, both read-only code and read/write data, the page must be marked as read/write, meaning that the code will be writable. As a result, device drivers or other kernel-mode code could, either maliciously or due to a bug, modify what is supposed to be read-only operating system or driver code without causing a memory access violation. If small pages are used to map the operating system's kernel-mode code, the read-only portions of Ntoskrnl.exe and Hal.dll can be mapped as read-only pages. Using small pages does reduce efficiency of address translation, but if a device driver (or other kernel-mode code) attempts to modify a read-only part of the operating system, the system will crash immediately with the exception information pointing at the offending instruction in the driver. If the write were allowed to occur, the system would likely crash later (in a harder-to-diagnose way) when some other component tried to use the corrupted data.

If you suspect you are experiencing kernel code corruptions, enable Driver Verifier (described in Chapter 6, "I/O system"), which will disable the use of large pages.

Note The term *page* used in this and later chapters refers to a small page unless otherwise indicated or apparent by context.

Examining memory usage

The Memory and Process performance-counter categories provide access to most of the details about system and process memory utilization. Throughout this chapter, we'll include references to specific performance counters that contain information related to the component being described. We've included relevant examples and experiments throughout the chapter. One word of caution, however: Different utilities use varying and sometimes inconsistent or confusing names when displaying memory information. The following experiment illustrates this point. (We'll explain the terms used in this example in subsequent sections.)

EXPERIMENT: Viewing system memory information

The Performance tab in the Windows Task Manager, shown in the following screenshot from a Windows 10 version 1607 system (click the **Memory** tab on the left in the **Performance** tab), displays basic system memory information. This information is a subset of the detailed memory information available through performance counters. It includes data on both physical and virtual memory usage. The table that follows shows the meaning of the memory-related values.

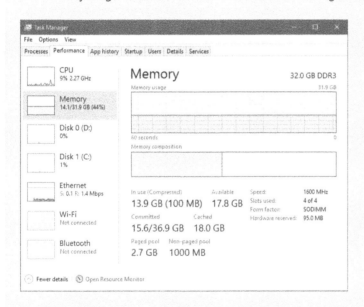

Task Manager Value	Definition
Memory usage histogram	The chart's line height reflects physical memory in use by Windows (not available as a performance counter). The area above the line is equal to the Available value in the bottom section. The total height of the graph is equal to the total value shown at the top right of the graph (31.9 GB in this example). This represents the total RAM usable by the operating system, and does not include BIOS shadow pages, device memory, and so on.
Memory composition	This details the relation between memory that is actively used, standby, modified, and free+zero (all described later in this chapter).

Task Manager Value	Definition
Total physical memory (top right of graph)	This shows the physical memory usable by Windows.
In Use (Compressed)	This is the physical memory currently being used. The amount of compressed physical memory is in parentheses. Hovering over the value shows the amount of memory saved by the compression. (Memory compression is discussed in the section "Memory compression" later in this chapter.)
Cached	This is the sum of the following performance counters in the Memory category: Cache Bytes, Modified Page List Bytes, Standby Cache Core Bytes, Standby Cache Normal Priority Bytes, and Standby Cache Reserve Bytes.
Available	This is the amount of memory that is immediately available for use by the operating system, processes, and drivers. It is equal to the combined size of the standby, free, and zero page lists.
Free	This shows the free and zero-page list bytes. To see this information, hover over the right-most part of the Memory Composition bar (assuming you have enough free memory to hover over it).
Committed	The two numbers shown here are equal to the values in the Committed Bytes and Commit Limit performance counters, respectively.
Paged Pool	This is the total size of the paged pool, including both free and allocated regions.
Non-Paged Pool	This is the total size of the non-paged pool, including both free and allocated regions.

To see the specific usage of the paged and non-paged pool, use the Poolmon utility, described later in this chapter in the "Monitoring pool usage" section.

The Process Explorer tool from Sysinternals can show considerably more data about physical and virtual memory. On its main screen, click the **View** menu, choose **System Information**, and click the **Memory** tab. Here is an example of a display from a 64-bit Windows 10 system. (We will explain most of these counters in the relevant sections later in this chapter.)

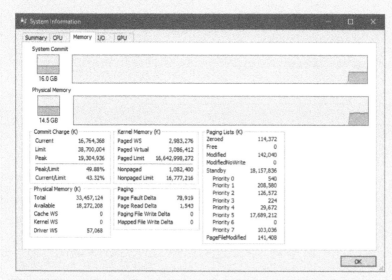

Two other Sysinternals tools show extended memory information:

- **VMMap**   This shows the usage of virtual memory within a process to a fine level of detail.

- **RAMMap**   This shows detailed physical memory usage.

These tools are featured in experiments found later in this chapter.

Finally, the `!vm` command in the kernel debugger shows the basic memory-management information available through the memory-related performance counters. This command can be useful if you're looking at a crash dump or hung system. Here's an example of its output from a 64-bit Windows 10 system with 32 GB of RAM:

```
lkd> !vm
Page File: \??\C:\pagefile.sys
  Current:    1048576 Kb  Free Space:    1034696 Kb
  Minimum:    1048576 Kb  Maximum:       4194304 Kb
Page File: \??\C:\swapfile.sys
  Current:      16384 Kb  Free Space:      16376 Kb
  Minimum:      16384 Kb  Maximum:      24908388 Kb
No Name for Paging File
  Current:   58622948 Kb  Free Space:   57828340 Kb
  Minimum:   58622948 Kb  Maximum:      58622948 Kb

Physical Memory:              8364281 (    33457124 Kb)
Available Pages:              4627325 (    18509300 Kb)
ResAvail Pages:              7215930 (    28863720 Kb)
Locked IO Pages:                   0 (           0 Kb)
Free System PTEs:         4295013448 ( 17180053792 Kb)
Modified Pages:                68167 (      272668 Kb)
Modified PF Pages:             68158 (      272632 Kb)
Modified No Write Pages:           0 (           0 Kb)
NonPagedPool Usage:              495 (        1980 Kb)
NonPagedPoolNx Usage:         269858 (     1079432 Kb)
NonPagedPool Max:         4294967296 ( 17179869184 Kb)
PagedPool 0 Usage:            371703 (     1486812 Kb)
PagedPool 1 Usage:             99970 (      399880 Kb)
PagedPool 2 Usage:            100021 (      400084 Kb)
PagedPool 3 Usage:             99916 (      399664 Kb)
PagedPool 4 Usage:             99983 (      399932 Kb)
PagedPool Usage:              771593 (     3086372 Kb)
PagedPool Maximum:        4160749568 ( 16642998272 Kb)
Session Commit:                12210 (       48840 Kb)
Shared Commit:                344197 (     1376788 Kb)
Special Pool:                      0 (           0 Kb)
Shared Process:                19244 (       76976 Kb)
Pages For MDLs:               419675 (     1678700 Kb)
Pages For AWE:                     0 (           0 Kb)
NonPagedPool Commit:          270387 (     1081548 Kb)
PagedPool Commit:             771593 (     3086372 Kb)
Driver Commit:                 24984 (       99936 Kb)
Boot Commit:                  100044 (      400176 Kb)
```

```
System PageTables:          5948 (      23792 Kb)
VAD/PageTable Bitmaps:     18202 (      72808 Kb)
ProcessLockedFilePages:      299 (       1196 Kb)
Pagefile Hash Pages:          33 (        132 Kb)
Sum System Commit:       1986816 (    7947264 Kb)
Total Private:           2126069 (    8504276 Kb)
Misc/Transient Commit:     18422 (      73688 Kb)
Committed pages:         4131307 (   16525228 Kb)
Commit limit:            9675001 (   38700004 Kb)
...
```

The values not in parentheses are in small pages (4 KB). We will describe many of the details of the output of this command throughout this chapter.

Internal synchronization

Like all other components of the Windows executive, the memory manager is fully reentrant and supports simultaneous execution on multiprocessor systems. That is, it allows two threads to acquire resources in such a way that they don't corrupt each other's data. To accomplish the goal of being fully reentrant, the memory manager uses several different internal synchronization mechanisms, such as spinlocks and interlocked instructions, to control access to its own internal data structures. (Synchronization objects are discussed in Chapter 8, "System mechanisms", in Part 2.)

Some of the system-wide resources to which the memory manager must synchronize access include:

- Dynamically allocated portions of the system virtual address space

- System working sets

- Kernel memory pools

- The list of loaded drivers

- The list of paging files

- Physical memory lists

- Image base randomization address space layout randomization (ASLR) structures

- Each individual entry in the page frame number (PFN) database

Per-process memory-management data structures that require synchronization include the following:

- **Working set lock**   This is held while changes are made to the working set list.

- **Address space lock**   This is held whenever the address space is being changed.

Both these locks are implemented using pushlocks. These are described in Chapter 8 in Part 2.

Services provided by the memory manager

The memory manager provides a set of system services to allocate and free virtual memory, share memory between processes, map files into memory, flush virtual pages to disk, retrieve information about a range of virtual pages, change the protection of virtual pages, and lock the virtual pages into memory.

Like other Windows executive services, memory-management services allow their caller to supply a process handle indicating the particular process whose virtual memory is to be manipulated. The caller can thus manipulate either its own memory or (with proper permissions) the memory of another process. For example, if a process creates a child process, by default it has the right to manipulate the child process's virtual memory. Thereafter, the parent process can allocate, deallocate, read, and write memory on behalf of the child process by calling virtual memory services and passing a handle to the child process as an argument. This feature is used by subsystems to manage the memory of their client processes. It is also essential for implementing debuggers because debuggers must be able to read and write to the memory of the process being debugged.

Most of these services are exposed through the Windows API. As shown in Figure 5-1, the Windows API has four groups of functions for managing memory in applications:

- **Virtual API** This is the lowest-level API for general memory allocations and deallocations. It always works on page granularity. It is also the most powerful, supporting the full capabilities of the memory manager. Functions include `VirtualAlloc`, `VirtualFree`, `VirtualProtect`, `VirtualLock`, and others.

- **Heap API** This provides functions for small allocations (typically less than a page). It uses the Virtual API internally, but adds management on top of it. Heap manager functions include `HeapAlloc`, `HeapFree`, `HeapCreate`, `HeapReAlloc` and others. The heap manager is discussed in the section "Heap manager" later in this chapter.

- **Local/Global APIs** These are leftovers from 16-bit Windows and are now implemented using the Heap API.

- **Memory-mapped files** These functions allow mapping files as memory and/or sharing memory between cooperating processes. Memory-mapped file functions include `CreateFileMapping`, `OpenFileMapping`, `MapViewOfFile`, and others.

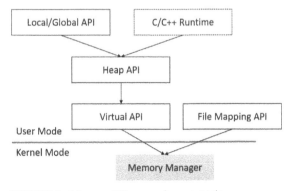

FIGURE 5-1 Memory API groups in user mode.

The dotted box shows a typical C/C++ runtime implementation of memory management (functions such as `malloc`, `free`, `realloc`, C++ operator `new` and `delete`) using the Heap API. The box is dotted because this implementation is compiler-dependent and certainly not mandatory (although quite common). The C runtime equivalents that are implemented in Ntdll.dll use the Heap API.

The memory manager also provides several services to other kernel-mode components inside the executive as well as to device drivers. These include allocating and deallocating physical memory and locking pages in physical memory for direct memory access (DMA) transfers. These functions begin with the prefix `Mm`. In addition, although not strictly part of the memory manager, some executive support routines that begin with `Ex` are used to allocate and deallocate from the system heaps (paged and non-paged pool) as well as to manipulate look-aside lists. We'll touch on these topics later in this chapter in the section "Kernel-mode heaps (system memory pools)."

Page states and memory allocations

Pages in a process virtual address space are either free, reserved, committed, or shareable. Committed and shareable pages are pages that, when accessed, ultimately translate to valid pages in physical memory. Committed pages are also referred to as private pages. This is because committed pages cannot be shared with other processes, whereas shareable pages can be (but might be in use by only one process).

Private pages are allocated through the Windows `VirtualAlloc`, `VirtualAllocEx`, and `VirtualAllocExNuma` functions, which lead eventually to the executive in the function `NtAllocateVirtualMemory` inside the memory manager. These functions are capable of committing memory as well as reserving memory. Reserving memory means setting aside a range of contiguous virtual addresses for possible future use (such as an array) while consuming negligible system resources, and then committing portions of the reserved space as needed as the application runs. Or, if the size requirements are known in advance, a process can reserve and commit in the same function call. In either case, the resulting committed pages can then be accessed by any thread in the process. Attempting to access free or reserved memory results in an access violation exception because the page isn't mapped to any storage that can resolve the reference.

If committed (private) pages have never been accessed before, they are created at the time of first access as zero-initialized pages (or *demand zero*). Private committed pages may later be automatically written to the paging file by the operating system if required by demand for physical memory. Private refers to the fact that these pages are normally inaccessible to any other process.

> **Note** Some functions, such as `ReadProcessMemory` and `WriteProcessMemory`, appear to permit cross-process memory access, but these are implemented by running kernel-mode code in the context of the target process. (This is referred to as *attaching to the process*.) They also require that the security descriptor of the target process grant the accessor the `PROCESS_VM_READ` or `PROCESS_VM_WRITE` right, respectively, or that the accessor holds the `SeDebugPrivilege`, which is by default granted only to members of the administrators group.

Shared pages are usually mapped to a view of a section. This in turn is part or all of a file, but may instead represent a portion of page file space. All shared pages can potentially be shared with other processes. Sections are exposed in the Windows API as file-mapping objects.

When a shared page is first accessed by any process, it will be read in from the associated mapped file unless the section is associated with the paging file, in which case it is created as a zero-initialized page. Later, if it is still resident in physical memory, the second and subsequent processes accessing it can simply use the same page contents that are already in memory. Shared pages might also have been prefetched by the system.

Two upcoming sections of this chapter, "Shared memory and mapped files" and "Section objects," go into much more detail about shared pages. Pages are written to disk through a mechanism called *modified page writing.* This occurs as pages are moved from a process's working set to a system-wide list called the *modified page list.* From there, they are written to disk or remote storage. (Working sets and the modified list are explained later in this chapter.) Mapped file pages can also be written back to their original files on disk with an explicit call to `FlushViewOfFile` or by the mapped page writer as memory demands dictate.

You can decommit private pages and/or release address space with the `VirtualFree` or `Virtual-FreeEx` function. The difference between decommittal and release is similar to the difference between reservation and committal. Decommitted memory is still reserved, but released memory has been freed; it is neither committed nor reserved.

Using the two-step process of reserving and then committing virtual memory defers committing pages—and, thereby, defers adding to the system commit charge described in the next section—until needed, but keeps the convenience of virtual contiguity. Reserving memory is a relatively inexpensive operation because it consumes very little actual memory. All that needs to be updated or constructed is the relatively small internal data structures that represent the state of the process address space. We'll explain these data structures, called *page tables* and *Virtual Address Descriptors* (*VADs*), later in this chapter.

One extremely common use for reserving a large space and committing portions of it as needed is the user-mode stack for each thread. When a thread is created, a stack is created by reserving a contiguous portion of the process address space. (The default size is 1 MB but you can override this size with the `CreateThread` and `CreateRemoteThread(Ex)` function calls or change it on an executable image basis by using the /STACK linker flag.) By default, the initial page in the stack is committed and the next page is marked as a guard page (which isn't committed) that traps references beyond the end of the committed portion of the stack and expands it.

EXPERIMENT: Reserved versus committed pages

You can use the `TestLimit` Sysinternals utility to allocate large amounts of reserved or private committed virtual memory. You can then observe the difference via Process Explorer. Follow these steps:

1. Open two command prompt windows.

2. Invoke TestLimit in one of the command prompt windows to create a large amount of reserved memory:

```
C:\temp>testlimit -r 1 -c 800

Testlimit v5.24 - test Windows limits
Copyright (C) 2012-2015 Mark Russinovich
Sysinternals - wwww.sysinternals.com

Process ID: 18468

Reserving private bytes 1 MB at a time ...
Leaked 800 MB of reserved memory (800 MB total leaked). Lasterror: 0
The operation completed successfully.
```

3. In the other command prompt window, create a similar amount of committed memory:

```
C:\temp>testlimit -m 1 -c 800

Testlimit v5.24 - test Windows limits
Copyright (C) 2012-2015 Mark Russinovich
Sysinternals - wwww.sysinternals.com

Process ID: 14528

Leaking private bytes 1 KB at a time ...
Leaked 800 MB of private memory (800 MB total leaked). Lasterror: 0
The operation completed successfully.
```

4. Run Task Manager, click the **Details** tab, and add a **Commit Size** column.

5. Find the two instances of TestLimit.exe in the list. They should look something like the following:

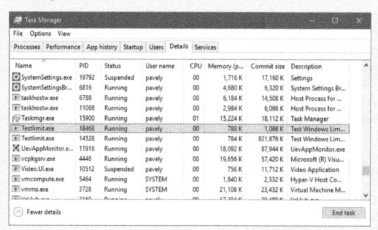

6. Notice that Task Manager shows the committed size but it has no counters that reveal the reserved memory in the other TestLimit process.

7. Open Process Explorer.

8. Click the **Process Memory** tab and enable the **Private Bytes** and **Virtual Size** columns.

9. Find the two TestLimit.exe processes in the main display:

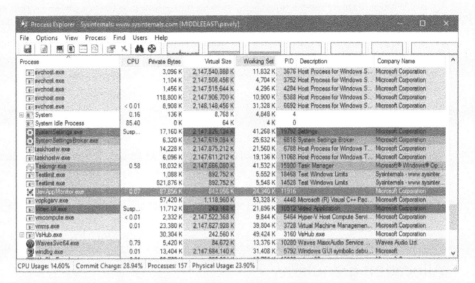

10. Notice that the virtual sizes of the two processes are identical, but only one shows a Private Bytes value that is comparable to the Virtual Size value. The large difference in the other TestLimit process (process ID 18468) is due to the reserved memory. You could make the same comparison in Performance Monitor by looking at the Virtual Bytes and Private Bytes counters in the Process category.

Commit charge and commit limit

On the Performance tab in Task Manager, on the Memory page, there is a Committed label with two numbers underneath it. The memory manager keeps track of private committed memory usage on a global basis, termed *commitment* or *commit charge*. This is the first of the two numbers, which represents the total of all committed virtual memory in the system.

There is a system-wide limit, called the *system commit limit* or simply the *commit limit*, on the amount of committed virtual memory that can exist at any one time. This limit corresponds to the current total size of all paging files plus the amount of RAM that is usable by the operating system. This is the second of the two numbers displayed under the Committed label. The memory manager can increase the commit limit automatically by expanding one or more of the paging files if they are not already at their configured maximum size.

Commit charge and the system commit limit are explained in more detail in the section "Commit charge and the system commit limit" later in this chapter.

Locking memory

In general, it's better to let the memory manager decide which pages remain in physical memory. However, there might be special circumstances when it might be necessary for an application or device driver to lock pages in physical memory. Pages can be locked in memory in two ways:

- Windows applications can call the VirtualLock function to lock pages in their process working set. Pages locked using this mechanism remain in memory until explicitly unlocked or until the process that locked them terminates. The number of pages a process can lock can't exceed its minimum working set size minus eight pages. If a process needs to lock more pages, it can increase its working set minimum with the SetProcessWorkingSetSizeEx function, discussed later in this chapter in the section "Working set management."

- Device drivers can call the MmProbeAndLockPages, MmLockPagableCodeSection, MmLockPagable-DataSection, or MmLockPagableSectionByHandle kernel-mode functions. Pages locked using this mechanism remain in memory until explicitly unlocked. The last three of these APIs enforce no quota on the number of pages that can be locked in memory because the resident available page charge is obtained when the driver first loads. This ensures that it can never cause a system crash due to overlocking. For the first API, quota charges must be obtained or the API will return a failure status.

Allocation granularity

Windows aligns each region of reserved process address space to begin on an integral boundary defined by the value of the system allocation granularity, which can be retrieved from the Windows Get-SystemInfo or GetNativeSystemInfo functions. This value is 64 KB, a granularity that is used by the memory manager to efficiently allocate metadata (for example, VADs, bitmaps, and so on) to support various process operations. In addition, if support were added for future processors with larger page sizes (for example, up to 64 KB) or virtually indexed caches that require system-wide physical-to-virtual page alignment, the risk of requiring changes to applications that made assumptions about allocation alignment would be reduced.

> **Note** Windows kernel-mode code isn't subject to the same restrictions. It can reserve memory on a single-page granularity (although this is not exposed to device drivers for the reasons detailed earlier). This level of granularity is primarily used to pack TEB allocations more densely. Because this mechanism is internal only, this code can easily be changed if a future platform requires different values. Also, for the purposes of supporting 16-bit and MS-DOS applications on x86 systems only, the memory manager provides the MEM_DOS_LIM flag to the MapViewOfFileEx API, which is used to force the use of single-page granularity.

Finally, when a region of address space is reserved, Windows ensures that the size and base of the region is a multiple of the system page size, whatever that might be. For example, because x86 systems use 4 KB pages, if you tried to reserve a region of memory 18 KB in size, the actual amount reserved on an x86 system would be 20 KB. If you specified a base address of 3 KB for an 18 KB region, the actual amount reserved would be 24 KB. Note that the VAD for the allocation would then also be rounded to 64 KB alignment/length, thus making the remainder of it inaccessible.

Shared memory and mapped files

As is true with most modern operating systems, Windows provides a mechanism to share memory among processes and the operating system. *Shared memory* can be defined as memory that is visible to more than one process or that is present in more than one process virtual address space. For example, if two processes use the same DLL, it would make sense to load the referenced code pages for that DLL into physical memory only once and share those pages between all processes that map the DLL, as illustrated in Figure 5-2.

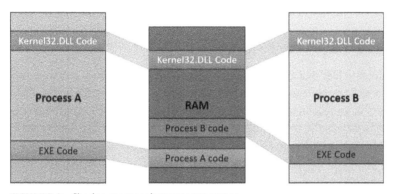

FIGURE 5-2 Sharing memory between processes.

Each process would still maintain its private memory areas to store private data but the DLL code and unmodified data pages could be shared without harm. As we'll explain later, this kind of sharing happens automatically because the code pages in executable images—EXE and DLL files, and several other types like screen savers (SCR), which are essentially DLLs under other names—are mapped as execute-only and writable pages are mapped as copy-on-write. (See the "Copy-on-write" section later in this chapter for more information.)

Figure 5-2 shows two processes, based on different images, that share a DLL mapped just once to physical memory. The images (EXE) code itself is not shared in this case because the two processes run different images. The EXE code would be shared between processes that run the same image, such as two or more processes running Notepad.exe.

The underlying primitives in the memory manager used to implement shared memory are called *section objects*, which are exposed as file-mapping objects in the Windows API. The internal structure and implementation of section objects are described later in this chapter in the section "Section objects."

This fundamental primitive in the memory manager is used to map virtual addresses whether in main memory, in the page file, or in some other file that an application wants to access as if it were in memory. A section can be opened by one process or by many. In other words, section objects don't necessarily equate to shared memory.

A section object can be connected to an open file on disk (called a *mapped file*) or to committed memory (to provide shared memory). Sections mapped to committed memory are called *page-file-backed sections* because the pages are written to the paging file (as opposed to a mapped file) if demands on physical memory require it. (Because Windows can run with no paging file, page-file-backed sections might in fact be "backed" only by physical memory.) As with any other empty page that is made visible to user mode (such as private committed pages), shared committed pages are always zero-filled when they are first accessed to ensure that no sensitive data is ever leaked.

To create a section object, call the Windows `CreateFileMapping`, `CreateFileMappingFromApp`, or `CreateFileMappingNuma(Ex)` function, specifying a previously opened file handle to map it to (or `INVALID_HANDLE_VALUE` for a page-file-backed section) and optionally a name and security descriptor. If the section has a name, other processes can open it with `OpenFileMapping` or the `CreateFileMapping*` functions. Or you can grant access to section objects through either handle inheritance (by specifying that the handle be inheritable when opening or creating the handle) or handle duplication (by using `DuplicateHandle`). Device drivers can also manipulate section objects with the `ZwOpenSection`, `ZwMapViewOfSection`, and `ZwUnmapViewOfSection` functions.

A section object can refer to files that are much larger than can fit in the address space of a process. (If the paging file backs a section object, sufficient space must exist in the paging file and/or RAM to contain it.) To access a very large section object, a process can map only the portion of the section object that it requires (called a *view* of the section) by calling the `MapViewOfFile(Ex)`, `MapViewOfFile-FromApp`, or `MapViewOfFileExNuma` function and then specifying the range to map. Mapping views permits processes to conserve address space because only the views of the section object needed at the time must be mapped into memory.

Windows applications can use mapped files to conveniently perform I/O to files by simply making them appear as data in memory within their address space. User applications aren't the only consumers of section objects; the image loader uses section objects to map executable images, DLLs, and device drivers into memory, and the cache manager uses them to access data in cached files. (For information on how the cache manager integrates with the memory manager, see Chapter 14 in Part 2.) The implementation of shared memory sections, both in terms of address translation and the internal data structures, is explained in the section "Section objects" later in this chapter.

EXPERIMENT: Viewing memory-mapped files

You can list the memory-mapped files in a process by using Process Explorer. To do so, configure the lower pane to show the DLL view. (Open the **View** menu, select **Lower Pane View**, and choose **DLLs**.) Note that this is more than just a list of DLLs—it represents all memory-mapped files in the process address space. Some of these are DLLs, one is the image file (EXE) being run, and additional entries might represent memory-mapped data files.

The following display from Process Explorer shows a WinDbg process using several different memory mappings to access the memory dump file being examined. Like most Windows programs, it (or one of the Windows DLLs it is using) is also using memory mapping to access a Windows data file called Locale.nls, which is part of the internationalization support in Windows.

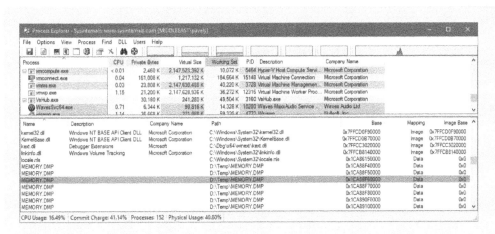

You can also search for memory-mapped files by opening the **Find** menu and choosing **Find Handle or DLL** (or pressing **Ctrl+F**). This can be useful when trying to determine which process(es) is using a DLL or a memory-mapped file that you are trying to replace.

Protecting memory

As explained in Chapter 1, "Concepts and tools," Windows provides memory protection so that no user process can inadvertently or deliberately corrupt the address space of another process or the operating system. Windows provides this protection in four primary ways.

- All system-wide data structures and memory pools used by kernel-mode system components can be accessed only while in kernel mode. User-mode threads can't access these pages. If they attempt to do so, the hardware generates a fault, which the memory manager reports to the thread as an access violation.

- Each process has a separate, private address space, protected from access by any thread belonging to another process. Even shared memory is not really an exception to this because each process accesses the shared regions using addresses that are part of its own virtual address space. The only exception is if another process has virtual memory read or write access to the process object (or holds SeDebugPrivilege) and thus can use the ReadProcessMemory or WriteProcessMemory function. Each time a thread references an address, the virtual memory hardware, in concert with the memory manager, intervenes and translates the virtual address into a physical one. By controlling how virtual addresses are translated, Windows can ensure that threads running in one process don't inappropriately access a page belonging to another process.

- In addition to the implicit protection offered by virtual-to-physical address translation, all processors supported by Windows provide some form of hardware-controlled memory protection such as read/write, read-only, and so on. (The exact details of such protection vary according to the processor.) For example, code pages in the address space of a process are marked read-only and are thus protected from modification by user threads. Table 5-2 lists the memory-protection options defined in the Windows API. (See the documentation for the VirtualProtect, Virtual-ProtectEx, VirtualQuery, and VirtualQueryEx functions.)

TABLE 5-2 Memory-protection options defined in the Windows API

Attribute	Description
PAGE_NOACCESS	Any attempt to read from, write to, or execute code in this region causes an access violation.
PAGE_READONLY	Any attempt to write to (and on processors with no execute support, execute code in) memory causes an access violation, but reads are permitted.
PAGE_READWRITE	The page is readable and writable but not executable.
PAGE_EXECUTE	Any attempt to write to code in memory in this region causes an access violation, but execution (and read operations on all existing processors) is permitted.
PAGE_EXECUTE_READ*	Any attempt to write to memory in this region causes an access violation, but executes and reads are permitted.
PAGE_EXECUTE_READWRITE*	The page is readable, writable, and executable. Any attempted access will succeed.
PAGE_WRITECOPY	Any attempt to write to memory in this region causes the system to give the process a private copy of the page. On processors with no-execute support, attempts to execute code in memory in this region cause an access violation.
PAGE_EXECUTE_WRITECOPY	Any attempt to write to memory in this region causes the system to give the process a private copy of the page. Reading and executing code in this region is permitted. (No copy is made in this case.)
PAGE_GUARD	Any attempt to read from or write to a guard page raises an EXCEPTION_GUARD_PAGE exception and turns off the guard page status. Guard pages thus act as a one-shot alarm. Note that this flag can be specified with any of the page protections listed in this table except PAGE_NOACCESS.
PAGE_NOCACHE	This uses physical memory that is not cached. This is not recommended for general usage. It is useful for device drivers—for example, mapping a video frame buffer with no caching.
PAGE_WRITECOMBINE	This enables write-combined memory accesses. When enabled, the processor does not cache memory writes (possibly causing significantly more memory traffic than if memory writes were cached), but it does try to aggregate write requests to optimize performance. For example, if multiple writes are made to the same address, only the most recent write might occur. Separate writes to adjacent addresses may be similarly collapsed into a single large write. This is not typically used for general applications, but it is useful for device drivers—for example, mapping a video frame buffer as write combined.
PAGE_TARGETS_INVALID and PAGE_TARGETS_NO_UPDATE (Windows 10 and Windows Server 2016)	These values control behavior of Control Flow Guard (CFG) for executable code in these pages. Both constants have the same value but are used in different calls, essentially acting as a toggle. PAGE_TARGETS_INVALID indicates indirect calls should fail CFG and crash the process. PAGE_TARGETS_NO_UPDATE allows VirtualProtect calls that change the page range to allow execution to not update CFG state. See Chapter 7, "Security," for more information on CFG.

*No execute protection is supported on processors that have the necessary hardware support (for example, all x64 processors) but not in older x86 processors. If unsupported, "execute" translates to "read."

- Shared memory section objects have standard Windows access control lists (ACLs) that are checked when processes attempt to open them, thus limiting access of shared memory to those processes with the proper rights. Access control also comes into play when a thread creates a section to contain a mapped file. To create the section, the thread must have at least read access to the underlying file object or the operation will fail.

Once a thread has successfully opened a handle to a section, its actions are still subject to the memory manager and the hardware-based page protections described earlier. A thread can change the page-level protection on virtual pages in a section if the change doesn't violate the permissions in the ACL for that section object. For example, the memory manager allows a thread to change the pages of a read-only section to have copy-on-write access but not to have read/write access. The copy-on-write access is permitted because it has no effect on other processes sharing the data.

Data Execution Prevention

Data Execution Prevention (DEP), or no-execute (NX) page protection, causes an attempt to transfer control to an instruction in a page marked as "no execute" to generate an access fault. This can prevent certain types of malware from exploiting bugs in the system through the execution of code placed in a data page such as the stack. DEP can also catch poorly written programs that don't correctly set permissions on pages from which they intend to execute code. If an attempt is made in kernel mode to execute code in a page marked as "no execute," the system will crash with the bug check code ATTEMPTED_ EXECUTE_OF_NOEXECUTE_MEMORY (0xFC). (See Chapter 15, "Crash dump analysis," in Part 2 for an explanation of these codes.) If this occurs in user mode, a STATUS_ACCESS_VIOLATION (0xC0000005) exception is delivered to the thread attempting the illegal reference. If a process allocates memory that needs to be executable, it must explicitly mark such pages by specifying the PAGE_EXECUTE, PAGE_ EXECUTE_READ, PAGE_EXECUTE_READWRITE, or PAGE_EXECUTE_WRITECOPY flags on the page-granularity memory-allocation functions.

On 32-bit x86 systems that support DEP, bit 63 in the page table entry (PTE) is used to mark a page as non-executable. Therefore, the DEP feature is available only when the processor is running in Physical Address Extension (PAE) mode, without which page table entries are only 32 bits wide. (See the section "x86 virtual address translation" later in this chapter.) Thus, support for hardware DEP on 32-bit systems requires loading the PAE kernel (%SystemRoot%\System32\Ntkrnlpa.exe), which currently is the only supported kernel on x86 systems.

On ARM systems, DEP is set to AlwaysOn.

On 64-bit versions of Windows, execution protection is always applied to all 64-bit processes and device drivers and can be disabled only by setting the nx BCD option to AlwaysOff. Execution protection for 32-bit programs depends on system configuration settings, described shortly. On 64-bit Windows, execution protection is applied to thread stacks (both user and kernel mode), user-mode pages not specifically marked as executable, the kernel paged pool, and the kernel session pool. For a description of kernel memory pools, see the section "Kernel-mode heaps (system memory pools)." However, on 32-bit Windows, execution protection is applied only to thread stacks and user-mode pages, not to the paged pool and session pool.

The application of execution protection for 32-bit processes depends on the value of the BCD nx option. To change the settings, open the **Data Execution Prevention** tab in the Performance Options dialog box (see Figure 5-3). (To open this dialog box, right-click **Computer**, select **Properties**, click **Advanced System Settings**, and choose **Performance Settings**.) When you configure no-execute protection in the Performance Options dialog box, the BCD nx option is set to the appropriate value. Table 5-3 lists the variations of the values and how they correspond to the Data Execution Prevention tab. The registry lists 32-bit applications that are excluded from execution protection under the HKLM\ SOFTWARE\Microsoft\Windows NT\CurrentVersion\AppCompatFlags\Layers key, with the value name being the full path of the executable and the data set to DisableNXShowUI.

FIGURE 5-3 Data Execution Prevention tab settings.

TABLE 5-3 BCD nx values

BCD nx Value	Option on Data Execution Prevention Tab	Explanation
OptIn	Turn on DEP for Essential Windows Programs and Services Only	This enables DEP for core Windows system images. It enables 32-bit processes to dynamically configure DEP for their life-time.
OptOut	Turn on DEP for All Programs and Services Except Those I Select	This enables DEP for all executables except those specified. It enables 32-bit processes to dynamically configure DEP for their lifetime. It also enables system compatibility fixes for DEP.
AlwaysOn	There is no dialog box option for this setting	This enables DEP for all components with no ability to exclude certain applications. It disables dynamic configuration for 32-bit processes and disables system compatibility fixes.
AlwaysOff	There is no dialog box option for this setting	This disables DEP (not recommended). It also disables dynamic configuration for 32-bit processes.

On Windows client versions (both 64-bit and 32-bit), execution protection for 32-bit processes is configured by default to apply only to core Windows operating system executables. That is, the nx BCD option is set to OptIn. This is to avoid breaking 32-bit applications that might rely on being able to execute code in pages not specifically marked as executable, such as self-extracting or packed applications. On Windows server systems, execution protection for 32-bit applications is configured by default to apply to all 32-bit programs. That is, the nx BCD option is set to OptOut.

Even if you force DEP to be enabled, there are still other methods through which applications can disable DEP for their own images. For example, regardless of which execution-protection options are enabled, the image loader will verify the signature of the executable against known copy-protection mechanisms (such as SafeDisc and SecuROM) and disable execution protection to provide compatibility with older copy-protected software such as computer games. (See Chapter 3 for more information about the image loader.)

EXPERIMENT: Looking at DEP protection on processes

Process Explorer can show you the current DEP status for all the processes on your system, including whether the process is opted in or benefiting from permanent protection. To look at the DEP status for processes, right-click any column in the process tree, choose **Select Columns**, and then select **DEP Status** on the **Process Image** tab. There are three possible values:

- **DEP (permanent)**   This means the process has enabled DEP because it is a "necessary Windows program or service."

- **DEP**   This means the process opted in to DEP. This may be due to a system-wide policy to opt in to all 32-bit processes, because of an API call such as SetProcessDEPPolicy, or because the /NXCOMPAT linker flag was set when the image was built.

- **Nothing**   If the column displays no information for this process, DEP is disabled because of either a system-wide policy or an explicit API call or shim.

Additionally, to provide compatibility with older versions of the Active Template Library (ATL) framework (version 7.1 or earlier), the Windows kernel provides an ATL thunk emulation environment. This environment detects ATL thunk code sequences that have caused the DEP exception and emulates the expected operation. Application developers can request that ATL thunk emulation not be applied by using the latest Microsoft C++ compiler and specifying the /NXCOMPAT flag (which sets the IMAGE_DLL-CHARACTERISTICS_NX_COMPAT flag in the PE header), which tells the system that the executable fully supports DEP. Note that ATL thunk emulation is permanently disabled if the AlwaysOn value is set.

Finally, if the system is in OptIn or OptOut mode and executing a 32-bit process, the SetProcess-DEPPolicy function allows a process to dynamically disable DEP or to permanently enable it. When it is enabled through this API, DEP cannot be disabled programmatically for the lifetime of the process. This function can also be used to dynamically disable ATL thunk emulation if the image wasn't compiled with the /NXCOMPAT flag. On 64-bit processes or systems booted with AlwaysOff or AlwaysOn, the function always returns a failure. The GetProcessDEPPolicy function returns the 32-bit per-process DEP policy (it fails on 64-bit systems, where the policy is always the same—enabled), while GetSystem-DEPPolicy can be used to return a value corresponding to the policies in Table 5-3.

Copy-on-write

Copy-on-write page protection is an optimization the memory manager uses to conserve physical memory. When a process maps a copy-on-write view of a section object that contains read/write pages, the memory manager delays the copying of pages until the page is written to instead of making a process private copy at the time the view is mapped. For example, in Figure 5-4, two processes are sharing three pages, each marked copy-on-write, but neither of the two processes has attempted to modify any data on the pages.

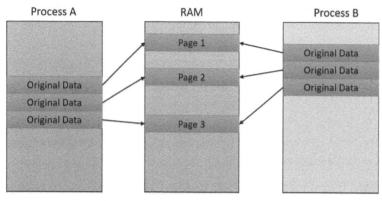

FIGURE 5-4 The "before" of copy-on-write.

If a thread in either process writes to a page, a memory-management fault is generated. The memory manager sees that the write is to a copy-on-write page, so instead of reporting the fault as an access violation, it does the following:

1. It allocates a new read/write page in physical memory.

2. It copies the contents of the original page to the new page.

3. It updates the corresponding page-mapping information (explained later in this chapter) in this process to point to the new location.

4. It dismisses the exception, causing the instruction that generated the fault to be re-executed.

This time, the write operation succeeds. However, as shown in Figure 5-5, the newly copied page is now private to the process that did the writing and isn't visible to the other process still sharing the copy-on-write page. Each new process that writes to that same shared page will also get its own private copy.

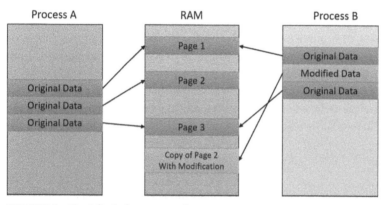

FIGURE 5-5 The "after" of copy-on-write.

One application of copy-on-write is to implement breakpoint support in debuggers. For example, by default, code pages start out as execute-only. If a programmer sets a breakpoint while debugging a program, however, the debugger must add a breakpoint instruction to the code. It does this by first changing the protection on the page to PAGE_EXECUTE_READWRITE and then changing the instruction stream. Because the code page is part of a mapped section, the memory manager creates a private copy for the process with the breakpoint set, while other processes continue using the unmodified code page.

Copy-on-write is one example of an evaluation technique called *lazy evaluation* that the memory manager uses as often as possible. Lazy-evaluation algorithms avoid performing an expensive operation until absolutely required. If the operation is never required, no time is wasted on it.

To examine the rate of copy-on-write faults, see the Write Copies/Sec performance counter in the Memory category of the Performance Monitor tool.

Address Windowing Extensions

Although the 32-bit version of Windows can support up to 64 GB of physical memory (refer to Table 2-2), each 32-bit user process has only a 2 GB virtual address space by default. (You can configure this to up to 3 GB when using the increaseuserva BCD option, described in the upcoming section "Virtual address space layouts.") An application that needs to make more than 2 GB (or 3 GB) of data easily available in a single process could do so via file mapping, remapping a part of its address space into various portions of a large file. However, significant paging would be involved upon each remap.

For higher performance (and more fine-grained control), Windows provides a set of functions called *Address Windowing Extensions* (*AWE*). These functions allow a process to allocate more physical memory than can be represented in its virtual address space. It then can access the physical memory by mapping a portion of its virtual address space into selected portions of the physical memory at various times.

You allocate and use memory via the AWE functions in three steps:

1. You allocate the physical memory to be used. The application uses the Windows functions AllocateUserPhysicalPages or AllocateUserPhysicalPagesNuma. (These require the SeLockMemoryPrivilege.)

2. You create one or more regions of virtual address space to act as windows to map views of the physical memory. The application uses the Win32 VirtualAlloc, VirtualAllocEx, or VirtualAllocExNuma function with the MEM_PHYSICAL flag.

3. Steps 1 and 2 are, generally speaking, initialization steps. To actually use the memory, the application uses MapUserPhysicalPages or MapUserPhysicalPagesScatter to map a portion of the physical region allocated in step 1 into one of the virtual regions, or windows, allocated in step 2.

Figure 5-6 shows an example. The application has created a 256 MB window in its address space and has allocated 4 GB of physical memory. It can then use MapUserPhysicalPages or MapUserPhysicalPagesScatter to access any portion of the physical memory by mapping the desired portion of memory into the 256 MB window. The size of the application's virtual address space window determines the amount of physical memory the application can access with any given mapping. To access another portion of the allocated RAM, the application can simply remap the area.

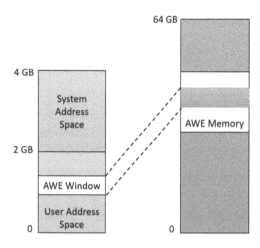

FIGURE 5-6 Using AWE to map physical memory.

The AWE functions exist on all editions of Windows and are usable regardless of how much physical memory a system has. However, AWE is most useful on 32-bit systems with more than 2 GB of physical memory because it provides a way for a 32-bit process to access more RAM than its virtual address space would otherwise allow. Another use is for security purposes. Because AWE memory is never paged out, the data in AWE memory can never have a copy in the paging file that someone could examine by rebooting into an alternate operating system. (VirtualLock provides the same guarantee for pages in general.)

Finally, there are some restrictions on memory allocated and mapped by the AWE functions:

- Pages can't be shared between processes.

- The same physical page can't be mapped to more than one virtual address.

- Page protection is limited to read/write, read-only, and no access.

AWE is less useful on 64 bit Windows systems because these systems support 128 TB of virtual address space per process, while allowing a maximum of only 24 TB of RAM (on Windows Server 2016 systems). Therefore, AWE is not necessary to allow an application to use more RAM than it has virtual address space; the amount of RAM on the system will always be smaller than the process virtual address space. AWE remains useful, however, for setting up non-pageable regions of a process address space. It provides finer granularity than the file-mapping APIs. (The system page size is 4 KB rather than 64 KB.)

For a description of the page table data structures used to map memory on systems with more than 4 GB of physical memory, see the section "x86 virtual address translation."

Kernel-mode heaps (system memory pools)

At system initialization, the memory manager creates two dynamically sized memory pools, or heaps, that most kernel-mode components use to allocate system memory:

- **Non-paged pool** This consists of ranges of system virtual addresses that are guaranteed to reside in physical memory at all times. Thus, they can be accessed at any time without incurring a page fault—meaning they can be accessed from any IRQL. One of the reasons a non-paged pool is required is because page faults can't be satisfied at DPC/dispatch level or above. Therefore, any code and data that might execute or be accessed at or above DPC/dispatch level must be in non-pageable memory.

- **Paged pool** This is a region of virtual memory in system space that can be paged into and out of the system. Device drivers that don't need to access the memory from DPC/dispatch level or above can use paged pool. It is accessible from any process context.

Both memory pools are in the system part of the address space and are mapped in the virtual address space of every process. The executive provides routines to allocate and deallocate from these pools. For information on these routines, see the functions that start with `ExAllocatePool`, `ExAllocate-PoolWithTag`, and `ExFreePool` in the Windows Development Kit (WDK) documentation.

Systems start with four paged pools, which are combined to make the overall system paged pool, and two non-paged pools. More are created—as many as 64—depending on the number of NUMA nodes on the system. Having more than one paged pool reduces the frequency of system code blocking on simultaneous calls to pool routines. Additionally, the different pools created are mapped across different virtual address ranges that correspond to different NUMA nodes on the system. The different data structures, such as the large page look-aside lists, to describe pool allocations are also mapped across different NUMA nodes.

In addition to the paged and non-paged pools, there are a few other pools with special attributes or uses. For example, there is a pool region in session space that is used for data that is common to all processes in the session. Allocations from another pool, called *special pool*, are surrounded by pages marked as "no access" to help isolate problems in code that accesses memory before or after the region of pool it allocated.

Pool sizes

A non-paged pool starts at an initial size based on the amount of physical memory on the system and then grows as needed. For a non-paged pool, the initial size is 3 percent of system RAM. If this is less than 40 MB, the system will instead use 40 MB as long as 10 percent of RAM results in more than 40 MB. Otherwise, 10 percent of RAM is chosen as a minimum. Windows dynamically chooses the maximum size of the pools and allows a given pool to grow from its initial size to the maximums shown in Table 5-4.

TABLE 5-4 Maximum pool sizes

Pool Type	Maximum on 32-Bit Systems	Maximum on 64 bit Systems (Windows 8, Server 2012)	Maximum on 64-Bit Systems (Windows 8.1, 10, Server 2012 R2, 2016)
Non-paged	75 percent of physical memory or 2 GB, whichever is smaller	75 percent of physical memory or 128 GB, whichever is smaller	16 TB
Paged	2 GB	384 GB	15.5 TB

Four of these computed sizes are stored in kernel variables in Windows 8.*x* and Server 2012/R2. Three of these are exposed as performance counters and one is computed only as a performance counter value. Windows 10 and Server 2016 moved the global variables into fields in a global memory management structure (MI_SYSTEM_INFORMATION) named MiState. Within this lies a variable named Vs (of type _MI_VISIBLE_STATE) where this information resides. The global variable MiVisibleState also points to that Vs member. These variables and counters are listed in Table 5-5.

TABLE 5-5 System pool size variables and performance counters

Kernel Variable	Performance Counter	Description
MmSizeOfNonPagedPoolInBytes	Memory: Pool non-paged bytes	This is the size of the initial non-paged pool. It can be reduced or enlarged automatically by the system if memory demands dictate. The kernel variable will not show these changes, but the performance counter will.
MmMaximumNonPagedPoolInBytes (Windows 8.x and Server 2012/R2)	Not available	This is the maximum size of a non-paged pool.
MiVisibleState->MaximumNonPagePool InBytes (Windows 10 and Server 2016)	Not available	This is the maximum size of a non-paged pool.
Not available	Memory: Pool paged bytes	This is the current total virtual size of paged pool.
WorkingSetSize (number of pages) in the MmPagedPoolWs struct (type MMSUPPORT) (Windows 8.x and Server 2012/R2)	Memory: Pool paged resident bytes	This is the current physical (resident) size of paged pool.
MmSizeOfPagedPoolInBytes (Windows 8.x and Server 2012/R2)	Not available	This is the maximum (virtual) size of a paged pool.
MiState.Vs.SizeOfPagedPoolIn Bytes (Windows 10 and Server 2016)	Not available	This is the maximum (virtual) size of a paged pool.

EXPERIMENT: Determining the maximum pool sizes

You can obtain the pool maximums by using either Process Explorer or live kernel debugging (explained in Chapter 1). To view pool maximums with Process Explorer, select the **View** menu, choose **System Information**, and then click the **Memory** tab. The pool limits are displayed in the Kernel Memory section, as shown here:

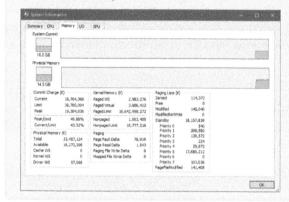

Note For Process Explorer to retrieve this information, it must have access to the symbols for the kernel running on your system. For a description of how to configure Process Explorer to use symbols, see the experiment "Viewing process details with Process Explorer" in Chapter 1.

To view the same information by using the kernel debugger, you can use the `!vm` command as was shown previously in this chapter.

Monitoring pool usage

The Memory performance counter object has separate counters for the non-paged pool and paged pool (both virtual and physical). In addition, the Poolmon utility (in the WDK Tools directory) allows you to monitor the detailed usage of non-paged and paged pool. When you run Poolmon, you should see a display like the one shown in Figure 5-7.

```
C:\Program Files (x86)\Windows Kits\10\Tools\x64\poolmon.exe
Memory:33457124K Avail:14121052K PageFlts:980013301   InRam Krnl:36936K P:4522264K
Commit:25130464K Limit:34505700K Peak:25253232K         Pool N:1747584K P:4579680K
System pool information
Tag  Type    Allocs         Frees          Diff    Bytes          Per Alloc

-UMD Nonp       4 (   0)       1 (   0)       3       144 (   0)        48
.UMD Nonp       4 (   0)       3 (   0)       1       128 (   0)       128
2920 Nonp       1 (   0)       0 (   0)       1       128 (   0)       128
2UuQ Nonp    1967 (   0)    1963 (   0)       4     16384 (   0)      4096
3DMN Paged      1 (   0)       0 (   0)       1       144 (   0)       144
4321 Nonp       1 (   0)       1 (   0)       0         0 (   0)         0
8042 Nonp      60 (   0)      56 (   0)       4      4048 (   0)      1012
8042 Paged     12 (   0)      12 (   0)       0         0 (   0)         0
9472 Nonp      17 (   0)      13 (   0)       4     91888 (   0)     22972
@CP  Nonp       7 (   0)       5 (   0)       2       160 (   0)        80
@GM2 Nonp  463473 (   0)  461901 (   0)    1572   2364288 (   0)      1504
@GM6 Nonp  420521 (   0)  418374 (   0)    2147   3229088 (   0)      1504
@GM7 Nonp      21 (   0)      21 (   0)       0         0 (   0)         0
@GM8 Nonp      21 (   0)      21 (   0)       0         0 (   0)         0
@GMM Nonp   14441 (   0)   14316 (   0)     125    128944 (   0)      1031
@GMa Nonp       6 (   0)       0 (   0)       6      9024 (   0)      1504
@GMb Nonp      54 (   0)      53 (   0)       1      1504 (   0)      1504
@GMe Nonp       5 (   0)       0 (   0)       5      7520 (   0)      1504
@GMf Nonp    3478 (   0)    3398 (   0)      80    120320 (   0)      1504
@GMg Nonp       1 (   0)       0 (   0)       1      1504 (   0)      1504
@GMn Nonp       1 (   0)       0 (   0)       1      1504 (   0)      1504
@GMn Nonp       1 (   0)       1 (   0)       0         0 (   0)         0
@GMo Nonp      16 (   0)       0 (   0)      16     24064 (   0)      1504
@GMp Nonp    6999 (   0)    6460 (   0)     539    810656 (   0)      1504
@GMq Nonp       1 (   0)       1 (   0)       0         0 (   0)         0
```

FIGURE 5-7 Poolmon output.

Any highlighted lines you might see represent changes to the display. (You can disable the highlighting feature by typing **/** while running Poolmon; type **/** again to re-enable highlighting.) Type **?** while Poolmon is running to bring up its help screen. You can configure which pools you want to monitor (paged, non-paged, or both) and the sort order. For example, by pressing the **P** key until only non-paged allocations are shown, and then the **D** key to sort by the Diff (differences) column, you can find out what kind of structures are most numerous in non-paged pool. Also, the command-line options are shown, which allow you to monitor specific tags (or every tag but one tag). For example, the command `poolmon –iCM` will monitor only CM tags (allocations from the configuration manager, which manages the registry). The columns have the meanings shown in Table 5-6.

TABLE 5-6 Poolmon columns

Column	Explanation
Tag	This is a four-byte tag given to the pool allocation.
Type	This is the pool type (paged or non-paged).
Allocs	This is a count of all allocations. The number in parentheses shows the difference in the Allocs column since the last update.
Frees	This is the count of all frees. The number in parentheses shows the difference in the Frees column since the last update.
Diff	This is the count of allocations minus frees.
Bytes	This is the total bytes consumed by this tag. The number in parentheses shows the difference in the Bytes column since the last update.
Per Alloc	This is the size in bytes of a single instance of this tag.

For a description of the meaning of the pool tags used by Windows, see the Pooltag.txt file in the Triage subdirectory where the Debugging tools for Windows are located. Because third-party device-driver pool tags are not listed in this file, you can use the –c switch on the 32-bit version of Poolmon that comes with the WDK to generate a local pool tag file (Localtag.txt). This file will contain pool tags used by drivers found on your system, including third-party drivers. (Note that if a device-driver binary has been deleted after it was loaded, its pool tags will not be recognized.)

Alternatively, you can search the device drivers on your system for a pool tag by using the Strings.exe tool from Sysinternals. For example, the following command displays drivers that contain the string "abcd":

```
strings %SYSTEMROOT%\system32\drivers\*.sys | findstr /i "abcd"
```

Device drivers do not necessarily have to be located in %SystemRoot%\System32\Drivers. They can be in any folder. To list the full path of all loaded drivers, follow these steps:

1. Open the **Start** menu and type **Msinfo32** (System Information should appear).

2. Run System Information.

3. Select **Software Environment**.

4. Choose **System Drivers**. If a device driver has been loaded and then deleted from the system, it will not be listed here.

An alternative way to view pool usage by device driver is to enable the pool-tracking feature of Driver Verifier, explained in Chapter 6. While this makes the mapping from pool tag to device driver unneces-sary, it does require a reboot (to enable Driver Verifier on the desired drivers). After rebooting with pool tracking enabled, you can either run the graphical Driver Verifier Manager (%SystemRoot%\System32\Verifier.exe) or use the Verifier /Log command to send the pool-usage information to a file.

Finally, you can view pool usage with the kernel debugger !poolused command. The !poolused 2 command shows non-paged pool usage sorted by pool tag using the most amount of pool. The !poolused 4 command lists paged-pool usage, again sorted by pool tag using the most amount of pool. The following example shows the partial output from these two commands:

```
lkd> !poolused 2
........
Sorting by NonPaged Pool Consumed
```

	NonPaged		Paged		
Tag	Allocs	Used	Allocs	Used	
File	626381	260524032	0	0	File objects
Ntfx	733204	227105872	0	0	General Allocation , Binary: ntfs.sys
MmCa	513713	148086336	0	0	Mm control areas for mapped files , Binary: nt!mm
FMsl	732490	140638080	0	0	STREAM_LIST_CTRL structure , Binary: fltmgr.sys
CcSc	104420	56804480	0	0	Cache Manager Shared Cache Map , Binary: nt!cc
SQSF	283749	45409984	0	0	UNKNOWN pooltag 'SQSF', please update pooltag.txt
FMfz	382318	42819616	0	0	FILE_LIST_CTRL structure , Binary: fltmgr.sys
FMsc	36130	32950560	0	0	SECTION_CONTEXT structure , Binary: fltmgr.sys
EtwB	517	31297568	107	105119744	Etw Buffer , Binary: nt!etw
DFmF	382318	30585440	382318	91756320	UNKNOWN pooltag 'DFmF', please update pooltag.txt
DFmE	382318	18351264	0	0	UNKNOWN pooltag 'DFmE', please update pooltag.txt
FSfc	382318	18351264	0	0	Unrecoginzed File System Run Time allocations (update pooltag.w) , Binary: nt!fsrtl
smNp	4295	17592320	0	0	ReadyBoost store node pool allocations , Binary: nt!store or rdyboost.sys
Thre	5780	12837376	0	0	Thread objects , Binary: nt!ps
Pool	8	12834368	0	0	Pool tables, etc.

EXPERIMENT: Troubleshooting a pool leak

In this experiment, you will fix a real paged pool leak on your system so that you can use the techniques described in the previous section to track down the leak. The leak will be generated by the Notmyfault tool from Sysinternals. Follow these steps:

1. Run Notmyfault.exe for your OS bitness (for example, the 64 bit on a 64-bit system).

2. Notmyfault.exe loads the Myfault.sys device driver and presents a Not My Fault dialog box with the Crash tab selected. Click the **Leak** tab. It should look something like this:

3. Ensure that the **Leak/Second** setting is set to 1000 KB.

4. Click the **Leak Paged** button. This causes Notmyfault to begin sending requests to the Myfault device driver to allocate paged pool. Notmyfault will continue sending requests until you click the **Stop Paged** button. Paged pool is not normally released even when you close a program that has caused it to occur (by interacting with a buggy device driver). The pool is permanently leaked until you reboot the system. However, to make testing easier, the Myfault device driver detects that the process was closed and frees its allocations.

5. While the pool is leaking, open Task Manager, click the **Performance** tab, and select the **Memory** label. Notice the **Paged Pool** value climbing. You can also check this with Process Explorer's System Information display (select the **View** menu, choose **System Information**, and click the **Memory** tab).

6. To determine which pool tag is leaking, run Poolmon and press the **B** key to sort by the number of bytes.

7. Press **P** twice so that Poolmon shows only paged pool. Notice the Leak pool tag climbing to the top of the list. (Poolmon shows changes to pool allocations by highlighting the lines that change.)

8. Click the **Stop Paged** button so that you don't exhaust paged pool on your system.

9. Using the technique described in the previous section, run Strings (from Sysinternals) to look for driver binaries that contain the Leak pool tag. This should display a match on the file Myfault.sys, thus confirming it as the driver using the Leak pool tag.

```
Strings %SystemRoot%\system32\drivers\*.sys | findstr Leak
```

Look-aside lists

Windows provides a fast memory-allocation mechanism called *look-aside lists*. The basic difference between pools and look-aside lists is that while general pool allocations can vary in size, a look-aside list contains only fixed-sized blocks. Although the general pools are more flexible in terms of what they can supply, look-aside lists are faster because they don't use any spinlocks.

Executive components and device drivers can create look-aside lists that match the size of frequently allocated data structures by using the ExInitializeNPagedLookasideList (for non-paged allocations) and ExInitializePagedLookasideList (for paged allocation) functions, as documented in the WDK. To minimize the overhead of multiprocessor synchronization, several executive subsystems such as the I/O manager, cache manager, and object manager create separate look-aside lists for each processor for their frequently accessed data structures. The executive also creates a general per-processor paged and non-paged look-aside list for small allocations (256 bytes or less).

If a look-aside list is empty (as it is when it's first created), the system must allocate from the paged or non-paged pool. But if it contains a freed block, the allocation can be satisfied very quickly. (The list grows as blocks are returned to it.) The pool-allocation routines automatically tune the number of freed buffers that look-aside lists store according to how often a device driver or executive subsystem allocates from the list. The more frequent the allocations, the more blocks are stored on a list. Look-aside lists are automatically reduced in size if they aren't being allocated from. (This check happens once per second when the balance set manager system thread wakes up and calls the ExAdjustLookasideDepth function.)

EXPERIMENT: Viewing the system look-aside lists

You can display the contents and sizes of the various system look-aside lists with the kernel debugger !lookaside command. The following excerpt is from the output of this command:

```
lkd> !lookaside

Lookaside "nt!CcTwilightLookasideList" @ 0xfffff800c6f54300  Tag(hex): 0x6b576343 "CcWk"
    Type            =       0200  NonPagedPoolNx
    Current Depth   =          0  Max Depth   =          4
    Size            =        128  Max Alloc   =        512
    AllocateMisses  =     728323  FreeMisses  =     728271
    TotalAllocates  =    1030842  TotalFrees  =    1030766
    Hit Rate        =        29%  Hit Rate    =        29%

Lookaside "nt!IopSmallIrpLookasideList" @ 0xfffff800c6f54500  Tag(hex): 0x73707249 "Irps"
    Type            =       0200  NonPagedPoolNx
    Current Depth   =          0  Max Depth   =          4
    Size            =        280  Max Alloc   =       1120
    AllocateMisses  =      44683  FreeMisses  =      43576
    TotalAllocates  =     232027  TotalFrees  =     230903
    Hit Rate        =        80%  Hit Rate    =        81%
```

```
Lookaside "nt!IopLargeIrpLookasideList" @ 0xfffff800c6f54600  Tag(hex): 0x6c707249 "Irpl"
    Type          =        0200  NonPagedPoolNx
    Current Depth =           0  Max Depth   =         4
    Size          =        1216  Max Alloc   =      4864
    AllocateMisses =       143708  FreeMisses  =    142551
    TotalAllocates =       317297  TotalFrees  =    316131
    Hit Rate      =         54% Hit Rate    =        54%
...


Total NonPaged currently allocated for above lists =          0
Total NonPaged potential for above lists          =      13232
Total Paged currently allocated for above lists   =          0
Total Paged potential for above lists             =       4176
```

Heap manager

Most applications allocate smaller blocks than the 64-KB minimum allocation granularity possible using page-granularity functions such as VirtualAlloc. Allocating such a large area for relatively small allocations is not optimal from a memory usage and performance standpoint. To address this, Windows provides a component called the *heap manager*, which manages allocations inside larger memory areas reserved using the page-granularity memory-allocation functions. The allocation granularity in the heap manager is relatively small: 8 bytes on 32-bit systems, and 16 bytes on 64-bit systems. The heap manager has been designed to optimize memory usage and performance in the case of these smaller allocations.

The heap manager exists in two places: Ntdll.dll and Ntoskrnl.exe. The subsystem APIs (such as the Windows heap APIs) call the functions in Ntdll.dll, and various executive components and device drivers call the functions in Ntoskrnl.exe. Its native interfaces (prefixed with Rtl) are available only for use in internal Windows components or kernel-mode device drivers. The documented Windows API interfaces to the heap (prefixed with Heap) are forwarders to the native functions in Ntdll.dll. In addition, legacy APIs (prefixed with either Local or Global) are provided to support older Windows applications. These also internally call the heap manager, using some of its specialized interfaces to support legacy behavior. The most common Windows heap functions are:

- **HeapCreate or HeapDestroy**   These create or delete, respectively, a heap. The initial reserved and committed size can be specified at creation.

- **HeapAlloc**   This allocates a heap block. It is forwarded to **RtlAllocateHeap** in Ntdll.dll.

- **HeapFree**   This frees a block previously allocated with HeapAlloc.

- **HeapReAlloc**   This changes the size of an existing allocation, growing or shrinking an existing block. It is forwarded to RtlReAllocateHeap in Ntdll.dll.

- **HeapLock and HeapUnlock**   These control mutual exclusion to heap operations.

- **HeapWalk**   This enumerates the entries and regions in a heap.

Process heaps

Each process has at least one heap: the default process heap. The default heap is created at process startup and is never deleted during the process's lifetime. It defaults to 1 MB in size, but you can make it bigger by specifying a starting size in the image file by using the /HEAP linker flag. This size is just the initial reserve, however. It will expand automatically as needed. You can also specify the initial committed size in the image file.

The default heap can be explicitly used by a program or implicitly used by some Windows internal functions. An application can query the default process heap by making a call to the Windows GetProcessHeap function. Processes can also create additional private heaps with the HeapCreate function. When a process no longer needs a private heap, it can recover the virtual address space by calling HeapDestroy. An array with all heaps is maintained in each process, and a thread can query them with the Windows GetProcessHeaps function.

A Universal Windows Platform (UWP) app process includes at least three heaps:

- The default process heap just described.

- A shared heap used to pass large arguments to the process' session Csrss.exe instance. This is created by the CsrClientConnectToServer Ntdll.dll function, which executes early in the process initialization done by Ntdll.dll. The heap handle is available in the global variable CsrPortHeap (in Ntdll.dll).

- A heap created by the Microsoft C runtime library. Its handle is stored in the global variable _crtheap (in the msvcrt module). This heap is the one used internally by the C/C++ memory-allocation functions such as malloc, free, operator new/delete, and so on.

A heap can manage allocations either in large memory regions reserved from the memory manager via VirtualAlloc or from memory-mapped file objects mapped in the process address space. The latter approach is rarely used in practice (and is not exposed by the Windows API), but it's suitable for scenarios where the content of the blocks needs to be shared between two processes or between a kernel-mode and a user-mode component. The Win32 GUI subsystem driver (Win32k.sys) uses such a heap for sharing GDI and USER objects with user mode. If a heap is built on top of a memory-mapped file region, certain constraints apply with respect to the component that can call heap functions:

- The internal heap structures use pointers, and therefore do not allow remapping to different addresses in other processes.

- The synchronization across multiple processes or between a kernel component and a user process is not supported by the heap functions.

- In the case of a shared heap between user mode and kernel mode, the user-mode mapping should be read-only to prevent user-mode code from corrupting the heap's internal structures, which would result in a system crash. The kernel-mode driver is also responsible for not putting any sensitive data in a shared heap to avoid leaking it to user mode.

Heap types

Until Windows 10 and Server 2016, there was just one heap type, which we'll call the *NT heap*. The NT heap is augmented by an optional front-end layer, which if used, consists of the *low-fragmentation heap (LFH)*.

Windows 10 introduced a new heap type called *segment heap*. The two heap types include common elements but are structured and implemented differently. By default, the segment heap is used by all UWP apps and some system processes, while the NT heap is used by all other processes. This can be changed in the registry as described in the section "The segment heap" later in this chapter.

The NT heap

As shown in Figure 5-8, the NT heap in user mode is structured in two layers: a front-end layer and the heap back end (sometimes called the heap core). The back end handles the basic functionality and includes the management of blocks inside segments, the management of the segments, policies for extending the heap, committing and decommitting memory, and management of large blocks.

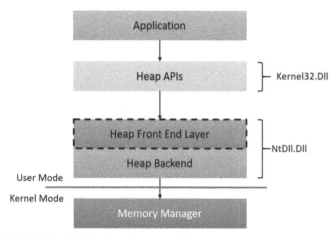

FIGURE 5-8 NT heap layers in user mode.

For user-mode heaps only, a front-end heap layer can exist on top of the core functionality. Windows supports one optional front end layer, the LFH, described in the upcoming section "The low-fragmentation heap."

Heap synchronization

The heap manager supports concurrent access from multiple threads by default. However, if a process is single threaded or uses an external mechanism for synchronization, it can tell the heap manager to avoid the overhead of synchronization by specifying the `HEAP_NO_SERIALIZE` flag either at heap creation or on a per-allocation basis. If heap synchronization is enabled, there is one lock per heap that protects all internal heap structures.

A process can also lock the entire heap and prevent other threads from performing heap operations for operations that would require consistent states across multiple heap calls. For instance, enumerating the heap blocks in a heap with the Windows function `HeapWalk` requires locking the heap if multiple threads can perform heap operations simultaneously. Locking and unlocking a heap can be done with the `HeapLock` and `HeapUnlock` functions, respectively.

The low-fragmentation heap

Many applications running in Windows have relatively small heap memory usage—usually less than 1 MB. For this class of applications, the heap manager's best-fit policy helps keep a low memory footprint for each process. However, this strategy does not scale for large processes and multiprocessor machines. In these cases, memory available for heap usage might be reduced due to heap fragmentation. Performance can suffer in scenarios where only certain sizes are often used concurrently from different threads scheduled to run on different processors. This happens because several processors need to modify the same memory location (for example, the head of the look-aside list for that particular size) at the same time, thus causing significant contention for the corresponding cache line.

The LFH avoids fragmentation by managing allocated blocks in predetermined different block-size ranges called *buckets*. When a process allocates memory from the heap, the LFH chooses the bucket that maps to the smallest block large enough to hold the required size. (The smallest block is 8 bytes.) The first bucket is used for allocations between 1 and 8 bytes, the second for allocations between 9 and 16 bytes, and so on, until the 32nd bucket, which is used for allocations between 249 and 256 bytes, followed by the 33rd bucket, which is used for allocations between 257 and 272 bytes, and so on. Finally, the 128th bucket, which is the last, is used for allocations between 15,873 and 16,384 bytes. (This is known as a *binary buddy* system.) If the allocation is larger than 16,384 bytes, the LFH simply forwards it to the underlying heap back end. Table 5-7 summarizes the different buckets, their granularity, and the range of sizes they map to.

TABLE 5-7 LFH buckets

Buckets	Granularity	Range
1–32	8	1–256
33–48	16	257–512
49–64	32	513–1,024
65–80	64	1,025–2,048
81–96	128	2,049–4,096
97–112	256	4,097–8,192
113–128	512	8,193–16,384

The LFH addresses these issues by using the core heap manager and look-aside lists. The Windows heap manager implements an automatic tuning algorithm that can enable the LFH by default under certain conditions, such as lock contention or the presence of popular size allocations that have shown better performance with the LFH enabled. For large heaps, a significant percentage of allocations is frequently grouped in a relatively small number of buckets of certain sizes. The allocation strategy used by LFH is to optimize the usage for these patterns by efficiently handling same-size blocks.

To address scalability, the LFH expands the frequently accessed internal structures to a number of slots that is two times larger than the current number of processors on the machine. The assignment of threads to these slots is done by an LFH component called the *affinity manager*. Initially, the LFH starts using the first slot for heap allocations; however, if a contention is detected when accessing some internal data, the LFH switches the current thread to use a different slot. Further contentions will spread threads on more slots. These slots are controlled for each size bucket to improve locality and minimize the overall memory consumption.

Even if the LFH is enabled as a front-end heap, the less frequent allocation sizes may continue to use the core heap functions to allocate memory, while the most popular allocation classes will be performed from the LFH. Once the LFH is enabled for a specific heap, it cannot be disabled. The `HeapSetInformation` API with the `HeapCompatibilityInformation` class that was able to remove the LFH layer in Windows 7 and earlier versions of Windows is now ignored.

The segment heap

Figure 5-9 shows the architecture of the segment heap, introduced in Windows 10.

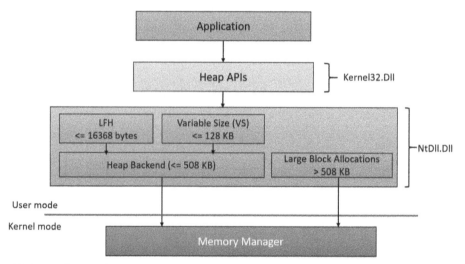

FIGURE 5-9 Segment heap.

The actual layer that manages an allocation depends on the allocation size as follows:

- For small sizes (less than or equal to 16,368 bytes), the LFH allocator is used, but only if the size is determined to be a common one. This is a similar logic to the LFH front layer of the NT heap. If the LFH has not kicked in yet, the variable size (VS) allocator will be used instead.

- For sizes less than or equal to 128 KB (and not serviced by the LFH), the VS allocator is used. Both VS and LFH allocators use the back end to create the required heap sub-segments as necessary.

- Allocations larger than 128 KB and less than or equal to 508 KB are serviced directly by the heap back end.

- Allocations larger than 508 KB are serviced by calling the memory manager directly (`Virtual-Alloc`) since these are so large that using the default 64 KB allocation granularity (and rounding to the nearest page size) is deemed good enough.

Here is a quick comparison of the two heap implementations:

- In some scenarios, the segment heap may be somewhat slower than the NT heap. However, it's likely that future Windows versions would make it on par with the NT heap.

- The segment heap has a lower memory footprint for its metadata, making it better suited for low-memory devices such as phones.

- The segment heap's metadata is separated from the actual data, while the NT heap's metadata is interspersed with the data itself. This makes the segment heap more secure, as it's more difficult to get to the metadata of an allocation given just a block address.

- The segment heap can be used only for a growable heap. It cannot be used with a user-supplied memory mapped file. If such a segment heap creation is attempted, an NT heap is created instead.

- Both heaps support LFH-type allocations, but their internal implementation is completely different. The segment heap has a more efficient implementation in terms of memory consumption and performance.

As mentioned, UWP apps use segment heaps by default. This is mainly because of their lower memory footprint, which is suitable for low-memory devices. It's also used with certain system processes based on executable name: csrss.exe, lsass.exe, runtimebroker.exe, services.exe, smss.exe, and svchost.exe.

The segment heap is not the default heap for desktop apps because there are some compatibility concerns that may affect existing applications. It's likely that in future versions, however, it will become the default. To enable or disable the segment heap for a specific executable, you can set an Image File Execution Options value named `FrontEndHeapDebugOptions` (DWORD):

- Bit 2 (4) to disable segment heap

- Bit 3 (8) to enable segment heap

You can also globally enable or disable the segment heap by adding a value named `Enabled` (DWORD) to the HKLM\ SYSTEM\CurrentControlSet\Control\Session Manager\Segment Heap registry key. A zero value disables the segment heap and a non-zero value enables it.

EXPERIMENT: Viewing basic heap information

In this experiment, we'll examine some heaps of a UWP process.

1. Using Windows 10, run the Windows calculator. (Click the **Start** button and type **Calculator** to find it.)

2. The calculator in Windows 10 has been turned into a UWP app (Calculator.Exe). Run WinDbg and attach to the calculator process.

3. Once attached, WinDbg breaks into the process. Issue the !heap command to get a quick summary of heaps in the process:

```
0:033> !heap
        Heap Address         NT/Segment Heap

        2531eb90000          Segment Heap
        2531e980000              NT Heap
        2531eb10000          Segment Heap
        25320a40000          Segment Heap
        253215a0000          Segment Heap
        253214f0000          Segment Heap
        2531eb70000          Segment Heap
        25326920000          Segment Heap
        253215d0000              NT Heap
```

4. Notice the various heaps with their handle and type (segment or NT). The first heap is the default process heap. Because it's growable and not using any preexisting memory block, it's created as a segment heap. The second heap is used with a user-defined memory block (described earlier in the "Process heaps" section). Because this feature is currently unsupported by the segment heap, it's created as an NT heap.

5. An NT heap is managed by the NtDll!_HEAP structure. Let's view this structure for the second heap:

```
0:033> dt ntdll!_heap 2531e980000
   +0x000 Segment          : _HEAP_SEGMENT
   +0x000 Entry            : _HEAP_ENTRY
   +0x010 SegmentSignature : 0xffeeffee
   +0x014 SegmentFlags     : 1
   +0x018 SegmentListEntry : _LIST_ENTRY [ 0x00000253'1e980120 -
0x00000253'1e980120 ]
   +0x028 Heap             : 0x00000253'1e980000 _HEAP
   +0x030 BaseAddress      : 0x00000253'1e980000 Void
   +0x038 NumberOfPages    : 0x10
   +0x040 FirstEntry       : 0x00000253'1e980720 _HEAP_ENTRY
   +0x048 LastValidEntry   : 0x00000253'1e990000 _HEAP_ENTRY
   +0x050 NumberOfUnCommittedPages : 0xf
   +0x054 NumberOfUnCommittedRanges : 1
   +0x058 SegmentAllocatorBackTraceIndex : 0
```

```
    +0x05a Reserved        : 0
    +0x060 UCRSegmentList  : _LIST_ENTRY [ 0x00000253'1e980fe0 -
0x00000253'1e980fe0 ]
    +0x070 Flags           : 0x8000
    +0x074 ForceFlags      : 0
    +0x078 CompatibilityFlags : 0
    +0x07c EncodeFlagMask  : 0x100000
    +0x080 Encoding        : _HEAP_ENTRY
    +0x090 Interceptor     : 0
    +0x094 VirtualMemoryThreshold : 0xff00
    +0x098 Signature       : 0xeeffeeff
    +0x0a0 SegmentReserve  : 0x100000
    +0x0a8 SegmentCommit   : 0x2000
    +0x0b0 DeCommitFreeBlockThreshold : 0x100
    +0x0b8 DeCommitTotalFreeThreshold : 0x1000
    +0x0c0 TotalFreeSize   : 0x8a
    +0x0c8 MaximumAllocationSize : 0x00007fff'fffdefff
    +0x0d0 ProcessHeapsListIndex : 2
    ...
    +0x178 FrontEndHeap    : (null)
    +0x180 FrontHeapLockCount : 0
    +0x182 FrontEndHeapType : 0 ''
    +0x183 RequestedFrontEndHeapType : 0 ''
    +0x188 FrontEndHeapUsageData : (null)
    +0x190 FrontEndHeapMaximumIndex : 0
    +0x192 FrontEndHeapStatusBitmap : [129]  ""
    +0x218 Counters        : _HEAP_COUNTERS
    +0x290 TuningParameters : _HEAP_TUNING_PARAMETERS
```

6. Notice the FrontEndHeap field. This field indicates whether a front-end layer exists. In the preceding output, it's null, meaning there is no front-end layer. A non-null value indicates an LFH front-end layer (since it's the only one defined).

7. A segment heap is defined with the NtDll!_SEGMENT_HEAP structure. Here's the default process heap:

```
0:033> dt ntdll!_segment_heap 2531eb90000
    +0x000 TotalReservedPages : 0x815
    +0x008 TotalCommittedPages : 0x6ac
    +0x010 Signature       : 0xddeeddee
    +0x014 GlobalFlags     : 0
    +0x018 FreeCommittedPages : 0
    +0x020 Interceptor     : 0
    +0x024 ProcessHeapListIndex : 1
    +0x026 GlobalLockCount : 0
    +0x028 GlobalLockOwner : 0
    +0x030 LargeMetadataLock : _RTL_SRWLOCK
    +0x038 LargeAllocMetadata : _RTL_RB_TREE
    +0x048 LargeReservedPages : 0
    +0x050 LargeCommittedPages : 0
    +0x058 SegmentAllocatorLock : _RTL_SRWLOCK
    +0x060 SegmentListHead : _LIST_ENTRY [ 0x00000253'1ec00000 -
```

```
0x00000253'28a00000 ]
    +0x070 SegmentCount    : 8
    +0x078 FreePageRanges  : _RTL_RB_TREE
    +0x088 StackTraceInitVar : _RTL_RUN_ONCE
    +0x090 ContextExtendLock : _RTL_SRWLOCK
    +0x098 AllocatedBase    : 0x00000253'1eb93200  ""
    +0x0a0 UncommittedBase  : 0x00000253'1eb94000  "--- memory read error at
address 0x00000253'1eb94000 ---"
    +0x0a8 ReservedLimit    : 0x00000253'1eba5000  "--- memory read error at
address 0x00000253'1eba5000 ---"
    +0x0b0 VsContext        : _HEAP_VS_CONTEXT
    +0x120 LfhContext       : _HEAP_LFH_CONTEXT
```

8. Notice the Signature field. It's used to distinguish between the two types of heaps.

9. Notice the SegmentSignature field of the _HEAP structure. It is in the same offset (0x10). This is how functions such as RtlAllocateHeap know which implementation to turn to based on the heap handle (address) alone.

10. Notice the last two fields in the _SEGMENT_HEAP. These contain the VS and LFH allocator information.

11. To get more information on each heap, issue the !heap -s command:

```
0:033> !heap -s

                                     Process    Total      Total
                            Global   Heap Reserved  Committed
  Heap Address  Signature   Flags    List     Bytes      Bytes
                                     Index     (K)        (K)

    2531eb90000  ddeeddee     0        1       8276       6832
    2531eb10000  ddeeddee     0        3       1108        868
    25320a40000  ddeeddee     0        4       1108         16
    253215a0000  ddeeddee     0        5       1108         20
    253214f0000  ddeeddee     0        6       3156        816
    2531eb70000  ddeeddee     0        7       1108         24
    25326920000  ddeeddee     0        8       1108         32


********************************************************************************
*************
                        NT HEAP STATS BELOW
********************************************************************************
*************
LFH Key                 : 0xd7b666e8f56a4b98
Termination on corruption : ENABLED
Affinity manager status:
    - Virtual affinity limit 8
    - Current entries in use 0
    - Statistics:  Swaps=0, Resets=0, Allocs=0


          Heap     Flags   Reserv  Commit  Virt   Free  List   UCR  Virt
Lock  Fast
```

cont. heap		(k)	(k)	(k)	(k) length		blocks
000002531e980000 00008000 0		64	4	64	2	1	1	0
00000253215d0000 00000001 N/A		16	16	16	10	1	1	0

12. Notice the first part of the output. It shows extended information on segment heaps (if any). The second part shows extended information on NT heaps in the process.

The !heap debugger command provides a multitude of options for viewing, investigating, and searching heaps. See the "Debugger Tools for Windows" documentation for more information.

Heap security features

As the heap manager has evolved, it has taken an increased role in early detection of heap usage errors and in mitigating effects of potential heap-based exploits. These measures exist to lessen the security effect of potential vulnerabilities in applications. Both the NT-heap and the segment-heap implementations have multiple mechanisms that reduce the likelihood of memory exploitation.

The metadata used by the heaps for internal management is packed with a high degree of randomization to make it difficult for an attempted exploit to patch the internal structures to prevent crashes or conceal the attack attempt. These blocks are also subject to an integrity-check mechanism on the header to detect simple corruptions such as buffer overruns. Finally, the heap uses a small degree of randomization of the base address or handle. By using the HeapSetInformation API with the Heap-EnableTerminationOnCorruption class, processes can opt in for an automatic termination in case of detected inconsistencies to avoid executing unknown code.

As an effect of block metadata randomization, using the debugger to simply dump a block header as an area of memory is not that useful. For example, the size of the block and whether it is busy are not easy to spot from a regular dump. The same applies to LFH blocks. They have a different type of metadata stored in the header, also partially randomized. To dump these details, the !heap –i command in the debugger does all the work to retrieve the metadata fields from a block, also flagging checksum or free-list inconsistencies if they exist. The command works for both LFH and regular heap blocks. The total size of the blocks, the user-requested size, the segment owning the block, and the header partial checksum are available in the output, as shown in the following sample. Because the randomization algorithm uses the heap granularity, the !heap –i command should be used only in the proper context of the heap containing the block. In the example, the heap handle is 0x001a0000. If the current heap context were different, the decoding of the header would be incorrect. To set the proper context, the same !heap –i command with the heap handle as an argument must be executed first.

```
0:004> !heap -i 000001f72a5e0000
Heap context set to the heap 0x000001f72a5e0000

0:004> !heap -i 000001f72a5eb180
Detailed information for block entry 000001f72a5eb180
Assumed heap        : 0x000001f72a5e0000 (Use !heap -i NewHeapHandle to change)
Header content      : 0x2FB544DC 0x1000021F (decoded : 0x7F01007E 0x10000048)
Owning segment      : 0x000001f72a5e0000 (offset 0)
Block flags         : 0x1 (busy )
Total block size    : 0x7e units (0x7e0 bytes)
Requested size      : 0x7d0 bytes (unused 0x10 bytes)
Previous block size: 0x48 units (0x480 bytes)
Block CRC           : OK - 0x7f
Previous block      : 0x000001f72a5ead00
Next block          : 0x000001f72a5eb960
```

Segment heap-specific security features

The segment heap implementation uses many security mechanisms to make it harder to corrupt memory or to allow code injection by an attacker. Here are a few of them:

- **Fail fast on linked list node corruption**   The segment heap uses linked lists to track segments and sub-segments. As with the NT heap, checks are added in the list node insertion and removal to prevent arbitrary memory writes due to corrupted list nodes. If a corrupted node is detected, the process is terminated via a call to RtlFailFast.

- **Fail fast on red-black (RB) tree node corruption**   The segment heap uses RB trees to track free back-end and VS allocations. Node insertion and deletion functions validate the nodes involved or, if corrupted, invoke the fail-fast mechanism.

- **Function pointer decoding**   Some aspects of the segment heap allow for callbacks (in VsContext and LfhContext structures, part of the _SEGMENT_HEAP structure). An attacker can override these callbacks to point to his or her own code. However, the function pointers are encoded by using a XOR function with an internal random heap key and the context address, both of which cannot be guessed in advance.

- **Guard pages**   When LFH and VS sub-segments and large blocks are allocated, a guard page is added at the end. This helps to detect overflows and corruption of adjacent data. See the section "Stacks" later in this chapter for more information on guard pages.

Heap debugging features

The heap manager includes several features to help detect bugs by using the following heap settings:

- **Enable tail checking**   The end of each block carries a signature that is checked when the block is released. If a buffer overrun destroys the signature entirely or partially, the heap will report this error.

- **Enable free checking**   A free block is filled with a pattern that is checked at various points when the heap manager needs to access the block, such as at removal from the free list to satisfy an allocate request. If the process continues to write to the block after freeing it, the heap manager will detect changes in the pattern and the error will be reported.

- **Parameter checking**   This function consists of extensive checking of the parameters passed to the heap functions.

- **Heap validation**   The entire heap is validated at each heap call.

- **Heap tagging and stack traces support**   This function supports the specification of tags for allocation and/or captures user-mode stack traces for the heap calls to help narrow the possible causes of a heap error.

The first three options are enabled by default if the loader detects that a process is started under the control of a debugger. (A debugger can override this behavior and turn off these features.) You can specify the heap debugging features for an executable image by setting various debugging flags in the image header using the Gflags tool. (See the next experiment and the section "Windows global flags" in Chapter 8 in Part 2.) Alternatively, you can enable heap debugging options using the !heap command in the standard Windows debuggers. (See the debugger help for more information.)

Enabling heap-debugging options affects all heaps in the process. Also, if any of the heap-debugging options are enabled, the LFH will be disabled automatically and the core heap will be used (with the required debugging options enabled). The LFH is also not used for heaps that are not expandable (because of the extra overhead added to the existing heap structures) or for heaps that do not allow serialization.

Pageheap

Because the tail and free checking options described in the preceding sections might discover corruptions that occurred well before the problem was detected, an additional heap debugging capability, called *pageheap*, is provided. Pageheap directs all or part of the heap calls to a different heap manager. You can enable pageheap using the Gflags tool (part of the Debugging Tools for Windows). When enabled, the heap manager places allocations at the end of pages and reserves the page that immediately follows. Because reserved pages are not accessible, any buffer overruns that occur will cause an access violation, making it easier to detect the offending code. Optionally, pageheap allows for the placement of blocks at the beginning of the pages, with the preceding page reserved, to detect buffer underrun problems (a rare occurrence). Pageheap also can protect freed pages against any access to detect references to heap blocks after they have been freed.

Note that using the pageheap can cause you to run out of address space (in 32-bit processes) because of the significant overhead added for small allocations. Also, performance can suffer due to the increase of references to demand zero pages, loss of locality, and additional overhead caused by frequent calls to validate heap structures. A process can reduce the impact by specifying that the pageheap be used only for blocks of certain sizes, address ranges, and/or originating DLLs.

EXPERIMENT: Using pageheap

In this experiment, you'll turn on pageheap for Notepad.exe and see its effects.

1. Run Notepad.exe.

2. Open Task Manager, click to the **Details** tab, and add the **Commit Size** column to the display.

3. Notice the commit size of the notepad instance you just launched.

4. Run Gflags.exe, located in the folder where Debugging Tools for Windows is installed (requires elevation).

5. Click the **Image File** tab.

6. In the **Image** text box, type **notepad.exe**. Then press the **Tab** key. The various check boxes should be selected.

7. Select the **Enable Page Heap** check box. The dialog box should look like this:

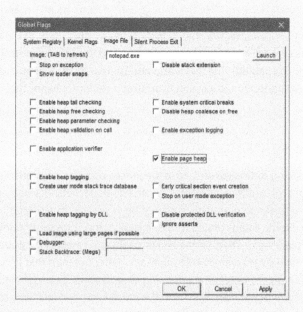

8. Click **Apply**.

9. Run another instance of Notepad. (Don't close the first one.)

10. In Task Manager, compare the commit size of both notepad instances. Notice that the second instance has a much larger commit size even though both are empty notepad processes. This is due to the extra allocations that pageheap provides. Here's a screenshot from 32-bit Windows 10:

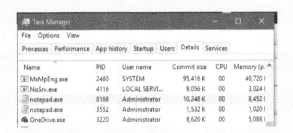

11. To get a better sense of the extra memory allocated, use the VMMap Sysinternals tool. While the notepad processes are still running, open VMMap.exe and select the notepad instance that is using pageheap:

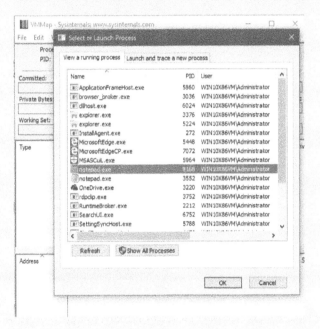

12. Open another instance of VMMap and select the other notepad instance. Place the windows side by side to see both:

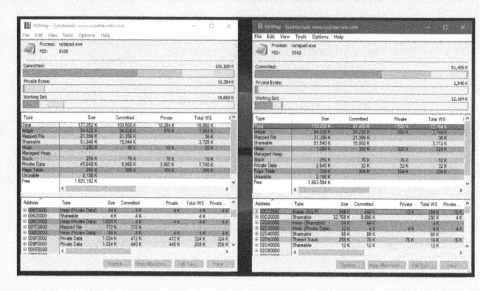

13. Notice that the difference in the commit size is clearly visible in the Private Data (yellow) part.

14. Click the **Private Data** line in the middle display on both VMMap instances to see its parts in the bottom display (sorted by size in the screenshot):

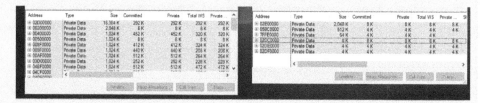

15. The left screenshot (notepad with pageheap) clearly consumes more memory. Open one of the 1,024 KB chunks. You should see something like this:

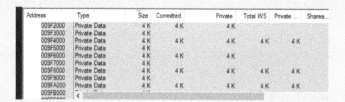

16. You can clearly see the reserved pages between committed pages that help catch buffer overruns and underruns courtesy of pageheap. Uncheck the **Enable Page Heap** option in Gflags and click **Apply** so future instances of notepad will run without pageheap.

For more information on pageheap, see the "Debugging Tools for Windows" help file.

Fault-tolerant heap

Microsoft has identified the corruption of heap metadata as one of the most common causes of application failures. Windows includes a feature called the *fault-tolerant heap* (*FTH*) to mitigate these problems and to provide better problem-solving resources to application developers. The FTH is implemented in two primary components:

- The detection component (FTH server)
- The mitigation component (FTH client)

The detection component is a DLL called Fthsvc.dll that is loaded by the Windows Security Center service (Wscsvc.dll), which in turn runs in one of the shared service processes under the local service account. It is notified of application crashes by the Windows Error Reporting (WER) service.

Suppose an application crashes in Ntdll.dll with an error status indicating either an access violation or a heap-corruption exception. If it is not already on the FTH service's list of watched applications, the service creates a "ticket" for the application to hold the FTH data. If the application subsequently crashes more than four times in an hour, the FTH service configures the application to use the FTH client in the future.

The FTH client is an application-compatibility shim. This mechanism has been used since Windows XP to allow applications that depend on a particular behavior of older Windows systems to run on later systems. In this case, the shim mechanism intercepts the calls to the heap routines and redirects them to its own code. The FTH code implements numerous mitigations that attempt to allow the application to survive despite various heap-related errors.

For example, to protect against small buffer overrun errors, the FTH adds 8 bytes of padding and an FTH reserved area to each allocation. To address a common scenario in which a block of heap is accessed after it is freed, HeapFree calls are implemented only after a delay. "Freed" blocks are put on a list, and freed only when the total size of the blocks on the list exceeds 4 MB. Attempts to free regions that are not actually part of the heap, or not part of the heap identified by the heap handle argument to HeapFree, are simply ignored. In addition, no blocks are actually freed once exit or RtlExitUser-Process has been called.

The FTH server continues to monitor the failure rate of the application after the mitigations have been installed. If the failure rate does not improve, the mitigations are removed.

You can observe the activity of the fault-tolerant heap in the Event Viewer. Follow these steps:

1. Open a Run prompt and type **eventvwr.msc**.

2. In the left pane, choose **Event Viewer**, select **Applications and Services Logs**, choose **Microsoft**, select **Windows**, and click **Fault-Tolerant-Heap**.

3. Click the **Operational** log.

4. The FTH may be disabled completely in the registry. in the HKLM\Software\Microsoft\FTH key, set the Enabled value to 0.

That same key contains the various FTH settings, such as the delay mentioned earlier and an exclusion list of executables (which includes by default system processes such as smss.exe, csrss.exe, wininit. exe, services.exe, winlogon.exe and taskhost.exe). A rule list is also included (RuleList value), which lists the modules and exception type (and some flags) to watch for in order for FTH to kick in. By default, a single rule is listed, indicating heap problems in Ntdll.dll of type STATUS_ACCESS_VIOLATION (0xc0000005).

The FTH does not normally operate on services, and it is disabled on Windows server systems for performance reasons. A system administrator can manually apply the shim to an application or service executable by using the Application Compatibility Toolkit.

Virtual address space layouts

This section describes the components in the user and system address space, followed by the specific layouts on 32-bit (x86 and ARM) and 64-bit (x64) systems. This information will help you to understand the limits on process and system virtual memory on these platforms.

Three main types of data are mapped into the virtual address space in Windows:

- **Per-process private code and data** As explained in Chapter 1, each process has a private address space that cannot be accessed by other processes. That is, a virtual address is always evaluated in the context of the current process and cannot refer to an address defined by any other process. Threads within the process can therefore never access virtual addresses outside this private address space. Even shared memory is not an exception to this rule, because shared memory regions are mapped into each participating process, and so are accessed by each process using per-process addresses. Similarly, the cross-process memory functions (Read-ProcessMemory and WriteProcessMemory) operate by running kernel-mode code in the context of the target process. The process virtual address space, called *page tables*, is described in the "Address translation" section. Each process has its own set of page tables. They are stored in kernel-mode-only accessible pages so that user-mode threads in a process cannot modify their own address space layout.

- **Session-wide code and data** Session space contains information that is common to each session. (For a description of sessions, see Chapter 2.) A session consists of the processes and other system objects such as the window station, desktops, and windows that represent a single user's logon session. Each session has a session-specific paged pool area used by the kernel-mode portion of the Windows subsystem (Win32k.sys) to allocate session-private GUI data structures. In addition, each session has its own copy of the Windows subsystem process (Csrss.exe) and logon process (Winlogon.exe). The Session Manager process (Smss.exe) is responsible for creating new sessions, which includes loading a session-private copy of Win32k.sys, creating the session-private object manager namespace (see Chapter 8 in Part 2 for more details on the object manager), and creating the session-specific instances of the Csrss.exe and Winlogon.exe processes. To virtualize sessions, all session-wide data structures are mapped into a region of system space called *session space*. When a process is created, this range of addresses is mapped to the pages associated with the session that the process belongs to.

- **System-wide code and data** System space contains global operating system code and data structures visible by kernel-mode code regardless of which process is currently executing. System space consists of the following components:

  - **System code** This contains the OS image, HAL, and device drivers used to boot the system.

  - **Nonpaged pool** This is the non-pageable system memory heap.

  - **Paged pool** This is the pageable system memory heap.

  - **System cache** This is virtual address space used to map files open in the system cache. (See Chapter 11, "Startup and shutdown," in Part 2 for detailed information.)

  - **System page table entries (PTEs)** This is the pool of system PTEs used to map system pages such as I/O space, kernel stacks, and memory descriptor lists. You can see how many system PTEs are available by using Performance Monitor to examine the value of the Memory: Free System Page Table Entries counter.

  - **System working set lists** These are the working set list data structures that describe the three system working sets: system cache, paged pool, and system PTEs.

  - **System mapped views** This is used to map Win32k.sys, the loadable kernel-mode part of the Windows subsystem, as well as kernel-mode graphics drivers it uses. (See Chapter 2 for more information on Win32k.sys.)

  - **Hyperspace** This is a special region used to map the process working set list and other per-process data that doesn't need to be accessible in arbitrary process context. Hyperspace is also used to temporarily map physical pages into the system space. One example of this is invalidating page table entries in page tables of processes other than the current one, such as when a page is removed from the standby list.

  - **Crash dump information** This is reserved to record information about the state of a system crash.

  - **HAL usage** This is system memory reserved for HAL-specific structures.

Now that we've described the basic components of the virtual address space in Windows, let's examine the specific layout on the x86, ARM, and x64 platforms.

x86 address space layouts

By default, each user process on 32-bit versions of Windows has a 2 GB private address space. (The operating system takes the remaining 2 GB.) However, for x86, the system can be configured with the `increaseuserva` BCD boot option to permit user address spaces up to 3 GB. Two possible address space layouts are shown in Figure 5-10.

The ability of a 32-bit process to grow beyond 2 GB was added to accommodate the need for 32-bit applications to keep more data in memory than could be done with a 2 GB address space. Of course, 64-bit systems provide a much larger address space.

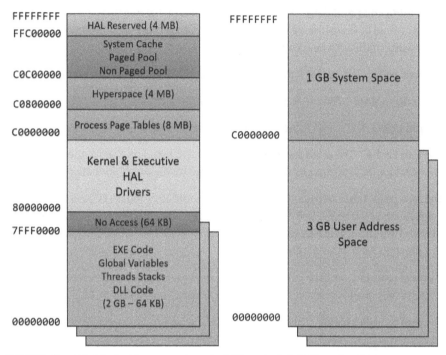

FIGURE 5-10   x86 virtual address space layouts (2 GB on the left, 3 GB on the right).

For a process to grow beyond 2 GB of address space, the image file must have the IMAGE_FILE_
LARGE_ADDRESS_AWARE flag set in the image header (in addition to the global increaseuserva setting). Otherwise, Windows reserves the additional address space for that process so that the application won't see virtual addresses greater than 0x7FFFFFFF. Access to the additional virtual memory is
opt-in because some applications assume they'll be given at most 2 GB of the address space. Because
the high bit of a pointer referencing an address below 2 GB is always zero (31 bits are needed to reference a 2 GB address space), these applications would use the high bit in their pointers as a flag for their
own data—clearing it, of course, before referencing the data. If they ran with a 3 GB address space,
they would inadvertently truncate pointers that have values greater than 2 GB, causing program errors,
including possible data corruption. You set this flag by specifying the /LARGEADDRESSAWARE linker flag
when building the executable. Alternatively, use the Property page in Visual Studio (choose **Linker**,
select **System**, and click **Enable Large Addresses**). You can add the flag to an executable image even
without building (no source code required) by using a tool such as Editbin.exe (part of the Windows
SDK tools), assuming the file is not signed. This flag has no effect when running the application on a
system with a 2 GB user address space.

Several system images are marked as large address space aware so that they can take advantage of
systems running with large process address spaces. These include the following:

- **Lsass.exe**   The Local Security Authority Subsystem
- **Inetinfo.exe**   Internet Information Server
- **Chkdsk.exe**   The Check Disk utility

- **Smss.exe** The Session Manager

- **Dllhst3g.exe** A special version of Dllhost.exe (for COM+ applications)

EXPERIMENT: Checking whether an application is large address aware

You can use the Dumpbin utility from the Visual Studio Tools (and older versions of the Windows SDK) to check other executables to see if they support large address spaces. Use the /headers flag to display the results. Here's a sample output of Dumpbin on the Session Manager:

```
dumpbin /headers c:\windows\system32\smss.exe
Microsoft (R) COFF/PE Dumper Version 14.00.24213.1
Copyright (C) Microsoft Corporation.  All rights reserved.
Dump of file c:\windows\system32\smss.exe
PE signature found
File Type: EXECUTABLE IMAGE
FILE HEADER VALUES
             14C machine (x86)
               5 number of sections
        57898F8A time date stamp Sat Jul 16 04:36:10 2016
               0 file pointer to symbol table
               0 number of symbols
              E0 size of optional header
             122 characteristics
                   Executable
                   Application can handle large (>2GB) addresses
                   32 bit word machine
```

Finally, memory allocations using `VirtualAlloc`, `VirtualAllocEx`, and `VirtualAllocExNuma` start with low virtual addresses and grow higher by default. Unless a process allocates a lot of memory or has a very fragmented virtual address space, it will never get back very high virtual addresses. Therefore, for testing purposes, you can force memory allocations to start from high addresses by using the `MEM_TOP_DOWN` flag to the `VirtualAlloc*` functions or by adding a DWORD registry value named `AllocationPreference` to the HKLM\SYSTEM\CurrentControlSet\Control\Session Manager\Memory Management key and setting its value to 0x100000.

The following output shows runs of the TestLimit utility (shown in previous experiments) leaking memory on a 32-bit Windows machine booted without the `increaseuserva` option:

```
Testlimit.exe -r

Testlimit v5.24 - test Windows limits
Copyright (C) 2012-2015 Mark Russinovich
Sysinternals - www.sysinternals.com

Process ID: 5500

Reserving private bytes (MB)...
Leaked 1978 MB of reserved memory (1940 MB total leaked). Lasterror: 8
```

The process managed to reserve close to the 2 GB limit (but not quite). The process address space has the EXE code and various DLLs mapped, so naturally it's not possible in a normal process to reserve the entire address space.

On that same system, you can switch to a 3 GB address space by running the following command from an administrative command window:

```
C:\WINDOWS\system32>bcdedit /set increaseuserva 3072

The operation completed successfully.
```

Notice that the command allows you to specify any number (in MB) between 2,048 (the 2 GB default) to 3,072 (the 3 GB maximum). After you restart the system so that the setting can take effect, running TestLimit again produces the following:

```
Testlimit.exe -r

Testlimit v5.24 - test Windows limits
Copyright (C) 2012-2015 Mark Russinovich
Sysinternals - www.sysinternals.com

Process ID: 2308

Reserving private bytes (MB)...
Leaked 2999 MB of reserved memory (2999 MB total leaked). Lasterror: 8
```

TestLimit was able to leak close to 3 GB, as expected. This is only possible because TestLimit was linked with /LARGEADDRESSAWARE. Had it not been, the results would have been essentially the same as on the system booted without increaseuserva.

 Note To revert a system to the normal 2 GB address space per process, run the bcdedit / deletevalue increaseuserva command.

x86 system address space layout

The 32-bit versions of Windows implement a dynamic system address space layout by using a virtual address allocator. (We'll describe this functionality later in this section.) There are still a few specifically reserved areas, as shown in Figure 5-10. However, many kernel-mode structures use dynamic address space allocation. These structures are therefore not necessarily virtually contiguous with themselves. Each can easily exist in several disjointed pieces in various areas of system address space. The uses of system address space that are allocated in this way include the following:

- Non-paged pool

- Paged pool

- Special pool

- System PTEs

- System mapped views

- File system cache

- PFN database

- Session space

x86 session space

For systems with multiple sessions (which is almost always the case, as session 0 is used by system processes and services, while session 1 is used for the first logged on user), the code and data unique to each session are mapped into system address space but shared by the processes in that session. Figure 5-11 shows the general layout of session space. The sizes of the components of session space, just like the rest of kernel system address space, are dynamically configured and resized by the memory manager on demand.

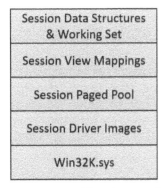

| Session Data Structures & Working Set |
| Session View Mappings |
| Session Paged Pool |
| Session Driver Images |
| Win32K.sys |

FIGURE 5-11   x86 session space layout (not proportional).

EXPERIMENT: Viewing sessions

You can display which processes are members of which sessions by examining the session ID. You can do this using Task Manager, Process Explorer, or the kernel debugger. Using the kernel debugger, you can list the active sessions with the !session command as follows:

```
lkd> !session
Sessions on machine: 3
Valid Sessions: 0 1 2
Current Session 2
```

You can then set the active session using the !session -s command and display the address of the session data structures and the processes in that session with the !sprocess command:

```
lkd> !session -s 1
Sessions on machine: 3
```

```
Implicit process is now d4921040
Using session 1

lkd> !sprocess
Dumping Session 1

_MM_SESSION_SPACE d9306000
_MMSESSION          d9306c80
PROCESS d4921040  SessionId: 1  Cid: 01d8    Peb: 00668000  ParentCid: 0138
    DirBase: 179c5080  ObjectTable: 00000000  HandleCount:   0.
    Image: smss.exe

PROCESS d186c180  SessionId: 1  Cid: 01ec    Peb: 00401000  ParentCid: 01d8
    DirBase: 179c5040  ObjectTable: d58d48c0  HandleCount: <Data Not Accessible>
    Image: csrss.exe

PROCESS d49acc40  SessionId: 1  Cid: 022c    Peb: 03119000  ParentCid: 01d8
    DirBase: 179c50c0  ObjectTable: d232e5c0  HandleCount: <Data Not Accessible>
    Image: winlogon.exe

PROCESS dc0918c0  SessionId: 1  Cid: 0374    Peb: 003c4000  ParentCid: 022c
    DirBase: 179c5160  ObjectTable: dc28f6c0  HandleCount: <Data Not Accessible>
    Image: LogonUI.exe

PROCESS dc08e900  SessionId: 1  Cid: 037c    Peb: 00d8b000  ParentCid: 022c
    DirBase: 179c5180  ObjectTable: dc249640  HandleCount: <Data Not Accessible>
    Image: dwm.exe
```

To view the details of the session, dump the MM_SESSION_SPACE structure using the dt command, as follows:

```
lkd> dt nt!_mm_session_space d9306000
   +0x000 ReferenceCount   : 0n4
   +0x004 u                : <unnamed-tag>
   +0x008 SessionId        : 1
   +0x00c ProcessReferenceToSession : 0n6
   +0x010 ProcessList      : _LIST_ENTRY [ 0xd4921128 - 0xdc08e9e8 ]
   +0x018 SessionPageDirectoryIndex : 0x1617f
   +0x01c NonPagablePages  : 0x28
   +0x020 CommittedPages   : 0x290
   +0x024 PagedPoolStart   : 0xc0000000 Void
   +0x028 PagedPoolEnd     : 0xffbfffff Void
   +0x02c SessionObject    : 0xd49222b0 Void
   +0x030 SessionObjectHandle : 0x800003ac Void
   +0x034 SessionPoolAllocationFailures : [4] 0
   +0x044 ImageTree        : _RTL_AVL_TREE
   +0x048 LocaleId         : 0x409
   +0x04c AttachCount      : 0
   +0x050 AttachGate       : _KGATE
   +0x060 WsListEntry      : _LIST_ENTRY [ 0xcdcde060 - 0xd6307060 ]
   +0x080 Lookaside        : [24] _GENERAL_LOOKASIDE
   +0xc80 Session          : _MMSESSION
...
```

EXPERIMENT: Viewing session space utilization

You can view session space memory utilization with the `!vm 4` command in the kernel debugger. For example, the following output was taken from a 32-bit Windows client system with a remote desktop connection, resulting in three sessions—the default two sessions plus the remote session. (The addresses are for the `MM_SESSION_SPACE` objects shown earlier.)

```
lkd> !vm 4
...
Terminal Server Memory Usage By Session:

Session ID 0 @ d6307000:
Paged Pool Usage:      2012 Kb
NonPaged Usage:         108 Kb
Commit Usage:          2292 Kb

Session ID 1 @ d9306000:
Paged Pool Usage:      2288 Kb
NonPaged Usage:         160 Kb
Commit Usage:          2624 Kb

Session ID 2 @ cdcde000:
Paged Pool Usage:      7740 Kb
NonPaged Usage:         208 Kb
Commit Usage:          8144 Kb

Session Summary
Paged Pool Usage:     12040 Kb
NonPaged Usage:         476 Kb
Commit Usage:         13060 Kb
```

System page table entries

System page table entries (PTEs) are used to dynamically map system pages such as I/O space, kernel stacks, and the mapping for memory descriptor lists (MDLs, discussed to some extent in Chapter 6). System PTEs aren't an infinite resource. On 32-bit Windows, the number of available system PTEs is such that the system can theoretically describe 2 GB of contiguous system virtual address space. On Windows 10 64 bit and Server 2016, system PTEs can describe up to 16 TB of contiguous virtual address space.

EXPERIMENT: Viewing system PTE information

You can see how many system PTEs are available by examining the value of the Memory: Free System Page Table Entries counter in Performance Monitor or by using the `!sysptes` or `!vm` command in the debugger. You can also dump the `_MI_SYSTEM_PTE_TYPE` structure as part of the memory state (`MiState`) variable (or the `MiSystemPteInfo` global variable on Windows 8.x/2012/R2). This will also show you how many PTE allocation failures occurred on the system. A high count indicates a problem and possibly a system PTE leak.

```
kd> !sysptes
System PTE Information
  Total System Ptes 216560
    starting PTE: c0400000
  free blocks: 969    total free: 16334    largest free block: 264

kd> ? MiState
Evaluate expression: -2128443008 = 81228980


kd> dt nt!_MI_SYSTEM_INFORMATION SystemPtes
   +0x3040 SystemPtes : _MI_SYSTEM_PTE_STATE

kd> dt nt!_mi_system_pte_state SystemViewPteInfo 81228980+3040
   +0x10c SystemViewPteInfo : _MI_SYSTEM_PTE_TYPE

kd> dt nt!_mi_system_pte_type 81228980+3040+10c
   +0x000 Bitmap          : _RTL_BITMAP
   +0x008 BasePte         : 0xc0400000 _MMPTE
   +0x00c Flags           : 0xe
   +0x010 VaType          : c ( MiVaDriverImages )
   +0x014 FailureCount    : 0x8122bae4  -> 0
   +0x018 PteFailures     : 0
   +0x01c SpinLock        : 0
   +0x01c GlobalPushLock  : (null)
   +0x020 Vm              : 0x8122c008 _MMSUPPORT_INSTANCE
   +0x024 TotalSystemPtes : 0x120
   +0x028 Hint            : 0x2576
   +0x02c LowestBitEverAllocated : 0xc80
   +0x030 CachedPtes      : (null)
   +0x034 TotalFreeSystemPtes : 0x73
```

If you are seeing lots of system PTE failures, you can enable system PTE tracking by creating a new DWORD value in the HKLM\SYSTEM\CurrentControlSet\Control\Session Manager\Memory Management key called TrackPtes and setting its value to 1. You can then use !sysptes 4 to show a list of allocators.

ARM address space layout

As shown in Figure 5-12, the ARM address space layout is nearly identical to the x86 address space. The memory manager treats ARM-based systems exactly as x86 systems in terms of pure memory management. The differences are at the address translation layer, described in the section "Address translation" later in this chapter.

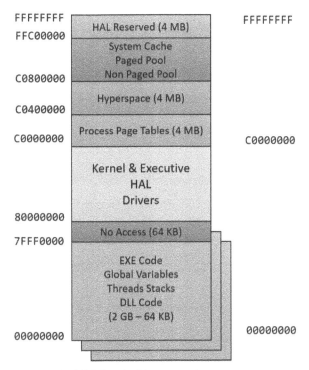

FIGURE 5-12   ARM virtual address space layout.

64-bit address space layout

The theoretical 64-bit virtual address space is 16 exabytes (EB), or 18,446,744,073,709,551,616 bytes. Current processor limitations allow for 48 address lines only, limiting the possible address space to 256 TB (2 to the 48th power). The address space is divided in half, where the lower 128 TB are available as private user processes and the upper 128 TB are system space. System space is divided into several different-sized regions (Windows 10 and Server 2016), as shown in Figure 5-13. Clearly, 64 bits provides a tremendous leap in terms of address space sizes as opposed to 32 bit. The actual starts of various kernel sections are not necessarily those shown, as ASLR is in effect in kernel space in the latest versions of Windows.

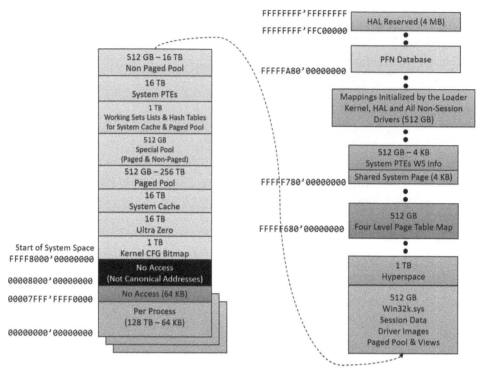

FIGURE 5-13 x64 address space layout.

Note Windows 8 and Server 2012 are limited to 16 TB of address space. This is because of Windows implementation limitations, described in Chapter 10 of the sixth edition of *Windows Internals Part 2*. Of these, 8 TB is per process and the other 8 TB is used for system space.

Thirty-two–bit images that are large address space aware receive an extra benefit while running on 64-bit Windows (under Wow64). Such an image will actually receive all 4 GB of user address space available. After all, if the image can support 3 GB pointers, 4 GB pointers should not be any different, because unlike the switch from 2 GB to 3 GB, there are no additional bits involved. The following output shows TestLimit running as a 32-bit application, reserving address space on a 64-bit Windows machine.

```
C:\Tools\Sysinternals>Testlimit.exe -r

Testlimit v5.24 - test Windows limits
Copyright (C) 2012-2015 Mark Russinovich
Sysinternals - www.sysinternals.com

Process ID: 264

Reserving private bytes (MB)...
Leaked 4008 MB of reserved memory (4008 MB total leaked). Lasterror: 8
Not enough storage is available to process this command.
```

These results depend on TestLimit having been linked with the /LARGEADDRESSAWARE option. Had it not been, the results would have been about 2 GB for each. Sixty-four–bit applications linked without /LARGEADDRESSAWARE are constrained to the first 2 GB of the process virtual address space, just like 32-bit applications. (This flag is set by default in Visual Studio for 64-bit builds.)

x64 virtual addressing limitations

As discussed, 64 bits of virtual address space allow for a possible maximum of 16 EB of virtual memory —a notable improvement over the 4 GB offered by 32-bit addressing. Obviously, neither today's computers nor tomorrow's are even close to requiring support for that much memory.

Accordingly, to simplify chip architecture and avoid unnecessary overhead—particularly in address translation (described later)—AMD's and Intel's current x64 processors implement only 256 TB of virtual address space. That is, only the low-order 48 bits of a 64-bit virtual address are implemented. However, virtual addresses are still 64 bits wide, occupying 8 bytes in registers or when stored in memory. The high-order 16 bits (bits 48 through 63) must be set to the same value as the highest-order implemented bit (bit 47), in a manner similar to sign extension in two's complement arithmetic. An address that conforms to this rule is said to be a *canonical address*.

Under these rules, the bottom half of the address space starts at 0x0000000000000000 as expected, but ends at 0x00007FFFFFFFFFFF. The top half of the address space starts at 0xFFFF800000000000 and ends at 0xFFFFFFFFFFFFFFFF. Each canonical portion is 128 TB. As newer processors implement more of the address bits, the lower half of memory will expand upward toward 0x7FFFFFFFFFFFFFFF, while the upper half will expand downward toward 0x8000000000000000.

Dynamic system virtual address space management

Thirty-two–bit versions of Windows manage the system address space through an internal kernel virtual allocator mechanism, described in this section. Currently, 64-bit versions of Windows have no need to use the allocator for virtual address space management (and thus bypass the cost) because each region is statically defined (refer to Figure 5-13).

When the system initializes, the MiInitializeDynamicVa function sets up the basic dynamic ranges and sets the available virtual address to all available kernel space. It then initializes the address space ranges for boot loader images, process space (hyperspace), and the HAL through the MiInitialize-SystemVaRange function, which is used to set hard-coded address ranges (on 32-bit systems only). Later, when non-paged pool is initialized, this function is used again to reserve the virtual address ranges for it. Finally, whenever a driver loads, the address range is relabeled to a driver-image range instead of a boot-loaded range.

After this point, the rest of the system virtual address space can be dynamically requested and released through MiObtainSystemVa (and its analogous MiObtainSessionVa) and MiReturnSystemVa. Operations such as expanding the system cache, the system PTEs, non-paged pool, paged pool, and/or special pool; mapping memory with large pages; creating the PFN database; and creating a new session all result in dynamic virtual address allocations for a specific range.

Each time the kernel virtual address space allocator obtains virtual memory ranges for use by a certain type of virtual address, it updates the MiSystemVaType array, which contains the virtual address type for the newly allocated range. The values that can appear in MiSystemVaType are shown in Table 5-8.

TABLE 5-8   System virtual address types

Region	Description	Limitable
MiVaUnused (0)	Unused	N/A
MiVaSessionSpace (1)	Addresses for session space	Yes
MiVaProcessSpace (2)	Addresses for process address space	No
MiVaBootLoaded (3)	Addresses for images loaded by the boot loader	No
MiVaPfnDatabase (4)	Addresses for the PFN database	No
MiVaNonPagedPool (5)	Addresses for the non-paged pool	Yes
MiVaPagedPool (6)	Addresses for the paged pool	Yes
MiVaSpecialPoolPaged (7)	Addresses for the special pool (paged)	No
MiVaSystemCache (8)	Addresses for the system cache	No
MiVaSystemPtes (9)	Addresses for system PTEs	Yes
MiVaHal (10)	Addresses for the HAL	No
MiVaSessionGlobalSpace (11)	Addresses for session global space	No
MiVaDriverImages (12)	Addresses for loaded driver images	No
MiVaSpecialPoolNonPaged (13)	Addresses for the special pool (non-paged)	Yes
MiVaSystemPtesLarge (14)	Addresses for large page PTEs	Yes

Although the ability to dynamically reserve virtual address space on demand allows better management of virtual memory, it would be useless without the ability to free this memory. As such, when the paged pool or system cache can be shrunk, or when special pool and large page mappings are freed, the associated virtual address is freed. Another case is when the boot registry is released. This allows dynamic management of memory depending on each component's use. Additionally, components can reclaim memory through MiReclaimSystemVa, which requests virtual addresses associated with the system cache to be flushed out (through the dereference segment thread) if available virtual address space has dropped below 128 MB. Reclaiming can also be satisfied if initial non-paged pool has been freed.

In addition to better proportioning and better management of virtual addresses dedicated to different kernel memory consumers, the dynamic virtual address allocator also has advantages when it comes to memory footprint reduction. Instead of having to manually pre-allocate static page table entries and page tables, paging-related structures are allocated on demand. On both 32-bit and 64-bit systems, this reduces boot-time memory usage because unused addresses won't have their page tables allocated. It also means that on 64-bit systems, the large address space regions that are reserved don't need to have their page tables mapped in memory. This allows them to have arbitrarily large limits, especially on systems that have little physical RAM to back the resulting paging structures.

EXPERIMENT: Querying system virtual address usage (Windows 10 and Server 2016)

You can look at the current and peak usage of each system virtual address type by using the kernel debugger. The global variable MiVisibleState (of type MI_VISIBLE_STATE) provides information available in the public symbols. (The example is on x86 Windows 10.)

1. To get a sense of the data provided by MiVisibleState, dump the structure with values:

```
lkd> dt nt!_mi_visible_state poi(nt!MiVisibleState)
   +0x000 SpecialPool      : _MI_SPECIAL_POOL
   +0x048 SessionWsList     : _LIST_ENTRY [ 0x91364060 - 0x9a172060 ]
   +0x050 SessionIdBitmap   : 0x8220c3a0 _RTL_BITMAP
   +0x054 PagedPoolInfo     : _MM_PAGED_POOL_INFO
   +0x070 MaximumNonPagedPoolInPages : 0x80000
   +0x074 SizeOfPagedPoolInPages : 0x7fc00
   +0x078 SystemPteInfo     : _MI_SYSTEM_PTE_TYPE
   +0x0b0 NonPagedPoolCommit : 0x3272
   +0x0b4 BootCommit        : 0x186d
   +0x0b8 MdlPagesAllocated : 0x105
   +0x0bc SystemPageTableCommit : 0x1e1
   +0x0c0 SpecialPagesInUse : 0
   +0x0c4 WsOverheadPages   : 0x775
   +0x0c8 VadBitmapPages    : 0x30
   +0x0cc ProcessCommit     : 0xb40
   +0x0d0 SharedCommit      : 0x712a
   +0x0d4 DriverCommit      : 0n7276
   +0x100 SystemWs          : [3] _MMSUPPORT_FULL
   +0x2c0 SystemCacheShared : _MMSUPPORT_SHARED
   +0x2e4 MapCacheFailures  : 0
   +0x2e8 PagefileHashPages : 0x30
   +0x2ec PteHeader         : _SYSPTES_HEADER
   +0x378 SessionSpecialPool : 0x95201f48 _MI_SPECIAL_POOL
   +0x37c SystemVaTypeCount : [15] 0
   +0x3b8 SystemVaType      : [1024] ""
   +0x7b8 SystemVaTypeCountFailures : [15] 0
   +0x7f4 SystemVaTypeCountLimit : [15] 0
   +0x830 SystemVaTypeCountPeak : [15] 0
   +0x86c SystemAvailableVa : 0x38800000
```

2. Notice the last arrays with 15 elements each, corresponding to the system virtual address types from Table 5-8. Here are the SystemVaTypeCount and SystemVaType-CountPeak arrays:

```
lkd> dt nt!_mi_visible_state poi(nt!mivisiblestate) -a SystemVaTypeCount
   +0x37c SystemVaTypeCount :
    [00] 0
    [01] 0x1c
    [02] 0xb
    [03] 0x15
    [04] 0xf
    [05] 0x1b
```

```
        [06] 0x46
        [07] 0
        [08] 0x125
        [09] 0x38
        [10] 2
        [11] 0xb
        [12] 0x19
        [13] 0
        [14] 0xd
lkd> dt nt!_mi_visible_state poi(nt!mivisiblestate) -a SystemVaTypeCountPeak
   +0x830 SystemVaTypeCountPeak :
        [00] 0
        [01] 0x1f
        [02] 0
        [03] 0x1f
        [04] 0xf
        [05] 0x1d
        [06] 0x51
        [07] 0
        [08] 0x1e6
        [09] 0x55
        [10] 0
        [11] 0xb
        [12] 0x5d
        [13] 0
        [14] 0xe
```

EXPERIMENT: Querying system virtual address usage (Windows 8.x and Server 2012/R2)

You can look at the current and peak usage of each system virtual address type by using the kernel debugger. For each system virtual address type described in Table 5-8, the MiSystemVa-TypeCount, MiSystemVaTypeCountFailures, and MiSystemVaTypeCountPeak global arrays in the kernel contain the sizes, count failures, and peak sizes for each type. The size is in multiples of a PDE mapping (see the "Address translation" section later in this chapter), which is effectively the size of a large page (2 MB on x86). Here's how you can dump the usage for the system, followed by the peak usage. You can use a similar technique for the failure counts. (The example is from a 32-bit Windows 8.1 system.)

```
lkd> dd /c 1 MiSystemVaTypeCount L f
81c16640    00000000
81c16644    0000001e
81c16648    0000000b
81c1664c    00000018
81c16650    0000000f
81c16654    00000017
81c16658    0000005f
81c1665c    00000000
81c16660    000000c7
```

```
81c16664   00000021
81c16668   00000002
81c1666c   00000008
81c16670   0000001c
81c16674   00000000
81c16678   0000000b
lkd> dd /c 1 MiSystemVaTypeCountPeak L f
81c16b60   00000000
81c16b64   00000021
81c16b68   00000000
81c16b6c   00000022
81c16b70   0000000f
81c16b74   0000001e
81c16b78   0000007e
81c16b7c   00000000
81c16b80   000000e3
81c16b84   00000027
81c16b88   00000000
81c16b8c   00000008
81c16b90   00000059
81c16b94   00000000
81c16b98   0000000b
```

Theoretically, the different virtual address ranges assigned to components can grow arbitrarily in size if enough system virtual address space is available. In practice, on 32-bit systems, the kernel allocator implements the ability to set limits on each virtual address type for the purposes of both reliability and stability. (On 64-bit systems, kernel address space exhaustion is currently not a concern.) Although no limits are imposed by default, system administrators can use the registry to modify these limits for the virtual address types that are currently marked as limitable (see Table 5-8).

If the current request during the `MiObtainSystemVa` call exceeds the available limit, a failure is marked (see the previous experiment) and a reclaim operation is requested regardless of available memory. This should help alleviate memory load and might allow the virtual address allocation to work during the next attempt. Recall, however, that reclaiming affects only system cache and non-paged pool.

EXPERIMENT: Setting system virtual address limits

The `MiSystemVaTypeCountLimit` array contains limitations for system virtual address usage that can be set for each type. Currently, the memory manager allows only certain virtual address types to be limited, and it provides the ability to use an undocumented system call to set limits for the system dynamically during run time. (These limits can also be set through the registry, as described at *http://msdn.microsoft.com/en-us/library/bb870880.aspx*.) These limits can be set for those types marked in Table 5-8.

You can use the MemLimit utility (found in this book's downloadable resources) on 32-bit systems to query and set the different limits for these types and to see the current and peak virtual address space usage. Here's how you can query the current limits with the -q flag:

```
C:\Tools>MemLimit.exe -q

MemLimit v1.01 - Query and set hard limits on system VA space consumption
Copyright (C) 2008-2016 by Alex Ionescu
www.alex-ionescu.com

System Va Consumption:

Type                   Current            Peak              Limit
Non Paged Pool          45056 KB          55296 KB           0 KB
Paged Pool             151552 KB         165888 KB           0 KB
System Cache           446464 KB         479232 KB           0 KB
System PTEs             90112 KB         135168 KB           0 KB
Session Space           63488 KB          73728 KB           0 KB
```

As an experiment, use the following command to set a limit of 100 MB for paged pool:

```
memlimit.exe -p 100M
```

Now use the Sysinternals TestLimit tool to create as many handles as possible. Normally, with enough paged pool, the number should be around 16 million. But with the limit to 100 MB, it's less:

```
C:\Tools\Sysinternals>Testlimit.exe -h

Testlimit v5.24 - test Windows limits
Copyright (C) 2012-2015 Mark Russinovich
Sysinternals - www.sysinternals.com

Process ID: 4780

Creating handles...
Created 10727844 handles. Lasterror: 1450
```

See Chapter 8 in Part 2 for more information about objects, handles, and page-pool consumption.

System virtual address space quotas

The system virtual address space limits described in the previous section allow for the limiting of system-wide virtual address space usage of certain kernel components. However, they work only on 32-bit systems when applied to the system as a whole. To address more specific quota requirements that system administrators might have, the memory manager collaborates with the process manager to enforce either system-wide or user-specific quotas for each process.

You can configure the PagedPoolQuota, NonPagedPoolQuota, PagingFileQuota, and WorkingSetPagesQuota values in the HKLM\SYSTEM\CurrentControlSet\Control\Session Manager\Memory Management key to specify how much memory of each type a given process can use. This information is read at initialization, and the default system quota block is generated and then assigned to all system processes. (User processes get a copy of the default system quota block unless per-user quotas have been configured, as explained next.)

To enable per-user quotas, you can create subkeys under the HKLM\SYSTEM\CurrentControlSet\ Session Manager\Quota System registry key, each one representing a given user SID. The values mentioned previously can then be created under this specific SID subkey, enforcing the limits only for the processes created by that user. Table 5-9 shows how to configure these values (which can be done at run time or not) and which privileges are required.

TABLE 5-9 Process quota types

Value Name	Description	Value Type	Dynamic	Privilege
PagedPoolQuota	This is the maximum size of paged pool that can be allocated by this process.	Size in MB	Only for processes running with the system token	SeIncreaseQuotaPrivilege
NonPagedPoolQuota	This is the maximum size of nonpaged pool that can be allocated by this process.	Size in MB	Only for processes running with the system token	SeIncreaseQuotaPrivilege
PagingFileQuota	This is the maximum number of pages that a process can have backed by the page file.	Pages	Only for processes running with the system token	SeIncreaseQuotaPrivilege
WorkingSetPagesQuota	This is the maximum number of pages that a process can have in its working set (in physical memory).	Pages	Yes	SeIncreaseBasePriorityPrivilege unless operation is a purge request

User address space layout

Just as address space in the kernel is dynamic, the user address space is also built dynamically. The addresses of the thread stacks, process heaps, and loaded images (such as DLLs and an application's executable) are dynamically computed (if the application and its images support it) through the ASLR mechanism.

At the operating system level, user address space is divided into a few well-defined regions of memory, as shown in Figure 5-14. The executable and DLLs themselves are present as memory-mapped image files, followed by the heap(s) of the process and the stack(s) of its thread(s). Apart from these regions (and some reserved system structures such as the TEBs and PEB), all other memory allocations are run-time dependent and generated. ASLR is involved with the location of all these run time–dependent regions and, combined with DEP, provides a mechanism for making remote exploitation of a system through memory manipulation harder to achieve. Because Windows code and data are placed at dynamic locations, an attacker cannot typically hard-code a meaningful offset into either a program or a system-supplied DLL.

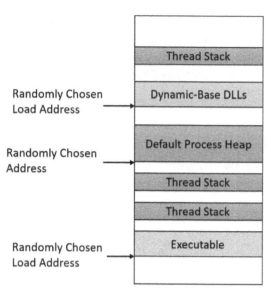

Randomly Chosen
Load Address

Randomly Chosen
Address

Randomly Chosen
Load Address

FIGURE 5-14   User address space layout with ASLR enabled.

EXPERIMENT: Analyzing user virtual address space

The VMMap utility from Sysinternals can show you a detailed view of the virtual memory being used by any process on your machine. This information is divided into categories for each type of allocation, summarized as follows:

- **Image**   This displays memory allocations used to map the executable and its dependencies (such as dynamic libraries) and any other memory-mapped image (portable executable format) files.

- **Mapped File**   This displays memory allocations for memory mapped data files.

- **Shareable**   This displays memory allocations marked as shareable, typically including shared memory (but not memory-mapped files, which are listed under either Image or Mapped File).

- **Heap**   This displays memory allocated for the heap(s) that this process owns.

- **Managed Heap**   This displays memory allocated by the .NET CLR (managed objects). It would show nothing for a process that does not use .NET.

- **Stack**   This displays memory allocated for the stack of each thread in this process.

- **Private Data**   This displays memory allocations marked as private other than the stack and heap, such as internal data structures.

The following shows a typical view of Explorer (64 bit) as seen through VMMap:

Depending on the type of memory allocation, VMMap can show additional information such as file names (for mapped files), heap IDs and types (for heap allocations), and thread IDs (for stack allocations). Furthermore, each allocation's cost is shown both in committed memory and working set memory. The size and protection of each allocation is also displayed.

ASLR begins at the image level, with the executable for the process and its dependent DLLs. Any image file that has specified ASLR support in its PE header (IMAGE_DLL_CHARACTERISTICS_DYNAMIC_BASE), typically specified by using the /DYNAMICBASE linker flag in Microsoft Visual Studio, and contains a relocation section will be processed by ASLR. When such an image is found, the system selects an image offset valid globally for the current boot. This offset is selected from a bucket of 256 values, all of which are 64 KB aligned.

Image randomization

For executables, the load offset is calculated by computing a delta value each time an executable is loaded. This value is a pseudo-random 8-bit number from 0x10000 to 0xFE0000, calculated by taking the current processor's time stamp counter (TSC), shifting it by four places, and then performing a division modulo 254 and adding 1. This number is then multiplied by the allocation granularity of 64 KB discussed earlier. By adding 1, the memory manager ensures that the value can never be 0, so executables will never load at the address in the PE header if ASLR is being used. This delta is then added to the executable's preferred load address, creating one of 256 possible locations within 16 MB of the image address in the PE header.

For DLLs, computing the load offset begins with a per-boot, system-wide value called the *image bias*. This is computed by `MiInitializeRelocations` and stored in the global memory state structure (MI_SYSTEM_INFORMATION) in the `MiState.Sections.ImageBias` fields (`MiImageBias` global variable in Windows 8.*x*/2012/R2). This value corresponds to the TSC of the current CPU when this function was called during the boot cycle, shifted and masked into an 8-bit value. This provides 256 possible values on 32 bit systems; similar computations are done for 64-bit systems with more possible values as the address space is vast. Unlike executables, this value is computed only once per boot and shared across the system to allow DLLs to remain shared in physical memory and relocated only once. If DLLs were remapped at different locations inside different processes, the code could not be shared. The loader would have to fix up address references differently for each process, thus turning what had been shareable read-only code into process-private data. Each process using a given DLL would have to have its own private copy of the DLL in physical memory.

Once the offset is computed, the memory manager initializes a bitmap called `ImageBitMap` (`MiImageBitMap` global variable in Windows 8.*x*/2012/R2), which is part of the MI_SECTION_STATE structure. This bitmap is used to represent ranges from 0x50000000 to 0x78000000 for 32-bit systems (see the numbers for 64-bit systems below), and each bit represents one unit of allocation (64 KB, as mentioned). Whenever the memory manager loads a DLL, the appropriate bit is set to mark its location in the system. When the same DLL is loaded again, the memory manager shares its section object with the already relocated information.

As each DLL is loaded, the system scans the bitmap from top to bottom for free bits. The `ImageBias` value computed earlier is used as a start index from the top to randomize the load across different boots as suggested. Because the bitmap will be entirely empty when the first DLL (which is always Ntdll. dll) is loaded, its load address can easily be calculated. (Sixty-four–bit systems have their own bias.)

- **32 bit**   *0x78000000 – (ImageBias + NtDllSizein64KBChunks) * 0x10000*

- **64 bit**   *0x7FFFFFFF0000 – (ImageBias64High + NtDllSizein64KBChunks) * 0x10000*

Each subsequent DLL will then load in a 64 KB chunk below. Because of this, if the address of Ntdll. dll is known, the addresses of other DLLs could easily be computed. To mitigate this possibility, the order in which known DLLs are mapped by the Session Manager during initialization is also randomized when Smss.exe loads.

Finally, if no free space is available in the bitmap (which would mean that most of the region defined for ASLR is in use), the DLL relocation code defaults back to the executable case, loading the DLL at a 64 KB chunk within 16 MB of its preferred base address.

EXPERIMENT: Calculating the load address of Ntdll.dll

With what you learned in the previous section, you can calculate the load address of Ntdll.dll with the kernel variable information. The following calculation is done on a Windows 10 x86 system:

1. Start local kernel debugging.

2. Find the ImageBias value:

```
lkd> ? nt!mistate
Evaluate expression: -2113373760 = 820879c0
lkd> dt nt!_mi_system_information sections.imagebias 820879c0
   +0x500 Sections      :
      +0x0dc ImageBias      : 0x6e
```

3. Open Explorer and find the size of Ntdll.dll in the System32 directory. On this system, it's 1547 KB = 0x182c00, so the size in 64 KB chunks is 0x19 (always rounding up). The result is 0x78000000 − (0x6E + 0x19) * 0x10000 = 0x77790000.

4. Open Process Explorer, find any process, and look at the load address (in the Base or Image Base columns) of Ntdll.dll. You should see the same value.

5. Try to do the same for a 64-bit system.

Stack randomization

The next step in ASLR is to randomize the location of the initial thread's stack and, subsequently, of each new thread. This randomization is enabled unless the StackRandomizationDisabled flag was enabled for the process, and consists of first selecting one of 32 possible stack locations separated by either 64 KB or 256 KB. You select this base address by finding the first appropriate free memory region and then choosing the xth available region, where x is once again generated based on the current processor's TSC shifted and masked into a 5-bit value. (This allows for 32 possible locations.)

When this base address has been selected, a new TSC-derived value is calculated—this one 9 bits long. The value is then multiplied by 4 to maintain alignment, which means it can be as large as 2,048 bytes (half a page). It is added to the base address to obtain the final stack base.

Heap randomization

ASLR randomizes the location of the initial process heap and subsequent heaps when created in user mode. The RtlCreateHeap function uses another pseudo-random TSC-derived value to determine the base address of the heap. This value, 5 bits this time, is multiplied by 64 KB to generate the final base address, starting at 0, giving a possible range of 0x00000000 to 0x001F0000 for the initial heap. Additionally, the range before the heap base address is manually deallocated to force an access violation if an attack is doing a brute-force sweep of the entire possible heap address range.

ASLR in kernel address space

ASLR is also active in kernel address space. There are 64 possible load addresses for 32-bit drivers and 256 for 64-bit drivers. Relocating user-space images requires a significant amount of work area in kernel space, but if kernel space is tight, ASLR can use the user-mode address space of the System process for this work area. On Windows 10 (version 1607) and Server 2016, ASLR is implemented for most system memory regions, such as paged and non-paged pools, system cache, page tables, and the PFN database (initialized by MiAssignTopLevelRanges).

Controlling security mitigations

As you've seen, ASLR and many other security mitigations in Windows are optional because of their potential compatibility effects: ASLR applies only to images with the IMAGE_DLL_CHARACTERISTICS_ DYNAMIC_BASE bit in their image headers, hardware no-execute (DEP) can be controlled by a combination of boot options and linker options, and so on. To allow both enterprise customers and individual users more visibility and control of these features, Microsoft publishes the Enhanced Mitigation Experience Toolkit (EMET). EMET offers centralized control of the mitigations built into Windows and adds several more mitigations not yet part of the Windows product. Additionally, EMET provides notification capabilities through the event log to let administrators know when certain software has experienced access faults because mitigations have been applied. Finally, EMET enables manual opt-out for certain applications that might exhibit compatibility issues in certain environments, even though they were opted in by the developer.

> **Note** EMET is in version 5.51 at the time of this writing. Its end of support has been extended to the end of July 2018. However, some of its features are integrated in current Windows versions.

EXPERIMENT: Looking at ASLR protection on processes

You can use Process Explorer from Sysinternals to look over your processes (and, just as important, the DLLs they load) to see if they support ASLR. Even if just one DLL loaded by a process does not support ASLR, it can make the process much more vulnerable to attacks.

To look at the ASLR status for processes, follow these steps:

1. Right-click any column in the process tree and choose **Select Columns**.

2. Select **ASLR Enabled** on the Process Image and DLL tabs.

3. Notice that all in-box Windows programs and services are running with ASLR enabled, but third-party applications may or may not run with ASLR.

In the example, we have highlighted the Notepad.exe process. In this case, its load address is 0x7FF7D76B0000. If you were to close all instances of Notepad and then start another, you would find it at a different load address. If you shut down and reboot the system and then try the experiment again, you will find that the ASLR-enabled DLLs are at different load addresses after each boot.

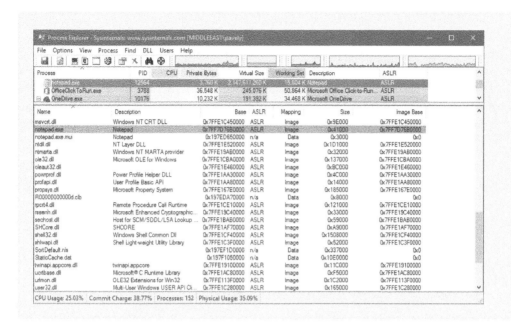

Address translation

Now that you've seen how Windows structures the virtual address space, let's look at how it maps these address spaces to real physical pages. User applications and system code reference virtual addresses. This section starts with a detailed description of 32-bit x86 address translation in PAE mode (the only mode supported in recent versions of Windows) and continues with a description of the differences on the ARM and x64 platforms. The next section describes what happens when such a translation doesn't resolve to a physical memory address (page fault) and explains how Windows manages physical memory via working sets and the page frame database.

x86 virtual address translation

The original x86 kernel supported no more than 4 GB of physical memory, based on the CPU hardware available at the time. The Intel x86 Pentium Pro processor introduced a memory-mapping mode called *Physical Address Extension* (*PAE*). With the proper chipset, the PAE mode allows 32-bit operating systems access to up to 64 GB of physical memory on current Intel x86 processors (up from 4 GB without PAE) and up to 1,024 GB of physical memory when running on x64 processors in legacy mode (although Windows currently limits this to 64 GB due to the size of the PFN database required to describe so much memory). Since then, Windows has maintained two separate x86 kernels—one that did not support PAE and one that did. Starting with Windows Vista, an x86 Windows installation always installs the PAE kernel even if the system's physical memory is not higher than 4 GB. This allows Microsoft to maintain a single x86 kernel, as the benefits of the non-PAE kernel in terms of performance and memory footprint became negligible (and is required for hardware no-execute support). Thus, we'll describe only x86 PAE address translation. Interested readers can read the relevant section in the sixth edition of this book for the non-PAE case.

Using data structures that the memory manager creates and maintains called *page tables*, the CPU translates virtual addresses into physical addresses. Each page of virtual address space is associated with a system-space structure called a *page table entry* (*PTE*), which contains the physical address to which the virtual one is mapped. For example, Figure 5-15 shows how three consecutive virtual pages might be mapped to three physically discontiguous pages on an x86 system. There may not even be any PTEs for regions that have been marked as reserved or committed but never accessed, because the page table itself might be allocated only when the first page fault occurs. (The dashed line connecting the virtual pages to the PTEs in Figure 5-15 represents the indirect relationship between virtual pages and physical memory.)

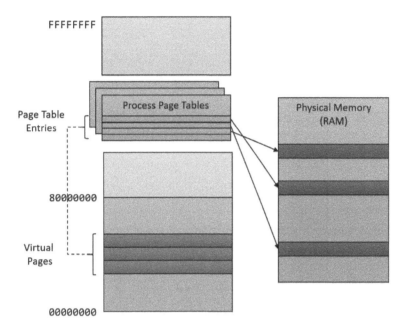

FIGURE 5-15   Mapping virtual addresses to physical memory (x86).

> **Note**   Even kernel-mode code (such as device drivers) cannot reference physical memory addresses directly, but it may do so indirectly by first creating virtual addresses mapped to them. For more information, see the memory descriptor list (MDL) support routines described in the WDK documentation.

The actual translation process and the layout of the page tables and page directories (described shortly), are determined by the CPU. The operating system must follow suit and build the structures correctly in memory for the whole concept to work. Figure 5-16 depicts a general diagram of x86 translation. The general concept, however, is the same for other architectures.

As shown in Figure 5-16, the input to the translation system consists of a 32-bit virtual address (since this is the addressable range with 32 bit) and a bunch of memory-related structures (page tables, page directories, a single page directory pointer table [PDPT], and translation lookaside buffers, all described shortly). The output should be a 36-bit physical address in RAM where the actual byte is located. The number 36 comes from the way the page tables are structured and, as mentioned, dictated by the processor. When mapping small pages (the common case, shown in Figure 5-16), the least significant 12 bits from the virtual address are copied directly to the resulting physical address. 12 bits is exactly 4 KB—the size of a small page.

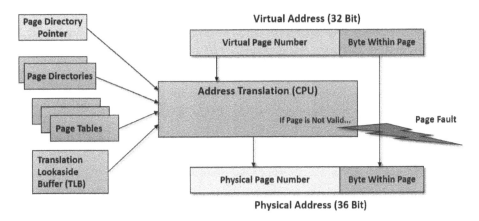

FIGURE 5-16 Virtual address translation overview.

If the address cannot be translated successfully (for example, the page may not be in physical memory but resides in a page file), the CPU throws an exception known as a *page fault* that indicates to the OS that the page cannot be located. Because the CPU has no idea where to find the page (page file, mapped file, or something else), it relies on the OS to get the page from wherever it's located (if possible), fix the page tables to point to it, and request that the CPU tries translation again. (Page faults are described in the section "Page files" later in this chapter.)

Figure 5-17 depicts the entire process of translating x86 virtual to physical addresses.

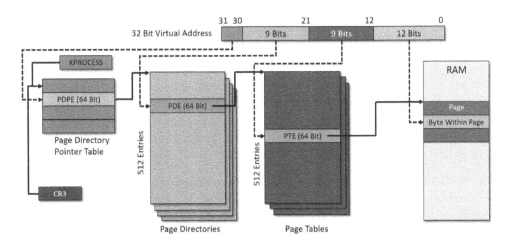

FIGURE 5-17 x86 virtual address translation.

The 32-bit virtual address to be translated is logically segregated into four parts. As you've seen, the lower 12 bits are used as-is to select a specific byte within a page. The translation process starts with a single PDPT per process, which resides in physical memory at all times. (Otherwise, how would the system locate it?) Its physical address is stored in the KPROCESS structure for each process. The special x86 register CR3 stores this value for the currently executing process (that is, one of its threads made the access to the virtual address). This means that when a context switch occurs on a CPU, if the new thread is running under a different process than the old thread, then the CR3 register must be loaded with the new process's page directory pointer address from its KROCESS structure. The PDPT must be aligned on a 32-byte boundary and must furthermore reside in the first 4 GB of RAM (because CR3 on x86 is still a 32-bit register).

Given the layout in Figure 5-17, the sequence of translating a virtual address to a physical one goes as follows:

1. The two most significant bits of the virtual address (bits 30 and 31) provide an index into the PDPT. This table has four entries. The entry selected—the page directory pointer entry (PDPE)—points to the physical address of a page directory.

2. A page directory contains 512 entries, one of which is selected by bits 21 to 29 (9 bits) from the virtual address. The selected page directory entry (PDE) points to the physical address of a page table.

3. A page table also contains 512 entries, one of which is selected by bits 13 to 28 (9 bits) from the virtual address. The selected page table entry (PTE) points to the physical address of the start of the page.

4. The virtual address offset (lower 12 bits) is added to the PTE pointed-to address to give the final physical address requested by the caller.

Every entry value in the various tables is also called a page frame number (PFN) because it points to a page-aligned address. Each entry is 64 bits wide—so the size of a page directory or page table is no larger than a 4 KB page—but only 24 bits are strictly necessary to describe a 64 GB physical range (combined with the 12 bits of the offset for an address range with a total of 36 bits). This means there are more bits than needed for the actual PFN values.

One of the extra bits in particular is paramount to the whole mechanism: the valid bit. This bit indicates whether the PFN data is indeed valid and therefore whether the CPU should execute the procedure just outlined. If the bit is clear, however, it indicates a page fault. The CPU raises an exception and expects the OS to handle the page fault in some meaningful way. For example, if the page in question was previously written to disk, then the memory manager should read it back to a free page in RAM, fix the PTE, and tell the CPU to try again.

Because Windows provides a private address space for each process, each process has its own PDPT, page directories, and page tables to map that process's private address space. However, the page directories and page tables that describe system space are shared among all processes (and session space is shared only among processes in a session). To avoid having multiple page tables describing the same virtual memory, the page directory entries that describe system space are initialized to point to the existing system page tables when a process is created. If the process is part of a session, session space page tables are also shared by pointing the session space page directory entries to the existing session page tables.

Page tables and page table entries

Each PDE points to a page table. A page table is a simple array of PTEs. So, too, is a PDPT. Every page table has 512 entries and each PTE maps a single page (4 KB). This means a page table can map a 2 MB address space (512 x 4 KB). Similarly, a page directory has 512 entries, each pointing to a page table. This means a page directory can map 512 x 2 MB or 1 GB of address space. This makes sense because there are four PDPEs, which together can map the entire 32-bit 4 GB address space.

For large pages, the PDE points with 11 bits to the start of a large page in physical memory, where the byte offset is taken for the low 21 bits of the original virtual address. This means such a PDE mapping a large page does not point to any page table.

The layout of a page directory and page table is essentially the same. You can use the kernel debugger !pte command to examine PTEs. (See the upcoming experiment "Translating addresses.") We'll discuss valid PTEs here and invalid PTEs in the section "Page fault handling." Valid PTEs have two main fields: the PFN of the physical page containing the data or of the physical address of a page in memory, and some flags that describe the state and protection of the page. (See Figure 5-18.)

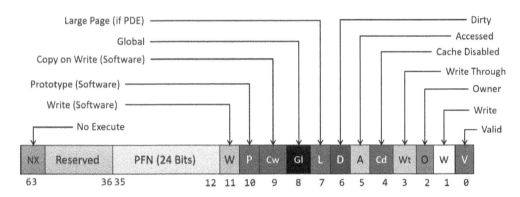

FIGURE 5-18 Valid x86 hardware PTEs.

The bits labeled "Software" and "Reserved" in Figure 5-18 are ignored by the memory management unit (MMU) inside the CPU regardless of whether the PTE is valid. These bits are stored and interpreted by the memory manager. Table 5-10 briefly describes the hardware-defined bits in a valid PTE.

TABLE 5-10 PTE status and protection bits

Name of Bit	Meaning
Accessed	The page has been accessed.
Cache disabled	This disables CPU caching for that page.
Copy-on-write	The page is using copy-on-write (described earlier).

TABLE 5-10   PTE status and protection bits *(continued)*

Name of Bit	Meaning
Dirty	The page has been written to.
Global	Translation applies to all processes. For example, a translation buffer flush won't affect this PTE.
Large page	This indicates that the PDE maps a 2 MB page. (Refer to the section "Large and small pages" earlier in this chapter.)
No execute	This indicates that code cannot execute in the page. (It can be used for data only.)
Owner	This indicates whether user-mode code can access the page or whether the page is limited to kernel-mode access.
Prototype	The PTE is a prototype PTE, which is used as a template to describe shared memory associated with section objects.
Valid	This indicates whether the translation maps to a page in physical memory.
Write through	This marks the page as write-through or, if the processor supports the page attribute table, write-combined. This is typically used to map video frame buffer memory.
Write	This indicates to the MMU whether the page is writable.

On x86 systems, a hardware PTE contains two bits that can be changed by the MMU: the dirty bit and the accessed bit. The MMU sets the accessed bit whenever the page is read or written (provided it is not already set). The MMU sets the dirty bit whenever a write operation occurs to the page. The operating system is responsible for clearing these bits at the appropriate times. They are never cleared by the MMU.

The x86 MMU uses a write bit to provide page protection. When this bit is clear, the page is read-only. When it is set, the page is read/write. If a thread attempts to write to a page with the write bit clear, a memory-management exception occurs. In addition, the memory manager's access fault handler (described later in the section "Page fault handling") must determine whether the thread can be allowed to write to the page (for example, if the page was really marked copy-on-write) or whether an access violation should be generated.

Hardware versus software write bits in page table entries

The additional write bit implemented in software (refer to Table 5-10) is used to force an update of the dirty bit to be synchronized with updates to Windows memory management data. In a simple implementation, the memory manager would set the hardware write bit (bit 1) for any writable page. A write to any such page will cause the MMU to set the dirty bit in the PTE. Later, the dirty bit will tell the memory manager that the contents of that physical page must be written to backing store before the physical page can be used for something else.

In practice, on multiprocessor systems, this can lead to race conditions that are expensive to resolve. At any time, the MMUs of the various processors can set the dirty bit of any PTE that has its hardware write bit set. The memory manager must, at various times, update the process working set list to reflect the state of the dirty bit in a PTE. The memory manager uses a pushlock to synchronize access to the working set list. But on a multiprocessor system, even while one processor is holding the lock, the dirty bit might be changed by MMUs of other CPUs. This raises the possibility of missing an update to a dirty bit.

To avoid this, the Windows memory manager initializes both read-only and writable pages with the hardware write bit (bit 1) of their PTEs set to 0 and records the true writable state of the page in the software write bit (bit 11). On the first write access to such a page, the processor will raise a memory-management exception because the hardware write bit is clear, just as it would be for a true read-only page. In this case, though, the memory manager learns that the page actually *is* writable (via the software write bit), acquires the working set pushlock, sets the dirty bit and the hardware write bit in the PTE, updates the working set list to note that the page has been changed, releases the working set pushlock, and dismisses the exception. The hardware write operation then proceeds as usual, but the setting of the dirty bit is made to happen with the working set list pushlock held.

On subsequent writes to the page, no exceptions occur because the hardware write bit is set. The MMU will redundantly set the dirty bit, but this is benign because the "written-to" state of the page is already recorded in the working set list. Forcing the first write to a page to go through this exception handling may seem to be excessive overhead. However, it happens only once per writable page as long as the page remains valid. Furthermore, the first access to almost any page already goes through memory-management exception handling because pages are usually initialized in the invalid state (the PTE bit 0 is clear). If the first access to a page is also the first write access to the page, the dirty bit handling just described will occur within the handling of the first-access page fault, so the additional overhead is small. Finally, on both uniprocessor and multiprocessor systems, this implementation allows flushing of the translation look-aside buffer (described in the next section) without holding a lock for each page being flushed.

Translation look-aside buffer

As you've learned, each hardware address translation requires three lookups:

- One to find the right entry in the PDPT

- One to find the right entry in the page directory (which provides the location of the page table)

- One to find the right entry in the page table

Because doing three additional memory lookups for every reference to a virtual address would quadruple the required bandwidth to memory, resulting in poor performance, all CPUs cache address translations so that repeated accesses of the same addresses don't have to be repeatedly translated. This cache is an array of associative memory called the *translation lookaside buffer* (*TLB*). Associative memory is a vector whose cells can be read simultaneously and compared to a target value. In the case of the TLB, the vector contains the virtual-to-physical page mappings of the most recently used pages, as shown in Figure 5-19, and the type of page protection, size, attributes, and so on applied to each page. Each entry in the TLB is like a cache entry whose tag holds portions of the virtual address and whose data portion holds a physical page number, protection field, valid bit, and usually a dirty bit indicating the condition of the page to which the cached PTE corresponds. If a PTE's global bit is set (as is done by Windows for system space pages that are visible to all processes), the TLB entry isn't invalidated on process context switches.

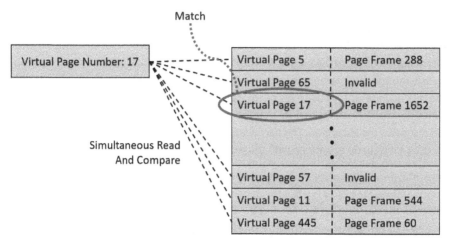

Match

Virtual Page Number: 17		Virtual Page 5	Page Frame 288

Simultaneous Read
And Compare

FIGURE 5-19 Accessing the TLB.

Frequently used virtual addresses are likely to have entries in the TLB, which provides extremely fast virtual-to-physical address translation and, therefore, fast memory access. If a virtual address isn't in the TLB, it might still be in memory, but multiple memory accesses are needed to find it, which makes the access time slightly slower. If a virtual page has been paged out of memory or if the memory manager changes the PTE, the memory manager is required to explicitly invalidate the TLB entry. If a process accesses it again, a page fault occurs, and the memory manager brings the page back into memory (if needed) and re-creates its PTE (which then results in an entry for it in the TLB).

EXPERIMENT: Translating addresses

To clarify how address translation works, this experiment shows an example of translating a virtual address on an x86 PAE system using the available tools in the kernel debugger to examine the PDPT, page directories, page tables, and PTEs. In this example, you'll work with a process that has virtual address 0x3166004, currently mapped to a valid physical address. In later examples, you'll see how to follow address translation for invalid addresses with the kernel debugger.

First convert 0x3166004 to binary and break it into the three fields used to translate an address. In binary, 0x3166004 is 11.0001.0110.0110.0000.0000.0100. Breaking it into the component fields yields the following:

31 30 29	21 20	12 11	0
00	00.0011.000	1.0110.0110	0000.0000.0100
Page Directory Pointer Index (0)	Page Directory Index (24)	Page Table Index (0x166 or 358)	Byte Offset (4)

To start the translation process, the CPU needs the physical address of the process's PDPT. This is found in the CR3 register while a thread in that process is running. You can display this address by looking at the `DirBase` field in the output of the `!process` command, as shown here:

```
lkd> !process -1 0
PROCESS 99aa3040  SessionId: 2  Cid: 1690     Peb: 03159000  ParentCid: 0920
    DirBase: 01024800  ObjectTable: b3b386c0  HandleCount: <Data Not Accessible>
    Image: windbg.exe
```

The `DirBase` field shows that the PDPT is at physical address 0x1024800. As shown in the preceding illustration, the PDPT index field in the sample virtual address is 0. Therefore, the PDPT entry that contains the physical address of the relevant page directory is the first entry in the PDPT, at physical address 0x1024800.

The kernel debugger `!pte` command displays the PDE and PTE that describe a virtual address, as shown here:

```
lkd> !pte 3166004
                     VA 03166004
PDE at C06000C0         PTE at C0018B30
contains 0000000056238867  contains 800000005DE61867
pfn 56238     ---DA--UWEV pfn 5de61     ---DA--UW-V
```

The debugger does not show the PDPT, but it is easy to display given its physical address:

```
lkd> !dq 01024800 L4
# 1024800 00000000'53c88801 00000000'53c89801
# 1024810 00000000'53c8a801 00000000'53c8d801
```

Here we have used the debugger extension command `!dq`. This is similar to the `dq` command (display as quadwords—64 bit values) but lets us examine memory by physical rather than virtual address. Because we know the PDPT is only four entries long, we added the L 4 length argument to keep the output uncluttered.

As illustrated, the PDPT index (the two most significant bits) from the sample virtual address equal 0, so the PDPT entry you want is the first displayed quadword. PDPT entries have a format similar to PDEs and PTEs, so you can see that this one contains a PFN of 0x53c88 (always page-aligned), for a physical address of 0x53c88000. That's the physical address of the page directory.

The `!pte` output shows the PDE address 0xC06000C0 as a virtual address, not physical. On x86 systems, the first process page directory starts at virtual address 0xC0600000. In this case, the PDE address is 0xC0—that is, 8 bytes (the size of an entry) times 24 added to the page directory start address. Therefore, the page directory index field of the sample virtual address is 24. That means you're looking at the 25th PDE in the page directory.

The PDE provides the PFN of the needed page table. In this example, the PFN is 0x56238, so the page table starts at physical address 0x56238000. To this the MMU will add the page table index field (0x166) from the virtual address multiplied by 8 (the size of a PTE in bytes). The resulting physical address of the PTE is 0x56238B30.

The debugger shows that this PTE is at *virtual* address 0xC0018B30. Notice that the byte offset portion (0xB30) is the same as that from the physical address, as is always the case in address translation. Because the memory manager maps page tables starting at 0xC0000000, adding 0xB30 to 0xC0018000 (the 0x18 is entry 24 as you've seen) yields the virtual address shown in the kernel debugger output: 0xC0018B30. The debugger shows that the PFN field of the PTE is 0x5DE61.

Finally, you can consider the byte offset from the original address. As described, the MMU concatenates the byte offset to the PFN from the PTE, giving a physical address of 0x5DE61004. This is the physical address that corresponds to the original virtual address of 0x3166004...at the moment.

The flags bits from the PTE are interpreted to the right of the PFN number. For example, the PTE that describes the page being referenced has flags of ---DA--UW-V. Here, A stands for accessed (the page has been read), U for user-mode accessible (as opposed to kernel-mode accessible only), W for writable page (rather than just readable), and V for valid (the PTE represents a valid page in physical memory).

To confirm the calculation of the physical address, look at the memory in question via both its virtual and its physical addresses. First, using the debugger's dd (display dwords) command on the virtual address, you see the following:

```
1kd> dd 3166004 L 10
03166004   00000034 00000006 00003020 0000004e
03166014   00000000 00020020 0000a000 00000014
```

And with the !dd command on the physical address just computed, you see the same contents:

```
1kd> !dd 5DE61004 L 10
#5DE61004 00000034 00000006 00003020 0000004e
#5DE61014 00000000 00020020 0000a000 00000014
```

You could similarly compare the displays from the virtual and physical addresses of the PTE and PDE.

x64 virtual address translation

Address translation on x64 is similar to x86, but with a fourth level added. Each process has a top-level extended page directory called the *page map level 4 table* that contains the physical locations of 512 third-level structures, called *page directory pointers*. The page parent directory is analogous to the x86 PAE PDPT, but there are 512 of them instead of just one, and each page parent directory is an entire page containing 512 entries instead of just four. Like the PDPT, the page parent directory's entries contain the physical locations of second-level page directories, each of which in turn contains 512 entries providing the locations of the individual page tables. Finally, the page tables, each of which contains 512 page table entries, contain the physical locations of the pages in memory. All the "physical locations" in the preceding description are stored in these structures as PFNs.

Current implementations of the x64 architecture limit virtual addresses to 48 bits. The components that make up this 48-bit virtual address and the connection between the components for translation purposes are shown in Figure 5-20, and the format of an x64 hardware PTE is shown in Figure 5-21.

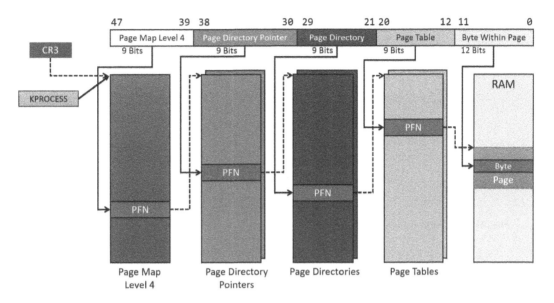

FIGURE 5-20   x64 address translation.

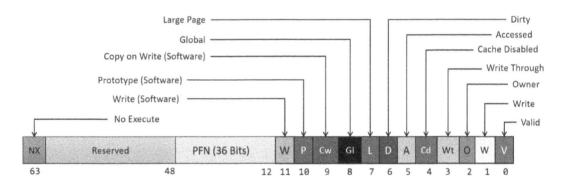

FIGURE 5-21   x64 hardware PTE.

ARM virtual address translation

Virtual address translation on ARM 32-bit processors uses a single page directory with 1,024 entries, each 32 bits in size. The translation structures are shown in Figure 5-22.

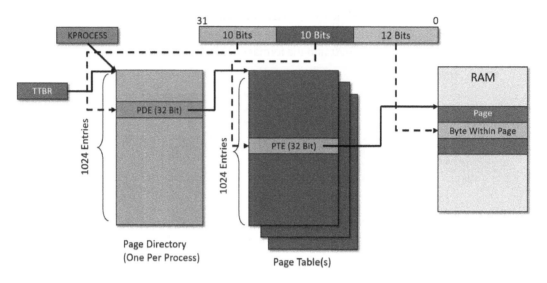

FIGURE 5-22 ARM virtual address translation structures.

Every process has a single page directory, with its physical address stored in the TTBR register (similar to the CR3 x86/x64 register). The 10 most significant bits of the virtual address select a PDE that may point to one of 1,024 page tables. A specific PTE is selected by the next 10 bits of the virtual address. Each valid PTE points to the start of a page in physical memory, where the offset is given by the lower 12 bits of the address (just as in the x86 and x64 cases). The scheme in Figure 5-22 suggests that the addressable physical memory is 4 GB because each PTE is smaller (32 bits) than the x86/x64 case (64 bits), and indeed only 20 bits are used for the PFN. ARM processors do support a PAE mode (similar to x86), but Windows does not use this functionality. Future Windows versions may support the ARM 64-bit architecture, which will alleviate the physical address limitations as well as dramatically increase the virtual address space for processes and the system.

Curiously, the layout of valid PTE, PDE, and large page PDE are not the same. Figure 5-23 shows the layout of a valid PTE for ARMv7, currently used by Windows. For more information, consult the official ARM documentation.

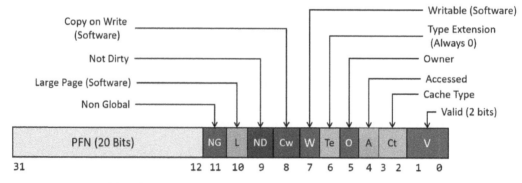

FIGURE 5-23 ARM valid PTE layout.

Page fault handling

Earlier, you saw how address translations are resolved when the PTE is valid. When the PTE valid bit is clear, this indicates that the desired page is for some reason not currently accessible to the process. This section describes the types of invalid PTEs and how references to them are resolved.

 Note   Only the 32-bit x86 PTE formats are detailed in this section. PTEs for 64-bit and ARM systems contain similar information, but their detailed layout is not presented.

A reference to an invalid page is called a *page fault*. The kernel trap handler (see the section "Trap dispatching" in Chapter 8 in Part 2) dispatches this kind of fault to the memory manager fault handler function, MmAccessFault, to resolve. This routine runs in the context of the thread that incurred the fault and is responsible for attempting to resolve the fault (if possible) or raise an appropriate exception. These faults can be caused by a variety of conditions, as listed in Table 5-11.

TABLE 5-11   Reasons for access faults

Reason for Fault	Result
Corrupt PTE/PDE	Bug-check (crash) the system with code 0x1A (MEMORY_MANAGEMENT).
Accessing a page that isn't resident in memory but is on disk in a page file or a mapped file	Allocate a physical page and read the desired page from disk and into the relevant working set.
Accessing a page that is on the standby or modified list	Transition the page to the relevant process, session, or system working set.
Accessing a page that isn't committed (for example, reserved address space or address space that isn't allocated)	Access violation exception.
Accessing a page from user mode that can be accessed only in kernel mode	Access violation exception.
Writing to a page that is read-only	Access violation exception.
Accessing a demand-zero page	Add a zero-filled page to the relevant working set.
Writing to a guard page	Guard-page violation (if there is a reference to a user-mode stack, perform automatic stack expansion).
Writing to a copy-on-write page	Make a process-private (or session-private) copy of the page and use it to replace the original in the process, session, or system working set.
Writing to a page that is valid but hasn't been written to the current backing store copy	Set the dirty bit in the PTE.
Executing code in a page that is marked as no execute	Access violation exception.
PTE permissions don't match enclave permissions (see the section "Memory enclaves" later in this chapter and the Windows SDK documentation for the CreateEnclave function)	User mode: access violation exception. Kernel mode: bug-check with code 0x50 (PAGE_FAULT_IN_NONPAGED_AREA).

The following section describes the four basic kinds of invalid PTEs that are processed by the access fault handler. Following that is an explanation of a special case of invalid PTEs, called *prototype PTEs*, which are used to implement shareable pages.

Invalid PTEs

If the valid bit of a PTE encountered during address translation is zero, the PTE represents an invalid page—one that will raise a memory-management exception, or page fault, upon reference. The MMU ignores the remaining bits of the PTE, so the operating system can use these bits to store information about the page that will assist in resolving the page fault.

The following list details the four kinds of invalid PTEs and their structure. These are often referred to as *software PTEs* because they are interpreted by the memory manager rather than the MMU. Some of the flags are the same as those for a hardware PTE, as described in Table 5-10, and some of the bit fields have either the same or similar meanings to corresponding fields in the hardware PTE.

- **Page file**   The desired page resides within a paging file. As illustrated in Figure 5-24, 4 bits in the PTE indicate in which of 16 possible page files the page resides, and 32 bits provide the page number within the file. The pager initiates an in-page operation to bring the page into memory and make it valid. The page file offset is always non-zero and never all ones (that is, the very first and last pages in the page file are not used for paging) to allow for other formats, described next.

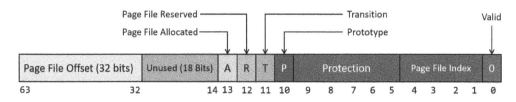

FIGURE 5-24   A PTE representing a page in a page file.

- **Demand zero**   This PTE format is the same as the page file PTE shown in the previous entry but the page file offset is zero. The desired page must be satisfied with a page of zeroes. The pager looks at the zero page list. If the list is empty, the pager takes a page from the free list and zeroes it. If the free list is also empty, it takes a page from one of the standby lists and zeroes it.

- **Virtual Address Descriptor**   This PTE format is the same as the page file PTE shown previously but in this case the page file offset field is all one. This indicates a page whose definition and backing store, if any, can be found in the process's Virtual Address Descriptor (VAD) tree. This format is used for pages that are backed by sections in mapped files. The pager finds the VAD that defines the virtual address range encompassing the virtual page and initiates an in-page operation from the mapped file referenced by the VAD. (VADs are described in more detail in the section "Virtual address descriptors" later in this chapter.)

- **Transition**   The transition bit is one. The desired page is in memory on either the standby, modified, or modified-no-write list or not on any list. The pager will remove the page from the list (if it is on one) and add it to the process working set. This is known as a *soft page fault* because no I/O is involved.

- **Unknown**   The PTE is zero or the page table doesn't yet exist. (The PDE that would provide the physical address of the page table contains zero.) In both cases, the memory manager must examine the VADs to determine whether this virtual address has been committed. If so, page tables are built to represent the newly committed address space. If not—that is, if the page is reserved or hasn't been defined at all—the page fault is reported as an access violation exception.

Prototype PTEs

If a page can be shared between two processes, the memory manager uses a software structure called *prototype page table entries* (*prototype PTEs*) to map these potentially shared pages. For page-file–backed sections, an array of prototype PTEs is created when a section object is first created. For mapped files, portions of the array are created on demand as each view is mapped. These prototype PTEs are part of the segment structure (described in the section "Section objects" later in this chapter).

When a process first references a page mapped to a view of a section object (recall that VADs are created only when the view is mapped), the memory manager uses the information in the prototype PTE to fill in the real PTE used for address translation in the process page table. When a shared page is made valid, both the process PTE and the prototype PTE point to the physical page containing the data. To track the number of process PTEs that reference a valid shared page, a counter in its PFN database entry is incremented. Thus, the memory manager can determine when a shared page is no longer referenced by any page table and thus can be made invalid and moved to a transition list or written out to disk.

When a shareable page is invalidated, the PTE in the process page table is filled in with a special PTE that points to the prototype PTE that describes the page, as shown in Figure 5-25. Thus, when the page is accessed, the memory manager can locate the prototype PTE using the information encoded in this PTE, which in turn describes the page being referenced.

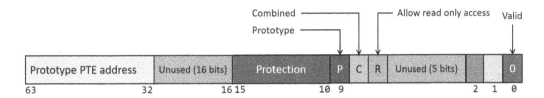

FIGURE 5-25 Structure of an invalid PTE that points to the prototype PTE.

A shared page can be in one of six different states, as described by the prototype PTE:

- **Active/valid** The page is in physical memory because of another process that accessed it.

- **Transition** The desired page is in memory on the standby or modified list (or not on any list).

- **Modified-no-write** The desired page is in memory and on the modified-no-write list. (Refer to Table 5-11.)

- **Demand zero** The desired page should be satisfied with a page of zeroes.

- **Page file** The desired page resides within a page file.

- **Mapped file** The desired page resides within a mapped file.

Although the format of these prototype PTEs is the same as that of the real PTEs described earlier, the prototype PTEs aren't used for address translation. They are a layer between the page table and the PFN database and never appear directly in page tables.

By having all the accessors of a potentially shared page point to a prototype PTE to resolve faults, the memory manager can manage shared pages without needing to update the page tables of each process sharing the page. For example, a shared code or data page might be paged out to disk at some point. When the memory manager retrieves the page from disk, it needs only to update the prototype PTE to point to the page's new physical location. The PTEs in each of the processes sharing the page remain the same, with the valid bit clear and still pointing to the prototype PTE. Later, as processes reference the page, the real PTE will get updated.

Figure 5-26 illustrates two virtual pages in a mapped view. One is valid and the other is invalid. As shown, the first page is valid and is pointed to by the process PTE and the prototype PTE. The second page is in the paging file—the prototype PTE contains its exact location. The process PTE (and any other processes with that page mapped) points to this prototype PTE.

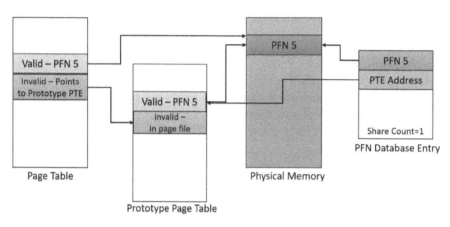

FIGURE 5-26 Prototype page table entries.

In-paging I/O

In-paging I/O occurs when a read operation must be issued to a file (paging or mapped) to satisfy a page fault. Also, because page tables are themselves pageable, the processing of a page fault can incur additional I/O if necessary when the system is loading the page table page that contains the PTE or the prototype PTE that describes the original page being referenced.

The in-page I/O operation is synchronous—that is, the thread waits on an event until the I/O completes—and isn't interruptible by asynchronous procedure call (APC) delivery. The pager uses a special modifier in the I/O request function to indicate paging I/O. Upon completion of paging I/O, the I/O system triggers an event, which wakes up the pager and allows it to continue in-page processing.

While the paging I/O operation is in progress, the faulting thread doesn't own any critical memory management synchronization objects. Other threads within the process can issue virtual memory functions and handle page faults while the paging I/O takes place. But there are a few interesting conditions that the pager must recognize when the I/O completes are exposed:

- Another thread in the same process or a different process could have faulted the same page (called a *collided page fault* and described in the next section).

- The page could have been deleted and remapped from the virtual address space.

- The protection on the page could have changed.

- The fault could have been for a prototype PTE, and the page that maps the prototype PTE could be out of the working set.

The pager handles these conditions by saving enough state on the thread's kernel stack before the paging I/O request such that when the request is complete, it can detect these conditions and, if necessary, dismiss the page fault without making the page valid. When and if the faulting instruction is reissued, the pager is again invoked and the PTE is reevaluated in its new state.

Collided page faults

The case when another thread in the same process or a different process faults a page that is currently being in-paged is known as a *collided page fault*. The pager detects and handles collided page faults optimally because they are common occurrences in multithreaded systems. If another thread or process faults the same page, the pager detects the collided page fault, noticing that the page is in transition and that a read is in progress. (This information is in the PFN database entry.) In this case, the pager may issue a wait operation on the event specified in the PFN database entry. Alternatively, it can choose to issue a parallel I/O to protect the file systems from deadlocks. (The first I/O to complete "wins," and the others are discarded.) This event was initialized by the thread that first issued the I/O needed to resolve the fault.

When the I/O operation completes, all threads waiting on the event have their wait satisfied. The first thread to acquire the PFN database lock is responsible for performing the in-page completion operations. These operations consist of checking I/O status to ensure that the I/O operation completed successfully, clearing the read-in-progress bit in the PFN database, and updating the PTE.

When subsequent threads acquire the PFN database lock to complete the collided page fault, the pager recognizes that the initial updating has been performed because the read-in-progress bit is clear and checks the in-page error flag in the PFN database element to ensure that the in-page I/O completed successfully. If the in-page error flag is set, the PTE isn't updated, and an in-page error exception is raised in the faulting thread.

Clustered page faults

The memory manager prefetches large clusters of pages to satisfy page faults and populate the system cache. The prefetch operations read data directly into the system's page cache instead of into a working set in virtual memory. Therefore, the prefetched data does not consume virtual address space, and the size of the fetch operation is not limited to the amount of virtual address space that is available.

Also, no expensive TLB-flushing inter-processor interrupt (IPI) is needed if the page will be repurposed. The prefetched pages are put on the standby list and marked as in transition in the PTE. If a prefetched page is subsequently referenced, the memory manager adds it to the working set. However, if it is never referenced, no system resources are required to release it. If any pages in the prefetched cluster are already in memory, the memory manager does not read them again. Instead, it uses a dummy page to represent them so that an efficient single large I/O can still be issued, as shown in Figure 5-27.

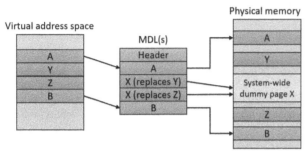

Pages Y and Z are already in memory, so the corresponding
MDL entries point to the system-wide dummy page

FIGURE 5-27 Usage of dummy page during virtual-address-to-physical-address mapping in an MDL.

In the figure, the file offsets and virtual addresses that correspond to pages A, Y, Z, and B are logically contiguous, although the physical pages themselves are not necessarily contiguous. Pages A and B are nonresident, so the memory manager must read them. Pages Y and Z are already resident in memory, so it is not necessary to read them. (In fact, they might already have been modified since they were last read in from their backing store, in which case it would be a serious error to overwrite their contents.) However, reading pages A and B in a single operation is more efficient than performing one read for page A and a second read for page B. Therefore, the memory manager issues a single read request that comprises all four pages (A, Y, Z, and B) from the backing store. Such a read request includes as many pages as it makes sense to read, based on the amount of available memory, the current system usage, and so on.

When the memory manager builds the MDL that describes the request, it supplies valid pointers to pages A and B. However, the entries for pages Y and Z point to a single system-wide dummy page X. The memory manager can fill the dummy page X with the potentially stale data from the backing store because it does not make X visible. However, if a component accesses the Y and Z offsets in the MDL, it sees the dummy page X instead of Y and Z.

The memory manager can represent any number of discarded pages as a single dummy page, and that page can be embedded multiple times in the same MDL or even in multiple concurrent MDLs that are being used for different drivers. Consequently, the contents of the locations that represent the discarded pages can change at any time. (See Chapter 6 for more on MDLs.)

Page files

Page files store modified pages that are still in use by some process but have had to be written to disk because they were unmapped or memory pressure resulted in a trim. Page file space is reserved when the pages are initially committed, but the actual optimally clustered page file locations cannot be chosen until pages are written out to disk.

When the system boots, the Session Manager process (Smss.exe) reads the list of page files to open by examining the HKLM\SYSTEM\CurrentControlSet\Control\Session Manager\Memory Management\ PagingFiles registry value. This multistring registry value contains the name, minimum size, and maximum size of each paging file. Windows supports up to 16 paging files on x86 and x64 and up to 2 page files on ARM. On x86 and x64 systems, each page file can be up to 16 TB in size, while the maximum is 4 GB on ARM systems. Once open, the page files can't be deleted while the system is running because the System process maintains an open handle to each page file.

Because the page file contains parts of process and kernel virtual memory, for security reasons, the system can be configured to clear the page file at system shutdown. To enable this, set the `ClearPage-FileAtShutdown` registry value in the HKLM\SYSTEM\CurrentControlSet\Control\Session Manager\ Memory Management key to 1. Otherwise, after shutdown, the page file will contain whatever data happened to have been paged out while the system was up. This data could then be accessed by someone who gained physical access to the machine.

If the minimum and maximum paging file sizes are both zero (or not specified), this indicates a system-managed paging file. Windows 7 and Server 2008 R2 used a simple scheme based on RAM size alone as follows:

- **Minimum size**   Set to the amount of RAM or 1 GB, whichever is larger
- **Maximum size**   Set to 3 * RAM or 4 GB, whichever is larger

These settings are not ideal. For example, today's laptops and desktop machines can easily have 32 GB or 64 GB of RAM, and server machines can have hundreds of gigabytes of RAM. Setting the initial page file size to the size of RAM may result in a considerable loss of disk space, especially if disk sizes are relatively small and based on solid-state device (SSD). Furthermore, the amount of RAM in a system is not necessarily indicative of the typical memory workload on that system.

The current implementation uses a more elaborate scheme to derive a "good" minimum page file size based not only on RAM size, but also on page file history usage and other factors. As part of page-file creation and initialization, Smss.exe calculates page file minimum sizes based on four factors, stored in global variables:

- **RAM (`SmpDesiredPfSizeBasedOnRAM`)**   This is the recommended page file size based on RAM.
- **Crash dump (`SmpDesiredPfSizeForCrashDump`)**   This is the recommended page file size needed to be able to store a crash dump.
- **History (`SmpDesiredPfSizeBasedOnHistory`)**   This is the recommended page file size based on usage history. Smss.exe uses a timer that triggers once an hour and records the page file usage.

- **Apps (SmpDesiredPfSizeForApps)** This is the recommended page file for Windows apps.

- These values are computed as shown in Table 5-12.

TABLE 5-12 Base calculation for page file size recommendation

Recommendation Base	Recommended Page File Size
RAM	If RAM <= 1 GB, then size = 1 GB. If RAM > 1 GB, then add 1/8 GB for every extra gigabyte of RAM, up to a maximum of 32 GB.

Crash dump	If a dedicated dump file is configured, then no page file is required for storing a dump file, and the size = 0. (You can configure this for a dedicated dump file by adding the value DedicatedDumpFile in the HKLM\System\CurrentControlSet\Control\CrashControl key.) If the dump type configured is set to Automatic (the default), then:
	    If RAM < 4 GB, then size = RAM / 6.
	    Otherwise, size = 2/3 GB + 1/8 GB for each extra gigabyte above 4 GB, capped to 32 GB.
	If there was a recent crash for which the page file was not large enough, then recommended size is increased to RAM size or 32 GB, whichever is smaller.
	If a full dump is configured, returned size = RAM size plus additional information size present in a dump file.
	If a kernel dump is configured, then size = RAM.

History	If enough samples have been logged, returns the 90th percentile as the recommended size. Otherwise, returns the size based on RAM (above).
Apps	If it's a server, return zero. The recommended size is based on a factor that the Process Lifecycle Manager (PLM) uses to determine when to terminate an app. Current factor is 2.3 * RAM, which was considered with RAM = 1 GB (rough minimum for mobile devices). The recommended size (based on the mentioned factor) is around 2.5 GB. If this is more than RAM, RAM is subtracted. Otherwise, zero is returned.

The maximum page file size for a system-managed size is set at three times the size of RAM or 4 GB, whichever is larger. The minimum (initial) page file size is determined as follows:

- If it's the first system-managed page file, then the base size is set based on page file history (refer to Table 5-12). Otherwise, the base size is based on RAM.

- If it's the first system-managed page file:

  - If the base size is smaller than the computed page file size for apps (SmpDesiredPfSizeForApps), then set the new base as the size computed for apps (refer to Table 5-12).

  - If the (new) base size is smaller than the computed size for crash dumps (SmpDesiredPfSizeForCrashDump), then set the new base to be the size computed for crash dumps.

EXPERIMENT: Viewing page files

To view the list of page files, look in the registry at the PagingFiles value in the HKLM\SYSTEM\CurrentControlSet\Control\Session Manager\Memory Management key. This entry contains the paging file configuration settings modified through the Advanced System Settings dialog box. To access these settings, follow these steps:

1. Open Control Panel.

2. Click **System and Security** and then click **System**. This opens the System Properties dialog box, which you can also access by right-clicking on **Computer** in Explorer and selecting **Properties**.

3. Click **Advanced System Settings**.

4. In the Performance area, click **Settings**. This opens the Performance Options dialog box.

5. Click the **Advanced** tab.

6. In the Virtual Memory area, click **Change**.

EXPERIMENT: Viewing page file recommended sizes

To view the actual variables calculated in Table 5-12, follow these steps (this experiment was done using an x86 Windows 10 system):

1. Start local kernel debugging.

2. Locate Smss.exe processes:

```
1kd> !process 0 0 smss.exe
PROCESS 8e54bc40  SessionId: none  Cid: 0130    Peb: 02bab000  ParentCid:
0004
    DirBase: bffe0020  ObjectTable: 8a767640  HandleCount: <Data Not
Accessible>
    Image: smss.exe

PROCESS 9985bc40  SessionId: 1  Cid: 01d4    Peb: 02f9c000  ParentCid: 0130
    DirBase: bffe0080  ObjectTable: 00000000  HandleCount:   0.
    Image: smss.exe

PROCESS a122dc40  SessionId: 2  Cid: 02a8    Peb: 02fcd000  ParentCid: 0130
    DirBase: bffe0320  ObjectTable: 00000000  HandleCount:   0.
    Image: smss.exe
```

3. Locate the first one (with a session ID of none), which is the master Smss.exe. (Refer to Chapter 2 for more details.)

4. Switch the debugger context to that process:

```
1kd> .process /r /p 8e54bc40
Implicit process is now 8e54bc40
Loading User Symbols
..
```

5. Show the four variables described in the previous section. (Each one is 64 bits in size.)

```
1kd> dq smss!SmpDesiredPfSizeBasedOnRAM L1
00974cd0  00000000'4fff1a00
```

```
1kd> dq smss!SmpDesiredPfSizeBasedOnHistory L1
00974cd8  00000000'05a24700
1kd> dq smss!SmpDesiredPfSizeForCrashDump L1
00974cc8  00000000'1ffecd55
1kd> dq smss!SmpDesiredPfSizeForApps L1
00974ce0  00000000'00000000
```

6. Because there is a single volume (C:\) on this machine, a single page file would be cre-
    ated. Assuming it wasn't specifically configured, it would be system managed. You can
    look at the actual file size of C:\PageFile.Sys on disk or use the !vm debugger command:

```
1kd> !vm 1
Page File: \??\C:\pagefile.sys
  Current:      524288 Kb  Free Space:      524280 Kb
  Minimum:      524288 Kb  Maximum:        8324476 Kb
Page File: \??\C:\swapfile.sys
  Current:      262144 Kb  Free Space:      262136 Kb
  Minimum:      262144 Kb  Maximum:        4717900 Kb
No Name for Paging File
  Current:   11469744 Kb  Free Space:    11443108 Kb
  Minimum:   11469744 Kb  Maximum:       11469744 Kb
...
```

Notice the minimum size of C:\PageFlle.sys (524288 KB). (We'll discuss the other page file
entries in the next section). According to the variables, `SmpDesiredPfSizeForCrashDump` is the
largest, so must be the determining factor (0x1FFECD55 = 524211 KB), which is very close to the
listed value. (Page file sizes round up to multiple of 64 MB.)

To add a new page file, Control Panel uses the internal `NtCreatePagingFile` system service defined
in Ntdll.dll. (This requires the `SeCreatePagefilePrivilege`.) Page files are always created as non-
compressed files, even if the directory they are in is compressed. Their names are *PageFile.Sys* (except
some special ones described in the next section). They are created in the root of partitions with the
Hidden file attribute so they are not immediately visible. To keep new page files from being deleted, a
handle is duplicated into the `System` process so that even after the creating process closes the handle
to the new page file, a handle is nevertheless always open to it.

The swap file

In the UWP apps world, when an app goes to the background—for example, it is minimized—the
threads in that process are suspended so that the process does not consume any CPU. The private
physical memory used by the process can potentially be reused for other processes. If memory pressure is high, the private working set (physical memory used by the process) may be swapped out to disk
to allow the physical memory to be used for other processes.

Windows 8 added another page file called a *swap file*. It is essentially same as a normal page file
but is used exclusively for UWP apps. It's created on client SKUs only if at least one normal page file
was created (the normal case). Its name is *SwapFile.sys* and it resides in the system root partition—for
example, C:\SwapFile.Sys.

After the normal page files are created, the HKLM\System\CurrentControlSet\Control\Session Manager\Memory Management registry key is consulted. If a DWORD value named SwapFileControl exists and its value is zero, swap file creation is aborted. If a value named SwapFile exists, it's read as a string with the same format as a normal page file, with a filename, an initial size, and a maximum size. The difference is that a value of zero for the sizes is interpreted as no swap file creation. These two registry values do not exist by default, which results in the creation of a SwapFile.sys file on the system root partition with a minimum size of 16 MB on fast (and small) disks (for example, SSD) or 256 MB on slow (or large SSD) disks. The maximum size of the swap file is set to 1.5 * RAM or 10 percent of the system root partition size, whichever is smaller. See Chapter 7 in this book and Chapter 8, "System mechanisms," and Chapter 9, "Management mechanisms," in Part 2 for more on UWP apps.

Note The swap file is not counted against the maximum page files supported.

The virtual page file

The !vm debugger command hints at another page file called "No Name for Paging File." This is a virtual page file. As the name suggests, it has no actual file, but is used indirectly as the backing store for memory compression (described later in this chapter in the section "Memory compression"). It is large, but its size is set arbitrarily as not to run out of free space. The invalid PTEs for pages that have been compressed point to this virtual page file and allow the memory compression store to get to the compressed data when needed by interpreting the bits in the invalid PTE leading to the correct store, region, and index.

EXPERIMENT: Viewing swap file and virtual page file information

The !vm debugger command shows the information on all page files, including the swap file and the virtual page file:

```
1kd> !vm 1
Page File: \??\C:\pagefile.sys
  Current:     524288 Kb  Free Space:      524280 Kb
  Minimum:     524288 Kb  Maximum:        8324476 Kb
Page File: \??\C:\swapfile.sys
  Current:     262144 Kb  Free Space:      262136 Kb
  Minimum:     262144 Kb  Maximum:        4717900 Kb
No Name for Paging File
  Current:   11469744 Kb  Free Space:    11443108 Kb
  Minimum:   11469744 Kb  Maximum:       11469744 Kb
```

On this system, the swap file minimum size is 256 MB, as the system is a Windows 10 virtual machine. (The VHD behind the disk is considered a slow disk.) The maximum size of the swap file is about 4.5 GB, as the RAM on the system is 3 GB and disk partition size is 64 GB (the minimum of 4.5 GB and 6.4 GB).

Commit charge and the system commit limit

We are now in a position to more thoroughly discuss the concepts of commit charge and the system commit limit.

Whenever virtual address space is created—for example, by a `VirtualAlloc` (for committed memory) or `MapViewOfFile` call—the system must ensure that there is room to store it, either in RAM or in backing store, before successfully completing the create request. For mapped memory (other than sections mapped to the page file), the file associated with the mapping object referenced by the `MapViewOfFile` call provides the required backing store. All other virtual allocations rely on system-managed shared resources for storage: RAM and the paging file(s). The purpose of the system commit limit and commit charge is to track all uses of these resources to ensure they are never overcommitted—that is, that there is never more virtual address space defined than there is space to store its contents, either in RAM or in backing store (on disk).

> **Note** This section makes frequent references to paging files. It is possible (though not generally recommended) to run Windows without any paging files. Essentially, this means that when RAM is exhausted, there is no room to grow and memory allocations fail, generating a blue screen. You can consider every reference to paging files here to be qualified by "if one or more paging files exist."

Conceptually, the system commit limit represents the total committed virtual address space that can be created in addition to virtual allocations that are associated with their own backing store—that is, in addition to sections mapped to files. Its numeric value is simply the amount of RAM available to Windows plus the current sizes of any page files. If a page file is expanded or new page files are created, the commit limit increases accordingly. If no page files exist, the system commit limit is simply the total amount of RAM available to Windows.

Commit charge is the system-wide total of all committed memory allocations that must be kept in either RAM or in a paging file. From the name, it should be apparent that one contributor to commit charge is process-private committed virtual address space. However, there are many other contributors, some of them not so obvious.

Windows also maintains a per-process counter called the *process page file quota*. Many of the allocations that contribute to commit charge also contribute to the process page file quota. This represents each process's private contribution to the system commit charge. Note, however, that this does not represent current page file usage. It represents the potential or maximum page file usage, should all these allocations have to be stored there.

The following types of memory allocations contribute to the system commit charge and, in many cases, to the process page file quota. (Some of these will be described in detail in later sections of this chapter.)

- **Private committed memory** This is memory allocated with the `VirtualAlloc` call with the `MEM_COMMIT` option. This is the most common type of contributor to the commit charge. These allocations are also charged to the process page file quota.

- **Page-file-backed mapped memory**   This is memory allocated with a `MapViewOfFile` call that references a section object, which in turn is not associated with a file. The system uses a portion of the page file as the backing store instead. These allocations are not charged to the process page file quota.

- **Copy-on-write regions of mapped memory (even if it is associated with ordinary mapped files)**   The mapped file provides backing store for its own unmodified content. However, should a page in the copy-on-write region be modified, it can no longer use the original mapped file for backing store. It must be kept in RAM or in a paging file. These allocations are not charged to the process page file quota.

- **Non-paged and paged pool and other allocations in system space that are not backed by explicitly associated files**   Even the currently free regions of the system memory pools contribute to commit charge. The non-pageable regions are counted in the commit charge even though they will never be written to the page file because they permanently reduce the amount of RAM available for private pageable data. These allocations are not charged to the process page file quota.

- **Kernel stacks**   Threads' stacks when executing in kernel mode.

- **Page tables**   Most of these are themselves pageable, and they are not backed by mapped files. However, even if they are not pageable, they occupy RAM. Therefore, the space required for them contributes to commit charge.

- **Space for page tables that are not yet actually allocated**   As you'll see, where large areas of virtual space have been defined but not yet referenced (for example, private committed virtual space), the system need not actually create page tables to describe it. However, the space for these as-yet-nonexistent page tables is charged to commit charge to ensure that the page tables can be created when they are needed.

- **Allocations of physical memory made via the Address Windowing Extension (AWE) APIs**   As discussed previously, consume physical memory directly.

For many of these items, the commit charge may represent the potential use of storage rather than its actual use. For example, a page of private committed memory does not actually occupy either a physical page of RAM or the equivalent page file space until it's been referenced at least once. Until then, it is a *demand-zero page* (described later). But commit charge accounts for such pages when the virtual space is first created. This ensures that when the page is later referenced, actual physical storage space will be available for it.

A region of a file mapped as copy-on-write has a similar requirement. Until the process writes to the region, all pages in it are backed by the mapped file. However, the process may write to any of the pages in the region at any time. When that happens, those pages are thereafter treated as private to the process. Their backing store is, thereafter, the page file. Charging the system commit for them when the region is first created ensures that there will be private storage for them later, if and when the write accesses occur.

A particularly interesting case occurs when reserving private memory and later committing it. When the reserved region is created with `VirtualAlloc`, system commit charge is not charged for the actual virtual region. On Windows 8 and Server 2012 and earlier versions, it is charged for any new page table pages that will be required to describe the region, even though these might not yet exist or even be eventually needed. Starting with Windows 8.1 and Server 2012 R2, page table hierarchies for reserved regions are not charged immediately; this means that huge reserved memory regions can be allocated without exhausting page tables. This becomes important in some security features, such as Control Flow Guard (CFG, see Chapter 7 for more details). If the region or a part of it is later committed, system commit is charged to account for the size of the region (and page tables), as is the process page file quota.

To put it another way, when the system successfully completes, for example, a `VirtualAlloc` commit or `MapViewOfFile` call, it makes a commitment that the necessary storage will be available when needed, even if it wasn't needed at that moment. Thus, a later memory reference to the allocated region can never fail for lack of storage space. (Of course, it could still fail for other reasons, such as page protection, the region being deallocated, and so on.) The commit charge mechanism allows the system to keep this commitment.

The commit charge appears in the Performance Monitor counters as Memory: Committed Bytes. It is also the first of the two numbers displayed on the Task Manager's Performance tab with the legend Commit (the second being the commit limit), and it is displayed by Process Explorer's System Information Memory tab as Commit Charge – Current.

The process page file quota appears in the performance counters as Process: Page File Bytes. The same data appears in the Process: Private Bytes performance counter. (Neither term exactly describes the true meaning of the counter.)

If the commit charge ever reaches the commit limit, the memory manager will attempt to increase the commit limit by expanding one or more page files. If that is not possible, subsequent attempts to allocate virtual memory that uses commit charge will fail until some existing committed memory is freed. The performance counters listed in Table 5-13 allow you to examine private committed memory usage on a system-wide, per-process, or per-page-file, basis.

TABLE 5-13 Committed memory and page file performance counters

Performance Counter	Description
Memory: Committed Bytes	This is the number of bytes of virtual (not reserved) memory that has been committed. This number doesn't necessarily represent page file usage because it includes private committed pages in physical memory that have never been paged out. Rather, it represents the charged amount that must be backed by page file space and/or RAM.
Memory: Commit Limit	This is the number of bytes of virtual memory that can be committed without having to extend the paging files. If the paging files can be extended, this limit is soft.
Process: Page File Quota	This is the process's contribution to Memory: Committed Bytes.
Process: Private Bytes	This is the same as Process: Page File Quota.
Process: Working Set – Private	This is the subset of Process: Page File Quota that is currently in RAM and can be referenced without a page fault. It is also a subset of Process: Working Set.
Process: Working Set	This is the subset of Process: Virtual Bytes that is currently in RAM and can be referenced without a page fault.
Process: Virtual Bytes	This is the total virtual memory allocation of the process, including mapped regions, private committed regions, and private reserved regions.
Paging File: % Usage	This is the percentage of the page file space that is currently in use.
Paging File: % Usage Peak	This is the highest observed value of Paging File: % Usage.

Commit charge and page file size

The counters in Table 5-13 can assist you in choosing a custom page file size. The default policy based on the amount of RAM works acceptably for most machines, but depending on the workload, it can result in a page file that's unnecessarily large or not large enough.

To determine how much page-file space your system really needs based on the mix of applications that have run since the system booted, examine the peak commit charge in the Memory tab of Process Explorer's System Information display. This number represents the peak amount of page file space since the system booted that would have been needed if the system had to page out the majority of private committed virtual memory (which rarely happens).

If the page file on your system is too big, the system will not use it any more or less. In other words, increasing the size of the page file does not change system performance. It simply means the system can have more committed virtual memory. If the page file is too small for the mix of applications you are running, you might get a "system running low on virtual memory" error message. In this case, check to see whether a process has a memory leak by examining the process private bytes count. If no process appears to have a leak, check the system paged pool size. If a device driver is leaking paged pool, this might also explain the error. Refer to the "Troubleshooting a pool leak" experiment in the "Kernel-mode heaps (system memory pools)" section for information on troubleshooting a pool leak.

EXPERIMENT: Viewing page file usage with Task Manager

You can view committed memory usage with Task Manager. To do so, click its **Performance** tab. You'll see the following counters related to page files:

The system commit total is displayed under the **Committed** label as two numbers. The first number represents *potential* page file usage, not actual page file usage. It is how much page file space would be used if all the private committed virtual memory in the system had to be paged out all at once. The second number displayed is the *commit limit*, which is the maximum virtual memory usage that the system can support before running out of virtual memory. (This includes virtual memory backed in physical memory as well as by the paging files.) The commit limit is essentially the size of RAM plus the current size of the paging files. It therefore does not account for possible page file expansion.

Process Explorer's System Information display shows an additional piece of information about system commit usage—namely, the percentage of the peak as compared to the limit and the current usage as compared to the limit:

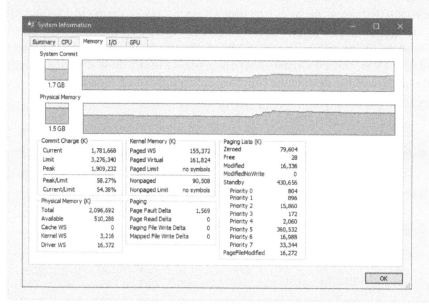

Stacks

Whenever a thread runs, it must have access to a temporary storage location in which to store function parameters, local variables, and the return address after a function call. This part of memory is called a *stack*. On Windows, the memory manager provides two stacks for each thread: the user stack and the kernel stack, as well as per-processor stacks called DPC stacks. Chapter 2 briefly discussed how system calls cause the thread to switch from a user stack to its kernel stack. Now we'll look at some extra services the memory manager provides to efficiently use stack space.

User stacks

When a thread is created, the memory manager automatically reserves a predetermined amount of virtual memory, which by default is 1 MB. This amount can be configured in the call to the Create-Thread or CreateRemoteThread(Ex) function or when compiling the application by using the / STACK:reserve switch in the Microsoft C/C++ compiler, which stores the information in the image header. Although 1 MB is reserved, only the first page of the stack will be committed (unless the PE header of the image specifies otherwise), along with a guard page. When a thread's stack grows large enough to touch the guard page, an exception occurs, causing an attempt to allocate another guard. Through this mechanism, a user stack doesn't immediately consume all 1 MB of committed memory but instead grows with demand. (However, it will never shrink back.)

EXPERIMENT: Creating the maximum number of threads

With only 2 GB of user address space available to each 32-bit process, the relatively large memory that is reserved for each thread's stack allows for an easy calculation of the maximum number of threads that a process can support: a little less than 2,048, for a total of nearly 2 GB of memory (unless the increaseuserva BCD option is used and the image is large address space aware). By forcing each new thread to use the smallest possible stack reservation size, 64 KB, the limit can grow to about 30,000 threads. You can test this for yourself by using the TestLimit utility from Sysinternals. Here is some sample output:

```
C:\Tools\Sysinternals>Testlimit.exe -t -n 64

Testlimit v5.24 - test Windows limits
Copyright (C) 2012-2015 Mark Russinovich
Sysinternals - www.sysinternals.com

Process ID: 17260

Creating threads with 64 KB stacks...
Created 29900 threads. Lasterror: 8
```

If you attempt this experiment on a 64-bit Windows installation (with 128 TB of user address space available), you would expect to see potentially hundreds of thousands of threads created (assuming sufficient memory was available). Interestingly, however, TestLimit actually creates fewer threads than on a 32-bit machine. This has to do with the fact that Testlimit.exe is a 32-bit application and thus runs under the Wow64 environment. (See Chapter 8 in Part 2 for more information on Wow64.) Each thread will therefore have not only its 32-bit Wow64 stack but also its 64-bit stack, thus consuming more than twice the memory, while keeping only 2 GB of address space. To properly test the thread-creation limit on 64-bit Windows, use the Testlimit64. exe binary instead.

You will need to terminate TestLimit with Process Explorer or Task Manager. You cannot use Ctrl+C to break the application because this operation itself creates a new thread, which will not be possible once memory is exhausted.

Kernel stacks

Although user stack sizes are typically 1 MB, the amount of memory dedicated to the kernel stack is significantly smaller: 12 KB on 32-bit systems and 16 KB on 64-bit systems, followed by another guard page, for a total of 16 or 20 KB of virtual address space. Code running in the kernel is expected to have less recursion than user code, as well as contain more efficient variable use and keep stack buffer sizes low. Because kernel stacks live in system address space (which is shared by all processes), their memory usage has a bigger impact of the system.

Although kernel code is usually not recursive, interactions between graphics system calls handled by Win32k.sys and its subsequent callbacks into user mode can cause recursive re-entries in the kernel on the same kernel stack. As such, Windows provides a mechanism for dynamically expanding and shrinking the kernel stack from its initial size. As each additional graphics call is performed from the same thread, another 16 KB kernel stack is allocated. (This happens anywhere in system address space. The memory manager provides the ability to jump stacks when nearing the guard page.) Whenever each call returns to the caller (unwinding), the memory manager frees the additional kernel stack that had been allocated, as shown in Figure 5-28. This mechanism allows reliable support for recursive system calls as well as efficient use of system address space. It is provided for use by driver developers when performing recursive callouts through the `KeExpandKernelStackAndCallout(Ex)` APIs, as necessary.

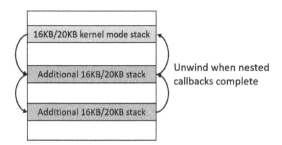

FIGURE 5-28 Kernel stack jumping.

EXPERIMENT: Viewing kernel-stack usage

You can use the RamMap tool from Sysinternals to display the physical memory currently being occupied by kernel stacks. Here's a screenshot from the **Use Counts** tab:

To view kernel-stack usage, try the following:

1. Repeat the previous TestLimit experiment, but don't terminate TestLimit yet.

2. Switch to RamMap.

3. Open the **File** menu and select **Refresh** (or press **F5**). You should see a much higher kernel stack size:

Running TestLimit a few more times (without closing previous instances) would easily exhaust physical memory on a 32-bit system, and this limitation results in one of the primary limits on system-wide 32-bit thread count.

DPC stack

Windows keeps a per-processor DPC stack available for use by the system whenever DPCs are executing. This approach isolates the DPC code from the current thread's kernel stack. (This is unrelated to the DPC's actual operation because DPCs run in arbitrary thread context. See Chapter 6 for more on DPCs.) The DPC stack is also configured as the initial stack for handling the `sysenter` (x86), `svc` (ARM), or `syscall` (x64) instruction during a system call. The CPU is responsible for switching the stack when these instructions are executed, based on one of the model-specific registers (MSRs on x86/x64). However, Windows does not want to reprogram the MSR for every context switch because that is an expensive operation. Windows therefore configures the per-processor DPC stack pointer in the MSR.

Virtual address descriptors

The memory manager uses a demand-paging algorithm to know when to load pages into memory, waiting until a thread references an address and incurs a page fault before retrieving the page from disk. Like copy-on-write, demand paging is a form of *lazy evaluation*—waiting to perform a task until it is required.

The memory manager uses lazy evaluation not only to bring pages into memory but also to construct the page tables required to describe new pages. For example, when a thread commits a large region of virtual memory with `VirtualAlloc`, the memory manager could immediately construct the page tables required to access the entire range of allocated memory. But what if some of that range is never accessed? Creating page tables for the entire range would be a wasted effort. Instead, the memory manager waits to create a page table until a thread incurs a page fault. It then creates a page table for that page. This method significantly improves performance for processes that reserve and/or commit a lot of memory but access it sparsely.

The virtual address space that would be occupied by such as-yet-nonexistent page tables is charged to the process page file quota and to the system commit charge. This ensures that space will be available for them should they actually be created. With the lazy-evaluation algorithm, allocating even large blocks of memory is a fast operation. When a thread allocates memory, the memory manager must respond with a range of addresses for the thread to use. To do this, the memory manager maintains another set of data structures to keep track of which virtual addresses have been reserved in the process's address space and which have not. These data structures are known as *Virtual Address Descriptors* (*VADs*). VADs are allocated in non-paged pool.

Process VADs

For each process, the memory manager maintains a set of VADs that describes the status of the process's address space. VADs are organized into a self-balancing AVL tree (named after its inventors, Adelson-Velsky and Landis, where the heights of the two child subtrees of any node differ by at most 1; this makes the insertion, lookup, and deletion very fast). On average, this results in the fewest comparisons when searching for a VAD corresponding with a virtual address. There is one VAD for each virtually contiguous range of not-free virtual addresses that all have the same characteristics (reserved versus committed versus mapped, memory access protection, and so on). Figure 5-29 shows a diagram of a VAD tree.

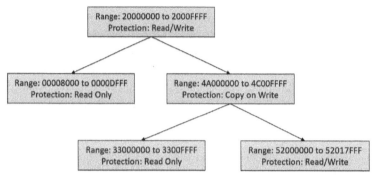

FIGURE 5-29 VADs.

When a process reserves address space or maps a view of a section, the memory manager creates a VAD to store any information supplied by the allocation request, such as the range of addresses being reserved, whether the range will be shared or private, whether a child process can inherit the contents of the range, and the page protection applied to pages in the range.

When a thread first accesses an address, the memory manager must create a PTE for the page containing the address. To do so, it finds the VAD whose address range contains the accessed address and uses the information it finds to fill in the PTE. If the address falls outside the range covered by the VAD or in a range of addresses that are reserved but not committed, the memory manager knows that the thread didn't allocate the memory before attempting to use it and therefore generates an access violation.

EXPERIMENT: Viewing VADs

You can use the kernel debugger's !vad command to view the VADs for a given process. First find the address of the root of the VAD tree with the !process command. Then specify that address to the !vad command, as shown in the following example of the VAD tree for a process running Explorer.exe:

```
1kd> !process 0 1 explorer.exe
PROCESS ffffc8069382e080
    SessionId: 1  Cid: 43e0    Peb: 00bc5000  ParentCid: 0338
    DirBase: 554ab7000  ObjectTable: ffffda8f62811d80  HandleCount: 823.
    Image: explorer.exe
    VadRoot ffffc806912337f0 Vads 505 Clone 0 Private 5088. Modified 2146. Locked 0.
...
```

```
lkd> !vad ffffc8068ae1e470
VAD             Level      Start      End Commit
ffffc80689bc52b0  9        640        64f      0 Mapped        READWRITE
Pagefile section, shared commit 0x10
ffffc80689be6900  8        650        651      0 Mapped        READONLY
Pagefile section, shared commit 0x2
ffffc80689bc4290  9        660        675      0 Mapped        READONLY
Pagefile section, shared commit 0x16
ffffc8068ae1f320  7        680        6ff     32 Private       READWRITE
ffffc80689b290b0  9        700        701      2 Private       READWRITE
ffffc80688da04f0  8        710        711      2 Private       READWRITE
ffffc80682795760  6        720        723      0 Mapped        READONLY
Pagefile section, shared commit 0x4
ffffc80688d85670 10        730        731      0 Mapped        READONLY
Pagefile section, shared commit 0x2
ffffc80689bdd9e0  9        740        741      2 Private       READWRITE
ffffc80688da57b0  8        750        755      0 Mapped        READONLY
\Windows\en-US\explorer.exe.mui
...
Total VADs: 574, average level: 8, maximum depth: 10
Total private commit: 0x3420 pages (53376 KB)
Total shared commit:  0x478 pages (4576 KB)
```

Rotate VADs

A video card driver must typically copy data from the user-mode graphics application to various other system memory, including the video card memory and the AGP port's memory, both of which have different caching attributes as well as addresses. To quickly allow these different views of memory to be mapped into a process, and to support the different cache attributes, the memory manager implements rotate VADs, which allow video drivers to transfer data directly by using the GPU and to rotate unneeded memory in and out of the process view pages on demand. Figure 5-30 shows an example of how the same virtual address can rotate between video RAM and virtual memory.

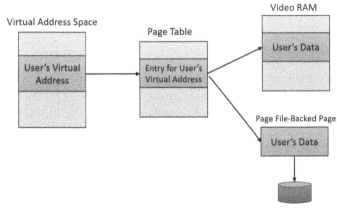

FIGURE 5-30 Rotate VADs.

NUMA

Each new release of Windows provides new enhancements to the memory manager to make better use of non-uniform memory architecture (NUMA) machines, such as large server systems as well as Intel i7 and AMD Opteron SMP workstations. The NUMA support in the memory manager adds intelligent knowledge of node information such as location, topology, and access costs to allow applications and drivers to take advantage of NUMA capabilities, while abstracting the underlying hardware details.

When the memory manager is initializing, it calls the `MiComputeNumaCosts` function to perform various page and cache operations on different nodes. It then computes the time it took for those operations to complete. Based on this information, it builds a node graph of access costs (the distance between a node and any other node on the system). When the system requires pages for a given operation, it consults the graph to choose the most optimal node (that is, the closest). If no memory is available on that node, it chooses the next closest node, and so on.

Although the memory manager ensures that, whenever possible, memory allocations come from the ideal processor's node (the *ideal node*) of the thread making the allocation, it also provides functions that allow applications to choose their own node, such as the `VirtualAllocExNuma`, `CreateFileMappingNuma`, `MapViewOfFileExNuma`, and `AllocateUserPhysicalPagesNuma` APIs.

The ideal node isn't used only when applications allocate memory but also during kernel operation and page faults. For example, when a thread running on a non-ideal processor takes a page fault, the memory manager won't use the current node. Instead, it will allocate memory from the thread's ideal node. Although this might result in slower access time while the thread is still running on this CPU, overall memory access will be optimized as the thread migrates back to its ideal node. In any case, if the ideal node is out of resources, the closest node to the ideal node is chosen and not a random other node. Just like user-mode applications, however, drivers can specify their own node when using APIs such as `MmAllocatePagesForMdlEx` or `MmAllocateContiguousMemorySpecifyCacheNode`.

Various memory manager pools and data structures are also optimized to take advantage of NUMA nodes. The memory manager tries to evenly use physical memory from all the nodes on the system to hold the non-paged pool. When a non-paged pool allocation is made, the memory manager uses the ideal node as an index to choose a virtual memory address range inside non-paged pool that corresponds to physical memory belonging to this node. In addition, per-NUMA node pool free lists are created to efficiently leverage these types of memory configurations. Apart from non-paged pool, the system cache and system PTEs are also similarly allocated across all nodes, as well as the memory manager's look-aside lists.

Finally, when the system needs to zero pages, it does so in parallel across different NUMA nodes by creating threads with NUMA affinities that correspond to the nodes in which the physical memory is located. The logical prefetcher and SuperFetch (described in the section "Proactive memory management [SuperFetch]") also use the ideal node of the target process when prefetching, while soft page faults cause pages to migrate to the ideal node of the faulting thread.

Section objects

As noted earlier in this chapter in the "Shared memory and mapped files" section, the *section object*, which the Windows subsystem calls a *file mapping object*, represents a block of memory that two or more processes can share. A section object can be mapped to the paging file or to another file on disk.

The executive uses sections to load executable images into memory, and the cache manager uses them to access data in a cached file. (See Chapter 14 in Part 2 for more information on how the cache manager uses section objects.) You can also use section objects to map a file into a process address space. The file can then be accessed as a large array by mapping different views of the section object and reading or writing to memory rather than to the file—an activity called *mapped file I/O*. When the program accesses an invalid page (one not in physical memory), a page fault occurs and the memory manager automatically brings the page into memory from the mapped file or page file. If the application modifies the page, the memory manager writes the changes back to the file during its normal paging operations. (Alternatively, the application can flush a view explicitly by using the Windows `FlushViewOfFile` function.)

Like other objects, section objects are allocated and deallocated by the object manager. The object manager creates and initializes an object header, which it uses to manage the objects; the memory manager defines the body of the section object. (See Chapter 8 in Part 2 for more on the object manager). The memory manager also implements services that user-mode threads can call to retrieve and change the attributes stored in the body of section objects. The structure of a section object is shown in Figure 5-31. Table 5-14 summarizes the unique attributes stored in section objects.

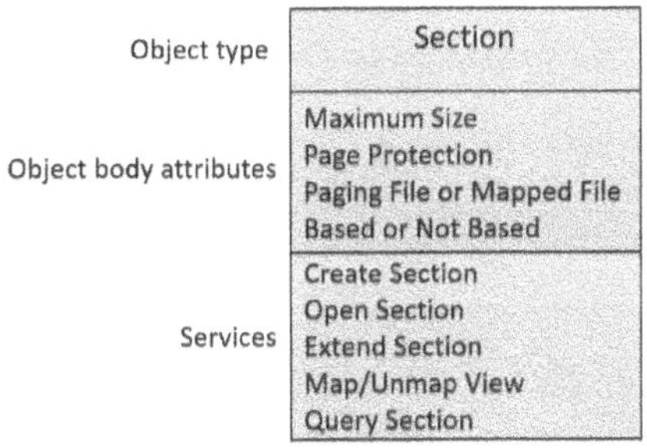

FIGURE 5-31   A section object.

TABLE 5-14   Section object body attributes

Attribute	Purpose
Maximum size	This is the largest size to which the section can grow in bytes. If mapping a file, this is the maximum size of the file.
Page protection	This is page-based memory protection assigned to all pages in the section when it is created.
Paging file or mapped file	This indicates whether the section is created empty (backed by the paging file—as explained earlier, page-file-backed sections use page-file resources only when the pages need to be written out to disk) or loaded with a file (backed by the mapped file).
Based or not based	This indicates whether a section is a based section, which must appear at the same virtual address for all processes sharing it, or a non-based section, which can appear at different virtual addresses for different processes.

EXPERIMENT: Viewing section objects

You can use Process Explorer from Sysinternals to see files mapped by a process. Follow these steps:

1. Open the **View** menu, choose **Lower Pane View**, and select **DLLs**.

2. Open the **View** menu, choose **Select Columns**, choose **DLL**, and enable the **Mapping Type** column.

3. Notice the files marked as Data in the Mapping column. These are mapped files rather than DLLs and other files the image loader loads as modules. Section objects that are backed by a page file are indicated in the Name column as <Pagefile Backed>. Otherwise, the file name is shown.

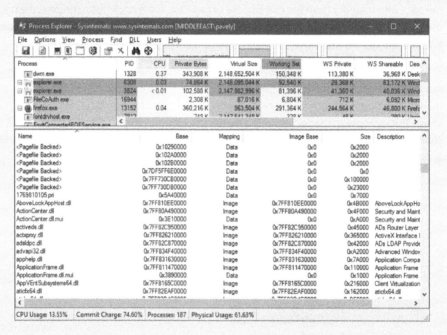

Another way to view section objects is to switch to handle view (open the **View** menu, choose **Lower Pane View**, and select **Handles**) and look for objects of type Section. In the following screenshot, the object name (if it exists) is shown. This is not the file name backing the section (if any); it's the name given to the section in the object manager's namespace. (See Chapter 8 in Part 2 for more on the object manager.) Double-clicking the entry shows more information on the object, such as the number of open handles and its security descriptor.

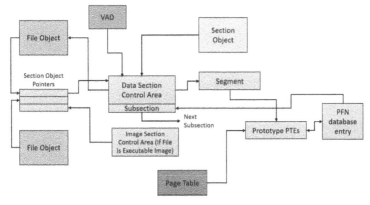

The screenshot shows Process Explorer with process and handle listings.

The data structures maintained by the memory manager that describe mapped sections are shown in Figure 5-32. These structures ensure that data read from mapped files is consistent regardless of the type of access (open file, mapped file, and so on). For each open file (represented by a file object), there is a single section object pointers structure. This structure is the key to maintaining data consistency for all types of file access as well as to providing caching for files. The section object pointers structure points to one or two control areas. One control area is used to map the file when it is accessed as a data file and the other is used to map the file when it is run as an executable image. A control area in turn points to subsection structures that describe the mapping information for each section of the file (read-only, read/write, copy-on-write, and so on). The control area also points to a segment structure allocated in paged pool, which in turn points to the prototype PTEs used to map to the actual pages mapped by the section object. As described earlier in this chapter, process page tables point to these prototype PTEs, which in turn map the pages being referenced.

FIGURE 5-32 Internal section structures.

Although Windows ensures that any process that accesses (reads or writes) a file will always see the same consistent data, there is one case in which two copies of pages of a file can reside in physical memory. (Even in this case, all accessors get the latest copy and data consistency is maintained.) This duplication can happen when an image file has been accessed as a data file (having been read or written) and is then run as an executable image. (An example might be when an image is linked and then run; the linker had the file open for data access, and then when the image was run, the image loader mapped it as an executable.) Internally, the following actions occur:

1. If the executable file was created using the file-mapping APIs or the cache manager, a data control area is created to represent the data pages in the image file being read or written.

2. When the image is run and the section object is created to map the image as an executable, the memory manager finds that the section object pointers for the image file point to a data control area and flushes the section. This step is necessary to ensure that any modified pages have been written to disk before accessing the image through the image control area.

3. The memory manager creates a control area for the image file.

4. As the image begins execution, its (read-only) pages are faulted in from the image file or copied directly over from the data file if the corresponding data page is resident.

Because the pages mapped by the data control area might still be resident (on the standby list), this is the one case in which two copies of the same data are in two different pages in memory. However, this duplication doesn't result in a data consistency issue. This is because, as mentioned, the data control area has already been flushed to disk, so the pages read from the image are up to date (and these pages are never written back to disk).

EXPERIMENT: Viewing control areas

To find the address of the control area structures for a file, you must first get the address of the file object in question. You can obtain this address through the kernel debugger by dumping the process handle table with the !handle command and noting the object address of a file object. Although the kernel debugger !file command displays the basic information in a file object, it doesn't display the pointer to the section object pointers structure. Then, using the dt command, format the file object to get the address of the section object pointers structure. This structure consists of three pointers: a pointer to the data control area, a pointer to the shared cache map (explained in Chapter 14 in Part 2), and a pointer to the image control area. From the section object pointers structure, you can obtain the address of a control area for the file (if one exists) and feed that address into the !ca command.

For example, if you open a PowerPoint file and use !handle to display the handle table for that process, you will find an open handle to the PowerPoint file (you can do a text search). (For more information on using !handle, see the "Object manager" section in Chapter 8 in Part 2 or the debugger documentation.)

```
lkd> !process 0 0 powerpnt.exe
PROCESS ffffc8068913e080
```

```
    SessionId: 1  Cid: 2b64    Peb: 01249000  ParentCid: 1d38
    DirBase: 252e25000  ObjectTable: ffffda8f49269c40  HandleCount: 1915.
    Image: POWERPNT.EXE
lkd> .process /p ffffc8068913e080
Implicit process is now ffffc806'8913e080
lkd> !handle
...
0c08: Object: ffffc8068f56a630  GrantedAccess: 00120089 Entry: ffffda8f491d0020
Object: ffffc8068f56a630  Type: (ffffc8068256cb00) File
    ObjectHeader: ffffc8068f56a600 (new version)
        HandleCount: 1  PointerCount: 30839
        Directory Object: 00000000  Name: \WindowsInternals\7thEdition\Chapter05\
diagrams.pptx {HarddiskVolume2}
...
```

Taking the file object address (FFFFC8068F56A630) and formatting it with dt results in this:

```
lkd> dt nt!_file_object ffffc8068f56a630
    +0x000 Type             : 0n5
    +0x002 Size             : 0n216
    +0x008 DeviceObject     : 0xffffc806'8408cb40 _DEVICE_OBJECT
    +0x010 Vpb              : 0xffffc806'82feba00 _VPB
    +0x018 FsContext        : 0xffffda8f'5137cbd0 Void
    +0x020 FsContext2       : 0xffffda8f'4366d590 Void
    +0x028 SectionObjectPointer : 0xffffc806'8ec0c558 _SECTION_OBJECT_POINTERS
...
```

Taking the address of the section object pointers structure and formatting it with dt results in this:

```
lkd> dt nt!_section_object_pointers 0xffffc806'8ec0c558
    +0x000 DataSectionObject : 0xffffc806'8e838c10 Void
    +0x008 SharedCacheMap    : 0xffffc806'8d967bd0 Void
    +0x010 ImageSectionObject : (null)
```

Finally, you can use !ca to display the control area using the address:

```
lkd> !ca 0xffffc806'8e838c10
ControlArea  @ ffffc8068e838c10
  Segment       ffffda8f4d97fdc0  Flink       ffffc8068ecf97b8  Blink
ffffc8068ecf97b8
    Section Ref           1  Pfn Ref           58  Mapped Views         2
    User Ref              0  WaitForDel         0  Flush Count          0
    File Object  ffffc8068e5d3d50  ModWriteCount      0  System Views         2
    WritableRefs          0
    Flags (8080) File WasPurged  \WindowsInternalsBook\7thEdition\Chapter05\diagrams.pptx

Segment @ ffffda8f4d97fdc0
    ControlArea     ffffc8068e838c10  ExtendInfo    0000000000000000
    Total Ptes             80
    Segment Size        80000  Committed                 0
    Flags (c0000) ProtectionMask
```

```
Subsection 1 @ ffffc8068e838c90
  ControlArea  ffffc8068e838c10  Starting Sector       0  Number Of Sectors   58
  Base Pte     ffffda8f48eb6d40  Ptes In Subsect      58  Unused Ptes          0
  Flags                      d   Sector Offset         0  Protection           6
  Accessed
  Flink        ffffc8068bb7fcf0  Blink   ffffc8068bb7fcf0  MappedViews         2

Subsection 2 @ ffffc8068c2e05b0
  ControlArea  ffffc8068e838c10  Starting Sector      58  Number Of Sectors   28
  Base Pte     ffffda8f3cc45000  Ptes In Subsect      28  Unused Ptes        1d8
  Flags                      d   Sector Offset         0  Protection           6
  Accessed
  Flink        ffffc8068c2e0600  Blink   ffffc8068c2e0600  MappedViews         1
```

Another technique is to display the list of all control areas with the !memusage command. The following excerpt is from the output of this command. (The command might take a long time to complete on a system with a large amount of memory.)

```
1kd> !memusage
 loading PFN database
loading (100% complete)

Compiling memory usage data (99% Complete).

            Zeroed:     98533 (  394132 kb)
              Free:      1405 (    5620 kb)
           Standby:    331221 ( 1324884 kb)
          Modified:     83806 (  335224 kb)
  ModifiedNoWrite:       116 (     464 kb)
      Active/Valid:   1556154 ( 6224616 kb)
        Transition:         5 (      20 kb)
         SLIST/Bad:      1614 (    6456 kb)
           Unknown:         0 (       0 kb)
             TOTAL:   2072854 ( 8291416 kb)

Dangling Yes Commit:       130 (     520 kb)
 Dangling No Commit:    514812 ( 2059248 kb)
  Building kernel map
  Finished building kernel map

 (Master1 0 for 1c0)

 (Master1 0 for e80)

 (Master1 0 for ec0)

 (Master1 0 for f00)
Scanning PFN database - (02% complete)

 (Master1 0 for de80)
Scanning PFN database - (100% complete)
```

```
   Usage Summary (in Kb):
Control      Valid Standby Dirty Shared Locked PageTables  name
ffffffffd 1684540    0     0     0 1684540     0    AWE
ffff8c0b7e4797d0    64     0     0     0     0     0  mapped_file( Microsoft-
Windows-Kernel-PnP%4Configuration.evtx )
ffff8c0b7e481650     0     4     0     0     0     0  mapped_file( No name for file )
ffff8c0b7e493c00     0    40     0     0     0     0  mapped_file( FSD-{ED5680AF-
0543-4367-A331-850F30190B44}.FSD )
ffff8c0b7e4a1b30     8    12     0     0     0     0  mapped_file( msidle.dll )
ffff8c0b7e4a7c40   128     0     0     0     0     0  mapped_file( Microsoft-
Windows-Diagnosis-PCW%4Operational.evtx )
ffff8c0b7e4a9010    16     8     0    16     0     0  mapped_file( netjoin.dll
)8a04db00    ...
ffff8c0b7f8cc360  8212     0     0     0     0     0  mapped_file( OUTLOOK.EXE )
ffff8c0b7f8cd1a0    52    28     0     0     0     0  mapped_file( verdanab.ttf )
ffff8c0b7f8ce910     0     4     0     0     0     0  mapped_file( No name for file )
ffff8c0b7f8d3590     0     4     0     0     0     0  mapped_file( No name for file )
...
```

The Control column points to the control area structure that describes the mapped file. You can display control areas, segments, and subsections with the kernel debugger !ca command. For example, to dump the control area for the mapped file Outlook.exe in this example, type the !ca command followed by the Control column number, as shown here:

```
lkd> !ca ffff8c0b7f8cc360

ControlArea @ ffff8c0b7f8cc360
  Segment      ffffdf08d8a55670  Flink      ffff8c0b834f1fd0  Blink
ffff8c0b834f1fd0
  Section Ref                 1  Pfn Ref              806  Mapped Views        1
  User Ref                    2  WaitForDel             0  Flush Count      c5a0
  File Object  ffff8c0b7f0e94e0  ModWriteCount          0  System Views     ffff
  WritableRefs          80000161
  Flags (a0) Image File

      \Program Files (x86)\Microsoft Office\root\Office16\OUTLOOK.EXE

Segment @ ffffdf08d8a55670
  ControlArea    ffff8c0b7f8cc360  BasedAddress   0000000000be0000
  Total Ptes              1609
  Segment Size         1609000  Committed              0
  Image Commit              f4  Image Info     ffffdf08d8a556b8
  ProtoPtes      ffffdf08dab6b000
  Flags (c20000) ProtectionMask

Subsection 1 @ ffff8c0b7f8cc3e0
  ControlArea  ffff8c0b7f8cc360  Starting Sector        0  Number Of Sectors   2
  Base Pte     ffffdf08dab6b000  Ptes In Subsect        1  Unused Ptes         0
  Flags                      2  Sector Offset          0  Protection          1

Subsection 2 @ ffff8c0b7f8cc418
  ControlArea  ffff8c0b7f8cc360  Starting Sector        2  Number Of Sectors 7b17
```

```
       Base Pte      ffffdf08dab6b008   Ptes In Subsect      f63   Unused Ptes            0
       Flags                        6   Sector Offset          0   Protection             3

  Subsection 3 @ ffff8c0b7f8cc450
    ControlArea   ffff8c0b7f8cc360   Starting Sector     7b19   Number Of Sectors 19a4
    Base Pte      ffffdf08dab72b20   Ptes In Subsect      335   Unused Ptes            0
    Flags                        2   Sector Offset          0   Protection             1

  Subsection 4 @ ffff8c0b7f8cc488
    ControlArea   ffff8c0b7f8cc360   Starting Sector     94bd   Number Of Sectors  764
    Base Pte      ffffdf08dab744c8   Ptes In Subsect       f2   Unused Ptes            0
    Flags                        a   Sector Offset          0   Protection             5

  Subsection 5 @ ffff8c0b7f8cc4c0
    ControlArea   ffff8c0b7f8cc360   Starting Sector     9c21   Number Of Sectors    1
    Base Pte      ffffdf08dab74c58   Ptes In Subsect        1   Unused Ptes            0
    Flags                        a   Sector Offset          0   Protection             5

  Subsection 6 @ ffff8c0b7f8cc4f8
    ControlArea   ffff8c0b7f8cc360   Starting Sector     9c22   Number Of Sectors    1
    Base Pte      ffffdf08dab74c60   Ptes In Subsect        1   Unused Ptes            0
    Flags                        a   Sector Offset          0   Protection             5

  Subsection 7 @ ffff8c0b7f8cc530
    ControlArea   ffff8c0b7f8cc360   Starting Sector     9c23   Number Of Sectors  c62
    Base Pte      ffffdf08dab74c68   Ptes In Subsect      18d   Unused Ptes            0
    Flags                        2   Sector Offset          0   Protection             1

  Subsection 8 @ ffff8c0b7f8cc568
    ControlArea   ffff8c0b7f8cc360   Starting Sector     a885   Number Of Sectors  771
    Base Pte      ffffdf08dab758d0   Ptes In Subsect       ef   Unused Ptes            0
    Flags                        2   Sector Offset          0   Protection             1
```

Working sets

Now that you've looked at how Windows keeps track of physical memory and how much memory it can support, we'll explain how Windows keeps a subset of virtual addresses in physical memory.

As you'll recall, a subset of virtual pages resident in physical memory is called a *working set*. There are three kinds of working sets:

- **Process working sets**   These contain the pages referenced by threads within a single process.

- **System working sets**   These contain the resident subset of the pageable system code (for example, Ntoskrnl.exe and drivers), paged pool, and the system cache.

- **Session's working set**   Each session has a working set that contains the resident subset of the kernel-mode session-specific data structures allocated by the kernel-mode part of the Windows subsystem (Win32k.sys), session paged pool, session mapped views, and other session-space device drivers.

Before examining the details of each type of working set, let's look at the overall policy for deciding which pages are brought into physical memory and how long they remain.

Demand paging

The Windows memory manager uses a demand-paging algorithm with clustering to load pages into memory. When a thread receives a page fault, the memory manager loads into memory the faulted page plus a small number of pages preceding and/or following it. This strategy attempts to minimize the number of paging I/Os a thread will incur. Because programs—especially large ones—tend to execute in small regions of their address space at any given time, loading clusters of virtual pages reduces the number of disk reads. For page faults that reference data pages in images, the cluster size is three pages. For all other page faults, the cluster size is seven pages.

However, a demand-paging policy can result in a process incurring many page faults when its threads first begin executing or when they resume execution at a later point. To optimize the startup of a process (and the system), Windows has an intelligent prefetch engine called the *logical prefetcher*, described in the next section. Further optimization and prefetching is performed by another component, called *SuperFetch*, described later in the chapter.

Logical prefetcher and ReadyBoot

During a typical system boot or application startup, the order of faults is such that some pages are brought in from one part of a file, then perhaps from a distant part of the same file, then from a different file, then perhaps from a directory, and then again from the first file. This jumping around slows down each access considerably. Indeed, analysis shows that disk seek times are a dominant factor in slowing boot and application startup times. By prefetching batches of pages all at once, you can achieve a more sensible ordering of access without excessive backtracking, thus improving the overall time for system and application startup. The pages that are needed can be known in advance because of the high correlation in accesses across boots or application starts.

The prefetcher tries to speed the boot process and application startup by monitoring the data and code accessed by boot and application startups and using that information at the beginning of a subsequent boot or application startup to read in the code and data. When the prefetcher is active, the memory manager notifies the prefetcher code in the kernel of page faults—those that require that data be read from disk (hard faults) and those that simply require data already in memory to be added to a process's working set (soft faults). The prefetcher monitors the first 10 seconds of application startup. For boot, the prefetcher by default traces from system start through the 30 seconds following the start of the user's shell (typically Explorer) or, failing that, through 60 seconds following Windows service initialization or through 120 seconds, whichever comes first.

The trace assembled in the kernel notes faults taken on the NTFS master file table (MFT) metadata file (if the application accesses files or directories on NTFS volumes), referenced files, and referenced directories. With the trace assembled, the kernel prefetcher code waits for requests from the prefetcher component of the `Superfetch` service (%SystemRoot%\System32\Sysmain.dll), running in an instance of Svchost. The `Superfetch` service is responsible for both the logical prefetching component in the kernel and the SuperFetch component that we'll talk about later. The prefetcher signals the `\KernelObjects\` `PrefetchTracesReady` event to inform the `Superfetch` service that it can now query trace data.

> **Note** You can enable or disable prefetching of the boot or application startups by editing the DWORD registry value `EnablePrefetcher` in the HKLM\SYSTEM\CurrentControlSet\ Control\Session Manager\Memory Management\PrefetchParameters key. Set it to 0 to disable prefetching altogether, 1 to enable prefetching of only applications, 2 for prefetching of boot only, and 3 for both boot and applications.

The `Superfetch` service (which hosts the logical prefetcher, although it is a completely separate component from the actual SuperFetch functionality) performs a call to the internal `NtQuerySystem-` `Information` system call requesting the trace data. The logical prefetcher post-processes the trace data, combining it with previously collected data, and writes it to a file in the %SystemRoot%\Prefetch folder. (See Figure 5-33.) The file's name is the name of the application to which the trace applies followed by a dash and the hexadecimal representation of a hash of the file's path. The file has a .pf extension. An example would be NOTEPAD.EXE-9FB27C0E.PF.

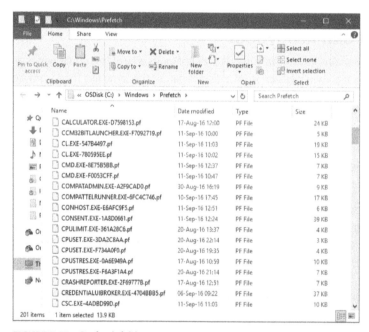

FIGURE 5-33 Prefetch folder.

There is an exception to the file name rule for images that host other components, including the Microsoft Management Console (%SystemRoot%\System32\Mmc.exe), the service hosting process (%SystemRoot%\System32\Svchost.exe), the RunDLL component (%SystemRoot%\System32\Rundll32.exe), and Dllhost (%SystemRoot%\System32\Dllhost.exe). Because add-on components are specified on the command line for these applications, the prefetcher includes the command line in the generated hash.

Thus, invocations of these applications with different components on the command line will result in different traces.

For a system boot, a different mechanism is used, called *ReadyBoot*. ReadyBoot tries to optimize I/O operations by creating large and efficient I/O reads and storing the data in RAM. When system components require the data, it's serviced through the stored RAM. This especially benefits mechanical disks, but can be also useful for SSDs. Information on the files to prefetch is stored after boot in the ReadyBoot subdirectory of the Prefetch directory shown in Figure 5-33. Once boot is complete, the cached data in RAM is deleted. For very fast SSDs, ReadyBoot is off by default because its gains are marginal, if any.

When the system boots or an application starts, the prefetcher is called to give it an opportunity to prefetch. The prefetcher looks in the prefetch directory to see if a trace file exists for the prefetch scenario in question. If it does, the prefetcher calls NTFS to prefetch any MFT metadata file references, reads in the contents of each of the directories referenced, and finally opens each file referenced. It then calls the memory manager function `MmPrefetchPages` to read in any data and code specified in the trace that's not already in memory. The memory manager initiates all the reads asynchronously and then waits for them to complete before letting an application's startup continue.

EXPERIMENT: Watching prefetch file reads and writes

If you capture a trace of application startup with Process Monitor from Sysinternals on a client edition of Windows (Windows Server editions disable prefetching by default), you can see the prefetcher check for and read the application's prefetch file (if it exists). In addition, you can see the prefetcher write out a new copy of the file roughly 10 seconds after the application starts. Here is a capture of Notepad startup with an `Include` filter set to `prefetch` so that Process Monitor shows only accesses to the %SystemRoot%\Prefetch directory:

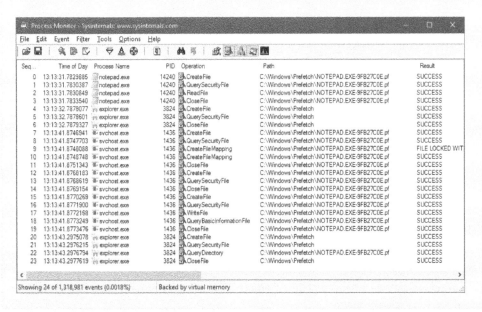

Lines 0–3 show the Notepad prefetch file being read in the context of the Notepad process during its startup. Lines 7–19 (which have time stamps 10 seconds later than the first four lines) show the Superfetch service—running in the context of a Svchost process—writing out the updated prefetch file.

To minimize seeking even further, every three days or so, during system idle periods, the Superfetch service organizes a list of files and directories in the order that they are referenced during a boot or application start and stores it in a file named %SystemRoot%\Prefetch\Layout.ini (see Figure 5-34). This list also includes frequently accessed files tracked by Superfetch.

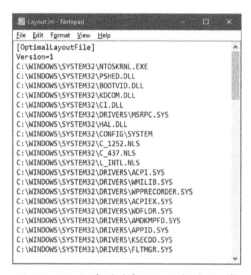

```
[OptimalLayoutFile]
Version=1
C:\WINDOWS\SYSTEM32\NTOSKRNL.EXE
C:\WINDOWS\SYSTEM32\PSHED.DLL
C:\WINDOWS\SYSTEM32\BOOTVID.DLL
C:\WINDOWS\SYSTEM32\KDCOM.DLL
C:\WINDOWS\SYSTEM32\CI.DLL
C:\WINDOWS\SYSTEM32\DRIVERS\MSRPC.SYS
C:\WINDOWS\SYSTEM32\HAL.DLL
C:\WINDOWS\SYSTEM32\CONFIG\SYSTEM
C:\WINDOWS\SYSTEM32\C_1252.NLS
C:\WINDOWS\SYSTEM32\C_437.NLS
C:\WINDOWS\SYSTEM32\L_INTL.NLS
C:\WINDOWS\SYSTEM32\DRIVERS\ACPI.SYS
C:\WINDOWS\SYSTEM32\DRIVERS\WMILIB.SYS
C:\WINDOWS\SYSTEM32\DRIVERS\WPPRECORDER.SYS
C:\WINDOWS\SYSTEM32\DRIVERS\ACPIEX.SYS
C:\WINDOWS\SYSTEM32\DRIVERS\WDFLDR.SYS
C:\WINDOWS\SYSTEM32\DRIVERS\AMDKMPFD.SYS
C:\WINDOWS\SYSTEM32\DRIVERS\APPID.SYS
C:\WINDOWS\SYSTEM32\DRIVERS\KSECDD.SYS
C:\WINDOWS\SYSTEM32\DRIVERS\FLTMGR.SYS
```

FIGURE 5-34 Prefetch defragmentation layout file.

It then launches the system defragmenter with a command-line option that tells the defragmenter to defragment based on the contents of the file instead of performing a full defrag. The defragmenter finds a contiguous area on each volume large enough to hold all the listed files and directories that reside on that volume and then moves them in their entirety into that area so that they are stored one after the other. Thus, future prefetch operations will even be more efficient because all the data read in is now stored physically on the disk in the order it will be read. Because the files defragmented for prefetching usually number only in the hundreds, this defragmentation is much faster than full-volume defragmentations.

Placement policy

When a thread receives a page fault, the memory manager must determine where in physical memory to put the virtual page. The set of rules it uses to determine the best position is called a *placement policy*. Windows considers the size of CPU memory caches when choosing page frames to minimize unnecessary thrashing of the cache.

If physical memory is full when a page fault occurs, Windows uses a replacement policy to determine which virtual page must be removed from memory to make room for the new page. Common replacement policies include least recently used (LRU) and first in, first out (FIFO). The LRU algorithm (also known as the *clock algorithm*, as implemented in most versions of UNIX) requires the virtual memory system to track when a page in memory is used. When a new page frame is required, the page that hasn't been used for the greatest amount of time is removed from the working set. The FIFO algorithm is somewhat simpler: It removes the page that has been in physical memory for the greatest amount of time, regardless of how often it's been used.

Replacement policies can be further characterized as either global or local. A global replacement policy allows a page fault to be satisfied by any page frame, regardless of whether that frame is owned by another process. For example, a global replacement policy using the FIFO algorithm would locate the page that has been in memory the longest and would free it to satisfy a page fault. A local replacement policy would limit its search for the oldest page to the set of pages already owned by the process that incurred the page fault. Be aware that global replacement policies make processes vulnerable to the behavior of other processes. For example, an ill-behaved application can undermine the entire operating system by inducing excessive paging activity in all processes.

Windows implements a combination of local and global replacement policies. When a working set reaches its limit and/or needs to be trimmed because of demands for physical memory, the memory manager removes pages from working sets until it has determined there are enough free pages.

Working set management

Every process starts with a default working set minimum of 50 pages and a working set maximum of 345 pages. Although it has little effect, you can change these working set limits with the Windows SetProcessWorkingSetSize function, although you must have the increase scheduling priority (SeIncreaseBasePriorityPrivilege) privilege to do this. However, unless you have configured the process to use hard working set limits, these limits are ignored. That is, the memory manager will permit a process to grow beyond its maximum if it is paging heavily and there is ample memory. (Conversely the memory manager will shrink a process below its working set minimum if it is not paging and there is a high demand for physical memory on the system.) You can set hard working set limits using the SetProcessWorkingSetSizeEx function along with the QUOTA_LIMITS_HARDWS_MAX_ENABLE flag, but it is almost always better to let the system manage your working set.

On 32 bit systems, the maximum working set size can't exceed the system-wide maximum calculated at system initialization time, stored in the MiMaximumWorkingSet kernel variable. On x64 systems, physical memory would be the practical upper limit, as the virtual address space is so vast. The working set maximums are listed in Table 5-15.

TABLE 5-15   Upper limit for working set maximums

Windows Version	Working Set Maximum
x86, ARM	2 GB—64 KB (0x7FFF0000)
x86 versions of Windows booted with increaseuserva	2 GB—64 KB + user virtual address increase
x64 (Windows 8, Server 2012)	8,192 GB (8 TB)
X64 (Windows 8.1, 10, Server 2012 R2, 2016)	128 TB

When a page fault occurs, the process's working set limits and the amount of free memory on the system are examined. If conditions permit, the memory manager allows a process to grow to its working set maximum (or beyond if the process does not have a hard working set limit and there are enough free pages available). However, if memory is tight, Windows replaces rather than adds pages in a working set when a fault occurs.

Windows attempts to keep memory available by writing modified pages to disk. Still, when modified pages are being generated at a very high rate, more memory is required to meet memory demands. Therefore, when physical memory runs low, the working set manager, a routine that runs in the context of the balance set manager system thread (described in the next section), initiates automatic working set trimming to increase the amount of free memory available in the system. You can also initiate working set trimming of your own process—for example, after process initialization—with the aforementioned Windows `SetProcessWorkingSetSizeEx` function.

The working set manager examines available memory and decides which, if any, working sets need to be trimmed. If there is ample memory, the working set manager calculates how many pages could be removed from working sets if needed. If trimming is needed, it looks at working sets that are above their minimum setting. It also dynamically adjusts the rate at which it examines working sets and arranges the list of processes that are candidates to be trimmed into an optimal order. For example, processes with many pages that have not been accessed recently are examined first; larger processes that have been idle longer are considered before smaller processes that are running more often; the process running the foreground application is considered last; and so on.

When the working set manager finds processes that are using more than their minimums, it looks for pages to remove from the working sets, making the pages available for other uses. If the amount of free memory is still too low, the working set manager continues removing pages from processes' working sets until it achieves a minimum number of free pages on the system.

The working set manager tries to remove pages that haven't been accessed recently by checking the accessed bit in the hardware PTE to see whether a page has been accessed. If the bit is clear, the page is said to be *aged*. That is, a count is incremented indicating that the page hasn't been referenced since the last working set trim scan. Later, the age of pages is used to locate candidate pages to remove from the working set.

If the hardware PTE accessed bit is set, the working set manager clears it and goes on to examine the next page in the working set. In this way, if the accessed bit is clear the next time the working set manager examines the page, it knows that the page hasn't been accessed since the last time it was examined. This scan for pages to remove continues through the working set list until either the number of desired pages has been removed or the scan has returned to the starting point. The next time the working set is trimmed, the scan picks up where it left off last.

EXPERIMENT: Viewing process working set sizes

You can use Performance Monitor to examine process working set sizes by looking at the performance counters shown in the following table. Several other process viewer utilities (such as Task Manager and Process Explorer) also display the process working set size.

Counter	Description
Process: Working Set	This notes the current size of the selected process's working set in bytes.
Process: Working Set Peak	This tracks the peak size of the selected process's working set in bytes.
Process: Page Faults/Sec	This indicates the number of page faults for the process that occur each second.

You can also get the total of all the process working sets by selecting the _Total process in the instance box in Performance Monitor. This process isn't real; it's simply a total of the process-specific counters for all processes currently running on the system. The total you see is larger than the actual RAM being used, however, because the size of each process working set includes pages being shared by other processes. Thus, if two or more processes share a page, the page is counted in each process's working set.

EXPERIMENT: Working set versus virtual size

Earlier in this chapter, you used the TestLimit utility to create two processes: one with a large amount of memory that was merely reserved, and one in which the memory was private committed. You then examined the difference between them with Process Explorer. Now we will create a third TestLimit process—one that not only commits the memory but also accesses it, thus bringing it into its working set. Follow these steps:

1. Create a new TestLimit process.

   ```
   C:\Users\pavely>testlimit -d 1 -c 800

   Testlimit v5.24 - test Windows limits
   Copyright (C) 2012-2015 Mark Russinovich
   Sysinternals - www.sysinternals.com

   Process ID: 13008

   Leaking private bytes with touch 1 MB at a time...
   Leaked 800 MB of private memory (800 MB total leaked). Lasterror: 0
   The operation completed successfully.
   ```

2. Open Process Explorer.

3. Open the **View** menu, choose **Select Columns**, and click the **Process Memory** tab.

4. Enable the **Private Bytes**, **Virtual Size**, **Working Set Size**, **WS Shareable Bytes**, and **WS Private Bytes** counters.

5. Find the three instances of TestLimit, as shown in the display:

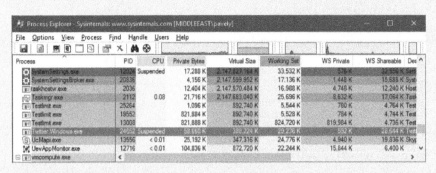

The new TestLimit process is the third one shown, PID 13008. It is the only one of the three that actually referenced the memory allocated, so it is the only one with a working set that reflects the size of the test allocation.

Note that this result is possible only on a system with enough RAM to allow the process to grow to such a size. Even on this system, not quite all of the private bytes (821,888 K) are in the WS Private portion of the working set. A small number of the private pages have been pushed out of the process working set due to replacement or have not been paged in yet.

EXPERIMENT: Viewing the working set list in the debugger

You can view the individual entries in the working set by using the kernel debugger !wsle command. The following example shows a partial output of the working set list of WinDbg (32-bit system):

```
lkd> !wsle 7

Working Set Instance @ c0802d50
Working Set Shared @ c0802e30

    FirstFree      f7d  FirstDynamic      6
    LastEntry     203d  NextSlot          6  LastInitialized   2063
    NonDirect        0  HashTable         0  HashTableSize        0

Reading the WSLE data ........................................................
.......

Virtual Address        Age  Locked  ReferenceCount
        c0603009         0     0        1
        c0602009         0     0        1
        c0601009         0     0        1
        c0600009         0     0        1
        c0802d59         6     0        1
        c0604019         0     0        1
        c0800409         2     0        1
        c0006209         1     0        1
        77290a05         5     0        1
        7739aa05         5     0        1
        c0014209         1     0        1
```

c0004209	1	0	1
72a37805	4	0	1
b50409	2	0	1
b52809	4	0	1
7731dc05	6	0	1
bbec09	6	0	1
bbfc09	6	0	1
6c801805	4	0	1
772a1405	2	0	1
944209	1	0	1
77316a05	5	0	1
773a4209	1	0	1
77317405	2	0	1
772d6605	3	0	1
a71409	2	0	1
c1d409	2	0	1
772d4a05	5	0	1
77342c05	6	0	1
6c80f605	3	0	1
77320405	2	0	1
77323205	1	0	1
77321405	2	0	1
7ffe0215	1	0	2
a5fc09	6	0	1
7735cc05	6	0	1

...

Notice that some entries in the working set list are page table pages (the ones with addresses greater than 0xC0000000), some are from system DLLs (the ones in the 0x7nnnnnnn range), and some are from the code of Windbg.exe itself.

Balance set manager and swapper

Working set expansion and trimming take place in the context of a system thread called the *balance set manager* (KeBalanceSetManager function). The balance set manager is created during system initialization. Although the balance set manager is technically part of the kernel, it calls the memory manager's working set manager (MmWorkingSetManager) to perform working set analysis and adjustment.

The balance set manager waits for two different event objects: an event that is signaled when a periodic timer set to fire once per second expires and an internal working set manager event that the memory manager signals at various points when it determines that working sets need to be adjusted. For example, if the system is experiencing a high page fault rate or the free list is too small, the memory manager wakes up the balance set manager so that it will call the working set manager to begin trimming working sets. When memory is more plentiful, the working set manager permits faulting processes to gradually increase the size of their working sets by faulting pages back into memory. However, the working sets will grow only as needed.

When the balance set manager wakes up because its 1-second timer has expired, it takes the following steps:

1. If the system supports Virtual Secure Mode (VSM, Windows 10 and Server 2016), then the secure kernel is called to do its periodic housekeeping (`VslSecureKernelPeriodicTick`).

2. Calls a routine to adjust IRP credits to optimize the usage of the per-processor look-aside lists used in IRP completion (`IoAdjustIrpCredits`). This allows better scalability when certain processors are under heavy I/O load. (See Chapter 6 for more on IRPs.)

3. Checks the look-aside lists and adjusts their depths (if necessary) to improve access time and reduce pool usage and pool fragmentation (`ExAdjustLookasideDepth`).

4. Calls to adjust the Event Tracing for Windows (ETW) buffer pool size to use ETW memory buffers more efficiently (`EtwAdjustTraceBuffers`). (For more on ETW, see Chapter 8 in Part 2.)

5. Calls the memory manager's working set manager. The working set manager has its own internal counters that regulate when to perform working set trimming and how aggressively to trim.

6. Enforces execution time for jobs (`PsEnforceExecutionLimits`).

7. Every eighth time the balance set manager wakes up because its 1-second timer has expired, it signals an event that wakes up another system thread called the *swapper* (`KeSwapProcessOrStack`). It attempts to outswap kernel stacks for threads that have not executed for a long time. The swapper thread (which runs at priority 23) looks for threads that have been in a user mode wait state for 15 seconds. If it finds one, it puts the thread's kernel stack in transition (moving the pages to the modified or standby lists) to reclaim its physical memory, operating on the principle that if a thread has been waiting that long, it's going to be waiting even longer. When the last thread in a process has its kernel stack removed from memory, the process is marked to be entirely outswapped. That's why, for example, processes that have been idle for a long time (such as Wininit or Winlogon) can have a working set size of zero.

System working sets

Just as processes have working sets that manage pageable portions of the process address space, the pageable code and data in the system address space is managed using three global working sets, collectively known as the *system working sets*. These global working sets are as follows:

- **System cache working set**   This contains pages that are resident in the system cache.

- **Paged pool working set**   This contains pages that are resident in the paged pool.

- **System PTEs working set**   This contains pageable code and data from loaded drivers and the kernel image and pages from sections that have been mapped into the system space.

Table 5-16 shows where these system working set types are stored.

TABLE 5-16 System working sets

System Working Set Type	Stored in (Windows 8.x, Server 2012/R2)	Stored in (Windows 10, Server 2016)
System cache	`MmSystemCacheWs`	`MiState.SystemVa.SystemWs[0]`
Paged pool	`MmPagedPoolWs`	`MiState.SystemVa.SystemWs[2]`
System PTEs	`MmSystemPtesWs`	`MiState.SystemVa.SystemWs[1]`

You can examine the sizes of these working sets or the sizes of the components that contribute to them with the performance counters or system variables shown in Table 5-17. (Note that the performance counter values are in bytes, whereas the system variables are measured in pages.)

TABLE 5-17 System working set performance counters

Performance Counter (in Bytes)	System Variable (in Pages)	Description
Memory: Cache Bytes Memory: System Cache Resident Bytes	`WorkingSetSize` member	This is the physical memory consumed by the file system cache.
Memory: Cache Bytes Peak	`PeakWorkingSetSize` member (Windows 10 and 2016) `Peak` member (Windows 8.x and 2012/R2)	This is the peak system working set size.
Memory: System Driver Resident Bytes	`SystemPageCounts.SystemDriverPage` (global, Windows 10 and Server 2016) `MmSystemDriverPage` (global, Windows 8.x and Server 2012/R2)	This is the physical memory consumed by pageable device driver code.
Memory: Pool Paged Resident Bytes	`WorkingSetSize` member	This is the physical memory consumed by paged pool.

You can also examine the paging activity in the system cache working set by examining the Memory: Cache Faults/Sec performance counter. This counter describes page faults that occur in the system cache working set (both hard and soft). The `PageFaultCount` member in the system cache working set structure contains the value for this counter.

Memory notification events

Windows provides a way for user-mode processes and kernel-mode drivers to be notified when physical memory, paged pool, non-paged pool, and commit charge are low and/or plentiful. This information can be used to determine memory usage as appropriate. For example, if available memory is low, the application can reduce memory consumption. If available paged pool is high, the driver can allocate more memory. Finally, the memory manager also provides an event that permits notification when corrupted pages have been detected.

User-mode processes can be notified only of low or high memory conditions. An application can call the `CreateMemoryResourceNotification` function, specifying whether low or high memory notification is desired. The returned handle can be provided to any of the wait functions. When memory is low (or high), the wait completes, thus notifying the thread of the condition. Alternatively, the `QueryMemoryResourceNotification` can be used to query the system memory condition at any time without blocking the calling thread.

Drivers, on the other hand, use the specific event name that the memory manager has set up in the \ KernelObjects object manager directory. This is because notification is implemented by the memory manager signaling one of the globally named event objects it defines, shown in Table 5-18. When a given memory condition is detected, the appropriate event is signaled, thus waking up any waiting threads.

TABLE 5-18 Memory manager notification events

Event Name	Description
HighCommitCondition	This event is set when the commit charge is near the maximum commit limit—in other words, memory usage is very high, very little space is available in physical memory or paging files, and the operating system cannot increase the size of its paging files.
HighMemoryCondition	This event is set whenever the amount of free physical memory exceeds the defined amount.
HighNonPagedPoolCondition	This event is set whenever the amount of non-paged pool exceeds the defined amount.
HighPagedPoolCondition	This event is set whenever the amount of paged pool exceeds the defined amount.
LowCommitCondition	This event is set when the commit charge is low relative to the current commit limit—in other words, memory usage is low and a lot of space is available in physical memory or paging files.
LowMemoryCondition	This event is set whenever the amount of free physical memory falls below the defined amount.
LowNonPagedPoolCondition	This event is set whenever the amount of free non-paged pool falls below the defined amount.
LowPagedPoolCondition	This event is set whenever the amount of free paged pool falls below the defined amount.
MaximumCommitCondition	This event is set when the commit charge is near the maximum commit limit—in other words, memory usage is very high, very little space is available in physical memory or paging files, and the operating system cannot increase the size or number of paging files.
MemoryErrors	This indicates that a bad page (non-zeroed zero page) has been detected.

 Note You can override the high and low memory values by adding the LowMemoryThreshold or HighMemoryThreshold DWORD registry value under HKLM\SYSTEM\CurrentControlSet\ Session Manager\Memory Management. This specifies the number of megabytes to use as the low or high threshold. You can also configure the system to crash when a bad page is detected instead of signaling a memory error event by setting the PageValidationAction DWORD registry value in the same key to 1.

EXPERIMENT: Viewing the memory resource notification events

To see the memory resource notification events, run WinObj from Sysinternals and click the **KernelObjects** folder. You will see both the low and high memory condition events shown in the pane on the right:

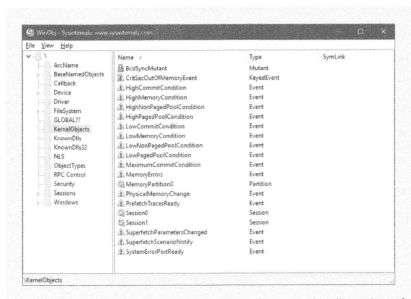

If you double-click either event, you can see how many handles and/or references have been made to the objects. To see whether any processes in the system have requested memory resource notification, search the handle table for references to LowMemoryCondition or HighMemoryCondition. To do so, use Process Explorer's **Find** menu (choose **Find Handle or DLL**) or use WinDbg. (For a description of the handle table, see the section "Object manager" in Chapter 8 in Part 2.)

Page frame number database

Several previous sections concentrated on the virtual view of a Windows process—page tables, PTEs, and VADs. The remainder of this chapter will explain how Windows manages physical memory, starting with how Windows keeps track of physical memory. Whereas working sets describe the resident pages owned by a process or the system, the PFN database describes the state of each page in physical memory. The page states are listed in Table 5-19.

TABLE 5-19 Physical page states

Status	Description
Active (also called valid)	The page is part of a working set (either a process working set, a session working set, or a system working set), or it's not in any working set (for example, a non-paged kernel page) and a valid PTE usually points to it.
Transition	This is a temporary state for a page that isn't owned by a working set and isn't on any paging list. A page is in this state when an I/O to the page is in progress. The PTE is encoded so that collided page faults can be recognized and handled properly. (This use of the term transition differs from the use of the word in the section on invalid PTEs. An invalid transition PTE refers to a page on the standby or modified list.)
Standby	The page previously belonged to a working set but was removed or was prefetched/clustered directly into the standby list. The page wasn't modified since it was last written to disk. The PTE still refers to the physical page but it is marked invalid and in transition.

TABLE 5-19   Physical page states *(continued)*

Status	Description
Modified	The page previously belonged to a working set but was removed. However, the page was modified while it was in use and its current contents haven't yet been written to disk or remote storage. The PTE still refers to the physical page but is marked invalid and in transition. It must be written to the backing store before the physical page can be reused.
Modified no-write	This is the same as a modified page except that the page has been marked so that the memory manager's modified page writer won't write it to disk. The cache manager marks pages as modified no-write at the request of file system drivers. For example, NTFS uses this state for pages containing file system metadata so that it can first ensure that transaction log entries are flushed to disk before the pages they are protecting are written to disk. (NTFS transaction logging is explained in Chapter 13, "File systems," in Part 2.)
Free	The page is free but has unspecified dirty data in it. For security reasons, these pages can't be given as a user page to a user process without being initialized with zeroes, but they can be overwritten with new data (for example, from a file) before being given to a user process.
Zeroed	The page is free and has been initialized with zeroes by the zero page thread or was determined to already contain zeroes.
Rom	The page represents read-only memory.
Bad	The page has generated parity or other hardware errors and can't be used (or used as part of an enclave).

The PFN database consists of an array of structures that represent each physical page of memory on the system. The PFN database and its relationship to page tables are shown in Figure 5-35. As this figure shows, valid PTEs usually point to entries in the PFN database (and the PFN index points to the page in physical memory), and the PFN database entries (for non-prototype PFNs) point back to the page table that is using them (if it is being used by a page table). For prototype PFNs, they point back to the prototype PTE.

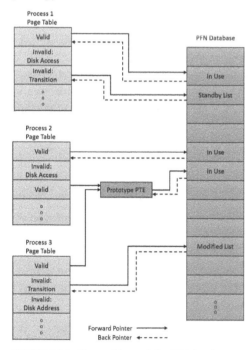

FIGURE 5-35   Page tables and the PFN database.

Of the page states listed in Table 5-19, six are organized into linked lists so that the memory manager can quickly locate pages of a specific type. (Active/valid pages, transition pages, and overloaded "bad" pages aren't in any system-wide page list.) Additionally, the standby state is associated with eight different lists ordered by priority. (We'll talk about page priority later in this section.) Figure 5-36 shows an example of how these entries are linked together.

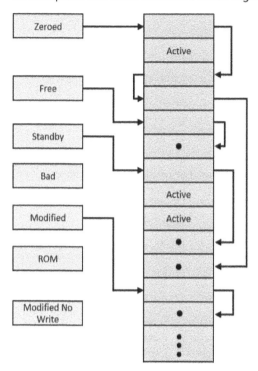

FIGURE 5-36 Page lists in the PFN database.

In the next section, you'll find out how these linked lists are used to satisfy page faults and how pages move to and from the various lists.

EXPERIMENT: Viewing the PFN database

You can use the MemInfo tool from the *Windows Internals* book's website to dump the size of the various paging lists by using the –s flag. The following is the output from this command:

```
C:\Tools>MemInfo.exe -s
MemInfo v3.00 - Show PFN database information
Copyright (C) 2007-2016 Alex Ionescu
www.alex-ionescu.com

Initializing PFN Database... Done

PFN Database List Statistics
            Zeroed:    4867 (    19468 kb)
```

```
        Free:    3076 (   12304 kb)
     Standby: 4669104 (18676416 kb)
    Modified:    7845 (   31380 kb)
ModifiedNoWrite:  117 (     468 kb)
Active/Valid: 3677990 (14711960 kb)
  Transition:       5 (      20 kb)
         Bad:       0 (       0 kb)
     Unknown:    1277 (    5108 kb)
       TOTAL: 8364281 (33457124 kb)
```

Using the kernel debugger !memusage command, you can obtain similar information, although this will take considerably longer to execute.

Page list dynamics

Figure 5-37 shows a state diagram for page frame transitions. For simplicity, the modified-no-write, bad and ROM lists aren't shown.

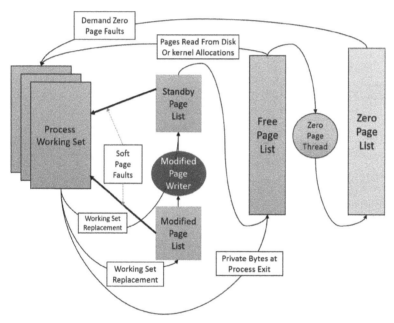

FIGURE 5-37   State diagram for physical pages.

Page frames move between the paging lists in the following ways:

■   When the memory manager needs a zero-initialized page to service a demand-zero page fault (a reference to a page that is defined to be all zeroes or to a user-mode committed private page that has never been accessed), it first attempts to get one from the zero page list. If the list is empty, it gets one from the free page list and zeroes the page. If the free list is empty, it goes to the standby list and zeroes that page.

One reason zero-initialized pages are needed is to meet security requirements such as the Common Criteria (CC). Most CC profiles specify that user-mode processes be given initialized page frames to prevent them from reading a previous process's memory contents. Thus, the memory manager gives user-mode processes zeroed page frames unless the page is being read in from a backing store. In that case, the memory manager prefers to use non-zeroed page frames, initializing them with the data off the disk or remote storage. The zero page list is populated from the free list by the zero page thread system thread (thread 0 in the System process). The zero page thread waits on a gate object to signal it to go to work. When the free list has eight or more pages, this gate is signaled. However, the zero page thread will run only if at least one processor has no other threads running, because the zero page thread runs at priority 0 and the lowest priority that a user thread can be set to is 1.

Note When memory needs to be zeroed as a result of a physical page allocation by a driver that calls MmAllocatePagesForMdl(Ex), by a Windows application that calls AllocateUserPhysicalPages or AllocateUserPhysicalPagesNuma, or when an application allocates large pages, the memory manager zeroes the memory by using a higher-performing function called MiZeroInParallel that maps larger regions than the zero page thread, which only zeroes a page at a time. In addition, on multiprocessor systems, the memory manager creates additional system threads to perform the zeroing in parallel (and in a NUMA-optimized fashion on NUMA platforms).

- When the memory manager doesn't require a zero-initialized page, it goes first to the free list. If that's empty, it goes to the zeroed list. If the zeroed list is empty, it goes to the standby lists. Before the memory manager can use a page frame from the standby lists, it must first backtrack and remove the reference from the invalid PTE (or prototype PTE) that still points to the page frame. Because entries in the PFN database contain pointers back to the previous user's page table page (or to a page of prototype PTE pool for shared pages), the memory manager can quickly find the PTE and make the appropriate change.

- When a process must give up a page out of its working set either because it referenced a new page and its working set was full or the memory manager trimmed its working set, the page goes to the standby lists if the page was clean (not modified) or to the modified list if the page was modified while it was resident.

- When a process exits, all the private pages go to the free list. Also, when the last reference to a page-file-backed section is closed, and the section has no remaining mapped views, these pages also go to the free list.

EXPERIMENT: The free and zero page lists

You can observe the release of private pages at process exit with Process Explorer's System Information display. Begin by creating a process with numerous private pages in its working set. We did this in an earlier experiment with the TestLimit utility:

```
C:\Tools\Sysinternals>Testlimit.exe -d 1 -c 1500

Testlimit v5.24 - test Windows limits
Copyright (C) 2012-2015 Mark Russinovich
Sysinternals - www.sysinternals.com

Process ID: 13928

Leaking private bytes with touch 1 MB at a time...
Leaked 1500 MB of private memory (1500 MB total leaked). Lasterror: 0
The operation completed successfully.
```

The –d option causes TestLimit to not only allocate the memory as private committed, but to touch it—that is, to access it. This causes physical memory to be allocated and assigned to the process to realize the area of private committed virtual memory. If there is sufficient available RAM on the system, the entire 1,500 MB should be in RAM for the process. The process will now wait until you cause it to exit or terminate (perhaps by pressing **Ctrl+C** in its command window). After you do, follow these steps:

1. Open Process Explorer.

2. Open the **View** menu, choose **System Information**, and click the **Memory** tab.

3. Observe the size of the Free and Zeroed lists.

4. Terminate or exit the TestLimit process.

You *may* see the free page list briefly increase in size. We say "may" because the zero page thread is awakened as soon as there are only eight pages on the free list, and it acts very quickly. Process Explorer updates this display only once per second, and it is likely that most of the pages were already zeroed and moved to the zeroed page list before it happened to "catch" this state. If you can see the temporary increase in the free list, you will then see it drop to zero, and a corresponding increase will occur in the zeroed page list. If not, you will simply see the increase in the zeroed list.

EXPERIMENT: The modified and standby page lists

You can observe the movement of pages from process working set to the modified page list and then to the standby page list with the VMMap and RAMMap Sysinternals tools and the live kernel debugger. Follow these steps:

1. Open RAMMap and observe the state of the quiet system. This is an x86 system with 3 GB of RAM. The columns in this display represent the various page states shown in Figure 5-37 (a few of the columns not important to this discussion have been narrowed for ease of reference).

RamMap - Sysinternals: www.sysinternals.com

File   Empty   Help

Use Counts | Processes | Priority Summary | Physical Pages | Physical Ranges | File Summary | File Details

Usage	Total	Active	Standby	Modified	Zeroed	Free
Process Private	448,284 K	404,448 K	13,412 K	30,424 K		
Mapped File	1,631,144 K	97,088 K	1,533,328 K	728 K		
Shareable	48,876 K	32,840 K	1,044 K	14,992 K		
Page Table	23,060 K	23,060 K				
Paged Pool	145,792 K	144,860 K	848 K	84 K		
Nonpaged Pool	66,108 K	66,096 K				
System PTE	27,964 K	27,964 K				
Session Private	12,416 K	12,416 K				
Metafile	297,956 K	9,816 K	288,036 K	104 K		
AWE						
Driver Locked	988 K	988 K				
Kernel Stack	10,912 K	10,672 K		240 K		
Unused	431,768 K	8,016 K			5,064 K	418,688 K
Large Page						
Total	3,145,268 K	838,264 K	1,836,668 K	46,572 K	5,064 K	418,688 K

2. The system has about 420 MB of RAM free (sum of the free and zeroed page lists). About 580 MB is on the standby list (hence part of "available," but likely containing data recently lost from processes or being used by SuperFetch). About 830 MB is "active," being mapped directly to virtual addresses via valid page table entries.

3. Each row further breaks down into page state by usage or origin (process private, mapped file, and so on). For example, at the moment, of the active 830 MB, about 400 MB is due to process private allocations.

4. Now, as in the previous experiment, use the TestLimit utility to create a process with a large number of pages in its working set. Again, we will use the –d option to cause TestLimit to write to each page, but this time we will use it without a limit, so as to create as many private modified pages as possible:

```
C:\Tools\Sysinternals>Testlimit.exe -d

Testlimit v5.24 - test Windows limits
Copyright (C) 2012-2015 Mark Russinovich
Sysinternals - www.sysinternals.com

Process ID: 7548

Leaking private bytes with touch (MB)...
Leaked 1975 MB of private memory (1975 MB total leaked). Lasterror: 8
```

5. TestLimit has now created 1975 allocations of 1 MB each. In RAMMap, use the **File** | **Refresh** command to update the display (because of the cost of gathering its information, RAMMap does not update continuously).

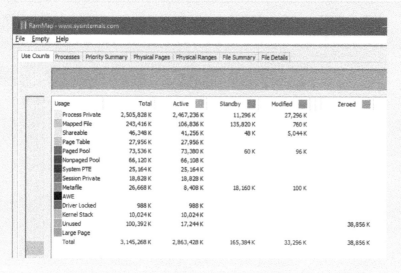

6. You will see that over 2.8 GB are now active, of which 2.4 GB are in the Process Private row. This is due to the memory allocated and accessed by the TestLimit process. Note also that the standby, zeroed, and free lists are now much smaller. Most of the RAM allocated to TestLimit came from these lists.

7. Next, in RAMMap, check the process's physical page allocations. Change to the **Physical Pages** tab, and set the filter at the bottom to the **Process** column and the value **Testlimit.exe**. This display shows all the physical pages that are part of the process working set.

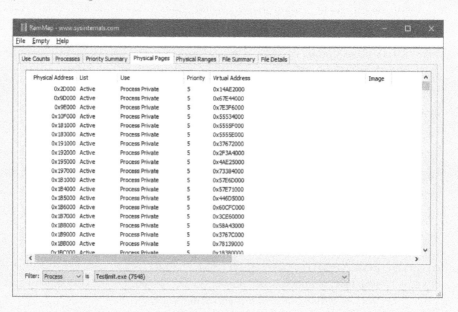

8. We would like to identify a physical page involved in the allocation of virtual address space done by TestLimit's –d option. RAMMap does not give an indication about which virtual allocations are associated with RAMMap's `VirtualAlloc` calls. However, we can get a good hint of this through the VMMap tool. Using VMMap on the same process, we find the following:

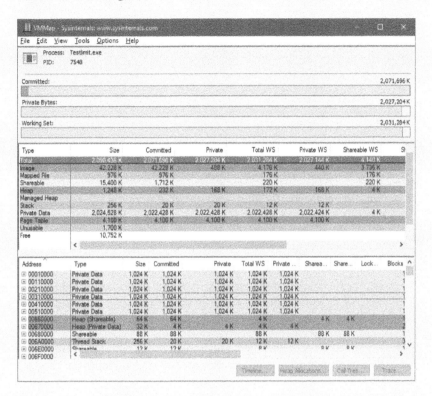

9. In the lower part of the display, we find hundreds of allocations of process private data, each 1 MB in size and with 1 MB committed. These match the size of the allocations done by TestLimit. One of these is highlighted in the preceding screenshot. Note the starting virtual address, 0x310000.

10. Now go back to RAMMap's physical memory display. Arrange the columns to make the Virtual Address column easily visible, click it to sort by that value, and you can find that virtual address:

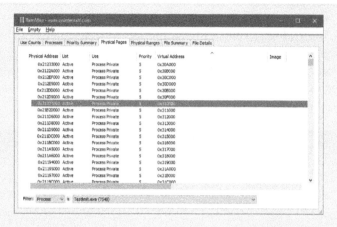

11. This shows that the virtual page starting at 0x310000 is currently mapped to physical address 0x212D1000. TestLimit's –d option writes the program's own name to the first bytes of each allocation. We can demonstrate this with the !dc (display characters using physical address) command in the local kernel debugger:

```
1kd> !dc 0x212d1000
#212d1000 74736554 696d694c 00000074 00000000 TestLimit.......
#212d1010 00000000 00000000 00000000 00000000 ................
...
```

12. If you're not quick enough, this may fail—the page may be removed from the working set. For the final leg of the experiment, we will demonstrate that this data remains intact (for a while, anyway) after the process working set is reduced and this page is moved to the modified and then the standby page list.

13. In VMMap, having selected the TestLimit process, open the **View** menu and choose **Empty Working Set** to reduce the process's working set to the bare minimum. VMMap's display should now look like this:

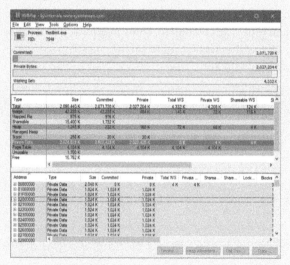

14. Notice that the Working Set bar graph is practically empty. In the middle section, the process shows a total working set of only 4 KB, and almost all of it is in page tables. Now return to RAMMap and refresh it. On the Use Counts tab, you will find that active pages have been reduced tremendously, with a large number of pages on the modified list and some on the standby list:

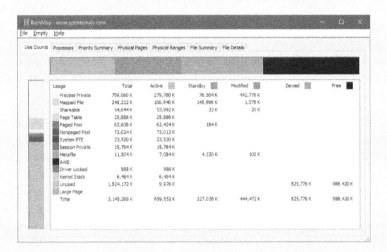

15. RAMMap's Processes tab confirms that the TestLimit process contributed most of those pages to those lists:

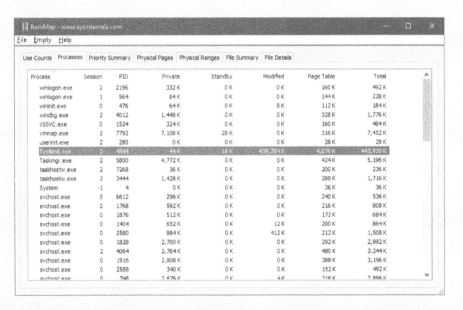

Page priority

Every physical page in the system has a page priority value assigned to it by the memory manager. The page priority is a number in the range 0 to 7. Its main purpose is to determine the order in which pages are consumed from the standby list. The memory manager divides the standby list into eight sublists that each stores pages of a particular priority. When the memory manager wants to take a page from the standby list, it takes pages from low-priority lists first.

Each thread and process in the system is also assigned a page priority. A page's priority usually reflects the page priority of the thread that first causes its allocation. (If the page is shared, it reflects the highest page priority among the sharing threads.) A thread inherits its page-priority value from the process to which it belongs. The memory manager uses low priorities for pages it reads from disk speculatively when anticipating a process's memory accesses.

By default, processes have a page-priority value of 5, but the SetProcessInformation and SetThreadInformation user-mode functions allow applications to change process and thread page-priority values. These functions call the native NtSetInformationProcess and NtSetInformation-Thread functions. You can look at the memory priority of a thread with Process Explorer (per-page priority can be displayed by looking at the PFN entries, as you'll see in an experiment later in the chapter). Figure 5-38 shows Process Explorer's Threads tab displaying information about Winlogon's main thread. Although the thread priority itself is high, the memory priority is still the standard 5.

FIGURE 5-38 Process Explorer's Threads tab.

The real power of memory priorities is realized only when the relative priorities of pages are understood at a high level, which is the role of SuperFetch, covered at the end of this chapter.

EXPERIMENT: Viewing the prioritized standby lists

You can use Process Explorer to look at the size of each standby paging list by opening the System Information dialog box and selecting the **Memory** tab:

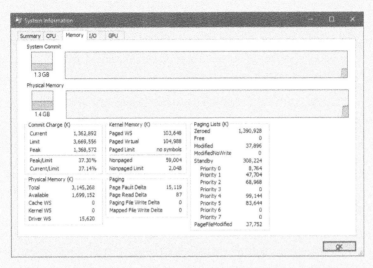

On the recently started x86 system used in this experiment, there is about 9 MB of data cached at priority 0, about 47 MB at priority 1, about 68 MB at priority 2, etc. The following shows what happens when we use the TestLimit tool from Sysinternals to commit and touch as much memory as possible:

```
C:\Tools\Sysinternals>Testlimit.exe -d
```

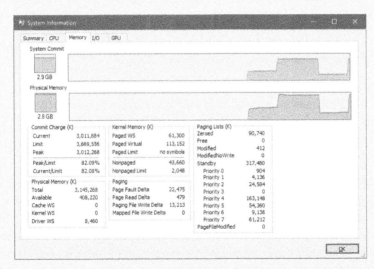

Note how the lower-priority standby page lists were used first (shown by the repurposed count) and are now much smaller, while the higher lists still contain valuable cached data.

Modified page writer and mapped page writer

The memory manager employs two system threads to write pages back to disk and move those pages back to the standby lists (based on their priority). One system thread writes out modified pages (MiModifiedPageWriter) to the paging file, and a second one writes modified pages to mapped files (MiMappedPageWriter). Two threads are required to avoid creating a deadlock. This would occur if the writing of mapped file pages caused a page fault that in turn required a free page when no free pages were available, thus requiring the modified page writer to create more free pages. By having the modified page writer perform mapped file paging I/Os from a second system thread, that thread can wait without blocking regular page file I/O.

Both threads run at priority 18, and after initialization they wait for separate event objects to trigger their operation. The mapped page writer waits on 18 event objects:

- An exit event, signaling the thread to exit (not relevant to this discussion).

- The mapped writer event, stored in the global variable MiSystemPartition.Modwriter. MappedPageWriterEvent (MmMappedPageWriterEvent on Windows 8.*x* and Server 2012/R2). This event can be signaled in the following instances:

  - During a page list operation (MiInsertPageInList); this routine inserts a page into one of the lists (standby, modified, etc.) based on its input arguments. The routine signals this event if the number of file-system-destined pages on the modified page list has reached more than 16 and the number of available pages has fallen below 1024.

  - In an attempt to obtain free pages (MiObtainFreePages).

  - By the memory manager's working set manager (MmWorkingSetManager), which runs as part of the kernel's balance set manager (once every second). The working set manager signals this event if the number of file-system-destined pages on the modified page list has reached more than 800.

  - Upon a request to flush all modified pages (MmFlushAllPages).

  - Upon a request to flush all file-system-destined modified pages (MmFlushAllFilesystemPages). Note that in most cases, writing modified mapped pages to their backing store files does not occur if the number of mapped pages on the modified page list is less than the maximum write cluster size, which is 16 pages. This check is not made in MmFlushAllFilesystemPages or MmFlushAllPages.

- An array of 16 events associated with 16 mapped page lists, stored in MiSystemPartition. PageLists.MappedPageListHeadEvent (MiMappedPageListHeadEvent on Windows 8.*x* and Server 2012/R2). Each time a mapped page is dirtied, it is inserted into one of these 16 mapped page lists based on a bucket number, stored in MiSystemPartition.WorkingSetControl->CurrentMappedPageBucket (MiCurrentMappedPageBucket on Windows 8.*x* and Server 2012/R2). This bucket number is updated by the working set manager whenever the system considers that mapped pages have gotten old enough, which is currently 100 seconds (stored in the WriteGapCounter variable in the same structure [MiWriteGapCounter on Windows 8.*x* and Server 2012/R2] and incremented whenever the working set manager runs). The reason for these additional events is to reduce data loss in the case of a system crash or power failure by eventually writing out modified mapped pages even if the modified list hasn't reached its threshold of 800 pages.

The modified page writer waits on two events: the first is an Exit event, and the second stored in `MiSystemPartition.Modwriter.ModifiedPageWriterEvent` (on Windows 8.*x* and Server 2012/R2 waits on a kernel gate stored in `MmModifiedPageWriterGate`), which can be signaled in the following scenarios:

- A request to flush all pages has been received.

- The number of available pages—stored in `MiSystemPartition.Vp.AvailablePages` (`MmAvailablePages` on Windows 8.*x* and Server 2012/R2)—drops below 128 pages.

- The total size of the zeroed and free page lists drops below 20,000 pages, and the number of modified pages destined for the paging file is greater than the smaller of one-sixteenth of the available pages or 64 MB (16,384 pages).

- When a working set is being trimmed to accommodate additional pages, if the number of pages available is less than 15,000.

- During a page list operation (`MiInsertPageInList`). This routine signals this event if the number of page-file-destined pages on the modified page list has reached more than 16 pages and the number of available pages has fallen below 1,024.

Additionally, the modified page writer waits on two other events after the preceding event is signaled. One is used to indicate rescanning of the paging file is required (for example, a new page file may have been created), stored in `MiSystemPartition.Modwriter.RescanPageFilesEvent` (`MiRescanPageFilesEvent` on Windows 8.*x* and Server 2012/R2). The second event is internal to the paging file header (`MiSystemPartition.Modwriter.PagingFileHeader` [`MmPagingFileHeader` on Windows 8.*x* and Server 2012/R2]), which allows the system to manually request flushing out data to the paging file when needed.

When invoked, the mapped page writer attempts to write as many pages as possible to disk with a single I/O request. It accomplishes this by examining the original PTE field of the PFN database elements for pages on the modified page list to locate pages in contiguous locations on the disk. Once a list is created, the pages are removed from the modified list, an I/O request is issued, and, at successful completion of the I/O request, the pages are placed at the tail of the standby list corresponding to their priority.

Pages that are in the process of being written can be referenced by another thread. When this happens, the reference count and the share count in the PFN entry that represents the physical page are incremented to indicate that another process is using the page. When the I/O operation completes, the modified page writer notices that the reference count is no longer 0 and doesn't place the page on any standby list.

PFN data structures

Although PFN database entries are of fixed length, they can be in several different states, depending on the state of the page. Thus, individual fields have different meanings depending on the state. Figure 5-39 shows the formats of PFN entries for different states.

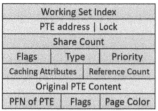

PFN for a page in a working set

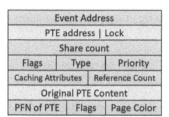

PFN for a page on the standby or modified list

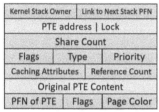

PFN for a page belonging to a kernel stack

PFN for a page with I/O in progress

FIGURE 5-39   States of PFN database entries (specific layouts are conceptual).

Several fields are the same for several PFN types, but others are specific to a given type of PFN. The following fields appear in more than one PFN type:

- **PTE address**   This is the virtual address of the PTE that points to this page. Also, since PTE addresses will always be aligned on a 4-byte boundary (8 bytes on 64-bit systems), the two low-order bits are used as a locking mechanism to serialize access to the PFN entry.

- **Reference count**   This is the number of references to this page. The reference count is incremented when a page is first added to a working set and/or when the page is locked in memory for I/O (for example, by a device driver). The reference count is decremented when the share count becomes 0 or when pages are unlocked from memory. When the share count becomes 0, the page is no longer owned by a working set. Then, if the reference count is also zero, the PFN database entry that describes the page is updated to add the page to the free, standby, or modified list.

- **Type**   This is the type of page represented by this PFN. (Types include active/valid, standby, modified, modified-no-write, free, zeroed, bad, and transition.)

- **Flags**   The information contained in the flags field is shown in Table 5-20.

- **Priority**   This is the priority associated with this PFN, which will determine on which standby list it will be placed.

- **Original PTE contents**   All PFN database entries contain the original contents of the PTE that pointed to the page (which could be a prototype PTE). Saving the contents of the PTE allows it to be restored when the physical page is no longer resident. PFN entries for AWE allocations are exceptions; they store the AWE reference count in this field instead.

- **PFN of PTE**   This is the physical page number of the page table page containing the PTE that points to this page.

- **Color**   Besides being linked together on a list, PFN database entries use an additional field to link physical pages by "color," which is the page's NUMA node number.

- **Flags**   A second flags field is used to encode additional information on the PTE. These flags are described in Table 5-21.

TABLE 5-20   Flags within PFN database entries

Flag	Meaning
Write in progress	This indicates that a page write operation is in progress. The first DWORD contains the address of the event object that will be signaled when the I/O is complete.
Modified state	This indicates whether the page was modified. (If the page was modified, its contents must be saved to disk before removing it from memory.)
Read in progress	This indicates that an in-page operation is in progress for the page. The first DWORD contains the address of the event object that will be signaled when the I/O is complete.
ROM	This indicates that this page comes from the computer's firmware or another piece of read-only memory such as a device register.
In-page error	This indicates that an I/O error occurred during the in-page operation on this page. (In this case, the first field in the PFN contains the error code.)
Kernel stack	This indicates that this page is being used to contain a kernel stack. In this case, the PFN entry contains the owner of the stack and the next stack PFN for this thread.
Removal requested	This indicates that the page is the target of a remove (due to ECC/scrubbing or hot memory removal).
Parity error	This indicates that the physical page contains parity or error correction control errors.

TABLE 5-21   Secondary flags within PFN database entries

Flag	Meaning
PFN image verified	This indicates that the code signature for this PFN (contained in the cryptographic signature catalog for the image being backed by this PFN) has been verified.
AWE allocation	This indicates that this PFN backs an AWE allocation.
Prototype PTE	This indicates that the PTE referenced by the PFN entry is a prototype PTE. For example, this page is shareable.

The remaining fields are specific to the type of PFN. For example, the first PFN in Figure 5-39 represents a page that is active and part of a working set. The share count field represents the number of PTEs that refer to this page. (Pages marked read-only, copy-on-write, or shared read/write can be shared by multiple processes.) For page table pages, this field is the number of valid and transition PTEs in the page table. As long as the share count is greater than 0, the page isn't eligible for removal from memory.

The working set index field is an index into the process working set list (or the system or session working set list, or zero if not in any working set) where the virtual address that maps this physical page resides. If the page is a private page, the working set index field refers directly to the entry in the working set list because the page is mapped only at a single virtual address. In the case of a shared page, the working set index is a hint that is guaranteed to be correct only for the first process that made the page valid. (Other processes will try to use the same index where possible.) The process that initially sets this field is guaranteed to refer to the proper index and doesn't need to add a working set list hash entry referenced by the virtual address into its working set hash tree. This guarantee reduces the size of the working set hash tree and makes searches faster for these entries.

The second PFN in Figure 5-39 is for a page on either the standby or the modified list. In this case, the forward and backward link fields link the elements of the list together within the list. This linking allows pages to be easily manipulated to satisfy page faults. When a page is on one of the lists, the share count is by definition 0 (because no working set is using the page) and therefore can be overlaid with the backward link. The reference count is also 0 if the page is on one of the lists. If it is non-zero (because an I/O could be in progress for this page—for example, when the page is being written to disk), it is first removed from the list.

The third PFN in Figure 5-39 is for a page that belongs to a kernel stack. As mentioned earlier, kernel stacks in Windows are dynamically allocated, expanded, and freed whenever a callback to user mode is performed and/or returns, or when a driver performs a callback and requests stack expansion. For these PFNs, the memory manager must keep track of the thread actually associated with the kernel stack, or if it is free it keeps a link to the next free look-aside stack.

The fourth PFN in Figure 5-39 is for a page that has an I/O in progress (for example, a page read). While the I/O is in progress, the first field points to an event object that will be signaled when the I/O completes. If an in-page error occurs, this field contains the Windows error status code representing the I/O error. This PFN type is used to resolve collided page faults.

In addition to the PFN database, the system variables in Table 5-22 describe the overall state of physical memory.

TABLE 5-22 System variables that describe physical memory

Variable (Windows 10 and Server 2016)	Variable (Windows 8.x and Server 2012/R2)	Description
MiSystemPartition.Vp.NumberOfPhysicalPages	MmNumberOfPhysicalPages	This is the total number of physical pages available on the system.
MiSystemPartition.Vp.AvailablePages	MmAvailablePages	This is the total number of available pages on the system—the sum of the pages on the zeroed, free, and standby lists.
MiSystemPartition.Vp.ResidentAvailablePages	MmResidentAvailablePages	This is the total number of physical pages that would be available if every process was trimmed to its minimum working set size and all modified pages were flushed to disk.

EXPERIMENT: Viewing PFN entries

You can examine individual PFN entries with the kernel debugger !pfn command. You need to supply the PFN as an argument. (For example, !pfn 0 shows the first entry, !pfn 1 shows the second, and so on.) In the following example, the PTE for virtual address 0xD20000 is displayed, followed by the PFN that contains the page directory, and then the actual page:

```
lkd> !pte d20000
                      VA 00d20000
PDE at C0600030             PTE at C0006900
contains 000000003E989867   contains 8000000093257847
pfn 3e989      ---DA--UWEV  pfn 93257      ---D---UW-V


lkd> !pfn 3e989
    PFN 0003E989 at address 868D8AFC
    flink        00000071  blink / share count 00000144  pteaddress C0600030
    reference count 0001    Cached      color 0    Priority 5
    restore pte 00000080  containing page 0696B3  Active      M
    Modified
lkd> !pfn 93257
    PFN 00093257 at address 87218184
    flink        000003F9  blink / share count 00000001  pteaddress C0006900
    reference count 0001    Cached      color 0    Priority 5
    restore pte 00000080  containing page 03E989  Active      M
    Modified
```

You can also use the MemInfo tool to obtain information about a PFN. MemInfo can sometimes give you more information than the debugger's output, and it does not require being booted into debugging mode. Here's MemInfo's output for those same two PFNs:

```
C:\Tools>MemInfo.exe -p 3e989

0x3E989000 Active      Page Table      5   N/A          0xC0006000 0x8E499480


C:\Tools>MemInfo.exe -p 93257

0x93257000 Active      Process Private 5   windbg.exe   0x00D20000 N/A
```

From left to right, the information shown includes the physical address, type, page priority, process name, virtual address, and potential extra information. MemInfo correctly recognized that the first PFN was a page table and that the second PFN belongs to WinDbg, which was the active process when the !pte d20000 command was used in the debugger.

Page file reservation

We have already seen some mechanisms used by the memory manager to attempt to reduce physical memory consumption and thus reduce accessing page files. Using the standby and modified list is one such mechanism, and so is memory compression (see the "Memory compression" section later in this chapter). Another optimization the memory uses is directly related to accessing page files themselves.

Rotational hard disks have a moving head that travels to a target sector before the disk can actually read or write. This seek time is relatively expensive (in the order of milliseconds) and so the total disk activity is the seek time added to the actual read/write time. If the amount of data accessed contiguously from the seek position is large, then the seek time may be negligible. But if the head must seek a lot while accessing scattered data on the disk, the aggregated seek time becomes the main issue.

When the Session Manager (Smss.exe) creates a page file, it queries the disk of the file's partition to find whether it's a rotational disk or a solid-state drive (SSD). If it's rotational, it activates a mechanism called *page file reservations* that tries to keep contiguous pages in physical memory contiguous in the page file as well. If the disk is an SSD (or a hybrid, which for the sake of page file reservation is treated as SSD), then page file reservation adds no real value (since there is no moving head), and the feature is not utilized for this particular page file.

Page file reservation is handled in three locations within the memory manager: working set manager, modified page writer, and page fault handler. The working set manager performs working set trimming by calling the MiFreeWsleList routine. The routine takes a list of pages from a working set and for each page it decrements its share count. If it reaches zero, the page can be placed on the modified list, changing the relevant PTE into a transition PTE. The old valid PTE is saved in the PFN.

The invalid PTE has two bits related to page file reservation: page file reserved and page file allocated (refer to Figure 5-24). When a physical page is needed and is taken from one of the "free" page lists (free, zero or standby) to become an active (valid) page, an invalid PTE is saved into the Original PTE field of the PFN. This field is the key for tracking page file reservation.

The MiCheckReservePageFileSpace routine tries to create page file reservation cluster starting from a specified page. It checks if page file reservation is disabled for the target page file and if there is already page file reservation for this page (based on the original PTE), and if any of these conditions is true, the function aborts further processing for this page. The routine also checks if the page type is of user pages, and if not, it bails out. Page file reservation is not attempted for other page types (such as paged pool), because it was not found to be particularly beneficial (because of unpredictable usage patterns, for example), which led to small clusters. Finally, MiCheckReservePageFileSpace calls MiReservePageFileSpace to do the actual work.

The search for page file reservation starts backward from the initial PTE. The goal is to locate eligible consecutive pages where reservation is possible. If the PTE that maps the neighboring page represents a decommitted page, a non-paged pool page, or if it's already reserved, then the page cannot be used; the current page will become the lower limit of the reservation cluster. Otherwise, the search continues backward. Then the search starts from the initial page forward, trying to gather as many eligible pages as possible. The cluster size must be at least 16 pages for the reservation to take place (the maximum cluster size is 512 pages). Figure 5-40 shows an example of a cluster bound by invalid page on one hand and an existing cluster on the other (note that it can span page tables within the same page directory).

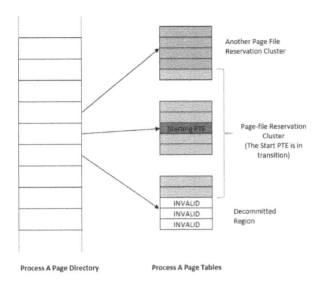

Another Page File
Reservation Cluster

Page-file Reservation
Cluster
(The Start PTE is in
transition)

Starting PTE

INVALID
INVALID
INVALID

Decommitted
Region

Process A Page Directory   Process A Page Tables

FIGURE 5-40 Page file reservation cluster.

Once the page cluster is computed, free page file space must be located to be reserved for this cluster of pages. Page file allocations are managed by a bitmap (where each set bit indicates a used page in the file). For page file reservation, a second bitmap is used that indicates pages that have been reserved (but not necessarily written to yet—this is the job of the page file allocation bitmap). Once there is page file space that is not reserved and not allocated (based on these bitmaps), the relevant bits are set in the reservation bitmap only. It is the job of the modified page writer to set these bits in the allocation bitmap when it writes the contents of the pages to disk. If not enough page file space could be found for the required cluster size, page file expansion is attempted, and if that already happened (or the maximum page file size is the expanded size), then the cluster size is reduced to fit in the reservation size that was located.

Note The clustered pages (except the original starting PTE) are not linked to any of the physical page lists. The reservation information is placed in the Original PTE of the PFN.

The modified page writer needs to handle writing pages that have reservations as a special case. It uses all the gathered information described previously to build an MDL that contains the correct PFNs for the cluster that is used as part of writing to the page file. Building the cluster includes finding contiguous pages that can span reservation clusters. If there are "holes" between clusters, a dummy page is added in between (a page that contains all bytes with 0xFF value). If the dummy page count is above 32, the cluster is broken. This "walk" is done going forward and then backward to build the final cluster to write. Figure 5-41 shows an example of the state of pages after such a cluster has been built by the modified page writer.

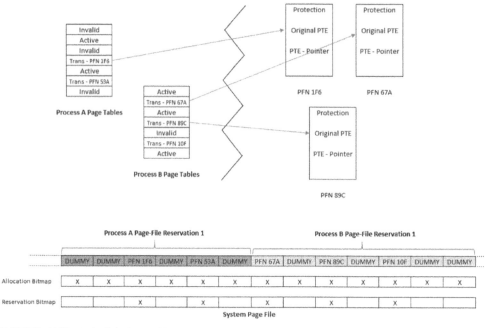

FIGURE 5-41 Cluster built before writing.

Finally, the page fault handler uses the built information from the reservation bitmap and the PTEs to determine the start and end points of clusters, to efficiently load back needed pages with minimal seeking of the mechanical disk head.

Physical memory limits

Now that you've learned how Windows keeps track of physical memory, we'll describe how much of it Windows can actually support. Because most systems access more code and data than can fit in physical memory as they run, physical memory is essentially a window into the code and data used over time. The amount of memory can therefore affect performance because when data or code that a process or the operating system needs is not present, the memory manager must bring it in from disk or remote storage.

Besides affecting performance, the amount of physical memory affects other resource limits. For example, the amount of non-paged pool is backed by physical memory, thus obviously constrained by physical memory. Physical memory also contributes to the system virtual memory limit, which is the sum of roughly the size of physical memory plus the current configured size of all paging files. Physical memory also can indirectly limit the maximum number of processes.

Windows support for physical memory is dictated by hardware limitations, licensing, operating system data structures, and driver compatibility. The following URL shows the memory limits of the various Windows editions: *https://msdn.microsoft.com/en-us/library/windows/desktop/aa366778.aspx*. Table 5-23 summarizes the limits in Windows 8 and higher versions.

TABLE 5-23 Limitations on physical memory support in Windows

Operating System Version/Edition	32-Bit Maximum	64-Bit Maximum
Windows 8.x Professional and Enterprise	4 GB	512
Windows 8.x (all other editions)	4 GB	128 GB
Windows Server 2012/R2 Standard and Datacenter	N/A	4 TB
Windows Server 2012/R2 Essentials	N/A	64 GB
Windows Server 2012/R2 Foundation	N/A	32 GB
Windows Storage Server 2012 Workgroup	N/A	32 GB
Windows Storage Server 2012 Standard Hyper-V Server 2012	N/A	4 TB
Windows 10 Home	4 GB	128 GB
Windows 10 Pro, Education and Enterprise	4 GB	2 TB
Windows Server 2016 Standard and Datacenter	N/A	24 TB

At the time of this writing, the maximum supported physical memory is 4 TB on some Server 2012/R2 editions and 24 TB on Server 2016 editions. The limitations don't come from any implementation or hardware limitation, but because Microsoft will support only configurations it can test. As of this writing, these were the largest tested and supported memory configurations.

Windows client memory limits

64-bit Windows client editions support different amounts of memory as a differentiating feature, with the low end being 4 GB increasing to 2 TB for Enterprise and Professional editions. All 32-bit Windows client editions, however, support a maximum of 4 GB of physical memory, which is the highest physical address accessible with the standard x86 memory management mode.

Although client SKUs support PAE addressing modes on x86 systems in order to provide hardware no-execute protection (which would also enable access to more than 4 GB of physical memory), testing revealed that systems would crash, hang, or become unbootable because some device drivers, commonly those for video and audio devices found typically on clients but not servers, were not programmed to expect physical addresses larger than 4 GB. As a result, the drivers truncated such addresses, resulting in memory corruptions and corruption side effects. Server systems commonly have more generic devices, with simpler and more stable drivers, and therefore had not generally revealed these problems. The problematic client driver ecosystem led to the decision for client editions to ignore physical memory that resides above 4 GB, even though they can theoretically address it. Driver developers are encouraged to test their systems with the nolowmem BCD option, which will force the kernel to use physical addresses above 4 GB only if sufficient memory exists on the system to allow it. This will immediately lead to the detection of such issues in faulty drivers.

Although 4 GB is the licensed limit for 32-bit client editions, the effective limit is actually lower and depends on the system's chipset and connected devices. This is because the physical address map includes not only RAM but device memory, and x86 and x64 systems typically map all device memory below the 4 GB address boundary to remain compatible with 32-bit operating systems that don't know how to handle addresses larger than 4 GB. Newer chipsets do support PAE-based device remapping, but client editions of Windows do not support this feature for the driver compatibility problems explained earlier. (Otherwise, drivers would receive 64-bit pointers to their device memory.)

If a system has 4 GB of RAM and devices such as video, audio, and network adapters that implement windows into their device memory that sum to 500 MB, then 500 MB of the 4 GB of RAM will reside above the 4 GB address boundary, as shown in Figure 5-42.

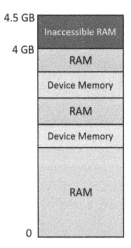

FIGURE 5-42   Physical memory layout on a 4 GB system.

The result is that if you have a system with 3 GB or more of memory and you are running a 32-bit Windows client, you may not get the benefit of all the RAM. You can see how much RAM Windows has detected as being installed in the System Properties dialog box, but to see how much memory is *really* available to Windows, you need to look at Task Manager's Performance page or the Msinfo32 utility. For example, on a Hyper-V virtual machine configured with 4 GB of RAM, with 32-bit Windows 10 installed, the amount of physical memory available is 3.87 GB, as shown in the Msinfo32 utility:

```
Installed Physical Memory (RAM)   4.00 GB
Total Physical Memory             3.87 GB
```

You can see the physical memory layout with the MemInfo tool. The following output is from MemInfo when run on a 32-bit system, using the –r switch to dump physical memory ranges:

```
C:\Tools>MemInfo.exe -r
MemInfo v3.00 - Show PFN database information
Copyright (C) 2007-2016 Alex Ionescu
www.alex-ionescu.com

Physical Memory Range: 00001000 to 0009F000 (158 pages, 632 KB)
Physical Memory Range: 00100000 to 00102000 (2 pages, 8 KB)
Physical Memory Range: 00103000 to F7FF0000 (1015533 pages, 4062132 KB)
MmHighestPhysicalPage: 1015792
```

Note the gap in the memory address range from A0000 to 100000 (384 KB), and another gap from F8000000 to FFFFFFFF (128 MB).

You can use Device Manager on your machine to see what is occupying the various reserved memory regions that can't be used by Windows (and that will show up as holes in MemInfo's output). To check Device Manager, follow these steps:

1. Run Devmgmt.msc.

2. Open the **View** menu and select **Resources by Connection**.

3. Expand the **Memory** node. On the laptop computer used for the output shown in Figure 5-43, the primary consumer of mapped device memory is, unsurprisingly, the video card (Hyper-V S3 Cap), which consumes 128 MB in the range F8000000–FBFFFFFF.

```
∨ 📱 Memory
    📱 [00000000 - 0009FFFF]  System board
    📱 [000A0000 - 000BFFFF]  PCI Bus
    📱 [000C0000 - 000DFFFF]  System board
    📱 [000E0000 - 000FFFFF]  System board
    📱 [00100000 - F7FFFFFF]  System board
  ∨ 📱 [E0000000 - FFFFFFFF]  PCI Bus
        📱 [FF800000 - FFFFFFFF]  Microsoft Hyper-V Video
    ∨ 📱 [F8000000 - FFFBFFFF]  PCI Bus
        📱 [F8000000 - FBFFFFFF]  Microsoft Hyper-V S3 Cap
        📱 [FEBFF000 - FEBFFFFF]  Intel 21140-Based PCI Fast Ethernet Adapter (Emulated)
        📱 [FEC00000 - FEC00FFF]  Motherboard resources
        📱 [FEE00000 - FEE00FFF]  Motherboard resources
    📱 [FFFC0000 - FFFFFFFF]  System board
```

FIGURE 5-43   Hardware-reserved memory ranges on a 32-bit Windows system.

Other miscellaneous devices account for most of the rest, and the PCI bus reserves additional ranges for devices as part of the conservative estimation the firmware uses during boot.

Memory compression

The Windows 10 memory manager implements a mechanism that compresses private and page-file-backed section pages that are on the modified page list. The primary candidates for compression are private pages belonging to UWP apps because compression works very well with the working set swapping and emptying that already occurs for such applications if memory is tight. After an application is suspended and its working set is outswapped, the working set can be emptied at any time and dirty pages can be compressed. This will create additional available memory that may be enough to hold another application in memory without making the first application's pages leave memory.

> **Note**   Experiments have shown that pages compress to around 30–50 percent of their original size using Microsoft's Xpress algorithm, which balances speed with size, thus resulting in considerable memory savings.

The memory compression architecture must adhere to the following requirements:

- A page cannot be in memory in a compressed and an uncompressed form because this would waste physical memory due to duplication. This means that whenever a page is compressed, it must become a free page after successful compression.

- The compression store must maintain its data structures and store the compressed data such that it is always saving memory for the system overall. This means that if a page doesn't compress well enough, it will not be added to the store.

- Compressed pages must appear as available memory (because they can really be repurposed if needed) to avoid creating a perception issue that compressing memory somehow increases memory consumption.

Memory compression is enabled by default on client SKUs (phone, PC, Xbox, and so on). Server SKUs do not currently use memory compression, but that is likely to change in future server versions.

 Note In Windows 2016, Task Manager still shows a number in parentheses for compressed memory, but that number is always zero. Also, the memory compression process does not exist.

During system startup, the Superfetch service (sysmain.dll, hosted in a svchost.exe instance, described in the upcoming "Proactive memory management (SuperFetch)" section) instructs the Store Manager in the executive through a call to NtSetSystemInformation to create a single system store (always the first store to be created), to be used by non-UWP applications. Upon app startup, each UWP application communicates with the Superfetch service and requests the creation of a store for itself.

Compression illustration

To get a sense of how memory compression works, let's look at an illustrative example. Assume that at some point in time, the following physical pages exist:

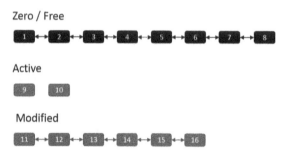

The zero and free page lists contain pages that have garbage and zeroes, respectively, and can be used to satisfy memory commits; for the sake of this discussion, we'll treat them as one list. The active pages belong to various processes, while the modified pages have dirty data that has not yet been written to a page file, but can be soft-faulted without an I/O operation to a process working set if that process references a modified page.

Now assume the memory manager decides to trim the modified page list—for example, because it has become too large or the zero/free pages have become too small. Assume three pages are to be removed from the modified list. The memory manager compresses their contents into a single page (taken from the zero/free list):

Zero / Free

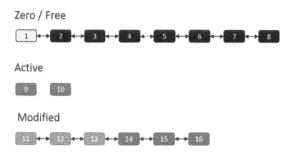

Active

Modified

Pages 11, 12 and 13 are compressed into page 1. After that's done, page 1 is no longer free and is in fact active, part of the working set of the memory compression process (described in the next section). Pages 11, 12, and 13 are no longer needed and move to the free list; the compression saved two pages:

Zero / Free

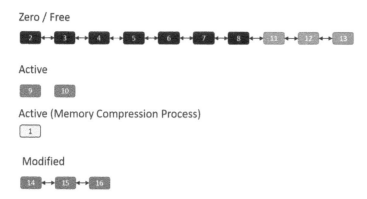

Active

Active (Memory Compression Process)

Modified

Suppose the same process repeats. This time, pages 14, 15, and 16 are compressed into (say) two pages (2 and 3) as shown here:

Zero / Free

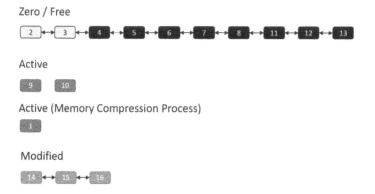

Active

Active (Memory Compression Process)

Modified

The result is that pages 2 and 3 join the working set of the memory compression process, while pages 14, 15, and 16 become free:

Zero / Free

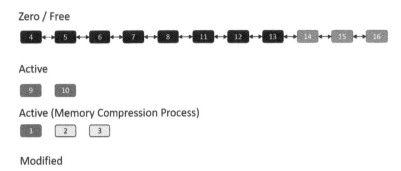

Active

Active (Memory Compression Process)

Modified

Suppose the memory manager later decides to trim the working set of the memory compression process. In that case, such pages are moved to the modified list because they contain data not yet written to a page file. Of course, they can at any time be soft-faulted back into their original process (decompressing in the process by using free pages). The following shows pages 1 and 2 being removed from the active pages of the memory compression process and moved to the modified list:

Zero / Free

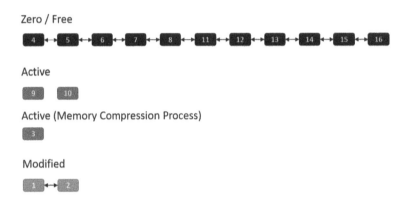

Active

Active (Memory Compression Process)

Modified

If memory becomes tight, the memory manager may decide to write the compressed modified pages to a page file:

Zero / Free

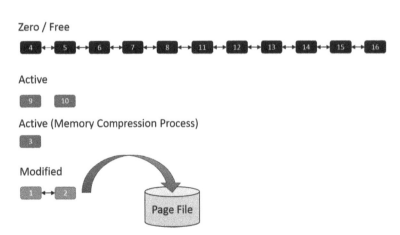

Active

Active (Memory Compression Process)

Modified

Finally, after such pages have been written to a page file, they move to the standby list because their content is saved, so they can be repurposed if necessary. They can also be soft-faulted (as when they are part of the modified list) by decompressing them and moving the resulting pages to the active state under the relevant process working set. When in the standby list, they are attached to the appropriate sub-list, depending on their priority (as described in the "Page priority and rebalancing" section later in this chapter):

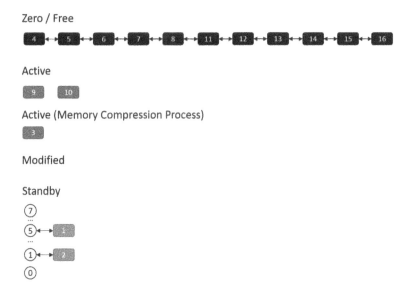

Compression architecture

The compression engine needs a "working area" memory to store compressed pages and the data structures that manage them. In Windows 10 versions prior to 1607, the user address space of the System process was used. Starting with Windows 10 Version 1607, a new dedicated process called *Memory Compression* is used instead. One reason for creating this new process was that the System process memory consumption looked high to a casual observer, which implied the system was consuming a lot of memory. That was not the case, however, because compressed memory does not count against the commit limit. Nevertheless, sometimes perception is everything.

The Memory Compression process is a minimal process, which means it does not load any DLLs. Rather, it just provides an address space to work with. It's not running any executable image either—the kernel is just using its user mode address space. (See Chapter 3, "Processes and jobs," for more information on minimal processes.)

Note By design, Task Manager does not show the Memory Compression process in its details view, but Process Explorer does. Using a kernel debugger, the compression process image name is `MemCompression`.

For each store, the Store Manager allocates memory in regions with a configurable region size. Currently, the size used is 128 KB. The allocations are done by normal VirtualAlloc calls as needed. The actual compressed pages are stored in 16 byte chunks within a region. Naturally, a compressed page (4 KB) can span many chunks. Figure 5-44 shows a store with an array of regions and some of the data structures associated with managing such a store.

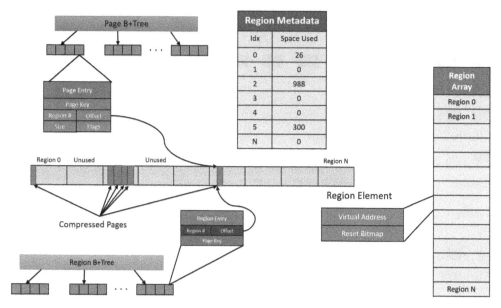

FIGURE 5-44   Store data structures.

As shown in Figure 5-44, pages are managed with a B+Tree—essentially a tree where a node can have any number of children—where each page entry points to its compressed content within one of the regions. A store starts with zero regions, and regions are allocated and deallocated as needed. Regions are also associated with priorities, as described in the "Page priority and rebalancing" section later in this chapter.

Adding a page involves the following major steps:

1. If there is no current region with the page's priority, allocate a new region, lock it in physical memory, and assign it the priority of the page to be added. Set the current region for that priority to the allocated region.

2. Compress the page and store it in the region, rounding up to the granularity unit (16 bytes). For example, if a page compresses to 687 bytes, it consumes 43 16-byte units (always rounding up). Compression is done on the current thread, with low CPU priority (7) to minimize interference. When decompression is needed, it's performed in parallel using all available processors.

3. Update the page and region information in the Page and Region B+Trees.

4. If the remaining space in the current region is not large enough to store the compressed page, a new region is allocated (with the same page priority) and set as the current region for that priority.

Removing a page from the store involves the following steps:

1. Find the page entry in the Page B+Tree and the region entry in the Region B+Tree.

2. Remove the entries and update the space used in the region.

3. If the region becomes empty, deallocate the region.

Regions become fragmented over time as compressed pages are added and removed. The memory for a region is not freed until the region is completely empty. This means some kind of compaction is necessary to reduce memory waste. A compaction operation is lazily scheduled with aggressiveness depending on the amount of fragmentation. Region priorities are taken into account when consolidating regions.

EXPERIMENT: Memory compression

There is very little visibility to the memory compression going on in the system. You can view the memory compression process with Process Explorer or a kernel debugger. The following figure shows the Performance tab in the properties of the Memory Compression process in Process Explorer (which must run with admin privileges):

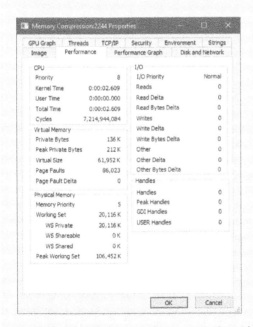

Notice that the process has no user time (since only kernel threads "work" within this process), and its working set is private only (not shared). This is because the compressed memory is not sharable in any sense. Compare that to the Memory view in Task Manager:

Here, the compressed memory in parentheses should correlate with the working set of the Memory Compression process—this screenshot was taken about a minute after the previous one—because this is the amount of space that the compressed memory is consuming.

Memory partitions

Traditionally, virtual machines (VMs) are used to isolate applications so that separate VMs can run completely isolated applications (or groups of applications) at least from a security standpoint. VMs cannot interact with each other, providing strong security and resource boundaries. Although this works, VMs have a high resource cost in terms of hardware that hosts the VMs and management costs. This gave a rise to container-based technologies, such as Docker. These technologies attempt to lower the barrier for isolation and resource management by creating sandbox containers that host applications, all on the same physical or virtual machine.

Creating such containers is difficult, as it would require kernel drivers that perform some form of virtualization on top of the regular Windows. Some of these drivers are the following (a single driver can encompass all these functionalities):

- File system (mini) filter that would create an illusion of an isolated file system

- Registry virtualization driver, creating an illusion of a separate registry (CmRegisterCallbacksEx)

- Private object manager namespace, by utilizing silos (see Chapter 3 for more details)

- Process management for associating processes with the correct container by using process create/notifications (PsSetCreateNotifyRoutineEx)

Even with these in place, some things are difficult to virtualize, specifically memory management. Each container may want to use its own PFN database, its own page file, and so on. Windows 10 (64-bit versions only) and Windows Server 2016 provide such possible memory control through Memory Partitions.

A memory partition consists of its own memory-related management structures, such as page lists (standby, modified, zero, free, etc.), commit charge, working set, page trimmer, modified page writer, zero-page thread, and so on, but isolated from other partitions. Memory partitions are represented in the system by Partition objects, which are securable, nameable objects (just like other executive objects). One partition always exists, called the *System Partition*, and it represents the system as a whole and is the ultimate parent of any explicitly created partition. The system partition's address is stored in a global variable (`MiSystemPartition`) and its name is `KernelObjects\MemoryPartition0`, visible with tools such as WinObj from Sysinternals as shown in Figure 5-45.

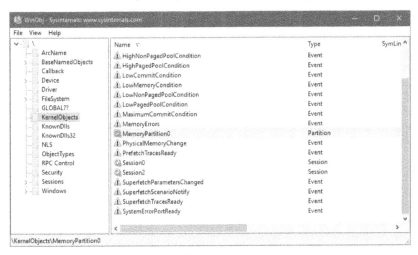

FIGURE 5-45 The System Partition in WinObj.

All partition objects are stored in global list, where the current maximum partition count is 1024 (10 bits), because the partition index must be encoded in PTEs for quick access to partition information where applicable. One of these indices is the system partition and two other values are used as special sentinels, leaving 1021 partitions available.

Memory partitions can be created from user mode or kernel mode by using the `NtCreatePartition` internal (and undocumented) function; user mode callers must have the `SeLockMemory` privilege for the call to succeed. The function can accept a parent partition, which initial pages will come from and eventually return to, when the partition is destroyed; the system partition is the default parent if none is specified. `NtCreatePartition` delegates the actual work to the internal memory manager `MiCreatePartition` function.

An existing partition can be opened by name using `NtOpenPartition` (no special privilege required for this as the object can be protected by ACLs as usual). The actual manipulation of a partition is reserved for the `NtManagePartition` function. This is the function that can be used to add memory to the partition, add a paging file, copy memory from one partition to another, and generally obtain information about a partition.

EXPERIMENT: Viewing memory partitions

In this experiment, you'll use the kernel debugger to look at partition objects.

1. Start local kernel debugging and issue the !partition command. It lists all the parti-
    tion objects in the system.

    ```
    lkd> !partition
    Partition0 fffff803eb5b2480 MemoryPartition0
    ```

2. By default, the always existing system partition is shown. The !parti-
    tion command can accept the address of a partition object and show more
    details:

    ```
    lkd> !partition fffff803eb5b2480
    PartitionObject @ ffffc808f5355920 (MemoryPartition0)
    _MI_PARTITION 0 @ fffff803eb5b2480
      MemoryRuns: 0000000000000000
      MemoryNodeRuns: ffffc808f521ade0
      AvailablePages:         0n4198472 ( 16 Gb 16 Mb 288 Kb)
      ResidentAvailablePages: 0n6677702 ( 25 Gb 484 Mb 792 Kb)
          0 _MI_NODE_INFORMATION @ fffff10000003800
              TotalPagesEntireNode:   0x7f8885
                              Zeroed                      Free
              1GB               0 ( 0)                          0 (
      0)
              2MB              41 ( 82 Mb)                      0 (
      0)
              64KB           3933 ( 245 Mb 832 Kb)             0 (
      0)
              4KB           82745 ( 323 Mb 228 Kb)             0 (
      0)
              Node Free Memory:    ( 651 Mb 36 Kb )
              InUse Memory:        ( 31 Gb 253 Mb 496 Kb )
              TotalNodeMemory:     ( 31 Gb 904 Mb 532 Kb )
    ```

The output shows some of the information stored in the underlying MI_PARTITION structure
(whose address is given as well). Notice that the command shows memory information on a
NUMA node basis (just one in this case). Since this is the system partition, the numbers related
to used, free, and total memory should correspond to the values reported by tools such as Task
Manager and Process Explorer. You can also examine the MI_PARTITION structure with the usual
dt command.

Future scenarios may leverage the memory partitioning capability for specific processes (through
job objects) to be associated with a partition, such as when exclusive control over physical memory may
be beneficial. One such scenario slated for the Creators Update release is game mode (more information on game mode is included in Chapter 8 in Part 2).

Memory combining

The memory manager uses several mechanisms in an attempt to save as much RAM as possible, such as sharing pages for images, copy-on-write for data pages, and compression. In this section, we'll take a look at yet another such mechanism called *memory combining*.

The general idea is simple: Find duplicates of pages in RAM and combine them into one, thus removing the rest of the duplicates. Clearly there are a few issues to resolve:

- What are the "best" pages to use as candidates for combining?
- When is it appropriate to initiate memory combining?
- Should combining be targeted at a particular process, a memory partition, or the entire system?
- How can the combining process be made quick so it does not adversely impact normally executing code?
- If a writeable combined page is later modified by one of its clients, how would it get a private copy?

We'll answer these questions throughout this section, starting with the last. The copy-on-write mechanism is used here: as long as a combined page is not written to, do nothing. If a process tries to write to the page, make a private copy for the writing process, and remove the copy-on-write flag for that newly allocated private page.

> **Note** Page combining can be disabled by setting a DWORD value named DisablePageCombining to 1 in the HKLM\System\CurrentControlSet\Control\Session Manager\Memory Management registry key.

> **Note** In this section, the terms *CRC* and *hash* are used interchangeably. They indicate a statistically unique (with high probability) 64-bit number referencing a page's contents.

The memory manager's initialization routine, `MmInitSystem`, creates the system partition (see the previous section on memory partitions). Within the `MI_PARTITION` structure that describes a partition lies an array of 16 AVL trees that identify the duplicated pages. The array is sorted by the last 4 bits of a combined page CRC value. We'll see in a moment how this fits into the algorithm.

Two special page types are called *common pages*. One includes an all zero bytes, and the other includes an all one bits (filled with the byte 0xFF); their CRC is calculated just once and stored. Such pages can easily be identified when scanning pages' contents.

To initiate memory combining, the `NtSetSystemInformation` native API is called with the `System-CombinePhysicalMemoryInformation` system information class. The caller must have the `SeProfile-SingleProcessPrivilege` in its token, normally granted to the local administrators group. The argument to the API provides the following options through a combination of flags:

- Perform memory combining on the entire (system) partition or just the current process.

- Search for common pages (all zeros or all ones) to combine only, or any duplicate pages regardless of content.

The input structure also provides an optional event handle that can be passed in, and if signaled (by another thread), will abort the page combining. Currently, the Superfetch service (see the section "SuperFetch" at the end of this chapter for more information) has a special thread, running in low priority (4) that initiates memory combining for the entire system partition when the user is away, or if the user is busy, every 15 minutes.

In the Creators Update, if the amount of physical memory is higher than 3.5 GB (3584 MB), most built-in Svchost-ed services host a single service in each Svchost process. This creates dozens of processes out of the box but removes the likelihood of one service affecting another (either because of some instability or security issues). In this scenario, the Service Control Manager (SCM) uses a new option of the memory combining API, and initiates page combining in each of the Svchost processes every three minutes by utilizing a thread pool timer running with base priority of 6 (ScPerformPage-CombineOnServiceImages routine). The rationale is to try to reduce RAM consumption that may be higher than with fewer Svchost instances. Note that non-Svchost services are not page combined, nor are services running with per-user or private user accounts.

The MiCombineIdenticalPages routine is the actual entry point to the page combining process. For each NUMA node of the memory partition, it allocates and stores a list of pages with their CRC inside the page combing support (PCS) structure, which is the one managing all the needed information for the page combining operation. (That's the one holding the AVL trees array mentioned earlier.) The requesting thread is the one doing the work; it should run on CPUs belonging to the current NUMA node, and its affinity is modified accordingly if needed. We'll divide the memory combining algorithm into three stages to simplify the explanation: search, classification, and page sharing. The following sections assume that a complete page combining is requested (rather than for the current process) and for all pages (not just the common pages); the other cases are similar in principle, and somewhat simpler.

The search phase

The goal of this initial stage is to calculate the CRC of all the physical pages. The algorithm analyses each physical page that belongs to the active, modified, or standby list, skipping the zeroed and free pages (since they are effectively unused).

A good page candidate for memory combining should be an active non-shared page that belongs to a working set, and that should not map a paging structure. The candidate could be even in the standby or modified state, but needs to have a reference counter of 0. Basically, the system identifies three types of pages for combining: user process, paged pool, and session space. Other types of pages are skipped.

To correctly calculate the CRC of the page, the system should map the physical page to a system address (because the process context is mostly different from the calling thread, making the page inaccessible in low user-mode addresses) using a new system PTE. The CRC of the page is then calculated with a customized algorithm (MiComputeHash64 routine), and the system PTE freed (the page is now unmapped from system address space).

The classification phase

When all the hashes of the pages that belong to a NUMA node have been successfully calculated, the second part of the algorithm commences. The goal of this phase is to process each CRC/PFN entry in the list and organize them in a strategic way. The page sharing algorithm must minimize the process contexts switches, and be as fast as possible.

The `MiProcessCrcList` routine starts by sorting the CRC/PFN list by hash (using a quick sort algorithm). Another key data structure, *combine block*, is used to keep track of all the pages that share the same hash, and, more importantly, to store the new prototype PTE that will map the new combined page. Each CRC/PFN of the new sorted list is processed in order. The system needs to verify if the current hash is common (belongs to a zeroed or a complete-filled page) and if it's equal to the previous or next hash (remember that the list is sorted). If this is not the case, the system checks if a combine block already exists in the PCS structure. If so, it means that a combined page has been already identified in a previous execution of the algorithm or in another node of the system. Otherwise it means that the CRC is unique and the page couldn't be combined, and the algorithm continues to the next page in the list.

If the found common hash has never been seen before, the algorithm allocates a new empty combine block (used for the master PFN) and inserts it in a list used by the actual page-sharing code (next stage). Otherwise if the hash already existed (the page is not the master copy), a reference to the combine block is added in the current CRC/PFN entry.

At this point, the algorithm has prepared all the data that the page-sharing algorithm needs: a list of combine blocks used to store the master physical pages and their prototype PTEs, a list of CRC/PFN entries organized by the owning working set, and some physical memory needed to store the content of the new shared pages.

The algorithm then obtains the address of the physical page (that should exist, due to the initial check performed previously by the `MiCombineIdenticalPages` routine) and searches a data structure used to store all the pages that belongs to the specific working set (from now on we will call this structure *WS CRC node*). If this doesn't exist, it allocates a new one and inserts it in another AVL tree. The CRC/PFN and virtual address of the page are linked together inside the WS CRC node.

After all the identified pages have been processed, the system allocates the physical memory for the new master shared pages (using an MDL), and processes each WS CRC node; for performance reasons, the candidate pages located inside the node are sorted by their original virtual address. The system is now ready to perform the actual page combining.

The page combining phase

The page combining phase starts with a WS CRC node structure that contains all the pages that belong to a specific working set and are all candidates for combining, and with a list of free combine blocks, used to store the prototype PTE and the actual shared page. The algorithm attaches to the target process and locks its working set (raising IRQL to dispatch level). In this way, it will be able to directly read and write each page without the need to remap it.

The algorithm processes every CRC/PFN entry in the list, but since it's running at dispatch level IRQL and execution could take some time, it checks if the processor has some DPCs or scheduled items in its queue (by calling KeShouldYieldProcessor) before analyzing the next entry. If the answer is yes, the algorithm does the right thing and takes appropriate precautions to maintain state.

The actual page sharing strategy expects three possible scenarios:

- The page is active and valid, but it contains all zeroes, so rather than combining, it replaces its PTE with a demand-zero PTE. Recall that this is the initial state of normal VirtualAlloc-like memory allocation.

- The page is active and valid, but it is not zeroed out, meaning it has to be shared. The algorithm checks if the page has to be promoted as the master: if the CRC/PFN entry has a pointer to a valid combine block, it means that it's not the master page; otherwise, the page is the master copy. The master page hash is rechecked and a new physical page assigned for the sharing. Otherwise, the already existing combine block is used (and its reference count incremented). The system is now ready to convert the private page into a shared one, and calls the MiConvert-PrivateToProto routine to perform the actual job.

- The page is in the modified or standby list. In this case, it's mapped to a system address as a valid page and its hash recalculated. The algorithm performs the same step as the previous scenario, with the only difference being that the PTE is converted from shared to prototype using the MiConvertStandbyToProto routine.

When the sharing of the current page ends, the system inserts the combine block of the master copy into the PCS structure. This is important because the combine block becomes the link between each private PTE and the combined page.

From private to shared PTE

The goal of MiConvertPrivateToProto is to convert a PTE of an active and valid page. If the routine detects that the prototype PTE inside the combine block is zero, it means that the master page must be created (together with the master shared prototype PTE). It then maps the free physical page into a system address and copies the content of the private page into the new shared one. Before actually creating the shared PTE, the system should free any page file reservation (see the section "Page file reservation" earlier in this chapter) and fill the PFN descriptor of the shared page. The shared PFN has the prototype bit set, and the PTE frame pointer set to the PFN of the physical page that contains the Prototype PTE. Most importantly, it has the PTE pointer set to the PTE located inside the combine block, but with the 63rd bit set to zero. This signifies to the system that the PFN belongs to a page that has been combined.

Next, the system needs to modify the PTE of the private page so that its target PFN is set to the shared physical page, its protection mask changed to copy-on-write, and the private page PTE is marked as valid. The prototype PTE inside the combine block is marked as a valid hardware PTE too: the content is identical to the new PTE of the private page. Finally, the page file space allocated for the private page is freed and the original PFN of the private page is marked as deleted. The TLB cache is flushed and the private process working set size is decremented by one page.

Otherwise (the prototype PTE inside the combine block is non-zero), it means that the private page should be a copy of the master one. Only the active PTE of the private page must be converted. The PFN of the shared page is mapped to a system address and the content of the two pages is compared. This is important because the CRC algorithm does not produce unique values in the general case. If the two pages don't match, the function stops processing and returns. Otherwise, it unmaps the shared page and sets the page priority of the shared PFN to the higher of the two. Figure 5-46 shows the state where only a master page exists.

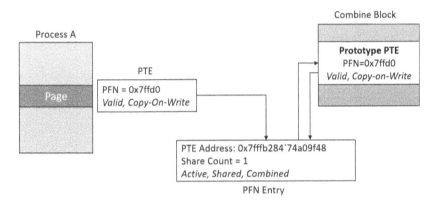

FIGURE 5-46 Combined master page.

The algorithm now calculates the new invalid software prototype PTE that should be inserted into the process private page table. To do that, it reads the address of the hardware PTE that maps the shared page (located in the combine block), shifts it, and sets the Prototype and Combined bits. A check is made that the share count of the private PFN is 1. If it is not, processing is aborted. The algorithm writes the new software PTE in the private page table of the process and decrements the share count of the page table of the old private PFN (keep in mind that an active PFN always has a pointer to its page table). The target process working set size is decremented by one page and the TLB is flushed. The old private page is moved into the transition state, and its PFN is marked for deletion. Figure 5-47 shows two pages, where the new page points to the prototype PTE but is not yet valid.

Finally, the system uses another trick to prevent working set trimming on the shared pages by simulating a page fault. That way the share count of the shared PFN is again incremented, and no fault would occur at a time the process will try to read the shared page. The end result is that the private PTE is again a valid hardware PTE. Figure 5-48 shows the effect of a soft page fault on the second page, making it valid and incrementing the share count.

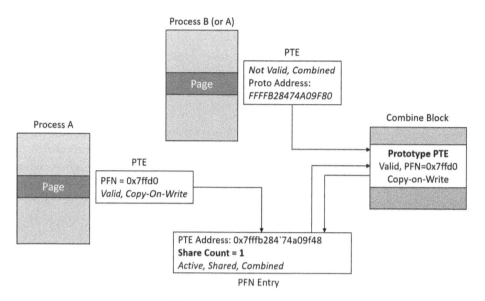

FIGURE 5-47 Combined pages before simulated page fault.

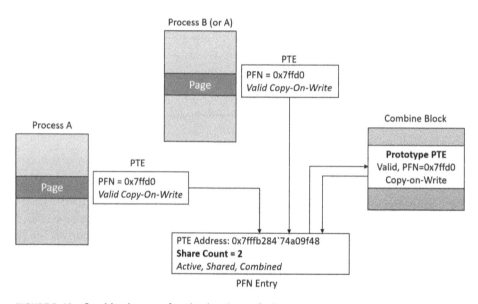

FIGURE 5-48 Combined pages after simulated page fault.

Combined pages release

When the system needs to free a particular virtual address, it first locates the address of the PTE that maps it. The pointed PFN of a combined page has the prototype and combined bits set. The free request for a combined PFN is managed exactly like the one for a prototype PFN. The only difference is that the system (if the combined bit is set) calls `MiDecrementCombinedPte` after processing the prototype PFN.

`MiDecrementCombinedPte` is a simple function that decrements the reference count of the combine block of the Prototype PTE. (Keep in mind that at this stage the PTE is in transition because the memory manager has already dereferenced the physical page that it maps. The share count of the physical page has already dropped to zero, and so the system put the PTE in transition.) If the reference count drops to zero, the prototype PTE will be freed, the physical page put in the free list, and the combine block returned to the combine free list of the PCS structure of the memory partition.

EXPERIMENT: Memory combining

In this experiment, you will see the effects of memory combing. Follow these steps:

1. Start a kernel debugging session with a VM target (as described in Chapter 4, "Threads").

2. Copy the MemCombine32.exe (for 32 bit targets) or MemCombine64.exe (for 64 bit targets), and MemCombineTest.exe executables from this book's downloadable resources to the target machine.

3. Run MemCombineTest.exe on the target machine. You should see something like the following:

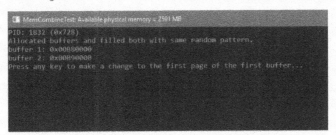

4. Note the two addresses shown. These are two buffers filled with a random generated pattern of bytes, repeated so that each page has the same content.

5. Break into the debugger. Locate the `MemCombineTest` process:

```
0: kd> !process 0 0 memcombinetest.exe
PROCESS ffffe70a3cb29080
    SessionId: 2  Cid: 0728    Peb: 00d08000  ParentCid: 11c4
    DirBase: c7c95000  ObjectTable: ffff918ede582640  HandleCount: <Data Not
Accessible>
    Image: MemCombineTest.exe
```

6. Switch to the located process:

```
0: kd> .process /i /r ffffe70a3cb29080
You need to continue execution (press 'g' <enter>) for the context
to be switched. When the debugger breaks in again, you will be in
the new process context.
0: kd> g
Break instruction exception - code 80000003 (first chance)
nt!DbgBreakPointWithStatus:
fffff801'94b691c0 cc                      int     3
```

7. Use the !pte command to locate the PFN where the two buffers are stored:

```
0: kd> !pte b80000
                                            VA 0000000000b80000
PXE at FFFFA25128944000    PPE at FFFFA25128800000    PDE at
FFFFA25100000028    PTE at FFFFA20000005C00
contains 00C0000025BAC867  contains 0FF00000CAA2D867  contains
00F000003B22F867  contains B9200000DEDFB867
pfn 25bac    ---DA--UWEV  pfn caa2d    ---DA--UWEV  pfn 3b22f    ---DA--
UWEV  pfn dedfb    ---DA--UW-V


0: kd> !pte b90000
                                            VA 0000000000b90000
PXE at FFFFA25128944000    PPE at FFFFA25128800000    PDE at
FFFFA25100000028    PTE at FFFFA20000005C80
contains 00C0000025BAC867  contains 0FF00000CAA2D867  contains
00F000003B22F867  contains B9300000F59FD867
pfn 25bac    ---DA--UWEV  pfn caa2d    ---DA--UWEV  pfn 3b22f    ---DA--
UWEV  pfn f59fd    ---DA--UW-V
```

8. Notice the PFN values are different, indicating that these pages are mapped to different physical addresses. Resume the target.

9. On the target, open an elevated command window, navigate to the directory where you copied MemCombine(32/64), and run it. The tool forces a full memory combining, which may take a few seconds.

10. When it's finished, break into the debugger again. Repeat steps 6 and 7. You should see the PFNs change:

```
1: kd> !pte b80000
                                            VA 0000000000b80000
PXE at FFFFA25128944000    PPE at FFFFA25128800000    PDE at
FFFFA25100000028    PTE at FFFFA20000005C00
contains 00C0000025BAC867  contains 0FF00000CAA2D867  contains
00F000003B22F867  contains B9300000EA886225
pfn 25bac    ---DA--UWEV  pfn caa2d    ---DA--UWEV  pfn 3b22f    ---DA--
UWEV  pfn ea886    C---A--UR-V


1: kd> !pte b90000
                                            VA 0000000000b90000
PXE at FFFFA25128944000    PPE at FFFFA25128800000    PDE at
FFFFA25100000028    PTE at FFFFA20000005C80
contains 00C0000025BAC867  contains 0FF00000CAA2D867  contains
00F000003B22F867  contains BA600000EA886225
pfn 25bac    ---DA--UWEV  pfn caa2d    ---DA--UWEV  pfn 3b22f    ---DA--
UWEV  pfn ea886    C---A--UR-V
```

11. Notice the PFN values are the same, meaning the pages are mapped to the exact same address in RAM. Also note the C flag in the PFN, indicating copy-on-write.

12. Resume the target and press any key in the MemCombineTest window. This changes a single byte in the first buffer.

13. Break into the target again and repeat steps 6 and 7 yet again:

```
1: kd> !pte b80000
                                        VA 0000000000b80000
PXE at FFFFA25128944000    PPE at FFFFA25128800000    PDE at
FFFFA25100000028    PTE at FFFFA20000005C00
contains 00C0000025BAC867  contains 0FF00000CAA2D867  contains
00F000003B22F867  contains B9300000813C4867
pfn 25bac    ---DA--UWEV pfn caa2d    ---DA--UWEV pfn 3b22f    ---DA--
UWEV pfn 813c4    ---DA--UW-V

1: kd> !pte b90000
                                        VA 0000000000b90000
PXE at FFFFA25128944000    PPE at FFFFA25128800000    PDE at
FFFFA25100000028    PTE at FFFFA20000005C80
contains 00C0000025BAC867  contains 0FF00000CAA2D867  contains
00F000003B22F867  contains BA600000EA886225
pfn 25bac    ---DA--UWEV pfn caa2d    ---DA--UWEV pfn 3b22f    ---DA--
UWEV pfn ea886    C---A--UR-V
```

14. The PFN for the first buffer has changed, and the copy-on-write flag was removed. The page has changed and was relocated to a different address in RAM.

Memory enclaves

Threads executing in a process have access to the entire process address space (as determined by page protection, which can be changed). This is desirable most of the time; however, in case malicious code manages to get itself injected into a process, it has the exact same power. It can freely read data that may contain sensitive information and even change it.

Intel has created a technology called Intel Software Guard Extensions (SGX) that allows the creation of protected memory enclaves—secure zones in a process address space where code and data are protected by the CPU from code running outside the enclave. Conversely, code running inside an enclave has full (normal) access to process address space outside the enclave. Naturally, the protection extends to access from other processes and even code running in kernel mode. A simplified diagram of memory enclaves is shown in Figure 5-49.

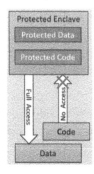

FIGURE 5-49 Memory enclaves.

Intel SGX is supported by sixth generation Core processors ("Skylake") and later generations. Intel has its own SDK for application developers that can be used on Windows 7 and later systems (64 bit only). Starting with Windows 10 version 1511 and Server 2016, Windows provide an abstraction using Windows API functions that removes the need to use Intel's SDK. Other CPU vendors may create similar solutions in the future, and these will also be wrapped by the same API, providing a relatively portable layer for application developers to use for creating and populating enclaves.

Note   Not all sixth generation Core processors support SGX. Also, an appropriate BIOS update must be installed on the system for SGX to work. Consult the Intel SGX documentation for more information. The Intel SGX website can be found at *https://software.intel.com/en-us/sgx*.

Note   At the time of this writing, Intel produced two versions of SGX (versions 1.0 and 2.0). Windows currently supports version 1.0 only. The differences are outside the scope of this book; consult the SGX documentation for more information.

Note   Current SGX versions do not support enclaves in ring 0 (kernel mode). Only ring 3 (user mode) enclaves are supported.

Programmatic interface

From an application developer's perspective, creating and working with an enclave consists of the following steps. (The internal details are described in the following sections.)

1.   Initially the program should determine whether memory enclaves are supported by calling `IsEnclaveTypeSupported`, passing a value representing the enclave technology, which currently can only be `ENCLAVE_TYPE_SGX`.

2.   A new enclave is created by calling the `CreateEnclave` function, which is similar in its arguments to `VirtualAllocEx`. For example, it's possible to create an enclave in a different process than the caller process. The complication in this function is the need to provide a vendor-specific configuration structure, which for Intel means a 4 KB data structure called *SGX Enclave Control Structure* (*SECS*), which Microsoft does not define explicitly. Instead, developers are expected to create their own structure based on the particular technology used and defined in its documentation.

3.   Once an empty enclave is created, the next step is to populate the enclave with code and data from outside of the enclave. This is accomplished by calling `LoadEnclaveData` where an external memory to the enclave is used to copy data to the enclave. Multiple calls to `LoadEnclaveData` may be used to populate the enclave.

4. The last step that is required to "activate" the enclave is achieved with the `InitializeEnclave` function. At that point, code that was configured to execute within the enclave can start executing.

5. Unfortunately, executing the code in the enclave is not wrapped by the API. Direct use of assembly language is required. The `EENTER` instruction transfers execution to the enclave and the `EEXIT` instruction causes return to the calling function. Abnormal termination of the enclave execution is also possible with Asynchronous Enclave Exit (AEX), such as due to a fault. The exact details are beyond the scope of this book, as they are not Windows-specific. Consult the SGX documentation to get the fine details.

6. Finally, to destroy the enclave, a normal `VirtualFree(Ex)` function can be used on the pointer to the enclave obtained in `CreateEnclave`.

Memory enclave initializations

During boot, Winload (the Windows Boot Loader) calls `OslEnumerateEnclavePageRegions`, which first checks if SGX is supported using the CPUID instruction. If it is, it issues instructions to enumerate Enclave Page Cache (EPC) descriptors. EPC is the protected memory provided by the processor for creating and using enclaves. For each enumerated EPC, `OslEnumerateEnclavePageRegions` calls `BlMm-AddEnclavePageRange` to add the page range information to a sorted list of memory descriptors with a type value of `LoaderEnclaveMemory`. This list is eventually stored in the `MemoryDescriptorListHead` member of the `LOADER_PARAMETER_BLOCK` structure used to pass information from the boot loader to the kernel.

During phase 1 initialization, the memory manager routine `MiCreateEnclaveRegions` is called to create an AVL tree for the discovered enclave regions (allowing quick lookups when needed); the tree is stored in the `MiState.Hardrware.EnclaveRegions` data member. The kernel adds a new enclave page list, and a special flag passed to `MiInsertPageInFreeOrZeroedList` enables functionality to utilize this new list. However, since the memory manager has actually run out of list identifiers (3 bits are used for a maximum of 8 values, all taken), the kernel actually identifies these pages as being "bad" pages currently suffering an in-page error. The memory manager knows never to use bad pages, so calling enclave pages "bad" keeps them from being used by normal memory management operations, and so such pages end up in the bad page list.

Enclave construction

The `CreateEnclave` API ends up calling `NtCreateEnclave` in the kernel. As noted, a SECS structure must be passed in, documented by Intel SGX as shown in Table 5-24.

`NtCreateEnclave` first checks if memory enclaves are supported by looking at the root of the AVL tree (not by using the slower CPUID instruction). It then creates a copy of the passed-in structure (as is usual for kernel functions obtaining data from user mode) and attaches to the target process (`KeStackAttachProcess`) if the enclave is to be created in a different process than the caller's. Then it transfers control to `MiCreateEnclave` to begin the actual work.

TABLE 5-24 SECS structure layout

Field	Offset (bytes)	Size (bytes)	Description
SIZE	0	8	Size of enclave in bytes; must be power of 2
BASEADDR	8	8	Enclave base linear address must be naturally aligned to size
SSAFRAMESIZE	16	4	Size of one SSA frame in pages (including XSAVE, pad, GPR, and conditionally MISC)
MRSIGNER	128	32	Measurement register extended with the public key that verified the enclave. See SIGSTRUCT for proper format
RESERVED	160	96	
ISVPRODID	256	2	Product ID of enclave
ISVSVN	258	2	Security version number (SVN) of the enclave
EID	Implementation dependent	8	Enclave identifier
PADDING	Implementation dependent	352	Padding pattern from the signature (used for key derivation strings)
RESERVED	260	3836	Includes EID, other non-zero reserved field and must-be-zero fields

The first thing `MiCreateEnclave` does is allocate the Address Windowing Extension (AWE) information structure that AWE APIs also utilize. This is because similar to the AWE functionality, an enclave allows a user-mode application to directly have access over physical pages (that is to say, the physical pages that are EPC pages based on the detection described earlier). Anytime a user-mode application has such direct control over physical pages, AWE data structures and locks must be used. This data structure is stored in the `AweInfo` field of the EPROCESS structure.

Next, `MiCreateEnclave` calls `MiAllocateEnclaveVad` to allocate an enclave-type VAD describing the enclave virtual memory range. This VAD has the `VadAwd` flag (as all AWE VADs) but also an additional `Enclave` flag, to differentiate it from a true AWE VAD. Finally, as part of VAD allocation, this is where the user-mode address for the enclave memory will be chosen (if not explicitly specified in the original `CreateEnclave` call).

The next step in `MiCreateEnclave` is to acquire an enclave page regardless of the enclave size or initial commitment. This is because, as per Intel's SGX documentation, all enclaves require at least a one-page control structure to be associated with them. `MiGetEnclavePage` is used to obtain the required allocation. This function simply scans the enclave page list described earlier, and extracts one page as needed. The returned page is mapped using a system PTE stored as part of the enclave VAD; the `MiInitializeEnclavePfn` function sets up the related PFN data structure and marks it `Modified` and `ActiveAndValid`.

There are no actual bits that would help you differentiate this enclave PFN from any other active region of memory (such as non-paged pool). This is where the enclave regions AVL tree comes into play, and `MI_PFN_IS_ENCLAVE` is a function that the kernel uses whenever it needs to check if a PFN is indeed describing an EPC region.

With the PFN initialized, the system PTE is now converted to a final global kernel PTE, and its resulting virtual address is computed. The final step in `MiCreateEnclave` is to call `KeCreateEnclave`, which will now do the low-level kernel enclave creation steps, including communication with the actual SGX hardware implementation. One job that `KeCreateEnclave` is responsible for is filling in the base address required by the SECS structure if the caller did not specify one, as it must be set in the SECS structure before communicating with the SGX hardware to create an enclave.

Loading data into an enclave

Once an enclave has been created, it's time to load information into it. The `LoadEnclaveData` function is exposed for that purpose. The function merely forwards the request to the underlying executive function, `NtLoadEnclaveData`. The function resembles a combination of a memory copy operation with some `VirtualAlloc` attributes (such as page protection).

If the enclave created with `CreateEnclave` doesn't yet have any committed enclave pages, they must first be obtained, which will result in zeroed out memory being added to the enclave, which can then be filled with non-zero memory from outside the enclave. Otherwise, if an initial pre-committed initialization size was passed in, then the enclave's pages can directly be filled in with non-zero memory from outside of the enclave.

Because enclave memory is described by a VAD, many of the traditional memory management APIs will function, at least partly, on this memory as well. For example, calling `VirtualAlloc` (ending up in `NtAllocateVirtualMemory`) on such an address with the `MEM_COMMIT` flag will result in `MiCommitEnclavePages` being called, which will validate that the protection mask for the new pages is compatible (i.e., a combination of read, write, and/or execute, without any special caching or write combining flags), and then call `MiAddPagesToEnclave`, passing a pointer to the enclave VAD associated with the address range, the protection mask that was specified to `VirtualAlloc`, and the PTE addresses that correspond to the virtual address range being committed.

`MiAddPagesToEnclave` first checks if the enclave VAD has any existing EPC pages associated with it, and if there's enough of them to satisfy the commit. If not, `MiReserveEnclavePages` is called to obtain a sufficient amount. `MiReserveEnclavePages` looks at the current enclave page list and counts the total. If there aren't enough physical EPC pages provided by the processor (based on the information obtained at boot), the function fails. Otherwise, it calls `MiGetEnclavePage` in a loop for the required amount of pages.

For each PFN entry that is retrieved, it is linked into the PFN array in the enclave VAD. Essentially, this means that once an enclave PFN is removed from the enclave page list and put into an active state, the enclave VAD acts as the list of active enclave PFNs.

Once the required committed pages have been obtained, `MiAddPagesToEnclave` translates the page protection passed to `LoadEnclaveData` into their SGX equivalents. Next, it reserves the appropriate number of system PTEs to hold paging information for each EPC pages that will be required. With this information in hand, it will eventually call `KeAddEnclavePage` that calls the SGX hardware to do the actual page adding.

One special page protection attribute is PAGE_ENCLAVE_THREAD_CONTROL, which indicates the memory is for a Thread Control Structure (TCS) defined by SGX. Each TCS represents a different thread that can execute independently within the enclave.

NtLoadEnclaveData validates parameters and then calls MiCopyPagesIntoEnclave to do the actual work, which may require getting committed pages as described earlier.

Initializing an enclave

Now that the enclave has been created and data has been transferred into it, there is another last step to perform before actual code in the enclave can execute. InitializeEnclave must be called to notify SGX that the enclave is in its final state before execution can begin. InitializeEnclave requires two SGX-specific structures to be passed in (SIGSTRUCT and EINITTOKEN; see the SGX documentation for the details).

The executive function NtInitializeEnclave called by InitializeEnclave does some parameter validation and makes sure the enclave VAD obtained has the correct attributes and then passed the structures along to the SGX hardware. Note that an enclave can only be initialized once.

The final step would be to use the Intel assembly instruction EENTER to start code execution (again, see the SGX documentation for the details).

Proactive memory management (SuperFetch)

Traditional memory management in operating systems has focused on the demand-paging model discussed thus far, with some advances in clustering and prefetching so that disk I/O can be optimized at the time of the demand-page fault. Client versions of Windows, however, include a significant improvement in the management of physical memory with the implementation of SuperFetch, a memory management scheme that enhances the least–recently accessed approach with historical file access information and proactive memory management.

The standby list management in older versions of Windows had two limitations. First, the prioritization of pages relies only on the recent past behavior of processes and does not anticipate their future memory requirements. Second, the data used for prioritization is limited to the list of pages owned by a process at any given point in time. These shortcomings can result in scenarios in which the computer is left unattended for a brief period of time, during which a memory-intensive system application runs (doing work such as an antivirus scan or a disk defragmentation) and then causes subsequent interactive application use (or launch) to be sluggish. The same thing can happen when a user purposely runs a data- and/or memory-intensive application and then returns to use other programs, which appear to be significantly less responsive.

This decline in performance occurs because the memory-intensive application forces the code and data that active applications had cached in memory to be overwritten by the memory-intensive activities—applications perform sluggishly as they have to request their data and code from disk. Client versions of Windows take a big step toward resolving these limitations with SuperFetch.

Components

SuperFetch has several components in the system that work hand in hand to proactively manage memory and limit the impact on user activity when SuperFetch is performing its work. These components include the following:

■ **Tracer** The tracer mechanisms are part of a kernel component (Pf) that allows SuperFetch to query detailed page-usage, session, and process information at any time. SuperFetch also uses the FileInfo mini-filter driver (%SystemRoot%\System32\Drivers\Fileinfo.sys) to track file usage.

■ **Trace collector and processor** This collector works with the tracing components to provide a raw log based on the tracing data that has been acquired. This tracing data is kept in memory and handed off to the processor. The processor then hands the log entries in the trace to the agents, which maintain history files (described next) in memory and persist them to disk when the service stops, such as during a reboot.

■ **Agents** SuperFetch keeps file page access information in history files, which keep track of virtual offsets. Agents group pages by attributes, such as the following:

- Page access while the user was active

- Page access by a foreground process

- Hard fault while the user was active

- Page access during an application launch

- Page access upon the user returning after a long idle period

■ **Scenario manager** This component, also called the *context agent*, manages the three Super-Fetch scenario plans: hibernation, standby, and fast-user switching. The kernel-mode part of the scenario manager provides APIs for initiating and terminating scenarios, managing the current scenario state, and associating tracing information with these scenarios.

■ **Rebalancer** Based on the information provided by the SuperFetch agents, as well as the current state of the system (such as the state of the prioritized page lists), the rebalancer—a specialized agent in the Superfetch user-mode service—queries the PFN database and reprioritizes it based on the associated score of each page, thus building the prioritized standby lists. The rebalancer can also issue commands to the memory manager that modify the working sets of processes on the system, and it is the only agent that actually takes action on the system. Other agents merely filter information for the rebalancer to use in its decisions. In addition to reprioritization, the rebalancer initiates prefetching through the prefetcher thread, which uses FileInfo and kernel services to preload memory with useful pages.

All these components use facilities inside the memory manager that allow for the querying of detailed information about the state of each page in the PFN database, the current page counts for each page list and prioritized list, and more. Figure 5-50 shows an architectural diagram of SuperFetch's multiple components. SuperFetch components also use prioritized I/O to minimize user impact. (See Chapter 8 in Part 2 for more on I/O priority.)

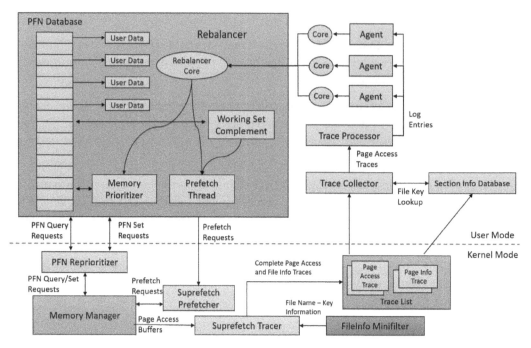

FIGURE 5-50 SuperFetch architectural diagram.

Tracing and logging

SuperFetch makes most of its decisions based on information that has been integrated, parsed, and post-processed from raw traces and logs, making these two components among the most critical. Tracing is like ETW in some ways because it uses certain triggers in code throughout the system to generate events, but it also works in conjunction with facilities already provided by the system, such as power-manager notification, process callbacks, and file-system filtering. The tracer also uses traditional page-aging mechanisms that exist in the memory manager, as well as newer working-set aging and access tracking implemented for SuperFetch.

SuperFetch always keeps a trace running and continuously queries trace data from the system, which tracks page usage and access through the memory manager's access bit tracking and working-set aging. To track file-related information, which is as critical as page usage because it allows prioritization of file data in the cache, SuperFetch leverages existing filtering functionality with the addition of the FileInfo driver. (See Chapter 6 for more information on filter drivers.) This driver sits on the file-system device stack and monitors access and changes to files at the stream level, which provides it with fine-grained understanding of file access. (For more information on NTFS data streams, see Chapter 13 in Part 2.) The main job of the FileInfo driver is to associate streams—identified by a unique key, currently implemented as the FsContext field of the respective file object—with file names so that the user-mode Superfetch service can identify the specific file stream and offset that a page in the standby list belonging to a memory-mapped section is associated with. It also provides the interface for prefetching file data transparently, without interfering with locked files and other file-system state.

The rest of the driver ensures that the information stays consistent by tracking deletions, renaming operations, truncations, and the reuse of file keys by implementing sequence numbers.

At any time during tracing, the rebalancer might be invoked to repopulate pages differently. These decisions are made by analyzing information such as the distribution of memory within working sets, the zero page list, the modified page list and the standby page lists, the number of faults, the state of PTE access bits, the per-page usage traces, current virtual address consumption, and working set size.

A given trace can be a page-access trace, in which the tracer uses the access bit to keep track of which pages were accessed by the process (both file page and private memory). Or, it can be a name-logging trace, which monitors the file name–to–file key mapping updates to the actual file on disk. These allow SuperFetch to map a page associated with a file object.

Although a SuperFetch trace only keeps track of page accesses, the `Superfetch` service processes this trace in user mode and goes much deeper, adding its own richer information such as where the page was loaded from (for example, in resident memory or a hard page fault), whether this was the initial access to that page, and what the rate of page access actually is. Additional information, such as the system state, is also kept, as well as information about recent scenarios in which each traced page was last referenced. The generated trace information is kept in memory through a logger into data structures, which—in the case of page-access traces—identify traces, a virtual address–to–working set pair, or, in the case of a name-logging trace, a file-to-offset pair. SuperFetch can thus keep track of which range of virtual addresses for a given process have page-related events and which range of offsets for a given file have similar events.

Scenarios

One aspect of SuperFetch that is distinct from its primary page reprioritization and prefetching mechanisms (covered in more detail in the next section) is its support for scenarios, which are specific actions on the machine for which SuperFetch strives to improve the user experience. These scenarios are as follows:

- **Hibernation**   The goal of hibernation is to intelligently decide which pages are saved in the hibernation file other than the existing working-set pages. The idea is to minimize the amount of time it takes for the system to become responsive after a resume.

- **Standby**   The goal of standby is to completely remove hard faults after resume. Because a typical system can resume in less than 2 seconds, but can take 5 seconds to spin up the hard drive after a long sleep, a single hard fault could cause such a delay in the resume cycle. SuperFetch prioritizes pages needed after a standby to remove this chance.

- **Fast user switching**   The goal of fast user switching is to keep an accurate priority and understanding of each user's memory. That way, switching to another user will cause the user's session to be immediately usable, and won't require a large amount of lag time to allow pages to be faulted in.

Each of these scenarios has different goals, but all are centered around the main purpose of minimizing or removing hard faults.

Scenarios are hardcoded, and SuperFetch manages them through the `NtSetSystemInformation` and `NtQuerySystemInformation` APIs that control system state. For SuperFetch purposes, a special information class, `SystemSuperfetchInformation`, is used to control the kernel-mode components and to generate requests such as starting, ending, and querying a scenario or associating one or more traces with a scenario.

Each scenario is defined by a plan file, which contains, at minimum, a list of pages associated with the scenario. Page priority values are also assigned according to certain rules (described next). When a scenario starts, the scenario manager is responsible for responding to the event by generating the list of pages that should be brought into memory and at which priority.

Page priority and rebalancing

You've already seen that the memory manager implements a system of page priorities to define which standby list pages will be repurposed for a given operation and in which list a given page will be inserted. This mechanism provides benefits when processes and threads have associated priorities—for example, ensuring that a defragmenter process doesn't pollute the standby page list and/or steal pages from an interactive foreground process. But its real power is unleashed through SuperFetch's page-prioritization schemes and rebalancing, which don't require manual application input or hardcoded knowledge of process importance.

SuperFetch assigns page priority based on an internal score it keeps for each page, part of which is based on frequency-based usage. This usage counts how many times a page was used in given relative time intervals, such as by hour, day, or week. The system also keeps track of time of use, recording how long it's been since a given page was accessed. Finally, data such as where this page comes from (which list) and other access patterns is used to compute this score.

The score is translated into a priority number, which can be anywhere from 1 to 6. (A priority of 7 is used for another purpose, described later.) Going down each level, the lower standby page list priorities are repurposed first, as shown in the "Viewing the prioritized standby lists" experiment. Priority 5 is typically used for normal applications, while priority 1 is meant for background applications that third-party developers can mark as such. Finally, priority 6 is used to keep a certain number of high-importance pages as far away as possible from repurposing. The other priorities are a result of the score associated with each page.

Because SuperFetch "learns" a user's system, it can start from scratch with no existing historical data and slowly build an understanding of the different page accesses associated with the user. However, this would result in a significant learning curve whenever a new application, user, or service pack was installed. Instead, by using an internal tool, Windows can pre-train SuperFetch to capture SuperFetch data and then turn it into prebuilt traces. These prebuilt traces were generated by the SuperFetch team, who traced common usages and patterns that all users will probably encounter, such as clicking the Start menu, opening Control Panel, or using the File Open/Save dialog box. This trace data was then saved to history files (which ship as resources in Sysmain.dll) and is used to prepopulate the special priority 7 list. This list is where the most critical data is placed and is rarely repurposed. Pages at priority 7 are file pages kept in memory even after the process has exited and even across reboots (by being repopulated at the next boot). Finally, pages with priority 7 are static, in that they are never reprioritized, and SuperFetch will never dynamically load pages at priority 7 other than the static pretrained set.

The prioritized list is loaded into memory (or prepopulated) by the rebalancer, but the actual act of rebalancing is handled by both SuperFetch and the memory manager. As shown, the prioritized standby page list mechanism is internal to the memory manager, and decisions as to which pages to throw out first and which to protect are innate, based on the priority number. The rebalancer does its job not by manually rebalancing memory but by reprioritizing it, which causes the memory manager to perform the needed tasks. The rebalancer is also responsible for reading the actual pages from disk, if needed, so that they are present in memory (prefetching). It then assigns the priority that is mapped by each agent to the score for each page, and the memory manager ensures that the page is treated according to its importance.

The rebalancer can take action without relying on other agents—for example, if it notices that the distribution of pages across paging lists is suboptimal or that the number of repurposed pages across different priority levels is detrimental. The rebalancer can also trigger working-set trimming, which might be required for creating an appropriate budget of pages that will be used for SuperFetch prepopulated cache data. The rebalancer will typically take low-utility pages—such as those that are already marked as low priority, that are zeroed, or that have valid content but not in any working set and have been unused—and build a more useful set of pages in memory, given the budget it has allocated itself. After the rebalancer has decided which pages to bring into memory and at which priority level they need to be loaded (as well as which pages can be thrown out), it performs the required disk reads to prefetch them. It also works in conjunction with the I/O manager's prioritization schemes so that I/Os are performed with very low priority and do not interfere with the user.

The memory consumption used by prefetching is backed by standby pages. As described in the discussion of page dynamics, standby memory is available memory because it can be repurposed as free memory for another allocator at any time. In other words, if SuperFetch is prefetching the wrong data, there is no real impact on the user because that memory can be reused when needed and doesn't actually consume resources.

Finally, the rebalancer also runs periodically to ensure that pages it has marked as high priority have actually been recently used. Because these pages will rarely (sometimes never) be repurposed, it is important not to waste them on data that is rarely accessed but may have appeared to be frequently accessed during a certain period. If such a situation is detected, the rebalancer runs again to push those pages down in the priority lists.

A special agent called the *application launch agent* is involved in a different kind of prefetching mechanism, which attempts to predict application launches and builds a Markov chain model that describes the probability of certain application launches given the existence of other application launches within a time segment. These time segments are divided across four different periods of roughly 6 hours each—morning, noon, evening, and night—and by weekday or weekend. For example, if on Saturday and Sunday evening a user typically launches Outlook after having launched Word, the application launch agent will likely prefetch Outlook based on the high probability of it running after Word during weekend evenings.

Because systems today have sufficiently large amounts of memory—on average more than 2 GB (although SuperFetch works well on low-memory systems, too)—the actual real amount of memory that frequently used processes on a machine need resident for optimal performance ends up being a manageable subset of their entire memory footprint. Often, SuperFetch can fit all the pages required into RAM. When it can't, technologies such as ReadyBoost and ReadyDrive can further prevent disk usage.

Robust performance

A final performance-enhancing functionality of SuperFetch is called *robustness,* or *robust performance.* This component—managed by the user-mode `Superfetch` service but ultimately implemented in the kernel (Pf routines)—watches for specific file I/O access that might harm system performance by populating the standby lists with unneeded data. For example, if a process were to copy a large file across the file system, the standby list would be populated with the file's contents, even though that file might never be accessed again (or not for a long period of time). This would throw out any other data within that priority—and if this was an interactive and useful program, chances are its priority would be at least 5.

SuperFetch responds to two specific kinds of I/O access patterns:

- **Sequential file access**   With this type of I/O access pattern, the system goes through all the data in a file.

- **Sequential directory access**   With this type of I/O access, the system goes through every file in a directory.

When SuperFetch detects that a certain amount of data past an internal threshold has been populated in the standby list as a result of this kind of access, it applies aggressive deprioritization (called *robustion*) to the pages being used to map this file. This occurs within the targeted process only so as not to penalize other applications. These pages, which are said to be *robusted,* essentially become reprioritized to priority 2.

Because this component of SuperFetch is reactive and not predictive, it does take some time for the robustion to kick in. SuperFetch will therefore keep track of this process for the next time it runs. Once SuperFetch has determined that it appears that this process always performs this kind of sequential access, it remembers this and robusts the file pages as soon as they're mapped instead of waiting for the reactive behavior. At this point, the entire process is now considered robusted for future file access.

Just by applying this logic, however, SuperFetch could potentially hurt many legitimate applications or user scenarios that perform sequential access in the future. For example, by using the Sysinternals Strings.exe utility, you can look for a string in all executables that are part of a directory. If there are many files, SuperFetch would likely perform robustion. Now, next time you run Strings.exe with a different search parameter, it would run just as slowly as it did the first time even though you'd expect it to run much faster. To prevent this, SuperFetch keeps a list of processes that it watches into the future, as well as an internal hard-coded list of exceptions. If a process is detected to later re-access robusted files, robustion is disabled on the process to restore the expected behavior.

The main point to remember when thinking about robustion—and SuperFetch optimizations in general—is that SuperFetch constantly monitors usage patterns and updates its understanding of the system to avoid fetching useless data. Although changes in a user's daily activities or application startup behavior might cause SuperFetch to pollute the cache with irrelevant data or to throw out data that it might think is useless, it will quickly adapt to any pattern changes. If the user's actions are erratic and random, the worst that can happen is that the system will behave in a similar state as if SuperFetch were not present at all. If SuperFetch is ever in doubt or cannot track data reliably, it quiets itself and doesn't make changes to a given process or page.

ReadyBoost

These days, RAM is easily available and relatively cheap compared to a decade ago. Still, it doesn't beat the cost of secondary storage such as hard disk drives. Unfortunately, mechanical hard disks contain many moving parts, are fragile, and, more importantly, are relatively slow compared to RAM, especially during seeking. As a result, storing active SuperFetch data on the drive would be as bad as paging out a page and hard-faulting it inside memory.

Solid state disks and hybrid drives offset some of these disadvantages but they are still pricier and slower compared to RAM. Portable solid state media such as USB flash disk (UFD), CompactFlash cards, and Secure Digital cards, however, provide a useful compromise. They are cheaper than RAM and available in larger sizes, but also have shorter seek times than mechanical hard drives because of the lack of moving parts.

Note In practice, CompactFlash cards and Secure Digital cards are almost always interfaced through a USB adapter, so they all appear to the system as USB flash disks.

Random disk I/O is especially expensive because disk head seek time plus rotational latency for typical desktop hard drives total about 10 milliseconds—an eternity for today's 3 or 4 GHz processors. Flash memory, however, can service random reads up to 10 times faster than a typical hard disk. Windows therefore includes a feature called *ReadyBoost* to take advantage of flash memory storage devices by creating an intermediate caching layer on them that logically sits between memory and disks.

ReadyBoost (not to be confused with ReadyBoot) is implemented with the aid of a driver (%SystemRoot%\System32\Drivers\Rdyboost.sys) that is responsible for writing the cached data to the non-volatile RAM (NVRAM) device. When you insert a USB flash disk into a system, ReadyBoost looks at the device to determine its performance characteristics and stores the results of its test in HKLM\SOFTWARE\Microsoft\Windows NT\CurrentVersion\Emdmgmt. (*Emd* is short for *external memory device*, the working name for ReadyBoost during its development.)

If the new device is between 256 MB and 32 GB in size, has a transfer rate of 2.5 MB per second or higher for random 4 KB reads, and has a transfer rate of 1.75 MB per second or higher for random 512 KB writes, then ReadyBoost will ask if you'd like to dedicate some of the space for disk caching. If you agree, ReadyBoost creates a file named *ReadyBoost.sfcache* in the root of the device, which it uses to store cached pages.

After initializing caching, ReadyBoost intercepts all reads and writes to local hard disk volumes (C:\, for example) and copies any data being read or written into the caching file that the service created. There are exceptions—for example, data that hasn't been read in a long while or data that belongs to Volume Snapshot requests. Data stored on the cached drive is compressed and typically achieves a 2:1 compression ratio, so a 4 GB cache file will usually contain 8 GB of data. Each block is encrypted as it is written using Advanced Encryption Standard (AES) encryption with a randomly generated per-boot session key to guarantee the privacy of the data in the cache if the device is removed from the system.

When ReadyBoost sees random reads that can be satisfied from the cache, it services them from there. However, because hard disks have better sequential read access than flash memory, it lets reads that are part of sequential access patterns go directly to the disk even if the data is in the cache. Likewise, when reading the cache, if large I/Os must be done, the on-disk cache will be read instead.

One disadvantage of depending on flash media is that the user can remove it at any time, which means the system can never solely store critical data on the media. (As you've seen, writes always go to the secondary storage first.) A related technology, ReadyDrive, covered in the next section, offers additional benefits and solves this problem.

ReadyDrive

ReadyDrive is a Windows feature that takes advantage of hybrid hard disk drives (H-HDDs). An *H-HDD* is a disk with embedded NVRAM. Typical H-HDDs include between 50 MB and 512 MB of cache.

Under ReadyDrive, the drive's flash memory does not simply act as an automatic, transparent cache, as does the RAM cache common on most hard drives. Instead, Windows uses ATA-8 commands to define the disk data to be held in the flash memory. For example, Windows saves boot data to the cache when the system shuts down, allowing for faster restarting. It also stores portions of hibernation file data in the cache when the system hibernates so that the subsequent resume is faster. Because the cache is enabled even when the disk is spun down, Windows can use the flash memory as a disk-write cache, which avoids spinning up the disk when the system is running on battery power. Keeping the disk spindle turned off can save much of the power consumed by the disk drive under normal usage.

Another consumer of ReadyDrive is SuperFetch. It offers the same advantages as ReadyBoost with some enhanced functionality, such as not requiring an external flash device and having the ability to work persistently. Because the cache is on the actual physical hard drive, which a user typically cannot remove while the computer is running, the hard drive controller typically doesn't have to worry about the data disappearing and can avoid making writes to the actual disk using solely the cache.

Process reflection

There are often cases where a process exhibits problematic behavior, but because it's still providing service, suspending it to generate a full memory dump or interactively debug it is undesirable. The length of time a process is suspended to generate a dump can be minimized by taking a minidump, which captures thread registers and stacks along with pages of memory referenced by registers, but that dump type has a very limited amount of information, which many times is sufficient for diagnosing crashes but not for troubleshooting general problems. With process reflection, the target process is suspended only long enough to generate a minidump and create a suspended cloned copy of the target, and then the larger dump that captures all of a process's valid user-mode memory can be generated from the clone while the target is allowed to continue executing.

Several Windows Diagnostic Infrastructure (WDI) components make use of process reflection to capture minimally intrusive memory dumps of processes their heuristics identify as exhibiting suspicious behavior. For example, the Memory Leak Diagnoser component of Windows Resource Exhaustion Detection and Resolution (also known as RADAR), generates a reflected memory dump of a process that appears to be leaking private virtual memory so that it can be sent to Microsoft via Windows Error Reporting (WER) for analysis. WDI's hung process detection heuristic does the same for processes that appear to be deadlocked with one another. Because these components use heuristics, they can't be certain the processes are faulty and therefore can't suspend them for long periods of time or terminate them.

The `RtlCreateProcessReflection` function in Ntdll.dll drives the implementation of process reflection. It works as follows:

1. It creates a shared memory section.

2. It populates the shared memory section with parameters.

3. It maps the shared memory section into the current and target processes.

4. It creates two event objects and duplicates them into the target process so that the current process and target process can synchronize their operations.

5. It injects a thread into the target process via a call to `RtlpCreateUserThreadEx`. The thread is directed to begin execution in Ntdll's `RtlpProcessReflectionStartup` function. (Because Ntdll.dll is mapped at the same address (randomly generated at boot) into every process's address space, the current process can simply pass the address of the function it obtains from its own Ntdll.dll mapping.)

6. If the caller of `RtlCreateProcessReflection` specified that it wants a handle to the cloned process, `RtlCreateProcessReflection` waits for the remote thread to terminate, otherwise it returns to the caller.

7. The injected thread in the target process allocates an additional event object that it will use to synchronize with the cloned process once it's created.

8. The injected thread calls `RtlCloneUserProcess`, passing parameters it obtains from the memory mapping it shares with the initiating process.

9. If the `RtlCreateProcessReflection` option that specifies the creation of the clone when the process is not executing in the loader, performing heap operations, modifying the process environment block (PEB), or modifying fiber-local storage is present, then `RtlCreateProcess-Reflection` acquires the associated locks before continuing. This can be useful for debugging because the memory dump's copy of the data structures will be in a consistent state.

10. `RtlCloneUserProcess` finishes by calling `RtlpCreateUserProcess`, the user-mode function responsible for general process creation, passing flags that indicate the new process should be a clone of the current one. `RtlpCreateUserProcess` in turn calls `ZwCreateUserProcess` to request the kernel to create the process.

When creating a cloned process, `ZwCreateUserProcess` executes most of the same code paths as when it creates a new process, with the exception that `PspAllocateProcess`, which it calls to create the process object and initial thread, calls `MmInitializeProcessAddressSpace` with a flag specifying that the address should be a copy-on-write copy of the target process instead of an initial process address space. The memory manager uses the same support it provides for the Services for Unix Applications `fork` API to efficiently clone the address space. Once the target process continues execution, any changes it makes to its address space are seen only by it, not the clone. This enables the clone's address space to represent a consistent point-in-time view of the target process.

The clone's execution begins at the point just after the return from `RtlpCreateUserProcess`. If the clone's creation is successful, its thread receives the STATUS_PROCESS_CLONED return code, whereas the cloning thread receives STATUS_SUCCESS. The cloned process then synchronizes with the target and, as its final act, calls a function optionally passed to `RtlCreateProcessReflection`, which must be implemented in Ntdll.dll. RADAR, for instance, specifies `RtlDetectHeapLeaks`, which performs heuristic analysis of the process heaps and reports the results back to the thread that called `RtlCreateProcess-Reflection`. If no function was specified, the thread suspends itself or terminates, depending on the flags passed to `RtlCreateProcessReflection`.

When RADAR and WDI use process reflection, they call `RtlCreateProcessReflection`, asking for the function to return a handle to the cloned process and for the clone to suspend itself after it has initialized. Then they generate a minidump of the target process, which suspends the target for the duration of the dump generation. Next, they generate a more comprehensive dump of the cloned process. After they finish generating the dump of the clone, they terminate the clone. The target process can execute during the time window between the minidump's completion and the creation of the clone, but for most scenarios any inconsistencies do not interfere with troubleshooting. The Procdump utility from Sysinternals also follows these steps when you specify the –r switch to have it create a reflected dump of a target process.

Conclusion

This chapter examined how the Windows memory manager implements virtual memory management. As with most modern operating systems, each process is given access to a private address space, protecting one process's memory from another's but allowing processes to share memory efficiently and securely. Advanced capabilities, such as the inclusion of mapped files and the ability to sparsely allocate memory, are also available. The Windows environment subsystem makes most of the memory manager's capabilities available to applications through the Windows API.

The next chapter covers another critical part of any operating system—the I/O system.

CHAPTER 6

I/O system

The Windows I/O system consists of several executive components that, together, manage hardware devices and provide interfaces to hardware devices for applications and the system. This chapter lists the design goals of the I/O system, which have influenced its implementation. It then covers the components that make up the I/O system, including the I/O manager, Plug and Play (PnP) manager, and power manager. Then it examines the structure and components of the I/O system and the various types of device drivers. It discusses the key data structures that describe devices, device drivers, and I/O requests, after which it describes the steps necessary to complete I/O requests as they move through the system. Finally, it presents the way device detection, driver installation, and power management work.

I/O system components

The design goals for the Windows I/O system are to provide an abstraction of devices, both hardware (physical) and software (virtual or logical), to applications with the following features:

- Uniform security and naming across devices to protect shareable resources. (See Chapter 7, "Security," for a description of the Windows security model.)

- High-performance asynchronous packet-based I/O to allow for the implementation of scalable applications.

- Services that allow drivers to be written in a high-level language and easily ported between different machine architectures.

- Layering and extensibility to allow for the addition of drivers that transparently modify the behavior of other drivers or devices, without requiring any changes to the driver whose behavior or device is modified.

- Dynamic loading and unloading of device drivers so that drivers can be loaded on demand and not consume system resources when unneeded.

- Support for Plug and Play, where the system locates and installs drivers for newly detected hardware, assigns them hardware resources they require, and allows applications to discover and activate device interfaces.

- Support for power management so that the system or individual devices can enter low-power states.

- Support for multiple installable file systems, including FAT (and its variants, FAT32 and exFAT), the CD-ROM file system (CDFS), the Universal Disk Format (UDF) file system, the Resilient File System (ReFS), and the Windows file system (NTFS). (See Chapter 13, "File systems," in Part 2 of this book for more specific information on file system types and architecture.)

- Windows Management Instrumentation (WMI) support and diagnosability so that drivers can be managed and monitored through WMI applications and scripts. (WMI is described in Chapter 9, "Management mechanisms," in Part 2.)

To implement these features, the Windows I/O system consists of several executive components as well as device drivers, which are shown in Figure 6-1.

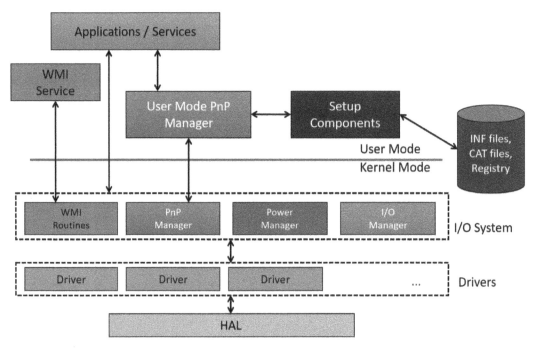

FIGURE 6-1 I/O system components.

- The I/O manager is the heart of the I/O system. It connects applications and system components to virtual, logical, and physical devices, and it defines the infrastructure that supports device drivers.

- A device driver typically provides an I/O interface for a particular type of device. A *driver* is a software module that interprets high-level commands, such as read or write commands, and issues low-level, device-specific commands, such as writing to control registers. Device drivers receive commands routed to them by the I/O manager that are directed at the devices they manage, and they inform the I/O manager when those commands are complete. Device drivers often use the I/O manager to forward I/O commands to other device drivers that share in the implementation of a device's interface or control.

- The PnP manager works closely with the I/O manager and a type of device driver called *a bus driver* to guide the allocation of hardware resources as well as to detect and respond to the arrival and removal of hardware devices. The PnP manager and bus drivers are responsible for loading a device's driver when the device is detected. When a device is added to a system that doesn't have an appropriate device driver, the executive Plug and Play component calls on the device-installation services of the user-mode PnP manager.

- The power manager also works closely with the I/O manager and the PnP manager to guide the system, as well as individual device drivers, through power-state transitions.

- WMI support routines, called the Windows Driver Model (WDM) WMI provider, allow device drivers to indirectly act as providers, using the WDM WMI provider as an intermediary to communicate with the WMI service in user mode.

- The registry serves as a database that stores a description of basic hardware devices attached to the system as well as driver initialization and configuration settings. (See the section "The registry" in Chapter 9 in Part 2 for more information.)

- INF files, which are designated by the .inf extension, are driver-installation files. INF files are the link between a particular hardware device and the driver that assumes primary control of that device. They are made up of script-like instructions describing the device they correspond to, the source and target locations of driver files, required driver-installation registry modifications, and driver-dependency information. Digital signatures that Windows uses to verify that a driver file has passed testing by the Microsoft Windows Hardware Quality Labs (WHQL) are stored in .cat files. Digital signatures are also used to prevent tampering of the driver or its INF file.

- The hardware abstraction layer (HAL) insulates drivers from the specifics of the processor and interrupt controller by providing APIs that hide differences between platforms. In essence, the HAL is the bus driver for all the devices soldered onto the computer's motherboard that aren't controlled by other drivers.

The I/O manager

The I/O manager is the core of the I/O system. It defines the orderly framework, or model, within which I/O requests are delivered to device drivers. The I/O system is packet driven. Most I/O requests are represented by an I/O request packet (IRP), which is a data structure that contains information completely describing an I/O request. The IRP travels from one I/O system component to another. (As you'll discover in the section "Fast I/O," fast I/O is the exception; it doesn't use IRPs.) The design allows an individual application thread to manage multiple I/O requests concurrently. (For more information on IRPs, see the section "I/O request packets" later in this chapter.)

The I/O manager creates an IRP in memory to represent an I/O operation, passing a pointer to the IRP to the correct driver and disposing of the packet when the I/O operation is complete. In contrast, a driver receives an IRP, performs the operation the IRP specifies, and passes the IRP back to the I/O manager, either because the requested I/O operation has been completed or because it must be passed on to another driver for further processing.

In addition to creating and disposing of IRPs, the I/O manager supplies code that is common to different drivers and that the drivers can call to carry out their I/O processing. By consolidating common tasks in the I/O manager, individual drivers become simpler and more compact. For example, the I/O manager provides a function that allows one driver to call other drivers. It also manages buffers for I/O requests, provides timeout support for drivers, and records which installable file systems are loaded into the operating system. There are about 100 different routines in the I/O manager that can be called by device drivers.

The I/O manager also provides flexible I/O services that allow environment subsystems, such as Windows and POSIX (the latter is no longer supported), to implement their respective I/O functions. These services include support for asynchronous I/O that allow developers to build scalable, high-performance server applications.

The uniform, modular interface that drivers present allows the I/O manager to call any driver without requiring any special knowledge of its structure or internal details. The operating system treats all I/O requests as if they were directed at a file; the driver converts the requests from requests made to a virtual file to hardware-specific requests. Drivers can also call each other (using the I/O manager) to achieve layered, independent processing of an I/O request.

Besides providing the normal open, close, read, and write functions, the Windows I/O system provides several advanced features, such as asynchronous, direct, buffered, and scatter/gather I/O, which are described in the "Types of I/O" section later in this chapter.

Typical I/O processing

Most I/O operations don't involve all the components of the I/O system. A typical I/O request starts with an application executing an I/O-related function (for example, reading data from a device) that is processed by the I/O manager, one or more device drivers, and the HAL.

As mentioned, in Windows, threads perform I/O on virtual files. A virtual file refers to any source or destination for I/O that is treated as if it were a file (such as devices, files, directories, pipes, and mailslots). A typical user mode client calls the CreateFile or CreateFile2 functions to get a handle to a virtual file. The function name is a little misleading—it's not just about files, it's anything that is known as a *symbolic link* within the object manager's directory called GLOBAL??. The suffix "File" in the CreateFile* functions really means a virtual file object (FILE_OBJECT) that is the entity created by the executive as a result of these functions. Figure 6-2 shows a screenshot of the WinObj Sysinternals tool for the GLOBAL?? directory.

As shown in Figure 6-2, a name such as C: is just a symbolic link to an internal name under the Device object manager directory (in this case, \Device\HarddiskVolume7). (See Chapter 8, "System mechanisms," in Part 2 for more on the object manager and the object manager namespace.) All the names in the GLOBAL?? directory are candidates for arguments to CreateFile(2). Kernel mode clients such as device drivers can use the similar ZwCreateFile to obtain a handle to a virtual file.

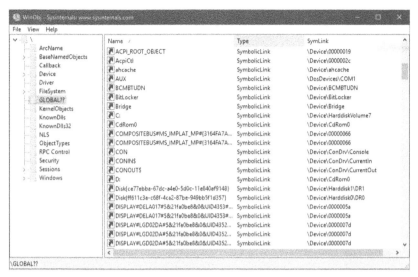

FIGURE 6-2 The object manager's GLOBAL?? directory.

Note Higher-level abstractions such as the .NET Framework and the Windows Runtime have their own APIs for working with files and devices (for example, the `System.IO.File` class in .NET or the `Windows.Storage.StorageFile` class in WinRT), but these eventually call `CreateFile(2)` to get the actual handle they hide under the covers.

Note The GLOBAL?? object manager directory is sometimes called DosDevices, which is an older name. `DosDevices` still works because it's defined as a symbolic link to *GLOBAL??* in the root of the object manager's namespace. In driver code, the ?? string is typically used to reference the GLOBAL?? directory.

The operating system abstracts all I/O requests as operations on a virtual file because the I/O manager has no knowledge of anything but files, therefore making it the responsibility of the driver to translate file-oriented comments (open, close, read, write) into device-specific commands. This abstraction thereby generalizes an application's interface to devices. User-mode applications call documented functions, which in turn call internal I/O system functions to read from a file, write to a file, and perform other operations. The I/O manager dynamically directs these virtual file requests to the appropriate device driver. Figure 6-3 illustrates the basic structure of a typical I/O read request flow. (Other types of I/O requests, such as write, are similar; they just use different APIs.)

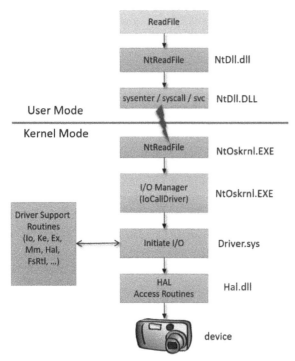

FIGURE 6-3 The flow of a typical I/O request.

The following sections look at these components more closely, covering the various types of device drivers, how they are structured, how they load and initialize, and how they process I/O requests. Then we'll cover the operation and roles of the PnP manager and the power manager.

Interrupt Request Levels and Deferred Procedure Calls

Before we proceed, we must introduce two very important concepts of the Windows kernel that play an important role within the I/O system: Interrupt Request Levels (IRQL) and Deferred Procedure Calls (DPC). A thorough discussion of these concepts is reserved for Chapter 8 in Part 2, but we'll provide enough information in this section to enable you to understand the mechanics of I/O processing that follow.

Interrupt Request Levels

The IRQL has two somewhat distinct meanings, but they converge in certain situations:

- **An IRQL is a priority assigned to an interrupt source from a hardware device**   This number is set by the HAL (in conjunction with the interrupt controller to which devices that require interrupt servicing are connected).

- **Each CPU has its own IRQL value**   It should be considered a register of the CPU (even though current CPUs do not implement it as such).

The fundamental rule of IRQLs is that lower IRQL code cannot interfere with higher IRQL code and vice versa—code with a higher IRQL can preempt code running at a lower IRQL. You'll see examples of how this works in practice in a moment. A list of IRQLs for the Windows-supported architectures is shown in Figure 6-4. Note that IRQLs are not the same as thread priorities. In fact, thread priorities have meaning only when the IRQL is less than 2.

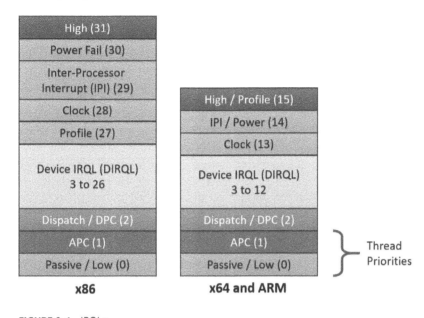

FIGURE 6-4   IRQLs.

> **Note**   IRQL is not the same as IRQ (interrupt request). IRQs are hardware lines connecting devices to an interrupt controller. See Chapter 8 in Part 2 for more on interrupts, IRQs, and IRQLs.

Normally, the IRQL of a processor is 0. This means "nothing special" is happening in that regard, and that the kernel's scheduler that schedules threads based on priorities and so on works as described in Chapter 4, "Threads." In user mode, the IRQL can only be 0. There is no way to raise IRQL from user mode. (That's why user-mode documentation never mentions the IRQL concept at all; there would be no point.)

Kernel-mode code can raise and lower the current CPU IRQL with the KeRaiseIrql and KeLower-Irql functions. However, most of the time-specific functions are called with the IRQL raised to some expected level, as you'll see shortly when we discuss a typical I/O processing by a driver.

The most important IRQLs for this I/O-related discussions are the following:

- **Passive(0)**   This is defined by the PASSIVE_LEVEL macro in the WDK header wdm.h. It is the normal IRQL where the kernel scheduler is working normally, as described at length in Chapter 4.

- **Dispatch/DPC (2) (`DISPATCH_LEVEL`)**   This is the IRQL the kernel's scheduler works at. This means if a thread raises the current IRQL to 2 (or higher), the thread has essentially an infinite quantum and will not be preempted by another thread. Effectively, the scheduler cannot wake up on the current CPU until the IRQL drops below 2. This implies a few things:

  - With the IRQL at level 2 or above, any waiting on kernel dispatcher objects (such as mutexes, semaphores, and events) would crash the system. This is because waiting implies that the thread might enter a wait state and another should be scheduled on the same CPU. However, because the scheduler is not around at this level, this cannot happen; instead, the system will bug-check (the only exception is if the wait timeout is zero, meaning no waiting is requested, just getting back the signaled state of the object).

  - No page faults can be handled. This is because a page fault would require a context switch to one of the modified page writers. However, context switches are not allowed, so the system would crash. This means code running at IRQL 2 or above can access only non-paged memory—typically memory allocated from non-paged pool, which by definition is always resident in physical memory.

- **Device IRQL (3–26 on x86; 3–12 on x64 and ARM) (`DIRQL`)**   These are the levels assigned to hardware interrupts. When an interrupt arrives, the kernel's trap dispatcher calls the appropriate interrupt service routine (ISR) and raises its IRQL to that of the associated interrupt. Because this value is always higher than `DISPATCH_LEVEL` (2), all rules associated with IRQL 2 apply for DIRQL as well.

Running at a particular IRQL masks interrupts with that and lower IRQLs. For example, an ISR running with IRQL of 8 would not let any code interfere (on that CPU) with IRQL of 7 or lower. Specifically, no user mode code is able to run because it always runs at IRQL 0. This implies that running in high IRQL is not desirable in the general case; there are a few specific scenarios (which we'll look at in this chapter) where this makes sense and is in fact required for normal system operation.

Deferred Procedure Calls

A Deferred Procedure Call (DPC) is an object that encapsulates calling a function at IRQL `DPC_LEVEL` (2). DPCs exist primarily for post-interrupt processing because running at DIRQL masks (and thus delays) other interrupts waiting to be serviced. A typical ISR would do the minimum work possible, mostly reading the state of the device and telling it to stop its interrupt signal and then deferring further processing to a lower IRQL (2) by requesting a DPC. The term *Deferred* means the DPC will not execute immediately—it can't because the current IRQL is higher than 2. However, when the ISR returns, if there are no pending interrupts waiting to be serviced, the CPU IRQL will drop to 2 and it will execute the DPCs that have accumulated (maybe just one). Figure 6-5 shows a simplified example of the sequence of events that may occur when interrupts from hardware devices (which are asynchronous in nature, meaning they can arrive at any time) occur while code executes normally at IRQL 0 on some CPU.

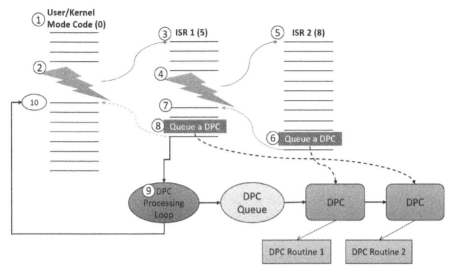

FIGURE 6-5 Example of interrupt and DPC processing.

Here is a rundown of the sequence of events shown in Figure 6-5:

1. Some user-mode or kernel-mode code is executing while the CPU is at IRQL 0, which is the case most of the time.

2. A hardware interrupt arrives with an IRQL of 5 (remember that Device IRQLs have a minimum value of 3). Because 5 is greater than zero (the current IRQL), the CPU state is saved, the IRQL is raised to 5, and the ISR associated with that interrupt is called. Note that there is no context switch; it's the same thread that now happens to execute the ISR code. (If the thread was in user mode, it switches to kernel mode whenever an interrupt arrives.)

3. ISR 1 starts executing while the CPU IRQL is 5. At this point, any interrupt with IRQL 5 or lower cannot interrupt.

4. Suppose another interrupt arrives with an IRQL of 8. Assume the system decides that the same CPU should handle it. Because 8 is greater than 5, the code is interrupted again, the CPU state is saved, the IRQL is raised to 8, and the CPU jumps to ISR 2. Note again that it's the same thread. No context switch can happen because the thread scheduler cannot wake up if the IRQL is 2 or higher.

5. ISR 2 is executing. Before it's done, ISR 2 would like to do some more processing at a lower IRQL so that interrupts with IRQLs less than 8 could be services as well.

6. As its final act, ISR 2 inserts a DPC initialized properly to point to a driver routine to do any post processing after the interrupt is dismissed by calling the `KeInsertQueueDpc` function. (We'll discuss what this post-processing typically includes in the next section.) Then the ISR returns, restoring the CPU state saved before entering ISR 2.

7. At this point, the IRQL drops to its previous level (5) and the CPU continues execution of ISR 1 that was interrupted before.

8. Just before ISR 1 finishes, it queues a DPC of its own to do its required post-processing. These DPCs are collected in a DPC queue that has not been examined yet. Then ISR 1 returns, restoring the CPU state saved before ISR 1 started execution.

9. At this point, the IRQL would want to drop to the old value of zero before all the interrupt handling began. However, the kernel notices that there are DPCs pending and so drops the IRQL to level 2 (DPC_LEVEL) and enters a DPC processing loop that iterates over the accumulated DPCs and calls each DPC routine in sequence. When the DPC queue is empty, DPC processing ends.

10. Finally, the IRQL can drop back to zero, restore the state of the CPU again, and resume execution of the original user or kernel code that got interrupted in the first place. Again, notice that all the processing described was done by the same thread (whichever one that may be). This fact implies that ISRs and DPC routines should not rely on any particular thread (and hence part of a particular process) to execute their code. It could be any thread, the significance of which will be discussed in the next section.

The preceding description is a bit simplified. It doesn't mention DPC importance, other CPUs that may handle DPCs for quicker DPC processing, and more. These details are not important for the discussion in this chapter. However, they are described fully in Chapter 8 in Part 2.

Device drivers

To integrate with the I/O manager and other I/O system components, a device driver must conform to implementation guidelines specific to the type of device it manages and the role it plays in managing the device. This section discusses the types of device drivers Windows supports as well as the internal structure of a device driver.

 Note Most kernel-mode device drivers are written in C. Starting with the Windows Driver Kit 8.0, drivers can also be safely written in C++ due to specific support for kernel-mode C++ in the new compilers. Use of assembly language is highly discouraged because of the complexity it introduces and its effect of making a driver difficult to port between the hardware architectures supported by Windows (x86, x64, and ARM).

Types of device drivers

Windows supports a wide range of device-driver types and programming environments. Even within a particular type of device driver, programming environments can differ depending on the specific type of device for which a driver is intended.

The broadest classification of a driver is whether it is a user-mode or kernel-mode driver. Windows supports a couple of types of user-mode drivers:

- **Windows subsystem printer drivers**   These translate device-independent graphics requests to printer-specific commands. These commands are then typically forwarded to a kernel-mode port driver such as the universal serial bus (USB) printer port driver (Usbprint.sys).

- **User-Mode Driver Framework (UMDF) drivers**   These are hardware device drivers that run in user mode. They communicate to the kernel-mode UMDF support library through advanced local procedure calls (ALPC). See the "User-Mode Driver Framework" section later in this chapter for more information.

In this chapter, the focus is on kernel-mode device drivers. There are many types of kernel-mode drivers, which can be divided into the following basic categories:

- **File-system drivers**   These accept I/O requests to files and satisfy the requests by issuing their own more explicit requests to mass storage or network device drivers.

- **Plug and Play drivers**   These work with hardware and integrate with the Windows power manager and PnP manager. They include drivers for mass storage devices, video adapters, input devices, and network adapters.

- **Non–Plug and Play drivers**   These include kernel extensions, which are drivers or modules that extend the functionality of the system. They do not typically integrate with the PnP manager or power manager because they usually do not manage an actual piece of hardware. Examples include network API and protocol drivers. The Sysinternals tool Process Monitor has a driver, and is an example of a non-PnP driver.

Within the category of kernel-mode drivers are further classifications based on the driver model to which the driver adheres and its role in servicing device requests.

WDM drivers

WDM drivers are device drivers that adhere to the Windows Driver Model (WDM). WDM includes support for Windows power management, Plug and Play, and WMI, and most Plug and Play drivers adhere to WDM. There are three types of WDM drivers:

- **Bus drivers**   These manage a logical or physical bus. Examples of buses include PCMCIA, PCI, USB, and IEEE 1394. A bus driver is responsible for detecting and informing the PnP manager of devices attached to the bus it controls and for managing the power setting of the bus. These are typically provided by Microsoft out of the box.

- **Function drivers**   These manage a particular type of device. Bus drivers present devices to function drivers via the PnP manager. The function driver is the driver that exports the operational interface of the device to the operating system. In general, it's the driver with the most knowledge about the operation of the device.

- **Filter drivers**   These logically layer either above function drivers (these are called *upper filters* or *function filters*) or above the bus driver (these are called *lower filters* or *bus filters*), augmenting or changing the behavior of a device or another driver. For example, a keyboard-capture utility could be implemented with a keyboard filter driver that layers above the keyboard function driver.

Figure 6-6 shows a device node (also called a *devnode*) with a bus driver that creates a physical device object (PDO), lower filters, a function driver that creates a functional device object (FDO), and upper filters. The only required layers are the PDO and FDO. The various filters may or may not exist.

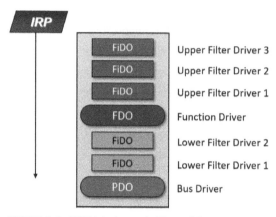

FIGURE 6-6 WDM device node (devnode).

In WDM, no one driver is responsible for controlling all aspects of a particular device. The bus driver is responsible for detecting bus membership changes (device addition or removal), assisting the PnP manager in enumerating the devices on the bus, accessing bus-specific configuration registers, and, in some cases, controlling power to devices on the bus. The function driver is generally the only driver that accesses the device's hardware. The exact manner in which these devices came to be is described in "The Plug and Play manager" section later in this chapter.

Layered drivers

Support for an individual piece of hardware is often divided among several drivers, each providing a part of the functionality required to make the device work properly. In addition to WDM bus drivers, function drivers, and filter drivers, hardware support might be split between the following components:

- **Class drivers**   These implement the I/O processing for a particular class of devices, such as disk, keyboard, or CD-ROM, where the hardware interfaces have been standardized so one driver can serve devices from a wide variety of manufacturers.

- **Miniclass drivers**   These implement I/O processing that is vendor-defined for a particular class of devices. For example, although Microsoft has written a standardized battery class driver, both uninterruptible power supplies (UPS) and laptop batteries have highly specific interfaces that differ wildly between manufacturers, such that a miniclass is required from the vendor. *Miniclass drivers* are essentially kernel-mode DLLs and do not perform IRP processing directly. Instead, the class driver calls into them and they import functions from the class driver.

- **Port drivers**   These implement the processing of an I/O request specific to a type of I/O port, such as SATA, and are implemented as kernel-mode libraries of functions rather than actual device drivers. Port drivers are almost always written by Microsoft because the interfaces are typically standardized in such a way that different vendors can still share the same port driver.

However, in certain cases, third parties may need to write their own for specialized hardware. In some cases, the concept of I/O port extends to cover logical ports as well. For example, Network Driver Interface Specification (NDIS) is the network "port" driver.

- **Miniport drivers** These map a generic I/O request to a type of port into an adapter type, such as a specific network adapter. Miniport drivers are actual device drivers that import the functions supplied by a port driver. Miniport drivers are written by third parties, and they provide the interface for the port driver. Like miniclass drivers, they are kernel-mode DLLs and do not perform IRP processing directly.

Figure 6-7 shows a simplified example for illustrative purposes that will help demonstrate how device drivers and layering work at a high level. As you can see, a file-system driver accepts a request to write data to a certain location within a particular file. It translates the request into a request to write a certain number of bytes to the disk at a particular (that is, the logical) location. It then passes this request (via the I/O manager) to a simple disk driver. The disk driver, in turn, translates the request into a physical location on the disk and communicates with the disk to write the data.

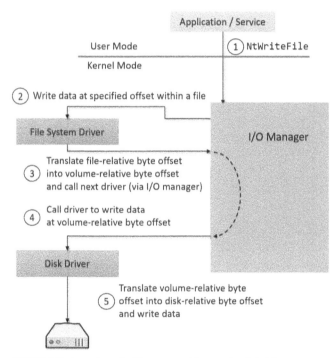

FIGURE 6-7   Layering of a file-system driver and a disk driver.

This figure illustrates the division of labor between two layered drivers. The I/O manager receives a write request that is relative to the beginning of a particular file. The I/O manager passes the request to the file-system driver, which translates the write operation from a file-relative operation to a starting location (a sector boundary on the disk) and a number of bytes to write. The file-system driver calls the I/O manager to pass the request to the disk driver, which translates the request to a physical disk location and transfers the data.

Because all drivers—both device drivers and file-system drivers—present the same framework to the operating system, another driver can easily be inserted into the hierarchy without altering the existing drivers or the I/O system. For example, several disks can be made to seem like a very large single disk by adding a driver. This logical volume manager driver is located between the file system and the disk drivers, as shown in the conceptual simplified architectural diagram presented in Figure 6-8. (For the actual storage driver stack diagram as well as volume manager drivers, see Chapter 12, "Storage management" in Part 2.)

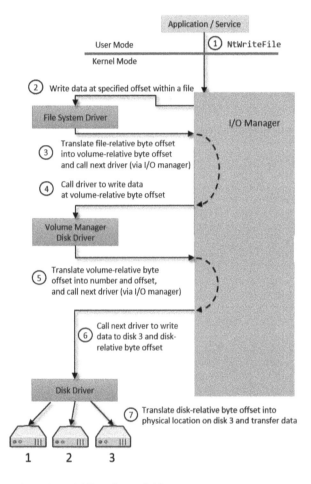

FIGURE 6-8 Adding a layered driver.

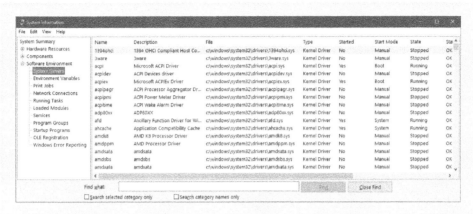

The list of drivers comes from the registry subkeys under HKLM\System\CurrentControlSet\Services. This key is shared between drivers and services. Both can be started by the Service Control Manager (SCM). The way to distinguish between a driver and a service for each subkey is by looking at the Type value. A small value (1, 2, 4, 8) indicates a driver, while 16 (0x10) and 32 (0x20) indicate a Windows service. For more information on the Services subkey, consult Chapter 9 in Part 2.

You can also view the list of loaded kernel-mode drivers with Process Explorer. Run Process Explorer, select the **System** process, and select **DLLs** from the **Lower Pane View** menu entry in the **View** menu:

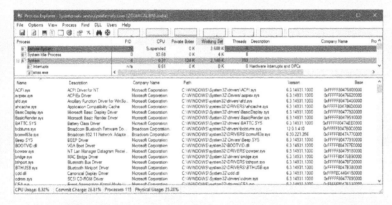

Process Explorer lists the loaded drivers, their names, version information (including company and description), and load address (assuming you have configured Process Explorer to display the corresponding columns).

Finally, if you're looking at a crash dump (or live system) with the kernel debugger, you can get a similar display with the kernel debugger lm kv command:

```
kd> lm kv
start    end        module name
80626000 80631000   kdcom      (deferred)
     Image path: kdcom.dll
```

```
                Image name: kdcom.dll
                Browse all global symbols  functions  data
                Timestamp:          Sat Jul 16 04:27:27 2016 (57898D7F)
                CheckSum:           0000821A
                ImageSize:          0000B000
                Translations:       0000.04b0 0000.04e4 0409.04b0 0409.04e4
    81009000 81632000    nt          (pdb symbols)              e:\symbols\ntkrpamp.
    pdb\A54DF85668E54895982F873F58C984591\ntkrpamp.pdb
                Loaded symbol image file: ntkrpamp.exe
                Image path: ntkrpamp.exe
                Image name: ntkrpamp.exe
                Browse all global symbols  functions  data
                Timestamp:          Wed Sep 07 07:35:39 2016 (57CF991B)
                CheckSum:           005C6B08
                ImageSize:          00629000
                Translations:       0000.04b0 0000.04e4 0409.04b0 0409.04e4
    81632000 81693000    hal         (deferred)
                Image path: halmacpi.dll
                Image name: halmacpi.dll
                Browse all global symbols  functions  data
                Timestamp:          Sat Jul 16 04:27:33 2016 (57898D85)
                CheckSum:           00061469
                ImageSize:          00061000
                Translations:       0000.04b0 0000.04e4 0409.04b0 0409.04e4
    8a800000 8a84b000    FLTMGR      (deferred)
                Image path: \SystemRoot\System32\drivers\FLTMGR.SYS
                Image name: FLTMGR.SYS
                Browse all global symbols  functions  data
                Timestamp:          Sat Jul 16 04:27:37 2016 (57898D89)
                CheckSum:           00053B90
                ImageSize:          0004B000
                Translations:       0000.04b0 0000.04e4 0409.04b0 0409.04e4
        ...
```

Structure of a driver

The I/O system drives the execution of device drivers. Device drivers consist of a set of routines that are called to process the various stages of an I/O request. Figure 6-9 illustrates the key driver-function routines, which are described next.

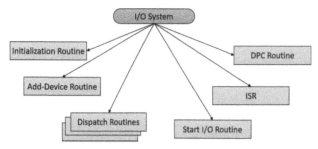

FIGURE 6-9   Primary device driver routines.

- **An initialization routine**   The I/O manager executes a driver's initialization routine, which is set by the WDK to `GSDriverEntry` when it loads the driver into the operating system. `GSDriverEntry` initializes the compiler's protection against stack-overflow errors (called a *cookie*) and then calls `DriverEntry`, which is what the driver writer must implement. The routine fills in system data structures to register the rest of the driver's routines with the I/O manager and performs any necessary global driver initialization.

- **An add-device routine**   A driver that supports Plug and Play implements an add-device routine. The PnP manager sends a notification to the driver via this routine whenever a device for which the driver is responsible is detected. In this routine, a driver typically creates a device object (described later in this chapter) to represent the device.

- **A set of dispatch routines**   Dispatch routines are the main entry points that a device driver provides. Some examples are open, close, read, write, and Plug and Play. When called on to perform an I/O operation, the I/O manager generates an IRP and calls a driver through one of the driver's dispatch routines.

- **A start I/O routine**   A driver can use a start I/O routine to initiate a data transfer to or from a device. This routine is defined only in drivers that rely on the I/O manager to queue their incoming I/O requests. The I/O manager serializes IRPs for a driver by ensuring that the driver processes only one IRP at a time. Drivers can process multiple IRPs concurrently, but serialization is usually required for most devices because they cannot concurrently handle multiple I/O requests.

- **An interrupt service routine (ISR)**   When a device interrupts, the kernel's interrupt dispatcher transfers control to this routine. In the Windows I/O model, ISRs run at device interrupt request level (DIRQL), so they perform as little work as possible to avoid blocking lower IRQL interrupts (as discussed in the previous section). An ISR usually queues a DPC, which runs at a lower IRQL (DPC/dispatch level) to execute the remainder of interrupt processing. Only drivers for interrupt-driven devices have ISRs; a file-system driver, for example, doesn't have one.

- **An interrupt-servicing DPC routine**   A DPC routine performs most of the work involved in handling a device interrupt after the ISR executes. The DPC routine executes at IRQL 2, which is a "compromise" between the high DIRQL and the low passive level (0). A typical DPC routine initiates I/O completion and starts the next queued I/O operation on a device.

Although the following routines aren't shown in Figure 6-9, they're found in many types of device drivers:

- **One or more I/O completion routines**   A layered driver might have I/O completion routines that notify it when a lower-level driver finishes processing an IRP. For example, the I/O manager calls a file-system driver's I/O completion routine after a device driver finishes transferring data to or from a file. The completion routine notifies the file-system driver about the operation's success, failure, or cancellation, and allows the file-system driver to perform cleanup operations.

- **A cancel I/O routine**   If an I/O operation can be canceled, a driver can define one or more cancel I/O routines. When the driver receives an IRP for an I/O request that can be canceled, it assigns a cancel routine to the IRP. As the IRP goes through various stages of processing, this routine can change or outright disappear if the current operation is not cancellable. If a thread that issues an I/O request exits before the request is completed or the operation is cancelled (for example, with the `CancelIo` or `CancelIoEx` Windows functions), the I/O manager executes the IRP's cancel routine if one is assigned to it. A cancel routine is responsible for performing whatever steps are necessary to release any resources acquired during the processing that has already taken place for the IRP as well as for completing the IRP with a canceled status.

- **Fast-dispatch routines**   Drivers that make use of the cache manager, such as file-system drivers, typically provide these routines to allow the kernel to bypass typical I/O processing when accessing the driver. (See Chapter 14, "Cache manager," in Part 2, for more information on the cache manager.) For example, operations such as reading or writing can be quickly performed by accessing the cached data directly instead of taking the I/O manager's usual path that generates discrete I/O operations. Fast dispatch routines are also used as a mechanism for callbacks from the memory manager and cache manager to file-system drivers. For instance, when creating a section, the memory manager calls back into the file-system driver to acquire the file exclusively.

- **An unload routine**   An unload routine releases any system resources a driver is using so that the I/O manager can remove the driver from memory. Any resources acquired in the initialization routine (`DriverEntry`) are usually released in the unload routine. A driver can be loaded and unloaded while the system is running if the driver supports it, but the unload routine will be called only after all file handles to the device are closed.

- **A system shutdown notification routine**   This routine allows driver cleanup on system shutdown.

- **Error-logging routines**   When unexpected errors occur (for example, when a disk block goes bad), a driver's error-logging routines note the occurrence and notify the I/O manager. The I/O manager then writes this information to an error log file.

Driver objects and device objects

When a thread opens a handle to a file object (described in the "I/O processing" section later in this chapter), the I/O manager must determine from the file object's name which driver it should call to process the request. Furthermore, the I/O manager must be able to locate this information the next time a thread uses the same file handle. The following system objects fill this need:

- **A driver object**   This represents an individual driver in the system (`DRIVER_OBJECT` structure). The I/O manager obtains the address of each of the driver's dispatch routines (entry points) from the driver object.

- **A device object**   This represents a physical or logical device on the system and describes its characteristics (`DEVICE_OBJECT` structure), such as the alignment it requires for buffers and the location of its device queue to hold incoming IRPs. It is the target for all I/O operations because this object is what the handle communicates with.

The I/O manager creates a driver object when a driver is loaded into the system. It then calls the driver's initialization routine (`DriverEntry`), which fills in the object attributes with the driver's entry points.

At any time after loading, a driver creates device objects to represent logical or physical devices—or even a logical interface or endpoint to the driver—by calling `IoCreateDevice` or `IoCreateDevice-Secure`. However, most Plug and Play drivers create devices in their add-device routine when the PnP manager informs them of the presence of a device for them to manage. Non–Plug and Play drivers, on the other hand, usually create device objects when the I/O manager invokes their initialization routine. The I/O manager unloads a driver when the driver's last device object has been deleted and no references to the driver remain.

The relationship between a driver object and its device objects is shown in Figure 6-10.

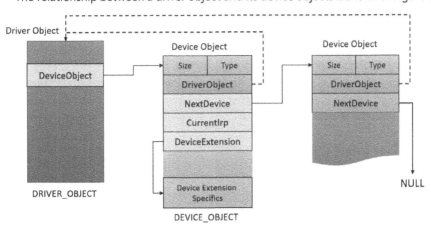

FIGURE 6-10 A driver object and its device objects.

A driver object holds a pointer to its first device object in the `DeviceObject` member. The second device object is pointed to by the `NextDevice` member of `DEVICE_OBJECT` until the last one points to `NULL`. Each device object points back to its driver object with the `DriverObject` member. All the arrows shown in Figure 6-10 are built by the device-creation functions (`IoCreateDevice` or `IoCreateDevice-Secure`). The `DeviceExtension` pointer shown is a way a driver can allocate an extra piece of memory that is attached to each device object it manages.

> **Note** It's important to distinguish driver objects from device objects. A driver object represents the behavior of a driver, while individual device objects represent communication endpoints. For example, on a system with four serial ports, there would be one driver object (and one driver binary) but four instances of device objects, each representing a single serial port, that can be opened individually with no effect on the other serial ports. For hardware devices, each device also represents a distinct set of hardware resources, such as I/O ports, memory-mapped I/O, and interrupt line. Windows is device-centric, rather than driver-centric.

When a driver creates a device object, the driver can optionally assign the device a name. A name places the device object in the object manager namespace. A driver can either explicitly define a name or let the I/O manager auto-generate one. By convention, device objects are placed in the \Device directory in the namespace, which is inaccessible by applications using the Windows API.

> **Note** Some drivers place device objects in directories other than \Device. For example, the IDE driver creates the device objects that represent IDE ports and channels in the \Device\ Ide directory. See Chapter 12 in Part 2 for a description of storage architecture, including the way storage drivers use device objects.

If a driver needs to make it possible for applications to open the device object, it must create a symbolic link in the \GLOBAL?? directory to the device object's name in the \Device directory. (The IoCreateSymbolicLink function accomplishes this.) Non–Plug and Play and file-system drivers typically create a symbolic link with a well-known name (for example, \Device\HarddiskVolume2). Because well-known names don't work well in an environment in which hardware appears and disappears dynamically, PnP drivers expose one or more interfaces by calling the IoRegisterDeviceInterface function, specifying a globally unique identifier (GUID) that represents the type of functionality exposed. GUIDs are 128-bit values that can be generated by using tools such as uuidgen and guidgen, which are included with the WDK and the Windows SDK. Given the range of values that 128 bits represents (and the formula used to generate them), it's statistically almost certain that each GUID generated will be forever and globally unique.

IoRegisterDeviceInterface generates the symbolic link associated with a device instance. However, a driver must call IoSetDeviceInterfaceState to enable the interface to the device before the I/O manager actually creates the link. Drivers usually do this when the PnP manager starts the device by sending the driver a start-device IRP—in this case, IRP_MJ_PNP (major function code) with IRP_MN_START_DEVICE (minor function code). IRPs are discussed in the "I/O request packets" section later in this chapter.

An application that wants to open a device object whose interfaces are represented with a GUID can call Plug and Play setup functions in user space, such as SetupDiEnumDeviceInterfaces, to enumerate the interfaces present for a particular GUID and to obtain the names of the symbolic links it can use to open the device objects. For each device reported by SetupDiEnumDeviceInterfaces, the application executes SetupDiGetDeviceInterfaceDetail to obtain additional information about the device, such as its auto-generated name. After obtaining a device's name from SetupDiGetDeviceInterface-Detail, the application can execute the Windows function CreateFile or CreateFile2 to open the device and obtain a handle.

EXPERIMENT: Looking at device objects

You can use the WinObj tool from Sysinternals or the !object kernel debugger command to view the device names under \Device in the object manager namespace. The following screenshot shows an I/O manager–assigned symbolic link that points to a device object in \Device with an auto-generated name:

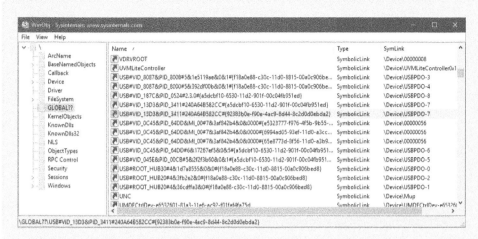

`\GLOBAL??\USB#VID_13D3&PID_3411#240A64B582CC#{92383b0e-f90e-4ac9-8d44-8c2d0d0ebda2}`

When you run the !object kernel debugger command and specify the \Device directory, you should see output similar to the following:

```
1: kd> !object \device
Object: 8200c530  Type: (8542b188) Directory
    ObjectHeader: 8200c518 (new version)
    HandleCount: 0  PointerCount: 231
    Directory Object: 82007d20  Name: Device

    Hash Address  Type            Name
    ---- -------  ----            ----
     00  d024a448 Device          NisDrv
         959afc08 Device          SrvNet
         958beef0 Device          WUDFLpcDevice
         854c69b8 Device          FakeVid1
         8befec98 Device          RdpBus
         88f7c338 Device          Beep
         89d64500 Device          Ndis
         8a24e250 SymbolicLink    ScsiPort2
         89d6c580 Device          KsecDD
         89c15810 Device          00000025
         89c17408 Device          00000019
     01  854c6898 Device          FakeVid2
         88f98a70 Device          Netbios
         8a48c6a8 Device          NameResTrk
         89c2fe88 Device          00000026
     02  854c6778 Device          FakeVid3
         8548fee0 Device          00000034
         8a214b78 SymbolicLink    Ip
         89c31038 Device          00000027
     03  9c205c40 Device          00000041
         854c6658 Device          FakeVid4
         854dd9d8 Device          00000035
         8d143488 Device          Video0
         8a541030 Device          KeyboardClass0
         89c323c8 Device          00000028
```

```
            8554fb50 Device                KMDF0
    04      958bb040 Device                ProcessManagement
            97ad9fe0 SymbolicLink          MailslotRedirector
            854f0090 Device                00000036
            854c6538 Device                FakeVid5
            8bf14e98 Device                Video1
            8bf2fe20 Device                KeyboardClass1
            89c332a0 Device                00000029
            89c05030 Device                VolMgrControl
            89c3a1a8 Device                VMBus
    ...
```

When you enter the !object command and specify an object manager directory object, the kernel debugger dumps the contents of the directory according to the way the object manager organizes it internally. For fast lookups, a directory stores objects in a hash table based on a hash of the object names, so the output shows the objects stored in each bucket of the directory's hash table.

As Figure 6-10 illustrates, a device object points back to its driver object, which is how the I/O manager knows which driver routine to call when it receives an I/O request. It uses the device object to find the driver object representing the driver that services the device. It then indexes into the driver object by using the function code supplied in the original request. Each function code corresponds to a driver entry point (called a *dispatch routine*).

A driver object often has multiple device objects associated with it. When a driver is unloaded from the system, the I/O manager uses the queue of device objects to determine which devices will be affected by the removal of the driver.

EXPERIMENT: Displaying driver and device objects

You can display driver and device objects with the !drvobj and !devobj kernel debugger commands, respectively. In the following example, the driver object for the keyboard class driver is examined, and one of its device objects viewed:

```
1: kd> !drvobj kbdclass
Driver object (8a557520) is for:
 \Driver\kbdclass
Driver Extension List: (id , addr)

Device Object list:
9f509648  8bf2fe20  8a541030
1: kd> !devobj 9f509648
Device object (9f509648) is for:
 KeyboardClass2 \Driver\kbdclass DriverObject 8a557520
Current Irp 00000000 RefCount 0 Type 0000000b Flags 00002044
Dacl 82090960 DevExt 9f509700 DevObjExt 9f5097f0
ExtensionFlags (0x00000c00)  DOE_SESSION_DEVICE, DOE_DEFAULT_SD_PRESENT
```

```
Characteristics (0x00000100)  FILE_DEVICE_SECURE_OPEN
AttachedTo (Lower) 9f509848 \Driver\terminpt
Device queue is not busy.
```

Notice that the !devobj command also shows you the addresses and names of any device objects that the object you're viewing is layered over (the AttachedTo line). It can also show the device objects layered on top of the object specified (the AttachedDevice line), although not in this case.

The !drvobj command can accept an optional argument that indicates more information to show. Here is an example with the most information to show:

```
1: kd> !drvobj kbdclass 7
Driver object (8a557520) is for:
 \Driver\kbdclass
Driver Extension List: (id , addr)

Device Object list:
9f509648  8bf2fe20  8a541030


DriverEntry:    8c30a010     kbdclass!GsDriverEntry
DriverStartIo:  00000000
DriverUnload:   00000000
AddDevice:      8c307250     kbdclass!KeyboardAddDevice


Dispatch routines:
[00] IRP_MJ_CREATE                    8c301d80     kbdclass!KeyboardClassCreate
[01] IRP_MJ_CREATE_NAMED_PIPE         81142342     nt!IopInvalidDeviceRequest
[02] IRP_MJ_CLOSE                     8c301c90     kbdclass!KeyboardClassClose
[03] IRP_MJ_READ                      8c302150     kbdclass!KeyboardClassRead
[04] IRP_MJ_WRITE                     81142342     nt!IopInvalidDeviceRequest
[05] IRP_MJ_QUERY_INFORMATION         81142342     nt!IopInvalidDeviceRequest
[06] IRP_MJ_SET_INFORMATION           81142342     nt!IopInvalidDeviceRequest
[07] IRP_MJ_QUERY_EA                  81142342     nt!IopInvalidDeviceRequest
[08] IRP_MJ_SET_EA                    81142342     nt!IopInvalidDeviceRequest
[09] IRP_MJ_FLUSH_BUFFERS             8c303678     kbdclass!KeyboardClassFlush
[0a] IRP_MJ_QUERY_VOLUME_INFORMATION  81142342     nt!IopInvalidDeviceRequest
[0b] IRP_MJ_SET_VOLUME_INFORMATION    81142342     nt!IopInvalidDeviceRequest
[0c] IRP_MJ_DIRECTORY_CONTROL         81142342     nt!IopInvalidDeviceRequest
[0d] IRP_MJ_FILE_SYSTEM_CONTROL       81142342     nt!IopInvalidDeviceRequest
[0e] IRP_MJ_DEVICE_CONTROL            8c3076d0     kbdclass!KeyboardClassDevice
Control
[0f] IRP_MJ_INTERNAL_DEVICE_CONTROL   8c307ff0     kbdclass!KeyboardClassPass
Through
[10] IRP_MJ_SHUTDOWN                  81142342     nt!IopInvalidDeviceRequest
[11] IRP_MJ_LOCK_CONTROL              81142342     nt!IopInvalidDeviceRequest
[12] IRP_MJ_CLEANUP                   8c302260     kbdclass!KeyboardClassCleanup
[13] IRP_MJ_CREATE_MAILSLOT           81142342     nt!IopInvalidDeviceRequest
[14] IRP_MJ_QUERY_SECURITY            81142342     nt!IopInvalidDeviceRequest
[15] IRP_MJ_SET_SECURITY              81142342     nt!IopInvalidDeviceRequest
[16] IRP_MJ_POWER                     8c301440     kbdclass!KeyboardClassPower
[17] IRP_MJ_SYSTEM_CONTROL            8c307f40     kbdclass!KeyboardClassSystem
Control
```

```
[18] IRP_MJ_DEVICE_CHANGE              81142342        nt!IopInvalidDeviceRequest
[19] IRP_MJ_QUERY_QUOTA                81142342        nt!IopInvalidDeviceRequest
[1a] IRP_MJ_SET_QUOTA                  81142342        nt!IopInvalidDeviceRequest
[1b] IRP_MJ_PNP                        8c301870        kbdclass!KeyboardPnP
```

The dispatch routines array is clearly shown, and will be discussed in the next section. Note that operations that are not supported by the driver point to an I/O manager's routine `IopInvalidDeviceRequest`.

The address to the `!drvobj` command is for a `DRIVER_OBJECT` structure, and the address for the `!devobj` command is for a `DEVICE_OBJECT`. You can view these structures directly using the debugger:

```
1: kd> dt nt!_driver_object 8a557520
   +0x000 Type              : 0n4
   +0x002 Size              : 0n168
   +0x004 DeviceObject      : 0x9f509648 _DEVICE_OBJECT
   +0x008 Flags             : 0x412
   +0x00c DriverStart       : 0x8c300000 Void
   +0x010 DriverSize        : 0xe000
   +0x014 DriverSection     : 0x8a556ba8 Void
   +0x018 DriverExtension   : 0x8a5575c8 _DRIVER_EXTENSION
   +0x01c DriverName        : _UNICODE_STRING "\Driver\kbdclass"
   +0x024 HardwareDatabase  : 0x815c2c28 _UNICODE_STRING "\REGISTRY\MACHINE\HARDWARE\
DESCRIPTION\SYSTEM"
   +0x028 FastIoDispatch    : (null)
   +0x02c DriverInit        : 0x8c30a010     long  +ffffffff8c30a010
   +0x030 DriverStartIo     : (null)
   +0x034 DriverUnload      : (null)
   +0x038 MajorFunction     : [28] 0x8c301d80     long  +ffffffff8c301d80
1: kd> dt nt!_device_object 9f509648
   +0x000 Type              : 0n3
   +0x002 Size              : 0x1a8
   +0x004 ReferenceCount    : 0n0
   +0x008 DriverObject      : 0x8a557520 _DRIVER_OBJECT
   +0x00c NextDevice        : 0x8bf2fe20 _DEVICE_OBJECT
   +0x010 AttachedDevice    : (null)
   +0x014 CurrentIrp        : (null)
   +0x018 Timer             : (null)
   +0x01c Flags             : 0x2044
   +0x020 Characteristics   : 0x100
   +0x024 Vpb               : (null)
   +0x028 DeviceExtension   : 0x9f509700 Void
   +0x02c DeviceType        : 0xb
   +0x030 StackSize         : 7 ''
   +0x034 Queue             : <unnamed-tag>
   +0x05c AlignmentRequirement : 0
   +0x060 DeviceQueue       : _KDEVICE_QUEUE
   +0x074 Dpc               : _KDPC
   +0x094 ActiveThreadCount : 0
   +0x098 SecurityDescriptor : 0x82090930 Void
   ...
```

There are some interesting fields in these structures, which we'll discuss in the next section.

Using objects to record information about drivers means that the I/O manager doesn't need to know details about individual drivers. The I/O manager merely follows a pointer to locate a driver, thereby providing a layer of portability and allowing new drivers to be loaded easily.

Opening devices

A *file object* is a kernel-mode data structure that represents a handle to a device. File objects clearly fit the criteria for objects in Windows: They are system resources that two or more user-mode processes can share; they can have names; they are protected by object-based security; and they support synchronization. Shared resources in the I/O system, like those in other components of the Windows executive, are manipulated as objects. (See Chapter 8 in Part 2 for more on object management.)

File objects provide a memory-based representation of resources that conform to an I/O-centric interface, in which they can be read from or written to. Table 6-1 lists some of the file object's attributes. For specific field declarations and sizes, see the structure definition for FILE_OBJECT in wdm.h.

TABLE 6-1 File object attributes

Attribute	Purpose
File name	This identifies the virtual file that the file object refers to, which was passed in to the CreateFile or CreateFile2 APIs.
Current byte offset	This identifies the current location in the file (valid only for synchronous I/O).
Share modes	These indicate whether other callers can open the file for read, write, or delete operations while the current caller is using it.
Open mode flags	These indicate whether I/O will be synchronous or asynchronous, cached or non-cached, sequential or random, and so on.
Pointer to device object	This indicates the type of device the file resides on.
Pointer to the volume parameter block (VPB)	This indicates the volume, or partition, that the file resides on (in the case of file system files).
Pointer to section object pointers	This indicates a root structure that describes a mapped/cached file. This structure also contains the shared cache map, which identifies which parts of the file are cached (or rather, mapped) by the cache manager and where they reside in the cache.
Pointer to private cache map	This is used to store per-handle caching information such as the read patterns for this handle or the page priority for the process. See Chapter 5, "Memory management," for more information on page priority.
List of I/O request packets (IRPs)	If thread-agnostic I/O (described in the section "Thread-agnostic I/O" later in this chapter) is used and the file object is associated with a completion port (described in the section "I/O completion ports"), this is a list of all the I/O operations that are associated with this file object.
I/O completion context	This is context information for the current I/O completion port, if one is active.
File object extension	This stores the I/O priority (explained later in this chapter) for the file and whether share-access checks should be performed on the file object, and contains optional file object extensions that store context-specific information.

To maintain some level of opacity toward driver code that uses the file object, and to enable extending the file object functionality without enlarging the structure, the file object also contains an extension field, which allows for up to six different kinds of additional attributes, described in Table 6-2.

TABLE 6-2 File object extensions

Extension	Purpose
Transaction parameters	This contains the transaction parameter block, which contains information about a transacted file operation. It's returned by `IoGetTransactionParameterBlock`.
Device object hint	This identifies the device object of the filter driver with which this file should be associated. It's set with `IoCreateFileEx` or `IoCreateFileSpecifyDeviceObjectHint`.
I/O status block range	This allows applications to lock a user-mode buffer into kernel-mode memory to optimize asynchronous I/Os. It's set with `SetFileIoOverlappedRange`.
Generic	This contains filter driver–specific information, as well as extended create parameters (ECPs) that were added by the caller. It's set with `IoCreateFileEx`.
Scheduled file I/O	This stores a file's bandwidth reservation information, which is used by the storage system to optimize and guarantee throughput for multimedia applications. (See the section "Bandwidth reservation (scheduled file I/O)" later in this chapter.) It's set with `SetFileBandwidthReservation`.
Symbolic link	This is added to the file object upon creation, when a mount point or directory junction is traversed (or a filter explicitly reparses the path). It stores the caller-supplied path, including information about any intermediate junctions, so that if a relative symbolic link is hit, it can walk back through the junctions. See Chapter 13 in Part 2 for more information on NTFS symbolic links, mount points, and directory junctions.

When a caller opens a file or a simple device, the I/O manager returns a handle to a file object. Before that happens, the driver responsible for the device in question is asked via its Create dispatch routine (`IRP_MJ_CREATE`) whether it's OK to open the device and allow the driver to perform any initialization necessary if the open request is to succeed.

> **Note** File objects represent open instances of files, not files themselves. Unlike UNIX systems, which use *vnodes*, Windows does not define the representation of a file; Windows file-system drivers define their own representations.

Similar to executive objects, files are protected by a security descriptor that contains an access control list (ACL). The I/O manager consults the security subsystem to determine whether a file's ACL allows the process to access the file in the way its thread is requesting. If it does, the object manager grants the access and associates the granted access rights with the file handle that it returns. If this thread or another thread in the process needs to perform additional operations not specified in the original request, the thread must open the same file again with a different request (or duplicate the handle with the requested access) to get another handle, which prompts another security check. (See Chapter 7 for more information about object protection.)

EXPERIMENT: Viewing device handles

Any process that has an open handle to a device will have a file object in its handle table corresponding to the open instance. You can view these handles with Process Explorer by selecting a process and checking **Handles** in the **Lower Pane View** submenu of the **View** menu. Sort by the **Type** column and scroll to where you see the handles that represent file objects, which are labeled as *File*.

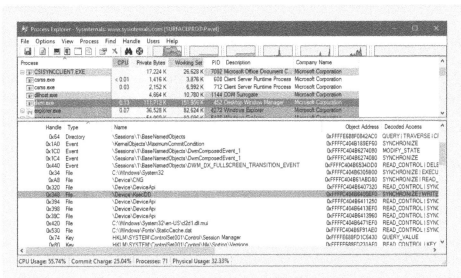

In this example, the Desktop Windows Manager (dwm.exe) process has a handle open to a device created by the kernel security device driver (Ksecdd.sys). You can look at the specific file object in the kernel debugger by first identifying the address of the object. The following command reports information on the highlighted handle (handle value 0xD4) in the preceding screenshot, which is in the Dwm.exe process that has a process ID of 452 decimal:

```
lkd> !handle 348 f 0n452

PROCESS ffffc404b62fb780
    SessionId: 1  Cid: 01c4    Peb: b4c3db0000  ParentCid: 0364
    DirBase: 7e607000  ObjectTable: ffffe688fd1c38c0  HandleCount: <Data Not Accessible>
    Image: dwm.exe

Handle Error reading handle count.

0348: Object: ffffc404b6406ef0  GrantedAccess: 00100003 (Audit) Entry: ffffe688fd396d20
Object: ffffc404b6406ef0  Type: (ffffc404b189bf20) File
    ObjectHeader: ffffc404b6406ec0 (new version)
        HandleCount: 1  PointerCount: 32767
```

Because the object is a file object, you can get information about it with the !fileobj command (notice it's also the same object address shown in Process Explorer):

```
lkd> !fileobj ffffc404b6406ef0

Device Object: 0xffffc404b2fa7230   \Driver\KSecDD
Vpb is NULL
Event signalled

Flags:  0x40002
        Synchronous IO
        Handle Created

CurrentByteOffset: 0
```

Because a file object is a memory-based representation of a shareable resource and not the resource itself, it's different from other executive objects. A file object contains only data that is unique to an object handle, whereas the file itself contains the data or text to be shared. Each time a thread opens a file, a new file object is created with a new set of handle-specific attributes. For example, for files opened synchronously, the current byte offset attribute refers to the location in the file at which the next read or write operation using that handle will occur. Each handle to a file has a private byte offset even though the underlying file is shared. A file object is also unique to a process—except when a process duplicates a file handle to another process (by using the Windows DuplicateHandle function) or when a child process inherits a file handle from a parent process. In these situations, the two processes have separate handles that refer to the same file object.

Although a file handle is unique to a process, the underlying physical resource is not. Therefore, as with any shared resource, threads must synchronize their access to shareable resources such as files, file directories, and devices. If a thread is writing to a file, for example, it should specify exclusive write access when opening the file to prevent other threads from writing to the file at the same time. Alternatively, by using the Windows LockFile function, the thread could lock a portion of the file while writing to it when exclusive access is required.

When a file is opened, the file name includes the name of the device object on which the file resides. For example, the name \Device\HarddiskVolume1\Myfile.dat may refer to the file Myfile.dat on the C: volume. The substring \Device\HarddiskVolume1 is the name of the internal Windows device object representing that volume. When opening Myfile.dat, the I/O manager creates a file object and stores a pointer to the HarddiskVolume1 device object in the file object and then returns a file handle to the caller. Thereafter, when the caller uses the file handle, the I/O manager can find the HarddiskVolume1 device object directly.

Keep in mind that internal Windows device names can't be used in Windows applications—instead, the device name must appear in a special directory in the object manager's namespace, which is \GLOBAL??. This directory contains symbolic links to the real, internal Windows device names. As was described earlier, device drivers are responsible for creating links in this directory so that their devices will be accessible to Windows applications. You can examine or even change these links programmatically with the Windows QueryDosDevice and DefineDosDevice functions.

I/O processing

Now that we've covered the structure and types of drivers and the data structures that support them, let's look at how I/O requests flow through the system. I/O requests pass through several predictable stages of processing. The stages vary depending on whether the request is destined for a device operated by a single-layered driver or for a device reached through a multilayered driver. Processing varies further depending on whether the caller specified synchronous or asynchronous I/O, so we'll begin our discussion of I/O types with these two and then move on to others.

Types of I/O

Applications have several options for the I/O requests they issue. Furthermore, the I/O manager gives drivers the choice of implementing a shortcut I/O interface that can often mitigate IRP allocation for I/O processing. In this section, we'll explain these options for I/O requests.

Synchronous and asynchronous I/O

Most I/O operations issued by applications are *synchronous* (which is the default). That is, the application thread waits while the device performs the data operation and returns a status code when the I/O is complete. The program can then continue and access the transferred data immediately. When used in their simplest form, the Windows `ReadFile` and `WriteFile` functions are executed synchronously. They complete the I/O operation before returning control to the caller.

Asynchronous I/O allows an application to issue multiple I/O requests and continue executing while the device performs the I/O operation. This type of I/O can improve an application's throughput because it allows the application thread to continue with other work while an I/O operation is in progress. To use asynchronous I/O, you must specify the `FILE_FLAG_OVERLAPPED` flag when you call the Windows `CreateFile` or `CreateFile2` functions. Of course, after issuing an asynchronous I/O operation, the thread must be careful not to access any data from the I/O operation until the device driver has finished the data operation. The thread must synchronize its execution with the completion of the I/O request by monitoring a handle of a synchronization object (whether that's an event object, an I/O completion port, or the file object itself) that will be signaled when the I/O is complete.

Regardless of the type of I/O request, I/O operations issued to a driver on behalf of the application are performed asynchronously. That is, once an I/O request has been initiated, the device driver must return to the I/O system as soon as possible. Whether or not the I/O system returns immediately to the caller depends on whether the handle was opened for synchronous or asynchronous I/O. Figure 6-3 illustrates the flow of control when a read operation is initiated. Notice that if a wait is done, which depends on the overlapped flag in the file object, it is done in kernel mode by the `NtReadFile` function.

You can test the status of a pending asynchronous I/O operation with the Windows `HasOverlapped-IoCompleted` macro or get more details with the `GetOverlappedResult(Ex)` functions. If you're using I/O completion ports (described in the "I/O completion ports" section later in this chapter), you can use the `GetQueuedCompletionStatus(Ex)` function(s).

Fast I/O

Fast I/O is a special mechanism that allows the I/O system to bypass the generation of an IRP and instead go directly to the driver stack to complete an I/O request. This mechanism is used for optimizing certain I/O paths, which are somewhat slower when using IRPs. (Fast I/O is described in detail in Chapter 13 and Chapter 14 in Part 2.) A driver registers its fast I/O entry points by entering them in a structure pointed to by the `PFAST_IO_DISPATCH` pointer in its driver object.

EXPERIMENT: Looking at a driver's registered fast I/O routines

The !drvobj kernel debugger command can list the fast I/O routines that a driver registers in its driver object. Typically, however, only file-system drivers have any use for fast I/O routines—although there are exceptions, such as network protocol drivers and bus filter drivers. The following output shows the fast I/O table for the NTFS file-system driver object:

```
lkd> !drvobj \filesystem\ntfs 2
Driver object (ffffc404b2fbf810) is for:
 \FileSystem\NTFS
DriverEntry:    fffff80e5663a030                          NTFS!GsDriverEntry
DriverStartIo: 00000000
DriverUnload:  00000000
AddDevice:     00000000

Dispatch routines:
...
Fast I/O routines:
FastIoCheckIfPossible          fffff80e565d6750
NTFS!NtfsFastIoCheckIfPossible
FastIoRead                     fffff80e56526430          NTFS!NtfsCopyReadA
FastIoWrite                    fffff80e56523310          NTFS!NtfsCopyWriteA
FastIoQueryBasicInfo           fffff80e56523140
NTFS!NtfsFastQueryBasicInfo
FastIoQueryStandardInfo        fffff80e56534d20          NTFS!NtfsFastQueryStdInfo
FastIoLock                     fffff80e5651e610          NTFS!NtfsFastLock
FastIoUnlockSingle             fffff80e5651e3c0          NTFS!NtfsFastUnlockSingle
FastIoUnlockAll                fffff80e565d59e0          NTFS!NtfsFastUnlockAll
FastIoUnlockAllByKey           fffff80e565d5c50
NTFS!NtfsFastUnlockAllByKey
ReleaseFileForNtCreateSection  fffff80e5644fd90          NTFS!NtfsReleaseForCreate
Section
FastIoQueryNetworkOpenInfo     fffff80e56537750          NTFS!NtfsFastQueryNetwork
OpenInfo
AcquireForModWrite             fffff80e5643e0c0
NTFS!NtfsAcquireFileForModWrite
MdlRead                        fffff80e5651e950          NTFS!NtfsMdlReadA
MdlReadComplete                fffff802dc6cd844
nt!FsRtlMdlReadCompleteDev
PrepareMdlWrite                fffff80e56541a10          NTFS!NtfsPrepareMdlWriteA
MdlWriteComplete               fffff802dcb76e48
nt!FsRtlMdlWriteCompleteDev
FastIoQueryOpen                fffff80e5653a520
NTFS!NtfsNetworkOpenCreate
ReleaseForModWrite             fffff80e5643e2c0
NTFS!NtfsReleaseFileForModWrite
AcquireForCcFlush              fffff80e5644ca60
NTFS!NtfsAcquireFileForCcFlush
ReleaseForCcFlush              fffff80e56450cf0
NTFS!NtfsReleaseFileForCcFlush
```

The output shows that NTFS has registered its `NtfsCopyReadA` routine as the fast I/O table's `FastIoRead` entry. As the name of this fast I/O entry implies, the I/O manager calls this function when issuing a read I/O request if the file is cached. If the call doesn't succeed, the standard IRP path is selected.

Mapped-file I/O and file caching

Mapped-file I/O is an important feature of the I/O system—one that the I/O system and the memory manager produce jointly. (See Chapter 5 for details on how mapped files are implemented.) *Mapped-file I/O* refers to the ability to view a file residing on disk as part of a process's virtual memory. A program can access the file as a large array without buffering data or performing disk I/O. The program accesses memory, and the memory manager uses its paging mechanism to load the correct page from the disk file. If the application writes to its virtual address space, the memory manager writes the changes back to the file as part of normal paging.

Mapped-file I/O is available in user mode through the Windows `CreateFileMapping`, `MapViewOf-File`, and related functions. Within the operating system, mapped-file I/O is used for important operations such as file caching and image activation (loading and running executable programs). The other major consumer of mapped-file I/O is the cache manager. File systems use the cache manager to map file data in virtual memory to provide better response time for I/O-bound programs. As the caller uses the file, the memory manager brings accessed pages into memory. Whereas most caching systems allocate a fixed number of bytes for caching files in memory, the Windows cache grows or shrinks depending on how much memory is available. This size variability is possible because the cache manager relies on the memory manager to automatically expand (or shrink) the size of the cache using the normal working set mechanisms explained in Chapter 5—in this case applied to the system working set. By taking advantage of the memory manager's paging system, the cache manager avoids duplicating the work that the memory manager already performs. (The workings of the cache manager are explained in detail in Chapter 14 in Part 2.)

Scatter/gather I/O

Windows supports a special kind of high-performance I/O called *scatter/gather*, available via the Windows `ReadFileScatter` and `WriteFileGather` functions. These functions allow an application to issue a single read or write from more than one buffer in virtual memory to a contiguous area of a file on disk instead of issuing a separate I/O request for each buffer. To use scatter/gather I/O, the file must be opened for non-cached I/O, the user buffers being used must be page-aligned, and the I/Os must be asynchronous (overlapped). Furthermore, if the I/O is directed at a mass storage device, the I/O must be aligned on a device sector boundary and have a length that is a multiple of the sector size.

I/O request packets

An *I/O request packet* (*IRP*) is where the I/O system stores information it needs to process an I/O request. When a thread calls an I/O API, the I/O manager constructs an IRP to represent the operation as it progresses through the I/O system. If possible, the I/O manager allocates IRPs from one of three per-processor IRP non-paged look-aside lists:

- **The small-IRP look-aside list** This stores IRPs with one stack location. (IRP stack locations are described shortly.)

- **The medium-IRP look-aside list** This contains IRPs with four stack locations (which can also be used for IRPs that require only two or three stack locations).

- **The large-IRP look-aside list** This contains IRPs with more than four stack locations. By default, the system stores IRPs with 14 stack locations on the large-IRP look-aside list, but once per minute, the system adjusts the number of stack locations allocated and can increase it up to a maximum of 20, based on how many stack locations have been recently required.

These lists are also backed by global look-aside lists as well, allowing efficient cross-CPU IRP flow. If an IRP requires more stack locations than are contained in the IRPs on the large-IRP look-aside list, the I/O manager allocates IRPs from non-paged pool. The I/O manager allocates IRPs with the `IoAllocate-Irp` function, which is also available for device-driver developers, because in some cases a driver may want to initiate an I/O request directly by creating and initializing its own IRPs. After allocating and initializing an IRP, the I/O manager stores a pointer to the caller's file object in the IRP.

> **Note** If defined, the DWORD registry value `LargeIrpStackLocations` in the HKLM\
> System\CurrentControlSet\Session Manager\I/O System key specifies how many stack
> locations are contained in IRPs stored on the large-IRP look-aside list. Similarly, the
> `MediumIrpStackLocations` value in the same key can be used to change the size of IRP stack
> locations on the medium-IRP look-aside list.

Figure 6-11 shows some of the important members of the IRP structure. It is always accompanied by one or more `IO_STACK_LOCATION` objects (described in the next section).

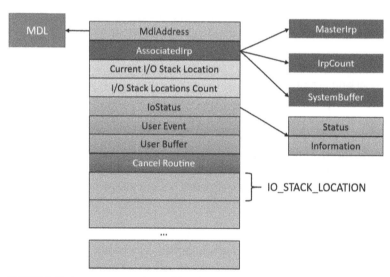

FIGURE 6-11 Important members of the IRP structure.

Here is a quick rundown of the members:

- **IoStatus**   This is the status of the IRP, consisting of two members; Status, which is the actual code itself and Information, a polymorphic value that has meaning in some cases. For example, for a read or write operation, this value (set by the driver) indicates the number of bytes read or written. This same value is the one reported as an output value from the functions ReadFile and WriteFile.

- **MdlAddress**   This is an optional pointer to a memory descriptor list (MDL). An MDL is a structure that represents information for a buffer in physical memory. We'll discuss its main usage in device drivers in the next section. If an MDL was not requested, the value is NULL.

- **I/O stack locations count and current stack location**   These store the total number of trailing I/O stack location objects and point to the current one that this driver layer should look at, respectively. The next section discusses I/O stack locations in detail.

- **User buffer**   This is the pointer to the buffer provided by the client that initiated the I/O operation. For example, it is the buffer provided to the ReadFile or WriteFile functions.

- **User event**   This is the kernel event object that was used with an overlapped (asynchronous) I/O operation (if any). An event is one way to be notified when the I/O operation completes.

- **Cancel routine**   This is the function to be called by the I/O manager in case the IRP is cancelled.

- **AssociatedIrp**   This is a union of one of three fields. The SystemBuffer member is used in case the I/O manager used the buffered I/O technique for passing the user's buffer to the driver. The next section discusses buffered I/O, as well as other options for passing user mode buffers to drivers. The MasterIrp member provides a way to create a "master IRP" that splits its work into sub-IRPs, where the master is considered complete only when all its sub-IRPs have completed.

I/O stack locations

An IRP is always followed by one or more I/O stack locations. The number of stack locations is equal to the number of layered devices in the device node the IRP is destined for. The I/O operation information is split between the IRP body (the main structure) and the current I/O stack location, where *current* means the one set up for the particular layer of devices. Figure 6-12 shows the important fields of an I/O stack location. When an IRP is created, the number of requested I/O stack locations is passed to IoAllocateIrp. The I/O manager then initializes the IRP body and the first I/O stack location only, destined for the topmost device in the device node. Each layer in the device node is responsible for initializing the next I/O stack location if it decides to pass the IRP down to the next device.

Here is a rundown of the members shown in Figure 6-12:

- **Major function**   This is the primary code that indicates the type of request (read, write, create, Plug and Play, and so on), also known as dispatch routine code. It's one of 28 constants (0 to 27) starting with IRP_MJ_ in wdm.h. This index is used by the I/O manager into the MajorFunction array of function pointers in the driver object to jump to the appropriate routine within a driver.

Most drivers specify dispatch routines to handle only a subset of possible major function codes, including create (open), read, write, device I/O control, power, Plug and Play, system control (for WMI commands), cleanup, and close. File-system drivers are an example of a driver type that often fills in most or all of its dispatch entry points with functions. In contrast, a driver for a simple USB device would probably fill in only the routines needed for open, close, read, write, and sending I/O control codes. The I/O manager sets any dispatch entry points that a driver doesn't fill to point to its own `IopInvalidDeviceRequest`, which completes the IRP with an error status indicating that the major function specified in the IRP is invalid for that device.

- **Minor function** This is used to augment the major function code for some functions. For example, `IRP_MJ_READ` (read) and `IRP_MJ_WRITE` (write) have no minor functions. But Plug and Play and Power IRPs always have a minor IRP code that specializes the general major code. For example, the Plug and Play `IRP_MJ_PNP` major code is too generic; the exact instruction is given by the minor IRP, such as `IRP_MN_START_DEVICE`, `IRP_MN_REMOVE_DEVICE`, and so on.

- **Parameters** This is a monstrous union of structures, each of which valid for a particular major function code or a combination of major/minor codes. For example, for a read operation (`IRP_MJ_READ`), the `Parameters.Read` structure holds information on the read request, such as the buffer size.

- **File object and Device object** These point to the associated `FILE_OBJECT` and `DEVICE_OBJECT` for this I/O request.

- **Completion routine** This is an optional function that a driver can register with the `IoSetCompletionRoutine(Ex)` DDI, to be called when the IRP is completed by a lower layer driver. At that point, the driver can look at the completion status of the IRP and do any needed post-processing. It can even undo the completion (by returning the special value `STATUS_MORE_PROCESSING_REQUIRED` from the function) and resend the IRP (perhaps with modified parameters) to the device node—or even a different device node—again.

- **Context** This is an arbitrary value set with the `IoSetCompletionRoutine(Ex)` call that is passed, as is, to the completion routine.

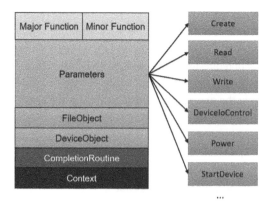

FIGURE 6-12 Important members of the `IO_STACK_LOCATION` structure.

The split of information between the IRP body and its I/O stack location allows for the changing of I/O stack location parameters for the next device in the device stack, while keeping the original request parameters. For example, a read IRP targeted at a USB device is often changed by the function driver to a device I/O control IRP where the input buffer argument of the device control points to a USB request packet (URB) that is understood by the lower-layer USB bus driver. Also, note that completion routines can be registered by any layer (except the bottom-most one), each having its own place in an I/O stack location (the completion routine is stored in the *next* lower I/O stack location).

EXPERIMENT: Looking at driver dispatch routines

You can obtain a list of the functions a driver has defined for its dispatch routines by using bit 1 (value of 2) with the `!drvobj` kernel debugger command. The following output shows the major function codes supported by the NTFS driver. (This is the same experiment as with fast I/O.)

```
1kd> !drvobj \filesystem\ntfs 2
Driver object (ffffc404b2fbf810) is for:
 \FileSystem\NTFS
DriverEntry:   fffff80e5663a030                        NTFS!GsDriverEntry
DriverStartIo: 00000000
DriverUnload:  00000000
AddDevice:     00000000

Dispatch routines:
[00] IRP_MJ_CREATE                    fffff80e565278e0    NTFS!NtfsFsdCreate
[01] IRP_MJ_CREATE_NAMED_PIPE         fffff802dc762c80    nt!IopInvalidDeviceRequest
[02] IRP_MJ_CLOSE                     fffff80e565258c0    NTFS!NtfsFsdClose
[03] IRP_MJ_READ                      fffff80e56436060    NTFS!NtfsFsdRead
[04] IRP_MJ_WRITE                     fffff80e564461d0    NTFS!NtfsFsdWrite
[05] IRP_MJ_QUERY_INFORMATION         fffff80e565275f0    NTFS!NtfsFsdDispatchWait
[06] IRP_MJ_SET_INFORMATION           fffff80e564edb80    NTFS!NtfsFsdSetInformation
[07] IRP_MJ_QUERY_EA                  fffff80e565275f0    NTFS!NtfsFsdDispatchWait
[08] IRP_MJ_SET_EA                    fffff80e565275f0    NTFS!NtfsFsdDispatchWait
[09] IRP_MJ_FLUSH_BUFFERS             fffff80e5653c9a0    NTFS!NtfsFsdFlushBuffers
[0a] IRP_MJ_QUERY_VOLUME_INFORMATION  fffff80e56538d10    NTFS!NtfsFsdDispatch
[0b] IRP_MJ_SET_VOLUME_INFORMATION    fffff80e56538d10    NTFS!NtfsFsdDispatch
[0c] IRP_MJ_DIRECTORY_CONTROL         fffff80e564d7080
NTFS!NtfsFsdDirectoryControl
[0d] IRP_MJ_FILE_SYSTEM_CONTROL       fffff80e56524b20
NTFS!NtfsFsdFileSystemControl
[0e] IRP_MJ_DEVICE_CONTROL            fffff80e564f9de0    NTFS!NtfsFsdDeviceControl
[0f] IRP_MJ_INTERNAL_DEVICE_CONTROL   fffff802dc762c80    nt!IopInvalidDeviceRequest
[10] IRP_MJ_SHUTDOWN                  fffff80e565efb50    NTFS!NtfsFsdShutdown
[11] IRP_MJ_LOCK_CONTROL              fffff80e5646c870    NTFS!NtfsFsdLockControl
[12] IRP_MJ_CLEANUP                   fffff80e56525580    NTFS!NtfsFsdCleanup
[13] IRP_MJ_CREATE_MAILSLOT           fffff802dc762c80    nt!IopInvalidDeviceRequest
[14] IRP_MJ_QUERY_SECURITY            fffff80e56538d10    NTFS!NtfsFsdDispatch
[15] IRP_MJ_SET_SECURITY              fffff80e56538d10    NTFS!NtfsFsdDispatch
[16] IRP_MJ_POWER                     fffff802dc762c80    nt!IopInvalidDeviceRequest
[17] IRP_MJ_SYSTEM_CONTROL            fffff802dc762c80    nt!IopInvalidDeviceRequest
[18] IRP_MJ_DEVICE_CHANGE             fffff802dc762c80    nt!IopInvalidDeviceRequest
```

```
[19] IRP_MJ_QUERY_QUOTA              fffff80e565275f0    NTFS!NtfsFsdDispatchWait
[1a] IRP_MJ_SET_QUOTA                fffff80e565275f0    NTFS!NtfsFsdDispatchWait
[1b] IRP_MJ_PNP                      fffff80e56566230    NTFS!NtfsFsdPnp

Fast I/O routines:
...
```

While active, each IRP is usually queued in an IRP list associated with the thread that requested the I/O. (Otherwise, it is stored in the file object when performing thread-agnostic I/O, which is described in the "Thread agnostic I/O" section, later in this chapter.) This allows the I/O system to find and cancel any outstanding IRPs if a thread terminates with I/O requests that have not been completed. Additionally, paging I/O IRPs are also associated with the faulting thread (although they are not cancellable). This allows Windows to use the thread-agnostic I/O optimization—when an asynchronous procedure call (APC) is not used to complete I/O if the current thread is the initiating thread. This means page faults occur inline instead of requiring APC delivery.

EXPERIMENT: Looking at a thread's outstanding IRPs

The !thread command prints any IRPs associated with the thread. The !process command does this as well, if requested. Run the kernel debugger with local or live debugging and list the threads of an explorer process:

```
lkd> !process 0 7 explorer.exe
PROCESS ffffc404b673c780
    SessionId: 1  Cid: 10b0    Peb: 00cbb000  ParentCid: 1038
    DirBase: 8895f000  ObjectTable: ffffe689011b71c0  HandleCount: <Data Not
Accessible>
    Image: explorer.exe
    VadRoot ffffc404b672b980 Vads 569 Clone 0 Private 7260. Modified 366527. Locked 784.
    DeviceMap ffffe688fd7a5d30
    Token                             ffffe68900024920
    ElapsedTime                       18:48:28.375
    UserTime                          00:00:17.500
    KernelTime                        00:00:13.484
    ...
    MemoryPriority                    BACKGROUND
    BasePriority                      8
    CommitCharge                      10789
    Job                               ffffc404b6075060

        THREAD ffffc404b673a080  Cid 10b0.10b4  Teb: 0000000000cbc000 Win32Thread:
ffffc404b66e7090 WAIT: (WrUserRequest) UserMode Non-Alertable
            ffffc404b6760740  SynchronizationEvent
        Not impersonating
    ...

        THREAD ffffc404b613c7c0  Cid 153c.15a8  Teb: 00000000006a3000 Win32Thread:
ffffc404b6a83910 WAIT: (UserRequest) UserMode Non-Alertable
```

```
            ffffc404b58d0d60  SynchronizationEvent
            ffffc404b566f310  SynchronizationEvent
    IRP List:
        ffffc404b69ad920: (0006,02c8) Flags: 00060800  Mdl: 00000000
...
```

You should see many threads, with most of them having IRPs reported in the IRP List section of the thread information (note that the debugger will show only the first 17 IRPs for a thread that has more than 17 outstanding I/O requests). Choose an IRP and examine it with the !irp command:

```
lkd> !irp ffffc404b69ad920
Irp is active with 2 stacks 1 is current (= 0xffffc404b69ad9f0)
 No Mdl: No System Buffer: Thread ffffc404b613c7c0:  Irp stack trace.
    cmd  flg cl Device   File     Completion-Context
>[IRP_MJ_FILE_SYSTEM_CONTROL(d), N/A(0)]
            5 e1 ffffc404b253cc90 ffffc404b5685620 fffff80e55752ed0-ffffc404b63c0e00
Success Error Cancel pending
                \FileSystem\Npfs       FLTMGR!FltpPassThroughCompletion
                            Args: 00000000 00000000 00110008 00000000
 [IRP_MJ_FILE_SYSTEM_CONTROL(d), N/A(0)]
            5  0 ffffc404b3cdca00 ffffc404b5685620 00000000-00000000
                \FileSystem\FltMgr
                            Args: 00000000 00000000 00110008 00000000
```

The IRP has two stack locations and is targeted at a device owned by the Named Pipe File System (NPFS) driver. (NPFS is described in Chapter 10, "Networking," in Part 2.)

IRP flow

IRPs are typically created by the I/O manager, and then sent to the first device on the target device node. Figure 6-13 shows a typical IRP flow for hardware-based device drivers.

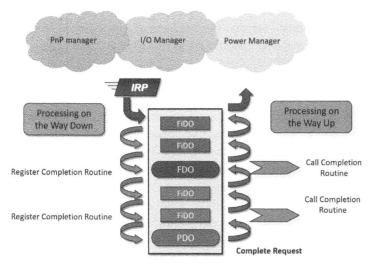

FIGURE 6-13 IRP flow.

The I/O manager is not the only entity that creates IRPs. The Plug and Play manager and the Power manager are also responsible for creating IRPs with major function code IRP_MJ_PNP and IRP_MJ_POWER, respectively.

Figure 6-13 shows an example device node with six layered device objects: two upper filters, the FDO, two lower filters, and the PDO. This means an IRP targeted at this devnode is created with six I/O stack locations—one for each layer. An IRP is always delivered to the highest layered device, even if a handle was opened to a named device that is lower in the device stack.

A driver that receives an IRP can do one of the following:

- It can complete the IRP then and there by calling IoCompleteRequest. This could be because the IRP has some invalid parameters (for example, insufficient buffer size or bad I/O control code), or because the operation requested is quick and can be accomplished immediately, such as getting some status from the device or reading a value from the registry. The driver calls IoGetCurrentIrpStackLocation to get a pointer to the stack location that it should refer to.

- The driver can forward the IRP to the next layer after optionally doing some processing. For example, an upper filter can do some logging of the operation and send the IRP down to be executed normally. Before sending the request down, the driver must prepare the next I/O stack location that would be looked at by the next driver in line. It can use the IoSkipCurrentIrp-StackLocation macro if it does not wish to make changes, or it can make a copy with IoCopy-IrpStackLocationToNext and make changes to the copied stack location by getting a pointer with IoGetNextIrpStackLocation and making appropriate changes. Once the next I/O stack location is prepared, the driver calls IoCallDriver to do the actual IRP forwarding.

- As an extension of the previous point, the driver can also register for a completion routine by calling IoSetCompletionRoutine(Ex) before passing down the IRP. Any layer except the bottom-most one can register a completion routine (there is no point in registering for the bottom-most layer since that driver must complete the IRP, so no callback is needed). After IoCompleteRequest is called by a lower-layer driver, the IRP travels up (refer to Figure 6-13), calling any completion routines on the way up in reverse order of registration. In fact, the IRP originator (I/O manager, PnP manager, or power manager) use this mechanism to do any post-IRP processing and finally free the IRP.

> **Note** Because the number of devices on a given stack is known in advance, the I/O manager allocates one stack location per device driver on the stack. However, there are situations in which an IRP might be directed into a new driver stack. This can happen in scenarios involving the filter manager, which allows one filter to redirect an IRP to another filter (for example, going from a local file system to a network file system). The I/O manager exposes an API, IoAdjustStackSizeForRedirection, that enables this functionality by adding the required stack locations because of devices present on the redirected stack.

EXPERIMENT: Viewing a device stack

The !devstack kernel debugger command shows you the device stack of layered device objects associated with a specified device object. This example shows the device stack associated with a device object, \device\keyboardclass0, which is owned by the keyboard class driver:

```
1kd> !devstack keyboardclass0
  !DevObj           !DrvObj             !DevExt           ObjectName
> ffff9c80c0424440  \Driver\kbdclass    ffff9c80c0424590  KeyboardClass0
  ffff9c80c04247c0  \Driver\kbdhid      ffff9c80c0424910
  ffff9c80c0414060  \Driver\mshidkmdf   ffff9c80c04141b0  0000003f
!DevNode ffff9c80c0414d30 :
  DeviceInst is "HID\MSHW0029&Col01\5&1599b1c7&0&0000"
  ServiceName is "kbdhid"
```

The output highlights the entry associated with KeyboardClass0 with the > character in the first column. The entries above that line are drivers layered above the keyboard class driver, and those below are layered beneath it.

EXPERIMENT: Examining IRPs

In this experiment, you'll find an uncompleted IRP on the system, and will determine the IRP type, the device at which it's directed, the driver that manages the device, the thread that issued the IRP, and what process the thread belongs to. This experiment is best performed on a 32-bit system with non-local kernel debugging. It will work with local kernel debugging as well, but IRPs may complete during the period between when commands are issued, so some instability of data should be expected.

At any point in time, there are at least a few uncompleted IRPs on a system. This occurs because there are many devices to which applications can issue IRPs that a driver will complete only when a particular event occurs, such as data becoming available. One example is a blocking read from a network endpoint. You can see the outstanding IRPs on a system with the !irpfind kernel debugger command (this may take some time; you can stop after some IRPs appear):

```
kd> !irpfind
Scanning large pool allocation table for tag 0x3f707249 (Irp?) (a5000000 : a5200000)

   Irp      [ Thread ] irpStack: (Mj,Mn)   DevObj   [Driver]         MDL Process
9515ad68 [aa0c04c0] irpStack: ( e, 5)   8bcb2ca0 [ \Driver\AFD] 0xaa1a3540
8bd5c548 [91deeb80] irpStack: ( e,20)   8bcb2ca0 [ \Driver\AFD] 0x91da5c40

Searching nonpaged pool (80000000 : ffc00000) for tag 0x3f707249 (Irp?)

86264a20 [86262040] irpStack: ( e, 0)   8a7b4ef0 [ \Driver\vmbus]
86278720 [91d96b80] irpStack: ( e,20)   8bcb2ca0 [ \Driver\AFD] 0x86270040
86279e48 [91d96b80] irpStack: ( e,20)   8bcb2ca0 [ \Driver\AFD] 0x86270040
862a1868 [862978c0] irpStack: ( d, 0)   8bca4030 [ \FileSystem\Npfs]
```

```
862a24c0 [86297040] irpStack: ( d, 0)  8bca4030 [ \FileSystem\Npfs]
862c3218 [9c25f740] irpStack: ( c, 2)  8b127018 [ \FileSystem\NTFS]
862c4988 [a14bf800] irpStack: ( e, 5)  8bcb2ca0 [ \Driver\AFD] 0xaa1a3540
862c57d8 [a8ef84c0] irpStack: ( d, 0)  8b127018 [ \FileSystem\NTFS] 0xa8e6f040
862c91c0 [99ac9040] irpStack: ( 3, 0)  8a7ace48 [ \Driver\vmbus] 0x9517ac40
862d2d98 [9fd456c0] irpStack: ( e, 5)  8bcb2ca0 [ \Driver\AFD] 0x9fc11780
862d6528 [9aded800] irpStack: ( c, 2)  8b127018 [ \FileSystem\NTFS]
862e3230 [00000000] Irp is complete (CurrentLocation 2 > StackCount 1)
862ec248 [862e2040] irpStack: ( d, 0)  8bca4030 [ \FileSystem\Npfs]
862f7d70 [91dd0800] irpStack: ( d, 0)  8bca4030 [ \FileSystem\Npfs]
863011f8 [00000000] Irp is complete (CurrentLocation 2 > StackCount 1)
86327008 [00000000] Irp is complete (CurrentLocation 43 > StackCount 42)
86328008 [00000000] Irp is complete (CurrentLocation 43 > StackCount 42)
86328960 [00000000] Irp is complete (CurrentLocation 43 > StackCount 42)
86329008 [00000000] Irp is complete (CurrentLocation 43 > StackCount 42)
863296d8 [00000000] Irp is complete (CurrentLocation 2 > StackCount 1)
86329960 [00000000] Irp is complete (CurrentLocation 43 > StackCount 42)
89feeae0 [00000000] irpStack: ( e, 0)  8a765030 [ \Driver\ACPI]
8a6d85d8 [99aa1040] irpStack: ( d, 0)  8b127018 [ \FileSystem\NTFS] 0x00000000
8a6dc828 [8bc758c0] irpStack: ( 4, 0)  8b127018 [ \FileSystem\NTFS] 0x00000000
8a6f42d8 [8bc728c0] irpStack: ( 4,34)  8b0b8030 [ \Driver\disk] 0x00000000
8a6f4d28 [8632e6c0] irpStack: ( 4,34)  8b0b8030 [ \Driver\disk] 0x00000000
8a767d98 [00000000] Irp is complete (CurrentLocation 6 > StackCount 5)
8a788d98 [00000000] irpStack: ( f, 0)  00000000 [00000000: Could not read device
object or _DEVICE_OBJECT not found
]
8a7911a8 [9fdb4040] irpStack: ( e, 0)  86325768 [ \Driver\DeviceApi]
8b03c3f8 [00000000] Irp is complete (CurrentLocation 2 > StackCount 1)
8b0b8bc8 [863d6040] irpStack: ( e, 0)  8a78f030 [ \Driver\vmbus]
8b0c48c0 [91da8040] irpStack: ( e, 5)  8bcb2ca0 [ \Driver\AFD] 0xaa1a3540
8b118d98 [00000000] Irp is complete (CurrentLocation 9 > StackCount 8)
8b1263b8 [00000000] Irp is complete (CurrentLocation 8 > StackCount 7)
8b174008 [aa0aab80] irpStack: ( 4, 0)  8b127018 [ \FileSystem\NTFS] 0xa15e1c40
8b194008 [aa0aab80] irpStack: ( 4, 0)  8b127018 [ \FileSystem\NTFS] 0xa15e1c40
8b196370 [8b131880] irpStack: ( e,31)  8bcb2ca0 [ \Driver\AFD]
8b1a8470 [00000000] Irp is complete (CurrentLocation 2 > StackCount 1)
8b1b3510 [9fcd1040] irpStack: ( e, 0)  86325768 [ \Driver\DeviceApi]
8b1b35b0 [a4009b80] irpStack: ( e, 0)  86325768 [ \Driver\DeviceApi]
8b1cd188 [9c3be040] irpStack: ( e, 0)  8bc73648 [ \Driver\Beep]
...
```

Some IRPs are complete, and may be de-allocated very soon, or they have been de-allocated, but because the allocation from lookaside lists, the IRP has not yet been replaced with a new one.

For each IRP, its address is given, followed by the thread that issued the request. Next, the major and minor function codes for the current stack location are shown in parentheses. You can examine any IRP with the !irp command:

```
kd> !irp 8a6f4d28
Irp is active with 15 stacks 6 is current (= 0x8a6f4e4c)
 Mdl=8b14b250: No System Buffer: Thread 8632e6c0:  Irp stack trace.
     cmd  flg cl Device   File      Completion-Context
```

```
[N/A(0), N/A(0)]
        0  0 00000000 00000000 00000000-00000000

                        Args: 00000000 00000000 00000000 00000000
[N/A(0), N/A(0)]
        0  0 00000000 00000000 00000000-00000000

                        Args: 00000000 00000000 00000000 00000000
[N/A(0), N/A(0)]
        0  0 00000000 00000000 00000000-00000000

                        Args: 00000000 00000000 00000000 00000000
[N/A(0), N/A(0)]
        0  0 00000000 00000000 00000000-00000000

                        Args: 00000000 00000000 00000000 00000000
[N/A(0), N/A(0)]
        0  0 00000000 00000000 00000000-00000000

                        Args: 00000000 00000000 00000000 00000000
>[IRP_MJ_WRITE(4), N/A(34)]
        14 e0 8b0b8030 00000000 876c2ef0-00000000 Success Error Cancel
           \Driver\disk           partmgr!PmIoCompletion
                        Args: 0004b000 00000000 4b3a0000 00000002
[IRP_MJ_WRITE(4), N/A(3)]
        14 e0 8b0fc058 00000000 876c36a0-00000000 Success Error Cancel
           \Driver\partmgr        partmgr!PartitionIoCompletion
                        Args: 4b49ace4 00000000 4b3a0000 00000002
[IRP_MJ_WRITE(4), N/A(0)]
        14 e0 8b121498 00000000 87531110-8b121a30 Success Error Cancel
           \Driver\partmgr        volmgr!VmpReadWriteCompletionRoutine
                        Args: 0004b000 00000000 2bea0000 00000002
[IRP_MJ_WRITE(4), N/A(0)]
        4 e0 8b121978 00000000 82d103e0-8b1220d9 Success Error Cancel
           \Driver\volmgr         fvevol!FvePassThroughCompletionRdpLevel2
                        Args: 0004b000 00000000 4b49acdf 00000000
[IRP_MJ_WRITE(4), N/A(0)]
        4 e0 8b122020 00000000 82801a40-00000000 Success Error Cancel
           \Driver\fvevol         rdyboost!SmdReadWriteCompletion
                        Args: 0004b000 00000000 2bea0000 00000002
[IRP_MJ_WRITE(4), N/A(0)]
        4 e1 8b118538 00000000 828637d0-00000000 Success Error Cancel pending
           \Driver\rdyboost       iorate!IoRateReadWriteCompletion
                        Args: 0004b000 3fffffff 2bea0000 00000002
[IRP_MJ_WRITE(4), N/A(0)]
        4 e0 8b11ab80 00000000 82da1610-8b1240d8 Success Error Cancel
           \Driver\iorate         volsnap!VspRefCountCompletionRoutine
                        Args: 0004b000 00000000 2bea0000 00000002
[IRP_MJ_WRITE(4), N/A(0)]
        4 e1 8b124020 00000000 87886ada-89aec208 Success Error Cancel pending
           \Driver\volsnap        NTFS!NtfsMasterIrpSyncCompletionRoutine
                        Args: 0004b000 00000000 2bea0000 00000002
```

```
[IRP_MJ_WRITE(4), N/A(0)]
            4 e0 8b127018 a6de4bb8 871227b2-9ef8eba8 Success Error Cancel
                \FileSystem\NTFS              FLTMGR!FltpPassThroughCompletion
                            Args: 0004b000 00000000 00034000 00000000
[IRP_MJ_WRITE(4), N/A(0)]
            4  1 8b12a3a0 a6de4bb8 00000000-00000000    pending
                \FileSystem\FltMgr
                            Args: 0004b000 00000000 00034000 00000000
```

Irp Extension present at 0x8a6f4fb4:

This is a monstrous IRP with 15 stack locations (6 is current, shown in bold above, and is also specified by the debugger with the > character). The major and minor functions are shown for each stack location along with information on the device object and completion routines addresses.

The next step is to see what device object the IRP is targeting by executing the !devobj command on the device object address in the active stack location:

```
kd> !devobj 8b0b8030
Device object (8b0b8030) is for:
 DR0 \Driver\disk DriverObject 8b0a7e30
Current Irp 00000000 RefCount 1 Type 00000007 Flags 01000050
Vpb 8b0fc420 SecurityDescriptor 87da1b58 DevExt 8b0b80e8 DevObjExt 8b0b8578 Dope
8b0fc3d0
ExtensionFlags (0x00000800)  DOE_DEFAULT_SD_PRESENT
Characteristics (0x00000100)  FILE_DEVICE_SECURE_OPEN
AttachedDevice (Upper) 8b0fc058 \Driver\partmgr
AttachedTo (Lower) 8b0a4d10 \Driver\storflt
Device queue is not busy.
```

Finally, you can see details about the thread and process that issued the IRP by using the !thread command:

```
kd> !thread 8632e6c0
THREAD 8632e6c0 Cid 0004.0058  Teb: 00000000 Win32Thread: 00000000 WAIT:
(Executive) KernelMode Non-Alertable
    89aec20c  NotificationEvent
IRP List:
    8a6f4d28: (0006,02d4) Flags: 00060043  Mdl: 8b14b250
Not impersonating
DeviceMap                 87c025b0
Owning Process            86264280       Image:         System
Attached Process          N/A            Image:         N/A
Wait Start TickCount      8083           Ticks: 1 (0:00:00:00.015)
Context Switch Count      2223           IdealProcessor: 0
UserTime                  00:00:00.000
KernelTime                00:00:00.046
Win32 Start Address nt!ExpWorkerThread (0x81e68710)
Stack Init 89aecca0 Current 89aebeb4 Base 89aed000 Limit 89aea000 Call 00000000
Priority 13 BasePriority 13 PriorityDecrement 0 IoPriority 2 PagePriority 5
```

I/O request to a single-layered hardware-based driver

This section traces I/O requests to a single-layered kernel-mode device driver. Figure 6-14 shows a typical IRP processing scenario for such a driver.

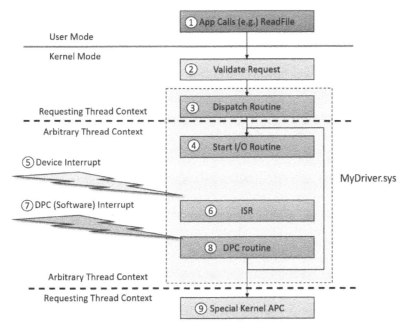

FIGURE 6-14 Typical single layer I/O request processing for hardware drivers.

Before we dig into the various steps outlined in Figure 6-14, some general comments are in order:

- There are two types of horizontal divider lines. The first (solid line) is the usual user-mode/kernel-mode divider. The second (dotted line) separates code that runs in the requesting thread context versus the arbitrary thread context. These contexts are defined as follows:

  - The requesting thread context region indicates that the executing thread is the original one that requested the I/O operation. This is important because if the thread is the one that made the original call, it means the process context is the original process, and so the user-mode address space that contains the user's buffer supplied to the I/O operation is directly accessible.

  - The arbitrary thread context region indicates that the thread running those functions can be any thread. More specifically, it's most likely *not* the requesting thread, and so the user-mode process address space visible is not likely to be the original one. In this context, accessing the user's buffer with a user-mode address can be disastrous. You'll see in the next section how this issue is handled.

 Note The explanations for the steps outlined in Figure 6-14 will prove why the divider lines reside where they are.

- The large rectangle consisting of the four blocks (labeled Dispatch Routine, Start I/O Routine, ISR, and DPC Routine) represents the driver-provided code. All other blocks are provided by the system.

- The figure assumes the hardware device can handle one operation at a time, which is true of many types of devices. Even if the device can handle multiple requests, the basic flow of operations is still the same.

Here is the sequence of events as outlined in Figure 6-14:

1. A client application calls a Windows API such as ReadFile. ReadFile calls the native NtReadFile (in Ntdll.dll), which makes the thread transition to kernel mode to the executive NtReadFile (these steps have already been discussed earlier in this chapter).

2. The I/O manager, in its NtReadFile implementation, performs some sanity checks on the request, such as whether the buffer provided by the client is accessible with the right page protection. Next, the I/O manager locates the associated driver (using the file handle provided), allocates and initializes an IRP, and calls the driver into the appropriate dispatch routine (in this case, corresponding to the IRP_MJ_READ index) using IoCallDriver with the IRP.

3. This is the first time the driver sees the IRP. This call is usually invoked using the requesting thread; the only way for that *not* to happen is if an upper filter held on to the IRP and called IoCallDriver later from a different thread. For the sake of this discussion, we'll assume this is not the case (and in most cases involving hardware devices, this does not happen; even if there are upper filters, they do some processing and call the lower driver immediately from the same thread). The dispatch read callback in the driver has two tasks on its hand: first, it should perform more checking that the I/O manager can't do because it has no idea what the request really means. For example, the driver could check if the buffer provided to a read or write operation is large enough; or for a DeviceIoControl operation, the driver would check whether the I/O control code provided is a supported one. If any such check fails, the driver completes the IRP (IoCompleteRequest) with the failed status and returns immediately. If the checks turn up OK, the driver calls its Start I/O routine to initiate the operation. However, if the hardware device is currently busy (handling a previous IRP), then the IRP should be inserted into a queue managed by the driver and a STATUS_PENDING is returned without completing the IRP. The I/O manager caters for such a scenario with the IoStartPacket function, that checks a busy bit in the device object and, if the device is busy, inserts the IRP into a queue (also part of the device object structure). If the device is not busy, it sets the device bit as busy and calls the registered Start I/O routine (recall that there is such a member in the driver object that would have been initialized in DriverEntry). Even if a driver chooses not to use IoStartPacket, it would still follow similar logic.

4. If the device is not busy, the Start I/O routine is called from the dispatch routine directly—meaning it's still the requesting thread that is making the call. Figure 6-14, however, shows that the Start I/O routine is called in an arbitrary thread context; this will be proven to be true in the general case when we look at the DPC routine in step 8. The purpose of the Start I/O routine is to take the IRP relevant parameters and use them to program the hardware device (for example,

by writing to its ports or registers using HAL hardware access routines such as `WRITE_PORT_UCHAR`, `WRITE_REGISTER_ULONG`, etc.). After the Start I/O completes, the call returns, and no particular code is running in the driver, the hardware is working and "does its thing." While the hardware device is working, more requests can come in to the device by the same thread (if using asynchronous operations) or other threads that also opened handles to the device. In this case the dispatch routine would realize the device is busy and insert the IRP into the IRP queue (as mentioned, one way to achieve this is with a call to `IoStartPacket`).

5. When the device is done with the current operation, it raises an interrupt. The kernel trap handler saves the CPU context for whatever thread was running on the CPU that was selected to handle the interrupt, raises the IRQL of that CPU to the IRQL associated with the interrupt (DIRQL) and jumps to the registered ISR for the device.

6. The ISR, running at Device IRQL (above 2) does as little work as possible, telling the device to stop the interrupt signal and getting the status or other required information from the hardware device. As its last act, the ISR queues a DPC for further processing at a lower IRQL. The advantage of using a DPC to perform most of the device servicing is that any blocked interrupt whose IRQL lies between the Device IRQL and the DPC/dispatch IRQL (2) is allowed to occur before the lower-priority DPC processing occurs. Intermediate-level interrupts are thus serviced more promptly than they otherwise would be, and this reduces latency on the system.

7. After the interrupt is dismissed, the kernel notices that the DPC queue is not empty and so uses a software interrupt at IRQL DPC_LEVEL (2) to jump to the DPC processing loop.

8. Eventually, the DPC is de-queued and executes at IRQL 2, typically performing two main operations:

   - It gets the next IRP in the queue (if any) and starts the new operation for the device. This is done first to prevent the device from being idle for too long. If the dispatch routine used `IoStartPacket`, then the DPC routine would call its counterpart, `IoStartNextPacket`, which does just that. If an IRP is available, the Start I/O routine is called from the DPC. This is why in the general case, the Start I/O routine is called in an arbitrary thread context. If there are no IRPs in the queue, the device is marked not busy—that is, ready for the next request that comes in.

   - It completes the IRP, whose operation has just finished by the driver by calling `IoCompleteRequest`. From that point, the driver is no longer responsible for the IRP and it shouldn't be touched, as it can be freed at any moment after the call. `IoCompleteRequest` calls any completion routines that have been registered. Finally, the I/O manager frees the IRP (it's actually using a completion routine of its own to do that).

9. The original requesting thread needs to be notified of the completion. Because the current thread executing the DPC is arbitrary, it's not the original thread with its original process address space. To execute code in the context of the requesting thread, a special kernel APC is issued to the thread. An APC is a function that is forced to execute in the context of a particular thread. When the requesting thread gets CPU time, the special kernel APC executes first (at IRQL APC_LEVEL=1). It does what's needed, such as releasing the thread from waiting, signaling an event that was registered in an asynchronous operation, and so on. (For more on APCs, see Chapter 8 in Part 2.)

A final note about I/O completion: the asynchronous I/O functions `ReadFileEx` and `WriteFileEx` allow a caller to supply a callback function as a parameter. If the caller does so, the I/O manager queues a user mode APC to the caller's thread APC queue as the last step of I/O completion. This feature allows a caller to specify a subroutine to be called when an I/O request is completed or canceled. User-mode APC completion routines execute in the context of the requesting thread and are delivered only when the thread enters an alertable wait state (by calling functions such as `SleepEx`, `WaitForSingleObjectEx`, or `WaitForMultipleObjectsEx`).

User address space buffer access

As shown in Figure 6-14, there are four main driver functions involved in processing an IRP. Some or all of these routines may need to access the buffer in user space provided by the client application. When an application or a device driver indirectly creates an IRP by using the `NtReadFile`, `NtWriteFile`, or `NtDeviceIoControlFile` system services (or the Windows API functions corresponding to these services, which are `ReadFile`, `WriteFile`, and `DeviceIoControl`), the pointer to the user's buffer is provided in the `UserBuffer` member of the IRP body. However, accessing this buffer directly can be done only in the requesting thread context (the client's process address space is visible) and in IRQL 0 (paging can be handled normally).

As discussed in the previous section, only the dispatch routine meets the criteria of running in the requesting thread context and in IRQL 0. And even this is not always the case—it's possible for an upper filter to hold on to the IRP and not pass it down immediately, possibly passing it down later on using a different thread, and could even be done when the CPU IRQL is 2 or higher.

The other three functions (Start I/O, ISR, DPC) clearly run on an arbitrary thread (could be any thread), and with IRQL 2 (DIRQL for the ISR). Accessing the user's buffer directly from any of these routine is mostly fatal. Here's why:

- Because the IRQL is 2 or higher, paging is not allowed. Since the user's buffer (or part of it) may be paged out, accessing the non-resident memory would crash the system.

- Because the thread executing these functions could be any thread, and thus a random process address space would be visible, the original user's address has no meaning and would likely lead to an access violation, or worse—accessing data from some random process (the parent process of whatever thread was running at the time).

Clearly, there must be a safe way to access the user's buffer in any of these routines. The I/O manager provides two options, for which it does the heavy lifting. These are known as Buffered I/O and Direct I/O. A third option, which is not really an option, is called Neither I/O, in which the I/O manager does nothing special and lets the driver handle the problem on its own.

A driver selects the method in the following way:

- For read and write requests (`IRP_MJ_READ` and `IRP_MJ_WRITE`), it sets the `Flags` member (with an OR boolean operation so as not to disturb other flags) of the device object (`DEVICE_OBJECT`) to `DO_BUFFERED_IO` (for buffered I/O) or `DO_DIRECT_IO` (for direct I/O). If neither flag is set, neither I/O is implied. (`DO` is short for *device object*.)

- For device I/O control requests (IRP_MJ_DEVICE_CONTROL), each control code is constructed using the CTL_CODE macro, where some of the bits indicate the buffering method. This means the buffering method can be set on a control code–by–control code basis, which is very useful.

The following sections describe each buffering method in detail.

Buffered I/O With buffered I/O, the I/O manager allocates a mirror buffer that is the same size as the user's buffer in non-paged pool and stores the pointer to the new buffer in the AssociatedIrp. SystemBuffer member of the IRP body. Figure 6-15 shows the main stages in buffered I/O for a read operation (write is similar).

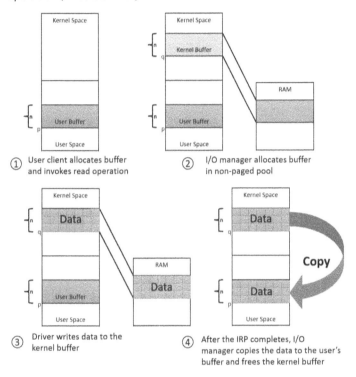

FIGURE 6-15 Buffered I/O.

The driver can access the system buffer (address q in Figure 6-15) from any thread and any IRQL:

- The address is in system space, meaning it's valid in any process context.

- The buffer is allocated from non-paged pool, so a page fault will not happen.

For write operations, the I/O manager copies the caller's buffer data into the allocated buffer when creating the IRP. For read operations, the I/O manager copies data from the allocated buffer to the user's buffer when the IRP completes (using a special kernel APC) and then frees the allocated buffer.

Buffered I/O clearly is very simple to use because the I/O manager does practically everything. Its main downside is that it always requires copying, which is inefficient for large buffers. Buffered I/O is commonly used when the buffer size is no larger than one page (4 KB) and when the device does not support direct memory access (DMA), because DMA is used to transfer data from a device to RAM or vice versa without CPU intervention—but with buffered I/O, there is always copying done with the CPU, which makes DMA pointless.

Direct I/O Direct I/O provides a way for a driver to access the user's buffer directly without any need for copying. Figure 6-16 shows the main stages in direct I/O for a read or write operation.

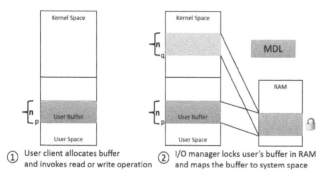

① User client allocates buffer and invokes read or write operation

② I/O manager locks user's buffer in RAM and maps the buffer to system space

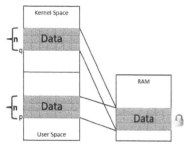

③ Driver reads/writes to the buffer using the system address

FIGURE 6-16 Direct I/O.

When the I/O manager creates the IRP, it locks the user's buffer into memory (that is, makes it non-pageable) by calling the MmProbeAndLockPages function (documented in the WDK). The I/O manager stores a description of the memory in the form of a memory descriptor list (MDL), which is a structure that describes the physical memory occupied by a buffer. Its address is stored in the MdlAddress member of the IRP body. Devices that perform DMA require only physical descriptions of buffers, so an MDL is sufficient for the operation of such devices. If a driver must access the contents of a buffer, however, it can map the buffer into the system's address space using the MmGetSystemAddressForMdlSafe function, passing in the provided MDL. The resulting pointer (*q* in Figure 6-16) is safe to use in any thread context (it's a system address) and in any IRQL (the buffer cannot be paged out). The user's buffer is effectively double-mapped, where the user's direct address (*p* in Figure 6-16) is usable only from the original process context, but the second mapping into system space is usable in any context. Once the IRP is complete, the I/O manager unlocks the buffer (making it pageable again) by calling MmUnlock-Pages (documented in the WDK).

Direct I/O is useful for large buffers (more than one page) because no copying is done, especially for DMA transfers (for the same reason).

Neither I/O With neither I/O, the I/O manager doesn't perform any buffer management. Instead, buffer management is left to the discretion of the device driver, which can choose to manually perform the steps the I/O manager performs with the other buffer-management types. In some cases, accessing the buffer in the dispatch routine is sufficient, so the driver may get away with neither I/O. The main advantage of neither I/O is its zero overhead.

Drivers that use neither I/O to access buffers that might be located in user space must take special care to ensure that buffer addresses are valid and do not reference kernel-mode memory. Scalar values, however, are perfectly safe to pass, although very few drivers have only a scalar value to pass around. Failure to do so could result in crashes or in security vulnerabilities, where applications have access to kernel-mode memory or can inject code into the kernel. The `ProbeForRead` and `ProbeForWrite` functions that the kernel makes available to drivers verify that a buffer resides entirely in the user-mode portion of the address space. To avoid a crash from referencing an invalid user-mode address, drivers can access user-mode buffers protected with structured exception handling (SEH), expressed with `__try/__except` blocks in C/C++, that catch any invalid memory faults and translate them into error codes to return to the application. (See Chapter 8 in Part 2 for more information on SEH.) Additionally, drivers should also capture all input data into a kernel buffer instead of relying on user-mode addresses because the caller could always modify the data behind the driver's back, even if the memory address itself is still valid.

Synchronization

Drivers must synchronize their access to global driver data and hardware registers for two reasons:

- The execution of a driver can be preempted by higher-priority threads and time-slice (or quantum) expiration or can be interrupted by higher IRQL interrupts.

- On multiprocessor systems (the norm), Windows can run driver code simultaneously on more than one processor.

Without synchronization, corruption could occur—for example, device-driver code running at passive IRQL (0) (say, a dispatch routine) when a caller initiates an I/O operation can be interrupted by a device interrupt, causing the device driver's ISR to execute while its own device driver is already running. If the device driver was modifying data that its ISR also modifies—such as device registers, heap storage, or static data—the data can become corrupted when the ISR executes.

To avoid this situation, a device driver written for Windows must synchronize its access to any data that can be accessed at more than one IRQL. Before attempting to update shared data, the device driver must lock out all other threads (or, in the case of a multiprocessor system, CPUs) to prevent them from updating the same data structure.

On a single-CPU system, synchronizing between two or more functions that run at different IRQLs is easy enough. Such function just needs to raise the IRQL (`KeRaiseIrql`) to the highest IRQL these functions execute in. For example, to synchronize between a dispatch routine (IRQL 0) and a DPC routine (IRQL 2), the dispatch routine needs to raise IRQL to 2 before accessing the shared data. If synchronization between a DPC and ISR is required, the DPC would raise IRQL to the Device IRQL (this information is provided to the driver when the PnP manager informs the driver of the hardware resources a device is connected to.) On multiprocessing systems, raising IRQL is not enough because the other routine—for example, ISR—could be serviced on another CPU (remember that IRQL is a CPU attribute, and not a global system attribute).

To allow high IRQL synchronization across CPUs, the kernel provides a specialized synchronization object: the spinlock. Here, we'll take a brief look at spinlocks as they apply to driver synchronization. (A full treatment of spinlocks is reserved for Chapter 8 in Part 2.) In principle, a spinlock resembles a mutex (also discussed in detail in Chapter 8 in Part 2) in the sense that it allows one piece of code to access shared data, but it works and is used quite differently. Table 6-3 summarizes the differences between mutexes and spinlocks.

TABLE 6-3 Mutexes versus spinlocks

	Mutex	Spinlock
Synchronization nature	One thread out of any number of threads that is allowed enters a critical region and accesses shared data.	One CPU out of any number of CPUs that is allowed enters a critical region and accesses shared data.
Usable at IRQL	`< DISPATCH_LEVEL (2)`	`>= DISPATCH_LEVEL (2)`
Wait kind	Normal. That is, it does not waste CPU cycles while waiting.	Busy. That is, the CPU is constantly testing the spinlock bit until it's free.
Ownership	The owner thread is tracked, and recursive acquisition is allowed.	The CPU owner is not tracked, and recursive acquisition will cause a deadlock.

A spinlock is just a bit in memory that is accessed by an atomic test and modify operation. A spinlock may be owned by a CPU or free (unowned). As shown in Table 6-3, spinlocks are necessary when synchronization is needed in high IRQLs (>=2), because a mutex can't be used in these cases as a scheduler is needed, but as we've seen the scheduler cannot wake up on a CPU whose IRQL is 2 or higher. This is why waiting for a spinlock is a busy wait operation: The thread cannot go to a normal wait state because that implies the scheduler waking up and switching to another thread on that CPU.

Acquiring a spinlock by a CPU is always a two-step operation. First, the IRQL is raised to the associated IRQL on which synchronization is to occur—that is, the highest IRQL on which the function that needs to synchronize executes. For example, synchronizing between a dispatch routine (IRQL 0) and a DPC (2) would need to raise IRQL to 2; synchronizing between DPC (2) and ISR (DIRQL) would need to raise IRQL to DIRQL (the IRQL for that particular interrupt). Second, the spinlock is attempted acquisition by atomically testing and setting the spinlock bit.

> **Note** The steps outlined for spinlock acquisition are simplified and omit some details that are not important for this discussion. The complete spinlock story is described in Chapter 8 in Part 2.

The functions that acquire spinlocks determine the IRQL on which to synchronize, as we shall see in a moment.

Figure 6-17 shows a simplified view of the two-step process of acquiring a spinlock.

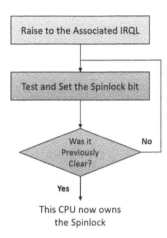

FIGURE 6-17 Spinlock acquisition.

When synchronizing at IRQL 2—for example, between a dispatch routine and a DPC or between a DPC and another DPC (running on another CPU, of course)—the kernel provides the KeAcquireSpin-Lock and KeReleaseSpinLock functions (there are other variations that are discussed in Chapter 8 in Part 2). These functions perform the steps in Figure 6-17 where the "associated IRQL" is 2. The driver in this case must allocate a spinlock (KSPIN_LOCK, which is just 4 bytes on 32-bit systems and 8 bytes on 64-bit systems), typically in the device extension (where driver-managed data for the device is kept) and initialize it with KeInitializeSpinLock.

For synchronizing between any function (such as DPC or a dispatch routine) and the ISR, different functions must be used. Every interrupt object (KINTERRUPT) holds inside it a spinlock, which is acquired before the ISR executes (this implies that the same ISR cannot run concurrently on other CPUs). Synchronization in this case would be with that particular spinlock (no need to allocate another one), which can be acquired indirectly with the KeAcquireInterruptSpinLock function and released with KeReleaseInterruptSpinLock. Another option is to use the KeSynchronizeExecution function, which accepts a callback function the driver provides that is called between the acquisition and release of the interrupt spinlock.

By now, you should realize that although ISRs require special attention, any data that a device driver uses is subject to being accessed by the same device driver (one of its functions) running on another processor. Therefore, it's critical for device-driver code to synchronize its use of any global or shared data or any accesses to the physical device itself.

I/O requests to layered drivers

The "IRP flow" section showed the general options drivers have for dealing with IRPs, with a focus on a standard WDM device node. The preceding section showed how an I/O request to a simple device controlled by a single device driver is handled. I/O processing for file-based devices or for requests to other layered drivers happens in much the same way, but it's worthwhile to take a closer look at a request targeted at file-system drivers. Figure 6-18 shows a very simplified illustrative example of how an asynchronous I/O request might travel through layered drivers for non–hardware based devices as primary targets. It uses as an example a disk controlled by a file system.

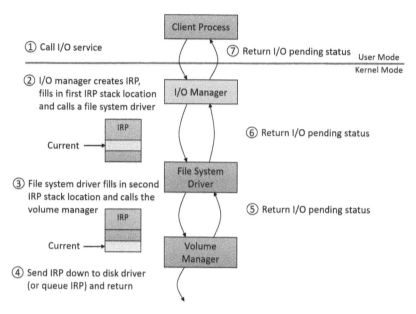

FIGURE 6-18 Queuing an asynchronous request to layered drivers.

Once again, the I/O manager receives the request and creates an IRP to represent it. This time, however, it delivers the packet to a file-system driver. The file-system driver exercises great control over the I/O operation at that point. Depending on the type of request the caller made, the file system can send the same IRP to the disk driver or it can generate additional IRPs and send them separately to the disk driver.

The file system is most likely to reuse an IRP if the request it receives translates into a single straightforward request to a device. For example, if an application issues a read request for the first 512 bytes in a file stored on a volume, the NTFS file system would simply call the volume manager driver, asking it to read one sector from the volume, beginning at the file's starting location.

After the disk controller's DMA adapter finishes a data transfer, the disk controller interrupts the host, causing the ISR for the disk controller to run, which requests a DPC callback completing the IRP, as shown in Figure 6-19.

As an alternative to reusing a single IRP, a file system can establish a group of associated IRPs that work in parallel on a single I/O request. For example, if the data to be read from a file is dispersed across the disk, the file-system driver might create several IRPs, each of which reads some portion of the request from a different sector. This queuing is illustrated in Figure 6-20.

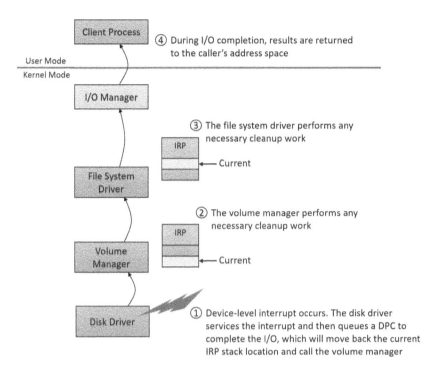

FIGURE 6-19 Completing a layered I/O request.

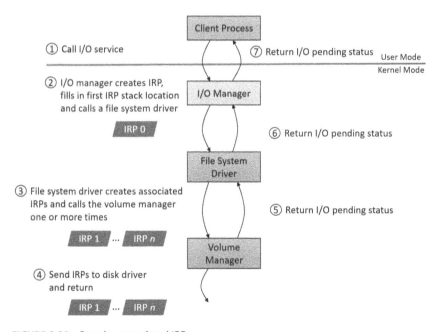

FIGURE 6-20 Queuing associated IRPs.

The file-system driver delivers the associated IRPs to the volume manager, which in turn sends them to the disk-device driver, which queues them to the disk device. They are processed one at a time, and the file-system driver keeps track of the returned data. When all the associated IRPs complete, the I/O system completes the original IRP and returns to the caller, as shown in Figure 6-21.

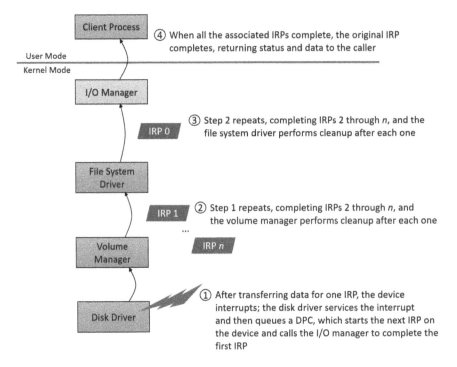

FIGURE 6-21 Completing associated IRPs.

> **Note** All Windows file-system drivers that manage disk-based file systems are part of a stack of drivers that is at least three layers deep. The file-system driver sits at the top, a volume manager in the middle, and a disk driver at the bottom. In addition, any number of filter drivers can be interspersed above and below these drivers. For clarity, the preceding example of layered I/O requests includes only a file-system driver and the volume-manager driver. See Chapter 12 in Part 2 for more information.

Thread-agnostic I/O

In the I/O models described thus far, IRPs are queued to the thread that initiated the I/O and are completed by the I/O manager issuing an APC to that thread so that process-specific and thread-specific context are accessible by completion processing. Thread-specific I/O processing is usually sufficient for the performance and scalability needs of most applications, but Windows also includes support for *thread-agnostic I/O* via two mechanisms:

- I/O completion ports, which are described at length in the section "I/O completion ports" later in this chapter

- Locking the user buffer into memory and mapping it into the system address space

With I/O completion ports, the application decides when it wants to check for the completion of I/O. Therefore, the thread that happens to have issued an I/O request is not necessarily relevant because any other thread can perform the completion request. As such, instead of completing the IRP inside the specific thread's context, it can be completed in the context of any thread that has access to the completion port.

Likewise, with a locked and kernel-mapped version of the user buffer, there's no need to be in the same memory address space as the issuing thread because the kernel can access the memory from arbitrary contexts. Applications can enable this mechanism by using `SetFileIoOverlappedRange` as long as they have the `SeLockMemoryPrivilege`.

With both completion port I/O and I/O on file buffers set by `SetFileIoOverlappedRange`, the I/O manager associates the IRPs with the file object to which they have been issued instead of with the issuing thread. The `!fileobj` extension in WinDbg shows an IRP list for file objects that are used with these mechanisms.

In the next sections, you'll see how thread-agnostic I/O increases the reliability and performance of applications in Windows.

I/O cancellation

While there are many ways in which IRP processing occurs and various methods to complete an I/O request, a great many I/O processing operations actually end in cancellation rather than completion. For example, a device may require removal while IRPs are still active, or the user might cancel a long-running operation to a device—for example, a network operation. Another situation that requires I/O cancellation support is thread and process termination. When a thread exits, the I/Os associated with the thread must be cancelled. This is because the I/O operations are no longer relevant and the thread cannot be deleted until the outstanding I/Os have completed.

The Windows I/O manager, working with drivers, must deal with these requests efficiently and reliably to provide a smooth user experience. Drivers manage this need by registering a cancel routine, by calling `IoSetCancelRoutine`, for their cancellable I/O operations (typically, those operations that are still enqueued and not yet in progress), which is invoked by the I/O manager to cancel an I/O operation. When drivers fail to play their role in these scenarios, users may experience unkillable processes, which have disappeared visually but linger and still appear in Task Manager or Process Explorer.

User-initiated I/O cancellation

Most software uses one thread to handle user interface (UI) input and one or more threads to perform work, including I/O. In some cases, when a user wants to abort an operation that was initiated in the UI, an application might need to cancel outstanding I/O operations. Operations that complete quickly might not require cancellation, but for operations that take arbitrary amounts of time—like large data transfers or network operations—Windows provides support for cancelling both synchronous and asynchronous operations.

- **Cancelling synchronous I/Os**   A thread can call `CancelSynchronousIo`. This enables even create (open) operations to be cancelled when supported by a device driver. Several drivers in Windows support this functionality. These include drivers that manage network file systems (for example, MUP, DFS, and SMB), which can cancel open operations to network paths.

- **Cancelling asynchronous I/Os**   A thread can cancel its own outstanding asynchronous I/Os by calling `CancelIo`. It can cancel all asynchronous I/Os issued to a specific file handle, regardless of which thread initiated them, in the same process with `CancelIoEx`. `CancelIoEx` also works on operations associated with I/O completion ports through the aforementioned thread-agnostic support in Windows. This is because the I/O system keeps track of a completion port's outstanding I/Os by linking them with the completion port.

Figure 6-22 and Figure 6-23 show synchronous and asynchronous I/O cancellation. (To a driver, all cancel processing looks the same.)

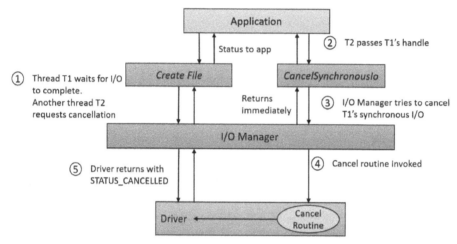

FIGURE 6-22   Synchronous I/O cancellation.

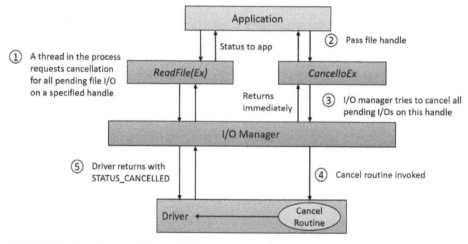

FIGURE 6-23   Asynchronous I/O cancellation.

I/O cancellation for thread termination

The other scenario in which I/Os must be cancelled is when a thread exits, either directly or as a result of its process terminating (which causes the threads of the process to terminate). Because every thread has a list of IRPs associated with it, the I/O manager can walk this list, look for cancellable IRPs, and cancel them. Unlike `CancelIoEx`, which does not wait for an IRP to be cancelled before returning, the process manager will not allow thread termination to proceed until all I/Os have been cancelled. As a result, if a driver fails to cancel an IRP, the process and thread object will remain allocated until the system shuts down.

> **Note** Only IRPs for which a driver sets a cancel routine are cancellable. The process manager waits until all I/Os associated with a thread are either cancelled or completed before deleting the thread.

EXPERIMENT: Debugging an unkillable process

In this experiment, we'll use Notmyfault from Sysinternals to force an unkillable process by causing the Myfault.sys driver, which Notmyfault.exe uses, to indefinitely hold an IRP without having registered a cancel routine for it. (Notmyfault is covered in detail in the "Crash dump analysis" section of Chapter 15, "Crash dump analysis," in Part 2.) Follow these steps:

1. Run Notmyfault.exe.

2. The Not My Fault dialog box appears. Click the **Hang** tab and choose **Hang with IRP**, as shown in the following screenshot. Then click the **Hang** button.

3. You shouldn't see anything happen, and you should be able to click the **Cancel** button to quit the application. However, you should still see the Notmyfault process in Task Manager or Process Explorer. Attempts to terminate the process will fail because Windows will wait forever for the IRP to complete given that the Myfault driver doesn't register a cancel routine.

4. To debug an issue such as this, you can use WinDbg to look at what the thread is currently doing. Open a local kernel debugger session and start by listing the information about the Notmyfault.exe process with the `!process` command (notmyfault64 is the 64-bit version):

```
lkd> !process 0 7 notmyfault64.exe
PROCESS ffff8c0b88c823c0
    SessionId: 1  Cid: 2b04    Peb: 4e5c9f4000  ParentCid: 0d40
    DirBase: 3edfa000  ObjectTable: ffffdf08dd140900  HandleCount: <Data Not
Accessible>
    Image: notmyfault64.exe
    VadRoot ffff8c0b863ed190 Vads 81 Clone 0 Private 493. Modified 8. Locked
0....
        THREAD ffff8c0b85377300  Cid 2b04.2714  Teb: 0000004e5c808000
Win32Thread: 0000000000000000 WAIT: (UserRequest) UserMode Non-Alertable
            fffff80a4c944018  SynchronizationEvent
        IRP List:
            ffff8c0b84f1d130: (0006,0118) Flags: 00060000  Mdl: 00000000
        Not impersonating
        DeviceMap                 ffffdf08cf4d7d20
        Owning Process            ffff8c0b88c823c0        Image:
notmyfault64.exe
...
        Child-SP          RetAddr           : Args to Child
: Call Site
        ffffb881'3ecf74a0 fffff802'cfc38a1c : 00000000'00000100
00000000'00000000 00000000'00000000 00000000'00000000 :
nt!KiSwapContext+0x76
        ffffb881'3ecf75e0 fffff802'cfc384bf : 00000000'00000000
00000000'00000000 00000000'00000000 00000000'00000000 :
nt!KiSwapThread+0x17c
        ffffb881'3ecf7690 fffff802'cfc3a287 : 00000000'00000000
00000000'00000000 00000000'00000000 00000000'00000000 :
nt!KiCommitThreadWait+0x14f
        ffffb881'3ecf7730 fffff80a'4c941fce : fffff80a'4c944018
fffff802'00000006 00000000'00000000 00000000'00000000 :
nt!KeWaitForSingleObject+0x377
        ffffb881'3ecf77e0 fffff802'd0067430 : ffff8c0b'88d2b550
00000000'00000001 00000000'00000001 00000000'00000000 : myfault+0x1fce
        ffffb881'3ecf7820 fffff802'd0066314 : ffff8c0b'00000000
ffff8c0b'88d2b504 00000000'00000000 ffffb881'3ecf7b80 : nt!IopSynchronousSer
viceTail+0x1a0
        ffffb881'3ecf78e0 fffff802'd0065c96 : 00000000'00000000
00000000'00000000 00000000'00000000 00000000'00000000 :
nt!IopXxxControlFile+0x674
        ffffb881'3ecf7a20 fffff802'cfd57f93 : ffff8c0b'85377300
fffff802'cfcb9640 00000000'00000000 fffff802'd005b32f :
nt!NtDeviceIoControlFile+0x56
        ffffb881'3ecf7a90 00007ffd'c1564f34 : 00000000'00000000
00000000'00000000 00000000'00000000 00000000'00000000 :
nt!KiSystemServiceCopyEnd+0x13 (TrapFrame @ ffffb881'3ecf7b00)
```

5. From the stack trace, you can see that the thread that initiated the I/O is now waiting for cancellation or completion. The next step is to use the same debugger extension command used in the previous experiments, !irp, and attempt to analyze the problem. Copy the IRP pointer, and examine it with !irp:

```
lkd> !irp ffff8c0b84f1d130
Irp is active with 1 stacks 1 is current (= 0xffff8c0b84f1d200)
 No Mdl: No System Buffer: Thread ffff8c0b85377300:  Irp stack trace.
     cmd  flg cl Device   File     Completion-Context
>[IRP_MJ_DEVICE_CONTROL(e), N/A(0)]
             5  0 ffff8c0b886b5590 ffff8c0b88d2b550 00000000-00000000
             \Driver\MYFAULT
                       Args: 00000000 00000000 83360020 00000000
```

6. From this output, it is obvious who the culprit driver is: \Driver\MYFAULT, or Myfault.sys. The name of the driver highlights the fact that the only way this situation can occur is through a driver problem—not a buggy application. Unfortunately, although you now know which driver caused the problem, there isn't much you can do about it apart from rebooting the system. This is necessary because Windows can never safely assume it is OK to ignore the fact that cancellation hasn't yet occurred. The IRP could return at any time and cause corruption of system memory.

 Tip If you encounter this situation in practice, you should check for a newer version of the driver, which might include a fix for the bug.

I/O completion ports

Writing a high-performance server application requires implementing an efficient threading model. Having either too few or too many server threads to process client requests can lead to performance problems. For example, if a server creates a single thread to handle all requests, clients can become starved because the server will be tied up processing one request at a time. A single thread could simultaneously process multiple requests, switching from one to another as I/O operations are started. However, this architecture introduces significant complexity and can't take advantage of systems with more than one logical processor. At the other extreme, a server could create a big pool of threads so that virtually every client request is processed by a dedicated thread. This scenario usually leads to thread-thrashing, in which lots of threads wake up, perform some CPU processing, block while waiting for I/O, and then, after request processing is completed, block again waiting for a new request. If nothing else, having too many threads results in excessive context switching, caused by the scheduler having to divide processor time among multiple active threads; such a scheme will not scale.

The goal of a server is to incur as few context switches as possible by having its threads avoid unnecessary blocking, while at the same time maximizing parallelism by using multiple threads. The ideal is for there to be a thread actively servicing a client request on every processor and for those threads not to block when they complete a request if additional requests are waiting. For this optimal process to work correctly, however, the application must have a way to activate another thread when a thread processing a client request blocks I/O (such as when it reads from a file as part of the processing).

The IoCompletion object

Applications use the `IoCompletion` executive object, which is exported to the Windows API as a completion port, as the focal point for the completion of I/O associated with multiple file handles. Once a file is associated with a completion port, any asynchronous I/O operations that complete on the file result in a completion packet being queued to the completion port. A thread can wait for any outstanding I/Os to complete on multiple files simply by waiting for a completion packet to be queued to the completion port. The Windows API provides similar functionality with the `WaitForMultipleObjects` API function, but completion ports have one important advantage: concurrency. *Concurrency* refers to the number of threads that an application has actively servicing client requests, which is controlled with the aid of the system.

When an application creates a completion port, it specifies a concurrency value. This value indicates the maximum number of threads associated with the port that should be running at any given time. As stated earlier, the ideal is to have one thread active at any given time for every processor in the system. Windows uses the concurrency value associated with a port to control how many threads an application has active. If the number of active threads associated with a port equals the concurrency value, a thread that is waiting on the completion port won't be allowed to run. Instead, an active thread will finish processing its current request, after which it will check whether another packet is waiting at the port. If one is, the thread simply grabs the packet and goes off to process it. When this happens, there is no context switch, and the CPUs are utilized nearly to their full capacity.

Using completion ports

Figure 6-24 shows a high-level illustration of completion-port operation. A completion port is created with a call to the `CreateIoCompletionPort` Windows API function. Threads that block on a completion port become associated with the port and are awakened in last in, first out (LIFO) order so that the thread that blocked most recently is the one that is given the next packet. Threads that block for long periods of time can have their stacks swapped out to disk, so if there are more threads associated with a port than there is work to process, the in-memory footprints of threads blocked the longest are minimized.

A server application will usually receive client requests via network endpoints that are identified by file handles. Examples include Windows Sockets 2 (Winsock2) sockets or named pipes. As the server creates its communications endpoints, it associates them with a completion port and its threads wait for incoming requests by calling `GetQueuedCompletionStatus(Ex)` on the port. When a thread is given a packet from the completion port, it will go off and start processing the request, becoming an active thread. A thread will block many times during its processing, such as when it needs to read or write data to a file on disk or when it synchronizes with other threads. Windows detects this activity and recognizes that the completion port has one less active thread. Therefore, when a thread becomes inactive because it blocks, a thread waiting on the completion port will be awakened if there is a packet in the queue.

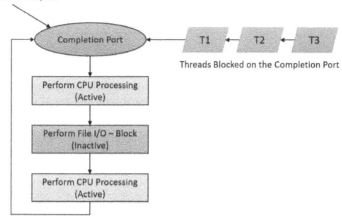

Incoming Client Request

Completion Port

Threads Blocked on the Completion Port

Perform CPU Processing (Active)

Perform File I/O – Block (Inactive)

Perform CPU Processing (Active)

FIGURE 6-24 I/O completion-port operation.

Microsoft's guidelines are to set the concurrency value roughly equal to the number of processors in a system. Keep in mind that it's possible for the number of active threads for a completion port to exceed the concurrency limit. Consider a case in which the limit is specified as 1:

1. A client request comes in and a thread is dispatched to process the request, becoming active.

2. A second request arrives, but a second thread waiting on the port isn't allowed to proceed because the concurrency limit has been reached.

3. The first thread blocks, waiting for a file I/O, so it becomes inactive.

4. The second thread is released.

5. While the second thread is still active, the first thread's file I/O is completed, making it active again. At that point—and until one of the threads blocks—the concurrency value is 2, which is higher than the limit of 1. Most of the time, the count of active threads will remain at or just above the concurrency limit.

The completion port API also makes it possible for a server application to queue privately defined completion packets to a completion port by using the PostQueuedCompletionStatus function. A server typically uses this function to inform its threads of external events, such as the need to shut down gracefully.

Applications can use thread-agnostic I/O, described earlier, with I/O completion ports to avoid associating threads with their own I/Os and associating them with a completion port object instead. In addition to the other scalability benefits of I/O completion ports, their use can minimize context switches. Standard I/O completions must be executed by the thread that initiated the I/O, but when an I/O associated with an I/O completion port completes, the I/O manager uses any waiting thread to perform the completion operation.

I/O completion port operation

Windows applications create completion ports by calling the CreateIoCompletionPort Windows API and specifying a NULL completion port handle. This results in the execution of the NtCreateIoCompletion system service. The executive's IoCompletion object contains a kernel synchronization object called a *kernel queue*. Thus, the system service creates a completion port object and initializes a queue object in the port's allocated memory. (A pointer to the port also points to the queue object because the queue is the first member of the completion port.) A kernel queue object has a concurrency value that is specified when a thread initializes it, and in this case the value that is used is the one that was passed to CreateIoCompletionPort. KeInitializeQueue is the function that NtCreateIoCompletion calls to initialize a port's queue object.

When an application calls CreateIoCompletionPort to associate a file handle with a port, the NtSetInformationFile system service is executed with the file handle as the primary parameter. The information class that is set is FileCompletionInformation, and the completion port's handle and the CompletionKey parameter from CreateIoCompletionPort are the data values. NtSetInformationFile dereferences the file handle to obtain the file object and allocates a completion context data structure.

Finally, NtSetInformationFile sets the CompletionContext field in the file object to point at the context structure. When an asynchronous I/O operation completes on a file object, the I/O manager checks whether the CompletionContext field in the file object is non-NULL. If it is, the I/O manager allocates a completion packet and queues it to the completion port by calling KeInsertQueue with the port as the queue on which to insert the packet (this works because the completion port object and queue object have the same address).

When a server thread invokes GetQueuedCompletionStatus, the NtRemoveIoCompletion system service is executed. After validating parameters and translating the completion port handle to a pointer to the port, NtRemoveIoCompletion calls IoRemoveIoCompletion, which eventually calls KeRemoveQueueEx. For high-performance scenarios, it's possible that multiple I/Os may have been completed, and although the thread will not block, it will still call into the kernel each time to get one item. The GetQueuedCompletionStatus or GetQueuedCompletionStatusEx API allows applications to retrieve more than one I/O completion status at the same time, reducing the number of user-to-kernel roundtrips and maintaining peak efficiency. Internally, this is implemented through the NtRemoveIoCompletionEx function. This calls IoRemoveIoCompletion with a count of queued items, which is passed on to KeRemoveQueueEx.

As you can see, KeRemoveQueueEx and KeInsertQueue are the engine behind completion ports. They are the functions that determine whether a thread waiting for an I/O completion packet should be activated. Internally, a queue object maintains a count of the current number of active threads and the maximum number of active threads. If the current number equals or exceeds the maximum when a thread calls KeRemoveQueueEx, the thread will be put (in LIFO order) onto a list of threads waiting for a turn to process a completion packet. The list of threads hangs off the queue object. A thread's control block data structure (KTHREAD) has a pointer in it that references the queue object of a queue that it's associated with; if the pointer is NULL, the thread isn't associated with a queue.

Windows keeps track of threads that become inactive because they block on something other than the completion port by relying on the queue pointer in a thread's control block. The scheduler routines that possibly result in a thread blocking (such as KeWaitForSingleObject, KeDelayExecutionThread, and so on) check the thread's queue pointer. If the pointer isn't NULL, the functions call KiActivate-WaiterQueue, a queue-related function that decrements the count of active threads associated with the queue. If the resulting number is less than the maximum and at least one completion packet is in the queue, the thread at the front of the queue's thread list is awakened and given the oldest packet. Conversely, whenever a thread that is associated with a queue wakes up after blocking, the scheduler executes the KiUnwaitThread function, which increments the queue's active count.

The PostQueuedCompletionStatus Windows API function results in the execution of the NtSet-IoCompletion system service. This function simply inserts the specified packet onto the completion port's queue by using KeInsertQueue.

Figure 6-25 shows an example of a completion port object in operation. Even though two threads are ready to process completion packets, the concurrency value of 1 allows only one thread associated with the completion port to be active, and so the two threads are blocked on the completion port.

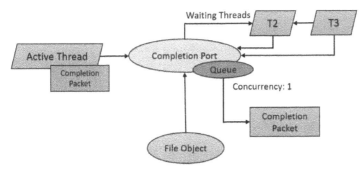

FIGURE 6-25   I/O completion port object in operation.

You can fine-tune the exact notification model of the I/O completion port through the SetFile-CompletionNotificationModes API, which allows application developers to take advantage of addition-al, specific improvements that usually require code changes but can offer even more throughput. Three notification-mode optimizations are supported, which are listed in Table 6-4. Note that these modes are per file handle and cannot be changed after being set.

TABLE 6-4   I/O completion port notification modes

Notification Mode	Meaning
Skip completion port on success (FILE_SKIP_ COMPLETION_PORT_ON_SUCCESS=1)	If the following three conditions are true, the I/O manager does not queue a completion entry to the port when it would ordinarily do so. First, a completion port must be associated with the file handle. Second, the file must be opened for asynchronous I/O. Third, the request must return success immediately without returning ERROR_ PENDING.

Continues...

TABLE 6-4 I/O completion port notification modes *(continued)*

Notification Mode	Meaning
Skip set event on handle (FILE_SKIP_SET_EVENT_ON_HANDLE=2)	The I/O manager does not set the event for the file object if a request returns with a success code or the error returned is ERROR_PENDING and the function that is called is not a synchronous function. If an explicit event is provided for the request, it is still signaled.
Skip set user event on fast I/O (FILE_SKIP_SET_USER_EVENT_ON_FAST_IO=4)	The I/O manager does not set the explicit event provided for the request if a request takes the fast I/O path and returns with a success code or the error returned is ERROR_PENDING and the function that is called is not a synchronous function.

I/O prioritization

Without I/O priority, background activities like search indexing, virus scanning, and disk defragmenting can severely impact the responsiveness of foreground operations. For example, a user who launches an application or opens a document while another process is performing disk I/O will experience delays as the foreground task waits for disk access. The same interference also affects the streaming playback of multimedia content like music from a disk.

Windows includes two types of I/O prioritization to help foreground I/O operations get preference: priority on individual I/O operations and I/O bandwidth reservations.

I/O priorities

The Windows I/O manager internally includes support for five I/O priorities, as shown in Table 6-5, but only three of the priorities are used. (Future versions of Windows may support High and Low.)

TABLE 6-5 I/O priorities

I/O Priority	Usage
Critical	Memory manager
High	Not used
Normal	Normal application I/O
Low	Not used
Very Low	Scheduled tasks, SuperFetch, defragmenting, content indexing, background activities

I/O has a default priority of Normal, and the memory manager uses Critical when it wants to write dirty memory data out to disk under low-memory situations to make room in RAM for other data and code. The Windows Task Scheduler sets the I/O priority for tasks that have the default task priority to Very Low. The priority specified by applications that perform background processing is Very Low. All the Windows background operations, including Windows Defender scanning and desktop search indexing, use Very Low I/O priority.

Prioritization strategies

Internally, the five I/O priorities are divided into two I/O prioritization modes, called *strategies*. These are the hierarchy prioritization and the idle prioritization strategies. Hierarchy prioritization deals with all the I/O priorities except Very Low. It implements the following strategy:

- All critical-priority I/O must be processed before any high-priority I/O.

- All high-priority I/O must be processed before any normal-priority I/O.

- All normal-priority I/O must be processed before any low-priority I/O.

- All low-priority I/O is processed after any higher-priority I/O.

As each application generates I/Os, IRPs are put on different I/O queues based on their priority, and the hierarchy strategy decides the ordering of the operations.

The idle prioritization strategy, on the other hand, uses a separate queue for non-idle priority I/O. Because the system processes all hierarchy prioritized I/O before idle I/O, it's possible for the I/Os in this queue to be starved, as long as there's even a single non-idle I/O on the system in the hierarchy priority strategy queue.

To avoid this situation, as well as to control back-off (the sending rate of I/O transfers), the idle strategy uses a timer to monitor the queue and guarantee that at least one I/O is processed per unit of time (typically, half a second). Data written using non-idle I/O priority also causes the cache manager to write modifications to disk immediately instead of doing it later and to bypass its read-ahead logic for read operations that would otherwise preemptively read from the file being accessed. The prioritization strategy also waits for 50 milliseconds after the completion of the last non-idle I/O in order to issue the next idle I/O. Otherwise, idle I/Os would occur in the middle of non-idle streams, causing costly seeks.

Combining these strategies into a virtual global I/O queue for demonstration purposes, a snapshot of this queue might look similar to Figure 6-26. Note that within each queue, the ordering is first-in, first-out (FIFO). The order in the figure is shown only as an example.

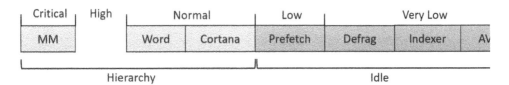

FIGURE 6-26 Sample entries in a global I/O queue.

User-mode applications can set I/O priority on three different objects. The functions `SetPriority-Class` (with the `PROCESS_MODE_BACKGROUND_BEGIN` value) and `SetThreadPriority` (with the `THREAD_MODE_BACKGROUND_BEGIN` value), set the priority for all the I/Os that are generated by either the entire process or specific threads (the priority is stored in the IRP of each request). These functions work only on the current process or thread and lower the I/O priority to Very Low. In addition, these also lower the scheduling priority to 4 and the memory priority to 1. The function `SetFileInformationByHandle` can set the priority for a specific file object (the priority is stored in the file object). Drivers can also set I/O priority directly on an IRP by using the `IoSetIoPriorityHint` API.

> **Note** The I/O priority field in the IRP and/or file object is a *hint*. There is no guarantee that the I/O priority will be respected or even supported by the different drivers that are part of the storage stack.

The two prioritization strategies are implemented by two different types of drivers. The hierarchy strategy is implemented by the storage *port* drivers, which are responsible for all I/Os on a specific port, such as ATA, SCSI, or USB. Only the ATA port driver (Ataport.sys) and USB port driver (Usbstor.sys) implement this strategy, while the SCSI and storage port drivers (Scsiport.sys and Storport.sys) do not.

> **Note** All port drivers check specifically for Critical priority I/Os and move them ahead of their queues, even if they do not support the full hierarchy mechanism. This mechanism is in place to support critical memory manager paging I/Os to ensure system reliability.

This means that consumer mass storage devices such as IDE or SATA hard drives and USB flash disks will take advantage of I/O prioritization, while devices based on SCSI, Fibre Channel, and iSCSI will not.

On the other hand, it is the system storage class device driver (Classpnp.sys) that enforces the idle strategy, so it automatically applies to I/Os directed at all storage devices, including SCSI drives. This separation ensures that idle I/Os will be subject to back-off algorithms to ensure a reliable system during operation under high idle I/O usage and so that applications that use them can make forward progress. Placing support for this strategy in the Microsoft-provided class driver avoids performance problems that would have been caused by lack of support for it in legacy third-party port drivers.

Figure 6-27 displays a simplified view of the storage stack that shows where each strategy is implemented. See Chapter 12 in Part 2 for more information on the storage stack.

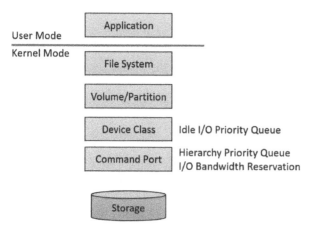

FIGURE 6-27 Implementation of I/O prioritization across the storage stack.

I/O priority inversion avoidance

To avoid I/O priority inversion, in which a high I/O priority thread is starved by a low I/O priority thread, the executive resource (ERESOURCE) locking functionality uses several strategies. The ERESOURCE was picked for the implementation of I/O priority inheritance specifically because of its heavy use in file system and storage drivers, where most I/O priority inversion issues can appear. (See Chapter 8 in Part 2 for more on executive resources.)

If an ERESOURCE is being acquired by a thread with low I/O priority, and there are currently waiters on the ERESOURCE with normal or higher priority, the current thread is temporarily boosted to normal I/O priority by using the PsBoostThreadIo API, which increments the IoBoostCount in the ETHREAD structure. It also notifies Autoboost if the thread I/O priority was boosted or the boost was removed. (Refer to Chapter 4 for more on Autoboost.)

It then calls the IoBoostThreadIoPriority API, which enumerates all the IRPs queued to the target thread (recall that each thread has a list of pending IRPs) and checks which ones have a lower priority than the target priority (normal in this case), thus identifying pending idle I/O priority IRPs. In turn, the device object responsible for each of those IRPs is identified, and the I/O manager checks whether a priority callback has been registered, which driver developers can do through the IoRegisterPriority-Callback API and by setting the DO_PRIORITY_CALLBACK_ENABLED flag on their device object. Depending on whether the IRP was a paging I/O, this mechanism is called *threaded boost* or *paging boost*. Finally, if no matching IRPs were found, but the thread has at least some pending IRPs, all are boosted regardless of device object or priority, which is called *blanket boosting*.

I/O priority boosts and bumps

Windows uses a few other subtle modifications to normal I/O paths to avoid starvation, inversion, or otherwise unwanted scenarios when I/O priority is being used. Typically, these modifications are done by boosting I/O priority when needed. The following scenarios exhibit this behavior:

- When a driver is being called with an IRP targeted to a particular file object, Windows makes sure that if the request comes from kernel mode, the IRP uses normal priority even if the file object has a lower I/O priority hint. This is called a *kernel bump*.

- When reads or writes to the paging file are occurring (through IoPageRead and IoPageWrite), Windows checks whether the request comes from kernel mode and is not being performed on behalf of Superfetch (which always uses idle I/O). In this case, the IRP uses normal priority even if the current thread has a lower I/O priority. This is called a *paging bump*.

The following experiment will show you an example of Very Low I/O priority and how you can use Process Monitor to look at I/O priorities on different requests.

EXPERIMENT: Very low versus normal I/O throughput

You can use the IO Priority sample application (included in this book's utilities) to look at the throughput difference between two threads with different I/O priorities. Follow these steps:

1. Launch **IoPriority.exe**.

2. In the dialog box, under Thread 1, check the **Low Priority** check box.

3. Click the **Start I/O** button. You should notice a significant difference in speed between the two threads, as shown in the following screenshot:

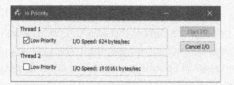

 Note If both threads run at low priority and the system is relatively idle, their throughput will be roughly equal to the throughput of a single normal I/O priority in the example. This is because low-priority I/Os are not artificially throttled or otherwise hindered if there isn't any competition from higher-priority I/O.

4. Open the process in Process Explorer and look at the low I/O priority thread to see the priorities:

5. You can also use Process Monitor to trace IO Priority's I/Os and look at their I/O priority hint. To do so, launch Process Monitor, configure a filter for IoPriority.exe, and repeat the experiment. In this application, each thread reads from a file named _File_ concatenated with the thread ID.

6. Scroll down until you see a write to File_1. You should see output similar to the following:

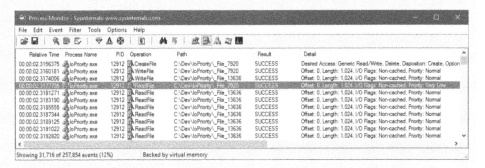

7. Notice that I/Os directed at _File_7920 in the screenshot have a priority of very low. Looking at the Time of Day and Relative Time columns, you'll also notice that the I/Os are spaced half a second from each other, which is another sign of the idle strategy in action.

EXPERIMENT: Performance analysis of I/O priority boosting/bumping

The kernel exposes several internal variables that can be queried through the undocumented `SystemLowPriorityIoInformation` system class available in `NtQuerySystemInformation`. However, even without writing or relying on such an application, you can use the local kernel debugger to view these numbers on your system. The following variables are available:

- `IoLowPriorityReadOperationCount` and `IoLowPriorityWriteOperationCount`

- `IoKernelIssuedIoBoostedCount`

- `IoPagingReadLowPriorityCount` and `IoPagingWriteLowPriorityCount`

- `IoPagingReadLowPriorityBumpedCount` and `IoPagingWriteHighPriorityBumpedCount`

- `IoBoostedThreadedIrpCount` and `IoBoostedPagingIrpCount`

- `IoBlanketBoostCount`

You can use the dd memory-dumping command in the kernel debugger to see the values of these variables (all are 32-bit values).

Bandwidth reservation (scheduled file I/O)

Windows I/O bandwidth-reservation support is useful for applications that desire consistent I/O throughput. For example, using the `SetFileBandwidthReservation` call, a media player application can ask the I/O system to guarantee it the ability to read data from a device at a specified rate. If the device can deliver data at the requested rate and existing reservations allow it, the I/O system gives the application guidance as to how fast it should issue I/Os and how large the I/Os should be.

The I/O system won't service other I/Os unless it can satisfy the requirements of applications that have made reservations on the target storage device. Figure 6-28 shows a conceptual timeline of I/Os issued on the same file. The shaded regions are the only ones that will be available to other applications. If I/O bandwidth is already taken, new I/Os will have to wait until the next cycle.

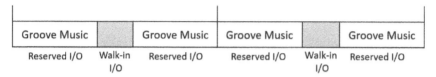

FIGURE 6-28 Effect of I/O requests during bandwidth reservation.

Like the hierarchy prioritization strategy, bandwidth reservation is implemented at the port driver level, which means it is available only for IDE, SATA, or USB-based mass-storage devices.

Container notifications

Container notifications are specific classes of events that drivers can register for through an asynchronous callback mechanism by using the `IoRegisterContainerNotification` API and selecting the notification class that interests them. Thus far, one such class is implemented in Windows: `IoSession-StateNotification`. This class allows drivers to have their registered callback invoked whenever a change in the state of a given session is registered. The following changes are supported:

- A session is created or terminated.

- A user connects to or disconnects from a session.

- A user logs on to or logs off from a session.

By specifying a device object that belongs to a specific session, the driver callback will be active only for that session. In contrast, by specifying a global device object (or no device object at all), the driver will receive notifications for all events on a system. This feature is particularly useful for devices that participate in the Plug and Play device redirection functionality that is provided through Terminal Services, which allows a remote device to be visible on the connecting host's Plug and Play manager bus as well (such as audio or printer device redirection). Once the user disconnects from a session with audio playback, for example, the device driver needs a notification in order to stop redirecting the source audio stream.

Driver Verifier

Driver Verifier is a mechanism that can be used to help find and isolate common bugs in device drivers or other kernel-mode system code. Microsoft uses Driver Verifier to check its own device drivers as well as all device drivers that vendors submit for WHQL testing. Doing so ensures that the drivers submitted are compatible with Windows and free from common driver errors. (Although not described in this book, there is also a corresponding Application Verifier tool that has resulted in quality improvements for user-mode code in Windows.)

Note Although Driver Verifier serves primarily as a tool to help device driver developers discover bugs in their code, it is also a powerful tool for system administrators experiencing crashes. Chapter 15 in Part 2 describes its role in crash analysis troubleshooting.

Driver Verifier consists of support in several system components: the memory manager, I/O manager, and HAL all have driver verification options that can be enabled. These options are configured using the Driver Verifier Manager (%SystemRoot%\System32\Verifier.exe). When you run Driver Verifier with no command-line arguments, it presents a wizard-style interface, as shown in Figure 6-29. (You can also enable and disable Driver Verifier, as well as display current settings, by using its command-line interface. From a command prompt, type **verifier /?** to see the switches.)

FIGURE 6-29 Driver Verifier Manager.

Driver Verifier Manager distinguishes between two sets of settings: standard and additional. This is somewhat arbitrary, but the standard settings represent the more common options that should be probably selected for every driver being tested, while the additional settings represent those settings that are less common or specific to some types of drivers. Selecting **Create Custom Settings** from the main wizard's page shows all options with a column indicating which is standard and which is additional, as shown in Figure 6-30.

Regardless of which options are selected, Driver Verifier always monitors drivers selected for verification, looking for a number of illegal and boundary operations, including calling kernel-memory pool functions at invalid IRQL, double-freeing memory, releasing spinlocks inappropriately, not freeing timers, referencing a freed object, delaying shutdown for longer than 20 minutes, and requesting a zero-size memory allocation.

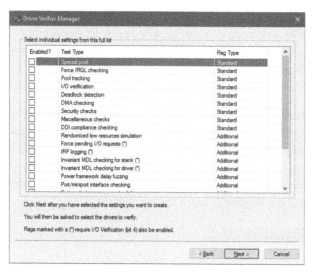

FIGURE 6-30 Driver Verifier settings.

Driver Verifier settings are stored in the registry under the HKLM\SYSTEM\CurrentControlSet\ Control\Session Manager\Memory Management key. The VerifyDriverLevel value contains a bitmask that represents the verification options that are enabled. The VerifyDrivers value contains the names of the drivers to monitor. (These values won't exist in the registry until you select drivers to verify in the Driver Verifier Manager.) If you choose to verify all drivers (which you should never do, since this will cause considerable system slowdown), VerifyDrivers is set to an asterisk (*) character. Depending on the settings you have made, you might need to reboot the system for the selected verification to occur.

Early in the boot process, the memory manager reads the Driver Verifier registry values to determine which drivers to verify and which Driver Verifier options you enabled. (Note that if you boot in safe mode, any Driver Verifier settings are ignored.) Subsequently, if you've selected at least one driver for verification, the kernel checks the name of every device driver it loads into memory against the list of drivers you've selected for verification. For every device driver that appears in both places, the kernel invokes the VfLoadDriver function, which calls other internal Vf* functions to replace the driver's references to a number of kernel functions with references to Driver Verifier–equivalent versions of those functions. For example, ExAllocatePool is replaced with a call to VerifierAllocatePool. The windowing system driver (Win32k.sys) also makes similar changes to use Driver Verifier–equivalent functions.

I/O-related verification options

The various I/O-related verification options are as follows:

- **I/O Verification** When this option is selected, the I/O manager allocates IRPs for verified drivers from a special pool and their usage is tracked. In addition, the Driver Verifier crashes the system when an IRP is completed that contains an invalid status or when an invalid device object is passed to the I/O manager. This option also monitors all IRPs to ensure that drivers mark them correctly when completing them asynchronously, that they manage device-stack locations correctly, and that they delete device objects only once. In addition, the Verifier randomly stresses drivers by sending them fake power management and WMI IRPs, changing the order in which devices are enumerated, and adjusting the status of PnP and power IRPs when they complete to test for drivers that return incorrect status from their dispatch routines. Finally, the Verifier also detects incorrect re-initialization of remove locks while they are still being held due to pending device removal.

■ **DMA Checking** DMA is a hardware-supported mechanism that allows devices to transfer data to or from physical memory without involving the CPU. The I/O manager provides several functions that drivers use to initiate and control DMA operations, and this option enables checks for the correct use of the functions and buffers that the I/O manager supplies for DMA operations.

■ **Force Pending I/O Requests** For many devices, asynchronous I/Os complete immediately, so drivers may not be coded to properly handle the occasional asynchronous I/O. When this option is enabled, the I/O manager randomly returns STATUS_PENDING in response to a driver's calls to IoCallDriver, which simulates the asynchronous completion of an I/O.

■ **IRP Logging** This option monitors a driver's use of IRPs and makes a record of IRP usage, which is stored as WMI information. You can then use the Dc2wmiparser.exe utility in the WDK to convert these WMI records to a text file. Note that only 20 IRPs for each device will be recorded—each subsequent IRP will overwrite the least recently added entry. After a reboot, this information is discarded, so Dc2wmiparser.exe should be run if the contents of the trace are to be analyzed later.

Memory-related verification options

The following are memory-related verification options supported by Driver Verifier. (Some are also related to I/O operations.)

Special Pool

Selecting the Special Pool option causes the pool allocation routines to bracket pool allocations with an invalid page so that references before or after the allocation will result in a kernel-mode access violation, thus crashing the system with the finger pointed at the buggy driver. Special pool also causes some additional validation checks to be performed when a driver allocates or frees memory. With special pool enabled, the pool allocation routines allocate a region of kernel memory for Driver Verifier to use. Driver Verifier redirects memory allocation requests that drivers under verification make to the special pool area rather than to the standard kernel-mode memory pools. When a device driver allocates memory from special pool, Driver Verifier rounds up the allocation to an even-page boundary. Because Driver Verifier brackets the allocated page with invalid pages, if a device driver attempts to read or write past the end of the buffer, the driver will access an invalid page, and the memory manager will raise a kernel-mode access violation.

Figure 6-31 shows an example of the special pool buffer that Driver Verifier allocates to a device driver when Driver Verifier checks for overrun errors.

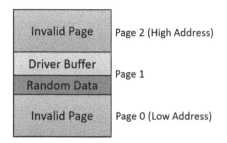

Invalid Page	Page 2 (High Address)
Driver Buffer	Page 1
Random Data	
Invalid Page	Page 0 (Low Address)

FIGURE 6-31 Layout of special pool allocations.

By default, Driver Verifier performs overrun detection. It does this by placing the buffer that the device driver uses at the end of the allocated page and filling the beginning of the page with a random pattern. Although the Driver Verifier Manager doesn't let you specify underrun detection, you can set this type of detection manually by adding the DWORD registry value PoolTagOverruns to the HKLM\SYSTEM\CurrentControlSet\Control\Session Manager\Memory Management key and setting it to 0 (or by running the Gflags.exe utility and selecting the **Verify Start** option in the Kernel Special Pool Tag section instead of the default option, Verify End). When Windows enforces underrun detection, Driver Verifier allocates the driver's buffer at the beginning of the page rather than at the end.

The overrun-detection configuration includes some measure of underrun detection as well. When the driver frees its buffer to return the memory to Driver Verifier, Driver Verifier ensures that the pattern preceding the buffer hasn't changed. If the pattern is modified, the device driver has underrun the buffer and written to memory outside the buffer.

Special pool allocations also check to ensure that the processor IRQL at the time of an allocation and deallocation is legal. This check catches an error that some device drivers make: allocating pageable memory from an IRQL at DPC/dispatch level or above.

You can also configure special pool manually by adding the DWORD registry value PoolTag in the HKLM\SYSTEM\CurrentControlSet\Control\Session Manager\Memory Management key, which represents the allocation tags the system uses for special pool. Thus, even if Driver Verifier isn't configured to verify a particular device driver, if the tag the driver associates with the memory it allocates matches what is specified in the PoolTag registry value, the pool allocation routines will allocate the memory from special pool. If you set the value of PoolTag to 0x2a or to the wildcard (*), all memory that drivers allocate will be from special pool, provided there's enough virtual and physical memory (drivers will revert to allocating from regular pool if there aren't enough free pages).

Pool tracking

If pool tracking is enabled, the memory manager checks at driver unload time whether the driver freed all the memory allocations it made. If it didn't, it crashes the system, indicating the buggy driver. Driver Verifier also shows general pool statistics on the Driver Verifier Manager's Pool Tracking tab (accessible from the main wizard UI by selecting **Display Information About the Currently Verified Drivers** and selecting **Next** twice). You can also use the `!verifier` kernel debugger command. This command shows more information than Driver Verifier and is useful to driver writers.

Pool tracking and special pool cover not only explicit allocation calls, such as `ExAllocatePoolWith-Tag`, but also calls to other kernel APIs that implicitly allocate memory from pools: `IoAllocateMdl`, `IoAllocateIrp`, and other IRP allocation calls; various `Rtl` string APIs; and `IoSetCompletionRoutineEx`.

Another driver verified function enabled by the Pool Tracking option pertains to pool quota charges. The call to `ExAllocatePoolWithQuotaTag` charges the current process's pool quota for the number of bytes allocated. If such a call is made from a DPC routine, the process that is charged is unpredictable because DPC routines may execute in the context of any process. The Pool Tracking option checks for calls to this routine from the DPC routine context.

Driver Verifier can also perform locked memory page tracking, which additionally checks for pages that have been left locked after an I/O operation completes and generates a `DRIVER_LEFT_LOCKED_PAGES_IN_PROCESS` crash code instead of `PROCESS_HAS_LOCKED_PAGES`—the former indicates the driver responsible for the error as well as the function responsible for the locking of the pages.

Force IRQL Checking

One of the most common device driver bugs occurs when a driver accesses pageable data or code when the processor on which the device driver is executing is at an elevated IRQL. The memory manager can't service a page fault when the IRQL is DPC/dispatch level or above. The system often doesn't detect instances of a device driver accessing pageable data when the processor is executing at a high IRQL level because the pageable data being accessed happens to be physically resident at the time. At other times, however, the data might be paged out, which results in a system crash with the stop code `IRQL_NOT_LESS_OR_EQUAL` (that is, the IRQL wasn't less than or equal to the level required for the operation attempted—in this case, accessing pageable memory).

Although testing device drivers for this kind of bug is usually difficult, Driver Verifier makes it easy. If you select the Force IRQL Checking option, Driver Verifier forces all kernel-mode pageable code and data out of the system working set whenever a device driver under verification raises the IRQL. The internal function that does this is `MiTrimAllSystemPagableMemory`. With this setting enabled, whenever a device driver under verification accesses pageable memory when the IRQL is elevated, the system instantly detects the violation, and the resulting system crash identifies the faulty driver.

Another common driver crash that results from incorrect IRQL usage occurs when synchronization objects are part of data structures that are paged and then waited on. Synchronization objects should never be paged because the dispatcher needs to access them at an elevated IRQL, which would cause a crash. Driver Verifier checks whether any of the following structures are present in pageable memory: `KTIMER`, `KMUTEX`, `KSPIN_LOCK`, `KEVENT`, `KSEMAPHORE`, `ERESOURCE`, and `FAST_MUTEX`.

Low Resources Simulation

Enabling Low Resources Simulation causes Driver Verifier to randomly fail memory allocations that verified device drivers perform. In the past, developers wrote many device drivers under the assumption that kernel memory would always be available, and that if memory ran out, the device driver didn't have to worry about it because the system would crash anyway. However, because low-memory conditions can occur temporarily, and today's mobile devices are not as powerful as larger machines, it's important that device drivers properly handle allocation failures that indicate kernel memory is exhausted.

The driver calls that will be injected with random failures include the functions ExAllocatePool*, MmProbeAndLockPages, MmMapLockedPagesSpecifyCache, MmMapIoSpace, MmAllocateContiguous-Memory, MmAllocatePagesForMdl, IoAllocateIrp, IoAllocateMdl, IoAllocateWorkItem, IoAllo-cateErrorLogEntry, IOSetCompletionRoutineEx, and various Rtl string APIs that allocate from the pool. Driver Verifier also fails some allocations made by kernel GDI functions (see the WDK documentation for a complete list). Additionally, you can specify the following:

- **The probability that allocation will fail**   This is 6 percent by default.

- **Which applications should be subject to the simulation**   All are by default.

- **Which pool tags should be affected**   All are by default.

- **What delay should be used before fault injection starts**   The default is 7 minutes after the system boots, which is enough time to get past the critical initialization period in which a low-memory condition might prevent a device driver from loading.

You can change these customizations with command line options to verifier.exe.

After the delay period, Driver Verifier starts randomly failing allocation calls for device drivers it is verifying. If a driver doesn't correctly handle allocation failures, this will likely show up as a system crash.

Systematic Low Resources Simulation

Similar to the Low Resources Simulation option, this option fails certain calls to the kernel and *Ndis.Sys* (for network drivers), but does so in a systematic way, by examining the call stack at the point of failure injection. If the driver handles the failure correctly, that call stack will not be failure injected again. This allows the driver writer to see issues in a systematic way, fix a reported issue, and then move on to the next. Examining call stacks is a relatively expensive operation, therefore verifying more than a single driver at a time with this setting is not recommended.

Miscellaneous checks

Some of the checks that Driver Verifier calls *miscellaneous* allow it to detect the freeing of certain system structures in the pool that are still active. For example, Driver Verifier will check for:

- **Active work items in freed memory**   A driver calls ExFreePool to free a pool block in which one or more work items queued with IoQueueWorkItem are present.

- **Active resources in freed memory**   A driver calls ExFreePool before calling ExDelete-Resource to destroy an ERESOURCE object.

- **Active look-aside lists in freed memory**   A driver calls ExFreePool before calling ExDelete-NPagedLookasideList or ExDeletePagedLookasideList to delete the look-aside list.

Finally, when verification is enabled, Driver Verifier performs certain automatic checks that cannot be individually enabled or disabled. These include the following:

- Calling `MmProbeAndLockPages` or `MmProbeAndLockProcessPages` on an MDL having incorrect flags. For example, it is incorrect to call `MmProbeAndLockPages` for an MDL that was set up by calling `MmBuildMdlForNonPagedPool`.

- Calling `MmMapLockedPages` on an MDL having incorrect flags. For example, it is incorrect to call `MmMapLockedPages` for an MDL that is already mapped to a system address. Another example of incorrect driver behavior is calling `MmMapLockedPages` for an MDL that was not locked.

- Calling `MmUnlockPages` or `MmUnmapLockedPages` on a partial MDL (created by using `IoBuild-PartialMdl`).

- Calling `MmUnmapLockedPages` on an MDL that is not mapped to a system address.

- Allocating synchronization objects such as events or mutexes from `NonPagedPoolSession` memory.

Driver Verifier is a valuable addition to the arsenal of verification and debugging tools available to device driver writers. Many device drivers that first ran with Driver Verifier had bugs that Driver Verifier was able to expose. Thus, Driver Verifier has resulted in an overall improvement in the quality of all kernel-mode code running in Windows.

The Plug and Play manager

The PnP manager is the primary component involved in supporting the ability of Windows to recognize and adapt to changing hardware configurations. A user doesn't need to understand the intricacies of hardware or manual configuration to install and remove devices. For example, it's the PnP manager that enables a running Windows laptop that is placed on a docking station to automatically detect additional devices located in the docking station and make them available to the user.

Plug and Play support requires cooperation at the hardware, device driver, and operating system levels. Industry standards for the enumeration and identification of devices attached to buses are the foundation of Windows Plug and Play support. For example, the USB standard defines the way that devices on a USB bus identify themselves. With this foundation in place, Windows Plug and Play support provides the following capabilities:

- The PnP manager automatically recognizes installed devices, a process that includes enumerating devices attached to the system during a boot and detecting the addition and removal of devices as the system executes.

- Hardware resource allocation is a role the PnP manager fills by gathering the hardware resource requirements (interrupts, I/O memory, I/O registers, or bus-specific resources) of the devices attached to a system and, in a process called *resource arbitration*, optimally assigning resources so that each device meets the requirements necessary for its operation. Because hardware devices can be added to the system after boot-time resource assignment, the PnP manager must also be able to reassign resources to accommodate the needs of dynamically added devices.

- Loading appropriate drivers is another responsibility of the PnP manager. The PnP manager determines, based on the identification of a device, whether a driver capable of managing the device is installed on the system, and if one is, it instructs the I/O manager to load it. If a suitable driver isn't installed, the kernel-mode PnP manager communicates with the user-mode PnP manager to install the device, possibly requesting the user's assistance in locating a suitable driver.

- The PnP manager also implements application and driver mechanisms for the detection of hardware configuration changes. Applications or drivers sometimes require a specific hardware device to function, so Windows includes a means for them to request notification of the presence, addition, or removal of devices.

- It provides a place for storing device state, and it participates in system setup, upgrade, migration, and offline image management.

- It supports network connected devices, such as network projectors and printers, by allowing specialized bus drivers to detect the network as a bus and create device nodes for the devices running on it.

Level of Plug and Play support

Windows aims to provide full support for Plug and Play, but the level of support possible depends on the attached devices and installed drivers. If a single device or driver doesn't support Plug and Play, the extent of Plug and Play support for the system can be compromised. In addition, a driver that doesn't support Plug and Play might prevent other devices from being usable by the system. Table 6-6 shows the outcome of various combinations of devices and drivers that can and can't support Plug and Play.

TABLE 6-6   Device and driver plug-and-play capability

Type of Device	Plug-and-Play Driver	Non–Plug and Play Driver
Plug and play	Full plug and play	No plug and play
Non–plug and play	Possible partial plug and play	No plug and play

A device that isn't Plug and Play–compatible is one that doesn't support automatic detection, such as a legacy ISA sound card. Because the operating system doesn't know where the hardware physically lies, certain operations—such as laptop undocking, sleep, and hibernation—are disallowed. However, if a Plug and Play driver is manually installed for the device, the driver can at least implement PnP manager–directed resource assignment for the device.

Drivers that aren't Plug and Play–compatible include legacy drivers, such as those that ran on Windows NT 4. Although these drivers might continue to function on later versions of Windows, the PnP manager can't reconfigure the resources assigned to such devices in the event that resource reallocation is necessary to accommodate the needs of a dynamically added device. For example, a device might be able to use I/O memory ranges A and B, and during the boot, the PnP manager assigns it range A. If a device that can use only A is attached to the system later, the PnP manager can't direct the first device's driver to reconfigure itself to use range B. This prevents the second device from obtaining required resources, which results in the device being unavailable for use by the system. Legacy drivers also impair a machine's ability to sleep or hibernate. (See the section "The power manager" later in this chapter for more details.)

Device enumeration

Device enumeration occurs when the system boots, resumes from hibernation, or is explicitly instructed to do so (for example, by clicking Scan for Hardware Changes in the Device Manager UI). The PnP manager builds a device tree (described momentarily) and compares it to its known stored tree from a previous enumeration, if any. For a boot or resume from hibernation, the stored device tree is empty. Newly discovered devices and removed devices require special treatment, such as loading appropriate drivers (for a newly discovered device) and notifying drivers of a removed device.

The PnP manager begins device enumeration with a virtual bus driver called *Root*, which represents the entire computer system and acts as the bus driver for non–Plug and Play drivers and the HAL. The HAL acts as a bus driver that enumerates devices directly attached to the motherboard as well as system components such as batteries. Instead of actually enumerating, however, the HAL relies on the hardware description the Setup process recorded in the registry to detect the primary bus (in most cases, a PCI bus) and devices such as batteries and fans.

The primary bus driver enumerates the devices on its bus, possibly finding other buses, for which the PnP manager initializes drivers. Those drivers in turn can detect other devices, including other subsidiary buses. This recursive process of enumeration, driver loading (if the driver isn't already loaded), and further enumeration proceeds until all the devices on the system have been detected and configured.

As the bus drivers report detected devices to the PnP manager, the PnP manager creates an internal tree called a *device tree* that represents the relationships between devices. Nodes in the tree are called *device nodes*, or *devnodes*. A devnode contains information about the device objects that represent the device as well as other Plug and Play–related information stored in the devnode by the PnP manager. Figure 6-32 shows an example of a simplified device tree. A PCI bus serves as the system's primary bus, which USB, ISA, and SCSI buses are connected to.

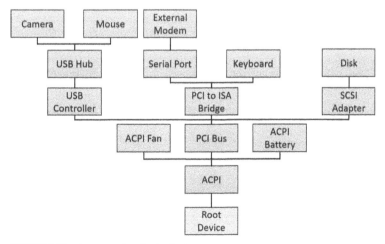

FIGURE 6-32 An example of a device tree.

The Device Manager utility, which is accessible from the Computer Management snap-in in the Programs/Administrative Tools folder of the Start menu (and also from the Device Manager link of the System utility in Control Panel), shows a simple list of devices present on a system in its default configuration. You can also select the Devices by Connection option from the Device Manager's View menu to see the devices as they relate to the device tree. Figure 6-33 shows an example of the Device Manager's Devices by connection view.

FIGURE 6-33 Device Manager, with the device tree shown.

EXPERIMENT: Dumping the device tree

A more detailed way to view the device tree than using Device Manager is to use the !devnode kernel debugger command. Specifying 0 1 as command options dumps the internal device tree devnode structures, indenting entries to show their hierarchical relationships, as shown here:

```
1kd> !devnode 0 1
Dumping IopRootDeviceNode (= 0x85161a98)
DevNode 0x85161a98 for PDO 0x84d10390
  InstancePath is "HTREE\ROOT\0"
  State = DeviceNodeStarted (0x308)
  Previous State = DeviceNodeEnumerateCompletion (0x30d)
  DevNode 0x8515bea8 for PDO 0x8515b030
  DevNode 0x8515c698 for PDO 0x8515c820
    InstancePath is "Root\ACPI_HAL\0000"
    State = DeviceNodeStarted (0x308)
```

```
      Previous State = DeviceNodeEnumerateCompletion (0x30d)
    DevNode 0x84d1c5b0 for PDO 0x84d1c738
      InstancePath is "ACPI_HAL\PNP0C08\0"
      ServiceName is "ACPI"
      State = DeviceNodeStarted (0x308)
      Previous State = DeviceNodeEnumerateCompletion (0x30d)
      DevNode 0x85ebf1b0 for PDO 0x85ec0210
        InstancePath is "ACPI\GenuineIntel_-_x86_Family_6_Model_15\_0"
        ServiceName is "intelppm"
        State = DeviceNodeStarted (0x308)
        Previous State = DeviceNodeEnumerateCompletion (0x30d)
      DevNode 0x85ed6970 for PDO 0x8515e618
        InstancePath is "ACPI\GenuineIntel_-_x86_Family_6_Model_15\_1"
        ServiceName is "intelppm"
        State = DeviceNodeStarted (0x308)
        Previous State = DeviceNodeEnumerateCompletion (0x30d)
      DevNode 0x85ed75c8 for PDO 0x85ed79e8
        InstancePath is "ACPI\ThermalZone\THM_"
        State = DeviceNodeStarted (0x308)
        Previous State = DeviceNodeEnumerateCompletion (0x30d)
      DevNode 0x85ed6cd8 for PDO 0x85ed6858
        InstancePath is "ACPI\pnp0c14\0"
        ServiceName is "WmiAcpi"
        State = DeviceNodeStarted (0x308)
        Previous State = DeviceNodeEnumerateCompletion (0x30d)
      DevNode 0x85ed7008 for PDO 0x85ed6730
        InstancePath is "ACPI\ACPI0003\2&daba3ff&2"
        ServiceName is "CmBatt"
        State = DeviceNodeStarted (0x308)
        Previous State = DeviceNodeEnumerateCompletion (0x30d)
      DevNode 0x85ed7e60 for PDO 0x84d2e030
        InstancePath is "ACPI\PNP0C0A\1"
        ServiceName is "CmBatt"
...
```

Information shown for each devnode includes the InstancePath, which is the name of the device's enumeration registry key stored under HKLM\SYSTEM\CurrentControlSet\Enum, and the ServiceName, which corresponds to the device's driver registry key under HKLM\SYSTEM\CurrentControlSet\Services. To see the resources assigned to each devnode, such as interrupts, ports, and memory, specify 0 3 as the command options for the !devnode command.

Device stacks

As devnodes are created by the PnP manager, driver objects and device objects are created to manage and logically represent the linkage between the devices that make up the devnode. This linkage is called a *device stack* (briefly discussed in the "IRP flow" section earlier in this chapter). You can think of the device stack as an ordered list of device object/driver pairs. Each device stack is built from the bottom to the top. Figure 6-34 shows an example of a devnode (a reprint of Figure 6-6), with seven device objects (all managing the same physical device). Each devnode contains at least two devices (PDO and FDO), but can contain more device objects. A device stack consists of the following:

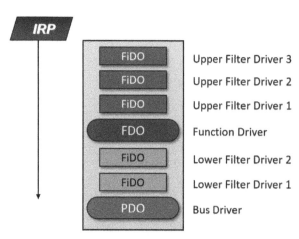

FIGURE 6-34 Devnode (device stack).

- A physical device object (PDO) that the PnP manager instructs a bus driver to create when the bus driver reports the presence of a device on its bus during enumeration. The PDO represents the physical interface to the device and is always at the bottom of the device stack.

- One or more optional filter device objects (FiDOs) that layer between the PDO and the functional device object (FDO; described in the next bullet), called *lower filters* (the term "lower" is always considered in relation to the FDO). These may be used for intercepting IRPs coming out of the FDO and towards the bus driver (which may be of interest to bus filters).

- One (and only one) functional device object (FDO) that is created by the driver, which is called a *function driver*, that the PnP manager loads to manage a detected device. An FDO represents the logical interface to a device, having the most "intimate" knowledge of the functionality provided by the device. A function driver can also act as a bus driver if devices are attached to the device represented by the FDO. The function driver often creates an interface (essentially a name) to the FDO's corresponding PDO so that applications and other drivers can open the device and interact with it. Sometimes function drivers are divided into a separate class/port driver and miniport driver that work together to manage I/O for the FDO.

- One or more optional FiDOs that layer above the FDO, called *upper filters*. These get first crack at an IRP header for the FDO.

 Note The various device objects have different names in Figure 6-34 to make them easier to describe. However, they are all instances of DEVICE_OBJECT structures.

Device stacks are built from the bottom up and rely on the I/O manager's layering functionality, so IRPs flow from the top of a device stack toward the bottom. However, any level in the device stack can choose to complete an IRP, as described in the "IRP flow" section earlier in this chapter.

Device-stack driver loading

How does the PnP manager find the correct drivers as part of building the device stack? The registry has this information scattered in three important keys (and their subkeys), shown in Table 6-7. (Note that *CCS* is short for *CurrentControlSet*.)

TABLE 6-7 Important registry keys for plug-and-play driver loading

Registry Key	Short Name	Description
HKLM\System\CCS\Enum	Hardware key	Settings for known hardware devices
HKLM\System\CCS\Control\Class	Class key	Settings for device types
HKLM\System\CCS\Services	Software key	Settings for drivers

When a bus driver performs device enumeration and discovers a new device, it first creates a PDO to represent the existence of the physical device that has been detected. Next, it informs the PnP manager by calling `IoInvalidateDeviceRelations` (documented in the WDK) with the `BusRelations` enumeration value and the PDO, indicating to the PnP manager that a change on its bus has been detected. In response, the PnP manager asks the bus driver (through an IRP) for the device identifier.

The identifiers are bus-specific; for example, a USB device identifier consists of a vendor ID (VID) for the hardware vendor that made the device and a product ID (PID) that the vendor assigned to the device. For a PCI device, a similar vendor ID is required, along with a device ID, to uniquely identify the device within a vendor (plus some optional components; see the WDK for more information on device ID formats). Together, these IDs form what Plug and Play calls a *device ID*. The PnP manager also queries the bus driver for an instance ID to help it distinguish different instances of the same hardware. The instance ID can describe either a bus-relative location (for example, the USB port) or a globally unique descriptor (for example, a serial number).

The device ID and instance ID are combined to form a device instance ID (DIID), which the PnP manager uses to locate the device's key under the Hardware key shown in Table 6-7. The subkeys under that key have the form <Enumerator>\<Device ID>\<Instance ID>, where the enumerator is a bus driver, the device ID is a unique identifier for a type of device, and the instance ID uniquely identifies different instances of the same hardware.

Figure 6-35 presents an example of an enumeration subkey of an Intel display card. The device's key contains descriptive data and includes values named `Service` and `ClassGUID` (which are obtained from a driver's INF file upon installation) that help the PnP manager locate the device's drivers as follows:

- The `Service` value is looked up in the Software key, and there the path to the driver (SYS file) is stored in the `ImagePath` value. Figure 6-36 shows the Software subkey named *igfx* (from Figure 6-35) where the Intel display driver can be located. The PnP manager will load that driver (if it's not already loaded), call its add-device routine, and there the driver will create the FDO.

- If a value named `LowerFilters` is present, it contains a multiple string list of drivers to load as lower filters, which can be located in the Software subkey. The PnP manager loads these drivers before loading the driver associated with the `Service` value above.

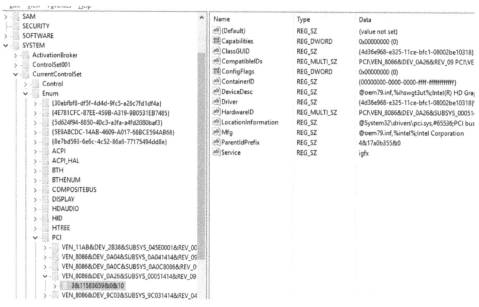

FIGURE 6-35 Example of a Hardware subkey.

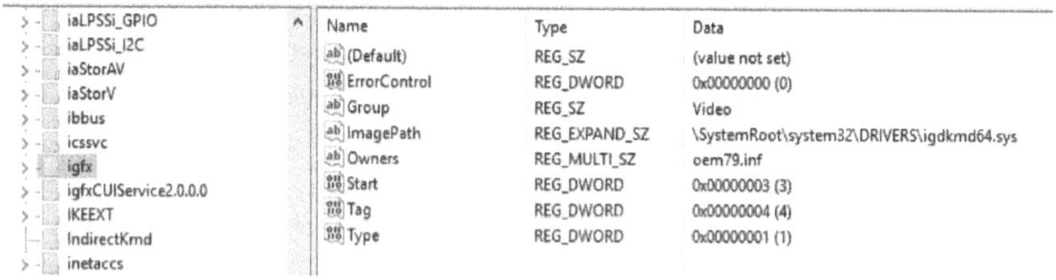

FIGURE 6-36 Example of a Software subkey.

- If a value named `UpperFilters` is present, it indicates a list of driver names (under the Software key, similar to `LowerFilters`) which the PnP manager will load in much the same way after it loads the driver pointed to by the `Service` value.

- The `ClassGUID` value represents the general type of device (display, keyboard, disk, etc.), and points to a subkey under the Class key (from Table 6-7). The key represents settings applicable to all drivers for that type of device. In particular, if the values `LowerFilters` and/or `UpperFilters` are present, they are treated just like the same values in the Hardware key of the particular device. This allows, for example, the loading of an upper filter for keyboard devices, regardless of the particular keyboard or the vendor. Figure 6-37 shows the class key for keyboard devices. Notice the friendly name (Keyboard), although the GUID is what matters (the decision on the particular class is provided as part of the installation INF file). An `UpperFilters` value exists, listing the system provided keyboard class driver that always loads as part of any keyboard devnode. (You can also see the `IconPath` value that is used as the icon for the keyboard type in the Device Manager's UI.)

Name	Type	Data
(Default)	REG_SZ	(value not set)
Class	REG_SZ	Keyboard
ClassDesc	REG_SZ	@%SystemRoot%\System32\SysClass.Dll,-3002
IconPath	REG_MULTI_SZ	%SystemRoot%\System32\setupapi.dll,-3
NoInstallClass	REG_SZ	1
UpperFilters	REG_MULTI_SZ	kbdclass

Left tree pane:
- {4d36e967-e325-11ce-bfc1-08002be
- {4d36e968-e325-11ce-bfc1-08002be
- {4d36e969-e325-11ce-bfc1-08002be
- {4d36e96a-e325-11ce-bfc1-08002be
- {4d36e96b-e325-11ce-bfc1-08002be
- {4d36e96c-e325-11ce-bfc1-08002be
- {4d36e96d-e325-11ce-bfc1-08002be
- {4d36e96e-e325-11ce-bfc1-08002be

FIGURE 6-37 The keyboard class key.

To summarize, the order of driver loading for a devnode is as follows:

1. The bus driver is loaded, creating the PDO.

2. Any lower filters listed in the Hardware instance key are loaded, in the order listed (multi string), creating their filter device objects (FiDOs in Figure 6-34).

3. Any lower filters listed in the corresponding Class key are loaded in the order listed, creating their FiDOs.

4. The driver listed in the Service value is loaded, creating the FDO.

5. Any upper filters listed in the Hardware instance key are loaded, in the order listed, creating their FiDOs.

6. Any upper filters listed in the corresponding Class key are loaded in the order listed creating their FiDOs.

To deal with multifunction devices (such as all-in-one printers or cell phones with integrated camera and music player functionalities), Windows also supports a container ID property that can be associated with a devnode. The container ID is a GUID that is unique to a single instance of a physical device and shared between all the function devnodes that belong to it, as shown in Figure 6-38.

Windows PC

Other devnode:
• ContainerID: {3dd3e49d-869d-489c-aad4-255bef9f0043}

Printer devnode properties:
• ContainerID: {a6858a00-5bc9-47ac-896d-ca96a44bc9ad}

Scanner devnode properties:
• ContainerID: {a6858a00-5bc9-47ac-896d-ca96a44bc9ad}

Fax devnode properties:
• ContainerID: {a6858a00-5bc9-47ac-896d-ca96a44bc9ad}

Other devnode:
• ContainerID: {5bdbf3d1-a63e-4fb1-903b-4f0f970c8da5}

Multifunction device container

Plug and Play devnodes

Multifunction device
• Printer
• Scanner
• Fax

FIGURE 6-38 All-in-one printer with a unique ID as seen by the PnP manager.

The container ID is a property that, similar to the instance ID, is reported back by the bus driver of the corresponding hardware. Then, when the device is being enumerated, all devnodes associated with the same PDO share the container ID. Because Windows already supports many buses out of the box—such as PnP-X, Bluetooth, and USB—most device drivers can simply return the bus-specific ID, from which Windows will generate the corresponding container ID. For other kinds of devices or buses, the driver can generate its own unique ID through software.

Finally, when device drivers do not supply a container ID, Windows can make educated guesses by querying the topology for the bus, when that's available, through mechanisms such as ACPI. By understanding whether a certain device is a child of another, and whether it is removable, hot-pluggable, or user-reachable (as opposed to an internal motherboard component), Windows is able to assign container IDs to device nodes that reflect multifunction devices correctly.

The final end-user benefit of grouping devices by container IDs is visible in the Devices and Printers UI. This feature is able to display the scanner, printer, and faxing components of an all-in-one printer as a single graphical element instead of three distinct devices. For example, in Figure 6-39, the HP 6830 printer/fax/scanner is identified as a single device.

FIGURE 6-39 The Devices and Printers Control Panel applet.

EXPERIMENT: Viewing detailed devnode information in Device Manager

The Device Manager applet shows detailed information about a device node on its Details tab. The tab allows you to view an assortment of fields, including the devnode's device instance ID, hardware ID, service name, filters, and power capabilities.

The following screen shows the selection combo box of the Details tab expanded to reveal some of the types of information you can access:

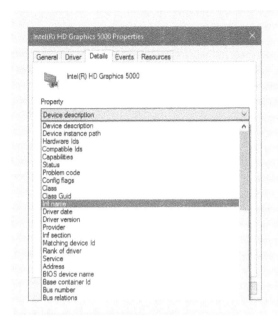

Driver support for Plug and Play

To support Plug and Play, a driver must implement a Plug and Play dispatch routine (IRP_MJ_PNP), a power-management dispatch routine (IRP_MJ_POWER, described in the section "The power manager" later in this chapter), and an add-device routine. Bus drivers must support Plug and Play requests that are different than the ones that function or filter drivers support, however. For example, when the PnP manager guides device enumeration during the system boot, it asks bus drivers for a description of the devices that they find on their respective buses through PnP IRPs.

Function and filter drivers prepare to manage their devices in their add-device routines, but they don't actually communicate with the device hardware. Instead, they wait for the PnP manager to send a start-device command (IRP_MN_START_DEVICE minor PnP IRP code) for the device to their Plug and Play dispatch routine. Before sending the start-device command, the PnP manager performs resource arbitration to decide what resources to assign the device. The start-device command includes the resource assignment that the PnP manager determines during resource arbitration. When a driver receives a start-device command, it can configure its device to use the specified resources. If an application tries to open a device that hasn't finished starting, it receives an error indicating that the device does not exist.

After a device has started, the PnP manager can send the driver additional Plug and Play commands, including ones related to the device's removal from the system or to resource reassignment. For example, when the user invokes the remove/eject device utility, shown in Figure 6-40 (accessible by clicking the USB connector icon in the taskbar notification area), to tell Windows to eject a USB flash drive, the PnP manager sends a query-remove notification to any applications that have registered for Plug and Play notifications for the device. Applications typically register for notifications on their handles, which they close during a query-remove notification. If no applications veto the query-remove request, the PnP manager sends a query-remove command to the driver that owns the device being ejected (IRP_MN_QUERY_REMOVE_DEVICE). At that point, the driver has a chance to deny the removal or to ensure that any pending I/O operations involving the device have completed, and to begin rejecting further I/O requests aimed at the device. If the driver agrees to the remove request and no open handles to the device remain, the PnP manager next sends a remove command to the driver (IRP_MN_REMOVE_DEVICE) to request that the driver stop accessing the device and release any resources the driver has allocated on behalf of the device.

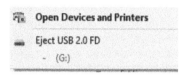

FIGURE 6-40 The remove/eject device utility.

When the PnP manager needs to reassign a device's resources, it first asks the driver whether it can temporarily suspend further activity on the device by sending the driver a query-stop command (IRP_MN_QUERY_STOP_DEVICE). The driver either agrees to the request (if doing so won't cause data loss or corruption) or denies the request. As with a query-remove command, if the driver agrees to the request, the driver completes pending I/O operations and won't initiate further I/O requests for the device that can't be aborted and subsequently restarted. The driver typically queues new I/O requests so that the resource reshuffling is transparent to applications currently accessing the device. The PnP manager then sends the driver a stop command (IRP_MN_STOP_DEVICE). At that point, the PnP manager can direct the driver to assign different resources to the device and once again send the driver a start-device command for the device.

The various Plug and Play commands essentially guide a device through an operational state machine, forming a well-defined state-transition table, which is shown in Figure 6-41. (The state diagram reflects the state machine implemented by function drivers. Bus drivers implement a more complex state machine.) Each transition in Figure 6-41 is marked by its minor IRP constant name without the IRP_MN_ prefix. One state that we haven't discussed is the one that results from the PnP manager's command (IRP_MN_SURPRISE_REMOVAL). This command results when either a user removes a device without warning, as when the user ejects a PCMCIA card without using the remove/eject utility, or the device fails. The command tells the driver to immediately cease all interaction with the device because the device is no longer attached to the system and to cancel any pending I/O requests.

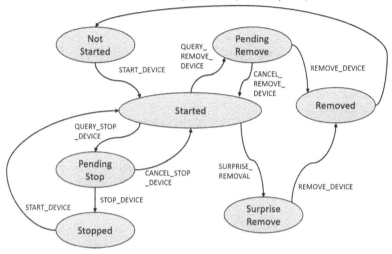

Device detected, driver loaded, DriverEntry called, AddDevice called

FIGURE 6-41 Device plug-and-play state transitions.

Plug-and-play driver installation

If the PnP manager encounters a device for which no driver is installed, it relies on the user-mode PnP manager to guide the installation process. If the device is detected during the system boot, a devnode is defined for the device, but the loading process is postponed until the user-mode PnP manager starts. (The user-mode PnP manager service is implemented in Umpnpmgr.dll hosted in a standard Svchost. exe instance.)

The components involved in a driver's installation are shown in Figure 6-42. Dark-shaded objects in the figure correspond to components generally supplied by the system, whereas lighter-shaded objects are those included in a driver's installation files. First, a bus driver informs the PnP manager of a device it enumerates using a Device ID (1). The PnP manager checks the registry for the presence of a corresponding function driver, and when it doesn't find one, it informs the user-mode PnP manager (2) of the new device by its Device ID. The user-mode PnP manager first tries to perform an automatic install without user intervention. If the installation process involves the posting of dialog boxes that require user interaction and the currently logged-on user has administrator privileges, the user-mode PnP manager launches the Rundll32.exe application (the same application that hosts classic .cpl Control Panel utilities) to execute the Hardware Installation Wizard (3) (%SystemRoot%\System32\Newdev. dll). If the currently logged-on user doesn't have administrator privileges (or if no user is logged on) and the installation of the device requires user interaction, the user-mode PnP manager defers the installation until a privileged user logs on. The Hardware Installation Wizard uses Setupapi.dll and CfgMgr32.dll (configuration manager) API functions to locate INF files that correspond to drivers that are compatible with the detected device. This process might involve having the user insert installation media containing a vendor's INF files, or the wizard might locate a suitable INF file in the driver store (%SystemRoot%\System32\DriverStore) that contains drivers that ship with Windows or others that are downloaded through Windows Update. Installation is performed in two steps. In the first, the third-party driver developer imports the driver package into the driver store, and in the second, the system performs the actual installation, which is always done through the %SystemRoot%\System32\Drvinst. exe process.

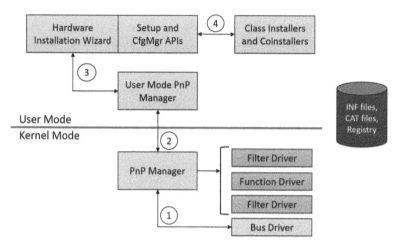

FIGURE 6-42 Driver installation components.

To find drivers for the new device, the installation process gets a list of hardware IDs (discussed earlier) and compatible IDs from the bus driver. Compatible IDs are more generic—for example a USB mouse from a specific vendor might have a special button that does something unique, but a compatible ID for a generic mouse can utilize a more generic driver that ships with Windows if the specific driver is not available and at least provide the basic, common functionality of a mouse.

These IDs describe all the various ways the hardware might be identified in a driver installation file (INF). The lists are ordered so that the most specific description of the hardware is listed first. If matches are found in multiple INFs, the following points apply:

- More-precise matches are preferred over less-precise matches.

- Digitally signed INFs are preferred over unsigned ones.

- Newer signed INFs are preferred over older signed ones.

 Note If a match is found based on a compatible ID, the Hardware Installation wizard can prompt for media in case a more up-to-date driver came with the hardware.

The INF file locates the function driver's files and contains instructions that fill in the driver's enumeration and class keys in the registry, copy required files, and the INF file might direct the Hardware Installation Wizard to (4) launch class or device co-installer DLLs that perform class-specific or device-specific installation steps, such as displaying configuration dialog boxes that let the user specify settings for a device. Finally, when the drivers that make up a devnode load, the device/driver stack is built (5).

EXPERIMENT: Looking at a driver's INF file

When a driver or other software that has an INF file is installed, the system copies its INF file to the %SystemRoot%\Inf directory. One file that will always be there is Keyboard.inf because it's the INF file for the keyboard class driver. View its contents by opening it in Notepad and you should see something like this (anything after a semicolon is a comment):

```
;
; KEYBOARD.INF  -- This file contains descriptions of Keyboard class devices
;
;
; Copyright (c) Microsoft Corporation.  All rights reserved.

[Version]
Signature  ="$Windows NT$"
Class      =Keyboard
ClassGUID  ={4D36E96B-E325-11CE-BFC1-08002BE10318}
Provider   =%MSFT%
DriverVer=06/21/2006,10.0.10586.0

[SourceDisksNames]
3426=windows cd

[SourceDisksFiles]
i8042prt.sys   = 3426
kbdclass.sys   = 3426
kbdhid.sys     = 3426
...
```

An INF has the classic INI format, with sections in square brackets and underneath are key/value pairs separated by an equal sign. An INF is not "executed" from start to end sequentially; instead, it's built more like a tree, where certain values point to sections with the value name where execution continues. (Consult the WDK for the details.)

If you search the file for .sys, you'll come across sections that direct the user-mode PnP manager to install the i8042prt.sys and kbdclass.sys drivers:

```
...
[i8042prt_CopyFiles]
i8042prt.sys,,,0x100

[KbdClass.CopyFiles]
kbdclass.sys,,,0x100
...
```

Before installing a driver, the user-mode PnP manager checks the system's driver-signing policy. If the settings specify that the system should block or warn of the installation of unsigned drivers, the user-mode PnP manager checks the driver's INF file for an entry that locates a catalog (a file that ends with the .cat extension) containing the driver's digital signature.

Microsoft's WHQL tests the drivers included with Windows and those submitted by hardware vendors. When a driver passes the WHQL tests, it is "signed" by Microsoft. This means that WHQL obtains a *hash*, or unique value representing the driver's files, including its image file, and then cryptographically signs it with Microsoft's private driver-signing key. The signed hash is stored in a catalog file and included on the Windows installation media or returned to the vendor that submitted the driver for inclusion with its driver.

EXPERIMENT: Viewing catalog files

When you install a component such as a driver that includes a catalog file, Windows copies the catalog file to a directory under %SystemRoot%\System32\Catroot. Navigate to that directory in Explorer, and you'll find a subdirectory that contains .cat files. For example, Nt5.cat and Nt5ph. cat store the signatures and page hashes for Windows system files.

If you open one of the catalog files, a dialog box appears with two pages. The page labeled "General" shows information about the signature on the catalog file, and the Security Catalog page has the hashes of the components that are signed with the catalog file. This screenshot of a catalog file for an Intel audio driver shows the hash for the audio driver SYS file. Other hashes in the catalog are associated with the various support DLLs that ship with the driver.

As it installs a driver, the user-mode PnP manager extracts the driver's signature from its catalog file, decrypts the signature using the public half of Microsoft's driver-signing private/public key pair, and compares the resulting hash with a hash of the driver file it's about to install. If the hashes match, the driver is verified as having passed WHQL testing. If a driver fails the signature verification, the user-mode PnP manager acts according to the settings of the system driver-signing policy, either failing the installation attempt, warning the user that the driver is unsigned, or silently installing the driver.

Note Drivers installed using setup programs that manually configure the registry and copy driver files to a system and driver files that are dynamically loaded by applications aren't checked for signatures by the PnP manager's signing policy. Instead, they are checked by the kernel-mode code-signing policy described in Chapter 8 in Part 2. Only drivers installed using INF files are validated against the PnP manager's driver-signing policy.

Note The user-mode PnP manager also checks whether the driver it's about to install is on the *protected driver list* maintained by Windows Update and, if so, blocks the installation with a warning to the user. Drivers that are known to have incompatibilities or bugs are added to the list and blocked from installation.

General driver loading and installation

The preceding section showed how drivers for hardware devices are discovered and loaded by the PnP manager. These drivers mostly load "on demand," meaning such a driver is not loaded unless needed—a device that the driver is responsible for enters the system; conversely, if all devices managed by a driver are removed, the driver will be unloaded.

More generally, the Software key in the registry holds settings for drivers (as well as Windows Services). Although services are managed within the same registry key, they are user-mode programs and have no connection to kernel drivers (although the Service Control Manager can be used to load both services and device drivers). This section focuses on drivers; for a complete treatment of services, see Chapter 9 in Part 2.

Driver loading

Each subkey under the Software key (HKLM\System\CurrentControlSet\Services) holds a set of values that control some static aspects of a driver (or service). One such value, `ImagePath`, was encountered already when we discussed the loading process of PnP drivers. Figure 6-36 shows an example of a driver key and Table 6-8 summarizes the most important values in a driver's Software key (see Chapter 9 in Part 2 for a complete list).

The `Start` value indicates the phase in which a driver (or service) is loaded. There are two main differences between device drivers and services in this regard:

- Only device drivers can specify `Start` values of boot-start (0) or system-start (1). This is because at these phases, no user mode exists yet, so services cannot be loaded.

- Device drivers can use the `Group` and `Tag` values (not shown in Table 6-8) to control the order of loading within a phase of the boot, but unlike services, they can't specify `DependOnGroup` or `DependOnService` values (see Chapter 9 in Part 2 for more details).

TABLE 6-8 Important values in a driver's registry key

Value Name	Description
ImagePath	This is the path to the driver's image file (SYS).
Type	This indicates whether this key represents a service or a driver. A value of 1 means a driver and a value of 2 means a file system (or filter) driver. Values of 16 (0x10) and 32 (0x20) mean a service. See Chapter 9 in Part 2 for more information.
Start	This indicates when the driver should load. The options are as follows: **0 (SERVICE_BOOT_START)** The driver is loaded by the boot loader. **1 (SERVICE_SYSTEM_START)** The driver is loaded after the executive is initialized. **2 (SERVICE_AUTO_START)** The driver is loaded by the service control manager. **3 (SERVICE_DEMAND_START)** The driver is loaded on demand. **4 (SERVICE_DISABLED)** The driver is not loaded.

Chapter 11, "Startup and shutdown, in Part 2 describes the phases of the boot process and explains that a driver Start value of 0 means that the operating system loader loads the driver. A Start value of 1 means that the I/O manager loads the driver after the executive subsystems have finished initializing. The I/O manager calls driver initialization routines in the order that the drivers load within a boot phase. Like Windows services, drivers use the Group value in their registry key to specify which group they belong to; the registry value HKLM\SYSTEM\CurrentControlSet\Control\ServiceGroupOrder\List determines the order that groups are loaded within a boot phase.

A driver can further refine its load order by including a Tag value to control its order within a group. The I/O manager sorts the drivers within each group according to the Tag values defined in the drivers' registry keys. Drivers without a tag go to the end of the list in their group. You might assume that the I/O manager initializes drivers with lower-number tags before it initializes drivers with higher-number tags, but such isn't necessarily the case. The registry key HKLM\SYSTEM\CurrentControlSet\Control\ GroupOrderList defines tag precedence within a group; with this key, Microsoft and device-driver developers can take liberties with redefining the integer number system.

 Note The use of Group and Tag is reminiscent from the early Windows NT days. These tags are rarely used in practice. Most drivers should not have dependencies on other drivers (only on kernel libraries linked to the driver, such as NDIS.sys).

Here are the guidelines by which drivers set their Start value:

■ Non–Plug and Play drivers set their Start value to reflect the boot phase they want to load in.

■ Drivers, including both Plug and Play and non–Plug and Play drivers, that must be loaded by the boot loader during the system boot specify a Start value of boot-start (0). Examples include system bus drivers and the boot file-system driver.

■ A driver that isn't required for booting the system and that detects a device that a system bus driver can't enumerate specifies a Start value of system-start (1). An example is the serial port driver, which informs the PnP manager of the presence of standard PC serial ports that were detected by Setup and recorded in the registry.

- A non–Plug and Play driver or file-system driver that doesn't have to be present when the system boots specifies a `Start` value of auto-start (2). An example is the Multiple Universal Naming Convention (UNC) Provider (MUP) driver, which provides support for UNC-based path names to remote resources (for example, \\RemoteComputerName\SomeShare).

- Plug and Play drivers that aren't required to boot the system specify a `Start` value of demand-start (3). Examples include network adapter drivers.

The only purpose that the `Start` values for Plug and Play drivers and drivers for enumerable devices have is to ensure that the operating system loader loads the driver—if the driver is required for the system to boot successfully. Beyond that, the PnP manager's device enumeration process determines the load order for Plug and Play drivers.

Driver installation

As we've seen, Plug and Play drivers require an INF file for installation. The INF includes the hardware device IDs this driver can handle and the instructions for copying files and setting registry values. Other type of drivers (such as file system drivers, file system filters and network filters) require an INF as well, which includes a unique set of values for the particular type of driver.

Software-only drivers (such as the one Process Explorer uses) can use an INF for installation, but don't have to. These can be installed by a call to the `CreateService` API (or use a tool such as sc.exe that wraps it), as Process Explorer does after extracting its driver from a resource within the executable (if running with elevated permissions). As the API name suggests, it's used to install services as well as drivers. The arguments to `CreateService` indicate whether it's installing a driver or a service, the `Start` value and other parameters (see the Windows SDK documentation for the details). Once installed, a call to `StartService` loads the driver (or service), calling `DriverEntry` (for a driver) as usual.

A software-only driver typically creates a device object with a name its clients know. For example, Process Explorer creates a device named PROCEXP152 that is then used by Process Explorer in a `Create-File` call, followed by calls such as `DeviceIoControl` to send requests to the driver (turned into IRPs by the I/O manager). Figure 6-43 shows the Process Explorer object symbolic link (using the WinObj Sysinternals tool) in the \GLOBAL?? directory (recall that the names in this directory are accessible to user mode clients) that's created by Process Explorer the first time it's running with elevated privileges. Notice that it points to the real device object under the \Device directory and it has the same name (which is not a requirement).

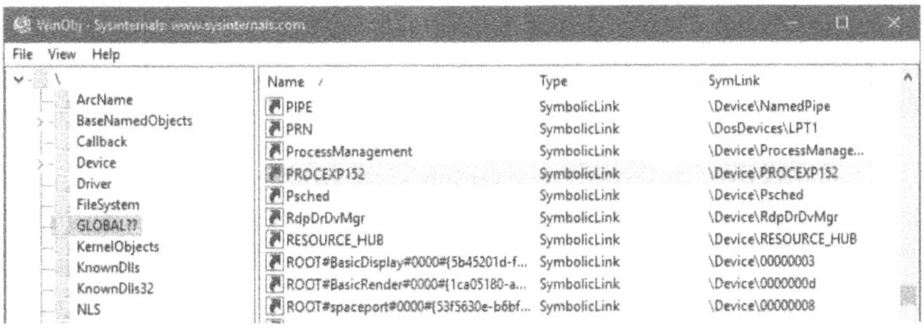

FIGURE 6-43 Process Explorer's symbolic link and device name.

The Windows Driver Foundation

The Windows Driver Foundation (WDF) is a framework for developing drivers that simplifies common tasks such as handing Plug and Play and Power IRPs correctly. WDF includes the Kernel-Mode Driver Framework (KMDF) and the User-Mode Driver Framework (UMDF). WDF is now open source and can be found at *https://github.com/Microsoft/Windows-Driver-Frameworks*. Table 6-9 shows the Windows version support (for Windows 7 and later) for KMDF. Table 6-10 shows the same for UMDF.

TABLE 6-9   KMDF versions

KMDF Version	Release Method	Included in Windows	Drivers Using It Run On
1.9	Windows 7 WDK	Windows 7	Windows XP and later
1.11	Windows 8 WDK	Windows 8	Windows Vista and later
1.13	Windows 8.1 WDK	Windows 8.1	Windows 8.1 and later
1.15	Windows 10 WDK	Windows 10	Windows 10, Windows Server 2016
1.17	Windows 10 version 1511 WDK	Windows 10 version 1511	Windows 10 version 1511 and later, Windows Server 2016
1.19	Windows 10 version 1607 WDK	Windows 10 version 1607	Windows 10 version 1607 and later, Windows Server 2016

TABLE 6-10   UMDF versions

UMDF Version	Release Method	Included in Windows	Drivers Using It Run On
1.9	Windows 7 WDK	Windows 7	Windows XP and later
1.11	Windows 8 WDK	Windows 8	Windows Vista and later
2.0	Windows 8.1 WDK	Windows 8.1	Windows 8.1 and later
2.15	Windows 10 WDK	Windows 10	Windows 10 and later, Windows Server 2016
2.17	Windows 10 version 1511 WDK	Windows 10 version 1511	Windows 10 version 1511 and later, Windows Server 2016
2.19	Windows 10 version 1607 WDK	Windows 10 version 1607	Windows 10 version 1607, Windows Server 2016

Windows 10 introduced the concept of Universal Drivers, briefly described in Chapter 2, "System architecture." These drivers use a common set of DDIs implemented in multiple editions of Windows 10—from IoT Core, to Mobile, to desktops. Universal drivers can be built with KMDF, UMDF 2.*x*, or WDM. Building such drivers is relatively easy with the aid of Visual Studio, where the Target Platform setting is set to Universal. Any DDI that is outside the boundaries of Universal will be flagged by the compiler.

UMDF versions 1.*x* used a COM based model for programming drivers, which is a very different programming model than KMDF, which is using object-based C. UMDF 2 has been aligned with KMDF and provides an almost identical API, reducing overall cost associated with WDF driver development; in fact, UMDF 2.*x* drivers can be converted to KMDF if the need arises with little work. UMDF 1.*x* will not be discussed in this book; consult the WDK for more information.

The following sections discuss KMDF and UMDF, which essentially behave in a consistent manner, no matter the exact OS they're running on.

Kernel-Mode Driver Framework

We've already discussed some details about the Windows Driver Foundation (WDF) in Chapter 2. In this section, we'll take a deeper look at the components and functionality provided by the kernel-mode part of the framework, KMDF. Note that this section will only briefly touch on some of the core architecture of KMDF. For a much more complete overview on the subject, please refer to the Windows Driver Kit documentation.

 Note Most of the details presented in this section are the same for UMDF 2.x, with the exceptions discussed in the next section.

Structure and operation of a KMDF driver

First, let's look at which kinds of drivers or devices are supported by KMDF. In general, any WDM-conformant driver should be supported by KMDF, as long as it performs standard I/O processing and IRP manipulation. KMDF is not suitable for drivers that don't use the Windows kernel API directly but instead perform library calls into existing port and class drivers. These types of drivers cannot use KMDF because they only provide callbacks for the actual WDM drivers that do the I/O processing. Additionally, if a driver provides its own dispatch functions instead of relying on a port or class driver, IEEE 1394, ISA, PCI, PCMCIA, and SD Client (for Secure Digital storage devices) drivers can also use KMDF.

Although KMDF provides an abstraction on top of WDM, the basic driver structure shown earlier also generally applies to KMDF drivers. At their core, KMDF drivers must have the following functions:

- **An initialization routine**   Like any other driver, a KMDF driver has a `DriverEntry` function that initializes the driver. KMDF drivers initiate the framework at this point and perform any configuration and initialization steps that are part of the driver or part of describing the driver to the framework. For non–Plug and Play drivers, this is where the first device object should be created.

- **An add-device routine**   KMDF driver operation is based on events and callbacks (described shortly), and the `EvtDriverDeviceAdd` callback is the single most important one for PnP devices because it receives notifications when the PnP manager in the kernel enumerates one of the driver's devices.

- **One or more `EvtIo*` routines**   Similar to a WDM driver's dispatch routines, these callback routines handle specific types of I/O requests from a particular device queue. A driver typically creates one or more queues in which KMDF places I/O requests for the driver's devices. These queues can be configured by request type and dispatching type.

The simplest KMDF driver might need to have only an initialization and add-device routine because the framework will provide the default, generic functionality that's required for most types of I/O processing, including power and Plug and Play events. In the KMDF model, *events* refer to run-time states to which a driver can respond or during which a driver can participate. These events are not related to the synchronization primitives (synchronization is discussed in Chapter 8 in Part 2), but are internal to the framework.

For events that are critical to a driver's operation, or that need specialized processing, the driver registers a given callback routine to handle this event. In other cases, a driver can allow KMDF to perform a default, generic action instead. For example, during an eject event (EvtDeviceEject), a driver can choose to support ejection and supply a callback or to fall back to the default KMDF code that will tell the user that the device does not support ejection. Not all events have a default behavior, however, and callbacks must be provided by the driver. One notable example is the EvtDriverDeviceAdd event just described that is at the core of any Plug and Play driver.

EXPERIMENT: Displaying KMDF and UMDF 2 drivers

The Wdfkd.dll extension that ships with the Debugging Tools for Windows package provides many commands that can be used to debug and analyze KMDF drivers and devices (instead of using the built-in WDM-style debugging extension, which may not offer the same kind of WDF-specific information). You can display installed KMDF drivers with the !wdfkd.wdfldr debugger command. In the following example, the output from a Windows 10 32-bit Hyper-V virtual machine is shown, displaying the built-in drivers that are installed.

```
1kd> !wdfkd.wdfldr
----------------------------------------------------------------
 KMDF Drivers
----------------------------------------------------------------
 LoadedModuleList      0x870991ec
-----------------------------------
LIBRARY_MODULE  0x8626aad8
  Version         v1.19
  Service         \Registry\Machine\System\CurrentControlSet\Services\Wdf01000
  ImageName       Wdf01000.sys
  ImageAddress    0x87000000
  ImageSize       0x8f000
  Associated Clients: 25

  ImageName                   Ver    WdfGlobals  FxGlobals   ImageAddress ImageSize
  umpass.sys                  v1.15  0xa1ae53f8  0xa1ae52f8  0x9e5f0000   0x00008000
  peauth.sys                  v1.7   0x95e798d8  0x95e797d8  0x9e400000   0x000ba000
  mslldp.sys                  v1.15  0x9aed1b50  0x9aed1a50  0x8e300000   0x00014000
  vmgid.sys                   v1.15  0x97d0fd08  0x97d0fc08  0x8e260000   0x00008000
  monitor.sys                 v1.15  0x97cf7e18  0x97cf7d18  0x8e250000   0x0000c000
  tsusbhub.sys                v1.15  0x97cb3108  0x97cb3008  0x8e4b0000   0x0001b000
  NdisVirtualBus.sys          v1.15  0x8d0fc2b0  0x8d0fc1b0  0x87a90000   0x00009000
  vmgencounter.sys            v1.15  0x8d0fefd0  0x8d0feed0  0x87a80000   0x00008000
  intelppm.sys                v1.15  0x8d0f4cf0  0x8d0f4bf0  0x87a50000   0x00021000
```

```
vms3cap.sys                    v1.15  0x8d0f5218  0x8d0f5118  0x87a40000   0x00008000
netvsc.sys                     v1.15  0x8d11ded0  0x8d11ddd0  0x87a20000   0x00019000
hyperkbd.sys                   v1.15  0x8d114488  0x8d114388  0x87a00000   0x00008000
dmvsc.sys                      v1.15  0x8d0ddb28  0x8d0dda28  0x879a0000   0x0000c000
umbus.sys                      v1.15  0x8b86ffd0  0x8b86fed0  0x874f0000   0x00011000
CompositeBus.sys               v1.15  0x8b869910  0x8b869810  0x87df0000   0x0000d000
cdrom.sys                      v1.15  0x8b863320  0x8b863220  0x87f40000   0x00024000
vmstorfl.sys                   v1.15  0x8b2b9108  0x8b2b9008  0x87c70000   0x0000c000
EhStorClass.sys                v1.15  0x8a9dacf8  0x8a9dabf8  0x878d0000   0x00015000
vmbus.sys                      v1.15  0x8a9887c0  0x8a9886c0  0x82870000   0x00018000
vdrvroot.sys                   v1.15  0x8a970728  0x8a970628  0x82800000   0x0000f000
msisadrv.sys                   v1.15  0x8a964998  0x8a964898  0x873c0000   0x00008000
WindowsTrustedRTProxy.sys      v1.15  0x8a1f4c10  0x8a1f4b10  0x87240000   0x00008000
WindowsTrustedRT.sys           v1.15  0x8a1f1fd0  0x8a1f1ed0  0x87220000   0x00017000
intelpep.sys                   v1.15  0x8a1ef690  0x8a1ef590  0x87210000   0x0000d000
acpiex.sys                     v1.15  0x86287fd0  0x86287ed0  0x870a0000   0x00019000
-----------------------------------
Total: 1 library loaded
```

If UMDF 2.x drivers were loaded, they would have been shown as well. This is one of the benefits of the UMDF 2.x library (see the UMDF section later in this chapter for more on this subject).

Notice that the KMDF library is implemented in Wdf01000.sys, which is the current version 1.x of KMDF. Future versions of KMDF may have a major version of 2 and will be implemented in another kernel module, Wdf02000.sys. This future module can live side by side with the version 1.x module, each loaded with the drivers that compiled against it. This ensures isolation and independence between drivers built against different KMDF major version libraries.

KMDF object model

The KMDF object model is object-based, with properties, methods and events, implemented in C, much like the model for the kernel, but it does not make use of the object manager. Instead, KMDF manages its own objects internally, exposing them as handles to drivers and keeping the actual data structures opaque. For each object type, the framework provides routines to perform operations on the object (called *methods*), such as WdfDeviceCreate, which creates a device. Additionally, objects can have specific data fields or members that can be accessed by Get/Set (used for modifications that should never fail) or Assign/Retrieve APIs (used for modifications that can fail), which are called *properties*. For example, the WdfInterruptGetInfo function returns information on a given interrupt object (WDFINTERRUPT).

Also unlike the implementation of kernel objects, which all refer to distinct and isolated object types, KMDF objects are all part of a hierarchy—most object types are bound to a parent. The root object is the WDFDRIVER structure, which describes the actual driver. The structure and meaning is analogous to the DRIVER_OBJECT structure provided by the I/O manager, and all other KMDF structures are children of it. The next most important object is WDFDEVICE, which refers to a given instance of a detected device on the system, which must have been created with WdfDeviceCreate. Again, this is analogous to the DEVICE_OBJECT structure that's used in the WDM model and by the I/O manager. Table 6-11 lists the object types supported by KMDF.

TABLE 6-11 KMDF object types

Object	Type	Description
Child list	WDFCHILDLIST	This is a list of child WDFDEVICE objects associated with the device. It is used only by bus drivers.
Collection	WDFCOLLECTION	This is a list of objects of a similar type, such as a group of WDFDEVICE objects being filtered.
Deferred Procedure Call	WDFDPC	This is an instance of a DPC object.
Device	WDFDEVICE	This is an instance of a device.
DMA common buffer	WDFCOMMONBUFFER	This is a region of memory that a device and driver can access for DMA.
DMA enabler	WDFDMAENABLER	This enables DMA on a given channel for a driver.
DMA transaction	WDFDMATRANSACTION	This is an instance of a DMA transaction.
Driver	WDFDRIVER	This is an object for the driver. It represents the driver, its parameters, and its callbacks, among other items.
File	WDFFILEOBJECT	This is an instance of a file object that can be used as a channel for communication between an application and the driver.
Generic object	WDFOBJECT	This allows driver-defined custom data to be wrapped inside the framework's object data model as an object.
Interrupt	WDFINTERRUPT	This is an instance of an interrupt that the driver must handle.
I/O queue	WDFQUEUE	This represents a given I/O queue.
I/O request	WDFREQUEST	This represents a given request on a WDFQUEUE.
I/O target	WDFIOTARGET	This represents the device stack being targeted by a given WDFREQUEST.
Look-aside list	WDFLOOKASIDE	This describes an executive look-aside list. (See Chapter 5.)
Memory	WDFMEMORY	This describes a region of paged or nonpaged pool.
Registry key	WDFKEY	This describes a registry key.
Resource list	WDFCMRESLIST	This identifies the hardware resources assigned to a WDFDEVICE.
Resource range list	WDFIORESLIST	This identifies a given possible hardware resource range for a WDFDEVICE.
Resource requirements list	WDFIORESREQLIST	This contains an array of WDFIORESLIST objects describing all possible resource ranges for a WDFDEVICE.
Spinlock	WDFSPINLOCK	This describes a spinlock.
String	WDFSTRING	This describes a Unicode string structure.
Timer	WDFTIMER	This describes an executive timer. (See Chapter 8 in Part 2 for more information.)
USB device	WDFUSBDEVICE	This identifies the one instance of a USB device.
USB interface	WDFUSBINTERFACE	This identifies one interface on the given WDFUSBDEVICE.
USB pipe	WDFUSBPIPE	This identifies a pipe to an endpoint on a given WDFUSBINTERFACE.
Wait lock	WDFWAITLOCK	This represents a kernel dispatcher event object.

Object	Type	Description
WMI instance	WDFWMIINSTANCE	This represents a WMI data block for a given WDFWMIPROVIDER.
WMI provider	WDFWMIPROVIDER	This describes the WMI schema for all the WDFWMIINSTANCE objects supported by the driver.
Work item	WDFWORKITEM	This describes an executive work item.

For each of these objects, other KMDF objects can be attached as children. Some objects have only one or two valid parents, while others can be attached to any parent. For example, a WDFINTERRUPT object must be associated with a given WDFDEVICE, but a WDFSPINLOCK or WDFSTRING object can have any object as a parent. This allows for fine-grained control over their validity and usage and the reduction of global state variables. Figure 6-44 shows the entire KMDF object hierarchy.

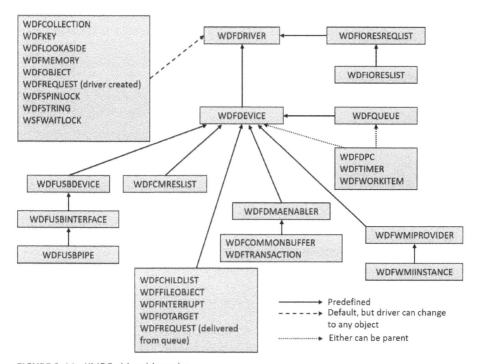

FIGURE 6-44 KMDF object hierarchy.

The associations mentioned earlier and shown in Figure 6-44 are not necessarily immediate. The parent must simply be on the *hierarchy chain*, meaning one of the ancestor nodes must be of this type. This relationship is useful to implement because object hierarchies affect not only an object's locality but also its lifetime. Each time a child object is created, a reference count is added to it by its link to its parent. Therefore, when a parent object is destroyed, all the child objects are also destroyed, which is why associating objects such as WDFSTRING or WDFMEMORY with a given object instead of the default WDFDRIVER object can automatically free up memory and state information when the parent object is destroyed.

Closely related to the concept of hierarchy is KMDF's notion of object context. Because KMDF objects are opaque (as discussed) and are associated with a parent object for locality, it becomes important to allow drivers to attach their own data to an object in order to track certain specific information outside the framework's capabilities or support. Object contexts allow all KMDF objects to contain such information. They also allow multiple object context areas, which permit multiple layers of code inside the same driver to interact with the same object in different ways. In WDM, the device extension custom data structure allows such information to be associated with a given device, but with KMDF even a spinlock or string can contain context areas. This extensibility enables each library or layer of code responsible for processing an I/O request to interact independently of other code, based on the context area that it works with.

Finally, KMDF objects are also associated with a set of attributes, shown in Table 6-12. These attributes are usually configured to their defaults, but the values can be overridden by the driver when creating the object by specifying a WDF_OBJECT_ATTRIBUTES structure (similar to the object manager's OBJECT_ATTRIBUTES structure that's used when creating a kernel object).

TABLE 6-12   KMDF object attributes

Attribute	Description
ContextSizeOverride	This is the size of the object context area.
ContextTypeInfo	This is the type of the object context area.
EvtCleanupCallback	This is the callback to notify the driver of the object's cleanup before deletion. (References may still exist.)
EvtDestroyCallback	This is the callback to notify the driver of the object's imminent deletion. (The reference count will be 0.)
ExecutionLevel	This describes the maximum IRQL at which the callbacks may be invoked by KMDF.
ParentObject	This identifies the parent of the object.
SynchronizationScope	Specifies whether callbacks should be synchronized with the parent, a queue, a device, or nothing.

KMDF I/O model

The KMDF I/O model follows the WDM mechanisms discussed earlier in this chapter. In fact, you can even think of the framework itself as a WDM driver, since it uses kernel APIs and WDM behavior to abstract KMDF and make it functional. Under KMDF, the framework driver sets its own WDM-style IRP dispatch routines and takes control of all IRPs sent to the driver. After being handled by one of three KMDF I/O handlers (described shortly), it then packages these requests in the appropriate KMDF objects, inserts them in the appropriate queues (if required), and performs driver callback if the driver is interested in those events. Figure 6-45 describes the flow of I/O in the framework.

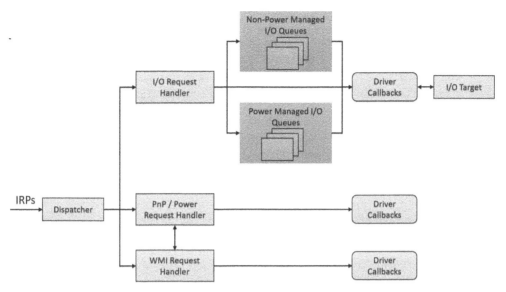

FIGURE 6-45 KMDF I/O flow and IRP processing.

Based on the IRP processing discussed previously for WDM drivers, KMDF performs one of the following three actions:

- It sends the IRP to the I/O handler, which processes standard device operations.

- It sends the IRP to the PnP and power handler that processes these kinds of events and notifies other drivers if the state has changed.

- It sends the IRP to the WMI handler, which handles tracing and logging.

These components then notify the driver of any events it registered for, potentially forward the request to another handler for further processing, and then complete the request based on an internal handler action or as the result of a driver call. If KMDF has finished processing the IRP but the request itself has still not been fully processed, KMDF will take one of the following actions:

- For bus drivers and function drivers, it completes the IRP with STATUS_INVALID_DEVICE_REQUEST.

- For filter drivers, it forwards the request to the next lower driver.

I/O processing by KMDF is based on the mechanism of queues (WDFQUEUE, not the KQUEUE object discussed earlier in this chapter). KMDF queues are highly scalable containers of I/O requests (packaged as WDFREQUEST objects) and provide a rich feature set beyond merely sorting the pending I/Os for a given device. For example, queues track currently active requests and support I/O cancellation, I/O concurrency (the ability to perform and complete more than one I/O request at a time), and I/O synchronization (as noted in the list of object attributes in Table 6-12). A typical KMDF driver creates at least one queue (if not more) and associates one or more events with each queue, as well as some of the following options:

- The callbacks registered with the events associated with this queue.

- The power management state for the queue. KMDF supports both power-managed and non–power managed queues. For the former, the I/O handler wakes up the device when required (and when possible), arms the idle timer when the device has no I/Os queued up, and calls the driver's I/O cancellation routines when the system is switching away from a working state.

- The dispatch method for the queue. KMDF can deliver I/Os from a queue in sequential, parallel, or manual mode. Sequential I/Os are delivered one at a time (KMDF waits for the driver to complete the previous request), while parallel I/Os are delivered to the driver as soon as possible. In manual mode, the driver must manually retrieve I/Os from the queue.

- Whether the queue can accept zero-length buffers, such as incoming requests that don't actually contain any data.

 Note The dispatch method only affects the number of requests that can be active inside a driver's queue at one time. It does not determine whether the event callbacks themselves will be called concurrently or serially. That behavior is determined through the synchronization scope object attribute described earlier. Therefore, it is possible for a parallel queue to have concurrency disabled but still have multiple incoming requests.

Based on the mechanism of queues, the KMDF I/O handler can perform various tasks upon receiving a create, close, cleanup, write, read, or device control (IOCTL) request:

- For create requests, the driver can request to be immediately notified through the `EvtDevice-FileCreate` callback event, or it can create a non-manual queue to receive create requests. It must then register an `EvtIoDefault` callback to receive the notifications. Finally, if none of these methods are used, KMDF will simply complete the request with a success code, meaning that by default, applications will be able to open handles to KMDF drivers that don't supply their own code.

- For cleanup and close requests, the driver will be immediately notified through `EvtFileClean-up` and `EvtFileClose` callbacks, if registered. Otherwise, the framework will simply complete with a success code.

- For write, read, and IOCTL requests, the flow shown in Figure 6-46 applies.

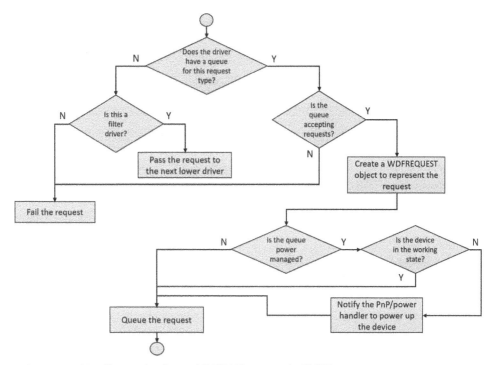

FIGURE 6-46 Handling read, write, and IOCTL I/O requests by KMDF.

User-Mode Driver Framework

Windows includes a growing number of drivers that run in user mode, using the User-Mode Driver Framework (UMDF), which is part of the WDF. UMDF version 2 is aligned with KMDF in terms of object model, programming model and I/O model. The frameworks are not identical, however, because of some of the inherent differences between user mode and kernel mode. For example, some KMDF objects listed in Table 6-12 don't exist in UMDF, including WDFCHILDLIST, DMA-related objects, WDFLOOKASIDELIST (look-aside lists can be allocated only in kernel mode), WDFIORESLIST, WDFIORES-REQLIST, WDFDPC, and WMI objects. Still, most KMDF objects and concepts apply equally to UMDF 2.*x*.

UMDF provides several advantages over KMDF:

- UMDF drivers execute in user mode, so any unhandled exception crashes the UMDF host process, but not the entire system.

- The UMDF host process runs with the Local Service account, which has very limited privileges on the local machine and only anonymous access in network connections. This reduces the security attack surface.

- Running in user mode means the IRQL is always 0 (PASSIVE_LEVEL). Thus, the driver can always take page faults and use kernel dispatcher objects for synchronization (events, mutexes, and so on).

- Debugging UMDF drivers is easier than debugging KMDF drivers because the debugging setup does not require two separate machines (virtual or physical).

The main drawback to UMDF is increased latency because of the kernel/user transitions and communication required (as described shortly). Also, some types of drivers, such as drivers for high-speed PCI devices, are simply not meant to execute in user mode and thus cannot be written with UMDF.

UMDF is designed specifically to support protocol device classes, which refers to devices that all use the same standardized, generic protocol and offer specialized functionality on top of it. These protocols currently include IEEE 1394 (FireWire), USB, Bluetooth, human interface devices (HIDs) and TCP/IP. Any device running on top of these buses (or connected to a network) is a potential candidate for UMDF. Examples include portable music players, input devices, cell phones, cameras and webcams, and so on. Two other users of UMDF are SideShow-compatible devices (auxiliary displays) and the Windows Portable Device (WPD) Framework, which supports USB-removable storage (USB bulk transfer devices). Finally, as with KMDF, it's possible to implement software-only drivers, such as for a virtual device, in UMDF.

Unlike KMDF drivers, which run as driver objects representing a SYS image file, UMDF drivers run in a driver host process (running the image %SystemRoot%\System32\WUDFHost.exe), similar to a service-hosting process. The host process contains the driver itself, the User-Mode Driver Framework (implemented as a DLL), and a run-time environment (responsible for I/O dispatching, driver loading, device-stack management, communication with the kernel, and a thread pool).

As in the kernel, each UMDF driver runs as part of a stack. This can contain multiple drivers that are responsible for managing a device. Naturally, because user-mode code can't access the kernel address space, UMDF also includes components that allow this access to occur through a specialized interface to the kernel. This is implemented by a kernel-mode side of UMDF that uses ALPC—essentially an efficient inter-process communication mechanism to talk to the run-time environment in the user-mode driver host processes. (See Chapter 8 in Part 2 for more information on ALPC.) Figure 6-47 shows the architecture of the UMDF driver model.

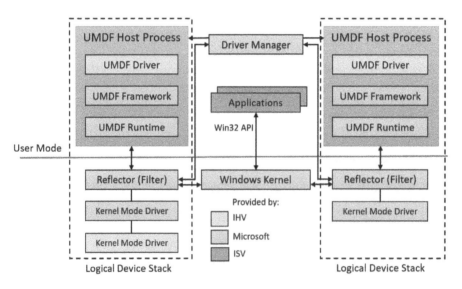

FIGURE 6-47 UMDF architecture.

Figure 6-47 shows two different device stacks that manage two different hardware devices, each with a UMDF driver running inside its own driver host process. From the diagram, you can see that the following components comprise the architecture:

- **Applications**   These are the clients of the drivers. They are standard Windows applications that use the same APIs to perform I/Os as they would with a KMDF-managed or WDM-managed device. Applications don't know (nor care) that they're talking to a UMDF-based device, and the calls are still sent to the kernel's I/O manager.

- **Windows kernel (I/O manager)**   Based on the application I/O APIs, the I/O manager builds the IRPs for the operations, just like for any other standard device.

- **Reflector**   The reflector is what makes UMDF "tick." It is a standard WDM filter driver (%SystemRoot%\System32\Drivers\WUDFRd.Sys) that sits at the top of the device stack of each device that is being managed by a UMDF driver. The reflector is responsible for managing the communication between the kernel and the user-mode driver host process. IRPs related to power management, Plug and Play, and standard I/O are redirected to the host process through ALPC. This enables the UMDF driver to respond to the I/Os and perform work, as well as be involved in the Plug and Play model, by providing enumeration, installation, and management of its devices. Finally, the reflector is responsible for keeping an eye on the driver host processes by making sure they remain responsive to requests within an adequate time to prevent drivers and applications from hanging.

- **Driver manager**   The driver manager is responsible for starting and quitting the driver host processes, based on which UMDF-managed devices are present, and also for managing information on them. It is also responsible for responding to messages coming from the reflector and applying them to the appropriate host process (such as reacting to device installation). The driver manager runs as a standard Windows service implemented in %SystemRoot%\System32\WUDFsvc.dll (hosted in a standard Svchost.exe), and is configured for automatic startup as soon as the first UMDF driver for a device is installed. Only one instance of the driver manager runs for all driver host processes (as is always the case with services), and it must always be running to allow UMDF drivers to work.

- **Host process**   The host process provides the address space and run-time environment for the actual driver (WUDFHost.exe). Although it runs in the local service account, it is not actually a Windows service and is not managed by the SCM—only by the driver manager. The host process is also responsible for providing the user-mode device stack for the actual hardware, which is visible to all applications on the system. Currently, each device instance has its own device stack, which runs in a separate host process. In the future, multiple instances may share the same host process. Host processes are child processes of the driver manager.

- **Kernel-mode drivers**   If specific kernel support for a device that is managed by a UMDF driver is needed, it is also possible to write a companion kernel-mode driver that fills that role. In this way, it is possible for a device to be managed both by a UMDF and a KMDF (or WDM) driver.

You can easily see UMDF in action on your system by inserting a USB flash drive with some content on it. Run Process Explorer, and you should see a WUDFHost.exe process that corresponds to a driver host process. Switch to DLL view and scroll down until you see DLLs like the ones shown in Figure 6-48.

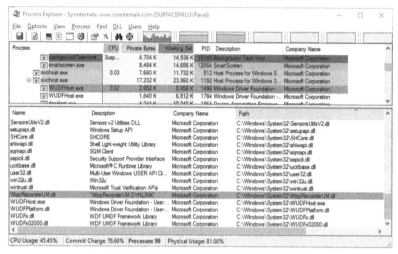

FIGURE 6-48   DLL in UMDF host process.

You can identify three main components, which match the architectural overview described earlier:

- **WUDFHost.exe**   This is the UMDF host executable.

- **WUDFx02000.dll**   This is the UMDF 2.x framework DLL.

- **WUDFPlatform.dll**   This is the run-time environment.

The power manager

Just as Windows Plug and Play features require support from a system's hardware, its power-management capabilities require hardware that complies with the Advanced Configuration and Power Interface (ACPI) specification, which is now part of the Unified Extensible Firmware Interface (UEFI). (The ACPI spec is available at *http://www.uefi.org/specifications*.)

The ACPI standard defines various power levels for a system and for devices. The six system power states are described in Table 6-13. They are referred to as S0 (fully on or working) through S5 (fully off). Each state has the following characteristics:

- **Power consumption**   This is the amount of power the system consumes.

- **Software resumption**   This is the software state from which the system resumes when moving to a "more on" state.

- **Hardware latency**   This is the length of time it takes to return the system to the fully on state.

TABLE 6-13 System power-state definitions

State	Power Consumption	Software Resumption	Hardware Latency
S0 (fully on)	Maximum	Not applicable	None
S1 (sleeping)	Less than S0, more than S2	System resumes where it left off (returns to S0)	Less than 2 seconds
S2 (sleeping)	Less than S1, more than S3	System resumes where it left off (returns to S0)	2 or more seconds
S3 (sleeping)	Less than S2; processor is off	System resumes where it left off (returns to S0)	Same as S2
S4 (hibernating)	Trickle current to power button and wake circuitry	System restarts from saved hibernation file and resumes where it left off before hibernation (returns to S0)	Long and undefined
S5 (fully off)	Trickle current to power button	System boot	Long and undefined

As noted in Table 6-13, states S1 through S4 are sleeping states, in which the system appears to be off because of reduced power consumption. However, in these sleeping states, the system retains enough information—either in memory or on disk—to move to S0. For states S1 through S3, enough power is required to preserve the contents of the computer's memory so that when the transition is made to S0 (when the user or a device wakes up the computer), the power manager continues executing where it left off before the suspend.

When the system moves to S4, the power manager saves the compressed contents of memory to a hibernation file named Hiberfil.sys, which is large enough to hold the uncompressed contents of memory, in the root directory of the system volume (hidden file). (Compression is used to minimize disk I/O and to improve hibernation and resume-from-hibernation performance.) After it finishes saving memory, the power manager shuts off the computer. When a user subsequently turns on the computer, a normal boot process occurs, except that the boot manager checks for and detects a valid memory image stored in the hibernation file. If the hibernation file contains the saved system state, the boot manager launches %SystemRoot%\System32\Winresume.exe, which reads the contents of the file into memory, and then resumes execution at the point in memory that is recorded in the hibernation file.

On systems with hybrid sleep enabled, a user request to put the computer to sleep will actually be a combination of both the S3 state and the S4 state. While the computer is put to sleep, an emergency hibernation file will also be written to disk. Unlike typical hibernation files, which contain almost all active memory, the emergency hibernation file includes only data that could not be paged in at a later time, making the suspend operation faster than a typical hibernation (because less data is written to disk). Drivers will then be notified that an S4 transition is occurring, allowing them to configure themselves and save state just as if an actual hibernation request had been initiated. After this point, the system is put in the normal sleep state just like during a standard sleep transition. However, if the power goes out, the system is now essentially in an S4 state—the user can power on the machine, and Windows will resume from the emergency hibernation file.

 Note You can disable hibernation completely and gain some disk space by running `power-cfg /h off` from an elevated command prompt.

The computer never directly transitions between states S1 and S4 (because that requires code execution, but the CPU is off in these states); instead, it must move to state S0 first. As illustrated in Figure 6-49, when the system is moving from any of states S1 through S5 to state S0, it's said to be *waking*, and when it's transitioning from state S0 to any of states S1 through S5, it's said to be *sleeping*.

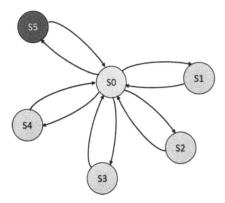

FIGURE 6-49   System power-state transitions.

Experiment: System power states

To view the supported power states, open an elevated command window and type in the command **powercfg /a**. You'll see output similar to the following:

```
C:\WINDOWS\system32>powercfg /a
The following sleep states are available on this system:
    Standby (S3)
    Hibernate
    Fast Startup

The following sleep states are not available on this system:
    Standby (S1)
        The system firmware does not support this standby state.

    Standby (S2)
        The system firmware does not support this standby state.

    Standby (S0 Low Power Idle)
        The system firmware does not support this standby state.

    Hybrid Sleep
        The hypervisor does not support this standby state.
```

Notice that the standby state is S3 and hibernation is available. Let's turn off hibernation and re-execute the command:

```
C:\WINDOWS\system32>powercfg /h off

C:\WINDOWS\system32>powercfg /a
```

```
The following sleep states are available on this system:
    Standby (S3)

The following sleep states are not available on this system:
    Standby (S1)
        The system firmware does not support this standby state.

    Standby (S2)
        The system firmware does not support this standby state.

    Hibernate
        Hibernation has not been enabled.

    Standby (S0 Low Power Idle)
        The system firmware does not support this standby state.

    Hybrid Sleep
        Hibernation is not available.
        The hypervisor does not support this standby state.

    Fast Startup
        Hibernation is not available.
```

For devices, ACPI defines four power states, from D0 through D3. State D0 is fully on, while state D3 is fully off. The ACPI standard leaves it to individual drivers and devices to define the meanings of states D1 and D2, except that state D1 must consume an amount of power less than or equal to that consumed in state D0, and when the device is in state D2, it must consume power less than or equal to that consumed in D1.

Windows 8 (and later) splits the D3 state into two sub-states, D3-hot and D3-cold. In D3-hot state, the device is mostly turned off, but is not disconnected from its main power source, and its parent bus controller can detect the presence of the device on the bus. In D3-cold, the main power source is removed from the device, and the bus controller cannot detect the device. This state provides another opportunity for saving power. Figure 6-50 shows the device states and the possible state transitions.

Figure 6-50 shows the device states and the possible state transitions.

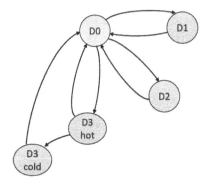

FIGURE 6-50 Device power-state transitions.

Before Windows 8, devices could only reach D3-hot state while the system is fully on (S0). The transition to D3-cold was implicit when the system went into a sleep state. Starting with Windows 8, a device's power state can be set to D3-cold while the system is fully on. The driver that controls the device cannot put the device into D3-cold state directly; instead, it can put the device into D3-hot state, and then, depending on other devices on the same bus entering D3-hot states, the bus driver and firmware may decide to move all the devices to D3-cold. The decision whether to move the devices to D3-cold states depends on two factors: first, the actual ability of the bus driver and firmware, and second on the driver that must enable the transition to D3-cold either by specifying that in the installation INF file or by calling the SetD3DColdSupport function dynamically.

Microsoft, in conjunction with the major hardware OEMs, has defined a series of power management reference specifications that specify the device power states that are required for all devices in a particular class (for the major device classes: display, network, SCSI, and so on). For some devices, there's no intermediate power state between fully on and fully off, which results in these states being undefined.

Connected Standby and Modern Standby

You may have noticed in the experiment above another system state called Standby (S0 Low Power Idle). Although not an official ACPI state, it is a variant of S0 known as *Connected Standby* on Windows 8.*x* and later enhanced in Windows 10 (desktop and mobile editions) and called *Modern Standby*. The "normal" standby state (S3 above) is sometimes referred to as *Legacy Standby*.

The main problem with Legacy Standby is that the system is not working, and therefore, for example, the user receives an email, the system can't pick that up without waking to S0, which may or may not happen, depending on configuration and device capabilities. Even if the system wakes up to get that email, it won't go immediately to sleep again. Modern Standby solves both issues.

Systems that support Modern Standby normally go into this state when the system is instructed to go to Standby. The system is technically still at S0, meaning the CPU is active and code can execute. However, desktop processes (non-UWP apps) are suspended, as well as UWP apps (most are not in the foreground and suspended anyway), but background tasks created by UWP apps are allowed to execute. For example, an email client would have a background task that periodically polls for new messages.

Being in Modern Standby also means that the system is able to wake to full S0 very quickly, sometimes referred to as *Instant On*. Note that not all systems support Modern Standby, as it depends on the chipset and other platform components (as can be seen in the last experiment, the system on which the experiment ran does not support Modern Standby and thus supports Legacy Standby).

For more information on Modern Standby, consult the Windows Hardware documentation at *https://msdn.microsoft.com/en-us/library/windows/hardware/mt282515(v=vs.85).aspx*.

Power manager operation

Windows power-management policy is split between the power manager and the individual device drivers. The power manager is the owner of the system power policy. This ownership means the power manager decides which system power state is appropriate at any given point, and when a sleep, hibernation, or shutdown is required, the power manager instructs the power-capable devices in the system to perform appropriate system power-state transitions.

The power manager decides when a system power-state transition is necessary by considering several factors:

- System activity level
- System battery level
- Shutdown, hibernate, or sleep requests from applications
- User actions, such as pressing the power button
- Control Panel power settings

When the PnP manager performs device enumeration, part of the information it receives about a device is its power-management capabilities. A driver reports whether its devices support device states D1 and D2 and, optionally, the latencies, or times required, to move from states D1 through D3 to D0. To help the power manager determine when to make system power-state transitions, bus drivers also return a table that implements a mapping between each of the system power states (S0 through S5) and the device power states that a device supports.

The table lists the lowest possible device power state for each system state and directly reflects the state of various power planes when the machine sleeps or hibernates. For example, a bus that supports all four device power states might return the mapping table shown in Table 6-14. Most device drivers turn their devices completely off (D3) when leaving S0 to minimize power consumption when the machine isn't in use. Some devices, however, such as network adapter cards, support the ability to wake up the system from a sleeping state. This ability, along with the lowest device power state in which the capability is present, is also reported during device enumeration.

TABLE 6-14 An example of system-to-device power mappings

System Power State	Device Power State
S0 (fully on)	D0 (fully on)
S1 (sleeping)	D1
S2 (sleeping)	D2
S3 (sleeping)	D2
S4 (hibernating)	D3 (fully off)
S5 (fully off)	D3 (fully off)

Driver power operation

When the power manager decides to make a transition between system power states, it sends power commands to a driver's power dispatch routine (IRP_MJ_POWER). More than one driver can be responsible for managing a device, but only one of the drivers is designated as the device power-policy owner. This is typically the driver that manages the FDO. This driver determines, based on the system state, a device's power state. For example, if the system transitions between state S0 and S3, a driver might decide to move a device's power state from D0 to D1.

Instead of directly informing the other drivers that share the management of the device of its decision, the device power-policy owner asks the power manager, via the PoRequestPowerIrp function, to tell the other drivers by issuing a device power command to their power dispatch routines. This behavior enables the power manager to control the number of power commands that are active on a system at any given time. For example, some devices in the system might require a significant amount of current to power up. The power manager ensures that such devices aren't powered up simultaneously.

EXPERIMENT: Viewing a driver's power mappings

You can use Device Manager to see a driver's system power state–to–driver power state mappings. To do so, open the Properties dialog box for a device, click the **Details** tab, click the **Property** drop-down list, and choose **Power Data**. The Properties dialog box also displays the current power state of the device, the device-specific power capabilities that it provides, and the power states from which it can wake the system:

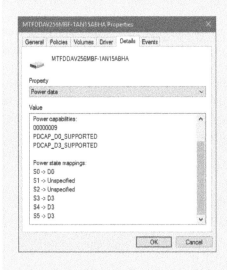

Many power commands have corresponding query commands. For example, when the system is moving to a sleep state, the power manager will first ask the devices on the system whether the transition is acceptable. A device that is busy performing time-critical operations or interacting with device hardware might reject the command, which results in the system maintaining its current system power-state setting.

EXPERIMENT: Viewing the system power capabilities and policy

You can view a computer's system power capabilities by using the !pocaps kernel debugger command. Here's the output of the command when run on an x64 Windows 10 laptop:

```
1kd> !pocaps
PopCapabilities @ 0xfffff8035a98ce60
  Misc Supported Features:  PwrButton SlpButton Lid S3 S4 S5 HiberFile FullWake
VideoDim
  Processor Features:       Thermal
  Disk Features:
  Battery Features:         BatteriesPresent
    Battery 0 - Capacity:        0  Granularity:        0
    Battery 1 - Capacity:        0  Granularity:        0
    Battery 2 - Capacity:        0  Granularity:        0
  Wake Caps
    Ac OnLine Wake:         Sx
    Soft Lid Wake:          Sx
    RTC Wake:               S4
    Min Device Wake:        Sx
    Default Wake:           Sx
```

The Misc Supported Features line reports that, in addition to S0 (fully on), the system supports system power states of S3, S4 and S5 (it doesn't implement S1 or S2) and has a valid hibernation file to which it can save system memory when it hibernates (state S4).

The Power Options page, which you open by selecting **Power Options** in the Control Panel, lets you configure various aspects of the system's power policy. The exact properties you can configure depend on the system's power capabilities.

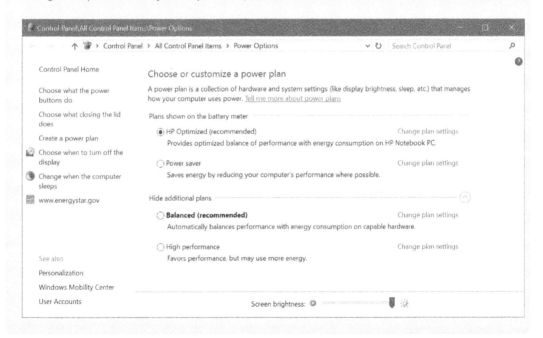

Notice that OEMs can add power schemes. These schemes can be listed by typing the **power-cfg /list** command as shown here:

```
C:\WINDOWS\system32>powercfg /list

Existing Power Schemes (* Active)
-------------------------------------
Power Scheme GUID: 381b4222-f694-41f0-9685-ff5bb260df2e  (Balanced)
Power Scheme GUID: 8759706d-706b-4c22-b2ec-f91e1ef6ed38  (HP Optimized
(recommended)) *
Power Scheme GUID: 8c5e7fda-e8bf-4a96-9a85-a6e23a8c635c  (High performance)
Power Scheme GUID: a1841308-3541-4fab-bc81-f71556f20b4a  (Power saver)
```

By changing any of the preconfigured plan settings, you can set the idle detection timeouts that control when the system turns off the monitor, spins down hard disks, goes to standby mode (moves to system power state S3 in the previous experiment), and hibernates (moves the system to power state S4). In addition, selecting the **Change Plan Settings** link lets you specify the power-related behavior of the system when you press the power or sleep buttons or close a laptop's lid.

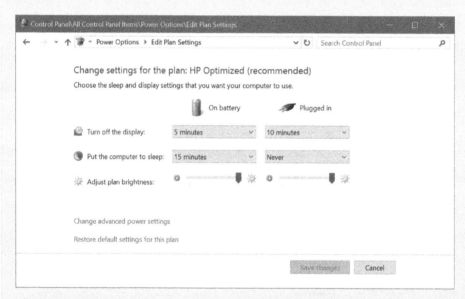

The Change Advanced Power Settings link directly affects values in the system's power policy, which you can display with the !popolicy debugger command. Here's the output of the command on the same system:

```
lkd> !popolicy
SYSTEM_POWER_POLICY (R.1) @ 0xfffff8035a98cc64
   PowerButton:      Sleep  Flags: 00000000  Event: 00000000
   SleepButton:      Sleep  Flags: 00000000  Event: 00000000
   LidClose:          None  Flags: 00000000  Event: 00000000
   Idle:             Sleep  Flags: 00000000  Event: 00000000
```

```
OverThrottled:        None  Flags: 00000000   Event: 00000000
IdleTimeout:             0  IdleSensitivity:        90%
MinSleep:               S3  MaxSleep:               S3
LidOpenWake:            S0  FastSleep:              S3
WinLogonFlags:           1  S4Timeout:               0
VideoTimeout:          600  VideoDim:                0
SpinTimeout:           4b0  OptForPower:             0
FanTolerance:           0%  ForcedThrottle:         0%
MinThrottle:            0%  DyanmicThrottle:   None (0)
```

The first lines of the display correspond to the button behaviors specified in the Power Options Advanced Settings window. On this system, both the power and the sleep buttons put the computer in a sleep state. Closing the lid, however, does nothing. The timeout values shown near the end of the output are expressed in seconds and displayed in hexadecimal notation. The values reported here directly correspond to the settings configured in the Power Options window. For example, the video timeout is 600, meaning the monitor turns off after 600 seconds (because of a bug in the debugging tools used here, it's displayed in decimal), or 10 minutes. Similarly, the hard disk spin-down timeout is 0x4b0, which corresponds to 1200 seconds, or 20 minutes.

Driver and application control of device power

In addition to responding to power manager commands related to system power-state transitions, a driver can unilaterally control the device power state of its devices. In some cases, a driver might want to reduce the power consumption of a device it controls if the device is left inactive for a period of time. Examples include monitors that support a dimmed mode and disks that support spin-down. A driver can either detect an idle device itself or use facilities provided by the power manager. If the device uses the power manager, it registers the device with the power manager by calling the PoRegisterDevice-ForIdleDetection function.

This function informs the power manager of the timeout values to use to detect whether a device is idle and, if so, the device power state that the power manager should apply. The driver specifies two timeouts: one to use when the user has configured the computer to conserve energy and the other to use when the user has configured the computer for optimum performance. After calling PoRegisterDeviceForIdleDetection, the driver must inform the power manager, by calling the PoSetDeviceBusy or PoSetDeviceBusyEx functions, whenever the device is active, and then register for idle detection again to disable and re-enable it as needed. The PoStartDeviceBusy and PoEndDeviceBusy APIs are available as well, which simplify the programming logic required to achieve the behavior just described.

Although a device has control over its own power state, it does not have the ability to manipulate the system power state or to prevent system power transitions from occurring. For example, if a badly designed driver doesn't support any low-power states, it can choose to remain on or turn itself completely off without hindering the system's overall ability to enter a low-power state—this is because the power manager only *notifies* the driver of a transition and doesn't ask for *consent*. Drivers do receive a power query IRP (IRP_MN_QUERY_POWER) when the system is about to transition to a lower power state.

The driver may veto the request, but the power manager does not have to comply; it may delay transition if possible (e.g., the device is running on a battery that is not critically low); transition to hibernation, however, can never fail.

Although drivers and the kernel are chiefly responsible for power management, applications are also allowed to provide their input. User-mode processes can register for a variety of power notifications, such as when the battery is low or critically low, when the machine has switched from DC (battery) to AC (adapter/charger) power, or when the system is initiating a power transition. Applications can never veto these operations, and they can have up to two seconds to clean up any state necessary before a sleep transition.

Power management framework

Starting with Windows 8, the kernel provides a framework for managing power states of individual components (sometimes called *functions*) within a device. For example, suppose an audio device has playback and recording components, but if the playback component is active and the recording component is not, it would be beneficial to put the recording component into a lower power state. The power management framework (PoFx) provides an API that drivers can use to indicate their components' power states and requirements. All components must support the fully-on state, identified as F0. Higher-number F-states indicate lower power states that a component may be in, where each higher F-state represents a lower power consumption and higher transition time to F0. Note that F-state management has meaning only when the device is in power state D0, because it's not working at all in higher D-states.

The power policy owner of the device (typically the FDO) must register with PoFx by calling the PoFxRegisterDevice function. The driver passes along the following information in the call:

- The number of components within the device.

- A set of callbacks the driver can implement to be notified by PoFx when various events occur, such as switching to active or idle state, switching the device to D0 state and sending power control codes (see the WDK for more information).

- For each component, the number of F-states it supports.

- For each component, the deepest F-state from which the component can wake.

- For each component, for each F-state, the time required to return from this state to F0, the minimum amount of time the component can be in this F-state to make the transition worthwhile, and the nominal power the component consumes in this F-state. Or, it can be set to indicate that the power consumption is negligible and is not worth considering when PoFx decides to wake several components simultaneously.

PoFx uses this information—combined with information from other devices and system-wide power state information, such as the current power profile—to make intelligent decisions for which power F-state a particular component should be in. The challenge is to reconcile two conflicting objectives: first, ensuring that an idle component consumes as little power as possible, and second, making sure a component can transition to the F0 state quickly enough so that the component is perceived as always on and always connected.

The driver must notify PoFx when a component needs to be active (F0 state) by calling `PoFxActivate-Component`. Sometime after this call, the corresponding callback is invoked by PoFx, indicating to the driver that the component is now at F0. Conversely, when the driver determines the component is not currently needed, it calls `PoFxIdleComponent` to tell PoFx, which responds by transitioning the component to a lower-power F-state and notifies the driver once it does.

Performance state management

The mechanisms just described allow a component in an idle condition (non-F0 states) to consume less power than in F0. But some components can consume less power even in state F0, related to the actual work a device is doing. For example, a graphic card may be able to use less power when showing a mostly static display, whereas it would need higher power when rendering 3D content in 60 frames per second.

In Windows 8.*x*, such drivers would have to implement a propriety performance state selection algorithm and notify an OS service called platform extension plug-in (PEP). PEP is specific to a particular line of processors or system on a chip (SoC). This makes the driver code tightly coupled to the PEP.

Windows 10 extends the PoFx API for performance state management, prompting the driver code to use standard APIs and not worry about the particular PEP on the platform. For each component, PoFx provides the following types of performance states:

- A discrete number of states in the frequency (Hz), bandwidth (bits per second), or an opaque number meaningful to the driver.

- A continuous distribution of states between a minimum and maximum (frequency, bandwidth, or custom).

An example of this is for a graphic card to define a discrete set of frequencies in which it can operate, thus indirectly affecting its power consumption. Similar performance sets could be defined for its bandwidth usage, if appropriate.

To register with PoFx for performance state management, a driver must first register the device with PoFx (`PoFxRegisterDevice`) as described in the previous section. Then, the driver calls `PoFxRegister-ComponentPerfStates`, passing performance details (discrete or range-based, frequency, bandwidth, or custom) and a callback when state changes actually occur.

When a driver decides that a component should change performance state, it calls `PoFxIssue-PerfStateChange` or `PoFxIssuePerfStateChangeMultiple`. These calls request the PEP to place the component in the specified state (based on the provided index or value, depending on whether the set is for a discrete state or range-based). The driver may also specify that the call should be synchronous, asynchronous or "don't care," in which case the PEP decides. Either way, PoFx will eventually call into the driver-registered callback with the performance state, which may be the requested one, but it can also be denied by the PEP. If accepted, the driver should make the appropriate calls to its hardware to make the actual change. If the PEP denies the request, the driver may try again with a new call to one of the aforementioned functions. Only a single call can be made before the driver's callback is invoked.

Power availability requests

Applications and drivers cannot veto sleep transitions that are already initiated. However, certain scenarios demand a mechanism for disabling the ability to initiate sleep transitions when a user is interacting with the system in certain ways. For example, if the user is currently watching a movie and the machine would normally go idle (based on a lack of mouse or keyboard input after 15 minutes), the media player application should have the capability to temporarily disable idle transitions as long as the movie is playing. You can probably imagine other power-saving measures that the system would normally undertake, such as turning off or even just dimming the screen, that would also limit your enjoyment of visual media. In legacy versions of Windows, `SetThreadExecutionState` was a user-mode API capable of controlling system and display idle transitions by informing the power manager that a user was still present on the machine. However, this API did not provide any sort of diagnostic capabilities, nor did it allow sufficient granularity for defining the availability request. Also, drivers could not issue their own requests, and even user applications had to correctly manage their threading model, because these requests were at the thread level, not at the process or system level.

Windows now supports power request objects, which are implemented by the kernel and are bona-fide object manager–defined objects. You can use the WinObj utility from Sysinternals (more details on this tool are in Chapter 8 in Part 2) and see the PowerRequest object type in the \ObjectTypes directory, or use the `!object` kernel debugger command on the \ObjectTypes\PowerRequest object type, to validate this.

Power availability requests are generated by user-mode applications through the `PowerCreate-Request` API and then enabled or disabled with the `PowerSetRequest` and `PowerClearRequest` APIs, respectively. In the kernel, drivers use `PoCreatePowerRequest`, `PoSetPowerRequest`, and `PoClear-PowerRequest`. Because no handles are used, `PoDeletePowerRequest` is needed to remove the reference on the object (while user mode can simply use `CloseHandle`).

There are four kinds of requests that can be used through the Power Request API:

- **System request** This type request asks that the system not automatically go to sleep due to the idle timer (although the user can still close the lid to enter sleep, for example).

- **Display request** This type of request does the same as a system request, but for the display.

- **Away-mode request** This is a modification to the normal sleep (S3 state) behavior of Windows, which is used to keep the computer in full powered-on mode but with the display and sound card turned off, making it appear to the user as though the machine is really sleeping. This behavior is normally used only by specialized set-top boxes or media center devices when media delivery must continue even though the user has pressed a physical sleep button, for example.

- **Execution required request** This type of request (available starting with Windows 8 and Server 2012) requests a UWP app process continue execution even if normally the Process Lifecycle Manager (PLM) would have terminated it (for whatever reason); the extended length of time depends on factors such as the power policy settings. This request type is only supported for systems that support Modern Standby, otherwise this request is interpreted as a system request.

EXPERIMENT: Viewing power availability requests

Unfortunately, the power request kernel object that's created with a call such as `PowerCreate-Request` is unavailable in the public symbols. However, the Powercfg utility provides a way to list power requests without any need for a kernel debugger. Here's the output of the utility while playing a video and a stream audio from the web on a Windows 10 laptop:

```
C:\WINDOWS\system32>powercfg /requests
DISPLAY:
[PROCESS] \Device\HarddiskVolume4\Program Files\WindowsApps\Microsoft.
ZuneVideo_10.16092.10311.0_x64__8wekyb3d8bbwe\Video.UI.exe
Windows Runtime Package: Microsoft.ZuneVideo_8wekyb3d8bbwe

SYSTEM:
[DRIVER] Conexant ISST Audio (INTELAUDIO\FUNC_01&VEN_14F1&DEV_50F4&SUBSYS_103C80D3&R
EV_1001\4&1a010da&0&0001)
An audio stream is currently in use.
[PROCESS] \Device\HarddiskVolume4\Program Files\WindowsApps\Microsoft.
ZuneVideo_10.16092.10311.0_x64__8wekyb3d8bbwe\Video.UI.exe
Windows Runtime Package: Microsoft.ZuneVideo_8wekyb3d8bbwe

AWAYMODE:
None.

EXECUTION:
None.

PERFBOOST:
None.

ACTIVELOCKSCREEN:
None.
```

The output shows six request types (as opposed to the four described previously). The last two—perfboost and active lockscreen—are declared as part of an internal power request type in a kernel header, but are otherwise currently unused.

Conclusion

The I/O system defines the model of I/O processing on Windows and performs functions that are common to or required by more than one driver. Its chief responsibilities are to create IRPs representing I/O requests and to shepherd the packets through various drivers, returning results to the caller when an I/O is complete. The I/O manager locates various drivers and devices by using I/O system objects, including driver and device objects. Internally, the Windows I/O system operates asynchronously to achieve high performance and provides both synchronous and asynchronous I/O capabilities to user-mode applications.

Device drivers include not only traditional hardware device drivers but also file-system, network, and layered filter drivers. All drivers have a common structure and communicate with each other and the I/O manager by using common mechanisms. The I/O system interfaces allow drivers to be written in a high-level language to lessen development time and to enhance their portability. Because drivers present a common structure to the operating system, they can be layered one on top of another to achieve modularity and reduce duplication between drivers. By using the Universal DDI baseline, drivers can target multiple devices and form factors with no code changes.

Finally, the role of the PnP manager is to work with device drivers to dynamically detect hardware devices and to build an internal device tree that guides hardware device enumeration and driver installation. The power manager works with device drivers to move devices into low-power states when applicable to conserve energy and prolong battery life.

The next chapter touches on one of the most important aspects of today's computer systems: security.

CHAPTER 7

Security

Preventing unauthorized access to sensitive data is essential in any environment in which multiple users have access to the same physical or network resources. An operating system, as well as individual users, must be able to protect files, memory, and configuration settings from unwanted viewing and modification. Operating system security includes obvious mechanisms such as accounts, passwords, and file protection. It also includes less obvious mechanisms, such as protecting the operating system from corruption, preventing less privileged users from performing actions (rebooting the computer, for example), and not allowing user programs to adversely affect the programs of other users or the operating system.

In this chapter, we explain how every aspect of the design and implementation of Microsoft Windows was influenced in some way by the stringent requirements of providing robust security.

Security ratings

Having software, including operating systems, rated against well-defined standards helps the government, corporations, and home users protect proprietary and personal data stored in computer systems. The current security rating standard used by the United States and many other countries is the Common Criteria (CC). To understand the security capabilities designed into Windows, however, it's useful to know the history of the security ratings system that influenced the design of Windows: the Trusted Computer System Evaluation Criteria (TCSEC).

Trusted Computer System Evaluation Criteria

The National Computer Security Center (NCSC) was established in 1981 as part of the U.S. Department of Defense's (DoD) National Security Agency (NSA). One goal of the NCSC was to create a range of security ratings, listed in Table 7-1, to indicate the degree of protection commercial operating systems, network components, and trusted applications offer. These security ratings, which can be found at *http://csrc.nist.gov/publications/history/dod85.pdf*, were defined in 1983 and are commonly referred to as the *Orange Book*.

TABLE 7-1 TCSEC rating levels

Rating	Description
A1	Verified design
B3	Security domains
B2	Structured protection
B1	Labeled security protection
C2	Controlled access protection
C1	Discretionary access protection (obsolete)
D	Minimal protection

The TCSEC standard consists of levels-of-trust ratings, where higher levels build on lower levels by adding more rigorous protection and validation requirements. No operating system meets the A1 (verified design) rating. Although a few operating systems have earned one of the B-level ratings, C2 is considered sufficient and the highest rating practical for a general-purpose operating system.

The following were the key requirements for a C2 security rating, and they are still considered the core requirements for any secure operating system:

■ **A secure logon facility** This requires that users be able to be uniquely identified and that they must be granted access to the computer only after they have been authenticated in some way.

■ **Discretionary access control** This allows the owner of a resource (such as a file) to determine who can access the resource and what they can do with it. The owner grants rights that permit various kinds of access to a user or to a group of users.

■ **Security auditing** This affords the ability to detect and record security-related events or any attempts to create, access, or delete system resources. Logon identifiers record the identities of all users, making it easy to trace anyone who performs an unauthorized action.

■ **Object reuse protection** This prevents users from seeing data that another user has deleted or from accessing memory that another user previously used and then released. For example, in some operating systems, it's possible to create a new file of a certain length and then examine the contents of the file to see data that happens to have occupied the location on the disk where the file is allocated. This data might be sensitive information that was stored in another user's file but had been deleted. Object reuse protection prevents this potential security hole by initializing all objects, including files and memory, before they are allocated to a user.

Windows also meets two requirements of B-level security:

■ **Trusted path functionality** This prevents Trojan horse programs from being able to intercept users' names and passwords as they try to log on. The trusted path functionality in Windows comes in the form of its Ctrl+Alt+Delete logon-attention sequence, which cannot be intercepted by nonprivileged applications. This sequence of keystrokes, which is also known as the secure attention sequence (SAS), always displays a system-controlled Windows security screen (if a user is already logged on) or the logon screen so that would-be Trojan horses can easily be recognized. (The SAS can also be sent programmatically via the SendSAS API if Group Policy and other restrictions allow it.) A Trojan horse presenting a fake logon dialog box will be bypassed when the SAS is entered.

- **Trusted facility management** This requires support for separate account roles for administrative functions. For example, separate accounts are provided for administration (Administrators), user accounts charged with backing up the computer, and standard users.

Windows meets all these requirements through its security subsystem and related components.

The Common Criteria

In January 1996, the United States, United Kingdom, Germany, France, Canada, and the Netherlands released the jointly developed Common Criteria for Information Technology Security Evaluation (CCITSE) specification. CCITSE, usually referred to as the Common Criteria (CC), is the recognized multinational standard for product security evaluation. The CC home page is at *http://www.niap-ccevs.org/cc-scheme*.

The CC is more flexible than the TCSEC trust ratings and has a structure closer to the ITSEC standard than to the TCSEC standard. The CC includes the concept of a Protection Profile (PP), used to collect security requirements into easily specified and compared sets, and the concept of a Security Target (ST), which contains a set of security requirements that can be made by reference to a PP. The CC also defines a range of seven Evaluation Assurance Levels (EALs), which indicate a level of confidence in the certification. In this way, the CC (like the ITSEC standard before it) removes the link between functionality and assurance level that was present in TCSEC and earlier certification schemes.

Windows 2000, Windows XP, Windows Server 2003, and Windows Vista Enterprise all achieved Common Criteria certification under the Controlled Access Protection Profile (CAPP). This is roughly equivalent to a TCSEC C2 rating. All received a rating of EAL 4+, the "plus" denoting "flaw remediation." EAL 4 is the highest level recognized across national boundaries.

In March 2011, Windows 7 and Windows Server 2008 R2 were evaluated as meeting the requirements of the US Government Protection Profile for General-Purpose Operating Systems in a Networked Environment, version 1.0 (GPOSPP) (*http://www.commoncriteriaportal.org/files/ppfiles/pp_gpospp_v1.0.pdf*). The certification includes the Hyper-V hypervisor. Again, Windows achieved Evaluation Assurance Level 4 with flaw remediation (EAL 4+). The validation report can be found at *http://www.commoncriteriaportal.org/files/epfiles/st_vid10390-vr.pdf*, and the description of the security target, giving details of the requirements satisfied, can be found at *http://www.commoncriteriaportal.org/files/epfiles/st_vid10390-st.pdf*. Similar certifications were achieved by Windows 10 and Windows Server 2012 R2 in June 2016. The report can be found at *http://www.commoncriteriaportal.org/files/epfiles/cr_windows10.pdf*.

Security system components

These are the core components and databases that implement Windows security. (All files mentioned are in the %SystemRoot%\System32 directory unless otherwise specified.)

- **Security reference monitor (SRM)**   This component in the Windows executive (Ntoskrnl.exe) is responsible for defining the access token data structure to represent a security context, performing security access checks on objects, manipulating privileges (user rights), and generating any resulting security audit messages.

- **Local Security Authority Subsystem Service (Lsass)**   This user-mode process runs the image Lsass.exe that is responsible for the local system security policy (such as which users are allowed to log on to the machine, password policies, privileges granted to users and groups, and the system security auditing settings), user authentication, and sending security audit messages to the event log. The Local Security Authority service (Lsasrv.dll), a library that Lsass loads, implements most of this functionality.

- **LSAIso.exe**   This is used by Lsass (if so configured on supported Windows 10 and Server 2016 systems), also known as Credential Guard (see the upcoming "Credential Guard" section for more on Credential Guard), to store users' token hashes instead of keeping them in Lsass's memory. Because Lsaiso.exe is a Trustlet (Isolated User Mode process) running in VTL 1, no normal process—not even the normal kernel—can access the address space of this process. Lsass itself stores an encrypted blob of the password hash needed when it communicates with Lsaiso (via ALPC).

- **Lsass policy database**   This database contains the local system security policy settings. It is stored in the registry in an ACL-protected area under HKLM\SECURITY. It includes such information as what domains are entrusted to authenticate logon attempts, who has permission to access the system and how (interactive, network, and service logons), who is assigned which privileges, and what kind of security auditing is to be performed. The Lsass policy database also stores "secrets" that include logon information used for cached domain logons and Windows service user-account logons. (See Chapter 9, "Management mechanisms," in *Windows Internals Part 2* for more information on Windows services.)

- **Security Accounts Manager (SAM)**   This service is responsible for managing the database that contains the user names and groups defined on the local machine. The SAM service, which is implemented in Samsrv.dll, is loaded into the Lsass process.

- **SAM database**   This database contains the defined local users and groups along with their passwords and other attributes. On domain controllers, the SAM does not store the domain-defined users, but stores the system's administrator recovery account definition and password. This database is stored in the registry under HKLM\SAM.

- **Active Directory** This is a directory service that contains a database that stores information about objects in a domain. A *domain* is a collection of computers and their associated security groups that are managed as a single entity. Active Directory stores information about the objects in the domain, including users, groups, and computers. Password information and privileges for domain users and groups are stored in Active Directory, which is replicated across the computers that are designated as domain controllers of the domain. The Active Directory server, implemented as Ntdsa.dll, runs in the Lsass process. For more information on Active Directory, see Chapter 10, "Networking," in Part 2.

- **Authentication packages** These include dynamic link libraries (DLLs) that run in the context of both Lsass process and client processes and implement Windows authentication policy. An authentication DLL is responsible for authenticating a user by checking whether a given user name and password match (or whatever mechanism was used to provide credentials), and if so, returning to Lsass information detailing the user's security identity, which Lsass uses to generate a token.

- **Interactive logon manager (Winlogon)** This is a user-mode process running Winlogon. exe that is responsible for responding to the SAS and for managing interactive logon sessions. Winlogon creates a user's first process when the user logs on, for example.

- **Logon user interface (LogonUI)** This is a user-mode process running the image LogonUI. exe that presents users with the user interface they can use to authenticate themselves on the system. LogonUI uses credential providers to query user credentials through various methods.

- **Credential providers (CPs)** These are in-process COM objects that run in the LogonUI process (started on demand by Winlogon when the SAS is performed) and used to obtain a user's name and password, smartcard PIN, biometric data (such as a fingerprint), or other identification mechanism. The standard CPs are authui.dll, SmartcardCredentialProvider.dll, BioCredProv. Dll, and FaceCredentialProvider.dll, a face-detection provider added in Windows 10.

- **Network logon service (Netlogon)** This is a Windows service (Netlogon.dll, hosted in a standard SvcHost) that sets up the secure channel to a domain controller, over which security requests—such as an interactive logon (if the domain controller is running Windows NT 4) or LAN Manager and NT LAN Manager (v1 and v2) authentication validation—are sent. Netlogon is also used for Active Directory logons.

- **Kernel Security Device Driver (KSecDD)** This is a kernel-mode library (%SystemRoot%\ System32\Drivers\Ksecdd.sys) of functions that implement the advanced local procedure call (ALPC) interfaces that other kernel mode security components, including the Encrypting File System (EFS), use to communicate with Lsass in user mode.

- **AppLocker** This mechanism allows administrators to specify which executable files, DLLs, and scripts can be used by specified users and groups. AppLocker consists of a driver (%SystemRoot%\ System32\Drivers\Appld.sys) and a service (AppIdSvc.dll) running in a standard SvcHost process.

Figure 7-1 shows the relationships among some of these components and the databases they manage.

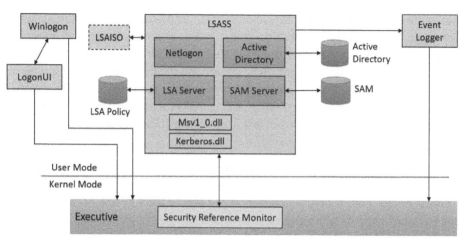

FIGURE 7-1 Windows security components.

EXPERIMENT: Looking inside HKLM\SAM and HKLM\Security

The security descriptors associated with the SAM and Security keys in the registry prevent access by any account other than the local system account. One way to gain access to these keys for exploration is to reset their security, but that can weaken the system's security. Another way is to execute Regedit.exe while running as the local system account. This can be done using the PsExec tool from Sysinternals with the –s option, as shown here:

```
C:\>psexec –s –i –d c:\windows\regedit.exe
```

The -i switch instructs PsExec to run the target executable under the interactive window station. Without it, the process would run in a non-interactive window station, on an invisible desktop. The -d switch just indicates PsExec should not wait until the target process exits.

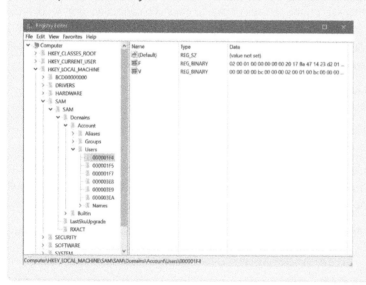

The SRM, which runs in kernel mode, and Lsass, which runs in user mode, communicate using the ALPC facility described in Chapter 8, "System mechanisms," in Part 2. During system initialization, the SRM creates a port, named SeRmCommandPort, to which Lsass connects. When the Lsass process starts, it creates an ALPC port named SeLsaCommandPort. The SRM connects to this port, resulting in the creation of private communication ports. The SRM creates a shared memory section for messages longer than 256 bytes, passing a handle in the connect call. Once the SRM and Lsass connect to each other during system initialization, they no longer listen on their respective connect ports. Therefore, a later user process has no way to connect successfully to either of these ports for malicious purposes. The connect request will never complete.

Virtualization-based security

It is common to refer to the kernel as *trusted*, due to its inherently higher level of privilege and isolation from user-mode applications. Yet, countless third-party drivers are written each month—Microsoft has stated that a million unique driver hashes are seen through telemetry, monthly! Each of these can contain any number of vulnerabilities, not to mention purposefully malicious kernel-mode code. In such a reality, the idea that the kernel is a small, protected component, and that user-mode applications are "safe" from attack, is clearly an unrealized ideal. This state of affairs leads to an inability to fully trust the kernel, and leaves key user-mode applications, which may contain highly private user data, open to compromise from other malicious user-mode applications (which exploit buggy kernel-mode components) or malicious kernel-mode programs.

As discussed in Chapter 2, "System architecture," Windows 10 and Server 2016 include a virtualization-based security (VBS) architecture that enables an additional orthogonal level of trust: the virtual trust level (VTL). In this section, you will see how Credential Guard and Device Guard leverage VTLs to protect user data and provide an additional hardware-trust-based layer of security for digital code-signing purposes. At the end of this chapter, you will also see how Kernel Patch Protection (KPP) is provided through the PatchGuard component and enhanced by the VBS-powered HyperGuard technology.

As a reminder, normal user-mode and kernel code runs in VTL 0 and is unaware of the existence of VTL 1. This means anything placed at VTL 1 is hidden and inaccessible to VTL 0 code. If malware is able to penetrate the normal kernel, it still cannot gain access to anything stored in VTL 1, including even user-mode code running in VTL 1 (which is called Isolated User Mode). Figure 7-2 shows the main VBS components we'll be looking at in this section:

- Hypervisor-Based Code Integrity (HVCI) and Kernel-Mode Code Integrity (KMCI), which power Device Guard

- LSA (Lsass.exe) and isolated LSA (Lsaiso.exe), which power Credential Guard

Additionally, recall that the implementation of Trustlets, which run in IUM, was shown in Chapter 3, "Process and jobs."

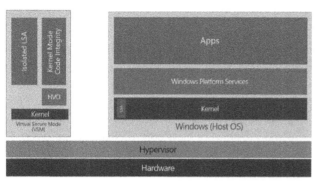

FIGURE 7-2 VBS components.

Of course, like any trusted component, VTL 1 also makes certain assumptions that the components it depends on can also be trusted. As such, VTL 1 requires Secure Boot (and thus, firmware) to function correctly, the hypervisor to not have been compromised, and hardware elements such as the IOMMU and Intel Management Engine to be free of VTL 0–accessible vulnerabilities. For more information on the hardware chain of trust and boot-related security technologies, see Chapter 11, "Startup and shutdown," in Part 2.

Credential Guard

To understand the security boundary and protection that Credential Guard provides, it is important to understand the various components that provide access to a user's resources and data or login capabilities on a networked environment:

- **Password** This is the primary credential used by interactive users to identify themselves on the machine. This credential is used for authentication and to derive the other components of the credential model. It is the most highly sought after piece of a user's identity.

- **NT one-way function (NT OWF)** This is a hash used by legacy components to identify the user (after a successful password logon) using the NT LAN Manager (NTLM) protocol. While modern networked systems no longer use NTLM to authenticate the user, many local components still do, as do some types of legacy network components (such as NTLM-based authenticating proxies). Because NTOWF is an MD4 hash, its algorithmic complexity in the face of today's hardware, and its lack of anti-repeatability protection, means that intercepting the hash leads to instant compromise and even possible recovery of the password.

- **Ticket-granting ticket (TGT)** This is the equivalent of the NTOWF when a much more modern remote authentication mechanism is used: Kerberos. This is the default on Windows Active Directory–based domains and is enforced on Server 2016. The TGT and a corresponding key are provided to the local machine after a successful logon (just like the NTOWF on NTLM), and intercepting both components will result in instant compromise of the user's credentials, although reuse and password recovery will not be possible.

Without Credential Guard enabled, some or all of these components of a user's authentication credentials are present in the memory of Lsass.

Note To enable Credential Guard on Windows 10 Enterprise and Server 2016 editions, open the Group Policy editor (**gpedit.msc**), choose **Computer Configuration**, select **Administrative Templates**, choose **System**, choose **Device Guard,** and select **Turn on Virtualization Based Security**. In the top-left part of the dialog box that appears, select **Enabled**. Finally, select one of the **Enabled** options in the Credential Guard Configuration combo box.

Protecting the password

The password, encrypted with a local symmetric key, is stored to provide single sign-on (SSO) capabilities over protocols such as digest authentication (WDigest, used for HTTP-based authentication since Windows XP) or Terminal Services/RDP. As these protocols use plaintext authentication, the password must be kept in memory, which is then accessible through code injection, debugger, or other exploit techniques, and decrypted. Credential Guard cannot change the nature of these inherently unsafe protocols. Therefore, the only possible solution, which Credential Guard employs, is to disable SSO functionality for such protocols. This causes a loss of compatibility and forces the user to re-authenticate.

Obviously, a preferable solution is to remove the usage of a password completely, which Windows Hello, described in the "Windows Hello" section later in this chapter, allows. Authenticating with biometric credentials such as a user's face or fingerprint removes the need to ever type a password, securing the interactive credential against hardware key loggers, kernel sniffing/hooking tools, and user mode–based spoofing applications. If the user never has a password to type, there is no password to steal. Another similar secure credential is the combination of a smart card and associated PIN. While a PIN may be stolen as its typed in, the smart card is a physical element whose key cannot be intercepted without a complex hardware-based attack. This is a type of two-factor authentication (TFA), of which many other implementations exist.

Protecting the NTOWF/TGT key

Even with protected interactive credentials, a successful login results in a domain controller's key distribution center (KDC) returning the TGT and its key, as well as the NTOWF for legacy applications. Later, the user simply uses the NTOWF for accessing legacy resources and uses the TGT and its key to generate a service ticket. This can then be used to access remote resources (such as files on a share), as shown in Figure 7-3.

FIGURE 7-3 Accessing remote resources.

Thus, with either the NTOWF or the TGT and its key (stored in Lsass) in the attacker's hands, access to resources is possible even without the smart card, PIN, or user's face or fingerprint. Protecting Lsass from access by an attacker is thus one option that can be used, and which is possible using the Protected Process Light (PPL) architecture described in Chapter 3.

Lsass can be configured to run protected by setting the DWORD value RunAsPPL in the HKLM\System\CurrentControlSet\Consol\Lsa registry key to 1. (This is not a default option, as legitimate third-party authentication providers [DLLs] load and execute in the context of Lsass, which would not be possible if Lsass would run protected.) Unfortunately, while this protection does guard the NTOWF and TGT key from user-mode attackers, it does not protect against kernel attackers or user-mode attackers that leverage vulnerabilities in any of the millions of drivers that are produced monthly. Credential Guard solves this problem by using another process, Lsaiso.exe, which runs as a Trustlet in VTL 1. This process therefore stores the user's s secrets in its memory, not in Lsass.

Secure communication

As shown in Chapter 2, VTL 1 has a minimal attack surface, as it does not have the full regular "NT" kernel, nor does it have any drivers or access to I/O of hardware of any kind. As such, isolated LSA, which is a VTL 1 Trustlet, cannot directly communicate with the KDC. This is still the responsibility of the Lsass process, which serves as a proxy and protocol implementer, communicating with the KDC to authenticate the user and to receive the TGT and the key and NTOWF, as well as communicating with the file server by using service ticket. This seemingly results in a problem: the TGT and its key/NTOWF transiently pass through Lsass during authentication, and the TGT and its key are somehow available to Lsass for the generation of service tickets. This leads to two questions: How does Lsass send and receive the secrets from isolated ISA, and how can we prevent an attacker from doing the same?

To answer the first question, recall that Chapter 3, "Processes and jobs," described which services are available to Trustlets. One was the Advanced Local Procedure Call (ALPC), which the Secure Kernel supports by proxying the NtAlpc* calls to the Normal Kernel. Then, the Isolated User Mode environment implements support for the RPC runtime library (Rpcrt4.dll) over the ALPC protocol, which allows a VTL 0 and VTL 1 application to communicate using local RPC just like any other application and service. In Figure 7-4, which shows Process Explorer, you can see the Lsaiso.exe process, which has a handle to the LSA_ISO_RPC_SERVER ALPC port. This is used to communicate with the Lsass.exe process. (See Chapter 8 in Part 2 for more information on ALPC.)

To answer the second question, some understanding of cryptographic protocols and challenge/response models is required. If you're already familiar with some of the basic concepts of SSL/TLS technology and its use in Internet communications to prevent man-in-the-middle (MitM) attacks, you can think of the KDC and isolated LSA protocol in a similar way. Although Lsass sits in the middle as a proxy would, it only sees encrypted traffic between the KDC and isolated LSA, without the ability to understand its contents. Because isolated LSA establishes a local "session key," which only lives in VTL 1, and then uses a secure protocol to send this session key encrypted with yet another key, which only the KDC has, the KDC can then respond with the TGT and its key after encrypting it with the isolated LSA session key. Therefore, Lsass sees an encrypted message to the KDC (which it can't decrypt) and an encrypted message from the KDC (which it can't decrypt).

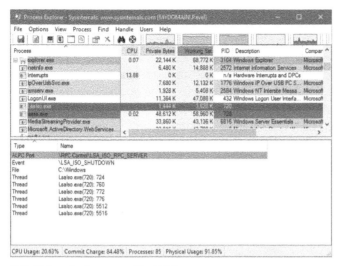

FIGURE 7-4 Lsalso.exe and its ALPC port.

This model can even be used to protect legacy NTLM authentication, which is based on a challenge/response model. For example, when a user logs in with a plaintext credential, LSA sends it to isolated LSA, which then encrypts it with its session key and returns the encrypted credential to Lsass. Later, when an NTLM challenge/response is required, Lsass sends the NTLM challenge and the previously encrypted credentials to isolated LSA. At this point, only isolated LSA has the encryption key, so it decrypts the credentials and generates an NTLM response based on the challenge.

Note, however, that four possible attacks exist in this model:

■ If the machine is already physically compromised, the plaintext password can be intercepted either as it is inputted or as it is sent to isolated LSA (if Lsass is already compromised). Using Windows Hello can mitigate against this.

■ As mentioned, NTLM does not have anti-replay properties. Therefore, if the NTLM response is captured, it can be replayed for the same challenge. Alternatively, if the attacker can compromise Lsass after logon, it can capture the encrypted credential and force isolated LSA to generate new NTLM responses for arbitrary NTLM challenges. This attack, however, only works until reboot, because isolated LSA generates a new session key at that point.

■ In the case of Kerberos logon, the NTOWF (which is not encrypted) can be intercepted and then reused, just like in a standard pass-the-hash attack. Again, however, this requires an already compromised machine (or physical network interception).

■ The user, with physical access, may be able to disable Credential Guard. In this situation, the legacy authentication model is used (a so-called "downgrade attack"), and older attack models can now be employed.

UEFI lock

Because disabling Credential Guard (which is ultimately nothing more than a registry setting) is trivial for an attacker, Secure Boot and UEFI can be leveraged to prevent a non-physically present administrator (such as malware with admin rights) from disabling Credential Guard. This is done by enabling Credential Guard with UEFI Lock. In this mode, an EFI runtime variable is written to firmware memory and a reboot is required. At the reboot, the Windows boot loader, which still operates in EFI Boot Services mode, will write an EFI boot variable (which has the property of not being readable or writeable once EFI Boot Services mode is exited) to record the fact that Credential Guard is enabled. Additionally, a Boot Configuration Database (BCD) option will be recorded.

When the kernel boots, it will automatically rewrite the required Credential Guard registry key in the presence of the BCD option and/or UEFI runtime variable. If the BCD option is deleted by an attacker, BitLocker (if enabled) and TPM-based remote attestation (if enabled) will detect the change and require physical input of the admin's recovery key before booting, which will then restore the BCD option based on the UEFI runtime variable. If the UEFI runtime variable is deleted, the Windows boot loader will restore it based on the UEFI boot variable. As such, without special code to delete the UEFI boot variable—which can only be done in EFI Boot Services mode—there is no way to disable Credential Guard in UEFI lock mode.

The only such code that exists is in a special Microsoft binary called SecComp.efi. This must be downloaded by the administrator, who must then either boot the computer from an alternate EFI-based device and manually execute it (which will require the BitLocker recovery key as well as physical access) or modify the BCD (which will require the BitLocker recovery key). At the reboot, SecComp.efi will require user confirmation while in UEFI mode (which can only be done by a physical user).

Authentication policies and armored Kerberos

Using a security model of "secure, unless already compromised before logon or by a physical administrator" is definitely an improvement over the traditional non–Credential Guard–based security model. However, some enterprises and organizations may want an even stronger security guarantee: that even a compromised machine cannot be used to fake or replay a user's credentials, and that if a user's credentials *have* been compromised, they cannot be used outside of specific systems. By leveraging a Server 2016 feature called Authentication Policies, and armored Kerberos, Credential Guard can operate in this heightened security mode.

In this mode, the VTL 1 Secure Kernel will collect, using the TPM (a file on disk can also be used, but makes the security moot), a special machine ID key. This key is then used to generate a machine TGT key during the initial domain join operation as the machine is provisioned (obviously, it is important to ensure the machine is in a trusted state during provisioning), and this TGT key is sent to the KDC. Once configured, when the user logs in with his or her credential, it is combined with the machine's credential (which only isolated LSA has access to), which forms a proof-of-origin key. The KDC will then reply with the NTOWF and user TGT and its key after encrypting it with the proof-of-origin key. In this mode, two security guarantees are provided:

- **The user is authenticating from a known machine**　If the user, or an attacker, has the original credentials, and attempts to use them on a different machine, its TPM-based machine credential will be different.

- **The NTLM response/user ticket is coming from isolated LSA and has not been manually generated from Lsass**   This guarantees that Credential Guard is enabled on the machine, even if the physical user can disable it in some way.

Unfortunately, once again, if the machine is compromised in such a way that the proof-of-origin–encrypted KDC response that contains the user TGT and its key is intercepted, it can be stored and used to request session key–encrypted service tickets from isolated LSA. This can then be sent to a file server (for example) to access it until a reboot is issued to wipe the session key. As such, on a system with Credential Guard, it is recommended to reboot each time a user logs off. Otherwise, an attacker may be able to issue valid tickets even after the user is no longer present.

Future improvements

As discussed in Chapter 2 and Chapter 3, the Secure Kernel in VTL 1 is currently undergoing improvements to add support for specialized classes of PCI and USB hardware, which can exclusively be communicated with only through the hypervisor and VTL 1 code using the Secure Device Framework (SDF). Combined with BioIso.exe and FsIso.exe, which are new Trustlets to securely obtain biometric data and video frames (from a webcam), a VTL 0 kernel mode–based component cannot intercept the contents of a Windows Hello authentication attempt (which we've classified as safe compared to a user's plaintext password, but still technically capturable through custom driver-based interception). Once released, Windows Hello credentials will be guaranteed at the hardware level to not ever be available to VTL 0. In this mode, Lsass will not need to be involved in a Windows Hello authentication. Isolated LSA will obtain the credentials directly from the isolated biometrics or isolated frame service.

> **Note**   The Secure Driver Framework (SDF) is the WDF-equivalent for VTL 1 drivers. This framework is not currently public, but is shared with Microsoft partners only for creating VTL 1 drivers.

Device Guard

While Credential Guard is concerned with safeguarding the user's credentials, Device Guard has a completely different goal: protecting the user's machine itself from different kinds of software- and hardware-based attacks. Device Guard leverages the Windows Code Integrity services, such as Kernel-Mode Code Signing (KMCS) and User-Mode Code Integrity (UMCI), and strengthens them through HyperVisor Code Integrity (HVCI). (See Chapter 8 in Part 2 for more information on Code Integrity.)

Additionally, Device Guard is fully configurable, thanks to Custom Code Integrity (CCI) and signing policies that are protected by Secure Boot and defined by the enterprise administrator. These policies, which are explained in Chapter 8, allow the enforcement of inclusion/exclusion lists that are based on cryptographically sound information (such as certificate signers or SHA-2 hashes) instead of file paths or file names as with AppLocker's policies. (See the section "AppLocker" later in this chapter for more on AppLocker.)

Therefore, while we won't describe here the different ways in which Code Integrity policies can be defined and customized, we will show how Device Guard enforces whatever these policies may be set to, through the following guarantees:

■ **If kernel-mode code signing is enforced, only signed code can load, regardless of the kernel itself being compromised**   This is because the kernel-loading process will notify the Secure Kernel in VTL 1 whenever it loads a driver, and only successfully load it once HVCI has validated its signature.

■ **If kernel-mode code signing is enforced, signed code cannot be modified once loaded, even by the kernel itself**   This is because the executable code pages will be marked as read-only through the hypervisor's Second Level Address Translation (SLAT) mechanism, which is further explained in Chapter 8 in Part 2.

■ **If kernel-mode code signing is enforced, dynamically allocated code is prohibited (a tautology of the first two bullets)**   This is because the kernel does not have the ability to allocate executable entries in the SLAT page table entries, even though the kernel's page tables themselves may mark such code as executable.

■ **If kernel-mode code signing is enforced, UEFI runtime code cannot be modified, even by other UEFI runtime code or by the kernel itself**   Additionally, Secure Boot should already have validated that this code was signed at the time it was loaded. (Device Guard relies on this assumption.) Furthermore, UEFI runtime data cannot be made executable. This is done by reading all the UEFI runtime code and data, enforcing the correct permissions, and duplicating them in the SLAT page table entries, which are protected in VTL 1.

■ **If kernel-mode code signing is enforced, only kernel-mode (ring 0) signed code can execute**   This may once again sound like a tautology of the first three bullets, but consider signed ring 3 code. Such code is valid from UMCI's perspective and has been authorized as executable code in the SLAT page table entries. The Secure Kernel relies on the Mode-Based Execution Control (MBEC) feature, if present in hardware, which enhances the SLAT with a user/kernel executable bit, or the hypervisor's software emulation of this feature, called Restricted User Mode (RUM).

■ **If user-mode code signing is enforced, only signed user-mode images can be loaded**   This means all executable processes must be signed (.exe) files as well as the libraries they load (.dll).

■ **If user-mode code signing is enforced, the kernel does not allow user-mode applications to make existing executable code pages writable**   Obviously, it is impossible for user-mode code to allocate executable memory or to modify existing memory without asking the kernel permission. As such, the kernel can apply its usual enforcement rules. But even in the case of a compromised kernel, the SLAT ensures that no user-mode pages will be executable without the Secure Kernel's knowledge and approval, and that such executable pages can never be writeable.

■ **If user-mode code signing is enforced, and hard code guarantees are requested by the signing policy, dynamically allocated code is prohibited**   This is an important distinction from the kernel scenarios. By default, signed user-mode code is allowed to allocate additional executable memory to support JIT scenarios unless a special enhanced key usage (EKU) is present in the application's certificate, which serves as a dynamic code generation entitlement. At present, NGEN.EXE (.NET Native Image Generation) has this EKU, which allows IL-only .NET executables to function even in this mode.

■ **If user-mode PowerShell constrained language mode is enforced, all PowerShell scripts that use dynamic types, reflection, or other language features that allow the execution or arbitrary code and/or marshalling to Windows/.NET API functions must also be signed** This prevents possibly malicious PowerShell scripts from escaping constrained mode.

SLAT page table entries are protected in VTL 1 and contain the "ground truth" for what permissions a given page of memory can have. By withholding the executable bit as needed, and/or withholding the writable bit from existing executable pages (a security model known as W^X, pronounced *double-you xor ex*), Device Guard moves all code-signing enforcement into VTL 1 (in a library called SKCI.DLL, or Secure Kernel Code Integrity).

Additionally, even if not configured explicitly on the machine, Device Guard operates in a third mode if Credential Guard is enabled by enforcing that all Trustlets have a specific Microsoft signature with a certificate that includes the Isolated User Mode EKU. Otherwise, an attacker with ring 0 privileges could attack the regular KMCS mechanism and load a malicious Trustlet to attack the isolated LSA component. Furthermore, all user-mode code-signing enforcements are active for the Trustlet, which executes in hard code guarantees mode.

Finally, as a performance optimization, it is important to understand that the HVCI mechanism will not reauthenticate every single page when the system resumes from hibernation (S4 sleep state). In some cases, the certificate data may not even be available. Even if this were the case, the SLAT data must be reconstructed, which means that the SLAT page table entries are stored in the hibernation file itself. As such, the hypervisor needs to trust the hibernation file has not been modified in any way. This is done by encrypting the hibernation file with a local machine key that is stored in the TPM. Unfortunately, without a TPM present, this key must be stored in a UEFI runtime variable, which allows a local attacker to decrypt the hibernation file, modify it, and re-encrypt it.

Protecting objects

Object protection and access logging are the essence of discretionary access control and auditing. The objects that can be protected on Windows include files, devices, mailslots, pipes (named and anonymous), jobs, processes, threads, events, keyed events, event pairs, mutexes, semaphores, shared memory sections, I/O completion ports, LPC ports, waitable timers, access tokens, volumes, window stations, desktops, network shares, services, registry keys, printers, Active Directory objects, and so on—theoretically, anything managed by the executive object manager. In practice, objects that are not exposed to user mode (such as driver objects) are usually not protected. Kernel-mode code is trusted and usually uses interfaces to the object manager that do not perform access checking. Because system resources that are exported to user mode (and hence require security validation) are implemented as objects in kernel mode, the Windows object manager plays a key role in enforcing object security.

You can view object protection with the WinObj Sysinternals tool (for named objects), shown in Figure 7-5. Figure 7-6 shows the Security property page of a section object in the user's session. Although files are the resources most commonly associated with object protection, Windows uses the same security model and mechanism for executive objects as it does for files in the file system. As far as access controls are concerned, executive objects differ from files only in the access methods supported by each type of object.

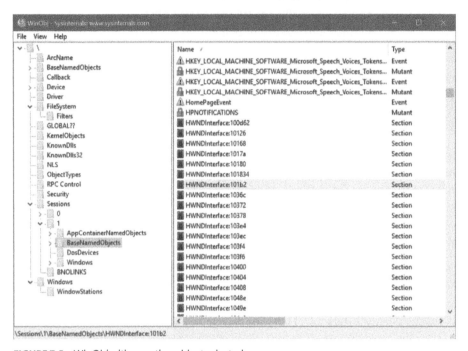

FIGURE 7-5 WinObj with a section object selected.

FIGURE 7-6 An executive object and its security descriptor, viewed by WinObj.

What is shown in Figure 7-6 is actually the object's discretionary access control list (DACL). We will describe DACLs in detail in the section "Security descriptors and access control."

You can use Process Explorer to view the security properties of objects by double-clicking a handle in the lower pane view (when configured to show handles). This has the added benefit of displaying objects that are unnamed. The Property page shown is the same in both tools, as the page itself is provided by Windows.

To control who can manipulate an object, the security system must first be sure of each user's identity. This need to guarantee the user's identity is the reason that Windows requires authenticated logon before accessing any system resources. When a process requests a handle to an object, the object manager and the security system use the caller's security identification and the object's security descriptor to determine whether the caller should be assigned a handle that grants the process access to the object it desires.

As discussed later in this chapter, a thread can assume a different security context than that of its process. This mechanism is called *impersonation*. When a thread is impersonating, security validation mechanisms use the thread's security context instead of that of the thread's process. When a thread isn't impersonating, security validation falls back on using the security context of the thread's owning process. It's important to keep in mind that all the threads in a process share the same handle table, so when a thread opens an object—even if it's impersonating—all the threads of the process have access to the object.

Sometimes, validating the identity of a user isn't enough for the system to grant access to a resource that should be accessible by the account. Logically, one can think of a clear distinction between a service running under the Alice account and an unknown application that Alice downloaded while browsing the Internet. Windows achieves this kind of intra-user isolation with the Windows integrity mechanism, which implements integrity levels. The Windows integrity mechanism is used by User Account Control (UAC) elevations, User Interface Privilege Isolation (UIPI) and AppContainers, all described later in this chapter.

Access checks

The Windows security model requires that a thread specify up front, at the time that it opens an object, what types of actions it wants to perform on the object. The object manager calls the SRM to perform access checks based on a thread's desired access. If the access is granted, a handle is assigned to the thread's process with which the thread (or other threads in the process) can perform further operations on the object.

One event that causes the object manager to perform security access validation is when a thread opens an existing object using a name. When an object is opened by name, the object manager performs a lookup of the specified object in the object manager namespace. If the object isn't located in a secondary namespace, such as the configuration manager's registry namespace or a file system driver's file system namespace, the object manager calls the internal function ObpCreateHandle once it locates the object. As its name implies, ObpCreateHandle creates an entry in the process handle table that becomes associated with the object. ObpCreateHandle first calls ObpGrantAccess to see if the thread has permission to access the object. If so, ObpCreateHandle calls the executive function ExCreateHandle to create the entry in the process handle table. ObpGrantAccess calls ObCheckObjectAccess to initiate the security access check.

ObpGrantAccess passes to ObCheckObjectAccess the security credentials of the thread opening the object, the types of access to the object that the thread is requesting (read, write, delete, and so forth, including object-specific operations), and a pointer to the object. ObCheckObjectAccess first locks the object's security descriptor and the security context of the thread. The object security lock prevents another thread in the system from changing the object's security while the access check is in progress. The lock on the thread's security context prevents another thread (from that process or a different process) from altering the security identity of the thread while security validation is in progress. ObCheckObjectAccess then calls the object's security method to obtain the security settings of the object. (See Chapter 8 in Part 2 for a description of object methods.) The call to the security method might invoke a function in a different executive component. However, many executive objects rely on the system's default security management support.

When an executive component defining an object doesn't want to override the SRM's default security policy, it marks the object type as having default security. Whenever the SRM calls an object's security method, it first checks to see whether the object has default security. An object with default security stores its security information in its header, and its security method is SeDefaultObjectMethod. An object that doesn't rely on default security must manage its own security information and supply a specific security method. Objects that rely on default security include mutexes, events, and semaphores. A file object is an example of an object that overrides default security. The I/O manager, which defines the file object type, has the file system driver on which a file resides manage (or choose not to implement) the security for its files. Thus, when the system queries the security on a file object that represents a file on an NTFS volume, the I/O manager file object security method retrieves the file's security using the NTFS file system driver. Note, however, that ObCheckObjectAccess isn't executed when files are opened because they reside in secondary namespaces. The system invokes a file object's security method only when a thread explicitly queries or sets the security on a file (with the Windows SetFileSecurity or GetFileSecurity functions, for example).

After obtaining an object's security information, ObCheckObjectAccess invokes the SRM function SeAccessCheck. SeAccessCheck is one of the functions at the heart of the Windows security model. Among the input parameters SeAccessCheck accepts are the object's security information, the security identity of the thread as captured by ObCheckObjectAccess, and the access that the thread is requesting. SeAccessCheck returns true or false, depending on whether the thread is granted the access it requested to the object.

Here is an example: Suppose a thread wants to know when a specific process exits (or terminates in some way). It needs to get a handle to the target process by calling the OpenProcess API, passing in two important arguments: the unique process ID (let's assume it's known or has been obtained in some way) and an access mask indicating the operations that the thread wants to perform using the returned handle. Lazy developers may just pass PROCESS_ALL_ACCESS for the access mask, specifying they want all possible access rights for the process. One of the following two results would occur:

- If the calling thread can be granted all the permissions, it would get back a valid handle and then could call `WaitForSingleObject` to wait for the process to exit. However, another thread in the process, perhaps with fewer privileges, can use the same handle to do other operations with the process, such as terminate it prematurely with `TerminateProcess`, because the handle allows all possible operations on the process.

- The call can fail if the calling thread does not have sufficient privileges to be granted all possible access and the result is an invalid handle, meaning no access to the process. This is unfortunate, because the thread just needed to ask for the SYNCHRONIZE access mask. That has a much better chance of succeeding than asking for PROCESS_ALL_ACCESS.

The simple conclusion here is that a thread should request the exact access it requires—no more, no less.

Another event that causes the object manager to execute access validation is when a process references an object using an existing handle. Such references often occur indirectly, as when a process calls on a Windows API to manipulate an object and passes an object handle. For example, a thread opening a file can request read permission to the file. If the thread has permission to access the object in this way, as dictated by its security context and the security settings of the file, the object manager creates a handle— representing the file—in the handle table of the thread's process. The types of accesses the threads in the process are granted through the handle are stored with the handle by the object manager.

Subsequently, the thread could attempt to write to the file using the `WriteFile` Windows function, passing the file's handle as a parameter. The system service `NtWriteFile`, which `WriteFile` calls via Ntdll.dll, uses the object manager function `ObReferenceObjectByHandle` (documented in the WDK) to obtain a pointer to the file object from the handle. `ObReferenceObjectByHandle` accepts the access that the caller wants from the object as a parameter. After finding the handle entry in the process handle table, `ObReferenceObjectByHandle` compares the access being requested with the access granted at the time the file was opened. In this example, `ObReferenceObjectByHandle` will indicate that the write operation should fail because the caller didn't obtain write access when the file was opened.

The Windows security functions also enable Windows applications to define their own private objects and to call on the services of the SRM (through the AuthZ user-mode APIs, described later) to enforce the Windows security model on those objects. Many kernel-mode functions that the object manager and other executive components use to protect their own objects are exported as Windows user-mode APIs. The user-mode equivalent of `SeAccessCheck` is the AuthZ API `AccessCheck`. Windows applications can therefore leverage the flexibility of the security model and transparently integrate with the authentication and administrative interfaces that are present in Windows.

The essence of the SRM's security model is an equation that takes three inputs: the security identity of a thread, the access that the thread wants to an object, and the security settings of the object. The output is either yes or no and indicates whether the security model grants the thread the access it desires. The following sections describe the inputs in more detail and then document the model's access-validation algorithm.

EXPERIMENT: Viewing handle access masks

Process Explorer can show the access mask associated with open handles. Follow these steps:

1. Open Process Explorer.

2. Open the **View** menu, choose **Lower Pane View**, and select **Handles** to configure the lower pane to show handles.

3. Right-click the column headers of the lower pane and choose **Select Columns** to open the dialog box shown here:

4. Select the **Access Mask** and **Decoded Access Mask** check boxes (the latter is available in version 16.10 and later) and click **OK**.

5. Select **Explorer.exe** from the process list and look at the lower pane handles. Each handle has an access mask, indicating the access granted using this handle. To help with interpreting the bits of the access mask, the decoded access mask column shows a textual representation of the access masks for many types of objects:

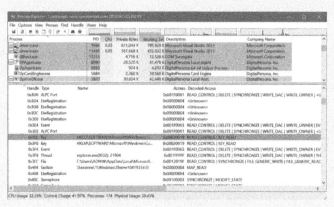

Notice there are generic access rights (for example, READ_CONTROL and SYNCHRONIZE) and specific ones (for example, KEY_READ and MODIFY_STATE). Most of the specific ones are shortened versions of the actual defines in the windows headers (for example, MODIFY_STATE instead of EVENT_MODIFY_STATE, TERMINATE instead of PROCESS_TERMINATE).

Security identifiers

Instead of using names (which might or might not be unique) to identify entities that perform actions in a system, Windows uses security identifiers (SIDs). Users have SIDs, as do local and domain groups, local computers, domains, domain members, and services. A SID is a variable-length numeric value that consists of a SID structure revision number, a 48-bit identifier authority value, and a variable number of 32-bit subauthority or relative identifier (RID) values. The authority value identifies the agent that issued the SID, and this agent is typically a Windows local system or a domain. Subauthority values identify trustees relative to the issuing authority, and RIDs are simply a way for Windows to create unique SIDs based on a common base SID. Because SIDs are long and Windows takes care to generate truly random values within each SID, it is virtually impossible for Windows to issue the same SID twice on machines or domains anywhere in the world.

When displayed textually, each SID carries an S prefix, and its various components are separated with hyphens like so:

S-1-5-21-1463437245-1224812800-863842198-1128

In this SID, the revision number is 1, the identifier authority value is 5 (the Windows security authority), and four subauthority values plus one RID (1128) make up the remainder of the SID. This SID is a domain SID, but a local computer on the domain would have a SID with the same revision number, identifier authority value, and number of subauthority values.

When you install Windows, the Windows Setup program issues the computer a machine SID. Windows assigns SIDs to local accounts on the computer. Each local-account SID is based on the source computer's SID and has a RID at the end. RIDs for user accounts and groups start at 1000 and increase in increments of 1 for each new user or group. Similarly, Domain Controller Promote (Dcpromo.exe), the utility used to create a new Windows domain, reuses the computer SID of the computer being promoted to domain controller as the domain SID and re-creates a new SID for the computer if it is ever demoted. Windows issues to new domain accounts SIDs that are based on the domain SID and have an appended RID (again starting at 1000 and increasing in increments of 1 for each new user or group). A RID of 1028 indicates that the SID is the twenty-ninth SID the domain issued.

Windows issues SIDs that consist of a computer or domain SID with a predefined RID to many predefined accounts and groups. For example, the RID for the Administrator account is 500, and the RID for the guest account is 501. A computer's local Administrator account, for example, has the computer SID as its base with the RID of 500 appended to it:

S-1-5-21-13124455-12541255-61235125-500

Windows also defines a number of built-in local and domain SIDs to represent well-known groups. For example, a SID that identifies any and all accounts (except anonymous users) is the Everyone SID: S-1-1-0. Another example of a group that a SID can represent is the Network group, which is the group that represents users who have logged on to a machine from the network. The Network group SID is S-1-5-2. Table 7-2, reproduced here from the Windows SDK documentation, shows some basic well-known SIDs, their numeric values, and their use. Unlike users' SIDs, these SIDs are predefined constants, and have the same values on every Windows system and domain in the world. Thus, a file that is accessible by members of the Everyone group on the system where it was created is also accessible to Everyone on any other system or domain to which the hard drive where it resides happens to be moved. Users on those systems must, of course, authenticate to an account on those systems before becoming members of the Everyone group.

TABLE 7-2 A few well-known SIDs

SID	Name	Use
S-1-0-0	Nobody	Used when the SID is unknown
S-1-1-0	Everyone	A group that includes all users except anonymous users
S-1-2-0	Local	Users who log on to terminals locally (physically) connected to the system
S-1-3-0	Creator Owner ID	A security identifier to be replaced by the security identifier of the user who created a new object (used in inheritable ACEs)
S-1-3-1	Creator Group ID	Identifies a security identifier to be replaced by the Primary group SID of the user who created a new object (used in inheritable ACEs)
S-1-5-18	Local System account	Used by services
S-1-5-19	Local Service account	Used by services
S-1-5-20	Network Service account	Used by services

> **Note** See Microsoft Knowledge Base article 243330 for a list of defined SIDs at *http://support.microsoft.com/kb/243330*.

Finally, Winlogon creates a unique logon SID for each interactive logon session. A typical use of a logon SID is in an access control entry (ACE) that allows access for the duration of a client's logon session. For example, a Windows service can use the `LogonUser` function to start a new logon session. The `LogonUser` function returns an access token from which the service can extract the logon SID. The service can then use the SID in an ACE (described in the section "Security descriptors and access control" later in this chapter) that allows the client's logon session to access the interactive window station and desktop. The SID for a logon session is S-1-5-5-X-Y, where the X and Y are randomly generated.

EXPERIMENT: Using PsGetSid and Process Explorer to view SIDs

You can easily see the SID representation for any account you're using by running the `PsGetSid` utility from Sysinternals. `PsGetSid`'s options allow you to translate machine and user account names to their corresponding SIDs and vice versa.

If you run `PsGetSid` with no options, it prints the SID assigned to the local computer. Because the Administrator account always has a RID of 500, you can determine the name assigned to the account (in cases where a system administrator has renamed the account for security reasons) simply by passing the machine SID appended with -500 as `PsGetSid`'s command-line argument.

To obtain the SID of a domain account, enter the user name with the domain as a prefix:

```
c:\>psgetsid redmond\johndoe
```

You can determine the SID of a domain by specifying the domain's name as the argument to PsGetSid:

```
c:\>psgetsid Redmond
```

Finally, by examining the RID of your own account, you know at least a number of security accounts (equal to the number resulting from subtracting 999 from your RID) have been created in your domain or on your local machine (depending on whether you are using a domain or local machine account). You can determine what accounts have been assigned RIDs by passing a SID with the RID you want to query to PsGetSid. If PsGetSid reports that no mapping between the SID and an account name was possible and the RID is lower than that of your account, you know that the account assigned the RID has been deleted.

For example, to find out the name of the account assigned the 28th RID, pass the domain SID appended with -1027 to PsGetSid:

```
c:\>psgetsid S-1-5-21-1787744166-3910675280-2727264193-1027
Account for S-1-5-21-1787744166-3910675280-2727264193-1027:
User: redmond\johndoe
```

Process Explorer can also show you information on account and group SIDs on your system through its Security tab. This tab shows you information such as who owns this process and which groups the account is a member of. To view this information, simply double-click any process (for example, Explorer.exe) in the Process list and then click the **Security** tab. You should see something similar to the following:

The information displayed in the User field contains the friendly name of the account owning this process, while the SID field contains the actual SID value. The Group list includes information on all the groups that this account is a member of (groups are described later in this chapter).

Integrity levels

As mentioned, integrity levels can override discretionary access to differentiate a process and objects running as and owned by the same user, offering the ability to isolate code and data within a user account. The mechanism of Mandatory Integrity Control (MIC) allows the SRM to have more detailed information about the nature of the caller by associating it with an integrity level. It also provides information on the trust required to access the object by defining an integrity level for it.

The integrity level of a token can be obtained with the GetTokenInformation API with the Token-IntegrityLevel enumeration value. These integrity levels are specified by a SID. Although integrity levels can be arbitrary values, the system uses six primary levels to separate privilege levels, as described in Table 7-3.

TABLE 7-3 Integrity level SIDs

SID	Name (Level)	Use
S-1-16-0x0	Untrusted (0)	Used by processes started by the Anonymous group. It blocks most write access.
S-1-16-0x1000	Low (1)	Used by AppContainer processes (UWP) and Protected Mode Internet Explorer. It blocks write access to most objects (such as files and registry keys) on the system.
S-1-16-0x2000	Medium (2)	Used by normal applications being launched while UAC is enabled.
S-1-16-0x3000	High (3)	Used by administrative applications launched through elevation when UAC is enabled, or normal applications if UAC is disabled and the user is an administrator.
S-1-16-0x4000	System (4)	Used by services and other system-level processes (such as Wininit, Winlogon, Smss, and so on).
S-1-16-0x5000	Protected (5)	Currently unused by default. Can be set by kernel-mode caller only.

Another, seemingly additional, integrity level is called *AppContainer*, used by UWP apps. Although seemingly another level, it's in fact equal to Low. UWP process tokens have another attribute that indicates they are running inside an AppContainer (described in the "AppContainers" section). This information is available with the GetTokenInformation API with the TokenIsAppContainer enumeration value.

EXPERIMENT: Looking at the integrity level of processes

You can use Process Explorer to quickly display the integrity level for the processes on your system. The following steps demonstrate this functionality.

1. Launch Microsoft Edge browser and Calc.exe (Windows 10).

2. Open an elevated command prompt window.

3. Open Notepad normally (without elevating it).

4. Open an elevated Process Explorer, right-click any column header in the Process list, and then click **Select Columns**.

5. Select the **Process Image** tab and select the **Integrity Level** check box. The dialog box should look similar to the one shown here:

6. Process Explorer shows you the integrity level of the processes on your system. You should see the Notepad process at medium, the Edge (MicrosoftEdge.exe) process at AppContainer, and the elevated command prompt at High. Also note that the services and system processes are running at an even higher integrity level, System.

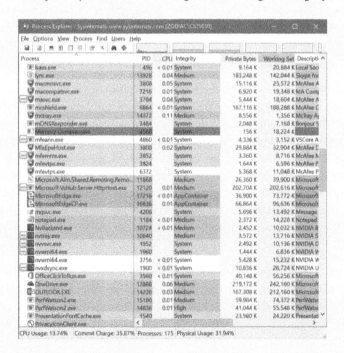

Every process has an integrity level that is represented in its token and propagated according to the following rules:

- A process normally inherits the integrity level of its parent (which means an elevated command prompt will spawn other elevated processes).

- If the file object for the executable image to which the child process belongs has an integrity level and the parent process's integrity level is medium or higher, the child process will inherit the lower of the two.

- A parent process can create a child process with an explicit integrity level lower than its own. To do this, it uses `DuplicateTokenEx` to duplicate its own access token, it uses `SetToken-Information` to change the integrity level in the new token to the desired level, and then it calls `CreateProcessAsUser` with that new token.

Table 7-3 lists the integrity level associated with processes, but what about objects? Objects also have an integrity level stored as part of their security descriptor, in a structure that is called the *mandatory label*.

To support migrating from previous versions of Windows (whose registry keys and files would not include integrity-level information), and to make it simpler for application developers, all objects have an implicit integrity level to avoid having to manually specify one. This implicit integrity level is medium, meaning that the mandatory policy (described shortly) on the object will be performed on tokens accessing this object with an integrity level lower than medium.

When a process creates an object without specifying an integrity level, the system checks the integrity level in the token. For tokens with a level of medium or higher, the implicit integrity level of the object remains medium. However, when a token contains an integrity level lower than medium, the object is created with an explicit integrity level that matches the level in the token.

Objects that are created by high- or system-integrity-level processes have a medium integrity level themselves so that users can disable and enable UAC. If object integrity levels always inherited their creator's integrity level, the applications of an administrator who disables UAC and subsequently re-enables it could fail because the administrator would not be able to modify any registry settings or files created when running at the high integrity level. Objects can also have an explicit integrity level that is set by the system or by the creator of the object. For example, processes, threads, tokens, and jobs are given an explicit integrity level by the kernel when it creates them. The reason for assigning an integrity level to these objects is to prevent a process for the same user, but one running at a lower integrity level, from accessing these objects and modifying their content or behavior (for example, DLL injection or code modification).

Apart from an integrity level, objects also have a mandatory policy, which defines the actual level of protection that's applied based on the integrity-level check. Three types are possible, shown in Table 7-4. The integrity level and the mandatory policy are stored together in the same ACE.

TABLE 7-4 Object mandatory policies

Policy	Present on, by Default	Description
No-Write-Up	Implicit on all objects	Used to restrict write access coming from a lower integrity level process to the object.
No-Read-Up	Only on process objects	Used to restrict read access coming from a lower integrity level process to the object. Specific use on process objects protects against information leakage by blocking address space reads from an external process.
No-Execute-Up	Only on binaries implementing COM classes	Used to restrict execute access coming from a lower integrity level process to the object. Specific use on COM classes is to restrict launch-activation permissions on a COM class.

EXPERIMENT: Looking at the integrity level of objects

You can use the AccessChk tool from Sysinternals to display the integrity level of objects on the system, such as files, processes, and registry keys. Here's an experiment showing the purpose of the LocalLow directory in Windows:

1. Browse to C:\Users\<UserName>\ in a command prompt window, where <username> is your user name.

2. Try running AccessChk on the AppData folder, as follows:

   ```
   C:\Users\UserName> accesschk -v appdata
   ```

3. Note the differences between the Local and LocalLow subfolders in your output, similar to that shown here:

   ```
   C:\Users\UserName\AppData\Local
     Medium Mandatory Level (Default) [No-Write-Up]
     [...]
   C:\Users\UserName\AppData\LocalLow
     Low Mandatory Level [No-Write-Up]
     [...]
   C:\Users\UserName\AppData\Roaming
     Medium Mandatory Level (Default) [No-Write-Up]
     [...]
   ```

4. Notice that the LocalLow directory has an integrity level set to Low, while the Local and Roaming directories have integrity levels of Medium (default). The default means the system is using an implicit integrity level.

5. Pass the -e flag to AccessChk so it displays only explicit integrity levels. If you run the tool on the AppData folder again, you'll notice only the LocalLow information is displayed.

The -o (object), -k (registry key), and -p (process) flags allow you to specify something other than a file or directory.

Tokens

The SRM uses an object called a *token* (or *access token)* to identify the security context of a process or thread. A security context consists of information that describes the account, groups, and privileges associated with the process or thread. Tokens also include information such as the session ID, the integrity level, and the UAC virtualization state. (We'll describe both privileges and UAC's virtualization mechanism later in this chapter.)

During the logon process (described later in this chapter), Lsass creates an initial token to represent the user logging on. It then determines whether the user logging on is a member of a powerful group or possesses a powerful privilege. The groups checked for in this step are as follows:

- Built-In Administrators
- Certificate Administrators
- Domain Administrators
- Enterprise Administrators
- Policy Administrators
- Schema Administrators
- Domain Controllers
- Enterprise Read-Only Domain Controllers
- Read-Only Domain Controllers
- Account Operators
- Backup Operators
- Cryptographic Operators
- Network Configuration Operators
- Print Operators
- System Operators
- RAS Servers
- Power Users
- Pre-Windows 2000 Compatible Access

Many of the groups listed are used only on domain-joined systems and don't give users local administrative rights directly. Instead, they allow users to modify domain-wide settings.

The privileges checked for are as follows:

- `SeBackupPrivilege`
- `SeCreateTokenPrivilege`
- `SeDebugPrivilege`
- `SeImpersonatePrivilege`

- `SeLabelPrivilege`

- `SeLoadDriverPrivilege`

- `SeRestorePrivilege`

- `SeTakeOwnershipPrivilege`

- `SeTcbPrivilege`

These privileges are described in detail in the section "Privileges," later in this chapter.

If one or more of these groups or privileges are present, Lsass creates a restricted token for the user (also called a *filtered admin token*) and creates a logon session for both. The standard user token is attached to the initial process or processes that Winlogon starts (by default, Userinit.exe).

Note If UAC has been disabled, administrators run with a token that includes their administrator group memberships and privileges.

Because child processes inherit a copy of the token of their creators by default, all processes in the user's session run under the same token. You can also generate a token by using the Windows `LogonUser` function. You can then use this token to create a process that runs within the security context of the user logged on through the `LogonUser` function by passing the token to the Windows `CreateProcessAsUser` function. The `CreateProcessWithLogonW` function combines these into a single call, which is how the `Runas` command launches processes under alternative tokens.

Tokens vary in size because different user accounts have different sets of privileges and associated group accounts. However, all tokens contain the same types of information. The most important contents of a token are represented in Figure 7-7.

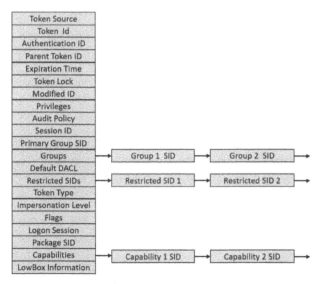

FIGURE 7-7 Access tokens.

The security mechanisms in Windows use two components to determine what objects can be accessed and what secure operations can be performed. One component comprises the token's user account SID and group SID fields. The SRM uses SIDs to determine whether a process or thread can obtain requested access to a securable object, such as an NTFS file.

The group SIDs in a token indicate which groups a user's account is a member of. For example, a server application can disable specific groups to restrict a token's credentials when the server application is performing actions requested by a client. Disabling a group produces nearly the same effect as if the group wasn't present in the token. (It results in a deny-only group, described in the section "Restricted tokens." Disabled SIDs are used as part of security access checks, described in the section "Determining access" later in the chapter.) Group SIDs can also include a special SID that contains the integrity level of the process or thread. The SRM uses another field in the token, which describes the mandatory integrity policy, to perform the mandatory integrity check described later in the chapter.

The second component in a token that determines what the token's thread or process can do is the privilege array. A token's privilege array is a list of rights associated with the token. An example of a privilege is the right of the process or thread associated with the token to shut down the computer. Privileges are described in more detail later in this chapter.

A token's default primary group field and default discretionary access control list (DACL) field are security attributes that Windows applies to objects that a process or thread creates when it uses the token. By including security information in tokens, Windows makes it convenient for a process or thread to create objects with standard security attributes because the process or thread doesn't need to request discrete security information for every object it creates.

Each token's type distinguishes a primary token (a token that identifies the security context of a process) from an impersonation token (a type of token that threads use to temporarily adopt a different security context, usually of another user). Impersonation tokens carry an impersonation level that signifies what type of impersonation is active in the token. (Impersonation is described later in this chapter.)

A token also includes the mandatory policy for the process or thread, which defines how MIC will behave when processing this token. There are two policies:

- **TOKEN_MANDATORY_NO_WRITE_UP**   Enabled by default, this sets the No-Write-Up policy on this token, specifying that the process or thread will not be able to access objects with a higher integrity level for write access.

- **TOKEN_MANDATORY_NEW_PROCESS_MIN**   Also enabled by default, this specifies that the SRM should look at the integrity level of the executable image when launching a child process and compute the minimum integrity level of the parent process and the file object's integrity level as the child's integrity level.

Token flags include parameters that determine the behavior of certain UAC and UIPI mechanisms, such as virtualization and user interface access. Those mechanisms will be described later in this chapter.

Each token can also contain attributes that are assigned by the Application Identification service (part of AppLocker) when AppLocker rules have been defined. AppLocker and its use of attributes in the access token are described later in this chapter.

A token for a UWP process includes information on the AppContainer hosting the process. First, it stores a package SID, identifying the UWP package the process originated from. The significance of this SID will be described in the "AppContainers" section later in this chapter. Second, UWP processes need to request capabilities for operations that require the user's consent. Examples of capabilities include network access, using the phone capabilities of the device (if any), accessing the camera on the device, and more. Each such capability is represented with a SID, stored as part of the token. (Capabilities will be discussed further in the "AppContainers" section.)

The remaining fields in a token serve informational purposes. The token source field contains a short textual description of the entity that created the token. Programs that want to know where a token originated use the token source to distinguish among sources such as the Windows Session Manager, a network file server, or the remote procedure call (RPC) server. The token identifier is a locally unique identifier (LUID) that the SRM assigns to the token when it creates the token. The Windows executive maintains the executive LUID, a monotonically increasing counter it uses to assign a unique numeric identifier to each token. A LUID is guaranteed to be unique only until the system is shut down.

The token authentication ID is another kind of LUID. A token's creator assigns the token's authentication ID when calling the LsaLogonUser function. If the creator doesn't specify a LUID, Lsass obtains the LUID from the executive LUID. Lsass copies the authentication ID for all tokens descended from an initial logon token. A program can obtain a token's authentication ID to see whether the token belongs to the same logon session as other tokens the program has examined.

The executive LUID refreshes the modified ID every time a token's characteristics are modified. An application can test the modified ID to discover changes in a security context since the context's last use.

Tokens contain an expiration time field that can be used by applications performing their own security to reject a token after a specified amount of time. However, Windows itself does not enforce the expiration time of tokens.

Note To guarantee system security, the fields in a token are immutable (because they are located in kernel memory). Except for fields that can be modified through a specific system call designed to modify certain token attributes (assuming the caller has the appropriate access rights to the token object), data such as privileges and SIDs in a token can never be modified from user mode.

EXPERIMENT: Viewing access tokens

The kernel debugger dt _TOKEN command displays the format of an internal token object. Although this structure differs from the user-mode token structure returned by Windows API security functions, the fields are similar. For further information on tokens, see the description in the Windows SDK documentation.

Here's a token structure on Windows 10:

```
lkd> dt nt!_token
   +0x000 TokenSource       : _TOKEN_SOURCE
   +0x010 TokenId           : _LUID
   +0x018 AuthenticationId  : _LUID
   +0x020 ParentTokenId     : _LUID
   +0x028 ExpirationTime    : _LARGE_INTEGER
   +0x030 TokenLock         : Ptr64 _ERESOURCE
   +0x038 ModifiedId        : _LUID
   +0x040 Privileges        : _SEP_TOKEN_PRIVILEGES
   +0x058 AuditPolicy       : _SEP_AUDIT_POLICY
   +0x078 SessionId         : Uint4B
   +0x07c UserAndGroupCount : Uint4B
   +0x080 RestrictedSidCount : Uint4B
   +0x084 VariableLength    : Uint4B
   +0x088 DynamicCharged    : Uint4B
   +0x08c DynamicAvailable  : Uint4B
   +0x090 DefaultOwnerIndex : Uint4B
   +0x098 UserAndGroups     : Ptr64 _SID_AND_ATTRIBUTES
   +0x0a0 RestrictedSids    : Ptr64 _SID_AND_ATTRIBUTES
   +0x0a8 PrimaryGroup      : Ptr64 Void
   +0x0b0 DynamicPart       : Ptr64 Uint4B
   +0x0b8 DefaultDacl       : Ptr64 _ACL
   +0x0c0 TokenType         : _TOKEN_TYPE
   +0x0c4 ImpersonationLevel : _SECURITY_IMPERSONATION_LEVEL
   +0x0c8 TokenFlags        : Uint4B
   +0x0cc TokenInUse        : UChar
   +0x0d0 IntegrityLevelIndex : Uint4B
   +0x0d4 MandatoryPolicy   : Uint4B
   +0x0d8 LogonSession      : Ptr64 _SEP_LOGON_SESSION_REFERENCES
   +0x0e0 OriginatingLogonSession : _LUID
   +0x0e8 SidHash           : _SID_AND_ATTRIBUTES_HASH
   +0x1f8 RestrictedSidHash : _SID_AND_ATTRIBUTES_HASH
   +0x308 pSecurityAttributes : Ptr64 _AUTHZBASEP_SECURITY_ATTRIBUTES_INFORMATION
   +0x310 Package           : Ptr64 Void
   +0x318 Capabilities      : Ptr64 _SID_AND_ATTRIBUTES
   +0x320 CapabilityCount   : Uint4B
   +0x328 CapabilitiesHash  : _SID_AND_ATTRIBUTES_HASH
   +0x438 LowboxNumberEntry : Ptr64 _SEP_LOWBOX_NUMBER_ENTRY
   +0x440 LowboxHandlesEntry : Ptr64 _SEP_LOWBOX_HANDLES_ENTRY
   +0x448 pClaimAttributes  : Ptr64 _AUTHZBASEP_CLAIM_ATTRIBUTES_COLLECTION
   +0x450 TrustLevelSid     : Ptr64 Void
   +0x458 TrustLinkedToken  : Ptr64 _TOKEN
   +0x460 IntegrityLevelSidValue : Ptr64 Void
   +0x468 TokenSidValues    : Ptr64 _SEP_SID_VALUES_BLOCK
   +0x470 IndexEntry        : Ptr64 _SEP_LUID_TO_INDEX_MAP_ENTRY
   +0x478 DiagnosticInfo    : Ptr64 _SEP_TOKEN_DIAG_TRACK_ENTRY
   +0x480 SessionObject     : Ptr64 Void
   +0x488 VariablePart      : Uint8B
```

You can examine the token for a process with the `!token` command. You'll find the address of the token in the output of the `!process` command. Here's an example for an explorer.exe process:

```
lkd> !process 0 1 explorer.exe
PROCESS ffffe18304dfd780
    SessionId: 1  Cid: 23e4    Peb: 00c2a000  ParentCid: 2264
    DirBase: 2aa0f6000  ObjectTable: ffffcd82c72fcd80  HandleCount: <Data Not
Accessible>
    Image: explorer.exe
    VadRoot ffffe18303655840 Vads 705 Clone 0 Private 12264. Modified 376410. Locked 18.
    DeviceMap ffffcd82c39bc0d0
    Token                               ffffcd82c72fc060
    ...

PROCESS ffffe1830670a080
    SessionId: 1  Cid: 27b8    Peb: 00950000  ParentCid: 035c
    DirBase: 2cba97000  ObjectTable: ffffcd82c7ccc500  HandleCount: <Data Not
Accessible>
    Image: explorer.exe
    VadRoot ffffe183064e9f60 Vads 1991 Clone 0 Private 19576. Modified 87095. Locked 0.
    DeviceMap ffffcd82c39bc0d0
    Token                               ffffcd82c7cd9060
    ...

lkd> !token ffffcd82c72fc060
_TOKEN 0xffffcd82c72fc060
TS Session ID: 0x1
User: S-1-5-21-3537846094-3055369412-2967912182-1001
User Groups:
 00 S-1-16-8192
    Attributes - GroupIntegrity GroupIntegrityEnabled
 01 S-1-1-0
    Attributes - Mandatory Default Enabled
 02 S-1-5-114
    Attributes - DenyOnly
 03 S-1-5-21-3537846094-3055369412-2967912182-1004
    Attributes - Mandatory Default Enabled
 04 S-1-5-32-544
    Attributes - DenyOnly
 05 S-1-5-32-578
    Attributes - Mandatory Default Enabled
 06 S-1-5-32-559
    Attributes - Mandatory Default Enabled
 07 S-1-5-32-545
    Attributes - Mandatory Default Enabled
 08 S-1-5-4
    Attributes - Mandatory Default Enabled
 09 S-1-2-1
    Attributes - Mandatory Default Enabled
 10 S-1-5-11
    Attributes - Mandatory Default Enabled
```

```
   11 S-1-5-15
      Attributes - Mandatory Default Enabled
   12 S-1-11-96-3623454863-58364-18864-2661722203-1597581903-1225312835-2511459453-
1556397606-2735945305-1404291241
      Attributes - Mandatory Default Enabled
   13 S-1-5-113
      Attributes - Mandatory Default Enabled
   14 S-1-5-5-0-1745560
      Attributes - Mandatory Default Enabled LogonId
   15 S-1-2-0
      Attributes - Mandatory Default Enabled
   16 S-1-5-64-36
      Attributes - Mandatory Default Enabled
Primary Group: S-1-5-21-3537846094-3055369412-2967912182-1001
Privs:
   19 0x000000013 SeShutdownPrivilege               Attributes -
   23 0x000000017 SeChangeNotifyPrivilege           Attributes - Enabled Default
   25 0x000000019 SeUndockPrivilege                 Attributes -
   33 0x000000021 SeIncreaseWorkingSetPrivilege     Attributes -
   34 0x000000022 SeTimeZonePrivilege               Attributes -
Authentication ID:          (0,1aa448)
Impersonation Level:        Anonymous
TokenType:                  Primary
Source: User32              TokenFlags: 0x2a00 ( Token in use )
Token ID: 1be803            ParentToken ID: 1aa44b
Modified ID:                (0, 43d9289)
RestrictedSidCount: 0    RestrictedSids: 0x0000000000000000
OriginatingLogonSession: 3e7
PackageSid: (null)
CapabilityCount: 0      Capabilities: 0x0000000000000000
LowboxNumberEntry: 0x0000000000000000
Security Attributes:
Unable to get the offset of nt!_AUTHZBASEP_SECURITY_ATTRIBUTE.ListLink
Process Token TrustLevelSid: (null)
```

Notice that there is no package SID for Explorer, since it's not running inside an AppContainer.

Run calc.exe under Windows 10, which spawns calculator.exe (now a UWP app), and examine its token:

```
lkd> !process 0 1 calculator.exe
PROCESS ffffe18309e874c0
    SessionId: 1  Cid: 3c18    Peb: cd0182c000  ParentCid: 035c
    DirBase: 7a15e4000  ObjectTable: ffffcd82ec9a37c0  HandleCount: <Data Not
Accessible>
    Image: Calculator.exe
    VadRoot ffffe1831cf197c0 Vads 181 Clone 0 Private 3800. Modified 3746. Locked 503.
    DeviceMap ffffcd82c39bc0d0
    Token                                 ffffcd82e26168f0
...

lkd> !token ffffcd82e26168f0
_TOKEN 0xffffcd82e26168f0
```

```
TS Session ID: 0x1
User: S-1-5-21-3537846094-3055369412-2967912182-1001
User Groups:
 00 S-1-16-4096
    Attributes - GroupIntegrity GroupIntegrityEnabled
 01 S-1-1-0
    Attributes - Mandatory Default Enabled
 02 S-1-5-114
    Attributes - DenyOnly
 03 S-1-5-21-3537846094-3055369412-2967912182-1004
    Attributes - Mandatory Default Enabled
 04 S-1-5-32-544
    Attributes - DenyOnly
 05 S-1-5-32-578
    Attributes - Mandatory Default Enabled
 06 S-1-5-32-559
    Attributes - Mandatory Default Enabled
 07 S-1-5-32-545
    Attributes - Mandatory Default Enabled
 08 S-1-5-4
    Attributes - Mandatory Default Enabled
 09 S-1-2-1
    Attributes - Mandatory Default Enabled
 10 S-1-5-11
    Attributes - Mandatory Default Enabled
 11 S-1-5-15
    Attributes - Mandatory Default Enabled
 12 S-1-11-96-3623454863-58364-18864-2661722203-1597581903-1225312835-2511459453-
1556397606-2735945305-1404291241
    Attributes - Mandatory Default Enabled
 13 S-1-5-113
    Attributes - Mandatory Default Enabled
 14 S-1-5-5-0-1745560
    Attributes - Mandatory Default Enabled LogonId
 15 S-1-2-0
    Attributes - Mandatory Default Enabled
 16 S-1-5-64-36
    Attributes - Mandatory Default Enabled
Primary Group: S-1-5-21-3537846094-3055369412-2967912182-1001
Privs:
 19 0x000000013 SeShutdownPrivilege              Attributes -
 23 0x000000017 SeChangeNotifyPrivilege          Attributes - Enabled Default
 25 0x000000019 SeUndockPrivilege                Attributes -
 33 0x000000021 SeIncreaseWorkingSetPrivilege    Attributes -
 34 0x000000022 SeTimeZonePrivilege              Attributes -
Authentication ID:        (0,1aa448)
Impersonation Level:      Anonymous
TokenType:                Primary
Source: User32            TokenFlags: 0x4a00 ( Token in use )
Token ID: 4ddb8c0         ParentToken ID: 1aa44b
Modified ID:              (0, 4ddb8b2)
```

```
RestrictedSidCount: 0        RestrictedSids: 0x0000000000000000
OriginatingLogonSession: 3e7
PackageSid: S-1-15-2-466767348-3739614953-2700836392-1801644223-4227750657-
1087833535-2488631167
CapabilityCount: 1      Capabilities: 0xffffcd82e1bfccd0
Capabilities:
 00 S-1-15-3-466767348-3739614953-2700836392-1801644223-4227750657-1087833535-
2488631167
    Attributes - Enabled
LowboxNumberEntry: 0xffffcd82fa2c1670
LowboxNumber: 5
Security Attributes:
Unable to get the offset of nt!_AUTHZBASEP_SECURITY_ATTRIBUTE.ListLink
Process Token TrustLevelSid: (null)
```

You can see there is one capability required by Calculator (which is in fact equal to its AppContainer SID RID, as described in the section "AppContainers" later in this chapter). Looking at the token of the Cortana process (searchui.exe) shows the following capabilities:

```
lkd> !process 0 1 searchui.exe
PROCESS ffffe1831307d080
    SessionId: 1  Cid: 29d8    Peb: fb407ec000  ParentCid: 035c
DeepFreeze
    DirBase: 38b635000  ObjectTable: ffffcd830059e580  HandleCount: <Data Not
Accessible>
    Image: SearchUI.exe
    VadRoot ffffe1831fe89130 Vads 420 Clone 0 Private 11029. Modified 2031. Locked 0.
    DeviceMap ffffcd82c39bc0d0
    Token                             ffffcd82d97d18f0
    ...


lkd> !token ffffcd82d97d18f0
_TOKEN 0xffffcd82d97d18f0
TS Session ID: 0x1
User: S-1-5-21-3537846094-3055369412-2967912182-1001
User Groups:
 ...
Primary Group: S-1-5-21-3537846094-3055369412-2967912182-1001
Privs:
 19 0x000000013 SeShutdownPrivilege              Attributes -
 23 0x000000017 SeChangeNotifyPrivilege          Attributes - Enabled Default
 25 0x000000019 SeUndockPrivilege                Attributes -
 33 0x000000021 SeIncreaseWorkingSetPrivilege    Attributes -
 34 0x000000022 SeTimeZonePrivilege              Attributes -
Authentication ID:         (0,1aa448)
Impersonation Level:       Anonymous
TokenType:                 Primary
Source: User32             TokenFlags: 0x4a00 ( Token in use )
Token ID: 4483430          ParentToken ID: 1aa44b
Modified ID:               (0, 4481b11)
RestrictedSidCount: 0      RestrictedSids: 0x0000000000000000
OriginatingLogonSession: 3e7
```

```
PackageSid: S-1-15-2-1861897761-1695161497-2927542615-642690995-327840285-
2659745135-2630312742
CapabilityCount: 32     Capabilities: 0xffffcd82f78149b0
Capabilities:
 00 S-1-15-3-1024-1216833578-114521899-3977640588-1343180512-2505059295-473916851-
3379430393-3088591068
    Attributes - Enabled
 01 S-1-15-3-1024-3299255270-1847605585-2201808924-710406709-3613095291-873286183-
3101090833-2655911836
    Attributes - Enabled
 02 S-1-15-3-1024-34359262-2669769421-2130994847-3068338639-3284271446-2009814230-
2411358368-814686995
    Attributes - Enabled
 03 S-1-15-3-1
    Attributes - Enabled
...
 29 S-1-15-3-3633849274-1266774400-1199443125-2736873758
    Attributes - Enabled
 30 S-1-15-3-2569730672-1095266119-53537203-1209375796
    Attributes - Enabled
 31 S-1-15-3-2452736844-1257488215-2818397580-3305426111
    Attributes - Enabled
LowboxNumberEntry: 0xffffcd82c7539110
LowboxNumber: 2
Security Attributes:
Unable to get the offset of nt!_AUTHZBASEP_SECURITY_ATTRIBUTE.ListLink
Process Token TrustLevelSid: (null)
```

There are 32 capabilities required by Cortana. This simply indicates the process is richer in features that need to be accepted by end users and validated by the system.

You can indirectly view token contents with Process Explorer's Security tab in the process Properties dialog box. The dialog box shows the groups and privileges included in the token of the process you examine.

EXPERIMENT: Launching a program at low integrity level

When you elevate a program, either by using the Run as Administrator option or because the program is requesting it, the program is explicitly launched at high integrity level. However, it is also possible to launch a program at low integrity level by using PsExec from Sysinternals:

1. Launch Notepad at low integrity level by using the following command:

    ```
    c:\psexec –l notepad.exe
    ```

2. Try opening a file (such as one of the XML files) in the %SystemRoot%\System32 directory. Notice that you can browse the directory and open any file contained within it.

3. In Notepad, open the **File** menu and choose **New**.

4. Enter some text in the window and try saving it in the %SystemRoot%\System32 directory. Notepad displays a dialog box indicating a lack of permissions and suggests saving the file in the Documents folder.

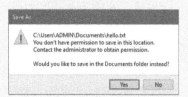

5. Accept Notepad's suggestion. You will get the same message box again, and repeatedly for each attempt.

6. Now try saving the file in the LocalLow directory of your user profile, shown in an experiment earlier in the chapter.

In the previous experiment, saving a file in the LocalLow directory worked because Notepad was running with low integrity level, and only the LocalLow directory also had low integrity level. All the other directories where you tried to save the file had an implicit medium integrity level. (You can verify this with AccessChk.) However, reading from the %SystemRoot%\System32 directory, as well as opening files within it, did work, even though the directory and its file also have an implicit medium integrity level.

Impersonation

Impersonation is a powerful feature Windows uses frequently in its security model. Windows also uses impersonation in its client/server programming model. For example, a server application can provide access to resources such as files, printers, and databases. Clients wanting to access a resource send a request to the server. When the server receives the request, it must ensure that the client has permission to perform the desired operations on the resource. For example, if a user on a remote machine tries to delete a file on an NTFS share, the server exporting the share must determine whether the user is allowed to delete the file. The obvious way to determine whether a user has permission is for the server to query the user's account and group SIDs and scan the security attributes on the file. This approach is tedious to program, prone to errors, and wouldn't permit new security features to be supported transparently. Thus, Windows provides impersonation services to simplify the server's job.

Impersonation lets a server notify the SRM that the server is temporarily adopting the security profile of a client making a resource request. The server can then access resources on behalf of the client, and the SRM carries out the access validation, but it does so based on the impersonated client security context. Usually, a server has access to more resources than a client does and loses some of its security credentials during impersonation. However, the reverse can be true: The server can gain security credentials during impersonation.

A server impersonates a client only within the thread that makes the impersonation request. Thread-control data structures contain an optional entry for an impersonation token. However, a thread's primary token, which represents the thread's real security credentials, is always accessible in the process's control structure.

Windows makes impersonation available through several mechanisms. For example, if a server communicates with a client through a named pipe, the server can use the `ImpersonateNamedPipeClient` Windows API function to tell the SRM that it wants to impersonate the user on the other end of the pipe. If the server is communicating with the client through Dynamic Data Exchange (DDE) or RPC, it can make similar impersonation requests using `DdeImpersonateClient` and `RpcImpersonateClient`. A thread can create an impersonation token that's simply a copy of its process token with the `ImpersonateSelf` function. The thread can then alter its impersonation token, perhaps to disable SIDs or privileges. A Security Support Provider Interface (SSPI) package can impersonate its clients with `ImpersonateSecurityContext`. SSPIs implement a network authentication protocol such as LAN Manager version 2 or Kerberos. Other interfaces such as COM expose impersonation through APIs of their own, such as `CoImpersonateClient`.

After the server thread finishes its task, it reverts to its primary security context. These forms of impersonation are convenient for carrying out specific actions at the request of a client and for ensuring that object accesses are audited correctly. (For example, the audit that is generated gives the identity of the impersonated client rather than that of the server process.) The disadvantage to these forms of impersonation is that they can't execute an entire program in the context of a client. In addition, an impersonation token can't access files or printers on network shares unless it is a delegation-level impersonation (described shortly) and has sufficient credentials to authenticate to the remote machine, or the file or printer share supports null sessions. (A null session is one that results from an anonymous logon.)

If an entire application must execute in a client's security context or must access network resources without using impersonation, the client must be logged on to the system. The `LogonUser` Windows API function enables this action. `LogonUser` takes an account name, a password, a domain or computer name, a logon type (such as interactive, batch, or service), and a logon provider as input, and it returns a primary token. A server thread can adopt the token as an impersonation token, or the server can start a program that has the client's credentials as its primary token. From a security standpoint, a process created using the token returned from an interactive logon via `LogonUser`, such as with the `CreateProcessAsUser` API, looks like a program a user starts by logging on to the machine interactively. The disadvantage to this approach is that a server must obtain the user's account name and password. If the server transmits this information across the network, the server must encrypt it securely so that a malicious user snooping network traffic can't capture it.

To prevent the misuse of impersonation, Windows doesn't let servers perform impersonation without a client's consent. A client process can limit the level of impersonation that a server process can perform by specifying a security quality of service (SQOS) when connecting to the server. For instance, when opening a named pipe, a process can specify SECURITY_ANONYMOUS, SECURITY_IDENTIFICATION, SECURITY_IMPERSONATION, or SECURITY_DELEGATION as flags for the Windows `CreateFile` function. These same options apply to other impersonation-related functions listed earlier. Each level lets a server perform different types of operations with respect to the client's security context:

- **SecurityAnonymous** This is the most restrictive level of impersonation. The server can't impersonate or identify the client.

- **SecurityIdentification** This lets the server obtain the identity (the SIDs) of the client and the client's privileges, but the server can't impersonate the client.

- **SecurityImpersonation** This lets the server identify and impersonate the client on the local system.

- **SecurityDelegation** This is the most permissive level of impersonation. It lets the server impersonate the client on local and remote systems.

Other interfaces such as RPC use different constants with similar meanings (for example, RPC_C_IMP_LEVEL_IMPERSONATE).

If the client doesn't set an impersonation level, Windows chooses the SecurityImpersonation level by default. The CreateFile function also accepts SECURITY_EFFECTIVE_ONLY and SECURITY_CONTEXT_TRACKING as modifiers for the impersonation setting:

- **SECURITY_EFFECTIVE_ONLY** This prevents a server from enabling or disabling a client's privileges or groups while the server is impersonating.

- **SECURITY_CONTEXT_TRACKING** This specifies that any changes a client makes to its security context are reflected in a server that is impersonating it. If this option isn't specified, the server adopts the context of the client at the time of the impersonation and doesn't receive any changes. This option is honored only when the client and server processes are on the same system.

To prevent spoofing scenarios in which a low-integrity process could create a user interface that captured user credentials and then used LogonUser to obtain that user's token, a special integrity policy applies to impersonation scenarios: a thread cannot impersonate a token of higher integrity than its own. For example, a low-integrity application cannot spoof a dialog box that queries administrative credentials and then attempt to launch a process at a higher privilege level. The integrity-mechanism policy for impersonation access tokens is that the integrity level of the access token that is returned by LsaLogonUser must be no higher than the integrity level of the calling process.

Restricted tokens

A restricted token is created from a primary or impersonation token using the CreateRestrictedToken function. The restricted token is a copy of the token it's derived from, with the following possible modifications:

- Privileges can be removed from the token's privilege array.

- SIDs in the token can be marked as deny-only. These SIDs remove access to any resources for which the SID's access is denied by using a matching access-denied ACE that would otherwise be overridden by an ACE granting access to a group containing the SID earlier in the security descriptor.

- SIDs in the token can be marked as restricted. These SIDs are subject to a second pass of the access-check algorithm, which will parse only the restricted SIDs in the token. The results of both the first pass and the second pass must grant access to the resource or no access is granted to the object.

Restricted tokens are useful when an application wants to impersonate a client at a reduced security level, primarily for safety reasons when running untrusted code. For example, the restricted token can have the shutdown-system privilege removed from it to prevent code executed in the restricted token's security context from rebooting the system.

Filtered admin token

As you saw earlier, restricted tokens are also used by UAC to create the filtered admin token that all user applications will inherit. A filtered admin token has the following characteristics:

- The integrity level is set to medium.

- The administrator and administrator-like SIDs mentioned previously are marked as deny-only to prevent a security hole if the group were to be removed altogether. For example, if a file had an access control list (ACL) that denied the Administrators group all access but granted some access to another group the user belongs to, the user would be granted access if the Administrators group was absent from the token, which would give the standard user version of the user's identity more access than the user's administrator identity.

- All privileges are stripped except Change Notify, Shutdown, Undock, Increase Working Set, and Time Zone.

EXPERIMENT: Looking at filtered admin tokens

You can make Explorer launch a process with either the standard user token or the administrator token by following these steps on a machine with UAC enabled:

1. Log on to an account that's a member of the Administrators group.

2. Open the **Start** menu, type **command**, right-click the **Command Prompt** option that appears, and choose **Run as Administrator** to run an elevated command prompt.

3. Run a new instance of cmd.exe, but this time do it normally (that is, not elevated).

4. Run Process Explorer elevated, open the Properties dialog boxes for the two command prompt processes, and click the **Security** tabs. Note that the standard user token contains a deny-only SID and a medium mandatory label, and that it has only a couple of privileges. The properties on the right in the following screenshot are from a command prompt running with an administrator token, and the properties on the left are from one running with the filtered administrator token:

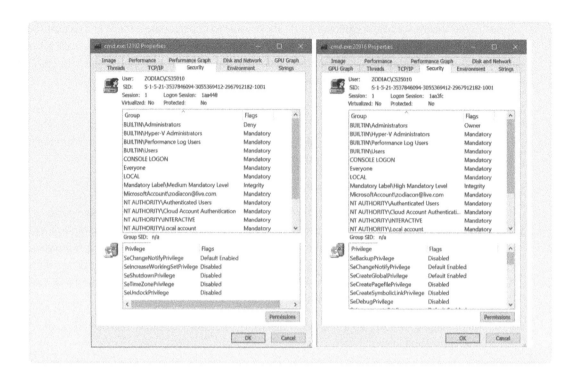

Virtual service accounts

Windows provides a specialized type of account known as a *virtual service account* (or simply *virtual account*) to improve the security isolation and access control of Windows services with minimal administrative effort. (See Chapter 9 in Part 2 for more information on Windows services.) Without this mechanism, Windows services must run under one of the accounts defined by Windows for its built-in services (such as Local Service or Network Service) or under a regular domain account. The accounts such as Local Service are shared by many existing services and so offer limited granularity for privilege and access control; furthermore, they cannot be managed across the domain. Domain accounts require periodic password changes for security, and the availability of services during a password-change cycle might be affected. Furthermore, for best isolation, each service should run under its own account, but with ordinary accounts this multiplies the management effort.

With virtual service accounts, each service runs under its own account with its own security ID. The name of the account is always NT SERVICE\ followed by the internal name of the service. Virtual service accounts can appear in access control lists and can be associated with privileges via Group Policy like any other account name. They cannot, however, be created or deleted through the usual account-management tools, nor assigned to groups.

Windows automatically sets and periodically changes the password of the virtual service account. Similar to the Local System and Other Service Accounts, there is a password, but the password is unknown to the system administrators.

EXPERIMENT: Using virtual service accounts

You can create a service that runs under a virtual service account by using the Service Control (Sc.exe) tool. Follow these steps:

1. In an Administrator command prompt, type the **create** command in the Sc.exe command-line tool to create a service and a virtual account in which it will run. This example uses the srvany service from the Windows 2003 resource kit, which you can download here: *https://www.microsoft.com/en-us/download/details.aspx?id=17657.*

   ```
   C:\Windows\system32>sc create srvany obj= "NT SERVICE\srvany" binPath=
   "c:\temp\srvany.exe"
   [SC] CreateService SUCCESS
   ```

2. The previous command created the service (in the registry and in the service controller manager's internal list) and created the virtual service account. Now run the Services MMC snap-in (services.msc), select the new service, and open its Properties dialog box.

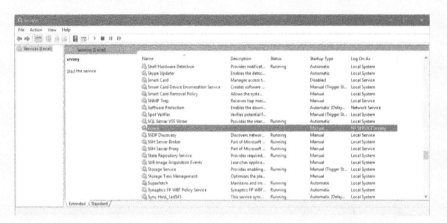

3. Click the **Log On** tab.

4. You can use the service's Properties dialog box to create a virtual service account for an existing service. To do so, change the account name to **NT SERVICE\servicename** in the This Account field and clear both password fields. Note, however, that existing services might not run correctly under a virtual service account because the account might not have access to files or other resources needed by the service.

5. If you run Process Explorer and view the Security tab in the Properties dialog box for a service that uses a virtual account, you can observe the virtual account name and its security ID (SID). To try this, in the Properties dialog box of the srvany service, enter the command-line arguments notepad.exe. (srvany can be used to turn normal executables into services, so it must accept some executable on the command line.) Then click the **Start** button to start the service.

6. The virtual service account can appear in an access control entry for any object (such as a file) the service needs to access. If you click the **Security** tab in a file's Properties dialog box and create an ACL that references the virtual service account, you will find that the account name you typed (for example, NT SERVICE\srvany) is changed to simply the service name (srvany) by the Check Names function, and it appears in the access control list in this shortened form.

7. The virtual service account can be granted permissions (or user rights) via Group Policy. In this example, the virtual account for the srvany service has been granted the right to create a pagefile (using the Local Security Policy editor, secpol.msc).

8. You won't see the virtual service account in user-administration tools like lusrmgr.msc because it is not stored in the SAM registry hive. However, if you examine the registry within the context of the built-in System account (as described previously), you will see evidence of the account in the HKLM\Security\Policy\Secrets key:

```
C:\>psexec -s -i -d regedit.exe
```

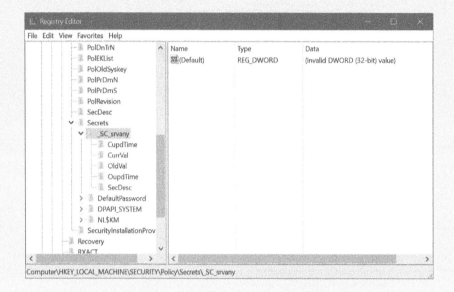

Security descriptors and access control

Tokens, which identify a user's credentials, are only part of the object security equation. Another part of the equation is the security information associated with an object, which specifies who can perform what actions on the object. The data structure for this information is called a *security descriptor*. A security descriptor consists of the following attributes:

- **Revision number** This is the version of the SRM security model used to create the descriptor.

- **Flags** These are optional modifiers that define the behavior or characteristics of the descriptor. These flags are listed in Table 7-5 (most are documented in the Windows SDK).

- **Owner SID** This is the owner's SID.

- **Group SID** This is the SID of the primary group for the object (used only by the POSIX subsystem, now unused since POSIX is no longer supported).

- **Discretionary access control list (DACL)** This specifies who has what access to the object.

- **System access control list (SACL)** This specifies which operations by which users should be logged in the security audit log and the explicit integrity level of an object.

TABLE 7-5 Security descriptor flags

Flag	Meaning
SE_OWNER_DEFAULTED	This indicates a security descriptor with a default owner security identifier (SID). Use this bit to find all the objects that have default owner permissions set.
SE_GROUP_DEFAULTED	This indicates a security descriptor with a default group SID. Use this bit to find all the objects that have default group permissions set.
SE_DACL_PRESENT	This indicates a security descriptor that has a DACL. If this flag is not set, or if this flag is set and the DACL is NULL, the security descriptor allows full access to everyone.
SE_DACL_DEFAULTED	This indicates a security descriptor with a default DACL. For example, if an object creator does not specify a DACL, the object receives the default DACL from the access token of the creator. This flag can affect how the system treats the DACL with respect to access control entry (ACE) inheritance. The system ignores this flag if the SE_DACL_PRESENT flag is not set.
SE_SACL_PRESENT	This indicates a security descriptor that has a system access control list (SACL).
SE_SACL_DEFAULTED	This indicates a security descriptor with a default SACL. For example, if an object creator does not specify a SACL, the object receives the default SACL from the access token of the creator. This flag can affect how the system treats the SACL with respect to ACE inheritance. The system ignores this flag if the SE_SACL_PRESENT flag is not set.
SE_DACL_UNTRUSTED	This indicates that the ACL pointed to by the DACL of the security descriptor was provided by an untrusted source. If this flag is set and a compound ACE is encountered, the system will substitute known valid SIDs for the server SIDs in the ACEs.
SE_SERVER_SECURITY	This requests that the provider for the object protected by the security descriptor be a server ACL based on the input ACL, regardless of its source (explicit or defaulting). This is done by replacing all the GRANT ACEs with compound ACEs granting the current server access. This flag is meaningful only if the subject is impersonating.
SE_DACL_AUTO_INHERIT_REQ	This requests that the provider for the object protected by the security descriptor automatically propagate the DACL to existing child objects. If the provider supports automatic inheritance, the DACL is propagated to any existing child objects, and the SE_DACL_AUTO_INHERITED bit in the security descriptor of the parent and child objects is set.
SE_SACL_AUTO_INHERIT_REQ	This requests that the provider for the object protected by the security descriptor automatically propagate the SACL to existing child objects. If the provider supports automatic inheritance, the SACL is propagated to any existing child objects, and the SE_SACL_AUTO_INHERITED bit in the security descriptors of the parent object and child objects is set.
SE_DACL_AUTO_INHERITED	This indicates a security descriptor in which the DACL is set up to support automatic propagation of inheritable ACEs to existing child objects. The system sets this bit when it performs the automatic inheritance algorithm for the object and its existing child objects.
SE_SACL_AUTO_INHERITED	This indicates a security descriptor in which the SACL is set up to support automatic propagation of inheritable ACEs to existing child objects. The system sets this bit when it performs the automatic inheritance algorithm for the object and its existing child objects.
SE_DACL_PROTECTED	This prevents the DACL of a security descriptor from being modified by inheritable ACEs.
SE_SACL_PROTECTED	This prevents the SACL of a security descriptor from being modified by inheritable ACEs.

TABLE 7-5 Security descriptor flags (*continued*)

Flag	Meaning
SE_RM_CONTROL_VALID	This indicates that the resource control manager bits in the security descriptor are valid. The resource control manager bits are 8 bits in the security descriptor structure that contains information specific to the resource manager accessing the structure.
SE_SELF_RELATIVE	This indicates a security descriptor in self-relative format, with all the security information in a contiguous block of memory. If this flag is not set, the security descriptor is in absolute format.

Security descriptors (SDs) can be retrieved programmatically by using various functions, such as GetSecurityInfo, GetKernelObjectSecurity, GetFileSecurity, GetNamedSecurityInfo, and other more esoteric functions. After retrieval, the SD can be manipulated and then the relevant Set function called to make the change. Furthermore, a security descriptor can be constructed using a string in a language called Security Descriptor Definition Language (SDDL), which is capable of representing a security descriptor using a compact string. This string can be converted to a true SD by calling ConvertStringSecurityDescriptorToSecurityDescriptor. As you might expect, the converse function exists as well (ConvertSecurityDescriptorToStringSecurityDescriptor). See the Windows SDK for a detailed description of the SDDL.

An access control list (ACL) is made up of a header and zero or more access control entry (ACE) structures. There are two types of ACLs: DACLs and SACLs. In a DACL, each ACE contains a SID and an access mask (and a set of flags, explained shortly), which typically specifies the access rights (read, write, delete, and so forth) that are granted or denied to the holder of the SID. There are nine types of ACEs that can appear in a DACL: access allowed, access denied, allowed object, denied object, allowed callback, denied callback, allowed object callback, denied-object callback, and conditional claims. As you would expect, the access-allowed ACE grants access to a user, and the access-denied ACE denies the access rights specified in the access mask. The callback ACEs are used by applications that make use of the AuthZ API (described later) to register a callback that AuthZ will call when it performs an access check involving this ACE.

The difference between allowed object and access allowed, and between denied object and access denied, is that the object types are used only within Active Directory. ACEs of these types have a globally unique identifier (GUID) field that indicates that the ACE applies only to particular objects or subobjects (those that have GUID identifiers). (A GUID is a 128-bit identifier guaranteed to be universally unique.) In addition, another optional GUID indicates what type of child object will inherit the ACE when a child is created within an Active Directory container that has the ACE applied to it. The conditional claims ACE is stored in a *-callback type ACE structure and is described in the section on the AuthZ APIs.

The accumulation of access rights granted by individual ACEs forms the set of access rights granted by an ACL. If no DACL is present (a null DACL) in a security descriptor, everyone has full access to the object. If the DACL is empty (that is, it has zero ACEs), no user has access to the object.

The ACEs used in DACLs also have a set of flags that control and specify characteristics of the ACE related to inheritance. Some object namespaces have containers and objects. A container can hold other container objects and leaf objects, which are its child objects. Examples of containers are directories in the file system namespace and keys in the registry namespace. Certain flags in an ACE control how the ACE propagates to child objects of the container associated with the ACE. Table 7-6, reproduced in part from the Windows SDK, lists the inheritance rules for ACE flags.

TABLE 7-6 Inheritance rules for ACE flags

Flag	Inheritance Rule
CONTAINER_INHERIT_ACE	Child objects that are containers, such as directories, inherit the ACE as an effective ACE. The inherited ACE is inheritable unless the NO_PROPAGATE_INHERIT_ACE bit flag is also set.
INHERIT_ONLY_ACE	This flag indicates an inherit-only ACE that doesn't control access to the object it's attached to. If this flag is not set, the ACE controls access to the object to which it is attached.
INHERITED_ACE	This flag indicates that the ACE was inherited. The system sets this bit when it propagates an inheritable ACE to a child object.
NO_PROPAGATE_INHERIT_ACE	If the ACE is inherited by a child object, the system clears the OBJECT_INHERIT_ACE and CONTAINER_INHERIT_ACE flags in the inherited ACE. This action prevents the ACE from being inherited by subsequent generations of objects.
OBJECT_INHERIT_ACE	Non-container child objects inherit the ACE as an effective ACE. For child objects that are containers, the ACE is inherited as an inherit-only ACE unless the NO_PROPAGATE_INHERIT_ACE bit flag is also set.

A SACL contains two types of ACEs: system audit ACEs and system audit-object ACEs. These ACEs specify which operations performed on the object by specific users or groups should be audited. Audit information is stored in the system audit log. Both successful and unsuccessful attempts can be audited. Like their DACL object-specific ACE cousins, system audit-object ACEs specify a GUID indicating the types of objects or sub-objects that the ACE applies to and an optional GUID that controls propagation of the ACE to particular child object types. If a SACL is null, no auditing takes place on the object. (Security auditing is described later in this chapter.) The inheritance flags that apply to DACL ACEs also apply to system audit and system audit-object ACEs.

Figure 7-8 is a simplified picture of a file object and its DACL. As shown, the first ACE allows USER1 to read the file. The second ACE denies members of the group TEAM1 write access to the file. The third ACE grants all other users (Everyone) execute access.

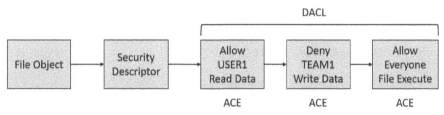

FIGURE 7-8 Discretionary access control list (DACL).

EXPERIMENT: Viewing a security descriptor

Most executive subsystems rely on the object manager's default security functionality to manage security descriptors for their objects. The object manager's default security functions use the security descriptor pointer to store security descriptors for such objects. For example, the process manager uses default security, so the object manager stores process and thread security descriptors in the object headers of process and thread objects, respectively. The security descriptor pointer of events, mutexes, and semaphores also store their security descriptors. You can use live kernel debugging to view the security descriptors of these objects once you locate their object header, as outlined in the following steps. (Note that both Process Explorer and AccessChk can also show security descriptors for processes.)

1. Start local kernel debugging.

2. Type **!process 0 0 explorer.exe** to obtain process information about Explorer:

```
lkd> !process 0 0 explorer.exe
PROCESS ffffe18304dfd780
    SessionId: 1  Cid: 23e4    Peb: 00c2a000  ParentCid: 2264
    DirBase: 2aa0f6000  ObjectTable: ffffcd82c72fcd80  HandleCount:
<Data Not Accessible>
    Image: explorer.exe

PROCESS ffffe1830670a080
    SessionId: 1  Cid: 27b8    Peb: 00950000  ParentCid: 035c
    DirBase: 2cba97000  ObjectTable: ffffcd82c7ccc500  HandleCount:
<Data Not Accessible>
    Image: explorer.exe
```

3. If more than one instance of explorer is listed, choose one. (It doesn't matter which.) Type **!object** with the address of the EPROCESS in the output of the previous command as the argument to show the object data structure:

```
lkd> !object ffffe18304dfd780
Object: ffffe18304dfd780  Type: (ffffe182f7496690) Process
    ObjectHeader: ffffe18304dfd750 (new version)
    HandleCount: 15  PointerCount: 504639
```

4. Type **dt _OBJECT_HEADER** and the address of the object header field from the previous command's output to show the object header data structure, including the security descriptor pointer value:

```
lkd> dt nt!_object_header ffffe18304dfd750
   +0x000 PointerCount      : 0n504448
   +0x008 HandleCount       : 0n15
   +0x008 NextToFree        : 0x00000000'0000000f Void
   +0x010 Lock              : _EX_PUSH_LOCK
   +0x018 TypeIndex         : 0xe5 ''
   +0x019 TraceFlags        : 0 ''
   +0x019 DbgRefTrace       : 0y0
   +0x019 DbgTracePermanent : 0y0
```

```
+0x01a InfoMask         : 0x88 ''
+0x01b Flags            : 0 ''
+0x01b NewObject        : 0y0
+0x01b KernelObject     : 0y0
+0x01b KernelOnlyAccess : 0y0
+0x01b ExclusiveObject  : 0y0
+0x01b PermanentObject  : 0y0
+0x01b DefaultSecurityQuota : 0y0
+0x01b SingleHandleEntry : 0y0
+0x01b DeletedInline    : 0y0
+0x01c Reserved         : 0x30003100
+0x020 ObjectCreateInfo : 0xffffe183'09e84ac0 _OBJECT_CREATE_INFORMATION
+0x020 QuotaBlockCharged : 0xffffe183'09e84ac0 Void
+0x028 SecurityDescriptor : 0xffffcd82'cd0e97ed Void
+0x030 Body             : _QUAD
```

5. Finally, use the debugger's !sd command to dump the security descriptor. The security descriptor pointer in the object header uses some of the low-order bits as flags, and these must be zeroed before following the pointer. On 32-bit systems there are three flag bits, so use & –8 with the security descriptor address displayed in the object header structure, as follows. On 64-bit systems there are four flag bits, so you use & –10 instead.

```
lkd> !sd 0xffffcd82'cd0e97ed & -10
->Revision: 0x1
->Sbz1    : 0x0
->Control : 0x8814
            SE_DACL_PRESENT
            SE_SACL_PRESENT
            SE_SACL_AUTO_INHERITED
            SE_SELF_RELATIVE
->Owner   : S-1-5-21-3537846094-3055369412-2967912182-1001
->Group   : S-1-5-21-3537846094-3055369412-2967912182-1001
->Dacl    :
->Dacl    : ->AclRevision: 0x2
->Dacl    : ->Sbz1        : 0x0
->Dacl    : ->AclSize     : 0x5c
->Dacl    : ->AceCount    : 0x3
->Dacl    : ->Sbz2        : 0x0
->Dacl    : ->Ace[0]: ->AceType: ACCESS_ALLOWED_ACE_TYPE
->Dacl    : ->Ace[0]: ->AceFlags: 0x0
->Dacl    : ->Ace[0]: ->AceSize: 0x24
->Dacl    : ->Ace[0]: ->Mask : 0x001fffff
->Dacl    : ->Ace[0]: ->SID: S-1-5-21-3537846094-3055369412-2967912182-1001

->Dacl    : ->Ace[1]: ->AceType: ACCESS_ALLOWED_ACE_TYPE
->Dacl    : ->Ace[1]: ->AceFlags: 0x0
->Dacl    : ->Ace[1]: ->AceSize: 0x14
->Dacl    : ->Ace[1]: ->Mask : 0x001fffff
->Dacl    : ->Ace[1]: ->SID: S-1-5-18

->Dacl    : ->Ace[2]: ->AceType: ACCESS_ALLOWED_ACE_TYPE
```

```
->Dacl     : ->Ace[2]: ->AceFlags: 0x0
->Dacl     : ->Ace[2]: ->AceSize: 0x1c
->Dacl     : ->Ace[2]: ->Mask : 0x00121411
->Dacl     : ->Ace[2]: ->SID: S-1-5-5-0-1745560

->Sacl     :
->Sacl     : ->AclRevision: 0x2
->Sacl     : ->Sbz1       : 0x0
->Sacl     : ->AclSize    : 0x1c
->Sacl     : ->AceCount   : 0x1
->Sacl     : ->Sbz2       : 0x0
->Sacl     : ->Ace[0]: ->AceType: SYSTEM_MANDATORY_LABEL_ACE_TYPE
->Sacl     : ->Ace[0]: ->AceFlags: 0x0
->Sacl     : ->Ace[0]: ->AceSize: 0x14
->Sacl     : ->Ace[0]: ->Mask : 0x00000003
->Sacl     : ->Ace[0]: ->SID: S-1-16-8192
```

The security descriptor contains three access-allowed ACEs: one for the current user (S-1-5-21-3537846094-3055369412-2967912182-1001), one for the System account (S-1-5-18), and the last for the Logon SID (S-1-5-5-0-1745560). The system access control list has one entry (S-1-16-8192) labeling the process as medium integrity level.

ACL assignment

To determine which DACL to assign to a new object, the security system uses the first applicable rule of the following four assignment rules:

1. If a caller explicitly provides a security descriptor when creating the object, the security system applies it to the object. If the object has a name and resides in a container object (for example, a named event object in the \BaseNamedObjects object manager namespace directory), the system merges any inheritable ACEs (ACEs that might propagate from the object's container) into the DACL unless the security descriptor has the SE_DACL_PROTECTED flag set, which prevents inheritance.

2. If a caller doesn't supply a security descriptor and the object has a name, the security system looks at the security descriptor in the container in which the new object name is stored. Some of the object directory's ACEs might be marked as inheritable, meaning they should be applied to new objects created in the object directory. If any of these inheritable ACEs are present, the security system forms them into an ACL, which it attaches to the new object. (Separate flags indicate ACEs that should be inherited only by container objects rather than by objects that aren't containers.)

3. If no security descriptor is specified and the object doesn't inherit any ACEs, the security system retrieves the default DACL from the caller's access token and applies it to the new object. Several subsystems on Windows have hard-coded DACLs that they assign on object creation (for example, services, LSA, and SAM objects).

4. If there is no specified descriptor, no inherited ACEs, and no default DACL, the system creates the object with no DACL, which allows everyone (all users and groups) full access to the object. This rule is the same as the third rule, in which a token contains a null default DACL.

The rules the system uses when assigning a SACL to a new object are similar to those used for DACL assignment, with some exceptions:

- Inherited system audit ACEs don't propagate to objects with security descriptors marked with the SE_SACL_PROTECTED flag (similar to the SE_DACL_PROTECTED flag, which protects DACLs).

- If there are no specified security audit ACEs and there is no inherited SACL, no SACL is applied to the object. This behavior is different from that used to apply default DACLs because tokens don't have a default SACL.

When a new security descriptor containing inheritable ACEs is applied to a container, the system automatically propagates the inheritable ACEs to the security descriptors of child objects. (Note that a security descriptor's DACL doesn't accept inherited DACL ACEs if its SE_DACL_PROTECTED flag is enabled, and its SACL doesn't inherit SACL ACEs if the descriptor has the SE_SACL_PROTECTED flag set.) The order in which inheritable ACEs are merged with an existing child object's security descriptor is such that any ACEs that were explicitly applied to the ACL are kept ahead of ACEs that the object inherits. The system uses the following rules for propagating inheritable ACEs:

- If a child object with no DACL inherits an ACE, the result is a child object with a DACL containing only the inherited ACE.

- If a child object with an empty DACL inherits an ACE, the result is a child object with a DACL containing only the inherited ACE.

- For objects in Active Directory only, if an inheritable ACE is removed from a parent object, automatic inheritance removes any copies of the ACE inherited by child objects.

- For objects in Active Directory only, if automatic inheritance results in the removal of all ACEs from a child object's DACL, the child object has an empty DACL rather than no DACL.

As you'll soon discover, the order of ACEs in an ACL is an important aspect of the Windows security model.

 Note Inheritance is generally not directly supported by the object stores, such as file systems, the registry, or Active Directory. Windows APIs that support inheritance, including SetEntriesInAcl, do so by invoking appropriate functions within the security inheritance support DLL (%SystemRoot%\System32\Ntmarta.dll) that know how to traverse those object stores.

Trust ACEs

The advent of protected processes and Protected Processes Light (PPL, discussed in Chapter 3) created a need for such a process to make objects as accessible by protected processes only. This is important to protect certain resources such as the KnownDlls registry key from tampering, even by admin-level code. Such ACEs are specified with well-known SIDs that provide the protection level and signer that is required to obtain access. Table 7-7 shows the SIDs and their level and meaning.

TABLE 7-7 Trust SIDs

SID	Protection Level	Protection Signer
1-19-512-0	Protected Light	None
1-19-512-4096	Protected Light	Windows
1-19-512-8192	Protected Light	WinTcb
1-19-1024-0	Protected	None
1-19-1024-4096	Protected	Windows
1-19-1024-8192	Protected	WinTcb

A *trust SID* is part of a token object that exists for tokens attached to protected or PPL processes. The higher the SID number, the more powerful the token is. (remember that Protected is higher than Protected Light).

EXPERIMENT: Viewing trust SIDs

In this experiment, you'll look at trust SIDs in tokens of protected processes.

Start local kernel debugging.

List Csrss.exe processes with basic information:

```
1kd> !process 0 1 csrss.exe
PROCESS ffff8188e50b5780
    SessionId: 0  Cid: 0358    Peb: b3a9f5e000  ParentCid: 02ec
    DirBase: 1273a3000  ObjectTable: ffffbe0d829e2040  HandleCount:
<Data Not Accessible>
    Image: csrss.exe
    VadRoot ffff8188e6ccc8e0 Vads 159 Clone 0 Private 324. Modified 4470.
Locked 0.
    DeviceMap ffffbe0d70c15620
    Token                           ffffbe0d829e7060
    ...
PROCESS ffff8188e7a92080
    SessionId: 1  Cid: 03d4    Peb: d5b0de4000  ParentCid: 03bc
    DirBase: 162d93000  ObjectTable: ffffbe0d8362d7c0  HandleCount:
<Data Not Accessible>Modified 462372. Locked 0.
    DeviceMap ffffbe0d70c15620
    Token                           ffffbe0d8362d060
    ...
```

Select one of the tokens and show its details:

```
1kd> !token ffffbe0d829e7060
_TOKEN 0xffffbe0d829e7060
TS Session ID: 0
User: S-1-5-18
...
Process Token TrustLevelSid: S-1-19-512-8192
```

That's a PPL with a WinTcb signer.

Determining access

Two methods are used for determining access to an object:

- The mandatory integrity check, which determines whether the integrity level of the caller is high enough to access the resource, based on the resource's own integrity level and its mandatory policy.

- The discretionary access check, which determines the access that a specific user account has to an object.

When a process tries to open an object, the integrity check takes place before the standard Windows DACL check in the kernel's SeAccessCheck function because it is faster to execute and can quickly eliminate the need to perform the full discretionary access check. Given the default integrity policies in its access token (TOKEN_MANDATORY_NO_WRITE_UP and TOKEN_MANDATORY_NEW_PROCESS_MIN, described previously), a process can open an object for write access if its integrity level is equal to or higher than the object's integrity level and the DACL also grants the process the accesses it desires. For example, a low-integrity-level process cannot open a medium-integrity-level process for write access, even if the DACL grants the process write access.

With the default integrity policies, processes can open any object—with the exception of process, thread, and token objects—for read access as long as the object's DACL grants them read access. That means a process running at low integrity level can open any files accessible to the user account in which it's running. Protected Mode Internet Explorer uses integrity levels to help prevent malware that infects it from modifying user account settings, but it does not stop malware from reading the user's documents.

Recall that process, thread, and token objects are exceptions because their integrity policy also includes No-Read-Up. That means a process integrity level must be equal to or higher than the integrity level of the process or thread it wants to open, and the DACL must grant it the access it wants for an attempt to open it to succeed. Assuming the DACLs allow the desired access, Table 7-8 shows the types of access that processes running at various integrity levels have to other processes and objects.

TABLE 7-8 Accessing objects and processes based on integrity level

Accessing Process	Access to Objects	Access to Other Processes
High integrity level	Read/write to all objects with integrity level of High or lower Read access to objects with integrity level of System	Read/write access to all processes with High or lower integrity level No read/write access to processes with System integrity level
Medium integrity level	Read/write to all objects with integrity level of Medium or Low Read access to objects with integrity level of High or System	Read/write access to all processes with Medium or Low integrity level No read/write access to processes with High or System integrity level
Low integrity level	Read/write to all objects with integrity level of Low Read access to objects with integrity level of Medium or higher	Read/write access to all processes with Low integrity level No read/write access to processes with Medium or higher integrity level

Note The read access to a process described in this section means full read access, such as reading the contents of the process address space. No-Read-Up does not prevent opening a higher-integrity-level process from a lower one for a more limited access, such as PROCESS_ QUERY_LIMITED_INFORMATION, which provides only basic information about the process.

User Interface Privilege Isolation

The Windows messaging subsystem also honors integrity levels to implement User Interface Privilege Isolation (UIPI). The subsystem does this by preventing a process from sending window messages to the windows owned by a process having a higher integrity level, with the following informational messages being exceptions:

- WM_NULL
- WM_MOVE
- WM_SIZE
- WM_GETTEXT
- WM_GETTEXTLENGTH
- WM_GETHOTKEY

- WM_GETICON
- WM_RENDERFORMAT
- WM_DRAWCLIPBOARD
- WM_CHANGECBCHAIN
- WM_THEMECHANGED

This use of integrity levels prevents standard user processes from driving input into the windows of elevated processes or from performing a shatter attack (such as sending the process malformed messages that trigger internal buffer overflows, which can lead to the execution of code at the elevated process's privilege level). UIPI also blocks window hooks (SetWindowsHookEx API) from affecting the windows of higher-integrity-level processes so that a standard user process can't log the keystrokes the user types into an administrative application, for example. Journal hooks are also blocked in the same way to prevent lower-integrity-level processes from monitoring the behavior of higher-integrity-level processes.

Processes (running with medium or higher integrity level only) can choose to allow additional messages to pass the guard by calling the ChangeWindowMessageFilterEx API. This function is typically used to add messages required by custom controls to communicate outside native common controls in Windows. An older API, ChangeWindowMessageFilter, performs a similar function, but it is per-process rather than per-window. With ChangeWindowMessageFilter, it is possible for two custom controls inside the same process to be using the same internal window messages, which could lead to one control's potentially malicious window message to be allowed through, simply because it happens to be a query-only message for the other custom control.

Because accessibility applications such as the On-Screen Keyboard (Osk.exe) are subject to UIPI's restrictions (which would require the accessibility application to be executed for each kind of visible integrity-level process on the desktop), these processes can enable UI access. This flag can be present in the manifest file of the image and will run the process at a slightly higher integrity level than medium (between 0x2000 and 0x3000) if launched from a standard user account, or at high integrity level if launched from an Administrator account. Note that in the second case, an elevation request won't actually be displayed. For a process to set this flag, its image must also be signed and in one of several secure locations, including %SystemRoot% and %ProgramFiles%.

After the integrity check is complete, and assuming the mandatory policy allows access to the object based on the caller's integrity, one of two algorithms is used for the discretionary check to an object, which will determine the outcome of the access check:

■ Determine the maximum access allowed to the object, a form of which is exported to user mode using the AuthZ API (described in the section "The AuthZ API" later in this chapter) or the older `GetEffectiveRightsFromAcl` function. This is also used when a program specifies a desired access of `MAXIMUM_ALLOWED`, which is what the legacy APIs that don't have a desired access parameter use.

■ Determine whether a specific desired access is allowed, which can be done with the Windows `AccessCheck` function or the `AccessCheckByType` function.

The first algorithm examines the entries in the DACL as follows:

1. If the object has no DACL (a null DACL), the object has no protection and the security system grants all access, unless the access is from an AppContainer process (discussed in the "AppContainers" section later in this chapter), which means access is denied.

2. If the caller has the take-ownership privilege, the security system grants write-owner access before examining the DACL. (Take-ownership privilege and write-owner access are explained in a moment.)

3. If the caller is the owner of the object, the system looks for an `OWNER_RIGHTS` SID and uses that SID as the SID for the next steps. Otherwise, read-control and write-DACL access rights are granted.

4. For each access-denied ACE that contains a SID that matches one in the caller's access token, the ACE's access mask is removed from the granted-access mask.

5. For each access-allowed ACE that contains a SID that matches one in the caller's access token, the ACE's access mask is added to the granted-access mask being computed, unless that access has already been denied.

When all the entries in the DACL have been examined, the computed granted-access mask is returned to the caller as the maximum allowed access to the object. This mask represents the total set of access types that the caller will be able to successfully request when opening the object.

The preceding description applies only to the kernel-mode form of the algorithm. The Windows version implemented by `GetEffectiveRightsFromAcl` differs in that it doesn't perform step 2, and it considers a single user or group SID rather than an access token.

Owner Rights

Because owners of an object can normally override the security of an object by always being granted read-control and write-DACL rights, a specialized method of controlling this behavior is exposed by Windows: the Owner Rights SID.

The Owner Rights SID exists for two main reasons:

■ **To improve service hardening in the operating system** Whenever a service creates an object at run time, the Owner SID associated with that object is the account the service is running in (such as local system or local service) and not the actual service SID. This means that any other service in the same account would have access to the object by being an owner. The Owner Rights SID prevents that unwanted behavior.

■ **To allow more flexibility for specific usage scenarios** For example, suppose an administrator wants to allow users to create files and folders but not to modify the ACLs on those objects. (Users could inadvertently or maliciously grant access to those files or folders to unwanted accounts.) By using an inheritable Owner Rights SID, the users can be prevented from editing or even viewing the ACL on the objects they create. A second usage scenario relates to group changes. Suppose an employee has been part of some confidential or sensitive group, has created several files while a member of that group, and has now been removed from the group for business reasons. Because that employee is still a user, he could continue accessing the sensitive files.

The second algorithm is used to determine whether a specific access request can be granted based on the caller's access token. Each open function in the Windows API that deals with securable objects has a parameter that specifies the desired access mask, which is the last component of the security equation. To determine whether the caller has access, the following steps are performed:

1. If the object has no DACL (a null DACL), the object has no protection and the security system grants the desired access.

2. If the caller has the take-ownership privilege, the security system grants write-owner access if requested and then examines the DACL. However, if write-owner access was the only access requested by a caller with take-ownership privilege, the security system grants that access and never examines the DACL.

3. If the caller is the owner of the object, the system looks for an OWNER_RIGHTS SID and uses that SID as the SID for the next steps. Otherwise, read-control and write-DACL access rights are granted. If these rights were the only access rights that the caller requested, access is granted without examining the DACL

4. Each ACE in the DACL is examined from first to last. An ACE is processed if one of the following conditions is satisfied:

   • The ACE is an access-deny ACE, and the SID in the ACE matches an enabled SID (SIDs can be enabled or disabled) or a deny-only SID in the caller's access token.

- The ACE is an access-allowed ACE, and the SID in the ACE matches an enabled SID in the caller's token that isn't of type deny-only.

- It is the second pass through the descriptor for restricted-SID checks, and the SID in the ACE matches a restricted SID in the caller's access token.

- The ACE isn't marked as inherit-only.

5. If it is an access-allowed ACE, the rights in the access mask in the ACE that were requested are granted. If all the requested access rights have been granted, the access check succeeds. If it is an access-denied ACE and any of the requested access rights are in the denied-access rights, access is denied to the object.

6. If the end of the DACL is reached and some of the requested access rights still haven't been granted, access is denied.

7. If all accesses are granted but the caller's access token has at least one restricted SID, the system rescans the DACL's ACEs looking for ACEs with access-mask matches for the accesses the user is requesting and a match of the ACE's SID with any of the caller's restricted SIDs. Only if both scans of the DACL grant the requested access rights is the user granted access to the object.

The behavior of both access-validation algorithms depends on the relative ordering of allow and deny ACEs. Consider an object with only two ACEs: one that specifies that a certain user is allowed full access to an object and one that denies the user access. If the allow ACE precedes the deny ACE, the user can obtain full access to the object, but if the order is reversed, the user cannot gain any access to the object.

Several Windows functions, such as SetSecurityInfo and SetNamedSecurityInfo, apply ACEs in the preferred order of explicit deny ACEs preceding explicit allow ACEs. For example, the security editor dialog boxes with which you edit permissions on NTFS files and registry keys use these functions. SetSecurityInfo and SetNamedSecurityInfo also apply ACE inheritance rules to the security descriptor on which they are applied.

Figure 7-9 shows an example of access validation demonstrating the importance of ACE ordering. In the example, access is denied to a user wanting to open a file even though an ACE in the object's DACL grants the access. This is because the ACE denying the user access (by virtue of the user's membership in the Writers group) precedes the ACE granting access.

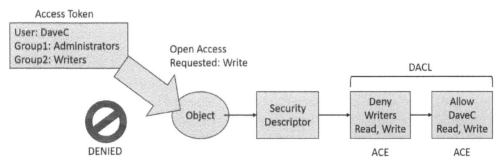

FIGURE 7-9 Access-validation example.

As stated, because it wouldn't be efficient for the security system to process the DACL every time a process uses a handle, the SRM makes this access check only when a handle is opened, not each time the handle is used. Thus, once a process successfully opens a handle, the security system can't revoke the access rights that have been granted, even if the object's DACL changes. Also keep in mind that because kernel-mode code uses pointers rather than handles to access objects, the access check isn't performed when the operating system uses objects. In other words, the Windows executive trusts itself (and all loaded drivers) in a security sense.

The fact that an object's owner is always granted write-DACL access to an object means that users can never be prevented from accessing the objects they own. If, for some reason, an object had an empty DACL (no access), the owner would still be able to open the object with write-DACL access and then apply a new DACL with the desired access permissions.

A warning regarding the GUI security editors

When you use the GUI permissions editors to modify security settings on a file, a registry, or an Active Directory object, or on another securable object, the main security dialog box shows you a potentially misleading view of the security that's applied to the object. If you allow Full Control to the Everyone group and deny the Administrator group Full Control, the list might lead you to believe that the Everyone group access-allowed ACE precedes the Administrator deny ACE because that's the order in which they appear. However, as we've said, the editors place deny ACEs before allow ACEs when they apply the ACL to the object.

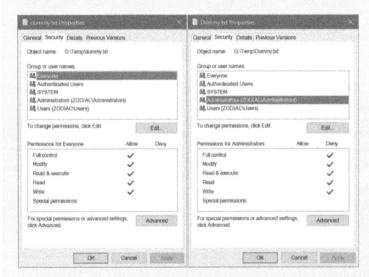

The Permissions tab of the Advanced Security Settings dialog box shows the order of ACEs in the DACL. However, even this dialog box can be confusing because a complex DACL can have deny ACEs for various accesses followed by allow ACEs for other access types.

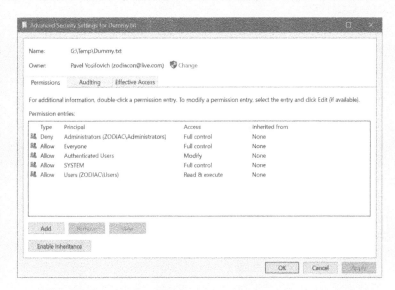

The only definitive way to know what access a particular user or group will have to an object (other than having that user or a member of the group try to access the object) is to use the **Effective Access** tab of the dialog box that is displayed when you click the **Advanced** button in the Properties dialog box. Enter the name of the user or group you want to check and the dialog box shows you what permissions they are allowed for the object.

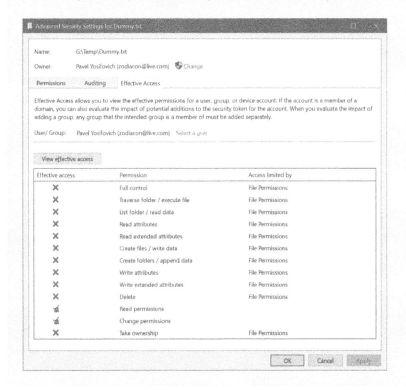

Dynamic Access Control

The discretionary access control mechanism discussed in previous sections has existed since the first Windows NT version and is useful in many scenarios. There are scenarios, however, where this scheme is not flexible enough. For example, consider a requirement that users accessing a shared file should be allowed to do so if they are using a computer in the workplace, but should not be allowed if accessing the file from their computer at home. There is no way to specify such a condition using an ACE.

Windows 8 and Server 2012 introduced Dynamic Access Control (DAC), a flexible mechanism that can be used to define rules based on custom attributes defined in Active Directory. DAC does not replace the existing mechanism, but adds to it. This means that for an operation to be allowed, both DAC and the classic DACL must grant the permission. Figure 7-10 shows the main aspects of Dynamic Access Control.

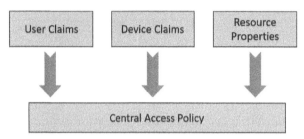

FIGURE 7-10   Dynamic Access Control components.

A claim is any piece of information about a user, device (computer in a domain), or resource (generic attribute) that has been published by a domain controller. Examples of valid claims are a user's title and department classification of a file. Any combination of claims can be used in expressions for building rules. These rules collectively become the central access policy.

DAC configuration is done in Active Directory and pushed through policy. The Kerberos tickets protocol has been enhanced to support authenticated transport of user and device claims (known as *Kerberos armoring*).

The AuthZ API

The AuthZ Windows API provides authorization functions and implements the same security model as the security reference monitor (SRM), but it implements the model totally in user mode in the %SystemRoot%\System32\Authz.dll library. This gives applications that want to protect their own private objects, such as database tables, the ability to leverage the Windows security model without incurring the cost of user mode–to–kernel mode transitions that they would make if they relied on the SRM.

The AuthZ API uses standard security descriptor data structures, SIDs, and privileges. Instead of using tokens to represent clients, AuthZ uses AUTHZ_CLIENT_CONTEXT. AuthZ includes user-mode equivalents of all access-check and Windows security functions—for example, AuthzAccessCheck is the AuthZ version of the AccessCheck Windows API that uses the SeAccessCheck SRM function.

Another advantage available to applications that use AuthZ is that they can direct AuthZ to cache the results of security checks to improve subsequent checks that use the same client context and security descriptor. AuthZ is fully documented in the Windows SDK.

This type of access checking, using a SID and security group membership in a static, controlled environment, is known as *Identity-Based Access Control* (*IBAC*), and it requires that the security system know the identity of every possible accessor when the DACL is placed in an object's security descriptor.

Windows includes support for *Claims Based Access Control* (*CBAC*), where access is granted not based upon the accessor's identity or group membership, but upon arbitrary attributes assigned to the accessor and stored in the accessor's access token. Attributes are supplied by an attribute provider, such as AppLocker. The CBAC mechanism provides many benefits, including the ability to create a DACL for a user whose identity is not yet known or dynamically calculated user attributes. The CBAC ACE (also known as a conditional ACE) is stored in a `*-callback` ACE structure, which is essentially private to AuthZ and is ignored by the system SeAccessCheck API. The kernel-mode routine SeSrpAccessCheck does not understand conditional ACEs, so only applications calling the AuthZ APIs can make use of CBAC. The only system component that makes use of CBAC is AppLocker, for setting attributes such as path or publisher. Third-party applications can make use of CBAC by taking advantage of the CBAC AuthZ APIs.

Using CBAC security checks allows powerful management policies, such as the following:

- Run only applications approved by the corporate IT department.

- Allow only approved applications to access your Microsoft Outlook contacts or calendar.

- Allow only people in a particular building on a specific floor to access printers on that floor.

- Allow access to an intranet website only to full-time employees (as opposed to contractors).

Attributes can be referenced in what is known as a *conditional ACE*, where the presence, absence, or value of one or more attributes is checked. An attribute name can contain any alphanumeric Unicode characters, as well as the following characters: colon (:), forward slash (/), and underscore (_). The value of an attribute can be one of the following: 64-bit integer, Unicode string, byte string, or array.

Conditional ACEs

The format of SDDL strings has been expanded to support ACEs with conditional expressions. The new format of an SDDL string is this: `AceType;AceFlags;Rights;ObjectGuid;InheritObjectGuid; AccountSid;(ConditionalExpression)`.

The AceType for a conditional ACE is either XA (for `SDDL_CALLBACK_ACCESS_ALLOWED`) or XD (for `SDDL_CALLBACK_ACCESS_DENIED`). Note that ACEs with conditional expressions are used for claims-type authorization (specifically, the AuthZ APIs and AppLocker) and are not recognized by the object manager or file systems.

A conditional expression can include any of the elements shown in Table 7-9.

TABLE 7-9 Acceptable Elements for a Conditional Expression

Expression Element	Description
AttributeName	Tests whether the specified attribute has a non-zero value.
exists AttributeName	Tests whether the specified attribute exists in the client context.
AttributeName Operator Value	Returns the result of the specified operation. The following operators are defined for use in conditional expressions to test the values of attributes. All these are binary operators (as opposed to unary) and are used in the form AttributeName Operator Value. The operators are Contains any_of , ==, !=, <, <=, >, >=.
ConditionalExpression || ConditionalExpression	Tests whether either of the specified conditional expressions is true.
ConditionalExpression && ConditionalExpression	Tests whether both of the specified conditional expressions are true.
!(ConditionalExpression)	The inverse of a conditional expression.
Member_of {SidArray}	Tests whether the SID_AND_ATTRIBUTES array of the client context contains all the security identifiers (SIDs) in the comma-separated list specified by SidArray.

A conditional ACE can contain any number of conditions. It is ignored if the resultant evaluation of the condition is false or applied if the result is true. A conditional ACE can be added to an object using the AddConditionalAce API and checked using the AuthzAccessCheck API.

A conditional ACE could specify that access to certain data records within a program should be granted only to a user who meets the following criteria (for example):

- Holds the Role attribute, with a value of Architect, Program Manager, or Development Lead, and the Division attribute with a value of Windows

- Whose ManagementChain attribute contains the value John Smith

- Whose CommissionType attribute is Officer and whose PayGrade attribute is greater than 6 (that is, the rank of General Officer in the US military)

Windows does not include tools to view or edit conditional ACEs.

Account rights and privileges

Many operations performed by processes as they execute cannot be authorized through object access protection because they do not involve interaction with a particular object. For example, the ability to bypass security checks when opening files for backup is an attribute of an account, not of a particular object. Windows uses both privileges and account rights to allow a system administrator to control what accounts can perform security-related operations.

A *privilege* is the right of an account to perform a particular system-related operation, such as shutting down the computer or changing the system time. An *account right* grants or denies the account to which it's assigned the ability to perform a particular type of logon, such as a local logon or interactive logon, to a computer.

A system administrator assigns privileges to groups and accounts using tools such as the Active Directory Users and Groups MMC snap-in for domain accounts or the Local Security Policy editor (%SystemRoot%\System32\secpol.msc). Figure 7-11 shows the User Rights Assignment configuration in the Local Security Policy editor, which displays the complete list of privileges and account rights available on Windows. Note that the tool makes no distinction between privileges and account rights. However, you can differentiate between them: Any user right that does not contain the words *log on* is an account privilege.

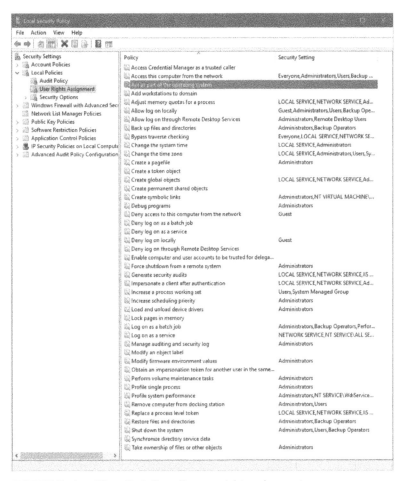

FIGURE 7-11   Local Security Policy editor user rights assignment.

Account rights

Account rights are not enforced by the SRM, nor are they stored in tokens. The function responsible for logon is LsaLogonUser. Winlogon, for example, calls the LogonUser API when a user logs on interactively to a computer, and LogonUser calls LsaLogonUser. LogonUser takes a parameter that indicates the type of logon being performed, which includes interactive, network, batch, service, and Terminal Server client.

In response to logon requests, the Local Security Authority (LSA) retrieves account rights assigned to a user from the LSA policy database at the time that a user attempts to log on to the system. The LSA checks the logon type against the account rights assigned to the user account logging on and denies the logon if the account does not have the right that permits the logon type or it has the right that denies the logon type. Table 7-10 lists the user rights defined by Windows.

TABLE 7-10 Account rights

User Right	Role
Deny logon locally, allow logon locally	Used for interactive logons that originate on the local machine
Deny logon over the network, allow logon over the network	Used for logons that originate from a remote machine
Deny logon through Terminal Services, allow logon through Terminal Services	Used for logons through a Terminal Server client
Deny logon as a service, allow logon as a service	Used by the service control manager when starting a service in a particular user account
Deny logon as a batch job, allow logon as a batch job	Used when performing a logon of type batch

Windows applications can add and remove user rights from an account by using the `LsaAddAccountRights` and `LsaRemoveAccountRights` functions, and they can determine what rights are assigned to an account with `LsaEnumerateAccountRights`.

Privileges

The number of privileges defined by the operating system has grown over time. Unlike user rights, which are enforced in one place by the LSA, different privileges are defined by different components and enforced by those components. For example, the debug privilege, which allows a process to bypass security checks when opening a handle to another process with the `OpenProcess` Windows API, is checked for by the process manager.

Table 7-11 is a full list of privileges and describes how and when system components check for them. Each privilege has a macro defined in the SDK headers, in the form SE_*privilege*_NAME, where *privilege* is a privilege constant—for example, SE_DEBUG_NAME for the debug privilege. These macros are defined as strings that start with Se and end with `Privilege`, as in SeDebugPrivilege. This may seem to indicate that privileges are identified by strings, but in fact they are identified by LUIDs, which naturally are unique for the current boot. Every access to a privilege needs to lookup the correct LUID by calling the `LookupPrivilegeValue` function. Note, however, that Ntdll and kernel code can identify privileges with integer constants directly without going through a LUID.

TABLE 7-11 Privileges

Privilege	User Right	Privilege Usage
`SeAssignPrimaryTokenPrivilege`	Replace a process-level token	Checked for by various components, such as `NtSetInformationJobObject`, that set a process's token.
`SeAuditPrivilege`	Generate security audits	Required to generate events for the Security event log with the `ReportEvent` API.

TABLE 7-11 Privileges (continued)

Privilege	User Right	Privilege Usage
SeBackupPrivilege	Back up files and directories	Causes NTFS to grant the following access to any file or directory, regardless of the security descriptor that's present: READ_CONTROL, ACCESS_SYSTEM_ SECURITY, FILE_GENERIC_READ, and FILE_ TRAVERSE. Note that when opening a file for backup, the caller must specify the FILE_FLAG_BACKUP_ SEMANTICS flag. Also allows corresponding access to registry keys when using RegSaveKey.
SeChangeNotifyPrivilege	Bypass traverse checking	Used by NTFS to avoid checking permissions on intermediate directories of a multilevel directory lookup. Also used by file systems when applications register for notification of changes to the file system structure.
SeCreateGlobalPrivilege	Create global objects	Required for a process to create section and symbolic link objects in the directories of the object manager namespace that are assigned to a different session than the caller.
SeCreatePagefilePrivilege	Create a pagefile	Checked for by NtCreatePagingFile, which is the function used to create a new paging file.
SeCreatePermanentPrivilege	Create permanent shared objects	Checked for by the object manager when creating a permanent object (one that doesn't get deallocated when there are no more references to it).
SeCreateSymbolicLinkPrivilege	Create symbolic links	Checked for by NTFS when creating symbolic links on the file system with the CreateSymbolicLink API.
SeCreateTokenPrivilege	Create a token object	NtCreateToken, the function that creates a token object, checks for this privilege.
SeDebugPrivilege	Debug programs	If the caller has this privilege enabled, the process manager allows access to any process or thread using NtOpenProcess or NtOpenThread, regardless of the process's or thread's security descriptor (except for protected processes).
SeEnableDelegationPrivilege	Enable computer and user accounts to be trusted for delegation	Used by Active Directory services to delegate authenticated credentials.
SeImpersonatePrivilege	Impersonate a client after authentication	The process manager checks for this when a thread wants to use a token for impersonation and the token represents a different user than that of the thread's process token.
SeIncreaseBasePriorityPrivilege	Increase scheduling priority	Checked for by the process manager and is required to raise the priority of a process.
SeIncreaseQuotaPrivilege	Adjust memory quotas for a process	Enforced when changing a process's working set thresholds, a process's paged and nonpaged pool quotas, and a process's CPU rate quota.
SeIncreaseWorkingSetPrivilege	Increase a process working set	Required to call SetProcessWorkingSetSize to increase the minimum working set. This indirectly allows the process to lock up to the minimum working set of memory using VirtualLock.

TABLE 7-11 Privileges *(continued)*

Privilege	User Right	Privilege Usage
SeLoadDriverPrivilege	Load and unload device drivers	Checked for by the NtLoadDriver and NtUnloadDriver driver functions.
SeLockMemoryPrivilege	Lock pages in memory	Checked for by NtLockVirtualMemory, the kernel implementation of VirtualLock.
SeMachineAccountPrivilege	Add workstations to the domain	Checked for by the Security Account Manager on a domain controller when creating a machine account in a domain.
SeManageVolumePrivilege	Perform volume maintenance tasks	Enforced by file system drivers during a volume open operation, which is required to perform disk-checking and defragmenting activities.
SeProfileSingleProcessPrivilege	Profile single process	Checked by Superfetch and the prefetcher when requesting information for an individual process through the NtQuerySystemInformation API.
SeRelabelPrivilege	Modify an object label	Checked for by the SRM when raising the integrity level of an object owned by another user, or when attempting to raise the integrity level of an object higher than that of the caller's token.
SeRemoteShutdownPrivilege	Force shutdown from a remote system	Winlogon checks that remote callers of the InitiateSystemShutdown function have this privilege.
SeRestorePrivilege	Restore files and directories	This privilege causes NTFS to grant the following access to any file or directory, regardless of the security descriptor that's present: WRITE_DAC, WRITE_OWNER, ACCESS_SYSTEM_SECURITY, FILE_GENERIC_WRITE, FILE_ADD_FILE, FILE_ADD_SUBDIRECTORY, and DELETE. Note that when opening a file for restore, the caller must specify the FILE_FLAG_BACKUP_SEMANTICS flag. Allows corresponding access to registry keys when using RegSaveKey.
SeSecurityPrivilege	Manage auditing and security log	Required to access the SACL of a security descriptor and to read and clear the security event log.
SeShutdownPrivilege	Shut down the system	Checked for by NtShutdownSystem and NtRaiseHardError, which presents a system error dialog box on the interactive console.
SeSyncAgentPrivilege	Synchronize directory service data	Required to use the LDAP directory synchronization services. It allows the holder to read all objects and properties in the directory, regardless of the protection on the objects and properties.
SeSystemEnvironmentPrivilege	Modify firmware environment variables	Required by NtSetSystemEnvironmentValue and NtQuerySystemEnvironmentValue to modify and read firmware environment variables using the hardware abstraction layer (HAL).
SeSystemProfilePrivilege	Profile system performance	Checked for by NtCreateProfile, the function used to perform profiling of the system. This is used by the Kernprof tool, for example.
SeSystemtimePrivilege	Change the system time	Required to change the time or date.

TABLE 7-11 Privileges *(continued)*

Privilege	User Right	Privilege Usage
SeTakeOwnershipPrivilege	Take ownership of files and other objects	Required to take ownership of an object without being granted discretionary access.
SeTcbPrivilege	Act as part of the operating system	Checked for by the SRM when the session ID is set in a token, by the Plug and Play manager for Plug and Play event creation and management, by BroadcastSystemMessageEx when called with BSM_ALLDESKTOPS, by LsaRegisterLogonProcess, and when specifying an application as a VDM with NtSetInformationProcess.
SeTimeZonePrivilege	Change the time zone	Required to change the time zone.
SeTrustedCredManAccessPrivilege	Access Credential Manager as a trusted caller	Checked by the Credential Manager to verify that it should trust the caller with credential information that can be queried in plaintext. It is granted only to Winlogon by default.
SeUndockPrivilege	Remove computer from a docking station	Checked for by the user-mode Plug and Play manager when either a computer undock is initiated or a device eject request is made.
SeUnsolicitedInputPrivilege	Receive unsolicited data from a terminal device	This privilege isn't currently used by Windows.

When a component wants to check a token to see whether a privilege is present, it uses the Privilege-Check or LsaEnumerateAccountRights APIs if running in user mode and SeSinglePrivilegeCheck or SePrivilegeCheck if running in kernel mode. The privilege-related APIs are not account-right aware, but the account-right APIs are privilege-aware.

Unlike account rights, privileges can be enabled and disabled. For a privilege check to succeed, the privilege must be in the specified token and it must be enabled. The idea behind this scheme is that privileges should be enabled only when their use is required so that a process cannot inadvertently perform a privileged security operation. Enabling or disabling privileges can be done with the AdjustTokenPrivileges function.

EXPERIMENT: Seeing a privilege get enabled

By following these steps, you can see that the Date and Time Control Panel applet enables the SeTimeZonePrivilege privilege in response to you using its interface to change the time zone of the computer (Windows 10):

1. Run Process Explorer elevated.

2. Right-click the clock in the system tray in the taskbar and choose **Adjust Date/Time**. Alternatively, open the Settings app and search for **time** to open the Date and Time settings page.

3. Right-click the **SystemSettings.exe** process in Process Explorer and choose **Properties**. Then click the **Security** tab in the Properties dialog box. You should see that the SeTimeZonePrivilege privilege is disabled.

4. Change the time zone, close the Properties dialog box, and then open it again. On the Security tab, you should now see that the SeTimeZonePrivilege privilege is enabled:

If you are a systems administrator, you must be aware of the Bypass Traverse Checking privilege (internally called SeNotifyPrivilege) and its implications. This experiment demonstrates that not understanding its behavior can lead to improperly applied security.

1. Create a folder and, within that folder, a new text file with some sample text.

2. Navigate in Explorer to the new file, open its Properties dialog box, and click the **Security** tab.

3. Click the **Advanced** button.

4. Deselect the **Inheritance** check box.

5. Select **Copy** when you are prompted as to whether you want to remove or copy inherited permissions.

6. Modify the security of the new folder so that your account does not have any access to the folder. To do so, select your account and check all the **Deny** boxes in the permissions list.

7. Run Notepad. Then open the **File** menu, choose **Open**, and browse to the new directory in the dialog box that appears. You should be denied access to the directory.

8. In the File Name field of the Open dialog box, type the full path of the new file. The file should open.

If your account does not have the Bypass Traverse Checking privilege, NTFS performs an access check on each directory of the path to a file when you try to open a file, which results in you being denied access to the file in this example.

Super privileges

Several privileges are so powerful that a user to which they are assigned is effectively a "super user" who has full control over a computer. These privileges can be used in an infinite number of ways to gain unauthorized access to otherwise off-limit resources and to perform unauthorized operations. However, we'll focus on using the privilege to execute code that grants the user privileges not assigned to the user, with the knowledge that this capability can be leveraged to perform any operation on the local machine that the user desires.

This section lists the privileges and discusses some of the ways they can be exploited. Other privileges, such as Lock Pages in Physical Memory (SeLockMemoryPrivilege), can be exploited for denial-of-service attacks on a system, but these are not discussed. Note that on systems with UAC enabled, these privileges will be granted only to applications running at high integrity level or higher, even if the account possesses them:

- **Debug programs (SeDebugPrivilege)**   A user with this privilege can open any process on the system (except for a protected process) without regard to the security descriptor present on the process. For example, the user could implement a program that opens the Lsass process, copy executable code into its address space, and then inject a thread with the CreateRemoteThread Windows API to execute the injected code in a more-privileged security context. The code could grant the user additional privileges and group memberships.

- **Take ownership (SeTakeOwnershipPrivilege)**   This privilege allows a holder to take ownership of any securable object (even protected processes and threads) by writing his own SID into the owner field of the object's security descriptor. Recall that an owner is always granted permission to read and modify the DACL of the security descriptor, so a process with this privilege could modify the DACL to grant itself full access to the object and then close and reopen the object with full access. This would allow the owner to see sensitive data and to even replace system files that execute as part of normal system operation, such as Lsass, with his own programs that grant a user elevated privileges.

- **Restore files and directories (SeRestorePrivilege)**   A user assigned this privilege can replace any file on the system with her own. She could exploit this power by replacing system files as described in the preceding paragraph.

- **Load and unload device drivers (SeLoadDriverPrivilege)**   A malicious user could use this privilege to load a device driver into the system. Device drivers are considered trusted parts of the operating system that can execute within it with System account credentials, so a driver could launch privileged programs that assign the user other rights.

- **Create a token object (SeCreateTokenPrivilege)**   This privilege can be used in the obvious way to generate tokens that represent arbitrary user accounts with arbitrary group membership and privilege assignment.

- **Act as part of operating system (SeTcbPrivilege)**   LsaRegisterLogonProcess, the function a process calls to establish a trusted connection to Lsass, checks for this privilege. A malicious user with this privilege can establish a trusted-Lsass connection and then execute LsaLogonUser, a function used to create new logon sessions. LsaLogonUser requires a valid user name and password and accepts an optional list of SIDs that it adds to the initial token created for a new logon session. The user could therefore use her own user name and password to create a new logon session that includes the SIDs of more privileged groups or users in the resulting token.

Note   The use of an elevated privilege does not extend past the machine boundary to the network because any interaction with another computer requires authentication with a domain controller and validation of domain passwords. Domain passwords are not stored on a computer either in plaintext or encrypted form, so they are not accessible to malicious code.

Access tokens of processes and threads

Figure 7-12 brings together the concepts covered so far in this chapter by illustrating the basic process and thread security structures. In the figure, notice that the process object and the thread objects have ACLs, as do the access token objects themselves. Also in this figure, thread 2 and thread 3 each have an impersonation token, whereas thread 1 uses the default process access token.

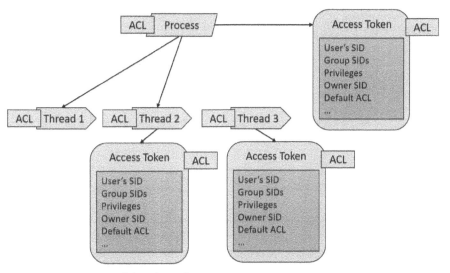

FIGURE 7-12 Process and thread security structures.

Security auditing

The object manager can generate audit events as a result of an access check, and Windows functions available to user applications can generate them directly. Kernel-mode code is always allowed to generate an audit event. Two privileges, `SeSecurityPrivilege` and `SeAuditPrivilege`, relate to auditing. A process must have the `SeSecurityPrivilege` privilege to manage the security event log and to view or set an object's SACL. Processes that call audit system services, however, must have the `SeAuditPrivilege` privilege to successfully generate an audit record.

The audit policy of the local system controls the decision to audit a particular type of security event. The audit policy, also called the Local Security Policy, is one part of the security policy Lsass maintains on the local system. It is configured with the Local Security Policy editor as shown in Figure 7-13. The audit policy configuration (both the basic settings under Local Policies and the Advanced Audit Policy Configuration) is stored in the registry as a bitmapped value in the HKEY_LOCAL_MACHINE\SECURITY\Policy\PolAdtEv key.

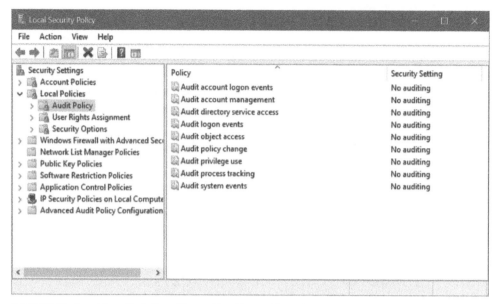

FIGURE 7-13 Local Security Policy editor audit policy configuration.

Lsass sends messages to the SRM to inform it of the auditing policy at system-initialization time and when the policy changes. Lsass is responsible for receiving audit records generated based on the audit events from the SRM, editing the records, and sending them to the event logger. Lsass (instead of the SRM) sends these records because it adds pertinent details, such as the information needed to more completely identify the process that is being audited.

The SRM sends audit records via its ALPC connection to Lsass. The event logger then writes the audit record to the security event log. In addition to audit records the SRM passes, both Lsass and the SAM generate audit records that Lsass sends directly to the event logger, and the AuthZ APIs allow for applications to generate application-defined audits. Figure 7-14 depicts this overall flow.

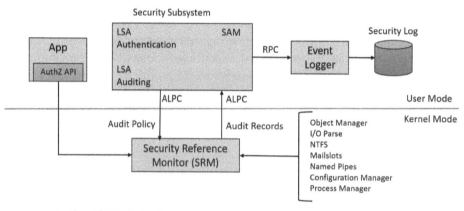

FIGURE 7-14 Flow of security audit records.

Audit records are put on a queue to be sent to the LSA as they are received. They are not submitted in batches. The audit records are moved from the SRM to the security subsystem in one of two ways. If the audit record is small (less than the maximum ALPC message size), it is sent as an ALPC message. The audit records are copied from the address space of the SRM to the address space of the Lsass process. If the audit record is large, the SRM uses shared memory to make the message available to Lsass and simply passes a pointer in an ALPC message.

Object access auditing

An important use of the auditing mechanism in many environments is to maintain a log of accesses to secured objects—in particular, files. To do this, the Audit object access policy must be enabled, and there must be audit ACEs in system access control lists that enable auditing for the objects in question.

When an accessor attempts to open a handle to an object, the SRM first determines whether the attempt is allowed or denied. If object access auditing is enabled, the SRM then scans the system ACL of the object. There are two types of audit ACEs: access allowed and access denied. An audit ACE must match any of the security IDs held by the accessor, it must match any of the access methods requested, and its type (access allowed or access denied) must match the result of the access check to generate an object access audit record.

Object access audit records include not just the fact of access allowed or denied, but also the reason for the success or failure. This "reason for access" reporting generally takes the form of an access control entry, specified in Security Descriptor Definition Language (SDDL), in the audit record. This allows for a diagnosis of scenarios in which an object to which you believe access should be denied is being permitted, or vice versa, by identifying the specific access control entry that caused the attempted access to succeed or fail.

As was shown in Figure 7-13, object access auditing is disabled by default (as are all other auditing policies).

EXPERIMENT: Object access auditing

You can observe object access auditing by following these steps:

1. In Explorer, navigate to a file to which you would normally have access (such as a text file), open its Properties dialog box, click the **Security** tab, and then select the **Advanced** settings.

2. Click the **Auditing** tab and click through the administrative privileges warning. The resulting dialog box allows you to add auditing of access control entries to the file's system access control list.

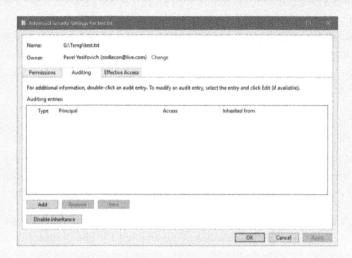

3. Click the **Add** button and choose **Select a Principal**.

4. In the resulting Select User or Group dialog box, enter your own user name or a group to which you belong, such as **Everyone**. Click **Check Names** and then click **OK**. This presents a dialog box for creating an Audit access control entry for this user or group for this file.

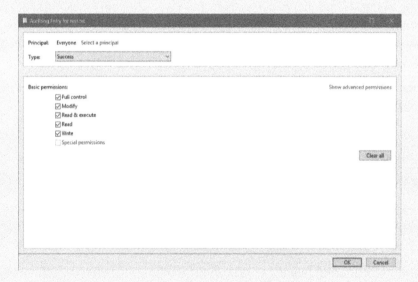

5. Click **OK** three times to close the file Properties dialog box.

6. In Explorer, double-click the file to open it with its associated program (for example, Notepad for a text file).

7. Click the **Start** menu, type **event**, and choose **Event Viewer**.

8. Navigate to the Security log. Note that there is no entry for access to the file. This is because the audit policy for object access is not yet configured.

9. In the Local Security Policy editor, navigate to **Local Policies** and choose **Audit Policy**.

10. Double-click **Audit Object Access** and click **Success** to enable auditing of successful access to files.

11. In Event Viewer, click **Action** (from the menu) and **Refresh**. Note that the changes to audit policy resulted in audit records.

12. In Explorer, double-click the file to open it again.

13. In Event Viewer, click **Action** and **Refresh**. Note that several file access audit records are now present.

14. Find one of the file access audit records for event ID 4656. This shows up as "a handle to an object was requested." (You can use the Find option to search for the file name you opened.)

15. Scroll down in the text box to find the Access Reasons section. The following example shows that two access methods, READ_CONTROL, SYNCHRONIZE, and ReadAttributes, ReadEA (extended attributes), and ReadData were requested. READ_CONTROL was granted because the accessor was the owner of the file. The others were granted because of the indicated access control entry.

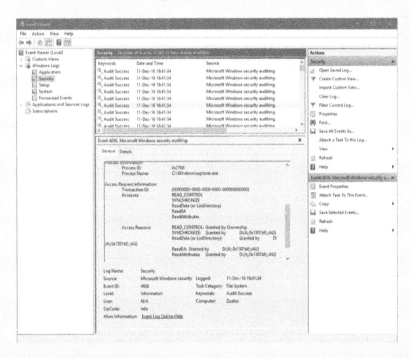

Global audit policy

In addition to object-access ACEs on individual objects, a global audit policy can be defined for the system that enables object-access auditing for all file-system objects, all registry keys, or for both. A security auditor can therefore be certain that the desired auditing will be performed, without having to set or examine SACLs on all the individual objects of interest.

An administrator can set or query the global audit policy via the AuditPol command with the /resourceSACL option. This can also be done programmatically by calling the AuditSetGlobalSacl and AuditQueryGlobalSacl APIs. As with changes to objects' SACLs, changing these global SACLs requires SeSecurityPrivilege.

EXPERIMENT: Setting global audit policy

You can use the AuditPol command to enable global audit policy.

1. If you didn't already do so in the previous experiment, open the Local Security Policy editor, navigate to the Audit Policy settings (refer to Figure 7-13), double-click **Audit Object Access**, and enable auditing for both success and failure. On most systems, SACLs specifying object access auditing are uncommon, so few if any object-access audit records will be produced at this point.

2. In an elevated command prompt window, enter the following command. This will produce a summary of the commands for setting and querying global audit policy.

    ```
    C:\> auditpol /resourceSACL
    ```

3. In the same elevated command prompt window, enter the following commands. On a typical system, each of these commands will report that no global SACL exists for the respective resource type. (Note that the File and Key keywords are case-sensitive.)

    ```
    C:\> auditpol /resourceSACL /type:File /view
    C:\> auditpol /resourceSACL /type:Key /view
    ```

4. In the same elevated command prompt window, enter the following command. This will set a global audit policy such that all attempts to open files for write access (FW) by the indicated user will result in audit records, whether the open attempts succeed or fail. The user name can be a specific user name on the system, a group such as Everyone, a domain-qualified user name such as domainname\username, or a SID.

    ```
    C:\> auditpol /resourceSACL /set /type:File /user:yourusername /success
    /failure /access:FW
    ```

5. While running under the user name indicated, use Explorer or other tools to open a file. Then look at the security log in the system event log to find the audit records.

6. At the end of the experiment, use the auditpol command to remove the global SACL you created in step 4, as follows:

    ```
    C:\> auditpol /resourceSACL /remove /type:File /user:yourusername
    ```

The global audit policy is stored in the registry as a pair of system access control lists in HKLM\SECURITY\Policy\GlobalSaclNameFile and HKLM\SECURITY\Policy\GlobalSaclNameKey. You can examine these keys by running Regedit.exe under the System account, as described in the "Security system components" section earlier in this chapter. These keys will not exist until the corresponding global SACLs have been set at least once.

The global audit policy cannot be overridden by SACLs on objects, but object-specific SACLs can allow for additional auditing. For example, global audit policy could require auditing of read access by all users to all files, but SACLs on individual files could add auditing of write access to those files by specific users or by more specific user groups.

Global audit policy can also be configured via the Local Security Policy editor in the Advanced Audit Policy settings, described in the next section.

Advanced Audit Policy settings

In addition to the Audit Policy settings described previously, the Local Security Policy editor offers a much more fine-grained set of audit controls under the Advanced Audit Policy Configuration heading, shown in Figure 7-15.

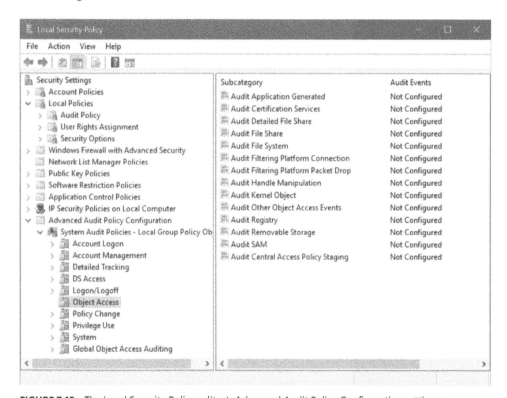

FIGURE 7-15 The Local Security Policy editor's Advanced Audit Policy Configuration settings.

Each of the nine audit policy settings under Local Policies (refer to Figure 7-13) maps to a group of settings here that provide more detailed control. For example, while the Audit Object Access settings under Local Policies allow access to all objects to be audited, the settings here allow auditing of access to various types of objects to be controlled individually. Enabling one of the audit policy settings under Local Policies implicitly enables all the corresponding advanced audit policy events, but if finer control over the contents of the audit log is desired, the advanced settings can be set individually. The standard settings then become a product of the advanced settings. However, this is not visible in the Local Security Policy editor. Attempts to specify audit settings by using both the basic and the advanced options can cause unexpected results.

You can use the Global Object Access Auditing option under Advanced Audit Policy Configuration to configure the global SACLs described in the previous section, using a graphical interface identical to that seen in Explorer or the Registry editor for security descriptors in the file system or the registry.

AppContainers

Windows 8 introduced a new security sandbox called an *AppContainer*. Although it was created primarily to host UWP processes, AppContainers can actually be used for "normal" processes as well (although there is no built-in tool to do that). This section will mostly cover the attributes of packaged AppContainers, which is the term that refers to AppContainers associated with UWP processes and their resulting .Appx format. A complete treatment of UWP apps is beyond the scope of this chapter. You can find more information in Chapter 3 of this book, and in Chapters 8 and 9 in Part 2. Here we'll concentrate on the security aspects of AppContainers and their typical usage as hosts of UWP apps.

Note The term *Universal Windows Platform* (*UWP*) *app* is the latest used to describe processes that host the Windows Runtime. Older names include *immersive app*, *modern app*, *metro app*, and sometimes simply *Windows app*. The *Universal* part indicates the ability of such apps to be deployed and run on various Windows 10 editions and form factors, from IoT core, to mobile, to desktop, to Xbox, to HoloLens. However, they are essentially the same as the ones first introduced in Windows 8. Therefore, the concept of AppContainers discussed in this section is relevant to Windows 8 and later versions of Windows. Note that Universal Application Platform (UAP) is sometimes used instead of UWP; it's the same thing.

Note The original codename for AppContainer was *LowBox*. You may see this term come up in many of the API names and data structures throughout this section. They refer to the same concept.

Overview of UWP apps

The mobile device revolution established new ways of obtaining and running software. Mobile devices normally get their applications from a central store, with automatic installation and updates, all with little user intervention. Once a user selects an app from the store, she can see the permissions the app requires to function correctly. These permissions are called *capabilities* and are declared as part of the package when it's submitted to the store. This way, the user can decide whether these capabilities are acceptable.

Figure 7-16 shows an example of a capabilities list for a UWP game (*Minecraft*, Windows 10 beta edition). The game requires internet access as a client and as a server and access to the local home or work network. Once the user downloads the game, she implicitly agrees the game may exercise these capabilities. Conversely, the user can be confident that the game uses *only* those capabilities. That is, there is no way the game could use other unapproved capabilities, such as accessing the camera on the device.

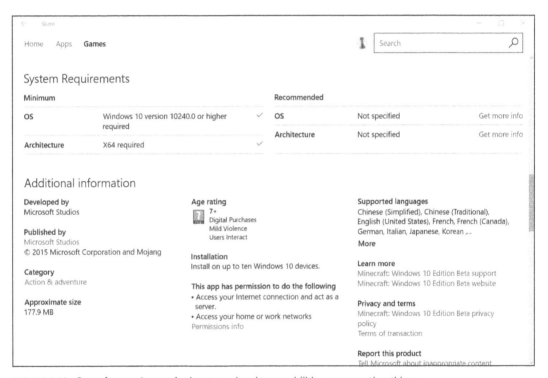

FIGURE 7-16 Part of an app's page in the store, showing capabilities, among other things.

To get a sense of the differences between UWP apps and desktop (classic) apps at a high level, consult Table 7-12. From a developer's perspective, the Windows platform can be seen as shown in Figure 7-17.

TABLE 7-12 High-level comparison of UWP and desktop apps

	UWP App	**Desktop (Classic) App**
Device Support	Runs on all Windows device families	Runs on PCs only
APIs	Can access WinRT, subset of COM, and subset of Win32 APIs	Can access COM, Win32, and subset of WinRT APIs
Identity	Strong app identity (static and dynamic)	Raw EXEs and processes
Information	Declarative APPX manifest	Opaque binaries
Installation	Self-contained APPX package	Loose files or MSI
App Data	Isolated per-user/per-app storage (local and roaming)	Shared user profile
Lifecycle	Participates in app resource management and PLM	Process-level lifecycle
Instancing	Single instance only	Any number of instances

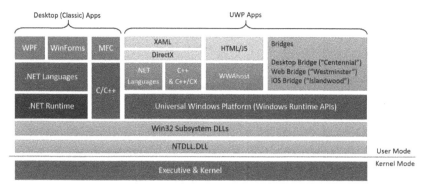

FIGURE 7-17 The Windows platform landscape.

A few items in Figure 7-17 are worth elaborating on:

- UWP apps can produce normal executables, just like desktop apps. Wwahost.exe (%SystemRoot%\ System32\wwahost.exe) is used to host HTML/JavaScript-based UWP apps, as those produce a DLL, not an executable.

- The UWP is implemented by the Windows Runtime APIs, which are based on an enhanced version of COM. Language projections are provided for C++ (through proprietary language extensions known as C++/CX), .NET languages, and JavaScript. These projections make it relatively easy to access WinRT types, methods, properties, and events from developers' familiar environments.

- Several bridging technologies are available, which can transform other types of applications into UWP. See the MSDN documentation for more information on utilizing these technologies.

- The Windows Runtime is layered on top of the Windows subsystem DLLs, just like the .NET Framework. It has no kernel components and is not part of a different subsystem because it still leverages the same Win32 APIs that the system offers. However, some policies are implemented in the kernel, as well as the general support for AppContainers.

- The Windows Runtime APIs are implemented in DLLs residing in the %SystemRoot%\System32 directory, with names in the form *Windows.Xxx.Yyy...*DII, where the file name usually indicates the Windows Runtime API namespace implemented. For example, Windows.Globalization.DII implements the classes residing in the `Windows.Globalization` namespace. (See the MSDN documentation for the complete WinRT API reference.)

The AppContainer

We've seen the steps required to create processes back in Chapter 3; we've also seen some of the extra steps required to create UWP processes. The initiation of creation is performed by the `DCOMLaunch` service, because UWP packages support a set of protocols, one of which is the Launch protocol. The resulting process gets to run inside an AppContainer. Here are several characteristics of packaged processes running inside an AppContainer:

- The process token integrity level is set to Low, which automatically restricts access to many objects and limits access to certain APIs or functionality for the process, as discussed earlier in this chapter.

- UWP processes are always created inside a job (one job per UWP app). This job manages the UWP process and any background processes that execute on its behalf (through nested jobs). The jobs allow the Process State Manager (PSM) to suspend or resume the app or background processing in a single stroke.

- The token for UWP processes has an AppContainer SID, which represents a distinct identity based on the SHA-2 hash of the UWP package name. As you'll see, this SID is used by the system and other applications to explicitly allow access to files and other kernel objects. This SID is part of the `APPLICATION PACKAGE AUTHORITY` instead of the `NT AUTHORITY` you've mostly seen so far in this chapter. Thus, it begins with S-1-15-2 in its string format, corresponding to `SECURITY_APP_PACKAGE_BASE_RID` (15) and `SECURITY_APP_PACKAGE_BASE_RID` (2). Because a SHA-2 hash is 32 bytes, there are a total of eight RIDs (recall that a RID is the size of a 4-byte `ULONG`) in the remainder of the SID.

- The token may contain a set of capabilities, each represented with a SID. These capabilities are declared in the application manifest and shown on the app's page in the store. Stored in the capability section of the manifest, they are converted to SID format using rules we'll see shortly, and belong to the same SID authority as in the previous bullet, but using the well-known `SECURITY_CAPABILITY_BASE_RID` (3) instead. Various components in the Windows Runtime, user-mode device-access classes, and kernel can look for capabilities to allow or deny certain operations.

- The token may only contain the following privileges: `SeChangeNotifyPrivilege`, `SeIncreaseWorkingSetPrivilege`, `SeShutdownPrivilege`, `SeTimeZonePrivilege`, and `SeUndockPrivilege`. These are the default set of privileges associated with standard user accounts. Additionally, the `AppContainerPrivilegesEnabledExt` function part of the `ms-win-ntos-ksecurity` API Set contract extension can be present on certain devices to further restrict which privileges are enabled by default.

- The token will contain up to four security attributes (see the section on attribute-based access control earlier in this chapter) that identify this token as being associated with a UWP packaged application. These attributes are added by the DcomLaunch service as indicated earlier, which is responsible for the activation of UWP applications. They are as follows:

  - **WIN://PKG** This identifies this token as belonging to a UWP packaged application. It contains an integer value with the application's origin as well as some flags. See Table 7-13 and Table 7-14 for these values.

  - **WIN://SYSAPPID** This contains the application identifiers (called *package monikers* or *string names*) as an array of Unicode string values.

  - **WIN://PKGHOSTID** This identifies the UWP package host ID for packages that have an explicit host through an integer value.

  - **WIN://BGKD** This is only used for background hosts (such as the generic background task host BackgroundTaskHost.exe) that can store packaged UWP services running as COM providers. The attribute's name stands for *background* and contains an integer value that stores its explicit host ID.

The TOKEN_LOWBOX (0x4000) flag will be set in the token's Flags member, which can be queried with various Windows and kernel APIs (such as GetTokenInformation). This allows components to identity and operate differently under the presence of an AppContainer token.

> **Note** A second type of AppContainer exists: a child AppContainer. This is used when a UWP AppContainer (or parent AppContainer) wishes to create its own nested AppContainer to further lock down the security of the application. Instead of eight RIDs, a child AppContainer has four additional RIDs (the first eight match the parents') to uniquely identify it.

TABLE 7-13 Package origins

Origin	Meaning
Unknown (0)	The package origin is unknown.
Unsigned (1)	The package is unsigned.
Inbox (2)	The package is associated with a built-in (inbox) Windows application.
Store (3)	The package is associated with a UWP application downloaded from the store. This origin is validated by checking if the DACL of the file associated with the main UWP application's executable contains a trust ACE.
Developer Unsigned (4)	The package is associated with an unsigned developer key.
Developer Signed (5)	The package is associated with a signed developer key.
Line-of-Business (6)	The package is associated with a side-loaded line-of-business (LOB) application.

TABLE 7-14 Package flags

Flag	Meaning
PSM_ACTIVATION_TOKEN_PACKAGED_APPLICATION (0x1)	This indicates that the AppContainer UWP application is stored in AppX packaged format. This is the default.
PSM_ACTIVATION_TOKEN_SHARED_ENTITY (0x2)	This indicates that this token is being used for multiple executables all part of the same AppX packaged UWP application.
PSM_ACTIVATION_TOKEN_FULL_TRUST (0x4)	This indicates that this AppContainer token is being used to host a Project Centennial (Windows Bridge for Desktop) converted Win32 application.
PSM_ACTIVATION_TOKEN_NATIVE_SERVICE (0x8)	This indicates that this AppContainer token is being used to host a packaged service created by the Service Control Manager (SCM)'s Resource Manager. See Chapter 9 in Part 2 for more information on services.
PSM_ACTIVATION_TOKEN_DEVELOPMENT_APP (0x10)	This indicates that this is an internal development application. Not used on retail systems.
BREAKAWAY_INHIBITED (0x20)	The package cannot create a process that is not itself packaged as well. This is set by using the PROC_THREAD_ATTRIBUTE_DESKTOP_APP_POLICY process-creation attribute. (See Chapter 3 for more information.)

EXPERIMENT: Viewing UWP process information

There are several ways to look at UWP processes, some more obvious than others. Process Explorer can highlight processes that use the Windows Runtime in color (cyan by default). To see this in action, open Process Explorer, open the **Options** menu, and choose **Configure Colors**. Then make sure the **Immersive Processes** check box is selected.

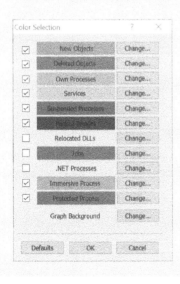

Immersive process is the original term used to describe WinRT (now UWP) apps in Windows 8. (They were mostly full screen, and therefore "immersive.") This distinction is available by calling the IsImmersiveProcess API.

Run Calc.exe and switch to Process Explorer. You should see several processes highlighted in cyan, including Calculator.exe. Now minimize the Calculator app and notice that the cyan highlight has turned gray. This is because Calculator has been suspended. Restore Calculator's window, and it's back to cyan.

You should have similar experiences with other apps—for example, Cortana (SearchUI.exe). Click or tap the **Cortana** icon on the taskbar and then close it. You should see the gray to cyan and back to gray transition. Or, click or tap the **Start** button. ShellExperienceHost.exe highlights in a similar fashion.

The presence of some cyan-highlighted processes might surprise you, such as Explorer.exe, TaskMgr.Exe, and RuntimeBroker.exe. These are not really apps, but use Windows Runtime APIs, and so are classified as immersive. (The role of RuntimeBroker will be discussed shortly.)

Finally, make sure the Integrity column is visible in Process Explorer and sort by that column. You'll find processes such as Calculator.exe and SearchUI.exe with AppContainer integrity level. Notice that Explorer and TaskMgr are not there, clearly showing they are not UWP processes, and so live under different rules.

Process	PID	CPU	Integrity ^	Private Bytes	Working Set	Description
Interrupts	n/a	0.74		0 K	0 K	Hardware Interrupt
Calculator.exe	11128		AppContainer	13,420 K	36,712 K	
Microsoft.Msn.Weather.exe	3040	Suspended	AppContainer	45,600 K	15,764 K	Weather
SearchUI.exe	3728	Suspended	AppContainer	43,508 K	102,564 K	Search and Cortana
ShellExperienceHost.exe	1872	Suspended	AppContainer	79,872 K	130,636 K	Windows Shell Exp
SkypeHost.exe	9624	Suspended	AppContainer	33,084 K	26,844 K	Microsoft Skype Pr
System Idle Process	0	92.57		0 K	4 K	
Twitter.Windows.exe	2084	Suspended	AppContainer	33,348 K	8,576 K	Twitter.Windows
Video.UI.exe	8772	Suspended	AppContainer	19,900 K	37,444 K	Video Application
firefox.exe	11856	0.31	Low	571,804 K	615,372 K	Firefox
ApntEx.exe	1060		Medium	1,844 K	5,960 K	Alps Pointing-devic
Apnlet.exe	0024	0.01	Medium	3,644 K	13,776 K	Alps Pointing-devic

EXPERIMENT: Viewing an AppContainer token

You can look at the properties of an AppContainer hosted process with several tools. In Process Explorer, the Security tab shows the capabilities associated with the token. Here's the Security tab for Calculator.exe:

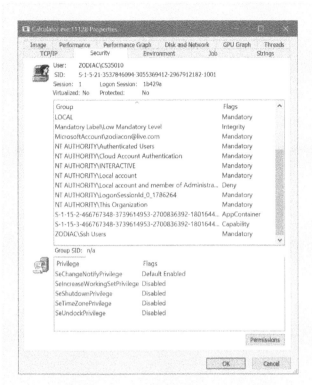

Notice two interesting pieces of information: the AppContainer SID, shown in the Flags column as AppContainer, and a single capability, right underneath the AppContainer SID. Except for the base RID (SECURITY_APP_PACKAGE_BASE_RID versus SECURITY_CAPABILITY_BASE_RID), the remaining eight RIDs are identical, and both refer to the package name in SHA-2 format as discussed. This shows you that there will always be one implicit capability, the capability of being the package itself, which really means Calculator requires no capabilities at all. The upcoming capabilities section covers a much more complex example.

EXPERIMENT: Viewing AppContainer token attributes

You can obtain similar information on the command line by using the AccessChk Sysinternals tool while also adding a full list of all of the token's attributes. For example, running AccessChk with the –p –f switches followed by the process ID for SearchUI.exe, which hosts Cortana, shows the following:

```
C:\ >accesschk -p -f 3728

Accesschk v6.10 - Reports effective permissions for securable objects
Copyright (C) 2006-2016 Mark Russinovich
Sysinternals - www.sysinternals.com

[7416] SearchUI.exe
```

```
    RW DESKTOP-DD6KTPM\aione
    RW NT AUTHORITY\SYSTEM
    RW Package
\S-1-15-2-1861897761-1695161497-2927542615-642690995-327840285-2659745135-2630312742
    Token security:
    RW DESKTOP-DD6KTPM\aione
    RW NT AUTHORITY\SYSTEM
    RW DESKTOP-DD6KTPM\aione-S-1-5-5-0-459087
    RW Package
\S-1-15-2-1861897761-1695161497-2927542615-642690995-327840285-2659745135-2630312742
    R  BUILTIN\Administrators
    Token contents:
      User:
        DESKTOP-DD6KTPM\aione
      AppContainer:
        Package
\S-1-15-2-1861897761-1695161497-2927542615-642690995-327840285-2659745135-2630312742
      Groups:
        Mandatory Label\Low Mandatory Level              INTEGRITY
        Everyone                                         MANDATORY
        NT AUTHORITY\Local account and member of Administrators group DENY
        ...
        Security Attributes:
      WIN://PKGHOSTID
          TOKEN_SECURITY_ATTRIBUTE_TYPE_UINT64
          [0] 1794402976530433
      WIN://SYSAPPID
          TOKEN_SECURITY_ATTRIBUTE_TYPE_STRING
          [0] Microsoft.Windows.Cortana_1.8.3.14986_neutral_neutral_cw5n1h2txyewy
          [1] CortanaUI
          [2] Microsoft.Windows.Cortana_cw5n1h2txyewy
      WIN://PKG
          TOKEN_SECURITY_ATTRIBUTE_TYPE_UINT64
          [0] 131073
      TSA://ProcUnique
          [TOKEN_SECURITY_ATTRIBUTE_NON_INHERITABLE]
          [TOKEN_SECURITY_ATTRIBUTE_COMPARE_IGNORE]
          TOKEN_SECURITY_ATTRIBUTE_TYPE_UINT64
          [0] 204
          [1] 24566825
```

First is the package host ID, converted to hex: 0x6600000000001. Because all package host IDs begin with 0x66, this means Cortana is using the first available host identifier: 1. Next are the system application IDs, which contain three strings: the strong package moniker, the friendly application name, and the simplified package name. Finally, you have the package claim, which is 0x20001 in hex. Based on the Table 7-13 and Table 7-14 fields you saw, this indicates an origin of Inbox (2) and flags set to PSM_ACTIVATION_TOKEN_PACKAGED_APPLICATION, confirming that Cortana is part of an AppX package.

AppContainer security environment

One of the biggest side-effects caused by the presence of an AppContainer SID and related flags is that the access check algorithm you saw in the "Access checks" section earlier in this chapter is modified to essentially ignore all regular user and group SIDs that the token may contain, essentially treating them as deny-only SIDs. This means that even though Calculator may be launched by a user John Doe belonging to the Users and Everyone groups, it will fail any access checks that grant access to John Doe's SID, the Users group SID, or the Everyone group SID. In fact, the only SIDs that are checked during the discretionary access check algorithm will be that of the AppContainer SID, followed by the capability access check algorithm, which will look at any capability SIDs part of the token.

Taking things even further than merely treating the discretionary SIDs as deny-only, AppContainer tokens effect one further critical security change to the access check algorithm: a NULL DACL, typically treated as an allow-anyone situation due to the lack of any information (recall that this is different from an empty DACL, which is a deny-everyone situation due to explicit allow rules), is ignored and treated as a deny situation. To make matters simple, the only types of securable objects that an AppContainer can access are those that explicitly have an allow ACE for its AppContainer SID or for one of its capabilities. Even unsecured (NULL DACL) objects are out of the game.

This situation causes compatibility problems. Without access to even the most basic file system, registry, and object manager resources, how can an application even function? Windows takes this into account by preparing a custom execution environment, or "jail" if you will, specifically for each AppContainer. These jails are as follows:

> **Note** So far we've implied that each UWP packaged application corresponds to one AppContainer token. However, this doesn't necessarily imply that only a single executable file can be associated with an AppContainer. UWP packages can contain multiple executable files, which all belong to the same AppContainer. This allows them to share the same SID and capabilities and exchange data between each other, such as a micro-service back-end executable and a foreground front-end executable.

- The AppContainer SID's string representation is used to create a subdirectory in the object manager's namespace under \Sessions\x\AppContainerNamedObjects. This becomes the private directory of named kernel objects. This specific subdirectory object is then ACLed with the AppContainer SID associated with the AppContainer that has an allow-all access mask. This is in contrast to desktop apps, which all use the \Sessions\x\BaseNamedObjects subdirectory (within the same session x). We'll discuss the implications of that shortly, as well as the requirement for the token to now store handles.

- The token will contain a LowBox number, which is a unique identifier into an array of LowBox Number Entry structures that the kernel stores in the g_SessionLowboxArray global variable. Each of these maps to a SEP_LOWBOX_NUMBER_ENTRY structure that, most importantly, contains an atom table unique to this AppContainer, because the Windows Subsystem Kernel Mode Driver (Win32k.sys) does not allow AppContainers access to the global atom table.

- The file system contains a directory in %LOCALAPPDATA% called Packages. Inside it are the package monikers (the string version of the AppContainer SID—that is, the package name) of all the installed UWP applications. Each of these application directories contains application-specific directories, such as TempState, RoamingState, Settings, LocalCache, and others, which are all ACLed with the specific AppContainer SID corresponding to the application, set to an allow-all access mask.

- Within the Settings directory is a Settings.dat file, which is a registry hive file that is loaded as an application hive. (You will learn more about application hives in Chapter 9 in Part 2.) The hive acts as the local registry for the application, where WinRT APIs store the various persistent state of the application. Once again, the ACL on the registry keys explicitly grants allow-all access to the associated AppContainer SID.

These four jails allow AppContainers to securely, and locally, store their file system, registry, and atom table without requiring access to sensitive user and system areas on the system. That being said, what about the ability to access, at least in read-only mode, critical system files (such as Ntdll.dll and Kernel32.dll) or registry keys (such as the ones these libraries will need), or even named objects (such as the \RPC Control\DNSResolver ALPC port used for DNS lookups)? It would not make sense, on each UWP application or uninstallation, to re-ACL entire directories, registry keys, and object namespaces to add or remove various SIDs.

To solve this problem, the security subsystem understands a specific group SID called ALL APPLICATION PACKAGES, which automatically binds itself to any AppContainer token. Many critical system locations, such as %SystemRoot%\System32 and HKLM\Software\Microsoft\Windows\CurrentVersion, will have this SID as part of their DACL, typically with a read or read-and-execute access mask. Certain objects in the object manager namespace will have this as well, such as the DNSResolver ALPC port in the \RPC Control object manager directory. Other examples include certain COM objects, which grant the execute right. Although not officially documented, third-party developers, as they create non-UWP applications, can also allow interactions with UWP applications by also applying this SID to their own resources.

Unfortunately, because UWP applications can technically load almost any Win32 DLL as part of their WinRT needs (because WinRT is built on top of Win32, as you saw), and because it's hard to predict what an individual UWP application might need, many system resources have the ALL APPLICATION PACKAGES SID associated with their DACL as a precaution. This now means there is no way for a UWP developer, for example, to prevent DNS lookups from their application. This greater-than-needed access is also helpful for exploit writers, which could leverage it to escape from the AppContainer sandbox. Newer versions of Windows 10, starting with version 1607 (Anniversary Update), contain an additional element of security to combat this risk: Restricted AppContainers.

By using the PROC_THREAD_ATTRIBUTE_ALL_APPLICATION_PACKAGES_POLICY process attribute and setting it to PROCESS_CREATION_ALL_APPLICATION_PACKAGES_OPT_OUT during process creation (see Chapter 3 for more information on process attributes), the token will not be associated with any ACEs that specify the ALL APPLICATION PACKAGES SID, cutting off access to many system resources that would otherwise be accessible. Such tokens can be identified by the presence of a fourth token attribute named WIN://NOALLAPPPKG with an integer value set to 1.

Of course, this takes us back to the same problem: How would such an application even be able to load Ntdll.dll, which is key to any process initialization? Windows 10 version 1607 introduces a new group, called ALL RESTRICTED APPLICATION PACKAGES, which takes care of this problem. For example, the System32 directory now also contains this SID, also set to allow read and execute permissions, because loading DLLs in this directory is key even to the most sandboxed process. However, the DNSResolver ALPC port does not, so such an AppContainer would lose access to DNS.

EXPERIMENT: Viewing AppContainer security attributes

In this experiment, we'll look at the security attributes of some of the directories mentioned in the previous section.

1. Make sure Calculator is running.

2. Open WinObj elevated from Sysinternals and navigate to the object directory corresponding to Calculator's AppContainer SID. (You saw it in a previous experiment.)

3. Right-click the directory, select **Properties**, and click the **Security** tab. You should see something like the following screenshot. Calculator's AppContainer SID has permission to list, add object, and add subdirectory (among others scrolled out of view), which simply means Calculator can create kernel objects under this directory.

4. Open Calculator's local folder by navigating to %LOCALAPPDATA%\Packages\ Microsoft.WindowsCalculator_8wekyb3d8bbwe. Then right-click the **Settings** sub-directory, select **Properties**, and click the **Security** tab. You should see Calculator's AppContainer SID having full permissions for the folder:

5. In Explorer, open the %SystemRoot% directory (for example, C:\Windows), right-click the **System32** directory, select **Properties,** and click the **Security** tab. You should see the read and execute permissions for all application packages and all restricted application packages (if using Windows 10 version 1607 or later):

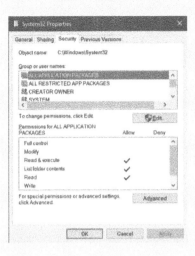

As an alternative, you can use the AccessChk Sysinternals command-line tool to view the same information.

EXPERIMENT: Viewing the AppContainer atom table

An atom table is a hash table of integers to strings that's used by the windowing system for various identification purposes, such as Window Class registration (`RegisterClassEx`) and custom Windows messages. The AppContainer private atom table can be viewed with the kernel debugger:

1. Run Calculator, open WinDbg, and start local kernel debugging.

2. Find the Calculator process:

```
lkd> !process 0 1 calculator.exe
PROCESS ffff828cc9ed1080
    SessionId: 1  Cid: 4bd8     Peb: d040bbc000  ParentCid: 03a4
DeepFreeze
    DirBase: 5fccaa000  ObjectTable: ffff950ad9fa2800  HandleCount:
<Data Not Accessible>
    Image: Calculator.exe
    VadRoot ffff828cd2c9b6a0 Vads 168 Clone 0 Private 2938. Modified 3332.
Locked 0.
    DeviceMap ffff950aad2cd2f0
    Token                                  ffff950adb313060
    ...
```

3. Use the token value with the following expressions:

```
lkd> r? @$t1 = @$t0->NumberOfBuckets
lkd> r? @$t0 = (nt!_RTL_ATOM_TABLE*)((nt!_token*)0xffff950adb313060)-
>LowboxNumberEntry->AtomTable
lkd> .for (r @$t3 = 0; @$t3 < @$t1; r @$t3 = @$t3 + 1) {  ?? (wchar_t*)@$t0-
```

```
>Buckets[@$t3]->Name }
wchar_t * 0xffff950a'ac39b78a
 "Protocols"
wchar_t * 0xffff950a'ac17b7aa
 "Topics"
wchar_t * 0xffff950a'b2fd282a
 "TaskbarDPI_Deskband"
wchar_t * 0xffff950a'b3e2b47a
 "Static"
wchar_t * 0xffff950a'b3c9458a
 "SysTreeView32"
wchar_t * 0xffff950a'ac34143a
 "UxSubclassInfo"
wchar_t * 0xffff950a'ac5520fa
 "StdShowItem"
wchar_t * 0xffff950a'abc6762a
 "SysSetRedraw"
wchar_t * 0xffff950a'b4a5340a
 "UIA_WindowVisibilityOverridden"
wchar_t * 0xffff950a'ab2c536a
 "True"
...
wchar_t * 0xffff950a'b492c3ea
 "tooltips_class"
wchar_t * 0xffff950a'ac23f46a
 "Save"
wchar_t * 0xffff950a'ac29568a
 "MSDraw"
wchar_t * 0xffff950a'ac54f32a
 "StdNewDocument"
wchar_t * 0xffff950a'b546127a
 "{FB2E3E59-B442-4B5B-9128-2319BF8DE3B0}"
wchar_t * 0xffff950a'ac2e6f4a
 "Status"
wchar_t * 0xffff950a'ad9426da
 "ThemePropScrollBarCtl"
wchar_t * 0xffff950a'b3edf5ba
 "Edit"
wchar_t * 0xffff950a'ab02e32a
 "System"
wchar_t * 0xffff950a'b3e6c53a
 "MDIClient"
wchar_t * 0xffff950a'ac17a6ca
 "StdDocumentName"
wchar_t * 0xffff950a'ac6cbeea
 "StdExit"
wchar_t * 0xffff950a'b033c70a
 "{C56C5799-4BB3-7FAE-7FAD-4DB2F6A53EFF}"
wchar_t * 0xffff950a'ab0360fa
 "MicrosoftTabletPenServiceProperty"
wchar_t * 0xffff950a'ac2f8fea
 "OLEsystem"
```

AppContainer capabilities

As you've just seen, UWP applications have very restricted access rights. So how, for example, is the Microsoft Edge application able to parse the local file system and open PDF files in the user's Documents folder? Similarly, how can the Music application play MP3 files from the Music directory? Whether done directly through kernel access checks or by brokers (which you'll see in the next section), the key lies in capability SIDs. Let's see where these come from, how they are created, and when they are used.

First, UWP developers begin by creating an application manifest that specifies many details of their application, such as the package name, logo, resources, supported devices, and more. One of the key elements for capability management is the list of capabilities in the manifest. For example, let's take a look at Cortana's application manifest, located in %SystemRoot%\SystemApps\Microsoft.Windows. Cortana_cw5n1h2txywey\AppxManifest.xml:

```
<Capabilities>
        <wincap:Capability Name="packageContents"/>
        <!-- Needed for resolving MRT strings -->
        <wincap:Capability Name="cortanaSettings"/>
        <wincap:Capability Name="cloudStore"/>
        <wincap:Capability Name="visualElementsSystem"/>
        <wincap:Capability Name="perceptionSystem"/>
        <Capability Name="internetClient"/>
        <Capability Name="internetClientServer"/>
        <Capability Name="privateNetworkClientServer"/>
        <uap:Capability Name="enterpriseAuthentication"/>
        <uap:Capability Name="musicLibrary"/>
        <uap:Capability Name="phoneCall"/>
        <uap:Capability Name="picturesLibrary"/>
        <uap:Capability Name="sharedUserCertificates"/>
        <rescap:Capability Name="locationHistory"/>
        <rescap:Capability Name="userDataSystem"/>
        <rescap:Capability Name="contactsSystem"/>
        <rescap:Capability Name="phoneCallHistorySystem"/>
        <rescap:Capability Name="appointmentsSystem"/>
        <rescap:Capability Name="chatSystem"/>
        <rescap:Capability Name="smsSend"/>
        <rescap:Capability Name="emailSystem"/>
        <rescap:Capability Name="packageQuery"/>
        <rescap:Capability Name="slapiQueryLicenseValue"/>
        <rescap:Capability Name="secondaryAuthenticationFactor"/>
        <DeviceCapability Name="microphone"/>
        <DeviceCapability Name="location"/>
        <DeviceCapability Name="wiFiControl"/>
</Capabilities>
```

You'll see many types of entries in this list. For example, the Capability entries contain the well-known SIDs associated with the original capability set that was implemented in Windows 8. These begin with SECURITY_CAPABILITY_—for example, SECURITY_CAPABILITY_INTERNET_CLIENT, which is part of the capability RID under the APPLICATION PACKAGE AUTHORITY. This gives us a SID of S-1-15-3-1 in string format.

Other entries are prefixed with uap, rescap, and wincap. One of these (rescap) refers to restricted capabilities. These are capabilities that require special onboarding from Microsoft and custom approvals before being allowed on the store. In Cortana's case, these include capabilities such as accessing SMS text messages, emails, contacts, location, and user data. Windows capabilities, on the other hand, refer to capabilities that are reserved for Windows and system applications. No store application can use these. Finally, UAP capabilities refer to standard capabilities that anyone can request on the store. (Recall that UAP is the older name for UWP.)

Unlike the first set of capabilities, which map to hard-coded RIDs, these capabilities are implemented in a different fashion. This ensures a list of well-known RIDs doesn't have to be constantly maintained. Instead, with this mode, capabilities can be fully custom and updated on the fly. To do this, they simply take the capability string, convert it to full upper-case format, and take a SHA-2 hash of the resulting string, much like AppContainer package SIDs are the SHA-2 hash of the package moniker. Again, since SHA-2 hashes are 32 bytes, this results in 8 RIDs for each capability, following the well-known SECURITY_CAPABILITY_BASE_RID (3).

Finally, you'll notice a few DeviceCapability entries. These refer to device classes that the UWP application will need to access, and can be identified either through well-known strings such as the ones you see above or directly by a GUID that identifies the device class. Rather than using one of the two methods of SID creation already described, this one uses yet a third! For these types of capabilities, the GUID is converted into a binary format and then mapped out into four RIDs (because a GUID is 16 bytes). On the other hand, if a well-known name was specified instead, it must first be converted to a GUID. This is done by looking at the HKLM\Software\Microsoft\Windows\CurrentVersion\DeviceAccess\CapabilityMappings registry key, which contains a list of registry keys associated with device capabilities and a list of GUIDs that map to these capabilities. The GUIDs are then converted to a SID as you've just seen.

> **Note** For an up-to-date list of supported capabilities, see *https://msdn.microsoft.com/en-us/windows/uwp/packaging/app-capability-declarations*.

As part of encoding all of these capabilities into the token, two additional rules are applied:

- As you may have seen in the earlier experiment, each AppContainer token contains its own package SID encoded as a capability. This can be used by the capability system to specifically lock down access to a particular app through a common security check instead of obtaining and validating the package SID separately.

- Each capability is re-encoded as a group SID through the use of the SECURITY_CAPABILITY_APP_RID (1024) RID as an additional sub-authority preceding the regular eight-capability hash RIDs.

After the capabilities are encoded into the token, various components of the system will read them to determine whether an operation being performed by an AppContainer should be permitted. You'll note most of the APIs are undocumented, as communication and interoperability with UWP applications is not officially supported and best left to broker services, inbox drivers, or kernel components. For example, the kernel and drivers can use the RtlCapabilityCheck API to authenticate access to certain hardware interfaces or APIs.

As an example, the Power Manager checks for the `ID_CAP_SCREENOFF` capability before allowing a request to shut off the screen from an AppContainer. The Bluetooth port driver checks for the `bluetoothDiagnostics` capability, while the application identity driver checks for Enterprise Data Protection (EDP) support through the `enterpriseDataPolicy` capability. In user mode, the documented `CheckTokenCapability` API can be used, although it must know the capability SID instead of providing the name (the undocumented `RtlDeriveCapabilitySidFromName` can generate this, however). Another option is the undocumented `CapabilityCheck` API, which does accept a string.

Finally, many RPC services leverage the `RpcClientCapabilityCheck` API, which is a helper function that takes care of retrieving the token and requires only the capability string. This function is very commonly used by many of the WinRT-enlightened services and brokers, which utilize RPC to communicate with UWP client applications.

EXPERIMENT: Viewing AppContainer capabilities

To clearly demonstrate all these various capability combinations and their population in the token, let's look at the capabilities for a complex app such as Cortana. You've already seen its manifest, so you can use that output to compare with the UI. First, looking at the Security tab for SearchUI.exe shows the following (sorted by the Flags column):

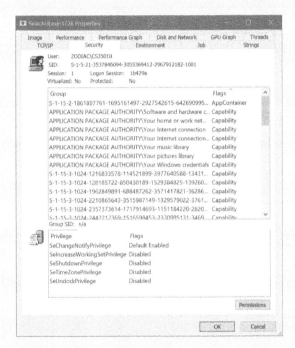

Clearly, Cortana has obtained many capabilities—all the ones in its manifest. Some are those that were originally in Windows 8 and are known to functions like `IsWellKnownSid`, for which Process Explorer shows a friendly name. Other capabilities are just shown using their SID, as they represent either hashes or GUIDs, as discussed.

To get the details of the package from which the UWP process was created, you can use the UWPList tool provided with the downloadable resources for this book. It can show all immersive processes on the system or a single process based on its ID:

```
C:\WindowsInternals>UwpList.exe 3728
List UWP Processes - version 1.1 (C)2016 by Pavel Yosifovich

Building capabilities map... done.

Process ID:   3728
------------------
Image name: C:\Windows\SystemApps\Microsoft.Windows.Cortana_cw5n1h2txyewy\SearchUI.exe
Package name: Microsoft.Windows.Cortana
Publisher: CN=Microsoft Windows, O=Microsoft Corporation, L=Redmond, S=Washington, C=US
Published ID: cw5n1h2txyewy
Architecture: Neutral
Version: 1.7.0.14393
AppContainer SID: S-1-15-2-1861897761-1695161497-2927542615-642690995-327840285-
2659745135-2630312742
Lowbox Number: 3
Capabilities: 32
cortanaSettings (S-1-15-3-1024-1216833578-114521899-3977640588-1343180512-
2505059295-473916851-3379430393-3088591068) (ENABLED)
visualElementsSystem (S-1-15-3-1024-3299255270-1847605585-2201808924-710406709-
3613095291-873286183-3101090833-2655911836) (ENABLED)
perceptionSystem (S-1-15-3-1024-34359262-2669769421-2130994847-3068338639-
3284271446-2009814230-2411358368-814686995) (ENABLED)
internetClient (S-1-15-3-1) (ENABLED)
internetClientServer (S-1-15-3-2) (ENABLED)
privateNetworkClientServer (S-1-15-3-3) (ENABLED)
enterpriseAuthentication (S-1-15-3-8) (ENABLED)
musicLibrary (S-1-15-3-6) (ENABLED)
phoneCall (S-1-15-3-1024-383293015-3350740429-1839969850-1819881064-1569454686-
4198502490-78857879-1413643331) (ENABLED)
picturesLibrary (S-1-15-3-4) (ENABLED)
sharedUserCertificates (S-1-15-3-9) (ENABLED)
locationHistory (S-1-15-3-1024-3029335854-3332959268-2610968494-1944663922-
1108717379-267808753-1292335239-2860040626) (ENABLED)
userDataSystem (S-1-15-3-1024-3324773698-3647103388-1207114580-2173246572-
4287945184-2279574858-157813651-603457015) (ENABLED)
contactsSystem (S-1-15-3-1024-2897291008-3029319760-3330334796-465641623-3782203132-
742823505-3649274736-3650177846) (ENABLED)
phoneCallHistorySystem (S-1-15-3-1024-2442212369-1516598453-2330995131-3469896071-
605735848-2536580394-3691267241-2105387825) (ENABLED)
appointmentsSystem (S-1-15-3-1024-2643354558-482754284-283940418-2629559125-
2595130947-547758827-818480453-1102480765) (ENABLED)
chatSystem (S-1-15-3-1024-2210865643-3515987149-1329579022-3761842879-3142652231-
371911945-4180581417-4284864962) (ENABLED)
smsSend (S-1-15-3-1024-128185722-850430189-1529384825-139260854-329499951-
1660931883-3499805589-3019957964) (ENABLED)
emailSystem (S-1-15-3-1024-2357373614-1717914693-1151184220-2820539834-3900626439-
4045196508-2174624583-3459390060) (ENABLED)
```

```
packageQuery (S-1-15-3-1024-1962849891-688487262-3571417821-3628679630-802580238-
1922556387-206211640-3335523193) (ENABLED)
slapiQueryLicenseValue (S-1-15-3-1024-3578703928-3742718786-7859573-1930844942-
2949799617-2910175080-1780299064-4145191454) (ENABLED)
S-1-15-3-1861897761-1695161497-2927542615-642690995-327840285-2659745135-2630312742
(ENABLED)
S-1-15-3-787448254-1207972858-3558633622-1059886964 (ENABLED)
S-1-15-3-3215430884-1339816292-89257616-1145831019 (ENABLED)
S-1-15-3-3071617654-1314403908-1117750160-3581451107 (ENABLED)
S-1-15-3-593192589-1214558892-284007604-3553228420 (ENABLED)
S-1-15-3-3870101518-1154309966-1696731070-4111764952 (ENABLED)
S-1-15-3-2105443330-1210154068-4021178019-2481794518 (ENABLED)
S-1-15-3-2345035983-1170044712-735049875-2883010875 (ENABLED)
S-1-15-3-3633849274-1266774400-1199443125-2736873758 (ENABLED)
S-1-15-3-2569730672-1095266119-53537203-1209375796 (ENABLED)
S-1-15-3-2452736844-1257488215-2818397580-3305426111 (ENABLED)
```

The output shows the package full name, executable directory, AppContainer SID, publisher information, version, and list of capabilities. Also shown is the LowBox number, which is just a local index of the app.

Lastly, you can inspect these properties in the kernel debugger with the !token command.

Some UWP apps are called *trusted*, and although they use the Windows Runtime platform like other UWP apps, they do not run inside an AppContainer, and have an integrity level higher than Low. The canonical example is the System Settings app (%SystemRoot%\ImmersiveControlPanel\ SystemSettings.exe); this seems reasonable, as the Settings app must be able to make changes to the system that would be impossible to do from an AppContainer-hosted process. If you look at its token, you will see the same three attributes—PKG, SYSAPPID, and PKGHOSTID—which confirm that it's still a packaged application, even without the AppContainer token present.

AppContainer and object namespace

Desktop applications can easily share kernel objects by name. For example, suppose process A creates an event object by calling CreateEvent(Ex) with the name MyEvent. It gets back a handle it can later use to manipulate the event. Process B running in the same session can call CreateEvent(Ex) or OpenEvent with the same name, MyEvent, and (assuming it has appropriate permissions, which is usually the case if running under the same session) get back another handle to the same underlying event object. Now if process A calls SetEvent on the event object while process B was blocked in a call to WaitForSingleObject on its event handle, process B's waiting thread would be released because it's the same event object. This sharing works because named objects are created in the object manager directory \Sessions\x\BaseNamedObjects, as shown in Figure 7-18 with the WinObj Sysinternals tool.

Furthermore, desktop apps can share objects between sessions by using a name prefixed with Global\. This creates the object in the session 0 object directory located in \BaseNamedObjects (refer to Figure 7-18).

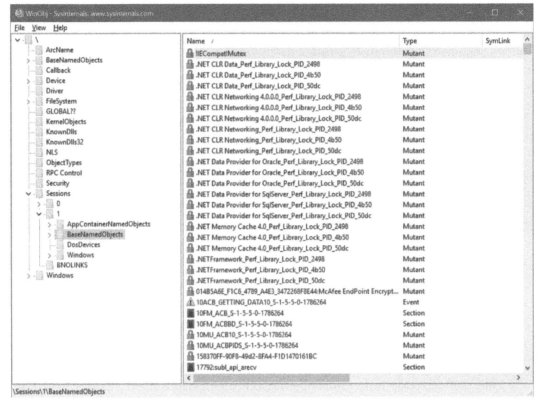

FIGURE 7-18 Object manager directory for named objects.

AppContainer-based processes have their root object namespace under \Sessions\x\AppContainer NamedObjects\<AppContainerSID>. Since every AppContainer has a different AppContainer SID, there is no way two UWP apps can share kernel objects. The ability to create a named kernel object in the session 0 object namespace is not allowed for AppContainer processes. Figure 7-19 shows the object manager's directory for the Windows UWP Calculator app.

UWP apps that want to share data can do so using well-defined contracts, managed by the Windows Runtime. (See the MSDN documentation for more information.)

Sharing kernel objects between desktop apps and UWP apps is possible, and often done by broker services. For example, when requesting access to a file in the Documents folder (and getting the right capability validated) from the file picker broker, the UWP app will receive a file handle that it can use for reads and writes directly, without the cost of marshalling requests back and forth. This is achieved by having the broker duplicate the file handle it obtained directly in the handle table of the UWP application. (More information on handle duplication appears in Chapter 8 in Part 2.) To simplify things even further, the ALPC subsystem (also described in Chapter 8) allows the automatic transfer of handles in this way through ALPC handle attributes. and the Remote Procedure Call (RPC) services that use ALPC as their underlying protocol can use this functionality as part of their interfaces. Marshallable handles in the IDL file will automatically be transferred in this way through the ALPC subsystem.

FIGURE 7-19 Object manager directory for Calculator.

Outside of official broker RPC services, a desktop app can create a named (or even unnamed) object normally, and then use the `DuplicateHandle` function to inject a handle to the same object into the UWP process manually. This works because desktop apps typically run with medium integrity level and there's nothing preventing them from duplicating handles into UWP processes—only the other way around.

> **Note** Communication between a desktop app and a UWP is not usually required because a store app cannot have a desktop app companion, and cannot rely on such an app to exist on the device. The capability to inject handles into a UWP app may be needed in specialized cases such as using the desktop bridge (Centennial) to convert a desktop app to a UWP app and communicate with another desktop app that is known to exist.

AppContainer handles

In a typical Win32 application, the presence of the session-local and global BaseNamedObjects directory is guaranteed by the Windows subsystem, as it creates this on boot and session creation. Unfortunately, the AppContainerBaseNamedObjects directory is actually created by the launch application itself. In the case of UWP activation, this is the trusted `DComLaunch` service, but recall that not all AppContainers are necessarily tied to UWP. They can also be manually created through the right process-creation attributes. (See Chapter 3 for more information on which ones to use.) In this case, it's possible for an untrusted application to have created the object directory (and required symbolic links within it), which would result in the ability for this application to close the handles from underneath the AppContainer application. Even without malicious intent, the original launching application might exit, cleaning up its handles and destroying the AppContainer-specific object directory. To avoid this situation, AppContainer tokens have the ability to store an array of handles that are guaranteed to exist throughout the lifetime of any application using the token. These handles are initially passed in when the AppContainer token is being created (through NtCreateLowBoxToken) and are duplicated as kernel handles.

Similar to the per-AppContainer atom table, a special SEP_CACHED_HANDLES_ENTRY structure is used, this time based on a hash table that's stored in the logon session structure for this user. (See the "Logon" section later in this chapter for more information on logon sessions.) This structure contains an array of kernel handles that have been duplicated during the creation of the AppContainer token. They will be closed either when this token is destroyed (because the application is exiting) or when the user logs off (which will result in tearing down the logon session).

EXPERIMENT: Viewing token stored handles

To view token stored handles, follow these steps:

1. Run Calculator and launch local kernel debugging.

2. Search for the calculator process:

```
lkd> !process 0 1 calculator.exe
PROCESS ffff828cc9ed1080
    SessionId: 1 Cid: 4bd8    Peb: d040bbc000   ParentCid: 03a4
DeepFreeze
    DirBase: 5fccaa000 ObjectTable: ffff950ad9fa2800  HandleCount:
<Data Not Accessible>
    Image: Calculator.exe
    VadRoot ffff828cd2c9b6a0 Vads 168 Clone 0 Private 2938. Modified 3332.
Locked 0.
    DeviceMap ffff950aad2cd2f0
    Token                               ffff950adb313060
    ElapsedTime                         1 Day 08:01:47.018
    UserTime                            00:00:00.015
    KernelTime                          00:00:00.031
    QuotaPoolUsage[PagedPool]           465880
    QuotaPoolUsage[NonPagedPool]        23288
    Working Set Sizes (now,min,max)  (7434, 50, 345) (29736KB, 200KB, 1380KB)
    PeakWorkingSetSize                  11097
    VirtualSize                         303 Mb
    PeakVirtualSize                     314 Mb
    PageFaultCount                      21281
    MemoryPriority                      BACKGROUND
    BasePriority                        8
    CommitCharge                        4925
    Job                                 ffff828cd4914060
```

3. Dump the token using the dt command. (Remember to mask the lower 3 or 4 bits if they are not zero.)

```
lkd> dt nt!_token ffff950adb313060
   +0x000 TokenSource      : _TOKEN_SOURCE
   +0x010 TokenId          : _LUID
   +0x018 AuthenticationId : _LUID
   +0x020 ParentTokenId    : _LUID
   ...
   +0x0c8 TokenFlags       : 0x4a00
   +0x0cc TokenInUse       : 0x1 ''
   +0x0d0 IntegrityLevelIndex : 1
   +0x0d4 MandatoryPolicy  : 1
   +0x0d8 LogonSession     : 0xffff950a'b4bb35c0 _SEP_LOGON_SESSION_REFERENCES
   +0x0e0 OriginatingLogonSession : _LUID
   +0x0e8 SidHash          : _SID_AND_ATTRIBUTES_HASH
   +0x1f8 RestrictedSidHash : _SID_AND_ATTRIBUTES_HASH
   +0x308 pSecurityAttributes : 0xffff950a'e4ff57f0 _AUTHZBASEP_SECURITY_
ATTRIBUTES_INFORMATION
   +0x310 Package          : 0xffff950a'e00ed6d0 Void
   +0x318 Capabilities     : 0xffff950a'e8e8fbc0 _SID_AND_ATTRIBUTES
   +0x320 CapabilityCount  : 1
   +0x328 CapabilitiesHash : _SID_AND_ATTRIBUTES_HASH
   +0x438 LowboxNumberEntry : 0xffff950a'b3fd55d0 _SEP_LOWBOX_NUMBER_ENTRY
   +0x440 LowboxHandlesEntry : 0xffff950a'e6ff91d0 _SEP_LOWBOX_HANDLES_ENTRY
   +0x448 pClaimAttributes : (null)
   ...
```

4. Dump the LowboxHandlesEntry member:

```
lkd> dt nt!_sep_lowbox_handles_entry 0xffff950a'e6ff91d0
   +0x000 HashEntry        : _RTL_DYNAMIC_HASH_TABLE_ENTRY
   +0x018 ReferenceCount   : 0n10
   +0x020 PackageSid       : 0xffff950a'e6ff9208 Void
   +0x028 HandleCount      : 6
   +0x030 Handles          : 0xffff950a'e91d8490  -> 0xffffffff'800023cc Void
```

5. There are six handles. Let's dump their values:

```
lkd> dq 0xffff950ae91d8490 L6
ffff950a'e91d8490  ffffffff'800023cc ffffffff'80001e80
ffff950a'e91d84a0  ffffffff'80004214 ffffffff'8000425c
ffff950a'e91d84b0  ffffffff'800028c8 ffffffff'80001834
```

6. You can see that these handles are kernel handles—that is, handle values starting with 0xffffffff (64 bit). Now you can use the !handle command to look at individual handles. Here are two examples from the six handles above:

```
lkd> !handle ffffffff'80001e80

PROCESS ffff828cd71b3600
    SessionId: 1  Cid: 27c4    Peb: 3fdfb2f000  ParentCid: 2324
```

```
      DirBase: 80bb85000  ObjectTable: ffff950addabf7c0  HandleCount:
<Data Not Accessible>
      Image: windbg.exe

Kernel handle Error reading handle count.

80001e80: Object: ffff950ada206ea0  GrantedAccess: 0000000f (Protected)
(Inherit) (Audit) Entry: ffff950ab5406a00
Object: ffff950ada206ea0  Type: (ffff828cb66b33b0) Directory
    ObjectHeader: ffff950ada206e70 (new version)
        HandleCount: 1  PointerCount: 32770
        Directory Object: ffff950ad9a62950  Name: RPC Control

    Hash Address            Type                    Name
    ---- -------            ----                    ----
        23  ffff828cb6ce6950 ALPC Port
OLE376512B99BCCA5DE4208534E7732
lkd> !handle ffffffff'800028c8

PROCESS ffff828cd71b3600
    SessionId: 1  Cid: 27c4    Peb: 3fdfb2f000  ParentCid: 2324
    DirBase: 80bb85000  ObjectTable: ffff950addabf7c0  HandleCount: <Data
Not Accessible>
    Image: windbg.exe

Kernel handle Error reading handle count.

800028c8: Object: ffff950ae7a8fa70  GrantedAccess: 000f0001 (Audit) Entry:
ffff950acc426320
Object: ffff950ae7a8fa70  Type: (ffff828cb66296f0) SymbolicLink
    ObjectHeader: ffff950ae7a8fa40 (new version)
        HandleCount: 1  PointerCount: 32769
        Directory Object: ffff950ad9a62950  Name: Session
        Flags: 00000000 ( Local )
        Target String is '\Sessions\1\AppContainerNamedObjects
\S-1-15-2-466767348-3739614953-2700836392-1801644223-4227750657
-1087833535-2488631167'
```

Finally, because the ability to restrict named objects to a particular object directory namespace is a valuable security tool for sandboxing named object access, the upcoming (at the time of this writing) Windows 10 Creators Update includes an additional token capability called *BNO isolation* (where *BNO* refers to BaseNamedObjects). Using the same SEP_CACHE_HANDLES_ENTRY structure, a new field, BnoIsolationHandlesEntry, is added to the TOKEN structure, with the type set to SepCachedHandlesEntryBnoIsolation instead of SepCachedHandlesEntryLowbox. To use this feature, a special process attribute must be used (see Chapter 3 for more information), which contains an isolation prefix and a list of handles. At this point, the same LowBox mechanism is used, but instead of an AppContainer SID object directory, a directory with the prefix indicated in the attribute is used.

Brokers

Because AppContainer processes have almost no permissions except for those implicitly granted with capabilities, some common operations cannot be performed directly by the AppContainer and require help. (There are no capabilities for these, as these are too low level to be visible to users in the store, and difficult to manage.) Some examples include selecting files using the common File Open dialog box or printing with a Print dialog box. For these and other similar operations, Windows provides helper processes, called *brokers*, managed by the system broker process, RuntimeBroker.exe.

An AppContainer process that requires any of these services communicates with the Runtime Broker through a secure ALPC channel and Runtime Broker initiates the creation of the requested broker process. Examples are %SystemRoot%\PrintDialog\PrintDialog.exe and %SystemRoot%\System32\PickerHost.exe.

EXPERIMENT: Brokers

The following steps show how broker processes are launched and terminated:

1. Click the **Start** button, type **Photos**, and select the **Photos** option to run the built-in Windows 10 Photos application.

2. Open Process Explorer, switch the process list to a tree view, and locate the Microsoft. Photos.exe process. Place both windows side by side.

3. In the Photos app, select a picture file, and click **Print** in the top ellipsis menu or right-click the picture and choose **Print** from the menu that appears. The Print dialog box should open, and Process Explorer should show the newly created broker (PrintDialog. exe). Notice they are all children of the same Svchost process. (All UWP processes are launched by the DCOMLaunch service hosted inside that process.)

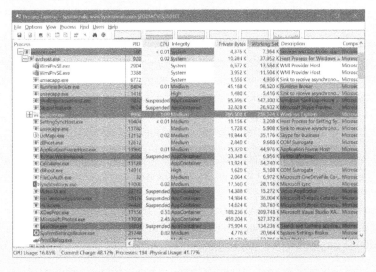

4. Close the Print dialog box. The PrintDialog.exe process should exit.

Logon

Interactive logon (as opposed to network logon) occurs through the interaction of the following:

- The logon process (Winlogon.exe)

- The logon user interface process (LogonUI.exe) and its credential providers

- Lsass.exe

- One or more authentication packages

- SAM or Active Directory

Authentication packages are DLLs that perform authentication checks. Kerberos is the Windows authentication package for interactive logon to a domain. MSV1_0 is the Windows authentication package for interactive logon to a local computer, for domain logons to trusted pre–Windows 2000 domains, and for times when no domain controller is accessible.

Winlogon is a trusted process responsible for managing security-related user interactions. It coordinates logon, starts the user's first process at logon, and handles logoff. It also manages various other operations relevant to security, including launching LogonUI for entering passwords at logon, changing passwords, and locking and unlocking the workstation. The Winlogon process must ensure that operations relevant to security aren't visible to any other active processes. For example, Winlogon guarantees that an untrusted process can't get control of the desktop during one of these operations and thus gain access to the password.

Winlogon relies on the credential providers installed on the system to obtain a user's account name or password. Credential providers are COM objects located inside DLLs. The default providers are authui.dll, SmartcardCredentialProvider.dll, and FaceCredentialProvider.dll, which support password, smartcard PIN, and face-recognition authentication, respectively. Allowing other credential providers to be installed enables Windows to use different user-identification mechanisms. For example, a third party might supply a credential provider that uses a thumbprint-recognition device to identify users and extract their passwords from an encrypted database. Credential providers are listed in HKLM\SOFTWARE\Microsoft\Windows\CurrentVersion\Authentication\Credential Providers, where each subkey identifies a credential provider class by its COM CLSID. (The CLSID itself must be registered at HKCR\CLSID like any other COM class.) You can use the CPlist.exe tool provided with the downloadable resources for this book to list the credential providers with their CLSID, friendly name, and implementation DLL.

To protect Winlogon's address space from bugs in credential providers that might cause the Winlogon process to crash (which, in turn, will result in a system crash, because Winlogon is considered a critical system process), a separate process, LogonUI.exe, is used to actually load the credential providers and display the Windows logon interface to users. This process is started on demand whenever Winlogon needs to present a user interface to the user, and it exits after the action has finished. It also allows Winlogon to simply restart a new LogonUI process should it crash for any reason.

Winlogon is the only process that intercepts logon requests from the keyboard. These are sent through an RPC message from Win32k.sys. Winlogon immediately launches the LogonUI application to display the user interface for logon. After obtaining a user name and password from credential providers, Winlogon calls Lsass to authenticate the user attempting to log on. If the user is authenticated, the logon process activates a logon shell on behalf of that user. The interaction between the components involved in logon is illustrated in Figure 7-20.

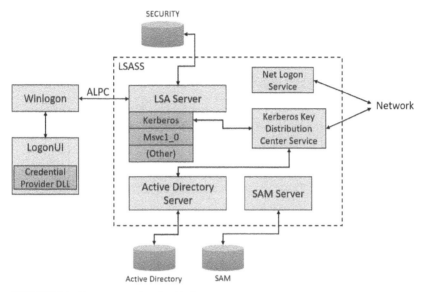

FIGURE 7-20 Components involved in logon.

In addition to supporting alternative credential providers, LogonUI can load additional network provider DLLs that need to perform secondary authentication. This capability allows multiple network providers to gather identification and authentication information all at one time during normal logon. A user logging on to a Windows system might simultaneously be authenticated on a Linux server. That user would then be able to access resources of the UNIX server from the Windows machine without requiring additional authentication. Such a capability is known as one form of single sign-on.

Winlogon initialization

During system initialization, before any user applications are active, Winlogon performs the following steps to ensure that it controls the workstation once the system is ready for user interaction:

1. It creates and opens an interactive window station (for example, \Sessions\1\Windows\WindowStations\WinSta0 in the object manager namespace) to represent the keyboard, mouse, and monitor. Winlogon creates a security descriptor for the station that has one and only one ACE containing only the system SID. This unique security descriptor ensures that no other process can access the workstation unless explicitly allowed by Winlogon.

2. It creates and opens two desktops: an application desktop (\Sessions\1\Windows\WinSta0\Default, also known as the interactive desktop) and a Winlogon desktop (\Sessions\1\Windows\WinSta0\Winlogon, also known as the Secure Desktop). The security on the Winlogon desktop is created so that only Winlogon can access that desktop. The other desktop allows both

Winlogon and users to access it. This arrangement means that any time the Winlogon desktop is active, no other process has access to any active code or data associated with the desktop. Windows uses this feature to protect the secure operations that involve passwords and locking and unlocking the desktop.

3. Before anyone logs on to a computer, the visible desktop is Winlogon's. After a user logs on, pressing the SAS sequence (by default, Ctrl+Alt+Del) switches the desktop from Default to Winlogon and launches LogonUI. (This explains why all the windows on your interactive desktop seem to disappear when you press Ctrl+Alt+Del, and then return when you dismiss the Windows Security dialog box.) Thus, the SAS always brings up a Secure Desktop controlled by Winlogon.

4. It establishes an ALPC connection with Lsass. This connection will be used for exchanging information during logon, logoff, and password operations, and is made by calling `LsaRegisterLogonProcess`.

5. It registers the Winlogon RPC message server, which listens for SAS, logoff, and workstation lock notifications from Win32k. This measure prevents Trojan horse programs from gaining control of the screen when the SAS is entered.

 Note The Wininit process performs steps similar to steps 1 and 2 to allow legacy interactive services running on session 0 to display windows, but it does not perform any other steps because session 0 is not available for user logon.

How SAS is implemented

The SAS is secure because no application can intercept the Ctrl+Alt+Del keystroke combination or prevent Winlogon from receiving it. Win32k.sys reserves the Ctrl+Alt+Del key combination so that whenever the Windows input system (implemented in the raw input thread in Win32k) sees the combination, it sends an RPC message to Winlogon's message server, which listens for such notifications. The keystrokes that map to a registered hot key are not sent to any process other than the one that registered it, and only the thread that registered a hot key can unregister it, so a Trojan horse application cannot deregister Winlogon's ownership of the SAS.

A Windows function, `SetWindowsHookEx`, enables an application to install a hook procedure that's invoked every time a keystroke is pressed, even before hot keys are processed, and allows the hook to squash keystrokes. However, the Windows hot key processing code contains a special case for Ctrl+Alt+Del that disables hooks so that the keystroke sequence can't be intercepted. In addition, if the interactive desktop is locked, only hot keys owned by Winlogon are processed.

Once the Winlogon desktop is created during initialization, it becomes the active desktop. When the Winlogon desktop is active, it is always locked. Winlogon unlocks its desktop only to switch to the application desktop or the screen-saver desktop. (Only the Winlogon process can lock or unlock a desktop.)

User logon steps

Logon begins when a user presses the SAS (Ctrl+Alt+Del). After the SAS is pressed, Winlogon starts LogonUI, which calls the credential providers to obtain a user name and password. Winlogon also creates a unique local logon SID for this user, which it assigns to this instance of the desktop (keyboard, screen, and mouse). Winlogon passes this SID to Lsass as part of the LsaLogonUser call. If the user is successfully logged on, this SID will be included in the logon process token—a step that protects access to the desktop. For example, another logon to the same account but on a different system will be unable to write to the first machine's desktop because this second logon won't be in the first logon's desktop token.

When the user name and password have been entered, Winlogon retrieves a handle to a package by calling the Lsass function `LsaLookupAuthenticationPackage`. Authentication packages are listed in the registry under HKLM\SYSTEM\CurrentControlSet\Control\Lsa. Winlogon passes logon information to the authentication package via `LsaLogonUser`. Once a package authenticates a user, Winlogon continues the logon process for that user. If none of the authentication packages indicates a successful logon, the logon process is aborted.

Windows uses two standard authentication packages for interactive username/password-based logons:

- **MSV1_0**   The default authentication package on a stand-alone Windows system is MSV1_0 (Msv1_0.dll), an authentication package that implements LAN Manager 2 protocol. Lsass also uses MSV1_0 on domain-member computers to authenticate to pre–Windows 2000 domains and computers that can't locate a domain controller for authentication. (Computers that are disconnected from the network fall into this latter category.)

- **Kerberos**   The Kerberos authentication package, Kerberos.dll, is used on computers that are members of Windows domains. The Windows Kerberos package, with the cooperation of Kerberos services running on a domain controller, supports the Kerberos protocol. This protocol is based on Internet RFC 1510. (Visit the Internet Engineering Task Force [IETF] website at *http://www.ietf.org* for detailed information on the Kerberos standard.)

MSV1_0

The MSV1_0 authentication package takes the user name and a hashed version of the password and sends a request to the local SAM to retrieve the account information, which includes the hashed password, the groups to which the user belongs, and any account restrictions. MSV1_0 first checks the account restrictions, such as hours or type of accesses allowed. If the user can't log on because of the restrictions in the SAM database, the logon call fails and MSV1_0 returns a failure status to the LSA.

MSV1_0 then compares the hashed password and user name to that obtained from the SAM. In the case of a cached domain logon, MSV1_0 accesses the cached information by using Lsass functions that store and retrieve "secrets" from the LSA database (the SECURITY hive of the registry). If the information matches, MSV1_0 generates a LUID for the logon session and creates the logon session by calling Lsass, associating this unique identifier with the session and passing the information needed to ultimately create an access token for the user. (Recall that an access token includes the user's SID, group SIDs, and assigned privileges.)

Note MSV1_0 does not cache a user's entire password hash in the registry because that would enable someone with physical access to the system to easily compromise a user's domain account and gain access to encrypted files and to network resources the user is authorized to access. Instead, it caches half of the hash. The cached half-hash is sufficient to verify that a user's password is correct, but it isn't sufficient to gain access to EFS keys and to authenticate as the user on a domain because these actions require the full hash.

If MSV1_0 needs to authenticate using a remote system, as when a user logs on to a trusted pre–Windows 2000 domain, MSV1_0 uses the Netlogon service to communicate with an instance of Netlogon on the remote system. Netlogon on the remote system interacts with the MSV1_0 authentication package on that system, passing back authentication results to the system on which the logon is being performed.

Kerberos

The basic control flow for Kerberos authentication is the same as the flow for MSV1_0. However, in most cases, domain logons are performed from member workstations or servers rather than on a domain controller, so the authentication package must communicate across the network as part of the authentication process. The package does so by communicating via the Kerberos TCP/IP port (port 88) with the Kerberos service on a domain controller. The Kerberos Key Distribution Center service (Kdcsvc.dll), which implements the Kerberos authentication protocol, runs in the Lsass process on domain controllers.

After validating hashed user-name and password information with Active Directory's user account objects (using the Active Directory server Ntdsa.dll), Kdcsvc returns domain credentials to Lsass, which returns the result of the authentication and the user's domain logon credentials (if the logon was successful) across the network to the system where the logon is taking place.

Note This description of Kerberos authentication is highly simplified, but it highlights the roles of the various components involved. Although the Kerberos authentication protocol plays a key role in distributed domain security in Windows, its details are outside the scope of this book.

After a logon has been authenticated, Lsass looks in the local policy database for the user's allowed access, including interactive, network, batch, or service process. If the requested logon doesn't match the allowed access, the logon attempt will be terminated. Lsass deletes the newly created logon session by cleaning up any of its data structures and then returns failure to Winlogon, which in turn displays an appropriate message to the user. If the requested access is allowed, Lsass adds the appropriate additional security IDs (such as Everyone, Interactive, and the like). It then checks its policy database for any granted privileges for all the SIDs for this user and adds these privileges to the user's access token.

When Lsass has accumulated all the necessary information, it calls the executive to create the access token. The executive creates a primary access token for an interactive or service logon and an impersonation token for a network logon. After the access token is successfully created, Lsass duplicates the token, creating a handle that can be passed to Winlogon, and closes its own handle. If necessary, the logon operation is audited. At this point, Lsass returns success to Winlogon along with a handle to the access token, the LUID for the logon session, and the profile information, if any, that the authentication package returned.

EXPERIMENT: Listing active logon sessions

As long as at least one token exists with a given logon session LUID, Windows considers the logon session to be active. You can use the LogonSessions tool from Sysinternals, which uses the `LsaEnumerateLogonSessions` function (documented in the Windows SDK) to list the active logon sessions:

```
C:\WINDOWS\system32>logonsessions

LogonSessions v1.4 - Lists logon session information
Copyright (C) 2004-2016 Mark Russinovich
Sysinternals - www.sysinternals.com


[0] Logon session 00000000:000003e7:
    User name:     WORKGROUP\ZODIAC$
    Auth package: NTLM
    Logon type:    (none)
    Session:       0
    Sid:           S-1-5-18
    Logon time:    09-Dec-16 15:22:31
    Logon server:
    DNS Domain:
    UPN:


[1] Logon session 00000000:0000cdce:
    User name:
    Auth package: NTLM
    Logon type:    (none)
    Session:       0
    Sid:           (none)
    Logon time:    09-Dec-16 15:22:31
    Logon server:
    DNS Domain:
    UPN:


[2] Logon session 00000000:000003e4:
    User name:     WORKGROUP\ZODIAC$
    Auth package: Negotiate
    Logon type:    Service
    Session:       0
    Sid:           S-1-5-20
    Logon time:    09-Dec-16 15:22:31
    Logon server:
    DNS Domain:
    UPN:
```

```
[3] Logon session 00000000:00016239:
    User name:    Window Manager\DWM-1
    Auth package: Negotiate
    Logon type:   Interactive
    Session:      1
    Sid:          S-1-5-90-0-1
    Logon time:   09-Dec-16 15:22:32
    Logon server:
    DNS Domain:
    UPN:

[4] Logon session 00000000:00016265:
    User name:    Window Manager\DWM-1
    Auth package: Negotiate
    Logon type:   Interactive
    Session:      1
    Sid:          S-1-5-90-0-1
    Logon time:   09-Dec-16 15:22:32
    Logon server:
    DNS Domain:
    UPN:

[5] Logon session 00000000:000003e5:
    User name:    NT AUTHORITY\LOCAL SERVICE
    Auth package: Negotiate
    Logon type:   Service
    Session:      0
    Sid:          S-1-5-19
    Logon time:   09-Dec-16 15:22:32
    Logon server:
    DNS Domain:
    UPN:

...
[8] Logon session 00000000:0005c203:
    User name:    NT VIRTUAL MACHINE\AC9081B6-1E96-4BC8-8B3B-C609D4F85F7D
    Auth package: Negotiate
    Logon type:   Service
    Session:      0
    Sid:          S-1-5-83-1-2895151542-1271406230-163986315-2103441620
    Logon time:   09-Dec-16 15:22:35
    Logon server:
    DNS Domain:
    UPN:

[9] Logon session 00000000:0005d524:
    User name:    NT VIRTUAL MACHINE\B37F4A3A-21EF-422D-8B37-AB6B0A016ED8
    Auth package: Negotiate
    Logon type:   Service
    Session:      0
    Sid:          S-1-5-83-1-3011463738-1110254063-1806382987-3631087882
    Logon time:   09-Dec-16 15:22:35
```

```
      Logon server:
      DNS Domain:
      UPN:

...
[12] Logon session 00000000:0429ab2c:
      User name:     IIS APPPOOL\DefaultAppPool
      Auth package: Negotiate
      Logon type:    Service
      Session:       0
      Sid:           S-1-5-82-3006700770-424185619-1745488364-794895919-4004696415
      Logon time:    09-Dec-16 22:33:03
      Logon server:
      DNS Domain:
      UPN:
```

Information reported for a session includes the SID and name of the user associated with the session, as well as the session's authentication package and logon time. Note that the Negotiate authentication package, seen in logon sessions 2 and 9 in the preceding output, will attempt to authenticate via Kerberos or NTLM, depending on which is most appropriate for the authentication request.

The LUID for a session is displayed on the Logon Session line of each session block. Using the Handle.exe utility (also from Sysinternals), you can find the tokens that represent a particular logon session. For example, to find the tokens for logon session 8 in the output just shown, you could enter this command:

```
C:\WINDOWS\system32>handle -a 5c203

Nthandle v4.1 - Handle viewer
Copyright (C) 1997-2016 Mark Russinovich
Sysinternals - www.sysinternals.com

System            pid: 4      type: Directory     1274: \Sessions\0\
DosDevices\00000000-0005c203
lsass.exe         pid: 496    type: Token          D7C: NT VIRTUAL MACHINE\
AC9081B6-1E96-4BC8-8B3B-C609D4F85F7D:5c203
lsass.exe         pid: 496    type: Token         2350: NT VIRTUAL MACHINE\
AC9081B6-1E96-4BC8-8B3B-C609D4F85F7D:5c203
lsass.exe         pid: 496    type: Token         2390: NT VIRTUAL MACHINE\
AC9081B6-1E96-4BC8-8B3B-C609D4F85F7D:5c203
svchost.exe       pid: 900    type: Token          804: NT VIRTUAL MACHINE\
AC9081B6-1E96-4BC8-8B3B-C609D4F85F7D:5c203
svchost.exe       pid: 1468   type: Token         10EC: NT VIRTUAL MACHINE\
AC9081B6-1E96-4BC8-8B3B-C609D4F85F7D:5c203
vmms.exe          pid: 4380   type: Token          A34: NT VIRTUAL MACHINE\
AC9081B6-1E96-4BC8-8B3B-C609D4F85F7D:5c203
vmcompute.exe     pid: 6592   type: Token          200: NT VIRTUAL MACHINE\
AC9081B6-1E96-4BC8-8B3B-C609D4F85F7D:5c203
vmwp.exe          pid: 7136   type: WindowStation  168: \Windows\WindowStations\
Service-0x0-5c203$
vmwp.exe          pid: 7136   type: WindowStation  170: \Windows\WindowStations\
Service-0x0-5c203$
```

Winlogon then looks in the registry at the value HKLM\SOFTWARE\Microsoft\Windows NT\Current Version\Winlogon\Userinit and creates a process to run whatever the value of that string is. (This value can be several EXEs separated by commas.) The default value is Userinit.exe, which loads the user profile and then creates a process to run whatever the value of HKCU\SOFTWARE\Microsoft\Windows NT\Current Version\Winlogon\Shell is, if that value exists. That value does not exist by default, however. If it doesn't exist, Userinit.exe does the same for HKLM\SOFTWARE\Microsoft\Windows NT\Current Version\Winlogon\Shell, which defaults to Explorer.exe. Userinit then exits (which is why Explorer.exe shows up as having no parent when examined in Process Explorer). For more information on the steps followed during the user logon process, see Chapter 11 in Part 2.

Assured authentication

A fundamental problem with password-based authentication is that passwords can be revealed or stolen and used by malicious third parties. Windows includes a mechanism that tracks the authentication strength of how a user authenticated with the system, which allows objects to be protected from access if a user did not authenticate securely. (Smartcard authentication is considered to be a stronger form of authentication than password authentication.)

On systems that are joined to a domain, the domain administrator can specify a mapping between an object identifier (OID) (a unique numeric string representing a specific object type) on a certificate used for authenticating a user (such as on a smartcard or hardware security token) and a SID that is placed into the user's access token when the user successfully authenticates with the system. An ACE in a DACL on an object can specify such a SID be part of a user's token in order for the user to gain access to the object. Technically, this is known as a *group claim*. In other words, the user is claiming membership in a particular group, which is allowed certain access rights on specific objects, with the claim based upon the authentication mechanism. This feature is not enabled by default, and it must be configured by the domain administrator in a domain with certificate-based authentication.

Assured authentication builds on existing Windows security features in a way that provides a great deal of flexibility to IT administrators and anyone concerned with enterprise IT security. The enterprise decides which OIDs to embed in the certificates it uses for authenticating users and the mapping of particular OIDs to Active Directory universal groups (SIDs). A user's group membership can be used to identify whether a certificate was used during the logon operation. Different certificates can have different issuance policies and, thus, different levels of security, which can be used to protect highly sensitive objects (such as files or anything else that might have a security descriptor).

Authentication protocols (APs) retrieve OIDs from certificates during certificate-based authentication. These OIDs must be mapped to SIDs, which are in turn processed during group membership expansion, and placed in the access token. The mapping of OID to universal group is specified in Active Directory.

As an example, an organization might have several certificate-issuance policies named Contractor, Full Time Employee, and Senior Management, which map to the universal groups Contractor-Users, FTE-Users, and SM-Users, respectively. A user named Abby has a smartcard with a certificate issued using the Senior Management issuance policy. When she logs in using her smartcard, she receives an additional group membership (which is represented by a SID in her access token) indicating that she is a member of the SM-Users group. Permissions can be set on objects (using an ACL) such that only members of the FTE-Users or SM-Users group (identified by their SIDs within an ACE) are granted access. If Abby logs in using her smartcard, she can access those objects, but if she logs in with just her user name and password (without the smartcard), she cannot access those objects because she will not have either the FTE-Users or SM-Users group in her access token. A user named Toby who logs in with a smartcard that has a certificate issued using the Contractor issuance policy would not be able to access an object that has an ACE requiring FTE-Users or SM-Users group membership.

Windows Biometric Framework

Windows provides a standardized mechanism for supporting certain types of biometric devices, such as fingerprint scanners, used to enable user identification via a fingerprint swipe: the Windows Biometric Framework (WBF). Like many other such frameworks, the WBF was developed to isolate the various functions involved in supporting such devices, so as to minimize the code required to implement a new device.

The primary components of the WBF are shown in Figure 7-21. Except as noted in the following list, all of these components are supplied by Windows:

- **The Windows Biometric Service (%SystemRoot%\System32\Wbiosrvc.dll** This provides the process-execution environment in which one or more biometric service providers can execute.

- **The Windows Biometric Driver Interface (WBDI)** This is a set of interface definitions (IRP major function codes, `DeviceIoControl` codes, and so forth) to which any driver for a biometric scanner device must conform if it is to be compatible with the Windows Biometric Service. WBDI drivers can be developed using any of the standard driver frameworks (UMDF, KMDF and WDM). However, UMDF is recommended to reduce code size and increase reliability. WBDI is described in the Windows Driver Kit documentation.

- **The Windows Biometric API** This allows existing Windows components such as Winlogon and LogonUI to access the biometric service. Third-party applications have access to the Windows Biometric API and can use the biometric scanner for functions other than logging in to Windows. An example of a function in this API is `WinBioEnumServiceProviders`. The Biometric API is exposed by %SystemRoot%\System32\Winbio.dll.

- **The fingerprint biometric service provider** This wraps the functions of biometric-type-specific adapters to present a common interface, independent of the type of biometric, to the Windows Biometric Service. In the future, additional types of biometrics, such as retinal scans or voiceprint analyzers, might be supported by additional biometric service providers. The biometric service provider in turn uses three adapters, which are user-mode DLLs:

  - **The sensor adapter** This exposes the data-capture functionality of the scanner. The sensor adapter usually uses Windows I/O calls to access the scanner hardware. Windows provides a sensor adapter that can be used with simple sensors, those for which a WBDI driver exists. For more complex sensors, the sensor adapter is written by the sensor vendor.

  - **The engine adapter** This exposes processing and comparison functionality specific to the scanner's raw data format and other features. The actual processing and comparison might be performed within the engine adapter DLL, or the DLL might communicate with some other module. The engine adapter is always provided by the sensor vendor.

- **The storage adapter** This exposes a set of secure storage functions. These are used to store and retrieve templates against which scanned biometric data is matched by the engine adapter. Windows provides a storage adapter using Windows cryptography services and standard disk file storage. A sensor vendor might provide a different storage adapter.

■ **The functional device driver for the actual biometric scanner device** This exposes the WBDI at its upper edge. It usually uses the services of a lower-level bus driver, such as the USB bus driver, to access the scanner device. This driver is always provided by the sensor vendor.

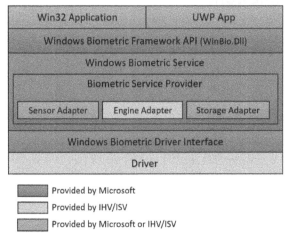

FIGURE 7-21 Windows Biometric Framework components and architecture.

A typical sequence of operations to support logging in via a fingerprint scan might be as follows:

1. After initialization, the sensor adapter receives from the service provider a request for capture data. The sensor adapter in turn sends a DeviceIoControl request with the IOCTL_BIOMETRIC_CAPTURE_DATA control code to the WBDI driver for the fingerprint scanner device.

2. The WBDI driver puts the scanner into capture mode and queues the IOCTL_BIOMETRIC_CAPTURE_DATA request until a fingerprint scan occurs.

3. A prospective user swipes a finger across the scanner. The WBDI driver receives notification of this, obtains the raw scan data from the sensor, and returns this data to the sensor driver in a buffer associated with the IOCTL_BIOMETRIC_CAPTURE_DATA request.

4. The sensor adapter provides the data to the fingerprint biometric service provider, which in turn passes the data to the engine adapter.

5. The engine adapter processes the raw data into a form compatible with its template storage.

6. The fingerprint biometric service provider uses the storage adapter to obtain templates and corresponding security IDs from secure storage. It invokes the engine adapter to compare each template to the processed scan data. The engine adapter returns a status indicating whether it's a match or not a match.

7. If a match is found, the Windows Biometric Service notifies Winlogon, via a credential provider DLL, of a successful login and passes it the security ID of the identified user. This notification is sent via an ALPC message, providing a path that cannot be spoofed.

Windows Hello

Windows Hello, introduced in Windows 10, provides new ways to authenticate users based on biometric information. With this technology, users can log in effortlessly just by showing themselves to the device's camera or swiping their finger.

At the time of this writing, Windows Hello supports three types of biometric identification:

- Fingerprint
- Face
- Iris

The security aspect of biometrics needs to be considered first. What is the likelihood of someone being identified as you? What is the likelihood of you *not* being identified as you? These questions are parameterized by two factors:

- **False accept rate (uniqueness)** This is the probability of another user having the same biometric data as you. Microsoft's algorithms make sure the likelihood is 1 in 100,000.

- **False reject rate (reliability)** This is the probability of you not being correctly recognized as you (for example, in abnormal lighting conditions for face or iris recognition). Microsoft's implementation makes sure there is less than 1 percent chance of this happening. If it does happen, the user can try again or use a PIN code instead.

Using a PIN code may seem less secure than using a full-blown password (the PIN can be as simple as a four-digit number). However, a PIN is more secure than a password for two main reasons:

- The PIN code is local to the device and is never transmitted across the network. This means that even if someone gets a hold of the PIN, they cannot use it to log in as the user from any other device. Passwords, on the other hand, travel to the domain controller. If someone gets hold of the password, they can log in from another machine into the domain.

- The PIN code is stored in the Trusted Platform Module (TPM)—a piece of hardware that also plays a part in Secure Boot (discussed in detail in Chapter 11 in Part 2)—so is difficult to access. In any case, it requires physical access to the device, raising the bar considerably for a potential security compromise.

Windows Hello is built upon the Windows Biometric Framework (WBF) (described in the previous section). Current laptop devices support fingerprint and face biometrics, while iris is only supported on the Microsoft Lumia 950 and 950 XL phones. (This will likely change and expand in future devices.) Note that face recognition requires an infrared (IR) camera as well as a normal (RGB) one, and is supported on devices such as the Microsoft Surface Pro 4 and the Surface Book.

User Account Control and virtualization

User Account Control (UAC) is meant to enable users to run with standard user rights as opposed to administrative rights. Without administrative rights, users cannot accidentally (or deliberately) modify system settings, malware can't normally alter system security settings or disable antivirus software, and users can't compromise the sensitive information of other users on shared computers. Running with standard user rights can thus mitigate the impact of malware and protect sensitive data on shared computers.

UAC had to address a couple of problems to make it practical for a user to run with a standard user account. First, because the Windows usage model has been one of assumed administrative rights, software developers assumed their programs would run with those rights and could therefore access and modify any file, registry key, or operating system setting. Second, users sometimes need administrative rights to perform such operations as installing software, changing the system time, and opening ports in the firewall.

The UAC solution to these problems is to run most applications with standard user rights, even though the user is logged in to an account with administrative rights. At the same time, UAC makes it possible for standard users to access administrative rights when they need them—whether for legacy applications that require them or for changing certain system settings. As described, UAC accomplishes this by creating a filtered admin token as well as the normal admin token when a user logs in to an administrative account. All processes created under the user's session will normally have the filtered admin token in effect so that applications that can run with standard user rights will do so. However, the administrative user can run a program or perform other functions that require full Administrator rights through UAC elevation.

Windows also allows certain tasks that were previously reserved for administrators to be performed by standard users, enhancing the usability of the standard user environment. For example, Group Policy settings exist that can enable standard users to install printers and other device drivers approved by IT administrators and to install ActiveX controls from administrator-approved sites.

Finally, when software developers test in the UAC environment, they are encouraged to develop applications that can run without administrative rights. Fundamentally, non-administrative programs should not need to run with administrator privileges; programs that often require administrator privileges are typically legacy programs using old APIs or techniques, and they should be updated.

Together, these changes obviate the need for users to run with administrative rights all the time.

File system and registry virtualization

Although some software legitimately requires administrative rights, many programs needlessly store user data in system-global locations. When an application executes, it can be running in different user accounts, and it should therefore store user-specific data in the per-user %AppData% directory and save per-user settings in the user's registry profile under HKEY_CURRENT_USER\Software. Standard user accounts don't have write access to the %ProgramFiles% directory or HKEY_LOCAL_MACHINE\ Software, but because most Windows systems are single-user and most users have been administrators until UAC was implemented, applications that incorrectly saved user data and settings to these locations worked anyway.

Windows enables these legacy applications to run in standard user accounts through the help of file system and registry namespace virtualization. When an application modifies a system-global location in the file system or registry and that operation fails because access is denied, Windows redirects the operation to a per-user area. When the application reads from a system-global location, Windows first checks for data in the per-user area and, if none is found, permits the read attempt from the global location.

Windows will always enable this type of virtualization unless:

- **The application is 64-bit** Because virtualization is purely an application-compatibility technology meant to help legacy applications, it is enabled only for 32-bit applications. The world of 64-bit applications is relatively new and developers should follow the development guidelines for creating standard user-compatible applications.

- **The application is already running with administrative rights** In this case, there is no need for any virtualization.

- **The operation came from a kernel-mode caller**

- **The operation is being performed while the caller is impersonating** For example, any operations not originating from a process classified as legacy according to this definition, including network file-sharing accesses, are not virtualized.

- **The executable image for the process has a UAC-compatible manifest** Specifying a `requestedExecutionLevel` setting, described in the next section.

- **The administrator does not have write access to the file or registry key** This exception exists to enforce backward compatibility because the legacy application would have failed before UAC was implemented even if the application was run with administrative rights.

- **Services are never virtualized**

You can see the virtualization status (the process virtualization status is stored as a flag in its token) of a process by adding the UAC Virtualization column to Task Manager's Details page, as shown in Figure 7-22. Most Windows components—including the Desktop Window Manager (Dwm.exe), the Client Server Run-Time Subsystem (Csrss.exe), and Explorer—have virtualization disabled because they have a UAC-compatible manifest or are running with administrative rights and so do not allow virtualization. However, 32-bit Internet Explorer (iexplore.exe) has virtualization enabled because it can host multiple ActiveX controls and scripts and must assume that they were not written to operate correctly with standard user rights. Note that, if required, virtualization can be completely disabled for a system using a Local Security Policy setting.

In addition to file system and registry virtualization, some applications require additional help to run correctly with standard user rights. For example, an application that tests the account in which it's running for membership in the Administrators group might otherwise work, but it won't run if it's not in that group. Windows defines a number of application-compatibility shims to enable such applications to work anyway. The shims most commonly applied to legacy applications for operation with standard user rights are shown in Table 7-15.

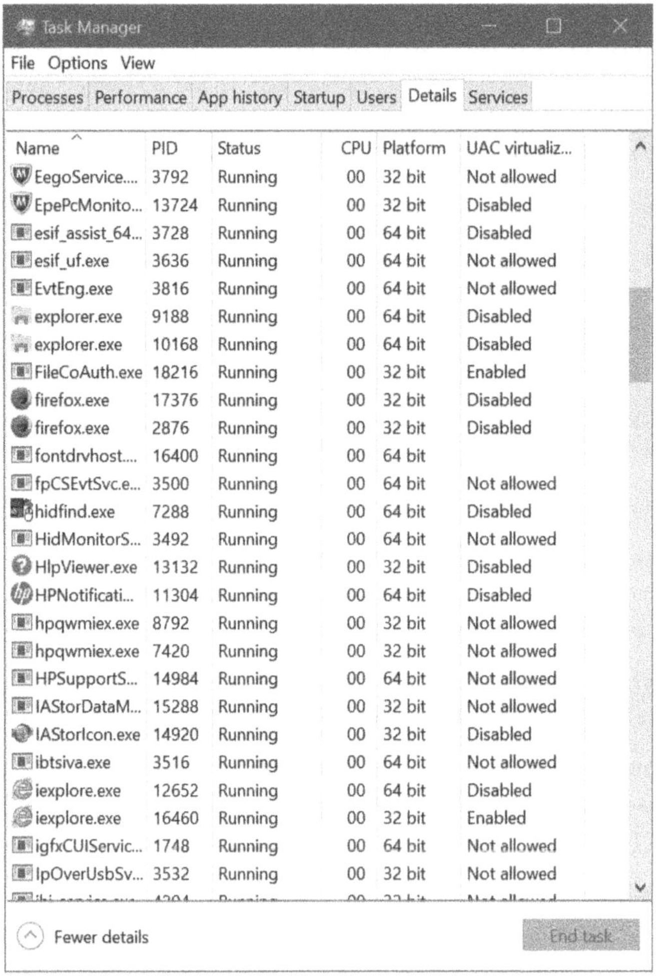

FIGURE 7-22 Using Task Manager to view virtualization status.

TABLE 7-15 UAC virtualization shims

Flag	Meaning
ElevateCreateProcess	This changes CreateProcess to handle ERROR_ELEVATION_REQUIRED errors by calling the application information service to prompt for elevation.
ForceAdminAccess	This spoofs queries of Administrator group membership.
VirtualizeDeleteFile	This spoofs successful deletion of global files and directories.
LocalMappedObject	This forces global section objects into the user's namespace.
VirtualizeHKCRLite	This redirects global registration of COM objects to a per-user location.
VirtualizeRegisterTypeLib	This converts per-machine typelib registrations to per-user registrations.

File virtualization

The file system locations that are virtualized for legacy processes are %ProgramFiles%, %ProgramData%, and %SystemRoot%, excluding some specific subdirectories. However, any file with an executable extension—including .exe, .bat, .scr, .vbs, and others—is excluded from virtualization. This means that programs that update themselves from a standard user account fail instead of creating private versions of their executables that aren't visible to an administrator running a global updater.

> **Note** To add extensions to the exception list, enter them in the HKLM\System\Current-ControlSet\Services\Luafv\Parameters\ExcludedExtensionsAdd registry key and reboot. Use a multistring type to delimit multiple extensions, and do not include a leading dot in the extension name.

Modifications to virtualized directories by legacy processes are redirected to the user's virtual root directory, %LocalAppData%\VirtualStore. The Local component of the path highlights the fact that virtualized files don't roam with the rest of the profile when the account has a roaming profile.

The UAC File Virtualization filter driver (%SystemRoot%\System32\Drivers\Luafv.sys) implements file system virtualization. Because this is a file system filter driver, it sees all local file system operations, but it implements functionality only for operations from legacy processes. As shown in Figure 7-23, the filter driver changes the target file path for a legacy process that creates a file in a system-global location but does not for a non-virtualized process with standard user rights. Default permissions on the \Windows directory deny access to the application written with UAC support, but the legacy process acts as though the operation succeeds when it really created the file in a location fully accessible by the user.

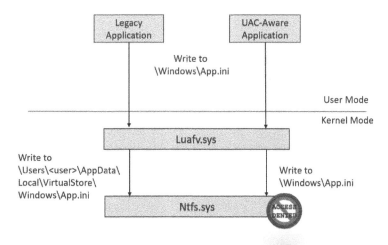

FIGURE 7-23 UAC File Virtualization filter driver operation.

EXPERIMENT: File virtualization behavior

In this experiment, you will enable and disable virtualization on the command prompt and see several behaviors to demonstrate UAC file virtualization:

1. Open a non-elevated command prompt (you must have UAC enabled for this to work) and enable virtualization for it. You can change the virtualization status of a process by right-clicking the process in the Task Manager Details tab and selecting **UAC Virtualization** from the shortcut menu that appears.

2. Navigate to the C:\Windows directory and use the following command to write a file:

   ```
   echo hello-1 > test.txt
   ```

3. List the contents of the directory. You'll see that the file appears.

   ```
   dir test.txt
   ```

4. Disable virtualization by right-clicking the process in the Task Manager Details tab and deselecting **UAC Virtualization**. Then list the directory as in step 3. Notice that the file is gone. However, a directory listing of the VirtualStore directory will reveal the file:

   ```
   dir %LOCALAPPDATA%\VirtualStore\Windows\test.txt
   ```

5. Enable virtualization again for this process.

6. To look at a more complex scenario, create a new command prompt window, but elevated this time. Then repeat steps 2 and 3 using the string `hello-2`.

7. Examine the text inside these files by using the following command in both command prompts. The screenshots that follow show the expected output.

   ```
   type test.txt
   ```

8. From your elevated command prompt, delete the test.txt file:

```
del test.txt
```

9. Repeat step 3 of the experiment in both windows. Notice that the elevated command prompt cannot find the file anymore, while the standard user command prompt shows the old contents of the file again. This demonstrates the failover mechanism described earlier: Read operations look in the per-user virtual store location first, but if the file doesn't exist, read access to the system location will be granted.

Registry virtualization

Registry virtualization is implemented slightly differently from file system virtualization. Virtualized registry keys include most of the HKEY_LOCAL_MACHINE\Software branch, but there are numerous exceptions, such as the following:

- HKLM\Software\Microsoft\Windows
- HKLM\Software\Microsoft\Windows NT
- HKLM\Software\Classes

Only keys that are commonly modified by legacy applications, but that don't introduce compatibility or interoperability problems, are virtualized. Windows redirects modifications of virtualized keys by a legacy application to a user's registry virtual root at HKEY_CURRENT_USER\Software\Classes\ VirtualStore. The key is located in the user's Classes hive, %LocalAppData%\Microsoft\Windows\ UsrClass.dat, which, like any other virtualized file data, does not roam with a roaming user profile. Instead of maintaining a fixed list of virtualized locations as Windows does for the file system, the virtualization status of a key is stored as a combination of flags, shown in Table 7-16.

You can use the Reg.exe utility included in Windows, with the flags option, to display the current virtualization state for a key or to set it. In Figure 7-24, note that the HKLM\Software key is fully virtualized, but the Windows subkey (and all its children) have only silent failure enabled.

TABLE 7-16 Registry virtualization flags

Flag	Meaning
REG_KEY_DONT_VIRTUALIZE	This specifies whether virtualization is enabled for this key. If the flag is set, virtualization is disabled.
REG_KEY_DONT_SILENT_FAIL	If the REG_KEY_DONT_VIRTUALIZE flag is set (virtualization is disabled), this key specifies that a legacy application that would be denied access performing an operation on the key is instead granted MAXIMUM_ALLOWED rights to the key (any access the account is granted) instead of the rights the application requested. If this flag is set, it implicitly disables virtualization as well.
REG_KEY_RECURSE_FLAG	This determines whether the virtualization flags will propagate to the child keys (subkeys) of this key.

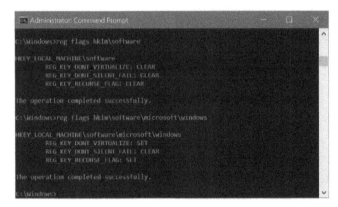

FIGURE 7-24 UAC registry virtualization flags on the Software and Windows keys.

Unlike file virtualization, which uses a filter driver, registry virtualization is implemented in the configuration manager. (See Chapter 9 in Part 2 for more information on the registry and the configuration manager.) As with file system virtualization, a legacy process creating a subkey of a virtualized key is redirected to the user's registry virtual root, but a UAC-compatible process is denied access by default permissions. This is shown in Figure 7-25.

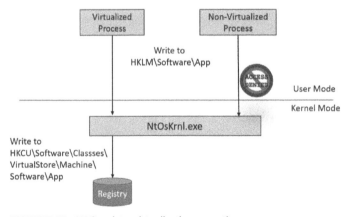

FIGURE 7-25 UAC registry virtualization operation.

Elevation

Even if users run only programs that are compatible with standard user rights, some operations still require administrative rights. For example, the vast majority of software installations require administrative rights to create directories and registry keys in system-global locations or to install services or device drivers. Modifying system-global Windows and application settings also requires administrative rights, as does the parental controls feature. It would be possible to perform most of these operations by switching to a dedicated administrator account, but the inconvenience of doing so would likely result in most users remaining in the administrator account to perform their daily tasks, most of which do not require administrative rights.

It's important to be aware that UAC elevations are conveniences and not security boundaries. A security boundary requires that security policy dictate what can pass through the boundary. User accounts are an example of a security boundary in Windows because one user can't access the data belonging to another user without having that user's permission.

Because elevations aren't security boundaries, there's no guarantee that malware running on a system with standard user rights can't compromise an elevated process to gain administrative rights. For example, elevation dialog boxes only identify the executable that will be elevated; they say nothing about what it will do when it executes.

Running with administrative rights

Windows includes enhanced "run as" functionality so that standard users can conveniently launch processes with administrative rights. This functionality requires giving applications a way to identify operations for which the system can obtain administrative rights on behalf of the application, as necessary (we'll say more on this topic shortly).

To enable users acting as system administrators to run with standard user rights but not have to enter user names and passwords every time they want to access administrative rights, Windows makes use of a mechanism called *Admin Approval Mode* (*AAM*). This feature creates two identities for the user at logon: one with standard user rights and another with administrative rights. Since every user on a Windows system is either a standard user or acting for the most part as a standard user in AAM, developers must assume that all Windows users are standard users, which will result in more programs working with standard user rights without virtualization or shims.

Granting administrative rights to a process is called *elevation*. When elevation is performed by a standard user account (or by a user who is part of an administrative group but not the actual Administrators group), it's referred to as an *over-the-shoulder* (*OTS*) *elevation* because it requires the entry of credentials for an account that's a member of the Administrators group, something that's usually completed by a privileged user typing over the shoulder of a standard user. An elevation performed by an AAM user is called a *consent elevation* because the user simply has to approve the assignment of his administrative rights.

Stand-alone systems, which are typically home computers, and domain-joined systems treat AAM access by remote users differently because domain-connected computers can use domain administrative groups in their resource permissions. When a user accesses a stand-alone computer's file share,

Windows requests the remote user's standard user identity. But on domain-joined systems, Windows honors all the user's domain group memberships by requesting the user's administrative identity. Executing an image that requests administrative rights causes the application information service (AIS, contained in %SystemRoot%\System32\Appinfo.dll), which runs inside a standard service host process (SvcHost.exe), to launch %SystemRoot%\System32\Consent.exe. Consent captures a bitmap of the screen, applies a fade effect to it, switches to a desktop that's accessible only to the local system account (the Secure Desktop), paints the bitmap as the background, and displays an elevation dialog box that contains information about the executable. Displaying this dialog box on a separate desktop prevents any application present in the user's account from modifying the appearance of the dialog box.

If an image is a Windows component digitally signed (by Microsoft or another entity), the dialog box displays a light blue stripe across the top, as shown at the left of Figure 7-26 (the distinction between Microsoft signed images and other signers has been removed in Windows 10). If the image is unsigned, the stripe becomes yellow, and the prompt stresses the unknown origin of the image (see the right of Figure 7-26). The elevation dialog box shows the image's icon, description, and publisher for digitally signed images, but it shows only the file name and "Publisher: Unknown" for unsigned images. This difference makes it harder for malware to mimic the appearance of legitimate software. The Show More Details link at the bottom of the dialog box expands it to show the command line that will be passed to the executable if it launches.

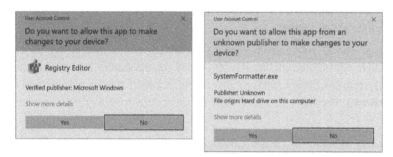

FIGURE 7-26 AAC UAC elevation dialog boxes based on image signature.

The OTS consent dialog box, shown in Figure 7-27, is similar, but prompts for administrator credentials. It will list any accounts with administrator rights.

FIGURE 7-27 OTS consent dialog box.

If a user declines an elevation, Windows returns an access-denied error to the process that initiated the launch. When a user agrees to an elevation by either entering administrator credentials or clicking Yes, AIS calls `CreateProcessAsUser` to launch the process with the appropriate administrative identity. Although AIS is technically the parent of the elevated process, AIS uses new support in the `CreateProcessAsUser` API that sets the process's parent process ID to that of the process that originally launched it. That's why elevated processes don't appear as children of the AIS service-hosting process in tools such as Process Explorer that show process trees. Figure 7-28 shows the operations involved in launching an elevated process from a standard user account.

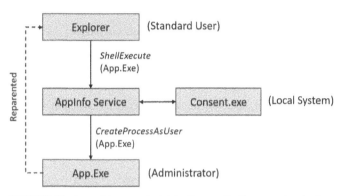

FIGURE 7-28 Launching an administrative application as a standard user.

Requesting administrative rights

There are a number of ways the system and applications identify a need for administrative rights. One that shows up in the Explorer user interface is the Run as Administrator context menu command and shortcut option. These items also include a blue and gold shield icon that should be placed next to any button or menu item that will result in an elevation of rights when it is selected. Choosing the Run as Administrator command causes Explorer to call the `ShellExecute` API with the `runas` verb.

The vast majority of installation programs require administrative rights, so the image loader, which initiates the launch of an executable, includes installer-detection code to identify likely legacy installers. Some of the heuristics it uses are as simple as detecting internal version information or whether the image has the words *setup*, *install*, or *update* in its file name. More sophisticated means of detection involve scanning for byte sequences in the executable that are common to third-party installation wrapper utilities. The image loader also calls the application-compatibility library to see if the target executable requires administrator rights. The library looks in the application-compatibility database to see whether the executable has the `RequireAdministrator` or `RunAsInvoker` compatibility flag associated with it.

The most common way for an executable to request administrative rights is for it to include a `requestedExecutionLevel` tag in its application manifest file. The element's level attribute can have one of the three values shown in Table 7-17.

TABLE 7-17 Requested elevation levels

Elevation Level	Meaning	Usage
As invoker	No need for administrative rights; never ask for elevation.	Typical user applications that don't need administrative privileges—for example, Notepad.
Highest available	Request approval for highest rights available. If the user is logged on as a standard user, the process will be launched as invoker; otherwise, an AAM elevation prompt will appear, and the process will run with full administrative rights.	Applications that can function without full administrative rights but expect users to want full access if it's easily accessible. For example, the Registry Editor, Microsoft Management Console, and the Event Viewer use this level.
Require administrator	Always request administrative rights. An OTS elevation dialog box prompt will be shown for standard users; otherwise, AAM.	Applications that require administrative rights to work, such as the Firewall Settings Editor, which affects system-wide security.

The presence of the `trustInfo` element in a manifest (which you can see in the manifest dump of eventvwr.exe) denotes an executable that was written with support for UAC and the `requestedExecutionLevel` element nests within it. The `uiAccess` attribute is where accessibility applications can use the UIPI bypass functionality mentioned earlier.

```
C:\>sigcheck -m c:\Windows\System32\eventvwr.exe
...
<trustInfo xmlns="urn:schemas-microsoft-com:asm.v3">
    <security>
        <requestedPrivileges>
            <requestedExecutionLevel
                level="highestAvailable"
                uiAccess="false"
            />
        </requestedPrivileges>
    </security>
</trustInfo>
<asmv3:application>
    <asmv3:windowsSettings xmlns="http://schemas.microsoft.com/SMI/2005/WindowsSettings">
        <autoElevate>true</autoElevate>
    </asmv3:windowsSettings>
</asmv3:application>
...
```

Auto-elevation

In the default configuration (see the next section for information on changing this), most Windows executables and control panel applets do not result in elevation prompts for administrative users, even if they need administrative rights to run. This is because of a mechanism called *auto-elevation*. Auto-elevation is intended to preclude administrative users from seeing elevation prompts for most of their work; the programs will automatically run under the user's full administrative token.

Auto-elevation has several requirements. One is that the executable in question must be considered as a Windows executable. This means it must be signed by the Windows publisher (not just by Microsoft; oddly, they are not the same—Windows-signed is considered more privileged than Microsoft-signed). It must also be in one of several directories considered secure: %SystemRoot%\

System32 and most of its subdirectories, %Systemroot%\Ehome, and a small number of directories under %ProgramFiles% (for example, those containing Windows Defender and Windows Journal).

There are additional requirements, depending on the type of executable. EXE files other than Mmc.exe auto-elevate if they are requested via an `autoElevate` element in their manifest. The manifest shown earlier of eventvwr.exe in the previous section illustrates this.

Mmc.exe is treated as a special case because whether it should auto-elevate or not depends on which system management snap-ins it is to load. Mmc.exe is normally invoked with a command line specifying an MSC file, which in turn specifies which snap-ins are to be loaded. When Mmc.exe is run from a protected administrator account (one running with the limited administrator token), it asks Windows for administrative rights. Windows validates that Mmc.exe is a Windows executable and then checks the MSC. The MSC must also pass the tests for a Windows executable, and furthermore must be on an internal list of auto-elevate MSCs. This list includes nearly all MSC files in Windows.

Finally, COM (out-of-process server) classes can request administrative rights within their registry key. To do so requires a subkey named `Elevation` with a DWORD value named `Enabled`, having a value of 1. Both the COM class and its instantiating executable must meet the Windows executable requirements, although the executable need not have requested auto-elevation.

Controlling UAC behavior

UAC can be modified via the dialog box shown in Figure 7-29. This dialog box is available under Change User Account Control Settings. Figure 7-29 shows the control in its default position.

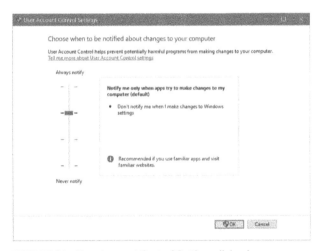

FIGURE 7-29 User Account Control Settings dialog box.

The four possible settings have the effects described in Table 7-18.

The third position is not recommended because the UAC elevation prompt appears not on the Secure Desktop but on the normal user's desktop. This could allow a malicious program running in the same session to change the appearance of the prompt. It is intended for use only in systems where the video subsystem takes a long time to dim the desktop or is otherwise unsuitable for the usual UAC display.

TABLE 7-18   UAC options

Slider Position	When administrative user not running with administrative rights...		Remarks
	...attempts to change Windows settings (for example, use certain Control Panel applets)	...attempts to install software or run a program whose manifest calls for elevation, or uses Run as Administrator	
Highest position (Always Notify)	A UAC elevation prompt appears on the Secure Desktop.	A UAC elevation prompt appears on the Secure Desktop.	This was the Windows Vista behavior.
Second position	UAC elevation occurs automatically with no prompt or notification.	A UAC elevation prompt appears on the Secure Desktop.	Windows default setting.
Third position	UAC elevation occurs automatically with no prompt or notification.	A UAC elevation prompt appears on the user's normal desktop.	Not recommended.
Lowest position (Never Notify)	UAC is turned off for administrative users.	UAC is turned off for administrative users.	Not recommended.

The lowest position is strongly discouraged because it turns UAC off completely as far as administrative accounts are concerned. All processes run by a user with an administrative account will be run with the user's full administrative rights in effect; there is no filtered admin token. Registry and file system virtualization are disabled as well for these accounts, and the Protected mode of Internet Explorer is disabled. However, virtualization is still in effect for non-administrative accounts, and non-administrative accounts will still see an OTS elevation prompt when they attempt to change Windows settings, run a program that requires elevation, or use the Run as Administrator context menu option in Explorer.

The UAC setting is stored in four values in the registry under HKLM\SOFTWARE\Microsoft\Windows\CurrentVersion\Policies\System, as shown in Table 7-19. ConsentPromptBehaviorAdmin controls the UAC elevation prompt for administrators running with a filtered admin token, and ConsentPromptBehaviorUser controls the UAC prompt for users other than administrators.

TABLE 7-19   UAC registry values

Slider Position	ConsentPrompt BehaviorAdmin	ConsentPrompt BehaviorUser	EnableLUA	PromptOnSecureDesktop
Highest position (Always Notify)	2 (display AAC UAC elevation prompt)	3 (display OTS UAC elevation prompt)	1 (enabled)	1 (enabled)
Second position	5 (display AAC UAC elevation prompt, except for changes to Windows settings)	3	1	1
Third position	5	3	1	0 (disabled; UAC prompt appears on user's normal desktop)
Lowest position (Never Notify)	0	3	0 (disabled; logins to administrative accounts do not create a restricted admin access token)	0

Exploit mitigations

Throughout this chapter, we've seen a number of technologies that help protect the user, guarantee the code-signing properties of executable code, and lock down access to resources through sandboxing. At the end of the day, however, all secure systems have failure points, all code has bugs, and attackers leverage increasingly complex attacks to exploit them. A security model in which all code is assumed to be bug-free, or in which a software developer assumes all bugs will eventually be found and fixed, is destined to fail. Additionally, many security features that provide code-execution "guarantees" do so at a cost of performance or compatibility, which may be unacceptable in such scenarios.

A much more successful approach is to identify the most common techniques used by attackers, as well as employ an internal "red team" (that is, an internal team attacking its own software) to discover new techniques before attackers do and to implement mitigations against such techniques. (These mitigations can be as simple as moving some data around or as complex as employing Control Flow Integrity [CFI] techniques.) Because vulnerabilities can number in the thousands in a complex code base such as Windows, but exploit techniques are limited, the idea is to make large classes of bugs very difficult (or in some cases, impossible) to exploit, without worrying about finding all the bugs.

Process-mitigation policies

While individual applications can implement various exploit mitigations on their own (such as Microsoft Edge, which leverages a mitigation called *MemGC* to avoid many classes of memory-corruption attacks), this section will cover mitigations that are provided by the operating system to all applications or to the system itself to reduce exploitable bug classes. Table 7-20 describes all mitigations in the latest version of Windows 10 Creators Update, the type of bug class they mitigate against, and mechanisms to activate them.

TABLE 7-20   Process mitigation options

Mitigation Name	Use Case	Enabling Mechanism
ASLR Bottom Up Randomization	This makes calls to `VirtualAlloc` subject to ASLR with 8-bit entropy, including stack-base randomization.	This is set with the PROCESS_ CREATION_MITIGATION_POLICY_ BOTTOM_UP_ASLR_ALWAYS_ON process-creation attribute flag.
ASLR Force Relocate Images	This forces ASLR even on binaries that do not have the /DYNAMICBASE linker flag.	This is set with `SetProcessMitigationPolicy` or the PROCESS_CREATION_ MITIGATION_POLICY_FORCE_ RELOCATE_IMAGES_ALWAYS_ON process-creation flag.
High Entropy ASLR (HEASLR)	This significantly increases entropy of ASLR on 64-bit images, increasing bottom-up randomization to up to 1 TB of variance (that is, bottom-up allocations may start anywhere between 64 KB and 1 TB into the address space, giving 24 bits of entropy).	Must be set through /HIGHENTROPYVA at link time or the PROCESS_CREATION_MITIGATION_ POLICY_HIGH_ENTROPY_ASLR_ ALWAYS_ON process-creation attribute flag.

TABLE 7-20 Process mitigation options *(continued)*

Mitigation Name	Use Case	Enabling Mechanism
ASLR Disallow Stripped Images	This blocks the load of any library without relocations (linked with the /FIXED flag) when combined with ASLR Force Relocate Images.	This is set with `SetProcessMitigationPolicy` or with the `PROCESS_CREATION_MITIGATION_POLICY_FORCE_RELOCATE_IMAGES_ALWAYS_ON_REQ_RELOCS` process-creation flag.
DEP: Permanent	This prevents the process from disabling DEP on itself. Only relevant on x86. Only relevant on 32-bit applications (and/or under WoW64)	This is set with the `SetProcessMitigationPolicy`, process-creation attribute or with `SetProcessDEPPolicy`.
DEP: Disable ATL Thunk Emulation	This prevents legacy ATL library code from executing ATL thunks in the heap, even if a known compatibility issue. Only relevant on 32-bit applications (and/or under WoW64)	This is set with the `SetProcessMitigationPolicy`, process-creation attribute or with `SetProcessDEPPolicy`.
SEH Overwrite Protection (SEHOP)	This prevents structure exception handlers from being overwritten with incorrect ones, even if the image was not linked with Safe SEH (/SAFESEH). Only relevant on 32-bit applications (and/or under WoW64).	This can be set with `SetProcessDEPPolicy` or with the `PROCESS_CREATION_MITIGATION_POLICY_SEHOP_ENABLE` process-creation flag.
Raise Exception on Invalid Handle	This helps catch handle reuse (use-after-handle-close) attacks in which a process uses a handle that is no longer the handle it expected (for example: `SetEvent` on a mutex) by crashing the process instead of returning a failure that the process might ignore.	This is set with `SetProcessMitigationPolicy` or the `PROCESS_CREATION_MITIGATION_POLICY_STRICT_HANDLE_CHECKS_ALWAYS_ON` process-creation attribute flag.
Raise Exception on Invalid Handle Close	This helps catch handle reuse (double-handle-close) attacks in which a process is attempting to close a handle that has already been closed, suggesting that a different handle may potentially be used in other scenarios, in which an exploit would be successful, ultimately limiting its universal effectiveness.	Undocumented, and can only be set through an undocumented API.
Disallow Win32k System Calls	This disables all access to the Win32 kernel-mode subsystem driver, which implements the Window Manager (GUI) and Graphics Device Interface (GDI) and DirectX. No system calls to this component will be possible.	This is set with `SetProcessMitigationPolicy` or the `PROCESS_CREATION_MITIGATION_POLICY_WIN32K_SYSTEM_CALL_DISABLE_ALWAYS_ON` process-creation attribute flag.
Filter Win32k System Calls	This filters access to the Win32k kernel-mode subsystem driver only to certain APIs allowing simple GUI and Direct X access, mitigating many of the possible attacks, without completely disabling availability of the GUI/GDI services.	This is set through an internal process-creation attribute flag, which can define one out of three possible sets of Win32k filters that are enabled. However, because the filter sets are hard-coded, this mitigation is reserved for Microsoft internal usage.

TABLE 7-20 Process mitigation options *(continued)*

Mitigation Name	Use Case	Enabling Mechanism
Disable Extension Points	This prevents a process from loading an input method editor (IME), a Windows hook DLL (`SetWindowsHookEx`), an app-initialization DLL (`AppInitDlls` value in the registry), or a Winsock layered service provider (LSP).	This is set with `SetProcessMitigationPolicy` or the `PROCESS_CREATION_MITIGATION_POLICY_EXTENSION_POINT_DISABLE_ALWAYS_ON` process-creation attribute flag.
Arbitrary Code Guard (CFG)	This prevents a process from allocating executable code or from changing the permission of existing executable code to make it writeable. It can be configured to allow a particular thread inside the process to request this capability or to allow a remote process from disabling this mitigation, which are not supported from a security point of view.	This is set with `SetProcessMitigationPolicy` or the `PROCESS_CREATION_MITIGATION_POLICY_PROHIBIT_DYNAMIC_CODE_ALWAYS_ON` and `PROCESS_CREATION_MITIGATION_POLICY_PROHIBIT_DYNAMIC_CODE_ALWAYS_ON_ALLOW_OPT_OUT` process-creation attribute flags.
Control Flow Guard (CFG)	This helps prevent memory corruption vulnerabilities from being used to hijack control flow by validating the target of any indirect CALL or JMP instruction against a list of valid expected target functions. Part of Control Flow Integrity (CFI) mechanisms described in the next section.	The image must be compiled with the `/guard:cf` option, and linked with the `/guard:cf` option. It can be set with the `PROCESS_CREATION_MITIGATION_POLICY_CONTROL_FLOW_GUARD_ALWAYS_ON` process-creation attribute flag in case the image does not support it, but CFG enforcement is still desirable for other images loading in the process.
CFG Export Suppression	This strengthens CFG by suppressing indirect calls to the exported API table of the image.	The image must be compiled with `/guard: exportsuppress`, and can also be configured through `SetProcessMitigationPolicy` or with the `PROCESS_CREATION_MITIGATION_POLICY_CONTROL_FLOW_GUARD_EXPORT_SUPPRESSION` process-creation attribute flag.
CFG Strict Mode	This prevents the loading of any image library within the current process that was not linked with the `/guard:cf` option.	This is set through `SetProcessMitigationPolicy` or with the `PROCESS_CREATION_MITIGATION_POLICY2_STRICT_CONTROL_FLOW_GUARD_ALWAYS_ON` process-creation attribute flag.
Disable Non System Fonts	This prevents the loading of any font files that have not been registered by Winlogon at user logon time, after being installed in the C:\windows\fonts directory.	This is set through `SetProcessMitigationPolicy` or the `PROCESS_CREATION_MITIGATION_POLICY_FONT_DISABLE_ALWAYS_ON` process-creation attribute flag.
Microsoft-Signed Binaries Only	This prevents the loading of any image library within the current process that has not been signed by a Microsoft CA—issued certificate.	This is set through the `PROCESS_CREATION_MITIGATION_POLICY_BLOCK_NON_MICROSOFT_BINARIES_ALWAYS_ON` process-attribute flag at startup time.

TABLE 7-20 Process mitigation options *(continued)*

Mitigation Name	Use Case	Enabling Mechanism
Store-Signed Binaries Only	This prevents the loading of any image library within the current process that has not been signed by the Microsoft Store CA.	This is set through the `PROCESS_CREATION_MITIGATION_POLICY_BLOCK_NON_MICROSOFT_BINARIES_ALLOW_STORE` process attribute flag at startup time.
No Remote Images	This prevents the loading of any image library within the current process that is present on a non-local (UNC or WebDAV) path.	This is set through `SetProcessMitigationPolicy` or the `PROCESS_CREATION_MITIGATION_POLICY_IMAGE_LOAD_NO_REMOTE_ALWAYS_ON` process-creation attribute flag.
No Low IL Images	This prevents the loading of any image library within the current process that has a mandatory label below medium (0x2000).	This is set through `SetProcessMitigationPolicy` or the `PROCESS_CREATION_MITIGATION_POLICY_IMAGE_LOAD_NO_LOW_LABEL_ALWAYS_ON` process-creation flag. It can also be set through a resource claim ACE called `IMAGELOAD` on the file of the process being loaded.
Prefer System32 Images	This modifies the loader's search path to always look for the given image library being loaded (through a relative name) in the %SystemRoot%\System32 directory, regardless of the current search path.	This is set through `SetProcessMitigationPolicy` or the `PROCESS_CREATION_MITIGATION_POLICY_IMAGE_LOAD_PREFER_SYSTEM32_ALWAYS_ON` process-creation attribute flag.
Return Flow Guard (RFG)	This helps prevent additional classes of memory-corruption vulnerabilities that affect control flow by validating, before the execution of a RET instruction, that the function was not called through a return-oriented programming (ROP) exploit by not having begun its execution correctly or by executing on an invalid stack. This is part of the Control Flow Integrity (CFI) mechanisms.	Currently still being implemented in a robust and performant way, this mitigation is not yet available, but is included here for completeness.
Restrict Set Thread Context	This restricts the modification of the current thread's context.	Currently disabled pending the availability of RFG, which makes the mitigation more robust, this mitigation may appear in a future version of Windows. It is included here for completeness.
Loader Continuity	This prohibits the process from dynamically loading any DLLs that do not have the same integrity level as the process, in cases where a signature policy mitigation above could not be enabled at startup time due to compatibility concerns. This specifically targets cases of DLL planting attacks.	This is set through `SetProcessMitigationPolicy` or the `PROCESS_CREATION_MITIGATION_POLICY2_LOADER_INTEGRITY_CONTINUITY_ALWAYS_ON` process-creation attribute flag.

TABLE 7-20 Process mitigation options *(continued)*

Mitigation Name	Use Case	Enabling Mechanism
Heap Terminate On Corruption	This disables the Fault Tolerant Heap (FTH) and the raising of a continuable exception in the case of heap corruption by terminating the process instead. This prevents the use of heap corruption as a way to force an attacker-controlled exception handler from executing, or in cases where the program ignores the heap exception, or cases where the exploit only sometimes causes heap corruption (limiting its universal effectiveness or reliability).	This is set through `HeapSetInformation` or by using the `PROCESS_CREATION_MITIGATION_POLICY_HEAP_TERMINATE_ALWAYS_ON` process-creation attribute flag.
Disable Child Process Creation	This prohibits the creation of child processes by marking the token with a special restriction, which should stop any other component from creating a process while impersonating the token of this process (for example, WMI process creation, or a kernel component creating the process).	This is set through the `PROCESS_CREATION_CHILD_PROCESS_RESTRICTED` process-creation attribute flag. It can be overridden to allow packaged (UWP) applications with the `PROCESS_CREATION_DESKTOP_APPX_OVERRIDE` flag.
All Application Packages Policy	This makes an application running under an AppContainer unable to access resources that have an ALL APPLICATION PACKAGES SID present, as was explained earlier in the "AppContainers" section. The presence of an ALL RESTRICTED APPLICATION PACKAGES SID will be required instead. Sometimes referred to as Less Privileged App Container (LPAC).	This is set through the `PROC_THREAD_ATTRIBUTE_ALL_APPLICATION_PACKAGES_POLICY` process-creation attribute.

Note that it is also possible to some of these mitigations on a per-application or per-system basis without the cooperation of the application developer. To do so, open the Local Group Policy Editor. Then expand **Computer Configuration**, then **Administrative Templates**, then **System**, and finally **Mitigation Options** (see Figure 7-30). In the Process Mitigation Options dialog box, enter the appropriate bit-number value that corresponds to the mitigations being enabled, using **1** to enable a mitigation, **0** to disable it, or **?** to leave it to its default or process-requested value (again, see Figure 7-30). The bit numbers are taken from the `PROCESS_MITIGATION_POLICY` enumeration found in the Winnt.h header file. This will result in the appropriate registry value being written in the Image File Execution Options (IFEO) key for the entered image name. Unfortunately the current version of Windows 10 Creators Update and earlier will strip out many of the newer mitigations. You can avoid this by manually setting the `REG_DWORD` `MitigationOptions` registry value.

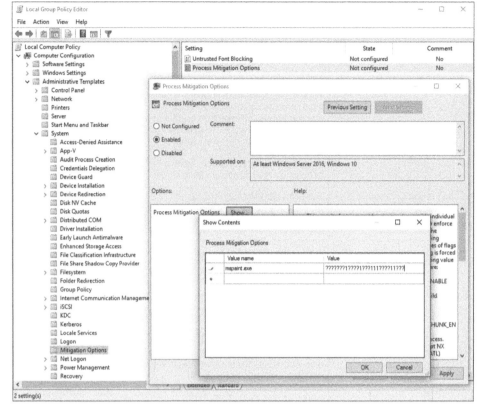

FIGURE 7-30 Customizing process-mitigation options.

Control Flow Integrity

Data Execution Prevention (DEP) and Arbitrary Code Guard (ACG) make it hard for exploits to place executable code on the heap or stack, to allocate new executable code, or to change existing executable code. As a result, memory/data-only attacks have become more interesting. Such attacks allow the modification of portions of memory to redirect control flow, such as modifying return addresses on the stack or indirect function pointers stored in memory. Techniques such as return-oriented-programming (ROP) and jump-oriented-programming (JOP) are often used to violate the regular code flow of the program and redirect it to known locations of interesting code snippets ("gadgets").

Because such snippets are often present in the middle or end of various functions, when control flow is redirected in this way, it must be redirected into the middle or end of a legitimate function. By employing Control Flow Integrity (CFI) technologies—which can, for example, validate that the target of an indirect JMP or CALL instruction is the beginning of a real function, or that a RET instruction is pointing to an expected location, or that a RET instruction is issued after the function was entered through its beginning—the operating system and compiler can detect and prevent most classes of such exploits.

Control Flow Guard

Control Flow Guard (CFG) is an exploit-mitigation mechanism first introduced in Windows 8.1 Update 3 that exists in enhanced version in Windows 10 and Server 2016, with further improvements released on various updates (up to and including the latest Creators Update). Originally implemented only for user-mode code, CFG now also exists as Kernel CFG (KCFG) on the Creators Update. CFG addresses the indirect CALL/JMP part of CFI by verifying that the target of an indirect call is at the start of a known function (more on that momentarily). If the target is not at the start of a known function, the process is simply terminated. Figure 7-31 shows the conceptual operation of CFG.

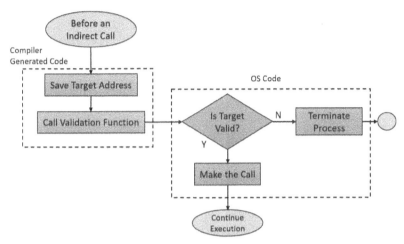

FIGURE 7-31 Conceptual view of Control Flow Guard.

CFG requires the cooperation of a supported compiler that will add the call to the validation code before indirect changes in control flow. The Visual C++ compiler has an option, /guard:cf, that must be set for images (or even on a C/C++ source file level) to be built with CFG support (this option is also available in Visual Studio's GUI in the C/C++/Code Generation/Control Flow Guard setting in the project's properties). This setting should also be set in the linker settings, as both components of Visual Studio are required to collaborate to support CFG.

Once those settings are present, images (EXEs and DLLs) that are compiled with CFG-enabled indicate this in their PE header. In addition, they contain a list of functions that are the valid indirect control flow targets in a .gfids PE section (by default merged by the linker with the .rdata section). This list is built by the linker and contains the relative virtual address (RVA) of all functions in the image. This includes those that might not be called by an indirect call by the code present in the image because there's no way of knowing if outside code does not somehow legitimately know the address of a function and is attempting to call it. This can be especially true of exported functions, which can be called after obtaining their pointer through GetProcAddress.

That being said, programmers can use a technique called *CFG suppression*, which is supported through the DECLSPEC_GUARD_SUPRESS annotation, and which marks the function in the table of valid functions with a special flag indicating that the programmer never expects such a function to be the target of any indirect call or jump.

Now that a table of valid function targets exists, all that a simple validation function would need to do is to compare the target of the CALL or JMP instruction with one of the functions in the table. Algorithmically, this would result in an O(n) algorithm, where the number of functions needed to check would be equivalent, in the worst case, to the number of functions in the table. Clearly, linearly scanning an entire array during every single indirect change in control flow would bring a program to its knees, so operating system support is needed to perform CFG checks efficiently. We'll see in the next section how Windows can achieve this.

EXPERIMENT: Control Flow Guard information

The DumpBin Visual Studio tool can show some basic CFG information. The following dumps header and loader configuration information for Smss:

```
c:\> dumpbin /headers /loadconfig c:\windows\system32\smss.exe
Microsoft (R) COFF/PE Dumper Version 14.00.24215.1
Copyright (C) Microsoft Corporation.  All rights reserved.
Dump of file c:\windows\system32\smss.exe
PE signature found
File Type: EXECUTABLE IMAGE
FILE HEADER VALUES
            8664 machine (x64)
               6 number of sections
        57899A7D time date stamp Sat Jul 16 05:22:53 2016
               0 file pointer to symbol table
               0 number of symbols
              F0 size of optional header
              22 characteristics
                   Executable
                   Application can handle large (>2GB) addresses


OPTIONAL HEADER VALUES
             20B magic # (PE32+)
           14.00 linker version
           12800 size of code
            EC00 size of initialized data
               0 size of uninitialized data
            1080 entry point (0000000140001080) NtProcessStartupW
            1000 base of code
       140000000 image base (0000000140000000 to 0000000140024FFF)
            1000 section alignment
             200 file alignment
           10.00 operating system version
           10.00 image version
           10.00 subsystem version
               0 Win32 version
           25000 size of image
             400 size of headers
           270FD checksum
               1 subsystem (Native)
            4160 DLL characteristics
```

```
                    High Entropy Virtual Addresses
                    Dynamic base
                    NX compatible
                    Control Flow Guard
...
Section contains the following load config:

            000000D0 size
                   0 time date stamp
                0.00 Version
                   0 GlobalFlags Clear
                   0 GlobalFlags Set
                   0 Critical Section Default Timeout
                   0 Decommit Free Block Threshold
                   0 Decommit Total Free Threshold
    0000000000000000 Lock Prefix Table
                   0 Maximum Allocation Size
                   0 Virtual Memory Threshold
                   0 Process Heap Flags
                   0 Process Affinity Mask
                   0 CSD Version
                0800 Dependent Load Flag
    0000000000000000 Edit List
    0000000140020660 Security Cookie
    00000001400151C0 Guard CF address of check-function pointer
    00000001400151C8 Guard CF address of dispatch-function pointer
    00000001400151D0 Guard CF function table
                  2A Guard CF function count
            00010500 Guard Flags
                     CF Instrumented
                     FID table present
                     Long jump target table present
                0000 Code Integrity Flags
                0000 Code Integrity Catalog
            00000000 Code Integrity Catalog Offset
            00000000 Code Integrity Reserved
    0000000000000000 Guard CF address taken IAT entry table
                   0 Guard CF address taken IAT entry count
    0000000000000000 Guard CF long jump target table
                   0 Guard CF long jump target count
    0000000000000000 Dynamic value relocation table


Guard CF Function Table

        Address
        --------
        0000000140001010   _TlgEnableCallback
        0000000140001070   SmpSessionComplete
        0000000140001080   NtProcessStartupW
        0000000140001B30   SmscpLoadSubSystemsForMuSession
        0000000140001D10   SmscpExecuteInitialCommand
        0000000140002FB0   SmpExecPgm
```

```
0000000140003620    SmpStartCsr
00000001400039F0    SmpApiCallback
0000000140004E90    SmpStopCsr
```
...

The CFG-related information is marked in bold in the preceding output. We will discuss that shortly. For now, open Process Explorer, right-click the process column header, choose **Select Columns.** Then, in the Process Image tab, select the **Control Flow Guard** check box. Also select **Virtual Size** in the Process Memory tab. You should see something like this:

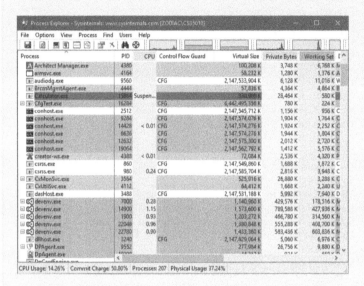

You should see most Microsoft-provided processes were built with CFG (including Smss, Csrss, Audiodg, Notepad, and many others). The virtual size for CFG-built processes is surprisingly high. Recall that the virtual size indicates the total address space used in the process, whether that memory is committed or reserved. In contrast, the Private Bytes column shows the private committed memory and is not even remotely close to the virtual size (although the virtual size includes non-private memory as well). For 64-bit processes, the virtual size is at least 2 TB, which we will shortly be able to rationalize.

The CFG bitmap

As you saw earlier, forcing the program to iterate through a list of function calls every few instructions would not be practical. Therefore, instead of an algorithm that requires linear time O(*n*), performance requirements dictate that an O(1) algorithm be used instead—one where a constant lookup time is used, regardless of how many functions are present in the table. This constant lookup time should be as small as possible. A clear winner of such a requirement would be an array that is indexable by the target function's address, which is an indication if this address is valid or not (such as a simple BOOL). With a 128 TB of possible addresses, though, such an array would itself have to be 128 TB * sizeof(BOOL), which is an unacceptable storage size—bigger than the address space itself. Can we do better?

First, we can leverage the fact that compilers ought to generate x64 function code on 16-byte boundaries. This reduces the size to the required array to only 8 TB * `sizeof(BOOL)`. But using an entire BOOL (which is 4 bytes in the worst case or 1 byte in the best) is extremely wasteful. We only need one state, valid or invalid, which only needs to use 1 bit. This makes the calculation 8 TB / 8, or simply 1 TB. Unfortunately, however, there's a snag. There's no guarantee that the compiler will generate *all* functions on a 16-byte binary. Hand-crafted assembly code and certain optimizations might violate this rule. As such, we'll have to figure out a solution. One possible option is to simply use another bit to indicate if the function begins *somewhere* on the next 15 bytes instead of on the 16-byte boundary itself. Thus, we have the following possibilities:

- **{0, 0}** No valid function begins inside this 16-byte boundary.

- **{1, 0}** A valid function begins exactly on this aligned 16-byte address.

- **{1, 1}** A valid function begins somewhere inside of this 16-byte address.

Thanks to this setup, if the attacker attempts to call inside a function that was marked as 16-byte aligned by the linker, the 2-bit state will be {1, 0}, while the required bits (that is, bits 3 and 4) in the address will be {1, 1} as the address won't be 16-byte aligned. Therefore, an attacker will only be able to call an arbitrary instruction in the first 16 bytes of the function if the linker did not generate the function aligned in the first place (bits would then be {1, 1}, as shown above). Even then, this instruction must somehow be useful to the attacker without crashing the function (typically some sort of stack pivot or gadget that ends in a `ret` instruction).

With this understanding in mind, we can apply the following formulas to compute the size of the CFG bitmap:

- **32-bit application on x86 or x64** 2 GB / 16 * 2 = 32 MB

- **32-bit application with /LARGEADDRESSAWARE, booted in 3 GB mode on x86** 3 GB / 16 * 2 = 48 MB

- **64-bit application** 128 TB / 16 * 2 = 2 TB

- **32-bit application with /LARGEADDRESSAWARE, on x64** 4 GB / 16 * 2 = 64 MB, plus the size of the 64-bit bitmap, which is needed to protect 64-bit Ntdll.dll and WoW64 components, so 2 TB + 64MB

Allocating and filling out 2 TB of bits on every single process execution is still a tough performance overhead to swallow. Even though we have fixed the execution cost of the indirect call itself, process startup cannot be allowed to take so long, and 2 TB of committed memory would exhaust the commit limit instantly. Therefore, two memory-saving and performance-helping tricks are used.

First, the memory manager will only reserve the bitmap, basing itself on the assumption that the CFG validation function will treat an exception during CFG bitmap access as an indication that the bit state is {0,0}. As such, as long as the region contains 4 KB of bit states that are all {0, 0}, it can be left as reserved, and only pages with at least one bit set {1, X} need to be committed.

Next, as described in the ASLR section of Chapter 5, "Memory management," the system performs the randomization/relocation of libraries typically only once at boot, as a performance-saving measure to avoid repeated relocations. As such, after a library that supports ASLR has been loaded once at a given address, it will always be loaded at that same address. This also therefore means that once the relevant bitmap states have been calculated for the functions in that library, they will be identical in all other processes that also load the same binary. As such, the memory manager treats the CFG bitmap as a region of pagefile-backed shareable memory, and the physical pages that correspond to the shared bits only exist in RAM once.

This reduces the cost of the committed pages in RAM and means that only the bits corresponding to private memory need to be calculated. In regular applications, private memory is not executable except in the copy-on-write case where someone has patched a library (but this will not happen at image load), so the cost of loading an application, if it shares the same libraries as other previously launched applications, is almost nil. The next experiment demonstrates this.

EXPERIMENT: Control Flow Guard bitmap

Open the VMMap tool and select a Notepad process. You should see a large reserved block in the Sharable section like so:

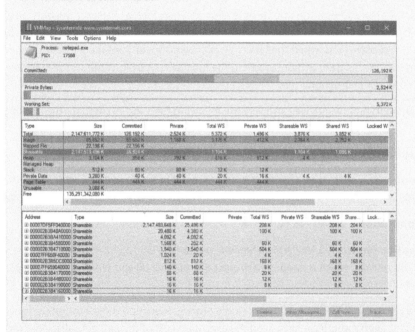

You can sort the lower pane by size and quickly locate the large chunk used for the CFGBitmap, as shown. Additionally, if you attach to the process and use the `!address` command on the process, you will see WinDBG identifying the CFG bitmap for you:

```
+       7df5'ff530000 7df6'0118a000 0'01c5a000    MEM_MAPPED MEM_RESERVE
Other   [CFG Bitmap]
        7df6'0118a000 7df6'011fb000 0'00071000    MEM_MAPPED MEM_COMMIT PAGE_NOACCESS
Other   [CFG Bitmap]
        7df6'011fb000 7ff5'df530000 1ff'de335000 MEM_MAPPED MEM_RESERVE
Other   [CFG Bitmap]
```

```
    7ff5'df530000 7ff5'df532000 0'00002000   MEM_MAPPED MEM_COMMIT PAGE_READONLY
Other  [CFG Bitmap]
```

Note how large regions are marked as MEM_RESERVE, in between regions that are MEM_COMMIT, representing that at least one valid bit state {1, X} is set. Also, all (or almost all) the regions will be MEM_MAPPED, since they belong to the shared bitmap.

CFG bitmap construction

Upon system initialization, the MiInitializeCfg function is called to initialize support for CFG. The function creates one or two section objects (MmCreateSection) as reserved memory with size appropriate for the platform, as shown earlier. For 32-bit platforms, one bitmap is enough. For x64 platforms, two bitmaps are required—one for 64-bit processes and the other for Wow64 processes (32-bit applications). The section objects' pointers are stored in a substructure within the MiState global variable.

After a process is created, the appropriate section is securely mapped into the process's address space. *Securely* here means that the section cannot be unmapped by code running within the process or have its protection changed. (Otherwise, malicious code could just unmap the memory, reallocate, and fill everything with 1 bits, effectively disabling CFG, or simply modify any bits by marking the region read/write.)

The user mode CFG bitmap(s) are populated in the following scenarios:

- During image mapping, images that have been dynamically relocated due to ASLR (see Chapter 5, for more on ASLR) will have their indirect call target metadata extracted. If an image does not have indirect call target metadata, meaning it was not compiled with CFG, it is assumed that every address within the image can be called indirectly. As explained, because dynamically relocated images are expected to load at the same address in every process, their metadata is used to populate the shared section that is used for the CFG bitmap.

- During image mapping, special care is needed for non-dynamically relocated images and images not being mapped at their preferred base. For these image mappings, the relevant pages of the CFG bitmap are made private and are populated using the CFG metadata from the image. For images whose CFG bits are present in the shared CFG bitmap, a check is made to ensure that all the relevant CFG bitmap pages are still shared. If this is not the case, the bits of the private CFG bitmap pages are populated using the CFG metadata from the image.

- When virtual memory is allocated or re-protected as executable, the relevant pages of the CFG bitmap are made private and initialized to all 1s by default. This is needed for cases such as just-in-time (JIT) compilation, where code is generated on the fly and then executed (for example, .NET or Java).

Strengthening CFG protection

Although CFG does an adequate job to prevent types of exploits that leverage indirect calls or jumps, it could be bypassed through the following ways:

- If the process can be tricked or an existing JIT engine abused to allocate executable memory, all the corresponding bits will be set to {1, 1}, meaning that all memory is considered a valid call target.

- For 32-bit applications, if the expected call target is __stdcall (standard calling convention), but an attacker is able to change the indirect call target to __cdecl (C calling convention), the stack will become corrupt, as the C call function will not perform cleanup of the caller's arguments, unlike a standard call function. Because CFG cannot differentiate between the different calling conventions, this results in a corrupt stack, potentially with an attacker-controlled return address, bypassing the CFG mitigation.

- Similarly, compiler-generated setjmp/longjmp targets behave differently from true indirect calls. CFG cannot differentiate between the two.

- Certain indirect calls are harder to protect, such as the Import Address Table (IAT) or Delay-Load Address Table, which is typically in a read-only section of the executable.

- Exported functions may not be desirable indirect function calls.

Windows 10 introduces advancements to CFG that address all these issues. The first is to introduce a new flag to the VirtualAlloc function called PAGE_TARGETS_INVALID and one to VirtualProtect called PAGE_TARGETS_NO_UPDATE. With these flags set, JIT engines that allocate executable memory will not see all their allocations' bits set to the {1, 1} state. Instead, they must manually call the SetProcess-ValidCallTargets function (which calls the native NtSetInformationVirtualMemory function), which will allow them to specify the actual function start addresses of their JITed code. Additionally, this function is marked as a suppressed call with DECLSPEC_GUARD_SUPPRESS, making sure that attackers cannot use an indirect CALL or JMP to redirect into it, even at its function start. (Because it's an inherently dangerous function, calling it with a controlled stack or registers could result in the bypassing of CFG.)

Next, improved CFG changes the default flow you saw in the beginning of this section with a more refined flow. In this flow, the loader does not implement a simple "verify target, return" function, but rather a "verify target, call target, check stack, return" function, which is used in a subset of places on 32-bit applications (and/or running under WoW64). This improved execution flow is shown in Figure 7-32.

Next, improved CFG adds additional tables inside of the executable, such as the Address Taken IAT table and the Long Jump Address table. When longjmp and IAT CFG protection are enabled in the compiler, these tables are used to store destination addresses for these specific types of indirect calls, and the relevant functions are *not* placed in the regular function table, therefore not figuring in the bitmap. This means that if code is attempting to indirect jump/call to one of these functions, it will be treated as an illegal transition. Instead, the C Runtime and linker will validate the targets of, say, the longjmp function, by manually checking this table. Although it's more inefficient than a bitmap, there should be little to no functions in these tables, making the cost bearable.

Finally, improved CFG implements a feature called *export suppression*, which must be supported by the compiler and enabled by process-mitigation policy. (See the section "Process-mitigation policies" for more on process level mitigations.) With this feature enabled, a new bit state is implemented (recall that bulleted list had {0, 1} as an undefined state). This state indicates that the function is valid but export-suppressed, and it will be treated differently by the loader.

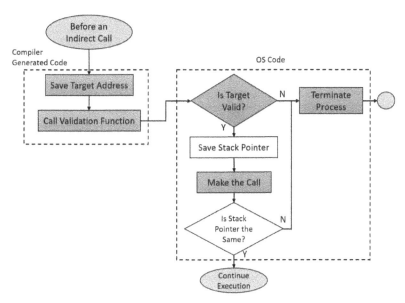

FIGURE 7-32 Improved CFG.

You can determine which features are present in a given binary by looking at the guard flags in the Image Load Configuration Directory, which the DumpBin application used earlier can decode. For reference, they are listed in Table 7-21.

TABLE 7-21 Control Flow Guard flags

Flag Symbol	Value	Description
IMAGE_GUARD_CF_INSTRUMENTED	0x100	This indicates CFG support is present for this module.
IMAGE_GUARD_CFW_INSTRUMENTED	0x200	This module performs CFG and write integrity checks.
IMAGE_GUARD_CF_FUNCTION_TABLE_PRESENT	0x400	This module contains CFG-aware function lists.
IMAGE_GUARD_SEURITY_COOKIE_UNUSED	0x800	This module does not make use of the security cookie emitted with the compiler /GS flag.
IMAGE_GUARD_PROTECT_DELAYLOAD_IAT	0x1000	This module supports read-only delay-load Import Address Tables (IATs).
IMAGE_GUARD_DELAYLOAD_IAT_IN_ITS_OWN_SECTION	0x2000	Delay-load IAT is its own section, so it can be re-protected if desired.
IMAGE_GUARD_CF_EXPORT_SUPPRESSION_INFO_PRESENT	0x4000	This module contains suppressed export information.
IMAGE_GUARD_CF_ENABLE_EXPORT_SUPPRESSION	0x8000	This module enables suppression of exports.
IMAGE_GUARD_CF_LONGJUMP_TABLE_PRESENT	0x10000	This module contains longjmp target information.

Loader interaction with CFG

Although it is the memory manager that builds the CFG bitmap, the user-mode loader (see Chapter 3 for more information) serves two purposes. The first is to dynamically enable CFG support only if the feature is enabled (for example, the caller may have requested no CFG for the child process, or the process itself might not have CFG support). This is done by the LdrpCfgProcessLoadConfig loader function, which is called to initialize CFG for each loaded module. If the module DllCharacteristics flags in the optional header of the PE does not have the CFG flag set (IMAGE_DLLCHARACTERISTICS_ GUARD_CF), the GuardFlags member of IMAGE_LOAD_CONFIG_DIRECTORY structure does not have the IMAGE_GUARD_CF_INSTRUMENTED flag set, or the kernel has forcibly turned off CFG for this module, then there is nothing to do.

Second, if the module is indeed using CFG, LdrpCfgProcessLoadConfig gets the indirect checking function pointer retrieved from the image (the GuardCFCheckFunctionPointer member of IMAGE_LOAD_CONFIG_DIRECTORY structure) and sets it to either LdrpValidateUserCallTarget or LdrpValidateUserCallTargetES in Ntdll, depending on whether export suppression is enabled. Additionally, the function first makes sure the indirect pointer has not been somehow modified to point outside the module itself.

Furthermore, if improved CFG was used to compile this binary, a second indirect routine is available, called the *dispatch CFG routine*. It is used to implement the enhanced execution flow described earlier. If the image includes such a function pointer (in the GuardCFDispatchFunctionPointer member of the abovementioned structure), it is initialized to LdrpDispatchUserCallTarget, or LdrpDispatchUserCallTargetES if export suppression is enabled.

> **Note** In some cases, the kernel itself can emulate or perform indirect jumps or calls on behalf of user mode. In situations where this is a possibility, the kernel implements its own MmValidateUserCallTarget routine, which performs the same work as LdrpValidate- UserCallTarget.

The code generated by the compiler when CFG is enabled issues an indirect call that lands in the LdrpValidateCallTarget(ES) or LdrpDispatchUserCallTarget(ES) functions in Ntdll. This function uses the target branch address and checks the bit state value for the function:

- If the bit state is {0, 0}, the dispatch is potentially invalid.

- If the bit state is {1, 0}, and the address is 16-byte aligned, the dispatch is valid. Otherwise, it is potentially invalid.

- If the bit state is {1, 1}, and the address is not 16-byte aligned, the dispatch is valid. Otherwise, it is potentially invalid.

- If the bit state is {0, 1}, the dispatch is potentially invalid.

If the dispatch is potentially invalid, the RtlpHandleInvalidUserCallTarget function will execute to determine the appropriate action. First, it checks if suppressed calls are allowed in the process, which is an unusual application-compatibility option that might be set if Application Verifier is enabled, or through the registry. If so, it will check if the address is suppressed, which is why it was not inserted into the bitmap (recall that a special flag in the guard function table entry indicates this). If this is the case, the call is allowed through. If the function is not valid at all (meaning it's not in the table), then the dispatch is aborted and the process terminated.

Second, a check is made to see if export suppression is enabled. If it is, the target address is checked against the list of export-suppressed addresses, which is once again indicated with another flag that is added in the guard function table entry. If this is the case, the loader validates that the target address is a forwarder reference to the export table of another DLL, which is the only allowed case of an indirect call toward an image with suppressed exports. This is done by a complex check that makes sure the target address is in a different image, that its image load directory has enabled export suppression, and that this address is in the import directory of that image. If these checks match, the kernel is called through the `NtSetInformationVirtualMemory` call described earlier, to change the bit state to {1, 0}. If any of these checks fail, or export suppression is not enabled, then the process is terminated.

For 32-bit applications, an additional check is performed if DEP is enabled for the process. (See Chapter 5 for more on DEP.) Otherwise, because there are no execution guarantees to begin with, the incorrect call is allowed, as it may be an older application calling into the heap or stack for legitimate reasons.

Finally, because large sets of {0, 0} bit states are not committed to save space, if checking the CFG bitmap lands on a reserved page, an access violation exception occurs. On x86, where exception handling setup is expensive, instead of being handled as part of the verification code, it is left to propagate normally. (See Chapter 8 in Part 2 for more on exception dispatching.) The user-mode dispatcher handler, `KiUserExceptionDispatcher`, has specific checks for recognizing CFG bitmap access violation exceptions within the validation function and will automatically resume execution if the exception code was `STATUS_IN_PAGE_ERROR`. This simplifies the code in `LdrpValidateUserCallTarget(ES)` and `LdrpDispatchUserCallTarget(ES)`, which don't have to include exception handling code. On x64, where exception handlers are simply registered in tables, the `LdrpICallHandler` handler runs instead, with the same logic as above.

Kernel CFG

Although drivers compiled with Visual Studio and `/guard:cf` also ended up with the same binary properties as user-mode images, the first versions of Windows 10 did not do anything with this data. Unlike the user-mode CFG bitmap, which is protected by a higher, more trusted entity (the kernel), there is nothing that can truly "protect" the kernel CFG bitmap if one were to be created. A malicious exploit could simply edit the PTE that corresponded to the page containing the desired bits to modify, mark it as read/write, and proceed with the indirect call or jump. Therefore, the overhead of setting up such a trivially bypassable mitigation was simply not worth it.

With a greater number of users enabling VBS features, once again, the higher security boundary that VTL 1 provides can be leveraged. The SLAT page table entries come to the rescue by providing a second boundary against PTE page protection changes. While the bitmap is readable to VTL 0 because the SLAT entries are marked as read only, if a kernel attacker attempts to change the PTEs to mark them read/write, they cannot do the same to the SLAT entries. As such, this will be detected as an invalid

KCFG bitmap access which HyperGuard can act on (for telemetry reasons alone—since the bits can't be changed anyway).

KCFG is implemented almost identically to regular CFG, except that export suppression is not enabled, nor is `longjmp` support, nor is the ability to dynamically request additional bits for JIT purposes. Kernel drivers should not be doing any of these things. Instead, the bits are set in the bitmap based on the "address taken IAT table" entries, if any are set; by the usual function entries in the guard table each time a driver image is loaded; and for the HAL and kernel during boot by `MiInitializeKernelCfg`. If the hypervisor is not enabled, and SLAT support is not present, then none of this will be initialized, and Kernel CFG will be kept disabled.

Just like in the user-mode case, a dynamic pointer in the load configuration data directory is updated, which in the enabled case will point to `__guard_check_icall` for the check function and `__guard_dispatch_icall` for the dispatch function in enhanced CFG mode. Additionally, a variable named `guard_icall_bitmap` will hold the virtual address of the bitmap.

One last detail on Kernel CFG is that unfortunately, dynamic Driver Verifier settings will not be configurable (for more information on Driver Verifier, see Chapter 6, "I/O system"), as this would require adding dynamic kernel hooks and redirecting execution to functions that may not be in the bitmap. In this case, STATUS_VRF_CFG_ENABLED (0xC000049F) will be returned, and a reboot is required (at which time the bitmap can be built with the Verifier Driver hooks in place).

Security assertions

Earlier, we described how Control Flow Guard will terminate the process. We also explained how certain other mitigations or security features will raise an exception to kill the process. It is important to be accurate with what *exactly* happens during these security violations because both these descriptions hide important details about the mechanism.

In fact, when a security-related breach occurs, such as when CFG detects an incorrect indirect call or jump, terminating the process through the standard `TerminateProcess` mechanism would not be an adequate path. There would be no crash generated, and no telemetry sent to Microsoft. These are both important tools for the administrator to understand that a potential exploit has executed or that an application compatibility issue exists, as well as for Microsoft to track zero-day exploitation in the wild. On the flip side, while raising an exception would achieve the desired result, exceptions are callbacks, which can be:

■ Potentially hooked by attackers if /SAFESEH and SEHOP mitigations are not enabled, causing the security check to be the one that gives control to an attacker in the first place—or an attacker can simply "swallow" the exception.

■ Potentially hooked by legitimate parts of the software through an unhandled exception filter or vectored exception handler, both of which might accidentally swallow the exception.

■ Same as above, but intercepted by a third-party product that has injected its own library into the process. Common to many security tools, this can also lead in the exception not being correctly delivered to Windows Error Reporting (WER).

- A process might have an application recovery callback registered with WER. This might then display a less clear UI to the user, and might restart the process in its current exploited state, leading anywhere from a recursive crash/start loop to the exception being swallowed whole.

- Likely in a C++-based product, caught by an outer exception handler as if "thrown" by the program itself, which, once again, might swallow the exception or continue execution in an unsafe manner.

Solving these issues requires a mechanism that can raise an exception that cannot be intercepted by any of the process's components outside of the WER service, which must itself be guaranteed to receive the exception. This is where security assertions come into play.

Compiler and OS support

When Microsoft libraries, programs, or kernel components encounter unusual security situations, or when mitigations recognize dangerous violations of security state, they now use a special compiler intrinsic supported by Visual Studio, called __fastfail, which takes one parameter as input. Alternatively, they can call a runtime library (Rtl) function in Ntdll called RtlFailFast2, which itself contains a __fastfail intrinsic. In some cases, the WDK or SDK contain inline functions that call this intrinsic, such as when using the LIST_ENTRY functions InsertTailList and RemoveEntryList. In other situations, it is the Universal CRT (uCRT) itself that has this intrinsic in its functions. In yet others, APIs will do certain checks when called by applications and may use this intrinsic as well.

Regardless of the situation, when the compiler sees this intrinsic, it generates assembly code that takes the input parameter, moves it into the RCX (x64) or ECX (x86) register, and then issues a software interrupt with the number 0x29. (For more information on interrupts, see Chapter 8 in Part 2.)

In Windows 8 and later, this software interrupt is registered in the Interrupt Dispatch Table (IDT) with the handler KiRaiseSecurityCheckFailure, which you can verify on your own by using the !idt 29 command in the debugger. This will result (for compatibility reasons) in KiFastFailDispatch being called with the STATUS_STACK_BUFFER_OVERRUN status code (0xC0000409). This will then do regular exception dispatching through KiDispatchException, but treat this as a second-chance exception, which means that the debugger and process won't be notified.

This condition will be specifically recognized and an error message will be sent to the WER error ALPC port as usual. WER will claim the exception as non-continuable, which will then cause the kernel to terminate the process with the usual ZwTerminateProcess system call. This, therefore, guarantees that once the interrupt is used, no return to user mode will ever be performed within this process again, that WER will be notified, and that the process will be terminated (additionally, the error code will be the exception code). When the exception record is generated, the first exception argument will be the input parameter to __fastfail.

Kernel-mode code can also raise exceptions, but in this case KiBugCheckDispatch will be called instead, which will result in a special kernel mode crash (bugcheck) with code 0x139 (KERNEL_SECURITY_CHECK_FAILURE), where the first argument will be the input parameter to __fastfail.

Fast fail/security assertion codes

Because the `__fastfail` intrinsic contains an input argument that is bubbled up to the exception record or crash screen, it allows the failing check to identify what part of the system or process is not working correctly or has encountered a security violation. Table 7-22 shows the various failure conditions and their meaning or significance.

TABLE 7-22   `__fastfail` failure codes

Code	Meaning
Legacy OS Violation (0x0)	An older buffer security check present in a legacy binary has failed, and has been converted to a security assertion instead.
V-Table Guard Failure (0x1)	The Virtual Table Guard Mitigation in Internet Explorer 10 and higher has encountered a corrupted virtual function table pointer.
Stack Cookie Check Failure (0x2)	The stack cookie generated with the /GS compiler option (also called a stack canary) has been corrupted.
Corrupt List Entry (0x3)	One of the macros for manipulating LIST_ENTRY structures has detected an inconsistent linked list, where the grandparent or grandchild entry does not point to the parent or child entry of the item being manipulated.
Incorrect Stack (0x4)	A user-mode or kernel-mode API that is often potentially called from ROP-based exploits while operating on an attacker-controlled stack has been called, and the stack is therefore not the expected one.
Invalid Argument (0x5)	A user-mode CRT API (typically) or other sensitive function has been called with an invalid argument, suggesting potential ROP-based use or an otherwise corrupted stack.
Stack Cookie Init Failure (0x6)	The initialization of the stack cookie has failed, suggesting image patching or corruption.
Fatal App Exit (0x7)	The application has used the FatalAppExit user-mode API, which has been converted into a security assertion to grant it the advantages this has.
Range Check Failure (0x8)	Additional validation checks in certain fixed array buffers to check if the array element index is within expected bounds.
Unsafe Registry Access (0x9)	A kernel-mode driver is attempting to access registry data from a user-controllable hive (such as an application hive or user profile hive) and is not using the RTL_QUERY_REGISTRY_TYPECHECK flag to protect itself.
CFG Indirect Call Failure (0xA)	Control Flow Guard has detected an indirect CALL or JMP instruction to a target address that is not a valid dispatch per the CFG bitmap.
CFG Write Check Failure (0xB)	Control Flow Guard with write protection has detected an invalid write to protected data. This feature (/guard:cfw) is not supported outside of testing at Microsoft.
Invalid Fiber Switch (0xC)	The SwitchToFiber API was used on an invalid fiber or from a thread which has not been converted to a fiber.
Invalid Set of Context (0xD)	An invalid context record structure was detected while attempting to restore it (due to an exception or SetThreadContext API), in which the stack pointer is not valid. Checked only when CFG is active on the process.
Invalid Reference Count (0xE)	A reference countered object (such as the OBJECT_HEADER in kernel-mode or a Win32k.sys GDI object) has underflowed its reference count below 0 or overflowed beyond its maximum capacity back to 0.
Invalid Jump Buffer (0x12)	A longjmp attempt is being made with a jump buffer that contains an invalid stack address or invalid instruction pointer. Checked only when CFG is active on the process.

TABLE 7-22 __fastfail failure codes *(continued)*

Code	Meaning
MRDATA Modified (0x13)	The mutable read-only data heap/section of the loader has been modified. Checked only when CFG is active on the process.
Certification Failure (0x14)	One or more Cryptographic Services APIs has encountered an issue parsing a certificate or an invalid ASN.1 stream.
Invalid Exception Chain (0x15)	An image linked with /SAFESEH, or with the SEHOP mitigation, has encountered an invalid exception handler dispatch.
Crypto Library (0x16)	CNG.SYS, KSECDD.SYS, or their equivalent APIs in user mode have encountered some critical failure.
Invalid Call in DLL Callout (0x17)	An attempt to call dangerous functions while in the user-mode loader's notification callback has occurred.
Invalid Image Base (0x18)	An invalid value for __ImageBase (IMAGE_DOS_HEADER structure) was detected by the user-mode image loader.
Delay Load Protection Failure (0x19)	The delay-loaded IAT has been found to be corrupted while delay-loading an imported function. Checked only when CFG is active on the process, and delay-load IAT protection is enabled.
Unsafe Extension Call (0x1A)	Checked when certain kernel-mode extension APIs are called, and the caller state is incorrect.
Deprecated Service Called (0x1B)	Checked when certain no-longer supported, and undocumented system calls, are called.
Invalid Buffer Access (0x1C)	Checked by the runtime library functions in Ntdll and the kernel when a generic buffer structure is corrupt in some way.
Invalid Balanced Tree (0x1D)	Checked by the runtime library functions in Ntdll and the kernel when an RTL_RB_TREE or RTL_AVL_TABLE structure has invalid nodes (where siblings and/or parent nodes do not match up with the grandparent's, similar to the LIST_ENTRY checks).
Invalid Next Thread (0x1E)	Checked by the kernel scheduler when the next thread to schedule in the KPRCB is invalid in some way.
CFG Call Suppressed (0x1F)	Checked when CFG is allowing a suppressed call due to compatibility concerns. In this situation, WER will mark the error as handled, and the kernel will not terminate the process, but telemetry will still be sent to Microsoft.
APCs Disabled (0x20)	Checked by the kernel when returning to user-mode and kernel APCs are still disabled.
Invalid Idle State (0x21)	Checked by the kernel power manager when the CPU is attempting to enter an invalid C-state.
MRDATA Protection Failure (0x22)	Checked by the user-mode loader when the Mutable Read-Only Heap Section has already been unprotected outside of the expected code path.
Unexpected Heap Exception (0x23)	Checked by the heap manager whenever the heap is corrupted in ways that indicate potential exploitation attempts.
Invalid Lock State (0x24)	Checked by the kernel when certain locks are not in their expected state, such as if an acquired lock is already in a released state.
Invalid Longjmp (0x25)	Checked by longjmp when called, and CFG is active on the process with Longjmp Protection enabled, but the Longjmp Table is corrupt or missing in some way.
Invalid Longjmp Target (0x26)	Same conditions as above, but the Longjmp Table indicates that this is not a valid Longjmp target function.

TABLE 7-22 __fastfail failure codes *(continued)*

Code	Meaning
Invalid Dispatch Context (0x27)	Checked by the exception handler in kernel-mode when an exception is attempted to be dispatched with an incorrect CONTEXT record.
Invalid Thread (0x28)	Checked by the scheduler in kernel-mode when the KTHREAD structure is corrupt during certain scheduling operations.
Invalid System Call Number (0x29)	Similar to Deprecated Service Called, but WER will mark the exception as handled, resulting in the process continuing and therefore only used for telemetry.
Invalid File Operation (0x2A)	Used by the I/O Manager and certain file systems, as another telemetry-type failure as above.
LPAC Access Denied (0x2B)	Used by the SRM's access check function when a lower-privilege AppContainer attempts to access an object that does not have the ALL RESTRICTED APPLICATION PACKAGES SID and tracing of such failures is enabled. Once more, results only in telemetry data, not a process crash.
RFG Stack Failure (0x2C)	Used by Return Flow Guard (RFG), although this feature is currently disabled.
Loader Continuity Failure (0x2D)	Used by the process-mitigation policy of the same name, shown earlier, to indicate that an unexpected image with a different signature or no signature has been loaded.
CFG Export Suppression Failure (0x2D)	Used by CFG when enabled with export suppression to indicate that a suppressed export has been the target of an indirect branch.
Invalid Control Stack (0x2E)	Used by RFG, although this feature is currently disabled.
Set Context Denied (0x2F)	Used by the process-mitigation policy of the same name, shown earlier, although this feature is currently disabled.

Application Identification

Historically, security decisions in Windows have been based on a user's identity (in the form of the user's SID and group membership), but a growing number of security components (AppLocker, firewall, antivirus, anti-malware, Rights Management Services, and others) need to make security decisions based on what code is to be run. In the past, each of these security components used their own proprietary method for identifying applications, which led to inconsistent and overly complicated policy authoring. The purpose of Application Identification (AppID) is to bring consistency to how the security components recognize applications by providing a single set of APIs and data structures.

 Note This is not the same as the AppID used by DCOM/COM+ applications, where a GUID represents a process that is shared by multiple CLSIDs, nor is it related to UWP application ID.

Just as a user is identified when she logs in, an application is identified just before it is started by generating the main program's AppID. An AppID can be generated from any of the following attributes of the application:

- **Fields**   Fields within a code-signing certificate embedded within the file allow for different combinations of publisher name, product name, file name, and version. APPID://FQBN is a fully qualified binary name, and it is a string in the following form: `{Publisher\Product\Filename,Version}`. `Publisher` is the Subject field of the x.509 certificate used to sign the code, using the following fields:

- **O** Organization
- **L** Locality
- **S** State or province
- **C** Country

- **File hash** there are several methods that can be used for hashing. The default is `APPID://SHA256HASH`. However, for backward compatibility with SRP and most x.509 certificates, SHA-1 (`APPID://SHA1HASH`) is still supported. `APPID://SHA256HASH` specifies the SHA-256 hash of the file.

- **The partial or complete path to the file** `APPID://Path` specifies a path with optional wildcard characters (*).

> **Note** An AppID does not serve as a means for certifying the quality or security of an application. An AppID is simply a way of identifying an application so that administrators can reference the application in security policy decisions.

The AppID is stored in the process access token, allowing any security component to make authorization decisions based on a single consistent identification. AppLocker uses conditional ACEs (described earlier) for specifying whether a particular program is allowed to be run by the user.

When an AppID is created for a signed file, the certificate from the file is cached and verified to a trusted root certificate. The certificate path is reverified daily to ensure the certificate path remains valid. Certificate caching and verification are recorded in the system event log at Application and Services Logs\Microsoft\Windows\AppID\Operational.

AppLocker

Windows 8.1 and Windows 10 (Enterprise editions) and Windows Server 2012/R2/2016 support a feature known as *AppLocker*, which allows an administrator to lock down a system to prevent unauthorized programs from being run. Windows XP introduced Software Restriction Policies (SRP), which was the first step toward this capability, but SRP was difficult to manage, and it couldn't be applied to specific users or groups. (All users were affected by SRP rules.) AppLocker is a replacement for SRP, and yet co-exists alongside SRP, with AppLocker's rules being stored separately from SRP's rules. If both AppLocker and SRP rules are in the same Group Policy object (GPO), only the AppLocker rules will be applied.

Another feature that makes AppLocker superior to SRP is AppLocker's auditing mode, which allows an administrator to create an AppLocker policy and examine the results (stored in the system event log) to determine whether the policy will perform as expected—without actually performing the restrictions. AppLocker auditing mode can be used to monitor which applications are being used by one or more users on a system.

AppLocker allows an administrator to restrict the following types of files from being run:

- Executable images (EXE and COM)
- Dynamic-link libraries (DLL and OCX)
- Microsoft Software Installer (MSI and MSP) for both install and uninstall
- Scripts
- Windows PowerShell (PS1)
- Batch (BAT and CMD)
- VisualBasic Script (VBS)
- Java Script (JS)

AppLocker provides a simple GUI rule-based mechanism, which is very similar to network firewall rules, for determining which applications or scripts are allowed to be run by specific users and groups, using conditional ACEs and AppID attributes. There are two types of rules in AppLocker:

- Allow the specified files to run, denying everything else.
- Deny the specified files from being run, allowing everything else. Deny rules take precedence over allow rules.

Each rule can also have a list of exceptions to exclude files from the rule. Using an exception, you could create a rule to, for example, allow everything in the C:\Windows or C:\Program Files directories to be run except RegEdit.exe.

AppLocker rules can be associated with a specific user or group. This allows an administrator to support compliance requirements by validating and enforcing which users can run specific applications. For example, you can create a rule to allow users in the Finance security group to run the finance line-of-business applications. This blocks everyone who is not in the Finance security group from running finance applications (including administrators) but still provides access for those who have a business need to run the applications. Another useful rule would be to prevent users in the Receptionists group from installing or running unapproved software.

AppLocker rules depend upon conditional ACEs and attributes defined by AppID. Rules can be created using the following criteria:

- **Fields within a code-signing certificate embedded within the file, allowing for different combinations of publisher name, product name, file name, and version**   For example, a rule could be created to allow all versions greater than 9.0 of Contoso Reader to run or allow anyone in the Graphics group to run the installer or application from Contoso for GraphicsShop as long as the version is 14.*. For example, the following SDDL string denies execute access to any signed programs published by Contoso for the RestrictedUser user account (identified by the user's SID):

```
D:(XD;;FX;;;S-1-5-21-3392373855-1129761602-2459801163-1028;((Exists APPID://FQBN)
&& ((APPID://FQBN) >= ({"O=CONTOSO, INCORPORATED, L=REDMOND,
S=CWASHINGTON, C=US\*\*",0}))))
```

- ■ **Directory path, allowing only files within a particular directory tree to run**   This can also be used to identify specific files. For example, the following SDDL string denies execute access to the programs in the directory C:\Tools for the RestrictedUser user account (identified by the user's SID):

```
D:(XD;;FX;;;S-1-5-21-3392373855-1129761602-2459801163-1028;(APPID://PATH
Contains "%OSDRIVE%\TOOLS\*"))
```

- ■ **File hash**   Using a hash will also detect if a file has been modified and prevent it from running. This can also be a weakness if files are changed frequently because the hash rule will need to be updated frequently. File hashes are often used for scripts because few scripts are signed. For example, this SDDL string denies execute access to programs with the specified hash values for the RestrictedUser user account (identified by the user's SID):

```
D:(XD;;FX;;;S-1-5-21-3392373855-1129761602-2459801163-1028;(APPID://SHA256HASH
Any_of {#7a334d2b99d48448eedd308dfca63b8a3b7b44044496ee2f8e236f5997f1b647,
#2a782f76cb94ece307dc52c338f02edbbfdca83906674e35c682724a8a92a76b}))
```

AppLocker rules can be defined on the local machine using the Security Policy MMC snap-in (secpol. msc, see Figure 7-33) or a Windows PowerShell script, or they can be pushed to machines within a domain using Group Policy. AppLocker rules are stored in multiple locations within the registry:

- ■ **HKLM\Software\Policies\Microsoft\Windows\SrpV2**   This key is also mirrored to HKLM\SOFTWARE\Wow6432Node\Policies\Microsoft\Windows\SrpV2. The rules are stored in XML format.

- ■ **HKLM\SYSTEM\CurrentControlSet\Control\Srp\Gp\Exe**   The rules are stored as SDDL and a binary ACE.

- ■ **HKEY_CURRENT_USER\Software\Microsoft\Windows\CurrentVersion\Group Policy Objects\{GUID}Machine\Software\Policies\Microsoft\Windows\SrpV2**   AppLocker policy pushed down from a domain as part of a GPO are stored here in XML format.

Certificates for files that have been run are cached in the registry under the key HKLM\SYSTEM\ CurrentControlSet\Control\AppID\CertStore. AppLocker also builds a certificate chain (stored in HKLM\SYSTEM\CurrentControlSet\Control\AppID\CertChainStore) from the certificate found in a file back to a trusted root certificate.

There are also AppLocker-specific PowerShell commands (cmdlets) to enable deployment and testing via scripting. After using the Import-Module AppLocker to get AppLocker cmdlets into PowerShell, several cmdlets are available. These include `Get-AppLockerFileInformation`, `Get-AppLockerPolicy`, `New-AppLockerPolicy`, `Set-AppLockerPolicy`, and `Test-AppLockerPolicy`.

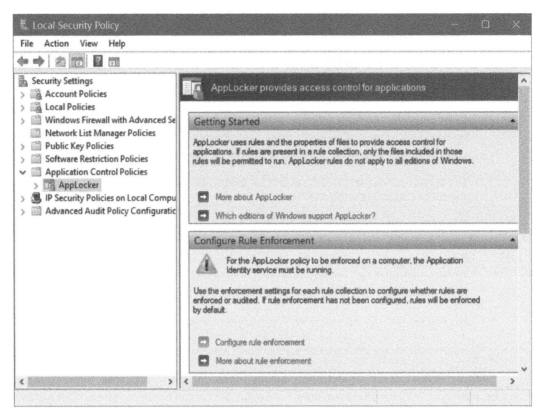

FIGURE 7-33 AppLocker configuration page in Local Security Policy.

The AppID and SRP services coexist in the same binary (AppIdSvc.dll), which runs within an SvcHost process. The service requests a registry change notification to monitor any changes under that key, which is written by either a GPO or the AppLocker UI in the Local Security Policy MMC snap-in. When a change is detected, the AppID service triggers a user-mode task (AppIdPolicyConverter.exe), which reads the new rules (described with XML) and translates them into binary format ACEs and SDDL strings, which are understandable by both the user-mode and kernel-mode AppID and AppLocker components. The task stores the translated rules under HKLM\SYSTEM\CurrentControlSet\Control\Srp\ Gp. This key is writable only by System and Administrators, and it is marked read-only for authenticated users. Both user-mode and kernel-mode AppID components read the translated rules from the registry directly. The service also monitors the local machine trusted root certificate store, and it invokes a user-mode task (AppIdCertStoreCheck.exe) to reverify the certificates at least once per day and whenever there is a change to the certificate store. The AppID kernel-mode driver (%SystemRoot%\System32\ drivers\AppId.sys) is notified about rule changes by the AppID service through an APPID_POLICY_ CHANGED DeviceIoControl request.

An administrator can track which applications are being allowed or denied by looking at the system event log using Event Viewer (once AppLocker has been configured and the service started). See Figure 7-34.

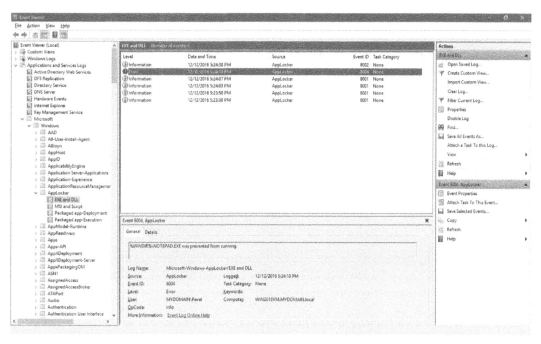

FIGURE 7-34 Event Viewer showing AppLocker allowing and denying access to various applications. Event ID 8004 is denied; 8002 is allowed.

The implementations of AppID, AppLocker, and SRP are somewhat blurred and violate strict layering, with various logical components coexisting within the same executables, and the naming is not as consistent as one would like.

The AppID service runs as LocalService so that it has access to the Trusted Root Certificate Store on the system. This also enables it to perform certificate verification. The AppID service is responsible for the following:

- Verification of publisher certificates

- Adding new certificates to the cache

- Detecting AppLocker rule updates and notifying the AppID driver

The AppID driver performs the majority of the AppLocker functionality and relies on communication (via DeviceIoControl requests) from the AppID service, so its device object is protected by an ACL, granting access only to the NT SERVICE\AppIDSvc, LOCAL SERVICE and BUILTIN\Administrators groups. Thus, the driver cannot be spoofed by malware.

When the AppID driver is first loaded, it requests a process-creation callback by calling PsSetCreateProcessNotifyRoutineEx. When the notification routine is called, it is passed a PPS_CREATE_NOTIFY_INFO structure (describing the process being created). It then gathers the AppID attributes that identify the executable image and writes them to the process's access token. Then it calls the undocumented routine SeSrpAccessCheck, which examines the process token and the conditional ACE AppLocker rules, and determines whether the process should be allowed to run. If the process should not be allowed to run, the driver writes STATUS_ACCESS_DISABLED_BY_POLICY_OTHER to the Status field of the PPS_CREATE_NOTIFY_INFO structure, which causes the process creation to be canceled (and sets the process's final completion status).

To perform DLL restriction, the image loader sends a DeviceIoControl request to the AppID driver whenever it loads a DLL into a process. The driver then checks the DLL's identity against the AppLocker conditional ACEs, just like it would for an executable.

> **Note** Performing these checks for every DLL load is time-consuming and might be noticeable to end users. For this reason, DLL rules are normally disabled, and they must be specifically enabled via the Advanced tab in the AppLocker properties page in the Local Security Policy snap-in.

The scripting engines and the MSI installer have been modified to call the user-mode SRP APIs whenever they open a file, to check whether a file is allowed to be opened. The user-mode SRP APIs call the AuthZ APIs to perform the conditional ACE access check.

Software Restriction Policies

Windows contains a user-mode mechanism called *Software Restriction Policies* (*SRP*) that enables administrators to control what images and scripts execute on their systems. The Software Restriction Policies node of the Local Security Policy editor, shown in Figure 7-35, serves as the management interface for a machine's code execution policies, although per-user policies are also possible using domain group policies.

FIGURE 7-35 Software Restriction Policy configuration.

Several global policy settings appear beneath the Software Restriction Policies node:

- **Enforcement**   This policy configures whether restriction policies apply to libraries, such as DLLs, and whether policies apply to users only or to administrators as well.

- **Designated File Types**   This policy records the extensions for files that are considered executable code.

- **Trusted Publishers**   This policy controls who can select which certificate publishers are trusted.

When configuring a policy for a particular script or image, an administrator can direct the system to recognize it using its path, its hash, its Internet zone (as defined by Internet Explorer), or its cryptographic certificate, and can specify whether it is associated with the Disallowed or Unrestricted security policy.

Enforcement of SRPs takes place within various components where files are treated as containing executable code. Some of these components are listed here:

- The user-mode Windows `CreateProcess` function in Kernel32.dll enforces it for executable images.

- The DLL loading code in Ntdll enforces it for DLLs.

- The Windows command prompt (Cmd.exe) enforces it for batch file execution.

- Windows Scripting Host components that start scripts—Cscript.exe (for command-line scripts), Wscript.exe (for UI scripts), and Scrobj.dll (for script objects)—enforce it for script execution.

- The PowerShell host (PowerShell.exe) enforces it for PowerShell script execution.

Each of these components determines whether the restriction policies are enabled by reading the `TransparentEnabled` registry value in the HKLM\Software\Policies\Microsoft \Windows\Safer\ CodeIdentifiers key, which if set to 1 indicates that policies are in effect. Then it determines whether the code it's about to execute matches one of the rules specified in a subkey of the CodeIdentifiers key and, if so, whether the execution should be allowed. If there is no match, the default policy, as specified in the `DefaultLevel` value of the CodeIdentifiers key, determines whether the execution is allowed.

Software Restriction Policies are a powerful tool for preventing the unauthorized access of code and scripts, but only if properly applied. Unless the default policy is set to disallow execution, a user can make minor changes to an image that's been marked as disallowed so that he can bypass the rule and execute it. For example, a user can change an innocuous byte of a process image so that a hash rule fails to recognize it, or copy a file to a different location to avoid a path-based rule.

Kernel Patch Protection

Some device drivers modify the behavior of Windows in unsupported ways. For example, they patch the system call table to intercept system calls or patch the kernel image in memory to add functionality to specific internal functions. Such modifications are inherently dangerous and can reduce system stability and security. Additionally, it is also possible for such modifications to be made with malicious intent, either by rogue drivers or through exploits due to vulnerabilities in Windows drivers.

Without the presence of a more privileged entity than the kernel itself, detecting and protecting against kernel-based exploits or drivers from within the kernel itself is a tricky game. Because both the detection/protection mechanism and the unwanted behavior operate in ring 0, it is not possible to define a security boundary in the true sense of the word, as the unwanted behavior could itself be used to disable, patch, or fool the detection/prevention mechanism. That being said, even in such conditions, a mechanism to react to such unwanted operations can still be useful in the following ways:

- By crashing the machine with a clearly identifiable kernel-mode crash dump, both users and administrators can easily see that an unwanted behavior has been operating inside of their kernel and they can take action. Additionally, it means that legitimate software vendors will not want to take the risk of crashing their customers' systems and will find supported ways of extending kernel functionality (such as by using the filter manager for file system filters or other callback-based mechanisms).

- Obfuscation (which is not a security boundary) can make it costly—either in time or in complexity—for the unwanted behavior to disable the detection mechanism. This added cost means that the unwanted behavior is more clearly identified as potentially malicious, and that its complexity results in additional costs to a potential attacker. By shifting the obfuscation techniques, it means that legitimate vendors will be better off taking the time to move away from their legacy extension mechanisms and implement supported techniques instead, without the risk of looking like malware.

- Randomization and non-documentation of which specific checks the detection/prevention mechanism makes to monitor kernel integrity, and non-determinism of when such checks are executed, cripple the ability of attackers to ensure their exploits are reliable. It forces them to account for every possible non-deterministic variable and state transition that the mechanism has through static analysis, which obfuscation makes nearly impossible within the timeframe required before another obfuscation shift or feature change is implemented in the mechanism.

- Because kernel mode crash dumps are automatically submitted to Microsoft, it allows the company to receive telemetry of in-the-wild unwanted code, and to either identify software vendors whose code is unsupported and is crashing systems, or to track the progress of malicious drivers in the wild, or even zero-day kernel-mode exploitations, and fix bugs that may not have been reported, but are actively exploited.

PatchGuard

Shortly after the release of 64-bit Windows for x64 and before a rich third-party ecosystem had developed, Microsoft saw an opportunity to preserve the stability of 64-bit Windows, and to add telemetry and exploit-crippling patch detection to the system, through a technology called *Kernel Patch Protection* (*KPP*), also referred to as *PatchGuard*. When Windows Mobile was released, which operates on a 32-bit ARM processor core, the feature was ported to such systems, too, and it will be present in 64-bit ARM (AArch64) systems as well. Due to the existence of too many legacy 32-bit drivers that still use unsupported and dangerous hooking techniques, however, this mechanism is not enabled on such systems, even on Windows 10 operating systems. Fortunately, usage of 32-bit systems is almost coming to an end, and server versions of Windows no longer support this architecture at all.

Although both *Guard* and *Protection* imply that this mechanism will protect the system, it is important to realize that the only guard/protection offered is the crashing of the machine, which prevents further execution of the unwanted code. The mechanism does not *prevent* the attack in the first place, nor mitigate against it, nor undo it. Think of KPP as an Internet-connected video security system, or CCTV, with a loud alarm (the crash) inside the vault (the kernel), not as an impenetrable lock on the vault.

KPP has a variety of checks that it makes on protected systems, and documenting them all would both be impractical (due to the difficulty of static analysis) and valuable to potential attackers (reducing their research time). However, Microsoft does document certain checks, which we generalize in Table 7-23. When, where, and how KPP makes these checks, and which specific functions or data structures are affected, is outside of the scope of this analysis.

TABLE 7-23 Generalized description of elements protected by KPP

Component	Legitimate Usage	Potential Unwanted Usage
Executable code in the kernel, its dependencies, and core drivers, as well as the Import Address Table (IAT) of these components	Standard Windows components key to operation of kernel-mode usage.	Patching code in these components can modify their behavior and introduce unwanted back doors to the system, hide data or unwanted communications from the system, as well as reduce the stability of the system, or even add additional vulnerabilities through buggy third-party code.
Global Descriptor Table (GDT)	CPU hardware protection for the implementation of ring privilege levels (ring 0 versus ring 3).	Modification of expected permissions and mappings between code and ring levels, allowing ring 3 code ring 0 access.
Interrupt Descriptor Table (IDT) or Interrupt Vector Table	Table read by the CPU to deliver interrupt vectors to the correct handling routine.	Hooking of keystrokes, network packets, paging mechanism, system calls, hypervisor communication, and more, which can be used for back-dooring, hiding malicious data or communications, or accidentally adding vulnerabilities through buggy third-party code.
System Service Descriptor Table (SSDT)	Table containing the array of pointers for each system call handler.	Hooking of all user-mode communications with the kernel. Same issues as above.
Critical CPU registers such as Control Registers, Vector Base Address Register, and Model Specific Registers	Used for system calls, virtualization, enabling CPU security features such as SMEP, and more.	Same as above, plus disabling of key CPU security features or hypervisor protection.
Various function pointers in the kernel	Used as indirect calls to various internal functionality.	Can be used to hook certain internal kernel operations, leading to back doors and/or instability.
Various global variables in the kernel	Used to configure various parts of the kernel, including certain security features.	Malicious code would disable these security features, such as through an exploit from user mode allowing arbitrary memory overwrites.
Process and module list	Used to show the user, in tools such as Task Manager, Process Explorer, and the Windows Debugger, which processes are active, and which drivers are loaded.	Malicious code can hide the existence of certain processes or drivers on the machine, making them invisible to the user and most applications such as security software.
Kernel stacks	Store function arguments, the call stack (where a function should return), and variables.	Operating on a non-standard kernel stack is often the sign of a return-oriented programming (ROP) exploit operating on a pivoted stack as part of the attack.
Window Manager, graphical system calls, callbacks, and more	Provides the GUI, GDI, and DirectX services.	Same hooking abilities as described earlier, but specifically targeting the graphics and window-management stack. Same issues as other types of hooks.
Object types	Definitions for the various objects (such as processes and files) that the system supports through the object manager.	Can be used as another hooking technique, which does not target indirect function pointers in binaries' data sections, nor patching code directly. Same issues.

TABLE 7-23 Generalized description of elements protected by KPP *(continued)*

Component	Legitimate Usage	Potential Unwanted Usage
Local APIC	Used to receive hardware interrupts on the processor, receive timer interrupts, and inter-processor interrupts (IPI).	Can be used to hook timer execution, IPIs, or interrupts, or as a way for persistent code to covertly maintain liveness on the machine, executing on a periodic basis.
Filter and third-party notification callbacks	Used by legitimate third-party security software (and Windows Defender) to receive notifications about system actions, and in some cases even block/defend against certain actions. Exists as the supported way to achieve much of what KPP prevents.	Could be used by malicious code to hook all the filterable operations, as well as maintain liveness on a machine, executing on a periodic basis.
Specialized configuration and flags	Various data structures, flags, and elements of legitimate components that provide security and/or mitigation guarantees to them.	Could be used by malicious code to bypass certain mitigations or violate certain guarantees or expectations that user-mode processes might have, such as unprotecting a protected process.
KPP engine itself	Code related to bug-checking the system during a KPP violation, executing the callbacks associated with KPP, and more.	By modifying certain parts of the system used by KPP, unwanted components could attempt to silence, ignore, or otherwise cripple KPP.

As mentioned, when KPP detects unwanted code on the system, it crashes the system with an easily identifiable code. This corresponds to bugcheck code 0x109, which stands for CRITICAL_STRUCTURE_CORRUPTION, and the Windows Debugger can be used to analyze this crash dump. (See Chapter 15, "Crash dump analysis," in Part 2 for more information.) The dump information will contain *some* information about the corrupted or scrumptiously modified part of the kernel, but any additional data must be analyzed by Microsoft's Online Crash Analysis (OCA) and/or Windows Error Reporting (WER) teams and is not exposed to users.

For third-party developers who use techniques that KPP deters, the following supported techniques can be used:

- **File system (mini) filters** Use these to hook all file operations, including loading image files and DLLs, that can be intercepted to purge malicious code on-the-fly or block reading of known bad executables or DLLs. (See Chapter 13, "File systems," in Part 2 for more information on these.)

- **Registry filter notifications** Use these to hook all registry operations. (See Chapter 9 in Part 2 for more information on these notifications.) Security software can block modification of critical parts of the registry, as well as heuristically determine malicious software by registry access patterns or known bad registry keys.

- **Process notifications** Security software can monitor the execution and termination of all processes and threads on the system, as well as DLLs being loaded or unloaded. With the enhanced notifications added for antivirus and other security vendors, they also can block process launch. (See Chapter 3 for more information on these notifications.)

- **Object manager filtering**   Security software can remove certain access rights being granted to processes and/or threads to defend their own utilities against certain operations. (These are discussed in Chapter 8 in Part 2.)

- **NDIS Lightweight Filters (LWF) and Windows Filtering Platform (WFP) filters**   Security software can intercept all socket operations (accept, listen, connect, close, and so on) and even the packets themselves. With LWF, security vendors have access to the raw Ethernet frame data that is going from the network card (NIC) to the wire.

- **Event Tracing for Windows (ETW)**   Through ETW, many types of operations that have interesting security properties can be consumed by a user-mode component, which can then react to data in near real-time. In certain cases, special secure ETW notifications are available to anti-malware-protected processes under NDA with Microsoft and participation in various security programs, which give access to a greater set of tracing data. (ETW is discussed in Chapter 8 in Part 2.)

HyperGuard

On systems that run with virtualization-based security (described earlier in this chapter in the section "Virtualization-based security"), it is no longer true that attackers with kernel-mode privileges are essentially running at the same security boundary as a detection/prevention mechanism. In fact, such attackers would operate at VTL 0, while a mechanism could be implemented in VTL 1. In the Anniversary Update of Windows 10 (version 1607), such a mechanism does indeed exist, which is appropriately named *HyperGuard*. HyperGuard has a few interesting properties that set it apart from PatchGuard:

- It does not need to rely on obfuscation. The symbol files and function names that implement HyperGuard are available for anyone to see, and the code is not obfuscated. Complete static analysis is possible. This is because HyperGuard is a true security boundary.

- It does not need to operate non-deterministically because this would provide no advantage due to the preceding property. In fact, by operating deterministically, HyperGuard can crash the system at the precise time unwanted behavior is detected. This means crash data will contain clear and actionable data for the administrator (and Microsoft's analysis teams), such as the kernel stack, which will show the code that performed the undesirable behavior.

- Due to the preceding property, it can detect a wider variety of attacks, because the malicious code does not have the chance to restore a value back to its correct value during a precise time window, which is an unfortunate side-effect of PatchGuard's non-determinism.

HyperGuard is also used to extend PatchGuard's capabilities in certain ways, and to strengthen its ability to run undetected by attackers trying to disable it. When HyperGuard detects an inconsistency, it too will crash the system, albeit with a different code: 0x18C (HYPERGUARD_VIOLATION). As before, it might be valuable to understand, at a generic level, what kind of things HyperGuard will detect, which you can see in Table 7-24.

TABLE 7-24 Generalized description of elements protected by HyperGuard

Component	Legitimate Usage	Potential Unwanted Usage
Executable code in the kernel, its dependencies, and core drivers, as well as the Import Address Table (IAT) of these components	Refer to Table 7-23.	Refer to Table 7-23.
Global Descriptor Table (GDT)	Refer to Table 7-23.	Refer to Table 7-23.
Interrupt Descriptor Table (IDT) or Interrupt Vector Table	Refer to Table 7-23.	Refer to Table 7-23.
Critical CPU registers such as Control Registers, GDTR, IDTR, Vector Base Address Register, and Model Specific Registers	Refer to Table 7-23.	Refer to Table 7-23.
Executable code, callbacks, and data regions in the Secure Kernel and its dependencies, including HyperGuard itself	Standard Windows components key to operation of VTL 1 and secure kernel-mode usage.	Patching code in these components implies the attacker has access to some sort of vulnerability in VTL 1, either through hardware or the hypervisor. Could be used to subvert Device Guard, HyperGuard, and Credential Guard.
Structures and features used by Trustlets	Sharing data between one Trustlet to another, or Trustlets and the kernel, or Trustlets and VTL 0.	Implies that some vulnerability might exist in one or more Trustlets, which could be used to hamper features such as Credential Guard or Shielded Fabric/vTPM.
Hypervisor structures and regions	Used by the hypervisor to communicate with VTL 1.	Implies a potential vulnerability in a VTL 1 component or the hypervisor itself, which may be accessible from ring 0 in VTL 0.
Kernel CFG bitmap	Used to identify valid kernel functions that are the subject of indirect function calls or jumps, as described earlier.	Implies that an attacker has been able to perform a modification to the VTL 1-protected KCFG bitmap through some sort of hardware or hypervisor exploit.
Page verification	Used to implement HVCI-related work for Device Guard.	Implies that an attacker has somehow attacked SKCI, which could result in Device Guard compromise or non-authorized IUM Trustlets.
NULL page	None.	Implies that an attacker has somehow coerced the kernel and/or secure kernel to allocate virtual page 0, which can be used to exploit NULL-page vulnerabilities in either VTL 0 or VTL 1.

On systems with VBS enabled, there is another security-related feature that is worth describing, which is implemented in the hypervisor itself: Non-Privileged Instruction Execution Prevention (NPIEP). This mitigation targets specific x64 instructions that can be used to leak the kernel-mode addresses of the GDT, IDT, and LDT, which are SGDT, SIDT, and SLDT. With NPIEP, these instructions are still allowed to execute (due to compatibility concerns), but will return a per-processor unique number that is not actually the kernel address of these structures. This serves as a mitigation against Kernel ASLR (KASLR) information leaks from local attackers.

Finally, note that there is no way to disable PatchGuard or HyperGuard once they are enabled. However, because device-driver developers might need to make changes to a running system as part of debugging, PatchGuard is not enabled when the system boots in debugging mode with an active remote kernel-debugging connection. Similarly, HyperGuard is disabled if the hypervisor boots in debugging mode with a remote debugger attached.

Conclusion

Windows provides an extensive array of security functions that meet the key requirements of both government agencies and commercial installations. In this chapter, we've taken a brief tour of the internal components that are the basis of these security features. In Chapter 8 of Part 2, we'll look at various mechanisms that are spread out throughout the Windows system.

Index

Symbols

! (exclamation points), 40
.NET Framework, 6–7
64-bit address space layouts, 357–359
64-bit extended systems, 50

A

AAM (Admin Approval Mode), 729
access
    access checks, 621–624
    access masks, 624
    access tokens, 20, 677
    ACEs (access control entries). *See* ACEs
    ACLs (access control lists). *See* ACLs
    object access auditing, 679–681
access checks, 621–624
access control entries. *See* ACEs
access control lists. *See* ACLs
access masks, 624
access tokens, 20, 677
accounting (quantums), 233
accounts
    privileges, 668–675
        Bypass Traverse Checking privilege, 675
        super privileges, 675–676
    rights, 668–670
    User Account Control. *See* UAC
ACEs (access control entries)
    conditional ACEs, 667–668
    GUI security editors, 664–665
    overview, 650–653
    trust SIDs, 657–658
ACLs (access control lists)
    assigning, 656–657
    determining access, 659–665
    GUI security editors, 664–665
    inheritance, 656–657
    overview, 650–653
    Owner Rights SIDs, 662
activation contexts, 163
address spaces
    64-bit address space layouts, 357–359
    ARM address space layouts, 356–357
    canonical addresses, 359
    creating processes, 140–142
    dynamic allocation, 359–365
    image bias, 368
    PTEs, 355–356
    quotas, 364–365
    sessions, 353–355
    setting address limits, 363–364
    types of data, 348–349

user address spaces. *See* user address
    spaces
    viewing address usage, 361–363
    x64 virtual address limitations, 359
    x86 address space layouts, 349–352
    x86 session space, 353–355
    x86 system address space layouts, 352–353
address translation
    ARM virtual address translation, 381–382
    overview, 371
    page tables, 375–376
    PTEs, 375–376
    TLB, 377–378
    viewing, 378–380
    write bits, 376–377
    x64 virtual address translation, 380–381
    x86 virtual address translation, 371–375
Address Windowing Extensions (AWE), 22,
    323–324
addresses, canonical, 359
Admin Approval Mode (AAM), 729
administrative rights (UAC), 729–732
advanced audit policy, 683–684
affinity manager, 336
affinity masks
    extended affinity masks, 276–277
    symmetric multiprocessing, 53
    threads, 275–277
allocating
    address spaces
        dynamic allocation, 359–365
        quotas, 364–365
    memory, 310–315
API Sets (image loader), 173–176
APIs (application programming interfaces)
    API Sets (image loader), 173–176
    AuthZ, 666–667
    COM (component object model), 5
    .NET Framework, 6–7
    overview, 4
    Windows Runtime, 5–6
AppContainers
    brokers, 709
    capabilities, 699–703
    handles, 705–708
    lowboxes, defined, 134
    object namespaces, 703–705
    overview, 684
    security environment. *See* security
        environment
    tokens, 690–692
    UWP apps, 685–687
    UWP processes, 687–692
AppIDs, 756–757
application programming interfaces. *See* APIs

applications. *See also* processes
    APIs. *See* APIs
    AppContainers. *See* AppContainers
    AppIDs, 756–757
    AppLocker, 757–762
    classic apps, 103
    desktop apps, 103
    immersive apps, 103
    large address spaces, 351
    modern apps, 103
    UWP apps, 685–687
AppLocker, 757–762
applying priority boosts, 249
architecture
    components, 61–62
    kernel mode, 47–49
    overview, 47–49, 61–62
    user mode, 47–49
    VBS, 59–61
ARM address space layouts, 356–357
ARM virtual address translation, 381–382
ASLR. *See* address spaces
assertions
    compilers, 753
    fast fail failure codes, 754–756
    operating system, 753
    overview, 752–753
assigning
    ACLs, 656–657
    processors (groups), 271–273
assured authentication, 718–719
asymmetric multiprocessing, 51
asynchronous I/O, 511
atom tables, 697–698
attributes
    AppContainer security, 695–697
    converting, 131–135
    trustlets, 125
auditing (security)
    advanced audit policy, 683–684
    global audit policy, 682–683
    object access auditing, 679–681
    overview, 677–679
authentication
    policies (Credential Guard), 616–617
    users, 713–718
        Kerberos, 714–715
        MSV1_0, 713–714
        viewing active logon sessions,
            715–717
AuthZ API, 666–667
Autoboost, 254
auto-elevation (UAC), 732–733
AWE (Address Windowing Extensions), 22,
    323–324

771